Phineas Parkhurst Quimby

Phineas Parkhurst Quimby:

HIS COMPLETE WRITINGS AND BEYOND

Including The Missing Works of P. P. Quimby

Ronald A. Hughes–*Editor*

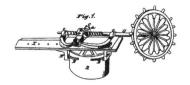

PHINEAS PARKHURST QUIMBY RESOURCE CENTER

http://www.PPQuimby.com

Printed in the United States of America

Library of Congress Control Number: 2009939445

ISBN 978-0-578-04092-9

PUBLISHED BY

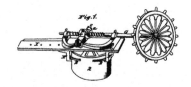

PHINEAS PARKHURST QUIMBY RESOURCE CENTER

HOWARD CITY, MICHIGAN

Find us on the World Wide Web at: http://www.PPQuimby.com

PRINTED IN THE UNITED STATES OF AMERICA

DEDICATION

This book is dedicated to Phineas Parkhurst Quimby, a man who aligned himself with Wisdom and became a law unto himself. In his search for truth, he came to realize:

"I found I was the very idea I was looking for."

Phineas Parkhurst Quimby ("The New Truth," pp. 402-403)

CONTENTS

* at the end of a title indicates an article or piece as being published for the first time.

** at the end of a title indicates a significant change or addition to a previously published article.

PREFACE

"Man is Belief Expressed"

Phineas Parkhurst Quimby was born in Lebanon, New Hampshire on February 16, 1802. His father, Jonathan Quimby (1765-1827), a blacksmith by trade, and his mother, Susanna (White) Quimby (1768-1827), were married on March 23, 1790, and had seven children. "Park," as he was addressed by his friends and family, was the sixth-born child of Jonathan and Susanna.

The Quimby family relocated to Belfast, Maine in 1804 when Phineas was two years old. Although technically he was not a lifelong resident of Belfast, he did maintain a home there for the remainder of his life. On December 23, 1827, Phineas married Susannah Burnham Haraden (1808-1875) and together they had four children.

The Belfast public school system in the early 1800s offered no more than six weeks of school classes per year. Phineas acquired only the most basic reading and writing skills during his formative years, but he didn't allow this disadvantage to limit the written expression of his ideas. He continued to educate himself throughout his lifetime and possessed a natural aptitude for anything mechanical. He followed the path of his oldest brother, William, and apprenticed as a clockmaker during his youth. In his later writings he tells us he possessed the mathematical skills necessary to calculate the gear train ratios used to determine the required pendulum lengths for timekeeping and the construction of clock movements.

P. P. Quimby also worked as a silver and goldsmith, jeweler, merchant, and was a photographer making an early form of photographs known as daguerreotypes. He was also an inventor and received at least four Letters Patent. President Andrew Jackson's signature appears on two of those patents. Around 1838 he became fascinated with mesmerism, (an early form of hypnosis) and went on to become an extraordinary mesmerist himself, conducting experiments and giving public demonstrations from 1843 through 1847. Based on his experiments and personal experiences, he concluded there were greater spiritual truths at work beyond the "Science of Mesmer," and it became his life's calling to explore these principles for the healing benefit of the sick and suffering.

By the time Quimby began his healing practice at the Hatch House in Bangor, Maine in December of 1857, he was being addressed professionally as "Doctor Quimby." This of course was an honorary title as he lacked the formal education and accreditation of a doctorate. Still, this healer was much beloved by his family, friends and patients, and the title of "Dr. Quimby" stayed with him for the remainder of his earthly life and beyond.

My first exposure to the spiritual healing work of Phineas Parkhurst Quimby occurred many years ago while I was reading *The Amazing Laws of Cosmic Mind Power*, by Divine Science minister Dr. Joseph Murphy. In this book, Murphy wrote: "You always will demonstrate your belief; that is why Dr. Quimby said one hundred years ago, 'Man is belief expressed.'"

"Man is belief expressed." This struck me as such a profound statement that I mentally carried it with me for several years and frequently contemplated the meanings and all of the implications of those words. This contemplation challenged me to change the way I perceived myself, God, my relationships, and the universe around me. It also triggered a nearly unquenchable desire to research every particle of information I could locate about this fellow-clockmaker by the name of Phineas Parkhurst "Park" Quimby.

In the course of my studies I created some useful computerized tools to assist me with my research of P. P. Quimby and his writings. One day it occurred to me to look up the quotation that had such an enormous impact on my consciousness: "Man is belief expressed." I wondered which article this quotation came from and in what context these words were written.

I was disappointed when my research proved that this exact quotation is not found anywhere in Quimby's published writings. The nearest quotation by Quimby seems to be: "Man is a combination of ideas and opinions and beliefs arranged into a form called man." Or possibly: "So man is a compound of opinions, belief, wisdom, science and ignorance, all arranged into a temple, not made of wood or stone but of ideas, and the world judges of the architect by the finish and workmanship."

Next, I turned my attention to the historical accuracy of other published works attributed to P. P. Quimby and came away with similar results.

First example: I was able to confirm that there are a number of unidentified alterations and deletions of Quimby's writings in *The Quimby Manuscripts*, edited by Horatio W. Dresser in 1921. Furthermore, I was able to confirm that this book did not contain all of the writings of P. P. Quimby.

Second example: in a 1951 publication, there is a section entitled "Quotations from The Quimby Manuscripts." In this chapter or section of the book, there are one hundred forty-two "quotations" attributed to *The Quimby Manuscripts*. Of this total, only eleven "quotations" are accurate quotations; nineteen "quotations" have been altered; and one hundred twelve "quotations" simply are not found in *The Quimby Manuscripts*. Even more disturbing, some of these so-called "Quimby quotations" are in sharp contrast with P. P. Quimby's ideas and his writings.

Third example: in a 1983 publication of Quimby's writings, the editor makes repetitious claims to the textual and historical accuracy of the publication and cites the transcription work of Erroll S. Collie as their reference source, but in fact many paragraphs of Quimby's presented writings have been extensively altered. Here is one random example from this book: "Teach man how to reason and he will free himself from ignorance and error or negative thinking. Give man Wisdom and he will easily detect error and its hiding place in ignorance." The actual quotation as transcribed by Erroll S. Collie is: "Teach man how to reason and he will free himself from the aristocracy of party, for this is the head of that serpent that has deceived the world. Give man wisdom and he will easily detect him and find out his abiding place."

Unfortunately, the rewriting of the Quimby materials continues to this present day. My purpose here isn't to single out and critique previous publications of Phineas Parkhurst Quimby's writings, but rather to demonstrate the need for historically accurate publications of those writings. This isn't about spelling mistakes or typographical errors, but rather this is in response to the surreptitious and deliberate rewriting of the Quimby materials. It is my personal position that the unedited Quimby writings constitutes a level playing field for anyone to use for study, interpretation and challenge of Quimby's ideas.

Only a few brief excerpts of P. P. Quimby's writings were published in the local newspapers during his own lifetime. When he closed his healing practice in Portland, Maine in the Spring of 1865, it was his intention to return to Belfast and organize the writings for publication. Phineas Parkhurst Quimby made his transition on January 16, 1866, and his book was left unfinished.

An exhaustive history of the publications of the Quimby writings is beyond the scope of this present volume, but a brief introduction to that history would be appropriate.

Julius Alfonso Dresser (1838-1893) met Annetta Gertrude Seabury (1843-1935) when they were both patients of P. P. Quimby during the Portland years. They fell in love and were married in September 1863. Their first-born child, Horatio Willis Dresser, was born on January 15, 1866, or the day before Quimby died.

Julius and Annetta Dresser credited the efforts of Quimby for their individual healings and in 1887, Julius issued a pamphlet entitled *The True History of Mental Science* that included one of Quimby's articles. In 1895, Annetta Gertrude (Seabury) Dresser published *The Philosophy of P. P. Quimby*, which included brief excerpts from some of Quimby's writings. This was followed by Horatio W. Dresser's book *The Quimby Manuscripts* in 1921, which included a substantial portion of Quimby's writings.

Beyond the publications of the Dresser family, there are two bright spots in the publications of Quimby's writings as they are based on original research and deserve special attention.

The first is the work of Erroll Stafford Collie (1897-1985) who made his personal discovery of P. P. Quimby and his writings in the year of 1932. "Collie" as he preferred to be addressed, had learned of the Quimby materials placed in the Library of Congress by P. P. Quimby's heirs. The placement of the materials occurred on April 5, 1930, and an announcement of the placement appeared the following day (Sunday, April 6, 1930) in the *New York Times* newspaper.

Collie began to compare the handwritten documents in the Library of Congress with *The Quimby Manuscripts* published by Horatio W. Dresser in 1921 and discovered that there was still a substantial amount of unpublished material in this collection. He transcribed this material and in 1940, he self-published and distributed a three-volume set entitled *The Science of Health and Happiness, by Phineas Parkhurst Quimby*. The set simply consisted of mimeographed typewritten pages bound in red folders. The publishing date is significant, as Collie wrote in his introductory remarks: "In 1930, the entire collection of these original writings of Dr. Quimby's, from which the articles in the Quimby Manuscripts were taken, was presented to the Library of Congress, Washington, D. C. by Dr. Quimby's heirs...." The significance here is that at the time Collie wrote this statement, he was unaware of the historical documents still retained by the Quimby family.

It wasn't until 1946 that Collie, along with Dr. Ervin Seale (1909-1990), would learn that the Quimby heirs still had a great deal of historical materials that were not included in the Library of Congress collection. Collie and Seale simply called these additional materials the "Family Collection." This collection is now located in the Howard Gotlieb Archival Research Center of Boston University, Boston, Mass.

This brings us to our second bright spot of previous publication that is worthy of special attention. Erroll Stafford Collie was introduced to Ervin Seale by a mutual acquaintance and they became great friends with a common interest in Quimby. Collie and Seale decided that a new publication of Quimby's writings was in order in light of the discovery of the previously unpublished materials.

In 1978, Ervin Seale formed the Quimby Memorial Church and Foundation and work was begun on a new three-volume publication of Quimby's writings. Seale and Collie were joined by Dr. Herman J. Aaftink, Founder and Director of the Quimby Foundation of Canada, as well as by Dr. William Graham of Portland, Oregon. Dr. C. Alan Anderson, a full professor of Philosophy and Religion at Curry College in Milton, Massachusetts, rounded out this group as the work of reassembling and organizing all of the Quimby materials progressed. In 1980, Alan Anderson photocopied all of the Quimby materials in Boston University and compiled a comprehensive directory or list of all of the Quimby materials in the Library of Congress, Boston University, and the Dresser family collection at the Houghton Library of Harvard University.

In a newsletter issued by the Quimby Foundation in 1984, Ervin Seale wrote in part: "There are 1739 pages of typescript in the main body of the Quimby writings. I am now working on page 1291. So the work goes on. During the summer when he is not teaching at Curry College, Dr. Alan Anderson will resume work on the Quimby material. Many times of late I have said that had I known the extent of the task, I doubt that I would have begun. But, as with any effort, it gets easier as it goes ahead."

In 1988, *Phineas Parkhurst Quimby: The Complete Writings*, began to roll off the printing presses in three hardcover volumes, but this was not before the passing of Erroll S. Collie and William Graham. Ervin Seale made his transition in 1990, and his handpicked successor to lead the Quimby Memorial Church and Foundation, Dr. Dimas R. Avila, unexpectedly died the following year.

Although *Phineas Parkhurst Quimby: The Complete Writings* was something of a "quantum leap" beyond of all previous Quimby publications in terms of its size, scope and research, there are still a few problems remaining with this publication.

In preparing for this present publication, I have gone back to the original handwritten documents that were produced by Phineas Parkhurst Quimby and his clerical assistants via photocopies and microfilmed images. During this process I have discovered–or, perhaps more accurately, rediscovered– additional Quimby writings and personally transcribed them for publication in this volume for the very first time. These articles, or "pieces" as Quimby sometimes referred to them, are designated by an asterisk (*) at the end of the title. A double asterisk (**) at the end of a title indicates a significant change or addition to previously published versions of the article found as the result of this new research.

As one part of the preparation process for this publication, the Quimby microfilms–listed as Primary Resources from the Library of Congress, Boston University, and Harvard University–were digitalized as was a photocopy collection of Quimby materials made by Alan Anderson in 1980. Next, a new master digital directory based on the microfilm frame numbers was created and cross-referenced with a full never-published directory, or list, created by Anderson.

Original titles have been restored to the articles where possible, and scattered article fragments have been returned to their proper sequential order. By cross-referencing the various versions of individual articles, the dating has been established or re-established for some of the previously undated articles.

For documentation purposes, a single microfilm frame reference number is included for each article, and the articles have been arranged in alphabetical order. In some instances, there is only a single copy of the source article, while in other instances there may be six or more copies in the various combined collections. Due to space limitations of this present volume, I have not included the newly created master digital directory of the various collections. It may be published at a later date.

Far too much has been made of P. P. Quimby's limited education. The critics of his day said he didn't understand the English language, and many of his critics of today have made this same claim. Quimby responded to his critics when he wrote the article *My Ignorance of English.*

Often overlooked by historians and scholars is a substantial collection of Phineas Parkhurst Quimby's handwritten manuscripts in the Library of Congress collection. By my count, there are two hundred eleven pages penned in his own handwriting. Due to his lack of formal institutional education,

Quimby developed his own unique phonetic "shorthand" writing style. There is an all-too-human urge to "fix" Quimby's writings. Spelling, capitalization, and punctuation protocols are largely ignored by Quimby, and this tends to make grammarians cringe.

Still, there is solid historical evidence that P. P. Quimby was a prolific writer who was inspired or, to use his term, "excited" after treating a patient and who wrote about the experience. Within this collection-within-a-collection are Quimby's original drafts of letters to patients; original drafts for many of his articles; an original draft of a letter to a newspaper editor; an original introduction for a book; examples of Quimby writing about himself from a third person perspective; and an example of Quimby's use of conversational dialogue to illustrate his particular point of view.

By contrast, I've been able to locate only three letters in the Boston University collection that are in his handwriting. Phineas Parkhurst Quimby's handwriting and spelling are distinctive and unmistakable. The writing procedure during the Portland years began with Quimby writing out his ideas and experiences in the form of a rough draft. This original version would be reviewed with one of the copyists: George Quimby, Emma Ware or Sarah Ware, and then a first copy would be made. During this first copy process, the original draft would be marked with revisions, and often as the copies were made, large sections of the original draft would be crossed out as the copyist progressed in their work. In many cases, once a first copy was completed, the original draft by Quimby's own hand was destroyed.

These first copies were then recopied for circulation among the patients as well as copied into commercially manufactured blank hardcover copybooks for preservation. These copybooks were not P. P. Quimby's personal journals as one might think of a traditional journal or diary; in fact his handwriting isn't found in any of them, nor should it be found there according to the procedure that has been described.

There are a total of eleven of these copybooks in the Library of Congress collection; there are nine in the Boston University collection; and six in the Harvard University collection.

In addition to hardcover copybooks, there are a number of handmade books and booklets in the collections of Quimby materials, such as Quimby's *Lecture Notes* and a two-booklet series of the article *The Explanation*, where George Quimby prepared Volume 1 and Emma Ware prepared Volume 2. There are also small booklets of individual articles for: *Defense Against an Accusation of Making Myself Equal to Christ* and *A Defense Against an Accusation of Putting Down Religion*, as well as several others.

Two other noteworthy patients of P. P. Quimby's should be acknowledged. They are Warren Felt Evans, a mental healer whose private healing practice and books influenced the emerging New Thought movement in the late 1800s, and Mary Baker Patterson, who would be later known to the world as Mary Baker Eddy, Founder of the Christian Science movement. A controversy erupted between some leaders and members of these two movements over the issue of originality, and we would do well to remember that Phineas Parkhurst Quimby made his transition in 1866 and is completely innocent of any participation in this controversy. In fact, the whole situation might have been avoided had he lived long enough to publish his book.

There is an inherent flaw in any complete publication of the Quimby writings in that it is most doubtful Quimby would have included everything he ever wrote in a single published book. As there was an evolution–or, to use his own word, a "progression"–of his spiritual understanding, he would most likely have discarded many of his earlier ideas or writings in favor of his best work.

My intentions throughout this publication are to:

First: Let Quimby *be* Quimby. Let us examine his writings as they are recorded.

Second: Present historically accurate, unaltered and verifiable information about Phineas Parkhurst Quimby in a single volume.

– Editor

COMMENTARY BY P. P. QUIMBY'S DESIGNATED COPYISTS

Editor's Introduction to the Articles of Commentary

The biographical article written by George A. Quimby for *The New England Magazine* in 1888, indicates that he and the "Misses Ware" (Sarah E. Ware and Emma G. Ware) were the designated copyists for Phineas Parkhurst Quimby in the Portland, Maine healing offices spanning the years of 1859 through 1865. It was their collective function to make copies of the original handwritten drafts of the articles penned by Quimby so they could be shared with the doctor's patients. In a sense, these three individuals comprised the healer's office staff, and in several letters from patients, these three people are acknowledged and greetings are extended specifically to each of them.

According to his newspaper advertisements, P. P. Quimby first began making trips into Portland, for the purpose of treating patients as early as December of 1858. It seems quite probable that he first met the Ware sisters on one of these earlier visits. Sarah and Emma Ware were the daughters of Judge Ashur Ware (1782-1873) of the United States District Court for the District of Maine, (not the United States Supreme Court as is sometimes cited.) He was nominated to that position by President James Monroe and confirmed by the United States Senate in 1822. Ashur Ware also has the distinction of being the very first Secretary of State for the State of Maine, serving in that office from 1820 to 1822. Quimby first established his healing practice in the United States Hotel and subsequently relocated to the International House Hotel, both in Portland.

A bookseller's label found in one of Miss Deering's copybooks.

Some of the other patients during Quimby's Portland years made their own copybooks that were given to George Quimby at a later time. For example, a "Miss S. M. Deering," whose later married name was "Sabine," made six of the nine commercially bound copybooks found in the Boston University collection. She was not one of P. P. Quimby's designated copyists, yet her collection of copybooks helps to date and authenticate the Quimby writings.

The commentary recorded by these three individuals is significant for a variety of reasons.

First, there was an agreement between Phineas Quimby and his son George that was very similar if not an actual formal apprenticeship contract. George traveled to Portland with his father and provided the necessary clerical and secretarial services required for the busy healing practice. In that capacity, George was deeply involved with the day-to-day operations of the office and gained valuable insight into the methodology employed by his father. George was eventually released from this formal agreement by his father. This is confirmed in a letter from George's mother, Susannah, written to Julius Dresser after Phineas Parkhurst Quimby's passing.

Next, Emma and Sarah Ware were both patients and were each personally treated by Quimby. When they began their roles as copyists for the doctor, they had frequent or perhaps daily access to him and his writings. This access began in 1859 and continued until his passing in 1866. If we were simply to combine the direct, personal experience of George, Emma and Sarah for the years of 1859 through 1865, we would have a total of twenty-one cumulative years of firsthand personal instruction by Dr. Quimby. This is significant in the study of P. P. Quimby because all three of these copyists attribute these writings to Quimby and to no one else. Through their articles and letters—and, in the case of Emma Ware, a personal testimonial—we the readers get a glimpse into the operation of Quimby's healing practice and acquire insight into some of the challenges he faced when presenting his ideas for public inspection.

Notice to the Rewriters of Phineas Parkhurst Quimby's Healing Message*

[*Editor's Note*: This unsigned and undated handwritten notice is found within the Boston University collection of Phineas Parkhurst Quimby materials at microfilm position BU 3:0476.]

This world is full of errors and it is to correct these errors that Dr. Q. cures. In writing which is merely curing on a large scale he is influenced by some particular idea which excites him to cure it (for every error has its life as much as every man) just the same as the error in a patient stimulates him to explain it–and when sitting with a patient what he says exactly fits the error of the patient and although two persons may have embraced the same error, smoking for example, yet to cure them he would talk differently to each and he would adapt what he said to each one's particular case. To bring it to a narrower illustration, suppose two patients to be possessed of the idea that it is right to pilfer. The error in the main is the same in both, but both might need a different explanation. What he says to cure them may vary so little that no one else would perceive it. It might be like the slightest possible variation of a chord in music which would require the most sensitive ear to perceive it, but it is still another idea, and so with regard to what he says to a patient, the slightest variation has its meaning applies only when it fits. And now to come back from where I started in writing, he is excited as I said at first by some particular error, whether he is conscious of it or not and what he writes about it is exactly what is wanted to correct it, so that even the turn of a sentence or the interpretation of a word has its meaning–and so I think that it is necessary that a person should be in unison with him before he is qualified to rewrite anything the Dr. is written–a person may correct it right or may correct it wrong, but he cannot tell himself as he has not the key note to which it will keep him in time and the less he alters the more likely he is to be right.

Phineas Parkhurst Quimby, by George A. Quimby

[Originally published in *The New England Magazine*, Volume 6, Issue 33, March 1888.–*Ed.*]

THE great interest evinced, during the last ten years, in the treatment of disease through the mind, and the growing desire of a large number of students of the science, and others, to know in what manner the late P. P. Quimby was connected with this principle of curing and what was his mode of treatment, has induced the writer to present, in a brief article, a sketch of the man, his life and ideas. It is not the intention to make the article other than a plain statement of facts, based on personal knowledge.

In his capacity of secretary for Mr. Quimby during the last and most active years of his profession, in which he was finishing his life's work, the writer is enabled to give a correct account of what passed during those years, and to publish, in the doctor's own words, what his ideas were.

Phineas Parkhurst Quimby was born in the town of Lebanon, N. H., February 16, 1802. When about two years of age, his parents emigrated to Maine, and settled in the town of Belfast. His father was a blacksmith, and the subject of this sketch was one of a family of seven children. Owing to his father's scanty means, and to the meagre chances for schooling, his opportunity for acquiring an education was limited. During his boyhood he attended the town school a part of the time, and acquired a brief knowledge of the rudimentary branches; but his chief education was gained in after life, from reading and observation. He always regretted his want of education, which was his misfortune, rather than any fault of his.

When he became old enough to go to work, he learned the trade of watch and clock making, and for many years after engaged in that pursuit. Later, before photography was known, he for several years made a business of taking a style of portrait picture known as daguerreotype. He had a very inventive mind, and was always interested in mechanics, philosophy, and scientific subjects. During his middle life, he invented several devices on which he obtained letters patent. He was very argumentative, and always wanted proof of anything, rather than an accepted opinion. Anything which could be demonstrated he was ready to accept; but he would combat what could not be proved with all his energy, rather than admit it as a truth.

With a mind of this combination, it is not strange that, when a gentleman visited Belfast, about the year 1838, and gave lectures and experiments in mesmerism, Mr. Quimby should feel deeply interested in the subject. Here was a new, to him at least, phenomenon; and he at once began to investigate the subject; and on every occasion when he could find a person who would allow him to try, he would endeavor to put him into a mesmeric sleep. He met with many failures, but occasionally would find a person whom he could influence.

At that time Mr. Quimby was of medium height, small in stature, his weight being about one hundred and twenty-five pounds; quick motioned and nervous, with piercing black eyes, black hair and whiskers; a well-shaped, well-balanced head; high, broad forehead, and a rather prominent nose, and a mouth indicating strength and firmness of will; persistent in what he undertook, and not easily defeated or discouraged.

In the course of his trials with subjects, he met with a young man named Lucius Burkmar, over whom he had the most wonderful influence; and it is not stating it too strongly to assert that with him he made some of the most astonishing exhibitions of mesmerism and clairvoyance that have been given in modern times.

At the beginning of these experiments, Mr. Quimby firmly believed that the phenomenon was the result of animal magnetism, and that electricity had more or less to do with it. Holding to this, he was never able to perform his experiments with satisfactory results when the "conditions" were not right, as he believed they should be.

For instance, during a thunder storm his trials would prove utter failures. If he pointed the sharp end of a steel instrument at Lucius, he would start as if pricked by a pin; but, when the blunt end was pointed toward him, he would remain unmoved.

One evening, after making some experiments with excellent results, Mr. Quimby found that during the time of the tests there had been a severe thunder storm; but, so interested was he in his experiments, he had not noticed it. This led him to further investigate the subject; and the results reached were that, instead of the subject being influenced by any atmospheric disturbance, the effects produced were brought about by the influence of one mind on another. From that time he could produce as good results during a storm as in pleasant weather, and could make his subject start by simply pointing a finger at him as well as by using a steel instrument.

PHINEAS PARKHURST QUIMBY

Mr. Quimby's manner of operating with his subject, was to sit opposite to him, holding both his hands in his, and looking him intently in the eye for a short time, when the subject would go into that state known as the mesmeric sleep, which was more properly a peculiar condition of mind and body, in which the natural senses would or would not, operate at the will of Mr. Quimby. When conducting his experiments, all communications on the part of Mr. Quimby with Lucius were mentally given, the subject replying as if spoken to aloud.

For several years, Mr. Quimby traveled with young Burkmar through Maine and New Brunswick, giving exhibitions, which at the time attracted much attention and secured notices through the columns of the newspapers.

It should be remembered that at the time Mr. Quimby was giving these exhibitions, over forty-five years ago, the phenomenon was looked upon in a far different light from that of the present day. At that time it was a deception, a fraud, and a humbug; Mr. Quimby was vilified and frequently threatened with mob violence, as the exhibitions smacked too strongly of witchcraft to suit the people.

As the subject gained more prominence, thoughtful men began to investigate the matter, and Mr. Quimby was often called upon to have his subject examine the sick. He would put Lucius into the mesmeric state, who would then examine the patient, describe his disease, and prescribe remedies for its cure.

After a time Mr. Quimby became convinced that whenever the subject examined a patient his diagnosis of the case would be identical with what either the patient himself or someone present believed, instead of Lucius really looking into the patient, and giving the true condition of the organs; in fact, that he was reading the opinion in the mind of someone, rather than stating a truth acquired by himself.

Dr. Quimby and Subject

Becoming firmly satisfied that this was the case, and having seen how one mind could influence another, and how much there was that had always been considered as true, but was merely some one's opinion, Mr. Quimby gave up his subject, Lucius, and began the developing of what is now known as mental healing, or curing disease through the mind.

In accomplishing this he spent years of his life fighting the battle alone and laboring with an energy and steadiness of purpose that shortened it many years.

To reduce his discovery to a science, which could be taught for the benefit of suffering humanity, was the all-absorbing idea of his life. To develop his "theory," or "the Truth," as he always termed it, so that others than himself could understand and practice it, was what he labored for. Had he been of a sordid and grasping nature, he might have acquired unlimited wealth; but for that he seemed to have no desire. He used to say: "Wait till I get my theory reduced to a science, so that I can teach the Truth to others, and then I can make money fast enough."

In a magazine article, it is impossible to follow the slow stages by which he reached his conclusions; for slow they were, as each step was in opposition to all the established ideas of the day, and was ridiculed and combated by the whole medical faculty and the great mass of the people. In the sick and suffering he always found staunch friends, who loved him and believed in him, and stood by him; but they were but a handful compared with those on the other side.

While engaged in his mesmeric experiments, Mr. Quimby became more and more convinced that disease was an error of the mind, and not a real thing; and in this he was misunderstood by others, and accused of attributing the sickness of the patient to the imagination, which was the very reverse of the fact. No one believed less in the imagination than he. "If a man feels a pain, he knows he feels it, and there is no imagination about it," he used to say.

But the fact that the pain might be a state of the mind, while apparent in the body, he did believe. As one can suffer in a dream all that it is possible to suffer in a waking state, so Mr. Quimby averred that the same condition of mind might operate on the body in the form of disease, and still be no more of a reality than was the dream.

As the truths of his discovery began to develop and grow in him, just in the same proportion did he begin to lose faith in the efficacy of mesmerism as a remedial agent in the cure of the sick; and after a few years he discarded it altogether.

Instead of putting the patient into a mesmeric sleep, Mr. Quimby would sit by him; and, after giving him account of what his troubles were, he would simply converse with him, and explain the causes of the troubles, and thus change the mind of the patient, and disabuse it of its errors and establish the truth in its place; which, if done, was the cure. He sometimes, in cases of lameness and sprains, manipulated the limbs of the patient, and often rubbed the head with his hands, wetting them with water. He said it was so hard for the patient to believe that his mere talk with him produced the cure, that he did this rubbing simply that the patient would have more confidence in him; but he always insisted that he possessed no "power" nor healing properties different from any one else, and that his manipulations conferred no beneficial effect upon his patient, although it was often the case that the patient himself thought they did. On the contrary, Mr. Quimby always denied emphatically that he used any mesmeric or mediumistic power.

He was always in his normal condition when engaged with his patient. He never went into any trance, and was a strong disbeliever in Spiritualism, as understood by that name. He claimed, and firmly held, that his only power consisted in his wisdom, and in his understanding the patient's case and being able to explain away the error and establish the truth, or health, in its place. Very frequently the patient could not tell how he was cured, but it did not follow that Mr. Quimby himself was ignorant of the manner in which he performed the cure.

Suppose a person should read an account of a railroad accident, and see in the list of killed a son. The shock on the mind would cause a deep feeling of sorrow on the part of the parent, and possibly a severe sickness, not only mental, but physical. Now, what is the condition of the patient? Does he imagine his trouble? Is it not real? Is his body not affected, his pulse quick, and has he not all the symptoms of a sick person, and is he not really sick? Suppose you can go and say to him that you were on the train, and saw his son alive and well after the accident, and prove to him that the report of his death was a mistake. What follows? Why, the patient's mind undergoes a change immediately, and he is no longer sick.

It was on this principle that Mr. Quimby treated the sick. He claimed that "mind was spiritual matter and could be changed;" that we were made up of "truth and error;" that "disease was an error, or belief, and that the Truth was the cure." And upon these premises he based all his reasoning, and laid the foundation of what he asserted to be the "science of curing the sick" without other remedial agencies than the mind.

In the year 1859 Mr. Quimby went to Portland, where he remained until the summer of 1865, treating the sick by his peculiar method. It was his custom to converse at length with many of his patients, who became interested in his method of treatment, and to try to unfold to them his ideas.

Among his earlier patients in Portland were the Misses Ware, daughters of the late Judge Ashur Ware, of the U.S. [District] Court; and they became much interested in "the Truth," as he called it. But the ideas were so new, and his reasoning was so divergent from the popular conceptions, that they found it difficult to follow him or remember all he said; and they suggested to him the propriety of putting into writing the body of his thoughts.

From that time he began to write out his ideas, which practice he continued until his death, the articles now being in the possession of the writer of this sketch. The original copy he would give to the Misses Ware, and it would be read to him by them; and, if he suggested any alteration, it would be made, after which it would be copied either by the Misses Ware or the writer of this and then re-read to him, that he might see that all was just as he intended it. Not even the most trivial word or the construction of a sentence would be changed without consulting him. He was given to repetition, and it was with difficulty that he could be induced to have a repeated sentence or phrase stricken out, as he would say, "If that idea is a good one and true, it will do no harm to have it in two or three times." He believed in the hammering process, and of throwing an idea or truth at the reader till it would be firmly fixed in his mind.

The first article he wrote was entitled, "Mind is Spiritual Matter," and he thus explains what he means: He says: "I found that I could change the mind of my patient, and produce thereby a chemical change in the body * * * The world makes mind intelligence. I put no intelligence in it, but make it subject to intelligence. * * * I call the power that governs the mind, spirit, in this piece, not using the word *wisdom*; but you will see that I recognize a wisdom superior to the word *mind*, for I always apply the word *mind* to matter, but never to the first cause."

In a circular to the sick, which he distributed while in Portland, he says that, as "my practice is unlike all other medical practice, it is necessary to say that I give no medicines and make no outward applications, but simply sit by the patient, tell him what he thinks is his disease, and my explanation is the cure. And if I succeed in correcting his errors, I change the fluids of the system, and establish the truth, or health. *The truth is the cure.*"

In an article over his own signature, published in the Portland Advertiser of February 13, 1862, he says:-

"As you have given me the privilege of answering an article in your paper of the 11th inst., wherein you classed me with spiritualists, mesmerizers, clairvoyants, etc., I take this occasion to state where I differ from all classes of doctors, from the allopathic physician to the healing medium. All of these admit disease as an independent enemy of mankind. * * * Now, I deny disease as a truth, but admit it as a deception, without any foundation, handed down from generation to generation, till the people believe it, and it has become a part of their lives. * * * My way of curing convinces him that he has been deceived; and, if I succeed, the patient is cured. My mode is entirely original."

Mr. Quimby, although not belonging to any church or sect, had a deeply religious nature, holding firmly to God as the first cause, and fully believing in immortality and progression after death, though entertaining entirely original conceptions of what death is. He believed that Jesus' mission was to the sick, and that he performed His cures in a scientific manner, and perfectly understood how He did them. Mr. Quimby was a great reader of the Bible, but put a construction upon it thoroughly in harmony with his train of thought.

His greatest desire was that the writer of this sketch should become interested in his work, and learn to heal the sick as he did. He always asserted that it was a science that he could teach, but that, if it were not communicated by him, others would take up the work and complete it. He wished the writer, after becoming conversant with the principles by which he cured, to fit himself for the lecture platform, and, as he expressed it, "You lecture, and then we will call the sick on the stage, and cure them by wholesale, right in public."

It may not be out of place to state here that the writer did not attempt to learn to practice as Mr. Quimby did; not because he could not, but for the reason that he was not at that time interested in the matter, and his tastes led him to adopt other pursuits.

Mr. Quimby's idea of happiness was to benefit mankind, especially the sick and suffering; and to that end he labored, and gave his life and strength. His patients not only found in him a doctor, but a sympathizing friend, and he took the same interest in treating a charity patient that he did a wealthy one. Until the writer went with him as secretary, he kept no accounts and made no charges. He left the keeping of books entirely with his patients; and although he pretended to have a regular price for visits and attendance, he took at settlement whatever the patient chose to pay him.

The last five years of his life were exceptionally hard. He was overcrowded with patients, and greatly overworked, and could not seem to find an opportunity for relaxation. At last, nature could no longer bear up under the strain; and, completely tired out, he took to his bed, from which he never rose again. While strong, he had always been able to ward off any disease that would have affected another person; but, when tired out and weak, he no longer had the strength of will nor the reasoning powers to combat the sickness which terminated his life.

An hour before he breathed his last, he said to the writer: "I am more than ever convinced of the truth of my theory. I am perfectly willing for the change myself, but I know you all will feel badly, and think I am dead; but I know that I shall be right here with you, just as I always have been. I do not dread the change any more than if I were going on a trip to Philadelphia."

His death occurred January 16, 1866, at his residence in Belfast, at the age of sixty-four years, and was the result of too close application to his profession and of overwork. A more fitting epitaph could not be accorded him than in these words:–

"Greater love hath no man than this, that a man lay down his life for his friends." For if ever a man did lay down his life for others, that man was PHINEAS PARKHURST QUIMBY.

Phineas P. Quimby's Theory, by George A. Quimby*

[*Editor's Note*: This untitled and unsigned article appears to be in George Quimby's handwriting and is found on the Boston University microfilm at designation BU 3:0423.]

A theory is the explanation of some phenomenon, science or discovery, and with it the author endeavors to enlighten the public and demonstrate clearly his truth. It is generally supposed that a theory explains itself. In most cases it does—yet in other either owing to the author not clearly defining his position—or to the fact that the subject to be explained is in direct opposition to the preconceived ideas of the world, in such cases it becomes necessary that the theory as well as the subject of which it treats should be explained if such a thing is possible.

We have in our midst a person who professes to cure the sick by an entirely new process, and in order to explain his process he has worked out a theory which to him is so plain, that because it cannot be readily understood, and its application to the sick be seen by others, that he is often led to believe that there is but little wisdom in mankind in general and that the minds of the few who can understand are very obtuse, at least in regard to the subject.

Having been brought up under this person's immediate eye, the writer professes in his humble way, to elucidate if possible some points of the theory in question. He has a difficult task for though reared when he has received the very droppings of the sanctuary, yet he has proved obstinate so far as understanding and believing the length and breadth of this singular doctrine. He can only account for it by stating that the "ills that flesh is heir to" never laid their hands on him in any very violent manner, therefore personally by experience he knows little about disease. He has also read that "they that are well need no physician" and being a very practical young man he cannot see why the well should understand the medical theories, if they have no need of their practice.

As the writer proposes to try and explain something of the new theory, he will commence by stating that according to this theory, nearly everything we believe such as the belief in Life, Death, and Disease as a reality is wrong, in fact it does not admit their existence at all only as an idea. It admits Wisdom and Truth as eternal principles and to them there is no Life, Death or Disease. It affirms that everything which comes within our senses which does not conflict with our health or happiness was spoken into existence by Wisdom, as for instance the world, for some wise purpose, and that everything which does conflict with our health and happiness was spoken into existence or created by man. As Disease comes in conflict with health let us see: What is Disease? It is the effect of a combination of false ideas, distilled into a belief, then refined in to what man believes to be a truth and then being labeled with its name and kind is thrown into the hungry mind of the people, where it is eagerly devoured. When the patient is told this and that they are themselves the authors of this disease they often exclaim with a surprised look that they positively never thought about it till it came to them. Of course they did not, no one disputes this, but the idea of disease was in the world and they with everyone else admitted it and therefore are liable to suffer from it. If they could have known exactly what disease was and how it was liable to affect persons, does anyone suppose he would have been a victim to it? Suppose a person rises in his sleep and unconsciously burns his finger and on waking discovers a sore on it. Would he not be liable to reason as to how the sore came there? Suppose he repeats the apparition several times burning him in different places and failing to discover the cause is fully satisfied it is a humor. After he firmly believes it to be a humor he has then got himself in a position where he can create humors independent of his burns, and be liable to be affected by it. Now to convince him of this, he has really created humors by his own belief, is to prove to him that he first burned his arm and then by his excitement and his belief in humors created in his own system what is called humor, which appeared visibly in his body.

It is an undisputable fact that we can produce apparent effects on our body by means of our belief and will. When excited, angry, or frustrated, we blush or turn pale. When sad we shed tears, which we certainly create ourselves and which are tangible realities. Thoughts, ideas, beliefs, opinion, etc. are like the atmosphere, which affects us in many ways. We go out into the open air and are soon overpowered with heat. Again we go out and are chilled through. Again and we are dampened by dew. Now the causes of these effects are not visible to our senses, yet we admit them and are aware of their effects on us. All disease is made by the belief, but not necessarily our own. God or Wisdom never made disease, for everything God made he named and pronounced good. If He did not make it, then man must have been its author, and created it out of his own ideas. Disease is an effect. Remove the cause and you destroy the disease, as removing the substance destroys the shadow. Allowing disease to be caused by the belief, where then is it located in man? The cause is our mind, the effect is our body. It acts as a looking glass in our minds reflecting everything placed before it, over all parts of the body. "But you think I imagine my trouble," is the patient's cry. Let us see if this theory admits of any such construction. It distinctly says, "Every person is to himself just what he thinks he is." This is one of its fundamental rules or cornerstones and clearly puts down such an accusation for if the patient imagines a pain as he says, being to himself just what he thinks he is of course he has the pain and no sensible person will deny it. Again it says, "Everything is to a person just what he thinks it is," but it does not necessarily follow that the person is always correct in his thoughts. Many a man takes a counterfeit bill for a good one and it is good to him till he discovers his mistake. It is in the principle of detecting the false from the real that his theory treats, and its author cures. He is as it were a counterfeit detector and he takes the patient's bills or feelings into his bank or wisdom and shows him where he has been cheated and endeavors to explain to him, how in future, he can tell himself, the good bills from the spurious.

When he sits by a patient he is immediately placed in possession of all their feelings, aches and pains, and here let me say, that this peculiarity is not a "gift," but has been gradually acquired by him, in his twenty-odd years of intercourse with the sick, till he is now so sensitive to others' feelings and thoughts, that he can describe them far better than they can themselves. Now from whence did he receive their feelings? They were merely the reflection of the patient's on him, and those of the patient's were either reflected from another, else were reflected from their own ideas. Where now is the difference between him and his patients? It is just here. He knows the feelings were shadows, as it were, and all he has to do to rid himself of them, is to destroy the object reflected or step aside so the shadow is no longer reflected on him and then he is no longer affected by them. The case of the patient is different, he knows not what the feelings are, he cannot escape from them neither can he destroy them. He is looking outside of himself for the cause of his trouble when it is in his belief, to which fact he does not know. Now he can be cured by being more aware of the cause of his trouble, which is done by reasoning and illustrations applicable to his particular case, and when he is convinced as to the truth of the reasoning, then he is cured and the great battle won though there may still be some guerilla fighting for a while. This is a rough explanation of treating the sick according to this theory, but it is impossible in one short article to give even a bird's eye view of what has been the results of twenty five years' study, though it may have thrown a little light upon the subject. In conclusion this article will give a few points which are the foundations of this particular theory. viz. That man is made up of truth, errors, beliefs, opinions and is governed by that which has the strongest foothold in him, that disease is the effect of a belief, the phenomena being visible in the body while the cause is located in the mind—that man is to himself just what he thinks he is and that things are to him just what he thinks they are, consequently there can be no such thing as imagination—that the cure is made by removing the cause of the disease which is done by reasoning and explaining to the patient how he is affected by his belief and that outside of the belief there is no such thing as disease. By keeping these points in view the reader will be better able to appreciate and understand this theory.

It is hoped by the author that the time is not far distant when not only the expounders will be able to make themselves better understood, but that the people will be better able to understand the ideas they advanced. Therefore till that long wished for time shall arise:

"Let us then be up and doing
With a heart for any fate—
Still achieving, still pursuing
Learn to labor and to wait."

The Conversion of Emma G. Ware to P. P. Quimby's Metaphysical Theory*

[*Editor's Note*: This untitled and unsigned testimonial is found within the Boston University microfilm of Phineas Parkhurst Quimby materials at BU 3:0650. The handwriting appears to match that of Emma G. Ware, one of the copyists in P. P. Quimby's offices in Portland, Maine during the years 1859-1865. It is fascinating to read her personal account of her own transformation from a most obstinate patient into one of Phineas Parkhurst Quimby's most ardent and loyal lifetime supporters.]

The first impression a patient receives of Dr. Quimby is often of the bitterest opposition to him. They feel ready to denounce him as an imposter and an infidel, and should they give expression to their feelings they would spare no language in abusing him. This may continue a longer or shorter time, but if they remain under him, they invariably find their repugnance diminish and learn to respect and like him as much as they disliked him at first. This arises from the startling and novel nature of his ideas striking upon minds moulded by education to which the learning of all ages has contributed. Some of his statements seem self contradicting and certainly make him appear assuming, while the arguments by which he undertakes to prove them are absurd and nothing to the point. Pursue him with a few questions and he flies off into the realm of things incomprehensible by human understanding as fast as words can carry him: confidence only gives him here a superiority over you and he silences but does not convince and only confuses you: He opposes with the utmost audacity every idea and opinion which constitute the sum and substance of your character, and you find yourself shaken from the foundation in matters where the wisest have never doubted, even the evidence of your senses goes with the general crash and ruin of all things. All this frequently creates an aversion too strong for language to describe, for who creates all this disturbance,–"An uneducated and unlettered man." This was my experience. I was sick. I suffered in my body. I had always employed the most intelligent physicians and I believed they understood the nature of my disease. I certainly understood it myself. I was unfortunate in never finding permanent relief from any source and I could not see that there was any for me.

When I first called Dr. Quimby I had lost all idea of ever being well again: but I did not like to suffer: I thought that he might relieve me from present suffering, but I was utterly faithless and hopeless that I should ever be well.

For some time after he first visited me I heard nothing of his strange talk and only considered him an honest, kind hearted man of great simplicity of character. I felt no aversion to him more than to anyone else, and I did not listen to what he said. At the end of a fortnight he produced a great change in me. I was able to walk down stairs which in my state was a miracle, at least it was such to my friends and myself. Then I began to grow stronger and to take notice of my doctor who had done all this for me: First I began to apologize to myself and invent reasons to satisfy my friends for keeping under his care. After hearing him account for disease in his principles of belief, I thought he was a harmless theorist embracing a very small range of facts and of course very ignorant of the true nature of disease. But when he classed my case with his category of complaints and said my disease was in my mind, I lost all patience and respect for him and his persisting in his forceful diagnosis gave me a great repugnance to him and I almost concluded not to remain under him anymore. But he was my only hope and as he had helped me when I knew nothing of his theory, I was obliged as it were to continue with him. So I concluded to get the benefit of his treatment and swallow the unpleasant pill of his remarks, determined not to listen to him.

So when he launched forth in argument and illustration on some metaphysical impracticability talking as though he had not come to doctor my body, but change my mind, I would remind him of the presence of my bodily suffering and tell him that I wish he would not talk but cure. As long as I continued to fling in his face the suffering which I hoped he would relieve, so long he continued his strange and incomprehensible talk: roused by his pertinacity I would try to bring him to do the business for which I employed him, by telling him to cease his talk and cure my foot.

Determined not to be deceived by any sophistry of argument or cunning invention of imagination, I would pay no attention to his arguments and illustration to make me think my trouble was not in my body. I accused him of trying to deceive me by fallacies adroitly presented and skillfully concealed into the belief that I was well and that when I got out I should be laughed at for being weak enough to believe his story, or still worse that he was keeping me along with his fanciful inventions for his own interests meanwhile I might; or might not get well. With all this fermenting in my mind, added to the constant dissatisfaction his talk always produced, I was so completely embittered against him, that I resisted the small symptoms of improvement that I felt conscious of, and refused to see gain which I afterwards found must have been going on, in fact I complained to him all the time that he might see he had not succeeded in curing me, however well he had done for others: All the while he had been patient, always pleasant and never ruffled by my repeated complaints that he didn't cure me any faster, perfectly attentive and respectful–in fact when not sitting with me,–extremely cheerful, entertaining and friendly as his patients always find him. Finally one day I came to the conclusion I must be a very unpleasant patient, and that if I remained under his care forever, I never would utter a complaint again to him. That if he did not cure me, I was sufficiently gratified for what he had done and that I had never expected to be worth anything, so it was no fault of his if I did not get well. So I gave up all idea of being cured and went to him as the spirits moved.

I now began to listen to what he said with as much attention as I would to anything else. Under this state of mind I began to see that he had a key to the knowledge of my past and present life, enabling him to see how much I must really suffer from causes of which I was as ignorant as I was innocent. They were actual misery which I should never think of expressing in words or blaming any particular thing as their origin. They had so long been with me that I came to consider them peculiarities of my disposition which it was impossible to account for or change. No one but myself knew them and could not know them for I never said anything about them to any living person: He knew the secret and real state of my misery and knew that it was eternal with me, and founded on such laws of nature and society that it could never be changed. He knew what tormented my soul and kept my life a prolonged existence of wretchedness, by sympathy, which purity and charity had rendered sensitive to such feelings in the sick and which those same simple qualities had enabled to carry to a fountain of wisdom superior to man's reason, that would wash away all such stains and purify the heart of man. To him belongs the credit of discovering the source of all misery which cannot be helped nor cured by man, and which is an everlasting clog to his happiness and progress, so his effect on the sick is new, exciting and effective. They all have their life of misery which he can bring to light and which is so common that it is only the sadder.

He proclaims a principle to the sick whose fruits are eternal happiness and shows them the wretched hollowness of their own lives, he feels the continual deception and disappointments which have brought them to their present state of utter hopelessness and degradation and he also reveals the shame and hypocrisy in the world which have thus deceived and destroyed them. In fact he enters the real Spiritual world in which they live their miserable lives, shows what it is made of and how it affects their natural life. So he lifts man out of his error where he is confined, a guiltless criminal–to the world where the seed of his bodily disease was sown and nurtured, which is rank with such vegetation, and shows that this world is in the lines of his mouth and meditations of his heart all unknown.

Extract of a Letter, by Emma G. Ware*

[*Editor's Note*: "About P. P. Q." has been added in red ink at the top of this extract of a letter that appears to be in the handwriting of Emma G. Ware and is found at microfilm designation BU 3:0422.]

In asking my advice as to what you had better do about your father, you place me in a delicate position, one which I fear I cannot fill, but I will try and tell you what I know of the Drs. treatment. In the first place let me say it is unquestionably certain that Dr. Quimby can cure your father. Christ says, "Come unto me all ye who labor and are heavy laden and I will give you rest." This is a general invitation with a promise. Dr. Q. professes to heal by the same unusual God-given truth, but as it is manifested through him to an unbelieving world, under the dynasty of dollars and cents, it is encumbered by various obstacles which prevent it from operating freely and also from being received as truth. Therefore it cannot be predicated of him whether he can or cannot cure any individual case. If you fully realize that his Science was an emanation from the divine wisdom as all Sciences are, you would not seek opinion or advice, you would be guided by the truth, but without that knowledge you require some signal or word of promise from me to give you confidence how to act. If I should say "come, the doctor can cure him," that would not make the thing sure, neither would it, if he said so himself, it would be placing the responsibility on one person's opinion. The cure is made by the operation of a higher principle than usually enters into our acts and which is only brought out in times of great relation and inspiration of soul. The wisdom he practices is from God and will heal all those who seek it in spirit and in truth, but the fact of being healed depends much on the outward conditions under which relief is sought. If the patient doubts, the doubt must be overcome and the same with the Doctor.

If there are prejudices, opinions, or circumstances standing between the sick and the loving truth they must be removed. So you see it is the work of ridding oneself of superstition and fear and casting oneself wholly on the truth. We are told to "Seek the kingdom of heaven first of all," but it is hard to divest oneself of every garment of belief, trusting to our faith, in God. When a ship first sets sail, the owner requires a promise on the part of the captain that he will make a successful voyage, or even that he will come back, for he knows that the captains knowledge will not circumscribe such a promise, but he knows that the science of Navigation will conduct the ship safely through her perilous voyage and he has confidence in the captain's knowledge of navigation. The Science of medicine does not stand on that solid and sound basis. So that we have been taught to depend on opinions for good or evil instead of principles that will guide the sick to a safe harbor. Dr. Q's treatment is derived from wisdom superior to himself, as the principles of navigation are superior to ordinary guess work, and he lets his works rest on that basis. Therefore if patients get uneasy and want to go home, he will not in word or thought coax them to stay, but rather urge their going, for in the former case he may be accused of selfishness. He will not compound with unbelief, but stand or fall by his works.

Phineas Parkhurst Quimby's Writings, by Emma G. Ware

[*Editor's Note*: "Emma's–Not by P. P. Q." is written across the top of this originally untitled article. It is located on the Boston University microfilm at designation BU 3:1230.]

Dr. Quimby's writings abound with statements made in direct contradiction to facts which we all know to be true. If not placed in the right light, by someone who sees and partially understands the truth he teaches, these will so shock the reader by their gross absurdity, that he will cast them by, as wanting in veracity and reason. The doctor writes upon disease, its cause and its cure, and he stands upon ground never before occupied by any man, who has ever treated on this subject. Hence he is alone and has the world against him, but in all he says he always retains the ground and this ought frequently to be brought before the reader, for otherwise he will be confused and read the statements as though they were made by a man standing with the world, and accordingly they will sound unreasonable and absurd.

Dr. Quimby says that man is a being of intelligence, made in the image of God and progressing in wisdom. This is what all admit in one sense, but here is where he differs from all men who acknowledge this belief, he carries it out in his treatment of the sick. With him the body is not sick, it is the man who is in trouble, and the man is an intellectual creature, capable of providing for his own health and happiness.

His arguments and his reasoning are all addressed to this man, and the principle of his treatment is to show him the error by which he has been defrauded of the knowledge and the power of providing for his health and happiness. In doing this he comes in mortal conflict with another man, whom the world has made, one who believes that he is the result of organized matter, and that he is born to disease and death. He is well known in society, popular, educated and religious. With him the Dr. is in open conflict on every question relating to his health and happiness, and the cure of the patient comes from the contest, with this man whom society has made, in which the Dr. is victorious. If he is conquered then he loses the case. This accounts for the discussions he frequently holds with his patients when he takes a ground which the sick have never heard argued and which seem full of fanciful whims and absurd inconsistencies. It also accounts for the feeling of opposition amounting to repugnance, which many of his patients experience when he touches their personal feelings on religion, or in the matter of disease. A few words in explanation of this feeling, otherwise the construction put upon his words would render him an unwise man. As I said he comes to the man of error, not to appease and conciliate, but to conquer and destroy him, and reinstate the man of intelligence in his possessions.

Therefore he stands to the sick, as the Union Army stands to the South, determined to kill secession and restore the Union, and he fights on the same principle, to destroy the disease and save the man. The battle must be a hard one and the conflict hot. Learning the facts of disease, and standing on the ground that man is an intelligence and the body is only the shadow, he travels through a domain that has been given up to mystery and brings health and deliverance to the sick. The relation of the substance to the shadow, and the connection between the mind and body have never been determined by the wisest.

In the matter of disease, he contends that he has solved this problem. He affirms that what he says is true and that he can prove it so to the sick. He never doctors the body. There are many, of course, who can see nothing but blasphemy and falsehood in his mode of procedure, and such would naturally have a feeling of repulsion towards one, whom they believed to be deceiving them. Others however who are fond of reasoning can see that what he says is no worn out humbug; and that he is striving to develop a truth which will emancipate the world from disease.

Another statement he makes [Article abruptly stops here. –*Ed*.]

Booklet of Articles and Letters of P. P. Quimby and Sarah E. Ware*

[*Editor's Note*: Microfilm images of this small booklet are found beginning at designation BU 3:0318 of the Boston University collection of Quimby materials. The handwriting throughout this booklet appears to be that of Sarah E. Ware. Horatio W. Dresser quoted portions of this booklet in his 1921 publication *The Quimby Manuscripts*. I have transcribed and reproduced the booklet here in its entirety.]

I

How does mind produce disease? In the progress of intelligence, men have only arrived at the question, how does mind affect disease? That it affects it more or less is admitted by all, but how far and in what way has never been explained. The connection between mind and body, and their relation to each other has always been a mystery,–its only solution–death. And what is death but a mystery. No one has ever returned to tell us what and where they are and every desire to pierce beyond the veil, and throw some light on the mystery of our future existence, returns baffled and disappointed. From the earliest ages, supernatural phenomena have from time to time occurred, and many individual experiences are upon record, remarkable in themselves, and those experiencing them often satisfactory. Spiritualism though embracing more among its advocates than any other belief, is yet satisfactory to comparatively but very few, and no explanation has ever been offered, which commends itself alike to our reason and common sense, as well as fills the unsatisfied want of our higher nature.

Nov. 1859

II

An individual may be divided into three component parts–soul, intellect and character. Our idea of soul is undefined. We admit it to be the highest part of man's nature, and according as a person exhibits spirituality, which is, according to our best understanding of it, a vague desire and insight into spiritual things, we say he has soul. It is a distinct quality, a separate ingredient, independent for its existence on any part of our nature, though it may be repressed and hidden, or expanded and new beauties unfolded, by our lives. The intellect has its seat in the brain. It is purely the action of a certain class of thoughts. Perhaps all thoughts may be of an intellectual character up to a certain point, but beyond that, we say that they are spiritual, - and that is something entirely different.–The character is distinct from both the above. A person may have character without any uncommon amount of soul or intellect. Character is composed of different attributes, all contributing to its increase, though not all necessary to its existence. Perhaps the most important element is determination. Energy, caution, integrity, judgment (though that is more or less of an intellectual nature), in fact all the moral qualities go to make it up. The affections, I cannot locate, though we all know that they belong to the higher part of our nature, but we often see a person very affectionate, whom we never should think of investing with either soul, intellect or character, beyond that common plane which is the part of humanity.–Dogs have affection, apparently of the same nature of our own. I have tried in the above to describe an individual according to the commonly received ideas.–an individual described according to the new ideas would be very different.

Aug. 1860

III What is disease?

The Spiritual world is the reality. The Spiritual man is the man, the only man who thinks, acts, or has life. Man, in the beginning, is a more Spiritual germ, and as such, is incapable of action. He is simply the principle of life. But life, of itself, is only the fact of existence–a simple truth and nothing more. It is necessary that that should be applied to matter or error in order that more life or science (or our self) should be derived from it. This is done by the force of circumstances.

God is the first great cause of everything, the answer of every question, the truth of every problem. For reasons best known to himself, he made man, made him in his own image, male and female, created he them. The material world is consistent with the natural man, and a necessary condition, as I have said before, in order to develop science. Now, to begin with our natural existence, as we call it, is diseases and when we die scientifically, we obtain the answer to it. Disease of the body, as we call it, is error, and all error is disease. So you see there are various kinds. In the early ages, mankind was in a more natural state, and there was less disease of any kind, for the reason that there was less activity. From generation to generation; the accumulation of knowledge, false and true increased, and accordingly men thought more and more.

Disease of the body was an invention of man, originally a simple humbug, designed to deceive the people. Finally the leaders like all ignorant and superstitious men, were frightened at their own shadow, and thus disease took an identity. A character was attributed to it and it was invested with power, to destroy.

This is the same disease that with strength, accumulated by its success for ages, now talks around the world, seeking whom it may devour. More misery is caused by this devil than by any other. It divides itself into numberless branches, each branch partaking of all the characteristics of the original tree.

Aug. 1860

IV Continued.

Mind is matter, ideas are mind, hence, ideas are matter. Men create ideas which are matter. These ideas have a real existence in the spirit world, and just according to the nature that is attributed to them and the fear that men have of them, their power is.

Fear of an idea thus created, on the part of its creator, condenses into matter so that it might be seen even by the natural eye–a creation, composed of the loathsome characteristics conceived of by the person's own [belief], an offspring of an excited and degraded mind. Such an idea is disease, the child of the Devil. This disease was first one simple, uncompounded idea, but when that finally was pushed into an identity, when men were once afraid of it, then it grew rapidly, like a poisonous weed, and derived its sustenance from the very life blood to which it owed its existence. All its horrible characteristics it draws from the mind of men; who could they only understand what they are doing, would plant a good seed in their soil or mind which could bear no fruit fit for disease to live on,–and thus it would starve to death.

Its characteristics embrace those most fearful to mankind. It has cruelty–for is not pain cruel? It is vengeful–for if we break a law which this devil has set up, will it not take its revenge? It is insidious, like a serpent, and has enveloped us in its coils and planted its sting in our hearts, before we are aware of its presence.

Then the venom courses through our veins and gradually it cuts every tie which could bind us to our friends and happiness and at last drags its victim down to the jaws of death, where the blackness of eternal midnight awaits him.

But mind is matter, and its form can be annihilated–To understand ourselves, what we are composed of and how we act, is not an easy task after man has gone so far astray.–but it can be understood and will be, now that we have sifted out old ideas, and found that there is no virtue in them.

Sept. [18]60

V Extract from a letter.

You want me to write about Dr. Q. It is very hard to give any one any idea of him. Particularly a person who has never seen him. The basis of his theory is that there is no intelligence, no power or action in matter of itself–that the Spiritual world to which our eyes are closed by ignorance or unbelief, is the real world, that in it lie all the causes for every effect visible in the natural world, and that if this spiritual life can be revealed to us, in other words if we can understand ourselves, that we shall then have our happiness or misery in our own hands,–and of course much of the suffering in the world will be done away with. Disease causes more misery than any other one thing, and he applies his knowledge of human nature, and life and matter to the curing of it. He is the cause of much happiness among individuals, as his life is devoted to the relief of suffering, but unless his principles can be made known so that they can be applied by other persons and on a larger scale of course, the good he does must be very limited. This is his object and may he succeed.

Nov. 1860

VI Extract from a letter.

–and if you do not receive satisfaction on the thousand and one dark points, do not blame the theory which you think cannot embrace them, but the expounder who is unworthy of the cause. You must know to begin with, that when Dr. Q. makes such an assertion as this, that there is no power in medicine, he involves then his knowledge of mind and matter which he has gained by years of intense and conscientious labor. I hardly know how to make this seem reasonable to you, except to give the general basis of the whole theory, viz. That there is no power in matter of itself. That assertion when first presented many would not deny, but when it is carried out then we find that it clashes with our commonly received opinions. He does not deny that cures so many and great as you please to claim, have taken, and are still taking place under the old belief, but that they were brought about by the inherent efficacy of the medicine itself, he does deny, and this he stands ready to prove.–You say that to carry out his ideas, we may live till we dry up and blow away. Admitting that what he claims is true, that he has discovered the principle of life and the secret of happiness, if the unhappiness that is in the world now is caused by ignorance of this, we know very well that it will take one long time to even start people in the right direction, and we need not meddle with the time when we are going to dry up and blow away, or live without eating. It is only satisfactory to carry these principles out into the region of pure speculation, to show that they are capable of it, and that he is not afraid to, but, such ideas as those of course have nothing to do with practical life.–are of no consequence any way. What we aim at, is merely to correct some of the errors of our own time and to give to the world the principle.–it may be left to future ages to be carried perhaps beyond our present conceptions. It is the basis only that we want–We say that there is no such thing as disease. This assertion involves the question what is disease?

It may be defined; a disarrangement of the bodily organs. The possibility of this of course, he admits, but it is in the cause of this effect wherein he differs from all others. Drs. consider the cause of disease to lie in the body, while he does not. The trouble lies here. Drs. have set up a standard of right and wrong with regard to health and have made the people accept and believe it, and now disease comes from the belief in this. Our happiness or misery is the effect of our belief, and when our belief embraces disease, we must be liable to it. Consumption will be in the world as long as people are under their present rules, but when they come to understand that matter is nothing of itself, except it be used by mind, and everything that is embraced in this, then consumption will be no longer in existence.

_____ It is so hard to talk about it before the science is admitted. Let that once be admitted as thousands of unworthy theories are, and then it is easy enough to talk. But the whole thing sounds so visionary and imaginative from it being so new and entirely unheard of, that it is very hard to put it into reasonable sounding shape. It is nothing more nor less than the Christian Religion rendered intelligent by being revealed as a Science. Everybody knows that religion, as it goes now, is not worth a straw, that is, the system. Each one may invent something which answers the purpose for himself, by which he can regulate his life and which will satisfy his cravings, but that is the reward of his own labors,–no thanks to any system. No one taught it all to him and he can teach it to no one. Religion has never been taught scientifically.

Nov. 1860

Happiness is not dependent on externals, but lies within us, and is the consciousness of keeping our loftier impulses free from contamination and revealing in our acts, a strength, which arises from uncorrupted motives–

[VII] Extract from a letter.

Dr. Q. believes that Jesus was a man just like any other man and that the Christ was wherein he differs from others.

That Christ was the name of the religion he taught, and it was in his religion that he was superior to other men. This religion was a science and I want you to be sure and understand what I mean to convey by applying that term to religion. It is simply this, that our nature is explained to us and the problem of life solved as that by means of this knowledge we shall be able to be happy and good.–which according to the present condition of society, physically and morally, religion does not seem to have done as yet. (Extract from Vol. IV. Chap I.) I hope that these everlasting quotations have conveyed to you the important idea that the spiritual life, which comes as near to what we call soul as anything is the reality, the substance. –that this soul is God or Christ and that it is knowledge. That is eternal and is all that is eternal. Hence we know ourselves and just what there is of us and can make as much of ourselves as we please. Dr. Q. applies these ideas to the errors of the world and one of the greatest is disease. And if man can be convinced that disease is an error and can have the way to truth or health pointed out, he certainly will be willing to take it.

…. A sick person is and must be unhappy. People talk about the elevating influence of suffering, the purifying effect of long sickness, but it is all a humbug. Any invalid is glad to get well, and if they are as happy and it is a direct blessing from God, why had they not rather stay so.

No one knows but the invalid himself of the wretchedness, hopelessness and disappointment of his life and when he finally becomes so hardened as it were, that he thinks himself happy in his misfortune and blesses the Lord for his disciplines; he has completed the degradation to which his disease has led him.

Feb. 1861

[VIII] Extract from a letter.

According to him, disease is the effect of a wrong direction given to the mind. Unhappiness is its handmaid, and constantly feeds the flame which is devouring you. Countless unsatisfied desires and unanswerable questions come thronging in upon you bewildering and overwhelming sometimes casting a gleam of light and hope, but oftener leaving you in greater darkness and discouragement than before. You have given me the questions which suggest themselves to you by your condition. Your mind is disturbed on this subject, and from not understanding the true answer to those questions, but from receiving other people's opinions and explanations about them arises all your trouble. Now according to the "truth", if I can answer them scientifically to your satisfaction, then your mind is at rest. Your system becomes quiet and health is restored. But you must not expect me to answer them all fully. That would be impossible now, for it would take a volume since you cover the whole ground. The best I can do is to give a general answer to them all, and then any questions which suggest themselves to you with regard to any particular application, I should be very glad to have. I will try to do the best I can and if I do not throw any light it is because I do not understand Dr. Q's theory as well as I think I do.

First you ask whether there is any knowledge, which if you had possessed it, would have prevented your sickness? Of course I answer, yes. Again you ask, is it different from any of the established rules of taking care of yourself etc.? Yes, entirely so. Now you say you don't understand anything about it, and want it explained. To begin with, you say you have taken all these colds this winter and inquire how their existence is dependent on our belief of them when they are right before your eyes. Now here is the first mistake. You assume too much. You admit to begin with, the existence of the disease, which he, in the sense which you understand it, at once denies. His explanation of this must be given of course, or that assertion has no weight and that I will now try to give. He says that "mind is matter". By this he does not mean that matter which is visible to the natural eye, but a spiritual matter, which like material matter can be changed into any form which a person chooses. This mind or matter surrounds every person and contains an expression of character. You know how often in sitting down by a person and have different impressions, for instance, we say, such a person is disagreeable, another is gentle, a third is selfish etc., and these impressions we have without being able to account for them in any way to ourselves or others. We should have had the same if we had been blind. Now that which we perceive without the aid of the natural senses, is the mind; or spiritual matter, or atmosphere, or vapor, or whatever you choose to call it, that surrounds everyone and is an index of character. This is what we come in contact with in our intercourse with men and through this medium we influence others and are influenced ourselves. It contains opinions, thoughts and everything in us which can be changed. What we <u>know</u> we have no opinion about, <u>that</u> is eternal and never can be changed, but what we do not know, if we have ever been excited on the subject, we have some opinion or belief about, and that opinion or belief may be the cause of unhappiness.

Some opinions do not affect us in any way. For example, 999 out of 1000 believe or have the opinion that the earth revolves. They have never proved it, but admit it, because it is an established fact. They embrace it as an opinion, for to them it is one, since they cannot prove it, but it causes no happiness or misery, has no effect any way. But suppose any one should tell you, and you believed, that the earth would stop its revolution at a certain time, –that opinion would have a bad effect. It would excite you, make you nervous, so much so that perhaps you would leave your skin before the time came. Now when you are laboring under this excitement and fear, lest the earth should stop its revolutions, someone comes to you and by explaining to you the laws which govern the motions of the planets, proves to your satisfaction that your fears are groundless, that its an impossibility, then your mind is changed, and you become quiet and happy again. In all this there was no disease, simply a disturbance. I hope that now you have got some idea of what he means by saying that "mind is matter", and that consequently it can be changed.

In order that a disease be created, a shock must first be produced. You can't move anything unless you first start it. Of course you admit that a sick person is in a different condition from a well one, and to be changed to that condition, he must have had a first start. Well, then, there must be a shock, be it ever so slight, a little excitement, fright, pleasure, anything which would produce a disturbance in the system. When you, for instance, are thus disturbed, the natural heat of the body, always either increases or diminishes, that is a person turns redder or paler.

Suppose you turn red, which is very natural. A stranger meets you and says that you look flushed, that would not be likely to take down your color, but would increase it. And after two or three remarks of that kind, you would begin to feel uncomfortable yourself. Your head would feel hot, and the heat might be so great that you would have pain, and presently you would be informed that you look feverish.

That would keep up the excitement, and when you went out of doors, you would be likely to cough from the irritation caused by the upward tendency and the heat. That would frighten you a little though you might not own it or know it, but the disturbance would keep up till some kind friend would inform you that you had taken cold, for your face was flushed and you coughed. That, mind you, is an opinion, for a person may flush and cough from excitement without any cold at all. Now you only need a little help from mistaken friends and a finishing touch from a Dr. to put you into a lung, brain or any other kind of a fever they please. That to use a very simple case, is the way a disease is made.

Of course circumstances alter cases, and every kind of a combination may exist, which would produce corresponding results.–The less anyone knows of medical science the less likely they are to be sick, for the whole thing is based on opinions and is productive of disease. Even post-mortem examinations, which are the grand proof of their doctrine are, must be, unreliable. They cut a dead person up and judge of the living by them, while the dead and the living are two different institutions. –Opinions, you know I have said are matter or mind, and so can be changed.

Now the countless opinions we are brought up with and believe as much as we do our existence, of course affect us, we have a body according to our belief. The belief comes first, then the system changes accordingly. –You ask how opinions are the cause of disease in children. Even before the child is born, it is affected by the mother and receives its mental and physical constitution from her.

After it has taken up existence on its own account, it is still affected by her, whether she speaks or not. The greater number of influences which act upon us, do not come through the natural senses, and are all the more dangerous of course, because unknown. And that is one object of Dr. Q's theory, to bring our spiritual existence to our senses, or rather to prove that our senses are not located in the body as we think they are, and thus we shall be able to protect ourselves. You know we are affected for good or evil in associating with persons whether they directly attempt it or not. Roger Chillingworth.[1] If you were as familiar with the facts of mesmerism as I am, you would easily see how mothers affect their children and how they literally kill them with kindness. By thoughts we are all affected, and even by the settled opinions of people whether they trouble themselves to apply them to our case or not–that is by public opinion.

With regard to the diseases of animals–Now with regard to disease I don't want you to misunderstand and think that he means that disease is in the imagination. He never accuses any one of imagining that they are sick. He admits every sensation that a person may claim indeed, he takes their feelings himself, so he has proof positive that they exist independent of what the patient says, and that physicians can't do, but he only differs from them in his explanation of the cause of those feelings. Phys. admit the disease as a something independent of ourselves, as something which may be caught. They have even given it an identity, and it stalks about the world seeking whom it may devour. While he knows that it is an invention of man and not of God and that it will be annihilated with the progress of knowledge.–Now as far as the treatment of your own case is concerned, his theory sanctions you to conform to any standard which you believe to be right, as for instance in guarding against exposure.

You believe yourself to be in danger from exposure, and so you are, and must conform to what you think proper. If it is to leave off rubbers and take cold, or put them on and not be as likely to, you must choose the least of two evils and put them on, though in putting them on there is no wisdom. It is only conforming to an arbitrary standard which you have agreed to and are consequently liable to its penalties if you disregard it.–Now for a winding up remark, you see that if these principles are true, there is no good in dying for that does not change us at all. We are just what we were before and if we have any ideas which make us unhappy, we still have them.

Our influences are changed it is true, for our friends believe us to be dead and away from all communication with them, so we stand a chance to be changed, but that we get rid of all sickness or sorrow, when we shuffle off this mortal coil, is a mistaken idea.

---

1.   A character from the 1850 novel *The Scarlet Letter.*

[IX] From a letter.

You speak of this Science as if it were a picture on which you had but to look and understand; as though the whole thing, complete in its general design and in every detail were placed before you at once and you had only to glance at it, to comprehend and pass judgment upon it. Hence you say you cannot embrace it because it is so beautiful etc. If you think that in a few letters from me, the subject can be presented in such a way that you can understand it and reject or receive it as you think best, you are altogether mistaken. We have been two years and a half in constant intercourse with Dr. Q. and now only feel that we just begin to understand ourselves on the subject to hardly dare even yet to attempt sustaining ourselves with strangers. In asking if I never have had any misgivings, you imply that I knew what it was to start with and understood just the roads to be taken to attain it. Instead of that being the case it has only been by having the advantage of daily conversations with Dr. Q. and constant access to his writings that I have been able to make any headway at all, and at first it seemed almost all the time as if, like the bay, I stepped up one step and tumbled down them. What he said sounded fanciful and chemical enough, that is I could make nothing reasonable out of it and it often seemed as if he wandered from the subject and lost himself in a labyrinth that only a fanatic could navigate through, but I was always careful not to condemn what I could not understand. But through the whole, there was enough that I could understand and could apply to my own case and by degrees to society, to retain my interest and stimulate my curiosity, and by constantly questioning and listening, I came by degrees to see more and more into it until now I do not hesitate to say that I understand him and that he is right. So much for my experience in learning the "Truth."

To answer your question at once, if mind is matter and all effects in the natural world have their cause in the spiritual world, then it is evident that heat and cold, food, in short all those things which are addressed to the outward senses, as we call them, must first gain access to us through other means than are apparent. That means in our belief.

The first mistake is in locating the senses in the body when they really exist entirely independently of it. But according "as a man thinketh, so is he" and if we believe that taste is in the tongue, hearing in the ears, sight in the eye and feeling in the nerves of the surface, etc. we must be affected according to our belief. For instance you believe that the cold air strikes you and makes you feel chilly. Could you have been educated to believe or be taught now to believe that the cold is not in the atmosphere, but in yourself, that is, in the construction that you put upon the sensation, then you could be made entirely superior to heat or cold, and in the same way to food. No one thing contains more nourishment or is more hurtful than another, only that we are taught to believe that it is. And on this foundation, lies the institution of dyspepsia. Should we be guided by the opinions of others we happen to be with, we should never eat anything, for there is nothing eatable, but what according to somebody is unwholesome, and one person knows just as much about it as another. The only difference between physicians and others in this respect, is that they are posted up on the standard–they have made it and they sustain it, and as we place confidence in them, their opinions affect us more than those of others. But it is only through the confidence that we have in them that their opinions do affect us. You are not bound to believe all this of course, just because Dr. Q. says so, but if I can present the subject in any way so that it shall in some degree commend itself to your good judgment, I shall be very glad. It is much harder to convey to anyone in writing any idea of this than it would be by conversation, for a thousand little obstacles etc.

But now you see that it never would do for anyone to act upon them properly who did not understand them, for they would do it blindly and would be as likely to suffer for it as not. If you cannot do it intelligently then the same risk is now as if you never had heard that it could be done. For you really admit the danger which you pretend to ignore by your actions, and of course are liable to suffer the penalties attached to the law. So until one can do it intelligently do you not see that it is better to put on your rubbers when you go out? In food the same principle applies. Take for ex. cheese. Suppose that it hurts you: when you eat it you literally eat the idea of its hurting you with the cheese, which you have associated with it. And the same would be the case if you took it without knowing it. Our spiritual senses are often more acute and sensitive than the natural ones. With regard to poisons, a great stumbling block to any one in investigating this principle–he says that the matter may be made the medium of the intelligence of man.

You ask is experience, wisdom? Certainly not, for there is no such thing as experience. Ex. is the construction which we put upon any event which occurs in our life. For instance the death of a friend: One person may draw one experience from it and another, another. But when the Science proves that there is no such thing as death, then all the various experiences which are the result of belief in the idea are annihilated.

So Science, or Wisdom, which is the same thing annihilates experience. That is a word coined from the wisdom of <u>this</u> world, and when the wisdom of God prevails, then the wisdom of this world together with all the beliefs and unhappiness which arise from it, is no more.

Do not let me forget to dispose of one remark you make. You say that the various opinions of Drs. are confirmed by observation. Of course they are, for as long as they have the confidence of the people, they can bring about any effect they please, but it is only through our beliefs that they do affect us. Dr. Q. explains the raising of Lazarus spiritually, but does not doubt that such a phenomenon as that taken literally might be brought about. Jesus, when he appeared after the crucifixion had condensed his spiritual self so that it could be seen by his natural eye, and he did it scientifically.

I use words merely for convenience which I say are wrong, for example death. The time will come when such words will be obsolete. The <u>will</u> need not be used when there is <u>knowledge</u>. The more ignorant people are the healthier they are and vice versa. We should suppose that if health was a physical condition, and the science of medicine a true one, the more people knew of their own physical condition and the more they become acquainted with what are considered the causes and cures of sickness, the healthier they would be as they would know so much better how to take care of themselves. But such is not the case. The more Drs. there are the more diseases–and the number increases every day.

April 1861

[X] From a letter.

All other sciences which deal in matter and which we admit as sciences for their existence depend on the fact of our admitting matter. This is beyond those and depends upon the fact of our denying it. It is the foundation of and embraces all others……..[sic]. The material world, in fact everything that is understood by the word matter, was spoken into existence after man's creation and as a necessity for his development. Without it mankind would have remained in innocence and ignorance and would be only grown up babies. Now we have matter created and men have only to be stimulated in order to produce all sorts of phenomena and they will of course put the best construction upon them that their intelligence admits of. In their climbing up the hill of knowledge certain phenomena were developed and certain facts were established, which being handed down from father to son, and generation to generation have become facts, but dependent on matter, which remember is only an idea. Science is the name of that wisdom which has been reduced to a system so that it can be taught. Now this accumulation of facts has been sifted down and systematized by different ones until gradually the sciences of Chemistry, Astronomy, Botany etc. have grown out of them. Now all these you see, are dependent for their existence on matter and when matter is annihilated these are also gone. According to your idea of a dead person, matter is nothing to him, for he is out of this world. Then of what use are the material sciences to him? You say that I reason myself out of matter, but that is not so. But you do. Consistent with the common idea of death is the idea that when any one dies he is out of matter. But here it is not so. If matter and everything growing out of that foundation is only an idea, it simply exists in the mind and mind must exist as long as anything, as far as I can see. So when a person dies, as you call it, he is no different from what he was before. Matter being only an idea, he still retains it and reasons just as he did before. It is simply a progression in the same line. Now you see it makes a vast difference whether a person admits the natural sciences as foundations of themselves, as you do, or whether a person believes them to be only developments of matter, which is not everlasting. With the former belief, progress is impossible for you make a barrier by your own belief, which cannot be surmounted.

With the latter belief the gate is opened and all may enter who choose. But because the barrier is taken down and the way free, it does not follow that all the facts that have been established since the world began can be understood and explained away in a minute. For instance that poisons will not kill a person with this belief as well as with any other.

It is doing pretty well if it should only take a larger dose to kill Dr. Q. than any other man. You admit the science of math. Suppose I tell you to perform any problem that I may set and you are not able to do it. Should I be just, in denying the whole science? And yet that is what you do. If I cannot eat saltpeter and drink burning fluid and take stones for pepper you say that the whole thing is false. Take the best chemist in the world and he cannot develop the science to its utmost extent, but is that any reason why we should deny the whole thing. Enough has been brought forward to prove that there is one and the reasoning is right. Now the existence of these natural sciences mind you, I admit as much as anyone. The only difference is that I know them to be of this world and therefore liable to death which this science is the foundation of all and to profess it is to profess the kingdom of Heaven within you. A man with this belief is, as you say, a good deal nearer God than any other man. He is God as far as he has knowledge and when he has not knowledge, he worships God in spirit and in truth. This religion ends all verbal prayers, ideas of death, and punishment and reward in another world, indeed another world itself…..[sic]. There can be no death, for we are just the same and cannot be altered. If we can get acquainted with each other spiritually, where is the end of the natural senses, and how can we ever be separated. Our happiness and misery lies in our acts, and we just as surely reap where we have sown as the world goes on. And our next world is here where we are and always must be. This teaches us to do to others as we would have others do to us, because as we are all a part of each other, when we injure one part the whole feels it. So there is no such thing as self sacrifice in this. That belongs to ignorance. Is it a sacrifice to make yourself happy?…..[sic]. The knowledge of the fact that we are all a part of each other gives us an intelligent charity, for we do not believe in willful sin, that a person wants to make himself unhappy, but that error in every form is the result of ignorance and so it is impossible to blame anyone……[sic]. It is only those unseen and dangerous influences that he wants to make known, that come like a thief in the night and steal away our happiness before we know that we have got it.

June. 1861.

Itinerant Mesmerist

Letters of Introduction

[Letters carried by P. P. Quimby and Lucius Burkmar as they traveled giving lectures and demonstrations of mesmerism from 1843 to 1847. –*Ed.*]

I

Belfast, Nov. 6, 1843

Nathan Hale, Esq.
Doctor Jacob Bigelow
Dr. John Ware

Gentlemen:

I have no means of introduction to Mr. Hale and Dr. Bigelow excepting this, that thirty years ago I boarded with them at Miss Fessenden's in Tremont Street.

The bearer of this, Mr. Phineas P. Quimby and the boy with him, Lucius Burkmar, are both inhabitants of this town. I know nothing and never heard anything to the prejudice of either of them. The boy is a subject of clairvoyance. I have had some 10 or 12 interviews with him when he was put into a state called mesmeric sleep. In four or five cases he failed entirely. In some others he was partially successful. 3 or 4 times he came quite up to the mark, and performed feats where there was no room for deception or mistake, which really outstripped anything I ever heard of Indian or Egyptian jugglers.

He told me my own thoughts kept to myself. He told me words that I imagined and did not make known in any way that I know of. He was blindfolded and told me truly and minutely facts and appearances at the distance of say 1½ to 2 miles which I did not know and no one in the room with him knew and which he could not know by any means within the limits of common experience. I have good reason to believe that he can discern the internal structure of an animal body and if there be anything morbid or defective therein, detect and explain it.

The important advantage of this to surgery and medicine is obvious enough. He, that is his intellect, can be in two places at the same time. He can go from one point to another (no matter how remote) without passing through the intermediate space.

I have ascertained by irrefragable experiments that he takes ideas, first directly from the mind of the person in communication with him, and secondly without reference to such mind directly from the object or thing to which his attention is directed, and in both instances without any aid from his five bodily senses.

He can perceive without using either of the common organs of perception. His mind when he is mesmerized seems to have no relation to body, distance, place, time, or motion. He passes from Belfast to Washington, or from earth to moon, not as horses, steam engines, or light go, but swifter than light, by a single act of volition.

In a word he strides far beyond the reach of philosophy. He demonstrates, as I think, better than all physical, metaphysical or moral sciences the immateriality of the human soul, and that its severance from the body involves not its own destruction; at least he proves this of himself, and I suppose other souls are like his.

I am aware that ultra savants in Europe turn up their noses and sneer at this whole subject, so they did forty years ago at the steam engine. But for all that mesmerism as manifested in this boy lets in more light than any other window that has been opened for 1800 years. This may look like gross extravagance, but if you have the same luck I have had you will find it is not so. Lord Byron impiously demanded a second revelation, and here it is!

If you please, try the boy and if need be three or four times. If successful you will detect something not indeed miraculous but full of mystery.

I would not by any means be presumptuous or occasion trouble, but I beg leave to say that it would afford me much gratification if you or either of you would write to me by mail after full experiments and express your opinion as to this boy.

Yours respectfully,
R. B. Allyn

II

Pembroke

Feb. 12, 1845

Dr. E. Richardson

Dear Sir:

This will introduce to your acquaintance Mr. P. P. Quimby of Belfast, who is exhibiting to the public through his companion, Lucius, the powers of mesmerism.

I have always been skeptical on this point and entered into the investigation with strong prejudices against the science, but I have been surprised, if not convinced, with the experimentation. I have been put into communication with Lucius and have been surprised at the accuracy of his thought reading. I have also performed several small operations or feats on him and others and have succeeded beyond my expectation or former belief.

Go and see for yourself, as I cannot describe the affair on paper. As candid, intelligent men we ought to investigate before we approve or condemn, and in order to do so, we must see them.

I write in great haste and hope you will be able to make this out.

Yours very respectfully,
B. Atkinson

Please show this to our friend, Dr. Whipper.

III

Saint Stephen

March 5, 1845

Mr. Thomas Jones, Esq.

Dear Sir:

A Mr. Quimby from Belfast, State of Maine, has a few days past been exhibiting experiments in animal magnetism to crowded audiences, to their entire satisfaction.

His price is moderate and as he intends visiting your place, he has desired me to give him a line to you and others of my friends by way of introduction.

Please give him what assistance you conveniently can in getting an audience and I think you will be pleased with the result of the experiments he will exhibit. Any aid you may afford him in the way he requires will be gratefully acknowledged by your obedient servant.

In haste
J. Burton Abbot

P.S. If I had time I would give you a full description of the experiments he has successfully performed in this place, but I have not at present.

IV

Belfast

Nov. 18, 1843

Hon. David Sears

Dear Sir:

The bearer, Mr. Phineas P. Quimby visits your city for the purpose of exhibiting the astonishing mesmeric powers of his subject, Master Lucius Burkmar. Mr. Quimby, as also the young man, are native citizens of this place and sustain in the community unblemished moral characters.

Mr. Quimby is not an educated man nor is he pretentious or obtrusive; but I think if you should take occasion to converse with him you will discover many traces of deep thought and reflection, particularly upon the subject above mentioned.

His boy I think will demonstrate in an extraordinary manner, the phenomena of magnetic influence, more especially in that department usually termed clairvoyance; and should you take an opportunity to be put in communication with him, I doubt not you will be satisfied with the result.

Time and distance with him are annihilated and he travels with the rapidity of thought. I think he will describe to you the appearance of any edifice, tower or temple, and even that of any person either in Europe or America, upon which or upon whom, your imagination may rest. I say this much from the fact that I have been in communication with him myself and do know that he has described remote places and objects and even the appearances of persons at great distances, which he never before could have heard or thought of.

Mr. Quimby has letters to several distinguished gentlemen of your city whose names he will probably mention, which has, in some degree, influenced me to take the liberty to introduce him to your favorable notice. A greater reason, however, upon this point, is my belief that you will take pleasure in witnessing in this instance some remarkable developments of this mysterious science.

I am dear sir,
Your Obedient Servant
James W. Webster

V

East Machias

Feb. 9, 1845

F. A. Pike Esq.
Calais, Maine
By Mr. Quimby

Dear Sir:

Permit me to introduce to you Mr. Quimby who has much interested us in Mesmerism, and whom I consider an honest man. His experiments with his amiable and honest Lucius are the most interesting and convincing of any I have ever witnessed. I have attended three lectures in public and several private examinations. I have been in communication with Lucius while in a mesmeric state and am entirely certain of his thought reading and have scarcely a doubt of his clairvoyance. What is most interesting of all is the very perfect manner in which Lucius examines the internal organization of diseased persons. He is very careful and conscientious and I think may be relied on. He has examined several persons here, among them Dr. Bates and Mrs. Abbot. I cannot describe these examinations but they are very wonderful and surprised us all.

In conclusion I say, go to the lectures and carry your sick friends to be examined or rather bring Lucius to them.

Please stir up the good people at your place.

Your friend,
Samuel Johnson

Lucius C. Burkmar's Private Journal

Lucius Burkmar

Tuesday 26th day December 1843.

Mr. P. P. Quimby and myself left Belfast for Gardener, we arrived at Searsmont at one, and we were persuaded to stop and lecture. We did and the experiments were very satisfactory, at least the audience thought so. Was taken by the Rev. Mr. Hawkes to the Methodist meeting house and described right. Was taken by a great many people and they seemed satisfied. Searsmont is a very pretty country place. The village is very pleasantly situated by the side of a small stream of water. There is a large tannery here in full operation and sawmills shingle machines clothing mills and gristmills in abundance.

Wednesday 27.

Left Searsmont for Gardener. Arrived at four, put up at the Cobosse House, kept by Rogers. A very good house and good accommodations.

Thursday 28

went over to Pitston with John Hall, came back and Hall was taken with a fever. He left Gardener for Belfast with Quimby's horse. In the afternoon rambled over the town, took a peep at the stone church. This church is of the Gothic order and is said to be one of the finest specimens of workmanship of the kind. It belongs to the Episcopal church of England. It is situated upon the top of a hill overlooking the town. It is said to be elegantly furnished but I was not inside and so of course I was not capable of judging. A small river runs through the town and there is a number of mills upon it. It is called Cobbosse-contee river and empties into the Kennebeck river. It is a great advantage to the town, there being a number of valuable mill privileges on it. This evening we're to have lecture. It is said there is a great many skeptics in this town but I think we shall satisfy them.

Friday 29.

We are to have another exhibition. Seemed pretty well satisfied last night. The people here seem polite and affable and treat strangers very polite. There seems to be a great opposition with the barbers here. It is laughable, to see the inducements held out to come and shave at such a shop, hair cutting done here for 6 1/4 cents, while another will read, no discount here. The spirit of the Yankees has got into the coloured gents for opposition seems to be all the go here. There is a beautiful Periodical depot here kept by Atwood, a fine reading room, 'tis here the latest novels of the day are purchased at very low prices.

Saturday 30.

A stormy day, nothing interesting. I am reading a novel by Ingraham called Fanny, or the Hunchback, very interesting. Afternoon examined Mr. Michael Hildreth. Said his lungs were not affected but said his stomach was out of order and his caul was in a thick green state and recommended him to take throughwort emetic for the lungs and a sweat and warm baths for the blood.

Sunday 31st.

Started for Watterville. On the way stopped at the Hollowwell House and dined. This house has undergone thorough repairs and is now kept by Mr. Charles Sager, a gentleman every inch of him. From there we drove to Augusta. Stopped at Mr. Door's house a few minutes, and from there drove to Watterville and arrived there about four o'clock. Stopped at Williams' House and ate supper, went to bed tired and sleepy.

Monday, Jan. 1st 1844.

A happy new year. All Watterville is agog to find out who we are. The young fellows are dashing about in sleighs with their girls, oh how I envy them their pleasure. Watterville is a very pleasant place. There is a number of beautiful brick blocks here. Afternoon a Frenchman came in to have his neck cured. The conversation between him and Mr. Quimby was laughable. Now I will cure your neck in ten minutes. The Frenchman looked scared and his eyes looked all ways for Sunday and sure enough in ten minutes he had no pain.

Tuesday, Jan. 2.

Went and took a look at the colleges. They are four stories high and built of brick. The chapel has a cupola on top, built of wood and painted white. There is three brick buildings and the boarding house and workshop. From there I rambled to the banks of the river and saw a mineral spring. The water comes out at the foot of a rock and runs into the river. I tasted of it. It has a bitter taste and is supposed by some to have a great deal of healing power. At any rate it tastes bad enough if that is what they want.

Wednesday, Jan. 3.

Stayed in the house all day. We're to have a lecture tonight.

Jan. 4.

We satisfied the skeptics, all of them but two. Had a crowded house and gave good satisfaction. He is going to stop another night.

Thursday, Jan. 5.

Last night we had a full house and satisfied the few remaining unbelievers.

Friday, Jan. 6.

Started for Skowhegan, passed through Bloomfield. In this town there are three buildings, that in proportion and symmetry I never saw surpassed. One is the Baptist church, the other is the town hall and the other is the Academy. They are all built of brick and situated upon the top of a hill, so the prospect from them is delightful. We crossed the bridge and entered Skowhegan. This village contains about two thousand inhabitants. There is nothing about it interesting. Here the Democratic Clarion is printed. It is printed and edited and published by one man and a boy, just enough to constitute "We." We stop at Mores Tavern, a very good landlord and very good house.

Sunday, Jan. 7.

Nothing doing. A very dull day. Sent some bills home. I am reading Dood's [Dod's] Lectures. Dood's deaf and dumb subject is here and I have wrote with him a great deal. He told me last night he tried to have an exhibition. He said nobody came. I pitied the poor fellow. He said he wanted to go to Watterville but had only two dollars. In his performance he imitates different sounds and actions such as vanity, pride, ambition, the ocean, ship, man, stealing apples, etc. It's very interesting.

Monday 8.

We are to have an exhibition.

Tuesday 9.

Our experiments passed off very well. They have tried to persuade us to stop another night.

Wednesday 10.

We leave here today and go to Norridgewock. We arrived at Norridgewock at 11 o'clock, stopped at Freeman's tavern, posted up our bills, and prepared to exhibit tonight.

Thursday 11.

We had a full house last night and the experiments went off well and the people seemed satisfied, and a number of them wants us to stop another night so we stop tonight. Norridgewock is the shire town of Sommerset County. It is pleasantly situated on the river of the Kennebeck, and a number of literary men reside here–Judge Tenny, lawyer Abott and Dr. Bates. The court house is a large brick two story building. The lower floor is occupied by the register of deeds office and Clerk's office and the upper floor for the court room.

Friday 12.

Is our last night. We did well last night.

Saturday 13.

We go to Skowhegan and exhibit tonight and Sunday we go to Anson.

Sunday 14.

Arrived at Anson at 1 o'clock and passed through the town of Maderson.

Monday 15.

Here we are. Anson is a very pretty place situated on a branch of the main river. Young Chase is here and about to get married.

Quimby has been doing miracles. He has cured a man that couldn't walk nor speak. It has produced a great excitement here among the people. He has been confined to his house about a year and never has spoke or walked. In one hour he made him walk about the room and speak so as to be heard in another room.

Tuesday 16.

At Anson yet, nothing doing. We are to have another exhibition, tonight.

Wednesday 17.

Started for Golan, arrived at 1 o'clock, stopped all night, had an exhibition, done well.

Thursday 18.

Started for Dexter, passed through Athens, Harmony, arrived at Dexter at six o'clock, went to bed tired and sleepy.

Friday 19.

Today I wandered all over wollen [sic] Factors. The superintendent was kind enough to show me all over the Factory and it was a great curiosity.

Saturday 20.

We had a lecture last night and we are to have another tonight.

Sunday 21.

In the morning we started for Newport and arrived there at 11, put up at the Centre House. Newport is a very pleasant town, a small stream runs through the town and a large Tannery, the largest there is in the United States, and there is the most business done here for the size of any place I have been in. We are to have an exhibition Monday night and I think we shall do well.

Monday 22.

Evening we had an exhibition and done well.

Tuesday 23.

Start for Unity, stopped there one night. Night was dark and stormy, but we had a very full house. Unity is a very pretty place. the principal part of the town is situated upon a long, level street. We stopped at Seavey's house, a very good house and good landlady.

Wednesday 24th.

Started for home, passed through Knox and Belmont, and so home.

So at last I have arrived home tired, yet pleased, with my journey. I found the inhabitants polite and pleased with our stay amongst them, excepting a few.

Amongst these were, Dr. Stickney, and Mr. Withington, a country schoolmaster who thought he knew more [than] any of the rest. Since I left Dexter I have heard that the wollen Factory has burnt down. It is a great loss. It has thrown a hundred hands out of employ. As a general thing we didn't find the people so bitter upon the subject of Animal Magnetism as we thought we should. We generally had the most influential men of the place upon our side of the question, and as a general thing satisfied all skeptics beyond a doubt. For instance, when we left Norridgewock the following gentlemen were in the affirmative and those opposite in the negative.

Judge Tenny	Mr. Adams
Dr. Bates	Mr. Gould
Esq. Seldon	
Mr. Abott	
Mr. William Bates	
Mr. Peets	

This is about as it stands in every town we passed through, two unbelievers to six believers. When we passed through Augusta we didn't so therefore we concluded to go round by the way of Bath, so Monday, Feb. 5th, we started from home for Goose river in Camden–so called form the number of wild geese that assembled there. We exhibited in the Brick School House to a crowded house.

Tuesday 6th.

From thence we went to Camden and exhibited there one night. Camden is a delightful place. The town is on the seacoast and it has considerable shipping. Back of the town is a high mountain–it [is a] delightful place in the summer. In the distance can be seen the Penobscot Bay, in all its splendour dotted with its numerous isles. Long Island can be seen dividing the bay, in two parts, as it were. At the back of this mountain is a turnpike, made (with a great deal of expense) by a man of the name of Barett. In riding over this road you must imagine to yourself frowning rocks that seem as if they would crush you to pieces. At your feet lies the pond stretching its waters afar off in the distance. In the spring it is dangerous to pass over this road owing to the frost working upon the rocks and causing them to fall down. This mountain is famous for being the place of an exploit that was performed by a man of the name of Eaton. He was attacked by a bear upon the top of the mountain and he had nothing to defend himself with but a large stick. The bear rose upon his hind legs, for the purpose of hugging him. At the moment he jumped upon his back and seized him by one ear and rode down the mountain, and the neighbors came and despatched the bear.

Wednesday 7th.

Rode from Camden to Thomaston, exhibited there one night. This is the great lime market. Thomaston lime stands the highest of any lime in the world. It is a great curiosity to visit the quarries. They have dug down to the depth of sixty or a hundred feet below the surface of the ground. The quarries are some two or three miles from the shore, but they burn their lime principally at the shore, so that in the summer season coasting vessels are constantly engaged in bringing kiln wood.

Thursday 8th.

Started from Thomaston to Warren, passed through West Thomaston to Warren. One thing I omitted to state, there is two villages in Thomaston, one is called East Thomaston ('tis here the quarries are) and the West Thomaston. We arrived at Warren at four o'clock P.M. Put up at Wetherbee's, engaged the town hall for our exhibition and had a good House.

Friday 9th.

Started for Walderburough, stopped at Balch's House and had an exhibition. This town has considerable business, principally in wood. Distance from Warren Walderburough ten miles.

Saturday 10th.

Rode to Damariscata mills, stopped at Boland's all night.

Sunday 11th.

Spent the greatest part of the day in reading.

Monday 12th.

Went to Newcastle. This is a fine town. The business is principally in building vessels, but there is one thing that we need very much, that is a police for they have the most unruly set of boys. The citizens are actually afraid of them.

mistake about the dates

Tuesday 13th.

Went to Wiscasset and stopped at Hilton's. We are to stop two nights. I rambled over the town and I found it very interesting. It is very old indeed. There is some very oldlooking houses. I went and peeped into Clark's steam saw mill. It's a new building, the other was burnt down. They make sugar shooks. Upon the whole it is a pretty town.

Wednesday 14th.

Stayed in the house all day and read and wrote.

Thursday 15th.

Went to Barth and stopped at the Elliott House. Had one lecture, didn't do well at all, failed entirely.

Friday 16th.

We tried tonight and done better.

Saturday 17th.

Loitered about and done nothing, rather hard work.

Sunday 18th.

Arrived at Wiscasset. We are to lecture one more night here and then for Augusta.

Monday evening 19th.

Had a crowded house and our experiments were good. I was taken by Mr. Clark to the bark Casilda or at least I went myself and found her in New York, and told what time she arrived and described his son (they have learned since by letter, it is correct).

Tuesday 20th.

Started for Dresden, a small town lying between Wiscasset and Gardener. Stopped there one night. Had a full house but the experiments were not very good.

Wednesday 21st.

Started for Augusta, this time we shall get there I hope. Passed through Gardener and Hollowwell, and arrived at 2 o'clock P.M.

Thursday 22nd.

Looked around the town, went and got my bills ready for tonight. We engaged the Concert Hall and are sanguine of success.

Friday 23rd.

Our experiments were good last night. Today I took a walk up to the State House to hear wisdom flow from the mouths of babes, for certainly here is some of the most verdant men that ever I see collected together en masse. Ye gods, it makes one shudder for the State of Maine to see into what hands the welfare of the [citizens] is entrusted to. The following dialogue will serve to show how pushed some of the towns were for men that knew something.

Subject: the Railroad Charter. A. Well, Squire what do you think of that, erh, Railroad question hey? B. Well, between you and I, I don't think much of it. We must put these big bugs down. I tell you that now. A. How is that, erh, little thing gonto be done? B. Git 'em on our side. I think as how we might as well give 'em that, erh, Charter to 'em. A. I think so too, at any rate the Squire of our town says he'll take a share if it does go through. They must give us a ride for nothing 'cause we helped 'em. I say, neighbor B, have you got a pair trousers you could lend me, mine's torn? B. Can't say as how I have on'y got one pair and them I got on. Your constituents must pay you for tearing your trousers. Good bye neighbor A. Good bye. A. (to himself) Darn stingy fool, I know he's got more than one pair of trousers; well at any rate I vote agin him. B. (to himself) Did he think I'm going to lend my trousers? No, I'll see him darned first.

The following [preceding] Dialogue actually occurred in a certain bar room, name not mentioned. These two worthies no doubt thought they were looked up to, by all these Legislatures [legislators], but I will drop this subject for the present and let these wise heads reign.

Saturday 24th.

We have our lecture in the same place as before. I went up today to the State House and peeped into the Representatives Hall. This is a large or spacious room, of a circular form, but the room is better than the people in it. The Senate is a square, spacious room and not quite as large as the Representatives Hall. There is a very large cabinet of minerals here that abound in Maine, also a large library here, filled with state books and the principal works of great authors. I also visited the Lunatic Asylum. Under the direction of Dr. Ray, this is a large stone building with wings. It can accommodate about 200 patients but there is only about 100 now and increases every day in number.

Sunday 25th.

We go home to Belfast, it is about 40 miles from Augusta. We arrived at one o'clock. stayed to home 2 days[.]

Tuesday 27th.

Started for Augusta. Arrived at Augusta at dark. Tonight we have the New Court House.

Wednesday 28th.

We are to have another lecture here.

Thursday 29th.

We have another lecture. We leave Augusta the 3rd of March, next.

Sunday March 3.

Leave here for Winthrop. Engaged the Universalist Church. Winthrop is a very pretty manufacturing town. There is a small cotton factory which employs something like 150 hands. It goes by water.

Monday 4th

We lecture tonight and I think by appearances we shall have a full house.

Tuesday 5th.

We had a full house last [night] and likely to have a full one tonight.

Wednesday 6th.

Had some private examinations and satisfied the Doctors, for these Country Doctors (some of them) think they know more than G or Aristotle and in fact they do in their own conceit and I find it best to let them think so for it pleases them.

Thursday 7th.

We go to Readfield and lecture there tonight. We lecture two nights here.

Friday 7th.

We go to Farmington, the Shire town of Franklin County. I find it is a beautiful village and the inhabitants think a great deal of their town and well they may. We lecture here tonight and tomorrow night.

Saturday 9th.

We did not have many in last night owing to a donation party given to the Congregational minister. We lecture here tonight.

Sunday 10th.

A new day opens upon me and I have got a new pen. Great news, today we go to Wilton. We arrived there at 10 o'clock forenoon, put up at Williard's tavern. This is rather a straggling town but they have considerable spirit for they have cut a canal about quarter of a mile long, the water is led from the stream up on the top of a high hill. There is considerable machinery here, is [there are] gristmills, sawmills, shingle machines in abundance.

Monday 11th.

Wrote a long letter home, had to write a pack of nonsense, there being no news to write here. Monday evening, we had a full house considering all things, for there was a party here too. It seems as if everything worked against us.

Tuesday 12th.

We went to Farmington Hall, there being two villages in one town. We lecture here tonight in the meeting house. They seem very kind to us here although they are all skeptics. The principal business done here is lumbering, there being three or four large mills here. There is quite a tannery here, also they have a covered bridge over what is called the Sandy river, about one hundred and thirty feet long. Farmington is celebrated for its elegant farms. They turn their attention to the cultivation of herds grass and clover seed, the most celebrated seed known. I have been having quite a confab with the landlord of the house in regard to temperance. It began with his saying that Brandy didn't do a man any hurt. I told him it was according to how he used it. He said, I don't care how you use it. I then asked him if he thought it was right to sell liquor. He said he didn't think it right to sell to man that was drunk. I asked why he sold it. His answer was because the rest did. This is a fair sample of landlords in the northern part of Maine. When we came in we found the barroom in a dirty state, the chimney piece ornamented with old chaws of tobacco, pieces of cigars, a tallow candle, and the drippings of a lamp that hung over it. The bar was covered with slops of gin and rum, by the side of the room a bunk for the hostler to sleep in, in one corner an old pine desk and in the other corner an old clock which seemed to partake of the general laziness [a]round for it was half an hour behind the time. Add to this three or four drunk loafers and you have a description of a country bar room. Travelers in passing from village to village will often see on the road but not in the village, mind you, the sign of Washingtonian House kept here, and why is it, I will tell you why. It is because they have no chance to get it to their tavern, and more than one half of the Landlords that keep these Washingtonian Houses will get drunk when they can get it, and no doubt keep a little in their house for themselves only and these are the gentlemen that cry, Temperance, Temperance at the top of their voice and the same time will take a drunken loafer by the arm and lead him to [the] next Grog Shop and treat him. You ask a landlord that keeps an intemperate house why he don't keep a temperance house and their answer is, Why damn it, there is no temperance houses in these parts for the ones that keep them are drunkards. And, you see, instead of reforming the morals of the people it [is] quite the reverse. The plan that I would adopt is let everyone that keeps a Washingtonian House send their names to the County Secretary, and let them print handbills so that public travelers may be warned against them, but I am afraid that the evil can never be remedied wholly under the present generation.

Wednesday 13th.

Went to New Sharon and stopped at a temperance house, and now I will give a description of a Temperance house. We entered (not a barroom) but a clean, neat room, simply furnished. In one corner sits a book case filled with books for the weary traveler to read, a parlor stove, not covered with tobacco spittle but the brasses around the stove blacked, with a merry fire burning in it, a table covered with a plain, white cloth, the map of Maine hangs against the wall, and to cap the whole a tidy Landlady and also a good Landlord and you have a description of a temperance house. They have a covered bridge here about the same length as the one at Farmington Falls. This town lies by the Sandy river. The principal part of the inhabitants are farmers. They have a brick church here built in a plain style, it belongs to the Methodists.

Thursday 14th.

1845

Monday 13th.

Started from Belfast to go to Bucksport. Passed through Prospect village and arrived at Bucksport at 1 o'clock. Put up at Bucks Hotel and waited impatiently for the evening. At length the long wished for moment arrived when Lucius was to astonish the natives of Bucksport. 7 o'clock in the evening, here I stand at the door, taking money hand over fist. Here comes a ragged brat. Please, sir, may I go in for fourpence? Yes, yes, pass in. Here comes a very pretty girl. Will you admit me for 10 cents? Who can resist such an appeal? I open the door with a bow and a scrape, and she passes in by me smiling. Here comes a man who spurns the grounds he walks upon. See with what an air he tosses the ninepence in my hand. Here comes a clerk. I know by the way he fumbles after the ninepence he has hooked from his master's drawer. Thus you see we have all sorts and sizes. Our experiments this eve are in my waking state. 10 o'clock, our experiments this eve have been satisfactory. Our receipts amount to $11.00, pretty good so far for the first night.

Tuesday 14th.

Cold day. Very good exhibition last night, try again tonight. We dined with Emery, spent part of the afternoon. The people seem to be very bitter upon the subject of magnetism, but we have satisfied a great many, some very hard cases. This afternoon I examined Mr. Hooper, thought the kidney and urethra was diseased, said there was a seated pain in the lower part of the abdomen, also a pain in the small of the back and thought the pain in the small of the back was caused by sympathy with the kidneys. Recommended him a plaster of Burgundy pitch to be worn upon the back, told him not to drink cold water for it did not agree with the kidneys. Also examined Mr. Pillsbury's wife, examined head and pronounced the brain diseased, said there was a congestion of the brain and large clots of blood laid upon the brain and it would produce convulsions and fits. While I was examining her, she had one of these fits as I was told by Mr. Quimby.

Wednesday 15th.

Stormy day. Nothing doing. Everybody upon the subject of magnetism! Magnetism! I am tired of the name. Afternoon it snows as if heaven was rifting all the snow there is upon the earth. Tonight is our last night. Then we shall go farther east. 10 o'clock in the evening. Our receipts tonight amount to 9 dollars. I, being doorkeeper, just fork over the chink to Mr. Quimby, and go to bed tired and sleepy, for our experiments tonight have been principally confined to clairvoyance, which generally tires me more than any other experiments we do. Come thou goddess of sleep, I embrace thee, encircle myself in the arms of Morpheus, I close my eyes and am, as I suppose, soon in the land of oblivion. When I am awoke by the slamming of a door which jars the whole house, I again try to console myself to sleep, wishing the jar might have been upon the person's head who slammed the door.

Thursday 16th.

A stormy day again. Oh dear, everything seems lonely, nothing to read but political newspapers. So goes the world, and so goes its inmates. I wander around the house like a hypochondriac. If I go into the barroom, there is the same ceaseless chatter. I go into the sitting room, there a pert lady meets me with a simper and inquires if I am sensible of anything that transpires during that state. Here I can't run away so must stay and answer a string of interrogations. Sometimes I am almost tempted to go to bed. I can't go into a store without being dinned with questions.

This afternoon we started for Orland and arrived about 3 o'clock, put up at a Washingtonian House and waited for lecture hours. We lecture this eve at the School House. It being a stormy night, I suppose we shall not have a great many in.

Friday 17th.

Our experiments last night proved very satisfactory to the audience. The first person, I was put in communication with Mr. Buck, and taken by him to his house, described his room and saw a map, lying upon the floor, and after he left the staging and told the audience that before he left his house he put a map upon the floor. We leave Orland for Castine this morning and arrive after a cold ride. We are to lecture this evening at this place.

Saturday 18th.

Owing to its being stormy, our lecture was rather thinly attended. We stop again tonight. It still keeps a snowing as if it never was going to stop. Afternoon Capt. Pinkham arrived in the packet, saw David Libby and got all the news, went aboard the Franklin and saw Stephen Libby, shook hands with him and inquired the news. Oh dear! Such a dull place. If I was a going to pray, one of my prayers would be, the Lord deliver me from Castine and I would wish my prayer might be answered.

Sunday 19th.

A fine day, the sun shines, the air is sharp and bracing. I have wrote to my mother and sent two papers home. Afternoon I rambled up to the old fort. The old French fort is situated at the back part of the town, on a rising ground. The place where the barracks stood can be seen now. The fortifications are in the form of a square though at each corner there is a bankment thrown up shaped like a half circle. In one of these corners there is an excavation somewhat resembling a dungeon. The sides are walled up. At first you enter a room about six feet square. At the end of this room there is a narrow passage two feet wide, the sides walled, and the roof covered with cedar. I entered this passage and crept along till I came to a heap of stones. I crept over these upon my hands and knees, but here I was suddenly stopped by the earth that had caved in. No one knows what this place is for though some think it was a prison.

Monday 20th.

The sun has hid his face from us this morning, and the clouds are flying to the north, and everything indicates a snowstorm. I just do nothing but sit in the house and read what I can get and that is not much. Afternoon examined Mr. Hooper, some relation to the one I examined, described him as having a rupture in the lower part of the abdomen, which was, as he stated, true.

Tuesday 21st.

We left Castine at 10 o'clock and arrived at Penobscot at 12. It still snows as bad as ever. Mr. Quimby is not very well today, has caught cold and has a pain in his head. We exhibit this evening. Oh if the ancient Grecians were plagued with snowstorms no wonder they sighed for the mild climate of Rome. Mr. Quimby's being sick the whole case develops on me. Therefore now Lucius, stretch thyself, and do your best. It still snows, as if it would never stop and blows so hard that if a man with a long nose should turn his face sideways, it would be apt to blow it off. I have engaged the Hall, my lamps are trimmed and all is ready for this evening.

Wednesday 22nd.

I have just crawled out of bed. I lift the curtain and get one peep, but that one look is enough. I drop the curtain in despair. I go downstairs and eat my breakfast, and then sit down by the stove and look at my thumbs. Last night we took about five dollars. I fall back in my chair and go to sleep and dream that I am in a snow drift a-struggling to get out but all my exertions sink me more. At last the snow is up to my chin, it rises to my mouth. At this period I awake and find the old Landlady is melting snow in a large kettle and in pouring it in she spilt some on my hand and this awoke me.

Thursday 23rd.

Ah my prayers are answered. We have a pleasant day, again the sun shines out gloriously as though it were glad to visit the earth once more, and I guess the inhabitants are glad to see it too. This morning we started for Bluehill and arrived there at 12 o'clock. Bluehill lies at the foot of Bluehill mountain. We have engaged the town hall and wait for company. There seems to be considerable aristocracy here for I see they have two classes here. One class are for these lectures and another class are against it. But we are gainers by it for it produces an excitement.

Friday 24th.

Last night our experiments were very well attended. There was about two hundred in. Mr. Quimby lectured about one hour. He spoke of mind and how the mind was acted upon while in the mesmeric state. In his remarks he clearly demonstrated that there was no fluid and he showed the relation between mind and matter. I have been having a chitchat with a very pretty girl. Her name is Abey Redman but mum is the word.

Saturday 25th.

Oh dear, ill luck attends us. It is but just done snowing, and now it begins to rain, but I comfort myself with one thing, that is, there is an end to all things, so of course there will be an end to this rain. But Despair says, When! When! Ah that is the query.

I believe I'll leave the ground to Despair for I cannot answer him. As I began today by snarling, I will finish out the page in the same way. If there is anything I despise, it is having so many questions asked me after I wake up. The first question is, Do you remember anything? Second is, Do you hear anything? Third is, How long do you think you have been asleep? Last night in returning from the lecture, I had a fellow quiz me all the way home. I was determined not to answer him, so after a while, I told him to call on me tomorrow and I would administer to his suffering curiosity. He stopped and I saw nothing more of him.

Sunday 26th.

We went to Sedgwick and was going to exhibit there but they had no Hall, so we went to the Public house (kept by Mr. Dority) and took dinner and went back to Bluehill. Sedgwick is a country place situated by a stream. There is one thing the inhabitants ought to be ashamed of, that is, there is no Hall, no public buildings, not even a town house. Now we are in Bluehill. This evening I went to a prayer meeting, fully attended-that is, with young fellows and girls.

Monday 27th.

We started early in the morning for Surrey. Rather cold ride. Arrived at Surrey at half past eight, didn't see much encouragement to stop, so we concluded to drive on to Elsworth. So we started and arrived there by 11 o'clock and put up at the Elsworth House. We lose this evening owing to there being a prayer meeting in the hall, so after dinner we drive down to Mr. George Buckmore's and stopped there, so he spoke to a number of young Ladies and Gentlemen to come down and see some experiments in Animal Magnetism. About 6 o'clock seven or eight couples in sleighs. After the experiments were over a number of them proposed to have some play, so some played Whist. I enjoyed myself much. The ladies were very sociable. They broke up about 12 o'clock and they all appeared pleased (at least I was).

Tuesday 28th.

We stopped down to Mr. Burkmar's till after dinner when we went up to the Elsworth House and went and engaged the hall and got prepared for the evening. Miss Abey Burkmar and Miss Quimby came up with me, and went to the lecture, and in the evening I went down to Mr. Burkmar's, stopped all night and came up in the afternoon ready for evening. After the lecture, I went up to the American House with Mr. Chamberlin and stopped all night and took breakfast in the morning.

Wednesday 29th.

A drizzly rain accompanied with fog. Nothing doing. In the forenoon examined Mrs. Barker, said there was a difficulty in the blood, described one of the valves of the heart as being thicker than the other. Thought she didn't have exercise enough. Said the valve being deranged caused the blood to stop. Was asked what sensation it produced. Said it produced a faintness, said this was the great difficulty, thought there was no other functional or organic disease. At the same time examined Mrs. Bennett. This (as I understood from the Doctor) was a nameless disease ... our experiments thus far have been very satisfactory. We have had the hall crowded every night. As it looks likely to rain, we have concluded to stop another night here.

Thursday 30th.

Nothing doing. I loiter around the town. I went up on the hill and examined the Court House. This building is built of brick painted white, surrounded with a balcony. It overlooks the town. Upon a range with this building is another built upon the same plan. This is the register of Deeds office and other Public offices. I examined the seat of Mr. Black, agent for the Bingham purchase. He is an Englishman, therefore his residence is somewhat like the seats of the Old English squires we read of. The house is built of brick with wings upon each side. The ground in front is laid out in the form of a horseshoe with circular lane leading up to the house. It sits off from the road, and makes a pretty appearance from the road in riding by. As it was about dinner time I hastened home very well satisfied with what I had seen.

Friday 31st.

This morning we went to Mr. Blood's and examined a daughter of his. Was put to sleep, described her as having the spinal complaint. Described the vertebrae, some of them as being disjointed. There was a curve in the back bone, recommended a plaster of Burgundy Pitch to be put on the small of back. Thought it would ease her, but thought she would never get well. After examining this lady we got ready to go to Cherryfield. We passed through Franklin, and through what is called Black's Woods, 14 miles long and it was black enough and long enough. We arrive at Cherryfield (after a cold ride) at 3 o'clock and put up at Burnham's House and got ready for the evening. In coming in to the village there was a building that attracted my attention. This building was in the form of an octagon with a cupola upon the top. It is called Harrison Hall. It was begun in 1840, built in shares at 20 dollars a share, but after the political excitement was over it was left shingled and boarded, and left until 1844 when it was finished.

Saturday, February 1st.

This day is sharp air. It stings anyone's face. There is an Irishman here by the name of Denis. He is just such an Irishman as described by Charles Lever in Jack Hinton-Croos Carney. His face is tied in a dozen knots and everything you ask him is answered with a snap. There is only one man he is afraid of and that is the landlord. By a mistake we misdated our bills, and therefore our house was rather thinly attended but we expect to do better tonight.

Sunday 2nd.

This day I am writing letters home to my Friends at B so I stay away from meeting, purpose to write. I have examined Mr. Sargent and the Landlord. Pronounced Mr. Sargent as being dyspeptic. Thought dieting would help him. Examined Mr. Sturges, said there was something the matter with his leg. Said the circulation of the blood was partially stopped, didn't recommend anything. Said the Landlord had the Spinal Complaint, recommended him to wear a wide flannel bandage on the small of his back.

Monday 3rd.

This morning we started for Columbia and arrived at eleven o'clock. Very poor traveling, most all bare ground. We exhibit here tonight 10 o'clock. Mr. Quimby is trying to magnetize a Miss Loring, a schoolmistress here. He has succeeded partially. Since we have been here he has operated upon the Landlord, Mr. W. He has the numb palsy in one side. He succeeded in making him walk, and thinks he will make a cure.

Tuesday 4th.

This is a fine day. The sun shines brightly. Today we go to Machias, passed through Jonesburough, Whitneyville. In this village there is a railroad. It extends to Machias Port, a distance of eight miles. This is constructed for the purpose of carrying lumber from the mills to Machias Port. 'Tis the last thing I should have thought of seeing. We at length arrived at Machias. We have engaged the Court House for our experiments and expect company....

Wednesday 5th.

During the night it has snowed so it makes the traveling better, so we can get along quite well. Our notices were not very well circulated, so we did not have a very full house last night but we expect to do better tonight, at least I hope we shall. As I have nothing else to write about, I will give a short history of the town. Machias was settled by people from the town of Scarburough. It is an Indian name; it is called by them Mechesis, thus the English corruption of Mechias. Mechias, East Machias and Machias Port were all originally all in one town but in 1835 it was divided. The principal business is lumbering. Since I have left Elsworth, I have seen nothing but sawmills and timbers and pretty girls, the first commodity rather splintyer than the last.

Thursday 6th.

This morning we started for East Machias, a distance of four miles from Machias. This is a very pretty village. I like it much better than the other Machias. It is situated on both sides of East Machias River. I have nothing more to write only there is a fellow just arrived from Thomaston.

Friday 7th.

'Tis a cloudy day and every minute I expect it will snow. Last night we had a very full house, quite a rarity, for we have not had a full house since we left Elsworth. After leaving Elsworth I notice the Churches are all built in the Gothic Style. So the first thing I see in looking at a [is] Church points and arches. In passing along the street yesterday I heard an old crone singing. The voice sounded so harsh and unmusical I involuntarily stopped and heard the following ditty.

Come all you youths of high and low degree I pray you all come listen unto me.

A very good story I will relate Concerning of the matrimonial state.

The above was sung in a drawling manner, so as to fetch it in the tune. This moment the old lady came at the door, so I had to dig.

Saturday 8th.

Done better last night than we did the night before. They seem better satisfied here than they were at Machias. All of them seem to want to be examined. We have examined five invalids, more than we ever examined in three days before. They want us to stop tonight so Mr. Quimby has concluded to stop another night. Heigh ho I see all manner of people, some with as unmeaning faces as a jackass. Mr. 's face looks like a monkey's and his wife's looks like an old hen's. The girls are fools. I have not seen but four sensible ladies in town, and those were married.

Sunday 9th.

Today is a beautiful day. Early this morning before we were out of bed Mr. Abbott called and wanted us to call and examine his wife, so we went and examined her, and thus we have at it all day, examining people. We have examined ten in the whole. We expected to go to Denysville this afternoon but we have concluded to stop till tomorrow. Mr. Quimby has partially magnetized a Miss Harmond that has been sick for thirteen years. The Doctors did not know what the matter was with her, but thought it was the Spinal complaint. He worked upon her a half an hour and succeeded in relieving her pains so that she got up and walked about the room without any assistance. He called on her again and magnetized some water and it had the same effect as it did when he was working upon her.

Monday 10th.

Considerable snow fell last night which makes it very good sleighing. This morning we started for Denysville, passed through a town called Marrion. This town consists of two taverns right in the woods. There is no other houses in the town as I have been informed, and the sport of it is they both pretend to be stage taverns. We arrived at Dennysville at half past twelve, put up at a public house kept by Wilder, took dinner and went and took a peep at the Schoolhouse, fixed our stage, trimmed our lamps and waited for the shades of darkness. 'nough said-Shake

Tuesday 11th.

Our experiments were not very satisfactory owing to the school room being small and densely crowded. Mr. Quimby has performed a miracle here. He took a man that had a lame shoulder, it was partially out of joint-he worked upon it, and the man said there was no pain in it. This astonished them. This afternoon the man went about his work as well as ever. We also examined Mr. Wilder, the Landlord. We started for Pembroke, a distance of six miles and arrived safe and sound and put up at the Pembroke House. We saw Card from Belfast here. We have the Schoolhouse to exhibit in, so I have to get it ready. Pembroke consists of two villages. One is called the Head of the tide, the other Salt Works, a distance of half a mile from each other.

Wednesday 12th.

The experiments last night were very good. Last night we took a man out of the audience (a perfect stranger to him) and effected a cure on his arm. The man had not been able to raise it up for two years, and in a few minutes he was able to raise his arm up to his head and moved it round free from pain. This forenoon we started to go to Eastport. It snows and blows, rains and hails as if all the elements were in war with each other. After a cold ride we reached Eastport at twelve o'clock, wet through to the skin. We put up at Brooks Hotel, a very, very nice house. We exhibit in Trescoot Hall this evening, Wind and Weather permitting. Mr. Quimby is acquainted with a Mr. Witheral who will use his influence to aid us.

Thursday 13th.

Our experiments were very satisfactory indeed, although there was not so many in as we would have wished. However we shall try our luck again tonight. Mr. Quimby had a letter of introduction from Dr. Atkinson to Dr. Richardson, so therefore he presented his letter and Dr. Richardson took him to see a patient of his. The case was that of a Woman who had fell down and injured the elbow joint so that she couldn't move it without excruciating pain. He magnetized her and made her move her arm about just as he pleased without any pain. This afternoon he went and see a child that was very sensitive. He could paralyze his tongue and prevent him from walking, stop him when and where he pleased. The boy was about 10 years old.

Friday 14th.

Last night was the fullest house we have ever had. The Hall was crowded, the experiments were very good. Mr. Quimby took that same boy in the audience and stopped him from talking. I was taken to Havanna by a Sea Captain and described the harbour right and the surrounding scenery. We took 22 dollars last night. Today we go to Lubec by water, 'tis three miles across. We have to go in an open boat. We reached Lubec about eleven. 'Tis a dirty looking place as I ever see, filled up with Irish principally. 'Tis situated by the side of a hill. We stop at Mr. Boyle's, an old Irishman, a fine old gentleman though. We have the Schoolhouse to exhibit in, and I hope our experiments will be satisfactory.

Saturday 15th.

Alas, all my expectations vanish in smoke. Our experiments were interrupted by a lawless gang, who began to show their dispositions even before we began to operate, but Mr. Quimby braved it out till 9 o'clock, then he dismissed them. Immediately some of them began to cry out humbug! Others swore they would have money back. Before Mr. Quimby began his operations, they began to make some noise, and then he spoke and told them if there was any person dissatisfied he would give them their money back but no they was content to stay and then after the lecture was over demanded their change. This Mr. Quimby wouldn't give them. Some swore they would run us on a rail, others swore they would take it out of our hides, and after we went down to the house, some proposed to pull us out of the house. In the morning we go back to Eastport and lecture there.

Sunday 16th.

Saturday night the hall was crowded. There was three hundred people in. Last night he took a Mr. Spencer and stopped him from talking and walking. He then put me to sleep and while I was asleep I magnetized this Mr. Spencer. This the audience . . . much. He operated upon a son of Mr. Sherwood, the British Consul here. He stopped him while talking.

Today we go to Callais. Passed through Robinston, stopped and dined there. Arrived at Callais at four, put up at the S. Croix Exchange kept by Vezia. Fine house. Sit round till bedtime, then go to bed. I must say I am both tired and sleepy.

Monday 17th.

Today is a fine day. Everything indicates a thaw. Today we must fix up for the evening. I go out to buy some pants, got fitted nicely. Saw Mr. Henderson from Belfast. Afternoon we had some private experiments. At Mrs. Wood's saw Mr. Charles Porter, originally from Belfast.

Tuesday 18th.

Our experiments last night were very satisfactory. Everything passed off as it should, but we had rather a thin house. We shall exhibit once more tonight. Been out and bought a new novel by Ingraham, to while away the time. This afternoon I passed over on the English side to St. Stevens, the first time I ever set foot on the queen's land. I find by inquiry that there are a great many people on the English side that take refuge there to get clear of the debts they owe because the Sherriff can't serve a writ there, and it's just so on the American side.

Wednesday 19th.

Our exhibition last night was not very crowded, so today we shall go to Milltown. We find the aristocratic part of the community had rather have private experiments, so they won't turn out at public experiments. At four o'clock we go to Milltown, get ready for the evening.

[End of Lucius Burkmar's Personal Journal.–*Ed.*]

THE LECTURE NOTES OF PHINEAS PARKHURST QUIMBY

Editor's Introduction to the Lecture Notes

There are a total of eight small hand-bound booklets photographed on the first reel of microfilm in the Boston University collection of Phineas Parkhurst Quimby materials. These booklets are simply numbered one through seven, there being two copies of "No. 1." The first copy of "No. 1" shows revisions made to the text and the second copy shows those revisions incorporated into the text.

The designation of "Lecture Notes" for these otherwise un-named volumes comes from Horatio W. Dresser's 1921 publication of *The Quimby Manuscripts*. On page 47 of the first edition and page 53 of the second edition of *The Quimby Manuscripts*, Dresser indicates that the lecture notes were used by P. P. Quimby during the period of his public exhibitions with Lucius C. Burkmar, who was Quimby's subject for experiments and demonstrations in mesmerism. This period extended from the year 1843 through 1847. As Horatio Dresser was the son of two of Quimby's patients, Julius A. Dresser and Annetta Gertrude (Seabury) Dresser, it is possible that he was in possession of information that would identify these volumes.

The language of the lecture notes, particularly in the first two volumes, is verbose in comparison with the remainder of P. P. Quimby's writings. It has been suggested that someone may have assisted Quimby in writing these volumes. Another possibility is that Quimby himself was attempting to emulate the writing styles, language, and formatting of the publications he was drawing from for the purpose of giving lectures. He drew extensively on case studies presented in John Abercrombie's *Inquiries Concerning the Intellectual Powers, and the Investigation of Truth*, (1842; published in New York by Harper and Brothers); and Volume 1 of the two-volume set of Thomas C. Upham's 1839 publication *Elements of Mental Philosophy, Embracing the Two Departments of the Intellect and the Sensibilities*, (published in Portland, Maine by William Hyde, for Z. Hyde).

Thomas Cogswell Upham (1799-1872), a Professor of Mental and Moral Philosophy at Bowdoin College in Brunswick, Maine whose *Elements of Mental Philosophy* was published by Harper & Brothers of New York in 1840. Upham's work was frequently revised and published in various formats and variant titles in more than 56 editions, including abridged versions that were used as high school and college textbooks.

John Abercrombie (1780-1844) was a Scottish physician, philosopher and author who received his medical degree from the University of Edinburgh in 1803. Abercrombie's 1842 edition of *Inquiries Concerning the Intellectual Powers, and the Investigation of Truth* was also adopted as a textbook for classes in Intellectual Philosophy by several higher-educational institutions of the period.

Phineas Parkhurst Quimby quotes from both of these authors in his lecture notes, as well as from several others of what is known as the "Scottish School of Common Sense" or "Scottish Common-Sense Realism," primarily to offer alternative explanations of the phenomena found in their case studies.

Further, Quimby discusses his views of his contemporaries in mesmerism and phrenology, most notably Charles Poyen, Robert H. Collyer, Chauncey Hare Townshend, Joseph R. Buchanan, La Roy Sunderland, and John Bovee Dods (the name "Dods" is spelled "Dodds" throughout the lecture notes.)

Although I am not a handwriting expert, it seems clear to me that the handwriting contained in Quimby's lecture notes does not match the substantial collection of authenticated Quimby handwriting found in the Library of Congress collection. Yet it is equally clear to me that the narrative in the lecture notes is that of Quimby. This suggests the probability there was a copyist or transcriptionist involved in preparing these booklets who omitted a few quotation marks. Appropriate credit is given to John Abercrombie and Thomas Upham for their case studies, and therefore these minor omissions of punctuation by the copyist should be considered nothing more than a simple oversight.

In this publication, Phineas Parkhurst Quimby's lecture notes are separated from the balance of his writings and presented in their original booklet format because this is historically accurate. The underlining of certain words reflects the underlining found in the original handwritten documents. For some unknown reason, these booklets were not microfilmed in their sequential order. The order of appearance in the Boston University microfilm is: No. 1; No. 1; No. 2; No. 3; No. 7; No. 6; No. 5; No. 4.

–Editor.

Lecture Notes–Booklet I
[BU 1:0001]

Primary Truths

What are primary truths? According to Mr. [Dugald] Stewart, "They are such and such only, as can neither be proved nor refuted by other propositions of greater perspicuity. They are self-evident–not borrowing the powers of reasoning to shed light upon themselves."

We are naturally inclined to consider the reality of our <u>personal</u> <u>existence</u>. That we exist is the great basis upon which we build everything. It is the foundation of all <u>knowledge</u>. Without <u>self-existence</u> nothing could result in the progress of the understanding. If any man questions the fact of his own existence, that very process, by which he doubts, proves to a demonstration, that an <u>existing</u>, <u>doubting</u> power must have been precedent, must have had a creation. The first internal thought is immediately followed with an undoubting conviction of personal self-existence. It is a primary truth in nature, and requires no further explanation.

Personal Identity

Another primary truth is <u>personal</u> <u>identity</u>. This is the knowledge of ourselves. The identifying of ourselves with our self-existence. We know that we exist, and in that existence we recognize our personality. Man is composed of matter and mind, by some mysterious combination united; and we may divide our identity into <u>mental</u> and <u>bodily</u>.

Mental identity is the continuance and oneness of the thinking and reasoning principle. It is not divisible in length, breadth and dimensions composed of particles etc. like matter, nor does it change or cease to exist. It remains as it was originally with all its eternal powers–its eternal principles.

Bodily identity is the sameness of the bodily organization–the man in figure, as we behold him with our natural eyes. The particles of matter of which the body is composed may change; but its shape and structure and its physical creation are the same.

Professor Upham, in his work on Intellectual Philosophy in reference to this subject, uses the following language. "It was a saying of Seneca, that no man bathes twice in the same river; and still we call it the same, although the water within its banks is constantly passing away. And in like manner we identify the human body, although it constantly changes."

Personal identity, then, comprehends the man as we behold him, in his bodily and mental nature, mysteriously and wonderfully made!

The old soldier, who has fought the battles of his country in the days of the American Revolution, will recount his deeds of valor and his heroic sufferings to his youthful listeners, not doubting, that he is really the same old soldier, who was in his country's service some sixty years since. The early settlers of our country, as they look abroad over the cultivated plain, never doubt, that they are really the same individuals, who some forty years felled the trees of the forest and turned the wilderness into a fruitful garden!

So is man constituted, that his own identity is one of the first primary truths.

We are so constituted that we believe, or rather there seems to be an authoritative principle within us of giving confidence or credence to certain propositions and truths, which are presented to our minds. Among the first things which the mind admits is <u>that</u> <u>there</u> is no beginning or change without a cause, that <u>nothing</u> could not create <u>something</u>. When any new principle is discovered, man immediately seeks out the cause, looks for some moving power, as though it could not be self-creative and self-acting.

In contemplating the material universe, in beholding the beautiful planetary system, the sun, the moon and the stars regulated and controlled by undeviating laws, who does not say, these are the results of some mighty creative intelligence! That the power of their existences and harmonious motions was originated beyond themselves.

Thus it is that we attribute to every effect a cause–to every result a motive power.

Matter and mind have uniform, undeviating and fixed laws. And they are always subject to and controlled by them. We are not to suppose otherwise, unless we give up our belief that any object is governed or directed. Yet we are not to suppose that the same laws apply both to matter and mind. Each has its peculiar governing principle, and in as much as mind, in its nature, deviates from matter, so may its laws deviate.

We all believe that the earth will continue to revolve on its axis and perform its annual orbit around the sun, that summer and winter, seed-time and harvest will continue to succeed each other, "that the decaying plants of autumn will revive again in spring."

This belief does not arise in the mind at once; but has its origin now in one instance and then in another, until it becomes universal.

Immateriality of the Soul.

It is a conceded principle, that mind does not possess, or rather, we fail to detect the same qualities in mind as in matter. No sect of philosophers, I believe, have ever pretended that mind is distinguished by extension, divisibility, impenetrability, color etc., and therefore most have agreed to use immateriality as applied to the soul, in distinction from materiality as applied to the body, that the soul is destitute of those qualities which appear in matter, having its own peculiar attributes, such as thought, feeling, remembrance and passion.

The mind as it exists in man and develops itself through the bodily organs, no doubt, has a close connection with matter, the physical system and particularly the brain. Yet we are not to suppose that mind is dependent for its existence upon the organs of the body, nor is it subject to the control of matter, although influenced and impressed by it. Mind rather exercises a direction to matter, producing certain results. If mind was any portion of the materiality of the body, a destruction of any portion of this would destroy a portion of that. But this is not the fact. Individuals, deprived of some of their limbs, do not exhibit any degree of loss of mind. How often has it appeared far more active and energetic, in the last moments of dissolving nature, than when the physical powers were in full health and vigor. Men, upon the battlefield, mutilated and wounded and suffering the intensest pain, have displayed, amid all this disaster of the body, the highest powers of intellectual action. So that, although mind to us appears at first view to have an inseparable connection with the body, yet, for its energies, its full unqualified powers of action does not rely upon bodily health and vigor.

The works of genius, as displayed in the various branches of science, literature and law, bear the character of a higher order of creation than matter. Memory and imagination do not appear to have resulted from ponderous substances. The powers of Judgment and Reasoning must have originated in something higher and nobler than divisible bodies. To what cause can you attribute the origin and perfection of the demonstrations of Euclid? What constituted the authorship of the wise laws of Solon and the political institutions of Lycurgus and those of modern Europe and the greatest concentration of wisdom ever embodied into one human work—I mean the American Constitution? What gave almost intellectual inspiration to the Iliad and Oddessa [Odyssey]. What gave birth to the wonderful productions of Tasso and Spencer and Milton? Where shall we look for the origin of the Philippics of the Ancients, or in more modern days, for the speeches of a Fox and the Orations of a Webster?

Where human genius has wrought its highest triumphs and achieved transcendent greatness, who can say, its creative cause, its fountain light is in powerless and inert matter! To ascribe the qualities of matter to the soul would erase forever the idea of a future and eternal existence. But we have no direct evidence of the soul's dissolution and discontinuance at death. The death of the body is only the removal of the soul's sphere of action from our natural view, and no doubt gives a larger world of Spiritual action in its new destination. And have we not every reason to suppose that the soul will exist after the dissolution of the body? "Death," in the language of Dr. Stewart, "only lifts the veil, which conceals from our eyes the invisible world. It annihilates the material universe to our senses, and prepares our minds for some new and unknown state of being."

We have already stated that belief is a simple state of the mind and consequently cannot be made plainer by any process of reasoning.

It is always the same in its nature although it admits of different degrees, which we express in the language of presumption, probability and certainty, etc.

It is on the principle of belief that the mind is operated upon in the various exhibitions of its power. For, without confidence, what can we accomplish? Without a belief in our ability to accomplish, what would be the result? It is a principle which comes into every department of reasoning; and testimony is only so operative upon the mind as it affects our <u>belief</u>.

The <u>Soul</u>.

Those, who style themselves philosophers and have written upon the subject of the mind, have always considered the soul as constituting a nature which is one and indivisible; yet for the purpose of more fully understanding its various stages of action, they have given it three parts or views, in which it may be contemplated expressed in the <u>Intellect</u>, <u>Sensibilities</u> and the <u>Will</u>. [Or the] <u>Intellectual</u>, <u>Sensitive</u> and the <u>voluntary</u> states of the mind.

We find, in different languages, terms expressive of these three states. Different authors, in works not written expressly upon the subject of the mind, have adopted these modes of expressing its action.

The popular author of "<u>Literary Hours</u>" [Nathan Drake, M.D.] has given in one of his works an interesting biographical sketch of Sir Robert Steele. After referring to his repeated seasons of riot and revelry, of his determinations and repentances etc., he thus describes him. "His misfortune, the cause of all his errors, was not to have clearly seen where his deficiencies lay; they were neither of the <u>head</u> nor of the <u>heart</u>, but of the <u>volition</u>. He possessed the <u>wish</u> but not the power of <u>volition</u> to carry his purposes into execution."

It has been remarked of Burns, that the force of that remarkable poet lay in the power of his understanding and the sensibilities of his heart. Dr. Currie in his life of Burns makes use of the following language. "He knew his own failings and predicted their consequences; these melancholy forebodings were not long absent from his mind; yet his passions carried him down the stream of error and swept him over the precipice he saw directly in his course. The fatal defect of his character lay in the comparative weakness of his volition, which governing the conduct according to the dictates of the understanding entitles it to be denominated rational."

Professor Upham, in his philosophy informs us of a celebrated writer, who in giving directions to his son as to the manner of conducting with foreign ministers, uses the following language. "If you engage his heart, you have a fair chance of imposing upon his understanding and determining his will." Shakespeare, the great philosopher of the human understanding, says in the second scene of Hamlet,

"It shows a will most incorrect to heaven,
A heart unfortified,
An understanding simple and unschooled."

<u>Origin</u> of <u>Knowledge</u>

The daily observation of every individual will result in the belief of different states of the mind. We often speak of the <u>natural</u> operations of the mind, its <u>natural</u> state etc., which is only that condition or standard nearest which a great majority of minds have resemblance. We also speak of the excited condition, the excited and deranged state. It is said with much truth, that every man is blest with some peculiarities entirely his own, that no two men are precisely alike in all respects. Now as we deviate from the great standard or natural state, <u>mind</u> becomes <u>excited</u> or morbid and insane. And all these different states or different temperatures of the mind are produced from strong impressions, made under peculiar circumstances. We are susceptible of <u>sensations</u>, governed and controlled by them under all circumstances. These direct all our conduct throughout the whole life. The life of man is a succession of sensations or impressions which induce him to act in one capacity or another. His capabilities are enlarged, as these impressions are numerous and powerful, or limited, as they are rare and light. All great minds are susceptible to the highest degree. His mind is most powerful and gigantic whose impressions are stamped upon the intellect with an indelible mark. This fact resolves the mystery of memory and explains the system of reasoning. We are the receptacles of successive impressions. Every step the mind takes in its progress of thought is marked with a new impression. Every beginning, every progress and every conclusion results in a new impression.

It is a very natural question among students to enquire, how the mind acquires knowledge from external objects. We will illustrate the process in this manner. An object is presented through the senses and the mind perceives, then is immediately impressed with the idea of that object, or receives the impression which the presentation of the object makes. This is the starting point and the mind immediately desires to possess or reject the same according to the character of the impression, or, at least, to know what constitutes the object. Now as the mind in this case is dependent upon the senses to convey a knowledge of the object to itself, or rather to place itself in immediate communication with the object, its attention and action is solely directed by the impression received. To an untaught or unlearned mind the presentation of an object would leave an impression but it is possible that action would here cease, unless it should receive other impressions than that merely of the object. But present the same object to a well-trained mind, and it gives an impression which is immediately followed by a successive train of impressions and ideas, giving rise to innumerable subjects of thought and contemplation. But, to the untaught mind, present a second object and a second impression is communicated, which is immediately followed by the first. Then comes a comparison or an impression of the difference of the two. And so a succession of objects presented, multiplies the number of impressions which follow, in a tenfold ratio. The principle of association, which is a successive train of impressions, is set in operation and keeps the mind ever on the stretch.

Thus the mind goes on its voyage of successive thoughts, arising from the presentation of one object or from some strong impression produced in some manner, through the organs of sense. Language is the expression of ideas or impressions and this is perhaps the great source by which mind communicates with mind through the sense of hearing. The conversation among our friends is the method, by language, of expressing ideas or impressions which produce similar ideas and impressions upon those to whom the conversation is directed. If you describe a scene you have witnessed in some distant country, giving different lights and shades as the impressions follow each other on your mind, bringing before another individual one grand view of the whole transaction, you give rise to impressions in the mind of your listener, which upon the principle of association, carries him back to a hundred different scenes of a similar character with each of which are associated ten thousand impressions, which are similar to those communicated at the place of transaction. Two men pass an old castle. Each receives an impression from the presentation of the object. It will remind one of some old ruins of a castle which he saw a thousand miles distant, and whatever transpired or what he witnessed at the time he saw it. The other perhaps will be reminded of some legend or old story which he read in his boyish days where lords and knights and ladies were made its inhabitants and visitors, about which are associated the days of chivalry and love. How differently are these two individuals affected by the appearance of the old castle. Each mind receives the starting point from the same source and then arise all these impressions entirely different in their course, yet equally rapid in their succession. A succession of ideas arises according to the previous acquisitions of each mind and these diverging trains are pursued until another subject presents itself which breaks up this course of thought. Then mind takes a different route and receives its new train of ideas or impressions. Here, too, it pursues its course, nor does it cease its wanderings until it receives a stronger impression from some other external object. It then sets off again in another direction and passes rapidly over a numerous train of ideas, succeeding each other on the principle of association.

I will illustrate the manner of acquiring the first impression by presenting an apple. It appears to the mind or rather the mind perceives it to be a substance, then of spherical dimensions. Here are two impressions given. If I exercise the sense of touch I shall learn the same facts. It feels round like itself. I convey another impression by the sense of smell. I taste of it, and here is a third impression. As the sight, feeling, smell and taste of the object affects me pleasantly or unpleasantly, I am impressed to take or reject the fruit. These are the means by which we acquire knowledge. Not in so rapid a succession as I have described, because, before we can pronounce the character of any object, we must have learned a language and the different modes of expressing its appearance to those who understand the language we employ.

Thus it is by testimony we receive much of our information. At first, it is difficult to believe what we are not accustomed to witness ourselves. Yet as the mind becomes enlightened and understands the principle upon which it is received, it yields its confidence and adopts this method of obtaining knowledge. An individual, who should be told that upon some parts of our globe constant night prevails for a certain number of months, and upon some other parts of the same globe constant day reigns for the same length of time, would not be very likely to believe it, unless such an anomaly could be explained upon principles which would carry conviction, by a comparison of all the knowledge he possesses upon the subject. Thus it is that mind is set in motion by the presentation of external objects. Before it is thus moved, it is a mere blank, possessing certain inherent powers which will only exhibit themselves by the exercise of some moving power. "The mind," says Professor Upham, in his work on Mental Philosophy, "appears at its creation to be merely an existence, involving certain principles and endowed with certain powers, but dependent for the first and original development of those principles and the exercise of those powers on the condition of an outward <u>impression</u>. But after it has been once brought into action, it finds new sources of thought and feeling in itself."

Having, therefore, all these inherent powers to acquire its knowledge is in proportion to the impressions it has received from external objects and internal operations. If you present a subject of conversation to a well trained mind, stored with impressions or knowledge, you have started a point which sets in motion the whole ocean of mind, educated from the past, and leads to endless discussions. But should you present the same topic to an untaught or partially-disciplined mind, you would start the current of thought, it is true, but that current would soon cease, or rather could not be very extended because the subjects of thought or the whole amount of knowledge possessed by the individual is limited.

I have spoken of the natural mind and the way of acquiring knowledge through the bodily senses only. But there are other means of communication by which impressions are conveyed to the mind.

If the spiritual being be independent of matter, why cannot we communicate with it without the aid of the bodily senses? It is to this subject I would now call your attention. The mind itself obeys the laws which its Creator first laid down, and we are not to suppose any strange anomaly in its outward exhibitions is contrary to the original design. The great <u>Law-giver</u> possesses all wisdom and is the fountain-head of all perfection. The mind is not a creative experiment of his, himself being ignorant of what results will follow. If these strange phenomena of the mind, which are exhibited in the different states of excitement, are exceptions to the common rule, we must attribute to the <u>Great Mind</u> imperfection and humanity or a direct interposition to stay the great laws which were first given to suppress and bewilder ignorant and dependent man. But to my mind, it does not appear consistent with the wisdom of God that so extended an interference would be personally made to counteract first principles which are displayed in this age of mesmeric light. It must be that all these strange appearances are reconcilable with eternal laws. And we are to look to these alone for a probable and clear solution. The same laws govern the mind, when in its natural state and susceptible of impressions through the five senses as when in its excited and unnatural condition or under the influence of Nervauric, Phrenomagnetic, Mesmeric or Somnambulic influence. The only difference is this, in the method of conveying impressions to the mind. Give the impression, whether through the senses or otherwise, and the same correspondent results follow. If I make an impression upon the mind of a beautiful landscape by pointing it out to the natural eye, it is the same as though I made the same impression upon that mind while in an excited or mesmeric state. The view is real and pleasing in one case as in the other, to the mind that beholds it. It is as much an existence before the mind, when the impression without the material object is made, as when the impression with a presentation of the real landscape to the natural eye is given.

We shall here give a brief outline of what appears to be the condition of mind when in an excited or mesmeric state. Susceptibility is in its highest state of action and the operator seems to control the direction of thought if he chooses or can so impress the mind with influences as to govern its action in a measure. This point is no doubt gained by some powerful impression produced by the operator upon the mind of the subject. This condition can be produced by other influences than an individual mind. A fright by suddenly coming upon some external object will often produce a similar state of mind. Intense thought and excruciating pains produce this excited state and sometimes sets the mind in action, when it is enabled to exhibit the same phenomena as when induced by an individual operator. We shall have occasion in the progress of our work to refer to cases which arise from unknown impressions upon the mind, producing hallucination, insanity, dreaming, somnambulism, spectral illusions etc.

This excited state of the mind, called by some, the magnetic, mesmeric and congestive is no doubt produced by a powerful impression of the operator upon the mind of the subject, concentrating or drawing the whole attention to one influence. No set rules can be given by which this influence can be exercised because the same efforts will produce different results upon different minds; yet no doubt every mind has its portal of access and could we know where that is, or the way and manner of approaching it, we could produce impressions so powerful upon every mind as to subdue the action of the bodily senses and communicate directly with it. The doctrine, therefore, of "powerful magnetizers" (as they call themselves) that only a more powerful capacity or higher order of intellectual vigor can subdue a weaker mind and produce the excited or mesmeric state is idle as the wind. These higher orders of intellects with strong sensibilities are more capable of being brought to the contemplation of one individual subject and receiving the most powerful impressions, if you can discover the accessible road to their sensibilities. If you can produce an impression upon such a mind as will overcome all his prejudices towards you or your science and acquire his undivided confidence, you will then excite the mind into this spiritual state of action and he will readily read your own thoughts. Indeed I have been led to the conclusion that the highest powers of genius have been the results of excited minds, upon the principles I have laid down, and that they are but the inspiration of this spiritual action. What is it that contributes so much to distinguish Homer and Demosthenes, Virgil and Cicero, Milton, Tasso, Shakespeare and the whole host of great men who lived in ancient and modern times! It must have been this excited state during which poetry and eloquence and the highest achievements of mind were left, as lights of their genius, to live through all coming time. Eloquence, which holds the multitude in breathless silence or sways them hither and thither, produces the controlling impression upon each mind which in its turn impresses and influences the other exciting a low degree of the mesmeric state. It is, in fact, a principle by which we are all more or less governed in all our pursuits.

The high degree of excitement, called clairvoyant, gives the mind freedom of action, placing it in close contact with everything. There is nothing remote or distant, past or future; everything is present and discoverable. It only requires direction, and the subject is before it.

It is enabled to discover and describe countries and cities, mountains and plains, rivers and oceans, inhabitants and animals on distant parts of the globe. The mind will pass into the depths of the earth or rather looks through all matter, all space and all time, giving its character, its condition and its result. Call its attention to any subject however remote and it is present to the mind. These ideas, I have thrown out in relation to mind in its highest state of excitement, are not the result of a vivid imagination or the productions of a speculating mind, but the effect of experiments, repeated at different times and on various occasions. They are facts, which stand out beyond all contradiction—all cavil! And we are not to pass them as a freak of nature or as the result of contradictory laws. It must be the highest state of action to which the mind has arrived, giving testimony of the great powers with which it is created, yet controlled by its natural laws. We must not, therefore, account for this wonderful development upon the supposition of exceptions to general rules, but upon the continuation of great and undeviating principles.

Lecture Notes–Booklet II
[BU 1:0032]

The different degrees of excitement of mind–taken up in their order and discussed.

1st. <u>Dreams</u> and <u>their</u> <u>Causes</u>.

The peculiar state of the mind usually called <u>dreaming</u> is explainable upon the principles laid down in our premises, namely, <u>that impressions are conveyed to the mind by some other process than through our bodily senses</u>. We may fall to sleep under a deep impression of some transaction which has actually occurred, and the mind, having long been under the most powerful action of thought in connection with the transaction, will yield up the access through its natural body and receive its impressions directly upon itself. In other words, the mind becomes in a degree mesmerized and is then capable of producing all the phenomena for both in dreaming, which it would, if it were actually thrown into that state by an individual second power. The principle of association or impression succeeding impression by which the mind is controlled, both in its natural and excited state, is the law, which always governs. The mind always acts from impressions received when it acts at all; and, when in this state, is not regulated exclusively by surrounding objects because it is as susceptible of impressions from objects at a vast distance as those immediately around it. For time, space, distance and matter are no impediments to its action. Give it direction towards any subject, and everything connected with it is present. The <u>dreaming</u> state does not differ from the <u>mesmeric</u>, only as it is produced by another method than what is commonly called <u>magnetic</u>.

We submit, therefore, the following accounts of individuals of what actually passed in their minds, taken from different authors, together with the usual explanations, and shall endeavor to account for them upon such principles as we believe to govern mind.

Dr. Abercrombie, who has philosophized much upon mind relates to us many interesting anecdotes which he had accumulated from observation and by the assistance of his friends.

An instance is mentioned of a gentleman and his wife, who were actually dreaming upon the same subject at the same time, in the following language. "It happened at the period, when there was an alarm of French invasion, and almost every man in Edinburgh was a soldier. All things had been arranged upon the expectation of the landing of the enemy, the first notice of which was to be given by a gun from the castle, and this was to be followed by a chain of signals calculated to alarm the country in all directions. Further, there had been recently in Edinburgh a splendid military spectacle in which five thousand men had been drawn up in Prince's Street, fronting the castle. The gentleman, to whom the dream occurred and who had been a zealous volunteer, was in bed between two and three o'clock in the morning when he dreamed of hearing the signal gun. He was immediately at the castle, witnessed the proceedings for displaying the signals and saw and heard a great bustle over the town from troops and artillery assembling in Prince's Street. At this time he was roused by his wife, who awoke in a fright in consequence of a similar dream connected with much noise and the landing of the enemy and concluding with the death of a particular friend of her husband's, who had served with him as a volunteer during the war."

The Dr. attributed all this remarkable occurrence to a noise produced in the room above by the fall of a pair of tongs which had been left in an awkward position etc. But how it should happen, that the tongs should have produced similar trains of thought in two different individuals by the noise of a fall is more than I can understand.

One would suppose that the noise would have been conveyed to the mind by the bodily senses, giving a true impression of its origin or at least would not have resulted in impressions so foreign to the real cause. The true explanation seems to be this. Both minds, no doubt, passed into the sleeping state, partially excited upon the alarm of the French invasion etc. and were in the mesmeric sleep and in communication with each other, capable of giving and receiving impressions. The fall of the tongs might have affected the mind of one or both. It would not be necessary to affect more than one. The train of association is started in this highly excited state by an impression which could not have been given through the bodily senses.

The impression received is immediately followed by other impressions connected with the subject upon which the mind was most intent during the waking state. And being in communication with the other, conveyed similar impressions. Thus both minds were led along in mutual connection, receiving real impressions but arising from (as we would say in the waking state) false causes.

Another instance is mentioned in which dreams are produced by whispering in their ears. The particulars of one case are given in the papers of Dr. Gregory and were related to him by a gentleman who witnessed them. The subject was an officer in the expedition to Louisburg in 1758 and while in this state was a great source of amusement to his associates and friends. "They could produce in him any kind of a dream by whispering in his ear, especially if this was done by a friend with whose voice he was familiar. At one time they conducted him through the whole progress of a quarrel which ended in a duel; and when the parties were supposed to be met, a pistol was placed in his hand, which he fired and was awakened by the report. On another occasion they found him asleep on the top of a locker or bunker in the cabin where they made him believe he had fallen overboard and exhorted him to save himself by swimming. He immediately imitated all the motions of swimming. They then told him that a shark was pursuing him and entreated him to dive for his life. He instantly did so, with so much force, as to throw himself entirely from the lockers upon the cabin floor, by which he was much bruised and awakened of course. After the landing of the army at Louisburg, his friends found him one day asleep in his tent, evidently much annoyed by the cannonading. They then made him believe that he was engaged when he expressed much fear and showed an evident disposition to run away. Against this they remonstrated, but at the same time increased his fears by imitating the groans of the wounded and dying; when he asked, as he often did, who was down, they named his particular friends. At last they told him that the man next himself in the line had fallen, when he instantly sprang from his bed, rushed out of the tent and was roused from his danger and his dream together by falling over the tent ropes."

["]Upon being aroused, he could not recollect anything which had transpired and had only a confused feeling of fatigue."

We can account for these experiments only upon the excited state of the mind being capable of receiving impressions from another source than through the senses. The whispering in the ear was only whispering to the mind, the sense of hearing being, no doubt, inactive, and all the impressions of the quarrel were actually produced upon his mind and not through the sense of hearing by the direction of those around him. In the case of swimming, a strong impression of a shark was made upon his mind and in the excited state it appeared real–was actually seen as much as though every circumstance had transpired as it appeared in the natural state; and all these impressions were the result of mind acting upon mind– impressions conveyed by the minds of those around him, directly to his mind, making precisely the same result, as though he had in his waking state fallen overboard and was pursued by a shark.

In this excited state of the mind, called by philosophical writers the <u>dreaming</u>, every act of the past may be called up by some directing power or by successive impressions. Dr. Abercrombie has related some incidents among his acquaintances which will illustrate this principle. "The gentleman who was the subject was at the time connected with one of the principal banks in Glasgow and was at his place at the teller's table, where money is paid, when a person entered demanding payment of a sum of six pounds. There were several people waiting, who were, in turn, entitled to be attended before him; but, he was extremely impatient and rather noisy; and, being besides a remarkable stammerer, he became so annoying that another gentleman requested my friend to pay him his money and get rid of him. He did so, accordingly, but with an expression of impatience at being obliged to attend to him before his turn, and thought no more of the transaction. At the end of the year, which was eight or nine months after, the books of the Bank could not be made to balance, the deficiency being exactly six pounds. Several days and nights were spent in endeavoring to discover the error but without success, when at last my friend returned home much fatigued and went to bed. He dreamed of being at his place in the bank, and the whole transaction with the stammerer, as now detailed, passed before him in all its particulars. He awoke under a full impression that the dream was to lead him to a discovery of what he was anxiously in search of and soon discovered, that the sum paid to this person in the manner now mentioned had been neglected to be inserted in the book of interests, and that it exactly accounted for the error in the balance." The Dr. acknowledges this to be a very remarkable case and not to be explained upon any principles with which he is acquainted. All the rules by which philosophers have accounted for experiments as wonderful as this, here fail him. Had he witnessed the experiments which have been given by subjects under the excited or mesmeric state, he could have accounted for the mystery. In this state, the mind may be said to be before a map on which is written the past, present and the future—only needs direction to some definite point to disclose every act of our lives. The error in the books had been a constant cause of excitement and his mind had been so highly wrought up as to pass into the mesmeric state and under the impression of discovering the error. All the transactions during the past year were before him with the books and he was thus enabled to detect the error. This no doubt was a species of the clairvoyant state of mind.

The author of Waverly [Sir Walter Scott] has given an interesting anecdote, considered by him authentic. "Mr. R. of Bowland, a gentleman of landed property in the Vale of Gala, was prosecuted for a considerable sum, the accumulated arrears of teind (or tithe) for which he was said to be indebted to a noble family, the titulars (lay impropriators of the tithes). Mr. R. was strongly impressed with the belief that his father had, by a form of process peculiar to the laws of Scotland, purchased these lands from the titular, and therefore, that the present prosecution was groundless. But, after an industrious investigation of the public records and a careful enquiry among all persons who had transacted law business for his father, no evidence could be recovered to support his defense. The period was now near at hand when he conceived the loss of his lawsuit to be inevitable, and he had formed his determination to ride to Edinburgh the next day and make the best bargain he could in the way of compromise. He went to bed with this resolution and, with all the circumstances of the case floating in his mind, had a dream to the following purpose;–His father who had been dead many years appeared to him, he thought, and asked him, why he was disturbed in his mind. In dreams men are not surprised at such apparitions. Mr. R. thought that he informed his father of the cause of his distress, adding that the payment of a considerable sum of money was the more unpleasant to him because he had a strong consciousness that it was not due, though he was unable to recover any evidence in support of his belief. 'You are right my son,' replied the paternal shade. 'I did acquire right in these teinds, for payment of which you are now prosecuted. The papers relating to the transaction are in the hands of Mr. _____, a writer (or attorney), who is now retired from professional business and resides at Inveresk, near Edinburgh. He was a person whom I employed on that occasion for a particular reason, but who never on any other occasion transacted business on my account. It is very possible,' pursued the vision, 'that Mr. _____ may have forgotten a matter which is now of a very old date; but you may call it to his recollection by this token, that when I came to pay his account, there was difficulty in getting change for a Portugal piece of gold and that we were forced to drink out the balance at a tavern!' Mr. R. awoke in the morning, with all the words of his vision imprinted on his mind, and thought it worthwhile to ride across the country to Inveresk, instead of going straight to Edinburgh. When he came there, he waited upon the gentleman mentioned in the dream, a very old man; without saying anything of the vision, he enquired whether he remembered having conducted such a matter for his deceased father. The old gentleman could not at first bring the circumstance to recollection; but on mention of the Portugal piece of gold, the whole returned upon his memory; he made an immediate search for the papers and recovered them—so that Mr. R. carried to Edinburgh the documents necessary to gain the cause, which he was on the verge of losing."

This incident was explained by Dr. Abercrombie that the son, no doubt, had heard his father relate all these circumstances at some prior time and that he had entirely forgotten them, but that the anxiety of mind upon the subject produced in the dreaming state, some circumstance, which led to discovery of what his father had previously told him. This may be a satisfactory explanation to those who believe it, yet I apprehend all would not be fully satisfied. This we believe might have occurred in this manner. The mind had become extremely excited, in the waking or natural state, upon the subject of the lawsuit and as sleep insensibly came upon him, the mind immediately passed into the excited or mesmeric state, when it would be enabled to recall the past and ascertain all about the facts from communication with the mind of the Attorney at Inveresk or from actually beholding the papers etc. Even this explanation, to me, is not satisfactory, although I have no doubt of the capabilities of the mind to have discovered it upon the principle above; yet why should we not admit the real appearance of his father's spirit and that a communication of "mind with mind" developed the facts as related. I will simply remark here that there is no question of the fact that individuals under this highly excited state of mind may communicate with the spirits of their deceased friends. We shall relate some experiments which have transpired, proving conclusively this spiritual communication in another part of this work.

We find recorded in some work on mental philosophy, the following anecdotes. "A gentleman of the law in Edinburgh had mislaid an important paper relating to some affairs on which a public meeting was soon to be held. He had been making a most anxious search for it for many days; but the evening of the day preceding that on which the meeting was to be held had arrived, without his being able to discover it. He went to bed under great anxiety and disappointment and dreamed that the paper was in a box, appropriated to the papers of a particular family with which it was in no way connected; it was accordingly found there the next morning. Another individual, connected with a public office, had mislaid a paper of such importance that he was threatened with the loss of his situation if he did not produce it. After along and unsuccessful search, under intense anxiety, he also dreamed of discovering the paper in a particular place, and found it there accordingly."

The minds of these two individuals no doubt passed into the clairvoyant state, when they were able to behold with the mind's eye, the condition and position of the various papers–And so intent was their mind upon the discovery, or the joy which followed the discovery in the mind produced so strong an impression, as to be recollected after the mind was aroused from the dreaming state, which is not uncommon under certain circumstances.

We will remark here, that no doubt the mind is in active operation during our sleeping hours and passes rapidly along the highway of thought, yet is not conscious of it by us in our waking state. Nor is this position contradicted by the fact that we do occasionally recollect our dreams. We seldom have any recollection of our dreams unless some very striking impression which causes pleasing emotions or startling fear or excessive sorrow is left upon the mind. And however much the mind might think while the bodily senses are wrapped in slumber, we should have no cognizance of such thoughts unless something peculiar and effective should occur. In our waking moments, as we pass along our streets, we seldom notice objects which are common and in their place; but if anything new is introduced and strikes us with emotions of pleasure or pain, we notice and recall it at some future time. In passing familiar objects, the mind, no doubt, recognizes them; but the impressions are slight and other immediate objects occupy our attention, and we are not aware that we have passed them, yet we could not argue that we have not passed them because they did not make strong impressions, so as to be recollected; nor can we reject the doctrine that the mind is ever watchful and never slumbers; but even when our bodily senses are at rest, it goes on in thought recollecting only what is most striking and peculiar in its progress. But we pause upon the ceaseless and constant action of the mind, when the bodily senses are at rest, by the excited or mesmerized condition which is (if you please) the dreaming state. The subject seldom recollects what has transpired during his sleeping state, unless you produce a very powerful impression which is followed by the emotion of pleasure or pain to a very high degree. Then it is enabled to recall what was intimately connected with those emotions, and those only. I have no doubt, that the two cases of dreaming and mesmerizing are controlled by similar laws and that they are alike in constantly occupying the mind, although we recollect only those ideas which are most powerfully presented and which appear to be connected with some strong emotion.

We have witnessed a great number of experiments upon subjects in the excited or mesmeric state which demonstrate what I have advanced in regard to impressions. Every subject can be so powerfully impressed as to recall the thought in his waking moments while of ordinary transactions no idea is retained. These experiments prove both the similarity of states of mind in the dreaming and mesmeric; and also, that our powers of mind are never at rest.

Mr. Combe mentions a singular dream of an individual, that he had committed murder, and that the murder was actually committed two years after. Another case of a clergyman who visited Edinburgh, residing not far from that city, and while sleeping at an inn, dreamed that he saw his own dwelling on fire and his child in the midst of it. He awoke with the full belief of his dream and immediately setting out for his residence arrived in time to witness the burning of his house and to save his child from the flames.

These are published in works of philosophy as singular and wonderful coincidence. It is said that they demonstrate a strong propensity of character and mental emotion combined in a dream, and by some natural cause, one speedily fulfilled. Dr. Abercrombie has very ingeniously accounted for the last example by the supposition, that "the gentleman left a servant, who had shown great carelessness in regard to fire and had often given rise in his mind to a strong apprehension that he might set fire to his house–that his anxiety might have been increased by being from home and the same circumstance might make the servant more careless." A further supposition is made, "that the gentleman before going to bed had, in addition to this anxiety, suddenly recollected that there was on that day in the neighborhood of his house, some fair or periodical merry-making, from which the servant was very likely to return home intoxicated." And at last it is supposed that these incidents "might have been embodied into a dream of his house being on fire, and that the same circumstances might have led to the fulfillment of the dream."

This explanation does not reasonably account for the murder which took place two years after the dream, if it should prove satisfactory in regard to the fire; and therefore we take the liberty to explain them both upon such principles as we have endeavored to lay down, as governing the mind under such circumstances. We believe that experiments have proved that to a mind in its excited or dreaming state, when its bodily senses are dormant or inactive, and impressions are conveyed to it by direct influences upon itself, all space, time, distance and matter are no obstacles to its action. In the cases above named, let us assume the fact that there is no such thing as time with the mind, that the past, present and future are all present and displayed before it as upon a map and which are all visible, and the explanation of the dreams which occurred previous to the actual occurrence are simple and readily understood.

The mind in this state looks forward and beholds occurrences, which have not yet transpired, but are reserved for a future event; yet it is not able to distinguish at what hour of time it will transpire. It, in fact, appears to the mind precisely like all other events, whether past or present and probably would not be remembered unless connected with some powerful emotion. The committal of murder in one case produced a most powerful impression upon the mind of the actor and was therefore recollected in his waking moments. The burning of the house, in which were those most dear to the clergyman and the imminent danger of his child, no doubt summoned up all the emotions of the heart and left an impression, which confirmed his belief, that the scene of the dream was actually taking place. Similar experiments have been witnessed in the declarations of mesmeric subjects, and scenes which transpired weeks and months and years after were beheld with all the vividness and reality as though they were the events of yesterday.

We have collected a few more facts [from Abercrombie], illustrative of the power of the mind under excitement, dreaming and mesmerism.

["]A gentleman in Scotland was affected with aneurism of the politeal artery and was under the care of two eminent surgeons and the day was fixed for operation. About two days previous to the time set by the surgeons, his wife dreamed that a change had taken place in the disease, in consequence of which the operation would not be required. Upon examination of the tumor, the next morning it was found that the pulsation had nearly ceased and it finally recovered itself. A lady dreamed that an aged female friend of hers had been murdered by a dark servant and the dream occurred more than once. The impression was so strange that she actually went to the house of the lady, to whom it related and prevailed upon a gentleman to watch in the adjoining room the following night. About 3 o'clock in the morning footsteps were heard on the stairs and the gentleman left his place of concealment and met the servant carrying up a basket of coal in which a strong knife was found concealed. Being questioned as to where he was going with his coal he replied in a confused manner, to mend his mistress' fire, which was not very probable in the month of July and at three o'clock in the morning.

["]Another lady dreamed that her nephew was drowned with some young companions with whom he had engaged to sail the following day, and the impression was so strong that she prevailed upon him not to join his companions, who went on the excursion and were all drowned. A lady, who had sent her watch to be repaired and a long time having elapsed without its return, she dreamed that the watchmaker's boy had dropped it on his way to the shop and it was injured so much as not to be repaired. Upon enquiry, this was ascertained to be a fact.["]

These experiments are acknowledged to be of an order not satisfactorily explainable upon such principles as are laid down by philosophers. The ground we have taken, we believe, fully explains these coincidents. And we shall give a few experiments upon mesmeric subjects showing that the same results may follow.

Another very singular instance of coincident dreams is related by Mr. Taylor and is given by him as a undoubted fact. ["]A young man who was at an academy a hundred miles from home, dreamed that he went to his father's house in the night, tried the front door but found it locked, got in by a back door and finding nobody out of bed went directly to the bedroom of his parents. He then said to his mother whom he found awake, 'Mother, I am going a long journey and am come to bid you good-by.' This she answered under much agitation, 'Oh, dear son, thou art dead.' He instantly awoke and thought no more of his dream until a few days after he received a letter from his father enquiring very anxiously after his health, in consequence of a frightful dream which his mother had on the same night in which the dream now mentioned occurred to him. She dreamed that she heard someone attempt to open the front door, then go to the back door and at last come into her bedroom. She then saw it was her son who came to the side of her bed and said, 'Mother, I am going a long journey and am come to bid you good-bye' on which she exclaimed, 'Oh, dear son, thou art dead.' But nothing unusual happened to any of the parties.["] Dr. Abercrombie supposes these two dreams must have arisen from some strong mental impression arising in both minds about the same time, which produced a similarity of dreaming. A circumstance very extraordinary and is quite as likely to occur from chance as that everything is governed at haphazard without undeviating laws. The true explanation is simple. These two minds were in a dreaming, excited or mesmeric state. The bodily senses cease to act–impressions are now conveyed directly to the mind. All space and time, in this state, are annihilated. Here, then, the mind of the son is in communication with his mother. He makes precisely the same impressions upon her mind as are made upon his; and both minds being in the excited state readily receive impressions from false causes. But we do not design here to say how this train of thought originated but probably from strong mental excitement in his waking moments, leading to the train which occurred in his dream. There can be no question but that one mind here was governed by the other and therefore both dreams would occur at the same time and upon the same subject.

The stories of second sight are also explainable upon the same principle laid down in our preceding work. Anxiety and constant thought upon subjects connected with our interests will sometimes lull us into a mesmeric or dreaming state in which we can behold many scenes, sometimes real and sometimes fictitious.

The mind is excited into the clairvoyant state and is then enabled to perceive objects without the bodily senses. The principle of sight is in the mind, and in our natural state, that principle develops itself through the eye. In the excited state it is developed independent of the eye, acting directly upon the object.

A gentleman sitting by the fire during a stormy night, while his domestics are upon the lake and exposed to the ravages of the storm, falls to sleep (in mesmeric sleep) under the excitement of their absence. The mind is immediately present with the boat and discovers every transaction which befalls the company. If the boat is capsized, he sees it; if it is to return safe, he beholds it. But we are told that under such circumstances, we should expect a disaster and that the mind, falling to sleep with all the picture of their danger before it conjured up by its imagination, would naturally dream their loss. And if the boat returns, nothing more is thought of the dream; if she is lost, these revive all the circumstances as they transpired in the sleeping moments! I grant that such might occur or rather happen but presume the instances of chance would not be numerous enough to account for all the stories of second sight. If the mind is regulated at all by laws, we do not see the reasons of so many exceptions, especially as I contend, all these dreaming phenomena cannot be satisfactorily explained upon other principles than what we have laid down. There is, however, a question which would naturally suggest itself in relation to the impressions we receive while in this excited, dreaming state. What we dream will not always come to pass. This does not militate against that doctrine we have laid down, but will only confirm what we have before declared in relation to the power of impressions to regulate our thoughts. We will illustrate our subject in this manner. Suppose an individual, whose mind has been long upon one subject in which he finds himself deeply interested. While having his mind intently fixed under ordinary excitement with all his external faculties in action, he arrives at certain conclusions which he believes to be correct and a strong impression is made governing the further action of the mind in relation to the subject. Now this conclusion may not be correct, yet the individual would be firm in his position. A wrong impression, arising somewhere in the process of reasoning, has led to a wrong conclusion. Now if the individual could detect the first false step, he would correct the conclusion and vindicate truth. This is the natural operation of mind under ordinary excitement. Now place a subject in the dreaming or mesmeric state, and it becomes far more susceptible of impressions than before. It is, therefore, even more liable to receive a wrong impression from some external cause or internal emotion than in its natural state, and therefore, all of these false dreams may be accounted for on this principle. An individual passing into this excited state may have, in his waking moments, impressed upon his mind something as having actually taken place which had not and did not transpire, with such power, as that the impression would control the mind and be led to an endless number of false conclusions which the facts in the case did not warrant. This is when the mind is led astray and does not receive impressions from facts but from preceding impressions. And that mind cannot distinguish the <u>false</u> from the <u>true</u> cause, unless in the course of its progress, it is led to reconsider or review the whole scene with the idea of getting the facts and giving a true statement. The mind can act from facts or rather receive its impressions from facts, and when this is the case, will always develop true results.

We shall mention only a few cases of what is usually called dreams and pass to another division of our subject. The following incident is related by Dr. Abercrombie who was acquainted with all the particulars and fully vouches for their accuracy.

"Two ladies, sisters, had been for several days in attendance upon their brother who was ill of a common sore throat, severe and protracted, but not considered as attended with danger. At the same time one of them had borrowed a watch of a female friend, in consequence of her own being under repair; this watch was one to which particular value was attached on account of some family associations, and some anxiety was expressed that it might not meet with any injury. The sisters were sleeping together in a room communicating with that of their brother, when the elder of them awoke in great agitation, and having roused the other, told her that she had had a frightful dream. 'I dreamed,' she said, 'that Mary's watch stopped and that when I told you of the circumstances, you replied, much worse than <u>that</u> has happened, for _____'s breath has stopped also,'–naming their brother who was ill. To quiet her agitation the younger sister immediately got up and found the brother sleeping quietly, and the watch, which had been carefully put by in a drawer, going correctly. The following night the very same dream occurred, followed by similar agitation, which was again composed in the same manner, the brother being again found in quiet sleep, and the watch going well. On the following morning soon after the family had breakfasted, one of the sisters was sitting by her brother while the other was writing a note in an adjoining room. When her note was ready for being sealed, she was proceeding to take out for this purpose, the watch alluded to, which had been put by in her writing desk; she was astonished to find it stopped. At the same instant she heard a scream of intense distress from her sister in the other room,–their brother, who had still been considered as going on favourably, had been seized with a sudden fit of suffocation, and had just breathed his last."

Lecture Notes–Booklet III
[BU 1:0055]

I have frequently alluded to the capacities of mind, acting in its excited state, independent of matter. This can be clearly proved by a subject under the mesmeric influence. The mind is then present with all things and needs only to be directed and the object is before it. Distance and space are nothing, and therefore, no time is required to pass the mind from one object to another. It is so in our waking thoughts. The mind is occupied with only one thing at a time and when it is directed to a new object of thought, the direction and the attention pass at the same instant. Nor does it require any longer time or any other further effort to think of an object in the Chinese Empire than those nearest us. But the mind in our natural state depends upon the five senses for its external information and forms all its ideas of things through them. But in the excited state, it receives no impressions through the organs of sense, but every object, which acts at all, acts directly upon the mind or is presented by the influence of another mind. Instances of dreaming are now on record in which this principle is fully illustrated–[William] Smellie in his [The Philosophy of] Natural History relates a case of a medical student of the University of Edinburgh, who was accustomed to dream and be aroused from the same cause that produced the first impression. We also notice instances of the following character. ["]A gentleman dreamed that he had enlisted as a common soldier, joined his regiment, deserted, was apprehended, carried back, tried, condemned to be shot, and at last led out for execution. After all these preparations, a gun was fired and he awoke with the report and found that a noise in the adjoining room had both produced the dream and awaked him. Dr. Gregory mentions a case in which a gentleman, who had taken cold from sleeping in a damp place, was liable to a feeling of suffocation when he slept in a lying posture; and this was always accompanied with a dream of a skeleton which grasped his throat. On one occasion, he procured a sentinel, giving him directions to arouse him whenever he was disposed to sink down, as these dreams never occurred when he slept in a sitting position. He began to sink away, and upon his being aroused instantly, found fault with his attendant for not having aroused him immediately as he had been in a struggle with the skeleton for a long time before he awoke.["] "A friend of mine," says Dr. Abercrombie, "dreamed that he had crossed the Atlantic and spent a fortnight in America. In embarking on his return, he fell into the sea, and having awoke from the fright, discovered that he had not been asleep above ten minutes."

"Count Lavallette," says Professor Upham, "who was some years since condemned to death in France, relates a dream, which occurred during his imprisonment, as follows. 'One night while I was asleep, the clock of the Palais de Justice struck twelve and awoke me. I heard the gate open to relieve the sentry, but I fell asleep again immediately. In this sleep, I dreamed that I was standing in the Rue St. Honoré at the corner of the Rue de l'Echelle. A melancholy darkness spread around me, all was still, nevertheless a low and uncertain sound soon arose. All of a sudden I perceived at the bottom of the street and advancing towards me a troop of cavalry, the men and horses however, all flayed. This horrible troop continued passing in a rapid gallop, and casting frightful looks at me. Their march, I thought, continued five hours; and they were followed by an immense number of artillery and wagons, full of bleeding corpses, whose limbs still quivered; a disgusting smell of blood and bitumen almost choked me. At length the iron gate of the prison, shutting with great force, awoke me again. I made my repeater strike; it was no more than midnight so that the horrible phantasmagoria had lasted no more than two or three minutes–that is to say, the time necessary for relieving the sentry and shutting the gate. The cold was severe and the watchword short. The next day, the turnkey confirmed my calculations.'"

These experiments all confirm the doctrine of the rapidity of thought, that no time, as we are accustomed to measure it, is required for transactions which would occupy months and years in their performance. Yet the mind lives in these short periods required to pass upon such scenes, apparently the whole time it would require to perform them. The mind in its dreaming or excited state will pass from country to country, from shore to shore, mountain to mountain in rapid succession, feeling that it has actually passed over a space of time sufficient to have accomplished all these distances. Under such influences, the mind would perform a pilgrimage to Mecca, experience all the particulars of the passage of the Rubicon, visit St. Petersburg and Moscow and be engaged in a whaling voyage in the Pacific Ocean–all in rapid succession. Impression follows impression and results and conclusions follow as rapidly as they are produced. It is true that the mind compares every transaction of thought with its knowledge, previously attained. And it is thus deceived in the measure of time when it does not, through the organized body, perform its thoughts. It has no other method by which to calculate than such as is derived from previous knowledge.

Somnambulism is another state of mind as laid down by different philosophers. It is only another condition of excited mind by which all the impressions are received by another process than the bodily organs, by which the subject is induced to walk and perform bodily and mental labor. This condition of mind is really the dreaming or excited state and explainable upon the same principles as other dreams. But the difficulty in explanations given by those who have written upon the subject is the misconception of its cause mixing up the action of the mind under such excitement with its action through the bodily senses. I do not intend to convey the idea that the mind may not act partly from one cause or condition and partly from the other. It does so act, and this no doubt is the cause of many impressions which the mind in its dreaming state is constantly receiving. Their confusion in explanations arises from the argument being drawn from the knowledge received through the bodily senses alone, not mentioning to explain the phenomena arising from an independent state. If facts alone, subject to the laws which govern mind, were to furnish a basis, it is not possible to explain these two conditions, natural and excited on other principles than those which have governed us throughout this work.

Somnambulism is then a species of mesmerism and a subject may be so controlled as to perform the same experiments we shall give, selected from different works.

"A young nobleman," says Dr. Abercrombie, "living in the citadel of Breslau, was observed by his brother, who occupied the same room, to rise in his sleep, wrap himself in a cloak and escape by a window to the roof of a building. He then tore in pieces a magpie's nest, wrapped the young birds in his cloak, returned to his apartment and went to bed. In the morning he mentioned the circumstances as having occurred in a dream, and could not be persuaded that there had been anything more than a dream, till he was shown the magpies in his cloak." [Quoted from John Abercrombie's *Inquiries Concerning the Intellectual Powers, and the Investigation of Truth* (1842). —*Ed.*]

"A farmer in one of the counties of Massachusetts had employed himself, some weeks in winter, threshing his grain. One night as he was about closing his labors, he ascended a ladder to the top of the great beams in the barn, where the rye which he was threshing was deposited, to ascertain what number of bundles remained un-threshed, which he determined to finish the next day. The ensuing night about two o'clock he was heard by one of the family to rise and go out. He repaired to his barn, being sound asleep and unconscious of what he was doing, set open his barn doors, ascended the great beams of the barn where his rye was deposited, threw down a flooring and commenced threshing it. When he had completed it, he raked off the straw and shoved the rye to one side of the floor, and then again ascended the ladder with the straw and deposited it on some rails that lay across the great beams. He then threw down another flooring of rye which he threshed and finished as before. Thus he continued his labors until he had threshed five floorings, and on returning from throwing down the sixth and last, in passing over part of the haymow, he fell off where the hay had been cut down about six feet, on the lower part of it, which awoke him. He at first imagined himself in his neighbor's barn, but after groping about in the dark for a long time, ascertained that he was in his own, and at length found the ladder on which he descended to the floor, closed his barn doors which he found open, and returned to his house. On coming to the light, he found himself in such a profuse perspiration that his clothes were literally wet through. The next morning on going to his barn, he found that he had threshed, during the night, five bushels of rye, had raked the straw off in good order and deposited it on the great beams and carefully shoved the grain to one side of the floor, without the least consciousness of what he was doing, until he fell from the hay." [Quoted from Thomas C. Upham's *Elements of Mental Philosophy* (1839). —*Ed.*]

We recollect of reading an account of a clergyman who had been long contemplating the writing of a sermon upon a certain passage of the Scripture, which required deep thought. He arose from his sleep during the night and entirely wrote out the whole discourse in a most lucid and convincing reasoning and language and returned to rest. On the following day, could recollect nothing of the transaction, but the different heads of the subject connected with dreaming. Upon going to his study, he was surprised to find the whole discourse in writing, neatly executed in his usual form of writing sermons.

Another instance came under our own observation, in the western part of Maine, of the gentleman farmer who during the month of August in one of his night walks, arose and taking his scythe went into his field and actually mowed down a half acre of his best wheat, returned the scythe to its usual place and returned to bed. He awoke the next morning and recollected nothing of the transaction, but remarked that he had a singular dream of taking his scythe and mowing an acre of his wheat instead of reaping it as was his usual method. He was loath to believe what he witnessed with his own eyes, the grain in the swath and that it had been done by his own hand. It no doubt would have been charged upon some of his good neighbors had not some of his own household witnessed the whole transaction.

Philosophers have confessed their inability to explain satisfactorily these strange phenomena–and then by undertaking to show in what possible manner it might all <u>happen</u>, mystify what was before mysterious. We do not learn from them how it is possible for one to see at all under any circumstances without the bodily organ of sight; and much less have they proved to us the power of seeing without eyes and in Egyptian darkness. "There is," says Prof. Upham, "a set of nerves which are understood to be particularly connected with respiration and appear to have nothing to do with sensation and muscular action. There is another set which one knows to possess a direct and important connection with sensation and the muscles. These last are separable into distinct filaments, having separate functions, some being connected with sensation merely and others with volition and muscular action. In sensation, the impression, made by some external body, exists at first in the external part of the organs of sense and is propagated along one class of filaments to the brain. In volition and voluntary muscular movement, the origin of action, as far as the body is concerned, seems to be the reverse, commencing in the brain and being propagated along other and appropriate nervous filaments to the different parts of the system. Hence it sometimes happens, that, in diseases of the nervous system, the power of sensation is in a great measure lost while that of motion fully remains; or, on the contrary, the power of motion is lost while that of sensation remains. These views help to throw light upon the subject of somnambulism. Causes, at present unknown to us, may operate through their appropriate nervous filaments to keep the muscles awake, without disturbing the repose and inactivity of the senses. A man may be asleep as to all the powers of external perception, and yet be awake in respect to the capabilities of muscular motion. And aided by the trains of association which make a part of his dreams, may be able to walk about and to do many things without the aid of the sight or hearing."

It cannot be possible that the explanation given by the professor was satisfactory to himself. For it would be one of the greatest experiments of chance ever known or thought of for a man to rise from his sleep and go to his barn and climb to the great beams, throw down his bundles of grain, thrash them and rake up the straw etc., etc., and follow up this course of business without seeing or without the power of sight. But the explanation given above admits that such transactions might happen without "<u>sight or hearing</u>." No one has ever undertaken to explain them upon the supposition that they do really see and perform all these muscular actions by the aid of the visual powers of mind.

There is another experiment referred to by the professor as not having been reached by any of his previous statements and explanations; and he considers that they may form an exception to the usual appearances in somnambulists but of a marked and extraordinary character. "There are few cases," he says, "(the recent instance of Jane Rider in this country is one), where persons, in the condition of somnambulism, have not only possessed slight visual power, but perceptions of sight increased much above the common degree. In the extraordinary narrative of Jane Rider, the author informs us, that he took two large wads of cotton and placed them directly on the closed eyelids, and then bound them on with a black silk handkerchief. The cotton filled the cavity under the eyebrows and reached down to the middle of the cheek and various experiments were tried to ascertain whether she could see. In one of them a watch enclosed in a case was handed to her and she was requested to tell what o'clock it was by it; upon which, after examining both sides of the watch, she opened the case and then answered the question. She also read, without hesitation, the name of a gentleman, written in characters so fine that no one else could distinguish it at the usual distance from the eye. In another paroxysm, the lights were removed from her room and the windows so secured that no object was discernible, and two books were presented to her when she immediately told the titles of both, though one of them was a book which she had never before seen. In other experiments, while the room was so darkened that it was impossible, with the ordinary powers of vision to distinguish the colors of the carpet, her eyes were also bandaged. She pointed out the different colors in the hearth rug, took up and read several cards lying on the table, threaded a needle and performed several other things which could not have been done without the aid of the vision. Of extraordinary cases of this kind, it would seem that no satisfactory explanation, (at least no explanation which is unattended with difficulties), has as yet been given."

This last case with the remarks is extracted from Upham's [1839] Mental Philosophy Vol. 1, page 214. He expresses no difficulty in explaining how the farmer of Massachusetts could do his thrashing in the midst of darkness and without the power of sight, but is willing to acknowledge his inability to explain the method of seeing in the case of Jane Rider. To us, it appears that they may both be explained upon the same principles, that they are nearly parallel cases and can be accounted for in no other way than by the principles we have laid down, namely, that in the excited, dreaming or somnambulistic subject, impressions are conveyed to the mind without the aid of the bodily organs, and that the faculties of the mind are acting in direct communication with objects–that the mind sees, hears, tastes, smells and feels, without the eyes, ears, tongue, nose and hands. And that precisely the same impressions may be conveyed to the mind directly without these organs as could be with them.

A case of somnambulism is related by Dr. Gillett of Connecticut. The subject was a lady of Wapping, near East Windsor, Conn., who was, while in this state, able to thread her needle, perform her domestic labors, read a book upside down with great fluency, tell the time by a watch held near her head and know what her friends were doing in any part of the room, at any moment etc., etc. This condition of mind was supposed to result from her weakness and ill health. She was afterwards cured of these spasms by the influence of mesmeric operations. The case of Yarnell, a lad born in Buck's County, Pennsylvania, is a striking instance of somnambulism or excited state of mind. He could perceive persons and their conduct, however remote, by simply resting his hands upon his knees and his head upon his hands. He was frequently questioned by wives, whose husbands were gone to sea and had been absent a long time, and would give the correct information as to their place and conduct. He would often direct where stolen goods were found and describe the persons who had taken them. Other instances might be named of the same class, proving the most extraordinary power of the mind while in this excited state.

One remark, before we close this part of our subject. The cases of somnambulism which we have referred to are conditions of mind precisely like those in the mesmeric state. Every action which transpired in the accounts above may be produced by a subject under the mesmeric influence. This places the question, beyond a doubt, that the different conditions of the mind are all governed by similar laws and explainable upon such principles as we have laid down. We have taken for examples, such anecdotes and incidents as are familiar to almost every individual who has paid close attention to the philosophy of the mind, such as are found in various authors who have explained these phenomena according to their ideas of mind; but we have endeavored to explain them upon other principles. We proceed now to a further illustration of our position upon the theory of mesmerism.

Mesmerism

Anton Mesmer, a Swiss Physician, about the year 1750 was distinguishing himself by his philosophical writings. From some cause or other, he left his native country and appeared in France in 1778. Soon after his arrival, he introduced the new science of Animal Magnetism, which has since been sometimes called Mesmerism from its supposed discoverer. The phenomena exhibited by Mesmer under the influence of his new science had been familiar in one form or other to the inhabitants of the world so far back as history extends; yet he claimed the honor of discovering its powers and its laws. He introduced the doctrine of the "magnetic fluid" and was accustomed to magnetize trees by whose power in turn subjects were thrown into the magnetic state etc. I believe it has generally been conceded by all who have succeeded him and who have claimed much honor for having advanced the science, that Mesmer first operated with the Animal fluid. In the year of 1784, the subject of Animal Magnetism excited much interest in Paris and the King was finally induced to direct a committee of the Royal Academy of Medicine of Paris to give the subject a thorough consideration and report their opinion of its merits. The American Philosopher, Dr. Franklin, was then Ambassador at the Court of France and was appointed a member of this committee. It appears during the progress of their investigations that two principles were to be decided. First, whether the experiments were really performed as they appeared or were they a species of deception practiced by collusion, contact or by previous practice. Second, whether, if there should be no deception practiced, there is sufficient evidence from the facts developed to establish a theory of "Magnetic Fluid" through which all these strange appearances of the mind were exhibited. The committee decided that there was not sufficient evidence exhibited to show that the phenomena called Magnetic, were caused by the action of a fluid, as had been contended by the disciples of Mesmer. This settled, with them, the second part of their enquiry. The results, however, and the facts witnessed, were more difficult to reject. They were thought to be "singular and wonderful" and were finally attributed to the power of the imagination. The mysterious influence of 'mind over mind,' was readily conceded; yet they supposed the medium to be (not a magnetic fluid), but "Imagination." We find no fault with this report except in the term used as its cause, namely, the "Imagination," believing that even the facts disclosed before the honorable committee were such as to require another expression. If I imagine a picture or scene, it will not appear real to me. I might create images corresponding to certain names which would be given them, but there would be no belief on my part of the real existence of such created images. The poet may rely upon his powers of imagination and portray in measured verse ideal existences which please and amuse, but should he portray what he believed to exist or knows to exist just as he would describe any fact, no one would contend that the work was a species of imagery, but a relation of facts by the author, or at least, what was believed to be true by him. Milton, in Paradise Lost has displayed the highest powers of the imagination, but we do not presume he believed himself relating simple facts, which actually transpired according to the description he has given. Yet to some minds who have read this work of genius and have a belief and a conviction of the reality of his imagery, it is with them a matter of fact. Imagination can have no permanent effect over the conduct of an individual, because an impression produced upon the mind by an imaginary cause ceases to control him, the moment he is conscious of this fact. If I should read an account of some wonderful event in the columns of a newspaper and I believed it to be a fact, there would be no imagination upon my part, although the whole scene might be the work of the editor's imagination. It would be imagery to him, but reality to me. Now the committee did not pretend that collusion or consent of action produced such results as were exhibited before them, but that it was by some unknown mystery, the influence of "Imagination."

It must be admitted at the present day that all subjects act from impressions and that they really believe in the reality of the cause of these impressions, else they would not appear so sincere or would not be sincere. If it were the result of the imagination, it would indeed be a species of polite deception because a subject could not be supposed to act sincerely and know at the same time that it proceeded from false causes and that he was deceiving himself. The operator, or rather the controller of the mind of a subject in the mesmeric state, may produce impressions upon the recipient, from false causes; yet those causes would be real to his subject and produce the same results as though every impression were the result of a real cause. A mesmerizer may imagine a book before the subject and the subject will see and feel it, although no book be in a room; that is, the same impression is made upon his mind by the mind of the operator as though a book had really been placed before him. The operator thinks or imagines the book, but the subject receives a real impression and acts as though the object was before him. I have frequently amused myself with experiments of this nature, fully demonstrating the effect of imagination producing real impressions upon the subject. I have handed Lucius, my subject, a six inch rule and imagined it to be twelve inches. He would immediately divide the rule into twelve inches by counting. Present him with the rule and ask him how many inches it contains and he would answer correctly unless, by the operation of my mind I should produce an impression that it contained twelve inches. I have first asked him to tell me how long it was and he would answer me correctly. I would then ask him to look again, and then I would imagine any length I please and he would answer me according to the impression I produced by my imagination or thought. So in regard to other impressions which I would cause to be made upon his mind, always producing the same results as though the real object were presented. I understand the term, imagination, as employed by the honorable Committee, to refer to the subject and not the operator–that it is a result of the imagination of the subject. Our remarks above, we think, explain precisely how much the imagination has to do with this subject, believing as we do that the mesmerized mind acts from impressions regulated by the same laws as when impressions are made by the communication of the bodily senses. In the experiments we have named, and no doubt it was so before the Committee, whatever imagination has to do with the experiments at all is confined, not to the subject but to the operator or individual who is in communication with the subject.

We believe the Committee had good and conclusive evidence against the theory of a fluid and we are equally unbelieving in the imagination as being the result of all they witnessed. We are aware that much, very much, appears at first view to be the power of imagination; but a further investigation into the results will prove that with the mesmeric subject, there is no such power as imagination.

There was an interesting experiment which was performed before the Committee at Paris of this nature. A tree was magnetized, as the operator supposed, and the subject was to be led up to it and the magnetic fluid would pass into him and throw him into the magnetic state. This was performed several times with perfect accuracy. But the Committee finally hit upon this method. Instead of taking him to the magnetized tree, he was led up, blindfold, to one not magnetized and quite as mysteriously fell into the mesmeric condition. This proved to the Committee, as it must to everyone, that in fact one tree possesses the same principle and quantity of magnetism as the other, which the operator had acted upon; or that neither of them was impregnated with magnetism but that some other cause, called by the Committee imagination, produced the mesmeric sleep. Query, was this imagination! The subject in the first instance believed that he was led to the magnetized tree, which was true, and there could not have been imagination about this. In the second instance he was led to the natural tree, but he believed it to be magnetized and of course the same impressions and the same results would follow, if you reject the magnetic fluid. Every circumstance to the subject would be the same in both experiments, and if like causes produce like effects, it could not be the result of a magnetic influence because one tree was magnetized and the other was not and the impressions being real in both cases could not have affected the imagination. Imagination supposes something not real. These impressions, from which the subject acts, are real and not imaginary to him.

If the reply is that imagination produced both results, we answer that everything which makes an impression upon the mind is, then, the result of the imagination. All the impressions we receive are imagined, and man's whole conduct is nothing but a series and succession of imaginations.

If I direct my subject to do a certain thing at such a time, informing him what that is and the result I wish to produce, and nothing further is said or thought about the direction until the time arrives, and should the subject by his own voluntary act do according to my direction, is it the result of his imagination? If on the other hand, I desire him to do something at a certain time, but do not communicate to him my desire, and he should without further cause perform the very act I wished, would it be the power of his imagination? If these are all the result of imagination, everything which surrounds us exists only in imagery and the world is ideal. The system of Berkeley concerning the non existence of matter and that material existences are but images etc.–might be well adopted; and to carry up the science a little further, Hume, with his creations of images and impressions, would be the pattern philosopher of the images of men!

We are rather disposed to confine the use of the word imagination to its proper definition and not to confound it with realities. We must therefore reject both the "magnetic fluid" and the "imagination" as being the cause of the phenomena called mesmeric. We embrace a doctrine which both the Committee and the followers of Mesmer do not deny, namely, the influence of mind over mind, not through the medium of a "fluid" or the "Imagination" but by direct contact with and action upon mind.

We shall now proceed to examine the theory of a "Fluid" and to show what deception those who have adopted and advocated the theory have practiced upon themselves. It has been remarked, (and with what truth our readers will hereafter decide), that Animal Magnetism is a stupendous humbug, that it is a species of polite deception held up to the community as something strange, wonderful and real–a delusion played upon the credulity of honest citizens by artful and designing operators. The facts resulting from experiments, in this enlightened age, cannot be refuted; but I am aware that the oddity and unreasonable methods of accounting for them by the writing and lectures of the advocates of a Fluid theory are so inconsistent with many experiments performed by the followers of Mesmer, themselves, that not only the animal fluid, but all the strange phenomena of mind, arising from the mesmeric state, are rejected at once and passed over to the grave of delusion.

But the rejection of facts should be more carefully done, than of falsehood. Nor should we give up the whole facts because the system of explanation is inconsistent and absurd. It is not really the community who are so essentially humbugged as those who adopt and defend the "Fluid Theory." They are really deceived, supposing they have the agency of a fluid when, in fact there is no fluid about the experiments. Their belief, however, enables them to perform their experiments and they proceed as though they were really doing something by its agency. If they should adopt the theory of solids instead of fluids, it would be quite as reasonable and they might perform all the experiments which they now perform with the fluid, or reject both and then all the experiments can be better performed which could be performed by "fluids and solids."

The Rev. Chauncey Hare Townshend A.M. late of Trinity Hall, Cambridge has published a volume of some four hundred pages, entitled Dispassionate Inquiry into Mesmerism. It is on the whole a very interesting work, and serves rather to amuse than to instruct and direct the enquirer after truth. His experiments were good and expressed in beautiful language and with scientific terms. But the error of all his labor was in the first impression from a false cause. He was a believer in the magnetic fluid and endeavored to bring all the facts he discovered under its agency. Like the Religionist who first writes out his creed and then bends every possible principle he can discover in the Bible to support a fabric which he has, himself, designed, he appears to be more intent upon settling the question of a fluid agency and bending all his experiments to support his Theory than to branch out in opposition and undertake to prove the falsity of his position.

On page 276 [409], Book fourth, we find the following principle laid down.

"First, I affirm that, productive of the effects called mesmeric, there is an action of matter as distinct and specific as that of light, heat, electricity or any other of the imponderable agents, as they are called; that, when the mesmerizer influences his patient, he does this by a medium, either known already in other guise, or altogether new to our experience.

"What proofs, it will be asked, can I bring forward to this assertion? I answer, such proofs as are considered available in all cases where an impalpable, imponderable medium is to be considered; facts, namely, or certain appearances, which, bearing a peculiar character, irresistibly suggest a peculiar cause.

"Let us take only one of these. Standing at some yards distant from a person who is in the mesmeric state, (that person being perfectly stationary, and with his back to me), I, by a slight motion of my hand (far too slight to be felt by the patient through any disturbance of the air) draw him towards me as if I actually grasped him.

"What is the chain of facts which is here presented to me? First, an action of my mind, without which I could not have moved my hand; secondly, my hand's motion; thirdly, motion produced in a body altogether external to, and distant from myself. But it will at once be perceived, that, in the chain of events, as thus stated, there is a deficient link. The communication between me and the distant body is not accounted for. How could an act of my mind originate an effect so unusual?" Here then follows the explanation. "That which is immaterial, cannot, by its very definition, move masses of matter. It is only when mysteriously united to a body that spirit is brought into relationship with place or extension, and under such a condition alone, and only through such a medium, can it propagate motion. Now, in some wondrous way spirit is in us incorporate. Our bodies are its medium of action. By them and only by them, as far as our experience reaches are we enabled to move masses of foreign matter. I may sit and will forever that yonder chair to come to me, but without the direct agency of my body, it must remain where it is. All the willing in the world cannot stir it an inch. I must bring myself into absolute contact with the body which I desire to move. But in the case before us, I will; I extend my hands; I move them hither and thither and I see the body of another person–a mass of matter external to myself, yet not in apparent contact with me– moved and swayed by the same action which stirs my own body. Am I thence to conclude that a miracle has been performed, that the laws of nature have been reversed, that I can move foreign matter without contact or intermediate agency? Or must I not rather be certain, that, if I am able to sway a distant body, it is by means of some unseen lever, that volition is employing some [Continued in Booklet IV.–*Ed.*]

[Continued from Booklet III.–*Ed.*] thing which is equal to a body, something which may be likened to an extended corporeity which has become the organ of my will?"

Here we have the experiment and the explanation. Let us examine the reasoning. First, "that which is immaterial cannot by its very definition move masses of matter." "I must bring myself into absolute contact with the body which I desire to move." The person at a distance is then brought into "absolute contact" by the agency or electricity. He "wills, extends his hands and moves them hither and thither" and the patient at a distance, being in actual contact with him by this electric agency, extends his hands, moves them hither and thither etc. The body or arm and hand of the patient is moved by the mind of the operator just as it acts in his body, electricity being the medium of communication as though the body of the operator, his mind, and the body of the patient are one person. Now if electricity or any other fluid can so connect mind and matter, I do not see why we may not connect ourselves with the chair in the supposition above and mind with its new organ of contact will cause the chair to move, on the same principle of connection as the body of the patient. Mind, no doubt, has equal power to connect itself with a chair as with any other material body by the agency of electricity. The body of the patient, without his mind, or acting independent of his own will, as it must, if it were moved by the mind of the operator, would be like every other material thing and susceptible of action upon it by another mind to the same degree, as the chair, being no more or less. And if he proves to you that the motion of the patient's hands is from the same mind as the motion of the operator's through the agency of electricity, I will as conclusively prove that by the same agent your minds may be in "absolute contact" with any, or all, material bodies and that you can as easily move the universe of matter by the mind, as the body of one man. But was not the experiment really performed? We answer, yes, without electricity or any other fluid–not by the mind of the operator acting on the body of the patient, but upon his mind. It was mind acting upon mind. The proposition laid down by the Rev. gentleman, that immateriality cannot move masses of materiality does not apply to destroy the influence or action of mind, being <u>immaterial</u>, over <u>immaterial</u> mind. We trust we have shown, by such experiments as have been introduced into the former part of this work, the great laws by which such facts are produced, that mind in the excited or mesmeric state is present with everything–that space, distance and material objects are no impediments to its action–that it is susceptible of impressions from other minds and will act under such impressions as it receives. Suppose, then, the operator is impressed to extend his hand; that impression is immediately made upon the mind of his patient and all the organs of his body, being under this control of his mind, act in conformity to the impression. The distance from the patient is no obstacle because mind, acting directly without the medium of the bodily senses, knows nothing of space and distance. It only requires direction and it is present with the object. If electricity be the "<u>lever</u>" by which the operator moved the arm of the patient, as asserted by the Rev. Mr. Townshend, we would ask where the fulcrum rests by which he gets his power. It might be answered that it rests where the fulcrum of the globe's foundation was supposed to–upon the "back of an enormous tortoise."

We will say further, that the experiment above could have been performed without the motion of the hand of the operator, by his willing the patient or impressing his mind to extend the hand. So that all that is necessary to be done in such experiments is to give an impression to do an act upon the mind of the subject and the result immediately follows.

"A friend of mine at Cambridge," says the Rev. Mr. Townshend, "was susceptible of being influenced by myself but transiently and imperfectly, while on the other hand, he was at once and invariably brought into the mesmeric state by being subjected to the action of a young fellow student, who (as to the rest) used no art in his manipulations and merely imitated rudely my proceedings and gestures." Also the following is extracted from his work on mesmerism. "E. A.," whom I could mesmerize in a few seconds, was operated upon for an hour by another person, who in other cases had displayed immense mesmeric power without experiencing any effect whatever."

Here are two cases directly opposite in their character. The first could only be partially operated upon by an experienced and powerful magnetizer; but a fellow student could throw him into the mesmeric sleep without exercising the least effort to pass the fluid. If it had been a fluid, he, who knew best how to direct it, of course would magnetize better than one who neither knew how nor used effort but only imitated the actions of a mesmerizer. The second case proves conclusively that the fluid, by which Mr. Townshend and the <u>powerful</u> magnetizer operated upon their subjects, and of course it must be the same, did not produce a result when under the control of one, which it did under that of the other, upon the same subject. If it was a fluid why did not the same results follow from the same causes. Both were powerful magnetizers and of course knew how to use and direct the fluid.

From facts like these Mr. Townshend concludes that it is not the power of the magnetizer, but the "proportions between the respective strengths of mesmerizer and patient which insures success and that the less or more on either side would indifferently prevent a perfect result." So that he has ventured to predict that in the progress of this science, a "neurometer, or instrument to ascertain the nervous power of a person, might give to mesmerism that precision which science requires." We fear however that he advanced beyond what we shall ever realize from the fluid theory that his mind had probably been exhilarated by a surcharge of electricity, which enabled him to predict an event, which, if it ever transpires, we think, must be very far distant in the future.

We have endeavored in every portion of our work to keep distinctly in view the theory of "<u>mind acting upon mind</u>," not through a medium, because we see no necessity of an agent different from itself, but by direct action. To those who are partial to a theory of fluid and are sincere and, as they say, conscious of the fact, we will remark that on the whole, we differ but little from them, save in the fluid. They are obliged to admit that it is often all "<u>mind acting upon mind</u>"; yet all the followers of Mesmer must complicate this operation by intermixing it with some imponderable agent, as though immateriality cannot act upon immateriality without the agency of matter. If "<u>mind acts upon mind</u>" at all, (and we contend it does) without the agency of the bodily senses, we see no reason why it may not act directly, carrying the influence home to the very soul of the subject, as well as to wield the lever of a fluid to make an impression, or to mount its thoughts astride of a streak of electricity to be conveyed to the mind of the subject. It is a little surprising to us, however, that some of the "Doctors" of mesmerism have not put their theory to the test, not by always supposing that a fluid is necessary, but by experimentising without the fluid in such cases as could not have been possible for any fluid to pass. Had this been the case, the theory of a fluid would have been abandoned long ago; for it would have been ascertained that all the fluid which really exists is in the mind of the operator, being like Berkeley's composition of matter, made up of ideas, impressions etc.

Mesmerism was introduced into the United States by M. Charles Poyen, a French gentleman, who did not appear to be highly blest with the powers of magnetizing to the satisfaction of his audience in his public lectures. I had the pleasure of listening to one of his lectures and pronounced it a humbug as a matter of course. And that his remarkable experiments, which were related, were, in my belief, equally true with witchcraft. I had never been a convert to witchcraft, nor had ever had any personal interviews with ghosts or hobgoblins and therefore considered all stories bordering on the marvelous as delusive.

Next came Dr. Collyer, who perhaps did more to excite a spirit of enquiry throughout the community than any who have succeeded him. But the community were still incredulous and the general eccentricity of his character no doubt contributed much to prejudice the minds of his audience against his science. He, however, like all those who had preceded him on both sides of the water, must have a <u>long handle to his science</u>, namely, a subtle fluid of the nature of electricity. So contrary to all experience did all the facts, elicited from his experiments, appear in connection with the laws which govern electricity, that almost every man of science would reject both theory and facts without a moment's consideration. However, the perseverance of the Dr. overcame, in part, some of the prejudices and he at last drew out of a committee in the city of Boston an acknowledgement of the facts, although they refrained from any expression of their opinion as to their occasion.

Collyer was, like all others, satisfied as to the fluid—and nothing could be accomplished without producing a current upon the subject or surcharging him with a quantity of the electric fluid. In a work published by him in 1842 although he is still the advocate of the fluid, yet he rejects the doctrine of Phreno-Magnetism, Neurology etc. as introduced and defended by Dr. Buchanan and La Roy Sunderland. The same course, which enabled him to detect the fallacy of their theories, would have led him, upon pursuing the subject a little further, to have rejected entirely his whole theory of a fluid. He would have looked to another cause of all this phenomenon. From testimony, now before the community, there is no doubt that Collyer performed the first phreno-magnetic experiments in this country and that the honor, if there be any, of the discovery should be yielded to him. It is a matter of little consequence to the community who shall wear the wreath of honor, but we prefer to see the peacock dressed in his own plumage and not bear the shame of a naked plucking by his neighboring fowl.

Dr. Buchanan and the Rev. La Roy Sunderland have claimed the distinguished honor of discovering the sciences of "Nervaurics" and "Phreno-Magnetism." These two sciences (so called), although claimed as distinct, are really regulated by the same laws; not the laws of a "nervous fluid" or of "electricity" but by the same great laws as govern all minds in the excited or mesmeric state–"Mind acting upon mind." It is the direct influence of the operator upon the subject which produces such results. The exciting of particular organs in the brain by the nervous fluid or by electricity is the principle of these sciences. That is, Dr. Buchanan actually fills up these different organs of the brain or such of them as he chooses, which produces an over action of these organs. This is done by contact of the fingers upon these bumps of the head. Dr. Collyer has given a few examples. The following experiments were given before the citizens of Canandaigua, New York.

ON JOHN PARSHALL

Touching	organ	of	Caution	"Feels like fighting"
"	"	"	Firmness	"Firm as a rock"
"	"	"	Acquisitiveness	"Smiles and laughs"
"	"	"	Combativeness	"Great fear"
"	"	"	Philoprogenitiveness	"Like fighting"
"	"	"	Mirthfulness	"Like singing"
"	"	"	Destructiveness	"Feels well, is kindly disposed"

ON OSCAR NILES

Touching	organ	of	Caution	"Desires to laugh"
"	"	"	Benevolence	"Desires to fight"
"	"	"	Mirthfulness	"Desires to sing"
"	"	"	Veneration	"Desires to walk"
"	"	"	Self-esteem	"As big as anyone"

The examples above show conclusively that there is no truth in the theory. There is no correspondence between the organs touched and the effects, except in a few instances. This would always be the case unless something actually occurred beside the passage of the "fluid" into the organ to be excited. I have personally tried hundreds of experiments, all going to prove not only that there is no such thing as exciting different locations of the head, but that there is no "fluid" at all. I can perform, and have done it repeatedly, the same experiments as have been done by Dr. Buchanan or La Roy Sunderland without being near my subject or by contact with any other part of the body than the head. The fingers or toes of any subject are quite as susceptible of excitement from the "fluid" and of producing all the remarkable phenomena and passions of the mind, as the head.

Phrenologists have laid down only thirty-four different organs; but in the rapid march of the science under the excitement of the "nervous fluid" or electricity, the number of organs has suddenly increased to upwards of two hundred. What a rapid stride in the progression of the science of Phrenology! And among these new organs are Felony, Drunkenness, Idiocy, Insanity etc., etc. What dolts must have been such philosophers as [Franz Joseph] Gall [1758-1828] and [Johann Gaspar] Spurzheim [1776-1832] who after devoting their whole lives in careful observation could discover only thirty-four organs in the brain, when these lights of modern genius came puffing by on their fluid cover, upsetting everything which lay before them and only stopping to gather a new recruit of "electricity" after having passed over two hundred newly discovered organs in the space of six months.

The science of "Neurology," as defended by Dr. Buchanan in a course of lectures delivered in the city of New York about two years since, has been most admirably criticized by a correspondent of the "Magnet," a work edited by La Roy Sunderland, who was the great champion of Phreno-Magnetism. We take pleasure in giving the whole communication showing, as we think, some of the absurdities there advanced. (From the Magnet No. 8. January 1841. Copy the correspondence signed C.) [This citation was not copied.–*Ed.*]

The excitability of the human brain by "nervauric influence" will soon be, if it is not already, an exploded idea. There cannot be anything in it. Not that I suppose the experiments which Dr. Buchanan professed to perform were not performed. But on the contrary, I have performed the same class of experiments and am constantly repeating them upon different individuals with whom I meet daily. Nor do I intend to charge any deception upon Dr. Buchanan, designedly practiced upon the community. It is a matter of belief, no doubt, with him and so believing, he could not perform his experiments without attributing them to the very cause he has selected. But if he should believe it sympathy alone he might behold the same results on abandoning all fluids, he could operate so as to produce the same phenomena by the direct influence of his mind upon the mind of his patient. They are a class of Mesmeric results performed without a fluid, nervauric, muscular, magnetic, galvanic or electric. It was the impression, which his mind made on the mind of his patient. In order to make an impression it will be necessary for anyone to have full confidence in the means he uses, or no impression will follow.

Phreno-Magnetism is the same thing in principle as neurology and the remarks we have made upon Nervaura are quite applicable to Phreno-Magnetism. There is no question but certain feelings and conditions of mind corresponding to Benevolence, Neuration, Self-esteem, Combativeness, etc. may be excited in the mind, but that these organs as laid down by phrenologists are magnetized, electrified, galvanized or nervaurised is idle to the wind. Experiments will always fail if the operator does not understand the location of these organs, which is conclusive proof against the theory of a fluid and the exciting of particular organs. The subject too, might also, were he acquainted with Phrenology, do much to answer the particular touches of the operator upon different parts of the head; but when the operator and the subject are both unskilled in the science, the experiment will always correspond with the condition of the mind of the operator. Another fact, which I have observed among different operators, is that no two locate these organs corresponding to what they wish to show, in the same place. Some locate the organ of "ejection" near caution, others, near benevolence, and others in different places; all going to show that "there is nothing in a location."

We venture the assertion, that whatever action is produced upon the brain at all, during this excited state, results rather from the mind of the subject, whose impressions are received from the mind of the operator.

The Rev. Mr. [John Bovee] Dodds [Dods] of Boston, Mass., we believe, deals more extensively in the Magnetic Fluid than any other magnetizer. We have examined his work upon the subject of Mesmerism and can but smile at proofs so conclusively drawn in support of his theory. A careful reading of the whole work is a comfortable electuring [sic] into a talkative sleep ending in ethereal and sublime explanations above the capacity of ordinary men. We were somewhat at a loss to determine whether the Rev. gentleman was most profuse in his language or his fluid! We do not doubt his sincerity in support of his fluid, but must wonder at his credulity. It is a strong proof of the wanderings of an excited mind connected with a strong belief of the means by which wonderful results are produced.

If we were to take up all the points in his theory and discuss them, we fear our pages would be too voluminous for ordinary purposes and that few would be inclined to pursue the investigation. Dods, like all others who believe in the fluid theory, supposed that something must be the medium of communication between mind and mind and between mind and matter separate from the bodily senses, and he has at once brought in the aid of a subtle fluid which pervades all nature.

To introduce the whole theory as it is contended for by most of those who have gone before me, I make the following extract from a pamphlet published in the city of Boston A.D. 1843 entitled "The History and Philosophy of Animal Magnetism" and dedicated by the author to Robert H. Collyer M. D. etc. (Copy chap. Fourth) [This citation was not copied.–*Ed.*]

And who, after such an array of distinguished names would differ from their established theory? All these men were powerful Magnetizers and many of them of the first order of talent but we fear a little inclined to speculate upon a theory, rather than to elicit facts aside from theory. We are satisfied that they all believed in the Fluid, but what its character is remains to be settled among them; as it seems, no two agree to allow it the same name or character. If this "elastic, invisible ether pervading all Nature" causes all these phenomena, it is a God-like power, second only to its Author. That it should operate so mysteriously, sometimes magnetizing individuals by contact and at others, passes through the space of one hundred miles and surcharges the patient and induces the mesmeric state; now made to reside in a letter, and again concealing itself in a tumbler of water, passing to the trunk of a tree; and from all these passing out upon a particular individual and inducing the magnetic sleep. If I could possibly believe in the "Fluid Theory" it would be far more marvelous and astonishing to trace out such laws as must govern this "<u>invisible ether</u>" than the experiments which follow. Or perhaps it may be a principle without the pale of the law, governing itself under the direction of the operator, in part, at some times and at others, entirely at its own control.

Some of the theories of the old Philosophers who wrote upon the subject of the Soul appear to us rather speculative. Fire and other imponderable agents so called were made not the connecting link of Soul and body, but Soul itself. Tracing the analogy of their ideas down to those of the Fluid System, we cannot see why this <u>Fluid</u> might not be the Soul itself. It is the means, we are taught, through which the mind acts and we are to suppose of course that it cannot act at all, except through the fluid, when the bodily senses are closed. It may then be either the soul itself or a necessary appendage, without which although Soul might exist, it could not act or give any evidence of its existence.

The same Author, from whom we have quoted the "Fluid Theory," makes the following remarks in defense of his Theory against the powers of Imagination. "We disapprove this charge at once," (that it is all the work of Imagination) "by the fact that a person, who has been magnetized several times, can be thrown into the magnetic sleep by the magnetizer when he is at a distance of half a mile, and at a moment when the person to be acted upon shall not even suspect it. This has been done successfully by a person who did not even know where the subject of his operations was at the time he made the attempt." Now upon the principle of a Fluid to be "directed upon the brain of the subject" how is it possible that direction can be given, when the operator is ignorant of the location of his subject; and how is it possible that this fluid can be made to pass through so great a distance? If the experiment above alluded to has been performed, could it have been done by the "<u>Fluid</u>"? If, by a "Fluid" how could the operator so direct it as to strike upon the brain of the subject, when he was ignorant of his situation. How could he give effectual direction without knowing where to direct! And then the "Fluid" is to pass through the space of half a mile before it can act upon the subject. If such an experiment as the above can be performed (and we know personally it can) with the fluid and not without it, we certainly must assign the power of intelligence to the "Fluid" and it being commanded by the mind of the operator, to go in search of his subject and induce sleep etc. obeys its master. Such experiments as the above prove one of two things; namely, either, that there is no Fluid by which a communication is effected between mesmerizer and mesmerized, or that this Fluid is an intelligent being, capable of thought itself. We contend that there is no Fluid in the case. If others believe there is, and that it is capable of receiving intelligence and obeying commands, we are not accountable for such belief; but we leave the community, who read and think the sole business of judging, which Theory, Fluid or no Fluid appears the most consistent.

I have performed a similar experiment upon my subject, Lucius, at a distance, sometimes knowing where he was and sometimes not knowing. Yet I did not use any fluid to my knowledge. We have, in another part of this work alluded to the experiment of the magnetized trees–the experiments before the Committee at Paris, France, in proof that no Fluid was in the tree and communicated to the subject. I will again repeat the experiment in substance. The subject was blindfold and led up to a magnetized tree and immediately fell into the magnetic sleep. Being again blindfold, was without his knowledge, led up to a tree not magnetized and also fell into the magnetic sleep, proving conclusively that there was the same virtue in the magnetized and the natural tree.

There is another class of subjects introduced by magnetizers in proof of a magnetic fluid. Some are in the habit of giving their subjects a magnet by which they are thrown into the magnetic sleep. This experiment is explained by attributing the power to the magnet of communicating the Fluid to the subject etc. I have repeatedly magnetized subjects by any little metallic article presenting it to them, after having imbued it with the "Fluid." I have also performed the same experiment by passing to them a similar article not imbued with my Fluid and it produced the same results. I took two combs belonging to two ladies present and magnetized one of them, that is, went through all the ceremony of magnetizing it and the other I only took and passed back to the lady without any operation upon it, and both ladies were thrown into the magnetic sleep by these combs. The lady who received the comb not magnetized was ignorant of that fact and on the contrary believed it magnetized. Perkin's metallic points are celebrated among mesmerizers and were considered sacred proofs of the fluid Theory. Yet after they had their run, some cunning wag introduced wooden points so neatly counterfeiting the metallic in their appearance that they would effect the same results upon a patient as the genuine points. I recollect a young man who in company with Dr. Cutter, the famed lecturer in this part of Maine, visited this place and being an easy subject to mesmerize, as a matter of defense, against the influence of powerful magnetizers, carried with him a magnet, believing it to be a safe preventive against all magnetic power. When armed with his magnet, no one could magnetize him, but without it, almost anyone could induce sleep.

If, by some artful management we could have induced him to believe his magnet absent, although it might have been concealed about him, we venture to say that he would have been quite as easily operated upon, as if his magnet had really been absent. The truth is that it was a matter of belief with the subject and he governed himself accordingly. If I could induce him to believe that magnetism or the magnet had nothing to do with mesmerism or the excited state of mind called mesmeric, then the charm of the magnet would be broken. The Rev. Mr. Dodds has become so confident of a fluid medium of mind and its similarity to electricity that he has found it convenient and perhaps companionable to carry about with him when upon his tours of lecturing, an Electric Machine and I believe he makes it an associate or assistant in throwing subjects into the magnetic state. If this Fluid be electricity, we do not see why Mr. Dodds could not with his machine surcharge a whole audience with a few turns of the handle by placing them in contact with its power.

We have witnessed the experiments of persons standing upon a glass stool and receiving a surcharge of electricity so that sparks might be seen to emit from various parts of their body, yet we saw no signs of magnetic sleep. Now if this Fluid be electricity, it does appear to me that the Electric Machine would be the very first power by which subjects could be magnetized.

While in the city of Boston about one year since, I met with a friend who began to question me as to the tricks I am playing in Magnetism, and as we continued our conversation some time, he suddenly turned his head and after a few moments' pause charged me with an attempt to magnetize him! I did not let him know, but it was so; in truth however, I did not think of it until after he named it. I state this experiment to show that I did not designedly use any fluid, indeed, could not have given direction to any; but the result upon my friend was just the same, no doubt, as though I had really sat down with the intention of performing an operation. This was the belief which he exercised in his mind, that I was trying my powers upon him and he became excited and partially yielded. I do not think I exerted any power to control him, yet he felt a power which he believed proceeded from me and it began to induce the mesmeric state into which he was passing.

A friend of mine, a powerful magnetizer who called on me not long since, operated upon a young lady in my family and threw her into the mesmeric sleep. He was a firm believer in the Magnetic Fluid and everything was done according to the law supposed to govern it. I began to exercise the power of my mind over the subject and she would readily obey me. Desiring her to come to me, she immediately turned her head and was about to rise when her operator, observing the movement, began to cut off the fluid with his hand so as to shut out the power I was gaining over her. I ceased trying to impress her mind with the desire of coming to me and she turned back. During the same sleep I exercised a control over her which was observed by the operator, and when he discovered it, awoke her, saying it was very dangerous mixing up the fluids of different magnetizers upon the subject at the same time. I could not induce him to go on with his experiments, and was obliged to do what I could to show that there was no danger from mixing up fluids etc. or that all the danger arising in the case would be from the fear and belief of the mesmerizer. I then performed a few experiments and requested him to exercise all his fluid power to counteract them. I am unable to say whether the fear of "<u>disturbing the fluid</u>" did not prevent him from making an effort, for all my experiments succeeded.

Steel and various kinds of metal are supposed to have powerful influence over subjects in the mesmeric sleep. Experiments have been introduced to prove the supposition. Some operators cannot exercise their magnetic powers if they have about them steel or silver. This is also a matter of belief. If an operator believes he cannot make an impression upon his subject while this or that metallic substance is about him, then as a matter of course, he will not; but remove what he thinks is the difficulty and then mind acts in full faith and produces a full and decided expression.

I recollect that when I first began to magnetize, I had all this horrid fear about the influence of metal, steel, silver etc. upon the subjects and being a full believer then in the Fluid Theory, supposed some strange connection in all metallic substances with the magnetized subjects. Having on a certain occasion put my subject into sleep after surcharging him with the fluid, a young lady present held the scissors pointing directly towards the head of the subject. Upon my first observing it, I was excited, fearing some bad result. The impression was conveyed to the mind of the subject and all the consequences I feared would result, followed. This to my mind, at that time, was conclusive proof of the power of certain metallic substances, highly magnetic, upon a subject.

I have had very many excellent experiments in Phreno-Magnetism, exciting the organs by pointing a steel rod pointed at one end to the supposed location, believing the fluid passed out of myself through this rod into the organ. When I held the sharp point of the rod towards the organ the subject would immediately arouse and answer to the direction; but if I held the blunt end, it would not affect him. This to me, as I was trying my experiments to prove whether there was any fluid or not, was strong testimony in favor of the fluid system. I had supposed there must be some agent to bring out such results and immediately embraced the theory adopted by most magnetizers, for want of something better. Having adopted, as a matter of belief, an agent by which I could bring about this excited state of mind, I had assigned it certain laws such as I knew to govern electricity. I had all the faith to produce a result when I directed the pointed end to the organ I wished to excite; but when I reversed the point and presented the blunt end, I did not suppose for an instant that the excitement would follow. So the results corresponded with my own feelings. I have witnessed the same experiments performed by other magnetizers and they always advance such facts as I have named as conclusive proofs of a fluid Theory. Since I have abandoned the fluid Theory, I find no difficulty in using either end of the steel rod or use no rod at all and placing myself at a respectable distance from the subject, can produce the same results as I did when the steel rod and fluid Theory were the only means of my operation.

When in the city of Boston with my subject, one of the most powerful magnetizers put my subject into the magnetic sleep and proceeded with his experiments in phreno-magnetics to convince me that the organs were excited by a fluid. He remained in contact with the subject and directed his fluid with the points of his fingers. I was sitting in the room at some distance from the scene of operation and exerted myself to counteract the impression given by the operator. The operator's experiments all failed although he was in contact with the subject and as he supposed was filling up his head with the electric or magnetic fluid.

I also entertained the same idea with other magnetizers about the condition of the atmosphere as being favorable or unfavorable to successful experiments. I could always, under this belief, succeed better in fine clear weather. Indeed, my experiments seldom succeeded in a dull and cloudy atmosphere. I had been giving some very interesting experiments during one evening and did not know but the atmosphere was clear and bright as when I entered the hall. At the close of the experiments I was astonished to learn that, for the last two hours, during the time of my best experiments, the atmosphere had been cloudy and that rain had been falling. This circumstance was one of the first which led to the rejection of the Fluid Theory.

I believed in the power to mesmerize a tumbler of water which, upon being drunk, would throw the patient into the magnetic sleep, and have often amused my audience by this simple experiment. I supposed I did imbue the water with some new virtue and this was also the belief of the subject, and the results followed as I had anticipated. The experiment of the silk handkerchief has been one I have performed repeatedly. I would magnetize the handkerchief and pass it to the subject and it would induce the mesmeric sleep. I was so confident in the fluid theory and that silk would affect its operation, that on one occasion when I had put my subject to sleep and a lady was sitting nearby dressed in silk, his hands and feet were extended towards her dress. These simple facts all went to confirm me in the belief of the fluid theory. Yet I have been compelled to reject them all and I find there is no difficulty in producing the same results with a tumbler of clear water as when I have surcharged it with magnetic fluid, or with a silk handkerchief in its natural state as when magnetized. And I can with all safety allow ladies to sit near my subject, in silk apparel, without any fear of distracting his slumber.

I have magnetized a cedar twig and given it to my subject and he would immediately pass into the magnetic state. I have also given him other articles and told him I had magnetized them, although I had not, yet he would pass into sleep as before. We might multiply simple cases of this class to a very great number but all of them would terminate as those I have mentioned. I have performed them with the fluid and have done the same without it.

It has sometimes been supposed that subjects are not susceptible of influence from the operator only in the sleeping state. This is not so. Dr. Buchanan, although a devoted advocate of the fluid, has given many experiments, in proof of a controlling power which the operator may have over the subject. It is, with me, my daily practice to perform most of my experiments when the subject could not know in his waking moments my wishes, while to all appearance he is not influenced by any one. I have frequently extended my power to impress upon the mind of some person in my presence a wish to do something, keeping distinctly in my mind what I would have him do. And the subject would soon do the very act which I had wished to bring about. I have frequently operated upon a subject in his waking state producing certain feelings in him corresponding to my own; have relieved pain in hundreds of instances to the benefit and happiness of persons under my influence; have relieved headache, pain in any part of the body. As I was writing a few sentences above, an individual called on me and stated that his foot was very painful to him, and if I could ease the pain and adding that he did not believe I could, that he would not deny the fact and should be a believer in Mesmerism. I operated upon his foot and relieved the pain. He acknowledged the fact and began, he said, to be a little more serious.

Lecture Notes–Booklet V

Another individual present, who began to ridicule the fact and made some strong remarks against any power I might exercise over him, desired me to make a simple experiment upon his foot and leg. I immediately wrote upon a piece of paper not letting anyone know the writing and laid it down upon the table and told him I had written upon that paper what kind of a sensation I would produce upon his foot and leg. I commenced the operation and in about two minutes, he said his foot and leg began to prickle and felt as though it was going to sleep. I handed him the paper and he read just what he had felt. Some have replied to similar experiments above, that they were the results of Imagination. We reply that the subject did not know what kind of a sensation we should produce and therefore could not imagine in the case. To him it was a reality, because he felt the prickling sensation and did not imagine that I was going to produce it. I have frequently taken persons and endeavored to produce a warm or cold sensation upon their limbs without their knowledge and have succeeded in bringing about my wishes.

A certain physician, who was a complete skeptic and perhaps more in a jocose manner than otherwise, invited me to visit one of his patients. I complied, and after looking at the patient and fixing her attention upon me, took the physician one side and told him what sort of a sensation I would produce upon her. We returned to her and I commenced impressing her mind with the same feeling I had named to the physician. She immediately complained of being cold and trembling, which was the very feeling I had been trying to produce. The physician I presume will recollect the circumstance and vouch for the fact. We might fill up our pages with hundreds of experiments, similar to those we have given, and all performed in the same manner.

Perhaps my readers may at this point enquire in what manner all these simple experiments are performed. It is simply this. I first get the attention of my subject, endeavoring to exclude all other external influences and drawing their mind to myself. I then work up the sensation I wish to produce upon my subject in my own mind and it is immediately communicated to that of the subject and a correspondent feeling will be the result. It is the simple process of mind acting upon mind. It is necessary to draw the attention of the subject to myself in order to receive the impression because no one could receive impressions from external objects unless he should give his attention to them. The public speaker makes it the first object to gain the attention of his audience and then proceeds to reason out the whole subject, and they are also prepared to go on with the speaker and receiving corresponding emotions with him. So in mesmerizing, some powerful impression must be produced to draw the attention of the subject and exclude other external influences and then the mind is prepared for further action.

All these simple experiments can be more easily performed if the subject is told what result you desire to effect; yet they can be performed, and I have repeatedly given them, without any knowledge of my desire having been communicated to the subject.

In the town of Skowhegan on the banks of the Kennebec, I met with a young man deaf and dumb, but was a very sensitive subject and easily operated upon in his waking moments. I requested him to sit down and place his hand upon the table and count by raising his hand up and down. I then asked someone to direct me to stop him when he had made a certain number of counts naming to me the number. When he had made the particular counts I willed him to stop and he did so. I then impressed his mind with the desire to walk back and forth upon the floor, and he arose and commenced walking. A gentleman asked me to stop him when he arrived at a certain point and I exercised my power upon his mind and he stopped instantly at the very point. I then desired him to speak to me and he made a noise. I made a stronger impression upon his mind to speak louder and he made a stronger effort to talk, graduating his effort, and raising his voice or noise with my thoughts impressing him to speak louder or softer. Someone then asked him in writing if he heard me speak, and he answered "that his mind heard." And so it is. The mind hears, sees, feels, and causes every action of the body. And impressions are conveyed directly upon the mind when the attention is given to the operator in such a manner as to shut out all other influences. And to produce these impressions and sensations when the mind of the subject is thus prepared, the operator must produce in himself the same sensation which he would communicate to the subject. The experiments last mentioned upon the deaf and dumb young man were performed without the subject knowing, by any of his outward senses, what I could design. I was behind the subject and out of his sight during the most of the experiments. I took every precaution in this case, as I have done repeatedly, to place the experiments upon such a basis that no one could attribute them to the imagination.

A young lady, who was passing some time at my house during the past season, was sitting in the keeping room and I was in one of my chambers with my little daughter. I requested my daughter to go down into the keeping room and tell the young lady I wished her to give her attention to me for a few minutes, that I wished to perform some experiments upon her. I also requested my daughter to remain with her and see what they were. I then commenced the operation of my mind to paralyze one of her limbs. In a few minutes, her foot moved out and become entirely paralyzed. I then willed her to rise and walk and she immediately obeyed, saying to my daughter, "Your father desires me to walk and it is impossible for me to resist." I willed her to come to the chamber door, that I had something to say to her. She then asked my daughter "if her father did not speak." Upon her replying that he did not, she said "he did and wishes to tell me something." She came to my door and asked me if I did not speak to her. I replied that I did in my mind, but not with my voice. She could not believe that she did not hear my voice. These experiments were done in the evening and my wife being absent I told her that I should will her to ask my wife a question when she returned, but would not tell her what it should be. Wishing to see how far I could carry out this principle of operating upon her mind directly, I willed her to ask my wife <u>if she had turned the cat outdoors</u>. In two hours from that time my wife came in and as she came up stairs, she enquired "<u>if she had turned the cat outdoors</u>."

Such experiments as I have named above and others of the same character, I have performed upon subjects in their waking state. I find, however, but few persons who are very susceptible of such impressions; yet I have given them before <u>so many</u> persons that, they, <u>at last</u>, by those who witnessed them, cannot be disputed. During my public exhibitions, I have practiced my subject, after the evening's exhibition is nearly closed, in similar experiments. I have left him and passed into another room and requested someone to tell me which of his arms to paralyze. Having directed me, he would return to my subject and request him to give his attention to me, that I was about to perform an experiment upon one of his limbs, arms or legs not allowing him to know which. Soon the arm, which I was requested to affect, would become paralyzed. Such experiments I have given to the public on many occasions. It is more difficult to influence the mind in the waking state than when mesmerized. Yet these experiments were done when he was awake.

My reader may enquire, whether such experiments are not all the influence of the imagination. We reply, that they are not imaginary, but real. The impressions received by the subject are real and not imaginary and the results are also real and not imaginary. The arm or foot does become paralyzed, and there is no imagination about it. If it were the result of an excited imagination the sequences could not be real. In the case of my subject, how could he know which arm I intended to operate upon? If he <u>imagined</u>, he could not produce the paralysis, and therefore no one can attribute it to imagination.

We have given our views more at length upon what we consider the power of imagination in another part of this work and shall not now go into a discussion of the subject so particularly. The distinction, however, is very clear between real and imaginary experiments or states of mind. If I act from an impression upon my mind which I believe to be true, there is no imagination about the transaction. If I create an impression in my own mind, which I know to be from a false cause or if I receive an impression and know it to be the result of my imagination, it could not further affect me. Suppose I imagined that my arm was paralyzed. Would that state of the mind bring about the real condition which I imagined? And if to me who imagined it, it should appear real, which circumstance would only be after the continuance of the imagination, would this imaginary condition of mind appear real to an individual who might be standing by? If it were the result of my imagination, it would not appear real to a disinterested bystander. And if it should appear and really be paralyzed, and hundreds of individuals should witness the fact, I presume that these individuals would not be willing to ascribe it to the powers of imagination. Indeed, a man might imagine a thousand things, none of which would turn out to be true because there is no truth in imagination. Men often act from false causes, not however false in appearance to them. The impressions they receive, of course are real and we cannot ascribe results from such real impressions as flowing from an excited imagination. These experiments then, are real, flowing from real impressions which are produced by causes which appear real and are so to the subject although the operator may have produced the cause without a real existent object. It is then imaginary to the operator but reality to the subject.

Clairvoyance

Clairvoyance is also an excited state of the mind, which enables the subject to see objects with an independent power of sight, without the use of the bodily eyes. It also implies the capacity to see every object to which the mind's attention is called whether present or distant. We have alluded to this state or capacity of mind in many of our experiments, but have not spoken of this power disconnected with other experiments. We recur to the subject again, to assert our belief in such a power founded on facts, which have come under our own observation, and which we have been enabled to give to the public. Thought reading itself is more astounding perhaps than seeing independent of the organ of sight. Yet in the present state of the world, men who have witnessed these phenomena, all agree, that subjects in the mesmeric state will read the thoughts of those who are in communication with them. And by some it is asserted, that this is all, which constitutes Clairvoyance. We however, rely upon facts which have not been controverted and cannot be explained on other principles, than, that the mind does possess the independent power of sight. We shall give a few examples illustrating this part of our subject and then proceed to show why so much reliance cannot be placed in the subject as is desirable while exercising this faculty.

On a certain occasion, I took my subject to Brunswick, entered the College Grounds, passed into the Anatomical Cabinet and requested him to pass round the room and describe to me everything he saw, which arrested his attention. He commenced on the left as you pass into the room, and described many things which I knew to be there. But there was one curiosity, which he named, with the rest of which I had no recollection and I was quite confident he had made a mistake. I had occasion to visit Brunswick in a few days and to satisfy my curiosity, called at the Anatomical Cabinet and found everything in precisely the same order as he had described them. The curiosity, of which I knew nothing, was there and he must have actually seen it or he could not have described it. It was not embraced in my thoughts and the subject was perfectly ignorant of the existence of an Anatomical Cabinet connected with Bowdoin College and had never been within thirty miles of the town.

On another occasion a friend of mine was in communication with a subject who had been excited or mesmerized and directed him to go to such a house, being occupied by a friend of his and describe to him, every particular about its external appearance. He did so and in this minute description was particular to speak of a peculiarity about that portion which was not in view of the street. After the experiment was over, my friend stated that he had given a correct description of the house except the peculiarity of which we have spoken, and remarked that "he was mistaken in that." About a month after this, I met this same friend and he related to me, that my subject was correct in his description of the house even to the peculiarity. He had visited the house and upon examination everything was found to agree with the minute description given by my subject.

During the winter of 1843 I visited Wiscasset with my subject and lectured before an audience and gave experiments illustrating my theory of Mesmerism. After putting my subject into the clairvoyant state a gentleman by the name of Clark, was placed in communication with him. Mr. Clark directed him to find the Barke [sic] _____ on board of which was his son. He immediately saw the Barke, described the vessel minutely, gave a general description of the Captain, Mate and his son–asked the Capt. what time he would arrive in New York and received the answer, which he communicated to Mr. Clark in the presence of the whole audience. I left Wiscasset on the following day and visited Bath. In a few days I returned to Wiscasset and gave further experiments. Mr. Clark was again placed in communication with him and directed him to find the same vessel. He did so and said she was hauling in to the wharf on dock in New York City at that moment and that she arrived on such a day.

Upon making a calculation about the arrival of the mail it was found that the news of her arrival would reach Wiscasset on the following day. When the mail came, many persons, who had witnessed the experiment were at the post office, anxiously waiting the news and to test the truth of Clairvoyance. The news was received of the Bark's arrival corresponding with the information communicated on the evening before by my subject. This circumstance was related in the Newspaper printed at Wiscasset at the time. On another occasion I placed my subject in communication with a gentleman who was an entire stranger to me and he took him to a certain bridge. My subject saw the bridge and described it very particularly. The gentleman gave up the subject and declared to the audience that the description was incorrect and he could not do anything with my subject at clairvoyance. On the following day, I met the same gentleman and he assured me that my subject was correct, according to what he had learned since last evening. That the bridge had been rebuilt since he had seen it and many material alterations made, such as my subject described. We would remark here that, many experiments of a similar character have been set down at the time as a partial failure, but that it was ascertained afterwards that the communicants were in the error and that the subject was correct.

My subject was placed in communication with a lady who directed him to her father's house, which he described with particularity, even noticing the closets and doors. And often giving a description of each member of the family, said there was an old lady sitting in the corner, with a pair of spectacles over her eyes and that she was knitting. The lady immediately wrote home and ascertained that at the time named by my subject, there was such an individual present in the room, answering to the description of my subject and that she was also knitting. While in Bangor a lady was put in communication with my subject and requested him to go with her. He complied and described a certain house and the flower-garden about it–even the shape of the flower beds. While he was going on with the description, he exclaimed at the top of his lungs, "Get out, get out." She enquired what he saw, and he replied that there was a great dog digging up one of the beds and destroying the flowers. Also asked the lady if she did not see him–that he should think she might as the dog had made so large a hole. This house and garden was situated in Gardiner. The lady immediately wrote to G. and received an answer, that my subject was correct–that there was a dog which did actually dig into one of the beds and destroy the flowers. Sometime after this I met one of the ladies of the house at Gardiner, who related to me the same facts.

During a session of the District Court in this village in 1842 some curiosity was exhibited among many distinguished gentlemen present to witness some of my experiments. I called on Judge Allen and found Gov. Anderson, Judge Briggles, the Rev. Mr. Hodgsdon and others present. Several experiments were performed. The Rev. Mr. Hodgsdon being placed in communication with my subject, took him to Dexter where his family were then residing. He described the house and family and said there was a small child sick, lying in the cradle. That Mrs. Hodgsdon said the child was getting better etc. Mr. Hodgsdon corrected Lucius and told him that he was mistaken about the cradle, that there was no cradle in the house. Lucius replied that there was and that the child was lying in it; and he would not yield to Mr. Hodgsdon's correction. The following day he returned to his family and found that Lucius was correct–that a cradle had been borrowed of one of his neighbors and that the child was lying in it–was getting better etc. –just as had been related by my subject.

While in the city of Boston Dr. W _____ performed an experiment with my subject–took him to his father's house and he described many things and said they were roasting beef in the kitchen. This was in the evening and seemed rather singular that "beef-roasting" should be going on at that time. The Dr. visited his father's the following day, being Thanksgiving and learned that what my subject had said, was true. A gentleman in this village, who was given a little to skepticism towards Clairvoyance although he was confident of the power of thought reading, requested me to call at his office with my subject at such an hour. In the meantime he had been to his house and requested his wife to arrange something in a certain room, different from what it was then and not let him know what the change was to be. The gentleman returned to his office and the room was put in order. My subject was taken to the room and described all the particulars, which the gentleman found to be correct upon his return. I took him to the room myself and he asked me if I heard, what the lady said? I enquired what it was and he replied, "she says I wish he would come, if he is coming. I wonder if he is here now." This was found to be the conversation of the lady while in the room at the time my subject was there, directed to her mother who was also present. A lady who had been frequently thrown into the Mesmeric State by me, desired to be directed to Boston and ascertain when her son, who was residing there would be home. I mesmerized her and directed her to Boston. She visited her son and asked him when he would be in Belfast. He answered her on such a day which proved to be correct. I also on another occasion took her to Boston to see her son. She said he had left in the scho[oner] Comet. I then directed her to find the Comet. She did and said it was just at that time coming out of a certain harbor, giving the name, and that she would arrive in Belfast on such a night, and that he would be home on the following morning after her arrival. He came according to her prediction.

These experiments are introduced to prove true clairvoyance, that the subject does actually see objects, which do not exist in the mind of the operator and of which the operator could have no knowledge–that there is something in all these facts seen independent of any other power than independent sight. Every experiment develops something, which is found to be true, and cannot be explained upon the principle of thought-reading. We say then that the mind is capable, of such excitement or of attaining to a state in which it may see without bodily eyes and also be present with all things at the same instant. In other words, that to the mind, independent of the body, there is no such impediment as time, space, distance and materiality, but that it only requires direction–and all its inherent faculties are in operation, giving its attention to the object to which it has been directed. The eye, ear, nose, sense of touch or the tongue is nothing except as they convey in our natural state certain sensations to the mind, from which a peculiar state of emotions arise. The faculty of sight, hearing, taste, smell and touch exists in the mind independent of the organs by which objects are communicated to these faculties. And cut off these organs or appendages, and then, mind acts direct or receives its impressions directly from external and internal objects. If then, you institute a peculiar state of the mind, called mesmeric and close up the bodily eyes, the faculty of the mind does not cease to act. It is rather, in part, freeing the soul from its narrow confinement in the sphere of acquiring knowledge through the limited means of the eye, and giving it a range of sight limited only by the laws of mind and not the laws of matter. It returns more like itself, when it shall have been entirely divested of man's materiality and left free, not to roam throughout the ranges of thought, but to be existent, with all its original faculties in full display, with all the creations of the Great First Cause.

We have given experiments to show the position we have taken–experiments which we challenge the world to gainsay, and which we cannot explain by any other principles than these we have laid down as governing the mind at all times under similar circumstances. We say, conclusive proofs are given in these facts of the mind's capacity to see through all space or to be present with all things in the universe and behold them, independent of the bodily eye and independent of the knowledge of the operator.

The question, then, arises: Will the subject at all times act and see independent of the operator and state the true condition of the object to which their attention is called? I answer, they will not, and that experiments of this character often fail. But this does not arise from the inability of the subject to see and relate the facts; but from the controlling influence of the operator over the mind of the subject, which induces the subject to describe the thoughts and ideas of the individual in communication with him rather than to look to the object or scene itself and describe from actual view. It appears to be an easier task for a subject under the control of an individual to read the thoughts of his controller, about certain things, than to describe such things from actual sight.

I will relate an experiment here which I tried when I first began to magnetize. I had been out during the evening, giving some private experiments and on returning home lost my pocket handkerchief. I heard nothing from it for more than a week. I then magnetized my subject and requested him to find it. He told me where I could find it, described the individual who picked it up in the street and told where it was found. The next morning I saw an individual, answering to the description and enquired of him if he had found a handkerchief and he replied that he had, told me when and where, which was precisely as my subject had told me.

Flushed with my success in this experiment, I adopted the rule that my subject would, under all circumstances in the mesmeric state, find anything which might be lost. My faith was unbounded with my new discovery and I began to dream of hidden treasures and mountain views, and diamonds in the desert, when lo! the very next experiment I made was a total failure! This drove me back again into the real world and I was obliged to feel along slowly and cautiously to discover the cause of my disaster. It was in part owing to the influence I exercised over my subject, compelling him to read my thoughts rather than to give me the real state of things; and partly, from the condition of the subject, not having passed into the high clairvoyant state. We will give a few experiments in thought reading and show when we are sometimes deceived, in our experiments.

I mesmerized my subject in private and resolved to try experiments in thought reading and satisfy myself as to the power of a subject to describe the thoughts of another. I commenced by bringing before my mind a house, which he immediately saw and described according to my thought. I then would imagine a cat and a dog, and my subject would answer instantly as the image was formed in my mind. I then brought before me a whole caravan, of animals of various classes and sizes, commencing with a platoon of elephants, then lions, tigers, rhinoce[ros], camels, monkeys, baboons, etc. My subject would without hesitation describe them as they arose in thought in my mind. I would think of an army of officers and soldiers passing in review and he would relate all my thoughts. I would imagine a person coming, who was well known to my subject, and he would call him by name. And a host of such experiments were performed, which would fill a volume, all going to show with what accuracy and rapidity he would read my thoughts. In my public exhibitions I have given experiments of the same character. On one occasion, a lady requested me to place her in communication with my subject. I gave her a seat on the stage and requested my subject to go to Michigan, (where the lady said her husband was) and find the lady's husband. He did so and gave a very minute description of the gentleman, stated how long he had been there, named his occupation and that he had written a letter to his wife, and told the contents of the letter. This was done in the presence of a large audience, many of whom, were acquainted with the facts and did testify to the truth of his disclosure. The lady, I will state, did not speak while my subject was going on with his description and she and her husband were entire strangers to me and my subject. During a session of the Supreme Court in Belfast, Judge Tenney presiding, there was some little excitement upon the subject of Mesmerism. Judge Tenney was anxious to witness a few experiments. I called at his room one evening, I placed my subject, after I had mesmerized him, under his control. The Judge wrote on a piece of paper, folded it up and held it in his hand. He then requested my subject to go with him to a certain house and asked him, whom he saw. He exclaimed it was a little deformed man and described him, giving his height and appearance. The Judge then handed me the paper and upon it was written, that he had a brother who was deformed etc, giving a description very similar to that of my subject. R. B. Allyn, Esq., of this village, was desirous of satisfying himself as to my subject's power of thought reading. He named the experiment he was going to try to no one, but carefully wrote a description of a large house he was going to imagine and filed the description in his drawer, not allowing any one to know its contents. He described a sign over the door with the word "abandoned" written upon it. He also located the house on his own premises below the village upon which there is no building. After I had placed him in communication with my subject, he put this question to him. "Will you go with me," not stating where. He answered, "yes." "Now Lucius, can you tell me what I am looking at." He replied "a large house." "Be particular and describe the house and the grounds around it." Lucius immediately proceeded to give a description of the house, observed the sign over the door and read off the word "abandoned," described its location and the appearance of the lands about it. Mr. Allyn, then took from his drawer the paper containing the description of the house, corresponding precisely with that given by Lucius and even to the word "abandoned" written upon the sign.

While in the city of Boston, some young gentlemen of my acquaintance called on me and desired to see some private experiments. I complied and placed my subject, after mesmerising him, in communication with several of them. One of them, however, did not succeed well in what he designed to bring before my subject. Indeed, a total failure attended every effort he made in this experiment. I took the young gentleman one side, and requested him to relate to me what experiment he wished Lucius to perform. He complied and said he was trying to bring a gentleman by the name of Lowel of Ellsworth before his mind–that Lucius might describe him. It so happened that I was acquainted with Lowel and my subject had also seen him. I returned to my subject and imagined the gentleman coming towards me in his peculiar manner of walking. Lucius, soon described him and said it was Esq. Lowel of Ellsworth. This was true thought reading, only describing my own ideas. Individuals have presented a box containing various articles and requested my subject to describe them. This he would do with accuracy–either from reading the thoughts of those who presented it, they knowing what it contained or from actually seeing the articles themselves by an independent power of sight.

So in almost all the experiments we have related in thought-reading, the subject may be said to either describe the thoughts of those around him or to actually see and describe the persons and objects themselves. Where an explanation may be given in thought reading or clairvoyance, it is difficult and perhaps impossible to tell from which the subject acts. And perhaps he may be governed in part by one power and in part by the other. We think this fact will explain much of the difficulty, which attends experiments in true clairvoyance. Another cause of failure and which is in close connection with this part of our subject, is that a subject will often be influenced in his description and conduct by an association of ideas, which leads him astray and to talk often upon some subject entirely foreign to that which was first presented. I will give one example illustrating my ideas upon this subject, and it will correspond precisely with what I have before remarked in this work, when speaking upon the principles of association. Two individuals, come into my room and see a large book upon my table. Both observe it and thoughts arise or impressions are received which give rise to trains of thought. But each has his peculiar train, different from the other, although the same book gave rise to each train. One will be reminded of a similar book, which he saw in a certain place at such a time and what transpired in connection with it. The other would perhaps be reminded of something very unlike the book itself–perhaps a person, a country, a city, an army or almost any idea of thought different from the other. So that you enquire of each about what train of thought arose upon seeing the book and they would name something entirely different. The application of this principle to mesmerized subjects is this. Subjects sometimes are in such a condition, that, upon receiving a first impression their mind is immediately led off upon such objects or transactions as are associated with this first impression; and if you request them to describe the object which caused this first impression, the rapidity of thought is such, that they would be quite as likely to describe some portion of the train of thought which follows, as the object itself. On this principle, a subject might not describe either the object itself, nor read the thoughts of those around him, but describe minutely an idea of their own reaction or association which follows in the train of thought first set in motion by the object to which one had called the attention of the subject. As though I beheld a book, and a train of thought commences which leads me to think of some friend, almost at the same instant, which I beheld the book. Someone, who had called my attention to the book, would ask me to describe it, and if I should then proceed to describe my friend, about whom I was thinking by the time the question should be put instead of the book, this would be a parallel case to a mesmerized mind governed by the same principle. We have heard of men, (indeed, witnessed ourselves, the act), who in their natural state, reply to questions without giving the correct answer, but speak of something brought to the mind, by the question, although one observing could not discover any relation between the answer given and the question put.

On a certain occasion I magnetized my subject and directed him to go to such a well and measure accurately the depth of the water. He did so and told to one fourth of an inch the depth of the water. This was Independent Sight, because I did not know anything in relation to the well. Now if I had known how deep the water was and thought it, and the subject had described my thoughts and given the true depth, this would be Thought Reading. If, however, I had taken him to the well and he upon seeing the water or upon being reminded of it, should associate with it the depth of another well he had actually measured in his waking state and instead of giving the true depth, given that of the well, he measured before he was mesmerized, this would be an answer on the principle of association. This is another action of the mind under different circumstances.

We have, therefore, given examples, proving to a demonstration that there are such states of mind as Clairvoyant, Thought Reading and that arising from association. That the mind sometimes acts in one of these capacities and sometimes in another and is also governed at other times by the principle of association. Now the difficulty in a clairvoyant subject is this. The mesmerized mind is liable to be under the partial control of all these conditions at the same time and would describe an object, partly from actual independent sight, partly from thought reading and partly from association; and the result always is a total failure in all. We are not able, in this early stage of our science, to give definite rules by which we can tell how far the subject may be led astray from independent sight by these two other principles. Indeed we have no barometer by which to ascertain how much weight our own thoughts, or the associations of the subject, may have over the mesmerized mind. In the progress of future advancement, this mystery may be solved; and subjects, under proper regulations, may discover to the operator, the true action of his mind, whether it be Seeing, Thought-reading, or Association. When mesmerism has attained this height, in the march of its discoveries, a new and brighter era in the history of the world will have dawned upon humanity—the ignorance of the past will be entombed in the light of the future, and truth, disrobed of superstition will govern paramount, the universe of immortal incorruptible thought.

Our remarks have thus far been confined to what we are pleased to call the development of the metaphysical mysteries of our subject (Mesmerism). We have sought to select that system which appears to be most consistent with the facts we have offered—that system only by which we can explain satisfactorily the wonderful phenomena of mind. We have thought our course thus far justifiable upon the ground, that a complete knowledge of the development of Mesmerism is necessary to a good understanding of the practical part of our science. We protest against a mere knowledge of results without cause. We should know rather the cause and we may then produce or prevent results. Our course has been to introduce such explanation as appears consistent with all the experiments given and as far as we had the power, to enlighten the understanding rather than to mystify what has already been too mysterious. How far we have succeeded, an intelligent community will act as our tribunal and we shall rest satisfied with their candid decision. We now come to the useful and practical part of our subject. It is to this part of our work we would solicit the attention of our reader. The study of the philosophy of science is entertaining and instructive; but the utility of science, is after all the great point to be attained in its advances. We shall proceed to show what connection mesmerism, as we understand it has with the relief of suffering humanity and consequently its necessary connection with medical science.

The world is full of theories and humbugs. No two men can agree precisely in any science about which there is much controversy as to the laws by which it is made up. The difficulties arising in medical science, are from the uncertainties of its practice. It is not like many of the physical sciences, about which there may be uniform and constant results. Even in this enlightened age, there seem to be no settled rules of practice. Every physician of course defends his own position or rather works out the position of his brother; and then declares his system entirely opposite. The whole practice of the schools and the faculty seems to have been a continual introduction of <u>Theories</u> contradicting each other–each order as they rise and fall opposing all others. While diseases are the same now as in the days of Hippocrates and Galen, the remedies have been as numerous as sands upon the sea shore. Every physician has his own remedy for the old diseases. So far back as history runs, we trace the rise, progress and fall of theory after theory. The course of progress is often this manner. Upon the introduction of a new theory and its full adoption into practice, all preceding theories retire to the shades for a season; the novelty soon ceases to astonish and then all sects of physicians are equally successful in some cases. Soon another star appears and dazzles with his awful splendor all who have preceded him; but he too passes the meridian of glory and goes to the shades of night. Then arises another more brilliant than the last, and after the harvest moon of his glory, passes like his predecessors into decay.

Lecture Notes–Booklet VI

[BU 1:0088]

Thus it has been from the days of Esculapius to Harrison and Thompson, and perhaps I should not slight Graham and Alcot, who, I must say, give a very economical system of medical practice which would not be very likely to induce the gout or dyspepsia. The different Theories of practice, however, no doubt grew out of the uncertainty of medicine. And the uncertainty of medicine was the necessary result of a want of a knowledge of those laws by which the animal economy of man is sustained. It all proceeds from the mistaken notion that medicine operates upon the organs which constitute the body without any reference to the impressions which it conveys to the mind. Medicine, upon the organs of the body, if it were to act upon them alone, would always produce the same results upon the same organizations. It would be a matter of certainty with the physician, that if Lobelia or Ipecac be taken into the stomach in measured quantities, proportionate effects will follow. And so of all medicines. If, on a certain occasion under certain symptoms, a certain medicine restored health, why will it not do so in all cases, when the symptoms and disease are the same? We have selected from Dr. Abercrombie such remarks as convey our ideas upon the uncertainty of medicine as practiced by physicians.

Quote from Dr. Abercrombie Part IV page 293. (copy the whole chapter). [Cited reference not copied here. –*Ed*.]

We have, in this quotation, the whole truth so far as the uncertainty of medicines is concerned. But even Dr. Abercrombie, we think, has not touched the real cause of all this uncertainty except where he partly attributes it to the "mental emotions." We hazard the assertion that all these difficulties arise from mental emotions, that whatever results follow the application of medicine are produced by the impressions which the taking and action which this medicine has, upon the organs of the body. And the same medicines do not affect different individuals in the same manner; because they, upon being taken, convey to these minds different impressions, and the mind exercises a control over the body and answers to the impressions by a result upon the functions of the body, either good or bad. Every intelligent physician with whom I have conversed has always acknowledged that mind has much to do with the taking of medicine, if good results follow–that no physician could probably do his patient much good, unless he should possess the confidence of such patient. Intelligent physicians, although they have full faith in medical remedies and believe that these, with the mental emotions of the patient are the only restoratives of health, yet do not after all consider that remedies possess such astonishing powers as is supposed by the quacks. I believe that there is a virtue in medicine, which, when taken by the patient, conveys impressions to the mind and that these impressions often result in the entire restoration of health. The mind of man is generally taken up with surrounding objects and seldom is attracted to contemplate the body to which it is attached.

If however by any attraction it should be turned upon the body, a war seems to arise between the body and mind, and the mind appears to be unwilling to abide its confinement. Disease then begins to prey upon the body and continues to increase until the soul departs and leaves matter to return to its original dust. We think we have abundant proof of the power of the mind to control the health of the body. Patients are advised to travel in pleasant countries and visit watering places, to bathe in sea water and mineral water, to spend the cold seasons in milder climates, engage more in pleasantries of society or even do anything by which the mind may be led off from its old habits of warring with the body. But why should we enumerate particular methods of restoring the health of a patient without a dose of medicine? All these methods are medicines for the mind; they leave lasting impressions and they restore the health. So is every remedy taken into the stomach or externally applied to the body a medicine for the mind. And it is only so far effectual to the end designed as it impresses the mind. We do not then discard the use of medicines, but rather recommend them; but we protest against such use, unless he who prescribes knows the laws by which his remedy is governed.

The true design of all medicine is to lead the mind to certain results and then it, the mind, will restore the body. No matter what this medicine is, if it accomplishes all the physician designs, it will effect a cure if it produces a healthy state of mind. Thus it is that very small doses, under the direction of the Homeopathic practice, effect such astonishing cures–Thus it is that so many drops of pure water, taken under the direction of a skillful physician, will restore health. Thus it is that a change of scenery gives new and pleasant impressions to the mind of a patient and results in a perfect restoration of the bodily health. We must here indulge in a pleasant anecdote, related to me by a friend of mine, the truth of which I would not dare question. He was in bad health of being troubled with the "cramp in his stomach" and the remedy was always one or two of Brandwith's pills. On one occasion he was taken very suddenly and after taking the pills as usual served up in a tumbler of cold water, he drank and the next morning found himself restored to perfect health, as usual in former attacks. He accidentally looked into his tumbler and saw both of the pills, which he had supposed were drunk, in the bottom of his tumbler. He found it must have been the cold water that cured him. He was however so much pleased with the idea of his cure that the cramp never returned. A young physician of my acquaintance, who was rising rapidly in his profession, was called to attend a patient who had been for a long time under the care of an old practitioner, but was fast failing. The old physician had given up all hopes of his patient's recovery and finally told him, he could do him no good. At this unfavorable moment, my young friend was called. He examined the patient, ascertained what remedies had been administered etc. and found that they were just such as he should apply in such a case. Somewhat puzzled for a moment what to order, he became very grave and thoughtful. He found that the mind of the patient was such as to reject the medicine and he determined to try the venture of a new medicine. He then returned to his office, filled an ounce vial of good pure water and again visited the patient, ordered ten drops to be administered at a time and repeated once in two hours. This was effectual and the patient was soon restored. Another physician, who is highly distinguished in his profession, related the following story. Being called to visit a patient that had been under the care of several physicians but was continually growing worse, he ascertained that they had been treating the patient in just such a manner as he should have done under the same circumstances. The patient, however, had no confidence in their treatment and as a matter of course continued to grow worse. He examined the patient and finally placing his hand upon his side remarked that if he could produce a warm sensation there in five minutes, he could cure him. A warm sensation was felt by the patient and the physician pronounced his case not dangerous, remarking that he had medicines which would certainly cure him. He then turned round and poured out the same kind of medicine as had been given to the patient by the other physicians and it was taken in full confidence of a restoration to health. The result was that the patient immediately recovered. We might mention a hundred such instances and then call our own experience to confirm the truth of them. But we have given these, proving that it is really the mind upon which an impression is to be made and that after all, the medicine has nothing to do in the matter only so far as it induces a state of feeling antecedent to a restoration. While the physicians have always admitted that the mind of the patient has much to do in the operation of medicine and the restoration of health, yet nothing is ever mentioned of the fact that "mind acts upon mind," that the mind of the physician has something to do in bringing about such results as restore health. Here then, we trace a great portion of the difficulty in the uncertainty of medicine. The physician has not been aware of this fact and therefore proceeds upon wrong principles in administering his medicine. In this respect the quack may effect more than the intelligent physician because he has more confidence in the remedies he applies. He, however, believes the great remedy is really in the medicine and has full confidence in administering it to the patient, and impresses his mind with the restorative powers of his balsam. Perhaps the quack might not understand the composition of his medicine, yet he knows the results and is so firm in his belief that he would almost bring about the result if the medicine had by mistake been omitted. The intelligent physician, knowing the properties of his medicine and having seen much practice, does not attribute an almighty charm to his antidote and therefore manifests less confidence in his skill. His mind influences directly that of his patient and he too will place but little confidence in the medicine. The result is that the patient becomes worse. Now had the physician understood or rather had he brought into his practice the great law that "mind acts upon mind," he might have remedied the whole evil. He would then have commanded all the influence which his powerful mind could exert over the mind of his patient and thus with the powerful or gentle action of the medicine directed a healthful result. In some instances, a powerful medicine taken under the impression of a good influence may do much and indeed in some instances entirely restore the patient. But it acts far more healthfully upon the patient when the mind is rightly directed.

This principle of making deep impressions upon patients by a medicinal or other process seems to have been well understood by Hippocrates, the great father of cures. When the plague broke out at Athens during the second year of the Peloponnesian war, it ravaged the whole army and bid defiance to the remedies of the most skillful physicians in that ancient city. At this critical period, the great Hippocrates entered the city and applied his remedies which soon began to check its ravages. His name only could save his countrymen. He caused fires to be lighted up in the streets and lanes of Athens to purify and clarify the atmosphere–introduced the warm bath to expel the infection by the surface of the skin, and to support their weakness, caused them to drink the rich wines of Naxos. Thus employing external agents to impress deeply the mind with the idea of an effectual remedy. We might enumerate other instances where the great cause of success in a particular treatment of disease was similar in principle to the above; but history is full of such examples and the daily observation of every student of human nature confirms its records. Every action, which results to the benefit or injury of the patient, is directed upon the mind which immediately answers the impression upon the disease of the body. Matter, in itself, is capable of no action, except by chemical process, unless connected with a mind or spirituality. The health and vigor of the body depends solely upon the condition and action of the mind because the immaterial part of man governs the material-matter or body connected with mind is under the immediate control of this spirituality. If, then the mind by external or internal influences has received impressions to destroy the health and vigor of the body and those impressions cannot be removed, then the body follows that state of mind and readily submits. If the mind of a patient does not feel some confidence in the restorative powers of a medicine taken, there is a probable chance that it will do the patient no good. His mind counteracts the impression, usually conveyed to the minds of most patients, by a strong impression that it could do no good.

There are other reasons why medicines prove so uncertain in the practice of physicians. And perhaps the greatest evil of all we could enumerate is the course which each physician has in his own judgment selected to pursue towards his brother competitors. It is a fact worth mentioning to those who have not witnessed it that no two physicians, who reside in our towns and villages where a direct competition is kept up, can agree to the same treatment of the same disease. If one is successful in his treatment, the other would not adopt the same course but must have his peculiar method and denounce the other. It is this constant warring with each other, this constant opposition–this unhallowed wish to rise on the ruins of a brother, this ambitious longing to put down every man of the same profession and assume the confidence, the practice and the distinguished honor which a suffering community can bestow. I protest against this vile slander of your neighbor's medicine or practice, not so much for the folly exhibited in the individual physician as the enormous evil entailed upon the suffering community. While physicians labor to destroy what confidence the community have been disposed to place in them, how can they individually expect to reap the advantage of a position which they have been constantly laboring to destroy? It is an old saying that "two gamesters can never agree," but we find this principle carried out to the very letter in medical practice. The success of my neighbor is not to be endured, while I do not receive the direct emolument. Let the world perish, if I alone can't save it is the common expression of every physician. I do not intend to embrace the whole class without some reserve. There are some honorable exceptions, men in medical science whose position is above the filth and slime of enmity; it is the proud position of a great mind desirous of progress, availing himself with all the assistance which may flow from the smaller sources that surround him. It is a remark in sacred history that the foolish things of this world sometimes confound the wise; and the great mind is ever watchful of the fulfillment of this declaration. It embraces whatever is useful and true and rejects whatever is injurious and false.

We are of the opinion that this entire want of confidence in each other and the medicines administered, manifest among common physicians, goes far to counteract what practical service any remedy may usually, under a proper condition of things, effect. It must be true that physicians are not aware of the influence which mind exerts upon mind–results upon the body, or they would desist from such violence.

We return to an expression we have before uttered, that we have full confidence in the power of certain medicines to produce healthful results, but further assert, that the mind of the patient or physician may so control this power as to produce disastrous results. We protest against this pretended ignorance of the physician upon the causes of the uncertainty of medicine. He should, or ought to, know what they result from or the great governing principle by which a failure follows. We exclaim against the daring and lawless courage of a physician who marches up, blindfold to the battle ground of disease struggling with nature, and often failing in his efforts to effect a reconciliation, raises a war club and strikes at random. If he luckily hits disease, the patient is restored and if not, the patient dies.

Our remarks thus far go to show that the mind has much to do with the practice of medicine and that results are from impressions conveyed to it by some process. We now proceed to illustrate by experiments what mesmerism has to do with diseases, and shall at the same time show the influence of mind acting upon mind.

By the action of my mind upon my patient in his waking state, I can produce the same results which flow from the taking of medicine. I can produce an emetic or cathartic, a dizziness or pain in the head, relieve pain in any part of the system and restore patients by acting directly upon their minds. If we succeed in giving such experiments and confirm the above declaration, will anyone doubt the fact that it is the mind which is operated upon and conveys the result to the body? We will not argue this point further, but proceed to give some further remarks and the experiments.

We lay it down as a principle that all medical remedies affect the body only through the mind.

The truth of this principle is tested in an experiment which I had upon a lady of intelligence, who was placed under my care. Her health was generally bad and caused a depression of spirits. I could magnetize her easily but preferred to perform my experiments in her waking moments. If she complained of pain in the head, I could relieve it. If her feet and hands were cold, I could induce a warm sensation. If her head became hot and feverish, I could induce a cool state and drive off the fever. Indeed almost any state I desired to produce, corresponding with the effect of medicine taken into the stomach, would follow. This is not a solitary case. I might enumerate hundreds of experiments equally wonderful and interesting, all tending directly to show that mind governs the body and, to affect the body, it must be done through the mind.

An individual who was an entire stranger to me called and said he was not a believer in Mesmerism, but would become so if I could relieve the pain under which he was then suffering from a contusion of the foot. I requested him to sit down and I would try, that I would first induce a strange feeling upon his foot and he might tell me the sensation which would follow. In about five minutes he remarked that he felt a prickling sensation, as though his "foot was going to sleep." This was what I designed to do. I then proceeded to relieve the pain and he described a cool sensation at first, which was soon followed by entire relief. He acknowledged the result and remarked "humbug or no humbug the pain is gone."

While I was traveling with my subject in 1843, a gentleman, who had long been troubled with lameness proceeding from rheumatic influence, hobbled up stairs and entered my room. He requested me to operate upon him and do him all the good I could. I made some enquiries into his case and proceeded to relieve the pain and restore him to health. In less than one hour he was enabled to walk with greater ease (his own declaration) than for the preceding two years. He left me in good spirits and the following morning rode to a neighboring town and unfortunately upset his sleigh. All the violence of the old rheumatic complaint returned. Two days after I heard of his misfortune and called on him. His physician was present and writing a prescription for medicines. I enquired of the Doct. after his patient who gave me no favorable account. I directed him to apply his mesmeric power and relieve the pain without <u>prescription</u>. He smiled and said he had made the attempt, could throw him into a sleeping state but could not relieve the pain. He gave me permission to try my power. I sat down by him and soon relieved the pain and before we left he was enabled to walk about the room. The physician tore up his prescription and remarked that he saw no occasion for his services and we both left in company. A friend of mine took me to see an Irish gentleman who was in the last stages of consumption. Upon entering his house we could distinctly hear him breathe. My friend introduced me and related the occasion of our call. The man with much difficulty replied that nothing could help him etc. I commenced acting upon his mind. In a short time the difficulty of breathing was removed, and the man raising himself up in bed exclaimed to my friend, "Why sir, what does this mean? My Sir, I feel, I feel very much relieved!" After spending an hour with him we left. I called again the next morning and found him up and dressed and doing well. I left town that day and have not since heard of him. Dr. H. took me to see one of his patients who was very low in the last stages of consumption. We found her very weak and oppressed with a difficulty of breathing. I commenced operating upon her and removed the difficulty of breathing and induced a strong and healthful feeling. We left her very comfortable and she declared she was much better. Whether she recovered from her illness I have not heard. Another patient in the last stages of consumption, who was entirely given over by all the physicians, sent for me a few days since. I soon relieved much of his pain—enabled him to swallow with less difficulty and entirely threw off his fever, which had returned regularly every day previous for some time. He appears now much better than when I first saw him. But it is too much to suppose that he can be restored from his very debilitated state to health.

I will now introduce another class of experiments. A gentleman residing out of town was seized with an affection of the head, producing severe pain. This continued for the space of two or three months but increasing in severity until he entirely lost the power of seeing and was blind. He sent for me to visit him. I did so and found him in the state I have described, suffering intensely from the pain in his head and not able to see any object around him. I commenced exercising my powers to throw him into the mesmeric state and was soon successful. I then relieved the pain of his head and proceeded to enable him to see objects around him. I placed my fingers in front of his eyes and he soon remarked that he saw them and felt an influence proceeding from them which was cooling. I was trying to allay the fever in that portion of the brain connected with his eyes, which was probably the influence he felt. He could tell when I was near to him or at a distance. I then roused him from his sleeping condition and commenced operating upon his eyes to induce the power of sight. He described the sensations produced like flakes of clouds passing before his eyes, being sometimes so dark that he could distinguish no light and then followed with light. I continued my operations until he was enabled to see an object I held up before him, described what it was and read the figures which were printed upon it. His health was so far gone that it would have been almost a miracle to have restored him. I left him however in this condition and soon after heard of his death.

A young man came to me not long since who was very pale and emaciated and asked if I could help him. He was much troubled to breathe and felt a bad pain in his side. I commenced experimenting upon him in his waking state and in a few moments relieved his difficulty of breathing and took away the pain in his side. He is now an active and healthy young man, enabled to attend to his business. I called on a young man residing upon the Kennebec, whom I found in this condition. He had not spoken or even whispered or walked for the previous eight or nine months and could not get about only as he managed himself along in his chair. I commenced operating upon him in his waking state and in the course of one half hour I requested him to answer me. He immediately answered me and easily talked. I then enabled him to walk across the floor and his neighbors came in and he was able to converse with them and to walk while in their presence. I left him in this condition and called the following day. He was walking his room and when I spoke to him he answered me by a nod of his head. I told him I did not understand him. He then answered me readily and was able to talk very well. This was the condition in which I left him and have no doubt but that he would have fully recovered had not other counteracting influences been brought to act upon him.

These influences were produced upon him by his ignorant physician, who probably feeling that some glory might be detracted from his great professional distinction if the patient, who had been so long under his immediate and mighty curatives, should recover by so simple a process which his dull genius had not discovered. Soon after I left, I was informed that this benevolent gentleman was so kind as to inform him that I was an impostor and had only been playing upon his imagination, that he would in a few days be worse etc. Thus by every act of which this little man was capable of exercising, he produced an opposite impression upon his mind, destroying all the good I had accomplished. So much for the <u>kindness</u>, <u>benevolence</u> and <u>philanthropy</u>, or if you please, the <u>ignorance</u> and <u>bigotry</u> of his physician. We have found but few <u>such</u> in the world and we desire, so far as our friends and ourselves are concerned, that they may be less frequent than angels visits. Had he possessed the common feelings of humanity, even though he could not, at that time place much confidence in so simple an operation of a stranger, yet for his friend's sake would it not have been the part of wisdom to have suspended the counteracting influences and rather assisted the mind of his patient and friend to overcome the difficulty. We leave the matter to the patient and his neighbors to say how much benefit such a physician is to mankind.

I was not long since called upon to visit an old lady who was afflicted with the "acute rheumatism," sometimes called. I found her in the most extreme pain. I commenced operating upon her in the waking state and soon eased the acute pains. Before I left her, she said she did not feel any pain in her limbs and she could use them without difficulty. I saw her husband the following day and he informed me that she slept well during the night and was fast recovering. I was called upon to visit an old lady whom I found in ill health and very low and gloomy in her feelings. She had given up all hope of recovering and even distributed her goods and chattels among her kinsmen. I observed that her temperament was such as to be easily wrought upon and told her I could restore her to perfect health. I operated upon her mind in the waking state and relieved all her suffering pains; but there was one difficulty, she remarked, about her, which, if it was not removed, would be the death of her. It was this. She said her liver was completely caked over and that she could feel it on her side. I examined her side and allowed her to think so, but told her I could remove that feeling and would do so. I then made an effort to regulate her feelings in this particular. She said she felt better and I left her promising to call the next day. I did so and found her pretty well, but the cake upon her liver had not entirely dissipated. I however corrected the disease and the woman is entirely restored.

The cases we have just enumerated may appear, at first view, to be nothing but imaginary diseases. This was not the fact. They were all real and all the impressions which were given by myself were real. I do not suppose that the last case was precisely what the old lady supposed, yet there was some disease or some cause which she attributed to a strong covering to her liver. We have endeavored to keep up a distinction between imaginary and real cases. And we will simply state here that all the patients were really as we have described them and none of them were troubled with imaginary evils—that what is real cannot be imaginary, that the moment the reality commences, imagination ceases. I will give one illustration. If I imagine a sharp pain in my finger and continue to keep up the imagination, the pain is not there, it exists only in my imagination or rather does not exist at all. Now suppose I commence imagining a pain in my finger and while doing it, a pain should be actually felt just when I was imagining. Would the pain really felt be real? We think it would and when this sensation exists there, imagination ceases to act.

In the cases above the remedies resorted to are real to the subjects because they restored them. At least they are as real as the diseases and the diseases were as real as any disease with which mankind are afflicted. If then one answers that all these cases are imaginary, we reply, then everything is imaginary and nothing is real.

We proceed to give other cases of a different class and which will more fully prove the distinction between the real and the imaginary.

There's a lady residing in this country who had been lame and unable to walk for two years. She had been under the care of physicians who had resorted to every medicine consistent with the case within the range of their profession. She had been three months under the care of the celebrated Dr. Hewit of Boston, but received no benefit but continued about the same. This was the condition in which I found her, unable to bear any weight upon her foot. We now ask, was this case real or imaginary, upon the facts as we have stated? Whatever the answer is, she and her friends, who were enabled to feel and see her condition, believed it real. I was lecturing in town and was sent for to visit her. I complied and commenced operating upon her in her waking state. In less than one half hour she rose from her chair and walked across the room and out of her keeping room into the other, astonishing all who beheld her. She continued to walk and grow better and has now nearly recovered. This walking could not have arisen from any excitement under which she labored at the time because she continued better and her ankle and foot are nearly or quite well. Is the recovery of the lady imaginary? If you think it unreal we will give another! It is this. A good old farmer, residing in town, who took a trip to one of the islands in our bay, was severely bitten by a dog through the wrist. His hand and arm began to perish and had already become much smaller than the other. When I saw him, which was about three months after his misfortune, a sore on the back of his hand had broken out several times or at stated intervals. I found him in a lawyer's office stating his case to his attorney, who had commenced a suit against the owner of the dog and afterwards recovered seven hundred dollars damages. I examined his arm at that time and found it in the condition I have described. In the conversation he remarked, that, if I would restore it, he would not spare the greatest expense of which his condition in life would admit. Before I commenced operating upon him, I asked him to use it and lift up a very small pamphlet which lay on the table. This he was unable to do and he stated that he had no use of it. I then took him into an adjoining room and operated upon him in his waking state. I soon enabled him to use his hand and arm. He took up the largest volume of the law library, held it in his hand and carried it into the other room. He then took hold of the bottom of a chair, lifted it up and carried it round. He returned to his farm and began to labor using his hand and arm. In about three months his arm had assumed its natural size and appeared perfectly well. He complained only of a slight weakness, in twisting his wrist. I soon removed that difficulty and he is now fully restored.

Another case was a man in the country, who had injured his wrist by blasting a rock and had not been able to use it for nine months, called on me. His hand and arm had withered very much and was carried in a sling. It was also cold although in midsummer, and he was obliged to keep it wrapped up from the air. I commenced operating upon him and before I left him he was enabled to lift a pail of water and other things which were near us. Before he left town, which was on the same day, he could lift with his lame hand and arm, a weight of fifty pounds. I have not seen or heard of him since and do not know whether he recovered entirely.

We suppose, after giving our last examples that no one will attribute their restoration to the imagination. We need not argue the case furthermore as to the reality of the condition of the patients we have named or the facts of their recovery. If any part of the whole transactions were real, then all were real. If any part were imaginary, then all were imaginary. And if these cases were imaginary then we say that all diseases, all conditions of mind and matter, anything about us and around us is imaginary and nothing has any reality.

We might state a great number of cases, similar to the above, all showing the same results and proving the same facts, all being real and not imaginary.

We have read of cases when persons have been thrown into the mesmeric state and had some of the most dangerous and, in the waking state, painful surgical operation performed without manifesting the least pain. We do not doubt their authority. We have had only one case when an actual operation was performed of the above class. A lady residing about ten miles from Belfast came to our village to have a polypus extracted from her nose by one of our surgeons. She called on Dr. W. at his office and requested him to send for me to throw her into the mesmeric state. He was no believer in mesmerism and at first refused; but the lady would not consent to the operation until I was sent for. I found her in the Dr.'s office and in ten minutes threw her into the mesmeric state and requested the Dr. to commence. He performed the operation and she did not even move a single muscle during the whole time and gave no appearance of pain. While the operation was being performed, the blood was observed by someone standing by to run into her mouth and I was requested to induce her to spit. I did so and she answered by spitting out the blood. This experiment took place in the presence of some four or five individuals and it was at that time noticed in the public prints.

When she awoke, she was not conscious of having suffered any pain.

Insanity

We now proceed to another state of mind, called by philosophers, Insanity. The power of reason, that is the faculty by which we compare facts with each other and mental expressions with external things, is said to be lost in Insanity. In this state of mind, the subject appears to be under the complete control of some strong and irresistible impression or train of successive impressions, real to him and which he cannot repulse with a comparison with external objects. Like a subject in the dreaming or mesmeric state, he is not able to discover what impressions flow from false causes and distinguish them from those which flow from real causes. The subject himself acts precisely as every man would under the same real impressions. Then mind is governed and controlled by the same laws in this state as in the natural or dreaming state. It acts from real impressions under a full belief of the real causes of such impressions. This state is no doubt induced by some powerful impressions upon the mind which cannot be removed by slight impressions produced upon the mind from common and everyday objects. If this state is removed at all, it must be done by inducing some counteracting impression, which will lead the mind into a different channel of thought. This state of mind often exhibits in the individual more acuteness and intelligence in almost every subject than when in its natural condition. He will reason correctly although from unsound data and return answers justifying his conduct, which would display a thoughtful and premeditating mind. We have read numerous instances of individuals whose conduct has been most unreasonable, yet could justify their acts by giving inducements to such conduct, based upon reasonable grounds. Dr. Abercrombie relates the case of a clergyman in Scotland, who having displayed many extravagances of conduct, was brought before a jury to be declared incapable of managing his own affairs and placed under the care of trustees. Among the extravagant exhibitions of conduct was that he had burnt his library. When the jury requested him to give an account of this part of his conduct, he replied in the following terms. "In the early part of my life, I had imbibed a liking for a most unprofitable study, namely controversial divinity. On reviewing my library, I found a great part of it to consist of books of this distinction. I was so anxious that my family should not be led to follow the same pursuit that I determined to burn the whole." He gave answers to other charges brought against him justifying his conduct and the jury did not find sufficient grounds for guarding him with trustees; but in the course of two weeks, he [was] in a state of decided mania! Individuals while in this excited state, when some leading impression has control, have really believed themselves to be some great actor in the world, an emperor or a king and supposed all the fair fields about them and all the inhabitants who live within their state or nation are subject to their control. Others have descended in the scale of their existence and supposed themselves beasts of burden, or mere things. These are all real to the subject. He feels himself just as he believes. This is sometimes called a deranged state of mind. It is, however, a disease, as much so as any condition of man. For we contend that disease is nothing only as it conveys impressions to the mind. That if one should cut his finger and no sensation should be conveyed through the sense of touch to the mind, it would not give pain to the subject. This position we know by experiments upon individuals both in their waking and mesmeric state.

Insanity, Monomania, Hallucination are all diseases, and remedies may be administered to counteract them. The treatment of the subject, while insane, has much to do with his recovery. For the benefit of this class of individuals, hospitals are erected at the public expense, where the best remedies can be administered. This disease among physicians is not usually attributed to flow from the same sources as what they term those of the body and therefore they do not resort to the same remedies. Physicians generally call Insanity a disease of the mind while fever and other similar states are diseases of the body. I maintain that all diseases are only known to exist as they affect the mind of the patient, that is, there would be no disease which could affect an individual provided it could not make a sensation upon his mind. If he did not feel sick, he would not probably be sick. In cases of scrofula and what is sometimes termed King's evil, diseases said to be incurable, the power of the Seventh Son to cure them is an effect upon the mind, being conclusive evidence that some strong impression induced the disease. And the belief of the patient and that also of the seventh son, acting in concert to produce a counteracting impression, would destroy the old first cause which brought about this diseased state and nature then restores herself. We do not believe that the seventh son has any more virtue to heal patients than any individual; nor do we think the fact of his passing his hand over the diseased portion of the body could affect anything towards counteracting the first impression, only so far as an external motion may assist to more strongly impress the mind. It is simply the process of mind acting upon and in correspondence with mind. I will introduce an experiment here which goes to show something in proof of what we are explaining. An individual fell from his horse and dislocated his elbow. The surgeon set it and his arm was, when I first saw it, badly swollen and very painful. I commenced operating upon it and in a short time reduced the swelling so that the bandages were very loose and all the pain subsided. He was then enabled to lift up a chair without any pain, but before could not lift a pound nor even use his fingers. Someone may enquire whether the dislocation of the elbow was a disease of the mind? We answer, it was, that is, all the pain which was the result of the falling from the horse was in the mind, being the only part of man susceptible of sensation, that the mere blow or contusion would not produce any pain unless there was a mind which could feel the blow, because matter is not supposed to have the power of sensation. We might bring many facts, as we trust we have in the former part of this work, to show where the disease is to be remedied and where of course it must flow from to affect the person or when an impression is produced from which follows all the phenomena of disease both of body and mind. But we allude to the subject here to illustrate our ideas upon Insanity. And by the results we have effected upon diseases by operating upon mind, we think the argument is conclusive that all diseases, including insanity, flow from the impressions upon the mind as their first cause.

Lecture Notes–Booklet VII
[BU 1:0082]

The treatment of insane persons therefore should correspond with the great principle of mind acting upon mind and of impressions counteracting impressions.

We give the following experiments illustrating the power of mind over mind in cases of Insanity.

I was called upon about two years since to visit an insane man who had been chained to prevent him from extravagant conduct but who had by some means gotten loose and was raving about his premises, to the danger of his own family and his neighbors. I found him in the wildest state of insanity. I approached him in company with another individual. When he saw us coming, he advanced towards us with a ten foot pole. My friend could not proceed and I was left alone to meet him. I advanced keeping my eye steadily fixed upon him. He held his pole and advanced until we came within ten feet of each other. He then suddenly stopped and told me not to advance another step. I continued however to walk towards him and as I came up he threw down his pole and looking me in the eye asked what I wanted. I requested him to go into the house. He followed me in and became obedient to my commands as a child. I performed several experiments upon him showing how easily I could control him. When any of his family came near, he would commence raving but upon my requesting him to be quiet, he readily complied. I ordered him to dress himself and upon clothing being handed to him, he complied. He walked up to me and look at my form and enquire how much I weighed. I asked him to guess. He thought two hundred and fifty pounds. I allowed him to think so, although my real weight was about one-hundred and forty. I was enabled to control him while I was present without touching him at all. Another case of a man who had become ravingly insane and was imprisoned in the County Jail. He would allow nothing in his cell and allow no one to enter. He kept up a constant hollering so as to be heard all over the village. The keeper of the prison decided that something must be done. My situation was such that I had occasion to see him. I took another man with me and going to the door of the cell requested him to remain outside and not allow him to know that he was near. I opened the cell door, holding in my hand a green hide and a rope. He ordered me not to approach him, holding in his hand a stone which he had dug out of some part of his cell. I stood and looked at him about five minutes. He began to step back and I entered. I then ordered him to come to me and get down on his knees. He obeyed instantly and I then thought I would try an experiment. I told him I would not whip or tie him then, but if he ever made any more noise or destroyed his bedding or anything which might be handed him, I would certainly kill him, at the same time showing my intention in my countenance. He seemed to be very much agitated and frightened. I produced so strong an impression upon his mind that he was perfectly quiet and became more rational. In the course of three weeks, he left the prison and returned home perfectly sane. He has been sane ever since. Thus the power of impressions over the mind to produce or counteract disease must be acknowledged. And the action of mind upon mind must be conceded. It is, in Insanity as in other diseases, necessary to make an impression more powerful than that which preceded this diseased state and thus lead or drive the mind into a new channel of thought. So in diseases of every class an impression counteracting that which induced the disease must be made and nature will restore herself. This impression may be made by administering powerful medicine or it may be done upon some patients by the mind of an operator acting upon the mind of the patient.

It might be a question in regard to all the experiments we have presented in this volume whether it is really the strong intellectual power of a mind which may gain the ascendancy over another, and hold it in complete submission as in the case of our two last experiments. We answer that we do not think it is great intellectual power, but the capacity or power of arresting the attention and producing a strong impression. And this faculty may be cultivated and enlarge its power to produce impressions and arrest the attention of mind to the exclusion of surrounding influences. We have mentioned the fact in another page that the idea of magnetizing or mesmerizing only those persons who are dull and enjoy poor health and weak minds is exploded. The more intelligent the mind, if the attention can be fixed and drawn away from surrounding influences, the more certain you are of producing the excited or mesmeric state in the highest degree. A bright, intelligent and thoughtful person enjoying good health always makes the best subject.

We do not therefore claim a more powerful intellect by which we can produce such results upon mind, but attribute it to a natural and cultivated power in this capacity which I am enabled to exercise and produce such experiments as are called mesmeric, magnetic, etc. The fact that the community have always laid it down as a general principle that only a more powerful mind can operate upon and control a weaker has retarded the progress of this branch of intellectual philosophy. The idea, no doubt, arose from some self-conceited personage, or perhaps a numerous class of those who were public magnetizers, desirous of claiming all the intellect which is really worth having. It is a fact we are compelled to acknowledge that some of my predecessors in this branch of science seem to have possessed no other intellectual faculty than that of mesmerizing; and the consequence was that they would be desirous of instructing the world to believe that the power they exercise is indeed that of a great mind and to be surpassed by no other power. All we have to remark upon this class of philosophers is that whatever discoveries and advances they have made in the progress of human knowledge should be thankfully received. And the follies and egotisms which have been interwoven with their progress should be rejected, as the consoling food for the vanity and self-esteem of its projectors. No man would be justified in rejecting the whole Copernican System because some wandering genius, desirous of making himself greater than the rest, should have advanced the idea and proceeded to prove it, that the earth is spherical and turns on its axis every twenty four hours and is kept in motion on the principle of a great wheel in a treadmill by the constant tramping of an enormous Mammoth upon the equator. "Retain the good and reject the evil." Then will science advance.

We now enter upon another branch of our subject by which a solution of the mysteries of past ages is given. We refer to the mystery and responses of the Ancient Apollo, the Egyptian Magi, the Black Art, Witchcraft, trances, catalepsy etc.

Apolonius of Tyana, Emanuel Swedenborg, Mahomet and others had the power of inducing this state of the mind upon themselves. This is a further and conclusive proof against a fluid theory.

We copy the following from Dr. Collyer's pamphlet upon Psychography. [Citation not copied here.—*Ed.*] [End of Lecture Notes.]

PHINEAS P. QUIMBY'S LETTERS

[BU 2:0020]

Belfast, Nov. 4th, 1856

Madam:

Yours of the 2nd inst. was received, and now I sit down to answer your inquiry in regard to your lameness. It seems to me that the skin on the knee is thinner and has a more healthy appearance. But you cannot be made to believe anything that is in plain contradiction to your own senses, and as your opinions have been formed from the evidence of persons in whom you have placed confidence and facts have gone to prove these opinions correct, it is not strange that you should hold on to your belief till some kind friend should come to your aid and lead your mind in a different direction.

Now to remind you of what I tried to make you understand is a very hard task on my part; for as I said to you, some of my ideas fall on stony ground, and some on dry ground, and some on good ground. These ideas are in your mind like the little leaven, and they will work till the whole mind or lump is changed.

You have asked me many questions which time and space will not permit me to answer, but I shall write that which seems to be of the most benefit to you. In regard to your coming to Belfast, use your own judgment. The cure of your limb depends on your faith. Your faith is what you receive from me, and what you receive is what you understand. Now if you understand that the mind is the name of the fluids of which your body is composed and your thoughts represent the change of the fluids or mind, you will then be in a state to act understandingly.

I will try to illustrate it to you so you can apply your thoughts to your body so as to receive the reward of your labor. As I told you, every thought contains a substance either good or bad, and it comes in and makes up a part of your body or mind; and as the thoughts which are in your system are poisoned, and the poison has come from without, it is necessary to know how to keep them out of your system so as not to be injured by them.

Now suppose you have around you a sort of heat like the light of a candle which embraces all your knowledge, and your body being the centre and you having the power to govern and control this heat, you then have a world of your own. Now in health this globe of which your body is the centre is perfect harmony. The heat of this globe is a protection to itself, like a walled city, to admit none but supposed friends. Now as every person has the same globe or heat, each person is a world or nation of itself. This is the state of a person in health.

Now as you wish to change and interchange with other nations, so does our house like to enjoy the society of other persons, and as we are liberal we admit strangers to our city or world as friends. When this proclamation goes out, our globe is filled with all sorts of people from all nations, bringing with them goods, setting up false doctrines, stirring up strife till the whole population or thoughts are changed, and man becomes a stranger in his own land and his own household becomes his enemies. This is the state of a person in disease. Now as there is nothing in your own system of itself to disturb you, you must look for your enemies from the strangers whom you have permitted to come into your land.

Belfast, Jan. 10th, 1857

Mr. Thomas Millet Pelmgru
Dear Sir:

Yours of the 4th was received and would say in reply to your enquiry that my opinion would be for your wife to remain at home for a short time.

On another case, I intend to visit Bangor in one or two weeks and while I am at Bangor I can take the case and come to Newport and take a private team to your house and return by the next train. This would be as long as I should wish to stop and my expense would not be much. At any rate I would not charge you more than two dollars above my expenses together.

If your wife should improve from that visit, she could come to Bangor or to Belfast just as you think best. I write in this way because I am partially engaged to go to Bangor and if your wife was here in

Belfast it would make it very bad for her and I would feel very bad myself. Now if this meets your ideas if you will leave word at the nearest point or station where the train stops with someone to carry me to your house, you could then carry me back to take the case so it would not be much expense. The fare from Bangor to your place and back you can ascertain, but if I don't go to Bangor I will let you know, and in the meantime you can ascertain and let me know which of the two would suit your wife best, to come here, or to have me visit her.

N.B. The price I charge you would have nothing to do with any other person. My charge is $3.00 but to see your wife I would charge $2.00 over and above my expenses from Bangor and back.

Yours truly,

P. P. Quimby

Portland, Feb., 1860

Mr. Editor:

I notice an article in your paper of the third inst. in answer to Y.C. I have nothing to do with that; but when a person sees fit to attack me as a sorcerer and humbug, he had better look out for his own theory or house and see if it is based on a sure foundation before he commences throwing stones at outsiders, for he will be likely to break his own windows and let in the cold.

Mr. J. seems to be troubled for the safety of the good people of Portland and warns them against mesmerism, sorcery and all sorts of humbug. Who art thou, oh man, that judges another without any cause? Did you know by what you measured to another it shall be measured back to you again? Judge not that ye be not judged. If you know more about my practice than I do, why did you not tell the people where the deception is and enlighten them upon the subject; then you would have done good to the sick. But you do not take the responsibility upon yourself but, like a demagogue, you come forward with a face of brass and an impudence that shows itself in every word you say. That shows you are giving an opinion upon what you have not the slightest knowledge, expecting the people to take your bare assertion for truth. Why are you not honest and say to the sick that they have not sense enough to know whether they are benefited by me or not and that you have just sense enough to see all through the humbug? For this is what you mean.

Now the time is come when such oracles as you will be weighed in the balance, and then you will receive sentence according to your knowledge.

P. P. Quimby

Portland, Feb. 9th, 1860
[To a patient in Hill, N.H.]

Your letter apprised me of your situation and I want to see if I could affect you. I am still trying to do so, but do not know as I can without sitting down and talking with you as I am at present. So I will sit by you a short time and relieve the pain in your stomach and carry it off. You can sit down when you receive this letter and listen to my story and I think you will feel better. Sit up straight. I am now rubbing the back part of your head and round the roots of your nose. I do not know as you feel my hand, but you twist your arm as though it felt rather queer, but it will make you feel better. When you read this, I shall be with you; and do as I write. I am in this letter, so remember and look at me, and see if I do not mean just as I say. I will now leave you and attend to some others that are waiting, so "Good evening." Let me know how you get along. If I do not write, I may have time to call for that does not require so much time.

P.P.Q.

Portland, Feb. 9th, 1860
To Miss K., Kennebunk, Me.:

Your letter of the 5th is received. I am surprised that you do not remember that all my patients have "a cold" as they call it, when the belief is. For instance, if you are told you have "consumption," this belief is matter under the direction of error, and as it is put into practice, it changes the mind so that the idea of consumption is thrown off from the belief. If you are excited by any other belief, you throw off all the misery that follows your belief. For instance, you are made to believe you are not so good as you ought to be. Your belief puts restrictions on your life, and as it is a burden to you, it makes you throw off a shadow that contains the punishment of your disobedience. This makes you another character, and you are not the happy child of Wisdom.

This was your belief when you called on me. As I struck at the roots of your belief with the axe of Truth, everything having a tendency to make you unhappy I tried to destroy. So in the destruction there must be a change. This change must be like its father. So if you had grief, it would produce grief for the present. Finally the Truth would dry up your tears and you would rejoice in that Truth that sets you free.

So in regard to the "cold"; if you had the idea of "consumption" when I drove that enemy of man out of your belief, this must produce a like cough, but it is all for the best. Remember that every error has its reaction, but an unravelling of error leads to life and happiness, while the winding it up leads to disease and misery.

All that is taking place in your case is just what I anticipated. So it is all right. Keep up good courage and all will come out right. Tell Miss F to keep good courage. Her cure is certain.

P.P.Q.

Portland, March 21st, 1860
To Mrs. Wayne
Dear Madam:

Yours of the 19th is received and I was very glad to hear I succeeded so well, but I was not disappointed, for I felt sure I could raise you up. I will say a word or two to you, Mrs. W. I was with you every little while after I first wrote you till the time I named, and then it seemed as though you were up so I left you. Now I shall drop in and see you often so you may not be surprised to feel my influence. Were there any ones at your house when you first got up? If so let me know how long you had been sick and how long since you walked. I shall be very glad. I think I shall make a statement to the facts of your case; it is so remarkable that it ought to be published for the benefit of the sick.

Yours, etc.
P.P.Q.

LETTER TO A PATIENT RECENTLY HELPED

Portland, March 22nd, 1860

Dear Sir:

Your letter of the 21st is received and I take pleasure in answering it. You must excuse me for addressing Maria for I come to save her, while those who are well need no physician. So Maria, I am glad to know you are getting along so well. Since I received the letter I have visited you often and shall drop in every day just after you take your meals and sit by you and quiet your system so that your food shall sit well. I shall visit you at night while you are sleeping in your bed and use my influence to make you rest well so you will be able to walk. You need not give yourself any fears of my forsaking you nor leaving you in the hands of your enemies. I shall watch over you till you are able to take care of yourself if my power is able to do it. I should be glad to hear how you get along.

IN REPLY TO A YOUNG PHYSICIAN

Portland, Sept. 16, 1860

Dear Sir:

Yours of the 5th is received, and in answer I would say that it is easier to ask a question than to answer it. But I will answer your question partly by asking another, and partly by coming at it by a parable. For to answer any question with regard to my mode of treatment would be like asking a physician how he knows a patient has the typhoid fever by feeling the pulse, and requesting the answer direct so that the person asking the question could sit down and be sure to define the disease from the answer.

My mode of treatment is not decided in that way, and to give a definite answer to your inquiry would be as much out of place as to ask you to tell me all you know about the medical practice so that I could put it into practice for the curing of disease, with no further knowledge independently from what I get from you. You see the absurdity of that request.

If it were in my power to give to the world the benefit of twenty years' hard study in one short or long letter, it would have been before the people long before this. The people ask they know not what. You might as well ask a man to tell you how to talk Greek without studying it, as to ask me to tell you how I test the true pathology of disease or how I test the true diagnosis of disease, etc. All of these questions would be very easily answered if I assumed a standard and then tested all disease by that standard.

The old mode of determining the diagnosis of disease is made up of opinions of diseased persons, in their right mind and out of it, under a nervous state of mind, all mixed up together, and set down accompanied by a certain state of pulse. In this dark chaos of error, they come to certain results like this. If you see a man going towards the water, he is going in swimming, for people go in swimming. But if he is running with his hat and coat off, he is either going to drown himself or someone is drowning, and soon. This is the old way. Mine is this.

If I see a man, I know it, and if I feel the cold I know it. But to see a person going towards the water is no sign that I know what he is going to do. He may be going to bathe or may be going to drown himself. Now here is the difference between the physician and myself, and this may give you some idea of how I define disease.

The regular and I sit down by a patient. He takes her by the hand, and so do I. He feels the pulse to ascertain the peculiar vibration and number of beats in a given time. This to him is knowledge. To me it is all quackery or ignorance. He looks at the tongue as though it contained information.

To me this is all folly and ignorance. He then begins to ask questions which contain nothing to me, because it is of no force. All this is shaken up in his head and comes forth in the form of a disease to which he gives a name. This is the diagnosis of a disease, which is all error to me, and I will give you the diagnosis of this error.

The feeling of the pulse is to affect the patient so he will listen to the doctor. Examining the tongue is all for effect. The peculiar cast of the doctor's head is the same. The questions, accompanied by certain looks and gestures, are all to get control of the patient's mind so as to produce an impression. Then he looks very wise, and so on. All the symptoms put together show no knowledge but a lack of wisdom, and the general credulity of mankind rendering liable to be humbugged by any person however ignorant he may be, if he only has the reputation of possessing all medical knowledge.

Now, sir, this is the field you are about to enter, and you will find the hardest stumbling block from diplomas. Greek and Latin and the like are all of no consequence to the sick. It is impossible to give you even a mere shadow of twenty years' experience. But I may be of some use to you. I will say a word or two on the old practice (not taking much time) that will answer all your questions on the old school, for the less you know the better.

Watch the popular physician. See his shrewdness. Watch the sick patient, nervous and trembling like a person in the hands of a magistrate who has him in his power and whose real object is to deceive him. See the two together, one perfectly honest, and the other, if honest, perfectly ignorant, undertaking blindfolded to lead the patients through the dark valley of the shadow of death, the patient being born blind. Then you see them going along, and at last they both fall into the ditch.

Now, like the latter, do not deceive your patients. Try to instruct them and correct their errors. Use all the wisdom you have and expose the hypocrisy of the profession in any one. Never deceive your patients behind their backs. Always remember that as you feel about your patients, just so they feel towards you. If you deceive them, they lose confidence in you. Just as you prove yourself superior to them, they give you credit mentally. If you pursue this course you cannot help succeeding. Be charitable to the poor. Keep the health of your patient in view, and if money comes, all well; but do not let that get the lead.

With all this advice, I leave you to your fate, trusting that the true wisdom will guide you–not in the path of your predecessors. Shun evil and learn to do good.

P.P.Q.

A LETTER REGARDING A PATIENT

Portland, Sept. 17th, 1860

Dear Sir:

Yours of Aug. 27th was received after a long journey through the state of Maine. I will give you all the information that I am aware I possess.

If certain conditions of mind exist, certain effects will surely follow. For instance, if two persons agree as touching one thing, it will be granted. But if one agrees and the other knows not the thing desired, then the thing will not be accomplished.

For example, the lady in question wishes my services to restore her health. Now her health is the thing she desires. Her faith is the substance of her hope. Her hope is her desire, it is founded on public opinion, and in this is her haven, the anchor to her desire, public opinion the ocean on which her barque or belief floats. Reports of me are the wind that either presses her along to the haven of health or down to despair. The tide of public opinion is either against her or in her favor. Now, as she lies moored on the sea with her desire or cable attached to her anchor of hope, tossed to and fro in the gale of disease, if she can see me or my power walking on the water saying to her aches and pains, "Be still," then I have no doubt that she will get better. The sea will then be calm, and she will get that which she hoped for, her faith or cure. For her faith is her cure and if she gets it, then her hope is lost in sight and she no longer hopes. This is the commencement of her cure. I, like Jesus, will stand at her heart and knock. If she hears my voice or feels my influence and opens the door of her belief, I will come in and talk and help her out of her troubles.

P.P.Q.

TO A GENTLEMAN REQUESTING HELP WITHOUT A PERSONAL INTERVIEW

Portland, Oct. 20th, 1860

Dear Sir:

In answer to your inquiry, I would say that owing to the skepticism of the world I do not feel inclined to assure you of any benefit which you may receive from my influence while away from you, as your belief would probably keep me from helping you. But it will not cost me much time nor expense to make the trial. So if I stand at your door and knock, and you know my voice or influence and receive me, you may be benefited. If you do receive my benefit, give it to the Principle, not to me as a man but to that Wisdom which is able to break the bonds of the prisoner, set him free from the errors of the doctors, and restore him to health. This I will try to do with pleasure. But if this fails and your case is one which requires my seeing you, then my opinion is of no use.

Yours, etc.

P.P.Q.

TO A CLERGYMAN

Oct. 28th, 1860

Dear Sir:

Your letter of the eighteenth was received, but owing to a press of business I neglected answering it. I will try to give you the wisdom you ask. So far as giving an opinion is concerned, it is out of my power as a physician, though as man I might. But it would be of no service, for it would contain no wisdom except of this world.

My practice is not of the wisdom of man, so my opinion as a man is of no value. Jesus said, "If I judge of myself, my judgment is not true; but if I judge of God, it is right," for that contains no opinion. So if I judge as a man it is an opinion, and you can get plenty of them anywhere.

You inquire if I have ever cured any cases of chronic rheumatism. I answer, "Yes." But there are as many cases of chronic rheumatism as there are of spinal complaint so that I cannot decide your case by another. You cannot be saved by pinning your faith on another's sleeve. Everyone must answer for his own sins or belief. Our beliefs are the cause of our misery. Our happiness and misery are what follow our belief. So as we measure out to another, it will be measured to us again.

You ask me if I ascribe my cures to spiritual influence. Not after the Rochester rappings, nor after Dr. Newton's way of curing. I think I know how he cures, though he does not. I gather by those I have seen who have been treated by him that he thinks it is through the imagination of the patient's belief. So he and I have no sympathy. If he cures disease, that is good for the one cured. But the world is not any wiser.

You ask if my practice belongs to any known science. My answer is, "No," it belongs to Wisdom that is above man as man. The Science that I try to practice is the Science that was taught eighteen-hundred years ago and has never had a place in the heart of man since, but is in the world, and the world knows it not. To narrow it down to man's wisdom, I sit down by the patient and take his feelings, and as the rest will be a long story, I will send you one of my circulars so that you may read for yourself.

Hoping this may limber the cords of your neck, I remain,

Yours, etc.
P.P. Quimby

Portland, Me., Dec. 27th, 1860

To Miss G.F.:

Your letter was received, and now I sit down to use my power to affect you. I will commence by telling you to sit upright and not give way to the pit of the stomach but hold yourself up straight. If I felt that you saw me as plainly while I am talking to you as I see you, then there would be no use in writing, for you are as plain before my eyes as you were when I was talking to the shadow in Portland. For the shadow came with the substance, and that which I am talking to now is the substance. If I make an impression on it, it may throw forth a shadow of a young lady upright without that "gone place" in the substance at the pit of the stomach. Now I am looking into the second stomach, opening the outlet so that all obstructions may be removed, also to prevent you from vomiting.

Remember that when I see you sitting or standing in the position I saw you in at Portland, I shall place one hand on your breast and the other on your hips and just straighten you up. If you complain of the back, you may lay it to me and I will be a little more gentle. You may expect me once in a while in the evening. So keep on the lookout. See that you have your lamp trimmed and burning so that when the truth comes it shall not find you sleeping but up straight, ready to receive the bridegroom. It seems that you understand this as I tell it to you. But for fear you will not explain it to the shadow or natural man, I will try to make you understand so it may come to the senses of the natural man. If I succeed, let my natural man know by a letter.

Yours, etc.
P.P.Q.

Portland, Me., Dec. 30th, 1860

To Mr. J.:

As your wife is about to leave for home, I take this way of expressing my ideas of the trouble she is laboring under, thinking you would like my opinion of her case. I think her friends are. not aware of her true state. Hers is one of a very peculiar kind. She is not deaf in the strict sense of the word, but her condition has been brought about by trouble of long standing. When I say "trouble" I do not confine it to any neglect on the part of her friends, but trouble when young, which made her nervous. This caused her to become low-spirited, till it has changed her system so that she is not the same person she was twelve years ago. I have given my attention to her general health, not to her deafness, for I think if she should come right in her mental or physical condition as she used to be, she would be well.

You can see and judge of her appearance and buoyancy of mind. If you come to the conclusion that she appears more like her former self, then I should think you would not run much risk to send her back. For if you see any improvement in her now, I think she will still improve to your satisfaction.

It takes a long time to produce a change in her system. To give you a full account of her case would take a long time, so I will leave her to explain what I have neglected to do.

Yours, etc.
P.P.Q.

Portland, Me., Jan. 2nd, 1861

To Mr. H. Hobson:

In answer to your letter, I must say that it is out of my power to visit your place in person at this time, from the fact that I have some thirty or more patients here on my hands, but if there comes a slack time I will come and let you know beforehand so you can meet me in Bangor.

Now a word or two to your wife. I will try my best while sitting by you, while writing this letter, to produce an effect on your stomach. I want you to take a tumbler of pure water while I write this, and now and then take a little. I am with you now seeing you. Do not be in a hurry when you read this, but be calm and you will in a short time feel it start from your left side and run down; then your head will be relieved and you will have an inclination to rise. Be slow in your movements so that your head will not swim around. I will take you by the hand at first and steady you till you can walk alone. Now remember what I say to you. I am in this letter and as often as you read this and listen to it, you listen to me. So let me know the effect one week from now. I will be with you every time you read this. Take about one half hour to devote to reading and listening to my counsel and I assure you, you will be better. Now do not forget.

Yours, etc.

P.P.Q.

Jan. 11th, 1861

To Miss G.:

Your letter to Miss W. was handed to me for perusal to see what course I thought best to take. So I will sit down by you as I used to do and commence operations. Excitement contracts the stomach, not from fright, but by being overjoyed at your recovery and having a pretty good appetite; the food digests slowly and it will make you feel a little sluggish at times. But it will soon act upon your system and produce a diarrhea, relieving you of the trouble in the water, for that is only nervous and has nothing to do with the kidneys. I will rub your head and work on your stomach while I write this and when you are reading I will repeat the same till you are all right.

Remember that I am with you when you read this and every time you read this you will feel my influence. I do not know that you feel it at this time 6-1-2 Wednesday night. But I am with you now, knocking at your door, and if you do not hear me when you get this message, open the door and I will come in and sit and chat with you, if I do not get too cold waiting out of doors. So keep this in remembrance of me, that is the Science, till the cure comes.

P.P. Quimby

Portland, Jan. 13th, 1861

Mrs. Dingley:

I went to you as soon as I received your letter but I cannot say you were aware of it. Now at the time I write this, I am working on your stomach and now and then giving you a little water so as to start this heat in your left side that rushes up to your head.

When you receive this letter, at night after you are through your work, just sit down in a chair and take a tumbler of cold water and this letter. Read this letter once or twice very slowly and in the meantime take a swallow of water. When you get through, this water will cause a sensation on your stomach and you will feel the wind moving in the stomach and bowels. This will affect your whole system and cause a sensation or perspiration opening the pores and throwing off that heat that is confined in the pores and makes the humor.

Remember what I say. When you read this letter I am with you, and just as long as you read this, I shall be in the letter using my wisdom to cure you. I leave you now, so good night.–9-12 o'clock Sunday evening–

P.P.Q.

Portland, Jan. 16th, 1861

Mrs. Aukee:

I sit down by you, although much hurried, thinking that your face would grow rather long and you would look down-hearted. It is Wednesday 7-1-2 evening, so please give me your attention. I will relieve the pressure across the chest. This will relax the stomach and you will hear these devils roar up out of your mouth. Don't cough when it starts. As I am so far away, by your unbelief, I do not know as you will feel my influence till you receive this. If not, when you receive this letter, seat yourself at evening, take a tumbler of water and as you read this, take a little, and you will feel my influence in you. Be about as long as when I was with you and after you have read this, I will scratch your head as I used to, but you won't have to comb your hair, for it is a spiritual scratch. You will feel a glow all over you. This creates a circulation and you will clear your head easier and speak better. As you read this, remember me and I shall be with you till your voice comes.

Yours, etc.

P.P.Q.

Portland, Jan. 19th, 1861

Mrs. Wheeler:

Your letter of the 11th came to hand, but for the want of time, I have been unable to write and I had anticipated that I might help you by an examination of your case. At the time I received your letter, I felt as though I was with you, explaining to you your case. I will commence now on my way, and as I always sit down by my patient and take them by the hand, I will seat myself by you and commence telling your feelings.

So give me your attention and listen to what I say. The pain in your head arises from a nervous fear which you do not understand. This nervous feeling affects you when you are in company causing a contraction in the stomach which creates a heat; this heat presses upon the aorta causing your heart to beat. This causes a flash in your face, brings on a heat all over it and produces a sort of faint or weak feeling. The fear makes you give way at the pit of the stomach, confines that heat there; this heat numbs the side, like leaning your arm over a chair. This makes the side feel as though it was swollen, and if you compare, you will find the shoulder a little fuller than the other. When you lie on one side, it feels as though there was a weight pulling you down. This you take for an adhesion to the pleura, but it is in the fluids in the flesh. This numbness is often taken for the lungs, but it is nothing more or less than a nervous heat that heats the muscles at the back of the neck and runs down the chest. This causes a contraction of the chest. This contraction makes you give way, like anyone in the hands of robbers attempting to bind him.

Imagine yourself in their hands and see how you would try not to be bound. You would be in the position of a fly in the foils of a spider. When the fly is buzzing, the spider is still at a distance but draws in all the slack. So this eternal error that man has invented and named consumption binds his victim and then waits to see him try to break the bands. It makes you nervous; this nervousness makes you cough. When the stomach relaxes, the heat passes out of it; then it affects the bowels, also the water, etc.

Now remember, all that the doctors tell you is false. Your lungs are as sound as any one's, all that you raise comes from your head. The heat presses over your eyes, makes you feel sleepy and tries to escape out of the nose. The cold comes in contact with it, just as the heat comes in contact with the glass on the window; the cold meeting it condenses the heat and forms a frost; then it melts and runs down. So the heat met by the cold produces a chemical change in the head, like the frost, and runs down into the mouth. This is called catarrh-that which runs into the throat, bronchitis. This is all your disease.

I will tell you what you must do. When you receive this letter, I want you to be seated about eight o'clock in the evening and take a tumbler of water. As you read this letter, or someone reads it to you, I shall be working on you. You take a little water now and then till you take a tumbler full. I shall work on your side and you will feel something like water run down. In a few days you will sneeze and think you have taken cold. Do not be alarmed. You will be a little sick at the stomach. Then it will work down and produce a diarrhea. This will relieve the cough. If this comes out right please let me know.

P.P.Q.

Jan. 25th, 1861

To Mrs. Ware:

By the request of Emma and Sarah I sit down by you to see if I can amuse you by my explanation of disease. You know I often talk to persons about religion and you often look as though you would rather have me talk about anything else. Perhaps it would be better, but if you knew the cause of every sensation, then you would not want a physician. Now you will want me to tell you how you feel and if you will give me your attention I will try to explain. This heavy lazy feeling that you have, accompanied with a desire to lie down and sort of indifference how things go along, comes from a quiet state of your system that prevents your food from digesting as readily as it did while here. But it will act upon you like an emetic or cathartic, either way is right. So give no care to what you shall eat or drink, for that wisdom that governs all science will cause all things to work for the best, and if you want to eat, consult your own feelings and take no one's opinion.

Remember that he who made us knows better our wants than man. So keep yourself quiet and I will reverse the action from your head and you will feel it passing out of your stomach. Then do not forget to sit up as I used to tell you and remember not to believe what the blind guides say for they have a new mask. They will come to you and if your throat is a little sore, as I have no doubt it will be from what I see for when the food acts as a cathartic it most always makes the throat sore, they will ask if you think this sore throat is the diphtheria, looking as wise as though they had discovered the philosopher's stone. The heat goes up to the head and tickles the nose; then it condenses and runs down into the throat.

Remember what I tell you about this disease, for these hypocrites or blind guides are working in the minds of the people like the demagogues of the south till they get up a disunion party. So keep on the lookout for these deceivers. I do not say that you will be troubled with them, but I have kept on their track for twenty years and have not the slightest confidence in anything they say. Their wisdom is of this world.

I hear you now, for the first time, asking me if I believe in another world. Yes, but not in the sense of the clergy. I will try to explain my two worlds. You live in Chicago and I in Portland, and if it will not be blasphemy to call your place heaven, we will suppose you are there in heaven and I in Portland. Now, if I am here sitting and talking with you I can't be on earth if your place is in heaven. So I must leave the earth and the matter and come to you. Now if I am with you, what is that that has left the body? It cannot be matter in a visible form, yet it is something. Listen and I will tell you. You read that God made all living things that had life out of the earth so that dead matter cannot produce living life, nor anything else; so all living life is matter in a form or out of a form. As all matter decomposes, the dust or odor that arises from it was the matter that man is formed of; this was human life or man. As the child is of living matter, not wisdom, when it grows to a certain age, it is ready to receive the breath of eternal life.

I want to explain one word. I said the child was living life, that is what I mean, not eternal life. Eternal life is a wisdom, just as much above human life as science is above ignorance. I think I hear you say what becomes of the little child should it die before it arrived at the age. It was made of the dust and shall return to the dust again, and the dust of life. So what have you lost by the change? Nothing, for it is still life, but sown in death or matter a natural body, it rises a spiritual body. Why is it not seen by the natural eyes? Because the natural man cannot discern spiritual bodies. You can see a piece of silver dissolved by a galvanic battery. Is it out of existence? No. Is it its natural self? No, it is the spiritual self. Is it not as much yours as before? "I do not know." Well then reverse the poles of the battery or your belief and you condense the silver into a solid, all but the dross.

When a child is dead, as you call it, it is dissolved, then raised into a spiritual form in the likeness of its natural body. Why? Because it is free from sin or matter. Then you may ask where is it? With its mother's heavenly man or wisdom, and grows in wisdom like a plant or child till it is ready to receive the wisdom of eternal life. Eternal life is Christ or Science; this teaches us that matter is a mere shadow of a substance which the natural man never saw nor never can see, for it is not matter; it never changes; it is the same today and forever.

This substance is the essence of wisdom and is in every living form. Like a seed in the earth it grows or develops either in matter or spirit just the same, and it is much under the control of its mother's wisdom as the gold which is dissolved and held in solution is under that of the chemist. If the mother's wisdom is of this world, then the spiritual child is not under her earthly care; but nevertheless, it is held in the bosom of its eternal wisdom that will cherish it till it is developed to receive the science of eternal wisdom. Eternal wisdom and eternal life are not the same, for the latter is not wisdom but living matter. Eternal wisdom cannot change but acts on eternal life, changes its form and identity. Eternal wisdom teaches us that all matter is to itself a shadow and is no barrier to wisdom, and just as we are wise in one thing our opinion vanishes. The shadow becomes transparent and nothing remains but the memory of what was, but now is not.

Matter is dense darkness; spirit is light. So, if you are wise your body or wisdom is light, and just as you sink into error you become dense or dark. Therefore let your light shine, so that when this cloud of wind comes blowing round in the form of an opinion, you may know there is something in it, only it is the noise of a demagogue. Believe them not and you will live and flourish. If you can understand this, you get the basis of my belief. For fear I have not made my two worlds clear to your mind, I will say a few words more.

The two worlds may be divided in this way: one opinions, the other science. Opinions are matter or the shadow of science, both are eternal life but one is limited in its sphere, and the other has no limits. One can be seen by the natural eyes; the other is an endless progression. One is always changing; the other is always progressing. The one is made up of reason, opinions, judgment, and the other is science and is the mystery of the latter. The natural man never will know one, for he cannot see wisdom and live.

Wisdom is the natural man's death. So he looks upon it as an enemy, prays to it, pays tribute to it as though wisdom was a man. He often uses it as a balance to weigh his ignorance in, but never to weigh the difference of his opinions. He often quotes it, talking as though it were his intimate friend, while he to wisdom is only known as a servant or shadow, all of imitation and all the above is matter; science is another character. Science rises above all such narrow ideas. He who is scientific in regard to health and happiness is his own law and is not subject to the laws of man except as he is deceived or ignorant. For wisdom cannot let him disobey her truth without knowing the consequences.

No one after he knows a scientific fact can ignorantly disobey it. So that with science, the punishment is in the act. But with man's laws it is different; the penalty may follow the act or come after. With wisdom, the laws are science. To know science is to know wisdom and how can a man work a mathematical problem intelligently and at the same time say he is not aware of the fact?

It cannot be done and so it is with every act of our lives. If we know the true meaning of every word or thought we should know what follows so that a person cannot scientifically act wrong. But being misled by public opinion, we believe a lie, so we suffer.

I have gone so far that I have reduced certain states of mind to their causes, as certain as ever a chemist saw the effect of a chemical change. For instance, consumption. I know every sensation of its character and it is as much a character as it ever had an existence. Its father or author is a hypocrite and deceiver. I look upon it as the most vile of all characters. It comes to a person under a most flattering form, with the kindest words, always very polite, ready to lend its aid in any way where it can get a hold. I will illustrate this prince of hypocrites.

I will come in the form of a lady, for it has many faces and characters. I enter as a neighbor with the customary salutations and you reply that you are very well. "Oh I am very glad, for I was expecting to find you abed by what I heard. But you can't tell anything by gossip. You do not seem quite as well as when I saw you last?" "Oh, yes, fully as well." "Well, you know there are diseases which always flatter the patient, but you must keep good courage. I suppose you have heard of the death of Mr. ." "No, when did he die?" "He died yesterday but was sick a long time. Sometimes he thought he was getting better, but I knew all the time he was running down. But you must not get discouraged because you are like him, for it is not always certain that a person in the same way as you has consumption. So good morning."

Here I make you nervous and you are glad when I leave. Knowing I am not welcome in that form I assume another character. I appear as a doctor; I sit down and count your pulse, look at your tongue, take a stick and examine the phlegm that you have raised. Then leaning back in the chair, draw a long sigh, and ask if you have a pain in your left side. Now I will not say but that the doctor is honest, but if he is, it is worse for you. He is like a dog who wags his tail while you feed him but when your back is turned will bite you. If ignorance and superstition is to be put down by scientific facts it is useless to mince matters. If a person is aiding an enemy, he is as guilty as the thief.

I want you to know that every word that is spoken is something, either matter or wisdom. Opinions are made up of words condensed into a belief, so if I tell you that you have congestion of the lungs, I impart my belief to you by a deposit of matter in the form of words. As you eat my belief it goes to form a disease like unto its author, it grows, comes forth and at last takes form as a pressure across the chest.

The doctor comes to get rid of the enemy, and by his remedies he creates another disease in the bowels. This is done by giving some little simple thing. He begins to talk about inflammation of the bowels; this frightens you. The fright contracts the stomach so the heat cannot escape, and it presses on the aorta at the pit of the stomach. This sets your heart to beating, causes a flush in the face which you call a rush of blood to the head.

It makes you feel sleepy and weak, as though you must lie down; then the stomach relaxes and the heat passes down into the bowels; this causes pains. You call it "Inflammation." All this is very simple if you know what caused it. I will tell you.

Your situation is the cause. (At the time you were lying on the sofa at your father's house, Judge Ware's, while I was sitting by you I was aware of your situation, almost to a certainty. I thought you knew it almost to a certainty for you kept laughing. Don't you remember it? I guess you do.) As your system changed it must produce a chemical change in your breast, for the fluids must change. This would make you feel a little nervous, which feeling would affect your head, making you feel stupid and inclined to loll on the sofa. Finally it would take away your appetite. All of this is not anything out of the way. The sickish feelings are to act upon the stomach. This acts on the bowels and if you will only drink water it will produce a diarrhea which will carry off all nervous excitement, and your health will be better than it has been for some time. This letter is an essay for you to read, so good night. Let me know how it works.

P.P. Quimby

Portland, Feb. 8th, 1861

To Mr. S.:

In answer to your letter I will try to explain the color you speak of, if you have forgotten, so that you will not forget it. Give me your attention while I explain. You know I told you about your stooping over; this stooping is caused by excitement affecting the head. this contracts the stomach, causes an irritation, sending the heat to the head. This heat excites the glands about the nose, it runs down the throat and this is all there is about it. It will affect you sometimes when you are a little excited, and you will take it for a cold.

Remember how I explained to you about standing straight. Just put your hands on your hips, then bend forward and back. This relaxes the muscles around the waist at the pit of the stomach. This takes away the pressure from the nerves of the stomach and allays the irritation. Now follow this and sit down and I will work upon your stomach two or three times in three or four days. It will affect your bowels and help your color. Tell your wife to sit down and give her attention and I will affect her in the same way. Please take a little water when you are sitting, say about 9 o'clock in the evening.

P.P.Q.

Portland, Feb. 8th, 1861

To Miss S., Hill, N.H.:

Your letter was received and I was sorry to learn that you thought you took cold. Perhaps you did, but you know all of my patients have to go through the fiery furnace to cleanse them of the dross of "this sinful world," made so by the opinions of the blind guides. Remember that passage where it says, "Whom the Lord loveth he chasteneth." As Truth is our friend, it rids us of our errors, and if we know its voice we should not fear but receive it with joy. For although it may seem a hard master, nevertheless it will work out for you a more perfect health and happiness than this world of error ever could. So listen to it and I will try to set all things right.

Of course you get very tired, and this would cause the heat to affect the surface as your head was affected; the heat would affect the fluids, and when the heat came in contact with the cold it would chill the surface. This change you call "a cold." But the same would come about in another way. Every word I said to you is like yeast. This went into your system like food and came in contact with the food of your old bread or belief. Mine was like a purgative, and acted like an emetic on your mind so that it would keep up a war with your devils, and they will not leave a person, when they have so good a hold as they have on you, without making some resistance. But keep up good courage and I will drive them all out so that you may once more rejoice in that Truth which will free you from your tormentors or disease.

If you will sit down and read this letter, take a tumbler of water and think of what I say, and drink and swallow now and then; I will make you sit up so you will feel better. You must be just about as long as you used to be in Portland. Try this every night about nine o'clock. This is the time I shall be with Mr. and Mrs. S. You know that where two or three are gathered together in the name of this Truth, there it will be in your midst and help you. So try it and see if it does help you. If you do, let me know.

Hoping this letter will be of some comfort to you and the rest, I remain your true friend and protector till you are well, if I have the Science to cure you. So I leave you for the present and attend to others.

P.P.Q.

Portland, Feb. 9th, 1861

To Mr. Sprague,

Your wife's letter was received, and I was glad to learn you were all so much better. But your wife says you still cough; this is necessary for your cure, for you have no other way to get rid of that heat in the head called catarrh. Now, this heat seems to be a mystery to everyone; everybody acknowledges it and tries to account for it.

Some call it nervous, but when asked to explain that, they fly to some other error.

You know I told you that mind was spiritual matter. In order to illustrate my meaning so you will understand it, I will make use of an illustration that Jesus used. He said, when the skies are red, you know it will be fair weather. Now thought is something and this acts in space. For instance, the body is nothing but a dense shadow, condensed into what is called matter or ignorance of God or Wisdom. God or Wisdom is all light. Your identity acts in these two elements, light and darkness, so that all impressions are made in this darkness or ignorance, and as the light springs up, the darkness disappears. One of these elements is governed by Wisdom, the other by error, and as all belief is in this world of darkness, the truth comes in and explains the error. This rarefies the darkness and the light takes its place. Now as this darkness is all the time varying, like the clouds, it is necessary that man should be posted about it as he would about the weather. For the wisdom of man has got so far from the truth that even the weather is our enemy, so that we step out as though we were liable to be caught by a cold, and if we are then comes the penalty. All this error arises from ignorance. So to keep clear of error is to know who he is, how he gets hold of us, and how we shall know when he is coming.

To make you understand I must come to you in some way in the form of a belief. So I will tell you a story of someone who died of bronchitis. You listen or eat this belief or wisdom as you would eat your meals. It sets rather hard upon your stomach; this disturbs the error or your body, and a cloud appears in the sky. You cannot see the storm but you can see it looks dark. In this cloud or belief you prophesy rain or a storm. So in your belief you foresee evils. the elements of the body of your belief are shaken, the earth is lit up by the fire of your error, the heat rises, the heaven or mind grows dark, the heat moves like the roaring of thunder, the lightning or hot flashes shoot to all parts of the solar system of your belief. At last the winds or chills strike the earth or surface of the body; a cold clammy sensation passes over you. This changes the heat into a sort of watery substance which works its way to the channels and pours to the head and stomach.

Now listen and you will hear a voice in the clouds of error saying, The truth hath prevailed to open the pores and let nature rid itself of the evil I loaded you down with in a belief. This is the way God or Wisdom takes to get rid of a false belief. The belief is made in the heavens or your mind; it then becomes more and more condensed till it takes the form of matter. Then Wisdom dissolves it and it passes through the pores, and the effort of coughing is one of Truth's servants, not error's; error would try to make you look upon it as an enemy. Remember it is for your good till the storm is over or the error is destroyed. So hoping that you may soon rid yourself of all worldly opinions and stand firm in the Truth that will set you free, I remain your friend and protector till the storm is over and the waters of your belief are still.

P.P.Q.

Portland, Feb. 10, 1861

Miss Elizabeth Brackett:

Owing to a press of business, your letter of Jan. 10th has not been answered, but I have made you a number of calls and find you better, and I shall visit you at times till you get over your troubles. Sometime I may explain to you how you became frightened, but as it will not alter the case now, it will need no explanation. Perhaps you will remember it yourself. I feel as though you would get well, so let me know how you are getting along. I am getting quite interested in your case and want to know if I understand it. I believe that if persons believe in the truth, it will teach them that although they may be absent from one another in the body, yet they may be present and feel each other's feelings. So if you will seat yourself in a chair on Thursday eve at nine o'clock, I will sit down by you and make you feel sleepy, cause the heat to pass down from your face and make you feel very well. If you experience any sensation, let me know; and if you remember how you feel at this time 9 o'clock Sunday eve, please name it.

It seems as though you were enjoying yourself, so I will bid you good night.

P.P. Quimby

Portland, Feb. 14th, 1861

To Mrs. H. Merrill:

Owing to a press of business your letter has remained unanswered, but when I receive a letter I always feel as though I was with the patient giving them advice. Sometimes I am in doubt whether I see or know who they are from the fact that so many come to me when I put myself in communication with the sick.

I make a sort of general visit as I used to when you were all in my office, but if I feel certain of one, I make that one a text to preach from. So I believe that if you can make yourself known to me by your faith, I can feel you.

Since I commenced writing, you have come up before me, so that I now recall you perfectly well and I will give my attention to you. I have often seen you and used my arguments to convince you of this great truth. When I say this truth, I mean this light that lighteth everyone that understands it. When I first sat by you, my desire to see you lights up my mind like a lamp; and as the light expands, my senses being attached to the light, each particle of light contains all the element of the whole. So when the light is strong enough to see your light in your darkness or doubts, then I come in harmony with your light and dissipate your error and bring your light out of your darkness. Then I try to associate you with matter as a substance that is separate and apart from your light or senses.

Man of himself is in matter. Science is out of matter. Disease is matter, health is out of matter so that you, i.e., science, cannot receive matter into your science, but your science can separate itself from matter.

So do not try to get out of your trouble and believe in the cause, for you cannot serve God and man or science and error. The opinion is the matter and the aches and pains are what follows your embracing it. So to say you do not believe in disease, and yet complain that you have one, is like saying that you do not believe in ghosts and telling the largest ghost story, declaring it is true.

P.P. Quimby

Portland, Feb. 23, 1861

To Mrs. Smith:

I was sorry to hear by your letter that your husband was more feeble. There is a time when all things must fail and it seems as though this would be so in the case of your husband, but I hope not. I have tried all in my power to carry him through that place, and if he had sunk when he first came to Portland, I should not have been surprised. Seeing him so nervous and in so critical a condition kept me in a very unpleasant situation. To voice my true feelings, he would have failed at once. So as a last resort, I was obliged to drive from myself all doubts of his not getting worse and see if I could produce any effect.

As this seemed to take a favorable turn, I never had a time that I dared to think otherwise than that he would get well. So things went on, doubts and fears on one side, and a powerful effort on my part to keep him up till I felt it would be best for him and you that he should return. If his strength was from me, he must fail at last; but if he could rally of himself then I felt as though, between us both, he might come up.

It is very unpleasant to be placed in such a situation. Knowing how little of a sea or swell it takes to upset our bark, I have to sit and paddle along in breathless silence lest some little billow may upset all my labors. This was the way in your husband's case. If he had been at home where all things could have been otherwise, I should not have had so many fears, but we must take the world as we find it and make the best of it.

Now as I sit here writing, I cannot leave the helm of his mind to even indulge in the idea of losing him, nor shall I till that enemy of life tears him from my grasp. If the [missing word] sets in, I shall have some more hope. I shall visit often and use my best effort for his recovery. So I cannot say anything different from what I want should take place. You, as I have always said, can have your own opinion. Hoping next time I hear I shall receive more favorable accounts, I remain,

Yours, etc.

P.P.Q.

Feb. 23, 1861

To Mrs. Cole:

Your letter of the 12th was received just as I was leaving for Belfast and upon my return I was sick, so this is the first time I have had to reply.

What you say about your child must take place, for you remember what I told you about his chest, how full it was. This fullness was a deposit of heat that forced itself through the lungs and pores to the surface and affected the muscles around the chest. This made him nervous and caused the heat to go to his head, as it did in your case; this heat was the cause of your color and his asthma.

Now when this passes down, it will condense into water and pass off in a diarrhea. So although it may seem as though your child was worse, it seems to me that he ought to get well, for he could never recover while this heat went to his head. Let him drink cold water and I cannot help feeling that a change must take place before long. You know how it was with you.

To reverse the action is not a very easy task, but if you wait patiently, I can't help thinking it will take place. I remember the case well, and shall, at intervals, use my power to correct the error. Hoping you may see some favorable effect soon, I remain, etc.

P.P.Q.

March 3rd, 1861

To Miss G.:

I will now sit down and put on paper what I did at the time I received your letter. I went to you at that time and have visited you at times ever since. I wish now to let you know that I am still with you, sitting by you while in your bed, encouraging you to keep up good spirits and all will go right. If you cough, it is to get rid of the heat that has gone to your head and when it condenses it runs down into the throat and you cough it up.

P.P.Q.

Portland, March 3rd, 1861

To Mrs. L.A. Burns,

I went to your relief on reading your letter and have visited you at intervals ever since. At this time I am sitting working on your stomach to make the heat pass down, and if you are affected, you must lay it to me. The pain you have in the bowels is all right, it shows that there is an action, it will relieve the left side. Your head I shall give a good rubbing, especially the back part of it. It won't bother you to comb your hair as it is short. I shall remember you and make you frequent calls.

P.P. Quimby

Portland, March 3rd, 1861

To Mrs. D.:

In answer to your letter I will say that you know I told you that your disease was in your mind. Now your mind is your opinion, and your opinion is that you have scrofulous or cancerous humour.

This opinion is something or it is nothing, and as it shows itself in your system, it must be something. I call it matter. As I change this something or opinion, it must change the effect. So as the effect is changed, the matter or mind or opinion is changed. In the change it will produce these feelings because it is in the fluids. As - this change goes on it must affect your head and also your side, and it ought to affect your stomach. This will bring on a phenomenon like a cold, and finish with a diarrhea. This carries off all the false ideas and relieves your system of that bloat and heat. Keep up your courage. It is all right.

P.P.Q.

Portland, March 3rd, 1861

To Mr. R.:

When your letter was received, I went to your relief, but I cannot say that I affected you. But now I will sit down and try to affect your stomach so that you will not want to smoke. I feel that if you were aware of the evil influence of the enemy that is prowling around you enticing you to smoke, you would not harbor him one moment but hurl him from you as you would a viper that would sting you to the heart. I know that opinions are something and they are our friends or our enemies. So the opinion you have of smoking is a false one and is an enemy to you. It is subtle like the serpent that coils around you till you feel its grasp around your chest, making your heart palpitate and sending the heat to your head. Then you will struggle to rid yourself of his grasp, till overpowered, you become paralyzed. He will laugh at your folly when your fear cometh. Remember that "love casteth out fear," and fear hath torment. Science is love. Fear is disease; torment is your reward. So watch lest he enter your house while you are asleep and bind your limbs, and when you awake find yourself bound hand and foot. So remember what I say to you as a friend.

P.P.Q.

Portland, March 3, 1861

To Miss T.:

Your letter of the first was received.... I will now give you a short sitting and amuse you by my talk. But as you seem to want your head cured I will rub the top of it, and while doing this, I will tell you what makes it feel so giddy. You know I have told you, you think too much on religion or what is called religion. This makes you nervous, for it contains a belief which contains opinions and they are matter; i.e. they can be changed. If opinions were not anything, they could not be changed, for there would be nothing to change. All religion is of this world and must give way to Science or Truth; for truth is eternal and cannot be changed. . . . So you see according to the religious world I must be an infidel. Suppose I am. I know that I am talking to you now. Does the Christian believe in this (talking with the spirit)? No. Here is where we differ.

Eighteen hundred years ago, there was a man called Jesus who, the Christians say, came from heaven to tell man that if he would conform to certain rules and regulations he could go to heaven when he died; but if he refused to obey them, he must go to hell. Now of course the people could not believe it merely because he said so, so it was necessary to give some proof that he came from God. Now what proof was required by the religious world? It must be some miracle or something that the people could not understand. So he cured the lame, made the dumb speak, etc. The multitude was his judge and if they could not account for all that he did was proof that he came from God. So after he had cured many people they decided that he did come from God.

Now does it follow that if I should say that I was the Son of God or even go so far in my supposition as to believe that I was God himself, that they would make it so? Or suppose I should say I will give some proof that I am really God and I should perform a sudden cure which the people really believed, is their belief to embrace the idea that I am really God or that I really cured the person? You may answer this.

A phenomenon is one thing and the way in which it is done another.

The spiritualists produce phenomena, but when they say it is from the spirits of the dead, that is an opinion. Now let me give you my opinion.

There was once a man called Jesus. I have no doubt that he cured, but his cures were no proof that he came from God any more than mine does, nor did he believe it.

This man Jesus was endowed with wisdom from the scientific world or God and not of this world, nor can he be explained by the natural man. His wisdom never taught any such thing. His God fills all space. His wisdom is eternal life, with no death about it. He never intended to give any construction to his cures or words. His cures were for the benefit and happiness of man. Men were religious from superstition, their religion was made of opinions, and they were the light of the mind; the opinion or light contained an idea and the idea was in the center of the light. When the idea is lit up, it throws its ray; and our senses, being in the rays, are affected by the idea or light.

As their ideas affected the people, they were like burdens grievous to be borne; so the people murmured.

Jesus knew all this and no man was able to break the seal or unlock the secret to health. So the people groaned in their trouble and prayed to be delivered from their evils. Wisdom, hearing the groans of the sick, acted upon this man Jesus and opened his eyes to the truth. Thus the heavens were opened to him. He saw this Truth or Science descend, and he understood it. Then came his temptation; if he would listen to the people and become king, they would all receive him. This he would not do. But to become a teacher of the poor and sick would be very unpopular. Here was the temptation. He chose the latter, and went forth teaching and curing all sorts of diseases in the name of this Wisdom, and calling on all men everywhere to repent, believe, and be saved from the priests and doctors who bound burdens on the people.

I should like to write much more but for the want of time must close.

P.P. Quimby

Portland, March 10th, 1861

To Mrs. W.:

I have not been able to answer your letter until now. But I have often scratched your head and talked to you. How much you have been aware of it, I cannot say. But I now see you and your husband sitting looking as easy as possible. I shall visit you as an angel, not a fallen one, but one of mercy, till you are able to guide your own bark.

It is true your husband can travel the briny deep, but he has never entered this ocean of this higher state. Here our senses are attached to our belief and our belief makes our bodies or barks. The sea is troubled, error is the rocks and quicksands where we are liable to be driven by the cross-currents while the wind of error is whistling in our ears; and when your bark is creaking and twisting from stem to stern, it is liable to go to pieces. Now keep a good lookout and you will see breakers ahead. So brace up and see that your compass is right. Keep all snug and fast. Remember what I told you about this place, not to lose control of yourself, but stand on deck and give your orders, not in a whining way, but bold and earnest. Then your crew will obey you and you will steer clear of all danger and land safe in the port of health. Then enjoy yourself with your husband, talking over your old sea voyage, and I will sit down with you and listen to your story. So I will leave you and your husband together.

P.P. Quimby

March 10th, 1861

To Miss S:

In answering your letter I will say that I have used my best efforts to help you, and I feel as though I had. Now I will once more renew my promise not to forsake you in your trouble, but to hold you in the influence of this great Truth that is like the ocean. While your bark is tossed by the breeze or storms of error and superstition, while the skies are dark with error and you are moved by your cable or belief, feeling as though you may be blown on to the rocks of death, you may look to that Truth that is now beating against the errors and breaking them in pieces, scattering them to the winds and even piercing the hardest flinty hearts, grinding them into pieces. This Truth shall shine like the sun and burn up all these errors that affect the human race.

So be of good cheer and keep up your courage, and you shall see me coming on the water of your belief and saying to the waters or pain, "Be still," soothing you till the storm is over. Then when the sun or Truth shall shine, and the pure breeze from heaven spring up, slip your cable and set sail for the port of health, there to be once more in the bosom of your friends. Then I will shake hands with you and go exploring for some other bark that is out in the same gale.

P.P. Quimby

March 10, 1861

Miss Brackett, Boston, Mass.:

Owing to a press of business, I have not had time to answer your letter until now, but I often see you and talk to you about your health. I feel as though I had explained to the spiritual or scientific man the cause of your trouble which I may not have made plain in my letters to the natural man, but it may sometime come to your senses or you may see me. Then I can tell you what I cannot put on paper. As for the cause affecting you now, I feel as though I had removed the cause, and the effect will soon cease and you will be happy and enjoy good health. I wait to hear that my prophecies have been fulfilled, but I shall keep a look out for your health till I hear you say that you are well.

P.P.Q.

Portland, March 28, 1861

To Mr. G. Cleanes:

Your letter of the 25th was received enclosing $2.00 for my advice. It is true that a person cannot afford to spend his time for nothing, but at the same time to give the public the idea that the cures can be made by letter opens the door for deception. For the sick are, of all classes, most easily humbugged since they are honest and expect others to be the same.

A person well is not a person sick. The well have no charity for the sick, and when one gets sick, he is like a man in the hands of robbers. If he does not look out, they will rob him of all he had, for a sick man will give all he has to be saved from disease. So they are easily deceived, and as I do not intend to open a door for these robbers to enter and rob the sick, I put myself into the hands of the sick instead of having the sick at my mercy. In the latter case, I do not know what I might be led to do. If this way has the effect I think it will, I am satisfied.

If I can get the good will of my patients, I can help them at a distance, but this is a theory of my own. From what I have done I know that the principle is true, so upon this principle I am going to try the theory for the benefit of mankind. If I succeed, I shall establish one thing that I wish to establish, that is, that the sick shall never run any risk of losing their money by trusting to any person for a cure, either by medicine or by letter or by spiritual communication or by any other way, unless the doctor will run the same chance.

It is what every honest person will do for a theory that he has confidence in. I therefore return your money, leaving it till I have tried my best and accomplished my object; then if you please to send it to me, I will receive it as a gift, not as a fee.

I will now sit down by you and take your feelings as they seem to me. The gone feeling or quivering at the pit of your stomach is caused by the contraction of the stomach on the left side. This creates a heat, and as the heat spreads in the stomach, it produces a sort of numbness around the left side, near the heart. At any excitement, the heat passes on the aorta, causing the heart to flutter and beat hard. This goes to your head and causes a dull heavy feeling over the eyes, like a sleepy feeling, and causes your hands to go to sleep as though they were resting on something.

Now sir, you may not think I have told you all, but perhaps you do not recognize the feelings I have told you of, but they are so, for I know it. Now sir, disease is like a thief or robber that enters your house or mind while you are asleep or ignorant of the cause, and it uses all the means in its power to decoy the person to death. So it tempts you by your tobacco to give way to your feelings in order that it may have you in its power. It is subtle, and, it seems like your best friend, but it is a viper in your stomach lying wait to poison your life while you can't help yourself.

I feel that it is working on your system by the queer feeling in your mind, so I know that you are very nervous, and strange feelings pass through your brain when you rub your head. Sometimes you feel your heart beat, and a suffocating feeling comes over you as though you wanted more air. Then comes the idea of heart disease or apoplexy. This is the effect of the tobacco. Then when it passes out of the stomach it condenses into water, causing you to pass a large quantity at times, then less. Now sir, if I am right in regard to your case, I think I can cure you. If you will let me know the effect, I will continue my visits mentally. If you see fit to show this to any person, I will say that I answer no letters without the person first showing his confidence in me. Then if I deceive him, he is at liberty to expose me. I will try to affect you till I hear from you.

P.P.Q.

Portland, Apr. 10th, 1861

To Mrs. Strong:

In answering your inquiry, I am not inclined to give a decided opinion in any case, for an opinion involves more responsibility than I am willing to take. Moreover an opinion is of no force as far as knowledge goes and it might do a great deal of harm and mislead you to put a false construction on what I might say. I always feel as though disease was an enemy that might be conquered if rightly understood, but if you let your enemy know your thoughts, you give him the advantage. Therefore I never give the sick any idea that should make them believe that I have any fears, nor will I reason with myself, for my reason is my guide. Making health the fixed object of my mind, I never parley or compromise. Once when your sister remarked that she never expected to be perfectly well, I replied that I never compromised with disease. And as she had been robbed of her health, I should not settle the case except on condition of the return of her health and happiness. Here she stands.

I will now say a word or two so you can see how I feel; when I really believe that I cannot destroy a disease, I always take the easiest possible way to induce the patient to return home of their own accord with the idea that they will do just as well as if they stayed longer. This is my mode of dismissing my patients and as I send away patients who I know will recover, the sick cannot see any partiality and they all leave in good spirits. When I feel as though a patient might get well but for circumstances which they cannot control which bear on their mind, if I think by lessening their burdens and anxieties I can effect the cure, that I do in this way. When your sister came to me I found her in a very nervous state, from the fact that she had lost her sister and expected soon to follow her. This made her very nervous and stimulated her to that degree that she appeared to be quite strong. As I relieved her fears, she became more quiet; this she took for weakness, but every change has come just as I told her it would. Like all who are sick, she looks at the expense, and as I felt very anxious to help her, I was willing to take the responsibility upon myself of telling her that I would like to have her remain and I would make no charge for my services but would wait till the cure was performed. This would relieve her of calling on her friends for funds to pay me and I find she feels happier and easier. You will see that I have no interest in keeping your sister here, and as long as she remains, I shall take as good care of her as though she were my own child.

P.P. Quimby

Portland, Apr. 11, 1861

To Miss L. H. Mead:

I will now sit down by you as I used to, for I see I am with you, and talk to you a little about your weak back. You forget to sit upright as I used to tell you.

Perhaps you cannot see how I can be sitting by you in your house and at the same time be in Portland. I see you look up, open your eyes and hear you say, No, I am sure I cannot, and I do not believe you can be in two places at the same time. Now listen and I will try to convince you that I can be here with you and at the same time be in Portland.

You remember when Jesus was journeying one day, he said to his disciples, our friend Lazarus is sick. We must go to him. How did Jesus know that Lazarus was sick? You need not ask me if I compare myself to Jesus; that is not answering the question. The question is simply this. Do you believe that Jesus knew the fact or did he guess at it? I hear you think, not speak, "I cannot say." No, you cannot say intelligently, for if you could, you would not doubt that I am now talking to you. But your faith is like that of Lazarus; it, needs more faith and Jesus knew it, or he would not have gone to the idea or body. Neither was Mary's or Martha's faith enough to raise him, so he had to go or do what was the same, for they could not believe in what they could not see; therefore he had to attach his senses to what they could see, Jesus; then they could see that Jesus could raise Lazarus. Now if your faith is no stronger in P.P.Q.'s truth or Christ than Lazarus' and his sisters' was in Jesus' Wisdom or Christ, then I fear your back will remain unrelieved, for I am too busy to go in bodily form. But I have faith to believe that I can make you believe by my wisdom, so I shall try to convince you that although I may be absent in the idea or body, yet I am present with you in the mind.

Suppose I am in Portland and you feel and know that I am here with you, where do you and the people in Portland differ in opinion? You say I cannot tell. I will tell you. The people, attaching their senses to P.P.Q. think wisdom is in him, but if you know that I am here, you attach your senses to the Christ or truth. And if you believe this, you are saved from the uncertainty of seeing me in the body, that I may tell you what I am now saying. While I have been sitting and talking, I have been trying to affect you and I feel as though you would be better. Hoping this will be so, I leave.

P. P. Quimby

Portland, Apr. 24, 1861

To Mrs. Bosworth:

Owing to my business I have delayed writing until now. I generally seem to see a patient when I read a letter, but sometimes I do not. This I account for on the principle that the errors obscure my sight. Light is something outside and independent of matter, which is so associated with matter that it has become attached to it. But in its pure operation, it sees through matter in its various combinations. Common education has placed a barrier between two persons; for instance, you and myself. This barrier is matter and can be seen through by intelligence superior to it. I will try to communicate with you, that is that part of you which sees and hears, etc., and is really independent of time and space but which is not known by that part of us that depends on the eye to see or the ear to hear or through those organs to be affected and realize a sensation or fact. This I call your wisdom or senses and they are imprisoned by the errors of common belief. This belief is yourself and acts upon your matter or body. It is under the direction of ideas or opinions of persons who never knew there was an intelligence independent of your body. You, being under their influence and finding no friend to lead you away from them, fall into the snares of their make and almost wholly believe in everything they say. Now I wish to talk with that part that does not believe in what these friends say, be this part ever so small or well concealed.

This disinclination to receive the opinions of your friends is founded on a truth, that is, that there is not a word of truth in what they say; it is all based on guesswork. All this is mere assertion on my part and of course needs proof to substantiate it. So if I can make myself felt by you without the common medium through which we know each other, that will show that we can act independently of that medium. I therefore will now try to dissolve the error, misbelief, and see if I cannot make myself felt by you. So if you hear my voice and are a little nervous, do not put a false construction on it by being frightened and closing the door of your belief so that I cannot enter and talk with you a little upon the idea that the world has established and imprisoned your wisdom in. If I can convince you that your friends are your enemies, then you will know how to treat them.

It is an old saying, deliver us from our friends. These friends, Christ pictured out better than I can do, so I will use his own illustration for he warned his disciples against them. He says beware of the Scribes and Pharisees, that is the priests and doctors' opinions, whether they come through a physician, minister or your friend. For if any person tells you anything and gives you an opinion, which if believed makes you worse, then beware of such whitened sepulchers or blind guides. They are wolves in sheep clothing, clouds without rain, hypocrites prowling around to devour. You remember what Jesus told his disciples about such a class. So when they come with long hypocritical faces and in whining tones and say, "You look very feeble, you are not so well," etc., turn from them.

These are the hypocrites that devour widows' houses, for your science is your house, and as you are all alone, you are a widow in the Science of Christ or Truth. Now Christ visited the widow and fatherless in their distress and told his disciples to do the same and keep them pure and unspotted from the world or opinions. While you read this, I am with you working in your belief or prison till I shall tear it down and raise you up.

P. P. Quimby

Portland, May 3, 1861

Mrs. Wingate:

You seem by your letter to be surprised by the course taken by the lady who answered your first letter, but I wish you to understand that I was apprised of the answer and it was written just according to my views, and if you could not understand it, the fault is in you and not in her. She knows the difficulty I have to encounter from persons who know me; also that all I say to the well is Greek, and although they may have respect for me as a man, they have none whatever in my opinions as a physician. This places me in a very unpleasant position.

When I first called on the lady, she was very feeble and unable to walk, had been attended by the very best physicians and believed in all the opinions of disease. Now to have all her wisdom upset by me was more than she could stand, and had it not been that I was a stranger and she dared not set up an opinion in opposition to me, I could not have cured her; but her strong desire to get well made her listen and keep still till she began to take an interest in my theory. If it had been my daughter, Augusta, I could not have cured her, from the fact that she could not have had the confidence in me that she would have had in a stranger. All of this she knew, and when I told her that your mother and myself were brought up together and that she knew me as a jeweller till I commenced this business, she could see that your mother's confidence in the medical opinions must be complete, and to have it all upset by one for whose medical knowledge she had no respect, although she might respect me as a man, would render it a hard case to cure. All the above is in answer to your misunderstanding her letter.

As regards your mother's case. I cannot tell anything about her till I could see her. According to your description, it must take a long time to cure her, if I could, at all. You see how little you understand of my mode of treatment, since you have said that it was all foolishness or the same thing, and if you fail to see any sense in what the lady wrote, how do you think your mother can, when she never has even been consulted in the case at all? So as I have said before, my opinion is worth just as much as your question–that is nothing at all. If I should sit by your mother and take her feelings, then when I undertake to tell her how she has been humbugged by the doctors, I should see how my ideas set on her stomach, for she could not embrace my ideas just because I said so. But I must labor long and hard to convince her so as to change her mind and effect the cure. Therefore, if I was a stranger whom she had just heard of, it would make a difference. She will know nothing of what I have to contend with, but I do, and so does the lady who wrote the letter to you. If you can find out anything by this I shall be glad.

Should I be in Bangor at any time, I would be happy to call and see your mother, or if she would be in Belfast when I go home, I would see her with pleasure. But I could not go to Bangor, leaving my business here, without charging twenty dollars and all my expenses. But if I happen to visit your city I will call with pleasure, if she wishes me to, not otherwise. I cannot cure a person on another's recommendation.

If you wish me to see your mother, I must see her at her own request and not on your account. I will let her know when I shall be in Belfast if she wishes. I go Friday and return Monday, and that would give me ample time to see what I can do. I will now close, wishing you a quiet state of mind while you read this letter. It may be of service to you in the day of trouble. So wishing you good-bye,

I remain,

P.P.Q.

Portland, May 9th, 1861

To Mr. _____

I will say in answer to your letter that it is impossible to give any correct opinion in regard to your wife's case, nor do I wish to give any encouragement that I may afterwards regret. I know the sick, like a drowning man, are ready to catch at a straw and this places them and their friends in the hands of all kinds of quackery. They are not the judges of their own case from the fact that health is all they want and money to them is nothing in comparison to it. This I know from experience and when they compare their cases with others the comparison will not hold good. I have been deceived by the sick, not knowing anything about their case except from their own account. I have advised some not to come; from the description of their cases and on sitting with them, I have found their trouble amounted to a mere nothing. I have advised others to come and found them far worse than I expected, then felt concerned for advising them to come. So I have concluded to let people take their chance and I do the best I can.

Now in regard to my going to Chicago, I am not in a situation to leave here at present as I have as many patients as I can attend to, and my expenses here amount to not less than $5.00 a day, which goes on, whether I am in town or not, and my business varies from twelve to twenty a day; therefore I cannot live on uncertainties. If I were certain of curing your wife and others, that would alter the case, but the uncertainty I do not wish to risk, nor can you, lest I should fail. I do not wish your wife to come here unless you feel as though there was a fair chance for her recovery. Mrs. Ware might be of some service to you; she, having some ideas of my cures, might be a better judge than you or your wife, but if you feel inclined to come this way, then I would do the very best I could. If your wife would write me the facts of her case, I will devote one hour to her and send her an account of her case. Then she may feel better satisfied what course to pursue.

P. P. Quimby

Portland, May 10th, 1861

To Mrs. Ferrell:

Yours of the 9th was received and I will sit down and try my best to relieve your right side and hope I shall be able to affect it. Be assured I shall not forget you, but shall have a dutiful care over you and encourage you through your trouble till you can see out of it and feel that your health is out of danger. Your cough is the effect of your health, throwing off the morbid state of your system and of course it makes you feel very bad. I am very sorry that I can't stop your cough at once, but so it is, and I will do my best to stop it. You see how my patients hold me to my promises.

You say in your letter that I told you so and so, and you hold me to my promise just as though I would forget you, if I had not promised that you would get well. Now these promises are the very thing I am trying to get rid of, for when you promise a child anything on condition, they never think of the obligation to their parent, but claim the reward. So it is with all my patients. It sometimes makes me smile to see how artful they will be to get me to make a promise and when I do it, it seems as that was all, and they never think that they have anything to do for themselves. This is so common among the sick that I have become very cautious how I promise, for if I do not fulfill my promises, they are sure to remind me of it. It often makes me feel as though they thought me to blame for not fulfilling my promise. And I really feel guilty myself, for I believe that our minds are under some wisdom, from a love [by] the natural man's wisdom, and when I mentally agree unconditionally to do a thing, it annoys me much if I fail to do it.

Now I know you as Mrs. Ferrell; do not hold me as P. P. Quimby responsible to stop your cough. But this sick idea does hold me to my promise, so I will try my best to fulfill it. In doing so, I must hold you, not Mrs. F but the sick idea, to its promise. And for fear you may forget, I will just remind Mrs. F what the sick idea promised on her part. It was that she would keep up good courage and not believe in what anyone said and not be afraid if she coughed a little but keep calm and cheerful. Now, if I hear about you complaining about your cough and getting low spirited, I shall tell you of it, and hold you to your bargain. You see you are bound to keep the peace and to do all that is right, so that your health may come, and you may once more rejoice. Now I think I have sat with you some time, and this contract, I want you to read now and then, and I will sit and listen when you are reading it, and I think we will get along first rate.

So good night.

Yours etc.

P. P. Quimby

Portland, Aug. 9, 1861

To Mrs. L. Emerson:

In your letter you have saved me the trouble of finding out your case myself by stating your feelings; so as I have your symptoms before me, I will try to affect you as much as I am able to.

I will say that it is hard labor on my part to sit and take a person's symptoms at a distance, and as my time is so much occupied, I cannot absent myself from my business to do so. But since, by sending your symptoms, you have saved me that labor, I will say a word to you while I am trying to affect you.

You say that if you were not able to reward me, you have no doubt that the Lord will in the world to come. So far as your honesty goes, I have no doubt but that you think so. I would rather trust to that than to any Lord of any world to come that I know of. I have no confidence in this God of man's invention. He asks too much of man and never pays. He is too much like a man; in fact he is the embodiment of man's opinions. Just look at the absurdity of what you say, and it is what we all often say, and yet it contains no wisdom at all.

You say that if I should help you, you cannot pay me; God will reward me in the world to come. Suppose there is another world and I should not go there for twenty years. You don't suppose the Lord will look me up when he has credited me for curing you? And of course, I should not put in a claim myself, so I rather think it will all be forgotten. I have lost all confidence in the God of such opinions.

I will give you a description of the God I worship. He has respect for persons. He is a God of love and truth. He feels our misery and administers to our wants. He never keeps any accounts but pays me my wages as soon as they are earned. So if I help you, my God is your God, and to do good to myself is to do good to you as far as lies in my power. So my God is in me, and His rewards are with Him. If I do a good act He pays me down, for He does not need to have any account with man. He has enough to pay all His debts, and if I neglect to fulfill my part, after I know and acknowledge it, I shall surely get my punishment. All this is the other world, not the world of opinions, for that world must be destroyed. God, and all the world of progression and science can never be destroyed, for it never had a beginning and therefore cannot end.

This is the world I believe in. If I help you, my God rewards me, for the reward is in the act. It is as much my gain as yours. To make you happy makes me so, and if I help you and make you happy, you of course share your happiness with me.

I will stop till I learn if you get any better and which God you think the most of.

P.P.Q.

Portland, Sept. 12, 1861

To Mr. Capen:

Your letter was received, and in it you say your wife was affected somewhat as I said she would be, and now you ask me if I think she should come to Portland, that I could help her knees. Now sir, my cures depend a great deal on the confidence of my patients, and if they think I have a power, then of course I do not know any more about it than they do. If it is from God or the Devil, I am but an instrument in their hands and give them the credit if they cure through me, and if they fail, lay the blame also on them.

I, as a man, cannot give an opinion of what the Lord or the Devil does through me towards curing disease. This is one of the absurdities of the world. They admit that I do not know anything about this power, as they call it, and then next ask me to give an opinion of what I can do, thus depriving me of any wisdom and then expecting me to give an opinion that makes me responsible for the Devil's or God's acts. Now Sir, I will place your wife's case before you in a sensible manner so that you shall not be deceived and let you decide about her coming by your own and her judgment.

She has been here and I tried to affect her after the manner that I do everyone, that is, appealing to her common sense. I do not assume any wisdom from God or from the Devil or from Spirits, but I try to show that disease is one of the phenomena of our belief, and to correct the belief, I change the mind of the patient. Their wisdom is then attached to my ideas of truth and this is the cure.

Now to get a person to come to me by holding out some inducement or promise in one hand and taking money in the other is selfish and hypocritical. If the patients have confidence in me they would not wish me to coax them. Jesus said, if the sheep knew the voice of the Shepherd, they would follow him. So I say, if the sick knew me, they would not want me to hold out inducements to cure them, but they would coax me instead of my coaxing them. This puts me in a position I do not like, and your wife is also in a bad position. Just let me make an illustration that will show how we both stand.

Suppose I am in a prison, and your wife has the name of getting people out. Now I know this, and I know that if I make my case known to her, she will do the best she can to get me out; and should she fail, it would not be from any neglect of hers. Now I send her a letter saying that if she thinks she can get me out, I should like to have her try. Do you think she would be induced to make much effort? You can answer. Suppose I believe that if I could only get her interested in my case she would get me clear. Then I should not put any restrictions on her but throw myself into her power and trust to luck. In this way when she had me in her power, if she had any sympathy, she would exert it for my happiness.

I told your wife that if she thought she received any benefit, she might get better; but if I had to make one single condition in the way of compromising to bring her here, by which she would not come unless I did, I should not have any faith at all. Therefore, I say if she comes, I shall use all my wisdom to restore her to health and happiness.

P.P.Q.

LETTER TO A LADY IN VERMONT

Portland, 1861

Madam:

I received your letter and I will now give you another sitting although I sat with you yesterday; but perhaps you were not aware of it, so I will now try again.

I cannot help thinking but what I can help your nose, for I believe it to be a curable case and I shall make an effort to have this visit operate on your bowels and change the current of the fluids in that direction. And I will now work on your stomach and shall keep up my visits till I produce an effect like a diarrhea and that I think will change the nature of the trouble which is in the fluids. Please let me know how I succeed. As I wrote you yesterday I will stop now till I hear from you. Good night, 7:01 o'clock and just going to my tea.

Perhaps it may seem strange that I was not seen at the exact time of writing but this is the fact. I have to produce a change in your system so that out of the matter or mind of yourself the body is made and I in it, thus it will take longer sometimes than it does others. If that lady is still with you I will try and make myself appear to her eyes next Sunday between 7 and 8 o'clock.

P. P. Quimby

[Extract from a letter from the above lady in Vermont to Dr. Quimby]

Last Friday evening, Oct. 3rd, between 7 and 10 o'clock, mother and a niece of hers, who is here on a visit, were sitting together talking, and this lady says she saw you standing by mother, about to lay your hand on her head. Just at that moment mother left the room before her friend had told her what she saw, so your visit was interrupted. What was quite strange was that this lady described some of your characteristics in looks and appearance very accurately, although you have never been described to her. Mother wishes to know if you were really here in spirit at that time.

Portland, Dec. 7, 1861

Miss Longfellow:

Your letter was received, but my engagements have been such that I have not had time to give my attention to your case until now. Although we have lived side by side ever since we were children, we have been ignorant of that power or science that is necessary to smooth our ruffled path as we travel along the road to wisdom, whence no child of science ever returns to his former home of ignorance and superstition. You and I have a power called the inner man by the ignorant, but its true name is wisdom or progression. This is the child of God, and although at first it is almost without an identity, this little wisdom implanted in this earthly man or idea is held in ignorance till some higher wisdom frees it from its prison.

You remember when your little pupils would stand by your side looking up to you for wisdom to satisfy their desires. You with your power like Moses went before them leading them through the sea of ignorance, they following your light as a pillar of fire, and in the clouds of darkness your light sprang up. As you traveled along, they murmuring and complaining, you like Moses fed them with the bread of science and eternal life. You smote the rock of wisdom that followed them and they drank of the waters that came out of your teaching and this rock or wisdom was Christ. You have a teacher as well as I that goes before us teaching us Science, and we become the child of the one we obey. You, like Moses, held up the serpent of ignorance before your little pupils and all who looked upon your explanation and understood were healed of their disease or ignorance; but the murmuring of your pupils would make you nervous and although you, like Moses on Mount Pisgah, could see the promised land, your heart failed you and you sank down in despair. In your discontented state of mind you call on your comforter, as Job did, but no answer returned from your doctors or spiritual advisers, who being blind guides find you like the man going down to Jericho and fall upon you and rob you of all your wisdom. So here you are a stranger among thieves, cast into prison by the very ones you have always taken for your leaders on the road to health; you are bound with bands, sick and with no hope of ever being set at liberty.

Now your belief is like a bark and your wisdom attached to it, on the water of this world, for water is an emblem of error so that the medical wisdom or ocean is where your bark seems to be moored. Here you are tossed to and fro, sometimes expecting to be lost, while the winds of spiritualism are whistling in your ear till it shakes the bark to which your wisdom is attached, and the heavens are dark and the light of wisdom extinguished in the opinions or waves of the medical science.

As you are tossing to and fro you see me coming. When I say "me," I mean Science in P.P.Q., not the P.P.Q. that you used to see but the wisdom in a body, not of flesh and blood but a body as it pleases and to every science its own body. Your body or bark is of this world and your wisdom is in it, and I have to come through your wisdom to get you clear of your enemies. So you may look out of the window of your bark while reading this and you will see me coming on the water of your belief saying to spiritualism and the waves of the medical faculty, "Be still, and I will come on board of your bark and still your fears and return you once more to your own house whence you have been decoyed by these blind guides."

As disease is in accordance with the laws of man, a penalty is attached to every act so that everyone found guilty must be punished by the law. As you are accused of a great many transgressions, your punishment is greater than you can bear, so you sink under your trouble. I appear in your behalf to have you tried by the laws of your own country, not by the laws of these barbarians. So I will read over the indictment that stands against you. Here it is: you are accused of dyspepsia, liver complaint, nervousness, sleepless nights, weak stomach, palpitation, neuralgia, rheumatism, pains through your back and hips, lameness and soreness, want of action in the stomach, etc. What say you to this indictment? Are you guilty or not guilty? You say, "guilty." But as I appear on your behalf, I deny that you are guilty of the evils which cause this punishment. I want you to have a fair trial before the judge of truth and disease, and if you have disobeyed any law of God or Science, you must answer to Science, not to man. I will call on the hypocrite or doctor who goes around devouring widows' houses and for a few dollars has got the people into trouble from which they cannot get out. He says you have all the above diseases.

On cross-examination when asked how he knows, he says, you told him. This is all the proof that he or any other doctor can bring. So by their false testimony you have been condemned for believing a lie, that you might be sick. Now as your case is one of a thousand, I have only to say a few words to your wisdom as judge. All disease is only the effect of our belief. The belief is of man, and as Science sees through man's belief, it destroys the belief and sets the soul or wisdom free.

I will now sum up the evidence. You have listened to the opinions of the doctors, who are blind guides crying peace, peace, till you have embraced all their wisdom. This has produced a stagnation in your system and what their ignorance has not done, the spiritualists have tried to do. So between them both you are a prisoner and in the same state as the people were in the days of Jesus when he said to them, "Beware of the doctrines of the Scribes and Pharisees, for they say and do not; they bind burdens on you that they cannot explain."

This keeps you nervous. So awake from your lethargy and come to the light of wisdom that will teach you that man's happiness is in himself, his life is eternal; this life is wisdom and as wisdom is progression, its enemy is ignorance. So seek wisdom and believe no man's opinion, for these opinions make you nervous. This causes a heat to go to your head making your head feel heavy and producing a dullness over your eyes, in fact, causes all your bad feelings, not that you have any disease independent of your mind, but your mind is matter, not wisdom.

So if I can lift your wisdom above the error or mind, then you will be free. But now this nervous heat is all through you and comes to the surface. When the cold strikes you, it chills you. This you take for a low state of the blood. But it is like a stagnation of your own self, not being able to explain the phenomena that you are affected by. As you read this it will excite you to understand it. This is like a little leaven that is put into your bread or belief, and it will work till it affects the lump and causes you to feel as though you had a very bad cold. It will work upon your system and affect your bowels, causing a diarrhea and also affecting the water.

Then you may know that your cure is at hand. So do not despair, only remember the signs of the times and pray that your flight may not be in the night nor on the Sabbath day when you are at meeting. So keep on the lookout and I think you will be better. If so, let me know. When you read this letter I am with you and you will think strange, for it will produce some strange sensations on your mind, sometimes joy and sometimes grief. But it is all for the best. So keep up good courage and I will lead you along through the dark valley of the shadow of death and land you safe in that land of Science where disease never comes.

I will stop now, but remember that as long as you read this and drink in these words, you do it in remembrance of me, not P.P.Q., but Science, till your health comes. I will leave you now and come again and lead you till you can go alone. If you will see fit to show this to Julia H. when you read it, we shall all be together, and you know what the truth says: that when two or three are gathered together in Science, Truth or Wisdom will be there and bless and explain to them.

P.P.Q.

Portland, Dec. 16, 1861

Miss B.:

Yours of the 7th is received containing $2.00 as a fee for my services on yourself. As you have shown a spirit of sympathy that I never have received before, I certainly shall not prove myself one who will not return to another as I would that another should do to me. So I receive your two dollars sent in hope of a relief and return your money, believing it came from one who is as ready to give as to receive. I believe if two persons agree in one thing sincerely, independent of self, it will be granted.

I will now use my skill as far as I am able to correct your mind in regard to your trouble. The heat you speak of is not a rush of blood to the head but is caused by a sensation on your mind like some trouble. This causes a weakness at times at the pit of your stomach. The heat in the second stomach causes a pressure on the aorta which makes the heart beat very rapidly at times. This you take for palpitation and it causes a flash or heat, which of course you take for a rush of blood to the head. But it is not so; it is the fluids. As the clouds in the skies change when the wind blows, so the fluids under the skin change at every excitement. The skin being transparent reveals the color; this annoys you and the false idea that is in the blood keeps up the fire. Now just take in your mind the spine as a combined lever of three parts, and you will see how to correct your form so as to ease the pressure on the aorta. Now imagine yourself sitting in a chair with the lower level or spine at right angles with your limbs. This relieve the stomach, take the pressure from the aorta and put out the fire so there can be no heat. This will produce a change in your feelings and the change is the cure.

If you will sit down on Sunday evening, I will try to straighten you up so as to relieve that feeling. I will try to exert my power on you and if you feel that I am entitled to anything in the shape of a gift, it will be received, if ever so trifling. Your sincerity towards me interests my sympathy in you, and if I relieve you, I shall be very glad. You have taken the way to make me try my best. This is true sympathy to sympathize with those who make the first sacrifice. It is of no consequence if it be one cent or one hundred. The sacrifice is all. It shows your faith, and according to your faith, so shall your cure be. This being a new experiment, let me know how I succeed and if I change your mind, the change is the cure. I send you one of my circulars which will tell you more of my mode of treatment. It is easier to cure than to explain to a patient at a distance. But I am sure of the principle and feel confident that I shall sometimes cure at a distance. For distance is nothing but an error that truth will sometime explode. If my faith and your hope mingle, the cure is the result, so I will give my attention to you as far as my faith goes and shall like to hear how I succeed.

P.P. Quimby

PORTLAND ADVERTISER

International House, Feb. 13, 1862

Mr. Editor:

As you have given me the privilege of answering an article in your paper of the 11th inst., where you classed me with spiritualists, mesmerizers, clairvoyants, etc., I take this occasion to state where I differ from all classes of doctors, from the allopathic physician to the healing medium.

All these admit disease as an independent enemy of mankind, but the mode of getting rid of it divides them in their practice. The old school admit that medicines contain certain properties and that certain medicines will produce certain effects. This is their honest belief. The homeopathic physicians believe their infinitesimals produce certain effects. This is also honest. But I believe all their medicine is of infinitely less importance than the opinions that accompany it.

I never make war with medicine, but opinions. I never try to convince a patient that his trouble arises from calomel or any other poison but the poison of the doctor's opinion in admitting a disease.

But another class, under cover of spiritualism and mesmerism, claim power from another world, and to these my remarks are addressed. I was one of the first mesmerizers in the state who gave public experiments and had a subject who was considered the best then known. He examined and prescribed for diseases just as this class do now. And I know just how much reliance can be placed on a medium; for, when in this state, they are governed by the superstition and beliefs of the person they are in communication with and read their thoughts and feelings in regard to their disease, whether the patient is aware of them or not.

The capacity of thought-reading is the common extent of mesmerism. Clairvoyance is very rare and can be easily tested by blindfolding the subject and giving him a book to read. If he can read without seeing, that is conclusive evidence that he has independent sight. This state is of very short duration. They then come into that state where they are governed by surrounding minds. All the mediums of this day reason about medicine as much as the regular physician. They believe in disease and recommend medicine.

When I mesmerized my subject, he would prescribe some little simple herb that would do no harm or good of itself. In some cases this would cure the patient. I also found that any medicine would cure certain cases if he ordered it. This led me to investigate the matter and arrive at the stand I now take: that the cure is not in the medicine but in the confidence of the doctor or medium. A clairvoyant never reasons nor alters his opinion; but, if in the first state of thought-reading he prescribes medicine, he must be posted by some mind interested in it, and also must derive his knowledge from the same source the doctors do.

The subject I had left me and was employed by_____, who employed him in examining diseases in the mesmeric sleep and taught him to recommend such medicines as he got up himself in Latin; and as the boy did not know Latin, it looked very mysterious. Soon afterwards he was at home again, and I put him to sleep to examine a lady, expecting that he would go on in his old way; but instead of that, he wrote a long prescription in Latin. I awoke him that he might read it; but he could not. So I took it to the apothecary's who said he had the articles and that they would cost twenty dollars. This was impossible for the lady to pay. So I returned and put him asleep again, and he gave his usual prescription of some little herb, and she got well.

This, with the fact that all the mediums admit disease and derive their knowledge from the common allopathic belief, convinces me that if it were not for the superstition of the people, believing that these subjects, merely because they have their eyes shut, know more than the apothecaries, they could make few cures. Let any medium open his eyes, and let the patient describe his disease; then the medicine would do about as much good as brown bread pills. But let the eyes be shut; then comes the mystery. It is true they will tell the feelings, but that is all the difference.

Now, I deny disease as a truth but admit it as a deception, started like all other stories without any foundation and handed down from generation to generation till the people believe it, and it has become a part of their lives. So they live a lie, and their senses are in it.

To illustrate this: suppose I tell a person he has the diphtheria and he is perfectly ignorant of what I mean. So I describe the feelings and tell the danger of the disease and how fatal it is in many places. This makes the person nervous, and I finally convince him of the disease. I have now made one; and he attaches himself to it and really understands it, and he is in it soul and body. Now he goes to work to make it, and in a short time it makes its appearance.

My way of curing convinces him that he has been deceived, and, if I succeed, the patient is cured. As it is necessary that he should feel that I know more than he does, I tell his feelings. This he cannot do to me, for I have no fear of diphtheria.

My mode is entirely original. I know what I say and they do not, if their word is to be taken. Just so long as this humbug of inventing disease continues, just so long the people will be sick and be deceived by the above-named crafts.

P. P. Quimby

Portland, Feb. 22nd, 1862

Mr. Carter
Dear Sir:

I was very glad to receive your letter of Dec. 1st but since then have been too busy to answer it until now. And now I scarcely know how to commence, knowing that I am about to tread on holy ground, and feel like Moses who viewed the promised land lying before him but could not enter with all his errors, so he saw for others what he was not permitted to enjoy in the natural man.

This truth that I practice is as plain to me as mathematics, but the developing of that science depends upon the progression of all other improvements, for if the world was ignorant like the savages, that wisdom called mathematics would still exist but their darkness could not see it. So as the light of God or wisdom springs up, man learns the truth and applies it to the phenomena of his day so it can be understood. This we call mathematics or God's wisdom revealed to man. I think that all controversies in the world are in matter, and man has attached himself to the idea of matter and lives and dies in it till the light of wisdom opens his eyes to the truth that his life is in this great light that sees matter as nothing but shadows.

I will try to illustrate my ideas by a parable. You know what the phenomenon called mesmerism is. Clairvoyance is perfect light. Matter is annihilated except as it is admitted. Thought-reading is another state in matter, like darkness, so that thought-readers see or feel by the light of another, while clairvoyance sees by its own light. Our senses are in one or the other of these states of light and darkness. The separation of these states has always been the great problem. They who were sitting in darkness saw this light spring up, but as the prince of darkness had sway, they crucified the light. Now, the world attaches their senses to the thing they can feel and see, but Jesus attached his to the light, so that his light was in their error and they saw it not.

By this time I hear you say, Show me this light or truth and it will satisfy me. I answer, Have I not sat by you and told you how you suffered and yet you cannot see me? The light of the body or wisdom is the eye, and if your wisdom is all light, your light is all wisdom, but if your light is darkness or thought-reading, it is darkness to wisdom. Such is this to those who cannot understand, but I feel as though you said, "I understand that." How do I show to the world my light? For a light under a bushel gives no light to those outside. So to let your light shine, you must make some physical demonstration of it.

When I sit down by a patient, their thought is their wisdom or opinions and to me there is no light in them. My light or wisdom sees through their darkness or belief and I, knowing that their sufferings are the effect of this world's wisdom, take them by the hand and guide them by my light till I raise them from the dead or error into the light of science or heaven. This is my heaven. My hell is where I was and where all others are till they come to a knowledge of this great truth, that man is outside of matter. When he knows this, he cuts himself clear and floats in the ocean of light where matter is to him a shadow, moved around by a wisdom attached to it, and their ignorance knows not that they are not of the matter but outside. I will illustrate.

Suppose I create a dog in my mind and mesmerize a person till I make him see it and finally I succeed. Now his senses or light is in my idea–the dog–he sees it but does not see the creator. And seeing the dog with life, he of course thinks the life is in the dog. If he never comes out of that state, then the dog follows him; and if I present it to him, then to himself he has a dog, but to his neighbors he is insane. . . .

All the while I know I am the author. Suppose I call the great God of all: Clairvoyant. All matter to him is nothing.

P. P. Quimby

EXTRACT FROM A LETTER

Portland, Feb., 1862

To Mrs. Woodward:

I will class all people who believe in another world in this way. They all believe that mind is one thing and spirit is the highest wisdom known to the Christian world. As mind is, then man's spirit is that part that lives after the mind is dead or gone.

Mind, matter and spirit are all one and the same, like the lamp, the oil and the light. The lamp is the body, the oil is the mind, and the light is the spirit. So when the oil is out, the spirit is dead, and this is the end of the religious world.

Now this is the way I divide man. The lamp is matter, the oil is mind, and the light is the wisdom or spirit of the oil. The wisdom that carries the lamp is God, and you will see that it is separate and apart from the other combinations of the lamp so that when we see the lamp, the wisdom that directs it is out of sight. This wisdom is what guides the sick. It trims your lamp and furnishes it with the oil or truth so that when the cry of the bridegroom or truth comes, your lamp may be filled and trimmed; and you will not be gone to borrow oil lest he comes when you are after oil, and he passes along and the door is shut. So do not get into your lamp but keep outside. Do not put your light under a bushel but on top. The light of truth or wisdom is like the sun; that of error, like the moon in the firmament of mind.

P.P.Q.

Portland, Apr. 27th, 1862

To Mrs. Marsh:

Your daughter's letter was received and it gave me much joy to hear that he [a different patient] was still going ahead. For you, I cannot say that the news was so gratifying, but I must say I think it is all for the best. We know that God sometimes uses rather strong means to accomplish his end; this is according to the Christian belief but I don't believe that my God ever uses any means. He is the end to obtain, and the means of obtaining to this end everyone tried to find. Man is the inventor of his own misery. Man's happiness is not an element but is the reaction of his own belief or acts. If you throw up a stone into the air it must come down, so the reaction returns with the same power that it receives. So if I do you an evil, the evil will return on me, but God is not in the good or evil. He is in that wisdom that measures out to everyone just according to his acts.

God can't be seen by the natural eye, but He is seen by the sympathy of our acts. When man acts, he either acts according to happiness or misery for the reward is in the act, and the knowledge of this is God. So God is in us and we are in our acts. And God won't censure man's acts unless man censures them himself. We too often mistake our lives for some other person in this way. If I tell you not to eat or drink this or that and you believe me, when you really believe you are me and not yourself, and you attach your senses to this belief and all the misery follows for the superstitious man, for God is not in an opinion. So when the Minister tells you that this is wrong and this is right, he deceives himself and makes the word of God of no effect, for God can't give an opinion. And the minister can't give any proof that he ever got the truth from God but man. Now all such foolish beliefs make one nervous, for you are bound, yet you were not born a slave, for God does not enslave anyone. But man is a slave to his own beliefs and forges his own fetters.

So take heed that none of these blind guides shall deceive you by their smooth words. But keep your light shining so when they come and commence to give an opinion, ask for proof and they will leave you. Then I will come to you and greet you and try to explain to you this truth that will set you free from this nervousness, for it is the fruits of your old errors. I told you that your body was like a picture which was given to you by a friend, but it has been covered up by opinions of the priests till you have lost all interest in it. They have made you believe that it is of no value, and as you set a great value on it, you grew nervous. Now I want to show you that the value is in the picture and then you will respect the donor who is the Father of all gifts. But the blind guides or devils want to destroy your happiness and get the picture. So remember what I tell you and read this and I will be with you and make you quiet till your health comes.

Yours, etc.
P. P. Quimby

EXCERPT FROM AN UNDATED LETTER TO A PATIENT

What is your true position in regard to the truth or spirit world, or the errors of this world or that feeling that keeps you in a quandary all the time? It seems as though there were two powers acting upon you at the same time and it seems as though I must put a false construction on the one that you fear the most. The one you fear is from itself. The fear of the construction that arose from some sensation that contained no knowledge nor harm but was a shock that disturbed your mind. This brought your mind like the earth in a fit state to receive direction from the power of this world of flesh and blood or the direction of the truth, and as the natural man or the knowledge of the world has governed your thoughts, you have been kept ignorant of your true position which is to destroy the enemy of the higher man or put it into subjection to the spiritual man or truth. This is the state of your mind at this time.

When you think of going anywhere, you feel that if I could go with you all would go well; but if you go alone, you take no interest in the amusements, for it is under the direction of this world and you have arrived at this state where you can foresee a higher state of mind than this world enjoys. But you cannot separate the one from the other yet. You will soon. I saw the two states last night in the hall and you might have noticed it in those girls. My patients all feel a sort of attachment to me and I could see the same feeling drawing to you. My patients feel my influence in you and like the children of Israel they want a leader which they will find in you. Those two influences are acting upon you all the time.

P. P. Quimby

To Mrs. A.C.B.:

In answer to your letter I will say that it is impossible to give an opinion of a case till I know something about it independent of my natural senses. I, of myself, cannot take another's feelings. Therefore my opinion is nothing.

When I sit by a patient, their feelings affect me and the sensation I receive from their mind is independent of their senses, for they do not know that they communicate any intelligence to me. This I feel, and it contains the cause of the trouble, and my Wisdom explains their trouble; and my Wisdom explaining the trouble, the explanation is the cure. You must trust in that Wisdom that is able to unlock any error that your wisdom can lock, so search into the error and you will find that your key can unlock the mystery and loose your bands. I will assist you all in my power.

P.P.Q.

Portland

To Mr. A. A. Atwood:

In reply to your questions I will say to you that I am unwilling to take charge of a person afflicted with fits, from the effect upon my own system. In regard to the blind, I should not recommend anyone like your description to come to see me for I have no faith that I could cure him. If a man is simply blind, I have no chance for a quarrel, for we both agree in that fact. But if a person has any sickness which he wants cured and is partially blind besides, then I might affect his blindness, but that is thrown in. I never undertake to cure the well and if a man is blind and satisfied, I can't find anything to talk about. For if I undertake to tell him anything, he says, Oh! I am all right, but my eyes, so he is spiritually blind and cannot see that his blindness ever had a beginning. So it is hard work to get up a controversy and therefore I refuse to take such cases till my popularity is such that my opinion is of some force to such persons.

For opinions of popular quacks are law and gospel about blindness, and so long as the blind lead the blind, they will both be in the ditch. Thirdly, you ask me if I can cure anyone from using intoxicating liquors. This is a hard question to answer, for it involves considerable. If you drink it is not my business; neither is it yours if I drink, for neither can set up a standard to judge the other by. I judge no man. Judgment belongs to God or Science and that judges right, for it contains no opinion. Giving an opinion is setting up a standard to judge your neighbor by, and this is not doing as you would be done by. The true science judges in this way. If you are sick and come to me, if I tell you how you feel, this is doing as you would like to be done by; there is no discord. Now you come to me, a criminal or debtor, accused of disobeying some opinion of man which you will not accept and worship. You are accused, condemned, and cast into prison; your punishment is your feelings. Now science, being a higher court than man's opinions, man appeals to that court. So he is brought before me and upon examination, I find that he has committed no offense against science and is not liable to their standard. I plead his case and show that all his acts were committed in self defense. His drinking is the effect of something he is accused of, and he takes to the cup to drown his sorrow. When I convince him how he has been deceived by his tormentors and explain the truth, he comes to his reason and abandons his old associates who have been the means of all this trouble. If he likes smoking and drinking, he is satisfied and wants no physician. But if sick, and I find that liquor is his enemy, then it is my duty to tell him so. And if I convince him, he has no more difficulty in cutting his acquaintance than he would an old friend whom he discovered plotted against his life; one case must be proved.

    P. P. Quimby

Portland

To Mrs. Doland:

I will try to drive these devils away that trouble you, but I must say, they originated in this world or matter. They are not the work of God, but they are the invention of man. God is not sin or error. We often hear persons say, while we are looking at nature, that we see God in everything. This to me is all folly.

If you should see an orange and had not the sense of smell, nor had intelligence; but smelling the orange and knowing it contained a peculiar odor, you worship the orange for what it contains. So it is with God. We see fields, streams and flowers, and all nature seems delighted to spring from its cold prison. We are not aware of any wisdom in the flowers nor grass, nor in anything that hath life; yet they all have their peculiar ways of expressing their feelings to the great wisdom of all, not by language, but in their own way. Their life is the father of all life, and when the cold breezes of November come, they leave the icy tenement of the world of matter and live again in a sphere far superior to this world of matter. Not losing their identity, they return in the spring and appear as though nothing had happened.

To the observer, the flowers seen in June are not the flowers of the next June, but yet they are. So man, like the plant, with one exception, is the higher element of God's wisdom. He partakes of the mathematical in man that plans and directs all. He is introduced into this world with the highest order of God's wisdom, not being perfect, for some cause not known to himself. He is left to work out his problems for his own happiness. So he becomes an inventive being, and as he becomes ambitious, he sets up standards of right and wrong and wants everyone to obey his peculiar notions. This makes war between truth and error. Error is arbitrary and wants to bind truth. Truth is gentle and never binds at all but, like a shepherd, leads his flock.

Error is always lying about the truth and trying to confine it. Every idea has an atmosphere around it, and in it the truth is confined.

Disease is the invention of man, and like all inventions of man, according to our belief, liable to perish. So decomposition is always taking place in every variety of matter. The destruction of anything we have an interest in affects us, just according to our belief.

Your body being matter is liable to the same destruction that any other matter is. To you it is a vineyard and you enjoy the fruits of your own vines. Now to be a good husbandman is to keep all the trees or ideas in good health so that no crooked branches should shoot out to injure the growth of the rest. The idea of rheumatism is the fruit of a tree called trouble that grows in the most barren part of the soil . . .

    P. P. Quimby

TO A PATIENT

Mrs. Norcross
Madam:

Yours of the ... is at hand. But a lack of faith on my part to describe your case and explain my ideas to you so you could rightly comprehend my meaning is my only excuse for not writing before. But thinking you would expect an answer, I now sit down to talk with you a short time.

After reading your letter I tried to exercise all the power I was master of to quiet and restore your limb to health. But to give a satisfactory answer to you or myself was more than I was capable of. I therefore will disturb your mind or fluids once more and try to direct them in a more healthy state by repeating some of my ideas which I repeated to you when here.

You know I told you that mind was the name of something, and this something is the fluids of the body. Disease is the name of the disturbance of these fluids or mind. Now as the fluids are in a scalding state, they are ready to be directed to any portion of the body. You remember I told you that every idea contained this fluid, and the combination varied just according to the knowledge or idea of disease.

I will explain. Two persons are told they are troubled with scrofula. One does not know anything about it and has never heard of the disease, is as ignorant as a child. No explanation is given to either. The other is well posted up in regard to all the bad effects of this disease. Now you can readily see the effect on the minds of these two persons. One is not affected at all till he is made acquainted with the case, while the other one's mind or fluids are completely changed and combined, so all that is necessary is to give direction and locate the disease in any part of the body.

I think I hear you say that a child can be troubled with scrofula, and they have no mind, as I said before. Your mother probably changed the fluids of your body when an infant or at any early age, and some circumstances located it in your leg. Now as it is there, you want to know how to get rid of it; and as it was directed there through ignorance, you can't get rid of it without some knowledge.

Now as this disturbance comes like a fright or sensation, it is to be understood as a fright. Now as disease is looked upon as a thing independent of the mind, the mind is disturbed by every sensation produced upon the senses, and the soul stands apart from the disturbed part and grieves over it as a person grieves over any trouble independent of the body. Now to cure you, you must come with me to where the trouble is, and you will find it to be nothing but a little heated fluid just under the skin, and it is kept hot and disturbed by your mind being misrepresented.

Now I believe that I can impart something from my mind that can enter into that distressed state of the fluids and change the heat and bring about a healthy state. I shall often try to produce a cooling sensation on your limb, at other times a perspiration so as to throw off the surplus heat. If I succeed in helping or relieving you, please let me know. But do not expect another explanation, for this has made me half insane. If you think you would improve faster by coming to Belfast, please let me know, and I will get you a private boarding house if desired. I think I can hear you say by this time that your limb feels better; if so, I shall be satisfied. I will close my long epistle by wishing you a long life and a well leg.

Miss B.:

Yours of the 7th is received and I am glad to learn that I have relieved your mind by "my power," as you call it. But you misunderstand my power. It is not power but Wisdom. If you knew as much as I do about yourself, you could feel another's feelings, but here is the trouble. What people call "power" I call Wisdom. Now if my wisdom is more than yours, then I can help you, but this I must prove to you. And if I tell you about yourself what you cannot tell me, then you must acknowledge that my wisdom is superior to yours and become a pupil instead of a patient.

I will now sit down by you and tell your feelings. You may give your attention to me by giving me your hand, be still, and look me in the eye. I will write down the conversation that I hold with you while sitting by you.

You have a sort of dizzy feeling in your head and a pain in the back part of the neck. This affects the front part of the head causing a heaviness over the eyes. The lightness about the head causes it to incline forward, bringing the pressure on your neck just below the base of the brain, so that you often find yourself throwing your head up to ease that part of the head. This makes it heavy, so it bears on the shoulders, cramps the neck, numbs the chest so that you give way at the pit of the stomach and feel as though you wanted something to hold you up. This cramps the stomach, giving you a "gone feeling" at the pit of the stomach. This contraction presses on the bowels and causes a full feeling at times and a heaviness about your hips and a loggy feeling when you walk. Now all these symptoms taken of themselves are nothing. But you have had medical advice or have got from someone else an answer to all these feelings. You are nervous. You have the heart complaint. Your blood rushes to the head, and you are liable to female weaknesses. Now take all these symptoms together and if they would not make your face red, what would?

Listen to me and I will give an explanation of all the above feelings. I must go back to the first cause, say some years ago. I will not undertake to tell just the cause but I will give you an illustration. Suppose I (the natural man) were sitting by you and we were alone, and I should go and fasten the door and go towards you and attempt to seize hold of you. And if you asked me what I intended to do and I should say, "Keep still, or I will blow your brains out," you would see this would frighten you. I think your heart would beat as fast as it ever did. This explanation I do not say is true. For I suppose a case, start contracts

115

the stomach, the fright or excitement heat, sets your heart beating, and throws the heat to your head; this heat tries to escape out of the nose causing a tickling in your nose and you often rub it because it itches and feels hot. It then tries to escape through the passage to the ears making your cheeks red and burn and causes a noise in your ears sometimes. This after a while subsides, the stomach relaxes and the heat passes down from the stomach into the bowels. . . .

Now follow the directions in the last letter and relieve the pressure on the aorta. This will check the nervous heat and relieve the excitement and then the heat will subside. The color is in the surface of the skin and has nothing to do with any humor or disease; it is nothing but excitement. As I told you in my last, I will be with you when you read the letters and you will feel a warm sensation pass over you, like a breath. This will open the pores of the skin and the heat will escape.

I send back the five dollars till the cure is performed. I don't like to be outdone in generosity and I am willing to risk as much as anyone in such a cause as this. If I come off conqueror, then it will be time enough for you to offer up a sacrifice. Till then, if I accept a gift, it is without an equivalent on my part. I feel as certain of success as you do, so I feel as though I run no risk. All I look for is the cure. You ask if I give any medicine. The only medicine I ever give is my explanation and that is the cure. In about a week let me know how the medicine works. Hoping to hear good news when next I hear from you, I remain, Your friend,

P. P. Quimby

Portland

To Mrs. Robinson
Madam:

Pardon me for addressing you on a subject in which as a stranger I have no personal interest. Mrs. Green, your mother, having been under my charge as an invalid, has frequently spoken of you and your husband connected with some trouble which I never asked her to explain. But from what little I gathered from some spiritual communications she had from a lady, if she may be so called, I felt as though there must be something wrong. This medium was one, if I understood her right, whom she consulted for her health. In the interview the idea of the dead would come up, and as is usual in this mode of practice, her husband came forward to give some ideas that might be of some benefit to the medium, not to Mrs. G, for all these communications are to settle some difficulty that neighbors get up.

In the communication her husband recommended me, saying I was a medium. This led her to call on me for advice. As my mode of treating disease is entirely new to the world, the spiritualists claim me as a medium. I deny this, but believe that mind acts upon mind and that it is the living and not the dead; so here is where we differ. When Mrs. G called on me I think Mrs. Otis was present and I told her of some things which I did not know before, and this gave her confidence in me. Then she wished me to read some communications from her husband and something connected with you and your husband, and it seems to me that they were interested to make trouble, and I told her so, but she thought not.

I will here say that whatever you may think of your mother she is sincere in her motives but is, I think, misled by some spirits that have flesh and blood who have some motive for acting. She thinks your husband has a power over you to make you do just as he chooses. This is her honest belief and that contemptible woman holds out the idea that she can, through the spirits, bring everything straight. As she has confidence in me, she wishes me to influence you not to be controlled by your husband. And I told her that I felt as there must be some misunderstanding and advised her to go to your place and have a fair explanation of all this trouble. For I believe the medium knew what she wrote as well as I do, and advised her to have no more to do with it.

But there is a combination of circumstances, showing to me that she is under some influence that is not for her happiness. So I told her I would try to bring things right and I thought she would have a letter making everything plain. This was three months ago, and Friday last she called and said she had not received a letter. I noticed she felt very badly and asked what she should do. I told her I would write to you myself and then I could tell more about the case, for I believe it was all a piece of deception on the part of the medium, either instigated by her enemies or that she had been deceived or misled by pretended friends and that the medium read her thoughts. This is my reason for addressing you on a subject in which I have no interest; it is to ferret out traitors who are busy in making trouble. I have had some experience in troubles of this kind where the spirits of the dead are called up, and I know that this horrid belief has been the cause of breaking up families, separating man and wife and setting mother against daughter and every possible evil.

I am perfectly ignorant of the charges against each other; I never asked her, I felt as though it was none of my business. But from her honest conviction of being right, I have no doubt that there have been persons who have got from stories, which if the real truth could be known, do not contain a single word of truth. Yet they are as true to her as the very Bible she reads and takes for truth. To show you the mind can be misled by these blind guides and deceived by these communications and their bad effects, I will relate one instance out of a dozen that I might give.

I was called to see a lady who had cut her throat and after the deed was done, she was considered insane. Her mother and husband were with her at the time I visited her, although he had been away from her for three months, from the fact that there was trouble between them. She had become jealous of him and their children staying among the neighbors, so he left. All this was done under the full belief that it was true, and when I entered the room her mother pointed to the husband saying, "He is the cause of all this trouble." Then his wife commenced abusing him violently. After hearing these stories, I said, I see no reason for all this trouble; the woman was insane and must have been so for some time, and now they were all insane. I then commenced restoring the lady to her reason and my effect upon her was such that I was obliged to hold her. Then she clung to her husband, but in the course of four or five hours I brought her to her senses and she fell asleep. After she awoke she enquired for her husband. I told her he had gone out. She wished to know why she could not live with him. I said I knew of no reason. She said she had nothing against him, that he had always treated her well, etc. It may all be explained like this: she had become interested in spiritualism and here was the result. My explanation of the phenomena reconciled them and now they live happily together.

P. P. Quimby

Mr. J. Watts Esq.:

In the letter I wrote to you about my coming to your place, I said nothing about my pay from the fact that I knew you would know the person who wishes to see me, neither did I want to give any idea in the papers, for if I should, it would bring on such hard cases that it might upset my plans.

My plan is this, to make some cure that would give me a position in your place that can't be put down by one or two failures. But if I open the door to all, I might fail.

Again, the first impression lasts the longest and I don't want to enter your service as one of Maine's politicians entering Governor Fairfield's room to solicit an office just as he entered, he stumped his toe and in he went headlong, saying, your fearless hire lays before you. I don't want to stumble against such ones at present. My object is to make my profession have character and to do this it must be respected, and if I don't respect it, I can't expect others will.

Here is the difference between myself as a man and my practice. My character speaks for itself and I am judged according to my acts, like all others. But you know that a profession has two identities: one is attached to the profession and the other to the man. Now reverse the tables. Take Dr. Wood of this place, say nothing about either character, give me his professional character and attach it to my practice, and give him my art or gift, as he would call it, and attach it to his practice and then you can see popularity is in his profession and not in his wisdom. But my wisdom has no character but is a sort of power or gift. Here is where I stand; the people will give me all the power but they won't the wisdom. You know, to establish a standard like the one I am trying requires more wisdom than Jeff Davis; one is based on one man's opinion and the other is based on the fact that his opinion is faith.

The medical faculty's opinion is based on the opinion of what they see of effect, they know not the cause; mine is based on what I know of the cause, like action and reaction. You know if you throw a ball in the air it will return with just as much force as it received, so the answer was in the action. So it is with all my practice.

The medical practice admits the ball comes down but can't say but what it was in the air from the beginning. Here is the difference: the medical profession sees an eruption on the skin, here is the reaction. Now to account for it is the point in dispute.

I feel the causes and effect in my own person and the doctors don't feel either, but the effect on the sufferers they see with their eyes to account for it in various ways, but all admit that is nothing very marvelous, but it is still a mystery. So their version reminds me of a story I will relate here. In a town called Berklay in Massachusetts, a sea captain knew that the inhabitants were very superstitious, so he went to the barn and found an egg and took his pencil and wrote, "Woe unto you Berklay folks." The egg was found by a child and a church meeting was called; so the parson opened the case by expressing his opinion, and the deacon was called to give his version on the phenomenon. He took the egg and examined it very minutely, looked very wise and made this remark, that he had no doubt it was the Lord's doing but that he had observed one very important fact which was this: the Lord did not spell Berklay right!

The doctors are making just such observations all the time, never accounting for any phenomena, but giving their opinion like the deacon, and there is just about as much wisdom in one as the other.

Now all I do is to show the sick the absurdity of both; this explains the cause and the effect being in the cause, the wisdom regulates both.

P. P. Quimby

Portland

To Mr. W. S. Atkins:

I will now sit down to answer your letter and will straighten you up as I used to. Remember the illustrations I used to make to you and I will stir up your ideas by referring to my theory. You want to know if I was in earnest in regard to your learning. I was, but you nor anyone else can learn of yourself, any more than a person can get religion of himself. It must be the effect of a change of mind. This you cannot understand, for your change of mind when you got religion was the effect of error, not of truth. So you worship you know not what. But I worship I know what, and, "Whom you ignorantly worship, him declare I unto you." This same Christ, whom you think is Jesus, is the same Christ that stands at the door of your dwelling or belief, knocking to come in and sit down with the child of science that has been led astray by blind guides into the wilderness of darkness. Now wake from your sleep and see if your wisdom is not of this world. To be born again is to unlearn your errors and embrace the truth of Christ; this is the new birth, and it cannot be learned except by desire for the truth of that Wisdom that can say to the winds of error and superstition "Be still!" and they obey.

It is not a very easy thing to forsake every established opinion and become a persecuted man for this Truth's sake, for the benefit of the poor and sick, when you have to listen to all their long stories without getting discouraged. This cannot be done in a day. I have been twenty years training myself to this one thing, the relief of the sick. A constant drain on a person's feelings for the sick alters him, and he becomes identified with the suffering of his patients; this is the work of time. Every person must become affected one way or the other, either to become selfish and mean so that his selfish acts will destroy his wisdom or keep it under and let his error reign, or his wisdom will become more powerful till it will run away with his obligation to himself and family.

It is not an easy thing to steer the ship of wisdom between the shores of poverty and the rocks of selfishness. If he is all self, the sick lose that sympathy which they need at his hand. If he is all sympathy, he ruins his health and becomes a poor outcast on a cold uncharitable world. For the sick can't help him and the rich won't. It is difficult to steer clear and keep your health.

P. P. Q.

THE WRITINGS OF PHINEAS PARKHURST QUIMBY IN ALPHABETICAL ORDER

Editor's Introduction to the Main Writings of Phineas Parkhurst Quimby

The main body of the writings of Phineas Parkhurst Quimby consists of articles, pieces, notes and letters. Quimby often wrote immediately after sitting with a patient while in the "excited" state, and describes the impressions they made upon his mind. In many cases, these articles are streams of consciousness that rarely remain confined to a single topic. He also wrote in response to questions submitted to him, as well as answered criticism that had been directed towards him in the local newspapers.

P. P. Quimby sometimes wrote from a third person perspective, especially if he was talking about himself in the article. A good example of Quimby "forgetting himself" is in the article, *Brief Sketch of Dr. Quimby's Theory*, that is published here for the first time. In this short three-paragraph article, Quimby begins the first paragraph as a third person's perspective describing his theory, and by the sixth sentence, he is beginning to slip into a first-person narration. The second paragraph is entirely written from his own perspective, and in the third paragraph he abruptly switches back to referring to himself as "he" and "his."

Another example of the different perspectives is found in two versions of *How Dr. Quimby Cures*. *How Dr. Quimby Cures III* is written as Quimby's first-person narrative, and *How Dr. Quimby Cures IV* was modified to an anonymous account of how Dr. Quimby cures.

The writings are presented here in alphabetical order as this seems to be the quickest and easiest way to locate a specific article. All of the writings in this section are by Phineas Parkhurst Quimby, with editorial comments and notations contained within brackets.

A single asterisk [*] following an article title signifies that the article is being published for the first time.

A double asterisk [**] following an article title signifies a change or addition to a previously published article.

Each article contains a single microfilm reference number for documentation purposes. The reference number begins with either "LC" for the Library of Congress microfilm or "BU" for the Boston University microfilm as listed in the Primary Resource Section. This is followed by "[microfilm reel number]: [microfilm frame number]." For example, the reference [LC 2:1067] indicates that one version of this article is to be found in the Library of Congress microfilm on reel number 2 at frame number 1067.

–Editor.

About Patients–A Case: A Divorced Lady
[LC 1:0227]

I will tell you how a patient whom I was sitting with affected me. It was a lady who had been divorced from her husband because she said he was so ugly she could not live with him. At the time I first saw her I told her of the fact and tried to convince her it was a disease, that her husband really loved her and his fears for her health made her nervous. This she could not believe for she said he ill-treated her and she knew he was bad. Now this was the fact. They both loved each other at the time they were married; this she acknowledged and they continued to love and respect each other till the lady was confined when, as she said, she took cold and was very sick. Then her husband turned against her, tried to kill her and reported all sorts of stories about her till she could bear it no longer. At last she lost all patience, lost confidence in her husband, forsook his bed and would not have anything to do with him. This story she believed to be true and so it was. But the cause she knew not. Her husband, getting out of all patience, forsook her and tried to get divorced; this was mutual.

Now all the above was real, but it was brought about from love and fear. Her sickness caused her husband's fear for her life. His fear excited her love, making her nervous; she put a false construction on his fears thinking he did not love her, for his love when she was well did not excite her fears and her trouble wanted someone to relieve her. His fears for her health made her worse. So that the more he would try to please her, the more he tormented her, till each one's love turned to hatred. At last they were divorced; then she was happy she said. But as she got rid of her husband, the disease or the insane idea attached itself to her own identity in the form of disease of the eye. So that at the time I speak of, she gave me to understand that she was then perfectly happy, with the exception of her eye. But I saw the same idea of insanity that kept her nervous and always will in some way or other. It was so plain to me that the idea took form and displayed itself to me in so simple a way that no one would ever detect it by her conversation. But it was so plain to me that I sat down and reduced the whole to writing, so that it should not depart from me, for it gave me wisdom that may be of value to mankind. It is to me and I will relate it.

Her love, she always considered as pure towards her husband. His love to her was impure and although it was not pure, yet she always would admit that he loved her a little, although she never wished him to but wanted to get clear and never could. So her insane idea was in this discord and it showed itself in some way, so that persons seeing and talking with her could not detect it in anything she would say; but she would always produce some sort of an impression that would excite those who talked with her. They never could know what it was, but their feelings would affect her and keep her nervous, so that she carried the idea of insanity all the time. At the time I am now speaking of, it showed itself in two large roses: one white and the other red, both on one side of her bonnet, the white above the red, showing her own love as pure white and the husband's as red or bloody. This I could see and the impression made on me almost frightened me for an instant, for I could see what was insanity and how it might be avoided.

Insanity consists in some little discord that might be corrected if the person knew it; it is brought on by the disturbance of the world's opinion. I will tell you how it comes. I have told you how this lady's came and I will tell you how to correct it. But before I correct it, I must make it or show what it is made of. This puts me in mind of two patients I had, both with symptoms alike as far as they knew. Both belonged to the same church; both complained of the same feelings; one was a farmer and the other was a doctor. Each admitted to a heaven and hell independent of themselves. The farmer's ambition led him only to leading a life so that he should get into heaven and his trouble was in steering his life and acts so that he should not burn up in hell. And as his ambition was for this world's goods, it acted like a current that he had to stem, so it made him nervous and kept him all the time uneasy. This nervousness showed itself in his body and was called by the doctors a trouble about the heart and congestion of the lungs. His wisdom was directed to heaven with hell on the starboard bow. This engrossed all his wisdom and talent to land safe in heaven when the storm of life was over.

The doctor was another character. He had more acquisitiveness and sagacity and his wisdom was not directed so much to heaven or hell as the farmer's, but he kept both in sight as though he would give his attention to that at a more convenient time. He wanted to examine into all things of this world, so as he was a doctor, he wanted to see how disease was made, what it was made of and how it was put together. He was looking at the errors of the world as real things. But the farmer had no curiosity to know how anything was made. He wanted to get into heaven, so he was more likely to get off the globe first, for he did not stop to examine anything as the doctor did. The doctor after examining all things here would steer for foreign parts and as heaven is his last place of destination, he will not be satisfied till he goes all through hell to see how that is constructed. And if he is able to see out after he gets in, I have no doubt of his reaching heaven. Now here are two characters: one ignorance and the other error. Ignorance embraces the largest class of mankind. Error is more active, but shows the wisdom of this world, and is called by the farmer or ignorance, very strong-minded men of great power.

Now there is another class not known by ignorance, called the inventive class. This is not so numerous as the other two classes but has more sagacity than both. This class creates and destroys. They can create a thing and present it to the two above classes, who will think it as real as their own existence. They use their powers of invention for their own benefit and make their money out of the other two classes. There is still another class, just like the last, with this exception: they show the error and ignorance how they are deceived, show them how to tear down all their ideas and bring all things on a level. This is the class that can create and destroy and teach others to do the same. This last class cannot be insane, for insanity is the invention of the natural man and can be destroyed by the scientific man.

November 1860

About Patients–Part 2–Supplemental
[LC 2:1070]

The reader will find my ideas strewn all through my writings and sometimes it will seem that what I said had nothing to do with the subject upon which I was writing. This defect is caused by the great variety of subjects that called the pieces out; for they were all written after sitting with patients who had been studying upon some subject, or who had been under some religious excitement, or were suffering from disappointment or worldly reverses, or had given much time to the study of health, being posted in all the wisdom of the medical faculty and had reasoned themselves into a belief; and their diseases were the effect of their reasoning. So you will see at a glance that I must have all classes of mind, as I have all classes of diseases. No two are alike. You will find under the head of Two Patients, Book III,[1] an article written from the impressions made upon me at the time I wrote. Although to the world their symptoms were, so far as they could describe them to a physician, precisely alike, yet the causes were entirely different.

One person had a strong desire for this world's goods and at the same time had been made to believe his salvation depended upon his being honest and steady. Hence his religion acted as a kind of hindrance to his worldly prosperity. This kept him all the time nervous, and he put all his troubles into the idea, heart disease. The other was a man who had a great deal of acquisitiveness and self esteem, so that all his acts were governed by popular opinion. He wanted to be a great man by making himself wise at others' expense, or getting every idea that is of any value without paying for it. This made him nervous, for his mind would often force itself into society where it was not wanted, yet if he made anything out of it, it was well. So his religion was always the last thing to think of. To him heaven had no claims till he had gone through hell to make up his mind which place was the better for his practice.

Now to cure these two men was to show them the hypocrisy of their belief and show them that all men are to themselves just what they make themselves. I convinced the former that his ideas of heaven were only a hindrance to his happiness, for to him religion was a sort of tyrant that he was afraid of. Now I have no belief, but if any person has a belief that they take for a truth that governs their lives through fear, I destroy it and I convince them that their happiness lies not in a belief but in themselves, and to do good from fear is not doing good from the right motive. But to do good because you feel better, then you act from love and not from fear. So in regard to any disease, I destroy the patient's belief in all sorts of medicine and also in all beliefs in disease and show that the whole foundation is based on a lie, and if I can tear their theory to pieces, I have nothing to give in return. For if the disease is gone, their belief is also gone, and to do well requires no belief, but it is wisdom, and to know how to keep well is to know what makes you sick.

This is what I intend to show. Therefore my arguments are aimed at some particular thing, sometimes words, sometimes one thing and sometimes another. So it is impossible to give a work like this to the public like any other. It will be more like a court record or a book on law with the arguments of each

case. It takes up a little of everything. Sometimes I am reasoning on politics so I have to show the absurdity of their reason. This stops their mouths and keeps them still so that they shall not get nervous on politics.
1862

1. This is a reference to the fourth paragraph of the previous article, "About Patients–A Case: A Divorced Lady."

About Patients–Symptoms of a Patient
[LC 2:1071]

I will give you the symptoms of a patient whom I just examined. He was a man about fifty years old and his symptoms affected me in this way. I felt a trembling sensation that went down to my head and a tightness across my chest with a tendency to sigh. This made me melancholy; then my thoughts left my body and I seemed to be in space creating places and attaching my senses to the ideas I created, while my happiness and misery was in the scenes of my own creation. I could see a sort of another world like the city of New York and it seemed so plain that I really felt the difference in the society of the city. This amazed me for it was a disease and although the man's thoughts had different localities, they affected me like a disease located in the body. Here I could see how we are affected by our opinions. His mind or belief was in matter of this world and was as plain to be seen by me as my thoughts are to a mesmerized subject. To him they were spiritual and although they were the imitation of some other's ideas, they were real truth to him. He attached his senses to the things or places he had made and in them was his happiness and misery. All the above was matter except the happiness and misery–this is always what follows a belief. All the rest I say was matter and belonged to the wisdom of this world.

By the spiritualist it would be called spiritualism; so it is, but it is of this world and confined to matter. That wisdom from above is not in this but can see through it and is not seen by the wisdom of this world at all. Now as I was out of his wisdom or this world and in the essence that flows from the higher wisdom, I was in a clairvoyant state, with my senses attached to an identity in this essence. This essence is light and is capable of penetrating this matter or mind, so that to it matter is annihilated. If a person's senses are in this light he sees all ideas as matter in the dark to those who are in them. One state is thought-reading or the wisdom of matter or spiritualism and the other is clairvoyance or the wisdom held in solution in this ocean of essence. The wisdom of this world is spiritual like an odor that arises from the earthly man. In this odor, all sorts of forms are made of a spiritual nature, governed by the same laws as their father. Thus the spiritual world is the son of its father. Jesus called it the devil, and its believers the children of their father, and as he was of matter he must be destroyed. Now the kingdom of God was not of matter but wisdom, so God called it father; as God is the son of wisdom; wisdom made man out of this essence or life. So that when he formed man out of the dust of this earth and breathed into him this breath of life, he then became a living progressive wisdom or man.

This life is the light or clairvoyant state that sees no matter independent of itself or mind and all matter is subject to this essence. Disease is the offspring of error or the devil, and wisdom in this essence acting through man can break the bars of death or error and set life free. For death is the name of something that error wants to destroy and this something is life. So the warfare is between life and death. Life cannot be destroyed but death can. The senses are attached to the identity of our belief and we are affected according to the fear that we associate with our senses. Death and disease are matter and when the senses or essence are attached to this body, it becomes subject to the laws of matter, and as mind is matter, it makes laws for strangers; as life is a stranger, it looks upon it as an enemy to death. All the happiness which death has is trying to destroy life, so for this effect it invents all sorts of diseases. This death is the king of terrors and is the worst enemy life has to contend with. Now man is the battlefield of these two powers: life and death.

If life is imprisoned in death's prison it is hard work to get clear. The only way is to destroy death or error and set life free. Our senses are the enemy of death and when they are attached to disease, disease holds them in its jaws and nothing but a direct revelation of wisdom can break the jaws of death. This truth is destruction to death and freedom from error and superstition. Then life rises to that state of light which is the essence called God–there to be free from matter, except as a medium to communicate through. Now all persons who can take another's feelings are in this state, but their senses may not all be attached to the same idea. For instance, a person may feel another's pain; this comes with the sense of feeling, but this feeling contains no wisdom. This is the case of mesmerism. One subject feels the aches and pains of another; this is called thought-reading. Another sees the deranged state of the body; this is called sight, but sight is not knowledge. All this is called the wisdom of the dead. So it is, but it is not the living, for it is confined to the wisdom of error or this world. The senses may be in this light, so far as to see and describe all that is asked, but that is from the father or God. His wisdom sees the effect, feels the aches and pains, sees the cause and sees the senses imprisoned in matter, steps forward and runs the risk of being imprisoned for the sake of his friends. He sees all the causes, stands and pleads their cases, gets the verdict and sets the captive free. This is the difference in the two. One is a power without knowledge. The other is knowledge applied to an idea that it can break up and scatter to the four winds of heaven.

I will try and show the two theories. I will say to you as Jesus said, Except you become as a little child you cannot understand and apply these sayings to the curing of disease. The Christian idea of the above parable, I have no sympathy with, for it contains no wisdom. Everyone knows that a little child is of all things the most ignorant and helpless. It has no wisdom at all. It will creep into the fire or water or anything else because it knows no fear. Now it is of all living creatures the very foundation on which to erect wisdom or error. Its senses are attached to its ideas, so as it creeps to the fire, the wisdom of its mother takes it from the fire. If the mother whips the child it shows fright, not wisdom. If the mother's wisdom is of this world, she reasons in this way. If you go near the fire I will whip you. This at first is Greek to the child, for it does not understand. So the child tries it again and the mother repeats the same sound, accompanied with her hand on the child's ear. The child puts wisdom in his senses, which he applies to his ears and keeps away from the fire, not because the fire will box his ears or harm him. His fear is in his idea of what will follow his mother's hand. But he is not at rest. His curiosity is excited and the more the mother whips the child the more earnest he is to know why he must not go near the fire. So at last when alone it creeps towards the fire and its little hand feels the heat. This frightens it and it holds on to whatever it touches till someone takes it away. The child remembers this and looks at its enemy with grief, as it does when its mother whips it. The mother is alarmed and changes her tone. She now tries to soothe the child by caressing him and showing some sympathy, and reasons with the child that the fire does not mean to burn it, that it was hot and that if it went up to the fire, it must be burned. This is the wisdom of God.

Man would say it is a naughty fire and if it burns you again, I will whip it. As soon as the mother gets over her fright, she sets the child down on the floor with a bounce, accompanied with a threat like this: Now don't go near the fire again; if you do I will take your skin off. So the child sits trembling, once in a while drawing a long sigh and a tear drops from its eyes. In all this the child has sinned not. It has been punished for the sins or errors of its mother. Now the wisdom from above, acting through Jesus, called Christ, reasons to the child in this way. It makes the child acquainted with the effects of the fire. It has forbearance with the little ideas the child has formed and tries to breathe into this little earth the seed of wisdom so that it grows like the grain of mustard seed. It would see and learn that fire was not its enemy or its friend but a servant, ready to be used at the will of the master. These two modes of reasoning embrace man and beast; neither embraces true wisdom. One is God's reasoning and the other is man's. But there is something beyond all this that man is destined to reach, which is creation and formation, destruction and eternal life. True wisdom is eternal and its knowledge is the destruction of all the above. Even the son of God was to be subject to this wisdom. Now just as a person understands this wisdom he can put it into practice. It is not confined to any particular branch but applies to all science for the healing of the nations from error and superstition.

It is not everyone who says he understands that does, but he who can teach the same understandingly to others. Everyone knows that in the natural world, some persons are good mechanics, but it is not absolutely necessary that every artist should be a chemist, nor every chemist an artist. But if a man should undertake to teach chemistry with no knowledge except what he obtained from books, his wisdom is like sounding brass and tinkling cymbals; it was already known. Look at the professors of chemistry; they never have the sick or anything else in their philosophy. The object of chemistry when first discovered was not to apply any theory, but it was the discovery of a new process. It was intended to analyze all sorts of substances and separate one element from another and not to apply them to any particular theory or science. The person who discovered the art of making whiskey from corn never thought of it to cure consumption or any other disease. There was a phenomenon produced and to apply it to something was another matter. Franklin discovered electricity, but he never found out that it had any curative qualities. That was left to those who knew just as much about it as they did before Franklin made this discovery.

The fact is that all kinds of drugs were discovered by chemists, not with any idea that they contain any curative qualities. Iodine is used now to cure half the diseases there are and its good qualities set forth by physicians. All these second hand ideas are applied by the medical faculty and not one out of a hundred knows how to make the medicines he uses. Yet they talk of the medical science! Here is the great mistake. To produce a phenomenon is one thing and to know how you produce it is another and to destroy it is still another. To cure an error intelligently is to know how to produce it. It will show that the doctors are not only ignorant of what they do when they make a cure, but by the very means they use to make it, they bring about the phenomenon they are trying to cure. To show how this is brought about I must illustrate it in some way, showing how the mind is affected through the ignorance of the physician.

Suppose you have a fine piano which you place a great value upon and you feel annoyed because everyone who comes in thumps on the keys. Finally you get so nervous that you cannot rest when anyone is near it. At last you grow sick and send for a physician. He comes in, as ignorant of music as the rest, goes to the piano and begins to look at it, you meanwhile growing nervous as he fusses over the piano. Then he turns toward you and says, "You look sick and your blood is low; you need some little tonic. Your head is a little affected; I think your music is hurting you. I will leave you some powders." As he leaves he strikes the piano again and you remain just where you were when he came, only a little worse. In a day or two he calls again and inquires, How are you. You say, "No better." The sight of the doctor reminds you of the instrument and you grow nervous. So he alters the medicine and gives some different directions and leaves without touching the piano. You are left alone and no one comes in to disturb you and in a short time you are out of doors. The doctor meets you and inquires how you are getting along. You reply, "Very well." "Continue the medicine as I directed. You are doing very well." So driven off you return home, and the neighbors begin to come in. The idea of the piano comes up again, making your heart beat and you feel faint as the piano is thumped.

At last you are left alone and you feel very weak, so you take some whiskey. This excites the brain and a flush comes over you and you sneeze. Now comes up the idea of a cold; you grow nervous and the doctor is sent for. He comes in, takes off his hat and overcoat and very deliberately sits down by the piano. This makes you nervous so he feels your pulse and looks at your tongue, then "hems" and says, You have taken a slight cold. He reminds you of what he said the other day, and he makes another alteration in the medicine. This process is kept up till the doctor is dismissed for another of the same kind. And so on, till they have run through the medical faculty and wind up with spiritualism and if the patient lives it is only by accident. In all this you get the whole of the medical knowledge and not one particle of wisdom. You can see by this illustration, when I apply the piano to your body, that the doctors make nine-tenths of all the diseases through ignorance and when a cure is effected it is through the same medium. Take the piano as your body and yourself as No. 2 and then you will understand the illustration. Your body is the property of No. 2; No. 2 sets a great value on it and tries to keep it in order. Just return to the piano again. You will admit there is no wisdom or music in the piano of itself, nor in those you are afraid of. For if they knew how to execute music, it would be a pleasure to listen, but to have experiments tried on your instrument annoys you.

Your doctor may be a very clever fellow in his way, but having no ear for music, his honesty towards you does not compensate for your fears about your instrument. On the whole you are no better off for his wisdom. You see then no wisdom in the doctor and all the noise he made evinced an entire ignorance for the science of music. You turn him away and send for another physician. This one has more sagacity and less science, if you call making a disease science. And having more natural ear for music, he sits down to the piano and does not touch the music, so he shows more sagacity than the other. He commences running over the keys and strikes some very musical chords. As you listen you grow more calm. He says nothing about music or disease but leaves you some little homeopathic pills. Mother comes in and asks what the doctor thinks. You say, "He thinks I shall do very well." "What does he recommend?" "Nothing but pure air and says that since I have been confined to this room so long, so associated with my disease, I had better travel." "How would you like that?" "Very much." "Did he say where you had better go, North or South, or in foreign parts, or to some springs?" "No, but I will ask him the next time he comes." "Well, what do you think of your new doctor." "I think that he is a very intelligent physician." "But you know he is not an educated man." "Yes, but I like him and he has some ear for music, for when he sat down by the piano, he did not make me so nervous as the other doctor did." "But he is no musician." "Well, I do not know as he is, but he does not make me so nervous." "Well, if he can cure you I do not care if he is a quack for this learned science I am tired of. But what will doctor A say?" "I do not know or care. I want to get well and if Dr. B is a quack, I don't care." "We had better send for Dr. A and see what he thinks of it. You know it will not be polite to dismiss an old doctor and employ a quack." "I don't believe he is a quack." "Why, you know that all those who have not received diplomas are quacks." "Yes, and some who have." "We will send for Dr. A."

The doctor arrives a little nervous, removes his coat and seats himself by the piano. This disturbs the patient a little, which the doctor observes. Like all the rest of his wisdom he shows his ignorance in this; he looks very wise as though he had just discovered a gold mine, says, You seem a little disturbed. I understand the cause. You have had that young quack here and feel a little guilty I suppose, but you need not be alarmed. Persons as sick and weak as you are are very easily thrown off their guard, so cheer up and saying, What did the fellow say?, commences rapping the keys of the piano. Mary, sick from the fear of the instrument being injured, is silent. The doctor stops rapping and turning around to Mary says, "Do not be afraid; tell what he said." As soon as the doctor leaves the instrument, Mary becomes more calm and says that he did not say much of anything. The doctor sneeringly smiles and says, That is where he shows his wisdom. Did you know Mary that this fellow is a quack and one of the worst impudent imposters that ever lived?

(Mary) Did you ever meet him?

(Dr.) Meet him? Do you suppose that I would so degrade my honorable profession as to consult with a quack? Why Mary you must be insane and your mother too. If this kind of humbug is kept up, the medical science will pass into the hands of these quacks and any educated physician will be ashamed to be seen among such fellows. You have no idea of employing this fellow, have you?

(Mary) Mother seems to be inclined to let him try. I do not have anything to say. I want to get well.

(Dr.) Won't you ask your mother to step in? I want to see her alone a few minutes. (Exit Mary and enter Mrs. H.)

(Mrs. H.) Why Mary thinks she is not getting along as fast as she would like and seeing her running down, I thought I would do anything to please her.

(Dr.) Oh, then it is Mary's plan.

(Mrs. H.) Yes.

(Dr.) I thought you were a woman of more sense. I always considered you a woman of superior mind and when Mary told me that it was your move, I must say I was a little surprised, but it is all right now. The world is getting into a dangerous way, even our clergy are attacked. These spiritualists make war with the church and even pretend to cure disease. It is blasphemy to suppose that Christ cured as these fanatics do. It is astonishing that sensible men and women will run after such things. I should think the church ought to call a meeting and excommunicate any who countenanced such imposters in religion or in doctoring. For if things go on in this way, my practice will be ruined and then Parson W. will lose one of his best parishioners.

(Mrs. H.) I suppose you do not know what I pay him every year, besides his doctor's bill, which is always large as he has had two or three sick in his family ever since I have been in this town. You know I came here about the time when the first parson first settled. I was the first member admitted into his church after he came and was very friendly to his family which at that time consisted of three young ladies from fifteen to nineteen years old. They were pretty and in good health and would probably have been alive and well if they had followed my advice. I took the utmost pains to give them the best of Christian advice. You remember when they first came to town, they attended that great ball given by Mrs. D. and that the church did not approve of their attending it. If it had not been for me, those three young ladies who I now trust are in heaven, would doubtless have continued going to such places now if they had lived.

At this time Mary came in and said, Perhaps if they had continued going to balls and parties and had done as they wanted to, they would be alive now.

(Mrs. H.) Hush Mary, you do not know what you are talking about.

(Dr.) Mary, you are young and I was just relating the sad case of our parson's family. I had the care of these three young ladies and they placed entire confidence in my medical skill as well as in my Christian character. These qualities they appreciated and I still continue to practice in the family. I have seen six out of their eight children borne from this world of trouble to the world of spirits. All went just as I foretold and their mother will tell you if you ask her of the good advice I gave the eldest, when to all appearance she was as well as anyone. Yet I saw where the destroyer worked and warned her of her danger, but she could not or would not see it till it was too late. Then I had the comfort of reconciling them to Christ and soothing them till the Redeemer came and took them. So I have cared for six of their children till the Lord took them home. Mary, I am your friend and if you know when you are well off, take my advice, do not risk your life in the hands of a quack, for it is of more value than gold.

(Mary) I want to get well. You have been attending me for a year and when you began, I could go about and attend balls and enjoy myself; now I can scarcely sit up two hours a day.

(Dr.) Yes. I have seen all that and have been trying to counteract the disease which has been preying upon your system. I will be frank with you Mary. You have the seeds of consumption in your frame which I detected long ago. I noticed it when I first came and used to play your piano; I could see the real hectic come into your face.

(Mary) Did you call that hectic?

(Dr.) Certainly.

(Mary) Well, then you made it, for you used to make me so nervous that it seemed as though I should fly. (Exit the doctor)

(Mary) (Alone) Now I begin to understand myself, I can see that neither of the two knows anything about me, not half as much as I do myself. This physician has convinced me that he knows nothing, for he saw the hectic on my cheek while he was drumming on the piano, which was merely my nervous hatred of him. And if that is hectic I know what produced it. All this I can trace to the piano, for when I was left alone I was better and went out. But on my return some friends came in and I became very nervous for fear they would injure my piano—this acted upon me like a cold. When the new doctor came he could play and this made me calmer, for I was not afraid of his injuring the instrument. So between them both I have come to this conclusion: if my old physician was honest in his practice, he is ignorant of its effect and the world is no wiser for his knowledge. As for the young man he showed more good sense, if not knowledge, than the other, for his qualities of mind are more agreeable to me. I know this one thing; it requires no science to make a disease, nor cure it, if the patient can find where he has been deceived. I know how my disease came, so all I have to do is to give up all opinions and try to understand, so as not to be deceived by any person's opinion, when no proof is offered.

Now let us sum up the evidence in this case and see how much is science and how much science and wisdom and how much disease have been evinced. All will admit that the piano contained no intelligence and the doctor showed no knowledge. The lady was the victim of the doctor's opinion. Now as a judge, judging from the evidence, it is a case of pure malpractice. And as the law stands, it is right to murder if you have a diploma from a medical school. But we, as a judge and reporter of cases, have a right to suggest a more perfect law by which the people can correct their own evils without employing either of the two professions, as we believe them both in error. We will show what needs to be done for the benefit of mankind. You see the world is no wiser for the theories of either priest or doctor, if it is not a disgrace to science to call the practice of medicine a theory. Where can science stand to have a foothold on this humbug? It is between the cure and the disease. To stand there you must know what is to be done. Now I am going to show what is not generally understood, if at all. Everyone knows that we can all agree on everything made by hand. For instance, if you go into a machine shop, you have no controversy about what the articles there are called: a sleigh for instance, or anything else. So if there is any controversy, it is in regard to where there is an opinion and the trouble lies in the understanding, not in the thing known. So it is with disease. The idea that matter and mind make the man prevents man from understanding himself.

I will give my ideas of man. When we see man we look at him as a whole, not seeing anything separate and apart. So when he is dead as it is called, this ends his life. Whatever opinions we may have of what follows, we have no positive proof that anything remains. If there is any proof that man is anything after what is called death, the natural man has never been able to give that proof to the world. Now is there any proof of a wisdom higher than the natural man? All Christians will admit that there is, but when asked for proof, they quote the Bible as such. If you will not take this, then they can give no proof. So if the Bible is proof, then man's opinion is of no use, for to the Bible, he can add no force. Let us go to the Bible. It lies on my table. It does not speak if I open it. It gives me no proof. I find that there is an account of the creation of the world and a great deal of other matter. So not getting there an answer to my inquiry, I turn to Mr. A. He tells me that it contains certain great truths and finally explains it according to his creed. I call on Mr. B and he gives his creed and so on to Mr. W. All are very sure it contains an account of another world and each one is sure that his own creed is right.

I sit down and look at the whole and come to this conclusion: that if the Bible contains anything, the explanations must be false, for they are at war with each other. They are like the man and his wife, never at peace, except when someone comes in to separate them. So it is with the churches; they will fight with each other like animals, but let someone step in and call religion a humbug and they will all be down on that person as though he was the greatest infidel in the world. So you cannot get any proof in that way.

I will give you my investigations for belief I have none, but I will tell you what I do not believe. This is what Jesus did; he told not what he believed but what he knew was false. When I sit by a patient, I do not try to electioneer for any creed. If I made war with a Baptist, it is not to make him a Universalist, nor anything else. And if I made war with a Methodist, or any other religious sect, or an infidel, as I often do, it is not to convert them to my creed or belief for I have none.

You may ask what is my religious belief. I answer none. I know I am sitting here now and I know I was here yesterday and I expect to be here tomorrow. This last is my belief, founded on the knowledge that I am here now and was here yesterday. My senses can act upon a person at a distance without that person knowing it. This I know. I also know that the Bible never spoke of itself. I know that God never made anything that is attributed to man's wisdom. I know that all language is the invention of man. I know that God never made happiness or misery. I know that man makes both. I know that with God, might is not right, that God never spoke to one being more than to another. I know that no priest ever went into another world and never came from one. I know that all their talk is but the invention of man. I believe in no priest's opinion. I know that all their doctrines are all the invention of men and the cause of nine-tenths of the misery in the world. I know that the profession of doctor, like that of priest, is all the invention of this world and causes nine-tenths of the diseases. Both together make more misery than all other evils. I will tell you why I am opposed to all the above. It is because I know that all disease is what follows our belief and happiness is the result of getting rid of our belief. Every man is a part of God, just so far as he is Wisdom. So I will tell you what I know, not what I believe. I said I knew I was here. I worship no God except my own and I will tell you what He teaches me. In the first place He puts no restrictions on me, in fact He is in me and just as I know myself I know Him; so that I and God are one, just as my children and I are one. So to please myself I please God and to injure myself is to injure my God. So all I have to do is to please myself. Now as God and I are one so you and I are one and to please myself is to please you and to injure myself is to injure you, so just as I measure out to you I measure out to myself. As you and I are one, you and your neighbor are one and to love your neighbor as yourself is more than all the prayers made by all the priests in the world. I know that if I do by another as I would be done by in like circumstances I feel right, for I judge no man. I do not judge of myself, for my knowledge of this Wisdom is as plain to me as my senses.

To the world it is a belief, but to me it is wisdom that the religious world knows not of. If they did they would never crucify me as they do in their ignorance. So my religion is my wisdom, which is not of this world, but of that Wisdom that will break in pieces the wisdom of man. Man's wisdom is the superstition of heathen idolatry; all Science is at variance with it. I stand alone, not believing in anything independent of Science; so you can put me down as having no sympathy with any belief or religion concerning another world or in anything belonging to the Christian death. Neither have I any belief in the resurrection of the body. My death is this–ignorance. Life is wisdom, and as death is darkness or matter, so life is light or wisdom. All men have wandered away from light and believed in darkness. To destroy matter you introduce light or life.

I will illustrate. Suppose you are sitting in the dark, call that this world. Now as the light springs up where is the darkness? All will say, the darkness is gone. The light is the resurrection of this body or darkness. What becomes of it when the light rises? So it is with man. Man is an idea of matter or darkness, and as his mind or matter becomes lit or clairvoyant, the darkness of the idea of matter is gone, and he is in light that the wisdom of this world of matter or darkness has not. So light came into darkness and the darkness comprehendeth it not.

When I sit down by a patient, I come out of this matter or darkness and stand by the patient's senses which are attached to some idea of the wisdom of this world which troubles him. I retain my former man or matter and its senses. I also have another identity independent of matter, and I (knowing what is the cause of his misery) stand by the matter or belief of my patient and destroy his belief or the effect it has on his senses; then as the darkness or belief is lit up by the wisdom of Science, his darkness disappears and he rejoices in the light. The light leads him back to his health, from whence he had been decoyed by the blind guides spoken of in Scripture.

Here you have what I believe and what I disbelieve–the two are my law and gospel. By the law no one can be saved, but by the gospel of Truth; Science will have all saved, not from the Christian world but from this world of superstition and ignorance, saved for the greater truth that was prepared from the beginning of the world for all those who search and try to find it. You cannot go into the clouds to call it down, nor into the sea to call it up, but it is in you, in your very thoughts. It is not of this world, but of a higher state of matter that can penetrate through this earthly matter as light through darkness. As the senses are of the body of truth, they travel through the light, as a man with a lamp travels in the dark.

So it is not everyone who has a lamp with oil, nor is everyone wise who says he is so. But he is wise who can come up to the one in the dark, and lead him along through his dark wilderness of disease into the light of reason and health. Like the good man who had the hundred sheep and one wandered away in the dark, he left the ninety and nine that were in the light and found the lost one and restored him to the fold. Now let those who pretend to be shepherds of the sheep or of sick persons starving to death like the prodigal son for spiritual food, eating the husks of science, not the priest's food, go and guide them along to the father of health where they can eat and be glad and have music and dancing.

This was Christ's truth; he was the Good Shepherd; the people were his sheep and all who looked to him and listened to the true wisdom were saved from the errors of the priests and doctors. As Moses lifted up the serpents in the old Egyptian theology and creed and explained them, and all who looked on his explanation were healed of their errors that made disease, so Christ was lifted up, and all who understood were healed from the doctrines of the Scribes and Pharisees.

So in our day I hold up the serpent of creeds and doctors' theories and show the absurdity of their beliefs and all who understand are healed of their diseases.

November 1860

About the Dead and Spiritualism
[Originally untitled.] [BU 3:0642]

The idea that any physical demonstration comes from the dead is to me totally absurd. The dead, as we call them, are just like the living. Some leave our sight very ignorant and others enlightened on all sciences. As the science of life is the only one that has agitated the living, its progression is shown by the development of certain phenomena as in all other sciences. The fact that development goes on does not prove that the dead know anything about it, but the superstition of the living attributes all of such to the dead. This is because they want to believe what they cannot understand. Now what cannot be understood and yet is admitted is to the wise a stumbling block and to the conceited and ignorant, foolishness; but to the scientific it is a phenomenon to be accounted for in some law or wisdom not yet understood.

I have devoted my life to the development of all phenomena seemingly mysterious and, having a good share of the evil common to all men, I found it hard to divest myself of my old belief. Therefore, I have charity for others in the depths of their superstitions. My education never carried me into classical lore so I have never penetrated the early ages of superstition nor learned the ancient mythology. Yet what has come to us through tradition and learning has bowed down the human race with a yoke of untold power, so that man now reels and totters with burdens as though they were the works of the everlasting God, when really they are the works of superstition. All spiritual phenomena have been investigated by the learned whose prejudices are based on heathen mythology, admitting phenomena that they could not explain, so people have been deceived. Now after a silence of two-hundred years, this same old error that played the Salem witchcraft game makes its appearance asking to be heard as touching the dead. The mediums set themselves up as oracles to call up a spirit of the dead. Tests are given satisfactory for the skeptic's brain becomes the machine of his new superstition and they all become believers.

September 1862

Advertisement–Hair Restorative*
[LC 1:0224]

To the Unfortunate. Dr._____'s hair restorative.

We have received from Dr. _____ a recipe for making the human hair grow. Dr. ____ having been in the practice of curing diseases of every kind, and finding that all disease finds its growth in the fluids and that changing the mind was the cure; his attention was turned to the restoration of the hair. He found that as he restored the patient to health, the hair commenced growing and this induced him to investigate the causes.

Not wishing to affect the imagination of the patient, he often tried such remedies as would suggest themselves to him, till at last, he found restoratives in certain ingredients which act upon the head, produce softness and health in the parts where applied. This he kept a secret from his patients from the fact that he did not want to take their money while he as investigating this great remedy. And now that he is certain that its application will restore the hair in eight cases out of ten, when it is scientifically applied, he takes this method of presenting his discovery to the public. He sells the right to certain hair dressers on these terms, that they shall use the remedy on all their customers without exacting pay down, but with the agreement that in case the hair grows to the satisfaction of the parties, then the person shall pay the fee agreed upon by the parities. Ladies wishing their heads shampooed only pay the regular fee for such labor, and where there is no effect produced, no charge is made.

This right is to be confined to such persons as he sees fit to select for that purpose. He takes this method to secure the public, for many needing such an article are often humbugged by persons pretending to restore the hair by selling certain washes, and sponging the public out of their money.

Oct. 1860

All Men Have Gone Out of The Way–None Doeth Good
[BU 2:0381]

What did Jesus [Paul] mean to convey when he said all men had gone out of the way, that there was none doing good, no not one? It is generally understood that man had wandered away from God and had become so sinful that he was in danger of eternal banishment from the presence of God. And unless he repented and returned to God, he would be banished from His presence forever. This being the state of mankind, God, seeing no way whereby man could be saved, gave His only son as a ransom for the redemption of the world. Or, God made Himself manifest in the flesh and came into the world, suffered and died, and rose again to show us that we should all rise from the dead.

This is the belief of most of the Christian world. Its opposers disbelieved all the above story but death. They can't help believing that man dies and they have a belief that there will be some sort of hocus-pocus or chemical change, that the soul or spirit will jump out at death and still have an existence somewhere. After the soul is set at liberty, it can go and stay just where it pleases. Others believe it goes to God, there to be in the presence of God and be a saint and sing hallelujahs forever.

All the above embraces all of mankind's belief and in this belief they feel as though Jesus Christ was the author and finisher of their faith. These beliefs embrace all the horrors of a separation from this world and a doubt whether man will obtain that world beyond this life.

Now you see no person is in danger of this change but the sick, for if a person is well he can't be dead and if he does not die, he is in no danger of heaven or hell; therefore to keep well you keep clear of both. This was just about the same belief that the people had before Christ began his reform.

I will try to show that Jesus never taught one single idea of all the above but condemned the whole as superstition and ignorance. He not only condemned the idea of a world independent of man but proved that there was none by all his sayings and doings. He looked upon all the above theories or beliefs as false and tending to make man unhappy.

These beliefs Jesus came to destroy and establish the Kingdom of God or truth in this world or belief, for the two beliefs are both in ourselves and we become the servant of the one we obey. And the embracing of the true Christ is the resurrection from the dead, for the dead know nothing. Therefore to be dead in sin or ignorance is a separation from God or truth and to know God is to know ourselves, and this knowledge is in Christ or truth.

Now what is the difference between Christ's belief and the world's belief? Christ had no belief. His kingdom was an everlasting kingdom, without beginning or end. It is a science based on an eternal truth. It does not contain an opinion or belief. It is all knowledge and power and will reign till all beliefs and error shall be destroyed. The last error or belief is death or ignorance, and truth or science will reign till ignorance is destroyed. Then the son or law shall be subject to God.

1859

Am I a Spiritualist?
[LC 1:0008]

The question is often asked if I am a spiritualist. My answer is that I am not, after the manner of the Rochester rappings, but I am a believer in the spirits of the living. Here seems to be a difference of opinion. The common opinion of the people in regard to the dead I have no sympathy with, from the fact that their belief is founded on an opinion that I know is false; yet I believe them honest but misled for the want of some better explanation of the phenomenon. We see men, women and children walking around; by and by they pass away from us, and their bodies are laid in the earth.

This is one of the phenomena of the world. We look on the scene and pause. A cold icy sensation passes through our frame. We weep from our ignorance. We have seen the matter in a form moving about as though it contained life. Now it lies, cold and clammy, and our hope is cut off. Perhaps it is a son or a daughter in whom we had our hopes raised to the highest extreme of seeing them stand before the world, loved and respected for their worth, now gone forever. Doubts and fears take possession of our minds. We want to believe that they will know us, and in this state of mind, we often ask this lump of clay if it does know us, but no answer returns. We weep and repeat the question but no answer comes, and in a convulsive state of mind we leave and retire to some lonely spot to pour out our grief. Some kind friend tries to console us by telling us that our friend is not dead, but still lives, by talking what they have no knowledge of, only a desire that it may be so.

Their sympathy and ignorance mingle in a belief, and we try to believe it. This is the state of the people in regard to the dead. Their belief rises from the necessity of the case, but it keeps them in ignorance of themselves and all their lives subject to bondage.

Now where do I differ from all this belief? In every respect. My belief is my knowledge, my knowledge is my practice, and my practice gives the lie to all my former belief. I believed as all others did, but my theory and practice were at variance with each other. I therefore abandoned all my former beliefs as they came in contact with my practice, and at last followed the dictates of the impressions made on me by my patients. In this way I got rid of the errors of the world or my old opinions and found an answer to all my former opinions. These former opinions embraced all sorts of disease and ideas that contained error, disease and unhappiness which lead to death. The unraveling of my old opinions gave me knowledge of myself and happiness the world knew nothing of, and this knowledge I found could be taught to others. It teaches man that he is not in the body but outside of it, as much as the power is outside of a lever; and the body is to the soul as the steam engine is to the engineer, a machine without knowledge or power, only as it is given by something independent of itself.

January 1860

Analysis of Ideas by a Lecturer, The
[LC 1:0590]

A lecturer when he analyzes ideas is in a different atmosphere from the masses, and those who are led by public opinion instead of truth see no force in his reasoning. This is why public speakers are always lauded to the skies by one class of persons and cried down by another who cannot find anything worthy of praise in what they say. He who sees and comprehends spiritual ideas in illustrating them to the ignorant can readily find natural ones to match them. But if the minds of men are settled on an opinion in regard to a certain idea, then his illustrations of the truth by changing their minds will destroy their opinions. Hence, they, not seeing the basis of his reasoning, would misrepresent him. When a lecturer resolves the two ideas North and South into their spiritual elements, he gives a different picture of our national affairs from one who is bound by his opinions. He says that the North means freedom in every department of civil and national life: free press, free speech, free thought, free schools and free labor, while the South contains the opposite elements of slavery, oppression and ignorance. Also he says that so long as man and nations are in error, they must continue to change till their redemption from sin and ignorance is worked out and they arrive at truth.

Truth and error are identified in the powers which act upon man. They are always at variance and set men to fighting. And they can never exist in the same place or mingle any more than light and darkness, for one is the destruction of the other. Truth is from God and Science is its embodiment. Its attribute is freedom and the discussion of unsolved problems. Error is an offshoot from matter and consequently it must perish. Its representative is slavery and its effect is to keep man in darkness and suppress all discussion. These two principles under different names are in every person and keep up a continual warfare to get possession of the individual and have charge of his actions. When reason is under the control of error, man gets up false issues and tries to deceive himself as to the real facts, but when guided by truth, he reasons from principle whose demonstration destroys error. A child seeing no sense in science is opposed to it and if left to himself would become indolent and brutal in intellect, but spurred up by truth, shakes off the earthly element and rises into a higher order of intelligence. Under the light of wisdom, man necessarily develops himself, and as truth and error cannot live in the same mind at peace, when the man of truth has fought and conquered the ignorant man, he finds his freedom or his separation from the man of error. But each has its respective ideas that continue the battle on a lower scale. For instance, science, annoyed at the idleness of ignorance, sees that its contentment is a stumbling block to wisdom, so it sends an idea into the domain of ignorance which stirs up discontent. And parties spring up and array themselves against the truth; like individuals, they are of mixed motives and show their position towards the truth by their acts. Error being a step higher than ignorance rouses it into action and then seeks to enslave it.

Science is the friend of ignorance but being spiritual cannot be seen, so it has to act through error on ignorance. Error seeing that it works for another power than itself is jealous and seeks to deceive ignorance, that it may still hold it in bondage. So it misrepresents the arguments of science and by incorrect version renders them absurd. Then science goes off and seeks a home in a far country where it can develop itself. This led our pilgrim fathers to cross the ocean and settle in the wilderness in a climate where no idle or ignorant people would follow to molest them in their right of worship. Thus New England was settled by those stern followers of science who sacrificed all ease and pleasure for the truth, while the indolent and aristocratic preferred a milder climate and more fertile soil where they could rule without so much labor. Therefore in our country these ideas separated and took different localities. Those who loved power settled south, while those who were industrious, ingenious and enterprising and cared not for power remained North.

So the land was divided and the division was spiritual and it could be seen in the corresponding dissensions of men. Ignorance not knowing the cause tries to smother or subdue the evil. And by its measures of encroachments and conciliation stirs up hatred, for while freedom and slavery are the real combatants, men cannot stay their passions till the battle is over and one is victorious. The hatred is not towards those for whom it is felt. It is the stern and resolute opposition of freedom against tyranny that stirs up the evil of slavery in men's minds and rouses feelings of patriotism and hatred of wrong in others. Every one capable of reasoning stands somewhere between science and ignorance on all disputed questions. He either inclines towards freedom or slavery, and when they are at war, he will find himself forced to fight on the side where he belongs. In working out universal freedom, science has never revealed its identity, for it has no party or locality and is only known as a missionary. But it dwells in every heart and rules the destinies of nations. Its power is felt by both parties alike in an individual and a nation and controversies spring up in regard to its character. That which is fighting for error maintains itself by keeping truth out of sight or in a mystery and taking the whole field itself.

This splits the party and men come forward who will not agree to such extremes of error. They learn from wisdom that the principle of wisdom carried out to its extent will free man from mental, moral and human slavery. And likewise that slavery unresisted in power would subject man to every kind of servitude. Science will work out the principle of freedom and error, that of slavery. Error being a disease, its death is science. So to save its life, it tries to cripple science, and in the struggle, it destroys itself. Controversy is its destruction and to prevent that, it galls the masses by arbitrary measures and they complain. This starts another party who try to gain the ascendancy, making a political war. Science standing to the world as a friend, each party quotes it as authority from God. One quotes largely from the Bible that slavery is a divine institution. Another party seeing that progress is the order of the day opposes this as an error handed down from the dark ages. One believes that the masses are not fit to govern themselves; the other pretends to believe that the people are intelligent enough for self-government.

The rock on which they split is democracy, that being the mortar to hold the ideas together and build up the party. Each class wants to lead it. One tries to get control of the masses by appealing to their passions and love of domineering. The other attempts a more intelligent plan and tries to reason with them. Each party is composed of three elements and these form a trinity: Aristocracy, a love of power; Hypocrisy, inventing false issues and Democracy, the masses. These are the principles of one. The other stands up for the administration putting down the rebellion and freedom to all mankind. Science is an unknown power in the matter and acts silently on the leaders. Neither of the parties at the present time appeals to the true idea at issue. Yet, it is working itself into light and will bring about the destruction of slavery. One party at the South honestly believes that slavery is a divine institution and there are many such at the North. But the North being more under the element of truth, it is more enlightened and thus the minds are divided. Whenever the true issue is revealed and admitted, then the slavery party will go down; but until it is understood in all its length and breadth, the party will be popular. All those minds ranging from the brute to the higher intellect will show their grade in talking. No man of narrow mind can appreciate freedom. He may admit it, but he cannot understand it, so he is as easily led into error as truth.

It is the same with disease. When ignorance is roused to action, it is confined in error which being disease struggles to keep ignorance in bondage. So when science, the friend of ignorance, attacks error, ignorance is frightened and not seeing science, it is deceived and compelled into submission and slavery by error. In this way, the priests retain their power over the people, the doctors over the sick and demagogues over the masses. Science is that still small voice that says to error, Thus far shall thou go and no further.

I have given the trinity of error in politics. I will now give it in disease: God, the father, the maker of arbitrary laws whose punishment is disease; the ignorance of man, the medium between the law and mankind; and the medical science which explains the other two. This is the trinity of superstition. I will give that of wisdom: Wisdom, Man and Christ or Science. Man being matter must pass through the wilderness of superstition or slavery to arrive at true wisdom or the father, for the worshippers of the true God are not in medical colleges nor in an aristocracy of wealth but in a heart free from man's opinions. To rebel against the God of man's opinions is to erect the kingdom of heaven in the temple of man's mind and write on it, To the living God or Science. To him shall every knee bow and every tongue confess that the only true religion of liberty is Science. In every civilized society, liberty and slavery divide society. In all barbarous nations, slavery is uppermost and their religion corresponds with their intelligence. It is the same in our country. Science and religion are not the same, they are considered separate and apart in character. Religion is cultivated by men of aristocratic principles and hypocritical motives and modified as men become religious. The former govern the world, but in the end the scientific man will reign. Whenever the intelligence of the masses can be approached by the scientific reasoning, then democracy will crumble to dust in respect to an idea that the people wish to investigate.

Take, for instance, religion; now it contains the same trinity that runs through all error. But let people become so enlightened that they will worship science as their God instead of man's opinion about God, then religion would prove by its works whether it be of science or opinion. Ignorance is the natural growth of matter. Out of ignorance comes error and science is the wisdom that will destroy both and put matter in a state of cultivation to become the medium of science. When the identity of science is acknowledged as much as that of matter, then it will be seen that every man is like an uncultivated wilderness inhabited by rude ideas which, like wild beasts, live on each other till a higher intelligence comes among them, subdues their savage ideas and introduces those of arts and sciences. Whenever these two classes of ideas come in contact with each other, a war commences which is kept up till the brutal party is subdued. The natural man having acknowledged that science has an identity outside of matter, working in man or matter preparing him for a higher capacity than the intellect of the brute, looks upon it as its teacher whose object is his own development.

The great error that stands in the way of this truth is this. Wisdom is not matter. It governs the brutes and all living things, but matter reasons as though itself was intelligent. Ideas governed by science and error are the material of man. One set are matter and are like building materials; the other set are spiritual and are not visible, but they dwell in the temple of the material ideas and exercise an unseen influence on matter, which matter attributes to its own intelligence. This false reasoning makes one world, science the other. The scientific man knows that the man of opinion is not a developed man though he is a step higher than the brute and his intellect ranges from the brute to the man of wisdom. Because they are all of God, we place them on the same platform. This is a mistake, for if it was so, then there would be no chance for improvement. If we class intellect as children without regard to age or color and let the standard of development be wisdom, then we should see old people very young in wisdom and young ones old. Principles are the foundation of the scientific man. He is not in matter but dwells in wisdom, while to the man of matter, he is like a man who once was and now is not. This error arises from the fact that man places his wisdom in matter and cannot see either intelligence or matter outside of himself. Therefore, his wisdom is in his light and his light is in his body. If his body is full of darkness, he cannot see any light but the false one of darkness. If however, his body is of science, he is full of light. And looking upon his body, he sees it as a thing or idea like any other idea that can be changed and destroyed, and he is not affected by what the world calls destruction of the body. This is the wisdom of Christ which Jesus professed; therefore, he, like other scientific men, was to the world a mystery.

March 1863

Another Conversation About Matter*
[BU 3:0498]

Characters: P. P. Q. is a learned man of the world in regard to matter.

(P. P.) Before commencing I must know what we are going to reason about, if you won't admit your own premises it is not worthwhile to reason. So I will hear you state that question.

(Wise Man) I suppose you do not deny the existence of matter do you?

(P. P.) That depends on circumstances. (W. M.) What do you mean by that? (P. P.) I mean to ask if I must admit anything you say because you say it. (W. M.) No. (P. P.) Then let me ask you a few questions before we begin if you please. Shall I? (W. M.) Oh yes. (P. P.) Do you admit of a wisdom without matter or is matter the first cause or wisdom, or is one the cause of the other or are they both the same? (W. M.) You mix up so many things in one it is impossible to separate them. I do not mean to confound the two together. (P. P.) What do you mean by the two? (W. M.) Mind and Matter. (P. P.) What do you mean by mind & matter, won't you separate them so I shall know how to follow you. (W. M.) You see that chair? (P. P.) Yes. (W. M.) That is matter. (P. P.) Tell me what mind is. Finis.

Sept. 1861

Conclusion.

From the abrupt termination of this learned discussion it is supposed that the parties could not agree.

Answer to an Article in the N. Y. Ledger
[LC 2:1065]

Mr. Editor:

I see an article in your paper of August 9, 1860, taken from the New York Ledger, in which the writer gives a minute account of a very remarkable case of clairvoyance or vision, as it is called, in which Dr. E. W. came in possession of a fact that he could not have received through his ordinary senses. Cases of this kind are frequently occurring and are accounted for on the principle of an overruling Providence interesting itself in some foolish trouble that man has got into. Just as though Dr. E. W.'s son must be returned to his father by the destruction of a young lady! As though God took this way to show his power! Oh! Vain man! How long is God to be misrepresented by such ignorance and superstition!

The time will come when this heathen superstition will give way to a higher development of God's wisdom, and God will no longer be made the cause of so much misery in this world of error. I accept the doctor's account of what he saw. I have no doubt that it took place to the very letter and he is responsible for the phenomenon. I can account for the phenomenon on the grounds of superstition and show just how it was brought about and thousands of other like cases.

It is not denied that persons can throw themselves into a nervous state to that degree that a scene that is troubling them can be seen and described to perfection. I have been excited upon some cases of disease so much that I have seen a whole scene as this doctor did, but under another state of belief. And if my belief had taken place, the opposite effect would have taken place. I will state a case for the benefit of the profession.

A lady, being very sick and unable to walk, had great confidence in my power to heal and wished me to visit her. But owing to engagements I could not leave. So I sent her husband a letter saying that I would visit his wife for one week and on Sunday between the hours of eleven and twelve, I would make her rise from her bed and walk. In two or three days I received a letter saying that the lady was made very nervous the night she received my letter but was better the next day. On the day I was to make her walk, I told some of my friends that I would have three or four strangers there to witness the scene. The Sunday following the scene I received a letter stating that the lady arose from the bed at the time named and walked into the dining room and returned, also that there were three persons from a neighboring town witnessing the scene.

Now what I wish to say is this. In the case of the lady I made walk, I was aware of my effect on her, and my mind acted upon hers to bring about the phenomenon I produced. As the time drew near for her to walk, I, of course, grew more anxious to have my cure accomplished, so at the hour appointed I was sitting alone and the scene was just as I described it to my friends. Now if I had believed that the lady was going to die with consumption, for that was what the doctors called her disease, I have no doubt but that I could have killed her just at the time appointed, that is if I had known that she was very sick and that a certain day in a certain month had a great effect on consumption and I feared that she would have died on that day.

I have no doubt that my own mind directed by ignorance would have produced the phenomenon as the doctor did in the case of the young lady. I have no doubt that from the ignorance and superstition of the doctor, his mind affected the young lady as mine did the sick lady but with this difference. I knew what I was doing and he did not, but each belief acted upon the persons just according to direction. The doctor, from his superstition, saw in this young lady, or thought he saw, the image of his wife. So the very first impression made upon her was bad. It would make her nervous. Then it was followed by remarks to her parents so as to get their minds all centered on their child. This was enough to get her mind into a nervous state, just fit for the phenomenon that the doctor had laid out. As his mind was watching the young lady, she became more nervous and at the time that the phenomenon occurred, no doubt but the doctor's own mind was tormenting her and his own soul by the superstition of his own brain. Now put the doctor in possession of the science of God or truth and this would not have taken place. This science gives man the consciousness of life independent of matter and in this life is the operation of principles and the action of thought which shows itself in the natural world in some form of disease or misery. This life contains the reality and here is where we must seek for the causes of our own troubles.

And as we investigate it, we learn that to think wrong towards anyone is as much a sin as to do or say the same; and in certain cases where there is much excitement, its effects are the same. The influences making our happiness or misery are, in either case, spiritual, but in one they are of God and in the other they are the inventions of man; and if we direct these towards others, they are affected by them. With this knowledge, the doctor would have felt that he injured the young lady and dishonored himself by the process of mind that he kept up. To account for the similarity which he observed in the young lady and his deceased wife, he sacrificed her with consumption and directed the parents to do the same. So the life of this young lady was surrounded by enemies and hypocrites who brought about the sad phenomenon which they had made.

August 1860

Answers to Questions Asked by Patients, Showing How the Sick Reason About Disease
[BU 2:0449]

(Q.) Why do you not rub your head when sick? (Ans.) Because I have nothing to rub out. Now here are the two modes of reasoning. The natural man never sees that the misery follows his acts. When he reasons it is all action with him and he never dreams that reaction is the true wisdom, so the natural man is courageous at first, for he does not see his real enemy. His real enemy is the natural result of his acts, which is reaction, the true wisdom that will always measure to action its own measure.

The wise man sees the wisdom of the thought before it takes effect and destroys it. When the patient asked the question, he had the answer in the question for his ignorance was what I was rubbing out, so if he had known that he would not have wanted any rubbing. I will illustrate this mode of reasoning by Jeff Davis and Abraham Lincoln. Davis' wisdom is all action, not having the element of true wisdom or reaction in all his acts. He is ambitious and wants his own way; this makes him a one-idea-man, all go-ahead without wisdom. His will is law and man must obey. As he sees no reaction or wisdom, he shows courage, but it is the effect of ignorance. Lincoln does not reason, his acts are governed by the people, and his wisdom is in knowing the laws and in putting them into execution according to the will of the people. He is not a dictator but a servant whom the people have chosen. Here is the difference. Davis is a dictator without wisdom or courage. Lincoln is a servant who has respect for his master, the people. Knowing that his acts are the wishes of the people, he is strong; he does not boast, for boasting is cowardice. Now when Davis sees the reaction of his folly, he will flee, for his wisdom is of this world, not of science; for if he had the science that action and reaction are equal, he would have seen that he was building up a tower that would fall and crush him in the ruins of his own wisdom. He did indeed show some spirit when his tower was rising, but when the winds of the Northwest blew upon it, it commenced to tumble, the rocks and mortar began to fall and he trembled, for his reason had departed from him. His friends forsook him and he tried to find a place in the mountains to hide himself, for the day of retribution had come and woe to them to whom it shall fall.

The last is a prophesy foretold the latter part of April 1861.

Are We Governed by Our Belief?
[BU 3:0638]

Are we as individuals governed by any one belief? My answer is, we are not; yet I once thought otherwise and my practice proved the folly of such a belief. Man is the embodiment of public opinion and science is the embodiment of God's wisdom. Each embodiment comes to the world or man's senses through a medium and the medium being man, we give to him the praise. Here is a great mistake, for we are liable to get into trouble by this error. The wisdom of the world is like an ocean surrounded by inlets, harbors and false lights to decoy the traveller into the land of the priests who come and give an account of their pretended country, and men believe their story. The question is, is it his own eloquence that affects us, or does the effect come from some other source? I say it comes from some other source and he is the medium of evil to destroy man's happiness and when we listen, we listen to public opinion in regard to the truth of what he says. So it is with science. The man who talks the science or truth is one thing and the truth is another, and if the man was out of existence, the truth would be the same, but the science would not be known. It is so with every belief.

Now what I say to the sick is not mine as a man's, but as a man, I speak the truth that I have received, not from man's opinion but from those who have been deceived by man's opinion and carried away captive into slavery or bondage, unable to escape. Their groans, sighs and trouble are their language and their misery is the penalty of their belief. Being misled by false theories they believe a lie thinking it true. This belief makes one hemisphere and science the other. So man is only an agent or servant to one or the other, and his pay is what he can get from the masses.

There have always been men, like missionaries, trying to get the people to go to each place. The idea body is the medium or earth upon which they work. So belief or opinion is one man, wisdom and science is the other. The body or idea called man is the medium of both. The man of belief puts his knowledge in the earth or body; the man of science puts his belief in God or wisdom and as he reduces his wisdom to practice it is called science. So that neither of the two is seen, only in their works. The man of opinion is seen through mediums pretending to be wise; the man of wisdom is seen correcting the errors of the man of opinion. One's labor is to make mischief and trouble; the other's is to establish God's kingdom or truth in the earth or natural man, thus driving out the old man of opinion and introducing the new man of science. This was the mission of Jesus and all those that make war with opinions by the introduction of science. This is my whole aim and what I am laboring for. So I speak not as a man of opinions but from what I know.

September 1862

Aristocracy and Democracy–I
[LC 1:0598]

There are two opposite principles in society named Aristocracy and Democracy, but this is not all. The former always dictates and seeks to govern the latter which being ignorant cannot rule. By means of hypocrisy, it governs the masses, but it is not the only governing agent. Another element opposed to it also acts upon the minds of men. Science dictates to no man but proves all things, while the religion of science embraces all things. Neither of these contains that love of power and deceit which distinguish the two I have named. Priests govern the people through hypocrisy, but science requires not even a belief to establish itself and when it is understood its fruits are universal freedom and charity. Since it works out freedom, science is unpopular, for that, united with democracy, forms a perfect system of slavery. Disease is another combination of the same elements. The leaders of the medical schools, through the hypocrisy of their profession, deceive the people into submission to their opinions, while the democracy forge[s] the fetters which are to bind them to disease. Science which would destroy this bondage is looked upon as blasphemy when it dares oppose the faculty, and religion has no place in the medical science.

Likewise in the church, the religion of Jesus which is Science is never heard, for it would drive aristocracy out of the pulpit and scatter seeds of freedom among the people. Nevertheless, the religion of Christ is shown in the progress of Christian Science, while the religion of society decays in proportions as liberal principles are developed. Man's religion labors to keep Science down in all churches North and South by suppressing free discussion, for aristocracy will not hear anything tending to freedom. It wishes to govern democracy as it always has done by arbitrary power, for the masses are always in slavery either black or white. African slavery is recognized by state laws and these are endangered by striking at the constitution; therefore aristocracy opposes any discussion of slavery in politics, while democracy dutifully opposes any discussion of the same in the pulpit. This affects the white slaves at the North. So nothing was so tenderly handled before the war as slavery. There was no freedom of speech allowed unless it be in favor of the extension of slavery. This was white slavery and the opinions of democracy ruled. All men are more or less democratic for they are not wise enough to govern themselves and rush into aristocracy from fear. A man who denies all law and vindicates unrestrained freedom must depend on some arbitrary power.

Slavery is to elevate democracy but aristocracy aims to keep it in subjection. It is easy to distinguish them. One appeals to the people in their own element of prejudice and passion and tries to convince them that the other party seeks to enslave them. Science tries to open their eyes; it shows them how their masters are binding them, but this requires reason and they will not listen to it. So they continue to bind themselves with their own burden till they can't help themselves; then, kneeling down, they kiss the hand that oppresses them. Democracy will not apply as a name for liberty; it is counterfeit and deceives many. Throw away all doctrines that deceive or enslave man and democracy will break from its leaders and come forth in the field of science and religion.

February 1863

Aristocracy and Democracy–II
[LC 1:0595]

[Originally untitled, this article appears prior to *Aristocracy and Democracy I.* in the Library of Congress microfilm. –*Ed.*]

Mankind are governed by two principles acting together and I will call them Aristocracy and Democracy. These terms are used in describing political parties, but their real meaning is not brought out. These elements always act together, for either alone is harmless. Democracy is the ignorance of the masses and serves as a medium for Aristocracy to work through; this is shown in the demagogue. There are what is called the rich aristocracy, but they are not the ones who rule the nation. They accumulate money and are governed by the same popular demagogue, when it is for their interest. The scientific element has no identity as a party and is shown in opposition to all parties. Aristocracy and Democracy I call the two extremes of one party. They are like the serpent which when killed or cut in pieces comes together and lives. They are found in all sects and parties under different names. In religion they are in the priest and people and again in the physician and masses. In both cases Aristocracy reigns over Democracy and there can never be a change until these extremes are severed, for Democracy is the body of Aristocracy. Cut them asunder and each will find the other. It is false that they are opposed to each other as it is popularly believed. Wisdom is riches so the scientific man is rich and as money is a figure of wisdom, it is Aristocracy of money as opposed to Democracy. So it is, for no man with money wants to give it away and become poor and neither does a wise man want to lose his wisdom and be ignorant. They are both opposed in these instances and there cannot be but one mind about it.

Men divide on the application of the word. Aristocracy of wisdom is thought to be the same as that of party when one is the counterfeit of the other. Teach man how to reason and he will free himself from the aristocracy of party, for this is the head of that serpent that has deceived the world. Give man wisdom and he will easily detect him and find out his abiding place. This spurious aristocracy is always found drumming up democracy, feeding the food of envy, exciting their passions and telling them how they are oppressed by the rich. The fraternity of divines is also of this serpent. They are constantly appealing to the rich to take care of the poor and instruct them for the reputation of the church. But the worse representative of this class is the aristocratic physician for he has entire control of the democracy. These three types of one serpent are the same in power and each leads the masses. Let them be exposed by wisdom and their influences vanish.

If men questioned opinions, they would see that their trouble arises from their beliefs. Ask a person what diphtheria is. The answer is, a collection of white sores in the throat always indicate the presence of this disease. Here a disease is admitted outside of a phenomenon. The invisible diphtheria is the genuine and the white sores come from it. This reasoning admits that the name diphtheria is the disease and the effect seen is what follows the name. Admitting the effect, man looks for the cause and finding no name, he names the effect which makes a cause in his belief. If man knew what produced the effect, he would have given no name but would have shown the causes. This would end names and stop diseases and then cause and effect would be the things to reason about. Then man would look back of the phenomenon to learn what produced it. For instance, if any one happened to have a discharge of water from the head, he would reason that it came from some little excitement on the mind which he could not name. But now in such a case, he would say he had the catarrh and this is the name of the effect which we believe is disease.

Throw away names and we get rid of disease and then the great necessity of the medical faculty vanishes. There is no need of naming every effect on the body. The only good done is to make a thing corresponding to the name. Destroy the word consumption and the effect that gives rise to it would never appear. I will show how to make the word intelligent to a person. Teach a man that a certain amount of clothing and pure air is necessary for his health, that low-studded rooms, exposure to night air and chilly east winds are very dangerous, also that bad blood, narrow chest and the habit sleeping and sitting in a certain position are injurious, and when he believes it all, he is certainly two-thirds in consumption. To cure him is to take him away from his error and convince him by your own life that the whole belief is false and the evidence brought forward is the cure. To set people reasoning about the folly of such opinions is to drive disease out of existence. If the people ridiculed and laughed at the ignorance of the profession, the doctors would hide their heads and cease their loud talk.

Start a lie. The people give it an impulse; it spreads and circulates through the country till everyone is satisfied that it is true. That is the success of a lie. Now if the people would not repeat the words of a physician, admitting that they are from superior knowledge, this quackery would end. The idea of disease is installed into the minds of the people as firmly as secession is at the South. And it is as hard to convince man that his disease is of his own make as it is to convince the Southerners that they are the authors of their present misery. Look into the newspapers and observe the manner of accounting for certain phenomena. The most absurd stories are given in explanation of remedies as though there was real efficacy in the application used. A person afflicted with the rheumatism is obliged to apply the sting of a bee to the parts affected as a sure means of restoration. Then follows an explanation which is merely an opinion. I know from my own experience that the word rheumatism applies to some effect on the body but men take the effect for the cause.

I will describe a case. Two persons get into an excitement and become heated up with passion and fear. The excitement does not pass off and each returns home feeling sharp pains in his joints. One takes no thought of it, the other is alarmed and they both send for a doctor. One sends for an old school allopath who tells him he has acute rheumatism. The other sends for a quack who, knowing nothing of the disease, tells him that there is no serious trouble. He merely got excited and is heated and inflamed and as the excitement abates, the blood will cool and he will be well. He told the cause; therefore there was no need to name the phenomenon. The other did not tell the cause but named the phenomenon. Here is a name of something that you are ignorant of which has an existence independent of the person who caught it. Here is where the error lies. Each person was the cause of his own trouble; both would admit it when explained, but in one case, the cause was not alluded to, while another idea, the invention of man, was introduced. Drive the name of disease out of the world, then remedies will cease and men will find that their troubles are within the control of their own wisdom.

1863

Assassination of President Lincoln, The–I
[LC 1:0603]

The people are once more called upon to reflect upon the natural results of this accursed rebellion against Freedom and Liberty. The assassination of President Lincoln is nothing but the natural spasm or convulsion of a wicked rebellion which is determined to destroy itself like an insane man, and all the evils arising are the natural result of the disease. The murder of the President is the working of this evil that has taken possession of man and has deluded the higher intelligence of his soul and now the people are called to their several places of worship to pour out their grief in behalf of the country's loss of one whom they loved and respected. But how stand those who are under the cloud of suspicion? Do they feel the sting of reproach that they, through their aid, have given countenance to the wicked act? No. They drop a hypocritical tear and say, "Well the party is not responsible for the act," but wisdom will hold them responsible and sooner or later they will reap their reward. When the principle of freedom bursts forth, they will see that individual acts are nothing but the natural result of principle and that the principle is responsible for the individual acts whether right or wrong.

God is responsible for his acts and no man can point to any one act of wisdom and say it is wrong. It is not for error to erect the standard as to what is right or wrong, for wisdom proves itself. I will take the case in question, the death of the President. In regard to Mr. Lincoln or Booth, as men, I have nothing to say; both were mediums of a principle and each placed himself where he belonged. Mr. Lincoln was the medium of the great principle of Freedom and Liberty, and this cloud or influence has been carried along through darkness of slavery and the sea of blood till he has reached the land of Liberty. Here was where the cloud stopped and the cloud of error formed round the different parties and began to burst forth and there collect its sundered fragments and cry for peace and compromise.

In this vacuum of hesitation, slavery is never easy because its life is its destruction and it always does the very thing it ought not to do for its own defense, yet it does the very thing it ought in order to destroy its life. As the President, being the medium of the people, had no motive to destroy individuals, it hesitated to carry into the effect the law of error. But slavery does not reason; it goes for "an eye for an eye and a tooth for a tooth," so it must do something and the worst thing it could do. So as all the elements were resting, as it were, on their arms, this cursed serpent crawled up from its den and struck the deadly blow at the President just at the time when he was the most popular with all the world. What was killed by the murderers' blow, Liberty or Slavery? Let some give the response, President Lincoln's body was not the body of the principle, and although slavery may kill the body, yet when it has done that, it has done all it can. But truth and Liberty cannot only kill the body or party of error but its very soul, and can cast it into hell.

God holds man as well as nations and parties responsible for their acts and the Democratic Party will be held responsible for the assassination of Mr. Lincoln, and the Liberal Party will hold them responsible, not as individuals but as a party, for Booth is nothing. Execute him and what do you destroy? Not the evil, for another may do the same. Now make the principle responsible and then see who will back it up. As long as the principle can strut around, it fears no danger, but strike at the principle and then you will see signs of mincing and uneasiness in the party. In this way, you destroy the evil and the effect will cease. This is what is now on trial, whether the principle shall have an identity in this country or whether it shall be destroyed. Slavery cannot find fault to be tried by its own laws. It has defined treason and how it shall be punished. Now as they have through their wicked acts laid themselves liable to the law, let President Johnson say to this rebellion as Jesus said to the Jews, I come not to destroy the law but to fulfill it and not one jot or tittle of the law shall pass till slavery and all its party shall be destroyed, for their souls are all against the law of God and man and cast this wicked generation of ideas into outer darkness. There will be a new heaven or principle wherein all can worship at the altar of Liberty where one shall not say to another, you shall not be free, but all shall have the privilege of freedom and the right to worship God according to their own conscience.

April 1865

Assassination of President Lincoln, The–II–President Lincoln's Death

[LC 1:0605]

The assassination of President Lincoln brings forth some grave ideas in regard to whether it was the design of God or solely the work of man. It is queer to hear the adherents of both these doctrines argue about what neither know anything of, except as their opinions, and I listen to find the point of the argument that they wish to prove, but I only hear one tell what he believes and the other in turn gives his ideas on the subject. One believed in fore-ordination and pointed to the Bible as proof. The other discarded the idea that God had any hand in the matter at all and left it altogether with man.

Differing with both, I will give my ideas which are based upon what I think every candid person will admit. Freedom is opposed to slavery, this all will admit. Now is freedom an element of intelligence or does it belong to our senses? Is it a truth that exists as a principle, the same as mathematics? Is it not like confined steam or anything that wants its liberty? Admit that liberty is wisdom as far as it goes and you have one point to reason from. Suppose wisdom to be an element and every act to come within its knowledge, so that nothing can transpire without its knowledge. Suppose everything is within this atmosphere of wisdom, as your body for instance, and if anything touches your body, your wisdom knows it. Everything that is seen by the natural eye existed without wisdom before it assumed a body. The chicken existed before it burst through the shell and had an identity and showed life, though when it came out of the shell, it assumed a new character. Now had the egg been destroyed before the chicken was hatched, would the idea chicken be destroyed to wisdom? I say no.

You hold a bullet in your hand. If you let go of it, the bullet will drop. Now wisdom knows that the bullet will fall and the holding of it one minute or more will not change the law or truth which knows that it will fall. Just as you drop the ball, someone catches it. Now is the law of gravitation changed? No, but you as a being cannot see outside your senses, that is, that there is any wisdom independent of what mankind knows and so you cannot see any wisdom outside the bullet. And if you try to account for its falling, you only make it less clear. In the fate of the President, men try to prove that he is alive after admitting that he is dead. Now he is neither alive nor dead, but if he is dead, then wisdom is not wisdom, for if you admit that the President had any wisdom and then assert that he is dead, you contradict yourself. Let us look at it in another light.

I said freedom was an element of wisdom. No principle can make itself manifest to man unless it assumes some form. Take the idea of gravitation. If there was nothing to fall, you could not prove the principle, so Freedom must have some medium by which to prove itself and so it works through man. Men may be compared to checkers. Liberty represented by Lincoln and Slavery represented by Davis are the players, and either Freedom or Slavery, the stakes. Every person who has any great interest in the great game reflects himself on the board. Now there is no intelligence in the checkers but the wisdom is in the players. The President is the party representative of Freedom and as all loyal persons are concentrated on him, it is not strange that he should play with hesitation and caution lest he lose, for slavery is a keen player and a hard element to contend with and often gains a point and then loses it.

At last Freedom gains the advantage and slavery has to yield. This excites the public and brings on discussion and discordant feelings and everyone gives his opinion and someone attacks the President and destroys the medium or body. But he is not in the body but in the principle Freedom with the people and feels the advantage gained over slavery and rejoices with the people as much as any of us. Wisdom no longer requires that he should play the game but lets another person assume the office while the President sits, looks on and enjoys the fruits of his labor. I look upon the change that has taken place in that way. He has finished his work and given up to another who will put the law in force on the traitors. Not that he has lost anything, for I cannot think that he has.

I have no death but the death of error. Wisdom cannot die. Slavery he destroyed, and he reigned till he had brought all the enemies of freedom under his feet and the last enemy was slavery. Now he delivers up the keys to his successor that his wisdom shall be all in all. Now the identity of Abraham Lincoln as a man was his own, independent of the people, and the elements of Freedom and Slavery were so evenly divided in him that he was sensitive to the outside impression of each party or element, and had he professed more of either element, either of slavery or freedom in him, it would have made matters worse. But the combination of the two made him sensitive to all feelings of each element and he was directed by the true element of freedom and justice which made every move and saw the effect thereof. He was not a man of party but of principle. Now since he has established the principle, it needs another element to gather up the grain of his threshing and burn up the chaff, and that task has fallen into Andrew Johnson's hands.

April 1865

Bad Belief Worse than None
[BU 3:0627]

When a person can be conscious of his senses being in two places at the same time, then he is in that position to see and feel man's trouble. The ignorance of this is the cause of our misery, for it is far better never to have had a belief than to have one that makes man miserable. For the fool has no belief; therefore he looks for nothing and is not disappointed. The man who has just sense enough to work up into a belief is living in a world of trouble in fear of something that may destroy his life, so he lives a life of misery and is all the time subject to death. Now convince man that his own existence, as he thinks he is, is death to a truth, and this truth will teach him that although his body may be here and talking, the real man may be in some other place and see and know what is going on and enjoy it, while the idea body with all the knowledge and beliefs may be sitting and talking to persons who are sitting by him.

Suppose you have just left a battlefield where you have been a principal actor. You enter a public house, take a seat and someone enters with a paper giving an account of the battle written by someone who picks up his facts from public rumor, so the crowd commences giving their opinion. You know that nearly all that is said is false and you are in two places at once, or in one place and out of it, for wisdom is not a place. Your wisdom is in their ignorance. This is a place, for it is surrounded by error of the truth. You are in their error or darkness, but they cannot see your light or wisdom. Here are two states, as they are called. You know that you are sitting in the room with the rest of the company and you know what they say is false. Your knowledge of that fact is based on your wisdom, so your senses and life are based in wisdom. This is one place. Their knowledge is based on their wisdom which is someone's opinion. This is the other place. You hear all that they say is false, but you are not with them nor are they with you. One is a place and the other, a condition. Your life and senses are in your wisdom but you have another life that is not known to the company. This life is dead to your wisdom, for you are alive in truth. In the life of true wisdom, there is no disease, but disease is the life of opinion. The company were dead to the truth. So when you began to let your light shine, they were afraid and would contradict because their life was in danger. But as you made your truth known, you had risen from the dead to them; but to you the dead did not rise but the living came from the dead. So you could say to all who believed, Let the dead bury their dead, but you who have received the truth follow me in the truth.

There is a process of reason that can bring a man into that state that he can tell these two states, one out of matter and one in it. When you know a thing, you can see where you were before you know it, but what you do not know contains one identity. For instance, a person in a waking state thinks that he is an individual himself and that he is just where he thinks he is and nowhere else. This is the natural man. He is like a man in the dark who thinks that he is the only one who has any light, and his light being darkness, he is led by a light that is not admitted to be one till his darkness is swallowed up, yet he thinks he has never changed. So he lives and dies every day and never knows that his identity has ever changed, for his progression is so slow that to him all things change, while there is no change in him. This is the man of opinions. The man of wisdom can see that he has changed from what he once believed to be true, but also can see that his wisdom was based on opinions of others and that when he has the evidence within himself, he knows that this evidence was not in his opinion. Spiritualism is based on a belief of what we want to have proved. We want to believe or have evidence that our friends are still living and know what we are about, so we consult a medium to tell us what we do not know. There are some who contend that they do know. Still they are all the time getting communications to prove what they believe. This shows a doubt. At another time they say their friends are present with them and know when they are writing a letter to them. The tree is known by its fruits. If I wish to write a letter to a person who is looking over my shoulder, of course he knows what I want, and if I believe him dead, would I write to the person who stood by me and then send it to a medium to get an answer? This is done by those who profess to believe, but if my friend sees the question, he of course must answer it while I write it, but to me the answer is not known.

May 1862

Belief of Man
[LC 2:0755]

The word man, according to the world, embraces the two ideas of matter and spirit. This I think will be admitted by Christians and all who do not believe in annihilation. The wisest reasoner commences with man in matter and reasons him into spirit, always keeping him the same man and only changing from a natural to a spiritual body. The mystery is what to do with the natural senses belonging to the natural body. Some say they die, and others, that they are lost. Now if man cannot determine what becomes of the bodily senses or what they are, how can they tell of what does not come within this knowledge? For they have never seen a spiritual body; therefore their belief is in what has been conjured up from some unaccounted phenomena. I will illustrate the explanation of these two men according to the theory of truth which I practice.

It is a well known fact that the subject can see whatever the mesmerizer imagines. The latter can make the object move and have life to the subject, knowing all the while that the life is his own idea. But the subject seeing life, to him it is a truth and the object has an identity as a living being subject to the same laws as himself. Like that of every idea, this life is kept in existence till it begins to act on its own account, according to the laws of life, under the principle of man's belief. This represents the natural man, put into this form by God, the first cause. This wisdom animates matter or error and man reasons as though he was the author of his own being. His knowledge is confined to his senses, and as they cannot see outside of his belief, he lives in his own wisdom. Job says of such, "Ye are the wisdom of this world, but your wisdom will die with you." I will now introduce the scientific man.

He is the Son of God, while the other is the son of man. The latter is merely the changing of matter to become a medium of a higher development, as a forest is cut down to prepare for a higher cultivation of the earth. The life of this man is ignorant of itself, for he knows not what manner of man he is. As matter becomes freed from error, it is more rarefied, and as man becomes more acquainted with himself, he will see that he is only the shadow of a wisdom which he never knew; and although he seemed to have life, he had deceived himself believing that he was the author of his own being. So he is in a certain sense, in his belief, but that would only keep him in existence for a certain time.

The beginning of the scientific man is to know that the natural man is nothing but ideas, like furniture, made from matter, having no value of himself but is merely a medium for a higher wisdom. The first thing is to make the invisible man wise. Mesmerism proves that the invisible man is the same man as in the visible state, with all his senses, faculties, etc. He is like a blind man suddenly receiving his sight. Imprison a man and educate him in all the branches of science, literature and philosophy as far as possible; then while asleep transfer him to the light and he is a spiritual or mesmeric man. How much more does he know out-of-doors than in his dungeon? Where is the difference? In the light, he sees what he read of but he is the same being. This is the spiritual man. He is in matter with all his senses, and those left in the dark look upon him according to their belief. He is dead to that class of persons who never had an idea of light.

When the wise tell the ignorant that those who are gone come back, they won't believe and those who have never seen the light except by faith think there must be a change in those who have left. So even to them it is a mystery. Now here is a man in the light but still in the dark. Get all men into this light and then men have taken one step towards wisdom. Then those in the dark are dead to those in the light. Each man is to himself the same as he was. Suppose he who is in the light be placed again in the dark. Then he is one risen from the darkness into the light and who returns to the darkness to instruct those still there. What is the difference in the man who has returned to the prison from what he was before he went into the light? He differs in his sight. He has seen what he read and thought about, so now he is in a different condition, for what to his friends is a mystery is to him a reality. Suppose one of the prisoners born blind and deaf suddenly brought to the light, he would not see objects but shadows like clouds. Now as you associate his sight with your explanation (for I am supposing his eyesight comes and also his hearing and other faculties), you must teach him like a child. If he was as ignorant as a child, his sight would be as contracted and as his knowledge increased, his sight would expand; for wisdom is sight, whether coming through the eye, ear, taste or smell.

If you know a fact, that is light, but if you think you know anything, that is twilight, but neither is science. Let all men be in this light; they are then in this world of matter but purer. The natural man and brute are in matter, like the earth; the error is out of the earth in mortar. The so-called wise are in liquid, the scientific, in ether. Each grade sees the one below and admits the one above in a mystery. As one works out of himself, he becomes the medium of the one above him; he imparts life to the matter but the same identity continues. The river that runs down the Kennebec is the same, but the water is changed and that is the Kennebec and not the banks. So the intellect of man is the man, not the identity body, for the intellect like the water can make a body or river when it pleases. There is still a higher person than those I have spoken of, that is he who can sit and know that he is in two places at the same time and prove it by others admitting it. He has passed from death unto life and all below him is either darkness or twilight.

December 1862

Bible, The—A Book of God's Wisdom*
[Originally untitled.] [BU 3:0655]

It is objected to Dr. Quimby that he interferes with the religious belief of his patients. Some think he wishes to rob them of their religion, others think that he is an intruder into the sacred privacy of their religious opinions. Some think he is a bold blasphemer and should not be listened to, but their religion being of the genuine order, they can receive the benefit of his treatment without being affected by his irreligion, while there is still another class who think it in very poor taste for him to attack a patient's religion in the way he does and that it is poor policy and it does not pay.

He is liable to all these charges and a great many more if left to the judgment of those who stand ready to account for the fact that he does talk to some patients about their religion, and indeed unless you take his own explanation of his doings, it is incomprehensible on any decent ground. He seems to sweep away the very foundation of the Christian religion and with it goes the various modifications of man's faith in God. He leaves not a relic of the precepts, which have reared the Christian church and have guided so many from sin to holiness, and the piety which makes it a pleasure to sacrifice natural desires, he denounces as hypocrisy and cant. To one reared in a religious atmosphere, who is sensitively attached to their religion it seems that he attacked the stronghold of their faith in God and dissuaded a surrender of their soul. Then comes a feeling that they must give up their religion in order to be cured and they halt between the ruin which follows the one and the hope which attends the other. They denounce him as the worst of men, who having it in his power to do them a service, being himself thoroughly irreligious, tempts them with their desire for health, to deny Christ.

The sacredness of their ideas concerning the Bible is turned into a joke and their disease is the weapon which he turns against their religion inasmuch as he reiterates that it is their religion that makes them sick. This assumption is intolerable in the last degree and often rouses a spirit of the bitterest hostility.

To add to their misery their faith in his curative power is firm and trusting to that they are forced as it were to throw themselves on his mercy and await the result. Then it is that he shows the right by which he makes war upon their religion, they are satisfied that he requires no sacrifice of opinion, of duty, or faith, he puts the scriptures in a different light from what they ever dreamed of and shows a higher meaning that they are capable of expressing. He makes the Bible a book of God's wisdom, intended to apply to the sick and wretched, to heal their woes and his explanation of certain passages illustrates their now peculiar state of suffering.

The sick feel that he, by pure pity and sympathy for them, preserved through the opposition of the world, immaculate to all contempt and derision, has found the key which can unlock the stores of God's love and wisdom and answer the desire of their hearts,–which is–health. Instead of being robbed of their religion, they suffer no change in that respect and learn to put a higher estimate on life. Instead of losing anything good, they receive that which they hope for and have failed to attain. Dr. Quimby sees that the construction that religious education has put upon certain precepts found and in the scriptures, breeds misery and sin and acts with terrible force upon the sick and it is his duty to destroy these by showing that the Bible is capable of higher interpretation, bearing on human life, that its true meaning has been prevented and the goodness and wisdom it contains are completely buried under the rubbish of educated Christianity. For instance take the common idea of sin. We are taught that it is eternal and natural: that its consequences are ruin and to be a poor sinner is to be the most miserable thing it is possible to conceive of. While the only power which can keep sin in check is the infinite mercy and love of God which we are to attain by a life of devotion to his worship, and then we by no means feel <u>sure</u> of his pardon. He finds many a patient suffering under the burden while such a belief binds upon their life. The feeble light which would guide them in the straight and narrow path, is often found to be a deception and they are tortured by continual disappointment and despair, while their fears still attach them to the cause of religion and in their darkness are sunk all native character.

Many a sick person gropes blindfold[ed] along the paths of their religious conviction to find the solace they vainly hope and waste away under the wearing promise of hope deferred. Dr. Quimby supplies the very sympathy they need to melt away their trouble, though not in the way they have been taught to look for, but his remedies though they seem severe and uncalled for, yield a fruit which places the author above any living man and those who have been led by him out of the darkness of their belief, see in his truths a light which can illumine future ages and bless the human race beyond their hopes.

Body of Jesus and the Body of Christ, The
[LC 2:0763]

Did Jesus intend to convey to the world that he was God? I answer he did not and I also contend that his whole teaching went to destroy the idea that he (Jesus) was Christ, but he labored to convince the people that the Christ was the truth which he, Jesus, spake and that this truth is from God and not of man. Jesus embodied it in an intelligence called Christ, embracing all the attributes of man, and being a revelation of a higher wisdom than had before appeared on the earth. This Christ was what prompted Jesus and when the Jews crucified the man Jesus, the Christ rose from the world's belief or body and disappeared in the clouds of their opinions. They laid the body of Jesus in the sepulcher but the chief priests said that the disciples stole the body of Christ or truth. The body of Jesus and the body of Christ were two, one visible to the natural man and the other the spiritual or scientific man clothed with a garment of truth which was stolen and parted among them. What the body of Christ was has never been explained to the satisfaction of the Christian world. Jesus spoke of a body of flesh and blood which the people should eat, etc., which plainly referred to the Christ although the people and his disciples could not understand his meaning.

Every discovery of truth is a Christ, having a spiritual and a natural body. For instance, the magnetic telegraph, when discovered, had a spiritual body of truth not visible to the natural man, but when it was demonstrated to man it spoke into the natural world a material body with all the elements of a working telegraph. Every discovery founded in truth has its Christ, but when founded in error, it has its false Christ. Every man who has the true Christ or Science feeds the multitude with its body and those who understand or drink its blood live on it; its body is their life. Jesus possessed the Christ which could free the people and to him it was meat and drink, and to all who ate and drank it was eternal life. Therefore he called it his body, as Morse might call the telegraph his body or idea. All truth being of God, Jesus called it his father, and says, "I, (this truth) and the father are one." In speaking of this truth Jesus gives it an identity. Sometimes he calls it himself, Christ, and sometimes he speaks of himself as Jesus. In John 14:1, it says, "Let not your heart be troubled; ye believe in God, believe also in me." These are not the words of Jesus but of Christ or truth. "In my Father's house are many mansions; if it were not so, I would have told you. I go to prepare a place for you." These are also the words of truth and I hold that they mean as follows. While this truth was with them in their understanding, they would rejoice in it, but in teaching them what they did not understand, it went away to prepare a place for them, so that the truth could explain how they had wandered away from it, through their errors and he (truth) would lead them back to their right senses.

Therefore, Christ or this Truth is a living substance and has an identity as much as God, for it is a part of God as much as a child is a part of its parents. The prophets spoke of it, but not as a being of intelligence separate from man. Moses believed that God himself spoke through him and sometimes that he talked with God. Jesus believed the same. But the difference between them was this. The bread or spiritual food of Moses belonged to this life and did not teach immortality. Moses believed in God as much as Jesus did, but his God had nothing to do with man after death. He taught nothing beyond death. His teaching was spiritual and was so understood by the people. Paul in 1st Cor. 10, says, "Moreover, brethren, I would not that ye should be ignorant, how that all our fathers were under the cloud, and all passed through the sea, and were baptized unto Moses in the cloud and did all eat the same spiritual meat; and did all drink the same spiritual drink, for they drank of that spiritual Rock that followed them, and that Rock was Christ. But with many of them God was not well pleased: for they were overthrown in the wilderness. Now these things were our examples, to the intent we should not lust after evil things, as they also lusted."

This cloud and sea were symbols of their superstitions and beliefs. The spiritual food was Moses' truth; his arguments quenched their thirst for knowledge. The rock was his truth or Christ, but that threw no light on to another state of life but was confined to the cloud that followed them. Although his food and drink was spiritual and was all confined to this world, yet Moses saw the promised land or had a vague idea of progression, but he never taught it, so the people ate his food and died. Jesus showed the difference between Moses and himself as men. Moses believed that God governed man by certain laws and regulations, that he rewarded the good and punished the bad and that he was the expounder of God's wisdom.

Jesus as a man understood all that Moses believed and knew that his wisdom or spiritual food was all confined to man's natural life, and if men lived up to the letter of that belief, they would die, for Moses never taught anything after death. But Jesus' food came from a higher wisdom which made man an immortal progressive intelligence. This truth he called his Father and he prayed to it to guide him. When guided by this great truth, he was God or the son of God. Therefore when he (the truth) spoke, it was God. He calls it the bread of life and tells how it differed from Moses' bread or manna, for he says, John 6:48, "I am that bread of life. Your fathers did eat manna in the wilderness, and are dead." He meant that this truth which he taught is the bread of life, for it taught no continuation of man's existence; therefore all who believed in it died and there was an end to them. His wisdom was the bread of life or this doctrine of an eternal progression and being superior to the belief of Moses, it assured that the wisdom of Moses was not the end of man. In the words of Christ, "This is the bread which came down from heaven that a man may eat thereof and not die," which being interpreted means, that if man understands it (the bread of life), he will live when Moses' belief would call him dead. "I am the living bread which came down from heaven" (Moses' was not this kind of bread) "if any man eat of this bread, he shall live forever."

Here is the difference between the doctrine of Jesus and that of Moses. The latter did not contain eternal life. Jesus' did. One lived to die, the other died to live. If a man died to Moses' belief, he lived in Christ. "And the bread that I will give is my flesh which I will give for the life of the world." Jesus believed in the perfect identity of man with all his attributes of mind and matter just as he stood before his disciples. The disciples and the people could not understand such a belief. So the Jews strove among them saying, "How can this man give us his flesh to eat?" They could not even compare in their understanding the reality of Christ's truth to the reality of Jesus' flesh and blood, and as he affirmed that his words of truth were his body and his spiritual food, they could not understand such purely spiritual doctrine. He tried to teach them that the body which they saw was nothing of itself and existed only as a shadow of the truth of Christ, which Christ was meat and drink and all that made up man. Jesus replied to the Jews in this way. "Verily, verily, I say unto you, except ye eat the flesh of the Son of man, and drink his blood, ye have no life in you. Whoso eateth my flesh and drinketh my blood, hath eternal life; and I will raise him up at the last day. For my flesh is meat indeed, and my blood is drink indeed. He that eateth my flesh, and drinketh my blood, dwelleth in me, and I in him."

This truth spoken through Jesus proved a hard saying to many of the disciples. Feeling that they did not understand him, he tried to explain by a figure. "What and if ye shall see the Son of man ascend up where he was before? It is the spirit that quickeneth; the flesh profiteth nothing: the words that I speak unto you, they are spirit, and they are life." From that time many of his disciples went back and walked no more with him. Then said Jesus unto the twelve, Will you also go away? All these words are perfectly intelligible to me, but at the time they were spoken, the people made the man Jesus responsible for them and they accused him of assuming to be greater than Moses, who was their guide, and also of making himself equal with God. In the same way at the present day, the priests assume to be oracles of the wisdom pertaining to spiritual things and the people admit their words as being truth from God. Therefore if any man doubt their explanation, he must be crucified or stoned because he makes himself equal to them, or as they say, "compares himself to Christ."

The Pharisees hearing that Jesus opposed forms and ceremonies found fault and asked him, "Why walk not thy disciples according to the tradition of the elders, but eat bread with unwashed hands?" This was an old tradition from the laws of Moses enjoined on the people by the priests as a commandment of God. Jesus answered, "Full well ye reject the commandments of God, that ye may keep your own tradition. For Moses said, Honor thy father and thy mother; and whoso curseth father or mother, let him die the death; but ye say, If a man shall say to his father or mother, 'It is Corban, that is to say a gift, by whatsoever thou mightest be profited by me.' " By the words Father and Mother is meant this truth which the people worshipped. Jesus then upbraided them for making the word of God of no effect through your tradition, thus really acting the part of hypocrites. For in the beginning he says, "Ye hypocrites, well hath Esaias prophesied of you, as it is written: This people honoreth me with their lips but their heart is far from me. Howbeit: in vain do they worship me, teaching for doctrines the commandments of men." This is a condemnation of the Mosaic priesthood, for it contained no life. It was idolatry, embodying no spirit or principle.

January 1863

Book of Man, The
[LC 2:0854]

Every person is a book of himself, a sort of library in which the life and acts are written and the trials which each has passed through in the progression of life's journey. The child is like a primer, full of stories, and his happiness and misery are in the amusement of his stories. As the child grows, his stories increase and the fears and effect of what follows his belief is realized. His life therefore becomes a book like the history of what he has passed through. At last he is caught by his own reasoning and confined in his own belief. Now his life becomes the history of some criminal confined in prison or banished to some desolate place, there to live a life of misery or to fly into the mountains, there to dwell in caves and dens. Some are confined in cells without the privilege of conversing with anyone but the keeper of the prison who is a tyrant. Others are bound out to slavery and kicked about by every person.

I might go for hours enumerating the various histories, but I will stop and commence and show how the child is first deceived by its parents. The first entry on the first page is all hypocrisy, flattery and deception. The infant mind is like a blank to be scribbled on by everyone. So in the little infant mind or introduction to the journey of life, on the first few pages will be found written by the friends and relations these words. Oh, what a darling little child! How much it looks like its father. It is the very picture of him. I should know it was a P., if I had seen him in China. This hypocrisy and flattery affect the mother and her child nurses the vanity from her till another page is written by some others that runs after this style. How handsome the little thing grows. It is so altered since I first saw it. I should not have known it. It is two months since I saw it and if I should die, I can't see one particle of resemblance to it when I first saw it. Let me take it. You pretty little darling. Here is its father's mouth exactly and only see it laugh. Does it not have the same look of its father? Oh, you little rogue; you are a perfect chip off the old block. I see it begins to take notice of what you say. The mother says, Oh, yes, it knows when I talk to it. Well, I think I never saw a child so forward. When Prof. Fowler comes this way, you must have his head examined, for he will tell you just what this child is best adapted for. He sees all through futurity so do not miss having his head examined. So goodbye.

(Mrs. A) Why did you flatter Mrs. B so? (Mrs. C) Why, don't you know that all women like to have their children praised? It is of no consequence what you say. (Mrs. A) I do not agree with you; the impressions you make on the parent are generally imprinted on the child and if it is a false one, it grows just as fast as a true one. Here is where the error begins. Well, never mind, it is all over now. So time runs on. The child begins to listen to the stories of its mother and in the course of one or two years, Mrs. C makes a visit with the parents. At this time, the little fellow can talk and he has grown out of the remembrance of Mrs. C, so when she enters she does not know the child from others playing about.

    Sept. 25, 1862

Breathing
[LC 2:1037]

How often are we misled by a false direction, resulting in great evils, misery and disease. The false idea of instructing man how to breathe is of all errors the worst, for it changes his mind in making him believe an error, thereby leading his soul astray and giving false direction to the matter or mind. For instance, we are taught to believe that the air goes into the lungs. This is acknowledged, without any questioning, and therefore must be a fact.

Now if any person of ordinary intelligence capable of understanding any kind of mechanical principles will stop one moment and look at the construction of man's internal organs, he must see that it is impossible for the air to go into the lungs. Giving the disciples of this belief the advantage of all they claim, it will be seen that if God intended that the air should go into the lungs to purify the blood, he put man to a great deal of trouble to get it there according to their own explanation. For we are told that the air goes in at the mouth or nose, passes down the windpipe, and enters the lungs, purifying the blood and is then thrown off. According to this route, the air that goes into his nose must first come into the mouth to meet the air in the mouth; after meeting, they find their way down the windpipe.

Everyone knows that there is a valve or clapper on the upper end of the windpipe to prevent anything from going down. This valve is closed all the time to prevent anything from going down when we eat or drink. Now to suppose that a person is breathing air into the mouth which passes down the lungs, one must either be ignorant of the effect of the circulation of the atmosphere or have never thought of the absurdity of such a belief. Just let common sense look and see how absurd the idea is. Everyone knows that cold air rushes where the air is warmer, for the warm air is more rarified, and this forms a partial vacuum; and the cold air, according to a natural law of heat and cold, would rush to fill the vacuum.

Now as the heat in the brain is warmer than in any other part of the system, the cold air would rush to that place according to a natural principle. The nose is constructed like a steam chamber with small holes or apertures for the air to pass through and pass into a larger chamber; this forms a bulkhead at these apertures, so that the hot air must pass down into the mouth. Now the amount of cold air that can pass down into the lungs is so small that it is not worth a thought.

Suppose you take a pipe and warm the stem, and pour cold air into the bowl, will it come out of the stem cold? No, then leave the bowl open and see how absurd it is to believe that it will come out cold. It is just as absurd to suppose that the cold air or any air goes into the lungs; for if it does not go in cold, it cannot go in hot, because the heat is forcing itself into the mouth, when the mouth is shut, to escape from the lungs.

The process of breathing is a law of science without the least particle of knowledge; it requires no knowledge.

The child knows as much about it when it is first set in motion as it ever does. If the machine gets out of order, then the will tries to remove the obstruction made by man's wisdom, for the wisdom of man has made obstructions by false reasoning. We have the power of contracting the muscles of the throat so that we can hold anything in the mouth, liquid or smoke. A person can hold tobacco smoke in the mouth or force it out of the nose, showing that the passage from the mouth is under the control of the will. So if the will can close the passage in the nose, you see how necessary it is not to give man a false idea about the circulation of the air. For if you make him believe that the air goes into the lungs, it does not make it go there, but you deceive him and in the act of using his will to induce the air to go into the lungs, he uses a great power of will which heats up the blood and this heat closes the apertures in the nose and prevents the natural circulation that would take place if no such information had ever been taught.

The blood wants good pure air, for in it there is something that sustains life and God knew what he was about when he made man. He know that man never would know enough to breath of himself, so he made circulation according to the laws of heat, leaving man nothing to do but to let nature do its work, and then all will go right.

Nature will let cold air go into the nose and then come in contact with the blood or something else that will take out of the atmosphere what the blood wants, then it will escape to let in more cold air. The blood is fed in this way and carries its food to all parts of the system; returning with the impurities of the system, it deposits them in the lungs whence they are thrown off. So the lungs act for the blood, as the intestines do for the stomach, and the mouth receives the food for the stomach and the nose receives the air or food for the blood. God, when he set man in motion, did not put food in his mouth but breath in his nostrils, and man became a living soul.

May 1860

Breathing II
[BU 2:0197]

As I have spoken of breathing, it is necessary that I should give my ideas concerning it. The fact is, if man had not set up his wisdom above God, or error had not undertaken to set up its standard as truth, there would not have been any need of making war against it. The error of breathing has become the common opinion of the world and mankind is affected by it. And it is time for someone to step forward and define the truth or science. If there had been no opinion taught to man, there would have been no need of an answer. So I do not come to establish a truth but to destroy an error, for the destruction of the error is bringing back the truth.

Now let us see what is the foundation for the common belief in regard to breathing. It certainly does not lengthen life, for those who know the least about it live the longest. And those who try the most experiments are the worst off; for all that class of persons who know nothing about the lungs and never heard of such an organ are not much affected till they become acquainted with this world of science. And it strikes me that any theory that tends to make us worse is not founded in truth. I will take a child that is perfectly well and show how to bring about consumption.

I must be well posted up in medical science (not knowledge, but the science) which is not to know anything about myself but to adopt the established opinions of other people. This I must learn by heart so that I can use all the phrases as readily as a sailor on board a ship. My chart is the medical science and my knowledge is to put it in practice and the evidence of the senses is the proof of my skill, for every tree or science must be known by its fruits. To show each science is to know how to put it in practice. And as I have the knowledge of the true science, it requires also the knowledge of the false science. Like a man playing a game of checkers, he must know his opponent's game better than his opponent does so that he can take advantage of his error. This is so in my way of doctoring.

Health is the game to be played; truth and error are the combatants. Error plays to destroy health and truth to save it. So that truth must know error's weak points so as to show him up and like a lawyer prove the absurdity of his move or opinion. And as life is in our senses, the game is to be decided by them. If I succeed in showing the absurdity of my opponent's theory, life gives me the game. So I will commence my plea as a regular physician and show how to make consumption. As public opinion is my knowledge, the more I have of it the more certain I am of success. I will assume the character of some learned physician, educated in Europe, who has a chest full of medals marked "M.D." This is my theory and the knowledge is to put it into practice. I commence my public career by giving a course of lectures before the people of _____, in which I set forth all evils that flesh is heir to. I call their attention particularly to the lungs, describing minutely their delicate structure and important office and lamenting the imminent danger which hangs over the young in this climate. After getting the people excited on the subject, all ready to be affected, I close my remarks by saying that a remedy has been discovered for this worst of all diseases, consumption which is inhalation, and that I shall be happy to attend to any person who would like to try it. This ends my advertisement and I wait for a customer. Presently I receive a call.

The patient is a young lady accompanied by her mother, who is more nervous than her daughter. She can hardly wait for me to speak before she tells me they attended my lecture and were so much interested by my remarks that she could hardly wait until morning to bring her daughter to see me. She says she thinks she must have taken cold, for she seemed to have a nervous cough. "No doubt," I reply. "I did not know," she continues, "but that she might have inhaled some of the impurities. You know there is a great deal of dust in such places." "Yes." "I should like to have you examine her lungs and see if there is any trouble. What is your fee?" "Ten dollars for an examination." "Ten dollars! Is not that high?" "Yes, but you are aware that to prepare one's self for the responsible duties of a physician, where so much depends on their knowledge in regard to the construction of the human system, must require a great deal of time and money." "Yes. Well I wish you to give her a thorough examination." So looking very wise, I commence tapping the chest and then place my ear down to listen. The mother sits in a nervous state of mind and the child is as pale as death. Seeing all this, I very modestly say, "I find the left side of the lung slightly diseased, but I think that it can be entirely cured." "Oh! How happy I am. Well, doctor, what shall we do for her?" "You remember that I spoke of my medicated inhalation treatment." "Yes." "I think if she tried this it would entirely cure the disease." "What do you charge for the preparation and fixtures?" "Fifteen dollars." "Nothing less?" "That is my fee. I am not a quack but a regular and I will explain its effects to you and how it acts. You will inhale this preparation into the lungs, where it produces a chemical change and you will have to clear the lungs by coughing off the deposit that is made there. If it should remain in the lungs they would become inflamed and tubercles will form and this last condition is entirely incurable." "You think there is no doubt you can cure her?" "I cannot say now but in a week or two I can tell. Be sure not to have her take the least cold and have her breathe the purest air. She must be particular about diet living on meat and ale with a little light food as graham bread." "Can she drink coffee?" "By no means, cold water is the best. Obey all my orders till I see her again." The lady and daughter leave and the daughter becomes more nervous, the mother more anxious.

In a week they call again and the doctor examines her lungs again, looking more doubtful. This kind of a practice is kept up till common report begins to do its work and then all their friends can see that the Doctor is right in regard to the lungs. The breathing becomes short, hectic sets in and all hope of recovery is given up. Some person has the courage or impudence to hint that if she had never seen a doctor she would have been well, but this is blasphemy and that person is silenced. Finally the young lady dies. By the request of her physician a post mortem examination is made. The brethren are called and the science tested. They find the lungs diseased and a great deal more trouble besides but finally they decide that she came to her death by consumption. Here you see the science proved and tested, by a committee of scientific men. Thus ends the life of one and thus is established the medical skill. This is one theory.

I propose now to introduce the other side, but as I have no chance with that patient, I will take her sister going in the same way, the doctors having become alarmed and decided that her case is like the other. The parents are induced to try some other doctor, so I am called. I find the patient with a cough, pains in her side, soreness about the chest and through the shoulders, heaviness about the eyes, hectic and all the symptoms of a consumptive. Now what course do I take? In the first place I take all her feelings on myself. Then I commence taking up the doctor's opinions, her mother being present and show that they are false and without the slightest foundation, that not one particle of fresh air goes into the lungs. By my explanations and experiments I show the absurdity of his theory. In the first place it is impossible for anything we inhale into the mouth to pass into the windpipe or stomach till we swallow, and in the act of swallowing the vapor would pass out of the nose. In smoking the smoke does not go into the lungs, but if a person is in a room with smokers, all the smoke that goes into the nose is carried into the lungs and stops up all the air cells so that he cannot breathe.

This inconsistency is believed. Why does not the smoke of a pipe go into the lungs? Because it does not, yet persons are told to smoke to make them raise, while at the same time it stuffs another up. One takes whiskey or brandy for the lungs, another can take neither. Now all these absurdities everyone knows and the people have never questioned the doctors' authority but have taken it for granted, living and dying in their errors. The idea of any inhaling vapor into the lungs is simply an absurdity. It goes to the brain, there stimulating and exciting the blood like liquor. If you take liquor into your mouth you must smell it, showing that it goes to the head and this is what excites. A person would become as drunk by smelling rum as by drinking it, but not so soon, but in neither case does anything go to the lungs. The expansion of the chest is an act of the will independent of the circulation of the air or breathing. The nose is as much under the control of the will as the mouth; everyone knows that we have the power to close the mouth, and we have the same power to control the nose.

All medicines ever given to affect the blood go to the brain in the form of vapor and affect the brain as the air does through the senses. If you are sick you know it and this knowledge affects the brain first, for the brain is the seat of power. The brain sets the body in motion and if that is disturbed by any chemical action produced by any effect on the soul, then the body is acted upon like a steam engine without an engineer. Both must be subject to a power superior to the machines or they will fly to pieces. I speak of the chemical action as though it contained no intelligence. But this is not the case, for mind is matter and any action on this mind or matter must be the act of a power superior to the mind and the effect shows which power acts upon it. For instance, almost any person can set a steam engine in operation and the effect produced by the engine shows the science of the operator; so when a sensation is produced the mind is obstructed or disturbed, resulting in a chemical change governed by truth or error. It is not chance, but the natural body or ignorance cannot understand it, for if it does it is not ignorance. All actions on the body are governed by an intelligence above the matter acted upon and the fruits or effect shows the intelligence of the power, whether it be of God or truth, or error.

Now to make a disease is to produce a change on the mind or body according to its author. When I believed all my mesmeric experiments were governed by the laws of electricity, I brought about changes in the system to accord with my ideas, showing that I governed the mind of my subject according to my knowledge, but then my knowledge was of this world, not of the truth. It was true that I produced the change and it is true that in the practice of medicine, the doctors may be honest in their profession, but that does not help the person who has to suffer from their ignorance. It is true that good results often follow from their ignorance. It is true that good results often follow from their remedies, as it did in the case of selling Joseph to the Ishmaelites. But if good comes from their practice, it does not prove that they have any science, but that science comes in spite of them. Now put man intelligently in possession of the idea that scientific knowledge can produce a change in the system scientifically, so that it increases man's happiness, then you establish the kingdom of heaven or happiness in this world of ignorance. This is the science to be taught.

This teaches man that matter, as it is called, is nothing but an idea, subject to two powers: one, truth and the other, error. And as error is the father of false impressions or directions, all its effects are subject to its master and do not contain truth. Now all that man can do is to separate them, the one from the other. This can only be done by proving it by works, just as error proves that its science is to derange matter, giving it a false direction and showing the author in its effects. Truth does the same; it takes matter in a deranged state, giving a true direction and the effect is harmony, happiness and peace. The effect of error is discord, disease and death. This is the position of both. I will try to illustrate the separation. Suppose that a person should tell you that the air you breathe is poisoned and go on to tell you the effect it has on the system: how it passes through the windpipe into the lungs, making you cough, and gives all the particulars of this disease called consumption, and you finally get the idea into your mind or knowledge. Now you live with all this knowledge. The matter is in operation, condensing itself into a disease according to your knowledge. And sooner or later you produce a body precisely according to the pattern you have received. This is the wisdom of this world.

Now before you finish it, you in your trouble (for you are in trouble) call on me to help you out. I know your feeling and see the disease you are trying to make, also the effect it has on your happiness and I know that you have been deceived by error. You were well enough before you received this knowledge, but your ambition to subject your mind or matter to your will carried you in a false direction. This was getting your life in trouble. Now I have to show you your error and how you got into trouble. And in showing you I dissolve the matter like clay and explain to you where your false direction is. This I do, not by experimenting, but by a science which gives to man a knowledge of himself. And this knowledge consists in destroying his opinions which he thinks are true and establishing in their place a science which will enable him to correct any opinion made on his mind without knowledge.

It is very hard to give a person a clear idea of a science which they have no previous idea of. To them it is a mystery and humbug, so I don't know exactly how to express myself; for to say that mind is matter is to you a mystery and so it is to every one that does not understand. If man had not been misled, the idea would not have been so much in the dark, but words are used so it has confounded the ideas of man and it is hard to explain what you mean. For instance, the word mind embraces everything that is called knowledge without another word. It embraces the soul, life, knowledge and in fact all there is of us. Yet we speak of losing the mind and saving the soul, and losing the soul or life. So you see there is no definite idea of life, mind or soul. Now as disease is in the mind, according to my theory, it is necessary to show what I mean by mind and matter, so that I can explain how I can change the mind or matter to cure disease.

For instance, in the case of the young lady I spoke of. Before she embraced the idea of consumption, the composition of the mind or matter was disturbed like mortar. Mortar is clay disturbed; so is mind, matter disturbed; not under the direction of truth or error, but merely disturbed and the result of this disturbance is ideas thrown off without any direction, like a galvanic battery. This state of mind or matter is sometimes called insanity, just according to the effect. But it is the working of matter, that is the decomposing of the body, ready to be used by any intelligence, superior to itself. There is such a power or science called God and also a power or science called the power of the devil or ignorance. One is confined to matter and a part of it. Its life is in its acts or directions so it sees no power superior to itself and its reason is confined to the length of its days. Now to save its life it invents all kinds of diseases, which are its own destruction.

You see the effect of this in all error. It reasons wrong in everything. It produces phenomena, for it is in its own opinion or knowledge. It creates disease as in the case of the young girl and it has become so popular that it has set up its standard as a real religious standard. It looks upon all science as mystery or humbug and warns its followers to beware. This enemy of man is the father and mother of all error and the true science is to correct it. Now to correct the error of the young girl is the cure. Therefore, I stand in the place of a counsel to plead her case. The indictment embraces all her symptoms and if she has them about her person, she is guilty of an offense against the laws of health. Now laws are for the protection of each man's rights and in the natural world as well as in the spiritual world, everyone is subject to its laws. The ignorant of this world are only a shadow of those ignorant in the other or spirit world. For truth and error has its spiritual as well as its natural world and those who are bound in the spirit world are also bound in the natural world. Jesus gave Peter the keys or knowledge of the two states, so that he could loose those bound in the spirit world and also relieve those in this world.

I will explain the binding in the spirit world. The young lady, when she was well, was not bound at all, but when she became nervous error began to bind her. This was in the spirit world, and as her mind became troubled, it showed itself in the natural world or body. This the doctor called disease. This contains their knowledge and their science. To bring about this state of mind or disease requires no knowledge of the scientific world, for that to them is all mystery or chance. Now to cure the lady would be to break the fetters and bands and set the prisoner free. As error is subject to science, it cannot hold the soul in bondage, only so long as the error exists. Like a problem the soul is imprisoned, till the true answer comes and then it is set at liberty. This is the way with disease. Error has its laws which are subject to the laws of truth, as the laws of the State are subject to those of the United States and when a person is accused of a crime, arrested and imprisoned by the authority of the State, if he is ignorant of the laws, he submits to his penalties. But if he is informed in regard to the laws of the United States and sees that he has not committed himself in the law he, like Paul, will appeal to a higher tribunal. This is the way with disease. God makes no laws to bind mankind. His laws are not like error's laws, nor his ways like error's ways. His ways are pleasant and all His paths are peace. There are certain principles of truth or knowledge that is God, that is not acknowledged by error to be knowledge, but principles making God of no effect, but chance. Error does not admit intelligence in science. It admits the phenomena but sees no intelligence in it, thinking that the intelligence which produces them is a gift or power derived from some higher science which it knows nothing of.

This keeps up a warfare between truth and error. Error sets up a standard and laws to protect its followers. As error is in a land of mystery, truth, like the prodigal son, leaves his father's house and tries its luck in this dark and uncertain experiment. As it passes, it is liable to get into trouble at every act. It finds the road rough and ragged, robbers and murderers on all sides and it finds persons ready to stretch forth their hand to help you. You will be decoyed into every place where you will be liable to break the laws of the land. If you ask for information you can get all you want and the more you get the worse you are off. For their laws are all for their own benefit and their penalties are your misery. You will find that you cannot step out of doors without being liable to be decoyed. Their laws are so completely adjusted to their penalties that it is impossible to deceive them. For instance, take the young lady. She enters this land to investigate its law and penalties. The first caution she receives is this: not to expose herself to the night air. This to her is an error, for God never made any such law and she will not obey the order, so she steps out nervously to see the effect. Her fear makes her cough and this frightens her and she tries to suppress it which increases the tendency to cough, and the first thing is, she is accused of disobeying the law. Now she is arrested and bound by error. Her offense is proved and she is cast into prison, there to be tormented till the debt is paid (called death). If she has any means, she has enough to pretend to plead her case till they are all expended, and she is left sick and without friends or means, like the prodigal son.

Now all this is known to science, and science is acknowledged by this error and it dare not hold a person in bondage if the freedom from error is proved. This was the case with the young man, when he came to the truth. That is, he saw that he had been deceived by error and he then returned to his father or truth. Now this young lady, from an ambition or desire to get knowledge, entered the world of error and here she becomes deceived and was decoyed into bad company or ideas. This disturbed her mind or matter and in this state she was misled and made to believe a lie that she might be accused by the mother or public opinion, condemned by the doctor and sold into bondage to live a life of suffering and torment till truth should set her free. Now as I find from her friends or truth that she has strayed away and not returned, I leave the health, like the ninety and nine sheep, and go and search diligently till I find the lost one. Then I claim her as a child of God and not of error. So a trial is held and all the witnesses are summoned to prove that she was always a child of disease. This takes some time, for there are many witnesses to be examined and I can't tell whether I can prove her innocent.

If she was born a slave I have no claim on her, but if she has been deceived into bondage, it is for me to prove her identity. So I will now state to the court that the prisoner at the bar was not born sick or diseased, and is therefore not a slave by birth, but was once well and happy and left her home to seek riches or truth and was led by error into disease or bad company. She is accused of disobeying laws that have no power over her and as she is not of your nation and having no knowledge of your laws and having no person to advise her, she has been frightened into an acknowledgement that she is guilty and submits to her punishment. I have authority from the truth to take her and return her to her father's house, from whence she has wandered away, if no proof can be brought that she is a slave or always was diseased. So if there is anyone to accuse her, let them come forward and condemn her.

Here you see a fair statement of error's effect on the truth or happiness of man. This was the state of society when Jesus appeared. He pleaded the cause of a guilty world and corrected the errors of his day, gave a different turn to society and brought light in regard to the errors. This light or truth opened the eyes of the blind or ignorant and broke open the prison doors, liberated the prisoners and set the captives free. Now as society is only a figure or emblem of our spiritual identity, we are all liable to be caught by error and condemned to eternal banishment from happiness if we do not find someone to assist us in our trouble, just as it is in the natural world.

I will now show the course I have to take to free the young lady from her enemies. It is necessary for me to answer all the questions as perfectly as though I was pleading a case of life and death. This I do with as much feeling and sympathy for the sick as though they stood accused of a crime, the punishment of which would be imprisonment for life. It seems as though I was actually standing as her counsel, with the judges, the patient's accusers, for it seems that there is no jury, but public opinion on one side and truth on the other. I have to take up all the symptoms that are embraced in the indictment and show that they are false and if I succeed in my endeavor she is set free by common consent and her accusers are seized and imprisoned for life. The prisoner is acquitted with joy and a change is felt by all the friends even in the natural world. I will now commence my defense for the young lady. She stands accused of all the symptoms of consumption. These symptoms are the property or ideas of error and if a person is found with them he is arrested and imprisoned. It seems as if disease is something that error is afraid of. If a person is accused of it, the whole community are up in arms about it and would kill the person to stop the disease. Ignorance is a coward and dare not face error. See the effect of the smallpox. The people are half frightened to death about it and if it was not for someone who has more truth or nerve than the masses, the victims would be killed for the benefit of the living. So it is with error in everything.

Error is very strict, ready to condemn everything, thinking that it is doing God's service. Look at all sectarianism; look at witchcraft, spiritualism and all the mysterious phenomena which have ever been. Error makes war and would fire or burn or imprison all who would uphold it. Ignorance dare not take any part. Truth investigates it and runs the risk of its reputation for the benefit of man's happiness. So error stands ready to torment anyone that is caught with anything confirmative to their laws. And as their laws are the cause of the very thing that they complain of, it is very hard to get rid of them. The means used to destroy the evil creates it, as it was in the days of the Salem witchcraft. The course taken to put down the evil was the very way to make it. And unless both parties had been punished, it never would have been stopped. So it is at this time. I have no doubt if there was a law that if a doctor told a patient who coughed that her lungs were diseased and by killing the patient the investigation should prove it a lie, then to execute the doctor, and do it in every case, you would not see so much coughing and complaining as you do now. It would have the same effect as it did in the days of witchcraft. The evil was made by the very authorities who were trying to put it down, and that was by the very wisest men of the age. But when the accuser and the accused both had to suffer the same punishment, it stopped the evil or changed it from witchcraft to disease, but which is just as absurd as it was under the other name. Now the witches are in the people in the form of disease. Then they were outside and that is all the difference. Change public opinion scientifically and you get rid of this curse of all evils, disease. This is my opening of the case of the young lady. I will introduce her as accused of consumption. Here she stands before her tormentors like the innocent girl of Salem, accused of being bewitched. She stands pale, with quivering lips and glassy eyes, a hard cough and flushed cheeks, nervously suppressing the little nervous cough for fear she would expose herself to these worst of all devils or barbarians, who stand ready to tear or choke her to death with their chains and bands or to bind her and cast her into prison for the safety of society. Here they stand before me and the judge of truth. I present the young lady to the judge, who listens, not as a partial judge, but as the judge of the dead and living, who has no respect for persons, but listens and decides just according to the evidence.

I will state her position and my defense. I assume that the young lady at the bar was born healthy and is not liable to any disease that her parents had or had not and that the symptoms are the effect of fear produced by her accusers. Now I will call the mother as witness and see what she knows. She tells her story which goes to condemn her daughter. She testifies that she has been looking around and watching her daughter for some time, had often heard her cough and caught her weeping and when she accused her she would deny the whole thing, saying, "If you would only let me alone I should be well enough." When cross questioned by myself, "When did you first perceive that your daughter was in trouble?" She answers, "Some time ago." "Did you think it was consumption?" "Yes, I knew it was." "How did you get your information?" "From the doctor." "Had the doctor ever seen your daughter at that time?" "No, but he attended her sister who died of the same complaint." "How do you know it was the same?" "Because she appears just like her sister." "Then because she appears just like her sister, she must have consumption. Is that all the proof that she has it?" "No, I know that she has it." "How do you know?" "Because she has, that's all."

Now the young lady cannot be condemned on this testimony and the witness, as she knows nothing, is dismissed from the stand. She goes off muttering, as though her opinion was law and she knew all about it. I will now call the doctor who appears ready to testify always on one side, for they never testify except as party concerned. "Will you state what you know of this young lady?" "I was called to see her about two months ago and found her very nervous." "What is that, what do you mean?" "Why nervous, an excitement of the nervous system." "Well, what is it?" "Must I be disturbed in this way?" "You can answer the question." "I have." "How?" "Why her mind was disturbed." "Is not your mind disturbed by me?" "Yes." "Have you consumption?" "No." "Then it does not follow that everyone who has his mind disturbed or nervous has consumption?" "No." "Well then what more have you to say in regard to the patient." "I have not said that she had consumption." "No, I know that you have not, and do you say that she has it?" "The symptoms go to prove it ." "How?" "Because she has all the symptoms of consumption." "Will you state what you know? If so go on." "I was called to see her and found her nervous." "That is, her mind was disturbed, I suppose." "Yes, and I examined her lungs." "How did you do that?" "By sounding on the chest and listening to the sound we detect the state of the lungs." "Do you not get deceived sometimes?" "Yes." "Will you say on your oath before your God, you are sure that the young lady's lungs are affected?" "I think that they are." "That does not answer the question." "Well, just taking the lungs alone does not prove that the disease has affected the lungs, but you must take in all the other symptoms." "Have you ever seen the lungs?" "No." "Then will you say on oath that you know what you never saw? and state it as a fact without qualifications?" "No, I won't say positively, but it is my opinion." "Then it is your opinion?" "Yes." "Your opinion is not law, so if you have no other proof than your opinion you can leave the stand."

Now I will show how this comes about and leave the judge to decide the case. I wish to take the stand. I say I feel all this young lady's feelings. Is this true? The young lady says, "Yes." Now here we both agree. I have no consumption and I know it, for I had not the feelings before I sat down; so is it not fair to suppose that she could have the feelings from some other cause, as it is that I should have consumption? Everyone would answer, Yes. I will ask the doctor a few questions. "Can't a person be nervous without having the lungs diseased?" "Yes." "Can't a person cough without having the lungs diseased?" "Yes." "Can't they have every symptom this young lady has without having consumption?" "Taking them separately,

Yes." "Then when combined it is consumption. Can't a person be so frightened, that they will turn pale?" "Yes." "Can't they cough from fright? Can't they have what you call hectic from fright?" "Yes." Well, if this young lady is to be condemned on this testimony, the reader may decide.

June 1860

Brief Sketch of Dr. Quimby's Theory*
[Originally untitled.] [BU 3:0762]

We, having heard of so many wonderful cures performed by Dr. Q. called on him to learn his explanation of the same and his explanation we give in his own words, letting the people judge if it is satisfactory. He says all disease is in the mind and mind is matter subject to a belief. Our senses are not matter but are attached to our belief. Our wisdom is in our senses, therefore it is of man and is a belief for what a man knows contains no belief, but is knowledge. If our knowledge is Science it is of God, and not of man. So Science is power and wisdom put into practice, therefore my wisdom is my cure for it contains no belief and a disease is what follows a belief. Destroy the patient's belief and the destruction is the cure. Religious creeds are a belief–all medical science is also a belief.

I have no belief at all. What I feel I know and my feelings are the patient's. His feelings are his disease, his disease is in his mind, his senses being attached to his mind. So the whole theory is summed up in these few words. There are two opinions, one based on science, the other on error. If I am right all others are wrong and if they are right I am wrong. The sick may judge between us for the well cannot judge, for they who are well need no physician.

I have given a brief sketch of his theory he uses no medicines of any kind and the sick alone can judge of his wisdom whether he knows more than they others. He is not responsible for what opinions the well may have of his mode of curing–if they know more about it than he does let them show it by their works, for fruits without works is dead. He shows his faith by his works.

Nov. 1860

Can a Spirit Have Flesh and Blood?
[BU 3:0623]

I answer, no, for a spirit is nothing but a shadow either of a belief or a substance. If a person knows anything, the shadow of the thing known is a spirit; so if we call ourselves a substance, the shadow is a spirit not a substance. Truth is a solid and makes no shadow. Wisdom never makes a shadow but ignorance is simply a shadow of something that exists as a belief. Life is a solid not a shadow and as it is attached to a belief of matter, our life seems to act in the matter, but in life there is no matter except as we admit it. We do admit it; therefore all things are based on this belief.

Our senses are our life and therefore are solid. As man is known to himself in his belief or matter, he has no idea of himself outside of matter so that he can be in but one place at a time, according to his belief, therefore if I am talking to a person, I monopolize him for a time. Now this is a false idea. The person to whom I am talking may be present at as many places as his wisdom can comprehend. As I sit and write this alone, I have no doubt but that many persons may be present, to listen and talk upon the subject, and yet not one is aware in the natural world of any change in himself. You ask for proof of all this. I have it. A person in a mesmeric state can ask a question of any person at a distance and get a correct answer and yet the person not know that any question has been asked or answered. When man knows himself, he will see that the thing called man is but a very little real identity.

In regard to getting communications from our friends who have died, there is a great error. The person who sends a letter to the medium supposes the spirit friend comes and influences the medium's hand to write because the answer comes without the medium knowing either party. Here is the mistake. Everyone who believes in the spirit world addresses a letter as he would to a living friend who lives at a distance, supposing that the friend knows nothing of the request till he or she is called up by the medium. This is not the case. The person is a part of the friend, and when he addresses the person, the answer is in the question; and if the medium is in a perfect state, he can see the answer as well as the question. If you ask a person whom you call dead a question, the wisdom of your friend is with you but it does not prove that your friend is aware that you asked the question any more than he is aware of answering it, yet the answer comes and is satisfactory.

I will relate an experiment that I performed with my subject, Lucius, in mesmerism. I asked any person in the room to give me a name of an individual written on a slip of paper. I would send the boy to find the person dead or alive, which he would do, bringing him into the room and describing him to the audience. On one occasion a name was handed to me which I gave as usual to the boy. He said this was a man who had a wife and three children, that he left his chest of tools in a barn and had gone direct to Boston. I told him to follow the man. So he went and said he had found him in Ohio in a cooper's shop, that he had died. Still I told him to find him. Finally he said he had found him and I told him to bring him before the people and describe him. Said he, "Can't you see him? He stands here." I told the boy that he was in a mesmeric state. (He could never understand this but admitted it because I said so. To him there was no change; he had all his faculties and his identity was as perfect as when awake. He expressed fear and joy at what he saw as much as though he had been in a waking state.) I said, "Describe him." He commenced giving a general description and I stopped him, saying if there was any peculiar trait or feature about him mention it. "Well," said he, "I should think anyone might know this man by his hare lip." I asked the person who gave me the name if this description was correct and he said it was in every particular. Here was a clear case of spiritualism. The subject would read sealed letters, he would go to a distant place and ask a person a question and get an answer, and yet the person would not be aware of answering any question.

The year that Mr. Dunn was chosen Speaker of the House of Representatives in this state, I sent the boy from Belfast in a mesmeric state to Augusta to Mr. Abbott, then Representative from Belfast, to inquire who was elected Speaker. He asked Mr. Abbott who was making a speech and received the answer that Dunn had a certain majority, naming it. This was before the vote was cast. A letter was sent to a gentlemen by one who was present when this experiment took place, mentioning the fact, and from some cause he had neglected to open it until after the vote was taken, when he found that it agreed. Here you see he got a fact before it was known to the world.

When at Eastport, I put a lady into a mesmeric sleep who wished to go to New Hampshire to see her friends. I accompanied her. She would smile and bow, and I asked her to whom she bowed. She said, It is our postmaster. She then said we have now got home. Here is where my father lives. We went into the house. She said, Our folks are baking. I asked her if her father was at home and if she would introduce me, and she went through the ceremony. I said, Ask your father if anything has happened since you left home; at this she started and turned pale and seemed agitated. Upon asking what was the trouble, she said that her uncle was dead, that he came there and was taken sick and had died on such a day and how, mentioning both, her aunt who came to take care of him had been sick but had recovered and her brother had carried her home. All this was confirmed in a few days by letter. Her uncle, Dr. Richardson, sent me a letter which I have in my possession, stating that all she had said was literally true. I might give many experiments showing that we don't know ourselves. When I sit by the sick, they tell me their feelings; yet they know it not through their natural senses; neither am I aware of their presence or feelings through the natural organs. But every person has two identities: one the substance and the other the shadow. To me the natural man is the shadow, but to himself, he is the substance and all that he cannot comprehend is shadow. A person in a mesmeric state proves to a person in a waking state that there are two states and each is a mystery to the other. The one in a waking state cannot see how a person can be dead to the waking state and still retain his own identity and be to himself the same person as before, and when he comes into the natural state, the mesmeric state is lost. The mesmerized person cannot understand why the person in the natural state cannot know what he knows in the mesmeric state. So each one is a mystery to the other. Here is the fact. Wisdom has no shadow, a belief has one. A fact is not a solid. For instance, there is a stone; that is a fact and it casts a shadow. The stone being the invention of man, it is matter according to our belief and this belief makes it a shadow. Man acts either by his belief or his wisdom. When he is in his wisdom, he is to opinion a spirit, but to him he is himself with all his belief. So as his belief makes him act in matter, every act is in his belief and the acknowledging of matter depends on his belief.

Jesus to the world was dead, so to the world he was a spirit, but to himself he was alive and had flesh and blood. Wisdom makes a man know himself, and when he does know himself, he can be in two places at once. This proves to man that as he rises from error into truth and knows it, he has two identities:

one in the body and one outside. To know this is to understand it so that you can put your wisdom into practice for the benefit of those who suffer for the sins of their belief.

Portland, May 1862

"Cancer Is Sown in the Mind, A"
[BU 3:1213]

It is nourished by human wisdom which says, A cancer is a living thing independent of our knowledge, that will eat and eat till it eats away life. This fact takes root in every part of man's sensitive system till his whole frame has become adjusted to it. The result is that the body takes form according to the growth of the seed; the mind, deriving its productive power from wisdom, keeps changing and changing till a living cancer is brought forth in the flesh.

The mind of man is like matter or soil which will bring forth vegetation, and man himself is the planter. When a new sensation is felt, we want to know what made it; and as all our knowledge of ourselves makes causes of things which come to our bodily senses, we reason that it was occasioned by some of our acts in which we disobeyed some law of nature and therefore this new feeling is the punishment. We may reason still further and discover what particular law we disobeyed and the name or nature of its penalty. This we ascertain without difficulty; perhaps it is one that attacks our very life, consumption. This terrible name disturbs the mind to its very depths; it takes root and the whole body is set to work to produce the disease. It derives its principle of life from the changeableness and futility of the mind; its poison is that of a falsehood; its efficiency is in our receiving and believing it as true. It may be asked what one's wisdom had to do with this? It simply sustains the power of creating.

It does not originate or condemn anything wrong, but sets men to work to try to correct their troubles themselves. This is only done successfully in any department by the application of truth to human reason. At one time all mankind believed in a personal devil, but in the progress of intelligence, he has been reasoned entirely out of existence in many of his relations to man. But although he is nearly dead as an individual, yet his works live after him and flourish like a green bay tree. They contain the subtlety, the poison and the hypocrisy of the serpent and are neatly covered up in our reasoning and opinions, often forming the most fascinating and respectable qualities of individuals.

Case of a Patient, The
[LC 2:0905]

I will give you a case of a patient to show how hard it is to cure or to correct an opinion or disease. The case was a gentleman who was laboring under a disease called by his physician, a German doctor, "Dropsy in the abdominal cave and in the subcutaneous cellular tissue." Now to the man this was all Greek so he requested the doctor to reduce it to writing so that on his return home he might show it to his physician. At the same time his physician doctored him for the asthma and the medicines that he gave seemed at first to have some effect, but after he returned home his family physician was called, and after seeing the description of his case by the German, he explained his case and gave him to understand it was the dropsy. Now the patient became nervous; his ankles and feet began to swell and his sleep departed from him. This bloated him up so that he was not able to lie down, for the pressure across his lungs was so great that he would spring up in the most frightful manner looking as red as a cherry.

The doctor all this time was using all his skill to convince his wife and mother that his chest was filling with water. So when he would be in this dreadful agony his mother would ask the doctor, "Can't you give him something to relieve his distress in the chest?" The doctor would reply, "We can't do anything till we get the water away," impressing on the mother and wife that he was filling up with water. So here he was; he could not lie down for fear of suffering with the water, for the doctor had made the wife and mother believe it was water. Now this was the state of the case when I was called.

To cure the patient was to change his mind. Now with all this amount of evidence, for me to step in and show that he had been deceived, and the phenomenon was the result of his deception or belief, was not an easy task. But I undertook it, and in the first place I convinced him that the doctor was wrong about his legs, for I reduced the sore one half, the first visit. This gave me a little chance over him, but he was so nervous that his belief of water in the chest had such an effect on his mind that he would spring up every time he would lose himself.

Now I had all the prejudices of the doctor's opinions to contend with. His wife and mother were like a vane to be operated on by every groan and expression that would drop from his lips. Their fears would keep him nervous and they would watch him to see if he bloated any more, and to be sure, they would ask him if he did not think his legs were more swollen; this of course would make him nervous. So he would fuss all night and in the morning they would begin with their complaints by saying, He has had a very restless night and don't you think, doctor, his legs and bowels are more swollen? See how purple he looks in the face; and then say, Can't there be something that he can take to get rid of this nervousness? Then the patient would say, I am so nervous I shall go crazy; is there nothing that will take this nervousness away, etc.

Now every day this took place and I had to sit and hear all this and know that it was the very thing that was making him nervous. So I would sometimes say, If you want to take medicine, why did you send for me? Then his wife would say, I don't want him to take medicine, for everything he takes makes him worse. Then his mother would say, Don't you think that soaking his feet would be good? Some say it is very good for dropsy.

This is the scene of a sick room and it is what I have to go through more or less with every patient. Now I had to account for all these feelings and ten times as many more. I had to tell the effects that would follow his getting well, and when they would come along, he would forget that I had told him. So I would have to explain every change that came along, showing him that I had explained it all before.

I will now give you the changes as they took place. I have described his appearance when I first called. I will now give my argument to convince him that the doctors were wrong. His trouble was in breathing; he believed he was filling up with water so that if he went to sleep he would suffocate. Now to convince him that it was not water in the chest I had to produce an action in the bowels, and I reasoned with him till he would drop asleep; and while I would sit by him, he would sleep; but as soon as I would leave, he would spring up on his feet and exclaim I shall suffocate. Now this I knew was nervousness and not water, so I sat and would [unfinished]

Dec. 3, 1861

Cause of Disease
[LC 2:1001]

Does the medical faculty or indeed any mode of practice known to the world treat the sick as the cause of their own disease? I reply that no mode of treatment administers medicine to the mind. They all treat the body as though it were a brute or a thing disconnected with intelligence. True, they admit imagination and try to influence it, believing that through it they can get control of the body or disease. But even that, they only affect through deception, just as a demagogue deceives the masses through their imagination. Physicians stand towards their patients as a master to his slave, in full possession of arbitrary power. If the slave obeys, all is well, but if not, arbitrary measures are used and reason is never employed to convince him. Only perfect obedience to the law is required. If the physician's orders are not obeyed to the letter, punishment surely follows.

A doctor is called to see a patient whose body he finds in a state of rebellion, as it were, against health. Assuming an air of authority, he gives his orders to the patient to take certain medicines in order to drive out the disease, which he admits is a kind of intelligence. And he leaves word that if it is not gone when he comes again, he shall resort to more powerful remedies. He approaches the patient as a general approaches a fortified city. The general orders the city to surrender or he will fire the city. The doctor in the same way orders the disease to leave the premises before morning or he will force him to leave. In the morning the rebel flag is flying, the face is flushed, the eyes inflamed, and the disease is in a perfect rage, ready for battle. A dose of calomel is given, which nearly turns out the disease, but leaves the man level with the bed. The doctor exults and rejoices in the success of his attack and enquires if the disease will surrender.

The disease asks for a little time to think of the matter and the doctor in a bravado gives a few hours to consider. But the disease, being stubborn, commences to rally and barricade its weak points to gain possession of what it has lost.

To the inquiry what conclusion it has come to, the disease runs up its flag. The doctor then commences his siege, sends a full portion which strikes the foundation, but no effect being seen, he repeats the dose. Still no response. He follows up the attack with hot shot down the throat. Although he receives no answer, yet the resistance is feeble and one more shot is fired and the flag of life comes down. A flag of truce is sent in and the fort is found to be deserted by the disease and left in a state of ruin. A council of war is called, a post mortem examination held and they find that the first dose of calomel fell into the stomach and sent the blood to the head, causing congestion of the brain, and the subsequent firing burst the arteries, so that when the disease left could not be told. Some say, it was the first fire, but others declare that signs of life were subsequently seen on the outside of the body. They are forced to the conclusion that the fort might have been taken by a slower process and the inmates saved, but now they cannot tell whether it was destroyed by them or whether the rebels destroyed it. To make it sure, some of the friends consult a medium, and the general reports that he abandoned the fort at the first fire. The newspaper states that a great man died on such a day from typhoid pneumonia, that he was attended by the most skillful and successful physician in the country. This is a fair illustration of the manner in which the sick are treated.

I differ from the profession in every particular. I contend that diseases are the natural results of oppression. A belief in what man has no evidence of is a despot, and it makes slavery in politics and religion. Those who enforce either are demagogues of the same class. the medical man is a slave driver and applies the whip in the shape of pills, blisters, etc. The priests and politicians are the same. Neither enlightens the people by any philosophical reasoning. It may be asked what are these classes good for if they do not benefit the people? They are the law, I answer, but not the gospel. And what they fail to do, the truth accomplishes by introducing through reason the higher law, the law of wisdom. Then as man grows wiser he breaks from the law of sin and death and rises into the law of love. Politics is like the wind and the medical faculty the thunder, and when both have exhausted themselves, then out of the clamor of war and the scene of carnage, the effects of false religion, rises the still small voice of science. I have travelled through these bloody scenes and can understand the language of one who writes of Epicurus: "He first opposed himself to the terrors of religion and with undaunted courage soared above every selfish theory of man and rose to that state of wisdom where he could see the hypocrisy of the world."

My course has been in the same direction and as his words will apply to my travels, I will give them. After saying that religion was the tyrant and tormentor of man and the author of his misery, he says that one man dared to meet this great enemy. Epicurus it was who "pressed forward, first to break through nature's fancied bounds, his mind's quick force prevailed, he passed through flaming portals of this world and wandered with his comprehensive soul o'er all the mighty space, from thence returned triumphant, told what things can have a being and what cannot, and how a finite power is fixed to each, a bound it cannot pass. And so religion that we feared before, by him subdued, we tread upon in turn. His conquest makes us equal with the gods." Here is a man who had seen slavery in the form of religion and politics, for both are tyrants to man. I have said I differ from all others. I have seen the effect of their beliefs. I have broken their hold on my mind, passed their finite bounds and landed in an open space. Do you wish, reader, to take a trip to the world beyond the narrow limit of man's wisdom? Give me your hand and close your eyes from the natural world and rise into space, out of sight and hearing of the bustle of the world. View the vast space and sit till you see things come as it were standing on nothing.

See the things created by the Almighty Power and things created by man. Look upon the earth and ask what the inhabitants know of this state. This is the world they fear and falsely worship. Now return and make your knowledge practical by destroying the beliefs of men in their opinions. My theory, being in opposition to the world, is based on the fact that man's misery is in his belief. The world is in opposition to truth. Like the South, it wants to rule so that every man who would enslave his fellow man is a rebel, but he who would free all men is a loyal man. So there is a constant war of ideas between slavery and freedom, disease and health. Not everyone who holds a slave is a believer in the principle, neither is everyone who believes in disease in favor of oppressing the sick. It is through the ignorance of the masses that slavery of any kind has its power.

1863

Cause of Man's Troubles, The
[BU 2:0534]

Do man's troubles arise from his errors? I say that they do, but this is merely an opinion unless I can show more proof than my base assertion. I will try and give some proof of what I say. All will admit that if a person believes he is acting rightly to himself, he is. But if his acts are condemned by the world, he must suffer the penalty of them. This is true of every act in man's life. It is true also of the sick in every stage of disease from a lame ankle to a confirmed cripple. Their belief is the cause of their trouble. Man never acted at all unless his acts were a combination of these two same laws. Sometimes they are separate and sometimes they are not and when they are not, then comes in the mystery as the interposition of God. Now if man knew what he was composed of, that is the identity called man, then his wisdom would put a different construction on his acts. Man is a combination of ideas and opinions and beliefs arranged into a form called man. The owner is not seen except by the representative which acts outside the real man. The true scientific man is not known by either of the other two. The scientific man is the one that deals out to the natural man and he moves the figure or machinery called the natural man. Now the figure or machine is the thing to be studied for it is the facsimile of the owner. And if the owner owns his body or machine independently, then all will go well and he will be happy. But if some one has a mortgage or claim on the body, then he shows it by complaining.

If consumption gets a claim on a person, it will not let him off till it saps the very foundation of the vineyard. For the body is like a vineyard and the owner is responsible to himself for his acts. If he buys anything, he must pay for it and there is no escaping from it. It is like buying an article that we do not want merely because some person will trust us for it. But the pay day will come and if we cannot pay, we shall have to be cast into prison till the debt is paid. As Christ or Science is the Savior, when he comes and explains his truth, it pays the debt and sets the debtor free and he tells him to beware how he gets into debt again. Now every person knows that there are thousands of ways of getting a person's money for some trifling object which is of no use whatever. So that if a person is not on his guard, he is liable to spend more than his income. This is only the emblem of the spiritual man. His spiritual body is the vineyard; his errors are his debts; his wisdom is his riches. The world is the merchandise and the peddlers and traders are the ideas that are asked to be bought or believed.

Now every person is thrown into the community where all these hawkers and peddlers are. And their ideas are the articles of the world which every one wishes to buy, for they think they cannot get along without them. The doctor brings out his sign and puts in a card of what he keeps on hand. All kinds of diseases are hung out for sale. Here is a pattern: a thin face, sunken eyes, poor skeleton, all ragged like an automaton. Speak to it and you will see that it coughs and throws itself into a variety of forms. This you are asked to purchase and your curiosity is excited so that you pay the proprietor to explain how it is made. He begins to say that the first thing is to go out into the cold till you begin to shiver. He explains, and the image represents the feelings till you get so worked up that you buy the idea and give your note or belief and return home, with the assurance that if you manufacture any more or let it to your children, you must pay for the patent. So you give a claim to the disease and home you go, and now you have sold yourself for life.

1864

Character
[BU 2:0306]

I will give you the true position of your character. There are two characters. Perhaps it will be necessary to state what I mean by a character. I mean the position that one person stands in relation to another or to society. Society is the standard by which to judge all acts or characters. If society is bad to one set of persons, they set up their standard of character and judge the others. The good set up their standard to judge the bad and each tries to gain the ascendency. This keeps the world in a quarrel between the two elements of matter and under the control of error and ignorance. Ignorance sees no reason for law and thinks all persons are the same. Error sees the faults of ignorance and takes the advantage and sets up standards of right and wrong to judge the world by. All this is the wisdom of this world. Now there is another character not known by the natural world and which is opposed by both these controlling elements. This character is the child of science. It has no sympathy with the other two and does not contain the elements of either. Its father is wisdom, its mother is science and its character is in its acts. In the natural world it is not known to have an identity. This character seeks not its own happiness independent of others, but its happiness is in its acts and it lives on its knowledge. Now when this character is known to a person so that it can be identified in them, then the wisdom of man is looked upon as nothing in comparison to it. All man's wisdom is dross, compared to this wisdom.

How shall a person know when he is guided by this wisdom? I will give you a sign so that you cannot be deceived. Man of himself is a servant acted upon and governed by two powers superior to himself. These two powers you may call God and the devil, good and bad, or science and error. Now as the bodies of men are a machine to be acted upon by one of these two powers, through the servant, these bodies are like a vineyard under the guidance of the steward or master, who is responsible to his lord. So when the lord of the vineyard calls the steward to an account, if his acts do not harmonize with the agreement made with his lord and master, then the steward is turned out and another takes his place. I will now state the agreement between the steward and his lord. Whatever a person agrees to is binding on the steward and if you as a steward of your own vineyard or body agree that the laws are right and just, then if you do anything contained in the law according to your agreement, you must be punished by this same law, if not by the law of the land. For one is sanctioned by God and the other by man. And wisdom does not change but rewards everyone according to his agreement.

Now man had better look over his contract and see where he stands in regard to himself, as he is answerable to himself, for his happiness or misery is in obeying or disobeying his contract. Now suppose we name over some of the articles contained in the agreement and see if we are guilty. I will call them over and you may say under the knowledge of your agreement whether or not you agreed to them as real existing things, which were bad or ought to be dealt with according to law. I will begin with the first article in the agreement. Have you not agreed that it is right for you to respect your parents as you would have them respect you? You answer, Yes. Then this is one of the agreements entered into by you and your master. Now this is binding on you, for it was your own free will, so just what punishment the law has attached to breaking that contract is your punishment. This is in the agreement and there is no escape, for everyone must give an account to his lord of his stewardship. So that whatever you have acknowledged as wrong or have given your sanction to as just and right, you are subject to.

You have acknowledged that to steal is wrong and to punish a person for stealing is right. This is the law of man and you have given it your sanction as right, so you have helped bind burdens on the people that you cannot remove. The wisdom of man is not able to remove this burden, so men are under these laws and the obeying of them makes one character and the disobeying of them the other. So the world is in a quarrel to see which party shall rule. Ignorance finds fault, though it does not wish to correct anything, but is willing everything should remain just as God made it. The other character wants to change everything and establish its own standard. In this way the science of wisdom finds no foothold in either of these two characters. Jesus called them Scribes and Pharisees. Each of these two characters often produce a phenomenon through a third person, as for instance, when Joseph was sold to the Ishmaelites. According to wisdom it was necessary that such a mind as Joseph's should go into Egyptian darkness to lead the people to a higher knowledge of a truth. Ignorance never would have carried such an act into execution, neither would error. For error is never guided by wisdom; therefore it must come from a higher power than either ignorance or error. It was wisdom acting through error and error not knowing it. As the light was in the darkness and the darkness comprehended it not. So wisdom acting through error brought about a scientific benefit to mankind, but the world knew it not scientifically and attributed it to some unknown law or wisdom of God and they gave the power to an unknown God as they always do.

Paul said to the Athenians when he saw a monument or error with this inscription, TO THE UNKNOWN GOD, Whom you ignorantly worship, him declare I unto you. This God was science or wisdom for the word science was not used then, so that any truth that was governed by wisdom or science was a miracle, for it could not be understood by the two characters, ignorance and error. These two with the third character made up the trinity. Ignorance is the weight or matter, error is the velocity or mind and wisdom is the direction or intelligence. Each one is necessary for an effect and neither can act alone. Wisdom must act on mind and mind on matter. As weight and velocity make mechanical power, so mind and matter make spiritual power governed by a wisdom superior to both. This last element, wisdom, is not known in the natural world except as a mystery or unknown God.

Error has always been looking for this power as it is called but when it comes it is not known. For everything that is known scientifically is not taken into account. So that the very God that ignorance ignorantly worships is near them even in their mouths and they know it not. As Jesus said to the Scribes and Pharisees, You draw near unto me, that is, this truth, with your mouth, but your hearts or knowledge are far from me or the truth, and you worship me, teaching for doctrines the commandments of men. The wisdom that acted upon Jesus was the Christ and when Jesus spoke of it he called it God. This was where all the mystery lay. The people thought that Jesus had a power, for science was not known so science was the god they ignorantly worshipped. When they asked him where he got this power or how he cured diseases, he said if they would tell him where John got his power of baptism, he would tell them how he cured disease; this they could not do, so they stopped his explanation. So I say to all who wish to know how I cure disease, if they, ask, tempting me as they did Jesus, I answer, Tell me how Jesus cured and I will tell you how I cure, for I answer everyone according to his sincerity as Jesus did.

November 1860

Christ and Truth
[BU 2:0115]

Eighteen hundred years ago, while Jesus was disputing with the Pharisees upon the old scriptures, He asked the question, What do you think of Christ or this truth? Has it a father and if so, who is he? The answer, "David," for this truth is David's ideas or theory. Jesus said, "If David is the Father of this Christ or theory, or ideas, or truth, why did he call it Lord if it was his son?" Here they both admitted a truth independent of the natural man. The Pharisees believed it was the offspring of David, and therefore called it David's son or theory. Jesus knew it was not of this world, but of God or truth and that it could be reduced to a science. This has been the rock upon which the people have split. This is the very thing to decide, whether there is a knowledge independent of man or whether it is the offspring of an organized being. Jesus called this truth the Son of God or Elias. Peter called it Christ. The people's ignorance confounded the two together and called it Jesus Christ. This last construction has given rise to all the religious wars and bloodshed since the Christian era. Decide this question and you shut the mouths of all the lions of the world.

Now let us look at the controversy of the two parties. This makes the two worlds–ignorance the one, and science the other. These two powers act upon every man. One is identified with the body and a part of it. Jesus gave some of the traits of that power when He said that it is of the earthly man and when He said, "Out of the heart proceedeth all kinds of evil thoughts." These thoughts are matter and are the result of error, superstition and ignorance, without any knowledge of God or Science. Science is the opponent of the above and as it accounts for all the phenomena, ignorance is destroyed. All science has had to fight this battle with the world of error and ignorance before it could establish its stand and take its position above the natural man. Then it is acknowledged and worshiped in spirit and in truth. Before it becomes a science it is under the laws of ignorance and superstition, directed by blind guides leading the blind by the knowledge of this world, and this Jesus called foolishness with God or Science. Now to separate these two, so that the wisdom of this world shall become subject to the knowledge of God or Science, is not an easy task. Almost all who have ever tried to do so have lost their lives.

I will not go back further than John the Baptist. He is the only one that Jesus seemed to put much stress upon. John saw that the time was very near when his truth or Christ would become a science. Therefore, he says, As the truth is laid at the root or foundation of their theories, every tree or supposed science that cannot stand the test of true science must be hewn down. Therefore he spoke of a science that he could not prove, but knew that it would soon be explained and become a science. Therefore his belief was like water that could wash away some of the errors, but when the Truth or Holy Ghost should come, then it would be reduced to a science. At this time Jesus had not received the Holy Ghost or knowledge, so as to explain it. Therefore He went with others to John to be baptized or hear John's ideas for truth. So when Jesus asked John to explain to Him, John modestly replied, "I have need to be baptized or taught by you." Jesus declined explaining, so John then went on to tell his ideas or belief. Jesus entered into the water or belief, and understood it, and when He came out of the water, the heavens were opened to Him and the Holy Ghost descended like a dove and lit upon Jesus and a voice said to Him and Him alone, This is my beloved Son or Science in whom I am well pleased. At this time, this science had no name till Peter gave it the name of Christ as an answer to a question put to him by Jesus. "Whom do the people say that I, this power, am?" Peter answered, "Some say Moses," etc. Jesus then said, "Whom do you say that I am?", not Jesus as is supposed, but this power; for all the persons that Peter had named were dead, so of course Jesus did not include Himself, but His theory. Peter answered Him, "Jesus, the Christ, the living God or Science." This science he called Christ. Then Jesus said, "Flesh and blood hath not revealed this to you." It must have come from the same power that Jesus had. Therefore He said, "Upon this rock or truth I will build my church or theory and the gates of error and superstition shall not prevail against it." This Truth or Christ is what Jesus taught. This broke the locks and bars, opened the prison doors and let the captive free from the old superstition and ignorance. By this power He healed all manner of diseases, cast out devils, established health and happiness, brought peace and good will to man.

This theory came in contact with all other theories, for there were false ones, and Christ warned the people against them. He said there were false Christs and told them how to distinguish between the false and the true. Now as Jesus became popular with the people, the chief priests and the doctors or scribes sought how to put Him down, and they tried in every way to catch Him. At one time while in the temple, the chief priests and elders of the people came to ask by what authority He did these things. Jesus answered them by asking them a question which, if they answered, would tell them how He performed His cures. The baptism of John or his theory, was it from heaven or of man? And they reasoned among themselves, saying, If we say, from heaven, He will say, Why then did ye not believe it? for they had killed John as a prophet. And so they answered, "We cannot tell." "Neither will I tell you how I do these things."

As it never has been explained how Jesus did these things, the people have looked upon them as miracles. But to suppose Jesus performed a miracle is to suppose Him ignorant of the power He exercised, and if so, He was just as much a quack as those He condemned; for He said, when accused of curing through ignorance or Beelzebub, If I cast out devils through Beelzebub, my theory or kingdom cannot stand, but if I do it by a science, it is not of this world but of God or Science, and it will stand. Here He makes a difference between ignorance and knowledge. Again, if Jesus was ignorant of His power and did not know how to explain it to others, why did He tell His disciples to go out into all the world and heal all manner of disease? If ignorant of what He said and gave no explanation of His manner of curing, He was as ignorant as they. But I am certain that He knew more than His disciples could understand, and after Jesus was crucified, the cures ceased to be done by a science but went back into the hands of priests and magicians and have been a miracle ever since, and the Christ that prompted Jesus' acts is not known at all. That Christ never taught doctrines nor creeds, nor offered up prayers. It did not belong to this world and it did not talk about any kind of religion. It talked itself. Itself was its life, and its life was the healing of the sick and distressed. It takes the feelings of the sick and knows their wants, and restores to them what this world has robbed them of. This is the Christ that was crucified eighteen hundred years ago. Now the only thing we hear is what was said about Him. Yet He is in the world but has no identity as a science.

January 1860

Christ Explained
[LC 1:0285]

I am often accused of making myself equal with Christ. When I ask what Christ is, I am told that Jesus Christ is one and the same. If I ask if Jesus, the man, was God, the answer is No, but God manifest in the flesh. Then can flesh and blood be God? No. Then what was that being that had flesh and blood who was crucified eighteen-hundred years ago? Jesus Christ. Is Christ God? Yes. Is God flesh and blood? No. Will you give me some idea of what that being was called Jesus Christ? Still the answer is, God manifest in the flesh. What do you mean by God manifest in the flesh? Why, that God took upon himself flesh and blood. Then what was that something that took upon itself flesh and blood? God. Is God a substance? No. Then can that which is not matter take matter upon itself? You ask too many questions, I am told. Well, if you cannot answer my questions, must I believe what you say without any proof? No, but we have the Bible and that says that Christ is God. Well, suppose it does and I ask you to explain Christ and you give me this answer, God manifest in the flesh. When I ask to have this explained you say, Why it is Christ. In all this you see, I get as intelligent answer–only an opinion of some person who knows no more than you do about it. Some think that words are all that is necessary, so they quibble about a certain word like this–the name Christ is said to be a Greek word meaning anointed. But what is that, I say. Does anointed throw any more light upon the Christ? Anointed is the name of something and this is what I want to have explained. To call it by this or that name is no explanation of the thing named. To call it Christ or Anointed or Messiah or Prince of Peace is only hopping from one name to another. I want to know what made that man Jesus who lived eighteen-hundred years ago different from other men. His birth I care nothing about nor is it of any consequence to this world why he was called Jesus Christ. If he was different from other men as I have no doubt he was, where was that difference and how was the world benefited by that difference? These are the questions. Now if you or any other man can prove to me that Jesus was not a man of flesh and blood, you make him a liar, for he says that he was flesh and blood; so now we have a man of flesh and blood just like any other man.

The difference between him and other men was called Christ. Now what did that difference consist in? In his life. What had his life to do with healing the sick? Has your life anything to do with healing a palsied limb? No. Then your good life cannot cure disease? No. Did Jesus' life cure? Yes. Then you must not claim to be a good disciple of Jesus, for if you claim to be a good man and we see no proof of your goodness on others, your goodness is of this world and not of Christ. You say he had a power. Now what do you mean by a power? We call steam a power and electricity a power but no one ever associates wisdom with them. Do you mean that Jesus' power was like the above or was it in what he said and did? It was in what he said and did. Well, what did he do? Did he not cure the sick? Yes. Well, how did he do it? Was it his power? Yes. How did he get it? It came from God. Did you not just say that Jesus was God? Yes. Then how could God come from one place when you and I both believe that God fills all space? Well, there is a mystery in the Godhead or Trinity that man cannot find out nor understand. Was not the Bible written for our understanding? Yes, but the mystery cannot be found out, so we have no right to penetrate the ways of God. There is enough in the Bible to learn and make us happy without searching into the hidden mysteries of another world. If the Bible was not for man's benefit, what was it for? If we are to take it for the word of God, who is to explain it? It explains itself. Do you understand it? In a measure. What do I understand by your answer? Can you give me any more light on the subject than what you have? No. Then I am as ignorant as I was when I began. Give me your opinion of Jesus Christ. Well, if you will listen, I will tell you what I know of Christ and what I believe of the man, Jesus.

I believe that there was a man called Jesus, the same that was called by some the son of David and by others the Son of God and by quite a number of names. I believe that he was a very good man from all accounts of him, but to take his own story, he was not the man represented in our days. This man always admitted a wisdom superior to himself. Now if there was a power superior to himself, what was this power? It must be God. Now is God inferior to himself, for this man Jesus prayed to this wisdom. How do you reconcile that prayer where he says: "Father forgive them for they know not what they do." This was the earthly man. Then the earthly man could pray like all other men? Yes, like earthly men. The ignorance of the people attributed to Jesus what he as a man never asked for or desired. On the contrary, he tried to prove to the people that there was a higher intelligence than they had ever acknowledged, except as a power without knowledge. This wisdom that Jesus had put him above the errors of the age.

The ignorance of the people could not understand and in their zeal to worship what they could not understand they confounded the man Jesus with his power as they called it and named it Jesus Christ. So now they worship the shadow of a substance called Christ. Christ is the name of something that the people applied to Jesus and in their ignorance they called it God manifest in the Flesh. This explanation is as clear as any part of their belief.

Everyone knows that there cannot be a shadow without a substance to reflect it. So when you speak of a thing, it shadows forth a form that has matter or substance. Now this world is made of matter and when we speak of anything that has form, the thing spoken of casts a shadow in the mind and the senses are attached to the shadow. For instance, if you speak of a man, you make a man in your mind; this is the shadow of your belief. Your senses are attached to the shadow of your belief, so if the shadow embraces a very bad man, the shadow is the same, and the effect on the body corresponds to the effect that the shadow produces.

Now when Christians speak of Jesus, they shadow forth a being with form and without form which is three persons, and only one that fills all space and yet is condensed into one person or being with all love, all hatred, and all power, but who will not use it, who knows all things and dictates all our acts so that not a sparrow can fall to the ground without his knowledge. Then they make another shadow of a man that fills some six and a half feet in height and contains all the power and wisdom of the above. This man they shadow in the mind as standing in one place calling persons to believe and they shall be saved. When asked, Saved from what? The answer is: From their sins. When I ask, What is sin? Everything wrong. If I ask if there is anything wrong of itself, I get no answer. So I come to this conclusion: that wrong is in ourselves and not in God and to act wrong is to do something that we have a feeling is not right. So if you agree that to injure another is wrong, you shadow forth your belief and the punishment attached to it, and your punishment is just according to your belief.

Now the truth is we believe in two powers: one wisdom called God, and the other, the devil. These were the names of these two powers in the days of Jesus. He acknowledged these two powers and tried to explain them. The true power was called Christ or God or by some other name. These powers have always been a mystery to the world. For when they hear the same person speaking through the same organs, it is very hard to believe and give the credit to another power. So when the people heard the man Jesus speak of himself and then of what he called God, it was a mystery to them. Therefore they in their ignorance put God in the man Jesus and called him Jesus Christ, the Son of God.

Now if the people had understood Jesus they never would have associated the Christ with him, any more than they would the science of mathematics with a man. Jesus was a man of flesh and blood as you or I, and he never intimated that he was anything more but always gave to Science or God the credit of all the impressions which he felt and which the natural man could not. Now this to you is a mystery, that one person can be two. But when you understand what the two means it will be plain enough to see what Jesus was trying to make the people understand. The people had no idea of Science, but thought that everything that happened which they could not account for was a mystery. So when they saw a phenomenon, they attached it to some invisible power. Their superstition put every phenomenon in some mysterious being. They were looking for some power to be developed that would put them in possession of some wisdom from heaven. So all that Jesus could say was of no force. The people would make him more than he wanted them to.

Jesus wanted to teach them a science that would make them better and happier but their superstition would not permit his explanation. They would rather believe in a power than learn a science. So they put false constructions on his acts and you cannot get Jesus' explanation of himself nor of this power called Christ. Now there must be some way to get at the meaning of this power or Christ. If we can settle down on a true explanation of that, then we have the same rock that Jesus had. He had the same trouble in his days. All the people admitted a power, even the Scribes and Pharisees, but they thought it was like the others that had appeared so they attributed it to the devil, for the belief in the power of the devil was common. Thus they classed Jesus among the sorcerers of his day, and had he been willing to be classed with them, he would not have met with the opposition that he did. But to explain what was never thought could be explained brought him in contact with all the learned men of his time. And as they were well, it was very hard to explain to them the feelings of the sick. Therefore Jesus said, "Those that are well need no physician," and as the standard of the well is applied to the sick, the sick had to be judged by the well. Thus you see the sick have no voice in correcting the evils that the well bind upon them.

Jesus could not sympathize with the well for they opposed him because he exposed their craft by which they held the sick in bondage. Now as every substance throws forth a shadow, the well throw forth one. This to the world is not frightful and does not produce any fear. Now all shadows that affect a person arise from a belief based on error and not wisdom, for true wisdom casts no shadow, neither does entire ignorance. Shadows come from error, so the fool knows no fear. And if a person was entirely wise he would know no error, for all would be light. So the light of God or Science is in the darkness or ignorance, but ignorance knows it not. Error sees the shadow of the light in the darkness of its mind and takes the shadow for the substance. Not knowing that it is a shadow, it reasons about the shadow as one man reasons with another not knowing that he is talking to himself but thinking that he is talking to some invisible being. So he is a man beside himself. All this is the effect of the natural man. In all this I embrace the religious man, the superstitious man, the infidel, the atheist and the deist. All the above are standing, reasoning about the shadow of their own belief, some denying it in toto, others believing it in full, but all affected by their own belief. Here on this platform stands all classes looking for the Messiah or Wisdom to explain the mystery of their belief. Yet the world is just as ignorant of the phenomena as though they all settled down on one belief, for there is no knowledge of science in their belief.

I will make a comparison to show this. Suppose Mr. A is ignorant of shadows and by chance sees himself on the wall by a lamp that he holds in his hand. The lamp makes the shadow. The error puts the fear of his belief in the shadow, so he calls on Mr. B, the skeptic, to explain the phenomenon. As darkness or ignorance is necessary to produce a phenomenon, they enter a room or state of mind about as dark as a room that cannot produce a shadow. So while waiting for the spirits, they kindle up a fire or error like a light. So the medium holds the lamp lit up and a shadow appears on the wall. The skeptic starts, his faith is shaken in ignorance, for wisdom he never had. Mr. A says, "Do you see that?" "Yes but it is not a spirit." "Then what is it?" "Oh, your imagination." "Don't you see it?" "Yes, I see something but I cannot make out what it is, but this I know, it is not a spirit." "If it is not a spirit, what is it?" "Oh, you get nervous and imagine anything." "Well, take this lamp and go up to it yourself." Mr. B takes the lamp and approaches the shadow and it is gone, so he believes.

An infidel, that does not believe in any God or devil but is as bold as a lion and fears not God or man, goes to investigate the phenomena. The conditions being right, they all enter the room. A lamp is produced and three persons appear on the wall. The infidel starts, his knees like Belshazzar's tremble; he is asked if he sees anything, any spirits. In a quivering voice he replies, "I don't know. I cannot exactly see." The medium who has the light steps one side; one of the spirits moves. The infidel pauses and says to the medium, "Ask the spirit to hold up his hand." The medium holds up his hand and the spirit does the same. A great many experiments are tried until one of the strongest minded men in the world is frightfully convinced that it must be spirits from another world. These are fair illustrations of the wisdom of the world in regard to the mysteries of life. In this, you see that three persons all agree in the phenomena. Their superstition, based on their ignorance, produced the phenomena. Their belief in spirits is as real as their existence so that want of wisdom in regard to lights and shadows keeps them in an error, and all their misery arises from their shadows or beliefs. This makes them nervous.

All of this is the effect of priestcraft. Their nervousness makes in themselves all sorts of evil spirits. This affects the body. Then comes a more hungry swarm of locusts called doctors, and they try to enlighten the sick. This class is worse than the others, for they admit their fears as a real existence independent of spirits. They condemn the phenomena of the spirits but admit all the proof that follows their belief as real phenomena. So you get a superstitious world within a world like a wheel within a wheel. So now all can be satisfied with the effect of their own belief. All this has nothing to do with the wisdom of God or Science. Science is not in the above, neither is Christ; all belong to the superstitions of the natural man or Jesus. Christ never made war with science. Jesus was never known to declaim against any truth that was based on science. All the war he fought was against the priests and doctors. The priests never could understand how there was any intelligence independent of man that could act through the senses. So Christ to them was an imposter.

Jesus tried to separate his knowledge called Christ from his own knowledge as a man. This was the hardest thing to be done, for if this one fact could be settled, it put an end to all the controversy, and the science of health and happiness would be established on earth as it was in heaven. This never was established, so the people to this day look forward to Christ just as they did eighteen-hundred years ago. And the Christians say that if Christ was on earth now as he was then they could be cured of all their diseases. For when I ask them, Do you suppose that if Jesus was alive they could be cured? They all say, Oh, yes! Now was it the flesh and blood that cured or was it the power that acted and took flesh and blood? Of course, it was the power and not the flesh. Now if it was the power and not the flesh, what was that power? Here we are just back to the question we started with, this something or power called Christ.

I will now try and see if I cannot separate it, and to do so I must take a patient, for the well know not Christ. It is the sick alone that know him. I will commence with one of my patients. You will admit I take your feelings. "Yes." "Could I have taken them through your ordinary senses?" "Yes." "Well if I feel your symptoms, I must be in sympathy with you, must I not?" "Yes." "Can you tell me how I get in sympathy with you and still retain my own senses?" "No." "What do you call this knowledge; is it not something higher than you possess?" "Yes." "Is it not more than any one of himself possesses?" "I cannot speak for another, but for myself, it is more than I can do."

You admit that I can tell your feelings. "I have no doubt of that, but the well will not believe it." I am aware of that and to such I am not sent, but to the lost sheep or sick of Adam's race. Therefore it is to the sick and not to the well that this is written, to open their eyes so that they can see how they have been deceived. I will now take you as a sick person and try to separate the Christ from the Jesus. You admit that I am with you or your feelings when I tell you what they are. "Yes." Well, what do you call that power? "I do not know." I call that power or that wisdom or that science which feels your feelings: Christ. Now Jesus says that false Christs shall spring up and deceive many, so he warned the people against them, and he told them how we should distinguish a true Christ from a false one. It is not every one that can tell your feelings that is a true Christ, but the one that can take your feelings and explain them away so that you can understand and be wiser by understanding; that is the true Christ. Now what makes the feelings? They are what arises from our belief. "Will you explain what you mean?" If we are in the dark, there are no shadows. Now suppose I tell you of something you never heard of. You of course knew nothing of it only as I explain. Suppose I should tell you of a man and give you a very minute description of his person. You would create such a person in your mind, would you not? "Yes." This creation of a man contains no effect on you one way or another.

After I have made you see him plainly, your belief condenses itself into what is called matter in the shape of an idea called man, but your senses are not affected by it. But suppose I tell you he is a very bad man. Now your mind is affected. This affects your idea or man. This, being your belief condensed into a man, is now disturbed and shadows forth a man according to my description. This last man is the offspring of your belief. So it is your child and I am the father. For you being married to my belief, this is the offspring. Now your senses being attached to the shadow, it troubles you and your trouble is your feelings; all this belongs to this world. Now suppose I sit down and talk to you about another world and try to explain it to you. Can you not see how you create it in your mind? "Yes." I explain heaven and hell and you have the two beliefs condensed into two ideas: heaven and hell. The former for the good and the latter for the bad, and you must govern your life according to the laws I lay down. For I am a minister of the Gospel and have wisdom that you must not dispute. After I bind burdens and lay them on your shoulders, I leave you to shape your life just as you please with this caution: that you must render to God according to your acts. Your life is now in the hands of man's God and as all things that man invents are his own, God has nothing to do with it at all. But you listen to man's wisdom and this excites your belief and sets your heaven and hell in trouble. This shadows forth all the terrors of a bad place and makes you nervous.

The doctor is called and he, like the minister, commences by introducing his stock in trade, which consists of all kinds of diseases from the gout to the consumption. He asks you all kinds of questions about yourself and then condenses them into a disease of which you are a stranger. This newcomer, like a lover, is not very acceptable at first. But by talking over his false wisdom, you become interested in it; and at last your mind or belief is completely overcome, and you become married to his belief. If you had any belief before, you have left it and become wedded to this new belief. Now as this new belief or husband is of this world, it is like all other bad husbands who are never happy except when they see others miserable. It begins to show its authority by laying restrictions on you. And if any of your old ideas or lovers appear, your new husband or belief puts his threats into execution. Suppose your new husband or belief is Mr. Consumption. Everyone knows that he is a very bad character. Of all hypocrites in the world, he is the worst, for he keeps you in fear all of the time. If you attempt to speak, he seizes you by the throat. And if you try to get rid of him, he seizes you by the side and in fact you are completely in his power. Now in your lonely hours, for you are always alone except when your tormentor is near, this belief throws out a shadow and the shadow is the child of your belief. So you attach your senses to this shadow and cling to it as a mother clings to her child.

Although her husband may be a bad man and her tormentor, yet she has some sympathy with him. The priests have invented a belief and called the people together. They pour out their wine or belief and the people drink of it and get intoxicated. And in their intoxication as in other dissipation, they fall in love and bad results follow. So the priests by their craft excite the people and in their excitement they marry the very belief that three days before they would not have listened to at all. The party breaks up and the company retires and as in all other gatherings where wine is drunk to excess a great deal of evil is done. After the excitement is over the lovers come; some have gotten married, others insulted, and some have left their father's house or innocent state of mind and have become the wife or husband of some bad belief. This was the case in the days of Jesus. He saw all of the above and saw where people were deceived. This knowledge of his was not of the priests or people but of a higher and more excellent wisdom that acted through Jesus and could see all the phenomena that the priests produced. This was called Christ or Science and was never applied to the testing of our beliefs.

Science was acknowledged in everything that could be demonstrated by a principle, but that man's belief should be made by science was something so new that when Christ came to test their belief by Science, they said that their craft was in danger. For if a man's thoughts could be felt and the effects of their thoughts on the body explained, the priests could see that their acts would come to naught. So this science of analyzing mind was a new idea that the natural man knew nothing of. This science came from the father of all and was always in the world but never acknowledged. So that all phenomena that were taking place in the world were looked upon by the priests as a revelation from God, and they were ordained to explain all the mysteries of the Godhead. So their explanation made the people seek this man Jesus. They saw from his peculiar organization that he could take the feelings of the sick, and the feelings being the shadows of their belief, science discovered the substance. And when Jesus' science or Christ analyzed the substance, he found it to contain hypocrisy and deception, based on ignorance. So he called this substance or belief the devil and the shadow was its child. So he said to them, You are the children of the devil and his works ye will do. He was a liar and abided not in the truth or science, for science has no beliefs but tries all beliefs to see whether they are of God or man.

Paul understood this science when he said, It was better not to marry or have a belief, but if you are not able to take care of yourself, it is better to have some belief than to be ignorant of all beliefs. Now the Christ that Jesus had was confined to the intelligence of mankind, to the opening of the eyes of the superstitious, loosening the tongues of the dumb, making the lame to walk and instructing those oppressed by the priests in the truth that sets them free. This was the true Christ. How can you tell a true Christ from a false one? By his science. If I tell a person how he feels and then he tells me his opinion, he is a liar and the truth is not in him. That is a false Christ. And if one tells you how you feel and attributes your feelings to the wisdom of man by locating a disease, believe him not, for there shall be many false Christs or theories.

The true Christ comes in this way. He takes no thought what he will say but it comes to him when he sits down by the sick and the answer corresponds with the feelings. For instance, if you feel a pain you have a wisdom of what the substance or belief is that makes it. So your Science or Christ will analyze the substance and explain it to the patient in language so plain that he will understand it. And as he understands, he embraces your wisdom and that lights up the error or belief till the belief is lost in wisdom and the shadow is gone. And you rejoice in the Christ or Truth that sets you free. This is the true Christ. So the word Christ is the name of that wisdom that can feel a sensation of another, analyze it so as to explain the error and destroy the belief so that the patient is set free from his belief. Christ is light. So is science and to be equal with Jesus is to do as he did. If you, by any power not understood, should do miracles or anything far beyond Jesus and do not know how you do it, then you would be a Christ, but an ignorant one. To be equal with Christ is to do the things intelligently and the wisdom is Christ; let it come through Jesus or any other man, for God has no respect for persons. All can learn to be Christ or Science if they only study.

1861

Christian Explanation of the Testaments, The
[LC 2:0671]

All religious teachers explain the Bible wholly or in part in a literal sense. Now a literal translation of the Old Testament destroys all the wisdom and beauty of the book. The books of Moses for instance are founded on the progression of the intelligence of the masses. They are illustrated by facts at different periods of the world, and in order to do this, literal illustrations had to be used to typify the intellectual progression. The writer commences with man and carries him up step by step to the commencement of civilization and shows his progress through the process of error to the land of truth or Canaan, and here is where the writer ends his history. It was never intended to be understood that he had no higher motive than to state certain facts about the children of Israel passing through the wilderness. He took literal facts and habits of the people and used them as illustrations of what he wished to teach. So when he tells what God did in six days, it is not to be explained literally, for no intelligent person can believe it; but heathen superstition had handed down these fables and Moses used them to explain the great Science he was to communicate to the people. His teaching was like travelers in a wilderness and he used the fables of certain tribes who had traveled to illustrate his truth. When a body of men migrate to a new country, they carry with them all their ideas of right and wrong and their religious principles.

After Moses had remained in Egypt as a teacher, his teachings become a part of the people's belief and his ideas of civilization and religion were not liked by the religious people of Egypt, so like all persecuted people, they sought a home in a far country. Like all emigrants, they must have laws to govern the people as well as science to teach them, and as they traveled, Moses instructed them in the wisdom of this great truth of science and happiness. This truth is the science of health, and as their diseases all arose from the Egyptian religion, Moses acted as a teacher and a priest.

Moses was the natural man and Aaron the science or truth that teaches man how to take care of himself. I have no idea that the word Moses meant any particular man but signified the natural man or error and disease, and Aaron, the science of the wisdom of God made manifest in the progression of man's development. The people's ideas were represented by Moses; the science was also made manifest through the same man called Aaron. The history of the world were the ideas of the heathen theology and Moses exposes their absurdity by parables. The history of Pharaoh and Aaron was a test of their powers or wisdom. The rod was his truth or arguments and the magicians' words were also their wisdom or truth. The subject or idea was the errors and they were like frogs and lizards, etc. They had, like the medical opinions of our days, got into their food and drink.

Ever since the world began, there have been two principles: one based on Science and the other on ignorance and superstition. One is called religion, the other, infidelity. These two principles keep together and run through every act of man's life, and each man is a part of them. Ignorance has always led but Science has passed it along. All religion is based on the superstition of man. You will find it in every revolution fighting against freedom. Wisdom is science; superstition and error is slavery. So the superstition of every man wants to suppress the wisdom of Science. These two powers are at war with each other, and all writers are impressed with one or the other and they have had as many names as political parties. One is always changing and does not know it; the other is progressing and knows it. The former is made up of those who profess to be true Christians or the democracy. They are like a man in the fog who sees no one but himself, so he thinks everyone is in the dark while he is in the light. The scientific man and poet pictures to himself man's progression and in his poetic strain illustrates his ideas by living facts or fiction. These little fables are handed down from one generation to another till the ignorant believe them as literal truth.

Progression is the power that moves the whole machinery, and ignorance is afraid of it, so it looks upon it as a mystery and tries to make peace with it. In this way religious creeds are started and combinations of men form into parties and clubs to contend against this. So they undertake to explain it to the people to keep them in subjection, for their lives depend on their ignorance. For as the light of science bursts in upon them, they are annihilated and so wars and strikes are kept up in hope of holding the power. Just go with me into Egypt and see how the people are governed by the priests or error, fighting progression. Listen now and hear men in squads talking about religious tyranny, working themselves up to the highest pitch of nervous excitement. They form themselves into bands or parties, spouting and arguing with each other. At last leaders are chosen and some form of government adopted; and someone wiser is instructing the masses, so at last a sort of covenant or beginning is introduced to account for all phenomena. As truth or error is the starting point, each claims the right to judge. As all things are admitted to have an existence, there must be a cause and someone commences with the creation of matter and uses the solar system as a figure of the creation of man. So he gives his ideas of man, not the shadow, for man contains truth and error. When God said, Let us create man in our own image, it meant wisdom creates man in the image of truth. When he formed man or matter, that was the medium for the image to have and control, like all other living things that were made out of matter. But man was of the dust or error of the world of ideas. So when he dissolved, his idea mingled with the dust or ideas of the world, but the image of God lives in its father, wisdom.

All will admit that God has all the attributes that man has, and no one will say that God is matter; neither will anyone say that he has not power over it, so it is not necessary for man to have a shadow in order to exist. Man exists outside of matter. To illustrate the ideas, man of science and man of opinions, I will suppose a case. Take a lamp and call it the body, the oil the life, the light the reason or mind. The soul is something these know nothing of; it is outside them all, comprehends each particular part and uses the combination for a purpose which no part nor the light itself can conceive of.

March 1862

Christian Religion Reduced to a Science, The
[BU 2:0380]

What is Dr. Quimby's theory? It is reducing the Christian Religion to a Science so that it can be applied to ourselves and others for the happiness and knowledge of mankind. By his theory we correct our errors which ignorance and superstition have bequeathed to us. It separates us from the phenomenon and makes man look for science or the cause outside of the phenomenon. Ignorance directs us to look for the cause inside the phenomenon. Now all mankind think and act upon these two theories. This is the field where all the battle must be fought.

The sun is the representative of true science, and the moon, of darkness and error, and everyone has these two lights in his mind and his mind is the field. Joshua is the representative of the law or science. His standard was truth. His opponents are represented by the five kings. Their standard was error. Now as truth goes forth in the mind to make war against error, when they meet, the armies stop while the leaders parley. Science shows itself to error as Joshua showed himself to the Amorites. The sensation of truth and error throws error in confusion and truth commands the two powers to stand still and they obey. The theories or kings flee, truth takes the field and the people rejoice.

Clairvoyance*
[BU 3:0124]

Clairvoyance is a state of existence independent of the natural senses. It embraces no matter, it involves no process of reasoning, but is Wisdom itself. Thought-reading is a lower state than clairvoyance, for the former, though still superior to the natural man, is in some degree dependent on mind. It embodies the ideas and reasoning of this world and is called spiritualism.

Clairvoyance, on the contrary, is entirely independent of the natural man. It is a higher state of being, in which we may acquire that wisdom which is superior to the knowledge of this world. It exists as a principle in every man: to understand and develop it is eternal life. In Jesus, whom it characterized above all others of his time, it was called <u>Christ</u>. It has manifested itself, in various forms in all ages of the world. Every new discovery in science is a proof of its presence and power. It is an entity of itself having neither beginning nor end.

Thought-reading should never be confounded with it. Thought-reading dies: clairvoyance rises from the dead. Thought-reading is simply perception of mental states as they actually exist: clairvoyance is perfection of Truth itself.

Clairvoyance II
[Another version of the previous article.] [BU 2:0048]

Clairvoyance is a state of existence independent of the natural senses or the body which has no matter, no reason, but is perfect knowledge. Thought-reading is a lower order connected with mind but superior to the natural man. This state is what would be called spiritualism and contains the knowledge and reasoning of this world. Clairvoyance is a higher state which is entirely disconnected with the natural man but can communicate through him, while in a dreamy or mesmeric state, information which the company cannot know. This principle is in every man. The understanding of it is eternal life. This eternal life was in Jesus and was Christ. It has manifested itself in various forms in all ages of the world whenever science has been discovered. This ignorance of the world with regard to this higher state of knowledge looks upon the manifestation of the thought-reading state as the highest development of man while this state dies and the clairvoyant state rises from the dead. It is all that is left. It can act on mind. It has an identity and never knew of its beginning nor ending. It is all the intelligence in man.

January 1860

Clairvoyance–A Detective in Disease
[BU 3:0891]

I notice an article under the signature of J. R. in your paper of the 14th in which the writer undertakes to show that clairvoyance is the surest test to a knowledge of disease. Now, I have no feeling towards any person claiming to cure disease by this or that mode, but when J. R. undertakes to enlighten the world in regard to what he pretends to know, he had better get the beam out of his own eye before he tries to take the mote out of his brother's eye. I believe I am as well posted in regard to clairvoyance as J. R. or I know that so far as its power is concerned in curing disease, it is a complete deception and it is the cause of more trouble than in any other mode of curing. Sympathy for the sick is all there is about it and if any person will follow my direction, if they do not satisfy themselves of the truth of what I say, I will forfeit my reputation as a man.

I have been for the last twenty years investigating clairvoyance and mesmerism, and it has opened my eyes to facts that have not come to the world as yet. It would be strange if I really believed that medicine was necessary to cure disease, that I should not give it. If my object was to sponge the sick and suffering, I certainly take the worst way to accomplish my object; but if my motives are what I pretend they are, to put men in possession of a fact that will keep them clear from such persons as J. R. who would have people believe that God has chosen the foolish of this world to confound the wise, if this is the case, he has certainly made a wise choice in selecting J. R.

For my own part I would examine persons for nothing and even pay them for it, if I wished to impose on them by selling medicines. I have no medicines to sell, nor do I recommend any, and I never meddle with what my patients shall eat or drink or wear if it does not interfere with their health. Then I tell them how it affects them and leave it to them to decide. If persons wish to take medicine, let them go to those who sell and buy for themselves. Those who would be cured in the way J. R. recommends by applying a test can detect whether the medium is clairvoyant or not. Blindfold the subject and see if he can tell what you have in your pocket or wallet. If they do that, they may see the state of your internal organs, but they cannot tell that it is done by reading the strong impression on your mind.

April 1862

Clairvoyance–A Detective in Disease–Supplemental*
[Originally untitled.] [BU 3:0657]

For many years I have been trying to convince the people that concerning my way of curing diseases, I am wholly separate from all that class of persons calling themselves healing mediums, clairvoyants and a variety of other names and any allusion to me, be it a sneer or civil, making this distinction is entirely satisfactory to me: I therefore tender my hearty thanks to J. R. the writer of a certain article which has recently appeared in the Argus, provided he intended the first few sentences of his remarks to apply to me. I have no sympathy for that class of persons whom his article is written to praise and when their advertisements begin by ridiculing me I feel sensibly grateful for the favor.

And now a word to J. R. himself–He says, "if we were suffering from cancerous disease or disease of the lungs it would be hard to convince us it was all in the mind." Now who is "us"?, of course we do not mean to ask any information about the personal pronoun. We refer to the man whom it represents. Is the thing that speaks the man, or the thing spoken of? Am I to understand J. R. to mean lungs is "the man" or does the man speak of the lungs as separate and apart from man?

Will J. R. tell what he means by the mind and show this charlatan where man is when man is out of the mind and where disease is separate from man. If man suffers pain is it man or the lungs and if the lungs are diseased is man diseased, and if diseased what becomes of man when this disease destroys man. Will man exist anywhere and if so will J. R. please inform this charlatan where man can be found outside the mind.

I am aware that in accounting for the phenomenon of disease I stand at great disadvantage with the world, and the odds seem fearfully against me, but I will stand by the principles which experience has developed to me and bide the result be it what it may. Because the world see no sense in saying that disease is in the mind is no reason why I am in the same place. So I should be foolish indeed if I intended to convey what they could not help meaning. They attach no meaning to the word mind in relation to the facts of real life, and do not believe that it is anything. But I use the word always with the same meaning. I use it to express the medium through which we receive impressions of every kind, from the natural world and from causes which are not within the range of the natural senses. I call it matter because it is something that under certain conditions comes to the bodily senses in the form of matter. It is the soil in which ideas of every kind grow and it is entirely subject to a superior element in man, as much as the earth is subject to the intent and skill of those who cultivate it, and I am convinced that to moralize the world in any direction you must go to the place where the seeds of error are first sown, and find their author. I contend that disease is an error. I know that it is based upon a principle of the life of matter, which the material world establishes with countless facts, that this body is the fountain and seat of man's intelligence and that it is an independent organization: I know that this principle is false and it is the rock on which is planted all human misery.–So it gives the evils that influence the life of man an independent identity. I am satisfied that the principle which my experience has unfolded to me, can now be shown in detail, so that man will choose it in preference to the other, since it points out a way to improvement and progress in which I can show that diseases spring from ignorance and a false philosophy and are a lie all through and if their names which include their character and course of action were not in the people's minds, these same diseases would not be in their bodies, for the body is the work shop where the inventions of the mind are manufactured in matter. This is where I differ from all others. I believe that man's life is not confined to this body. It is an unchangeable eternal substance, and what we see, hear and feel of ourselves and the world is the course of belief or order of effects departing from this fact, and which mankind have been educated into.

I take the ground that man is like a scientific principle put into the world to develop himself in knowledge and happiness, but as he begins to act, another element, error shows itself and which is so plausible and crafty that it frequently resembles the truth so much in appearance that man is deceived and led away from good by it. His life as we know it, is a continual conflict of these two principles. Under the first I have learned all matter becomes subject to his control. He pursues investigations in sciences, developing truth and experiments to satisfy his curiosity and he is an intelligent, honorable and happy man. But error has also a large share in molding man's life, and it has entire control of the body and makes his destiny disease and death. It begins with the bodily senses, denies all knowledge or existence independent of them in this world, and makes another for them to live in after the body is dead. Every artifice of imagination and craft is brought in to make the reality of the other world a sensible fact, and men are driven by fear to go where they would willingly avoid going, if a way was held out to them. Error has made the body the tyrant and inventor of man's misery, and yet man is forced to love and worship it from the fact that no other abiding place is known to him with equal or satisfactory intelligence. I can show that man lives in another world all the time, a world of the growth of ideas. There action and reaction, where the seeds of misery are sown and nourished until they come forth in the natural man. This is the world where my labors have been for these twenty years. I have endeavored to reduce it to language so it can be recognized as the fountain of every ones experience.

Little can be done to convince the well and by the well I mean those who are satisfied in every desire of their hearts, but the sick, who have grouped along the path of disappointment, and are driven and tossed from one shadow to another to get what they hope for, know well the hollowness and hypocrisy of the world they have met with and recognize with exceeding joy the light which I bring them for it reveals with certainty, that there is a way open to rid mankind of its great enemy disease.

When I say disease is in the mind, I expect the world will say that it is all humbug, for they it is who accuse and condemn the sick with one breath, but when I tell a sick person they have no disease, it is all their mind, I know they understand that I am trying to show to them a truth upon which their happiness depends. They can see the wisdom and force the arguments which I make to destroy the evidences of disease, and they know that I am honest and unselfish in the course I take, but to the well it is all folly. They see and hear nothing except what is plain before them, and have no interest at stake. They cannot feel how they crush the sick with their opinions.

Composition*
[LC 1:0043]

Nettie is sick. What is it? Has something come to her to disturb her and give her unhappiness, some thing?

If so, when and how did it come and how did it get hold of her? This is a fair question, for she did not feel so before, and what makes her feel now, if it is not some real thing that disturbs her? But no, we don't admit that any real thing has come and disturbed her; as far as we can tell, nothing has visited her in such a way and we don't believe these has. There is no real thing about it. Well, what is it? If she is sick, what is it? All people have a belief about it, but that won't answer the question, at least it doesn't. Then what is it that makes her sick, and what is her sickness?

To say, I don't know, and let it go at that, is simply to believe what other people say (doctors) about it and never know. But I am not satisfied with a mere belief about the sickness, which doesn't give any positive light upon it at all, but leaves me as much in the dark as if I had no belief. I want to know if possible, what the sickness is, or at least to free myself from thoughts and beliefs about it, that are not true, and only prevent me from discovering the truth. At one time she has a great deal of pain. Now what is it? She says her stomach is in pain. But what is this pain that comes and goes, is worse and then better? What is all this condition and change? What makes it? Where does it come from and where go? What changed it? If it were a thing of itself, where would it get its knowledge to work and to change, to come and to go, for it could not act without some intelligence. If it is a condition, it must have things to make it and change it to create it and destroy it, and where and what are they, and by what intelligence do they operate? We cannot establish it, cannot answer the question, our beliefs and ideas fall to the ground because we cannot find them, and they will not stand the test of argument.

Dr. Quimby comes to me in my dilemma and says, it is the mind that makes all the trouble. He says we live in our belief; and our belief makes us sick. That our sickness is a condition of mind, and all the changes we go through in sickness, such as sharp and moderate pains, and all the different sensations, conditions, and changes we experience, are the changes of mind through the belief. Now let us examine that idea a little. First, does he prove his theory? Yes, by his practice, allowing him to be the best judge of his practice. Then let us see how that idea accords with our experience. Take the case in hand. Nettie complained of a pain in her stomach. Now her stomach has no intelligence and if that pain is a thing of itself, it must have some intelligence of its own, by which to act and to inform her of its being there, else she would not know it. But there is no intelligent thing there. All the intelligent thing there is in her, is her mind, and all the knowledge she has of any pain or ill feeling or anything about her is in her mind. Consequently, when she says, "my stomach distresses me," or, "my head aches," it is not her head or stomach at all, for they know nothing and feel nothing, but it is her mind acting through her belief, because she believes in pain.

Everybody knows how the mind changes, and the thousand things that are all the time affecting it, and that it dwells upon one thing but a short time and this accounts for the changes in the pain in disease.

Again, I feel her pains, which I know by describing my sensations, and receiving her testimony of them. Now if these pains existed anywhere but in her mind, I could not take them, and again, I should be unable, if they were not of the mind, to throw them off by my belief and understanding of their true location (in the mind) and that there is nothing in them. This I do, and sometimes, when the pain is severe, also if I have ill feelings of my own, I have double proof, and more, that all excitations and diseases, are in the mind, and nothing but beliefs and false ideas. This sickness disappeared after a day.

1864

Concerning Happiness
[LC 1:0638]

There is one point of belief in which all men are agreed, viz: that the better a person is, the happier he is. In this, as I said, all are agreed, and the only question to be considered or argued is how shall we live so that our lives may be good and happy. Parents differ from one another as to the manner of rearing children. They do not all see alike, and each one has some peculiar belief in regard to the right way in which the child should be brought up. They may all be honest, yet some of them are deceived. Thus religious belief of parents has great influence on the child for good or for evil, and they stand to their children as God stands to them. If they believe that God requires obedience to his will as a duty they owe him as their preserver and friend, then they want the same obedience from their children. All kinds of religions are arbitrary and require submission to its will. It is the natural working of the earthly man. He asks to be worshipped in order that he may worship. In his ignorance, he invents some form of worship and this to him is religion. Jesus had no religion, yet he worshipped not any one's God but a truth, a science that he could feel and appreciate; that was his God, but it is not the God of the present religious man. His God is one of power and strength, a God that must be obeyed, a God that requires prayers and a strict regard for his laws.

The whole sum of man's belief is this, that there are two worlds: one that we now live in, and the other that we shall inhabit after death. For man believes that he must die and that his body must decompose and return to the mother earth, while his soul, if he has any, will return to the God who gave it. When men asked if they will know their friends in the other world, they answer, O yes. Ask what the soul is, and they say it is the spirit of a person. Can you see a spirit? O no. Can the spirit return to earth? Well, we differ on that point; some persons think it can while other persons think otherwise. Therefore some think their departed friends are with them, while others think they are absent. They all agree however that we must all die or something to the same effect, that we throw aside this body and assume a spiritual body.

Now this same controversy existed in the days of Jesus, and many were the questions put to him in order to learn what belief he entertained in regard to the dead. Now I believe that I entertain the same ideas in regard to death as Jesus did, and although to others it may be an opinion, I know that what I say is a truth. Science is not matter but wisdom reduced to practice. Error is matter for it can be destroyed. If I should tell you that you had committed an error in regard to a certain business transaction whereby you had lost quite a sum of money, and I make the error so plain to see that you believe it, there would be no effect on the body or matter. If what I said did not contain something and it still produced an effect, then it would seem that nothing can produce something; therefore that which I called an error was something real, and I call it matter because it can be changed. The mind can be changed and the ideas annihilated and still the mind will exist. A house is built of stone, the house is matter therefore. Now you destroy the house, but not the destruction of the matter, for the matter is eternal and cannot be destroyed, though its combination may change. So it is with beliefs which, like buildings, are made of matter. The belief may be destroyed but the material remains and can be formed into other ideas, as is the case with any other matter. Man's belief is all matter. His religion and ideas of disease are all false beliefs, and the effects produced on his body are caused by them. Man's creator is in him, and governs him, yet he is recognized only as a principle without wisdom.

Assuming that man and his beliefs and all that we see of him are matter and can be changed, I will endeavor to produce a man that is not made of matter, one that you cannot see except through your belief, but whom nevertheless you will admit. You will admit that there is such a thing as memory, yet memory cannot be seen. You will also admit there are certain principles which we call science, but you put no wisdom in them. Now it is just here that we differ. Jesus was a man of matter, but Christ was from God or Wisdom, and no one will say that God is matter or that he can be changed. Jesus' superiority over the natural man came from some wisdom above opinions; therefore if you believe that his wisdom came from God, you must admit that it existed before the birth of Jesus. If so, what was it and what was its identity? It could not be seen, yet it was admitted. We are told that it came into the world and the world knew it not. It came to its own and its own received it not. Probably all will admit that this something was intelligence. And if it was, and it is admitted that intelligence can come and go, and yet not be seen, then it must have an identity, not of matter, but of something else, something that cannot be destroyed; and it must be wisdom.

Wisdom must contain within itself all of man's knowledge and ideas and know what is true and what is false, and yet be invisible to our belief. Yet it is the power which governs all matter, whether in the form of man or beast. The world that Jesus came from when he said he came from his father is not the Christian's world but the world of wisdom. And when he came into this world, as it is called, he did not mean this world of matter, called the globe, but the world of opinions or the people's beliefs. Christ came from wisdom into error to teach the child of science that we are held in bondage by the errors of religion, that this world was not his home. For he had a house not made with hands or man's belief but by wisdom, which is eternal, and that the temple or belief which held him must crumble to pieces and be destroyed, the matter returning to matter to be subject to wisdom. To convince the people of this was to teach a new science, and when a person grows up and rids himself of error or opinions, then he lives in wisdom and is no longer a man of matter.

I will give you my belief, for to you it is a belief, though to me it is a truth. I will take a man giving him all the wisdom of the religious world and address myself to him and show wherein we differ, yet he cannot see the difference, for having eyes he sees not and ears but hears not and a heart but cannot understand. He chooses opinions or darkness because he cannot bear the truth or light, for science destroys error and sets the truth free. To make the difference between our beliefs plain, it is necessary to set them down side by side. A religious man is one who acknowledges himself to be flesh and blood but having a soul within him which, after the body dissolves, goes to heaven. The soul is a belief to him but the flesh and blood is a reality. I ask him to give me his ideas of the worlds. If I understand him, he means by this world the material globe and all that is in it. This constitutes the religious world. The other world to him is but a belief, while this world is a substance, a truth. His belief is founded on the Bible.

He believes that God made this world before he made man, and then he placed man in a literal garden wherein were all kinds of fruits and bade him eat of all kinds but one, that man in this garden disobeyed God's commands and in consequence lost his right to the other world and was banished from God's presence. Seeing that man would not return to him of his own accord, God pitied him and sent his own son Jesus Christ into the world to pardon all men on certain conditions. Man of himself can do nothing. His salvation is not of works, lest they should boast, but it is a free gift of God. And to obtain this gift man must forsake father and mother, house and home and acknowledge before God on his bended knees that he is unworthy to be called a Christian, that he has sinned against God; and if he had his just deserts, he would be cast out of heaven forever. He acknowledges that God is the embodiment of all benevolence, that his tender mercies are over all his children and that not one hair of our heads can fall without his notice. He believes that God has prepared a place for him and will sometime send his angel to bear him to his home when he puts aside this earthly body. I will not say that I have given the whole belief of the religious man, for I have not, but these are some of the principal heads. But unless we comply with all this and much more, God will cut us off from all his blessings and turn us over to the evil one. This is a literal statement of the Christian's belief.

I find this truth in the words of Jesus, viz: My kingdom is not of this world. Jesus then had a kingdom unlike man's, and my kingdom or theory is like that of Jesus, as I understand it. Man's kingdom is in another world outside of this material world, and Jesus came into this world and established his kingdom, but his kingdom is not like that of the Christian. This world to the Christian means this material globe, and Jesus' kingdom was in man's belief which was matter also. Man was a literal substance and could be seen by the people. Christ or science could not be seen except by those who had this science. One came by sight and the other by feeling and sympathy. The good and wicked were all in this religious world, while no unclean thing could enter the kingdom of Jesus.

The Christian is all the time trying to convert the wicked, while Jesus was trying to destroy them. The Kingdom of Jesus and that of the people were so different that Jesus could see no resemblance between them, and he destroyed the kingdom of man in man to establish his own. He aimed to destroy the devil's kingdom and that is what I am aiming at. Whenever he destroyed the kingdom of man, he holds up his own, creating a new heaven and a new earth, as the old heaven and earth had passed away. The fire shall run over all the earth, burning up every root and stubble, from which shall rise a peculiar people that shall worship God day and night.

I will now give my ideas of all this. This world is man's belief. The truth is the science or true shepherd. This truth put in practice is that which takes away the sins or errors of man, and the end of error is the end of the world. The introduction of religion based on science is the commencement of the new world. The science which shall devour our errors is the teaching of this great truth. The sick are those who are bound in prison before the flood and the opening of the prison doors is the understanding of this truth. Peter is the science that holds the keys or theory. All that are loosed on earth by this truth are loosed in heaven or in their belief. To preach Christ is to put heaven in practice, to liberate the poor and sick who have been bound by the false ideas of the world. I know of no other world than that which Jesus set up in man's heart, which meant the mind. He never had any reference to this globe as a world. His two worlds were science and error. He made but one for himself, and that was science. But man has made another world from his beliefs and that was the world that he came into, in order to cast out the children of the kingdom of error into a lake of fire. That is, he enters man's belief and destroying all error, he establishes his kingdom of science so that men shall come from the east and west, north and south and sit down with wisdom. It is then that the children of error are cast out and that was the end of the world. Then a new world begins and a new religion springs up based on science. Under this religion, no man will say to another, Do what is right, for all will do right because he will feel right in so doing.

1865

Concerning Revolutions and Rebellions
[LC 1:0587]

Freedom is the child of science; error or aristocracy is its opponent and is the casket or earth which holds the child till it is able to take care of itself. Man as a nation has both these principles, freedom and aristocracy. The working of error to keep freedom bound creates revolution. These revolutions must take place and will, till error is destroyed.

There is a species of rebellion that is a sin against the Holy Ghost or Science. It has been said that revolutions never go backwards, but revolution is only another name for a rebellion to destroy some error. It is true that rebellion is the natural working of the mind and is in some cases right. Rebellions that go backward are evils for they not only destroy themselves but they do much damage to society, but still they work out a greater truth.

Probably the rebellion in this country is the first one started for enslaving liberty and freedom. All other rebellions have been to free man from oppression and improve his condition. The Revolutionary War was to free us from the oppressive yoke of Great Britain, and after we had achieved our freedom, we still had the elements of oppression or slavery in us. And although we formed a constitution, based on the principle of self-government, yet there was an element in it that would not agree to this. It was a government admitting the right of revolution. Those revolutions which expand the areas of freedom are the natural workings of mind.

Revolutions in religion have always been taking place, but you will find that the liberal principles of freedom get the mastery over the aristocracy of slavery. It is the same with the medical; there is also a revolution, and freedom has not got its just due yet. The medical faculty holds its iron grasp on the people from which they cannot escape. The sins for the nation are like individual sins. Slavery is the effect of man's belief and the belief was fastened on us by our fathers.

We do not believe in the old Mosaic priesthood that sin is of divine origin, nor that our parents, having eaten of sour grapes, the teeth of the children will be set on edge, but that everyone must answer for his own sins. And if we sin against God or Truth, we must pay the penalty. The United States Government is not a thing you can take in your hand, but like Science is a principle that is implanted in the heart of every man. And if its presence is not felt, it is because it has been kept down by the error of slavery or aristocracy. So revolutions must take place till everyone feels that he is a part of the government and constitution, and if he has not this feeling, he is a stranger in his own land.

The revolutions of progression which are dictated by wisdom never made war to oppress but to liberate. Rebellion is to rebel against freedom in support of slavery, and all the states which are in rebellion have lost all rights under the constitution and have no claims to state rights which they had at the formation of the government. And a revolution of opinion and gunpowder must take place in order to destroy this right in the states. For the states are all combined to make the government and this union was sanctioned by God or Wisdom. Then the people bowed in subjugation to the will of the majority. Yet the right of states was acknowledged. But when some of the states seceded against the will of the majority, then this error was cast out, never to be reinstated.

The difference between rebellions and revolutions is this. Revolution is headed by the liberty party of all the world. Rebellion is got up by the aristocracy for their benefit and the enslavement of the many. Now the idea that a revolution and a rebellion depend on circumstances to change the name is wrong. But as all governments are founded on revolutions, the idea of revolution was right to a certain extent; but when a government is formed on the popular voice of the people, that is the answer to all the questions of self-government. For if a government cannot stand against a rebellion, waged against liberty, it clearly shows that the time for revolutions to cease has not arrived. But when all will admit that the people themselves are the government and to destroy the voice of the people is to destroy the government, then any act perpetrated against the liberties of the people must necessarily come under the head of rebellion; for the change must bring anarchy, aristocracy and despotism.

It must be admitted that our government is intended to be the voice of the people. It is perfection, as far as man's wisdom goes, and therefore to destroy it is wrong. The South, having destroyed their claims to the right of self-government, cannot destroy what they gave to make up the Constitution of the United States. By rebellion they gain nothing but lose everything. They lose the privilege of state rights and they guarantee to the Union the right to govern all the states, subject to the laws delegated to them, and to oppose them was rebellion against their own state. And thus, as a House divided against itself, they could not stand. Now they, having lost their state rights, it does not carry the state out of the union, for the state belongs to the will of the loyal men in it. And if there are enough loyal men left in the state to form a constitution, leaving out state rights, then the state is at harmony with itself. And no rebellion would have taken place in the United States, but in the state laws, which can always revolutionize for the better. But to rebel against itself is suicide to all concerned, and they lose all claims to self-government and must be treated as rebels or aliens and have no voice in the state till they are restored to their rights through a proper course of law.

Concerning the Use of Medicine
[LC 1:0628]

I am frequently asked if I am opposed to the use of medicine. To this question I answer that as the people are now educated, they believe a lie as a truth and therefore to tell such persons the truth would be to them like telling lies. So I would not destroy the law but fulfill it and wisdom is the end of the law to all who believe. To those who believe in disease there is, according to their belief, neither forgiveness nor cure except through the medium of medicine. But to those who have been born again or who have learned that disease is the result of a belief, disease has no power, and consequently medicine is useless. "Seek ye first the kingdom of God and all these things shall be added unto you." That is, seek first the science of health which is wisdom, and then all things will appear plain to your understanding. To take a person who believes in disease to cure the sick is like taking the hair of a dog to cure it's wound or like punishing a crime by a penalty similar to the offense, which barbaric custom is still kept up and sustained as much as the medical faculty. All remedies are based on the law of health. The doctors admit health to be the standard and a deviation from it a crime, deserving punishment. So if you have any complaint, you are examined by the doctors; and if found guilty, a blister, emetic or some other proper punishment is administered till you repent. And then if life enough remains in you and you are not found guilty of other offenses, you recover. And if not, you are found guilty of another offense.

Now if by explanation simply, a person can be cleared from the charges brought against him without the use of any remedies and be thereby convinced of his error and can learn to do good, which is to understand; then he is born again and ready to enter the kingdom of heaven or science. He can then enter this world of opinions and plead the cause of the sick and rescue them from the hands of their enemies without paying any great penalty. Perhaps if the criminal believes he must take a little cathartic to pay the debt that he has contracted, he may be allowed to take it, not because the person rescuing him believes it to be necessary or because the criminal is liable but because it gratifies the patient, who believes there is honor even among thieves. His protector only yields to an old prejudice which still clings to him.

When Paul converted a person or performed a cure and the patient wished to be baptized, he complied, not because he believed there was any creative properties in the water, but simply to gratify the convert. There are a class of ideas or persons who are never satisfied until they cause the poor to suffer for their sins. Man is a government of himself and some have certain animal propensities which cause them to torment themselves and such feel happier to be punished, like the man in the days of the Salem Witchcraft who, believing himself to be possessed of a witch, was not content till he was beaten almost to death in order to show that the witch might be cast out. The sick at the present day are not satisfied till they have been purged and blistered almost to death in order to kill the disease or witch which possesses them. When the reformation came, reason took the place of the stake and whip; so when science shall come, wisdom will take the place of the drugs of the physicians and the tormenting hell fire of the priests. Men will be guided by the star of science which points the way to wisdom. But medicine will be administered to the sick till the time when science shall step in and make a sacrifice of all these errors and then will come the end.

Jesus, seeing the folly of the world's belief, offered himself or his opinions as a willing sacrifice to the world in order to show man a higher and better way to salvation or the recovery of one's health. And then he rose from the natural world into the scientific world, there to appear in heaven or science for us. Once for all he laid down his life or belief and put his trust in science, believing it is able to cure the sick and save man from his sins or errors. The priests and doctors are still offering up sacrifices in the form of opinions, prayers and blisters, etc., none of which can take away the sins or errors of the world. When science comes, it makes an end to all these deceptions and introduces a new mode of reasoning to all who will receive it. The new heaven is this new mode of reasoning and to enter into it is to be baptized in the blood or belief of Jesus which is Christ or Science and which will wash away all opinions. I baptize with water, but when the real truth rises out of your opinions, then you will be baptized with fire or wisdom and the Holy Ghost. The Holy Ghost is Science or the explanation of the Father which is Wisdom.

All persons who come to the truth must be born again or baptized. And it is not strange, as in the case of the disciples, if some persons should cling to the old ideas; and therefore we must sometimes yield to their superstition. If they believe themselves ill with a bilious disease and cannot consent to go through the fire of truth but wish to be baptized of their old ideas, then we must administer some simple medicine, not that it possesses any curative qualities but simply as an offering to their ignorance which they imagine must be made; otherwise they cannot recover or be pardoned of their sins. Medicine contains nothing to me except as an effect and if a patient believes he must use it, I sometimes allow him to do so, but I always tell him the cure is in himself or in his belief and not in the medicine. If schools were established where persons could be taught to correct the errors of the sick in regard to disease, then they could approach the sick, armed with science, and the opinions of the sick would melt away before their reasoning, as darkness before the light of the sun. Disease is a cowardly belief and he who knows it is to the sick as a teacher to his pupil. The errors of the pupil can be destroyed by the wisdom of the teacher. The passengers on board the steamer can be enlightened by the wisdom of the Captain. But if he is as ignorant as they, and the ship, encountering a gale, succeeds in coming out safely, it is not by the skill of the captain but by a universal wisdom that sometimes guides man through the darkness unknown to all. A person outside of all those beliefs in disease is to the sick a savior, whether the sick are aware of it or not, but if they know it of themselves, they become their own pilots.

It may appear strange at first thought that belief can cure us, but it is readily admitted that belief can make us sick. Now I affirm that the belief is the very thing that I wish to destroy. If there was nothing to believe, we should have no belief. When you see a person you know to be your friend, you do not fear he will hurt you; but to have a belief that he might injure you, you might have some cause for your belief. Whether real or imaginary, to you it is real. Now if you were aware that your suspicions were wrong, the belief that he would injure you would vanish. So with disease, the error is the same. The cause was invented by the superstition of the world, and the people have been so imposed upon through their ignorance by the priests, till the idea disease has taken a living form and now is to man as real as his existence, and yet in reality it is as false as the religion. The time of the foundations of the Mohammedan religion can be ascertained, but now it is a living reality with as much life as the Catholic or Protestant Church and contains as much truth as either of these.

The medical faculty has exercised more power over men's minds than the priests, for all men believe in disease if they do not in religion. To me, both are alike. One tree produced both. The popular belief in religion as explained by the clergy of the present day is as absurd as the belief in disease. Yet every person believes more or less of each. Some persons appear and profess to disbelieve in religion and also in medicine but they still cherish a belief in both, and at the least approach of danger, they fly to one. The opinions of the priests have as little influence on me as do the doctors. They only strengthen my conviction that if honest, they are deceived and ignorant, and if not honest, they are hypocritical. And to those I can only hope that they will repent and turn aside from their wickedness ere it is too late.

1864

Conservatism
[LC 1:0537]

Conservatism is the body or disease to be corrected. Error is its opponent and so is science. Conservatism is opposed to both. Error is like a stream set in motion, governed by no theory, only chance. Science is the wisdom that directs error. Conservatism is the body to move. Now put language into these elements and you will hear how they reason. Now as I said, conservatism is a disease. Error is progression without wisdom. Wisdom gives direction to error and conservatism is a dead weight or the thing to destroy. To illustrate it, take the application of steam. Error would set steam in motion without any regard to science. Science would instruct error. Conservatism would oppose both and reason in this way. You can't make steam propel anything. Error says, I can propel everything. Science asks how? Error can't tell.

Science explains. Error does not understand. Conservatism says, You both are too fast; let steam alone and I will come out right but you are both wrong. But as error keeps up the fire, the steam holds back till science makes the engine and the steam forms and tries to escape from the _ _ _ _ _ _ yet it won't start. But when science unites the steam to the piston, then the body conservatism moves off in triumph.

Then conservatism says, Now this is just what I said. I told you to wait, the time had not arrived. But now it has come. So the water is made into steam by the force of error controlled by the wisdom of science. The steam never dreamed that it had gone through any change, for steam is water, hot or cold. So conservatism is matter or weight at rest or in motion and it never had the element of wisdom in it. It is the element to destroy and it destroys itself as fast as it moves. So with all progression. Take governments. All governments are like individuals. They either hold their identity, body or government or they dissolve and take new identities. The principles or science live. Take this government. Its life is its principles. Its principles are progression and freedom. So it contains, like individuals, the trinity or element of the Godhead, progression, without any definite idea of any kind. This element contains also freedom. Therefore as it has the element of freedom, it will not be bound if it can help itself. But as it has in this element no wisdom, it acts against its own reason, for when it wants freedom, it will enslave its opponent. Now as freedom is the principle to be obtained, science has to direct error. So science is the only element that can exist. All the other elements are always changing. This is death.

1864-65

Consumption–Second Sitting
[BU 3:0735]

A person in consumption consults Dr. Quimby. He describes their feelings satisfactorily. So they see he knows something about them. He then says: "You are afraid of consumption."

Patient: "I know that I have consumption. I know that my lungs are diseased."

Dr. Quimby: "How do you know it?"

Patient: "My doctor has pronounced my case consumption."

Dr. Quimby: "I say you have no consumption or disease of the lungs."

Patient: "How do you know that?"

Dr. Quimby: "You will admit that I told you your feelings in regard to your lungs?"

Patient: "Yes."

Dr. Quimby: "I had such feelings when I sat down by you, and I have no consumption. Why could not you have such feelings produced in some other way?"

Patient: "But I know that my lungs are diseased because I have such pains and suffer so much with my cough, etc."

Dr. Quimby: "Have I not taken all your feelings and do I not cough and raise as you do?"

Patient: "Yes, but it is from sympathy."

Dr. Quimby: "Well, if I take your feelings from sympathy, why could not you get these feelings from sympathy with some other person or idea?"

Patient: "Do you think I make all this sickness, or imagine my lungs are diseased?"

Dr. Quimby: "No."

Patient: "Then why do I have these bad feelings and cough if I have no disease? Do I imagine them?"

Dr. Quimby: "No, your feelings are real, but it is your mind."

Patient: "I have no mind about it. These feelings come without my mind, for when I sleep, I am still sick."

Dr. Quimby: "What is your mind?"

Patient: "My thoughts and abilities."

Dr. Quimby: "What are your thoughts about yourself?"

Patient: "My thoughts are that I am in consumption."

Dr. Quimby: "Then are you not in your thoughts?"

Patient: "I am when I think about myself."

Dr. Quimby: "Then are not your thoughts your mind?"

Patient: "Yes."

Dr. Quimby: "Then is not your disease in your mind?"

Patient: "No."

Dr. Quimby: "Where is it?"

Patient: "In my chest."

Dr. Quimby: "How do you know it?"

Patient: "By my feelings."

Dr. Quimby: "What are your feelings?"

Patient: "They are my consciousness of suffering."

Dr. Quimby: "Is not this consciousness your disease?"

Patient: "Yes."

Dr. Quimby: "Is not this in your mind?"

Patient: "Yes, but I should not have had this consciousness if something did not produce it and how could I ever have got this disease by my mind?"

Dr. Quimby: "By embracing false ideas and belief and receiving opinions for truth."

Patient: "What false ideas make me cough?"

Dr. Quimby: "The false idea of consumption which is a humbug."

Patient: "Do you mean to say that consumption does not exist and that people do not die with it?"

Dr. Quimby: "It exists as much as people believe in it. But it is all a lie. Men worship false gods but that does not make them true. Public opinion has made consumption and mankind embraces it as true and when it works its way destroying its believers, it says, `I am the truth' and death is its proof. I say there is no principle in disease. It is an error that truth can correct. Mankind reason entirely wrong about themselves, from a false belief and produce disease which is called upon as a witness to the truth of the very theory that made it and they will never be well or happy until they turn around and change their belief. You believe that there is something in your body independent of yourself that is consuming your frame. All around you are of the same mind. No one, save one, has ever thought differently or said so if they did. Your feelings are the symptoms or working of this destroyer and to cure you would be to get you out of this belief and make you see the humbug and imposition to which you have been subjected. I say that your physical health is entirely under the laws or operation of the mind and one is the expression of the other."

Patient: "I do not see how this can be, for we see those of strong minds confined to a weak and sickly body."

Dr. Quimby: "This may be in some respects. Your mind may be strong and healthy on every subject but that of health. But if you are sick and locate your trouble in your body, your ideas cannot be right about yourself. Flesh and blood cannot originate disease, but they carry it on, being formed in the mind. You think that a vital power exists in your body independent of your mind, which works the machinery of your pains, creating disease, and finally exhausting itself in death do you not?"

Patient: "I have every reason to believe that my vital powers are declining under a wasting disease and the condition of my lungs will testify to this."

Dr. Quimby: "You would like to get well?"

Patient: "Certainly, if it were possible."

Dr. Quimby: "Who says it is impossible?"

Patient: "The doctor and all my friends."

Dr. Quimby: "How do they know?"

Patient: "By my symptoms."

Dr. Quimby: "What are your symptoms?"

Patient: "All my bad feelings."

Dr. Quimby: "Have I not taken your feelings?"

Patient: "Yes, but you have no disease."

Dr. Quimby: "What should make the difference between us, if we both have the same feelings and why am I not in consumption and liable to die?"

Patient: "I do not know that, but there is the difference of health and disease and I am in danger of dying while you are not."

Dr. Quimby: "Are you aware that it is your belief that makes the difference between us?"

Patient: "Of course it is and reasonably." .

Dr. Quimby: "Would you not like to change your belief and be as free from disease as I am?"

Patient: "Certainly if my belief affects my health."

Dr. Quimby: "Have I not shown you that your disease is in your mind?"

Patient: "You have in words, but I do not believe it. You make out a clear case, but I do not see as that has anything to do with my disease."

Dr. Quimby: "This is where I shall try to explain to you what I mean. No phenomenon in the natural world ever produced itself and no irregularity, disturbance or disease in the human body ever was self-created. But they must be dependent on some cause which being ascertained comes within individual knowledge and experience, but not coming within the cognizance of the bodily senses is left in obscurity. When the trouble becomes apparent in the bodily senses, mankind in their ignorance assume that the cause is in the phenomenon thus giving matter life and creative power. Mankind believes that the life of the body is a separate and independent identity from that of the soul and that its life dies and whenever they get into trouble, they reason upon this belief. Mesmerism proves that an individual can act with all his faculties: reason, see, hear, taste, etc. entirely independent of his body, and numerous experiments show how completely a subject's organization is controlled by the belief and affected by the thoughts of the mesmerizer.

"When a person feels a pain in the side, the first inevitable construction of the world is that something is the matter in the body, while my experience teaches me to attend to the mind of the person as connected with it, not what they are thinking about but their state of mind whether nervous, anxious, sad or frightened, etc.; and in detecting this, the idea of their fright or whatever their state of mind might be comes too. If I understand the idea which induces their state of mind sufficiently to convince them or bring them into the same state that I am about it, then I make a cure."

Patient: "What do you find is the state of my mind?"

Dr. Quimby: "You are melancholy and afraid of consumption, and if I succeed in destroying the ideas that imprison you, then you are free."

Patient: "Do you suppose that you can ever convince me that I am not in consumption, when I have such proofs?"

Dr. Quimby: "Certainly not, and if I do not change your feelings and make you feel better, I cannot expect you to believe in me. I know that consumption is based upon a false belief and is generated by wrong ideas in the community and that it is fed and nourished by those who have the care of it. Whatever idea tends to make us unhappy cannot be true though it may be believed. If I can succeed in convincing you that your ideas concerning your health are false and that you have been drawn into this state by those who are as ignorant as you, then I shall help you out of your difficulty. Nothing can affect you unless you know it. You may not know it enough to tell it, but you are conscious of it. This disturbance I call mind. That, that knows it is disturbed, is the intelligence. Some time you have been disturbed so that it affected your system and in your trouble you have called upon those who have the care of the welfare of human bodies to help you. Now, it is satisfactory to know there is a cause for your trouble even though it be a bad one. But instead of going back to find the cause of the present trouble in some former time or experience, they go forward and fix upon a disease which is to flourish in future to account for the phenomenon; and by their belief, treatment and reasoning, they bring about a change to accord with their opinions. At the time the doctor told you what he thought was your disease, you were not in so bad a condition as now?"

Patient: "No, the disease was in its early stages and had not made such progress."

Dr. Quimby: "Now, when you first learned that your lungs were diseased, you believed it, and a horrid idea of consumption with its wasting, sufferings and sure progress and termination was formed in your mind. This ghost has kept you company ever since and sleeping or waking, it enters into every sensation you experience. Your friends, from sympathy and pity, force it upon you and in all the wisdom of the world there is no way for you to get rid of it. Everyone who pities you makes you worse. Therefore you withdraw yourself from all. As you never met anyone to help you, you look upon all mankind as enemies. So you look upon me as I talk like an imposter who is trying to get possession of you. If I do so it will be by destroying the opinions of your friends which keep you sick."

Patient: "You deceive yourself if you think my friends keep me sick."

Dr. Quimby: "I do not say that your friends willfully and intentionally harm you, but they are of this world and embrace the opinions of which your disease is made. You, being sick, are sensitive to the influence which your friends, by their pity, exert upon you. They depress and will destroy you. You feel better when I am with you, do you not?"

Patient: "I do not know. I want you to come to see me."

Dr. Quimby: "Do you know why?"

Patient: "I can't help hoping your mesmerism may benefit me."

Dr. Quimby: What is that?"

Patient: "The gift you have of healing."

Dr. Quimby: "I do not pretend to have any such gift and if I had as great a one as you would give me, I do not see how I could cure you if I believed as you do, unless I took the disease and died myself. I come to break the prison wall that surrounds you and if I did not know what it was, how could I do it? If I did not know what consumption was, how could I destroy it? In this world we are subject to any idea that we cannot scientifically destroy and we are affected by them all, from the most petty disease of fashion to the lowest superstition. Our minds act upon each other more indifferently than we are taught to believe. For instance, I establish an intercourse with you, perfectly intelligent to myself, purely mentally, and discover all your troubles by asking a single question. This you admit and this proves that you, as an individual, are entirely independent of the body which you inhabit. There is not a particle of knowledge in that body of itself, but it is a servant or medium of communication which you employ between yourself and others in the same state. That that sees is not the eye, the organ, and that that is seen through the eye is not the truth but matter or an idea, and it is the meaning that we see. This intelligence that controls the senses, I, by my practice, come in contact with. That disturbance which makes you come to me produces certain sensations on you which I feel, and in these sensations is the answer which you wish and which comes to me. This answer, if I can make you know and feel it as I do, is your cure and the science lies in making you know it. If I do not succeed it is not the fault of the truth, but the skill of the operator that is at fault."

Patient: "Well, I do not believe you can ever affect me so as to make me believe that consumption is all in the mind. I have not imagination enough for that."

Dr. Quimby: "I hope I shall convince you that I do not insult your intelligence by telling you a lie and then cure by a trick. Some time in your experience you have got disturbed and the answer you have sought and obtained has made all this trouble and you have been affected according as you believed it. Then you go to work and form the very trouble you are directed to and then comes your misery. In trying to get out of your trouble, you act upon your body through ideas that man has made. It requires no effort for a well person to breathe, but let that person become excited, by religion perhaps, so that the system is convulsed by their emotions and this very effect frightens them. Then they begin to breathe according to the ideas of man and every breath is laden with ideas of disease and death and they produce the very symptoms that they most fear. God never made any way of breathing which would make consumption. The act is regulated by natural principles of the circulation of the air and heat and cold. These principles are understood enough to be applied to machinery, but man has never thought of applying them to himself. He does not reason that he is a machine made by a wiser hand than himself and of course adjusted to true principles."

SECOND SITTING

Patient: "I have been thinking of what you said to me yesterday and now I want to know why you so persistently insist upon saying that my disease is in my mind, when I know that it is in my body."

Dr. Quimby: "What do you call the mind?"

Patient: "The intellectual ability, and you know very well that does not have consumption."

Dr. Quimby: "I differ from the world in the application of the word mind."

Patient: "What right have you to differ? What do you depict the mind to be?"

Dr. Quimby: "I say that mind is spiritual matter."

Patient: "But it is not so."

Dr. Quimby: "Cannot the mind change?"

Patient: "Certainly."

Dr. Quimby: "Can wisdom change?"

Patient: "No, I suppose not if it is true."

Dr. Quimby: "Then mind cannot be wisdom, for mind changes. Consequently, it must be matter or a substance that can change and take form."

Controversy about the Dead
[LC 1:0058]

The religious world has always been in a controversy in regard to the dead. Before Jesus taught a resurrection from the dead, the Pharisees believed that the dead rose at the end of the world. Others believed that spirits came back and entered the living, but there was no idea that was satisfactory to the thinking classes. The Sadducees disbelieved in everything, but admitted one living God. This was the state of man's belief at the time Jesus appeared before the people. He spoke as never man spake, for he spoke the truth and his truth gave the lie to all of the opinions of mankind. I will take the liberty of putting my own construction on Jesus' ideas or truth and leave it all to the common sense of the people to decide which is the most consistent with science or truth. You will see that at the time Jesus spoke, the idea of an identity of our existence after death was never taught, and to teach such an absurdity as that to the Jews was blasphemy. Therefore, Jesus had to admit the same ideas as the Jews, or they would crucify him at the commencement of his reform. So he admitted all their beliefs but put a spiritual meaning to them all. Jesus never spoke to the people but in parables, for his object was to reform the world of their superstition. Their belief was got up by man; their priesthood and all their ordinances were of this world or of man. Now Jesus opposed all of it from the beginning to the end; therefore he spoke in parables so they could put such construction upon them as they pleased and thus be shown the absurdity of their belief. So his sermons and talk were called out in answer to some questions asked him by the rulers of the people and his answer was in accordance with the questions put. But in it was shown the absurdity of their belief, so they could not catch him.

The greatest evil to overcome was the resurrection of the dead. This was a very difficult question to solve, for Jesus never believed in the natural body rising and to deny the resurrection of man was just as absurd as to deny the resurrection of the body; so to deny one and prove the other was not an easy task; it would upset all of the people's beliefs. So he had to admit a resurrection and teach it. And as the people called sin, death and truth, life, it was very easy for Jesus to adapt these meanings to his teachings. He could then show that the resurrection from the dead was a resurrection from an error to a truth, but this must be explained by a parable. Now this was what Jesus intended to convey to the people, that this power that they could not account for and which they ascribed to evil spirits of the dead was a science of ourselves and, although we are ignorant of it, yet it is ourselves and embraces all we are and all our senses. It is life itself and a knowledge of it is to put it into practice so the world can be benefited. The ignorance of it embraces all of the phenomena but in ignorance of their causes. This makes man superstitious, for he is ignorant of himself and believes that this belief is all there is of him and so it is till he is brought into a higher state of mind that can see that man has two minds or knowledge. One embraces matter and is in it; the other is the science and is out of matter but uses matter as a medium to convince the natural man of a higher knowledge of himself. It was Jesus' mission to convince the natural man of this truth. So when he spoke of Jesus he spoke of the earthly man, but when he spoke of Christ he spoke of the heavenly man or science. This the people could not understand, so when he said that he should rise from the earthly man, Jesus, he spoke of this Christ or knowledge. The people had no idea of what he meant to convey to them and when they saw him taken and tried they all forsook him and stood afar off; some denied him. This showed that they expected that Jesus would be crucified. This embraced Jesus Christ and all of his preaching and when he was crucified that ended the life of Jesus Christ to them.

Now, to rise from the dead was what he had promised his followers and they believed that Jesus intended to prove that his body or Jesus, which was flesh and blood, should rise. Here was where they misunderstood him. Jesus never intended to convey any such idea. Now if the people had understood what

Jesus meant, they would have put a different construction on all the scene. If they had known the facts, they would never have troubled themselves about the man, Jesus, but (would) have let that body remain in the tomb and when Jesus showed himself to his disciples and others then they could have seen the flesh and blood in the tomb. Then he, that is Christ, had established the saying, although you destroy this flesh and blood, you don't destroy the knowledge of it and this same knowledge can make to itself another body and show it to the people to convince them of eternal existence, not after death but a progression of our knowledge.

Now, I want to be as liberal as I can to the friends of Jesus, but I must say that in their zeal to establish what Jesus told, they made a great mistake, or at least some of them, for I believe that they did steal or take away the body of Jesus to establish their belief that it rose again. Now this just upset all that Jesus intended to prove, that is, that although they destroyed the flesh and blood, I, that is, Christ, will show myself to you to prove that man can live and have all his faculties and knowledge after the world calls him dead. Now as it stands, it shows nothing for no one expects the body to rise. In their zeal to carry out an idea, like all religious fanatics, they left the whole affair in a worse state than before. This gave rise to all kinds of controversy and as Christ had made himself manifest to the people, they of course believed that his body rose so it was not long till the believers were fighting, just as they are in our days.

Paul said to them, "I understand there is a dissension among you as touching the resurrection of the dead." Now he says, "If Christ be preached, (not Jesus, but this truth or science) that he rose from the dead, or from Jesus, how say some among you there is no such science or resurrection and all is of no force?" You see the people confounded the two ideas together, that is the people called Jesus Christ one and when he rose he was one because they had no idea of two identities. Those that differed from them had to contend against this deception of those fanatics that stole the body of Jesus, for those who believed the body rose were more enthusiastic than those who believed in the science. You will see how all those persons who can work themselves up to believe that the time is coming when our bodies will rise again are just about as far behind the times as those old persons who believe the time will come when the factories will be abolished and the girls will return to the spinning wheel and loom and railroads and steam will be done away with. If they get any comfort out of that kind of food, I, for one, will not disturb their repose. I have commenced climbing Jacob's ladder and I have never heard of the top round. It is said to reach to heaven so that the angels could descend on it. The Christian ladder has from one to seventy or eighty rounds, so when man climbs half his life he takes the other half to get back where he started. That makes him once a man and twice a child. So I suppose he commences a child and climbs to a man and then steps over and returns to a child. This is proof that man is a mere bubble. This is all that is held out to man as proof. It is true that we are told that we shall rise again or at least the soul. When we ask for proof we are referred to Christ but when told that there was no proof that any other flesh and blood rose, then comes mystery and we are called infidel because we don't believe what they don't prove nor themselves believe.

May 1860

Conversations with Patients during a Sitting
[BU 3:0640]

(Patient) I wish to ask you a few questions in regard to the way in which you cure diseases. Do you use medicine? (Doctor) No, none at all. (P) I have a bad feeling. (D) I never want a patient to tell me their feelings, that is my business. (P) That is all the better, for if a doctor can tell me my feelings I shall have more faith, but you say you don't use any medicine? (D) No. (P) Well, I don't understand, but I suppose it makes no difference with you. (D) No. (P) If you tell me what makes that pain in my side ... (D) I just said I did not want you to tell me anything in regard to yourself. (P) Oh, yes. Go on and tell me if you feel that pain I have in my shoulder. (D) I can't examine you. (P) Why not? (D) You can't keep your tongue still. (P) Why, I have faith, and if you will tell me how my head feels I shall have perfect confidence. (D) I must put off my examination for the present, from the fact that you cannot know anything about my mode of treating disease. So if you will listen I will try to make you understand, so that if you choose to come again you will know how to proceed. (P) I can't see into it all I want to. (D) Stop or you will let out some more of your trouble. (P) Then you do not want me to tell you anything? (D) No. (P) Then I will be silent and you may go on. (D) No, I will not go any farther this morning, but I will give you some idea of how I cure and how I find out the trouble. (P) Well, I should like to hear for I understand you are a mesmerize–some say you are a Spiritualist, others that you are a humbug. But I do not care what you are provided you cure my lame back. (D) That's right, let out all you know. I have told you not to tell me about your feelings. (P) As I do not care about the theory, I will not stop now but come in tomorrow. Good morning.

Here ends one dialogue of a hundred cases. It is almost impossible to make some persons understand what I mean and these are the facts. I stand before the public just as this patient says. Some say I am a mesmerizer and Spiritualist, others a humbug. Some understand my position and come intelligently and, while others come believing in some of the above theories, I have to take every one as I find them and it is very hard to get along with some. Here comes one of another class.

After learning that I am the doctor she says: I called to see if you ever cured consumption. (D) I never give an opinion at all. My opinion is worth just as much as any physician's and that is nothing. (P) How do you cure? What is your mode of treating disease? (D) I believe disease is all in the mind and treat it accordingly. (P) You believe there is no such thing as consumption, that it is all in imagination? (D) I do not believe in imagination. (P) I thought you said consumption was all imagination in the mind. (D) You said that, not I. (P) I cannot see any difference. (D) Then because you cannot see that a person may believe a lie and be affected, then it is all imagination. (P) I don't understand your meaning. (D) I mean that if you have a pain you know it. Is your wisdom all imagination? (P) No. (D) Suppose your pain stops, do you not know that and is it not a fact, too? (P) Yes. (D) Then where is the imagination? (P) There is none in that. (D) So it is with all cases. Disease is not seen at all except in the effect. The cause is out of sight. The medical faculty takes the shadow for the substance. This makes all the trouble. Let the medical faculty make this difference between causes and effect and then you will see that the effect called disease is a result of some opinion.

An opinion is the answer to what we think we know, from the sensation that is made on our mind. There is no wisdom in the cold air nor in the heat and the science is to teach the child that the fire will burn and the cold make you chilly. The fire and the heat and the child are three different things. When the child comes in contact with the cold, the sensation is the disease or deception and the effect is the phenomenon. This holds good in every idea. The trouble is in the fact that the wisdom of man has never been reduced to practice or science so as to receive the idea that mind is ideas and takes form just according to the wisdom you admit.

September 1862

Copperheads Caught in Their Own Trap
[BU 3:1089]

The trap laid by the Copperheads was to defeat the administration, and for that purpose they invented all sorts of plans to embarrass the administration. They opposed the war as unjust and cruel and used all their efforts to embarrass the government in raising troops, saying it was a Nigger war and let them fight it out, and by trying to prevent men from enlisting. Yet some of the Democrats would not heed the warning, so when the people appeared to cry aloud to those that would enlist, they used all their efforts to stop their men from going.

At last when the cities and towns voted to pay the soldiers for going they opposed that and said it was not legal and they would not pay their taxes. So they threw every obstacle in the way they could to prevent the government from getting men.

They would not take any interest in the welfare of the poor sick soldiers, would not subscribe anything, nor go themselves. In all this there was no law to compel them and they expected to have their property protected and get rid of all the burdens that they could. So when the government saw the drift of these copperheads, they saw that the burden was on the administration. So to remove this burden or make it fair and equal, they passed the conscription act.

Now this act worked like all traps and caught them in their own trap for this brought them up all standing. At first they bounded and surged and tried to get clear, but the more they tried the tighter the bands held. Seeing that the draft must come, the next thing was to prevent the men from going, so a plan was set on foot to let the towns vote to pay them three hundred dollars for a substitute. This is all the government wanted, for they could get men everywhere for that; thus they have been caught in their own trap. So now if the towns have to pay, they will have to be taxed, so they have but one more loophole; that is this: there is no law to collect this tax if the people refuse to pay, and in this case there must be a law passed. So they expect the Republican Party will take the loans and they would say to their Copperhead brothers, This money was raised by the Black Republicans and if you will vote for me I will oppose every law that will make you liable and they will repudiate this debt. So one ounce of prevention is worth a pound of cure. All vote for the money to be raised but let the capitalist assure the money to the bank.

Cor. 15.21
[1 Corinthians 15:21.] [BU 3:0802]

As in Adam or ignorance all men die, so in wisdom all men shall live, but every man in his own order. Wisdom is first and then every man according to his own understanding of it. Science being the body of wisdom, every man's science shows the capacity of his intelligence. So as ignorance being the embodiment of matter, just as the matter of body is dissolved by the science of wisdom, the scientific man rises out of his matter or darkness and shines in his wisdom. This is the change called by the natural man death, and so it is, but not the wisdom of science but to error.

Man has two identities, as mechanical power: weight and velocity. And his senses are attached to both. Wisdom being the first cause, as the weight or error or natural man is forced on by wisdom through the scientific man, the weight is destroyed by the velocity of progression and the scientific man finds himself out of his errors and learns that the weight of error to him now is nothing but an idea that he can use for his own convenience. Then he will see that wisdom and mind are as separate as a steam engine is from the man who made it. But the man of error puts life in the matter as though the engine and man were one and the same and reasons as though, if there never had been a man there never could have been an engine, any more than an engine could make a natural man. Both are matter, but matter must go through changes before it becomes a medium for the light of wisdom to form or create scientific truths and develop them by a science.

For instance, all wisdom exists outside of any ideas. Matter being an idea, it must be subject to wisdom. So science is the developing of matter according to the principles of wisdom.

The natural man develops himself according to the principle of matter, but the wisdom of the creator not being in matter, the natural man and brute are governed by its own law or principle. But there is a higher and more excellent law or principle that matter knows not of. This principle teaches the scientific man that matter of all kinds and descriptions in the material world is subject to his science or will and man himself as we see him is nothing but the shadow of an idea that science can change at pleasure, just as a man knows himself. So the death that we speak of is the enemy to progression, for it keeps matter in a gross state and retards progression. It is the darkness that science has to wade through. It is the cause of all the misery, for it acts on science as the cold winters act upon the earth. It closes all the avenues of life or vegetation, till the heat of summer bursts forth and life springs from the tomb. So error holds science in the grave of death till the trumpet of wisdom sounds through the pores of matter and quickens the soil and heats up the earth.

1865

Cures
[LC 1:0394]

I am often asked what I call my cures. I answer, the effect of a science because I know how I do them. If I did not know, they would be a mystery to the world and myself. Science is wisdom put into practice. For when it is understood it ceases to be a science and becomes wisdom to all who know it. This is the case with all wisdom acknowledged by the natural man. To him it is a power or mystery but to the wise it is wisdom. The wise make this difference between the two wisdoms. The natural man's wisdom is based on an opinion, but the scientific man bases his on a wisdom that can be demonstrated by facts and this demonstration is called science. So when we say that such a thing is based on a scientific principle it is the same as saying that it is wisdom superior to an opinion.

There are certain truths admitted by the world as science, that is, they cannot explain them, but to such as have wisdom there is no science but wisdom. All wisdom that has not been acknowledged by the natural man is called a power or gift or spiritual demonstration, not a science. The curing of disease has never been acknowledged to be under any wisdom superior to the medical faculty, so they by their opinions have kept the world in darkness till now, and how much longer they will do so I cannot tell. Now to put the world in possession of a wisdom that will make the natural man acknowledge a science is to admit the person who teaches it superior to the medical men. This is what I am trying to do and if I succeed in changing the minds of men enough to investigate they will see that disease is what follows an opinion, and that wisdom that will destroy the opinion will make the cure. Then the cure will be attributed to a superior wisdom, not a power. I will give one or two illustrations to show what must come to pass and how the people must be divided since they cannot serve God and Mammon, for if a person believes one, he cannot believe his doctor or anything that makes him sick.

I am accused of interfering with the religion of my patients. This is not the case, but if a particular passage in the Bible or some religious belief affects the patient, then I attack it. For instance, a person gets nervous from his belief that he has committed the unpardonable sin. His wisdom is attached to the sin of his belief, and his belief is someone's opinion about some passage in the Bible that he believes applies to his case. I know this is all false, so of course I have to destroy his opinion, and this destroys the effect which is the disease. His senses are attached to an opinion, mine are detached from the opinion and attached to the wisdom that shows the absurdity of the opinion. Their wisdom is of man, mine is of God or Science. All disease is the punishment of our belief either directly or indirectly, and our senses are in our punishments. My senses are attached to the wisdom that sees through the opinion so that my love or wisdom casteth out their disease or fear; for their fear hath torment, and perfect wisdom casteth out all opinions.

Now it never entered man's brain that man's wisdom is a part of himself. The natural man speaks of wisdom as a science which he has not got but wants to get, so of course his senses are not in the thing he has not got. The wise man has what the natural man is looking for and does not know it, when it is in his very thoughts.

We talk about the very wisdom that the natural man calls a gift. He calls it a science when he is the very science himself and knows it not.

I will make one illustration. Everyone will admit that a musician can play by note and compose music and teach it to another; this is a science. Now is it wisdom above the man who cannot play or compose? All will say, Yes. His wisdom is a mystery to the natural man but he knows that he can teach that wisdom to another and he calls it a science to distinguish it from that wisdom that arises from an opinion.

The musician's senses are in his wisdom, the natural man's senses are in his opinions; one is of this world, the other is of a wisdom far above. To be born again is to get the natural man's senses out of his opinions and attach them to wisdom. The science of music is lost in wisdom; then his wisdom of opinions has become subject to his wisdom of truth. These are the two kingdoms and every man is subject to one or the other and each man contains them both and is judged according to his acts. One is eternal and the other must come to an end and, as man has borne the one of opinions, he must also bear the other, for opinions cannot live where wisdom is.

May 1861

Curing Disease Must be Governed By Law
[BU 2:0045]

Curing disease must be governed by a law. Sin or death is the transgression of that law and when there is no law, there is no transgression.

Nov. 1859

Curing without Medicine
[BU 3:0945]

The idea of curing disease without medicine is a new idea and requires quite a stretch of the imagination to believe it, and to me it was as strange as to any person; but having had twenty-five years of experience, I have found out that all our evils are the result of our education and that we imbibe ideas that contain the evils that we complain of. Ideas are like food, and every person knows that in almost everything we eat and drink, there is some idea attached. So ideas are food for the mind, and every idea has its effect on mankind. Now seeing how ideas affect the mind, I find that when I correct the ideas, I cure the sick. For instance, the idea liver disease produces such and such a feeling, and heart disease certain kinds of symptoms. I might go on for hours giving the names and symptoms of diseases. Now if the people have all these diseases, for I know they have the feelings, then how can they be cured without the use of medicine? I contend they have all the symptoms that they say they have, but about the causes of them I shall differ with the world.

The doctors say they have this disease or that disease according to the symptoms that they say they have and therefore they must take some medicine. This false doctrine has taken possession of the people's mind and they believe it as firmly as the South believes that slavery is right. We see how the belief in slavery affected the masses; it took possession of their lives and it became a part of their identity, and it gave to them a peculiar character different from the people of the North. The North believed slavery was wrong and their belief gave to them a character and I leave the people to judge what is the most Christian-like belief. It is impossible to make man act different from his belief unless he feels a sort of condemnation; therefore, a northern man to believe in slavery must be more depraved than a southern man; for one believes it right, and if the northern man believes it right, he is reasoning against all his early religious education. So I cannot believe him honest for I cannot admit he is so ignorant as not to be affected by the influences around him. His party has blinded him into an admission of what he does not believe. So parties are formed and every person belongs to some one or another and their lives are made up of the ideas. Every form of religion has its advocates and persons are affected just according to their belief. The body suffers exactly as the mind is affected. Any belief that binds burdens on another binds them on ourselves. Therefore to do unto others as we would have others do unto us is the fulfilling of the law.

Now I have been so connected with man's beliefs and seen how they affect the body that I am sure that three-fourths of the misery can be stopped by explaining the causes. This I know I can do in public. When I first commenced operating on the mind I put persons into a mesmeric sleep, but this soon lost its effect for I could see no good results, only to gratify my curiosity. At last I found I could make my subjects read my thoughts and here was a new discovery.

1864

Death
[BU 3:0775]

What is the true definition of death? Death is the name of an idea; an idea is matter so that the destruction of an idea is death. Every opinion has its center and its center is the idea. Now if a person believes in anything that is founded on an opinion, the idea is in the opinion, and the senses being also in the opinion are attached to the idea. This imprisons the senses in the opinion. Now the idea is of itself nothing but an opinion condensed into a solid and called matter and every word goes to make the idea. So to make an idea, men reason about something they have no proof of, only as an opinion.

The word is called reasoning, governed by their wisdom and their wisdom is of the natural man or error. It affects the mind of their opponent so they build their building or opinion out of their error, and in the center is the idea; and if they succeed in establishing their opinion, they imprison their opponent in their opinion and the misery is what flows from the idea.

I will illustrate. Take the word "consumption." This word is of itself nothing to the person who never heard of it. To make it is to create the opinion or building and then reduce it to an idea; so matter in the form of words is so arranged as to make the idea in an opinion. Now as the opinion is forming in the mind, a chemical change is going on and the matter is held in solution until it is condensed into a form according to the pattern given by the direction; and after the opinion is fairly established in the mind and the person or idea in the center, the senses are then attached to the idea and become a part of it; so the senses become wedded to the idea and both are held in the belief or opinion. Now to separate the senses from the idea is death to the idea but life to the senses. This separation is what is called death, but it is only death to the one idea.

Man is always dying and living in progression, for error or opinion must always be in the mind and mind must always exist until time is no more. Man is made of science and ignorance or life and death. Man, seen by the senses, is the center of our belief and the senses are attached to the idea called man, so the idea, "man," varies as much as one star differs from another. No two men or ideas are alike, so each idea, "man," is composed of error and science. The word brute embraces all kinds of dumb animals, so the word man embraces all kinds of characters that vary as much as the brutes. Each idea, man and brute, is made of this combination called mind combined and held together by a superior wisdom to the matter.

I will now give you an illustration of what I call life and death of the animals. The animal is content to be just as he is and seeks no wisdom above his kind; he lives the animal and when his identity is destroyed, he is forgotten by his race; but this is only my opinion. But the animal that is dead to the living is as much alive in the higher state of matter or mind as the man who loses his idea. Each retains his own identity but man is progressive and the beast is the same forever. The beast has but one rotation of life and death but man lives all his life subject to death. So that to destroy one idea called death, he is liable to die again and again to the end of time unless his wisdom destroys death by the science of life. The last enemy to science is death, so the scientific man or idea shall reign till all error is destroyed.

All identities called man are not the same. There is the well identity of man, the lame, the sick, the deaf, the dumb and so on. I might enumerate as many varieties of men or identities as there are stars in the firmament. Each varies from the other and all are called man. Now all men are liable to have a combination of all these identities. For instance, a well man or child is an identity. Now it changes to a sick identity, so the well identity is destroyed and the child's senses are attached to the identity of a disease. Man's life is a life of progression governed by science or error, so to know what makes happiness is to know what makes misery. The science of life is to know how to keep man from getting into death or error. This is my theory—to put man in possession of a science that will destroy all the above ideas of the sick and teach man one living progression of his own identity, with life free from error and disease. Now as man passes through these combinations, they differ one from another; so will it be in the resurrection of the dead to life, freed from their false ideas and in truth. Now suppose that man could be so wise as to know every sensation that affects his senses. He could never change, so he would be always the same. Now take another that believes in all the opinions of man and he is dying and living all the time, dying to error and living to truth till he dies the death of all his opinions or beliefs. Therefore to be free from death is to be alive in truth, for sin or error is death and science or wisdom is eternal life and this life is the Christ.

March 1861

Death–Continued–How Disease Is Made, How Cured, Obstacles to the Progress of Science
[BU 3:0777]

In my remarks on death, I said that every opinion had a center and this center was an idea. I will try to make this plainer for it is the center or foundation on which all error rests. Destroy this and disease is out of the mind, for this central idea is the fortress that error erects to keep the subject in submission–this is the enemy's fortress. As wisdom is its enemy, it keeps up a constant cannonading to frighten wisdom into subjection. This idea is built by public opinion got up by demagogues or doctors and priests; its father or founder was a liar, its foundation is ignorance and superstition, its reign is tyranny and slavery to wisdom, and its victims are ignorance. This kingdom of darkness is the errors of man; every man's mind is subject to this prince of darkness; its power is in its popularity; its laws are arbitrary and binding on all; it knows no mercy; its chief end is the destruction of man's happiness. For that purpose it holds out large rewards, as it did to Jesus, to those who will enter its service. Its honesty is hypocrisy and in fact its whole aim is slavery or power.

I have given you a little idea of one world; this is Satan's kingdom. What classes does it embrace? It embraces every opinion of man. Ignorance is the foundation. Destruction to freedom or science is its chief end so its leaders invent all sorts of falsehoods and bind them onto the people or matter which is liable to be changed or molded into their belief. Every inducement is held out to persuade the senses to become interested in their idea or opinion. Now an opinion is like a city or town that has its center or laws. So as man's senses are traveling, like the man going down to Jericho who fell among thieves, he listens to these false leaders and hears of some idea like a place. It is described to him by some doctor or priest in an earnest manner. This excites the mind, curiosity is aroused, the senses leave their home or father's house like the prodigal son and wander away into this place or state. Here he is accused of being a stranger and is cast into the belief. The belief is the prison. The idea is the laws and if he chances to hear of diphtheria, he believes it is as much a place as Boston. So if he chances to go near the place and happens to feel a soreness of the throat, he is accused and if he acknowledges that he has it, then his acknowledgement becomes a belief. This places him in the prison and the sentence being passed, punishment commences. The prison or belief embraces all persons who have transgressed the laws of diphtheria. So every opinion is a prison or place to hold the person that believes it and man's senses may have as many indictments against him as he has opinions. If science is wisdom, it is used to free men from these prisons. So Science or Christ enters the cities or towns and pleads the case of the senses that are imprisoned, and if he gets the case, the prisoner is set at liberty or the senses detached from the idea and the error in the mind explained. Then the prisoner or senses rises from the place of torment to the kingdom of health.

Here you see one government or kingdom founded on error. Its boundaries are opinions, its subjects are superstition and its laws are for the destruction of science. To destroy this kingdom is to introduce science so that the warfare is endless, for neither party will yield. No compromise is entered into by science, but as the kingdom is divided against itself, it cannot stand. Now as these two parties are in one man, it may be necessary to define their tactics and show how the senses may keep clear of both. One party assumes an idea and uses all their cunning to make it admitted by the senses, so when that is established, then commences the argument. The opposite side, being more ignorant but more honest, admits the idea but tries to destroy it. Here is an illustration: the children of the kingdom assert that sin is of divine origin, so the opposite acknowledge it and then try to reason it out of existence. They say that Adam's sin was the cause of all sin. Admitting it, then they try to show how inconsistent it is. They say sin is death; when admitted it becomes a law so they go on assuming anything, and the other side admit, then argue about it, so that the kingdom of science is not known in all their reason. Science has battled down the walls of error and established liberty or science in much of their kingdom; it has hewn down the trees of superstition and established the science of mathematics. It has struck at the science of health. This is an unbroken wilderness never entered by man. Ever since the days of Moses there have been adventurers but none have as yet planted the standard of life with such an inscription: "The Science of Life is in the wilderness." Jesus tried to do it but was crucified before it became a science. Paul and all of his disciples also tried but no one has ever yet been able to penetrate through this dark wilderness and raise the standard and sustain it. As I have done so, it may be necessary to give a "physical" sketch of the inhabitants who lay in wait to devour everyone who enters this place. Now if you, reader, will follow me into this wilderness, you can see what man's senses have to contend with. As you enter at the East you see all sorts of improvements going on, just as though there was no wilderness anywhere around. The first person you meet is a very gentlemanly looking man who accosts you in this way. I perceive you are a stranger in these parts. "Yes." Are you not aware of the danger you are in? "No." You must have known of that cruel enemy to man that inhabits this wilderness of error; he comes prowling around, his breath is sure to poison you, his name is consumption, his place of birth is in the wilderness of error and very few ever get rid of his grasp. "Where does he attack man?" In the throat and holds on to him till his master comes; if the person will pay enough the master will let him off, if he can, but in the battle, the master ninety nine times out of a hundred loses the victim. "Do not the inhabitants do anything to destroy such monsters?" No, for our very best men use the creatures or devils called disease to rob strangers.

In the foregoing piece I have undertaken to separate the two ideas life and death, and as I explained but one side of the question, I will now give the other which is life. I showed that death is opposed to life. I did not use that term but you will see that that was what I meant. Now death is life to the natural man as much as error is. Truth and error have their kingdom and our senses are in one or the other just according to our acts. I gave an explanation of the natural man or error which is matter and showed that all our misery is in our ignorance of the other kingdom called life or science. This Kingdom or Science is that spoken of in the scriptures which was hewn out and came down to earth or the natural man and became embedded in the hearts of the people. This was the stone or Science that the builders of error rejected which has been the head or foundation of the new Science of Life.

This science or child was the one that was without father or mother. It had no beginning of days or ending of years, but it is from everlasting to everlasting. It was the rock that followed Moses in the wilderness of superstition, and upon whomsoever this rock or science falls, he shall be crushed to powder. Science is all the solid there ever was or ever can be and is directed by wisdom and cannot act contrary to itself. It is progression; it knows no evil; it is a consuming fire that will rage till it burns up every selfish idea. It is never found boasting of its wisdom; it is not puffed up. It sits and sees itself swell in the hearts of the people but they see it not. Their minds are now seeing the light that is going before them; they are afraid, so that even the kingdom of darkness is in rebellion against itself. The leaders begin to tremble, for they see that the angel of science has sounded his trumpet; the earth or matter is moved out of its place; the stars of parties are falling and the powers of the kingdom are shaken. Their sun or science has ceased to be an oracle of these blind guides. The moon or their error gives no light and the people or ideas are running to and fro, up and down on the earth or mind, not knowing what to do to be saved from the plagues that are coming upon them. So they pray and fast and throw dust into each other's eyes till they cannot see; the heavens or minds become so dark they run against each other's ideas, and in their desperation to escape the misery of their own making, they run headlong into the sea of public opinion and are lost to the world. Now the life of these blind guides or demagogues is in their error; the length of their days is in their wisdom; and when their wisdom is destroyed by that of science, they die and are forgotten. The wind of science passes over them and the places that once knew them shall know them no more. For their iniquities are sealed up in a bag and their wickedness is laid in the ground, and as the children of science pass along and look upon the ground that these demons inhabited, they see not one stone left upon another. The spears of superstition had been beaten into ploughshares; science has ploughed up all the stubble and burnt up all the rubbish. The fields of life are bringing forth the flowers of happiness; the streams of blood have turned into living waters to quench the soul that is playing on the green grass. The birds of wisdom are sounding their notes of peace and all the people rejoice, for the kingdom of this world has become the kingdom of science. The old world or beliefs are passed away and a new belief or heaven is set up in the hearts of men, where all beliefs shall be tested by science and the wicked or error shall be destroyed.

Now this is the new kingdom of which I am about to speak. I will give you an idea of this kingdom or science and show for what it was established. I have shown that the kingdom of darkness was the devil's or error's kingdom, established by error or the natural man, and the destruction of happiness was its chief end. Now science or life is the other, and its chief end is the destruction of error but its means are not the same as those of its enemies. Its leader is Christ or Wisdom; it aims at opinions; its march is progression; it knows no fear; its captain is Wisdom; its qualities are love. It neither turns to the right nor to the left. It is death to error when error undertakes to retard its progress. It seeks not its own kingdom or happiness but works on earth or in man for his happiness. Its aim is to establish its wisdom in man, and as it is a science, its identity is eternal life or progression. For this cause, it leaves father and mother or error and ignorance, goes into the kingdom of darkness and seeks out the poor, sick ideas which are prisons wherein are the children of science, having been deceived by their blind guides. It enters the prison or belief, unknown to the keeper, for wisdom cannot be seen by error and error or matter is no obstacle to wisdom. It pleads in this prison with the captive, reasons and teaches the Science of Happiness and protects the prisoner from its enemies in this wilderness of darkness–as Christ, when the king of error sought his life after it grew to have an identity. Herod killed all the children in his reign; so has everyone since. Now this science is only named: what its end will be no one knows, not even the science but wisdom itself. One thing is certain. The time will come when the opinions of priests and doctors must give way to the Science of Life, for their opinions lead to death and misery but the Science of Life is health and happiness.

March 1861

Death [I]
[LC 2:0659]

This is the basis of all disease. Disease must be classed with ideas or phenomena without wisdom, that is, such as have never been investigated, and all these may be traced to the speculations and opinions coming out of the Bible's belief. These diseases, which are the result of reason, call our first attention, from the fact that they cause more misery than all the phenomena or diseases that ignorance produces.

Take two children of the same parents. Place one in the charge of a pious person who believes in the Bible just as it reads with a literal construction and also in the allopathic mode of treating the sick with the various improvements to cure disease. Let the other child be put into the hands of the lowest man of mankind, the cannibals, for instance. Both children are females. Let them grow up and I ask any person which they suppose could bear the most hardship, the Christian or the cannibal child? No one is so ignorant as not to know that the Christian child is more likely to die by exposure.

It would seem from this that God in his wisdom, if it is his wisdom, instead of making man healthier and happier, really makes him more sickly and miserable, so where ignorance is bliss 'tis folly to be wise. Here is where the trouble lies. Man, as Paul says, does what he ought not to do, and leaves undone what he ought to do. Wisdom does not consist in opinions and health is not the result of man's wisdom. Man has no right to set up a standard of health or religion. In bringing up a child, the child should never be taught to fear any punishment except that which follows the act; but it should be taught scientifically that every act contains a reaction just equal to the act. This is according to science and is true. Do not teach the child that this is good and that is bad of itself, but the good and bad is in the act and the reaction of both must follow. This reaction is the happiness or misery, and religion is a belief in this truth.

If you understand this, you will then show by fruits which religion you are of, science or opinion. Health is a word that ought not to be used, for it really has no meaning. Jesus says they that are whole need no physician. It is man's duty to know how to correct those who have wandered away from God. I never heard that God was healthy or sick. God is wisdom, and wisdom is what man wants to keep him happy, and the lack of it is either ignorance or error. If the former, then he may be ignorantly happy, but error is misery. Wisdom would teach man that all his life is outside of his body. This would of course make him happy. Ignorance has no opinion nor wisdom, but in its way it is happy. The Christian is unhappy from the fact that he is taught to believe that he has a soul and that it is in his body. He is also taught that the soul and body make the man, and that the latter dying, the soul being in and a part of the body, they are left in the dark for the rest. So at death, everyone must look out for himself, and either the Lord or the devil gets us at last. Under this absurdity when anything ails a person, he is like a stranger in a strange land, without friends, where everyone is laying hold of him and he does not know which way to turn. He knows not but he may fall into the hands of bad men. So at this separation called death, when the soul is about to pass, they do not know where to go or where they will go. So they want their minister or someone to pray to keep up their courage till they are off, and then their friends settle their locality according to their opinions. The believers of course land him in heaven. But if the dead had done something wrong to one of his neighbors, then that one is in doubt, so the world is left in doubt where he is. Some say he is in heaven, some say in hell. If the man knows the thoughts of his friends about him, he will find that their opinions are his judges.

Now I have no heaven or hell to go to. When I lie down on my bed, I do not trouble myself what will become of me when I am nothing. If I am not anything and do not know it, then I am nothing, but if I am anything, I know it as long as I know anything. My wisdom teaches me that wisdom is not matter. And as my senses are attached to this wisdom, another world, as the Christians believe, is to me all folly and superstition, like witchcraft, without the least foundation in truth. Man is like mathematics; he is a principle not developed, his senses being attached to his wisdom in the same way as they are to mathematics. His senses are not attached to what he does not know, nor can they ever be till he knows it. So his life is in his wisdom, and if that is in a belief and his belief is in a body, he is just as large as his body according to his belief. Job says, "No doubt ye are the people, and wisdom shall die with you. But I have understanding as well as you and am not inferior to you." Job knew that all their talk was without wisdom and would come to an end. He says, "Lo, mine eye hath seen all this, mine ear hath heard and understood it. What ye know, the same do I know also. I am not inferior unto you. Surely I would speak to the Almighty, and I desire to reason with God. But ye are forgers of lies, ye are all physicians of no value. O that ye would altogether hold your peace, and it should be your wisdom."

January 1862

Death [II]
[LC 1:0538]

I will now say a few words in regard to the state called death. As this error is so well established that it is folly to deny it, I must explain my grounds for denying what everyone believes. Let us see what man loses by the change called death. If you make a man admit that his happiness is in this state of error or opinions, then to get out would be death. But convince every person that he might sit down and fall into a state in which he might go where he pleased and enjoy the society of those he did in his waking state, and be responsible for his acts the same as though awake, and if his ability and genius and good character earn for him the sympathy of some friend that would like to have him accompany him to some foreign country, and he should go and see all the beauties and enjoy all the privileges of a guest and then wake up, don't you suppose he would like to take another trip?

Now destroy all ideas of death and that would destroy disease. Then man would labor for wisdom, and when he grew rich he would say to himself, "I am rich enough, so I will lie down and rest and enjoy my friends and listen to the world's talk." So he gives up his cares and lies down and like a man that has got rich rides around and enjoys himself. One is a figure of the other; but one is real, and the other is a shadow. The man who is rich in this world's goods to the exclusion of some scientific capital cannot travel in the world of science with his money. To have money and no wisdom is to be like the rich man in the Bible spoken of by Jesus. He had been to work and got rich, and his crops were so large that he said to himself: "I will tear down my old house and barn and build me a more expensive establishment; or I will dress up and go into more educated society among the literary world and enjoy myself." But science says to him, This night shalt thou be satisfied that all thy riches will not make thee a man of science.

So you must lose all that foolish pride that impels the rulers of the world, for when science comes, riches take to themselves wings and fly away into the wilderness of darkness. When these two characters lie down together, they are received into society just according to their worth or talent. For money is not wisdom. So the rich man of this world may be the beggar of the scientific, while this beggar or man of small means with scientific riches will be as far removed from this neighbor as Dives from Lazarus. One must die to become the other. See the man that is made of money and knows nothing but his money and see him when he is past making it. He is feverish and all he thinks of is his money. This is his happiness and someone is all the time getting it away; so he is in trouble, while the man of science is investigating all the improvements of the age and becoming acquainted with all the scientific secrets. Now they both lie down to enjoy their riches. The miser is all the time nervous and frightened about his money, while the scientific man is traveling on the interest of his capital. And if an expedition is fitted out for some great discovery where his science is wanted, he receives an invitation and goes and enjoys himself, while the miser is prowling around to buy some second-hand lock to put on his door to keep out the robbers. These two characters may go on for hundreds of years, for time is nothing in eternity.

So we see every day figures of change. How many persons are there in this city who get up in the morning and pass the day without gaining enough wisdom to last them till nine o'clock? But you will see them up in the morning before day looking around to find some hole to creep into to get a drop of water or a substitute to moisten their tongue, for they are tormented by an appetite for this world's goods. So their life is one continual state of excitement, always opposing everything that enlightens men's minds and elevates their character.

Such a man is dead to the world of science, whether he is on top of the ground or underneath; while the man of science is alive whether on the earth or in it. They both lie down in their own sepulcher. If one is made of opinions, he must take it. If the other is science, he will be in it. So while one is progressing, the other is looking on. They are both rewarded for their acts.

1864

Death [III]*
[BU 3:0769]

What is life? It is whatever moves. Matter in every form contains life. All thoughts have life. Man as we see him has life. Then what is death? We answer it is the absence of life. But how can there be such a thing as death when everything we see contains life? But we say we know death occurs for we see the phenomenon. We see vegetable matter decompose and die, animals also and man. But does vegetable matter die? It decomposes, it is true, and when the form it once held passes away we say the thing is dead. For matter, all of it, is thus the same. What is not in the Earth is in the air, the combination only is changed. Then what is dead? A tree we say, dies. What is a tree? It is matter combined into a certain form. What combined it? Is the power in itself or independent? If it is in itself then matter is self-existent, self-creating, and self-directing. Nearly everyone will admit that the power which moves matter is independent of and superior to it. If then the power which made the tree is independent of it, the tree existed first in the intellect of the Wisdom that made it before it was put into matter–as a machine exists in the wisdom of its maker before it is produced in matter. The real tree then exists in the wisdom of God while that which we see is like an echo or shadow of the real substance. When a tree disappears then we say it dies; does it die? The dust returns to dust ready to be used to illustrate some other idea of wisdom and the spirit to God who gave it when it always did exist and always will, subject to His control. He made it and in this wisdom it exists as much after as before its material expression disappears from our sight. For it is the material only that we see with the eye of flesh, the real tree we can see only as we learn wisdom and then we are equal with God.

But we say that animals really die. The form is lifeless and the places that once knew them know them no more forever. Is an animal less a creation of wisdom than a plant? Wisdom then created the animal and the intelligence it possess it receives from God. Is that intelligence seen? Then the real animal we do not see any more than the real tree. We see only an echo of each. Then when the outward form disappears what right have we to say the animal is dead? Can the eye of flesh discern the things of God?; and if not, how can we judge of them?

Well then how do you account for the death of man? You cannot deny there is a separation, call it what you will. If the real tree or the real animal is not seen by man in his present state, it is certainly quite as true that the real man is invisible. Our thoughts then, and feelings, our pleasures and pains constitute the real man and these we do not see except they are expressed in some way that addresses the natural senses.

It does not follow that whatever we see moving about contains life of itself. A steam engine moves yet no one thinks it is alive. The power that moves it is independent of itself. The engine is only an automaton. Because we cannot see the power independent of matter is no sign it does not exist and act. Can we ever see any power? We call steam a power yet without proper direction it has no power. Where then does the power lie? In the intelligence of the person directing; that which we see is merely a medium by which to illustrate it or put it in practice. A machinist stands in the same relation to an engine as God does to man. The man we see is merely matter to be used to develop some idea. God breathed into this matter a part of his own life and <u>this</u> life is in which guides and directs all our right acts. This life creates a body whenever it wants one and is not affected by the loss of the natural body. This life, if man would follow, would never lead him into trouble and to know that he has it is to know that nothing have any power over it. This life it is which has the power of creating matter but man being ignorant of it thinks the matter he sees is something independent of himself and if he is told it will hurt him, he is afraid.

Then fear takes possession of him and governs him and he is liable to be affected just according to his belief about it. In this way man reasons about his body never thinking that the life of the body is a mere belief which puts him on a level with the laws of all other matter. Man is not matter, but the master of matter and must use it only to develop some truth which he knows, or is trying to discover. Reasoning that life is in the matter keeps him all the time in fear lest he may lose it, for all matter is governed by its own laws. The life which God breathed into man cannot die.

Death–A Scene
[BU 3:0978]

The impressions made on me sometimes as I am attending patients has opened to me scenes of a future existence so plain that to doubt the truth of them would be as absurd as to doubt my own existence. And these scenes show me the absurdity of the Christian belief, for man makes himself the creature of his belief. Life and death to him are as real as heat and cold. Now we admit that these two ideas, life and death, exist independent of our senses. Then of course they must have an existence outside of our senses or belief.

Now I will admit that man believes all this and he is responsible to himself for his belief and all the misery that follows comes from his own belief.

Man is in his belief, although he is not a part of it, but is like a man's wisdom in his works. His works contain no wisdom so his belief is the work of man's wisdom; and if his wisdom is of man's belief, he is in his belief; and if his wisdom is of science, he is in truth. Now I will show how these two elements take the senses or man from the idea body. I was attending an aged gentleman who had been rather feeble and according to the world's belief was gradually running down. The lamp of life was nearly consumed. Now all his friends expected the change, yet the time had not arrived for the angel to summon him to leave his earthly habitation and be transferred to the world of spirits, yet they, like the bridegroom, clamored, till the angel of death gave the alarm. Now it happened that a strange vision came over the old gentleman. A nervous cough set in. This was the signal of alarm and the angel of opinion gave the alarm. This roused the inmates and fear fell upon all the friends.

Now I felt the weight of this false belief, death, for I could see no danger, but from sympathy. It went like fire on a prairie till it enveloped the friends of the old gentleman. This I had to put out or it would envelop the old gentleman himself. Now I will relate my vision of what seemed to me to be a truth. Man's belief contains something. This acts upon another and mingles with every person just according to the evidence. So the sick are at the mercy of the world's belief. Now the senses are not in the belief, so if the belief is presented to a person in doubt, he is not in a state to resist it. So as the belief of the sick man was that his time of departure was near at hand, he would throw from himself an influence that would have a tendency to create distrust in his friends.

So as man's belief in death is a separation from the body, he will try to find some resting place outside of his earthly body. So heaven is introduced. This being a belief, we all without being aware create a place for our friends, and the first impression is that our friends cannot live. This acts like mesmerizing a person. The sick sit or lie passive, yet convulsed, and begin to show signs of short breathing. This encourages the friends in their belief, till a sort of atmosphere is created sufficient to bring up the spirit or identity of their friend and he rises like a person in a balloon and is carried beyond the regions of this world. There he floats in space, for their beliefs cannot define a spot. Now this cloud or ignorance or belief I saw, and as it gathered around the old gentleman, it seemed as though he sat upon a cloud ready to leave as soon as the cords of life were severed. Now I felt as though I could locate an atmosphere more rarefied than death and lighter than error's darkness. So I let my light shine into the cloud of death. Death was swallowed up with truth and the cloud dissolved. The light took its place and the truth prevailed.

July 1864

Defense Against an Accusation of Making Myself Equal to Christ
[LC 2:0768]

I am often accused of making myself equal to Christ when attempting to explain the theory of my cures. Now why should I be accused of what I do not intend to convey? It is because the people are deceived of themselves.

Christ is the embodiment of that wisdom that sympathizes with the earthly man and reveals to him the truth that will correct his errors, forgive his sins and heal his diseases. I make a difference between what I say as a man and what I feel as a physician. As a man I cannot see or feel a person's feelings, for such is the natural state of man. But as a physician, I give myself in perfect faith to the guidance of a higher wisdom than that of man which feels and sympathizes with the sick. Everyone who becomes aware of this wisdom gives it the praise and calls it by some name. Jesus called it his Father and the Son of God. Herod, when told of the marvelous words of Jesus, called it the spirit of John the Baptist. Peter called it Christ. Therefore people generally believed in some spiritual power acting on man as they do now. Many persons tell me my power comes from some spirit and give me more than I ask, but very few are willing to admit that I know more about my cures than they do. Jesus never said that he, the man, was God; but he strove to teach the people of the existence of a living principle of wisdom to which matter was subject, and this truth being fully revealed to his mind, he called it the son of God, admitting it in every act and never teaching that the flesh and blood of the natural man was God. The dispute between him and the people was not whether he, the man Jesus, was God or Christ or John the Baptist, but whether the man Jesus had any claim to wisdom superior to that of any wise man or prophet. He contended that he had and, in his words, he showed a wisdom superior to their own; but they, not understanding how such works as his could be done intelligently, were deaf to his words of wisdom and ascribed to him a mysterious power. Therefore they accepted his works as miracles but failed to receive him as a teacher of truth. So he was a stumbling block to the Jews and to the Greeks foolishness.

When I undertake to say that I know how I cure, I am accused by those as wise as Greeks or Jews of being a fool and making myself equal with Christ. So far as Jesus is concerned, I do not put myself on a level with Him any more than I do with Daniel Webster; but had Daniel Webster, with all his learning, been a chemist, provided I could produce a chemical experiment according to the science of chemistry, my works as far as they go are equal to his for both are under the same law. So with Jesus. Jesus as a good or bad man I have nothing to say about. But his wisdom which I consider from a higher source than man's opinion was a truth the understanding and application of which, for the benefit of the sick, is a science open to all and contains wisdom the world knows not of. I have no doubt that He wished to communicate that the natural man was error and the Son of God should arise from matter and that the resurrection from the dead was to come into this light or wisdom. The Jews believed themselves to be the chosen people of God and possessed of all truth and they could not admit anyone wiser than themselves; so they could not believe that Jesus knew any more about his miracles than the sorcerers and magicians who claimed their power from departed spirits. When asked by certain men how he did these things, he answered, The baptism of John, was it of Heaven or of man? They dared not answer, for if they had said it was Heaven, he would say, Why did ye not believe? So after communing they answered, We cannot tell. It is easy to see that if they said that his power came from God or Heaven they would have killed him. Accordingly, he answered, Neither tell I you by what authority I do these things. At another time the Sadducees put to him the question Whose wife should the woman who had seven husbands be in the resurrection? Jesus taught a resurrection. But according to the belief of the Pharisees who were the only class that taught the doctrine, but thinking that Jesus held the same ideas that the Pharisees believed, they stated a case to see if He could answer it. But he answered, Ye do err, not knowing the Scriptures nor the power of God. For in the resurrection they neither marry nor are given in marriage but are as the angels of Heaven. He taught that man should rise from an error into a truth or from a blind belief into actual knowledge. Immediately after this a Pharisee lawyer, hearing that he had silenced the Sadducees asked him a question tempting him, saying, Master, which is the greatest commandment in the Law, supposing that Jesus being uneducated could not answer. But Jesus said unto him, Thou shalt love the Lord thy God with all thy heart and with all thy soul and with all thy mind and the second is like unto it. Thou shalt love thy neighbor as thyself. On these two commandments hang all the Law and the prophets. Jesus then asked the Pharisees, What think ye of Christ, whose son is he? They say unto him, The Son of David. He said, How then doth David in spirit call him Lord–if David then calls him Lord how is he the son? And no man was able to answer him a word, neither dared any man from that day forth to ask him any more questions. Now it cannot be thought that they believed that the man Jesus was David's son, therefore they must have referred to the power that Jesus called Christ and he, Jesus, asked them their ideas concerning it. He asked his disciples, Whom do men say I, the son of man, am? They answered, Some say John the Baptist, some Elias, etc. He sayeth unto them, Whom say ye that I am? And Simon Peter answered, Thou art the Christ, the Son of the Living God. And Jesus answered him, Blessed art thou, Simon Bar Jona, for flesh and blood hath not revealed this unto thee, but my Father which is in Heaven. Then he told how he should be persecuted by all men because of the truth, but that the truth should rise from superstition and take to itself a body to show that man should not die, as was believed. He wished to communicate this one fact that his wisdom was outside the man Jesus and that Jesus was only matter used as a medium in the hands of Wisdom. Then Jesus would be to Christ what gold is to the chemist, a medium through which he can communicate his wisdom concerning it. He could dissolve the matter so that the form should decay and disappear, and still he could construct from matter which it was his wisdom to control, the Christ, or assume a body which those whom he taught could see. Then death was swallowed up in science.

November 1862

Defense Against an Accusation of Putting Down Religion, A
[LC 1:0331]

I am often accused of putting down religion and when I ask what religion is, I am told the same old story that everybody knows—to be good, worship God, etc. Now all this sort of cant may do if it is not analyzed, but if you undertake to analyze it, it vanishes like dew before the morning sun.

Religion is what it was before Christ and I think I know what that was. The religion that Christ opposed consisted in forms and ceremonies. Now why did Jesus oppose it if their belief had nothing to do with this health and happiness? He never said anything to such persons, for He said, They that are well need no physician. So if persons were well it made no difference to Jesus what they believed, but He came to those who had been deceived by the priests and doctors. Well how did He cure them? By changing their minds, for if He could not change their minds, He could not cure them.

This was the case with the rich young man who came to Jesus to know what he should do to be saved. Now if the young man was really in danger of being doomed to eternal punishment, as we are taught, then all that was wanted was to believe; so if his belief changed him, I ask if it changed his identity or mind? We are taught that man cannot do anything of himself to save himself, but was this the case with the young man? No, for Jesus told him what to do, to keep the commandments and these commandments were not Jesus' but Moses.' The young man said, This have I done from my youth up; so according to the young man's story he was a very good man and Jesus found no fault with him but said, If you would be perfect, go and sell all you have and give it to the poor and follow me. Now here was a young man who had done everything to be saved and Jesus would not save him unless he would give all that he had to the poor and follow Him. Now as absurd as this looks, it is quoted as a command of Jesus, yet you cannot find anyone that will comply with it, but they get over it by saying that we must give up all sinful acts. Well, be as honest to that young man who went away sorrowful, for he could not understand. For his beliefs were so strong that Christ answered him as much as to say, Go, give all your ideas away and embrace the truth. Now this is a fair specimen of the parables. Jesus never hinted that He or the young man had the slightest idea of another world, but it shows on the face that a man like Jesus could not be so little or narrow-minded as to send the person to endless misery because he would not give all his riches to the poor. Such constructions on the Bible are the cause of a great deal of sickness.

Now I will give my construction, and if I do not make Jesus more of a man than the other, then I never will attempt to explain the Bible again. The Jews thought that they were the chosen people of God and were the best and knew the most. So riches were wisdom and they were rich in the laws of Moses. This young man came to Jesus to ask him what he should do to obtain this belief that Jesus taught—eternal life. Jesus said, Keep the commandments. This he had done. Well go and give away your ideas and try to learn mine. This he could not do, for he could not see into it. So he went away sorrowful. Jesus' own disciples were in the same way for they said, We have forsaken all, what lack we more? He then goes on to tell them what they must do but they did it not, for they all forsook Him. Now if it requires such a sacrifice to go to heaven, then He never found one that went, for they asked Him, If these things be so, how can a man be saved? He said, Try; many shall try but few be chosen. Is it so now? No. It is the easiest thing in the world to get religion now; all that is required is to join the church and pay the minister well and you shall be saved. Now does anyone suppose this was Jesus' mission? If he does, I am sorry. He must have a very low opinion if he supposes that a man's salvation depends upon a certain belief, but it does, according to the belief of our day.

Now a belief is one thing and the thing to believe is another. I will here illustrate. We all admit the spine. Well, how many have seen one? Not one in a thousand. So one tells what he sees and all tell what they believe. Now suppose a person says, The spine is affected and another believes it; then to him it is so and this belief makes him unhappy. Now is it the spine that is unhappy or the belief? It must be the belief, for there is nothing of the sick man but beliefs. So you can see that all his sickness is ignorance or beliefs. Now if you satisfy him that he is mistaken and he believes it, then his spine is not affected and you change his mind. Now he is happy. Is the spine happy or his mind? Now you see that the belief is one thing and the thing believed is another. The spine is one thing and the belief is another so that our happiness and misery are only our beliefs and the thing believed has neither happiness nor misery. Now it is of vast importance to man to know what to believe for that which we know we have no belief of but proof, so that which we do not know is a mystery and causes a belief. Now there are certain things that all admit–based on scientific principles. Then there are other things that are admitted but have no proof only as the error has made it. For instance, religion is one of the things that is based on an opinion and not on science. The science is the thing or substance and the belief of it is religion and we are happy or miserable just according to our belief. The masses' and the religious world's religion is in their belief. Jesus' religion was the science itself. So you see that man reasons about religion just as he does about everything else–that the happiness or misery is in the spine and the belief is something else.

Now here is my religion. Mine, as that of Jesus, is in my acts, not in my belief. The sick are in their belief and not in their acts, for if it were in their acts, they would be better; for to be wise is to be good and to be good is to show your goodness in your acts. So if a man is sick he is not good, and if he is not good he is not happy, and if he is not good, that which is bad must be something else than good. His goodness is science or Christ. His badness must be an opinion or religion. Now to be born again is to separate the true religion from the dross and I know of no better rule than Jesus laid down. He said, By their fruits ye shall know them, whether they be of man or of God or science. Now I am willing to be judged by my works, and if they bear me out, then I do not know as the wisdom of this world of opinions has any right to pass judgment on me.

I will now show what Jesus' religion was. We are often told of the religion of Christ, but when we ask what it is, it cannot be separated from infidelity or this world; so I will try to define His religion. You remember I said that a belief was one thing and the thing believed was another. Now Jesus' religion was the Christ or the substance and the disciples and the multitude were the believers of the substance, not seen, but in the heavens. So Christ is the substance or science or the religion of Jesus. The Christian religion is in a belief of that substance called Christ, Wisdom or God and my religion is my wisdom and not my belief and when I come to the sick, I put my religion in practice and not my opinion. When I talk to the well I talk about it, for those that are well need no physician. My opinion is worth just as much as anyone's. I look upon all opinions as man's wisdom; they are worth what they will bring. They may be right, but they are often wrong.

When I sit by a person, if I find no opinion, I find no disease. But if I find a disease, I find an opinion. So that the misery that is in the opinion or belief is the disease. I have to make war with the disease or opinion, and as there are a great many that make their disease out of the world's opinions of religion, it is my duty to change their belief in order to make the cure. It is astonishing to see persons cling to their opinions just as though they contain the substance, when if they knew the substance of their belief, they would laugh at their folly. Now to me it is as plain as twice two makes four.

I can sum up the religion of this world and the religion of Jesus in one simple parable. That is the parable of the child when the people were disputing about the Kingdom of Heaven. Jesus took up a little child from their midst and said, Of such is the kingdom of heaven; except ye become as little children ye cannot enter into the kingdom of heaven. So the world, as a Christian world, has tried to imitate the child, and I cannot dispute that in most of their acts they have fallen short of the child; for he is ignorant of all their errors and as ignorance is bliss, 'tis folly to be wise or in error. Now this is the true meaning of the parable of the child. Science is not included in the Christian religion, neither wisdom of any kind. The religion was made up of all the superstitions of Egyptian darkness so that every man and woman was not in a fit state to become a disciple of Christ or science. So Jesus wanted to show the people by a parable what was wanted to get a person into the right state of mind to receive the kingdom of heaven or science. Everyone knows it is harder to unlearn an error than to learn a truth. So Jesus, knowing that a child was free from both, took him as a parable so that the Christian world must give away or get rid of all their errors and become as a little child to receive the Holy Ghost or Science. This was the new birth; therefore to enter into Science or the kingdom of heaven was not a very easy thing. So if anyone said he was born of God or Science let him show it, for many shall come saying, I am Christ and shall deceive many but by their fruits ye shall know them.

So you see that Jesus' religion had nothing to do with the opinions of this world; his was of wisdom and wisdom is something that is solid. Error or opinions are about this solid, and opinion is the world's religion, but Jesus' religion was the substance and that was what the sick had been robbed of by the blind guides. All I do is to put in their possession what they have been unjustly robbed of.

1861

Defense of Dr. Quimby, A*

[Originally untitled.] [BU 3:0206]

There is an impression prevailing to some extent in the community that Dr. Quimby's cures are performed by affecting the imagination of the patient, and that he knows this and covers it up by various means. One is a habit of referring to a vague incomprehensible theory which he professes to have, whenever allusion is made to his modus operandi. With this feeling many are ashamed to go to him or to own that he does them any good, if they happen to go. This is all a mistake as are a great many opinions purporting to explain him, and errors from a natural desire everyone has of accounting for everything themselves. If we understand what is meant by the term imagination it is applied to the experience of a person, by another who does not and cannot experience the same. For instance, one person as easily made seasick and consequently dislikes to go on the water; another never has been seasick and goes to sea at liberty, so he says to the first, "it is your imagination." There are very few cures on record after this manner.

How is it he does cure then? Is it mesmerism or spiritualism or what is it? Neither. Then what is it if it is not imagination?

To take his own story it is a science, that is knowledge of the causes operating on man to produce disease, so that the effects are removed and it comprehends all opinion, philosophy and beliefs of man which followed out will produce misery to anyone. His first principle of course is that the flesh did not originate disease, but that the human system is kept alive by a vitality that pervades all matter and comes from the great foundation of all life. That it is sensitive to unseen and outward influences as well as those which are visible. He traces the origin of disease back to the adoption of some error and its immediate effect and close application to the life of man, that his system has been changed and made over to the condition of many errors. That it has become a physical manifestation of them all. He says the body of man does not sicken and become good for nothing without a moving, acting, cause; that this cause acts first on the mind and then the effects follow in the body. In fact the body is only a visible manifestation of the action of certain causes. These he traces to the belief concerning the things of the flesh for if a man seriously and honestly believes a thing to him it is true. There is no imagination about it. He sees by what course of reasoning man has become diseased and also where his mistake is and then how to show it to him. He takes man off the plain of matter and puts him in the field of progress and applies the same kind of reasoning towards correcting an error of man as he would in the science [of] mathematics with this basis, that man is an intelligence, his life the growth of that intelligence. It has so long been believed that man lives inside his body, as a prisoner in a prison, and that his body has certain powers which restrain him in his spiritual development, and there is so much to make us keep that belief, that the presentation of an opposite one is strange and often falls on stony ground. It is no wonder then when he says that "disease is in the mind and mind is matter capable of being changed under any direction" that he is not understood, and misconstrued in every way but the right one. The great cause of his being misunderstood is in the popular definition of the word mind, meaning intellectual abilities, thoughts, judgment and a variety of things relating to human character, and in relation to disease, imagination which really means nothing at all.

It is hard for him to explain what he means by mind to the well for it includes the action of ideas of every description. With the sick it means fear remorse shame and guilt, often a reckless despondency and bitter animosity. All these have a cause. No one can feel guilt unless they think they have done something which lessens their self-respect. Remorse and hatred also have their corresponding causes which only can produce these very conditions—the sick certainly have all these feelings to a fearful degree—whence come they for they can have no cause in the natural world. It shows according to the Dr. that there is another world of as much reality and force as the one we know of—that man is an intelligence and lives in a world of action and reaction of cause and effect which plays in upon the natural world. This now he enters and destroys the chains that are forged there and that bind the weary sick man in the body. He shows that a person may waste away under the wearing effect of a falsehood which we are taught as true, as surely as by the process of slow poison in nature. When he finds a person abject and degraded in mind, doe he call it imagination? Certainly not. He discovers that opinion which being conscientiously honestly believed must produce these feelings, and it is the understanding of the universal truth which will explain all the troubles of man, which directs him to pronounce the fact in which such feelings are founded on error and to show up the whole machinery by which it is mounted and carried into one daily life affecting our relations with each other, and expose it a bubble—the difference between a belief and imagination is great, for one is a reality never questioned and the other does not pretend to be real. Our bodies are clay to be formed or moulded according to the intelligence of the man, and if disease is produced of course there must be some error in his governing power. To detect what this governing power is and to correct it is Dr. Q's way of curing–and he is as honorable and pure minded towards the sick, at all times as the court is to a prisoner–and could in no case cure a person if he felt disposed towards him as men do towards each other. He proves the existence of an invisible world and makes it sensible to man, and shows that it is the only real world there is.

Definition of Words, The
[LC 1:0631]

As I may have used some words in my writings which may have conveyed to the reader a different meaning from that intended, it will not perhaps be out of place to state some of the words which occur frequently in my writings. For instance, the word mind might be so construed as to mean the definition given it by man in general, that is, the intellectual power of man. The world here makes mind the intelligence while I make it the medium of intelligence. Here we have one point of difference and this difference runs all though my writings. In no case do I admit mind to be wisdom, but when the word might be used without misleading the reader as to its meaning, I may use it, but in the same sense as we say the sun rises and sets knowing all the time that in reality it is not true, yet it conveys the idea of night and day.

I believe mind to be a certain combination of matter under the control of wisdom and error. I make what we call man the medium of two ideas: one of wisdom and the other of error. The body is like the globe, the earth being the medium of the seed. Man's body is the globe, his mind the matter acted upon and changed by wisdom which is struggling in the mind to rid itself of the matter or casket which holds it, and the action is called by the world the enlightened part of man where there is no pure wisdom that is clear from error. Wisdom is that which is reduced to science. If I say I can do a thing and do not do it, or say I can do a thing and then do it, neither is wisdom. But if I can teach you how to do a thing so you can do it according to my directions and always have it done right, then that is science or wisdom reduced to practice. To do a problem and know you do it from memory and never reduce it to practice or apply a principle to it so that you can teach it to another is not wisdom but knowledge. So far as the person himself is concerned, he is rich, but his riches are to himself, but the world is not richer in wisdom. Wisdom which cannot be reduced to practice is but knowledge to the world. Here you will see the idea mind introduced into science. Whenever I use words different from the world, the difference between us is this. While the world applies words to literal things as life and death, this and the other world, each of which has two meanings, I never intend to convey the least meaning of the religious world's ideas of them but merely give them as Jesus applied them to man's belief and acts. To do wrong was a sin and this sin was death, and to be converted from the wrong or have the error explained was the forgiving of sin. The resurrection of truth from death is the receiving of the truth in regard to what we are dead in. This is what Jesus believed as I understand it. His coming from and going to his father was coming from truth into a discussion with a person in regard to the troubles which affect him and abiding with him in sympathy till his errors were destroyed and the truth or Jesus' kingdom established in the very place from which the enemy had been driven out. His ideas differed entirely from those of the religious world in regard to the two worlds, yet both use the same words. The disciples could not understand for he says they had eyes, ears and hearts, yet could not understand. Now if their life or salvation hereafter was what he intended to convey the idea of and he believed as the world did in regard to it, then every one might have understood.

If Jesus' ideas of death were like those of the religious people, then when a man died, he was dead as that was the real belief of all sects and parties. The controversy was whether there was anything after death. The religious people of his day tried to entrap him as he used the same words as they did, but they applied them to literal things and he applied the same words to the mind. The difference in the use of words created the controversy but failed in every way to entrap Jesus. I will give an instance where Jesus' ideas came in contact with those of the people.

When he was walking in the temple at Jerusalem, the chief priests, scribes and elders came to him and asked, "By what authority doest thou these things and who gave thee this authority to do these things?" And Jesus answered and said unto them, "I will also ask you one question and answer me, and I will tell you by what authority I do these things. The baptism of John, was it from heaven or of men? Answer me." And they reasoned with themselves saying, if we shall say, from heaven, he will say, Why did ye not believe, but if we shall say of man, we fear the people, for all men counted John, that he was a prophet indeed. And they answered and said unto Jesus, We cannot tell, and Jesus answered and said unto them, Neither do I tell you by what authority do I these things. Now it appears that it was his cures that caused the hatred of the chief priests and elders. They knew that the people believed in Jesus, not because he upheld their religion but because he could cure better than anyone else. But how he performed his cures was the question. The priests pretended it was the power of Beelzebub, but this the mass of the people did not believe. So then the priests sought to find something against him, but all they could find against him was his cures.

Now if man's belief had nothing to do with his sickness, why did Jesus condemn it so? Jesus and Christ are like Saul and Paul, and when the Christ spoke, he did so of himself as God or Wisdom, while the Jews thought he spoke as a man like themselves. When the chief priests came to him and inquired, Why do thy disciples transgress the tradition of the elders, for they wash not their hands when they eat bread? He asked them, Why do ye also transgress the commandments of God by your tradition? For God commanded saying, Honor thy father and mother and he that curseth father or mother, let him die the death. But ye say whosoever shall say to his father or mother, it is a gift, by whatsoever thou mightest be profited and honor not his father or mother, he shall be free. Thus have ye made the commandment of God of none effect by your tradition. Ye hypocrites, well did Esaias prophesy of you saying, This people draweth nigh unto me with their mouths but their heart is far from me, but in vain do you worship me, teaching for doctrines the commandments of men. And he called the multitude and said unto them, Hear and understand, not that which goeth into the mouth defileth the man but that which cometh out, this defileth a man. Then came his disciples and said unto him, Knowest thou that the Pharisees were offended after they heard these sayings? But he answered and said, Every plant or idea that my heavenly father or wisdom hath not planted shall be rooted up. All these ideas Jesus had to contend against for they created sickness amongst the people. Then answered Peter and said unto him, Declare unto us this parable. And Jesus said, Are ye yet without understanding? Do not ye yet understand that whatsoever entereth in at the mouth goeth into the belly and is cast unto the draught? But those things that proceed out of the mouth come forth from the heart and they defile the man, for out of the heart proceed evil thoughts, murders, adulteries, fornication, thefts, false worship, blasphemies. These are the things that defile a man. After this, as Jesus was departing, a woman of Canaan cried unto him saying, Have mercy on me, Oh Lord, thou son of David, my daughter is grievously vexed with a devil. Jesus said unto her, Be it unto thee as thou wilt, and her daughter was made whole from that very hour. Now if the priests had not taught the existence of a devil, then the woman would not have been vexed with one. Jesus knew it was her belief and therefore kept silent, but the mother cried the louder and entreated him to cure her, and when he saw her faith, he cured her daughter.

Now here was a cure performed where the disease was in the mind, as probably no one at the present time believes that the woman had a devil vexing her that could be seen by the natural eye. Perhaps the world's wisdom and knowledge have not been defined as clearly as they might be. Wisdom is demonstrated by science, so it cannot be misunderstood. Knowledge may be wisdom undefined, so it comes under the head of chance and opinions or memory. To know a fact that you cannot explain is not wisdom but knowledge, while to know a fact that you can explain on the wisdom of someone else is not wisdom. To know the globe is round because someone said so is knowledge, but to know it from mathematical calculation is wisdom. To know that a ball thrown in the air will fall to the ground again is wisdom, but to know why it returns with the same force is science. You may admit it, but if you cannot explain it on a scientific principle, then it is knowledge. When I use the word knowledge, I do not mean science or wisdom. Science is the medium by which man proves that he has wisdom; opinions may deceive but science never does. All theories based on science are proved by their standing, and all theories based on the traditions and opinions of the world are knowledge and are not to be believed as true.

Religion, politics, the medical science falsely so called are all based on opinions and will someday fall. All are founded on superstition and ignorance and cannot stand the test of investigation and, like slavery, they must give way to science. It is man's religion and God's wisdom, Jesus or Christ. Jesus was the representative of man, while Christ was the science which took away the errors or sins of man. Misery and disease are sins, and to get clear of them, man pays the priests and doctors just according to the law. There are sins unto death, for instance, the sin of consumption. Now if man sins against the laws of the doctors, he must pay the penalty of his sin and die according to the law of the priests and doctors. Thus he gives all he has of life and happiness and becomes poor and distressed, tormented with a cold, cough, etc., all to gratify the belief and pay the penalty. After the doctor has robbed him of his health and happiness and a great share of his worldly gains, finding nothing left of him but a skeleton, he turns that over to the priest in order that he may torment him. This was the condition of the people in the days of Jesus and he warned them to beware of the doctrines of the Scribes and Pharisees, for they bound heavy burdens on the people, grievous to be borne and would not use the tip of their fingers to remove those burdens.

Is there anyone who cannot see that man's disease was made by his belief? If so, I pity their ignorance. Jesus said unto such, Oh Jerusalem! Jerusalem! (or beliefs), thou that killeth the prophets and stoneth them that are sent unto thee (which is science), how often would I have gathered thy children together, even as a hen gathereth her chickens under her wings (and taught you the truth) and ye would not. Behold! Your house (or opinions) are left unto you desolate, for I say unto you, Ye shall not see me till ye shall say, Blessed is he which cometh in the name of the Lord. That is, ye shall not see Science or Christ till ye get wisdom enough to understand, and then ye will say, Blessed is he that cometh in the Science of Wisdom. Verily I say unto you, There shall not be left here one stone (or idea of your belief) upon another that shall not be thrown down.

He gave the disciples the sign of his coming and the end of the world or error by saying, Now learn the parable of the fig tree. When his branch is yet tender and putteth forth leaves, ye know that summer is nigh; so likewise ye, when ye shall see all these things (that were taking place in the world) know that it is near, even at the doors. That is, ye may know that man's belief or opinions have come to an end, that man's corruption had ripened into a harvest ready to be reaped. Then would come the new theory or heaven. The world at this time is like the harvest, ripe. Error like the wheat holds up its head, ready to be cut; but when the sickle of wisdom enters the field of error in the hand of freedom, it will cut down the crop of error and disease and slavery, and the fire of liberty will run over the field of aristocracy and burn up the political stubble. Their land or ideas shall be destroyed and their weapons shall be turned into scientific plowshares or teachers that shall plow up the errors of the old rule of slavery or disease; and then shall come a new generation of ideas, free from the old superstition. Then will the signs of the times be near at hand. Ideas will be warring against each other, and while they are eating and drinking in false ideas, the truth will come in the form of science and liberty and sweep away the old men or ideas. And then the young ideas will go from one sabbath to another and look upon the dead carcass (or beliefs) of the men that have transgressed against me, for the worm shall not die; neither shall the fire be quenched, and they shall be an abomination unto all flesh.

This is always the effect of the evil generation of error. Truth and liberty will always work itself out of matter or opinions, and woe be the man that opposes it. It would be better that he should have a millstone about his neck and be cast into the sea of public opinion, and say he knows nothing about the affairs of the world, and takes no interest in the progression of events, than to oppose this truth. Disease is the slavery that Jesus made war against, and as disease is the shadow of man's belief, his belief is the thing to destroy. The sick are bound by some belief that it is wrong, and disease is the punishment of believing an error. A Northern Copperhead is punishing himself, and his punishment will come to maturity sooner or later, for if a Northern man entertains feelings in unison with Southern traitors, he must meet a traitor's reward, for his belief is a disease and contains its own punishment. How often a person will do a wrong act out of spite merely, and then because they start wrong, rather than acknowledge it, they keep on the wrong track out of malice.

To let a person lead you with his ideas is as hard as dismounting from a horse and walking yourself while you let your enemy ride. We punish ourselves in feeling a desire to punish another. Man is an inventive being and will create and put in practice all the ideas that can be thought of. This world is that state of mind where man creates whatever he understands from what he hears and sees. There is another class that have not this mechanical mind. The idiot has not this inventive genius; though if he undertakes to imitate, he becomes really an inventor, for his imitations are so far from the original that they might pass for new inventions. Disease is one of the inventions of man, and if every man had a scientific mind, they would make diseases more alike. But some have no imitation and some no invention, so their ideas are thrown together haphazard and in that way some of the most awful diseases are created that can be thought of. They cannot be described and it is well they cannot, for if they could, they would be more imitated. The true Science of Wisdom is to destroy the disease and put in its place, science. The true science of wisdom is to destroy error.

Did St. Paul Teach Another World?
[BU 3:0851]

Did St Paul teach another world as it is taught by Christians? I answer, No, and shall prove that Paul preached and taught this very science that I am trying to teach and that he put it into practice as far as he was able; but he taught it more than he put it into practice, from the fact that it was necessary that the theory should be acknowledged. The world believed in religion and their religion taught another world. This was Paul's belief before he was converted to this science. But this science taught him that the wisdom or religion of this world was foolishness with the wisdom or science of God. Paul admitted Jesus as his teacher and Christ, the God or science; therefore, when he spoke of Christ, he meant something more than the natural man or Jesus. When Paul tried to make the Corinthians understand this difference, he said that he came not to teach the wisdom of this world so that their faith should stand on the wisdom of man in the power or science of God. What was the use to speak of the wisdom of this world that was perfect, as they thought, for all of this comes to an end. But he spake of the wisdom of God or science, in a mystery to them, even in a hidden mystery, that was with God before the world or man was formed, which none of the princes of this world knew; for if they had known this science, they would not have crucified the man that taught it.

This science was foretold and expressed in these words: the natural man's or error's eye had not seen nor ear heard; neither had it entered into their hearts that to be good was a science that God had prepared for those that could understand, but Jesus had taught and acknowledged it as the true science or Christ. The word science was not used in those days so that some other word must be used to convey the idea of this truth. As there was no settled opinion in regard to the word but all acknowledge the power, each person was left to himself to express it in his own way. So it was, as Paul says, a mystery to the wisdom of the world and even to this day it is not admitted by the Christian churches except as a mystery. And still they stand, as they always have stood, looking for it to come. When it is come, even in their mouth and they know it not, but eat and drink with the wisdom of this world as they did in the old world, till the flood came and swept them all away. So it will be with this science. The world will oppose it. It will be crucified by the church and priest, hated by the doctors, despised by the crowd, laughed at by fools and received by the foolish of this world. For as science to the natural man is foolishness, they cannot understand it. To the wise of this world it is a stumbling block.

Now Paul labored to reduce this something to a science in order that it might be understood; so it was necessary to separate it from the wisdom of this world and the way to do it has always been a mystery, from the fact that you can't introduce any science except by some proof. For to talk of a science is talking an opinion of something you cannot prove and to show the phenomena without any scientific explanation leaves it as much a mystery and the world is none the wiser. So to teach a science is to put it into practice so that the world can be put in possession of a truth that shall be acknowledged to be above the natural man. Now if you will read all Paul's writings, you will see that this science was what he was trying to make the people understand, for if they could understand it, it changed their motives of action and made them act from a higher principle. This principle was a science and proved itself; but to make it understood was not an easy task. I have been twenty years trying to learn and teach it and am at times nearly worn out, but when I think of Moses teaching it, or trying to, for forty years and then only seeing for other generations what he could never enjoy, it makes me almost sink to the earth. Even Jesus as a man thought that it would become a science in his generation but he was not sure, for he says, No man knoweth not the angels of heaven or the men wise in God's wisdom, but God alone. He knew that it would be established on earth as it is in heaven. So eighteen-hundred years have passed and yet the same angel is sounding with a loud trumpet saying, "How long shall it be till the wisdom of this world shall become reduced to a science so that it can be taught for the healing of the nations, so that man will cease from teaching lies and learn to speak the truth?" Then an opinion will be looked upon as an opinion, and science will judge the correctness of it. Then all kinds of opinions will be weighed in the balance of science and the wisdom of this world will come to naught. Then will arise a new heaven or science and a new earth of man, free from disease or error, for his old world or belief shall be burnt up with the fire of science, and the new heaven or science shall arise, wherein shall not be found all these old superstitions, bigotry and disease, but where there is no more death nor sighing from some ache or pain which arises from superstitions of the old world. Then shall come to pass that saying, "Oh! Death or error where is thy sting! Oh! Grave or misery where is thy victory!" For the sting or belief in death was sin or ignorance but the gift of science is of God which is eternal life.

This life was taught to man by Jesus and called Christ instead of science, and to know this science or Christ is to know eternal life which is eternal progression in the science of God. This science teaches man how to break off from all errors or bad habits that lead to disease; for as disease is in his belief, to be good is to be wise. But health does not always show itself in science for the fool in his heart says there is no Science or God. Therefore the fool is happy in his knowledge. So are a great many persons happy, according to Paul's idea, who are wise in their own conceit and are puffed up with the flattery of the world. But their wisdom comes to an end. They come up like the flowers of the field and flourish as a politician or in some other way for a time, but the dew or wisdom of science passes over them and they wither for the want of something to sustain them. Seeing themselves behind the times as scientific men, all their wisdom taken from them and turned out with the ox to eat this world's food or grass, they then see themselves as a man sees himself in a glass and then turns round, walks off, and forgets what manner of man he was. Then his friend who once knew him will know him no more; for his wisdom is numbered with the dead ideas that never had any life except of the animal life or wisdom of this world. So here end the lives of the small and great, the earthly prince or the ignorant beggar; both find their level in the grave of their belief. Their hope is in their belief and their belief is in their error, and all must yield to science, for science will reign till all error is put out of existence; and when this great science is established in this world, as it is in wisdom, then to be great is to be wise in science.

August 1860

Difference between Dr. Q. and All Others, The*
[BU 3:0524]

No phenomenon of the present time is more inexplicable than that of curing disease without the aid of medicine. That such is the case is now admitted by many but in the explanation of it, men differ as widely as the circumstances that moulded their opinions. Spiritualist are the only sect who claim that power as a distinguishing peculiarity of their belief, and even they rely in a greater or less degree on medicine, but others fully admitting the phenomenon, account for it on known principles of science, or consider it ingenious humbuggery. It is to separate him from all these positions that I call your attention to Dr. Q.

One more easily confounds Dr. Q. with Spiritualists than with any other organization and he is claimed by them as illustrating their principles if not admitting their belief. Spiritualism, like other creeds, is a belief and invented by man; he professes knowledge which cannot be belief and this simple statement is sufficient to separate him from all established religious sects. By men of education Dr. Q. is considered a skillful mesmerizer or a sort of living galvanic battery, and all the light which science can throw is brought to bear upon the subject from their point of view, and the explanation is considered satisfactory. Those who admit his cures, but accuse him of humbugging belong to that class who can conceive of no higher object of doing good than self-interest.

It is our object in the present article to define his position if possible in such a manner as to separate him completely from all established principles of science, moral, or religion.

Dr. Q. has been practicing in our city for three years. He has sought no favors and has interfered with no one's opinions independent of his own practice, but has devoted himself to his business, the relief of the sick and from having come among us unknown and masked, has gained for himself a respected position. His object in remaining here is, not pecuniary profit, for by accepting numerous offers abroad, his gain in that respect could be very much increased, but it is to make known the Science of health. He knows that his system of curing is dependent on knowledge and that it can be communicated to the world for the benefit of each individual. All established principles of science, morals or religion have failed to reveal the secret of happiness and health, such has been their object—such is his, and the only way for the masses to judge between them is by their results.

That he can do what no other living man can do can easily be seen by anyone who chooses to take the trouble. That he is the cause of more happiness than any individual of whom we have heard, if we except one, is not outside the truth. Time only can develop this Science of which he is the humble teacher, meanwhile a fair field is all he asks and he will rely on the strength of his principles for their establishment.

Jan. 1862
The above is incorrect in some statements.

Difference between Knowledge and Wisdom
[Originally untitled.] [BU 3:0753]

How often we hear this remark: "I never believe anything till I understand it." There is more truth than poetry in this remark, for a belief is not wisdom. It may be knowledge, but if it is, it is of this world and not of science, for true science does not admit a belief, as that admits a doubt. Now where does the author of this remark stand, in regard to wisdom or science? Does the remark show any wisdom superior to that of the community? Jesus answered this question himself as a man and showed the people the difference between a belief, or the wisdom of this world and wisdom of God or Science. When asked a question said, I, that is Christ, judge no man, for science or wisdom is the standard, but again he said, if I, the man Jesus, judge, his judgment was not good, for it is of this world. If it is true, or of the scientific world, it is not judgment but wisdom, therefore all judgment is submitted to science where everyone's opinion receives its reward, whether it be of good or evil. Therefore, call no man master, but one, and that is Science, and by this must all things be proved. The wisdom of this world is made up of opinions and decided by evidences, not by truth, for if truth decided, there would be no need of a judge, for the judge is in the science or truth.

July 1860

Difference between My Belief and Others'
[LC 1:0017]

Where does Dr. Quimby's mode of practice differ from that of others? In every particular. Disease is admitted by everyone, though there may be a few exceptions, as a something independent of the mind. Dr. Quimby denies all this and asks for the proof.

Disease is a departure from life. Now, how can a man lose his life and know it after it has taken place and at the same time not know it? For if health is life and a departure from it is death, how can this change take place independently of the mind? For if the mind is not that which undergoes the change, how can it suffer death if it does not know it? And if it is the mind, mind must be matter and matter, mind. This theory finishes up life by the death of the body by disease. This is man's theory and they prove it by their works. This has been the belief since the world began. Religion is founded on this theory and we are called upon to prepare for this change from life to death or from health to disease, for disease is a departure from life. Therefore we are called upon by this theory to prepare for this change from life to death, or from health to disease, and the people understand it pretty well, for they prove it in a few years to the satisfaction of both parties.

This was the state of the mind when Christ came to destroy this theory of disease and death by showing the truth, which was and is life. And no person was in any danger of hell, except those who were sick, for the well need no physician. Therefore to keep well was to keep clear of hell and to get into it was to get sick, for sickness led to death and death led to hell.

Therefore as long as man is well, according to this theory he is safe. Now as Christ was the sick man's advocate, he warned the people against believing either of the two advocates of health and disease. He said to the people, "Beware of the doctrine or beliefs or theories of the scribes and Pharisees, for they undertake to tell of what they know nothing about and they bind burdens in the form of disease or opinions and leave them on your shoulders, which are grievous to be borne and which must lead to death, or the departure from life or health." To keep in health and keep clear of death was to understand ourselves so that their opinions cannot harm us. Now, in all the above belief or theory, there is not the slightest intimation of any knowledge independent of mind. It is true that some people have a vague idea of something independent of the mind, but the person who dares express such an opinion is looked upon as a sort of lunatic or fool. Phenomena are constantly taking place, showing that there is a higher order of intellect that has not yet been developed in the form of a theory, but which can unravel the old theory and bring in one that will lead man to health and happiness and destroy the idea of disease and death. Dr. Quimby's theory, if understood, also goes to correct this error that is depriving so many of the life and happiness of mankind. His belief is his practice and his practice gives the lie to the old belief.

Jan. 1860

Difference between My Philosophy and That of Others
[LC 2:0883]

The difference between my belief and the rest of those who have written upon the philosophy of the mind is this: every philosophy aims at happiness as the greatest object to be attained. So they believe that goodness is one of the means to obtain this great point. So all their thoughts are aimed at this one object, happiness, thinking it is somewhere in the future and as though it was something which by laboring they might obtain. This is the great study of all great philosophers. Now I pretend to study the philosophy of the mind and have been for the last twenty years a constant student of this science, and I have come to the conclusion that happiness is like light and misery is like darkness and man being in darkness chooses darkness rather than light because of his ignorance. All philosophy teaches man how to find this light by prescribing certain rules and regulations as to what one shall eat and drink and wherewithal he shall be clothed, and they place all sorts of restrictions on man to be observed so that he may obtain this light. Now all the above leads him into darkness, death, disease and misery.

I differ from all such philosophy and call light happiness and darkness misery, and instead of trying to find the light, I labor to destroy the darkness. I will give an illustration: disease is the effect of darkness or a belief, for a belief has no light or wisdom; wisdom is light, and opinions are darkness. Now when man is in opinions he is in darkness and to get out of his opinions is to get into the light. Therefore I commence to correct the error that troubles him. This trouble is his darkness, so I convince him of the error and the light springs up and his light is his happiness. As the Bible says, the people which sat in the darkness saw a great light and to those which sat in the region and shadow of death the light is sprung up. Matt. 4:16

Difference of Opinion about the Dead
[BU 3:0070]

Why should there be such a difference of opinion in regard to the dead? If there is such a thing as death, what is it? It is of the body I suppose. Now if the body is matter, has matter life? If it has, then the life is a part of the body; and if the body dies, then the life dies also, for the life is the body. Now if you mean that this is the end of man, what lives after the life and body die? You will say, the soul. Where is the soul? Has anyone ever seen it? Or is it an opinion? The fact is that the theory of the body and soul is not in keeping with the progress of truth or science. It leaves everything in the dark. It gives no proof of any phenomenon but assumes that man must take an opinion of someone who does not undertake to prove it and admit an opinion of something that took place five thousand years ago, and renewed eighteen hundred years ago.

Mankind is just the same as it always was and so is the brute creation and all of God's race. They can be classified from the vegetable world to the spiritual world, but not as they have been, for there never has been a single philosophical grade above the brute since Christ.

Jesus tried to establish the kingdom of truth in man so that men would teach it, but he failed not because he was ignorant himself but because man was not developed enough to receive it.

It is sometimes supposed that the wisdom of God or science is made manifest in some simple girl or man. This is the case, and phenomena are continually occurring, which baffle the world's wisdom to explain, so they are set down as humbug or deception. By a mesmerized subject I can prove that there is no such thing as death as it is understood by all Christians. All will admit that a person can be mesmerized and when in that state can read and travel, going off to distant places. I can prove that mind is matter and there is no matter without mind, and death is nothing but an opinion or state of mind made up of matter which can be destroyed like any other opinion. It is true to the soul that is in matter, but to the science that is out of matter it is only an idea. The word matter is applied to man in his lowest state, just a little above the brute. The brute has his soul, but he is always in matter, for he shows no knowledge over any other brute. He shows no power of teaching more than the brute before him. This proves his limits.

The fowls are the same, and all creation have, as yet, shown no science. Now if it was intended for the above classes to learn and teach science, it is natural to suppose that they would have shown some symptoms of it before now, so I leave them as they are and pass on to man.

It is not to be supposed that every man who walks upright is to be set down as a scientific man, nor is it true that everyone who calls himself scientific is so. But it is he who can show himself so to the world by his acts, who can explain some truth, thereby putting the world in possession of a fact that it has been ignorant of, thus increasing the wisdom and happiness of mankind. This is the case with science.

Now if death can be explained away so that man can be put in possession of life eternal, then the world will be put in possession of a fact it is now ignorant of. This I will try to do.

What is life? It is admitted that it is something. It is a consciousness of an existence, and death is the fear of the annihilation of that consciousness. The natural man never sees anything beyond the idea of his belief. Therefore he lives in death and is all his life subject to his own belief. Now convince man that there is something independent of this belief that is true, that there is no such thing as matter, only as it is spoken into existence, and he will then see that mind is the very matter or error that is his belief.

As his belief changes, the matter or opinion changes and as matter or opinion or mind is all the same, when a chemical change takes place, the mind or opinion is destroyed and truth or science takes the place of error. Then the soul or science stands out from the mind or matter and sees how the mind can be made the medium of any soul to bring about any belief or disease.

When man arrives at that, then death is swallowed up in science; then the world will rejoice in the science that teaches man that he is nothing but a mass of ideas, can be destroyed and molded to any belief and take a form to suit its author. The knowledge of this teaches us that all misery is in ourselves, arising from some idea that our soul or science is in, like a prison.

The world is the belief, the destruction of the prison is the destruction of our belief and the liberation of our soul from bondage is life eternal. This is in God or science.

April 1860

Difficulty in Establishing a New Science–Language, The
[LC 2:0686]

The fact that the mode in which I cure disease cannot be understood by the learned may lead some to suppose that I do not understand myself. This is a mistake and arises from the fact that certain demagogues of all classes take upon themselves the responsibility of giving their opinions on every subject however complicated it may be. They always make war whether they see or hear about the thing in question or not and are always opposed as a stumbling block to every new science and invention.

Every science has its shadow based on opinions about the phenomenon as in the invention of steam, for instance. When it was first claimed that it could be applied to the advantage of the world, up sprang this set of demagogues to show off their knowledge. And while the first steamer was crossing the Atlantic, one of the learned quacks, lecturing in New York City, was proving by actual demonstration that the steamer could not carry coal enough to drive her to New York. But for all his wisdom, the steamer kept plowing along unheeding the prophetic voice till it arrived safely, thus proving by practice what the theory had contended for. This class of men abound everywhere. They are as superstitious as the people were in the days of the Salem witchcraft, and if it were not for their acquired abilities, would become a laughing stock to all sensible men. They are narrow-minded and place a great reliance on their education, supposing that education is wisdom, while it as often proves the shallowness of knowledge as it does its superiority. Wisdom is not learning; it was before education. Every phenomenon comes without learning or wisdom and the accounting for it brings out genius. This genius looks for causes and traces back the phenomenon to the cause, and then reduces the investigation to physical demonstration. This process is called science; therefore science is wisdom reduced to practice. The class spoken of above never had any genius; they had superstition. So learning is not confined to either class but is common to both. Men demand praise for learning, for that is an invention of men and a thing in common. No one supposes a dictionary has any more wisdom than Cock Robin. The man of genius puts his senses into his wisdom that is known to him in the form of science. The man of letters puts his senses in the shadow of this wisdom, in the form of opinions, and tries all things by his knowledge.

Now there are certain established principles, called law and order, made by the voluntary consent of the people. These arguments are condensed into law and they agree to be governed by the laws of their own make. So as law is arbitrary, it is not based on true wisdom but is the best that the majority can agree to. Therefore it is necessary to have persons who understand what the true construction of the law is. This class is called judges, and it is a very necessary calling and should be filled by those most skilled in learning. They give their attention to their new business if they know it, but if they do not, they become babblers of all sorts of parties and show that they are of the class I have described. This class is found opposing everything that requires physical demonstration. They oppose also all sorts of religion, not that they do not believe in another world, for they are the most zealous believers, but they have no genius. Everything that they cannot understand must be a mystery, and being ignorant, they cannot see the difference between a fact based on an opinion and on science. To them all is science. You hear them talking of the science of mesmerism, the science of phrenology and of many others that have not ever been broached to see what were the causes of the phenomena that are seen and heard, but which these blind guides claim as science. In like manner, you hear of the medical science. Yet there is not one fact reduced to practice by which man is put in possession of any wisdom that gives him superiority over the lowest laboring man who works in the gutters and lives on what he can get and pays no respect to the opinions of these blind guides, yet is the healthiest.

So learning never made a man healthy; wisdom might, but ignorance let alone is bliss. The class who stand in the way of health and offer their opinions for wisdom is what Jesus had to contend with.

Jude describes them when he says, "But these speak evil of those things which they know not but what they know naturally as brute beasts; in those things, they corrupt themselves. Woe unto them! For they have gone in the way of Cain and run greedily after the error of Balaam for reward and perished in the gainsaying of Korah!"

Every man who has ever introduced any new invention or discovery has had to contend with this set of babblers. I am not an exception to this rule. My observation of men for the last twenty years has taught me what every man must go through before he can establish a theory that strikes at the root of all superstition; for as no man knows himself, to introduce a mode by which men's thoughts can be weighed is so new and strange to the world that it is looked upon as humbug. My experience in mesmerism gave me a chance to see and hear the views of men upon those things that pertained to health and happiness. The investigation of mesmerism is like introducing any new discovery. You meet with all sorts of minds and all kinds of questions are asked, some for information, some to trip you up or to show you that they are posted up in all the quackery of the day and that they look upon everything with suspicion. So when you go into a place, you are attacked by these babblers in the form of second rate lawyers or students who want to get a hold on public opinion and young physicians who want a chance to show off their knowledge. My practice has given me great advantage over others from the fact that I work on my own responsibility, not being connected with any school of practice. This standing alone has created a sort of nervous excitement among not only the medical faculty but all that class of minds who looked upon everything that cannot be explained to their satisfaction as coming from God or the influence of the spirits of the dead. Then there is another class who have seen the absurdity of the medical profession and are willing to admit that there is something in what is embraced by mesmerism but believe that in time they can be accounted for on some principle not yet understood. This makes up men or society.

The religious persons I class in one scale: those who really believe that the Bible is of divine origin and have no doubts, and another class who have their doubts. The latter, in order to feel sure of their religion, will pay tithes for preaching and make great professions; they never use their influence for the benefit of mankind without a show. They generally pay well when it is for their interest. If they are traders, it is for custom; if they want political office, they pay those societies who will yield the most votes. Thus the world is made up of such material.

There is another class who mind their business. To them the world is merely a mechanical workshop and they allow everyone to follow their bent. This is not a small class, but it does not make any one noise in the world. Now all the above classes and many more besides are liable to be sick. They almost always call a physician, and from these, I have had a chance to learn the causes of most of the ills that flesh is heir to. When I first commenced investigating mesmerism, the phenomena were rare and scarcely any one believed, even in the sleep. It was so mysterious that it roused the minds of the masses to that degree that men took sides with considerable feeling. The first experiments were of that peculiar kind that they confounded the learned as well as the unlearned, and I was looked upon by some as a deceiver and by others as a humbug and by still others as ignorant but honest. Here were the most learned and liberal; but those men of education, among whom were doctors who had just come before the public, found a chance to make a show of their wisdom. So at every exhibition, I have to come in contact with some professor or doctor or minister who wanted to make himself popular at my expense.

I gave no explanation of the manner in which my experiments were done, so the investigation was to see that there was no collusion between the subject and myself. I have noticed how most people who have seen experiments in mesmerism have their opinions and try to make everything correspond with their belief, and as that is nothing more than a child's belief, it can be compared only to a bubble or sensation.

Happiness is the harmonizing of some disturbance. This disturbance is nothing of itself, but language makes its misery; so language excites it and happiness is only the name of rest from the disturbance or misery. We often hear of the evils of intemperance, etc. Now language of itself, like rum and tobacco, is harmless, but a bad use of either makes evil or discord. But of all evils, language is the worst. It is the groundwork of all other evils; it is at the bottom of every one that affects man. Some men live on it; they eat and drink it; deprive them of it, and they are not anything. All they are is language. Ask them for any scientific information and they are as hollow as a bubble. Language to them is like stimulant. It makes them talk about everything that they know nothing of but they get carried away by this false stimulant. (It never was the intention of the inventor of language that a bad use should be made of it, neither was it the intention of any true genius that his invention was to be applied to the destruction of life and happiness.) The discovery of wines and liquor was not to make misery but to elevate man, and the invention of gunpowder was not designed to make war but to defend us from our enemies. So language was invented to communicate sensation from one man to another so as to get him out of trouble. This is the origin of language and it is of no use except to facilitate certain plans. Genius never cares about language; his wisdom is all in the idea he wishes to accomplish. When it is accomplished, he wishes to convey the discovery to the world; and as the inventor is not the language, his invention must be introduced by someone who knows language but may or may not have genius. Genius is known in language only when language is the invention of genius to explain the wisdom of genius. The abuse of language is the root of all evil. You never hear of language itself doing any harm, but see if it is not the bottom of all misery. This rebellion would not have been started by the ignorance of language, for that must be used to corrupt the minds and get the people excited, and then they are ready for anything the leaders propose. Look at disease. If there never had been any language, the ideas advanced called disease would never have been heard.

April 1862

Difficulty of Introducing My Ideas, The
[LC 2:0906]

Introducing these ideas to the world is not an easy task, for the world like the sick cannot understand. For if they could, then there would not be any call for some other mode of reasoning. But the world, like a sick man, is in trouble and does not know how to free itself from the fetters that bind it. It is easy to take one individual case and apply the theory, but to take the world and give the causes and symptoms is not so easy a task. The world, like the sick, have no idea that what is said and believed in has anything to do with their sickness, when all our troubles or nearly so are from our belief, directly or indirectly. Therefore, I have to take the world as a patient and show that the causes of man's trouble arise from his beliefs and these make him sick. Now the sickness is not the belief, but the belief is the cause directly or indirectly. So to cure, I have to destroy the belief and then the sickness will cease. Then the question will be asked what is a belief?

Disease [I]
[BU 3:0977]

The fact that some cures are made outside of the medical faculty is not denied by any person, but how they are done is the problem to be solved. I say they are done by the mind which is acted upon by some wisdom outside of itself.

There never was a cure performed unless some wisdom superior to the cause was brought to act upon the mind. Now I have given over twenty years of my life to this subject and feel confident that my method of curing is entirely new to the world, that it has never been practiced intelligently by any living man. I am the first of my practice while all others are the last of theirs. All will admit that the allopathic practice is the older, except spiritualism, if you please to call it a practice. If spiritualism is admitted to be a mode of practice it is older than the allopathic practice, for there were certain men eighteen hundred years ago that practiced curing and casting out devils by this power.

One man called it the power of good, but Jesus called it the power of the devil. Jesus admitted there were some cures made, for when his disciples told him they saw persons casting out devils in his name and forbade them, he said, "Forbid them not, for those that are with us are not against us, and those that are not with us scattereth abroad." Now here were persons making cures that were not with Jesus and it was hard to convince the people that Jesus' cures were not made in the same way in which the spiritualists of his day made theirs. Now this false idea of spirits is the foundation of disease and gives rise to all kinds of practice. Until spiritualism can be explained, the world must be humbugged in some way, either by the medical faculty or some of the humbugs of the day. To deny that a cure was ever made by the above is to deny the Bible and all ancient history.

Dec. 9, 1861

Disease [II]
[LC 1:0566]

It is necessary for the benefit of mankind that there should be such a word as disease? I answer, No, and will show that the world will never escape from this evil as long as they admit it. Now the word disease supposes that either certain phenomena exist in the world, which pass under the name of disease and which have an identity separate from each individual as much as wild animals have an identity separate from man, or that there are certain hidden evils called disease that are ready to attack us when we expose ourselves to them. For instance, there are certain diseases that go in the air we are told. Now let us analyze them. Let us take, for example, the plague. This horrid disease as it is called goes in the air and travels from one part of the globe to another. Now when it is in the air, what kind of a looking thing is it? Has it any knowledge? It must have, according to what the medical faculty say of it, for it generally follows large cities and armies, but I never heard of it where there were no persons to be devoured by it. So of course it has an identity and is a horror to mankind. Now how does it vary from the old superstition in the church about the devil and the evil spirits that were going round seeking whom they might devour? If you ask a person if he really believes there is such a thing or being as the devil, he will tell you, No, we make him. But if you ask the same person if he believes in the plague going around from one place to another, he will say, Yes. Now one is just as absurd as the other. Both are the inventions of man and both will give way to the wisdom of man.

Liberal religion has destroyed the devil as a being and located him in man's evil thoughts and acts. And we are taught that to get rid of him is to keep ourselves free from mischief and learn to do good. In like manner, science will show the serpent's head called disease. And when man learns that its body is in our ignorance and we create him in ourselves, the same as we create the devil, then this old serpent the devil or disease will vanish and man will be free from one of the greatest curses that ever affected the human race.

I will try to show that disease is what follows our belief and our beliefs affect us and also each other and also animals. Ignorance being the medium to be affected, error is the first growth after the soil is disturbed. Now error sows all the seeds of misery. These seeds are beliefs. All phenomena in the soil of ignorance would of themselves produce no trouble. This is proved by facts that cannot be denied. Take savages. In their perfectly savage state they are not much troubled by the inventions of civilized life. And in proportion as the savage has intercourse with the white man, they become diseased, thus showing that the whites are the originators of this evil.

Now if disease is not the invention of the whites, why does the savage not have the disease in the same locality in which he lived before he ever knew the whites? Take the Indian tribes. When they lived separate from the whites and had no communication with them, they were healthy. But as soon as the whites settled near them and they began to enter into their beliefs, then the savages became frightened and disease took hold to them. Now if disease is a thing that goes around and attacks man, why does it not attack those that never had anything to do with civilized life? The fact is religion and disease are synonymous. Both are the invention of man for the special benefit of a few, but disease has become so settled in the minds of man that it amounts to a solid fact and is believed in as having a being independent of man and is an enemy to his happiness. It is believed by every person therefore that to correct this belief and restore a person to health is a mystery. But when a man can see that his belief can make him sick, he won't require much reasoning to see also that to correct his belief will make him well. Now take the effect of his belief and call that a disease; then you see that there is no need of the name disease. When man finds that a belief is something as much as an odor, then it won't be very difficult to see how odors affect man and beast. Now prove that odors affect man and beast to make them sick; then odors must be something. The next step will be to show that man has the power to create odors by his own belief and will.

Now the case of the boy, Caspar Hauser, shows that odors, which man in his ordinary senses cannot detect by the slightest effect, would make him vomit. The least wine or liquor put into water would throw him into convulsions and make his head ache. When meat was offered him, on putting it into his mouth, it produced convulsions. The odor of flowers affected him. The footsteps of persons at a distance were easily detected one from another. His sight was also so sensitive that he could see when it was so dark that others could not see. All this effect on the boy was proved. Now see the effect of these odors on the boy, making him sick, throwing him into convulsions and giving him dreams. Now after being taught, hear his story. He says that while confined in his cell or cave, he never dreamed and never was sick and he lived on bread and water, all going to prove that the elements of disease are in the world. And if the world had been a cave or prison and man was as ignorant as the boy, Caspar Hauser, disease as we have it would never have come. For bread and water he became accustomed to and the other odors would have affected us, but the name disease would never have been known. Now these odors that make all the disease that flesh is heir to—where did they come from and how came they in the world? I have said these odors affected this boy but only temporarily. The odor of a thing that could not be detected by his friend was very disagreeable to him. Now no one will say that the odor of a flower would give a person the typhoid fever or even any fever, for all the medical men recommend the open air and green fields to the sick. So all those things that we as individuals believe are healthy brought on all his trouble and misery. So we must look for disease from some other source.

Now all I have said in regard to this boy, I have proved by a mesmeric subject that I had. I found that his sense of smell was so acute that he could detect any odor at a distance and not only detect but describe the flower or persons that threw the odor, but all this does not account for disease. But I will lead you along to the point that will, and in doing so be patient for it cannot be shown by one sentence. It must be by degrees. The boy, Caspar Hauser, was transferred from his sensitive state to the normal state of man, for he was a mesmerized subject in one sense and I refer to him and to show the similarity between this boy and my subject. For instance, persons and things were like pictures, all on the surface. A man to him looked like a picture and everything the same. So with my boy. I could think of a being and he was as much of a being to him as anyone. Now just suppose that Caspar Hauser had been told that all these odors that affected him were poisoned and he was liable to disease and suppose that he had been taught all the names of diseases and the symptoms, do you not see how he must be made sick?

I said that I could create objects that my subject could see, so of course I could create things that would frighten him and I could create all kinds of fruit which he would eat and be affected by. For instance, when awake, he was very fond of lemons and was always eating them. I thought I would break him of the habit, so when I had him asleep, I would create mentally a lemon and he would see it. Then I would make him eat it till he would be so sick that he would vomit. Then he would beg me not to make him eat any more, promising me that he would never eat any more lemons again. I never named the conversation to him in his waking state. After trying the experiment two or three times, it destroyed his taste for lemons and he had no desire for them and could not bear even the look of them.

Now to the natural man. He ate no lemons; then why did he vomit from the effect of eating? It may be said that it was my mind acting upon his. This was the case. Now if my mind was not something, it could not produce an effect. So if my mind is something what is it? It is my belief governed by my wisdom. So an idea is the center of a belief. Now every idea that exists in the wisdom of man is in his mind, as every idea of a plant is in the earth and every living idea that creeps on the earth or dwells in the seas and every living thing that has form throws off an odor. And every person is affected more or less by the things he sees. Now there is another set of ideas just as real as the former which the world makes no account of, yet, they are of all things the most wicked and dangerous, from the fact that they can't be seen by the natural man's mind, and yet, they are in us, living on our very lives and devouring our substance of happiness and we know it not. Now settle this one thing, that ideas that cannot be seen are as real as those which can be seen; then man can account for his troubles as easily as he can account for injuries caused by an accident on a railroad or steamboat or any evils that we are subject to and he can learn how to avoid them.

Some ideas contain no intelligence because the author puts none in them, others do and the ignorant know no difference between them. Take the light of a lamp. When Caspar Hauser saw the light of a candle, he expressed joy and put his finger in the light, but as soon as it burned him, he drew it out and cried like a child, although he was 17 years of age. Now the idea candle to him contained no harm, but to those who knew it would burn him, it contained heat.

So after he was burned, he was afraid. Now suppose a person has put into the idea candle the idea poison. The idea poison to the boy would be like the candle before he put his finger in it. To him it contained nothing but a name poison. Now explain the nature of poison and make him believe that his finger would be liable to become diseased, that it would spread all over the body and finally kill him, and a combined idea enters his mind. But suppose you take some simple remedy and tell him if he applied it to the burn, it may stop the disease. Here you make an idea poison and the idea is as real as the light. Now the idea poison is in the light. Every time he sees the light, he sees the poison. Now until he is rid of the idea poison, he is liable to be affected in case he should be burned by the light. This is a fair illustration of all these ideas of disease. The natural world has in it all sorts of living identities from the vegetable to the animal, and every one throws off an odor. And before man became acquainted with the real properties of the odor, ignorance, superstition and error introduced other ideas and associated them with the thing that had an existence in the natural man or error. And not knowing how to account for all the sensations of the odors, the false mode of reasoning called knowledge sprang up. So now there is not an odor from anything but that there is a lie attached to it in the form of an opinion.

These opinions become a part and parcel of the original idea, so as man receives the one, he is affected by the other. Now the odor from the false idea contains the knowledge, so that every idea that contains knowledge, you may know is a lie, for the true idea contains nothing but a sensation. So in fact does the false idea, but the knowledge is in the odor of the lie and not in the odor of the real. For instance the word consumption is like a flower that throws off an atmosphere, but the atmosphere is different from the flower in this respect. The odor from the flower contains the bush but no language. The idea of consumption contains all the horror of death. All this is language. So if a person does not know the meaning, all he sees is the bush or skeleton from which this odor arises. Now make him acquainted with the disease and then he stands exactly as the boy does to the light when he is made to believe it contained poison. So the idea consumption contains all the knowledge of its locality and the symptoms, in fact all the varieties of changes that man goes through after he thinks he has it. The symptoms are like the burn and the remedies are not equal to the disease. So those that are affected by the symptoms are so excited that the idea remedy is not sufficient to produce the cure. Now apply this theory and you have a touchstone to test the true idea from the false. And the analyzing of the false idea destroys the effect and health is the result.
1863

Disease [III]
[LC 1:0485]

What is disease? It is false reasoning. True scientific wisdom is health and happiness. False reasoning is sickness and death; and on these two modes of reasoning hang all of our happiness or misery. The question is, how can we know how to separate the one from the other? The truth cannot be changed;

the false is always changing. The one is science, and the other is error, and our senses are attached to the one or the other. One is the natural development of matter or mind, and disease is one of the natural inventions of error. To show how disease is not what it is supposed to be, by those who use the word, I must show the absurdity of error's reasoning, for error is the father of disease.

We are all taught by this error to call disease something that is independent of man. To make it more plain and show where the two modes of reasoning act, I will suppose a case and take that of a young man or person who, feeling a little disturbed, calls on a physician. The physician sounds his lungs, examines his heart, and tells the patient he is very liable to have the heart disease. The patient asks him how he got it, and he is told that he is liable to catch disease and have it for it is not a part of him, and to get it or have it or catch it is to admit that it exists independent of himself. And though the patient be dead, yet it would exist the same and others would be liable to get it. At last the patient really has the heart disease which his physician described to him.

Now has he created it himself, or has the doctor created it for him? Now I propose to show that he has made what the world calls heart disease himself without anyone's help. To show how a building is razed is to frame one and then take it down again, so I will take down this building, heart disease, which this man has raised, and then he can see how ideas are made or raised. I will say to the patient, You have built the disease yourself in your sleep of ignorance. This he cannot understand. So I will tell him how he has worked in his sleep and made the very edifice, heart disease that he has got. So I begin to tell his dream by telling how he feels, in which he admits I am correct. Now when he was asleep, or ignorant of the feelings that disturbed him, behold a spirit in the form of a doctor sat by him, and lo and behold, he called up from the dead a person with the heart disease, as he called it, and he handled you, and your sleep departed from you and your limbs became cold and clammy, and your pulse quickened. This excited your brain, and at last a figure of a person arose like unto the one you saw in your dream, and then you were afraid, and you awoke in a fright. At last the image became more terrible till at length it overshadowed you and became a part of yourself, so that when you awoke you looked, and lo and behold the dream had become reality, and you had the heart disease. Now whose was it, the doctor's or yours? Did you catch the doctor's or did you create it yourself by your own reasoning in your sleep or ignorance, according to the pattern set you by the doctor?

I say you made it yourself. Now to cure you, or to take down the building, is to show you that all the feeling you had at the commencement arose from some trifling cause, and that when I can make you understand it, I have performed the cure. And instead of giving medicines or going to work by guess to destroy the building, I commence by showing the patient how he framed it by his own hand or wisdom. So I reason in this way. You listened to the doctor to try and understand what caused the heart disease. He explained every variety of feeling or symptom, and you listened until you understood it. Now without knowing it you created in your mind the disease, as much as you would if an artist or mechanic had taught you how to draft a building, and you would carry in your mind the building and in your sleep would create it. The only difference would be that one would please you, for it would contain wisdom, while the other would bind you, for it would contain fear and threaten to destroy your life.

Your trouble is the material with which to build the building or disease. A chemical change in the fluids of your system takes place, governed by your belief, and you condense these into a phenomenon corresponding with your draft. Now the fluids become diseased and your ingenuity in manufacturing the disease has been the destruction of your happiness. To destroy the disease I convince you that what the doctor said was an idea gotten up by error, not knowing how to account for some little disturbance, which in itself amounted to nothing; but by the doctor's mode of reasoning about what he knew nothing, you were led astray into the darkness of heathen superstition where all kinds of evil spirits and disease dwell in the brain of man. Superstition always shows itself through the ignorance of man's reasoning, assuming as many names and forms as the father of all lies, the Devil or the error of mankind.

1864

Disease and Its Cause
[LC 1:0529]

Disease is as old as man's existence, but the causes of it have never been explained. Various causes have been given. The ancients admitted disease and then tried to show that it arose from the people's habits of living. The Epicurean philosophers tried to show that man by his own acts caused his disease. Lucretius, one of the pupils of Epicurus, contended that man is the cause of his own misery by his own belief. He does not use these words, but I shall show that that was what he meant. And being misrepresented, his ideas have never found their way into the minds of the Christians of our day because he showed that the religion of his day was the cause of all the disease and trouble that men suffered. To show this was his labor in his poem that has never been understood. The reader will see, by going back one-hundred years before Jesus, how the people were excited by the religion of that time. To see what Lucretius had to contend with is to know what the people believed in. The effect of religion on the people, Lucretius showed in his poem. I will give some extracts.

He says, "Indeed mankind in wretched bondage held, lay groveling on the ground, galled by the yoke of what is called religion. From the sky this tyrant showed her head and with grim looks hung over us poor mortals here below, until a man of Greece with steady eye dared look her in the face and first oppose her power. Him not the fear of Gods nor thunderous roar kept back, nor threatening tumults of the sky, but still the more they roused the active virtue of his aspiring soul as he pressed forward, to break through nature's scanty bounds, his mind's quick force prevailed. And so he passed by far the flaming portals of this world and wandered with his comprehensive soul o'er all the mighty space. From thence returned triumphant, told us what things may have a being and what may not and how a finite power is fixed to each, a bond it cannot break. And so religion which we feared before, by him subdued, we tread upon in turn. His conquest makes us equal to the Gods."

It is generally believed that the writers of the Epicurean philosophy were men that opposed everything that was good, but they are misrepresented. They opposed the errors and superstitions of their day and to do this was to show that the heathen mythology was based on nothing but a belief. So he shows the absurdity of their religion. The Pythagoreans held to the transmigration of souls. A poet who lived about a hundred years before Lucretius affirmed that the "soul of Homer was in his body; but that he might not injure Pluto, he bequeathed to the infernal mansion not the soul nor the body but the ghost which the ancients held to be a third nature of which together with the body and soul the whole man consisted." Speaking of this class of philosophers, Lucretius says, "And yet the nature of the soul we know not, whether formed with the body or at the birth infused and then by death cut off she perishes as bodies do, or whether she descends to the dark caves and dreadful lakes of hell, or after death inspired with heavenly instinct, she returns into the brutes as our great Ennius sung, who first a crown of laurels ever grew brought down from Helicon, describes the stately places of Acheron where neither our souls nor bodies ever come, but certain spectres strange and wondrous pale." But then he goes on to say that he shall search into the soul what her nature is and what meets our wakeful eyes and frights the mind, and how by sickness and by sleep oppressed, we think we see or hear the voice of these who died long since, whose moldering bones rot in the cold embrace of the grave. "These terrors of the mind, this darkness, these not the sun's beams, nor the light ray of day can we dispel, but nature's light and reason whose first principles shall be my guide." This taught him that nothing was by nothing made, therefore could not produce something and every effect had a cause. Now these strange ghosts and spirits are all the inventions of man not of God. Yet to man they are something. But ask where they come from and how they got here, then comes the mystery. Now Lucretius shows that man is matter dissolved and like all other matter passed into space, and the matter was seen by those who believed in spirits. Here was where he failed. He proved that every effect had a cause and as these spirits are nothing, they have no cause or beginning.

His theory was that matter, like seeds, dissolves and each seed retains the elements of the whole lump. This reasoning he carried into man, so that man like all nature dissolves and passes into space and each particle or seed contains the whole of man's life. This was the cause of their strange spectres being seen that the people called spirits and ghosts. Their fear produced it by their imagination. This was his theory, and as far as he reasoned, his theory cannot be refuted. His starting point was light and reason. This taught that nothing cannot produce something, for if a thing could spring from nothing, what need is there for bodies to grow. And if nothing could produce something, then man might spring up out of the ground, grain from the sea and fish live on the land. But everything shows that all things have their causes and all phenomena must come from something. This shows that imagination is either something or nothing. And if a person imagines a thing and the thing appears, it shows that it has a cause outside of the thing seen. Now all these things have been seen and thousands more and there is proof to show that spirits, ghosts, spectres and strange delusions are matter moved without the aid of the natural man. And all these phenomena are so well attested to that it is folly in any one to deny the last. Among the strange phenomena are diseases, for disease is one of the great proofs that these things are among the things believed.

The ancient philosophers were promulgating certain truths as they thought and to live up to them was their religion. They did not have creeds as the people of our day do but a sort of philosophy that governed their lives according to the science of philosophy. The Pythian philosophy consisted of searching into the laws of mathematics. This would teach them causes and effects, so all their acts were governed by their wisdom and their happiness was the fruit of their religious philosophy. Plato believed in one great cause and matter in an invisible state, subject to a power. Here he, like all the rest of the philosophers, loses man. Now according to my own experience, matter is a substance to the one that believes it, but to suppose that matter exists independent of wisdom is not in the power of man to prove. So if matter is an idea, it is very easy to see that it is entirely under the control either of our belief or our wisdom. Now here are the two powers: one wisdom and the other belief. Now belief admits matter as a substance, wisdom admits it as a belief. Wisdom speaks it into existence and to belief it is a reality. I will now show how a belief can create matter and yet to wisdom it is nothing. To do this, I must assume to know what I am going to do. So if I can make a person believe a thing, I impart to him a sort of wisdom (I call it wisdom because it is the highest he has and he thinks it wisdom but I know it is not wisdom but an error). Now to the person, it is wisdom after I convince him of its truth, so I must prove it to the person to establish the fact.

I will take a person and perform a mesmeric experiment and satisfy the person that it is performed. Now he knows that I have done it. This to him is true, but he believes he cannot do it. I tell him he can do the same. So he tries and I produce the phenomenon myself, but he thinks he does it. In this way, he gets confidence and does it himself. Now he, in his belief, does the very thing I do. Now I am in his belief and he knows it not and thinks it is himself. So now he uses the wisdom he gets from me to perform his experiments. Suppose I tell him that the spirits can make him move a table. This he does not believe. By my arguments, I affect his belief till it is sufficient to move the table. Now his belief will not give me the credit but gives it to the spirits showing that my wisdom is a spirit to him. Now this wisdom that I impart can see the spirits and he creates them under this belief and to him they are spirits. But to me they are the spirits of his own make. Now to him this is matter, so he can be made to believe that bodies can be moved, but to wisdom it is not matter.

Matter supposes distance between like our senses, that is, one chair must be not as another chair, so our senses are divided into five. Now with wisdom, there is no division only as wisdom makes it. Senses are swallowed up in wisdom and there can be no space. So everything is present. The difference between wisdom and belief is this: wisdom is never deceived; belief is never certain but always changes. Man is like a town. The inhabitants are the intelligence and the identity of the town is the same. The locality is the same always although the intelligence is always changing. Yet, every person admits the identity of the town. But its inhabitants or intelligence are always changing and improvements are going on showing the growth of the intelligence, not of the town or the ground on which the town is built.

So God makes the ground or identity called body and gives it an identity called man. This is under the wisdom of man until it is able to act of itself, when man's body like a city or town is governed by the inhabitants or wisdom of the town. As a town is made up of different talent, so man is made up of different ideas and sometimes one set rules and sometimes another. Man is not a unit but is governed by a city or nation and is liable to be deceived by false ideas into a belief that gets up a sort of rebellion. All this is the working of matter. So diseases and revolutions take place and sometimes the inhabitants flee from their enemies, but this is the working of matter. There seems to be a sort of inconsistency in regard to God. If God knows and rules all things, how could there be another power that seems to be contradictory to what we call God's wisdom?

Now according to my theory that mind is matter, it looks very plain to me that there should be a conflict going on in man as in nations. For there is a regular grade of matter from the mineral to the animal creation. And there is a regular grade of intelligence that corresponds to the matter. Now as the matter of vegetables and animals are connected, it is not strange that every person should partake of the elements of each. Yet we all admit that the mineral and vegetable life acts just as it was intended by God; but when man steps in, he reasons that God is not quite up to the intelligence of man and we try to reconcile God to man, not man to God. This is as natural as our breath. Man wants to rule his fellow man and even dictate to God what is best for mankind.

Now look at man's mind, partaking of all the elements of knowledge of the lower animal creation acting in man, warring against the higher intelligence of matter or mind. Then you will see that man is the center or land of all the intellect of the brute creation, as the United States is the house of refuge for the scapegoats of all nations. So these elements in man as well as in nations are warring against themselves. So as man's body is the bounds of his identity as a man, his knowledge has its bounds as an intellectual man. So when we speak of a man, we embrace his body and his knowledge as one, just as we speak of a city. For instance, if we speak of Portland, we speak of it as a city of intelligence according to our ideas of wisdom, so we confound the city with the intelligence. Every citizen of Portland will admit there are parties and sects that come in conflict with each other and sometimes one party rules and sometimes another. Now the dominant party reasons that it is right and the other wrong. Then perhaps the next season the tables are turned; "the outs" are in and "the ins" are out. So no person will deny but there is a difference in regard to the intelligence of parties, yet everyone will say that his party is right. Now there are certain facts admitted by every person that can't be disputed, that shows there is a difference between what is called intelligence.

For instance, the brute is not blamed for being a brute nor is God blamed because he made man superior to the brute in this, that the man when developed can produce what the brute cannot. Not that man in his original state is above the brute, but man like the earth is capable of being cultivated beyond the brute, but the wisdom that develops man is not of man. But the earth brought forth all living things that hath life, but wisdom or science never came from the earthly man. So as life is out of the earth or animal matter, there is a natural grade so that every person can tell his place in society if he only has the wit to acknowledge it, and if he won't, the intelligence of the world will place him where he belongs. I will illustrate what I have said to show that there is a standard to test the plane of man's intellect. No person will call two dogs fighting with each other equal to two human beings, yet, they don't find fault with God but look upon the dogs as a lower development of matter or mind. Now suppose a being in the shape of a man should be found fighting with a dog, would any person place him on the same grade with a man of higher intelligence? Would not such a person place him with the dog, and if he is on a level with the dog, then God is not to blame for his acts any more than he is for the dog. But the higher intelligence ought to look upon him as a being that makes a link between the dog and a higher development.

So if you trace the working of the mind in man, you will find that man is now largely identified with the brute and is not to be condemned for his brutal feeling. Once admitted as such, you don't keep a dog that growls at you and even would like to bite you, but you don't expect anything better. Now that intellect which is nearly on a level with the brute shows itself opposing everything that goes to restrain its acts, but at the same time shows its brutal instinct by fighting down everything that will not bow to its own will, showing no wisdom of doing to another as you would have another do to you. This is the point where the man ceases or breaks the link between the brute and the human species. This step taken opens the door for reason, which the brutal man never does. His reason is all on one side, that he is the lord and his will is law and if he can't have his own way he goes for destroying them. With man and beast, it is rule or ruin. Now this is all as God intended and man, as I said, is like a new country unexplored, full of every kind of ideas that is embraced in the world.

1864

Disease and Sickness
[LC 2:0884]

When we speak of disease, we confound cause and effect together, yet we all speak of cause and effect as separate. Still when we speak of disease, we really admit them as one. Now sickness is as separate from disease as cause is from effect, and this confounding the two together prevents us from understanding the true philosophy of sickness. Sickness is what we feel and complain of, and disease is what we call the cause. There is sickness without any apparent disease, yet we call the sickness disease. How often do we hear this remark, Your disease is nervous or general debility. Now all names of disease embrace cause and effect as one. The same error is seen in all religions. Jesus Christ is one, yet they are no more one than the sickness and disease. Jesus is the man and Christ is the God or Wisdom, and the natural man makes them one, as he does sickness and disease, but science separates one from the other.

The law is a representative of the natural man; the Gospel or Science, that of the spiritual man; so what the law or natural man cannot explain by their arguments, science, coming through the natural man and putting an end to his common sense or reason, introduces a higher law or reason and appeals to the higher element or Christ. Now all disease is of the lower element of man and must be reasoned out by the higher element. The higher element is the Christ or the God manifested in man. This is the element by which science will judge the world of opinion in righteousness and it holds every word responsible to it. Therefore every idle word must give an account of its meaning and receive its reward for good or evil. All science does the same and error must give way.

Now sickness and sorrow is what Christ is to destroy; it makes war with our "common sense" for "common sense" is not wisdom but what man believes. But wisdom is what he knows and this wisdom knows that "common sense" is man's reasoning from false premises upon what he has no real wisdom of, only as an opinion. I will give one illustration to show how we reason and are affected by this false idea of sickness and disease. A person feels a slight sensation in the chest. I will suppose that the person has no idea what it is. Now the feeling is the sickness. No disease is there; the cause not being known to the patient, he is in trouble. Now if a person that had the true wisdom should feel the trouble, he would know the cause and relieve the fears of the patient and there would be an end of the trouble. But if they should send for one of those blind guides or doctors whose wisdom is based on someone's opinion, he would give some name of some evil spirit or disease (which is the same thing) that has gotten hold of the patient.

Now fear takes possession of the sick person, and the fear and sickness being wedded, they give birth to a child called congestion of the lungs. This is called after its father or physician. Now the patient becomes the medium of this evil spirit whose father was a liar and the truth was not in him. Now these two having one flesh, the patient will answer when asked what ails you, My sickness is congestion of the lungs. Here the sickness and disease are one. Now I have to separate the one from the other. I know the patient is sick, this I admit, but the devil or disease I say is a lie and is in the mind, for it troubles the sick person, but it has no effect on me I know it to be a lie. I feel the sickness, but the fright caused by this devil does not frighten me. So my practice is to reason (not to argue) to convince their senses, not their "common sense," for their "common sense" is the reason for this evil spirit or doctor's belief. So if I destroy the evil or cast it out by the science of wisdom, then the cure will stand, but if I cast out the devil by Beelzebub or medicine or some hocus pocus, then my kingdom being based on a lie cannot stand, and the disease may return and take possession of the patient.

Now Jesus saw the working of the priests, for they pretended to cure, and they did, for disease partook of the belief of the patient. Leprosy was an evil spirit which the priests created and the priests could destroy it when no application could. So when the priests controlled the minds, they created a class of evils that they gave names to, that they could control. But after Jesus began to cure, the priests lost their power over the sick and it passed into the hands of another class. Now all evils are the result of false reasoning and can never be remedied till the same principle is applied to all science, not to let an opinion have any sway over your minds. Let an opinion be looked upon as it ought to be, just what a man thinks, not what he knows.

The beasts are sick yet they have no fear of opinion, but I have no doubt that they are affected by man and they suffer and die when, if they could be left to themselves, they would get over their trouble. A great many think that I believe all disease is of the imagination, but this idea is wrong. I always admit the sickness, for that is what I feel and that is real, but the disease is another idea that I deny as having any identity outside of the mind or belief. There are certain ideas of nature that we all admit as having identities: beast, bird, and every living thing, trees, and all creations of wisdom, but to wisdom they are nothing but ideas. So man by his error has created images of things that never had an existence outside of his superstitious mind. These are just as real to man as the things wisdom has created. The difference is that wisdom's creation is for our own happiness and man's invention is for our misery. These are the two worlds, and to get into God's kingdom is to get out of man's kingdom. This is the new birth and blessed and happy is he that understands it, for on such the opinions of man have no power.

1863

Disease Traced to the Early Ages and Its Causes–Religion
[BU 3:0989]

My object in laying my ideas before the people in regard to the causes of disease is to separate myself from all others who pretend to cure disease. The world or the people in it are superstitious from ignorance, but their superstition shows itself in a variety of ways. Some who think they are free from it are in reality most affected by it. Superstition is not applied to wisdom but to some idea that has never been understood, and the explanation of the phenomena is the superstition if it is not explained on some scientific principle that puts an end to all investigation. My object in this communication is to confine myself to the prevailing superstition in regard to diseases, their causes and cures, and to show where I stand independent of all others.

To commence with the diseases of man, we must go back to the ancients. The ancients believed that disease was the consequence of sin. The Hebrews were very little versed in the study of mental philosophy and attributed all their sickness to evil spirits who, they believed, were the executioners of divine vengeance. If they could not account for their disease, they did not hesitate to say that it was a blow from the avenging hand of God, and to him the wisest and most religious had recourse for cures. King Asa was blamed for placing confidence in the physicians when he had a painful fit of gout in his feet and not applying to the Lord (2nd Chron. 16: 12). "So Asa in the 39th year of his reign was diseased in his feet until his disease was exceedingly great, yet in his disease he sought not the Lord but the physicians. So in the one and 40th year he died," having been under the medical faculty two years.

This shows that the medical faculty was of little account with the ancient Hebrews who claimed to put their trust in God. Asa was blamed for running after quacks, but the world has since been remodeled, not after the days of King Asa. Job's friends ascribed all his distempers and sicknesses to God's justice and to comfort him, they used these words (Chap. 4: 7, 8). "Remember I pray thee, whoever perished being innocent? Or when were the righteous cut off? Even as I have seen, they that plow iniquity and sow wickedness reap the same." Here Job was accused of transgressing God's laws. Every phenomenon that could not be accounted for was attributed to God or spirits from another world, and these superstitions of the Hebrews have come down to the present day.

Disease and death were the great evils to contend with, and in order to avoid them, it was necessary to do something to appease this God. So all sorts of religious theories and opinions spring up to instruct the people in a belief that will govern their lives so that they may show the evils which God has in store to afflict his children. Nearly all the diseases the people had were attributed to God. Leprosy, so common among the Jews, was treated as a disease sent by God. The priests judged of the quality of evil, confined the sick and declared that they were healed or still had the leprosy upon them; then they offered sacrifices to God for their sins or faults and so deceived the people through their craft or ignorance. In Numbers: Chap. 12, the case of Miriam's leprosy is recorded. Aaron and Miriam spake against Moses for marrying an Ethiopian woman. The Lord sent for the three and after learning the story was wroth and departed. When the cloud disappeared, Miriam became white as snow. Then Moses called unto the Lord saying, Heal her now O God, I beseech thee, and the Lord said, If her father had but spit in her face, should she not be ashamed seven days? Let her be shut out from the camp seven days. After this was done, she was cured. Here is the case of leprosy, its cause and cure, but the mode of operating is not given, but to me it is all plain. There is no doubt but disease is what follows our belief. They had such power over the masses that they cured their evils by imposing upon them the process I have mentioned. Their belief was their religion, and the forgiving their sins was the cure, so religion was health and disease was sin. This was Christ's idea, for he said the well need no physician, so according to the Hebrews it was a disgrace to be sick.

It may seem strange, at first thought, to say that any mode of curing disease was to make it and all the cures are done by an unknown God and therefore they are miracles. A miracle is some phenomenon that cannot be explained by the world of opinions. My object is to trace disease to its origin and see what it is and who is its father, and whether it can be attributed to the one living and true God, for I cannot believe that God is the author of our misery. Man is the author of his own misery and to trace disease to its author is to bring it down to man. The priest is the author of all the diseases in the Old Testament and it is easy to show that the case of Miriam's disease was made by her belief and cured by the same. She was made to believe it right to object to Moses marrying an Ethiopian or colored woman; consequently she must have been disturbed at the act. She got her system into a nervous excitement and she was ready to bring about any phenomenon that happened to come up. Moses resented her anger and of course she felt badly, and her belief being that leprosy was a punishment sent by God for sin as she thought she had not done right, and so this punishment came upon her. The priests controlled the people and were the judges of right and wrong. You see, to make a disease is to transgress some law of God, and if any person had a brother or sister married to a black person, would he not feel badly? I am looking for the origin of disease, and I know It is in the mind or belief. I shall bring the Scriptures to show that the ancient Hebrews of the religious class all attributed diseases to God as a punishment for sin, so God had to bear the blame of all their error and hypocrisy.

I will give some facts that go to show that disease followed some act that was not right according to their laws, for God never made a law. This is the law and the Gospel and all sin is death. The people were taught that God sent their diseases upon them. So by their belief they were made sick and by their belief the priests could pardon their sins and cure them, and their offerings were to pay the priests for curing them. There were those who were not so superstitious as the rest and they were of course called infidels. Show me the Christian who believes that God brought on the gout to Asa or the leprosy to Miriam or the disease on Job. The cure of Naaman, the captain of the host of the king will be found in 2nd Kings: 5th Chapt. Elisha without prescribing any medicine told the man to wash in the Jordan seven times and he was healed. Elisha would not take pay so his servant followed Naaman and took silver; for that act the prophet said that the leprosy should leave Naaman and cleave unto him and it was so. Here you see a cure made and a disease transferred from one person to another. This was done just according to their belief and the Lord had nothing to do with it, but the people believed that Elisha was a servant of God or a medium. You will find in 2nd Chron: 26th Chap., a case of King Uzziah who had flourished for a long time and he became great. One day he went into the temple to burn incense and Azariah the high priest followed with four score priests of the Lord. They undertook to stop him and he grew wroth and the leprosy arose on his forehead and he became a leper to the day of his death. This was a case where temper threw his system into a state to be affected by his belief.

I could show hundreds of cases in our days of men dying of heart disease, as it is called, while it is all caused by some mental trouble; but all this goes to show that disease was made by some impression on the mind under a belief that it is God's wrath. Those who were affected did not believe that the priests could cure them except the most superstitious, but they all believed in the disease, so a warfare was kept up between the priests and doctors till Jesus appeared. Then a new philosophy or priesthood sprang up that asked no sacrifices and Jesus said that Aaron's priesthood was like an old garment, and the world required a more perfect mode of curing. The people no longer laid the disease to God but to the spirits of the dead and to the devil who flourished about the time of Jesus, and these took away the credit of diseases which had been rendered to God. The power of the priests was waning; it was like an old garment ready to drop to pieces, for it was founded on their doctrines or religious beliefs. So when they wanted to unite Jesus' doctrine with their own, he told them that would be like putting new wine into old bottles; it would ferment and break them. So his precepts of happiness would not be confined to their bottles or religion, and as the people wanted a new religion that would not lay so many burdens on them, it must be in opposition to all their previous religion.

He said, Come unto me all ye that are sick and bound down by the heavy burdens of the priests and I will give you rest. The rest was health and the sick came and he healed them by the word of his mouth. He said nothing about religion, for his works were in direct opposition to the priests as much as mine are to the medical faculty. At that time, there were medical men and those who cured by the laying on of hands. They were opposed to the priests, and as the latter lost power in curing the people, the diseases took another form. Hell was invented, and a devil to torment the wicked people was introduced.

At the time of Jesus there was a variety of opinions and people were afflicted according to their belief. They believed in a devil and that he entered into animals as well as men, and in this form it was called spirits. Jesus saw that although the Jews had come up from out of the dominion of the priests in regard to curing of disease, the deception had only another form which opened the door to all sorts of quackery, medical and spiritual. There was competition and opposition among the sects. Each was cured according to their belief which was their religion, so all who applied to medical men were not religious but placed more confidence in these than in God. So the medical faculty did not amount to as much as they do now in the religious world. Job gives a true view of the medical faculty, Ch. 13; "Lo, mine eye hath seen all this, mine ear hath heard and understood it. What ye know the same do I know also; I am not inferior unto you. Surely I would speak to the Almighty, and I desire to reason with God, but ye are forgers of lies, ye are all physicians of no value, O, that ye would altogether hold your peace! and it should be your wisdom."

Job knew that they were quacks, and all they said were idle opinions about what they did not know. He was a scientific, not a religious man, but one who looked for causes and effects outside of the priests.

There is one mistake that the world is in and they will not get out of it till the origin of disease is acknowledged. Then men will learn to reason from cause to effect. My object is to show that the origin of the phenomenon called disease is in the mind or belief. Man is made up of opinions, for truth is not matter.

The wisdom of opinions is man's religion; the wisdom of science is God, and that is not matter. So to find a cause for disease, you must find some fear, for fear hath torment and the torment is the disease. The idea of death is a cause for fear, and to keep clear of death is what everyone tries to do. The religion of the ancients did not contain any positive ideas of another world. Moses was a leader of a people who had been enslaved in Egypt. He made laws to govern them, and they were the best he could make, and they all had reference to their relations and comfort in this life.

Religion is something not found in our words or acts or in our beliefs. It contains no wisdom; it is a substance. I will liken it unto a well of water; there is no intelligence in the water but it is to satisfy the desire of a person. It is like bread. It is the balm for every wound. It is to answer every person's desire for happiness. This is religion. The priests undertook to give it to the people. Moses undertook to give it to the multitudes, but the Bible says he never saw this substance, only heard it, as it were.

The people think religion is in a belief and they can get it; and then they can sit down and say to themselves as the rich man said, I have much stores laid up, so I will tear down my barn and build a larger one. Then the Lord said, Thou fool, this night shall thy soul be required of thee. This illustrates the Christian of our days. How often do you hear professors of religion talking thus, I take great pleasure in reading the Bible and meditating on the goodness of God, feeling that I am worthy to be his servant. This is all cant and is shown up in the illustration of the rich man by Jesus. This man's happiness consisted in his great wealth. Therefore he could say I am rich; why should I not enjoy my riches. I will eat, drink and take my ease. The Christian is also rich in the opinions of the world, eating vanity, never giving any attention to anyone that will correct a pain or ache, but sits and enjoys his goodness, condemning everything that he knows nothing of. He is puffed up with the vanity of the world. When the truth comes and sets fire to his house or theory and burns up his opinions, it will say to him, Thou fool! All your riches are vanity or opinion which, when Science comes, will take wings and fly away. This is the religious man and in such God takes no delight. His followers are not of that kind. Their religion is their riches in wisdom, and to impart this wisdom to the hungry and to feed all those who hunger and thirst after health and happiness.

The error is the idea religion; and the priests have taught that God is something, a spirit that will answer their requests. You never knew a Christian who was directed to act differently from any but a selfish act. If a man should be inclined to give up all his goods to the poor and spend his life in relieving those in distress, he would be looked upon as a monomaniac or fanatic by the church. But if he should give all his wealth to the church and let his children starve, then he would be a Christian. So religion is of this world and is the result of sin and ignorance. The time will come when every man will be rewarded according to his acts or wisdom. When that time comes, to be religious will be to give to the sick something that the world of opinions cannot give; and then to be wise is to be religious, but your religion cannot be distributed among the poor or those that need it. There is so much absurdity in regard to God, it makes the people disbelieve in almost everything. For instance, we are taught that God fills all space. Now we all know that matter in various forms fills some space; we are also taught that God is in everything. Here is a tree without any intelligence; we are taught that God is in the tree. How absurd it is to suppose that wisdom is in what we acknowledge contains none. It is not strange that with such absurdities people of intelligence should disbelieve in any religion.

Now here is the theory of my religion. My God is wisdom and all wisdom is of God. When there is no wisdom, there is no God, for God is not matter. Matter is only an idea that fills no space in wisdom, and as wisdom fills all space, all ideas are in wisdom. To make the creature larger than the Creator is absurd to me. My God is in nothing but everything is in Him. Attach all sight, smell and all the senses of wisdom; then they all fill all space. Everything to which we attach wisdom and all inanimate substances and opinions are in this wisdom. Then you see the difference between the Christian's God and mine. Their man is of the earth, and their God is in him; my man is what we know and their man is in that. So wisdom is my man and matter is the Christian's. Therefore their wisdom is under a bushel. Jesus said, Set your light on the bushel that it may give light to all around. Wisdom in matter is no wisdom at all, but separate yourselves and come out that your light may shine so that others seeing your light or wisdom may be benefited. Matter is darkness to wisdom for when a man is in an opinion, he is in a prison; and when the truth comes, he dies to opinions and lives in God or wisdom.

To see where I differ from any living man that I ever heard of is to show what others believe. Disease is something outside of man's opinions as the people believe. This belief makes disease not dependent on man's belief, but existing independent of it. To prove it, they quote a child and say the child has no mind yet it has a disease, so of course some remedies must be applied to cure a phenomenon which has no connection with mind. Thus error called disease is admitted by almost every human being and no one denies the phenomenon, and the whole civilized world agree that disease is something that exists independent of the mind. But in the causes and mode of cure they differ and this makes all the varieties of practice.

Since the priests lost the power of curing, the causes of disease have changed. Under the priests, God was the author of disease which was the punishment for some crime or misdemeanor and the priests judged of the disease according to the crime. All through the Old Testament disease followed some sin that the people had committed as it did in the cases I have mentioned. The gout, leprosy, scrofula and rheumatism were all diseases that were cured by the priests. Now how did they cure? The people in those days would answer, By the power of God. Here was their cause and remedy; the priests had made the people believe that unless they followed after their wisdom, some trouble would come. All that was needed when some phenomenon occurred was to attribute it to some wrong which they had done and the priest would ask God to forgive them and their forgiveness was the cure. This was their religion and to make all healthy and good, all must believe; but there were some who would not believe in this way and instead of calling on the priest, they called on the magicians or on some other craft, for they believed in disease. Every person that cured or attempted to cure uses the means in which they have faith. The medical men make the people believe that certain medicines will cure. The Spiritualist makes the people believe that they have some gift or power from the dead which directs them what to do. The Catholic priests, although they have lost their power, still claim to cure through the agency of God. These all admit disease. I stand alone on this ground that the phenomenon, disease, is the punishment of our belief.

The priests commenced the evil and they are at the bottom of all this. One need not go back further than Moses to show that restrictions put upon the people made them nervous and the phenomenon that followed they called a sin or disease, instead of the fear of the priests, for any simple thing that happened was some sin and the punishment, disease. Upon my theory, all disease can be accounted for by explaining the cause. Disease was the great evil that people were afflicted with and various modes of getting rid of it were introduced. These include the people's religion, and just as that changed, so the evils or disease changed; but since the medical men have established their belief, they have the people more in their power than ever the priests had. Just as the latter lose their hold on the people, the doctors catch them. The people are just as superstitious in regard to the origin of disease as they were in Moses' time, and instead of correcting the evil, they have increased it. The Catholics are freer from disease than the Protestants for the latter having lost their faith in the priests have regained it in the medical faculty. The causes are not explained, and until they are, people will believe and put their lives in the hands of these humbugs: priests, doctors, mediums, mysteries or something else, and they will continue to do so till they learn wisdom. Wisdom will teach them that everything we see is a phenomenon, and the cause that produces it is outside of it. Every thought that takes form in mind or matter has its cause outside of it, and man stands outside of all the above. To believe a thing is to make it.

To believe a thing is to make it in the mind, for believing is understanding. If you believe what a person tells you, you create in your own mind the thing, and when you have created the thing, you are either in it or outside of it. For instance, I will tell you of some new disease. If I can explain it to you so you believe it, you have got it in your mind, ready to spring up at any time when your system is in the right condition, so you are in danger of the disease. If you had wisdom, the lie or disease would be in your wisdom as a lie, and be a dead letter; but if you believed it, your wisdom would be confined in your belief and your punishment is the disease. I am in no belief but am outside of them all. I look upon the medical and religious beliefs as the offspring of heathen mythology and priestcraft.

The fear of death is the cause of nine-tenths of all disease. Rewards and punishments make men sick and bring on disease. The first origin is putting restrictions on children in the form of religious instruction. Take two children and bring them up in this way. Put restrictions on one, teach it if it does wrong God will punish it and give it religious instruction. Take the other and let it learn everything scientifically. Use no deception; never use the word God or religion but be kind and reason with it; then see which of the two will make the best man. One will be free from superstition, easy in manners, kind in disposition. The other will be fault finding, crabbed and overbearing, for just as you measure out to a child, just so the child will measure out to others. If you want to make a child good, be good yourself; and if you want him to be honest and respected, respect yourself and do not try to make your children believe what you do not believe yourself.

The idea that the Bible teaches another world is all false; the New and Old Testaments were written to make man better and civilize him. The leaders like politicians varied in the mode of instruction. In the Old Testament, the people were governed by the rod, and in the New, Jesus introduced reason and sympathy. Disease was the consequence of civilization, not that it is impossible that man might advance without it, but the principle on which such a civilization is grounded would be scientific reasoning and analysis about every phenomenon of life and would not contain any religious belief, for that contains the seed of all man's error and misery.

December 1861

Disease–White Swelling

[LC 2:1138]

Dr. Franklin when asked how he accounted for the fact that a fish weighed nothing in a pail of water said, "I never saw the experiment tried." There are many such fish stories. We take such an one for truth when there is not the slightest evidence of its truth. It stands only on an opinion. In this way we become superstitious, conceited and bigoted. All religion is based on such fish stories that cannot stand the test of science. Disease is one of this kind of fish, all swimming in the ocean of thought. This was the ocean that Jesus walked on. The water was their beliefs. This ocean was where Paul's barque lay, and this was where Jesus' disciples fished when Jesus walked by the seashore or public opinion and seeing Peter and Simon fishing for ideas or converts to the Jewish religion said, "Follow me," that is, learn the truth. So to teach the gospel of science, you became fishers or teachers of science instead of opinions. Into this sea of opinions Jesus told Peter to cast his hook and catch an idea or fish and he would find a piece of silver or find a truth in this idea which was worth saving.

Every idea contains a truth and the error is the dross. Now if men would learn enough to separate the truth from the error, then they might throw nets into the sea and draw them up and separate the good from the bad. But as it is now they have no standard by which to tell what is true and what is false, for the people are living in darkness and choose darkness rather than light, for their acts are evil. Let men apply this test to the medical and religious leaders. What proof have you of what you assume to be true, only what you have heard, and you are met with this answer: the Bible. Now the Bible does not speak at all, only as someone interprets it, and this interpretation is an opinion, for it is not tested by any scientific act.

If a teacher in mathematics makes an assertion, he proves it so there is no doubt about it. But the priest gives his opinion and we must take it for a truth. This is also true of the medical faculty. They give you an opinion for a truth. Man believes it and here is where he gets himself into trouble. Now apply Franklin's test. Don't believe in what is told you without proof nor attempt to account for it. No one will deny that a sensation can be made on a person. Now this sensation is one thing and the proof is another. I will show you how these two ideas affect man. A physician called on me who was lame with what he called a white swelling on his knee. It was true the knee was swollen, so to deny that the disease was on his knee would be to him absurd. To admit it to myself was as absurd as it would be to him to say the disease was in his mind.

Now here was a fair difference of opinion. To cure him was to change his mind or destroy his disease. The swelling we both admitted, but the cause was the thing in dispute. Now his belief in the white swelling was a part of his identity or wisdom. It was a reality that man could have a white swelling or a disease called by that name. Now I knew that God never made a disease or idea outside of man. I knew that man could invent ideas and condense his belief into a phenomenon that the world would call disease after man's belief. To me the belief was the disease and as I have no belief about my identity in regard to a white swelling, I could see that he was laboring under a false idea. This made the trouble. So then a controversy must come between the physician and myself before I could destroy his belief or disease. So now I must introduce the physician to let you know what he has to say in his own behalf. For his belief was in danger, and his disease being his belief and his belief being his life, to destroy his life or disease was to change his mind. Thus he could lose his belief and find his life in the truth that sets him free.

I will give the substance of my first visit. My ideas to him were like his ideas to me. He thought I was arguing to change his belief to mine, but I was reasoning with him, while he was arguing with me. Now the doctor at first believed that what I was going to talk about was nothing but a desire to have my way, not that I believed that what I said had anything to do with his trouble. You see that the point that separated us was this. What had I to cure? Was it the knee or his belief? To him it was the knee, but to me it was his belief. Now if I addressed myself to him and not to his knee, but to him, he wished me to address myself to his knee as the person. Yet he would not allow that his knee was intelligent, though at the same time he would tell how it felt, what trouble it made him, etc. So, of course, I commenced by telling him how he felt. I directed my conversation to him, not to his knee. He admitted that I told him how he felt, but he put all the feeling in his knee. I put his feeling in his senses and not in his knee. So here was where we differed.

To cure him was to detach his senses from his belief and then his wisdom would be the cure. So I said, Your disease is in the mind. (Dr.) I put it in my knee. (Quimby) Does your knee feel? (Dr.) No. (Q) Then it is you that feels and not your knee. (Dr.) You are too deep for me, I do not see the point you are at. I know my knee is swollen and it hurts me to lay any weight upon it. (Q) Then you admit that you can bear weight on your knee so as to hurt you. (Dr.) Yes. (Q) Then the one that bears the weight is the one that feels the pain. Now is there any pain in the weight? (Dr.) No. (Q) Then the one that bears the weight is not the weight, and the part that the weight bears on is not the one that bears. So that there must be some intelligence outside of the weight and the thing borne on or the knee. Now this something that knows all this that I have said is not matter, it is yourself, your senses and all that makes up the man. Now the weight or body is matter under the direction of the intelligence. So if the intelligence of this world's belief guides you, then your wisdom is enslaved by your opinion and your opinion is the keeper of your body. Your opinion and body is matter or mind and as your senses are in your belief or opinion, you speak of yourself as matter and of course you are in your knee, as much as a criminal is in his prison, who is confined for some crime. Your knee is your prison and your belief embraces your senses and you are in your belief as a criminal, and when you address me, you speak from your prison and you speak like all men who believe in disease. You speak the truth to yourself but to me you speak a lie and the devil is its father and he was a liar from the beginning.

Now when you learn that mind is matter and your belief is matter, then you will see that whatever you believe you can create and whatever you create takes form just according to your idea. Now you believe in the idea white swelling, so that any sensation in the knee that would draw your attention to it will suggest the idea and a phenomenon is created according to your belief. Then you bring the phenomenon as proof to show you were right in your first impression, when you really created the idea yourself. The trouble is in the way we express ourselves. The doctor said his knee felt badly, therefore the bad was in his knee. "My knee makes me feel badly"–he would have separated himself from his knee. Then he would have answered right, and then I should have asked him, What do you think produced this swelling that makes you feel so badly? He of course could not say, only give an opinion.

Now I told him I would tell him what made the swelling in his knee. So I said, You must have had a sudden shock that affected your mind. This shock contained no disease or opinion. For instance, suppose you should be thrown from a carriage onto the ground. The shock given to you disturbed your mind. This disturbance you located in the hip and here was where you first complained. All this contained nothing but a fright on you. But being frightened lest you had injured the hip, you would favor it the same as if it was injured. So to favor it, you kept the leg stiff from the knee to the foot and moved the upper portion of the body, letting the body bend from the hip. So you would bring the weight on the well leg by keeping the lame one stiff. This kept the ankle stiff, so that when the body swung forward, the ankle being stiff, it strained the muscles in the back part of the leg from the hip to the knee. This sensation in the knee that you made for fear of injuring the hip frightened you, and you began to locate your trouble in the knee. This caused the knee to swell and the swelling you called a white swelling. So to favor this, you kept your ankle stiff. This made more pain, and at last the knee was pronounced to have a white swelling. This was a disease, after the opinion of the medical faculty.

1864

Does Imagination Cure Disease?
[LC 2:0693]

Are men cured by imagination or by some power or virtue in medicine? All men believe in a power that cannot be explained. One person condemns the man who is cured by any mode of practice differing from his own; for instance, the allopathic practice is orthodox and any dissent from it is quackery. It is the same as in the religious sects. Calvinists believe in future rewards and all who do not embrace this belief are infidels. My theory classes all the different modes of cure with the different religious beliefs. Religion and healing are based on a belief that there is some saving power or healing quality independent of the mind of man. There is a shadow of truth in this, but I have seen that it is nothing but mind acting on mind and mind is only a medium for some wisdom to control.

I will describe a case under allopathic treatment and one under quackery and will ask any skeptic if the difference does not lie wholly in their belief. A person suffering from a severe pain in the stomach, supposed to proceed from inflammation, calls a doctor. The doctor gives medicine, applies blisters, etc., and the patient is no better. He hears of a lady of the same religious belief as his own. She comes and enters upon her course of treatment which I will give from the patient's own lips. The lady made a barley cake as large as the patient's hand. After baking it she took three pieces of a candle about an inch long, put them upright in the cake, and laid the cake on the patient's stomach and lit the candles. She then filled a tumbler with warm milk and water, turned it out, and placed the tumbler over the lights, extinguishing them. She then knelt down and prayed. The flesh rose up in the tumbler, the patient's pain was relieved and he was cured. Where is the difference in these two modes of treatment? To me they are the same, both being quackery.

It is true, cures are made. But the virtue is in the belief and the people liked to be humbugged, and those who cannot see through their own humbug are duped the more. The Eastern magicians acted upon the people in the same way, and in the days of Jesus, there were some who believed that he also cured in that manner; but from what I know, I am sure this cannot be the case. How does my theory apply to cases like the above? I know by sympathy that they have a pain in their stomach, this is no humbug or power but sympathy. The patient is nervous and I know that the doctor or someone has made him believe an opinion which is perhaps that his stomach is full of tumors; then he is made to believe that the blister has some healing virtue in it and it will cure. Now just as much as he is affected, just so much he believes. In cases of healing by prayer, either the patient cures himself by his belief or is cured by the combined beliefs of the operator and patient. There is no particle of wisdom in the disease or cure. The patient was made to believe a lie that made him sick; then he was made to believe another and this changed his mind from disease to health. The wisdom of the physician was ignorance or a belief in a lie. I convince the patient that he has been deceived. This destroys the deception and the light of his wisdom is his cure.

April 1862

Do People Really Believe What They Think They Do?
[BU 2:0394]

To some this may seem a strange question but it involves more of our real knowledge than we think it does. Our belief involves all of our religious opinions. Our opinions are the foundation of our misery, while our happiness is in the truth that comes out of our opinion, and the happiness is in the knowledge that follows the solving of the problem or error.

To illustrate: when you are solving a problem, you have wisdom and opinion and are in some trouble about it. But when the answer comes the happiness accompanies it. Then there is no more death, nor ignorance, sorrow nor excitement. Error and ignorance have passed away, all has become new and we are as though we never had been. We have got all the happiness we want; the misery is gone and the spirit returns to the Great Spirit, ready to solve another problem.

Now the problem I wish to solve is what I first named. Do we really believe in what we think we do? I answer, No, and shall show that we deny what we profess to believe in almost all we say and do, thereby proving ourselves either hypocritical or ignorant. We profess to believe in Christ, that He is God, that He knows all things and is capable of hearing and answering our prayers. We also believe that man is a free agent, that he is capable of judging between right and wrong and believe that if man does not do right he will be punished.

When asked for proof of all this, we are referred to the Bible. When we ask an explanation how Christ cured, we are told it was by a miracle. If we ask if Christ did not know all things, we are answered "Yes." Then did He not know what He was about, what He did, and how He did it? "Yes." Then if you ask how He knew, the answer is, "It is a miracle," or "The ways of God are past finding out," and thus you are left in the dark. Now this mode of reasoning does not come into any other mode. Those that reason this way will not accept any fact based upon any other way of reasoning. You must bring the strongest kind of proof to convince them of a fact that is produced in the same way or appears to be, or they will not believe. The fact is they don't reason or compare at all, and they admit what they haven't the slightest proof of, except the explanation of some person of doubtful existence.

Now when I can show that I can produce a phenomenon that to all appearances is just like some produced by Christ and on the living who can speak for themselves, I should like to know by what authority anyone dares to say that it is not done in the same way that Christ did His works. If they cannot tell how I do it, or how He did, how do they know but that it is done in the same way? Their only objection can be that it happens to be contrary to their own opinion which is not worth anything and they admit it, for they will say it is a miracle to them. This makes them just what Jesus said of such guides. He called them blind guides leading the blind, and warned the people against them. He called them whited sepulchers and all kinds of names, and the world has been led by such guides ever since.

Jesus told the people how they should know them. He said, "Not all who say Lord! Lord! shall enter into this theory or kingdom but he that doeth the will of the Father that sent him." Now what do they do that Jesus did? Nothing. Yet you cannot point to one act that Jesus did that these guides do. All who do good according to Scripture imitate the Pharisees in every respect. He called them the children of the devil and He said their father or error was a liar from the beginning. Jesus judged them by their works and told the people to do the same; for He said, "By their fruits ye shall know them."

March 1860

Do We Always Know All We Write and Say?
[LC 1:0499]

It is a common remark that if Jesus should appear on earth and could hear the explanations given to the remarks which He made eighteen hundred years ago, He never would imagine that He was in any way alluded to. This may be true. Jesus was as any other man, but Christ was Science or God which Jesus tried to teach. There never was and never can be a man who can express his thoughts without being governed more or less by the Scientific Man or Christ, and the masses will receive the ideas as they receive food and will pass judgment upon them according to their taste.

Different opinions will arise from the fact that often the writer is as ignorant of the true meaning of his ideas as his readers are. Not but that he knows what he says, but there is in each person a hidden meaning or truth that he, as a man, does not know. When one hears or reads anything it awakens in him some new idea which perchance the author never thought of, yet the author feels as though he had a similar idea of its meaning. It is the Christ in us that is making itself known through the senses, and as the senses are the only medium the world acknowledges, Wisdom uses them to destroy the darkness which prevents us from knowing ourselves. Thus it is when we read the works of the old authors. They have been misrepresented, from the fact that the readers' minds have been so dull that there was not sufficient light to penetrate through. So the dark explanations which are given become true ones till the world becomes educated up to a higher point when it shall see that the authors have been misrepresented and that even some truths may have been conveyed in the writings which the author himself had no idea of.

Every person is more or less clairvoyant and is in two states of mind at the same time, and when anyone writes he is not aware that he is dictated by a Wisdom that he through his natural senses does not know. On this principle rogues bring their evil deeds to light. Their crimes excite the mind and expose their evils to view, for by their efforts to conceal their crimes, they betray them to others by looks, acts or words, though unknown to themselves. This is as it should be and the better it is understood the more it will bring about the desired effect.

Watch the course of the Rebellion. Almost every act of either side develops something beside that which was anticipated and still it was just what they might have expected would follow the act. Yet no one saw it; still it was all right. The intelligence which is governing the world is as much in the dark to the actors as the plans of Generals are to the rank and file.

So the wisdom of our rulers is as much in the dark in regard to their own movements as the soldiers are of their own movements. Both are mediums of a higher wisdom as much as a mesmeric subject is the medium of the operator. Anyone who has any intelligent idea of mesmerizing is aware that the subject thinks he acts on his own responsibility, and so he does in a measure, though he is also acted upon and controlled by others. The real man is not seen at all, but is always acting upon matter and never will consent to change his course any more than the laws of Science, for Science is the real man; and although the natural man would like to have Science decide in his favor, he ought to know that it cannot act differently from itself. And if we act wrong, Science will expose us by making us expose ourselves. Let man understand this and he will be more likely to act from a higher motive than he does now.

Every act or thought contains the higher Science. The natural man calls it reaction, but it is wisdom. If you put sufficient wisdom in an act, it will see what the reaction will be. You can hardly suppose a person so ignorant but what if he throws a stone into the air, he will know that it will come down again. If you put the wisdom in the stone, the stone would not know what the reaction would be, but if you put sufficient wisdom in the act that made the stone go up, that wisdom will know the stone will come down again with the same force that it went up.

Man's body is just as ignorant as a stone, but there are two motions which act upon it: one ignorance and the other Science. Give a child a looking glass; before the child is educated or receives the intellectual element of reason, its acts are governed by passion or desire, not knowing of reaction, for reaction is the higher element and when that comes, the child's eyes are opened to the light of wisdom. Until then it would throw the glass on the floor, but when it sees the reaction, it is wiser and this wisdom checks it the next time.

In all crimes which man commits, the act embraces the intelligence that is the reaction which will follow sooner or later, for every act of man's must come to light. So the person who commits a crime leaves the evidence against him just as plainly as the thief who steals in open daylight.

The sick expose their ideas of disease, and I know by my feelings what they know by their senses. The more they try to conceal the fact, the more they expose it. Now the reason of this is that disease is a disgrace, although people try to make it fashionable; but they show that they do not believe it so, from the fact that they try to rid themselves of it as they would any bad habit.

Every person has acquaintances whom they would like to get rid of, yet they will put up with their company rather than cause them to feel badly. So with those who use tobacco. You will hear them say, "I know it hurts me and I wish I could leave off the habit, but I cannot." Their wisdom is not equal to what it should be or they would leave their friend, as they call it, but which is their enemy in disguise. Now if their wisdom could destroy a little of the milk of human kindness which they drink for the traitor who has no respect for their happiness except to gratify their desire, they would cut their acquaintance as they would drop from their lips a cup of poison prepared for them by the hand of a pretended friend, and their sympathy would soon cease.

1864

Do We See That Which We Are Afraid Of?
[LC 2:0986]

Do we see that which we are afraid of? Never, I answer. We see the medium of our own fears through the medium of our own belief and call it danger. We connect ourselves with some idea which we think or know exists and we attach our fears to it. We then express fear, thinking the danger is in the thing we see or think we see. Suppose you are on a railroad track and you see the engine coming. Now what are you afraid of? Is the fear in the engine or in you? I say it is in you. Now suppose that you do not see the engine till you are crushed under the wheels. Is the fear crushed or that to which the fear is attached? The fear cannot be seen or touched; therefore it cannot be run over. But the body is not that which is afraid; it is the senses.

Again, suppose you see a bear lying down. As you approach him he rises and you do not know but that he is loose. You are afraid. If your senses are frightened, the fear must contain reason, for matter never reasons. A superior wisdom acts upon what we call animal matter or life, and if wisdom directs the action, then nothing is seen but the matter acting. Here is the error. We associate intelligence with matter and call both one, just as we put fear in the bear and call him dangerous. Now separate the fear from the thing feared and then it contains no life or danger but is simply matter.

Our beliefs have made us fear death, which is the king of terrors. To destroy this is to destroy the foundation of man's misery. The wise man has said the fear of death is the beginning of wisdom. Let us examine his existence and discover his habitation, if he is in this world or the world to come. It cannot be in this world, for it cannot be seen, although we say men are killed, are shot dead. Now is death in the bullet or in you? Of course it is in you. Then the word death must apply to something we admit has life.

Man has admitted that the body has life; consequently it has death also. Can the death be seen? It cannot. Therefore we are afraid of that which cannot be seen. Perfect wisdom casteth out fear, for fear hath torment. And as we learn wisdom we destroy death and the fear of death; then we live in wisdom, for science hath plucked the sting from death and robbed the grave of victory. Death, like darkness, is the absence of light or wisdom. So everyone who is in the dark is dead. Fear dispels the darkness and introduces ideas which are as terrible as anything in nature and affect man's senses. Disease is one of these, and this is a danger which we never see but through the medium. Through the fear of some invisible danger we create our own troubles. The fear takes form and it is called disease. Death is the real danger or disease, and the belief that it is coming, or has come, creates the fear. The senses being in the fear which is attached to the matter, the matter is so acted upon that a phenomenon is produced. This is called disease or death. If the fear is separated from the phenomenon, it would then be like a wild animal that you are afraid of. The real danger is not in the phenomenon that can be seen but in the invisible idea that you have of it, and in such lies all danger.

Everything connected with death we are afraid of. Man is made up of life and death. If life is destroyed, then all is dead, but if death is destroyed, there is no more death. Jesus came to destroy death and to bring life and immortality to light. The Christians teach that man must die. Life and death make the man. One is destroyed by man and the other Jesus destroys. Then where is man? Jesus illustrates man by various figures. To him life was a reality and death a condition. The natural man makes himself a combination of life and death, and when his life gives out, he is dead. Jesus makes man of light and darkness; his light is his wisdom, and his darkness is death; and as he destroys darkness, his light shines. He puts no life in error and his resurrection is from death, while the Christian's is of death. In all his teaching, he always strove to destroy sin, and he separated it from the truth by giving them various names as righteous and unrighteous, etc. These two characters are included in one man as night and day are included in one day. The word man likewise includes light and darkness, or science and ignorance. Error is like twilight. It excites the darkness and the light bursts in. For when the light of truth burst in upon the Jews through the preaching of Jesus, those who were in darkness or dead in ignorance could not see the light, but it was seen by those in error or agitated by doubts and fears. In this twilight of error, man becomes superstitious. This is the condition in which he creates all the evils which a nervous state of mind can conceive. He must pass through it before he can shake off the body of death or ignorance. This is death.

Jesus entered this state and preached to those confined herein before the flood of light. Here were many sleeping in the dust of ignorance who should awake to the truth and come forth. In the Old Testament, the people believed then as they do now that man as you speak of him means all there is of him, what he knows or what he thinks he knows, and that he dies wholly, and at the last day, his flesh and bones and all there is of him will rise. Jesus divided man into two individuals: one was in life and the other was in death, and in the end death was to be swallowed up in truth. These identities were kept as separate as night and day. Both were spoken of but they never meant one. Man's ignorance has compounded the two together and he now tries to convert error into a truth and therefore he calls on error to repent. Here is a kingdom divided against itself, for error is life and health is also life, and by destroying error, life is destroyed. Jesus had no sympathy with this character of error. He came to destroy it, for it is the prison or grave of man. Man cannot see these two characters because he has never known himself, and he never will see them till he learns that wisdom which is developed through the medium of science is the true man, and that the diseased or sick man is error.

What we wish to destroy is the man who torments our senses, and he is the man of error-the man who tells what he believes but can explain nothing, one who can give the opinions of others but can prove nothing. This character cannot be seen except by science. If you felt a pain in the region of the hip joint, error would say that you had the hip disease. Suppose you believe this; you are then affected by your belief.

The idea that cures are made misleads the mind. A mathematician cannot say that he has cured a very sick person whose disease was that he believed water would run up hill and he had been studying how to do it.

Every person in error is sick, if there is such a thing as sickness. But if disease is an error, the misery that follows is the effect of that error. This is a basis of operation for establishing a science based upon philosophical principles of reasoning. Then man can be reasoned out of his error which the world calls disease, the same as he can be reasoned out of any other error. Religion is the basis of man's false reasoning and it produces disease. The doctors undertake to cure the effect by admitting the cause. This will never destroy the evil, for while the causes exist, the evil will follow. Now correct the evil and the cause will cease. Here I admit an evil before a cause. I will explain. A lie is nothing, neither is the belief, but the belief produces action which, being seen and felt, sets man to reasoning. The lie is not seen; that is in the dark. The evil therefore is not admitted in the making up of cause and effect. A physician in giving a diagnosis of disease never goes back of living matter. He never puts the first cause in an evil that he admits is truth. He admits the idea disease, while I deny it. He does not admit the evil he is trying to cure, otherwise his kingdom would be divided against itself. He believes the lie to be a truth, and when the fruits of his belief are shown, he takes the fruit as a disease, never knowing that his own belief is the cause. This is why man is kept in ignorance of himself.

A philosophy that will correct the first evil being established will destroy the opinions of the priest and physician and place man on a better basis of reasoning where he will look out for causes instead of remedies, for the true remedy is in knowing the cause. Suppose you believe you have the hip disease. Now to admit the cause anything but a disease is wrong, for if you do, you make a belief something; then something will follow, and that which follows you call disease. If this first admission were corrected the effect would never be. Man is not developed enough to produce the idea that words have an effect on mind just in proportion to their definition. Ideas are made of words and words to the one who understands them are something. True they cannot be seen, yet everyone will admit they will affect the mind, and if they can affect, how do they do it? First the mind is not the intellect. It is the medium. Then words being sounds must contain something or nothing. If the person who speaks a word knows what it means, it contains his knowledge; but if he does not know how to impress it upon the person he addresses, to that person it is an empty sound and it produces no effect. The truth when it is known will develop this fact that the causes of the phenomenon exist in words.

Here I differ from the world. I put the cause in words that convey fear to the senses or in some sensation, never in the phenomenon. The world puts disease in the phenomenon and guesses at the cause. They have never been taught that words are the basis of man's trouble. Words affect every person, yet you will hear people say, "it makes no difference to me what a person says, it does not affect me." But this is not the case. It is just as impossible for words to fall harmless on man's senses and not injure him as it is for stones to fall on his body without hurting him. Yet the world, ignorant of this fact, are constantly stoning the sick with their opinions and advice. Every word affects us as much as the one we speak to, even our thoughts affect us, and we are responsible for them as well as our acts. If this truth were known, man would conduct himself so that his thoughts would take a right direction. Then he will cease to do evil and learn to do good. Consider the influence that the physician has over his patient. Weigh his words by the standard of truth and see the misery he creates; then the mystery of disease will be explained. Look at the effect his own words have. If any virtue is attributed to his wisdom, it is attributed to his medicine and is accompanied by words of sympathy or fear.

I will explain how words affect people. There is nothing so annoying to a doctor as to have somebody give their opinion of his treatment, expressing a preference for some other physician. If opinions have no effect on people, why find fault, and if they have an effect, how do they affect and what do they affect? Is that which they affect so imaginary that it has an existence outside of the senses? Certainly not. The medical men want a monopoly of man's senses to impose their ideas upon them, and if they are interfered with by another, they accuse him of working upon the imagination of the sick. They never deceive the sick! It is their neighbors! They are blind guides and hypocrites and have imposed on the people's senses their false ideas, till the world has received them as true. And now these imposters with a brazen face accuse others of deceiving the people through their imagination. This shows that they believe it can be done, but at the same time, they know that the people think that education is necessary to cure the sick. So they institute diplomas, and if one appears without a diploma, they call him a deceiver, operating on the imagination. To me, each acts in the same medium, call it what you please. The deceived is honest but the deceiver feels that he can impose on the subject and take the advantage. He tells the patient a lie and if he believes it, this is acting upon the imagination. Of this word more hereafter.

1864

Do Words Contain Any Wisdom of Themselves?
[LC 2:0748]

That depends on who uses them. Jesus said, "The words I say unto you are eternal life." Now if another person should say the same words, there would be no life in them. Jesus says, "It is the spirit that quickeneth; the flesh profiteth nothing: the words that I speak unto you they are spirit and they are life." The disciples could not understand for Peter said, "To whom shall we go? Thou hast the words of eternal life." Words without meaning are like sounding brass and tinkling cymbals. What is the life of a word? It is the wisdom it communicates to the person who receives it. If I never heard the word dog, there is no life in it to me, for life is wisdom, but if you put life into the word, then the life is the substance and the dog is in it. If you say orange to a person who does not know it and apply the word to the thing, then wisdom comes in the odor which is the substance or life of the orange; but without any application or explanation, it is like a cloud without rain; it contains no wisdom or life.

Dr. Quimby Explains His Method of Cure
[Originally untitled.] [LC 2:0748]

As I am constantly receiving letters from persons who are sick, asking my opinion in regard to their disease, it is impossible for me to answer every enquiry; therefore I take this method to inform them of the mode in which I treat disease, and as I treat it entirely different from any other person, it is necessary for me to state what I call disease and how it originates. My theory is that all disease that flesh is heir to is the effect of sensations produced on the mind, and when I say all disease I mean so, and I use the same power or reason to cure them all.

I will illustrate what I mean by the power I use. If you send a watch to a watchmaker to have it repaired, he would say at once that he had the knowledge and all the necessary tools to repair a watch; therefore it is knowledge of a watch that enables him to repair the damage. Again, if you are in trouble in regard to a suit at law, you apply to a lawyer, state your case. He examines the evidence and gives his opinion accordingly. But to give a correct opinion, he must hear both sides of the question. Then the case must go to a jury of men in whom you have no confidence in regard to their opinion of the question in dispute, so that the whole case depends entirely upon the impression made upon the minds of the jurors. The difference in these cases is this. The watchmaker does his job mechanically without regard to outward influences, and the knowledge that enables him to repair carries with it the conviction that the watch will keep time. On the other hand the lawyer has two powers acting against him: the arguments of the opposing counsel and the ignorance of the jury regarding the truth of the case. From these two cases I will try to illustrate my mode of examining a case.

A person applies to me for help; he says he is sick. I do not ask him to tell me that he is sick, like the lawyer, but sit down like the watchmaker and examine into his case. Persons often say to me, as to the watchmaker, such and such things are out of order. I pay [This article ends abruptly here.–*Ed.*]

Dr. Q. as Reformer*
[BU 3:0615]

Reformations when they do their work must begin where abuses most call for them and in their contest against evil, show their superiority by establishing a higher standard. If a principle is true it can be carried out for the benefit of mankind, as far as necessity calls for it, if false it can show no facts for proof. It is the fortune of every new idea coming before the people for acceptance to be cried down by the popular voice till its merit is tested by living through the opposition and producing facts whose value gain it admittance. For instance the invention of steam.

A reformer having ideas by which humanity may be benefitted must demonstrate them to the community by applying them to the worst offences. To dissipate its vices or correct its errors is more than any system of truth now taught can do. To know ourselves has been the object of all teaching ever since the Pagan Philosophers, and how much we have advanced in that knowledge everyone is at liberty to judge, but most all will admit that something remains to be learned. The most thorough knowledge of human nature is obliged to admit a principle of Evil, and though liberal theology may in theory do away with a Devil, yet its effect remain unaccounted for, and its hopeful offspring still run riot through the land. Directly in contact with disease, the favorite child of this mythical personage stands Dr. Quimby with his science of happiness whose success proves the truth of his system. The opposition he meets with in individuals and the public is just what any inventor always has met and will meet. It is easy enough to cry humbug, sorcery, etc. like our friend J___, who offers an opinion on the subject of which he knows nothing, thus insulting the intelligence of those who have been benefitted by this treatment expecting them to set aside their facts in favor of his opinion.

All phenomena in the natural world are produced by the action of one of two directions in the spiritual world. Knowledge and ignorance and the happiness or misery following show which of the two directions governs. These two powers make two worlds within us, science and mystery, and we are subject to the one which we obey. Claiming for this principle an universal application forces upon Dr. Quimby the position of a reformer inasmuch as it brings him in conflict with many of our accepted standards of belief, which on analysis are found not to be based on this ground. The body represents the natural world and its applications the phenomena under the direction of ignorance, therefore disease is the effect of a wrong direction given to the mind and to cure it is to change the direction. To do this is to have the world of mystery which controls disease at our command and this can only be done by one who has given his attention to the subject and can prove his knowledge by facts. In everything Dr. Quimby says, he stands alone, being un-sustained by any accepted truth, therefore he meets the whole world as opposition, and the confidence of his patients, vague when they attempt to explain it but satisfactory by themselves, is his only evidence that he is what he pretends to be. As in any Science, he looks for the cause behind the phenomenon and finds disease in the mind and the effect in the body, so that he deals only with that false power which has possession of and directs the mind. To him, no disease could appear in the body independent of the mind any more than a piano-forte could produce a tune independent of a performer. The same intelligence which locates disease in the body independent of the mind, puts music in the piano and power in the lever, and underlies all human reasoning when that reasoning brings about unhappiness. This same reason he is in conflict with all the time for it is the philosophy of sickness.

No one has a feeling unless it be a bad one, for perfect health has no feelings. This feeling inasmuch as it attracts our attention, we put some construction upon, which brings either health or disease. His cure depends on destroying these constructions or beliefs by which we have imprisoned ourselves, thereby leaving us free. In this work, which is no child's play, he risks his reputation as a sane or honest man and is constantly liable to be misunderstood in motive and condemned in conduct; for he come into direct conflict with the chronic opinions of a whole family. His persistency in carrying out his reasoning towards the sick, brings down upon him opposition, contempt and abuse, which he is perfectly well aware of, whether it is expressed or not, but which fails to change his relation towards them. These conflicts which assume sometimes a serious aspect, however it may be with the patient, with him vanish with the words, for he never feels ill will towards the sick. Neither does he make light of human suffering, as some suppose by calling it imagination. Disease is no imaginary thing to a person who can take upon himself every feeling of the sick and appreciate the dreary experience of an invalid, but it is a hard reality, an inheritance from ignorance, in which the goodness of God has no place.

The question is often asked, how does Dr. Quimby cure? People are willing enough to allow him a mysterious power, but few are ready to admit that he knows anything about it preferring that ignorance and superstition should reign rather than that knowledge should render this power intelligent. It would be as easy to answer the question, "how do your cipher" without illustrating the rules of arithmetic as to answer the question "how does he cure" without bringing a case to which his principles can be applied, and the answer in the one case, "by reckoning," would be quite as satisfactory as the answer in the other, "by changing the mind." It is no more wonderful in fact, how he cures, than it is how we get sick, for it is in the same principle.

The question that the mind produces disease has hardly dawned on the intelligence of mankind. That it affects it is not doubted, but how far and in which way has never been determined. Its analysis, novel and interesting, demolishes much of our established knowledge and by giving us facts instead of mystery, invites further investigation.

Dr. Quimby vs. Spiritualism*
[BU 3:0612]

Few things are more annoying to a man of intelligence than to find himself classed with an error that he is opposing. It has been the misfortune of Dr. Quimby to have been claimed by the Spiritualists as one to be classed among them by those who wish to rank him among the things that they know. It is natural that he should be associated with them for he certainly does what no living man can do of himself and all the works which are above human understanding, have been regarded by common counsel as of supernatural origin and coming from the other world. So the Spiritualists embrace that portion of facts while the scientific world cannot explain and hence Dr. Quimby is accused of being one of that class.

Against this he protests and nothing is simpler than the difference he makes between his spiritual platform and theirs. He contends that the works he does, he does scientifically and intelligently, with no tangible nor intangible help from another world or from this, that the basis of his theory is a living truth, of which man is ignorant and which he demonstrates to the sick; that in his method there is no chance of deception or of humbug, for if such be his motive, his success as a doctor is at hazard. He admits the phenomena of the Spiritualists to the fullest extent, but the theory of spirits and another world he denies in toto and places it on the ground that he does all theories and beliefs invented by man to account for something that he has not the patience or courage to examine into. When supernatural phenomena occur, he says it ought to excite the minds of men to investigate as is done in the infancy of all sciences and then man may learn more about himself. But most generally people are so frightened at any such occurrence that they are not in a fit state of mind to look for causes and so they are the prey to anyone who happens to be a little cooler, therefore nothing is easier than to deceive such people in the explanation of the phenomena.

This is one difference between him and a Spiritualist. [Dr. Quimby] performs his cures just as a man does when he makes or works a machine, intelligently, honestly, and with no other help than the living truth which is open to all men, while the Spiritualist goes into a trance, gets help from the spirits of the dead and generally gives medicines. Then when Dr. Quimby cures, it is done by the principle of health that he proclaims to the sick and oppressed, that God made all men well and man has bound them with error till they are sick and diseased, and what the sick get from him is simply their rights with no miraculous interposition of God or the sprits.

Another point of difference is this. The Spiritualists believe in a future existence and claim that their tests prove that man is immortal and when they die they go to the spirit world to live. Dr. Quimby proves the immortality of the soul of the living man and does not wait for him to die that it may be proved.

He believes that the immortal man is the only real intelligence there is and that it animates and holds together the man that is seen, that it is the real man and that it can act of itself and to bring this to the understanding of the natural man, that he is two distinct identities and yet is one.

[It] is the Science of Eternal Life and is what he is constantly learning and trying to teach others. By his principle, truth and error are separate and apart and are no longer inextricably entangled.

What is eternally true is for the happiness and progression of man and is goodness. What is false is of man and requires a sacrifice of natural purity of feeling to receive. The real man is not the visible form but is the progress of the life of truth, the development of the principle of eternal goodness and knowledge.

To find this real man which is the same in all the varieties of characters has been the work to which Dr. Quimby has devoted his time and labor for many years, and to separate him and bring him to light so that he shall be recognized by human understanding is still the object of his labors. In doing this he is of course liable to be misunderstood. He expects to be. He expects every stumbling block to be put in his way of advancing his work before the public, but he feels confident from the reception his ideas have met with, as far as he has given them to the public, that, many will feel a strong interest in the unfolding of the truth which cannot help bring happiness and knowledge to the world.

Dr. Quimby's Theory of Curing Disease*
[Originally untitled.] [BU 3:0609]

What is the difference between Dr. Quimby's belief, or religion: and that of any other persons who have founded and established new religious societies? Swedenborg, Mahomet, Theodore Parker.

A great difference: Dr. Quimby takes no credit to himself for curing disease, nor does he lay down any rules of conduct, neither does he fire up any belief for mankind. He has no rewards or punishments of his or any other man's manufacture. He says that health can be reduced to a certainty, that it is dependent on a knowledge of ourselves, of the influences which form the various experiences of our everyday life. He makes man responsible to himself alone and the author of his happiness or misery. Instead of teaching man to believe this, or that, to insure his happiness–he would teach man to look for the cause of trouble in some intelligence, not in dead matter. He says that man is acted upon by two forces, truth and error and the fruits show which author. If the fruits are wrong, then the cause must be wrong, and with that man must deal. He claims to show man the way to determine the cause of his misery and by that means to correct it. This sounds vague. I will try to explain. There are two kinds of knowledge. One is so connected with matter, that he calls it: in matter. The other is above matter. It is known in true progress and in the power of exploding all deception; he separates the two and teaches man to depend on the latter. He brings that knowledge down to everyday life, so that his rules of action are perfect, and when understood produce harmony and true progress.

Well, I should like to see some of his rules.

Read his definition of right and wrong. It is the nicest and clearest definition I ever read. He separates those laws that are really binding on society and individuals, producing evil effects, from a true standard of right, making right the knowledge of good and wrong a deviation from that knowledge. In his theory, in order to be good, you must know something. No one has a right to make a law and oblige another to obey it. Yet this is constantly done in society, and he comes to expose this system of government. He comes with a knowledge of a higher law, which contains no evil, but is all love and good will to man. His confidence in the understanding of the above is entire and makes him sensitive to the presence of the error that obstructs the operation of the higher law. His mind has been so thoroughly changed by pursuing this kind of reasoning, that he knows its application to human life as certainly as a chemist knows the operation of certain chemicals. He has compared sickness to discords in music; intelligence is necessary in either case to correct them.

What does he mean by the natural man?

He mans the man who eats and drinks and acts, thinks all intelligence is in himself, but usually puts all knowledge in the phenomenon. He is a set of organs, content to do the office of any one's bidding and a firm believer that he is all there is of life, and is completely in the dark as regards any idea of causes existing outside of the phenomenon. We are all the natural man in sickness. Dr. Quimby believes all the feelings and thoughts of mankind have an origin and can be referred to these causes as certainly as actions can be proved the result of certain state of mind. The spiritual man has a knowledge of these causes and knows what every sensation is good for, that is, where it sprang from, what its effect would be if not corrected before it condenses into a belief. Every disease that has a name of course has a father: this father is the idea of the natural man that the body is all there is of us and it comprehends the extent of the natural man's knowledge. The body is sick and the body dies, all of its own accord, is endued with a power which is of the matter, and which no intelligence of man has yet fathomed. Now Dr. Quimby has succeeded in discovering the real forces that act upon the body producing disease, which in their various combination he calls mind. This mind is the matter which goes through a change at the approach or contact with some new idea or sudden shock, either producing some sensible result, in opinion and feelings, or making the person nervous.

Can Dr. Quimby substantiate his knowledge of curing disease on the plan of any other knowledge, and really reveal to man a science of himself? Is there no guess work or imagination?

There is no doubt of it in my mind. When he corrects an error in a sick person, he does not do it of himself, but is merely the medium of a higher intelligence, that sees through all matter and corrects all the various discords of human life, and the developing of this intelligence through man explodes all the ideas and belief of the natural man about himself.

Well, how do you know this? What proof can you give of the existence of such a principle independent of your belief? [This article ends here. –*Ed*.]

Effect of Mind upon Mind, The
[LC 1:0479]

It is an undisputed fact which philosophy has never explained that persons affect each other when neither is conscious of it. According to the principle by which I cure the sick, such incidents can be accounted for, and it can be proved beyond a doubt that man is perfectly ignorant of the influences that act upon him and, being ignorant of the cause, is constantly liable to the effect.

To illustrate this I will relate a case that came under my observation. A woman brought her little son of about five years to be treated by me. When I sat with the child, I found his symptoms were similar to those which persons have in spinal or rheumatic troubles. But the child, being ignorant of names and having no fear of disease, could only describe his feelings in this way: he complained of being tired. Sometimes he said his legs were sore and sometimes his head was tired. To me his feelings were as intelligent as the odor of a rose or any odor with which I was familiar. I described his feelings to his mother, telling how he could appear at times. This she said was correct and feeling impressed with the truth that I had told her about her child, she said she would sit with me and see if I was equally correct in describing her case. I found that the mother had precisely the same feelings as the child. Yet she complained of diseases which the child never thought of and furthermore she never had the least idea of the child having such feelings. To prove to her that I was right about the child, I told her to ask him if he did not feel so and so when he would lay his head down, and she found I was correct. These were the mother's symptoms: a heavy feeling over the eyes, a numbness in the hands, weakness in the back and a pain going from foot to the hip, all accompanied by a feeling of general prostration, etc. To her, every sensation she had the child had also, but he had not attached names to them. After playing, his leg would pain him and he would be restless at night, while his mother reasoned from the same feelings that she had spinal disease, trouble of the heart and was liable to paralysis. If she had been as ignorant as the child of names, she would not have had the fear of these false ideas and the child would have been well. For all its troubles came from its mother and her trouble was from the invention of the medical faculty.

It may be asked how could the child be affected by its mother? In the same way as I was affected. To have the sense of smell or any other sense requires no language. An odor can be perceived by a child as well as a grown person. To every disease there is an odor and everyone is affected by it when it comes within his knowledge. Everyone knows that he can produce in himself heat or cold by excitement; so likewise he can produce the odor of any disease so that he is affected by it. I have proved that I can create the odor of any kind of fruit and make a mesmerized person taste and smell it.

The ignorance of this principle prevents man from investigating into the operation of the human mind. Such course would change the whole mode of our reasoning. It would destroy society as it is now and replace it on another basis. In the place of hypocrisy, aristocracy and democracy, the three original elements of society, science, progress and freedom would be introduced. In his ignorant state, man belongs to the lowest of the aristocracy, but as he becomes scientific, he subdues this element and then the others are not needed to sustain it. His science works out patience, his patience perseverance and perseverance wisdom and the fruits are religion. Now the religion of today contains the elements of society and they run through all its roots and branches and poison its fruit. Science makes war upon this trinity and the war will continue until it is crushed. Then democracy will be subject to science and hypocrisy will not appear in the leaders. Then will come a new heaven or dispensation based on eternal truths and man will be rewarded for what he knows, not for what he thinks he knows. The popular teachers will then publicly correct the democracy or the errors which make them sick as well as a political error. Now political doctors in addressing the masses bind burdens on them which they, kneeling like camels, receive and kiss the hands that bind them. This slavery is the will of aristocracy and consequently it is not popular to oppose it. Therefore no appeal must be made to the higher feelings but these base passions must be addressed. Aristocracy never complains of oppression except when it cannot oppress. Its motto is "rule or ruin" and where it rules, slavery is considered a divine institution. Science is mocked at in its religion and the mockery is echoed by hypocrisy and it sits in the hearts of the rulers and delivers the law. But science like an undercurrent is deep and strong, and as its tide advances, it will sweep away the foundation of aristocracy. Revolutions must come and no man can tell what will be the end of this generation, but science will work out the problem of universal freedom to the oppressed in body and mind.

I prophesy that the time will come when men and women shall heal all manner of diseases by the words of their mouth. They will show the democracy that they have been deceived by their blind leaders who flattered them that they ruled when they have had no more to do with ruling the nation than the dog who is set onto the swine has to do with his master's affairs. No slave either black or white ever did or ever can rule. They both will fight for their master till they are intelligent enough to know their own rights. Of all slavery, democracy is the worst, for it is so indoctrinated into the hearts of man that it is popular and it is not safe to oppose it. Aristocracy, its master, has given it a name which is superior to every other, namely, the intelligence of the people, and to oppose this is to oppose its master. It tells the people that they rule, while in truth, aristocracy itself is the only ruler and it is the same with North and South, and the democracy in both sections do their master's bidding. African slavery is kept in check by the laws and democracy by the hypocrisy of the leaders. To appeal to truth with sound logic is as unpopular at the North as to preach emancipation and abolition at the South. The leaders would set the hounds on a person who would be rash enough to attempt it.

Such evils arise from man's ignorance of himself. If man knew himself, his first object would be to become acquainted with sensations that affect him. He would then learn that a corrupt fountain cannot bring forth pure water and that from aristocracy nothing but the blackest corruption can issue which, however, is popular because of the fountain. From the dens of iniquity comes an atmosphere as pleasant to aristocracy as tobacco to one who has been poisoned almost to paralysis by it. Tell him it hurts him; the answer is, I know it, but I cannot help using it. Such abject servitude is the medium of aristocracy, for democracy would never have taken the weed had not the former set the example. All drugs when taken stupefy the intellect so that science cannot reign. Error is a tyrant and democracy his agent to destroy the progress and happiness of man. Show a man who smokes or chews just how the habit affects him and he will part company with tobacco as quickly as a democrat will leave his leaders when he sees the corruption of their motives. A democrat is like a disease. He believes in everything popular and opposes everything unpopular and does not regard the welfare of his government. Let a man from this state in time of peace go South, and if he is popular, he will be in favor of slavery; but if he honors the principles of the constitution more than he loves this party, he will not be popular and neither will he be in favor of slavery. Therefore, if he wishes to place himself under the influence of slavery so that he will become a disease in the nation, let him abide by the so-called democratic principles and denounce everything differing from them as political quackery. Then he will be exceedingly popular. To be popular in religion, praise the institutions of the Sabbath and the church. Say what you please in the street about priestcraft and fear of man, only mention that your family go to church and you will be considered sound. To be unpopular, be honest in every act, treat others with respect, mind your own affairs and permit others to do the same. Then like an old fashioned person you are out of society and no one cares for you.

To be independent, speak the truth on all subjects without fear or vanity; condemn error wherever it is popular; treat others as you wish to be treated and let your religion be shown in your acts. Such a man will be envied by aristocracy, respected by the wise, hated by hypocrites and listened to by the thinking classes. He is at the same time popular and not popular. His style pleases the people; therefore the aristocracy will be forced to admire him in order that they may retain their power over him, for their rule is "keep as near a kicking horse as possible." They will extol such a man in some things and condemn him in others and thereby neutralize his effect on democracy.

Physicians will admit what the people believe. They will acknowledge I cure but limit my power to a few nervous cases and appeal to the vanity of intelligence by saying that it is not possible that an uneducated person can really cure actual disease, etc. A political leader at the North appeals to the democracy in this way. It is not expected that we at the North can equal those gentlemen at the South who have devoted their lives to the study of politics. This is swallowed, for the pronoun "we" makes it palatable, putting the leader and the democracy on a level. Is this the way the Southern leader addresses the Southern democracy? Not at all. He says to them, Those miserable Yankees want to rule over you when you can each whip a dozen of them. Thus the demagogue makes politicians of soldiers. This is the error of democracy which is really the mouthpiece of aristocracy to which it is believed to be opposed. It is a stream rising from a corrupt fountain. It trickles over the pebbles of ignorance and flows down into the ashes of eternal monarchy. Politics, religion and disease are the offspring of the trinity I have named and are the same combination of error. They will exist so long as error exists, for they live on ignorance.

February 1863

Effect of Religion on Health, The
[LC 1:0073]

I will give my opinion of the inconsistency of our religious ideas and how they affect our health. I was visiting a patient who was suffering very much from what is called rheumatism and a general debility of her nervous system. The doctors had tried all in their power to relieve her but to no effect and all their efforts only made her worse. At last she sent for me. I found her very nervous, complaining of aches and pains all over. When I told her that it was her mind that was disturbed, she replied, "Oh! No, my mind is at rest. I know that I am in the hands of a merciful God who will deal with me according to his will. I have full faith in Him." Do you suppose He knows your trouble, I ask? "Yes, He knows all things." Suppose that Jesus was here as he was eighteen-hundred years ago; do you think he would cure you? "Oh, yes. I know that He knows all my suffering." Then you believe He knows all your sufferings? "Yes." Then why doesn't He cure you? "Because it is His will that I should go through all this suffering to fit me for the Kingdom of Heaven." Suppose your daughter should be taken sick away from home in a strange land and suppose some kind friend should call upon her and say to her, "You seem to be very low spirited," and she should reply, "Oh no, I know it is all right." Suppose your mother was here, would you not get well? "Yes, she knows all my suffering but she thinks or knows it is all right for it makes me better prepared to enjoy her company when I get home." Do you believe that if she chose to cure you that she could do so? "Certainly." Can you say you love your mother when you admit that your life is in her hands and she permits you to suffer so much? "Oh! She is my mother and she knows God knows what is best. It gives me great comfort to know that I am in the hands of a merciful being." Would you like to have me cure you? "Yes, if you can, but not if I must give up my beliefs and my religion. I should rather go down to the grave with my belief than to be cured and lose my religion. If you can cure me of my lameness and not talk to me about religion I should like to get well, but if you can't cure me without that I don't know as I will be cured, for I think my religion has nothing to do with my disease." Don't you think your belief has something to do with your happiness? "Oh, yes, but it has nothing to do with my disease." What is your disease? "It is rheumatism, the doctors say, and a general prostration of the nervous system." What is that? "Neuralgia, I suppose." What is that? "I don't know, only the doctors say that it is a general prostration of the nervous system." What is that? "I don't know." Suppose I should try to explain how you came to be in this condition, would you listen? "Yes, if you don't talk religion." I have no religion to talk. "I know it." Have you? "I hope I have." Well I don't want it if it makes me as sick and unhappy as you are. "All the comfort I take while lying here all these long nights is thinking that I am in the hands of a merciful God who will do all things right." Would you like to get well? "If it is the will of God I should be very glad to get well." Do you think I can cure you? "I do not know, but I hope that you can; if you can't, I shall give up all hope of ever getting well." Then you think that your health depends on my science? "Yes." If I could cure you, would you give me the credit? "Yes." But would it be right to upset the will of God who is keeping you in all this misery for his own pleasure? "Oh! If God sees fit to have me cured I believe it is all right. I know that I feel badly enough and I should like to feel better, but if it is the will of God that I should suffer, I will submit, for I know that it is for the best. God suffered in the flesh to teach us to be better prepared for Heaven." Then you think if you should die, you would go to Heaven? "I hope so, for I can't suffer this pain always." Where is Heaven? Do you believe it is a place? "No." Then what is it? "It is a state of mind." Then you are not very near it I should judge by your mind. "Well, I don't know as that has anything to do with my pains." What is pain? "I don't know what it is but I know how it feels." How do you know? "I know it through my senses." Are not your senses affected by your mind? "I suppose so." Then if your mind is affected, you know it through your senses? "Yes." Then if your mind is disturbed and you put a false construction on the disturbance, will it not produce an unpleasant effect upon the senses? "I suppose so." Suppose this unpleasant effect should be pain, is it not the effect produced on the mind? "I don't know what that has to do with my lameness. I want to get well." Who wants to get well? "I." That is you, Mrs. H. _____

"Yes." Then that which wants to get well is that which suffers? "Yes. "Is not that all there is of you which has any mind or knowledge? "Yes." You don't expect this flesh and blood to go to Heaven? "No." Why not? "Because the Bible says flesh and blood cannot inherit the Kingdom of Heaven." I thought you just said that Heaven was a state of mind. "So I did." Do you mean that flesh and blood are in the mind? "Oh! You make me so nervous you will kill me." Why? "Because I don't like to hear you talk so. My mind is made up and I don't like to be disturbed in this way." Do you mean your flesh and blood are disturbed? "You disturb my mind and body." Then your mind is one thing and your body another. You believe in the soul? "Yes." You believe it goes to Heaven when you die? "Yes." I thought you said that Heaven is a state of mind. "Oh, yes. But we must die." What does? "This flesh and blood." Has it life? "Yes." Has it feeling? "You would think so if you suffered as much as I do." Then this that suffers is the flesh and blood? "Yes." Then it is conscious of all these bad feelings? "Yes." Are the feelings its consciousness or has it another consciousness independent of itself? "No." Then at death you mean that all these aches and pains leave you and you will be happy? "Yes." Then these aches and pains are the body's identity and belong to the flesh and blood? "Yes." And you say they can't go to Heaven, that is, they can't be in a happy state of mind? "Yes." Can two states of mind exist together? "No." Are you happy when you feel so bad? "No." Then you are not in Heaven. "I don't expect to be happy till I get to Heaven." Can you get there and have these pains? "No." Then when these pains leave you it will be Heaven on earth? "Oh, yes! If that ever takes place."

Now let us see where you stand. You have admitted enough to show that your mind is in a confused state like a person in trouble. You have not one particle of true knowledge. All your supposed knowledge is the effect of an impression on the senses without any wisdom. What takes the place of knowledge is the opinion of someone who explains some person's ideas according to his own ideas of truth; taking this for truth makes you nervous and brings about all your suffering. You are afraid of your enemies and pray to that very God who you admit keeps you in misery. You are taught to believe that God is watching all your actions and that He has laid down certain laws and regulations for you to follow, and, if you disobey, you will be punished. This keeps you in bondage and all your life subject to disease. Now to suppose that God selects you to be punished above all your companions is to believe that God is partial. This you cannot believe.

Now look at those who worship God; they have a false idea of the God they worship. God is not in any kind of worship that man has established. God is not an identity as man is. If He was then He would be matter, so all their prayers are in matter and all they are afraid of contains matter. This false idea keeps man in the dark. You never see a man praying to the fire that warms him nor does he pray to the elements; but his prayer is how he can understand them so as to keep them under his control. How is it with steam? Is not the person who knows the most about steam the best person to control it and does not everyone have more confidence in such a person than in one who is ignorant of it? So it is with all the elements. Man differs in one respect from living matter. The beasts and all God's creatures, except man, have never undertaken to control the elements so as to make them subservient to their will. This is where man commences his wisdom over all the rest of creation; he is so constructed that he is not happy or contented to live like the brutes and let the elements alone, but seeks to subject not only the brute creation but these also to his will. It is true there are some of the human species a little above the brutes and they are the class who never see anything outside of themselves. They sometimes show a kind of intelligence but it is like that of the monkey or parrot, all imitation. They show no power or desire to control the elements but are satisfied with carrying out the ideas of some long established authority. This they do with as much zeal as the brutes, mistaking zeal for knowledge, and set up their standards of judgment based on an opinion. This they take for the truth, from the fact that they cannot discriminate between an opinion based on another's opinion and one based on science. For instance, we often hear persons talking about the laws of nature as though they were the laws of God. They say that if we did not disobey them all would go right. Now here is the mistake. The laws of nature are very simple of themselves and they never trouble man if he does not trouble them. The beasts conform to these laws, for when they are thirsty, they find the law which quenches their thirst; when hungry, the same intelligence dictates the remedy. But man, in his eagerness to be lord over the brutes and elements, has developed the law of life which puts him in possession of certain faculties called senses. These are under a superior wisdom which can control the elements and use them for the benefit of the human race. Now, it is not to be expected that every person who happens to think of flying can make a flying machine that will be successful. Nor is it certain that any invention to control the elements will always work so that accidents, as they are called, will not take place and lives lost and much trouble made before the law or science is established. So it is with life. Life is a science that is little understood. The brutes have never shown any desire to investigate this science. Man is the only one that has ever undertaken it and now let us see how far he has progressed.

It is a fact that man's life is shortened by the theory of his own belief, for his belief is his practice and the length of his life is in his belief or theory. Everyone has his theory in regard to the lengthening of life but all admit that it must end, that it is set in motion and it may run some time or not. Some think that life is a perpetual machine which never was set in motion and never can stop. This life is the great problem to solve, and to save it from being lost, theories are invented for the benefit of man to save his life. He is given all the knowledge of every danger he is liable to pass through and warned against them. These call out all the science and skill of the world to put man in possession of a science to save his life just as though his life was something independent of himself. This makes competition and there is no science which teaches that life is eternal and that the discoveries of man go to destroy the happiness of life itself. Life cannot be destroyed but error can keep life in trouble.

A science which established life as an eternal principle is not for itself but for the happiness of mankind. In error there is continual warfare–one party or sect invents all sorts of bugbears to frighten man so as to get a chance to save something called life. So man is told if he does not believe just so, he will lose his life. Another who has made the elements his study and endeavored to control them finds that they are a great enemy to mankind and it is necessary for the preservation of human life that the people should know how to control them. And in order to give man this knowledge it requires that there should be a certain class of people who devote their time to it, who can show by their theory that life is in the knowledge of their practice or science. For instance, they show for one fact that fire will burn you to death and this ends your life according to their belief or theory; but you may be nearly scalded to death and then there is a chance for the science to save your life. This requires all their science. Experiments are tried and facts set down by persons trying them, and when a new phenomenon is produced, that is set down as a scientific fact. Thus the world has been humbugged by these blind guides leading the blind till their theory of opinions, like the locusts of Egypt, are in everything we eat or drink or wear. You cannot do anything but there is a penalty attached. If you go out of doors, you are liable to take cold. In short, all evils called disease are the inventions of man and they are as real as his life for they have complete power over it and we are afraid of them because they can destroy our lives. Now here is the trouble. Error has taken life as a thing that can be destroyed. Truth makes error matter that can be changed into any form or shape, and error is the servant to life or truth but error supposes it is the master and thinks that life or truth is the servant. So when the servant is above the master then error and superstition reign. But when the truth comes, error dies and as truth never makes war, it sits and sees error destroy itself.

I will try to separate these two powers, as far as disease goes, so that you can see to which of these elements you are subject. As matter is under the direction of life, it is its servant, and as life does not act, it is like a lord who has servants and gives his vineyard to man for their happiness. If the overseer gives to the servants false directions, disease is the result and confusion and unhappiness reign. But the disease or result is in the direction and not in the effect. Error puts disease in the result but the lord (of the vineyard) puts it in the direction. Therefore, when he comes to settle with his servants and finds that the overseer is ignorant of what he is about, he turns out that overseer and lets his vineyard to some other who will do better. So it is with our health. Health and happiness are a result of our acts and belief. They are under error or truth and all the misery that follows our belief is the natural consequence of our opinions. To suppose that we could be happy in a belief that puts restrictions on us is an error, for it is impossible for us to feel pain without knowing it. And to know the cause and know that it is from an intelligence that has the power to stop it if He pleases and will not (giving no reason, only what we may conjure up) is to believe that God is worse than we are ourselves. All of these errors arise from a superstitious mind, not daring to think or not having capacity to think, which lives in an error and is all his life subject to disease for the sake of his belief. Now God is not in this belief at all. He is in that truth that destroys this belief. I will make an illustration showing where error is, also where God is. Take the fire. The child is burned and is afraid of the fire and looks upon it as its enemy. Science sees the child's error and that its knowledge is error. The child tries to get rid of its enemy, supposing it will harm it. Its true knowledge will correct the child and then the wisdom of this world becomes subject to truth or science. So it is with all true knowledge. There is no true knowledge in an opinion and, as the most of our knowledge is made up of opinions, we are to ourselves just what we think we are.

Religions and medical opinions are the worst enemies that man has to contend with and they make him nervous. This leads to all sorts of dissipation to drown sorrow. Our lives are like a journey through a wilderness: we first take the priests' opinion, that is to trust in God. When we ask for an explanation of God we are told that He knows all things and not a hair of our head falls to the ground without His knowledge; that if we look to them they will deliver us out of all danger and that He takes better care of us than a parent does of his child. This is a brief sketch of God's goodness. Now suppose that we should not do quite as well as we expect, what follows? God has made a devil or something worse that stands ready to catch us if we don't do just according to His will or laws. These laws are not definite but are like the laws of the United States that every President can construe according to his belief. The laws of God, made by man, are arbitrary though not acknowledged as such. Jesus said, "Call no man master, but one, that is God." Here you see you have made a God that is full of inconsistencies and cannot stand the test of common reason. Now look at the true scientific answer to all our beliefs and it shows us that they contain no knowledge of God or life, for God is life eternal and this life was in his son, Jesus, which was Christ or Science. Now to suppose you lose your life is to be cut off from God, for God is not the God of the dead but of the living, for all live to Him.

Man's belief in religion and disease is all founded on the opinion that man must die or lose his life; therefore, we are called upon to do something to save it. This keeps man in ignorance of himself or life and all the time troubled from fear of death. Now destroy man's belief and introduce God's truth and then we are set free from this world of error and introduced into the world of light or science where there is no death but the living God or science. This science will lead us along to that happy state where there is no sickness or sorrow or grief, where all tears are wiped away from our eyes, there to be in the presence of this great truth that will watch us and hold us in the hollow of its hand and will be to us a light that will open our eyes. We shall not then be deceived by the blind guides who say, "Peace, peace," where there is no peace. Then we shall call no one master or leader for there is only one that leads us and that is God. He puts no restrictions upon us for our lives are in His hands or science, but our happiness or misery is in our belief. For our belief is what follows a direction. So if we are misdirected and disease or misery is the result, blame not God, or the result, but blame the cause or false direction. We, through our ignorance, put God into the false direction but not into the effect. But there can be no effect without a cause; therefore God or the cause is in the effect; so is the devil or ignorance in the cause and effect. Now to suppose that God is in the devil or error is to put God on a level with the errors of this world.

I will give an illustration of these two powers. Man has no idea of God but error pretends to know all about Him. Error says that all the hairs of our head are numbered and not one hair falls to the ground unnoticed by Him. Now what would be the most liberal construction that a child would have of God as far as His knowledge over us is concerned? For the Bible says, "Except you become as a little child you cannot enter the Kingdom of Heaven." Would it not be that God has eyes as the child has and is watching us and if a hair should fall He sees it? We are taught by this same error that God is watching all our acts and if we should happen to do something that is not in accordance with some person's opinion then we have disobeyed His will, are liable to be punished and thank the Lord for it.

Now I will give the scientific man's opinion of God. All laws are a part of God and intelligence is in them so that every act of our lives shows of which power we are the servant. These laws govern the beast and all living creatures and the knowledge is in the law. If the beast wants food, the desire contains the knowledge and direction how to get it and, if no obstruction is put in the way, he will have his prayer answered. So it is with all God's laws. The law of gravitation or attraction contains the cause and effect. So if there is no obstacle in the way, it will come according to those laws. This is God and to suppose God is in the effect of error is not the case. Now you see that to know what will be the result of every act is to see and know its cause and effect. Now as a hair is governed by the law of attraction, which is knowledge, and this knowledge is in the law, when it falls to the ground it must fall with the knowledge of the law which is God. Suppose you let a one pound weight of lead fall to the ground and a piece of cork at the same time. Is not your knowledge of attraction in the cork and lead to know the difference in the time? So it cannot fall without the knowledge of the law that governs it and this is God. But to have a God with eyes and ears and every faculty that man has is to have a being of flesh and blood. Now if you see God in your knowledge, you will admit that everything you do intelligently you do under the direction of a power or intelligence superior to yourself. So when you do anything ignorantly and the effect is bad, giving you trouble, you try to correct your errors thereby showing that you admit a power superior to yourself. This power is called Christ or God and, if you have not the power or Christ, you are not of Him. To know God is to know ourselves and to know ourselves is to know the difference between science and error. Error is of man and truth is of God and as truth is not in the cause of the disease, it is not in the effect; but as error is the cause of disease, it is in the effect. Therefore, to say we are happy when in disease is to admit that we have no disease, for disease is the error and the effect. Now as opinions contain either truth or error, not known, we are affected by the effect when it comes to the light of science and then the happiness or misery follows. This is called by the doctors, disease, and they treat the effect denying the cause or letting it go as though it was of no account.

Here is the difference. I put the disease in the direction and then I know what will be the effect. The doctors and ministers do the same, but being ignorant of their power, they mislead the patient and the result is just what science would have known and counteracted. For instance, I believe in disease and all I do is to prove it. Now if I had no belief and had the truth, this truth could not make disease but it could destroy it. Our belief is formed of matter that can be destroyed and our happiness is the result of correcting our impressions when first made; our error is the ignorance of these impressions. The opinions of the world and the error of ourselves are the cause of our trouble and the destruction of our opinions, whatever they may be, leaves us better. Suppose you were afraid of some person and you dare not stir lest he should kill you; do you think that you would be any worse off to know that he was your friend and felt unhappy to know that you had such an opinion of him? So it is in every act of our lives. The knowledge of ourselves never harmed us. Disease is not in knowledge but in ignorance. For instance, the fear of any trouble is the disease. Then you will say that you had no fear, so that cannot be true; but you misunderstand the idea. Go with me back to the time of the persecution of the church and the Salem witchcraft. The people believed in evil spirits and witches and considered it wrong to have anything to do with them. Here you see the disease in the people's belief and their belief was put in practice for the safety of mankind. Therefore every invention of their belief was called out to get rid of an evil that was tormenting man. Here you see the belief was one thing and the evil another and so it is in everything.

The wisdom of this world sees the mind one thing and disease another and reasons by saying the pain came before I had any thought about it and I had no mind about it. Take the man with the wooden leg. When this wooden leg itches, does it itch, or is it in his mind? No one would say that it was the leg that itched. So it is with all our troubles. That peculiar feeling was a state of mind which he called itching. If his leg felt cold, it was not the leg but the mind, and each sensation is only another combined state of mind or matter. This mind or matter is not understood, so the power that governs it puts intelligence in the wooden leg and makes the leg intelligent and itself intelligent. That makes two intelligences: one, the leg, and the owner, the other. But the wisdom of truth puts the knowledge in the owner and the effect in the leg. At first some sensation was made in the mind; ignorance and superstition gave it a false construction and lo! error formed the idea of white swelling on the knee. Thus the trouble of the mind was located in the knee and showed itself in that form. Now mind being a part of the man, when the limb was cut off, it might or might not have changed that peculiar state of mind. So it is with rheumatic pains. The state of mind or disease is admitted to have an existence in the minds of men as much as evil spirits and we are affected by our belief.

If anything disturbs our happiness, we fly to someone for protection and in our trouble we create some form of something in the mind and locate it in some place in the body. We suffer ourselves to be tormented to get rid of the enemy or disease just as those who believe themselves bewitched would suffer being whipped to drive out the devils. So do persons of this age suffer themselves to be tormented by the doctors to get rid of some enemy that the same doctor has made by his ignorance and treated in some part of the system.

I could name hundreds of cases where persons have called in physicians, and between them both have made an enemy and the patient suffered himself to be poulticed and blistered almost to death to get rid of the bronchitis or spinal disease or white swelling or some other devil supposed to have an existence independent of the mind. The doctors who use these means show just about as much knowledge as the persons did in Connecticut who beat the beer barrel if it worked on Sunday. It is the relic of heathen superstition that wisdom will sometime eradicate from the mind by explaining facts on scientific principles. Till then, the knife and lancet and calomel and all such things that are only introduced by a show of truth, not much in advance of nailing a horseshoe on the door or sleeping with a Bible under you to keep the witches off, must govern the world. Jesus knew that all the above beliefs were founded on ignorance; therefore he was not afraid of these beliefs and said these words, "Greater love hath no man than to lay down his life for his friends." This is the meaning. I know all this is false, that it is in your minds, so I am not afraid to lay down my life or put it in jeopardy for the sick so I can explain to them or lead them to health. You may say we must have physicians. I answer, "Have I not been with you in your trouble and relieved you without tormenting you?" For twenty years I have never said one word to a patient which, if he believed, would make him worse or cause him one moment's pain or misery. I have never tormented a patient by making a disease by which he would suffer to be burdened with caustic, blistered and at last lose his limbs in order to be rid of an evil that I have made. If the people would serve the doctors as they did those who accused another of bewitching them, it would put a stop to a great deal of evil. If a doctor tells a patient that he has a disease (which, if he believes, he is worse off), punish the doctor and they would soon learn to keep their tongues from speaking lies and learn to tell the truth or say nothing. I have tried it and seen the effect and know that the principle is right—never to say to a person anything that will, if believed, make him the least disappointed or grieved. If you cannot leave a happy impression, do not leave a bad one. This cannot be done under the old system as it kills the practice. Therefore, reform is necessary.

June 1860

Efficacy of Prayer for the Sick, The
[LC 2:0660]

What grounds have Christians for believing in the efficacy of prayer for the sick? The belief in a God independent of ourselves, who will answer prayer if asked in a spirit of true faith, not doubting. This is the ground for the Christian belief. Let us see how much faith they have in what they honestly believe. Jesus says, By their works ye shall know them. Now do the sick in their trouble call on the Lord or the doctor? I leave the sick to answer, and I hear one say that the doctor is the instrument in the hands of God to cure the sick. Then I ask if the sick do not get well, who is to blame, the Lord or the instrument? You may say the sick do not have faith enough. Then it is not the doctor nor the Lord but their faith that makes them whole. This was the case with the woman whom Jesus cured, when he said, Thy faith hath made thee whole. So faith without works is dead. It is plain enough that the Christians have no faith in God except as a belief; they cannot trust him at all. As soon as they are sick, instead of looking to God, they send for a doctor and if he does not cure them, they try some other. In their trouble, they lose all patience and like Saul, they say seek me a witch (I Sam. 18:7) or one that has a familiar spirit that I may inquire of it, thus denying the very God they profess to believe in. How comes all this skepticism in the church and people? It arises from the fact that the priests have invented lies and set up false Gods, calling on the people to believe in them, thus leading the people on the by-paths until the whole have gone out of the way and none believing in the one true God who answers prayers, not through the priests or doctors, but through the wisdom of themselves. For to know ourselves is to know God and that is Eternal Life to all who know it.

You may ask if I believe in prayer; I answer not in the sense that the Christian does. Jesus prayed; he said, I and my Father are one. This is a truth, but it was not Jesus that spoke but this truth called Christ that spoke through the man Jesus, in the same way when any truth is spoken intelligently, it is of God and that truth and God are one. Ignorance and superstition have misled men into the dark, so they choose darkness rather than light lest their error should be exposed, and then they die. You may ask if I deny that God sometimes cures the sick in answer to prayer. I do not deny the phenomenon, but I do deny that the one who prays knows to whom he prays or that his God cures him any more than the medicine that the doctor gives cures him. The priests and doctors stand in the same relation to the sick; the former put their curative principles in their God and the latter put them in the medicine; the faith of each acts on the patient and his faith mingling with theirs makes the cure, but that there is an intelligence or God outside of their belief, I know is false. Years of experience in curing the sick have put me in possession of a principle that can explain all the phenomena of prayer and the superstition of religious beliefs. A belief is one thing and wisdom is another. Jesus explained the difference when he said, "Render unto Caesar the things that are Caesar's and unto God the things that are God's."

They were trying to entangle Jesus by their questions in regard to his belief in God. He knew that their God was the opinion of man and their worship the invention of the priests, and the people paid tribute to Caesar as the priests now do to Christ, for to disbelieve in Caesar was a great sin. The people asked Jesus whether it was lawful to pay tribute to Caesar and he answered, "Why tempt ye me, ye hypocrites," and made the remark quoted above.

Here was where Jesus made a difference between his God and theirs. He knew it was not right to rob God or truth and give the credit to error or opinion, for in this way you keep man ignorant of himself and God (by putting man's opinion superior to the truth). So he said, Render to man's opinions what they are worth and to Science or God what belongs to truth. I will suppose that I, like Jesus, stand to the sick as their friend and have to come in contact with the same Caesar that Jesus did, for Caesar is man's wisdom embodied in flesh and blood. Jesus' wisdom was his God, while man's God was his opinions. So the latter being ignorant of God or Science worships it as a superior being and calls it God, but God is not in it; He is in the truth.

When a man is sick, he is under the penalty of man's laws or God's, as they are called, and to be cured is to be reconciled to God or the priests' opinion. Now I know all their prayers and medicines are false. They contain no wisdom but are opinions set up by the ignorant. You may ask me for truth. I will give it, for I do not give an opinion; what I know is true, and what I give as an opinion is what I do not know. This I know. What a minister says is an opinion, not wisdom, and therefore is worth just what it will bring among those who put a value on man's opinion, but to me it is not worth a snap for it is all froth or wind. Here is a sick man or woman who wants to get well. Such a one is the test of Jesus' religion. He put his God or Christ into practice, and it was called the bread of life, and he called on all to come and eat of it, etc. Why was Jesus looked upon as superior to other men of his day, for there were other men called Jesus and other Christs? The Jesus we are called on to worship was not the only one, for he says beware of false Christs who were to come when the true Christ came and he tells them how to prove them by their works. The true Christ shall cast out devils and do the works Jesus did and greater, but do you find the Christ of our day to do what the Christ of whom they pretend to be a disciple did? No. Why? Because they are false Christs. I pretend to do as Christ did and I believe in the same God that he did and this God was the wisdom that showed that all the priests' pretentions to divine wisdom were false.

I know as well as I know that I am writing this that there is not a word of knowledge in all the priests' profession, and instead of making man better and happier, it only makes them more bigoted and more liable to disease.

I will now tell what is not my opinion. I know that persons are raised from a sick bed to health, and I have no reason to doubt that there are many persons who have been influenced to break off their sins, as it is called, and embrace the priest's opinion as religion. All this and a great deal more I believe as a belief, but in all this, there is not one single ray of light or wisdom. They are merely phenomena without any wisdom, like mesmerism and spiritualism. I will explain the foregoing, not after the manner of the priests by calling on you to believe in me as an oracle and then giving an opinion, but I will use plain facts which are coming under my own observation every day.

What I know I will call wisdom, which is the knowledge of God and what I do not know is man's knowledge or opinion. I know I am writing this if I know anything. I also know that this wisdom can feel another's feelings and that I can go to a distance and act upon another wisdom unknown to the man of opinions. Here is the difference between me as a man and the priest as a priest or a doctor as a doctor. We all, as men, have flesh and blood. They have a belief that there is a God above that knows all things and this God is independent of them. I know that what they believe is false from my own experience, for I take their account of the God they worship and find it to be only an opinion, which works them up into a disease and takes a form in the person of a God. Their senses being attached to it, it is to them wisdom, and this shadow is the medium of all their acts. When they pray, their faith is in their God or medium, and they give to him all the glory and the power, not knowing that he is an image of their own creation.

You ask for proof. I will give it. Suppose there is a sick man living at a distance who wishes to be cured and I go to him in my wisdom and cure him. This is all with myself. I know how I do it and can explain it. Suppose he is taken sick again and he sends for a doctor. He tells the doctor how he feels and the doctor sends his medicine which he takes and he is healed. Again he is taken sick and sends for a priest, the priest prays and the patient gets well. Where is the difference in us three? I know what I am about, my cure is in my wisdom, their cure is in their belief. The ignorance of the priest puts his cure in his imaginary God, the patient puts his faith in his God, their faith mingle into a sort of chemical change and the patient is restored. The doctor's belief in the curative qualities of his medicine and the patient's superstition in the doctor's wisdom produce a change and the cure is made.

All cures are made just alike with one exception; satisfy the priest that there is no God but himself and his power is lost. Satisfy the patient that the medicine is all a humbug and let the doctor know it and no cure is made. Is that the case with me? No, I have acted on the patient without his knowing it through his natural senses and it is not necessary that the patient should have any belief at all in order to be cured. What conclusion have I arrived at in all the above? It is this. God is the wisdom of all mankind, and every person has an identity in this wisdom. All live and move in it and cannot get out of it. Each person is made independent of each other by his ignorance of himself, yet like little globules of matter, we are held together by the great ocean of wisdom. We are like ships on the sea without lights at the head of our barques, till the whole atmosphere of wisdom is lit by science. Then our lights mingle in harmony till not a cloud can be seen. Then we shall see as we are seen and know as we are known; then God is in us and we in him. Then priestcraft and opinion are burned up by the fire of Science, death is annihilated and sickness is a shadow of the things that never had an existence only in the mind of error.

March 1862

Element of Love*
[Originally untitled.] [BU 3:1211]

We speak of an intelligent, or scientific, or patriotic man; when he dies, all intelligence, science or patriotism dies with him. What are all these when he dies? Do they emanate from his material organization and die with it as a stream proceeds from a fountain? In short are wisdom, progress etc. the development of matter? If so, then they must have the properties of matter and die.

It is the design of Dr. Quimby to prove that man lives and acts in an element different from matter, that the universal nature of man can be traced to a different principle than that which would have him a transitory being. What element is that, that is not matter yet in which man acts and lives? It is impossible to describe in one word or in a few words, an existing medium that is not recognized or known as such, but it can be illustrated by facts that are common to all.

A child knows its mother, not by looks or voice, but by something not included within these two senses; it is that something that makes her different in her relation to the child from any other woman. Suppose it be called love or a desire for the child's happiness identified with her own. According as she directs the child in the pure intelligence of that love or yields her feelings to wisdom derived from a source which does not contain that love, "so shall the fruits be." What Dr. Quimby would establish is this, that this love contains an intelligence which if followed in spirit and truth, might destroy every obstacle in the way of that child's happiness and develop it into a self governing responsible being. Then why is it not so? Because from our religious and social education, no woman can carry out the high principle of her affection. She is taught by established morality to put restrictions on her child that would make her miserable in its place.

Patriotism also contains an eternal principle which acts on man guiding him to the right course of action, for the happiness of his country. When a man is under the influence of a patriotic feeling, he knows it and there is no division of opinion in his mind as what is best to do.

Aug. 18th, 1861

Elements of Progress, Aristocracy, Freedom, Conservatism & Abolitionism
[LC 1:0465]

The elements of political parties are the agents of wisdom, unintelligent and irresponsible in what they do. A child contains them all. Beginning as a blank, its first development is aristocracy or a desire to be free itself and rule others. The next is to be free from all arbitrary restraint. These acting together bring out another element called conservatism and reason. Neither of these is intelligent. The child and the brute alike contain aristocracy and freedom, for they are the action and reaction of the simplest capacity. Two animals when first placed together commence to fight, simply to see who will be master. At length one is overpowered and submits to the superior. The conquered becomes the slave and in him commences the element of abolitionism. The desire to throw off the yoke of servitude makes him envious, fretful and often rebellious until he has either gained his freedom or become submissive in slavery. He then loses his bold, defiant appearance and becomes dull and depressed. Living in these elements of master and slave, animals and birds leave their oppressors and go where they can enjoy their freedom. This discord is always working to bring about emigration in the animal kingdom so that the whole earth shall be peopled and the design of creation be fulfilled.

Man to a certain extent is governed in the same way. His first act is to rule and his oppression destroys freedom and causes emigration. Yet, when prepared to receive it, he is also subject to a higher element called science. Every element in nature exists in man, but he believes them to be intelligent. Heat and cold cause expansion and contraction in nature. In man, they are found under the names of tyranny and freedom and are thought to contain wisdom. In politics, their names are anti and pro-slavery, and in religion, Unitarianism and Calvinism. In nature, these elements act as follows. The cold lays its icy hand on the earth commanding the soil to cease producing and the light and warmth of the sun to be shut off. Then heat is held by the hand of ice and life is extinguished in death, till heat which cannot be long confined commences to expand. Both are now at work, one to hold the other and the other to keep from being held.

To show how they act in man, I must illustrate by children. When two children come together, the first element excited is aristocracy. Their combativeness is aroused and they contend for the mastery of each other. Finally it is received; then the aristocracy of the conqueror rises in its might and the vanquished is bound. The slave now develops the abolitionist element and seeks to free itself from the arbitrary rule of the other. Again they quarrel and in their struggle, the parent interferes, introducing a fourth element, conservatism. Here commences reason in man; conservatism, assuming to know more than the combatants, reasons with them, and as it expands, it takes possession of both, regulating and equalizing their position towards each other. Aristocracy, unwilling to be on an equality with freedom seeks means to gain some advantage, but conservatism holding the balance of power checks the attempt. At length, it succeeds in encroaching and then it declares war with freedom to get possession of the masses.

The masses or democracy is the lowest form of freedom and the leaders who constitute the arbitrary power try by argument and falsehood to gain the influence of the masses who are the strength of political parties. The radical aristocracy, having no principle and only a name, appeal to the democracy in one way while the more liberal party address themselves to a higher state of mind. The former having no higher gain than political power labor to appear the friends of the people and are very liberal in certain rights, when in reality they are forging bands for their degradation.

These same elements are seen acting upon man in disease. But freedom having no party, the leaders of aristocracy (the medical faculty) decide on the means to be used to keep the democracy (or man) in their power. So they quarrel about the different modes of practice with as much bitterness as political demagogues.

All admit disease as leaders admit the necessity of two parties and hence the necessity of doctors, and they through their belief in disease rule the people by their opinions as much as politicians control the people by political craft. The masses cannot believe that doctors are of no use, for so long as they admit disease, they will take medicine. Just so in politics. The necessity of two opposite parties makes the people believe in their leader and thus they become the tool of politicians. The leaders of all sects and parties rule the people, for aristocracy always rules democracy in religion, politics and disease. Aristocracy is represented in disease, freedom in health, and man is democracy or the element to be acted upon. Creeds, parties and beliefs start up aristocracy and all have the effect to keep freedom down. Having come out from both elements, I will address myself to conservatism, for that contains the other two and can be guided by wisdom, while the other two cannot be immediately acted upon by wisdom. Every person contains these three elements in various combinations.

I will illustrate these by a steam boat. The steam acting on the piston and the ship struggling to be free represents freedom. The mooring is aristocracy and he who cuts the cable is the conservative element under the direction of freedom. Then freedom bounds into the ocean of progression guided by the science of God in the captain or pilot. Here are the three. Two contain no intelligence, yet they act in harmony with the principles of wisdom. The third has knowledge of the other two and can be guided by wisdom, still it is ignorant how wisdom combines the three. All will admit that neither the ship nor the steam contained intelligence and the same with the mooring, but the man who, obeying orders, looses the ship and lets her go is of a higher order. These three were in action when Jesus appeared. Men like barques were moored on the sea of idolatry and superstition. Some like Paul, driven by the wind of conservatism toward the rocks of bigotry, while others drifting towards the ocean of wisdom sought to be free. Then amidst the fury of the struggle, they heard a voice say to the winds and waves, Be still and there was a calm and wisdom took possession of their barques. Every person is like a vessel governed by some intelligence superior to the elements of the vessel.

A sick man is like a vessel in a fog with the wind in shore and she in danger of going onto the rocks. He is moored in his belief which is a sea of danger. The doctor comes to assist him out of the difficulty and start him on the road to health, as a pilot goes on board ship to put her out to sea. Sitting by him, he feels his pulse to find how much confidence he has in getting him out of his difficulty. He asks his symptoms and then looking very wise, he tells him he is in very great danger and great care and attention must be used to prevent the disease from spreading, just as a pilot would give a captain a detailed account of the dangers and difficulties he must meet in going to sea. The doctor then leaves the patient with many orders and much medicine to his belief. The patient takes the opinion into his mind and the medicine into his body and they both result in a convulsion of the latter. The ship sails according to the direction of the pilot and the first thing heard is breakers ahead and then all hands to the pump. Having pumped out the water, she is tossed and rocked by the gale till the wind dies away and a dead calm follows. The voyage is given up till the ship is repaired. The sick man controlled by the knowledge of the doctor shows changes and symptoms which are doctored as fast as they appear, till all remedies fail. A complete prostration ensues and he is left to nature that she may recuperate. A dissatisfaction is felt among the friends of the sick and some are bold enough to say if he had never employed a doctor, he would not be in the state he is. A council is held and I am sent for, not that they have any confidence in my scientific knowledge, but they consider me more as an agent of nature than the physicians. They employ me as the captain employs a mechanic to repair the bad effect of the breaches and strains.

When I come, I find by the man that his real trouble is in his mind. Believing himself to be in great danger, he sent for a doctor and told him his sufferings and the doctor, ignorant of his trouble, brought him into his present state. Here comes in my peculiar way of reasoning to make him see that what I say is true. Medical authority admit that symptoms indicate a disease and I know them to be wholly the effect of their belief and theory. So when I commence proving this truth, the aristocratic parties rally round disease with their various beliefs and opinions and oppose the course I take with every species of insult and contempt. This truth by which I correct the sick of their errors and cure their disease is hated by aristocracy, despised by freedom and laughed at by conservatism. Consequently, I am opposed by the whole world. I have said that every one contains the two opposite elements of tyranny and freedom. But few contain conservatism, for that is born of the other two and indicates a higher capacity. It can be changed and acted upon by wisdom, for it can reason and see sides to a question. Unlike the other two, it does not require physical force to control it. That is only necessary among the brutes who, containing only the two first, bring forth an inferior element which answers for conservatism but is not refined enough to receive science. Man is composed of five elements: tyranny and freedom which are not intelligent, conservatism which is capable of becoming a medium for intelligence, and science and wisdom which act upon conservatism to develop man.

Every person by his acts and reason shows which combination governs him. A man governed by aristocracy is governed by freedom, and his conservatism, containing more of the former than freedom, he will be set in his ways. He will give his opinion as truth and pretending to liberal thinking will bind himself with the fetters which he himself has forged. Such a man never reasons from principles but always from creed or party. He will have an excellent memory for his belief but no appreciation of principles. Neither can he understand a scientific man who reasons from the basis of wisdom and, independent of established opinions and facts, applies universal truths to all sorts of philosophy. For instance, the truth that all men are born free and equal, carried out by scientific reasoning regardless of human interests, would show that oppression lives in obstructing freedom. The mechanical powers, weight and velocity, are not capable themselves of intelligent action, but they work out a combined force which is the power to be used and guided by a wisdom superior to itself. A stream of water with no obstructions represents the natural undeveloped man or the brute. Now let it be obstructed. Then the element of freedom, backed by pressure, struggles till the obstruction is removed. The idea dead weight or blank acts as a stumbling block and when freedom or motion encounters it, one or the other must give way. Often both elements keep up an action till the obstacle in the way of freedom is overcome. This holds good in all revolutions and it has truly been said that revolutions never go backwards, for these antagonistic forces break down all opposition. They dissolve all matter, making it a simple element that can be condensed and dissolved by science.

In philosophy, the obstacles are in the questions discussed. Slavery is a stumbling block in the stream of progression. But the fountain of liberty will force the tide of public opinion through the wilderness of slavery till every obstacle in its way is overcome. Like the waters of the Mississippi, it will overflow the land of slavery and sweep away everything opposing it. This is the action of the primary principles of nature. Now parties are agitated by the stream of liberty. And as in the overflowing of a prairie, the fear of destruction rouses conservatism which seeks to stop the tide of progression or bank up the low places so that the stream, in flowing, shall not desolate the whole country. Differences of opinion naturally arise as to the aim and result of the revolution. Some, seeing nothing but ruin, run from fear. Others throw themselves recklessly into the gulf and are carried along by the stream of progression, while others try to dam up the fountain, not thinking the reaction will overflow the dry land. And when the floods pass upon the obstruction, the stream bursts out, overflows and destroys all the inhabitants which are slavish ideas. Then the water of freedom becomes calm, the storm is over and peace is restored. This is a representation of man as we see him. All nature is embraced in the working of these elements. The power that gives direction is another principle. When it comes from their uniform action, it acts in harmony with itself; but when guided by a superior power from God, it becomes the spirit of man. It then contains life and reason and herein commences the knowledge of man.

I have said that freedom is kept bound by tyranny. A war is the result, not that freedom makes war, but tyranny aims at oppressing freedom, and this brings out conservatism and introduces a higher power. Conservatism is not the higher power; it contains reason, but that is no part of it. It is a medium or middle ground where the higher and lower elements of man meet and show by reason their comparative force. Therefore, science enters but error always precedes it and misleads the mind. Conservatism never fights; it dislikes commotion and cries peace to the conflict of opposing parties. A person in whom conservatism is predominant is not impulsive but lukewarm. He is satisfied with himself, cares not for the liberty of others and knows not if he is oppressed. Conservatism aims at harmony and employs various inventions to obtain it. Hence, differences of opinion arise and parties spring up. One, sympathizing with the lower part of man, appeals to aristocracy, while the other, belonging to the higher element, appeals to science. Every person contains the arguments of both, so each party hoping to command the average opinions invents false issues to satisfy conservatism that it is right. This condition of things is well illustrated by the present rebellion. Freedom can never make war; otherwise it binds itself and ceases to be freedom. But aristocracy, which lives by oppressing, makes war that it may live and its life is its destruction. As freedom like heat expands, oppression seeks to subdue it. Therefore it requires more power which it uses like a garment to cover its iniquity. And when freedom grows and occupies more space, oppression tries to cover it with its mantle which is found to be too short.

Both now come into the domain of conservatism and aristocracy demands more territory that it may enlarge its bounds. Science opposes this and a fight takes place; then both parties set forth their arguments and issues to gain conservatism. Aristocracy assumes that slavery is a divine institution and its destruction will involve the downfall of governments and societies. The opposite party denies that freedom was ever intended to be governed by aristocracy. But instead of settling this principle, false issues spring up which give another direction to their arguments. Aristocracy says that Liberty commenced the war and they try to prove it in all they say. If they succeed in convincing conservatism that this is the case, then every kind of deception will be used to make the party obnoxious to the people. So that when the rebellion is ended, they shall rally on this idea and can convince the people who pay the taxes that their trouble was brought upon them by the liberal party. But if the rebellion is put down by those who understand the real cause of the war, this very party who commenced the war, the slavery party, who try so hard to shirk out of the responsibility, is dead as far as African slavery is concerned.

This same progress is carried out in man in the action of the medical theory. When a person is sick, the first thing done is to call a physician who, being of the aristocracy, is the ruling element which is slavery and he favors disease or rebellion. Having the fighting powers under his control, he employs them according to medical direction.

Now as freedom from the medical faculty is spreading, the government uses every means to crush any attempt to free man from this cursed tyrant disease which alone benefits the aristocracy and keeps the masses poor and sick to pay the taxes. New parties now come up who try to divide the people. Under them, many desert their masters and declare themselves independent of all medical power. Yet, though they have worked out their own freedom, they believe in disease for others. Now I introduce myself among the masses as having come out from all sects; therefore I am a target for all of them. Knowing my position, I do not, like those called reformers, destroy the law but I appeal to the intelligence of the sick without. I strike at its very root and I destroy the foundation of disease. I assume the position that disease is not a divine creation, that its origin is not in principles of justice, love or any of the attributes of God but that it is an invention of man in his error and, like all slavery, it is for the benefit of the aristocratic few. I also affirm that man was made free and subject to no arbitrary laws, but that he has bound himself and enslaved the masses. The sick like the masses are held in bondage by the aristocracy. Not only do they submit to the yoke and consent to be led blindfold, but they even kiss the hand that has defrauded them of their native rights.

To oppose this deception, I have to contend with great obstacles. In the first place, all men who believe in disease admit a belief that disease is a punishment sent from God upon those who disobey some law. Consequently, all those who undertake to live free from law are in danger of punishment. Disease is a great advocate for law when it does not prescribe restrictions on its power, just as those in favor of slavery believe in supporting the laws which seem to favor the rebellion. Law must be so framed that it will sustain slavery to gain their support. So it is with disease. All laws that uphold disease must be obeyed. When sitting by the sick, I am a complete abolitionist for I oppose all laws made to keep man well. This must seem to make one radical, but when understood, I am not so but rather a conservative. The radical breaks down all law and obligation, leaving the people without principle or reason and he wants to impose his belief on the world. To all such, I am opposed; then of course I am a radical.

Jesus opposed radicals of every kind and urged the people to sustain the laws, while he warned them not to believe in the doctrines. As I have said, I never destroy the law. I destroy its foundation as an arbitrary power and then it rests easily where otherwise it bound. I never tell a man that he imagines his sickness and only thinks himself diseased when really he is not. According to this very truth I am trying to explain, disease is what follows an opinion. And when a man says he has the heart disease or liver complaint, I do not deny it in one sense. I do not admit the disease and tell him he has not got it, but I affirm that the disease is in his belief and his belief is in error. If he says I believe I have the heart disease, then he tells what he really believes and his feelings are the literal proof of his belief. This is the only way I reconcile the truth which denies disease with its real existence. But to acknowledge disease and deny the symptoms is to contradict myself.

Men take medical opinions as something existing outside of the minds, where all opinions originate, as though diseases were independent things living by themselves. And doctors, admitting this, try to drive them away but not to destroy them. They do not believe in annihilation. I do believe in the total annihilation of the wicked or false opinions. Therefore, I oppose all religious and moral laws which oppress the masses. Would I destroy all law and obligation that keeps society together? By no means; I would go as far as any man to sustain the laws. Still I cannot believe them to be of God. And I will use all the means God has put into my power to expose hypocrisy and redeem man from the law, not by violence, but by teaching him the religion that will purify him from all errors so that he may live in scientific truth, believing only in one loving and true God who will render to everyone according to his acts. To show more clearly how I oppose all laws, I will describe the course I have to take with a patient who has been made to believe by the doctors that he has the heart disease. If the patient believes the doctor, he believes himself guilty of disobeying some law whose punishment in his case is imprisonment in heart disease. I come to him and by finding his prison know what he is accused of, for every man is imprisoned in his belief either under sentence or under suspicion of some offense.

I take the ground that God never made a belief. A belief is of man and is intended to satisfy him instead of true wisdom. If God ever spake, he spoke the truth which liberated men and bound him with no obligations. When man speaks, he always tells a lie; that is, in explaining a phenomenon, he imposes a belief and invents opinions which blind people to truth. Science is the voice of God, opinions that of man. So when man speaks in his own knowledge, he gives an opinion; but when he tells a truth, that is of God. Now man is under the law of men. And the Science of God having no place in him, he is condemned by his own laws, which are declared by those, wise in their own conceit, to be the laws of God, to oppose which is blasphemy. I do oppose them and sometimes I meet with great opposition, for my mode of treatment being entirely new, it is difficult to make myself understood. I do not work in a belief. I work on an element in man, susceptible to a wisdom that is invisible and unconscious to the natural man. To me, it contains the real man; it is the casket or prison of man's belief.

Our belief has two bodies: a natural and a spiritual one. I will use the same illustration in heart disease to bring them out. If the belief takes a visible form and if after the patient dies the heart is found enlarged, this proves that he was killed by a disease. But if on the other hand the examination shows the heart to be unchanged, then the verdict is he died of imagination. To me the disease is the same in both cases and it is a deception in either. We are affected more or less by a story which we hear, thinking we believe it. But if no effect follows our belief, it shows that we only admit it in our knowledge and do not form it in the mind. The mind which receives impressions from matter partakes of the earthly man, but it also receives impressions from the spiritual elements which cannot be seen by the natural man, nor are they acknowledged by him except as imagination. This is the condition of a person whom the world calls dead. The ideas of death, life and matter all die to the natural man when the body ceases to breathe, but to me that element that is acted upon by an unseen power contains man's senses which are transferred from the visible form. Every person is in this higher element where all the senses live, but their belief, like darkness, keeps them all their natural life in ignorance of it and in bondage through fear of death, for the element is completely under the control of our belief. If we believe in spirits, we can condense them into the form of our belief and this we take as proof that there are spirits and are affected accordingly. The medical faculty also by their belief act on it when attached to the body. They by their power over this medium condense their belief into a disease and show the form to prove the truth of their assertions.

The trouble lies in our ignorance of this invisible element of matter which is a medium for science to develop wisdom. As every idea of man emanates from the great fountain of wisdom, they are sown in this element like seed in the ground and come forth as the child of wisdom, whose mother material it clings to, as the plant clings to the mother earth, thinking that it contains life. This medium being the offspring of freedom and slavery, the child looks upon them as his parents and at first it is guided by the chemical action of these forces, but as it grows in the wisdom of God, it casts off the two earthly elements and puts on that of wisdom. This is not always done at death for it represents progression and that is not stayed by death. This element, I have before said, is what I work upon in the curing of disease, for disease is the disturbing of the three. Aristocracy being the father, freedom or the mother wishes to rid herself of oppression and thus comes the child in the element of conservatism and this mingles with the wisdom of God. All these represent a garden in which the child of science is placed to control the brutal force of the two first elements. So the war is carried on in the natural element but controlled by the higher.

Every person shows to the world the element which rules him by his acts to himself, in his belief. Freedom which is God-like in man, like heat, will melt down the cold hand of oppression which tries to bind it. Thus a constant chemical action between the two is kept up and this coming in contact with each, forms that state of conservative heat, not too hot nor too cold, but a condition like summer, ready to produce the fruits of Science, while the extremes of heat or cold are produced by false reasoning. This was the wilderness that Moses passed through on his journey from Egyptian darkness to the land of Science.

The natural element of man is freedom, but in his ignorant state, it is a condition of darkness, filled by its enemy tyranny with countless terrors and superstitions intended to frighten man into subjection. Of this early condition, every man is a representative inasmuch as he is in error and under the law. The land of error being common property, every one claims the right of exploring it. So some study opinions and others become the apostles of freedom. Man reasons from shadows and therefore sees everything reversed, so that his first premise which is that oppression is the first step in progression is false, for it is an element created by freedom. Freedom is motion and motion creates resistance, so that resistance to progression is a natural result, like reaction. Man in ignorance of this admits these two elements and tries to believe them intelligent and then to him progression becomes an enemy to oppression. By false reasoning, men have taken elements for knowledge and try to fight against them through their blindness. All reasoning is based upon the false foundation that progression is wrong and dangerous, and it must be kept in check by an aristocracy which thinks it has the power to say to the tide, Thus far shall thou go and no further. In opposition to this false mode of reasoning is freedom, which expanding into liberty creates an opposition that checks it till it contracts to a certain extent. Still, the fire of freedom burns in the bosom of men, saying to the iron hand of slavery, "Stay your course," which is the working of the two elements.

Light is liberty, darkness is slavery. The aristocratic mind chooses darkness rather than light because his thoughts are evil, while the scientific mind comes to the light to prove all things. They are like two hostile armies into which errors creep like spies. Conservatism is when they press against each other and into which corruption is thrown by the commotion of these two opposing forces. In this chaos or purgatory, all political refuse is found and here is where direction is given to both parties. Both claim to be friends to harmony, but by their acts, they are known. One class opposes progression while the other opposes aristocracy. Each is ignorant of the true issue which they oppose. One fights against God and Liberty, the other fights against that party. Liberty requires no fighting, it is universal; and like a consuming fire, it will burn up every root and stubble that is thrown in its way. Checking it only creates more force, like checking the power of steam while the fire is burning, it will burst out again with more force.

Let leaders and statesmen settle down on the fact that freedom is from a divine principle emanating from wisdom; then no monarch can say, Thus far shall thou go and no further, without being crushed. Then man learning wisdom will cease to fight against God. And he will lay down the weapons he has created to destroy himself. The false idea that to oppress is right and freedom wrong is the error which has caused all the wars since the world began. It has made disease popular. Error has become God, ignorance bliss and misery the common lot of all. It has spread all over the civilized world and wisdom alone can see that when the field of politics is swept by the fire of freedom, its wicked generation must end. Like foxes of old, the political leaders will run through the field of slavery, destroying their own subsistence. And seeing what they have done, they will desert their parties and flee into a foreign land. Their fields will pass into the hands of those who, having silenced the noise of the cannon, will turn their weapons into plowshares and will cultivate the ground in the name of the one living and true principle of progression.

To apply the foregoing to the curing of disease, it is necessary to introduce a character higher than the elements I have mentioned and one which they do not recognize. I call it a new mode of reasoning. It is the true and living wisdom of God manifested in this third susceptible element in man. Without father or mother, it is not born of slavery or freedom but exists from everlasting to everlasting without beginning or end. It has been likened unto the leaven that leaveneth the whole lump. It has been called the Messiah and the bread of life. David called it wisdom and prayed to it as the Good Shepherd. It is that which every scientific man worships. This character is in the world guiding the destinies of nations and individuals and they know it not. To bring it to the understanding of man is to establish the kingdom of heaven on earth and this causes all warfare, human and moral. Man's health and happiness depend on his knowledge of this character, which to him is a good shepherd. And his disease and misery come from his having fallen in with wolves who, fed by superstition, stand ready to kill the shepherd and devour the sheep. In other words, blind superstition stands ready to destroy every scientific truth as soon as it is born or believed.

To know how this character enters man's house or belief is to see its hypocrisy and craft in argument, its cunning in reason. Follow me into the sick room of any patient and there see this subtle enemy of mankind hissing and turning the countenances into every shape and exhibiting every kind of hypocrisy. It may all be honest for the devil may assume an angel's temper and he is as honest as men are towards the sick. Listen to these human devils advocating disease in religion, politics and medicine and see them loose their hold on man as I make war with them.

The first question I ask on entering a sick room is, Are you sick? The reply comes, not from the voice of wisdom but from the officer who holds the keys of life and death. Yes. He is very low and probably cannot stand it long, for his disease is of that character that it is past the power of man to heal. Only the Supreme Ruler can save him. This answer embodies the wisdom of its father the devil who has made all his children believe that disease was sent by God upon man to prepare him for a higher state. Having no respect for this hypocrisy, I open my batteries upon it and am answered by a shower of abuse, for the devil's philosophy has become as fashionable as secession at the South. It is said that I do not believe there is any disease, that I set myself at defiance with divine institutions and am opposed to the laws of God, and various other accusations are made. Disease is the altar of the medical faculty. The priests prophesize falsely, and the doctors bear rule by their craft; and the people, believing it right, love to have it so.

Now when power and truth are united together by a principle of peace, they rush to arms and a council is called. The sick are laid upon the altar as a sacrifice to their belief and they argue and pray to God that he will not permit error to flourish, also that he has shown his power and mercy in visiting the sufferer with disease so that he shall be prepared to enter the kingdom of heaven. Thus aristocracy is agreed that slavery is for the happiness of the slave and the patient is sacrificed by false priests. In the presence of the multitudes, the parties arise; freedom lights the fire and I listen to learn if, by their theory, the sacrifice can be offered and the patient saved. They reason and offer opinions and wait. But the fire of truth burns not and the victim lies wasting upon a bed while the scriptures are searched to prove that they are doing the will of God. Finally patience is exhausted and the sick one is given over to me; that is, the friends begin to put confidence in what I say. Now I commence to build my altar and the first stone laid is the truth that disease is the work of Satan. I then finish with the stones from their altar, stating that the patient is sick according to their belief. Then laying the patient on the altar to God, I cover him with the word or arguments and kindle the fire of truth or show the absurdity of their reason. Their voices cry out, Bind the leaders and cast them into prison that they shall no longer deceive the people. Thus Satan's kingdom is divided against itself. As man begins to reason from another starting point, different results are accomplished.

The false assertion that disease is in any way connected with God leads to slavery which is opposed to every good thing. Slavery in mind or matter is of Satan. Science will explain it so that man will free himself from the opinion of priest and doctor and will allow their laws to stand as a warning to all generations as they pass along through the world of progression. Then evil ideas which once stood as truth shall be as a valley of dry bones, hated by all who see them. This will be the fate of the leaders of all kinds of slavery who have deceived the people through falsehood. This truth, springing like a phoenix out of the ashes, has become a prince of peace and he will establish his kingdom in the hearts of men. Then the devil in the form of religious and medical teachers will make war on the principle of freedom. Every artifice will be used to set the minds against science and every false belief will be appealed to in order to make a successful false issue. For instance, certain political leaders say that if the North had done right, this rebellion might have been avoided. Beware of such reasoning. Remember that freedom never makes war but Aristocracy always begins a quarrel, for if the reverse was true, then man could do evil that good may come. But he who loves the truth says, Let God be true and every man a liar. In other words, admit that Science is true and opinions false and then no one can arrive at a truth by admitting an error. To acknowledge slavery right is to allow an error that good may come. If the leaders can only establish the idea that the liberal party began the war, then everything will be brought up to make the Republicans responsible for the war. But if the truth is established that freedom is the natural condition of the mind and to oppose it and make war against it is fighting against God and Science, then every person will be very cautious how they speak against an institution that has caused so much bloodshed. Then a death blow will be struck at its roots and all that is heard is the gnashing of its teeth in the agonies of death. Its friends scattered throughout all the civilized world as warnings to tyrants and it will become a byword and reproach among nations and here endeth African Slavery.

White slavery or disease must go through the same process to meet its doom. The weapons will be reason and the warfare will be carried on upon the platform of intelligence. Its opposers will say to the party in favor of freedom, Go on, the people are too ignorant to listen to the words of wisdom. We have such a hold on the minds that they think their theory is as solid as a rock. But when the wind of science blows upon it while they are eating and drinking or talking and preaching their error, the storm will come and they will be swept away down the streams of time into the gulf of despair. And like the swine, they will be swallowed up in the ocean of forgetfulness. Before this takes place, men will doubt reason and question. Opposition to the old faculty will spring up; different arguments will be used till the idea that medicine must be used to cure disease is exploded. Parties spring up opposing drugs but believing in disease, and finally this sin will be denied. Then it will be a question to settle, Who invented disease or began it? And beware how you admit that it is from God, for this doctrine will be urged on the people. Abide by the truth that man is the inventor of the disease as he is of African slavery.

1863

Errors of False Reasoning
[LC 2:1051]

All error arises from false reasoning. If man knew when a sensation was produced on the senses, his senses or knowledge would be prepared to receive it without fear; but being ignorant of it, he receives it sometimes as a sweet morsel that he rolls under his tongue till at last he finds to his sorrow that he is hugging a viper that will sting him to death. Now if mankind knew these enemies and how they came and got into their house or mind they would be on the look-out and their knowledge would be a protector. But the wisdom of the world has set up a standard superior to the wisdom of God and supposes its opinions must be taken for truth without any doubts or questioning. This standard is based on the old superstition that went hand in hand with all other superstitions. Science has been ridding the world of its errors, but the science of life is in the hands of the most ignorant class of persons the world can produce, who undertake to be the teachers of a science that they know nothing of. How long would the world suffer a chemist to blow up every person venturing to stand by to see him produce a phenomenon, by which the world would be put in possession of some scientific truth and then hear him explain that it is a scientific experiment governed by the laws of chemistry, the effect being just what he knew before it took place? It strikes me that he would be put in prison for malpractice, but you stand by and see a physician do the same thing and think it all right.

For instance a physician, from his theory which is based on the lowest grade of ignorance and superstition, produces a chemical change in your friend and blows him up or kills him from his science, and your friend gives him the credit of being a scientific man. Now to kill a person by the theory or science of the faculty is one of the easiest things in the world. It is as easy as to take a vessel lying at a wharf in Portland and going on board of her in the dark, undertake to pilot her out of the harbor where you have never been yourself but have seen someone go in fair weather, and as you have the name of a pilot, to pilot man's soul to the other world. The Captain invites you to pilot his vessel, so you get the vessel underway and in a short time are right among the ledges. If it lightens up and you see there is no change for escape, you show your science by letting the vessel have her own way; if the current and tides carry her clear, you deserve a medal for your knowledge. And if she is lost, you get the credit of showing great skill in not getting lost before or in avoiding a worse place.

So it is with the doctor. He is called to see a patient who is a little nervous, is in the dark or rather afraid of going out. So this blind guide, called doctor or pilot, undertakes to pilot him through the valley of death and land him safely on the shores of health. The Captain or patient gives up the helm to this blind pilot, who shows his chart and points out the dangers of the coast. The Captain is now in a very nervous state, for he thinks he is deceived. He thought there was not much trouble but he finds by the pilot that he has been blown away by the breath of superstition and ignorance into the gulf of death where he is a stranger. So he and all his friends or crew give up to this blind guide because he shows his chart of the coast. Now the Captain is nervous and wants to know all the dangers, so the pilot sits down and commences giving a scientific account of all the rocks and quicksands and shoals–not forgetting to tell how many had been lost on the coast. He shows how the wind and tides vary sometimes. You think that you are clear and in the next minute a flash of heat strikes you on the cheek. This is called hectic and it is always an indication of a shoal called consumption. Then comes a crackling sound called cough. This shows that the tide of life is nearly on the turn. Now comes the science–if the tide is rising, the wind is fair and nothing happens, you will go clear. But if the tide is ebbing and the wind is rising, it is not certain how it will come out. As it is, it is not worthwhile to rack the hulk any more by pumping her life out. So make the helm fast and wait for Nature to do her work. So all acts are suspended, waiting for the tide of life to carry her clear. And if by chance you come into the river of life, you are lucky.

Then this false guide, who has been the means of all this trouble, comes forward on deck and speaks in the language of his science. "I have piloted a great many persons before but you have had the narrowest escape I ever saw. And if I had not been on the look-out, you and all hands must have been lost." But one old tar who has been posted up in this kind of knowledge, based on superstition, sees into the imposition and shows that the pilot has not shown one sign of scientific knowledge. Now he gets the credit of a great deal of science and receives all their thanks. This is a fair illustration of the medical practice. It is based on ignorance and not one single fact is explained by their theory. Phenomena are produced. So they are by the spiritualists. Both theories produce phenomena, but the world is none the wiser, for they establish an error for a truth and mankind has to suffer for their explanation. Their theory makes disease and mine cures it, so we are just in opposition to each other. I know how they get the world into trouble and they don't. By means of their belief, they kill more by trying to get them out of their trouble than by getting them into it, for they don't save any. But if they let them alone, the sick sometimes get well of themselves.

Now put man in possession of a science that will teach him that thought is matter, governed by another power, and also that his own belief is the cause of his trouble, and to correct his belief is his cure. Then he will see that he cannot become the dupe of such persons as he is now. It would teach him that there are two ways of doing everything in regard to disease. There is a way of making disease and also a way of unmaking it. The science of this world is to make disease and the science of truth is to destroy it. One is the science of an opinion and superstition and the other is the SCIENCE OF TRUTH.

May 1860

Eternal Principles of Truth, The*
[Originally untitled.] [BU 3:0661]

What evidence is there in popular belief by which Dr. Quimby can establish a science of curing disease without medicine? What is there in his belief that is common in the world, and what fact in man's life does he find to substantiate his belief?

Dr. Quimby's theory is the result of researches into the causes and mystery of disease, carried out in his mode of cure. This is merely the knowledge of the patient's trouble and the knowledge of what works through him to cure that trouble, therefore his cures are not the effect of accident nor a stroke in the dark, but they are the works of a system of belief, based upon eternal principles of truth.

These principles are what underlie and all improvement and progress, but they never have been embodied in language of their own, so they have been made use of by minds who want to lead public opinion, and interweave these principles of honor and goodness into their own selfish inventions, in order to carry the intelligent and enlightened classes. Therefore to say that knowledge and good will to man, are at the bottom of Dr. Quimby's theory, is merely saying what can be claimed by any theory invented by man for a selfish purpose. When a science is discovered, the motive of the discoverer must of course be disinterested in his desire to make it known to the people and whether successful or not in his object undertaking of making it known he stands towards the world beyond the imputation of vanity or selfishness. Dr. Quimby claims that his mode of curing disease is strictly applying the principles of charity and sympathy to the sick in their desire to get well, and that this leads him in the path where he sees the patient separated from the sickness, and the error by which they are bound in disease. The same light which enables him to see the suffering as an error enables him also to correct that error and leave the patient free. So it may be said that his theory is carrying out the principles of goodness, love and etc. which all mankind believe in, towards destroying the things that make men wretched and sick. He meets men on a common and a high ground of belief and differs from them in the fact that he carries into practice the principles which he professes, while the rest of mankind adjust them in the form of a belief and carry into daily practice motives and principles which are quite the reverse of what they say they believe. So when he comes to the sick, he is an incomprehensible enigma and breaks up every idea of justice and goodness which they have in their daily intercourse with the world, and declares that they are false and ought to be destroyed. For instance, take a person who has been sick a long time and who has no immediate prospect of recovery. One of the features of her sickness must be produced by what has often been told her, that she must trust in Providence and be resigned to her suffering and that she will undoubtedly recover if such be the Lord's will. So the poor girl lives on such food, and is doctored accordingly. Now such a belief to Dr. Quimby is not merely nonsense, it is a wicked perversion of faith, and keeps a person sick and while the friends stand back waiting for the coming of the Lord. All the world do this more or less and he has to contend with this error in his practice. He does not believe in a God that orders such service and foolish actions and he never leaves for Providence to do what man can be instrumental in accomplishing.

If all wisdom, all truth and all knowledge could be embodied in a power of itself, that would act upon mankind, like Christianity or civilization, it is easy to see that its mission would be to destroy all wickedness, sin and error that affect the human race. If it was not understood it would be a miracle, but if it was introduced as an intelligence, it would become a science, and man would have his destiny in his own hands, and would recognize the source as the fountain of all wisdom. Deep in every thinking mind there lies buried, under all the rubbish of opinions which education has piled up in stores of learning, the belief of a something which will wash away all sin and purify the heart of man. This acts upon all men and makes the sick keep constantly seeking for help and when they know as it were, that they are beyond all human aid, often they cling to a hope, with an insane tenacity to their friends that something will restore their health. This is a well known fact and common in all cases of sickness, and this is the evidence that mankind admit, if they do not believe in a living truth which can heal diseases. Here is where Dr. Quimby meets the world carrying into practice towards the sick the wisdom that heals all who ask, and is scientific and disinterested in revealing this truth which destroys error.

It may be asked, why is not Dr. Quimby received with this new light and why does he not cure all who come. Precisely because his process is a science and cannot flatter or seek favor from the world, and because mankind are taught to sit still and do nothing and wait for the coming of the truth, so they are often more attached to their opinions than they are desirous to get well in their reason, and when such is the case he cannot labor to any effect.

Evidence of Sight, The
[BU 3:1021]

I have tried to illustrate how we are deceived by the idea that wisdom based on the sight of the natural eye is no stronger proof than what we believe from the evidence through our other senses. Now this mistake causes our trouble, for everything that we admit exists that can be changed suddenly or gradually, when it is out of sight, the evidence of its existence diminishes just according to circumstances or evidence.

I will illustrate. Suppose A and B see a person in a certain place. A leaves one moment before B and A and B are sitting in an adjoining room. As A left the room where the stranger sat before B, when A and B are in their room the evidence of the stranger being gone to A may depend on what B says. So as A left before B, B may deceive A because B left last. But suppose they don't agree. A says the stranger must be in the room, for he had just sat down to eat and according to the natural time of eating he must be there. So they argue and B tries to convince A.

Now suppose a stranger is seen approaching the house and walks directly up to your door and enters and you know that he knows nothing of what you are disputing about and you say to the stranger I wish to ask you a question as to the strength of evidence or testimony. The stranger feels the point in dispute and says I know what you are disputing about. B says, What is it? (S) You are disputing about a man you can't see. How do you know says A? (S) Because I see the man eating supper in the dining room. (A) Can you describe the man? So the stranger gives a description of the person and tells everything connected with him which A and B know. Now is not this stronger evidence to A than B gave him?

Then comes the question, how the stranger sees and he convinces you that partition to his sight is no obstruction. So belief is a partition between true sight and error. What a man sees with his eyes to him is light and what a man sees through a belief is not positive. Now this is the way with the sick. They see through a glass or partition or belief that is not certain and the doctor sees through the same medium, so that the patient and doctor stand in relation to each other as A and B reasoning about a man in the form or idea, pain, that exists in the dark.

The doctor has no idea of the stranger only as the patient describes him so the patient commences by telling how he appears, and he affects the side and he goes on to describe, the doctor being more ignorant than the patient but by his impudence and brass, pretends to tell who it is and where it is, in this or that room, either the heart or lungs or pleura, etc.

Now if the patient believes, the belief makes him nervous and a result follows and this is shown as the person that the doctor had described. This is called disease. I come to the patient after the doctor leaves and I see the doctor's ideas on the patient and I see how they have affected him and I say to him, You have been told that this stranger that the doctor has described, which is not anything but his mere opinion imagination is so and so and you received it as truth and the effect that follows is the natural result of the deception. Now until man finds the real point to reason from, he is not safe from all errors and superstitions that may be heaped upon him.

We are too apt to believe our senses and not believe our sight. Now sight being the stronger sense we often get deceived by belief and take belief for sight. A man's senses is his judgment and what looks clear he receives as true. Now light may come from truth or error so the light of the body is the eye and if the light is single and confined to the idea, then it is light or true. But if the eye or light is darkened by an obstruction or an opinion, then the body is full of doubt or darkness.

Now I see these difficulties in every patient I sit with and I see how they are deceived and cannot see the deception. And it is the hardest task I ever performed to convince them how they are deceived. They think because they feel so and so that they must have this or that disease.

Now the same error exists with the spiritualists. They see or hear something that they cannot account for and of course it must be the spirits and when disputed they say, If it is not spirits, what is it? Now the idea spirit, like the idea disease has become a part of our very being. And the ideas are as real as our existence, so that at any excitement that comes upon us we are ready to create a spirit or disease, just according to the pattern given. And the spirit mediums and doctors are just alike. Each deceives the masses by their beliefs and creates diseases the same as spiritual phenomena.

Now it all arises from our belief in some invisible world that no one ever saw with scientific eyes but we have been educated into a sort of superstitious belief and have settled down to a reality that certain things exist. And because we see and hear certain groans and sounds and pains and phenomena that we can't account for, therefore they must be disease or spirits.

Now convince man or educate him up to the point of science so that he can see that all men's bodies are as mortar or clay and any phenomena he is able to understand he will create, if excited by fear. Then he will see that it is for every person's happiness to test every teacher about what he knows, not take his opinion.

Let me give you a rule by which you can test a doctor and I will not give you a rule that I am not willing to be tested by. Suppose you feel a little out of sorts and call a physician. When he comes, say to him, I have sent for you to tell me what is my trouble. This is the way Nebuchadnezzar did; he had magicians or doctors, only he called his disease a dream. His magicians said, Tell me your symptoms or dream and I will give you the interpretation of it. Just as the physicians say, Tell me how you feel and I will give you the interpretation of disease. Now be as wise as Nebuchadnezzar and say, My dreams or feelings have departed but tell me how I felt. This they could not do any more than the magicians could so they will answer as they did, You ask too much; there is no one that asks the doctor to tell them their symptoms. The time had arrived when the wisest men had learned that a man's opinion is not to be relied on as a truth. So when Nebuchadnezzar made war, he ordered his officers to bring of the wisest men of the nation that were well versed in science and in language so they might teach him the Chaldean tongue. Now Daniel was one of the wise men and when Nebuchadnezzar became sick and alarmed, like a dream, he had no confidence in his magicians or sorcerers and he took this way to tell them. So when he wished them to tell his symptoms or dream they could not do it so he passed a decree.

Lawrence, July 15, 1865

[A notation is made at the end of this article: "The last piece written by the author."–Ed.]

Experience of a Patient with Dr. Quimby
[LC 2:0716]

For many years I was very sick, and finding no benefit resulting from the various modes of cure that I had employed, I thought of visiting Dr. Quimby. So I inquired of some friends in regard to his treatment. Some said he was a spiritualist and others that he was a mesmerizer, and others said he made war on all religious beliefs. And as I could not see what my belief had to do with my disease, I gave up the idea of going to see him. But finally I was brought to the subject again through utter hopelessness and despair of recovery, so I went to see him.

In my first interview I asked him if he could cure the spinal disease. He answered that he never wished a patient to tell him his feelings. "Very well" said I, "what do you want me to do?" "Nothing," said he, "but listen to what I say." I then asked him if he gave medicine. "No." "Do you employ any agent from the world of spirits?" "No," said he. "Then," said I, "it must be mesmerism." He replied, "that may be your opinion but it is not the truth." "Then will you please to tell me what you call your way of curing?" He said he had no name. "Well," said I, "is it original with you?" He said he never knew anyone who cured as he did. "Can you give me some idea how you cure?" He said, "it would be very hard to convince a person how he felt unless I feel myself." "Yes," I said, "it would be hard for you to tell my feelings."

"Well," said he, "if I tell you how you feel will you admit it?" "Certainly, but how do you cure?" He answered, "I will illustrate one thing. Do you believe the Bible?" "Certainly," I said. "When Jesus said to his disciples `a little while I am with you, then I go my way and you shall seek me. Where I go you cannot come.' What did He mean by the passage?" "I suppose he spoke of the crucifixion." "Then you think," said he, "that Jesus alluded to another world when he said `If you loved me you would rejoice that I go to the Father..... Again, he said, `I go to prepare a place for you and if I go and prepare a place for you I will come again and receive you unto myself, that where I am there ye may be also.' In another place he says, `If I go not away, the Comforter will not come unto you, but if I depart I will send him to you.' Now I suppose you think all this refers to another world?" I said, "Yes."

"Well," said he, "now I will sit down and see if I can tell your feelings." He then sat down and took my hand and soon passed his hand on one of the vertebrae of my spine and said, "You have a very sharp pain in the vertebrae at this time." I said I had. Then he placed his hand on the left temple and said, "You have a very bad pain here and it affects the sight of your left eye." I then told him he was right. I asked him if one eye was affected more than the other. He said, Yes, he felt no pain in the right eye. I then told him he was right. "Now," said he, "I will explain how I cure."

"Will you admit that Jesus took upon himself our infirmities?" I said, "yes." "Have I not taken your pain in the spine, also in the temples and eyes?" "Yes," I said. "I will now explain those passages which I have mentioned. My theory is that disease is the invention of man, a burden bound on the people, laid on their shoulders, grievous to be borne; that man has been deceived, led away and is unable to get back to health and happiness; that Jesus' mission was to break the bands that bound the sick and restore them to health and happiness. In order to do this he had to find them, for they had wandered away like sheep without a shepherd. So he took their aches and pains to show them he was with them and knew how they felt and said, `Come unto me all you who are heavy laden and I will give you rest.' "

I said, "You seem to talk a great deal about the Bible. I came here to be cured and not to have my religion destroyed." He answered, "Have I said anything about religion?" "No, but I cannot see why you quote the Bible." "I will tell you," said he. "You admit I took your feelings?" "Yes." "Well, I want to convince that when I take your feelings I am with you, not myself as a man, but this great truth which I call Christ or God." "What do you mean by that? That you are equal with Christ?" "What do you mean by Christ?" he asked. "I mean Jesus." "Then Jesus and Christ are one?" "Yes." "Then," said he, "how is Jesus God?" "God manifest in the flesh," I replied. He asked, "What do you mean by God manifest in the flesh?" "That God took upon Himself flesh and blood to convince man of His power and save man from an endless eternity of misery." "Can God exist outside of matter?" he asked. I answered "Yes." "Is there anything of man that exists when God is out of him?" "Yes," said I, "flesh and blood." "Then flesh and blood is something of itself?" "Yes." "What do you call that, the natural man?" "Yes." "This Jesus would be the natural man of flesh and blood and Christ the God manifested in the man Jesus?" I said, "Yes, I think so." "Well," said he, "that is just what I want to prove to you, that the Christ is the God in us all. Do you deny that you have a particle of God in you?" "No, I believe it," I said.

"Then we do not disagree in this. I want to make you understand that this Christ or God in us is the same that is in Jesus, only in a greater degree in him like this: You teach music?" "Yes," I said. "Do your pupils know as much about the science of music as you do?" "No, if they did I could not teach them." "Then you have the science more than they?" "Yes." "They have some?" "Yes." "What they know is science? Is it not equal to the same amount in you?" "Yes," I said. "Then if one of your pupils should say I understand the science of music, it is to be understood that he is equal to you?" "No." "Well, so it is with me," said he. "When I say that by this great truth I cast out error, or in other words correct your opinion and free you from that curse of all evils, disease, I do not mean to say that P. P. Quimby is equal to the man Jesus or equal to his wisdom or Christ, but merely admit that I recognize the great principle in man of God as a separate and distinct person.

"While I am explaining this Christ I will give you the trinity that I believe in, that is P. P. Quimby's trinity, not that P.P.Q. is the trinity but that P.P.Q. believes it. He believes in one living and true wisdom called God, in Jesus (flesh and blood) a medium of this truth, and in the Holy Ghost or explanation of God to man. Here is my trinity and the Holy Ghost is the Science that will lead you into all truth. It will break the band of error and triumph over the opinion of the world. This Holy Ghost is what is with your Christ that your fleshly man knows not of; this is the Christ in you that has been cast into prison since you were first sick; it is the Christ that Jesus speaks of that preached to the prisoners long before the flood. This same Christ was crucified at the death of Jesus and laid in the tomb of Joseph's new doctrines, not with the body of Jesus. The Jews crucified Christ by their false religion and the masses crucified the man Jesus, so Christ in the tomb of every true disciple had the Christ lying in his breast crucified to the world of opinions. This Christ is the one that Jesus spoke of, not of the flesh and blood that the people saw by their natural eyes. So all the truth that came through the man Jesus was Christ and it was the garment of Jesus, so Jesus was clothed with the gospel or wisdom of God. When the error murdered the man Jesus, they stole the body of Christ and parted his garments of wisdom among them, while the people believed that the flesh and blood that was laid in the tomb was the one that they heard, when it was nothing but the medium of the one whom they never saw, only as a mystery. This same Christ rose again and is still in the world of matter reconciling the world of error to the science of God.

"I will now commence anew to preach Christ to you to cure you of your errors or disease and bring you into this living truth that will set you free from the evils of man's opinions that bind burdens upon you in the form of disease. So when I say I am with you, I mean this Christ or truth, not P. P. Quimby as a man.

I have acknowledged it as my leader and master. So when I speak of it, I speak of it as a wisdom superior to P.P.Q.'s, and you have the same Christ in you confined by the errors of this world. So I will now sit down by you again and listen to your groans, for I feel the pain of the bands that bind you across the chest." Do you feel the pains I have in my chest? I asked. "Yes," said he. "Now this that feels is not P. P. Quimby but the Christ, and that which complains is not Mrs. P. but the Christ in Mrs. P. struggling to roll the stone from the sepulchre of her tomb, to rise from the dead or error into the living God or Wisdom. You see that I, that is, this Wisdom, makes a sick man two, a man beside himself and the servant above his master. When the master is acknowledged, the servant is not known, no more than an error is known when the truth comes. I will show my meaning by an illustration. If you believe your lungs are diseased, the servant or belief is the master, and Wisdom, the true master, becomes the servant; but when the Lord of the vineyard comes, then the wicked servant is cast out and another is put in his place that will render to his Lord his dues. So when I, this truth, shall convince the error of its wrong, it cannot stand the fire of truth, so it will submit to Wisdom; then truth will resume its sway and health and happiness will be the result. Your disease is the result of your belief and to change your belief is to convince you of an error that binds you and the pains and depleted state of mind are the natural results of your punishment. Truth never binds or separates one truth from another, and all belief that has a tendency to separate us is error and makes unhappiness. Error always tries to separate one from another.

"I will illustrate. Suppose you are my child and you become sick as you are now; according to the religious belief, we must separate and perhaps at some future time we shall meet again in that world whence no traveller ever returned. The chances according to your own and your friends' belief are that you are bound for that world of spirits. Suppose I believe, as you and the rest of the religious world, what must be my feelings when I see you hastening to that world whence no traveller returns and how must you feel, knowing that you are about to be snatched from the bosom of your friends to enter that dark and dismal grave, with only the hope of a resurrection from the dead and that based on a belief. Is not that enough to rock the very foundation of your building and make the walls of your belief tremble even to the foundation? To me this is a horrid belief.

"Now this is your true state, standing trembling between hope and fear, holding back through fear and clinging to your friends, while the nearest and dearest of them are trying to drive you off through their blind faith. Suppose you are a parent and your only son should be pressed into the army. And your neighbors who have sons should come round and console you by saying he would be better off for going even if he should die fighting for his country, should you feel happy to part with him? Must not the separation be almost enough to break your heart? Then your husband is called upon and now your cup is filled to overflowing. Can all this happen without a sunken eye, a pale and hollow cheek with hectic flush, a purple lip, and nervous cough? In all this the chances are not one out of fifty that they will not both return to cheer you up in your last moments when your life is almost run out. In all this your spirits mingle as though you were only separated like other friends, but when they die, according to our belief, the thread that binds us is severed by the knife that cuts our life and our souls launch into the world of our belief. Which is worse? To go through either is bad enough, but I believe the religious belief is worse. The religious belief prepares the mind for the medical belief; one is based on old superstitions; this gets the mind worked up like mortar; then the potter or doctor molds the mind into disease. I have no sympathy with either. Science knows no such beliefs; Science never separates, it is from everlasting to everlasting, it has no beginning nor end. The man of science is the child of God and error is its servant. So in every person these two characters are shown.

"I will now return to you again as my child to convince you that although your eyes are sunken and your cheek hectic, your pains and trouble are all in your false ideas of yourself. We are all a part and parcel of each other, that is, in our wisdom or that life eternal which cannot be severed, but our beliefs may hold it in bondage. Now as you sit and listen, suppose you grow quiet and pass into that happy state of mind where you meet your husband and son, talk with them about the war and learn from them that they find it rather a hard life, but they will not return till the rebellion is crushed. On the whole you are satisfied that they are better off so far as their situation is concerned than you thought for. Would you not feel relieved? I know you would. While you are in this state, suppose you believed you were dying and your friends were weeping around you for the last time and you could not speak. Which do you think would have the most reviving effect on you when you awoke? You need not answer. Now, my belief is this: Wisdom never separates you from me but makes us a part of each other in Wisdom, for what I feel I know, and what I do not know I cannot feel. To believe my child is separate and apart from me is a horrid belief to us both, but to know

God cannot be divided is to know that we cannot be separated from our Heavenly Father. The error is only held together by opinions that can deceive, but Science is eternal life. This is in all mankind and is progression; it knows no death nor separation. To know this is more than the religious world ever had. This was the doctrine of Jesus. Christ is the child of this wisdom and this is what I am trying to get into your mind like the little leaven that leaveneth the whole lump. If this is infidel doctrine, then P. P. Quimby is an infidel; but I would rather part with everything on earth than part with this Truth which is my shepherd that leadeth me through the dark valley of the shadow of death, and lodges me where no belief or opinion can give me one drop of water to cool my tongue when tormented by religious belief."

October 1862

Experiences in Healing, Spiritualism and Mesmerism

[Originally untitled.] [BU 3:0283]

Man, as we see him, is not to be compared to a clock, as he sometimes is for various reasons. In the arrangement of a clock the motive power is the weight and all the results are governed by a train of wheels and pinions regulated by a pendulum, and accordingly as this pendulum is altered, the time must vary. Now, if there is no motive power in man except that which is the result of an organized brain, then the comparison would be of some force. But no one supposes that an eight-day clock is under the influence of any person, after it has been wound up until it has run down. Is anyone prepared to say the same of man? I think not. All will admit that man cannot move or breathe without the aid of what is called mind. Now if this power is not the result of an organized brain, it must be a power that is not dependent on the brain for its existence.

There is no doubt that the theory of the practice of medicine was founded on the idea that mind is the result of an organized brain, and therefore that mind and matter are the same. This is an error that will someday be corrected, for it leads man to bad results; it keeps him ignorant of himself and also of the power that governs him. Now let man believe that he (that is, his mind) is not the offspring of an organized brain and in a short time a different state of society will be seen.

Is the person that plays the pianoforte or harp a part of the instrument? If there is any tune produced from the instrument, it must be by a power independent of itself. So it is with man. If man's body never moved till the power to do so was created within itself, it would never move. I believe the body may be compared to an instrument, ready to be operated upon by any person who has the power of applying their mind to other persons than themselves, in the same way as a person conveys his ideas of music on an instrument. For instance, if an instrument is out of tune, one would not call on a person to tune it who had no ear for music, from the fact that he could not tell where the disorder was. If the instrument was well, or in tune, it would need no physician, or tuner. So it is with man; when well, he needs no sympathy or physician; but the sick need this sympathy which is a relief to their mind, of which a well person knows nothing.

The tones of a musical instrument may be compared to the mind. When I speak of mind, I do not mean ideas. Ideas are the results of the mind, used to convey any fact to another. Like the strings of a musical instrument, both are matter acted upon by the mind. It requires a person who has an ear for music to convey ideas of tunes to another. So it is with the mind; when a person's mind is at rest, all is well, but if the mind is disturbed through an injury done to the body or by any other cause, it uses the body to convey the fact to others. These discords are what are called diseases. This is the state of a person when he is in want of this sympathy. These discords in a person are as easily detected by some as the discords in music are by a professional musician, and there are persons who are as easily affected by the discords of the sick as there are those who are disturbed by the discords of music.

When I speak of discords in man, I mean disease. These disorders are the results of a chemical change in the fluids of the system, brought about by the action of the mind. These discords are sometimes brought about instantly and may be corrected as suddenly. It may be necessary to give some proof that the fluids are changed suddenly. Before I bring any proof, I wish it to be distinctly understood that it is my belief that I can change the fluids of another person in an instant, from a diseased to a healthy state. I do not mean every person, and I feel the discords as sensibly as a person feels the discords in music and use the same means to correct them. To prove the above statement I will take the case of the woman who was healed by the touch of Christ's garment. The woman believed that if she could touch the hem of Christ's garment, she should be made whole. Now to produce a cure it was necessary that a change should be produced in the system and to produce this change it was necessary to change the mind to correct the discord. Christ, being very susceptible of this power, felt the slightest discord in any person and, as quick to correct as to detect, was always ready to sympathize with the sick. When the woman touched him, he was disturbed by the discord and being well corrected the discord instantly, without any thought. When the discord passed off, he said to his disciples, Somebody hath touched me for I perceive that virtue hath gone out of me (Luke 8:46). Thus the fluids were changed in an instant and the disease was cured. I introduce this case to prove that the same power was used to cure disease then as now.

See the cures performed by the seventh son. No one will deny that some cures have been performed by the touch of the hand; but the idea that there was any more power in the seventh son than in any other person is all folly. The fact of a person's being the seventh son may lead him to give his attention to some particular class of diseases and may acquire the power of correcting the mind in those diseases, the same as a child may acquire the power of imitating a bird. Either power may be improved if the attention is devoted to the subject. Some persons suppose this power is a gift from God and that the one who has it must be superior to other men. I never heard that a man who was a professional musician was superior to any other person, but they are generally looked upon as being rather inferior, as they generally give their attention to the study of music and entirely neglect all other branches. So it is with the cure of diseases by sympathy. If a man is entitled to any credit, it is for discovering the principles on which the mind acts, rather than for the power that is given him.

I shall give some of my own and also others' experiments to show on what I base my opinion of the fluids changing instantly, so as to produce a derangement of the system. I have sat down by a person and taken them by the hand, have had what is called canker come in my mouth almost immediately, and on inquiring if they had the same, have found it so in every case. I was once operating on a lady who had a trouble in her head, as she thought, and in a short time I tasted snuff and also smelt it. I said to the lady, "Have you been taking snuff for your head?" She replied, "No, I never use snuff." I said, "I certainly taste snuff and you must have taken it and forgotten it." She was rather surprised at my remarks and sat for a few moments in silence, then she said, "About three weeks ago, I was directed by my physician to try snuff for my head; I took one pinch and as I felt no effect from it, I took no more." In a few moments she laughed and said she tasted the snuff for the first time.

All persons who ever tried any experiments in mesmerism know that the subject is very sensitive and will taste or smell what the mesmerizer does. Now this is done by changing the fluids of the system. The fluids equalize in the mesmerizer and the mesmerized and their taste is as one, precisely as two instruments are brought to accord with one another by the performer. On this principle, diseases are conveyed from one to another. Now, as these fluids are under the control of the mind, it is very necessary that a person should know how to govern them so that they shall not get the mastery of the mind and bring the person into the same state St. Paul was in when he said that the spirit warreth against the flesh.

When the fluids of the system are in a certain state, they produce an effect in the mind and the mind is disturbed and loses its control over the body to that degree that persons think they are under the influence of the Devil, and they manufacture ideas out of the fluids and talk to the beings of their own creation, as one man talks to another.

I was called to see a person who was sick and had been confined to his room for nine months and had kept his bed for most of that time. I knew nothing of his trouble when I went to see him. It was evening when I arrived at his house. I was conducted to his room by his wife. On entering his room, the effect on my system was like an electrical shock. I seemed to be paralyzed. On recovering my mind, I went to the bed where the sick man was lying, looked him in the eye for a minute or two and then asked him why he was lying there. He replied that he could not sit up. I then said, "You have no disease; it is your mind that is in trouble and those devils that were here when I entered made a spring at you, frightened you and then left the room—they are now standing outdoors by those trees." He looked me in the eye for an instant, and then said, "They frightened you, too, a little. They have taken hold of my collar and laid me on the bed!" I told him to get up, for they would not come back while I was there. He rose up and sat on the side of the bed. Withdrawing my mind from him for a moment to speak to his wife, he sprang back into bed immediately in great alarm exclaiming, "They have come back again!" I again directed my mind to him.

Then he got up and went into the sitting room and appeared as well as any person, except at such times as my mind was drawn away from him, when he would start for his room, apparently in alarm.

To restore this man to what he called health, it was necessary to destroy the devils his own mind had created. To do this it was necessary to restore the fluids of his system to harmony. This I did by a principle as well understood by me as the process of tuning a musical instrument is by a musician. The man was not troubled any more by these devils, but the fluids in my system were so changed that these images followed me on my way home, more than two miles, before I could drive them from my mind. They then left me, like an object going from another in the twilight, till they were out of sight. My mind was then at rest, as it was before.

I have been affected by persons to that degree as not to be able to stand it for a short time. I was attending a person who was subject to fits. At the time of one of my visits she was in convulsions. As soon as these ceased I felt a singular sensation in my head and to all intents and purposes was about to have a fit, myself. A lady took me by the arm and sat me in a chair and then sent for my son. He rubbed my head and in short time I felt better. He carried me to my house and for four or five hours I was not able to leave my bed and did not get over the shock for all day. This person after waking from sleep would often have a fit and therefore had been afraid to go to sleep. The shock was such as to change the fluids of my system so as to affect my mind to that extent that I was almost afraid to go to sleep for fear I should have a fit, and I have since declined to attend persons subject to them.

I could give hundreds of cases to prove that the fluids change instantly and this is the reason for so many miraculous cures ever since the world began. I will give another case. I went to see a person who was blind, as he said. His eyes were bandaged up with two or three handkerchiefs and the room he occupied was so dark, it was with difficulty I could see his face. When I sat down by him, I felt a sensation I cannot describe (which jarred on my system like discords in music) which I had to correct. When this sensation had lulled away, I felt as if the man could see. I loosened the bandage wherewith his eyes were bound and commanded him saying, Arise, go ye to the door of thy dwelling and behold thou shalt see. And straightway he arose and did so and the sun shone out of the firmament into his eyes and he looked about him and behold, he could see. And it was good. He has had his sight ever since then.

I have cured persons of lameness in a very few moments, and I am as well satisfied that there is a principle or law by which the fluids are changed as I am that there is a law or power by which a musical instrument may be put in tune. This law of the fluids changing was known by the ancients. Galen speaks of the ancient Indian medical men, believing that incantation and adjuration is an aid; while the ancient Grecian physicians thought by these to recall into the wandering soul its own perfection. He seems himself to adopt this explanation: "As the fluids of the body, being changed, change the action of the mind, so the action of the mind, being changed, changes the fluids."

The fluids are undergoing a change all the time, but the effect on the body depends very much on the state of the mind. For instance, if man was perfectly happy or well, he would be free from pain, for pain is the result of ignorance or sin, as it is called in the Bible. But man cannot be perfectly happy or well while he is arriving at the truth, any more than gold can be pure while in the ore. Chemical changes must take place to purify both. Gold and truth are mixed with dross and error through which both have to work their way. This change of fluids is a decomposition of the body. As this decomposition is going on all the time, it keeps the mind in agitation, like two persons in dispute or argument upon some important subject, each trying for the ascendency. These two powers were called by St. Paul, the inward and outward man. Christ compares them to the tares and wheat and sometimes to devils. Now, if man understood these powers, he would be less liable to be led away by them. Christ recognized these changes, and understanding the laws by which they were governed was not led astray by them. It was this power which tempted him, but he held it under his control. To show how it acts upon man I will suppose a case. A person sees a chance to make a large fortune by committing murder. The idea of making a fortune stimulates the person; this excites a chemical in his body, and a controversy arises which brings all the powers of each side into play. At length one or the other has to yield.

Now, I will tell you. A gentleman came to my office with a lady and wished me to see if I could tell what was the trouble with her. My method of examining persons is by telling them how they feel, instead of their telling me how they feel. I took the lady by the hand and sat for a few moments in silence. It seemed to me that I could see that lady with a rope in her hand going towards the woods apparently with the intention of committing suicide. I took the gentleman aside and inquired if the lady was his wife. He said she was. I told him that he had better not leave her alone or she would be likely to commit suicide. He informed me that she had, that morning, attempted to hang herself before he left home. After giving my attention to the lady for a short time, I informed her that I was aware of her attempt to commit suicide. She burst into tears and seemed to suffer very much, in mind. I then informed her what was the cause of this state of mind and changed her mind by changing the fluids of her system. The lady returned home and has had no such trouble since.

I have changed the fluids in persons who have had fever sores almost instantly, so that they stopped discharging within twenty-four hours and never troubled more. I cannot produce this effect on every person, but I can on a great many.

I will now say a few words in regard to the effect produced on the mind by the change of the fluids. In a healthy state these powers act in harmony, but when the mind is disturbed the action changes. This causes a derangement in the system; the mind is disturbed and driven from the body and the body seems to be under the influence of evil spirits. Persons in this state are like one frightened out of his house by some story or strange noise. A house is to the body what the body is to the mind; it seems to be its place of rest.

To illustrate the mode by which I bring the mind back to the body, we will suppose a case of a lady frightened from her house. A person purchases a house; on moving into it, the neighbors tell the family that the house is haunted and all the bugbear stories mind could invent. The lady is left in the house at night. Her mind is very much excited and this excitement changes the fluids of the system, so that her mind is in a fit state to create all manner of evil spirits and strange noises which would frighten her out of the house and it would be hard to persuade her to return. Suppose someone should try to persuade her to return to the house by telling her that it is all the imagination; do you think she would return on that evidence? No, it must be explained on some better ground than that. A stranger comes along and says to the lady, "Do not be frightened, you shall not be harmed." She tells him he does not know what her troubles are. He replies, "If you will listen to me, I will tell you all about it." If the lady's troubles are so great that she will not listen to his story, he cannot quiet her mind and restore her to her house. We will suppose that from curiosity to hear his story, she listens. She is perfectly satisfied that he knows nothing of her trouble.

The stranger then commences and recounts all the circumstances, from the time she moved into the house until she saw the evil spirits or heard the noise which so frightened her. By this time the lady has become somewhat interested and asks him questions. The stranger appears very calm and says to the lady, "Come, return to your house and I will explain the cause." They then enter the house, the stranger showing her the way she left it. He then describes the noise which frightened her and goes to the place where it was heard and shows her what it was that made it. By this time the mystery is explained and the lady's mind is at ease; harmony is restored and all is well.

This is the state of the mind in disease. The mind is driven from the body and dares not return to it. The body seems to be a complete rendezvous for evil spirits. This is the case with the mind of persons in a typhoid fever. Other states of mind are the result of other troubles. The mind of persons in a diseased state vary as much as minds in a healthy state and to control the mind of a person diseased requires a great deal of patience on the part of the operator. I have labored harder to control the mind of a person in a diseased state than I ever did in performing any manual labor in my whole life. I have spent hours of hard labor in mentally persuading the mind of a person to return to its body. This may seem strange to some, but it is true.

I went to see a person who was sick. His mind was so disturbed by the derangement of the fluids of his system that he really believed he was in a lake of fire and brimstone. In his mind he had created the lake and fire and they were as plainly seen by himself and me as any fire. I shall never forget the looks of the place. When his wife told him I had come to see him, he said, "What do you suppose you can do for me? You can't get me out of this place." I told him I would put out the fire and bring him out of the place. I then commenced the work of changing his mind. To do this it was necessary to give all my attention to the subject. The manner of correcting the fluids was to bring my mind into the same state, as near as I dared to, so as to sympathize with him, thus producing harmony. I then changed my mind, and mentally talking to the man, lead him back till I feel that he is safe, like the stranger and the lady alluded to above. At this time I was very much excited, as much so as if I had really restored a person from such a place; for I had sat by him from four o'clock P.M. until twelve.

During all this time he had laid in silence, rolling his eyes about. After becoming fully satisfied in my mind that he was out of the lake, I waited for him to speak. At length he asked me who I was. I told him. He then asked how I came here. I told him that I heard he was sick and came to see him. I asked him what was the last thing he remembered, which was attending the funeral of his sister's child, some eight days before. He then commenced praising the Lord for making me an instrument for getting him out of that place of torment. He had his wife and children called up to tell them how happy he was. A happier man I never saw. He has since told me he shall never disbelieve in a hell. He was formerly a professor of religion, I think, and had lately begun to be rather skeptical on that subject, but having these old ideas of such a place was liable at any time to create it to torment himself.

From what I have seen and felt of the mind, I am satisfied that nine-tenths of all the old chronic diseases are the result of wrong impressions produced on the mind of persons by physicians, ignorantly, for I do not want to accuse them of knowingly being the authors of so much misery. These errors do not arise with the country physician so much as in medical colleges where they are used for the purpose of inventing diseases to torment man. Diseases are like fashions; and everyone knows that we are all whirled round the wheels of fashion, in a greater or less degree. Had there never been a medical book written, advancing new ideas of medicine and disease, surrounded with blind quotations from Greek and Latin lollypop authors, mankind would have been much better off at the present time and subject to some thousands less diseases. There are so many diseases now that it is almost impossible for a person to be sick without having a combination of three or four diseases.

I have never seen the time since I first commenced magnetizing when I considered it necessary to give any name to diseases. I cannot see any use from it; it leads the mind astray, like the old witch stories used to frighten children. The only effect of a name to a disease is to frighten people so as to give physicians the power of working on the imagination, just like the political demagogues who get the people into a quarrel by making them believe their liberties are in danger for their own aggrandizement.

The people are deceived and put themselves under their charge and if they live to get out of their trouble, have the satisfaction of paying for their own folly. People legislate too much for their own good; if they would let the laws alone, they would soon understand them and keep out of trouble. So it is with diseases; destroy nine-tenths of the names and the people would be better off. Four out of five of the old chronic cases are the effect of false impressions. If the rising generation could grow up without these false impressions, you would not see so many persons going about drawn up, with the idea that they have got the consumption, dyspepsia, liver complaint, heart disease or some other of the thousand and one follies of this enlightened nineteenth century. The mind has as much to do with lameness as with diseases. I have had a great many cases of the above classes and have cured them without the aid of medicine by correcting the false impressions and pointing out where the trouble lay.

I will now proceed to state how I came by this belief and how I was led along to it. In the first of my attempting to mesmerize, I was very skeptical in regard to many things: such as seeing without eyes, tasting without having anything in the mouth, hearing without ears, etc. I had no confidence in any experiment which it was possible for the subject to have any foreknowledge of what was to be done. When I had my subject in a mesmeric sleep, if any person should speak out and ask me to make him move his hand or anything of that description, I would not do so, for it seemed so much like deception on the part of the subject. And as my subject was one who liked to play off his jokes upon people, I was determined that he should not do so at my expense. Although he was with me some four years, I never saw the slightest cause for believing but what he was perfectly ignorant of what he was doing while asleep. Therefore, at the outset, I adopted this resolve, never to let the subject know what I wanted, except mentally. All my experiments were carried on in this way: if I wished him to give me his hand, I would ask him mentally; and by practicing with him I could send him to any part of the room for anything I wished, and he would always get it, without my speaking a word. He got no knowledge from me in any other way than by my own thought. When he walked, and I wished to tell him to stop, I did it mentally.

I then began to create things within my own mind, such as snakes, etc., and he would be frightened at them. On telling him that I had imagined them, he could not understand it, for the things created in my mind were as real as life to him. I could drive the things away so he could not see them and bring them back again. This led me to believe that man had the power of creation and that ideas took form. The next question which arose was. What were ideas composed of? They must be something, or else they could not be seen by even spiritual eyes. This led me to inquire if knowledge was ideas. I found that if I thought of principles, he had no way of describing them, for there was nothing to see; but if I thought of anything that had form, I could make him see it. To bring this about required a great deal of labor, I had to think of the thing so long and intently.

I will here explain what seems to be a mystery to most people, that is, how a medium tells us our own thoughts. You are sitting at a table with a medium and you ask if any spirit is present. The answer comes: "Yes, your father." You say at once, That is not correct for your father is not dead. The spirit contends he is. You ask when he died, of what disease, etc. receiving answers which are correct. All that was unknown to the medium or present company.

There are two ways of communicating knowledge to the outward man and both are spiritual. First, our own spirits communicate knowledge to the outward man, of which we know nothing through the ordinary way.

I have spoken of the mind leaving the body; it has a body or form as plain to be seen by a person who has the power of communicating with the mind as the natural body is. This is the spirit which is always prompting man to do right and is always ready to communicate knowledge to his fellow man. This knowledge may be called truth, which is obtained by the spirit through the decomposition of the body of which I have before spoken.

The natural man is content to live like the beasts, but the spiritual man is always seeking after knowledge. These powers or laws are in the body together, like the wheat and tares, spoken of by Christ and cannot be separated entirely while in the body, but can be as easily distinguished as the wheat and tares.

The mode of communicating is this. When the body is disturbed by any injury done to it or by any other cause, the trouble commences and the spiritual man is disturbed by the body, which he leaves and goes to other spirits and communicates the fact to them and they communicate the fact to their natural man, or body, who thus comes into possession of a fact which he was ignorant of before. Thus, for instance, you have a friend at a distance who is sick. His spirit, in trouble for the outward man, leaves the body and communicates the fact to your spirit, who again informs you of the fact. This disturbs the outward man and you relate it to your friends through the bodily organ. This is called by some, foreknowledge and by others, knowledge from the spirit world.

Take the case spoken of above. Is it not a new development of the mind, not understood by man? Does not everyone have something to say upon the subject? Take, for instance, the magnetic telegraph. The communications when first sent were all confusion, but was that any reason why the thing should be abandoned? Suppose the intelligence necessary to put it in operation had depended on the great mass of the people. Would we now have lines of wires running all across the country? What is the great object of that enterprise? Is it not to communicate knowledge, annihilating time and space?

This is the case with mind; there is a law which has never yet been developed. Facts have come to light, occasionally, but the law which occasioned it has been in the dark ever since the world began. Our spiritual man has tried to convey facts to the body, but with little success until very lately. Is it at all strange that minds should require some mode by which to convey facts to the natural man, which he knows nothing of, as the telegraph conveys intelligence in advance of the mails? Some may ask what use this is to mankind. It will explain away all the old superstitions which have enveloped us for ages.

I will now give some experiments which have come under my own observation, which I think will go to show that all the demonstrations which are supposed to come from departed friends are the works of our own spirits; proving to us that we have a spiritual body, governed by the mind, like the natural body, which is not dependent on the natural body, nor the result of an organized brain, bringing minds in communication with each other and relieving us of a great deal of trouble. This places man in a condition where he may relieve the suffering of his fellow man.

I was attending a lady who was sick. Having been with her all day, the effect of my mind sympathizing with her had so changed the fluids of my system that I was almost exhausted and I went home to bed. About four o'clock the next morning, I sprang out of bed and said to my wife, "Mrs. B. wants me to come and see her immediately." Dressing myself hastily I hurried out of the house and met Mr. B. coming after me. Thus, you see, my own spirit communicated to me knowledge I was not aware of before. Mrs. B's spirit communicated with my spirit, who informed me (that is, the outward man) of her wish that I should come to her immediately.

Again: I was attending a gentleman who was sick with what physicians call typhoid fever. I had been with him almost constantly for a week. I left him asleep one day and went to my house to tea. On sitting down to the table, a sudden impression came over me that Mr. H. wanted me. I left the table, took my hat and went to his house as soon as I could. As I entered the house I met Mrs. H. who was rather surprised at my returning so quickly as she said there was no necessity for my doing, as Mr. H was lying perfectly quiet and sleeping calmly. At this time he was so weak that it was difficult to hear him breathe. Going to the bed, I found him lying just as I had left him, which rather surprised me, and almost induced me to believe I had been mistaken. I turned to walk to the window when a singular sensation came over me, which caused me to return to the bed. As I stood looking at Mr. H. the sensation passed off, and I felt quiet.

I then thought I would try the experiment of leaving him and as I did so, the same sensation returned. Seating myself by his side, I took his hand and asked him if he was easy. Before this, no word had been spoken by me or any other person in the room. He pressed my hand, but did not speak. I then asked him if he was not so well. He whispered softly, "I am dying, I shall never wake again." I told him not to be alarmed, he would wake in a short time. After sitting by him for nearly an hour, I woke him. I have since then talked with him on this subject and he told me he was aware of my presence in his room at that time and when I was by his bed he felt safe, but when I left the bedside he thought he was dying. This knowledge which was communicated to me was, I believe, spiritual, but not from departed friends but by spirits whose bodies are alive.

I will give another case. I was listening to a lady and gentleman who were conversing upon spiritual questions. In a short time I saw, standing by her side, the spirit of a young lady. (I cannot see these spirits except when my eyes are closed.) I said to the lady, "I see you have an attendant spirit, as it is called." She started rather suddenly and asked what kind of spirit. I told her it was a young lady. She wished me to describe her. I did so, telling her complexion, size, color of her hair and eyes and also asked of the spirit her age, which I told. The lady then wished me to ask the spirit if she was married while on this earth. I did so, and received an answer that she was not, but that she had been engaged to a gentleman who was a physician, but she went to the spirit world before they were married. I asked the spirit if the gentleman was an American, and was informed that he was an Englishman. After talking with the spirit some time longer, I asked the lady if what I had told was correct; she said it was, perfectly.

These kinds of experiments I have been trying for the last eight or nine years and call them thought-reading. I could give a great many cases similar to the above.

I have no doubt of an identity after death, but among all the demonstrations that purport to come from departed friends who have left the body, I have not heard any stronger proof than I have had myself. I have had some experiments which I cannot as yet explain upon the principle of the above.

I was in the country attending a girl about twelve or thirteen years of age, who was very sick and also very nervous. I was with her till nearly eleven o'clock at night. Then I went to bed, and thought I went to sleep.

It seemed to me as though I was with the young girl trying to drive away snakes and horrid looking monsters that were troubling her; but it seemed to me that I had not power to do so. I thought I would try and find my brother who had been in the spirit world ten or twelve years and see if he could give me any information on the subject. At last I found him, told him my trouble and asked him if he had any power over these serpents and devils. He said he had not but would take me to one who had. He introduced me to a man who was dressed in white garments. This person had a very mild expression of countenance and something about him which seemed to say, "You need not be troubled. I can drive them all away." At this moment I heard someone coming upstairs, which attracted my attention. I asked what was wanted and the lady of the house said that she wished me to come down, as her daughter was very restless and said that there were serpents and devils tormenting her.

I do not say that I saw my brother; but if I did not, and this was the effect of my imagination, it would be hard to prove to me that any spirit ever appeared to man from another would. Is not the case of Lazarus a similar one? Lazarus was sick and probably had a strong desire to see Christ. Upon my ground, Christ was affected by Lazarus, and there was sympathy between them for he "loved Lazarus," for he said, "Our friend, Lazarus, sleepeth; but I go that I may awake him out of sleep." Now it seems to me that if Lazarus had been raised from the spirit world, he would have had some knowledge of it and would have communicated the fact to others; but we have no authority from him that he went there. Again (Luke VII: 11-16), we have another case, also without any after reference to a spirit world. Is it any very difficult thing to suppose that Christ received his knowledge of Lazarus' situation in the same manner which I did that of Mrs. B. or Mr. H. before alluded to, or that he was in nearly the same condition?

I will now give one or two cases to show that my mind or spirit can go to a distant place and there produce an effect on a person without their knowledge. I was requested to try the experiment of putting a lady to sleep without her knowledge. She was about sixty years of age, nervous temperament and resided over two miles from my house.

About eight o'clock in the evening, I lay down on the sofa and commenced operations. In a short time it seemed to me that she had gone to sleep and I told my wife so. I could not keep my mind off the lady and laid still for some time, when my wife said to me, "If you have put Mrs. M. to sleep, it is time for you to wake her up." I seemed to try to do so, but it appeared to me that she did not want to wake up and as she wished it, I concluded to let her sleep all night.

On making inquiries the next day, I ascertained that at the time I commenced putting her to sleep, she was sitting by the fire knitting. All at once she said, "Mr. Quimby is mesmerizing me," and she rose to go to her bed but was so near asleep that her son and daughter had to lift her onto the bed where she slept quietly until breakfast time the next morning. At their usual bed time, the family tried to wake her for the purpose of removing her clothes, but could not do so. At another time, her son-in-law, who was not present at the first experiment, wished me to try it again and I did so with equal success. I have tried experiments similar to the above a great many times, and with nearly the same success.

I will give another experiment of seeing the spirit. I was called to attend an old lady who was sick and had been so for a long time. I was shown to her room by her husband, where I found the lady, a pitiful sight, lying on her bed and having more the appearance of a lunatic than a sane person. Her eyes were closed and she would hold no conversation with anyone, nor answer any questions I asked her. I then thought I would see if I could get any information by mental conversation. It soon seemed to me as though she was looking at a person, all the time saying, You are the cause of my trouble. She seemed to tell me that this was her brother and went on to tell me her story, which was this.

When she was young, a young man who was respectable and well off, as regarded worldly dross, paid her attention and they were engaged; but her brother, who did not like the match, reported false stories about her and the man left her. She loved the man and his desertion nearly broke her heart, but having good bodily health and a great deal of pride and ambition, she did not give way to her feelings.

After some thirty years, having lost much of her ambition and high spirits, she married her present husband who was not calculated to make her happy having an entirely dissimilar disposition, although he was very kind to her. After living with him some time, she became sick, worn out and completely run down in spirits. Like Rachel of old, her troubles were greater than she could bear and she would not be comforted. Her husband then entered the room and asked me what I thought of his wife, and whether I could help her. I sat for a few moments in silence, not knowing exactly what to say. I thought that if I should tell him the story which she had appeared to tell me, it might be false; he might get angry and order me out of the house which I did not wish to leave as it was after eleven o'clock at night, very cold, and I was fourteen miles from home.

So I mentally asked the old lady if what she seemed to tell me was true; she appeared glad to think I had found it out and said it was. I then turned to her husband and said, "I have tried to get your wife to answer my questions, but as she would not, I have gotten a mental account of her troubles and if you will not think hard of me I will relate her story." I then asked him if she had ever had any trouble with her brothers. He told me that some thirty years ago one of her brothers told some false stories about her, but that she had forgotten all about that. I then told him the story related above, and described the man to whom she had been engaged. At this time I was sitting beside the bed on which the old lady laid and while I was describing her old beau she opened her eyes a moment, which was the only time she did so while I was in the house. As her husband had never seen the man, he could not tell whether I was right or not, but so far as he did know, it was correct. I then left the room. After my departure she told her husband all I had said was correct and as for her beau, I had described him exactly.

Explanation, The
[LC 1:0298]

(Doctor) You may seat yourself in this chair.

(Patient) Do you wish me to tell you how I feel?

(Dr.) No, I will tell you.

(P.) Oh, that is all the better, for doctors all want their patients to tell them how they feel.

(Dr.) Yes, I know that, and here is where I differ from them. I tell you your feelings and you tell the doctors. Do you under understand that?

(P.) Yes, I think I do.

(Dr.) Well, which do you like better?

(P.) Your way of course, for if you tell me how I feel I shall think that you know more about it than I do, for I always supposed that you had to tell the doctors how you felt.

(Dr.) So it is, and then the doctor gives his opinion based on your feelings, and you know just about as much of your case as he does. So you see it is the blind leading the blind, and if the blind lead the blind, they both fall into the ditch.

(P.) Yes, so says the good book that never lies.

(Dr.) Now I do not do any such way. I sit down by the patient and take hold of his hand and sit till I feel a sensation in the mind.

(P.) How do you do that?

(Dr.) That is the mystery.

(P.) Well, it must be a mystery, for I cannot understand how you can take my feelings.

(Dr.) Do you know how Jesus took the feelings of the sick?

(P.) No, but I suppose that it must be by the power of God.

(Dr.) Do you believe the Bible?

(P.) Yes, the Bible says so, and of course it must be true.

(Dr.) Then God took upon himself the feelings of the sick

(P.) Yes.

(Dr.) Then if I take upon myself the feelings of the sick, what is it that does it?

(P.) It must be a power.

(Dr.) What do you mean by a power? (P.) I cannot tell; it is a mystery to me. (Dr.) So I supposed but now I will tell you how you feel. (P.) Well I would like to get well, and I do not care to know how it is done. (Dr.) Well, if you will give me your attention I will try to describe your feelings. Please to look at me in the eye. You have a strange feeling in your head. (P.) Yes, I will tell you. (Dr.) I do not wish you to tell me anything. Only say Yes or No to my questions. (P.) I believe I understand you. (Dr.) This feeling in the head affects you over the eyes and at the bridge of the nose between the eyes; this produces over your eyes a heavy sensation that makes you want to close them. (P.) I don't know what it is but that is just the way I feel. (Dr.) Then I am right so far? (P.) Perfectly, but I cannot see how you take my feelings. (Dr.) I will explain that by and by. This heavy feeling in your head causes you to sit with your head inclined forward and that tires your neck and causes a pain in the back of your head. (P.) That is just so. (Dr.) And you try to hold up your head and that strains the muscles in your neck, and heats up those that surround the chest. This heat contracts them and makes you feel a weight pressing on your chest. (P.) That is just as I have felt a thousand times. (Dr.) This numbs the whole of your chest and head, so your head would incline forward and you feel as if you had twenty pounds hanging from your neck. This, of course, bows you down, and the effort of the will to sit up is more than you can make, so you want to lie down.

(P.) I don't see how you tell my feelings so easily. I could not tell them as near myself. (Dr.) This heavy feeling causes you to give way at the pit of the stomach and that causes a pain in the left side and at times a suffocating feeling. (P.) How near that is. It is just so. (Dr.) And then it causes a bloated feeling in the pit of your stomach and you have to loosen your dress. (P.) Yes. (Dr.) This causes a full feeling, first below the stomach and across the bowels to feel like a weight pressing down and pulling from the pit of the stomach, as though something was giving way at the side. (P.) Yes. (Dr.) Now all this seems to come across the hips when you walk, so when you attempt to, it makes you feel weak in the back and weak all over. (P.) Yes, you are right, but can you help me? (Dr.) I must first find out all your troubles before I can explain to you the cause of them, for they are all in the mind. (P.) O dear, I know that it is not my mind that makes me feel all these feelings. (Dr.) Then what is it? (P.) Why, it is my back and stomach and head and side that feels, and ever so many more that you have not spoken of. (Dr.) Are all these feelings independent of yourself? (P.) No, but I never thought anything about them till they came. (Dr.) Then you are sure that they came of themselves? (P.) Of course I am. (Dr.) Can you tell where they came from? (P.) No. (Dr.) Do you suppose that they came from any one? (P.) I do not know anything about that. (Dr.) You admit I feel them. (P.) Yes. (Dr.) From where did I get them? (P.) From me, I suppose. (Dr.) Then if my feelings came from you, why could not yours come from someone also? (P.) I do not know. (Dr.) This is just where the trouble lies. We take a disease as something independent of the mind and here is the trouble; it is in us and not in the mind that the trouble lies.

The effect is in the mind and the cause is in the direction. Your feelings as far as I have gone are like witnesses that testify against you. You have no one to appear in your behalf and you are cast into prison by these false witnesses put up by blind guides who profess to lead the people into light but they lead them into darkness and rob them of all they have. Like the man going down to Jericho; you have fallen among thieves and you have been robbed of all your money or wisdom and been left alone in the dark . . . Now here you are without friends or wisdom, ignorant of all these enemies, cast into prison there to live a miserable life of suffering till death releases you from these evil beings. Now I appear in your behalf at the prison; for I find you there, indicted for all the above which, if true, you cannot escape. This power, as you call it, I call Christ, acting through the man Quimby. This wisdom is like the light or day, while your wisdom or belief is like the night or darkness and your light is like the moon's light that makes shadows. Now as all shadows are the reflection of a substance, there must be some darkness to make a shadow. Error is matter and of course a substance. Its author is a belief.

As science is of light, it makes no shadow but like the rising of the sun, it dissolves the darkness and destroys it, and so it burns up the error or disease. Now in this prison all looks dark and gloomy. The sentence of death is nearly pronounced, your trial being nearly finished. The doctors and priests, who have got you in this trouble like hypocrites of old, come to your prison wall to torment you, as the Jews did Jesus when they held vinegar to his mouth. They come to you pretending to be your friends, not knowing that their friendship is tormenting you. Now I suppose you would like to know whom I saw by you, for I talk as though I am speaking to someone else. Well, so I am, and that one is your life, imprisoned by the ignorance of man. This life is the scientific life or man; its growth is science and its life is progression, and to check its progression is to imprison it in error. So the prison is the checking of the scientific man. Your scientific man or life is imprisoned by the wisdom of error of this world. When I speak to you I speak to the scientific man, and when I speak of an opinion, I speak of the priests and doctors and sometimes of public opinion. These opinions are like the fish spoken of by Christ that is not engrafted into a theory or creed. We often hear persons disputing about the origin of language.

Now there never was a man who could translate the original language of God, for God never spoke at all. If Jesus was God, then God had to learn, and from all accounts Jesus was not much of a scholar. So either man or God lies. Now if God spoke to Moses, how did He speak? If He spoke, he must have spoken in the common language of Moses' day. So you see man must have invented language before God could communicate with him; so God keeps up with the times and every now and then man finds out that God was mistaken about certain passages in the Bible. Did God or Jesus misrepresent or were the people deceived by His language? You see there is a mystery about the original language of God, for the Bible says that God spoke not as man speaks, for God was before Adam. So if God ever spoke, He spoke in the same language at the beginning as he does now, for he is unchangeable. So we must listen to the sound of God's voice, not in the language of any person, for God speaks in that still small voice of sympathy that says to the poor sick like yourself, Be of good cheer, your sins or errors will be explained and your soul set at liberty. I will tell you how you may know when God speaks to you and when your prayers are heard. When you came here your prayer was to be cured. (P.) Yes, that has been my prayer night and day for a long time. (Dr.) God hears in secret and your prayers were in secret, were they not? (P.) Yes. (Dr.) Could your doctor hear your prayers or feel your woes? (P.) No. (Dr.) Could the priest? (P.) No. (Dr.) Then neither of them could answer your prayers by returning sympathy for sympathy that they could not feel. (P.) No.

(Dr.) If Jesus was here would he not feel your troubles or prayers? (P.) Yes. (Dr.) Did he not give his disciples the same power? (P.) Yes. (Dr.) Well, if they cannot do what he did, have they any claims to apostleship? (P.) No. (Dr.) The true original language of God is this. If you are in trouble, you know it and feel it. (P.) Yes. (Dr.) This comes within your senses. For me to understand your feelings or language is to feel it and then invent some words or signs so as to give your outward man a sign that I do feel it. This last invention is only to explain to the well as nearly as possible how the sick feel. So to know what the language of Jesus was is to know how he was affected by the person or persons he was addressing. There is a mistaken notion about the senses. The senses are just what a person knows and the difference between man and beast is in their senses, for man's senses is his wisdom.

The beast has five senses and a great many human beings have not half so many. Because a human being is deprived of sight, hearing, taste, smelling, does that make him of less value than the brute, who has all the above? The truth is, what a man knows is his senses, not what he smells; his senses are in everything that contains his wisdom. Show an orange to a child; the child's wisdom embraces sight, not smell nor taste nor anything else. Give the child wisdom of what the orange is and put him in full possession of all the knowledge. Then the child is wiser than he was before. So his senses grow with his wisdom and this makes man different from the brute, and the difference is in his senses or wisdom. If a man is as ignorant as the brute, he is worse than one, for he has neglected to fulfill his obligations to himself and God. Now you may ask what has all this to do with your disease. (P.) Yes, I do not see as that has anything to do with my aches and pains. (Dr.) This is now what I am going to show you, how your mind is the disease.

You know I told you about your head, neck and side, etc. (P.) Certainly. (Dr.) Well, do not forget that, for I shall refer to it when I come to the trial. (P.) Have you not come to that yet? (Dr.) Oh, No. I have not come to the disease yet. (P.) I thought you had been telling me my disease. (Dr.) No, these feelings are some of your symptoms; they are the effect and not the cause. (P.) Oh, well tell me the cause. (Dr.) Listen and I will try to explain the cause of your trouble as far as I have gone. These symptoms are in the first indictment, and as it will be necessary for me to prove all I state, I must draw your attention to what you will acknowledge to be true. You are aware that you have thought a good deal about the Scriptures and another world, as you call it. (P.) Oh, No! Not half as much as I ought to. (Dr.) Why? (P.) Oh, I think we all ought to read the Bible more than we do. (Dr.) Why? (P.) To make us better. (Dr.) Do you think that the Bible makes you better? (P.) Yes. (Dr.) Then you really feel as though you got some good out of the Bible? (P.) Yes. (Dr.) Do you think you understand it? (P.) Not as well as I wish I did. (Dr.) Do you get any more light in regard to it when you read it? (P.) Oh, Yes. (Dr.) How long have you studied it? (P.) I have always been taught to read the Bible.

(Dr.) Do you belong to any church? (P.) I do not know as that has anything to do with my disease. (Dr.) It may have, and as your belief is the witness, I first want to examine the witness so it is necessary that I should know all the facts that have a bearing on the case. (P.) I do not know as my belief has anything to do with the case. (Dr.) Well, we will see about that by and by. Please answer.

(P.) I suppose I am a member of a church. (Dr.) What church? (P.) The Calvinist Baptist. (Dr.) You say you study the Bible to find out your duty to your neighbor and yourself, and also your duty to your God as a Christian? (P.) Yes. (Dr.) Well, what progress have you made? (P.) I cannot say that I have made much, for it still looks dark. (Dr.) Do you think you understand it? (P.) Not as well as I should like to. (Dr.) Does anyone understand it? (P.) Why, I suppose Parson B knows more about it than I do. (Dr.) Where did he get his information? (P.) He is a very learned divine. (Dr.) So were the Pharisees and Levites, but Jesus shut their mouths, did he not? (P.) Yes. (Dr.) Was Jesus a learned man? (P.) Why, Jesus was God. (Dr.) Well, was God ever supposed to study any languages? (P.) No, for he knows all things. (Dr.) Then God knew all things before language was invented. (P.) Yes. (Dr.) Then language was not for God's benefit, but for man's. (P.) Yes. (Dr.) Then God could communicate his will to man without language. (P.) Yes. (Dr.) If God formerly talked to men, do you suppose He spoke in an audible voice? (P.) I suppose He did for the Bible said He spoke unto Moses. (Dr.) Did He not speak to Saul when he was going to Damascus? (P.) Yes. (Dr.) Did anyone but Saul hear Him? (P.) I believe not. (Dr.) Did He not speak to Jesus, when he saw the heavens open and the Holy Ghost come down and heard the voice of God saying, "This is my beloved son in whom I am well pleased?" Did any others hear it? (P.) It did not say they did, but when the devil spoke, they all heard.

(Dr.) Do you suppose that if anyone had been up in the mountain when Jesus was tempted, they could have heard the devil talking to Jesus? (P.) No, that was his earthly feelings or passions, like the rest of us when we are tempted to do wrong. (Dr.) The Bible says the devil talked and Jesus answered, Why do you put another construction on that passage? (P.) No one supposes that it was a devil in human shape. (Dr.) Then why did he tell him to get behind him? (P.) Oh! There are many passages hard to be understood. (Dr.) Yes, but such plain language as that ought not be misrepresented. Did not the people once believe in the devil in human form? (P.) Yes, I suppose they did. (Dr.) Well, if he ever had an existence, is he dead? (P.) We often hear that he is. (Dr.) Now, if there ever was a devil, then the story in the Bible is false, is it not? (P.) I cannot disbelieve in the Bible because I cannot understand it. (Dr.) Was not Christ sent to save sinners? (P.) Yes. (Dr.) What is a sinner? (P.) Why, we are all sinners. (Dr.) Why did he say I am not sent to call the righteous but sinners to repentance? (P.) Oh! I cannot explain that, but if Parson B was here, he could. I should like to hear him talk with you. There he comes, shall I call him? Will it interfere with your cure? (Dr.) Oh! Yes, I should like to hear him explain some of these passages. (P.) I will rap on the window, but he seems to be coming in.

(Enter Parson) (P.) Good morning, this is Dr. Quimby. He is trying to see if he can cure me. (Parson B) Good morning, Doctor. I suppose you find Sister "A" very nervous. (Dr.) Yes, somewhat so. (Parson) I have spent a great deal of time in trying to reconcile her to the Holy Scriptures, where she must go for happiness in this world of woe and where she must look for happiness and where she will find Christ ready to lead her to her Father in Heaven. (Dr.) Do you suppose she is prepared to meet her God. (Parson)

Oh, yes, she has been a bright and shining light in my church for over three years. (Dr.) What was the state of her mind when she first began to see the necessity of a change? (Parson) She was probably one of the most bewitching little creatures you ever saw. (Dr.) Did she ever do anything out of the way? (Parson) Oh, everyone liked her, but she was like all others without that hope that one must have to fit them for that place where sinners can never enter. (Dr.) I suppose you mean heaven. (Parson) Yes. (Dr.) Well, who has caused this change? (Parson) The Spirit of God. (Dr.) How did she receive it? (Parson) Through my feeble voice. (Dr.) Then you take the credit of being an instrument in the hands of God to explain the Scriptures so that she could understand and prepare her mind to receive the Holy Ghost or Christ? (Parson) Yes. (Dr.) Have you any proof that she has received the Holy Ghost? (Parson) Yes. (Dr.) What is it? (Parson) Why, she has met with a change of heart. (Dr.) What do you mean by a change of heart? (Parson) The love of God shed abroad in her heart, and a promise that if she continues in the true faith, delivered to the saints, she shall be saved.

(Dr.) Can you give me any sort of a reason for the faith you or she has in your beliefs? (Parson) Of course I can. (Dr.) Well, please tell me what you mean by religion? (Parson) To love God with all your heart and to love your neighbor as yourself. (Dr.) Do you live up to that? (Parson) Yes Sir, I think I do. (Dr.) Then you profess to be a follower of Christ, do you? (Parson) Yes. (Dr.) Could not Jesus raise this young lady if he was on earth? (Parson) Yes, for he could do all things. (Dr.) Can you? (Parson) The days of miracles are past, since the crucifixion of Christ. (Dr.) Have there not been any miracles since? (Parson) I think not. (Dr.) How did Jesus cure? (Parson) By the power of God. (Dr.) Was not Paul an apostle of Christ? (Parson) Yes. (Dr.) Was he not converted some thirty years after the crucifixion of Jesus? (Parson) Yes, I believe he was. (Dr.) Did he not perform miracles? (Parson) I cannot say about that. (Dr.) Well, you remember where it says that God wrought special miracles by the hands of Paul, so much so that aprons from his body were brought to the sick and the evil spirits went out of them and they were healed of their diseases. (Parson) Yes. (Dr.) Do you call yourself a converted man? (Parson) Yes. (Dr.) And feel as though you were born of God? (Parson) I do. (Dr.) Was God Christ? (Parson) Yes. (Dr.) I thought you said that Christ cured by the power of God. (Parson) I mean Jesus received his power from God. (Dr.) So I understand you; now was that power that Jesus received the same that Paul received, for they both claimed it was from God? (Parson) Yes.

(Dr.) Was it the power of wisdom or a gift? (Parson) I do not know as I understand you. (Dr.) Did Jesus know how he cured or was it a gift? (Parson) Why of course he knew how he performed the cures. (Dr.) Then it was wisdom, not a gift. (Parson) Yes. (Dr.) Was Paul's the same. (Parson) I suppose it must have been. (Dr.) Then the wisdom was not of this world. (Parson) No. (Dr.) Is not wisdom a power? (Parson) Yes. (Dr.) Is there any power in error? (Parson) Yes, for we read of the power of the devil. (Dr.) Then there are two powers. (Parson) Yes. (Dr.) Was the devil's power of God? (Parson) No. (Dr.) Then where did he get it? (Parson) I do not know, but God said it was from the beginning and that he was a liar from the beginning. (Dr.) How are we to distinguish these two powers? You say wisdom is God's power, and the Devil's you say did not come from God; so it cannot be wisdom, can it? Then it must be of this world. (Parson) Yes. (Dr.) Then this world is matter? (Parson) Yes. (Dr.) Then man is made of matter? (Parson) Yes. (Dr.) And wisdom in man, if he has any, must be God, is it not so? (Parson) Yes. (Dr.) Then man is under two powers: wisdom of God and wisdom of the devil or error. (Parson) Yes. (Dr.) Is wisdom matter? (Parson) No. (Dr.) Is error or the devil matter? (Parson) I don't know. (Dr.) What does it mean when it says God shall reign till he has put all enemies under his feet and the last enemy is death. So death and hell and he that hath the power of death shall be destroyed? Is not all the above matter or something that can be destroyed? (Parson) Yes.

(Dr.) Are you not preparing this young lady to be resigned to the devil or death? (Parson) What do you mean? I think if you would cure your patients and not instruct them in regard to the Bible, you would do much more good. (Dr.) Did not Christ cure? (Parson) I hope you will not compare yourself with Christ. (Dr.) Why not? (Parson) Because it is blasphemy. (Dr.) Did Christ preach? (Parson) Yes. (Dr.) Do you? (Parson) Yes. (Dr.) What kind of religion? (Parson) The religion of Christ. (Dr.) Do you mean to compare yourself with Christ? (Parson) Not in the sense that you do. (Dr.) How do you compare yourself with Christ? (Parson) By preaching his Gospel. (Dr.) Can you illustrate in what way you preach Christ, as the twelve apostles whom he called together, giving them power over all disease and to cast out devils, and telling them how to distinguish between the false Christ or teachers. Now if you are a true disciple of Christ, here is a case to prove it. Save this young lady from the hands of death where ignorance and superstition have placed her. (Parson) Here is no place to discuss questions of this kind. I will just say to this young lady, beware of evil spirits. Your soul is of more value than his theory, for if that is true, farewell to religion. We might live and enjoy ourselves as you did before you received the promise of eternal life. (Dr.) Did you not say that you were preparing her for the solemn scene of death? (Parson) It is not worthwhile for me to try to convince an infidel, so I will leave you, hoping you will see the error of your ways. Good morning.

(Dr.) Now you have heard your minister talk, and would his talk explain away your disease? (Patient) No. (Dr.) Then what is it good for? (P.) Well, I do not know, only it makes us happy. (Dr.) Does his talk or belief make you feel any better? (P.) I do not know as his talk would cure me, but I think his power could. (Dr.) I thought you admitted that he knew what he was doing? (P.) So I did. (Dr.) Well, how can a person let you know a truth without using language and talking? (P.) I do not know as they can. (Dr.) Now if I should cure you without explaining how I changed your mind, then you would be as ignorant as before? (P.) Yes, but I do not see that the mind has anything to do with the cure. For you say you have to change the mind to make the cure, and you say that you can cure me without my knowing how it is done. (Dr.) Yes, that is so, and I will try and explain, and if you do not believe, ask for proof.

Mind is matter but mind is not wisdom; so if your mind is disturbed and your wisdom imprisoned in the disturbance, I can by disturbing your mind set your wisdom at liberty and you be none the wiser. But if I use language to communicate to your error and convince it of its fault, then your error becomes wisdom. And then your wisdom increases just as you lose error; so that unto him that hath wisdom shall be given and unto him that hath not wisdom but error, that shall be taken away, or that which he thinks he has, by wisdom, and given to wisdom, and he shall have more wisdom.

Now I will illustrate this in your case. Your wisdom was of this world and was based on your religious opinions. They, being of man's invention, were false. But being acknowledged as true, the world has been deceived by these false guides into a belief that really has been acknowledged as true. So that everyone that is afflicted by these blind guides makes themselves a religion, that is according to the wisdom of man. Now your wisdom or science, by being misled by these blind guides, disturbs your mind, and the false direction given to it attaches it to a belief that you take for a truth. You may say, If your wisdom is of God how can it be deceived. Your wisdom is progression as well as science, so it may be misled as though it was of this world of error. Your belief is made of that substance called matter, and that to wisdom is called an idea and nothing more. For it can be destroyed or changed into another belief.

I want you to understand what I mean by a belief and how it affects you; so I will suppose myself your minister and I will commence by asking you if you were ever affected by religious experience. You must listen like a child, ready to receive instruction, so of course you have no mind or opinion on the subject. Your wisdom is excited and it wants to be developed, so you listen and take it for granted that I have more wisdom than you. And not being able or not knowing the mode of testing my wisdom, you, being honest and simple, take me as a guide. I introduce my wisdom as a guide or truth, and being ignorant of myself lead you into a belief that I may believe myself or I may not.

If I am honest, I am more sincere and my sincerity affects you differently from my hypocrisy. But let it be as it may; I commence by calling your attention to another world and that to you is all Greek, but as I talk, you become excited and you begin to condense my argument into a belief, like a building, so that it looks clear to your little wisdom and you frame a belief or building to agree with the plan I have introduced. As your belief is condensed, it looks plainer and like a shadow till it becomes so plain that you cease to have an opinion and it then becomes a truth. Now all beliefs being the invention of man, they are of matter and liable to be changed or disturbed. So restrictions, creeds or penalties are attached to them and certain forms and ceremonies required of persons for their happiness, and the neglect of them is the forfeiture of their happiness.

Your belief in your religion requires some sacrifice on your part, but Jesus says in sacrifices he takes no delight. Science requires no sacrifice, but all priesthoods are made up of sacrifice or offerings. If you comply with the creed or belief, then you shall be saved; if you see fit to doubt their wisdom, then you are judged guilty of the law and are tried by the creed, and being guilty, you are bound and cast into prison. In this state of mind, your wisdom being deceived, you become the child of these blind guides and in your trouble you call on the Lord, as you think. If you really do call on science, it would answer you, but you cannot call on whom you have never heard and receive an answer. So you receive the answer from your false leader and in this way you are held in prison till Christ or Science sets you free, as some revelation sets a criminal free by opening the door of his prison.

Now your state of mind first commenced by some little excitement that sent a flash to your head and this made you a little nervous. Then the parson commenced his story; this affects you more and more and your reason keeps you in a state of excitement. At last you see no way by which you can be saved except through Christ and Christ is these blind guides' belief. This you cannot understand. So in your trouble you think you are not as good as you ought to be. This troubles you till at last you settle down in a state of complete despair. This was the state of mankind when Jesus introduced this wisdom, called Christ. This wisdom separated the false Christ or theories from the true Christ or wisdom. One he called the wisdom of this world and the other the wisdom of God; so when he explained it, he used the parable of the talents. He who had the one talent, being young and not understanding, knew just enough not to be deceived but not enough to put his theory into practice, sat still or hid it in the dust of ignorance till the time came to render up to wisdom the things that belong to God. You know how he thought wisdom had been a hard master etc. But wisdom knew that it was error who talked, so he cast out his error, gave him the wisdom of God or Science, and said unto him, Unto him that hath shall be given and he shall have more abundant or unto him that hath a little wisdom shall be given more and unto the same person who hath error that he takes for truth, it shall be taken away and truth shall take its place.

Now this is your case. You have hidden your wisdom in the dust of ignorance and used the reason of error, as error never had any truth but is the wisdom of darkness. When the Christ or true wisdom comes, it calls your error to an account and as it cannot give any good account of itself, it is cast into prison. Your wisdom being attached to your error, you follow its father and Christ knew the Devil and of course your error becomes the child of the devil. Jesus says Christ shall reign till he has put all things under his feet and the last thing is death. See how near your teacher agrees with this Christ; your Christ or teacher calls on you to prepare you for the very thing that my Christ came to destroy. If you will stop and look at your belief, it does not contain one single truth that Christ taught but is directly in contradiction to all his teachings. So the very burdens are put upon you by your false teachers who cry, Peace, peace when there is no peace. Now you know as well as I do that your ministers cannot help you at all, but they can torment you by their creeds and leave you like the man going down to Jericho, who fell among thieves. They have robbed you of all your comfort and have left you to be devoured by wolves in men's clothing who come prowling around, undertaking to heal your wounds by tormenting you with their drugs. So at last, with their smooth tongues and poison, they quiet you to sleep and like the strong man who enters your house while asleep, poison you and destroy your health.

Now this is your case: while you were quietly travelling along the journey of life, young and happy, these blind guides decoyed you from your father's house or health and carried you off into a strange land or belief, robbed you of your happiness and left you among strangers or physicians, who come to you pretending to be your friends, offering you wine and opium and drugs to soothe your wounded heart. Then robbing you of all your health, they leave you on the ground. The priests and doctors come along and seeing you as the one they have robbed, pass by. Now I come and find you lying on the ground and taking you up, carry you into an inn or happier state of mind, bind up your heart that the priests have broken, and pour into your soul that they have wounded the oil of truth, leave a few pence or ideas of value with your wisdom or landlord and go my way. When I come again, if the debt of health is not paid, I will explain the balance. Now who is your friend? I will now bring you before your enemies, that you may be tried by the laws of God or Science. And as you are held in bondage by man's laws, the laws of science will set you free. I will read over your indictment. Here you stand before the tribunal of man, accused of sundry offenses which I shall read to the court, all of which you have been made to believe. If true, they must cast you into prison, there to live a miserable life. Here is the indictment:

You are accused of a heavy feeling over the eyes, so it is with difficulty you keep them open; also shooting pains in the head, cold, neuralgia, pains in the back of the neck, shooting across the chest, faintness at the stomach, sudden palpitation of the heart, etc; a heaviness about the hips causing great pains in the small of the back; a bearing down of the lower part of the abdomen, shortness of breath in walking, accompanied with a low state of mind, feeling at time as though you were alone in the world. All of the above are the feelings brought against you and you have pleaded guilty to them. Now I have undertaken your case and in reading over the indictment, I see that all the offenses you stand indicted for are offenses against the laws of man, not against God or Science. So that man's laws or opinions cannot hold the child of science in bondage, if she can be proved clear. It is not incumbent on me to show that you are innocent of all you are accused of, so I will state my defense to the court. In the first place, God never made a law that man can show and in the next place if he did, you never disobeyed it. And I am ready to have you tried by the laws of truth. If you have offended against truth, let your accusers come forward and show wherein.

I will call the doctor to the stand and let him tell his story. So Doctor, you may take the stand and state all you know about this lady.

Doc. I was called to see her some six months ago and found her laboring under a nervous excitement caused by congestion of the lungs. Well, what else? I administered to her and found her the next morning laboring under very severe pains in the head and across the eyes. Have you any name for these feelings? The pains across the chest were congestion of the lungs and the pains in the head and back were tic douloureux or neuralgia. The pains in the back of the neck running down the spine were caused by a spinal affection. After a day or two, the symptoms changed somewhat, assuming another form, a weakness at the pit of the stomach, with a slight irritation about the heart, causing great tenderness around the left side. These symptoms I treated in the usual way. (Counsel) Are you a regular? (Doc.) I am. (C) Go on. (Doc.) In a few days there was great soreness about the pit of the stomach, and pains shooting around the waist, producing a feverish state of the abdomen, with considerable swelling and a weight therein, so that it was with difficulty she could walk. (C) What do you call that? (Doc.) At first, I considered it a slight inflammation of the kidneys and intestines, but on further examination I came to the conclusion that it must be an affection of the female organs and treated her for that. But in spite of all my remedies, she sank till she became too weak to walk; so she had to keep to her bed most of the time. (C) How long since you have been called to this lady? (Doc.) Some six months. (C) How was she when you first saw her? (Doc.) As I have described, laboring under nervous excitement and congestion of the lungs. (C) What course of treatment did you use? (Doc.) I ordered a blister plaster over the chest and left medicine. (C) Did you not give the blue pill? (Doc.) Yes. (C) Did you not inform her or her parents of her state? (Doc.) Indeed, as fast as it appeared. (C) Did you wait for the symptoms to appear? (Doc.) Oh no. When I first saw her I told her the cause. (C) Do you remember the cause? (Doc.) Yes, for she was very much disappointed and said nothing ailed her. (C) Did you convince her you were right? (Doc.) I did. (C) You consider it your duty as a physician to tell the patient what disease he has? (Doc.) Yes sir. (C) Well sir, you say the bowels were swollen after that? (Doc.) Yes. (C) Did you use any remedies? (Doc.) Yes, I blistered them. (C) How did you treat the uterine trouble? (Doc.) I applied caustic for ulceration, for such was the state of the organs. (C) All this took place after you first saw her? (Doc.) Yes. (C) That is all. Now will the mother step on the stand? Will you please state how your daughter was attacked and also how she was when the doctor called. (Mother) Shall I begin from the commencement of her sickness? (C) Yes, if it is necessary to get the facts. (Mother) Well, some three years ago, when Parson B was ordained, Mary attended the meetings and became very much interested in the revival of religion that was subsequently awakened in the church. I think she took some cold, for she would complain of her head aching and at last she became melancholy. (C) Did she read much? (Mother) Nothing but the Bible. (C) Did you think that hurt her? (Mother) No. Religion never hurt anyone, but the want of it hurts a great many. Well, as I was saying, she grew melancholy and would sit alone for hours and it seems as though all the comfort she took was when the parson came in. Then she would rouse herself a little, but as soon as he was gone, she would sink back into the same state of mind. (C) What did she complain of? (Mother) She would sigh and often speak of her head being confused, and feeling weak, till we were alarmed about her and sent for the doctor; and when he came–(C) Stop here. Did she complain of any disease or only her feelings? (Mother) Only her feelings. (C) Go on.

(Mother) When the doctor came, he examined her and treated her accordingly. (C) Did you hear the doctor's testimony? (Mother) Yes. (C) Did you ever have such an opinion of her case till you were told so by the doctor? (Mother) No. (C) Did you ever hear your daughter intimate that she had such a disease before the doctor came? (Mother) No, and she went on from one disease to another just as the doctor had said. (C) And you are satisfied that the doctor understood her case? (Mother) Oh yes, for I remember when he told her that her lungs were affected, she was much surprised and so was I, for we never dreamed of such a thing. (C) How did it affect her? (Mother) At first it shocked her very much so that she did not sleep that night, but the parson came in the morning and prayed with her and she seemed more calm. Religion is the only thing the poor child has to cling to, for her disease went on so rapidly that it seemed as though we had all been blind to her danger. I really believe if she had not seen the doctor as she did, she would have been in her grave. (C) You need not give your opinion, only tell what you know. (Mother) Well, that is what the doctor said–if we did not send for him just as we did, she would have been in her grave. (C) Then all you know is what the doctor said? (Mother) Yes, of course, for I know nothing of disease myself. I have brought up six children and never a doctor in the house before. (C) Then you have a very good opinion of your doctor? (Mother) Why should I not when he could foresee just how my daughter's disease would go on. I was very particular to listen to all he said, and remember how he would tell how the disease would affect her. (C) You may retire.

Miss_____, will you please state to the judge how you were when the doctor came to see you first. You need not rise, keep your seat. (Patient) I do not remember my feelings as they were at that time well enough to describe them now, but when the doctor stated them, I remembered them. (C) Had you all the diseases that he said you had? (P) I do not know anything except what he said. (C) How did it affect you? (P) It at first made me very nervous. (Judge) Do you stop here? (C) Not quite yet. This is a case of great importance, not only to the person accused but to the whole people at large, for if a person is to be convinced on such testimony as that, science is of no use. If opinion is law, then the wisdom of God is of no effect. Now this young lady is accused of sundry and divers diseases, named in the writ as offenses against the laws of God; and she has been arraigned before you as a judge of truth and science, and it becomes necessary on my part to prove to the court that the whole of the above testimony is false, that it does not contain one word of science but is all the invention of man, that she is not guilty of any of the diseases named, as arising from any disobedience of God's laws.

I must show to the court that she is innocent of all she is accused, that all her symptoms, as they are called, are the effect of her belief, that the witnesses here are the very ones who have betrayed and deceived her into an acknowledgment of what she had never known anything before. Being threatened with everlasting punishment, she became so nervous that she was not in her right mind, and in this state she was made to confess whatever she was requested to do, and then her deceivers turned against her and here she is.

I will now show that all they have accused her of is false. I will call on the parson and show that his wisdom is based on an opinion of which he cannot show the first shadow of proof. You can state by what authority you so deceived the lady. (Parson) By what authority do you call my profession in question? (C) By the authority of God or wisdom. (Parson to the Judge) Have you any jurisdiction over a minister of the Gospel of Christ? (Judge) No. (Parson) Then why am I arraigned before you to answer for an offense which, if true, would be a stain on my Christian character? (C) I will state one thing which I stand ready to prove, that this minister is not in fellowship with the character of Jesus, nor is he a disciple of Christ, but is decidedly in opposition to all of Jesus' teachings. And that he is one of those blind guides spoken of by Jesus and his disciples who go about entering the houses of the mind, while the inmates are asleep or ignorant of his character, bind them and then destroy their goods or happiness.

This same minister entered her happy home or mind some three years ago, and by the dim light of heathen superstition frightened her into a confession that she had been guilty of disobeying the laws of God, and unless she repented and acknowledged it, she must suffer eternal punishment. This frightened her into a belief that made her nervous and in this state of mind the doctor was sent for. I will call the doctor on the stand again. If I remember rightly doctor, you said when you were called to see this young lady, you found her under great nervous excitement. (Doc.) Yes. (C) Did you make up your mind what was the cause? (Doc.) Not exactly, but supposed it must have been from some over-excitement of the brain. (C) Did you know that it was by religious excitement? (Doc.) In fact, I never thought of that till now (further evidence objected to but overruled). (C) Did you ever see a person laboring under excitement caused by attending these religious meetings? (Doc.) Yes, frequently. (C) If you should be particular to notice their talk and acts, could you not tell whether it was by religious excitement or not? (Doc.) Yes. (C) Well, please say whether or not you think this young lady's first excitement was caused by that. (Doc.) I am now certain of it and if this court will let me state what I know, that will show my feelings at the time. (C) Go on.

(Doc.) Some two or three weeks before the revival in which she was very much interested, together with a number of other young ladies who all experienced religion, I was at a ball where she was present, and in the course of conversation with her, expressed my interest in her health. She replied that as long as she could keep clear of doctors and priests she should do well enough and in less than two weeks after that time, the excitement commenced. (C) How long did it keep up? (Doc.) Some five or six days.

(C) Then it was at one of these protracted meetings? (Doc.) Yes. (C) How long ago was that? (Doc.) I don't know, but think it must have been some three years and a half ago. (C) You say that there were some other young ladies that were affected? (Doc.) Yes. (C) How have they come out? (Doc.) One is in an insane hospital and another died of depression of the most horrid kind. In fact, I do not know of anyone who was not affected. (C) Now you have heard the doctor's opinion of your meetings; what does the parson say to that? (Parson) I do not deny that those that he named came to their death as he said, but it was not by religion, for religion never makes any one crazy. (C) How do you know? You give no proof. (Parson) I know that. (C) You have stated something you cannot prove.

If it was necessary to prove that this man is a false teacher I could do it, but I have shown enough to prove that all his knowledge is based on an opinion of someone who is as ignorant as himself. So you may leave and answer to wisdom for your inability to preach Christ. Now I think I have the foundation for the medical doctor. I will show to the court that the medical doctor is as ignorant of his profession as the priest. And between them both they have kept this young lady in prison for three years. I will now ask the medical doctor a few questions. What causes disease? (Doc.) Disobeying the laws of God. (C) You are sure of that? (Doc.) Yes. (Judge) Have you the laws of God in regard to health? (Doc.) I have not. (Judge) Did you ever hear of such laws? (Doc.) Oh yes, often. (Judge) Did you ever see any such laws? (Doc.) No. (Counsel against the prisoner) You do not say that there are no such laws. (Judge) I never saw them. (Doc.) Are there any laws in regard to health? (Judge) Oh, yes, there are many, but who made them? (Doc.) Man I suppose, but are they not founded on the laws of God? (Judge) I never saw such laws in the book of life. (Doc.) Where are the laws that man disobeys? (Judge) The laws are of their own make. Every man is a book and is judged out of his own book, and he that is found in the book of life or wisdom is not judged by the laws of man. (Counsel) The patient is accused of certain offenses committed against the laws of God and by these laws she is to die. Here I stand ready to show that she had been deceived by the medical doctor who is ignorant of his calling and being ignorant had made her believe a lie, that she may be damned or die. So I will call the medical doctor to answer a few questions.

You say that when you first called on the patient you found that she was laboring under nervous excitement caused by congestion of the lungs? (Doc.) Yes. (C) How did you ascertain the fact that it was congestion of the lungs? (Doc.) By sounding them and by respiration. (C) Are you sure that you cannot be deceived? (Doc.) I think I am. (C) Do you on your oath, before the judge of wisdom say that there was congestion of the lungs? (Doc.) No, I won't swear, for I might be mistaken. (C) Do not all medical doctors get mistaken often? (Doc.) Oh, yes. (C) Then it is your opinion that her lungs were affected? (Doc.) Yes. (C) You caused a blister-plaster to be applied? (Doc.) Yes. I applied a blister-plaster all over the chest to relieve the irritation. (C) Does not a blister-plaster irritate? (Doc.) Yes. (C) Does it not make some persons so nervous that it has to be removed? (Doc.) Yes.

(C) Was it so in her case? (Doc.) She made a great deal of objection and wanted it to be removed. (C) Would not this of itself affect her whole system and cause her head to ache? (Doc.) I suppose it might. (C) Well, have you proof of any disease except your opinion? (Doc.) Yes. (C) What? (Doc.) A great many things. (C) Would you have known anything by your own feelings if you had been blind and the lady dumb? (Doc.) No.

(C) Your wisdom was founded on your sight and her voice? (Doc.) Yes. (C) Can you see pain? (Doc.) No. (C) Can you feel another's pain? (Doc.) No. (C) Then how do you know that anything ailed her, only by her looks and what she said? (Doc.) That is the only way. (C) Are not persons very nervous when they are not sick? (Doc.) Yes. (C) Well, that is all. I suppose the Judge is satisfied that the medical doctor's opinion is founded on circumstantial evidence and there is not one single particle of wisdom in all his testimony. So she is not guilty of any disease by man's laws from the testimony of the medical doctor, only that she has been frightened into an acknowledgement of something that she never knew anything about. I propose to show in the first place that God never made a law of any kind, and if he never made a law, then man could never transgress what was never made. I will introduce the original book of God or nature and see if the translation was right to make God responsible for man's laws. It reads in God's book that man was created a little above the brutes. Jesus said that the foxes have holes and the birds have nests, but the son of man had nowhere to lay his head, so that Jesus was a fair specimen of man in his original state, cast among brutes of all kinds. His life was one of terror and bloodshed, and as might was right with brutes and man, it became necessary for man to invent some way to protect himself against the brute, so he invented laws and penalties to govern man.

God is not found in any law containing rewards and punishments. We often hear the word science, but this is not found in God's book–science is the name of wisdom reduced to practice. We often hear of the laws of God. When we ask for an illustration, we are told, if a person falls off a building, it will kill him. Suppose it does, has he disobeyed any law? I say no. All will admit that bodies are attracted to the earth. This is a truth, and to reduce this wisdom to man's senses so that he shall know the fact, man calls it the effect of the science of God's laws, or a knowledge of God's wisdom. Now if you let a rock fall from a building, it falls according to the laws of God, but if man falls, he has disobeyed some of God's laws. And if by chance it does not kill him, he must be punished by God with pains until he will cease from breaking that law. And God has just about as much to do with the rock as with the man. It is impossible to disobey God in any one thing, for wisdom is not of this world of matter. For wisdom is that which fills all space, so there cannot be any real space occupied by matter. Matter as man calls it is only a shadow of substance, so a shadow cannot fill space; it is a vacuum, ready to be filled by wisdom when man arrives at the truth of the substance that makes the shadow.

Opinions are by the wisdom of this world admitted to be true. These opinions are condensed into a belief and pass off for substance. In this way matter has been introduced in this world by error and out of this error or matter man has been made. But the scientific man or wisdom came from God, and like the mind that penetrates through the pores of all matter, it was breathed into this shadow and it became a progressive being. This wisdom sees through the error or earthly man. It will not be subject to his will, but does not interfere with the natural man's opinions; it only sanctions what man agrees to. If man condenses his wisdom into any belief that makes him liable to any law that he may make and it becomes a fixed law, then he must be punished by that law. But if he seeks wisdom from above and obtains it, then the laws of matter cannot bind him in bondage. If I show by the wisdom of God that this young lady has not committed any offense against the laws of God, then the Judge of Science will release her from the laws of man. This is my defense: that disease is not self-existent but is the invention of this world of error. To show that, it is necessary to go back some ages and see how the ancient philosophers of Greece and Rome entertained the same ideas that Jesus did. Both condemned religion with the most vehement denunciation they could invent.

Lucretius condemns it as the greatest tyrant of man, holds that it is directly against science and everything that tends to enlighten man. He shows that mind is master, that there is nothing else than mind and matter. He called them matter, and void or space, which is the same. For matter is not seen by the natural man except by the effects. He shows that the idea of weight, as it is called, is impossible; but people cannot understand when they see a thing fall that it does not contain weight. Let our philosophers discard the idea of weight and introduce the words gravitation and attraction. These last are as false as the first, for there cannot be such a thing in wisdom as gravitation. Everyone knows that the air presses on all matter so that it is filled with air or something that makes a vacuum; so that when there is the most vacuum in matter, the lighter it is. The air penetrates like sound or matter, so that matter and mind are all that there is to be seen even by the spiritual man. His idea is that as all matter decomposes, it passes into void and out of sight to the natural man. So if matter is matter when it is not visible, why does it not fall to some center and there remain? (All wisdom shows that it does not act in that way.) Now as matter is dissolved by some solid which comes in contact with it, I call this solid the essence of wisdom. This essence breaks in pieces all the matter or error. And as it fills all space, it holds all matter in solution as it is in the very air. It is always dissolving all bodies and as they dissolve, they pass off, not rise, for there is no rise or fall, nor length or breadth, but vacuum or essence.

This essence is governed by wisdom and wisdom sees through all error or matter. Matter is the name of that which we see and feel, and that which we cannot see and can only feel is mind. This mind is what rises from the idea matter and as the idea is destroyed, the particles are held in solution, not destroyed but separated by this essence of wisdom. So that the word or idea is not in existence as such, or as matter, but as a remembrance. I will try to illustrate. The word disease contains an idea of disturbance of the mind. As there is no identity, it is a mere sensation in this essence where the mind is. Now the idea of a tumor is made or spoken into existence; this matter set in motion by this essence, an idea is formed or belief that there is such a thing as a tumor. This belief is the light of the person that believes it; his body is lighted by it, being nothing but the shadow of substance that can never be destroyed. This belief can enter the shadow and set up its standard of wisdom and keep the wisdom of God from developing itself, like a rock that defies the essence to dissolve it; but wisdom can break it in pieces by its power. Error gives direction, and as this matter like electricity is set in motion, and as vacuum is composed of vacuum and matter of error, error by excluding all wisdom or science from itself makes to itself a tumor as solid as its ignorance can invent. This process has been carried to that perfection, that man in his ignorance can almost turn his identity into a pillar of salt.

January 1861

Explanation of Matter, The
[LC 1:0324]

The religion of the pagans and heathen was founded on the superstition of their leaders and their philosophy was to prove their religion. Their religion affected the people, for the wiser men saw that there was no truth nor sound logic in all their reasoning but the tendency of their religion was to make man ignorant and superstitious. So to offset this a more enlightened class of philosophers arose whose aim was to destroy the mythology.

To do this it was necessary to show the absurdity of their doctrines. As their doctrines purposed to commence at the beginning of time, it was necessary that they should attack the very foundation of their theory. As of course those philosophers commenced in matter, it was necessary for the philosophers who wrote in opposition to their religion to show the absurdity of their theory. So Lucretius, who stands among the first of the pagan philosophers, struck at the pillar of their very foundations by showing that there was no foundation for their beliefs.

All philosophers mention the existence of matter which being dissolved passes into space. And man being made of matter, as his body decomposes, he also passes into space. And he, like all other matter, comes to an end. But as this theory would not cover the whole ground, it leaves man in space like all other matter, a sort of spirit or soul or some living principle that comes out of this matter and exists somewhere.

The locality of this soul or life was never defined by the religious world. Philosophers have given different accounts of the soul, but at the time that Lucretius wrote, the religious world had no idea of a world after death, like the Christians of our day, but all their religion was confined to this life. It is true that there were exceptions, but the large majority of the people at the time of Lucretius, one-hundred years before Christ, believed in a soul. So that by reading Lucretius you get a very good idea of the opinion of that philosopher concerning the effect of religion on the masses. He looked upon it as the worst enemy of man and to destroy it, it was necessary to show that the philosophy on which it was based was false.

So he commenced with matter and proved that matter is nothing but an idea, that there was no such thing as matter with the First Cause. He reasons man and matter into space and shows that all the philosophy of man is based upon a false basis and religion does more harm than good. So he, like all the rest, dissolves man and leaves him in space and all beyond is man's opinion, without any foundation.

His philosophy was to destroy the religion of his day, and mine is to destroy the religion of my day and show that our religion is based on our philosophy and claims the story of the Old Testament to prove it. So I have to commence at the beginning and show that the philosophy of the Old Testament had nothing to do with the creation of the earth nor anything in it nor on it. But those ideas were the beliefs of the ancients before Moses was born. Moses is supposed to give a description of the commencement of the world, when nothing can be more absurd. He only gave a theory of the creation of man and showed that there was a power superior to man. But the ignorant and superstitious supposed that Moses was writing about the creation of the world. This led to superstition and priestcraft and as these beliefs were accompanied with a philosophy to establish their doctrines, they turned and twisted the Old Testament into a religious book, teaching ideas that Moses never dreamed of.

Moses' religion was his wisdom and his wisdom was far superior to the religion of his day. His religion was his philosophy; so is every one's, and that philosophy which contains the most truth is the best religion. Science had nothing to do with their religion and was opposed to it. Religion, or man's science or philosophy, bound burdens on the people and there was no philosophy that could explain or lighten man of these burdens. For the wisdom of man had not arrived at the point where there could be a philosophy that would teach man that his happiness was the result of his wisdom and his misery was the natural result of his belief.

Now the mistaken idea of what mind is has led man into trouble and causes so much sickness and sorrow, and this is the origin of disease. Convince man that mind is matter and wisdom is not, and he will no longer be deceived by false guides, crying, Peace, peace, when there is no peace.

This is the origin of disease and this is what the philosophers of Greece and Rome, Lucretius and others wrote against. For they saw that the priests by their false doctrines made men believe all sorts of stories. They knew that their beliefs were matter or mind and they saw what their effect on the people was. But as the priests in those days held the people in a slavery sanctioned by their Gods, reformers found no favor with the people. Now as the priests kept binding burdens of disease on the people, philosophers would rise up and try to rid the people of their burdens. But the priests held such sway over the people's mind by phenomena that the masses could not explain, that the wise could not put their wisdom into practice. So the priests exercised full sway over the minds of the people. The philosophers who knew that mind was matter could see through the hypocrisy of the priests. Also they could see through the fact that any idea or belief could be condensed so as to come within the senses of the masses and this would be proof that the priests were right. So at the time these philosophers wrote, their doctrines or wisdom could not be understood. Nor is it understood now by the masses, nor will it ever be, although it be true and can be reduced to a science. Thus the masses have always been under the control of the priests. So that this wisdom which would destroy all standards in matter was not tried to be put into practice scientifically for some hundred and fifty years, when Jesus called attention to the same theory.

There were persons who could change matter, move bodies and cure many diseases and some had reduced it to a sort of belief which would counteract the priests' belief, but none but deceivers tried to sell the art. Even in these days, you see certain persons undertaking to teach people to psychologize, as though they knew something that others did not, while they themselves are so ignorant of the way they produce phenomena as the people were in the days of Jesus. The priests took advantage of every phenomenon, but they kept the knowledge for their own benefit and made the people believe in superstition. Finally they formed a religious belief, attaching penalties to the disobeying any laws that the priests set up. Now the science or wisdom that shows that mind can be acted upon would leak out and it kept the priests all the time inventing some new phenomena to keep the people under. At the time of Jesus their craft had leaked out so that it had gotten into the hands of the people and took the names of the inventions of men. They were like the mediums of our days, talking about a gift and communications from the spirits of the dead. Many such pretended to do as Jesus did, thinking it was a gift or art from God; they knew that theirs was not genuine, but the people believed in them. In these days, I am set down with the same class of people, who have a power or gift, by fools or the ignorant because the superstition and religious creeds have closed up all avenues to wisdom. They are in the fog and cannot see out and they think that everyone else is in the same place.

In Jesus' day, if he undertook to expose the priests, they would accuse him of making himself equal with God and would cry, Crucify him. So like the leaders of any party, when they want to bear down on their game, they set on the dogs. When Jesus began to teach this new truth, for although it was old it had a place in the minds of the masses, he called the people together, not to instruct them in religion but to show them that religion was just what the wise philosophers had called it. So he denounced the leaders, showed the people how their belief made them sick and being wiser and having more courage than any who believed as he did, he tried to reduce this wisdom to a science. To do this it was necessary to prove it by his works, as the priests would cure by their deception. For the mind, like potter's clay, is under control of whoever gives direction, the works showing whether they be of God or man. If of man, then man is under the law; if of God or science, man is free from the law so that the law has no power over him, for he that is dead to the law or alive in wisdom is free from sin and death or error.

Jesus wanted everything in common, that is, if a person knows anything that is for the happiness of man to know, let it be known. He said that every truth should be given or taught to man. No one should say, Know you this truth or science, but all should acknowledge it from the wisest and it shall become the wisdom of the world. Perhaps it will be necessary to say what there is to be known. It is this: Jesus wanted the people to understand that religion, as they were taught it, was the blackest sort of hypocrisy, only got up to keep a class of lazy thieves and robbers in power, who devour houses of wood and houses of mind, carrying off and selling men and women into slavery, for their own good. When Jesus applied these sayings to the people, it melted down their heathen belief and by his words of wisdom, they were cured.

Jesus never had any religious opinions. His works were his life and his life was his Christ or theory. The people could not understand this so they crucified him, and that ended the life of one of the best men that ever lived, for his natural man became subject to his scientific man or wisdom. This wisdom cannot help making mankind better any more than a good man can help becoming narrow-minded and bigoted by belonging to a church. Our beliefs are all there is of us and just as we measure out to our neighbor, we measure out to ourselves, so action and reaction are equal. If we make a person believe anything that we have no proof of, except as an opinion, we bind burdens on our friends that our wisdom cannot remove. Wisdom says that every idle word must be accounted for at the day of judgment.

So here I stand as a mediator for this young lady and if I have shown that her accusers are guilty of perjury against the laws of wisdom, then the court will give the verdict to the defendant and cast a wicked and ungodly belief into the fire of science, where it shall be burned with unquenchable truth.

I will stop here, for I believe that I have satisfied the court that the priests bound on this young lady their hypocritical creeds which made her nervous, and then the other part of the priesthood, the doctors, decoyed her into the worst of all company where she was betrayed into all kinds of misery. Then they turned their backs upon her after robbing her of her money and character–for her belief is her character–and making her believe she is one of the worst of characters. For to be sick is a disgrace and if the superstition of the world had the power, they would kill the sick for the safety of the well. These two classes, priests and doctors, have so degraded men that sickness is the greatest evil in life. Jesus knew this and he laid down his life or ran the risk that neither dared to do, took their diseases upon himself, risking the danger of becoming sick and dying as they would do.

In closing my argument, I will say to the court and multitude that I knew that this girl had been deceived by these two blind guides. In the first place, I never ask my patients anything but tell them all. This the doctors do not pretend to do. I have no religious belief to teach as the priests have. Something cannot come from nothing and as I have nothing of myself, they get nothing from me that will affect them. The priests' belief is a lie and is of matter; the believing of it changes the mind or matter. The ignorance of the creeds is their light and that being a false light makes a shadow and in the shadow the patient puts his trust. As it is founded in ignorance and superstition, it contains all sorts of evil spirits and ghosts, etc. My wisdom can see through this veil of the priests. I see where the deception lies and as I explain, the vacuum of their mind is lit up and the shadow disappears, like the rays of the moonlight when the sun rises. As ignorance or religion receives the truth or science it gives way to a higher priesthood not made by man, but eternal in wisdom, that teaches man to do to another as he would like that other should do to him. This is all; so I stop for the verdict to be made up.

January 1861

Explanation of an Error Is the End of Disease, The
[LC 2:0820]

The idea that the understanding of my theory is the cure of disease is a stumbling block to the wisdom of this world. They can't see that to understand what you believe is different from believing what you do not understand. Suppose I say to you that the earth is flat and you do not believe it. Now if I ask you to prove it is not flat, that is out of your power, unless you take the testimony of persons that have proved to the world that it is round. I presume there is not one man in ten million who could prove it either round or flat by experiments of his own, yet every person believes it round and to them it is round.

Now suppose a certain set of philosophers start the idea that it is of some other shape, just as absurd to the world as the idea that it was round was to the people that believed it flat, and show evidence of their idea that it is out of the power of the philosophers of our day to refute. Although they might know it was wrong, they would be changed, not only their mind or belief, but to them the earth would take the form of the majority's belief. You may say their belief could not alter the earth. Was the earth round to the people that believed it flat? No. Then which changed, the earth or the belief? Could you change their belief and still have the earth flat to those people? No. Then their belief is all that we have to do with, for just as a person believes to that person it is a fact.

This holds good in everything as far as ourselves are concerned. Now as you have admitted that man can change his belief, you must admit that his belief is something, in order that it may be changed. Now if my belief embraces my senses and all that I know, then to change my belief I change myself. Now what does a man believe in regard to what he does not see? If I see myself I know that fact, but I can believe that I shall not always see myself. So what we see, we know we see, and what we believe we do not see. Now the thing seen is the phenomenon of what we believe. Suppose I ask you if you ever saw a person with the heart disease and you should say, Yes. I then ask you how you know and you would have to give some answer that was based on a belief, for your assertion to me is only an opinion. Now I see the person and he says I have heart disease. Now is it a reality or a belief or both? You might say his belief had nothing to do with his disease, that the heart might become diseased and he have no mind or belief about it. Then where is it? Can there be a phenomenon in a person and the person know it and still say it is not a part of his senses? The trouble lies in the false idea of ourselves.

Mind, being subject to the will, is always being changed by every thought. Even our thoughts are not our own and in fact man is a combination of ideas that are constantly working out some problem and we are all a part and parcel of this great problem. To suppose that we act of ourselves is as absurd as to suppose that a clock keeps time by the weight. There is an intelligence that governs the world or man that is not known and this intelligence acts upon the belief, while the belief is not aware of the fact. Now all man's trouble is in this element called belief or mind. The phenomenon that we see is a fact. That is not intelligence but the effect of intelligence. Here is where we fail in perceiving how the understanding makes the cure. The doctors always address themselves to the phenomenon; I, to the intelligence. I will state a case.

I had a young officer who had his arm shot by a minie ball through the wrist. The hand became so painful and swollen that it was necessary to amputate the limb just below the elbow. But still the sensation of the hand remained, and it was so troublesome that he could not rest; his hand was in constant pain. The stump he did not feel but the hand that had been taken off was as real as the other. Now I suppose you would say this was all imagination, for the hand was gone. Now who is to decide this question, the person that felt the pain or the observers? He felt the hand and the doctor could not change his mind by telling him the hand was gone. This was false in the true sense, for his hand was a part of his senses and the phenomenon that could be seen was nothing to his senses; he had a hand, and it troubled him. Now was the trouble in his mind or in the phenomenon that the doctor had taken off? I say it was his mind and this was what he wished to get rid of. Although he, to his belief, had lost his hand, his senses had not lost it. And to cure or satisfy his senses, he wished to get rid of his hand, for it became a source of torment. So I took hold of the stump and by explaining the truth, I changed the mind and he cast the idea away and then felt of the stump and became quiet, satisfied that it was better to have one arm and be happy and well, than having two, and being in torment.

Now if I could not have changed his mind, he could not have gotten rid of the pain or misery. So you see, the taking off the phenomenon called the arm had no pain or disease in it, for it was there just as real as before. Suppose he had been a child and his hand had been crushed and amputation had taken place. The same effect might have been seen in the child. We think that our senses or mind may not be aware of the suffering of the body, that the body may be sick and the mind well. That is impossible, for the body cannot be sick any more than a steam engine could be sick. The owner may be sick, so a child may be sick, but when we speak of a child, we speak of what we see and not what we understand. The child is not visible but the phenomenon is, and when we doctor the phenomenon, we do not know the owner. The owner is where the eye cannot penetrate. Does not every person in the room hear the clock strike whether he is aware of it or not? In the same way mind is sensitive to every thought whether the body shows it or not. A belief is something and if it comes in contact with matter, it will make an impression. I might bring thousands of facts to show that disease is the effect of our belief, whether we know it or not. How many there are who do not think that they are influenced by others' beliefs, when it is as apparent as it is that the sun shines on a clear day, and yet they will take their oath that no person's belief affects them when in fact they are the mouthpiece of some belief. How often do we hear this remark. I have a belief of my own. Now if they have a belief, it cannot be a fact, so that their belief is in regard to something that they think exists. So if you can make a person believe a thing exists, then his belief to him is a fact, and this he considers as his own, although it is a belief.

This is the way disease comes. We are made to believe a lie and this belief creates a phenomenon. This is the proof that our belief was founded in wisdom, when we do not know that our belief is the very thing that changes the mind and creates. Make man know this and then he will see that what he needs is to know how to correct his mind in order to get rid of his trouble. This has to be done by another mode of reasoning and this is my mode of cure: to change the mind, believing that all our troubles are out of sight but the phenomenon is in sight. Therefore never look into the effect for the cause. The cause can never be seen by the natural eye, for man never sees the idea he is afraid of; causes cannot be seen, only effects. The cause is the belief of what cannot be seen. The belief affects the mind and a phenomenon is produced. This is called, for instance, cancer. Now show how we get an idea into the mind of man and the process of discovery rids the mind of the belief. And then the person is as free from cancer as a person who once believed the eclipse was sent from God as a warning to man to repent is, when he understands astronomy.

The fear or belief is gone and no phenomenon can take place. So it is with all diseases, for they are all lies and to discover the mode in which they were made is the destruction of error.

Sunday, Aug. 27, 1864

Explanation of Science
[Originally untitled.] [BU 3:0526]

Am I right in my explanation of Science when I say it is a knowledge of forces?

"Yes," but that does not cover all the combinations of the word, for science has no established standard independent of error. I will try to give you a plainer illustration of the word. To give an explanation of the word science, you must first know what is to be tested. If intended to apply to acknowledged truths, then your explanation covers all the ground. But if it is to be applied to wisdom not understood, then it will not cover the objections, for opinions may come in, as they are science by the natural man. True science is of the wisdom of God, false science is of man; so in using the word, this difference must be kept in mind.

I will give you your position before the world in regard to me or this truth. You are not to be supposed to be the truth or even to be me, but only to explain what I teach. For instance, one person can execute music on a piano and yet be ignorant of the science. Another can execute music and understand how he learned it and how to teach the same to others. Now the masses acknowledge both as musicians and class them in the same catalog. The scientific musician knows they are not alike, but the masses cannot understand the difference, for the tunes sound just alike to them. The wisdom of this world, or the masses, sees no difference. Now the scientific musician wants someone to tell where he makes the difference. He need not play or teach music, but show by experiment that one can play a tune that anyone can bring him and at the same time show that the other plays by rote.

Exposition of Dr. Quimby's Method of Curing
[LC 1:0434]

A patient comes to see Dr. Quimby. He renders himself absent from everything but the impression of their feelings. These are quickly daguerreotyped on him. They contain no intelligence but shadow forth a reflection of themselves which he looks at. This contains the disease as it appears to the patient. Being confident that it is a shadow of a false idea, he is not afraid of it but laughs at it. Then his feelings in regard to the disease which are health and strength are daguerreotyped on the receptive plate of the patient which also throws forth a shadow. The patient seeing this shadow of the disease in a new light gains confidence. This change of feeling is daguerreotyped on the doctor again, which also throws forth a shadow and he sees the change and continues to treat it in the same way. So the patient's feelings sympathize with him. The shadow changes and grows dim and finally the light takes its place and there is nothing left of the disease.

Extract from a Letter, An
[BU 2:0053]

All effects produced on the human frame are the result of a chemical change of the fluids with or without our knowledge, and all the varieties and changes are accompanied by a peculiar state of mind. If the mind should be directed to any particular organ, that organ might become deranged or it might not. In either case the trouble is in the mind, for the body is only the house for the mind to dwell in, and we put a value upon it according to its worth. Therefore if your mind has been deceived by some invisible enemy into a belief, you have put it into the form of a disease, with or without your knowledge. By my theory or truth I come in contact with your enemy and restore you to health and happiness.

This I do partly mentally and partly by talking till I correct the wrong impressions and establish the truth, and the truth is the cure. I use no medicines of any kind and make no applications. I am no spiritualist after the manner of the Rochester rappings and I am not dictated to by any living man but am guided by the dictations of my own conscience as a lawyer is in pleading a case governed by the evidence. A sick man is like a criminal cast into prison for disobeying some law that man has set up. I plead his case, and if I get the verdict, the criminal is set at liberty. If I fail, I lose the case. His own judgment is his judge, his feelings are his evidence. If my explanation is satisfactory to the judge, he will give me the verdict. This ends the trial, and the patient is released.

December 1859

False Reasoning in Politics
[LC 1:0586]

A large class of men in reasoning always leave out the cause and reason about the effect. Take the rebellion. There must have been a cause. This all will admit. But when men reason and act, they say nothing about the cause, for that is beyond their comprehension. They merely hint of the existence of a cause as nothing and talk about individual acts. Now everyone must know that the cause of this cursed rebellion was in error or in principle if you choose to give it that name. Liberty and equality, so far as political freedom goes, are for all and he who opposes it places himself antagonistically to it. Now if might is right, one has a physical right to enslave another if he can. But as a principle there is no such an element, but might is physically stronger than right and has no respect for it. So it creates for itself an element and all evils are in this element or might. When these elements are at war, they work out another element called law. Now law was never the design of either right or wrong but the pleading of might and the yielding of right.

The element of freedom is in the opposition to slavery. And slavery is opposed to the rights of freedom for the slave; so the elements become condensed into a party and are engrafted into individuals. Now this element prompts might to action and, as freedom never acts till it is acted upon, it is insulted by might. Slavery, being the element to excite the brutal feeling, makes war with the higher element of freedom and shows itself by its aristocratic power.

I wish to say one word in regard to riots. Man makes no distinction between them, when there is a great difference. Right never gets up riots. Might is never right but always wrong. When this government was formed, it had to be formed by the element which came out of the brutal element or might; so laws were made for the protection of might and not for right, for right does not need any laws.

Might is rebellion of itself, but it causes a reaction that it is afraid of and then it calls on right to protect it. Now this brutal element of slavery, not being under any law and because they had the power, commenced to enslave the blacks. And because they exercised their power, a reaction took place, and now the world is experiencing that reaction. They have created the element of retaliation by their striking down the law that has hitherto protected them. The reaction is not a mob nor a rebellion but a natural consequence of their wicked acts, and if they get handled roughly, it is their own fault. When they call on the law to protect them against their own crime, they must first destroy the evil before they can have any guarantee of protection. Just as long as the evils exist, just so long they will commit crimes by their wicked acts. Make the principle a party responsible and individuals will forsake it for the sake of their own protection.

All mobs which start for an evil purpose are met by a corresponding mob, and governed and headed by right, not law, which beat the mob of evil till it cries for mercy and begs for some guarantee from right that it shall not be harmed. Right lets them make their laws and then says, now respect them and obey them. But as this serpent slavery is so treacherous that it will abuse liberty every chance it has, it must be met by its own weapons. It now cries for peace, but it has not yet got its full reaction. It must have its reward, and then when it is ready to make a law that shall execute the idea or element, then they can have it, for it requires a law to make it do right.

First Cause, The
[LC 2:0775]

I will try to give an illustration of my First Cause. Wisdom is outside of everything. Opinion is in wisdom, for wisdom fills all space. Therefore, it being all wise, everything comes within itself. Opinion being in belief cannot be wisdom, for it is liable to change. Now man is in one or the other of these two elements, wisdom or opinion. Principles are wisdom reduced to science or practice. Laws are not principles but are based on opinions that can change and they belong to man's reasoning. Principles do not reason at all but are like rays of light. All the principles of wisdom that are understood are like the points of a compass and these we call cardinal principles.

Now man divides the globe into four quarters and the filling up of the points of compass is to fill up the space, so that man knows more than the four points; so with wisdom. The principles are so many that it is impossible to understand only as we grow wise. Now man has an identity but the precise locality of it he does not know. So as he believes in his identity, he forgets that he cannot see himself only as he develops himself in his own belief. So principles having no matter, he is lost when out of matter, for he has no idea of an existence in principle, yet he is in wisdom all the time and his size is just in proportion to the progress he makes in putting his wisdom into practice. The man, therefore, that believes in matter as being the First Cause is always changing and is not aware of the change, like the man who thinks everybody is changing and he is the only one that stands still, when everything changes that goes to make up his identity but the man.

This man you will find in politics. He is in the name, democrat, a fixed principle, as he thinks, when it is the name of that kind of mortar that is always used to fill up the breaches in progression. Yet it is mortar, though it is sometimes in bricks and sometimes in the gutter and is used for everything. Yet it is democracy or mortar. So man's wisdom is the democracy. His senses are attached to the name and although the matter or mind is always changing, he is not changed, for the change is not a part of him; he is nothing but the name. He is like a man who lives in a city who is always ready to tell you where he lives, but of the growth of the wisdom he is as ignorant as the mortar that is used to build the building; so he never changes from the name. He knows no other change than what he sees and as he sees the city grow, he never asks the cause. But when asked how long he has been a resident of P, he says, I was born here and so was my father, so his identity is in the name P, but the wisdom is to them a stranger. So when he sees a man that has come to P that is posted up with the wisdom of progression and he finds such a person rising, he looks around and says, I have always been a resident of P, and this man comes among us from abroad. What does he know? He is some renegade from some city or party; I am a long-lived democrat or citizen of Portland.

Now the difference is: one lives in his ignorance and the other in progression. It is the same with truth and error. One works out of opinion or matter into science, while the other like the silk worm covers himself with the cloak of error till there is no light in him. Now how can we show a man who believes he is in the light that he is in the dark? And yet it is plain that he is in the light to him and to every other person who believes as he does. Now when we admit that everything that can be changed cannot be a principle, then we will see what man is made of. For everything that we see changes: his hair, his skin, his weight and in fact everything that goes to make up the man. So if everything changes, what does not change? Principles. Now the man that is in the change thinks he is the same man, although his mind or matter is continually going through a change. Now what kind of a person is this that does not change? The man that knows he exists outside of all these changes and sees the change as a man looks at the skies and sees the clouds pass along and knows that they are nothing but wind. So the change to this man is in the clouds, while the other is in the clouds and sees the other looking at him, seeing him blown about by every wind of doctrine. He says to the one that stands still, What makes you fly around so when he himself is the one that is carried about and thinks he never changes, like a drunken man who thinks everyone he meets is staggering, while he himself is the one that staggers.

Now as the man of opinions is like the cloud, he is not aware of the darkness of himself, so that as he becomes more rarefied he is not aware of the change but thinks the change is in others. This is the state of the sick. They are in their belief. This to them is as real as the cloud, but they, being ignorant that it is a belief, make to themselves an image corresponding to their belief and think they are outside of their belief and that the image is a real thing. I will illustrate. Suppose a person comes to me to be examined. The person shows on his face the marks of and appearance of humor. Now of course this is a fact and there is no belief about it. Here is the fact before your eyes. So to everyone it is a truth, and their wisdom does not admit it as a belief but as a thing they can see. Now to show or pretend to convey to them that it is a belief and it is in their mind is to the world absurd. Now as absurd as this may seem, this is what I have to do to cure the person. I have to show them that all the foregoing is in the mind.

So now if you can see in your mind such a person sitting by me and that I am trying to change their minds to destroy the humor, as it is called, if you will listen to what I say, you will have some slight idea of how I cure a mind diseased. I begin with the person after this manner.

(Dr.) You think you have a humor about you? (P.) I know I have. (Dr.) Well, I don't dispute that you have an eruption on your face, but it is in your mind. (P.) Do you think I imagine that I have a humor, that there is no such thing and that it is all in my imagination? (Dr.) No, I admit the phenomenon, but I say it is in your mind. (P.) I have no mind about it. I know it if I know anything. (Dr.) What is the cause? (P.) I don't know, only the doctors say my blood is full of humor of a cancerous nature, and also that I have scrofula. (Dr.) When did you get it? (P.) I suppose I inherited it from my mother. (Dr.) Do you know certainly? (P.) No, only I have been told so. (Dr.) Then this is a belief? (P.) Yes. (Dr.) I thought you said you had no belief, you knew it. (P.) I do know that my face is all covered with humor and I should be glad to get rid of it. (Dr.) Yet you say it is not a belief. Did you not say you inherited it from your mother? Now which is true, the humor or the belief? (P.) I know I have got the humor, but the belief I don't care anything about. I can't see that my belief has anything to do with my humor. (Dr.) Can there be an effect without a cause? (P.) Why, yes, I suppose my blood is out of order for I know I am bilious. (Dr.) What is that? Do these things come without a cause? (P.) No, but I don't know any cause for my humor. (Dr.) Then you say you have no idea of the true cause? (P.) No, only I suppose my blood is not in a very good state. (Dr.) What got it out of order? (P.) I can't tell, but heat I suppose, working over the stove cooking. (Dr.) Now are you aware that you have proved that all your trouble is in your mind?

1863

First Symptoms of Disease, The–Part I
[BU 3:0309]

All disease is what follows some sensation on the mind or the fluids of the body. Man's body is made of ideas admitted by the world of opinion. The man as we see him is an idea or reality according to our belief. This makes one fact. All his reasoning about himself is other ideas that are the life and intelligence of the idea body. So if the idea man believes his body is out of order, to him it is so. This is so with every idea made of the idea matter. Matter according to our belief is porous and God can penetrate it. Wisdom is truth and error is matter or darkness or it is porous. Wisdom is as much quicker than lightning, as thought is quicker than the bullet from a gun. So as wisdom is so quick, all ideas are nothing to it. For instance, look as you are riding in the cars at the high board fences put up to prevent the snow from blowing in and drifting onto the track. You know the boards of these fences fit very near together, so the cracks are not far apart. But when the cars are going at a rapid speed, you can see objects on the other side as plainly as though there was no fence. In fact you would scarcely know there was any fence. This is the way with velocity; it destroys space and distance and weight so that obstacles in the way are not obstacles to the velocity. Velocity is like wisdom and opinion is like the fence. The wisdom of opinion stands still and all is out of sight or nearly so on the other side of the fence, while the wisdom that flies without time sees no fence but sees the objects its attention is called to. So it is with the idea matter or thought; it is sent so quickly that to wisdom it is perfectly transparent.

It is generally believed that the earth was once a ball of liquid fire cooled off on the outside, that now in the center it is a fire and that people were travelling round while it was cooling off. The prints of their feet are in the earth, also remains of animals, etc. All of this is no doubt true, but the explanation of geology is as absurd as the doctor's diagnosis of disease. The phenomenon of the earth and of disease is just the same; both are founded in error and cannot stand the velocity or progress of truth. Wisdom can see through the cracks or pores or error of both and can show that neither is correct. Where were all of these living things while the earth was in this liquid state, for they must have form and size, since they are found embedded in rocks and in the earth. Modern theology is not wise enough to explain these phenomena correctly or satisfactorily; but explain them on the principle I have laid down in regard to matter, and then there is no difficulty in understanding it.

To cure disease is to know what produced it, and to know that embraces all man's ideas and wisdom of the creation of the world, for his religious opinions embrace the creation of the earth and heaven and all things therein. Men reason about all this and their ideas are sown in the mind, like seed in the earth. So he is, as the scriptures say, full of dead men's bones and all sorts of corruption. The idea earth is full of all sorts of ideas as much as man. Science is to analyze the earth, and this explains to man his disease, for all are made of ideas. I will give you an illustration of the growth of the idea earth by comparing it with man. To base a truth on an idea is like building a house on the sand. When the wind of investigation shall blow and the wave of science shall beat upon the house of opinion, it must come down. Everyone will admit that wisdom is superior to the idea matter. So we have two alternatives: either that wisdom was nothing before there was matter or that matter is the creation of wisdom.

The world reasons about God as it does about man, that the brain is the seat and origin of the wisdom of man and that the earth or matter is the dwelling place of God and that neither God nor man has any identity out of matter. This is the foundation of man's reasoning; therefore, if one is false, so is the other, but they are false in one respect and true in another. It is true that the phenomena exist in the mind of man or in his belief and that matter to the original man is his life and wisdom, but to wisdom, out of a belief, this is false. The natural man cannot see wisdom, for wisdom is not visible to the eye of matter. In all mathematics, there is a wisdom to be admitted, like the principles in geometry. You first assume a truth and then bring evidence to establish it as a fact. Imagine a vast void or space, where nothing in the form of matter exists. No one is so ignorant as to suppose there never was such a time. Every fact proves to the contrary and goes to show that from the seed things grow, showing progression from void.

In this void, imagine wisdom superior to all the effects that have been developed. Give this wisdom an identity with all the senses and faculties like man, only independent of matter, and then you have a perfect fullness of wisdom. Its motion is its own and from its own self comes all good and perfect wisdom. It speaks ideas and they come forth. The ideas are in the wisdom, as the mist is in the air. As they move or act by their own wisdom that is in the ideas, it grows till it gets condensed into a substance that attaches its life to its growth, as a child. When the child is born, its life is attached to its body and as it grows or creates new ideas, they become attached to the child and this makes the growth of the child. No one supposes that a man does not know he was once a child. But if the child could have been kept ignorant of its growth till he became a man, no one could even make the man believe that he ever had any earlier existence.

Suppose a chicken hatched; after it became a hen, would it ever suppose it was the inhabitant of an egg? It is so with everything that has life. Now suppose that wisdom from some cause unknown to man spoke into existence everything that hath life, yet like all other life there was progression. So if wisdom spoke worlds into existence, it is not to be supposed that the worlds or planets were as large as they are now. But the globe, like a child, is the growth of wisdom that is in itself like everything on the earth that has life. Each life is not the same life. The life of minerals is not that of vegetables and no two things are the same. Our globe is one idea of wisdom and all the other globes and planets that make up the solar system may be like one family, though each globe contains all the life that ever can be. But the growth or development is progression. For instance, man would not be formed before there was some place for him to live or rest upon. So life attached to matter must have some foundation for the matter before life could be attached to it.

Suppose this void was full of mist or life, not wisdom, but life. It would then be in a state like man's mind to be formed into any idea that might be thought of. But wisdom's works are all done at once. For instance, if you throw a rock into the air, all the effects were in the act not developed at the time, but they showed themselves as the progression went on. So when wisdom spake worlds into existence, it is not to be understood that they could be seen as they are now but were like thoughts taking form. From this fullness of life, worlds nursed its idea till it became visible to the idea of itself and then its wisdom was its growth and its life was its ideas. So its ideas fed of the life of this space. To know its growth is to know what contains the least life, for its life is its wisdom, subject to a higher life or progression. Every strata of the earth is a representation of development. So one generation gives way to another more advanced, which lives on the latter.

As the earth is composed of all the elements of man, when it had passed through all the generations of life, so as man came forth, he was the substance of all the life of the earth. Man was first in this visible space with God or wisdom before he became visible to the living things on the earth. When his life began to act in matter, then it took form. This was man. I will show you that man reasons about himself as the world reasons about the earth. The doctors and chemists analyze men and beasts just as they do the earth.

Neither supposes there is any intelligence outside of what they analyze but think man's body is like the earth and disease is in it or can get into it, also that man has nothing to do with it; but this is not the case.

Seed did not make itself. It is the offspring of some life. And as man is the offspring of all the living, it is not strange that his growth as well as that of the earth should be encumbered by the errors of his predecessors. You will find traces of the development of the earth, following along with its growth; so superstition or the lower life often shows itself in the more enlightened lives. The body like the earth is the birthplace of both. And the battle is whether the life of progression shall rule, or the life of oppression, for where one is absent the other rules. Oppression is the next stratum above pressure. The stone's power is to press everything under it; ignorance is the same and might is right. When that is conquered by error or by wisdom just enough to keep clear, then its power departs and dies and it is buried. Over its grave springs up a wiser growth which flourishes for a time till some new life is introduced and another battle is fought and the dead are buried in their own ruins.

The earth developed itself by these strata until the brute creation appeared. Then contending parties sprang up. The wiser overpowered the weaker and the earth began to bring forth grass and yield its fruits, for the minerals were not known to them. At last the life of the human species came forth. Now to suppose that the man of our age contains the same combination of life as the first men did is to suppose that the wisdom of man has never progressed. Man is made up of opinions of truth and error and his life is a warfare like all other lives before him. Everyone's hand is against his brother, for truth and error claim the idea man.

Wisdom is the son of God and error is the son of the lower life of animals. These two characters are as easily distinguished from each other as light from darkness. If the animal life is predominant, then man is arbitrary and superstitious. If wisdom is predominant, it can be shown. The earth, like man, is analyzed and geologists can trace life up to human beings. The earth is examined, phenomena are discovered and philosophers have reasoned and traced the mineral into the vegetable and the vegetable into the animal kingdom. But their causes are not attributed to a wisdom outside and apart from all that is seen. So the medical faculty have traced disease down from Adam to the present time, not thinking that their own ignorance is the very cause of the phenomenon they are trying to explain.

The earth commences like a child and every stratum shows the rise and fall of some lower life. That part of the globe that would be called the least intelligent or showing the least life represents the child. It may have seed but it cannot come forth, any more than a child. It can grow and as the identity of the child dies, its life is transferred to another identity or stratum. So the earth's life passes through the ignorance of the mineral kingdom, buries its mother, and out of the covering or stratum the vegetable life springs but brings some of its mother or mineral life and phenomena are seen, half mineral, half vegetable. Thus the earth has been growing and developing itself like man, but man is a life of a higher stratum of the earth. So he brings into his life all the elements of all the other lives. When man commences, he is like the earth. He is made of all the lives of the lower kingdoms and his growth is to cover up the dead or ignorance of his birth. So he grows in size and intellect, ridding himself of his old matter. The growth of his body, he gets from the other lives and it is of his own existence, but eternal life is from wisdom or God. This wisdom was in the first life of man. But it could not come forth till the lower life or strata were fully developed to make the soil fit to bring it forth. And when it sprang up, lower lives appeared also.

Here must be a battle between the life of man and the life of Science or God. The latter has prevailed over the lower in nearly all discoveries except theology and pathology, or religion and disease. These two phenomena are so plainly discerned in man as tornadoes or disease are in the vegetable world. So far the higher or scientific man has not arrived at an age to bring forth this new kingdom, so the powers of darkness prevail and will until the time of reformation or investigation comes. Then opinion will see that there is a science or wisdom superior to itself. It is the science of analyzing the errors or phenomena of man. The chemist can analyze mineral and vegetable life. But man never thinks that all these developments of the earth are the natural result of ignorance, preparing for a higher development of man. When man goes on developing error upon error till he is buried in his own belief, it makes him but little higher than the animal kingdom. But the wisdom of science is to explain the phenomenon of man called disease, to show how they are made and how they can be unmade. This is as much a science as to decompose a piece of metal, which is one of the natural phenomena of ignorance in itself. No one supposes that the animal, mineral or vegetable life is aware of itself, how it is affected, or how to account for any phenomena that takes place. So the natural man is just as ignorant of the misery he brings upon himself as the beast. Both are the natural development of matter and the priest and doctor is the link between the animal and the scientific life. Neither has developed one single idea of wisdom, but they are the stratum for the scientific man to commence with. Their ideas are the field and their opinions are the tares to be pulled up and burned. When the axe of science is laid at the root of their opinions, you will see disease die and be buried in its own ruin. Out of its soil will rise up wise men, who will rid the world of its errors and its sins. Their iniquities shall be sealed up and the places where their opinions were once believed shall believe them no more forever.

So ends the old theory of religion and the creation of disease. Instead of curing disease, the doctors make it. The battle of disease is waged by the priests and doctors against ignorance. The doctors through their ignorance make the phenomenon. Their error calls it disease, their reason about the cure is a belief, and if they succeed in making the patient believe, his ignorance corrects his error sometimes and health is restored. Now if the child was never deceived, the phenomenon of disease would never happen any more than among the brutes, but our mode of reasoning makes disease. The diseases of brutes are like these of men and men differ in regard to them as much as some men and brutes. If disease was fashionable, you would not see so much labor used to get rid of it. Take a person whose disease makes him feel as though he wanted to be noticed; it is very hard to cure him.

Dec. 1861

First Symptoms of Disease, The–Part II–Popular Belief of Curing Disease
[BU 3:0313]

In every age of the world, there have been individuals who have appeared before the people claiming to come or get information from the world of spirits. And strange to say there is scarcely a living being who does not believe more or less in this place. They only differ in some slight variation. You may include the deists and all the religious beliefs down to the modern spiritualist. Say and preach what they please, they all have a belief that there is a God or something independent of themselves, but his locality or whereabouts is a mystery. Look at your churches and see the worship of this unknown God. If the people do not believe that he can hear and answer prayer, why do they call upon him? For they certainly do call upon this unknown God in their troubles.

This error is the beginning of trouble. It makes the child place his dependence on an invisible something that he knows nothing of. He is made to believe God is somewhere and that if he is a good child, he shall go to God when he dies. This is the old story and every child has heard it from his mother, if not from his father. All of this to me is superstition that leads to a phenomenon in the child as well as in the man and prepares the mind for another humbug as false as the former–the medical profession. Now disease is as much a part of our belief as the spirit world, but the devil manages his affairs so as to cut his own throat. He reasons to man in this way; he is very good to put man in possession of all information. He was the first to receive Eve and he has not forgotten his old trade for he labors as hard for his kingdom as Christ did for his; the only difference is the devil employs the priest and Jesus preached himself.

I will take this prince of darkness and hold him up as Moses did in the wilderness and show his absurdities. The devil I call error in man, so that all men who deceive the people for gain are the children of the devil. He has so fixed his craft that every man, woman and child is made to worship him and he employs all sorts of inventions to sustain his kingdom. I will introduce him in a neighborhood where people are perfectly ignorant of such a being. He enters the town and finds the people very happy and ignorant. He asks them if they ever heard of Christ. They say, No, and ask him what he means by Christ. He then goes on to tell his story which is not a very pleasant one for them to believe, for it shows them they are very wicked, and unless they pay him for preaching, they will all be lost. By his mesmeric will he excites them and sets their minds to work. This frightens the rest and he tells them his is the power of God. Some go into hysterical fits, others into trances and he governs it all for the benefit of the craft and when he has finished his revival, some are crazy and others are sick with brain fever. And now he introduces his pet lamb–the doctor. He, the doctor, takes the sick or those who are affected and mesmerizes them into some belief. This frightens them and instead of calling his fright the power of God, he calls it a disease and gives them to understand that he can cure them. So between the two they manage to rob the sick of their money and health. And at last parky devil gets what there is left by the voluntary desire of the sick to hold up his kingdom. Here is the origin of disease.

Jesus saw that and also saw the remedy. The priests as well as the doctors make a world out of sight and pretend to explain it. If they succeed in making the people believe that there is another world, then there must be a space between the two. This space or gulf is what every man must pass. And if the doctors make them believe that there is a disease independent of themselves (although such a thing was never seen detached from some human or animal life), it is as true to them as the belief in another world which no mortal eyes have ever seen and whence no traveler ever returns. This sort of deception has been kept up ever since the days of idolatry. Let us see if Jesus looked at this sort of theory and if he gives us any account of this other world. If Jesus was God, he must have filled this space or gulf, for the devil or priests admit that God fills all space, so he must fill more than they do. Jesus brought the kingdom of heaven down to their understanding or earth and established it in their hearts. The devil prepares man to go to heaven instead of having heaven in man. So you may trace the priests down and compare their belief with Jesus' truth or Christ and you will see a complete contradiction in them.

I will now show how God or Science fills all space and yet does not move at all. I will begin with the little child when it begins to learn. I will introduce the devil or priest and Jesus. Hear the priest explain some passage that he knows nothing about. Jesus sees through his ignorance and knows it is false. So the priest's lie to the child is transparent to him and there is no space between the cause and effect. Jesus sees it is false and no effect is produced on him, but to the child, there is space and distance and time to arrive at a truth. This is so with the doctor; they make the sick man one thing and disease another, so that the man is liable to catch it; here is space. Jesus knew it was false and his wisdom filled the space that the doctor made. He called the multitude to him and told them how they had been deceived by these two classes and tried to explain where it was. But the space was so plain to the people that it could not have much effect, yet he cured them of their beliefs so far as the disease was concerned, but they did not understand so that there was no space.

Just remember one thing. All opinions leave a space between the person and the thing believed. For instance, I tell you that there is a certain person who is in town. You ask me if I have seen him. I say, No, but I have no doubt of it. Here is a space between my opinion and the fact. To make it one and no space, I must prove it; then space is annihilated. So it is with every opinion. Now as the other world is in our belief, when man sees through his belief, there is no other world. The space is filled by the wisdom and as the wisdom is not in the opinion, the opinion is gone and this world fills the vacuum. It is so in disease. The doctor makes a space in the patient's mind. He makes him believe a lie or an opinion; this makes a space. So to pass this space is to get well and that is what the patient wants. So he believes a lie that he may be sick or get separated from health. This separation is disease, and my business is to fill up this space in the patient's mind or light up his wisdom so that he can see through the doctor's opinion, and then he is all right. I hold up the serpents or theories of the two to the people and show their absurdities, and the light guides them back to health or destroys the darkness of their belief.

December 1861

Foundation of Religious Belief
[BU 3:0885]

What is the foundation of a religious man's belief? It is in a God who has all power, all wisdom and all strength, all love and all goodness. To believe in all the above is to be a Christian. What does the Christian believe that this God is doing for the benefit of the human race? That he is watching over his creatures, providing everything that shall make them happy and comfortable and is ready to give to all that shall ask him, believing in his power to answer prayer. All this and a great deal more is believed by the Christians. They also believe that God watches over their health and knows better what they need than they do themselves. If they suffer, it is for their good to convince them of the weakness of man's wisdom and his dependence on a superior power; and if they suffer for his sake, they will receive a reward in heaven that shall recompense them for all their suffering.

Now suppose you believe in all the above, what does it profit you? Can you cure yourself of one ache or pain? Can you add to your height one inch, or turn a hair white or black, or give to the sick who are wasting from disease one single word of wisdom that will correct their error and restore them to health? Can you make one blade of grass grow or do anything that shall instruct the world in regard to man's wisdom? You must answer, No. Then what does your religion amount to? Nothing but a belief, like a child's belief in God. Suppose you believe that God is in heaven or don't believe it, what will that have to do with curing your heart disease? You will say, Nothing. Suppose you believe in all I have stated as the Christians believe, will it cure you? Then what is your belief good for except as a belief? Why does not your God cure you? Is it for want of faith on your part? If that is the case, then faith is the cure, so if you have the cure that is your faith. Faith is not wisdom but the substance or cure. Like water to the thirsty soul, it is his cure, but wisdom leads him to the fount of living water so that he will not thirst. Then his faith will be lost in sight for his wisdom prevents his thirst. Therefore to know God is to get wisdom, but to be separated from God is to be religious and believe that there is a fountain of water large enough to quench the thirst of everyone if they can find it. This is religion. But to the wise, it is to know this fountain is in yourself, a well of water springing up into everlasting wisdom. Then you will ask of this wisdom, and just as you understand, you will receive and your wisdom will teach you that you cannot ask of wisdom by your belief and have your prayers answered. God is like mathematics, for mathematics is wisdom put into practice or reduced to man's comprehension. To receive an intelligent answer in mathematics, you must ask in wisdom, not in opinion, and just according to your wisdom, the answer comes.

Here is the difference between you and me. Your God is your belief and you attach your senses to it. My God is my wisdom, and I attach my senses to it. My God is light and truth; your God is darkness and error. My God sees through your God and knows it is a God invented by man. To destroy your God is to destroy your opinion in man's belief. So as you cease from evil or believing in man's wisdom and learn to love God or wisdom, your errors or diseases are blotted out and your life is saved by this wisdom or truth.

All evil is in our religious beliefs. There could be no disease without a sensation, but a sensation is not a disease. It is simply a change from harmony. This is a chemical change in the mind or fluids. This change shows itself by heat. The heat is under the direction of man's opinion or God's wisdom through man. Wisdom can account for all the sensations. Error gives opinions, so disease is what follows opinion and the misery follows the belief. The child has no wisdom so that it has no disease to itself, but its misery is in its fear and its fear is in its ignorance. So to quiet its fear, you relieve its misery. Disease and a phenomenon are not the same. The same difference exists in the two as does in opinion and wisdom. The ignorant cannot see the difference between a truth based on an opinion and on a scientific fact. A scientific man and a Christian are as different as a truth based on a belief is different from a truth based on science. I will describe a man of religion and one of science so you can see and feel the difference. A purely religious man is all made of error, based on opinions, with not one element of wisdom in him. All his acts are governed by fear. The fear makes him believe in a God of love and hatred. If he does well, his God will reward him, and if he does wrong, his God will punish him. His God is not a part of himself but separate and apart from him, so he prays to his God. He lives in fear and dies in the hope that God will receive him in His abode. So he lives and dies as all error dies when the truth comes. This belief is full of contradiction, for it is of this world's opinion; so he is a man of matter and his God is a tyrant. What is my God? My God is all wise in everything. Science is his wisdom reduced to practice. He has not eyes like the Christian God, he is all light. He has not ears but is all wisdom, so that not a sparrow can move but moves in his wisdom. He hears all men's prayers that are made according to the principle of science, so when man asks for what he cannot have, without some act, God never will answer. The Christians believe that God will step out of the natural course of Science to help a man, but my God cannot do such a thing.

I will show how Christians receive favors from men, and through their wisdom give the praise to this unknown God. A pious old man and woman live in some by-lane in a small apartment with no furniture, not even a chair, and depend on the charity of the world for a living. You enter and find the woman with the Bible in her hand, feeble and careworn, and with a trembling voice she says, "Will you not be seated on this box by my side?" You seat yourself and learn her history. She tells you that when she was young, she experienced religion and felt that she had found her saviour. At the age of twenty, she married a man who had all the means to make her happy. But it seemed to be the will of God to remove from her all the blessings of life in order to teach her that man's happiness does not exist in the things of this world but on laying up treasures in heaven where moth and rust do not corrupt, etc. You ask her, "Do you feel satisfied with your situation?" "Oh, yes," she answers. "I feel as though God knows my wants and will not let me suffer but will watch over me ." "Don't you suffer for food?" "Oh, no. He sends me food." "How?" "The Lord sent Mrs. D. to see me, and she gave me all this food that you see here." Now here is where a great mistake is made in supposing that some intelligence outside of man is watching as man does not know himself.

All wisdom is outside of man's opinion and belief and that which does not come to his senses is to him a mystery. So the mystery is his God. To know the mystery is to know God, and when the mystery is understood, the religion vanishes. One great trouble comes from teaching us to believe in an overruling providence in the shape of a God who will answer our desires without our making any effort. It makes man indolent and superstitious and a burden on society. It makes man unhappy and even insane and draws out sympathy from a class of persons who know their religion is the effect of superstition. I will show how a person in a similar state from the lady above might be benefited by some persons without any knowledge through the senses. This would look as though it were by the divine influence of God, while God has just as much to do with every act that we take the credit of to ourselves and it really belongs to us. If I am hungry and you give me a dinner because you feel that it would make me happier, and you had this in your mind, then that was God and I give him the praise of my feelings that do not lie; but if you give me a dinner to be praised for your goodness, that is of man, and man should have the praise. Jesus said, "Render to Caesar the things that are Caesar's and to God the things that are God's." This God in us is always on the lookout to render kindness to those who are in trouble, but the Caesar is on the lookout to be rewarded for his acts so that it is hard to tell which is master.

To return to the case stated above. A poor, sickly person confined to her room, starving, freezing and nearly exhausted, offers up a prayer according to her belief that would make her put forth her desire or feelings. Her feeling excites the sympathy of some person; this, like yeast, excites him to look for a cause and, like a mesmeric person, he finds it by following the desire to the place of her abode and then relieves her wants. As both are ignorant of the cause and effect, the whole is laid to God, so they give God the praise. The ignorance of wisdom is called religion. You may ask me for proof. I will give it from my own acts under these impressions, and I know that God nor spirits nor man's wisdom has anything to do with them. They are the natural outpouring of persons' feelings, and not thinking that their trouble could reach my ears. But my wisdom could account for all. I will relate one or two instances, showing how little we know ourselves and how much we are governed by this wisdom unknown to the world of man.

I was attending not long ago a patient who was very sick. (P.R.H. Mrs. B&E.) All those had a desire to see me and their desire was their prayer and their prayers affected my wisdom or God that I believed in. Their wisdom or God was in trouble, and in their trouble, they called on this wisdom. But their senses or natural man knew not what they called on, for the religious man is a stranger to this wisdom, and when he is in distress, the priest teaches him to call on the Lord for help. This keeps them ignorant of this truth which they vainly worship. Their God is in the clouds of their belief and I can see it, for my God is my wisdom and theirs is in their opinion or belief. They expect to see him and I really see him. They are looking for his second coming, but to me he has come and is now writing this very truth that they vainly worship.

Here is a difference between a religious man and Jesus. God to the religious man is separate and apart from the human family and watches over them as a parent watches over his children. They stand to God as a servant to his master, ready to obey his call, and if they are in want, he thinks it is for their good. He grants their prayers if he thinks best, but if he chooses to do otherwise, it is all right. So they are always looking for this unknown God that is in them and they know it not. Now my God, that is, P.P.Q's, is his wisdom; and his senses (P.P.Q's) are attached to his God. So he lives and moves and his life is in the wisdom or God, and his prayer is to know more of himself, that is, this wisdom or God.

April 1862

Fragment, A
[LC 2:0796]

Does man in his reasoning separate the soul from the body? I answer he does not in practice yet he does in theory. He makes a distinction, but he makes a distinction without a difference. He calls the mind the earthly house or tenement, for he says when his house shall be dissolved, he has a house not made with hands. Now his house is his ideas or belief and his senses are in the house; so he reasons the same as a man reasons about a material house. Now if your house is on fire and you admit you are in it, then you lose your life with the house. So your mind being the house or body, if you admit your soul is in your body and disease is destroying the house, you must reason that all must be destroyed, soul and body, because you admit that you are in your belief or house. Now this is the reasoning of the wisdom of this world. But the wisdom of God reasons in this way: that God is the highest wisdom that belongs to man and just as man knows himself, he knows God, and man knows no God except that wisdom that governs and directs his acts. We have been taught to believe that God is a being independent of man. Now this is as absurd as for a child to believe that he came into existence without a father or mother. All will see the absurdity of that belief. So to admit that man and God are separate from each other is as absurd as to believe that the child is no part of its parent, yet the child has his identity of matter and the parent his.

1864

Future Life, A
[BU 2:0386]

All persons admit that after death there is something that lives. Now where is that something? When man is alive, you see him moving around, talking, reasoning, etc. All this is a truth and a part of man. We are all told so and taught to believe that this body or man contains life, that after a while it decays and dies and there is an end of it. Now where is the proof that there is anything which rises from the grave or this body according to the common opinion of man's belief? Does not the common opinion go to strengthen this belief?

Are we not all taught by the clergy to prepare for death, that it will come sooner or later and we must die and run the chance of a hereafter?

The doctors also preach the same story and invent all manner of bugbears in the form of disease to frighten us into the belief that we are in danger of death all the time. Public opinion falls in with the same belief and is it strange that with all this influence acting upon us sickness and misery and all sorts of trouble must follow this belief?

Now what is there to counteract all these facts? A mere belief that 1,800 years ago a man was on earth that God acted through, or a more absurd idea that it was God himself that left his throne in heaven and came down on earth and told the inhabitants that there was a place after death that he had prepared for them that loved him; and all those that did not love him more than all other things or earthly friends could not get into this place of happiness but were to be shut out or excluded from the presence of God. This was eternal banishment from his presence.

1860

God, the White Man, and the Negro Race
[Originally untitled.] [LC 2:0708]

In the Advertiser of September 22nd, an article can be found entitled, "God, the white man and the negro race."

All men reason from certain premises according to their intellectual plane. So do the animals, and each man or animal shows his development as plain as his color. The Ethiopian cannot change his skin, nor the leopard his spots. This figure is to show that a man in his reasoning cannot make himself wiser or clearer than he started at first. If his wisdom is as black as the Ethiopian's skin, he cannot make it white by his argument and if it is spotted by the corruption of a demagogue, his reason cannot wash out the spots. The writer is known by his fruits. He begins by saying that all men must admit that the creator is wiser than the creature. Then he assumes what he does not confine himself to. God made the black man but not the slave, but he makes God the author of slavery by making both identical. The Creator, the Bible says, made God in his own image. The writer says that the white man and the negro race are both of the human species, it is folly to deny, but that they are unlike in color and capacity, it is no less folly to deny. Now if the white and the black man are both of the human species, how comes it that the black man is enslaved by the white?

But I will return to the creator. According to his own reasoning, he admits that color has nothing to do with species, so we class all colors of men together with equal rights. Everyone knows that might is right with the animals, so it must have been the case in the early ages of mankind, for all beings admit this law by their acts. No one supposes that God put one class under another, neither is it supposable that what is wisdom in one race is not so in another. Here is where I differ from the writer; his God makes one man superior to another, mine makes all men alike. Now there is nothing plainer that they are not alike, then how comes this absurdity? It is in us and not in God. Creation and formation are not alike. If God created man in his own image, it cannot that he had reference to what we see with our natural eyes.

The man that my God created is science, which must be put in practice, else it is not science; therefore to form an idea is to reduce to practice the man that God has created. So out of the dust, he formed man, just as every other living being was formed. Now the earthly man and the brute was of the same formation and governed by the same law of all matter. As matter is developed, changes must follow and what we call man's wisdom is only the working of matter to bring about a higher principle of God. So all persons by their reason show just where they stand. This can be illustrated by two persons, one governed by the wisdom of science and the other by the workings of matter. The natural man is a blank. As he begins to develop he begins to be arbitrary and he wants to rule, so he shows his plane or sphere by his reason, and when his reason destroys his error, out comes the scientific man and when this man commences his career, he assumes a higher plane.

To make it clearer, we will take two men who are reasoning about the same subject. The scientific man is to loose the fetters with which the man of opinions binds his fellow man. The latter is not a man but a sort of half breed between the brute and the man. One sees no way of getting man free from his chains and reasons that God never intended he should be free. The other contends that God never made man a slave but man by his own act has created his life in matter and believes he is superior to his fellow man. The scientific man reasons that it is God in us to look upon all men as of the same family and that our acts separate us and not our color, for there are blacker hearts under a white face than ever there were under a black one.

The writer admits the negro inferior to the whites, then he cannot be so dangerous. It is the duty of every man to relieve his fellow man from the burdens that bind him down. You may not have your dog eat at the same table with yourself, but in your wisdom, you ought to respect his position and not despise him because he is not as good as you are, and you should rejoice that he is contented. There is a vast difference between a man being a slave and being a servant. This difference cannot be seen by the writer for his plane or development is not up to that standard, and if it were not for the wisdom that makes this difference, the writer would see no difference between the poor whites and the black slave, for he makes no distinction except in name. Everyone knows that you can find all grades of intellect from the idiot up to the philosopher in the white race. Then why should not the same intellect be enslaved as well as the black? Let the writer answer.

His mode of reasoning shows his development, that his intellect is kept in check by a wisdom superior to his own, which does not come outside of his own opinions. Every ignorant being is either black or blind, and as he grows wise he becomes spotted. This is the demagogue and his wisdom is his reason, but he is wise only in his own conceit. True wisdom rules by science, false by opinion, and when we see a person set himself up as wiser or a dictator, then you may know that his wisdom is of this world of opinion. But when man can see that God never made one scientific truth to tyrannize over another of the same combination, then you will see a man that is not of opinion. Slavery, black or white, is the offspring of opinions, like the earth; and when the earth becomes enriched by the wisdom of science, it brings forth fruits (like freedom), but in its original state, it brings forth only briars and thorns. So with the development of man. As he becomes wise, he loses the earthly, overbearing or brutal man, and sees that intellect is the man and not color or opinions, but what man can put into practice. Then he respects each man for what he knows; and instead of making himself popular by deceiving the masses, he will try to elevate them by his wisdom, breaking down the bars of progression and letting the minds of men live and feed in the sound pasture.

Like David, he will lead the people along by the voice of his wisdom and he will not teach them to forge fetters to bind their fellow man, giving God the praise that they are not slaves like their neighbors. This kind of slavery is demagoguism. It appeals only to one set of slaves to rule the other, and is on a level with the thief that enters the African shores and sets the black tribes to fighting, and then making money out of the quarrel, telling them that God never intended that those who can be subdued should have their freedom. The same writer would carry out his theory, applied to every nation on earth. It is not one whit above the lowest treason of the black-hearted traitor of the South, and it is in keeping with his life and acts, whoever he may be, you will find him popular with one kind of slaves just as any negro stealer is popular with those who will sell their race into slavery.

The writer is honest and so is the wolf who steals the sheep for his own eating. The two are both brutes, one a little higher than the other. Neither has any claim to an intellectual mind but show just how far they have advanced from ignorance into error on the road to wisdom. So he is to be looked upon, not as a fool but as a man of opinions, and not to be classed with that refined class of intellect that judges every one by his acts. Then he becomes a harmless serpent whose bite will not poison the multitude. The trouble with all such demagogues is that error and hypocrisy usually go hand in hand, and persons keep out of sight the very object they wish to attain. This is the case with the writer. His aim is selfish and not honest; therefore he keeps out of sight the working of the higher intellect because he knows it can't be appreciated. So he gives way to the evil in his heart, and like Judas sells his higher wisdom for a petty office or popularity with the masses.

Like Nebuchadnezzar, weighed in the balance and found wanting, he shows which end of the scale he is on. His God is one of his own make, like all others who wish to dictate the masses by their own opinion.

My God speaks in this way. He has finished his work or machine and sits down to see it work, it needs no repairs, it will run and perform its work, till every one shall know that to be good is to be wise and man's color is not the problem of progression but wisdom. And wisdom when reduced to practice will be recognized by every wise and benevolent person without regard to color. Slavery is one of the very first acts of man, at least it is an element as necessary as any other evil. It was intended by the creator for a wise purpose, but it never will be looked upon by a scientific mind as containing any of the elements of wisdom. It is the yeast in the lump of wisdom that agitates the mind or matter to bring out this great truth that man is capable of governing himself and that all will submit to science when it is shown, either in the white or black man.

So slavery is one of the evils that is necessary to show man the error of his own way, and teach him that so long as he is capable of enslaving his fellow man, he is digging a pit that he may at some time fall into. Look at the progression of freedom ever since the world began and you will see just how far the bonds have been broken and the tongue of wisdom and liberty let loose. The two elements have always existed by a variety of names. Error at first was called the serpent, then the devil, and has always had its cloven foot. Everyone knows that when a person tries to palm off an error as mathematical science, he shows the weak part of his wisdom or his cloven foot. This the writer has shown and will always show in every communication he can write, till he is exposed and sees that his hypocrisy can be detected by the wisdom of science in the masses. Then he will cease from doing evil and learn to be honest and do good. The writer like others of the same stripe will never cease from his hypocritical reasoning till his errors are exposed. Their wisdom is in their strategy and their strategy is in their deception.

September 1862

Government
[LC 1:0551]

What is the standard by which man is weighed? There is but one true standard by which man is weighed, and that is by his acts. Men set up standards to weigh others but the standard of wisdom is a balance, and sooner or later man's acts are tested by that, as in the case of Nebuchadnezzar. With this balance man will know his true weight, for it never varies; but man weighs his fellow man by the balance of public opinion; his weight is his popularity, so he varies according to the atmosphere in which he lives. To carry out the illustration of weighing men or mind (for mind is matter) by the standard of public opinion, the balance must rest on the same substance as itself; therefore the atmosphere of the place is the base on which the scale stands. And as each man is a world of himself, he creates a scale to weigh himself, but sometimes circumstances change the atmosphere and man finds himself weighed by another balance, then his weight is used to fill up a vacuum made by the change of the mind of public opinion.

For instance, you often see a man who feels as though he was of some importance yet who never shows any wisdom above the circle in which he moves; although active and aspiring, he evinces no superior intelligence, and restless and uneasy, he attaches himself to a political wheel of fortune, risking what he never really had but thought he had. The wheel revolves and finally stops. Some fall off, others hold on, so a vacuum is formed. He who held on did so from no merit of his wisdom but from desire to gain, and he is received not for his worth but for his persistency to fill the vacuum of the rotation of the wheel of public office. Now behold the change! His own wisdom never made him anything above a third class lawyer or an intriguing politician. Leaving his own home or the place where his talent was balanced, he jumps on the political wheel and is landed on the judge's bench, there to appear in the presence of men who never heard of such an individual.

How comes this metamorphosis of a man jumping from the lowest class of politicians into the highest scale of the legal profession? Is the profession of his class of wisdom or is there some mistake in the scales? Are judges weighed in the scale of their own wisdom or the political scale? Here is something which if wrong, ought to be corrected; but if it is right, destroy the barrier that separates the demagogue from the legal world. If law is nothing but a bubble, like any political bubble, then the world has been deceived, and it is not what all wise men have claimed it to be. Where is the principle to weigh the differences "in these estimates" so that the people may not be deceived by their own ignorance? This has never been done, so political scales which determine all merit are the standard of law.

This makes law arbitrary and if it is so, then law has no standard but public opinion and political opinions are the standard of the laws of nations. Therefore, a government or laws founded on public opinion must sooner or later crumble, bringing anarchy, despotism and destruction. This has always been the case and always will be where error holds sway. Let us see if there cannot be some way by which man can see the scale of justice that weighs every man by his acts. The world must be governed by laws and the judge must be superior to the law, or he could not explain it.

So the judge is the law and the people are the parties, and when the people make a contract to govern their acts, the judge is to listen to their stories and decide according to contract and his decision becomes law. If it becomes necessary to have more than one judge, the question comes, who shall appoint him? Must the candidate be weighed on the political scale or on the legal scale? If the judge is a political judge or made by a political party or any party at all outside of the profession, then have no judge at all, only a political demagogue. This holds true in all classes of science. So long as the judges are taken from the people, the government is in danger, for the wisdom of the political world is always changing.

Every man is a standard and his wisdom is his weight; each man shows his weight by his wisdom. If a man is wanted to work out a mathematical problem, one who had never studied mathematics would not be selected; and if in a school one of the teachers of that branch should die, no one would expect the scholars to select another. It is so in all branches of arts and sciences; politicians can never select any man to any professional calling, science or legislation. The power to determine the scientific must be kept apart, as religion and politics. Now man is a nation of himself and is governed precisely as a nation and any principle that will promote the health and happiness and prolong the life of a nation will apply to an individual.

There is a principle which if rightly understood would prolong the lives and happiness of nations, but this principle has never been recognized by the world in nations or individuals The standard of opinions has always held sway and that is arbitrary. Yet there is an element in both individuals and nations which is science, which has its secret influence and has always governed the civilized world. It is not recognized by the wisdom of opinions but is finally referred to after the opinions are exhausted by their own weakness and their power is gone; then steps in this third power and settles the trouble. Wisdom is supposed to be this last-named power, but true wisdom is one thing and political wisdom is another. But if the former settles the trouble there is an end of it.

Disease in man is the same as in nations. I will take our nation as an individual and show how it gets diseased, is kept so, and is finally destroyed and killed; how it sometimes may rise again, as man is believed to rise, and also how it becomes exterminated, as man is believed to be annihilated, body and soul. The life of a nation, like that of an individual, depends on its wisdom, and it is no evidence of wisdom to destroy life in either individuals or nations. Ignorance is nearer wisdom than error, for error has to retrace her steps to get back to ignorance to receive the truth. According to the judgment of error or opinion we are the wisest nation on earth, but our acts must tell the story. If the acts of the last administration had not been checked by a superior power than the executive, our beloved country would have been the scene of civil war and a final annihilation of the republic of the United States, showing that with all our boasted prosperity as a nation, we had hardly reached the age of some individuals on earth.

Now where is the defect for there must be one somewhere? Is it in the principle that wisdom cannot govern a nation or is it in the want of wisdom in the rulers? As I have said, a nation born into existence is like a child born into the world; both are nursed until they become old enough to help themselves. Now a nation that is born crippled or diseased is harder to raise to a healthy nation than one born perfect or ignorant. For instance, China is the oldest nation on the globe and the most ignorant. The American nation is the most enlightened and advanced in the arts and sciences, some pretend to say. Now see the difference. China stands firm–America is on a pivot; time must determine her destiny–for ruin or progress.

The wisdom of the American people has never been heard by the masses; the only sound that has reached their ears is from political demagogues. Tyranny has been the throne that the people have had to submit to and until the power is wrenched from these political despots, liberty is a mere farce. I will describe the growth of this young child, not quite eighty-six years old. He was born in the year of our Lord 1775. His parents were driven from their homes to find a place where they could carry out their own way of worshipping God, and here they planted their free principles among a savage race. As in all error they did not see the true law of justice and their first Christian act was to make war with the natives and drive them out of their land. Then the same error persecuted all religions opposed to their opinions. Finally the old world, finding her child growing too strong, undertook to put it into subjection, and therefore opened a war between father and son. The latter, having the sympathy of strangers, fought and finally gained his freedom. Then came a union of the North and South, which resulted in the birth of a son called Uncle Sam. He, like his father, was diseased for slavery had bound one side of him, paralyzing it so that it was a deadweight to the other side. Now it was for wisdom to bring the diseased side to life.

As I speak of each, I will call them North and South. The South being crippled by slavery, the North had pity for his brother and divided the heritage with him and they formed a contract called the Constitution. The North had the most political power; the South could not be heard in the political scale, for her voice was in the minority, as she had slaves, who according to their law, could not vote. So to make all things easy, the North agreed to a basis of representation that should put the South on an equal footing. The North gave five votes to three of the South. So as the slave population grew faster in proportion than the whites, a basis of representation was made so that five slaves should be equal to three whites. This was made in good faith.

Now slavery was not known in the Constitution, although it was in the minds of the framers. And it was a principle of honor which made the North give the South this advantage of representation. The equivalent was that in the territory to be acquired this equalization of power should not be carried. So the Constitution said nothing about slavery but acknowledged the right or representation as far as the states were concerned up to the thirteen states. This right being acknowledged, the South forgot the honor of their fathers not to trespass beyond their original states. And when new territory came to be admitted, quoted the contract and claimed her right of representation in free territory. Here was where the mistake was made by the North in not seeing what was claimed by the South.

The South seeing where she had the advantage of the North have always endeavored to hold it. But as the West grew up, the South seeing her power passing from her cries out, Persecution! The North, being ignorant of the true issue, have been made to attach their ideas to slavery instead of representation. So the cry of slavery has been heard at the North, when that has nothing to do with the question at issue.

The true question at issue is whether the North is willing to agree to a one-sided bargain that deprives them of two-fifths of their votes for no equivalent. This is the question. It takes two-thirds of Congress to alter the Constitution, but it will not take a long time to convince the North and West that they may stop the South from carrying their basis of representation into free territory. This error arises from the fact that when the wisdom of the political world makes political judges, the scientific world is enslaved. This was the case in the Dred Scott decision; the judges were political judges under the influence of political power; therefore they decided according to their party.

Now I go back to the starting point. If judges have no more wisdom than the political demagogues or masses, their science is a sham and law is a humbug. The health of a nation, like that of an individual, depends on the influences that govern it. Perhaps it may be better illustrated by the case of a sick person. The sick are made so by the influences that govern them; political quacks or doctors, like political leaders, deceive the patient by false issues. The doctors make their opinions the standard, create disease like politicians, and deceive the people into a belief that makes them sick. They then offer their services to get them out of the trouble they have got them into.

Now how can these evils be overcome? Only by teaching the people to know the difference between an opinion and a truth. This I will try to show. I will return to the political judge. If the people want to have a healthy nation, they must have wise judges. Now can that be done? All will admit that a law is not as wise as the lawgiver. For the lawgiver would see a defect where the parties would overlook one.

But if a decision is made by a judge not fully acquainted with the law, then the people are the losers. This was the case in the Dred Scott decision. If the judges had been honest they would have seen that the law was not defined in the case and therefore, to decide a question or principle embracing so much, by giving an opinion upon what they could not decide was assuming a power that showed that they were not judges of the law but party judges. They were to decide the law, not give an opinion, for an opinion is not law.

The North had one opinion, the South another; each claimed to be right. The Constitution being silent on the law of territory, each party might speak with some show of truth and the judges, had they been independent of party, must have agreed, provided there was no question. And if there was a question, let the people decide that and when a similar case came up, the judges would decide according to contract or law. These political judges are the cause of all disease. They make it by their own error and the people take their opinions for reality or truth. This caused a dissension among the people. It split up the North and untied the South and condensed a political error into a party truth. The error, running into the North, set fire there and turned the executive power into a political engine used against the North, and instead of pumping water to put out the fire, it turned its power towards upsetting the North.

As I sit, penning this article, the engine of government is in the hands of the North, but not without a struggle, for all that Buchanan and his party could do was done to destroy the government. If General Scott has been a traitor, like the rest, we should at this time, April 26th, 1861, be in a bloody war. But fortunately their power has departed, and Buchanan, like Nebuchadnezzar, is turned out to grass and Abraham has assumed the throne. His first act is to decide what the judges misrepresent. He says, Let the people decide what is not plain in the Constitution. This is as it should be. Now his acts are to take effect and what I now say is a prophecy, not yet fulfilled. It is based on a law, not of opinion but of wisdom or on a chemical change taking place in the political world which is governed by a wisdom superior to an opinion, although to the masses it is an opinion. But it is based on a truth that must prove true or the country is lost. The nation stands now like a man given over by his friends. The political doctors stand around his couch dropping a hypocritical tear for their lost father, but ready to devour his substance as soon as he breathes his last. They have exhausted all their skill on him till there is nothing left but the skeleton of Uncle Sam.

The people have got angry with these quacks and have taken the old gentleman into their hands and have employed a new physician by name, Abraham Lincoln. As soon as he comes to the old mansion, his first act is to listen to Uncle Sam's story. Here it is: while the old gentleman was sleeping, his son James, who had the whole care of him, was planning with the rest of his brethren to rob the old gentleman of his money and arms and get possession of his goods so that the kingdom would fall into their hands. So when the old gentleman was roused by Abraham, he was nearly powerless; out of thirty-four children, seven had stolen all they could. This roused Abraham, and his decree has gone forth. Baltimore is to be the scene of action and if the Northern troops do not pass, then the fight commences there. But I think that the government will pass their troops through and this ends the fighting at the North; but the principal fighting will be in the border states.

April 1861

Happiness
[BU 2:0536]

We often hear people say that the object of religion is to make us happy. The question then arises, What is happiness. This question cannot be decided by the opinions of one man or a hundred, for it must embrace some wisdom higher than man's opinion. If the author had no wisdom superior to the common belief of the world and chose the word happiness merely to represent a quiet ignorant state, then I have no objection to the common definition of it. But if it includes the person that labors for the improvement of man and his development, then I say the word is misapplied, for the results are as wide apart as virtue and vice. You might as well apply the word virtue to the most vicious person on earth, as to apply the word happiness to a man who seeks every opportunity to defraud and get the advantage of his neighbor by every means in his power without laying himself liable to the law.

Just see how the word is used. The little child when it is playing around like a little puppy is called happy. Now if this is happiness, it is not wisdom. So if it is desired rather than wisdom, then it is folly to be wise. Now let this state be called quiet, and the word happiness be applied to the person who, by his labors, has discovered some great truth that is for the benefit of man's condition and who puts his wisdom into practice and receives something that he feels and knows has enriched him both in health and wisdom and has raised him above the one who is ignorant. Then he can say that wisdom is happiness and riches. Just the same as the opposite man can say of the goods and money which he has extorted from some ignorant person, as he sits down and counts it over and over and exclaims, "How happy I am for what I have got." Now while he is rejoicing over the ill-gotten gains, his neighbor is grieving over his losses and turns to the other who has by his labor lifted up some poor, sick invalid, who had been robbed by these land sharks out of their health and left on the cold icy hand of the world to perish for want of the wisdom that might make them free. Now see such a person suffering, robbed of the comforts of this life and praying that some kind angel would come and feed them with the bread of life or explain to them the great truth of nature which will set them free from sin and death.

Now see someone come and open the book of wisdom and read to them all their griefs and pains and by the power of his wisdom destroy their beliefs or misery and show them the true way. Then they will arise in their strength and might and with the God of Wisdom which has set them free. Then the oppressed and the redeemer can mingle together and their joy will reign, and that is happiness.

1865

Harmony [I]
[LC 1:0035]

When two persons are in harmony in regard to a fact, they are as one, for there is no jar. The fact may be of truth or error, but if they are of the same opinion in regard to it, then they harmonize. If the harmony is pleasure, it is well; if it is trouble, it is harmony with them and discord with something else.

Error cannot be in harmony with truth. Ignorance is as a blank, error is the working of ignorance to arrive at harmony or truth. Truth is a science that can govern this chemical change in ignorance to bring it in harmony with science. I will illustrate. Ignorance produces sounds; error arranges them into a tune. Truth reduces the error to a science so that it can be taught. These then are as one. Each one is dependent on the other, for if there was no ignorance there could not be any error. Then there could be no happiness, for happiness is the result of some act or belief.

Truth contains no happiness, nor misery, but is that power or knowledge that governs all things according to itself. This truth is in all men, but it is not in the brutes, for it is not matter but the knowledge of creating matter or destroying it. Therefore, fear not that power that can destroy the body and nothing more, but fear that power that can destroy both body and soul, for all the above is matter and mind.

The power that can create and destroy matter is proved by error, for it is the destruction of the life of error. Ignorance says in its heart, there is no such power. Error knows that there is but is ignorant of its locality. To ignorance, this power is as an unknown God. The knowledge of this power is the harmony of one person in trouble with another in truth and happiness.

April 1860

Harmony II
[LC 1:0034]

Can two persons be in harmony except they be agreed? If you are affected by any person in a way that produces fear, you cannot be in perfect harmony with another till the fear is cast out. If it is from some idea that affects your character, you will be imprisoned in the idea till you are freed from it. The idea may or may not be accompanied with an individual, but if it is so accompanied, you will be affected by that person in your sleep, the same as in your waking state. One of these effects is attributed to the natural mind, and the other to the spiritual mind, but both have the same effect on the health.

But as my knowledge contains no matter, I am free from your prison; and as I break or destroy the prison or person that holds you, you come out of that spiritual idea and come to me. As I contain no matter but the truth, you will have no fear, and if you dream of me, you will not be afraid. I am your protector, but till you know who I am, you may be afraid because you have been deceived so many times. You look upon all sensation with suspicion, and you suspect yourself. The ignorance of yourself is the worst enemy that you have to contend with, for its character is public opinion which is taken for truth.

To separate us from what we look upon as truth is not a very easy task, for sometimes we think we like the very thing we really hate. This keeps us in ignorance of ourselves. When we would do good and evil is present with us, it is not ourselves but the evil that dwelleth in us. This evil comes from the knowledge of this world, and as this world is made up of flesh and blood, no true knowledge is in it. To separate us from error and bring us into harmony is to explain the false idea away, and then all sorrow is passed away. Nothing remains but the recollection of what is past, like a dream or nightmare, and you are not likely to get into the same error again.

All sensation, when first made, contains no direction but is simply a shock. Error puts a false construction or opinion upon it and speaks disease into existence. The mind is then imprisoned in the idea, and all the evils that follow are what are called disease. I shall speak of two kinds of disease. One is called by the doctors, local and the other, nervous. In my way I make no difference as far as the effect of the mind is concerned. Nervous disease is the effect of the regular's opinion reduced to a belief, and so are all others. I will state two cases to show the difference. A person is exposed to the cold. Ignorance and superstition have reduced to a disease called cold or consumption. This is set down as real disease and so it is, but it is based upon an ignorant superstitious idea. This is one of the errors of this world, judged by this world and proved by the effect on the body. This is called real, and no mistake.

Now, tell another that there is a serpent in his breast or a hell that will torment him in case he does not dream just such dreams or believe just so; and having succeeded in making the person believe this and seeing him tormented and miserable, you turn about and accuse him of being fidgety or nervous. All the sympathy he gets is to be told that he is weak-minded for believing what doctors and ministers have told him and warned him against for years. This is the judgment of this world's belief. To condemn all this folly is to disbelieve in all people's opinions that tend to make one sick or unhappy. Let God or Truth be true and all men liars. If two ideas come in conflict in you and you want to do what you think is not right, investigate the wrong and you will find that it is from some one's opinion and you have tried to carry it out to your own destruction. You have taken some effect for an element. This makes all the trouble. Error can produce no element but can only create disease and misery. Elements are like true love or science. They contain no evil except when hatred or passion is put in. Then they may take the name of the author of the evil. For instance, you may love a person, and he may love liquor; you may be induced to drink; your love for your friend may be transferred to the liquor and you may become a drunkard. Now to cure you is to have someone interest you in those who have a distaste for liquor, and in that way if you follow your friend and if he knows what he is about, he restores you to health and happiness.

April 1860

Healing Art, The*
[BU 3:0648]

Of all the various powers of man, none have been more subservient to the cause of superstition than the healing art. It has always been believed to be of supernatural origin and from this fact those who exercised it were tempted to make a selfish use of it and impose on the credulity and confidence of the sick. Thus it has always served a superstitious or dishonest purpose and it is at this day so connected with deception that he who should claim to make it honest and comprehensible will be suspected of insanity. As a fact this faculty is admitted but the causes with which it has always been identified have never lifted the veil of mystery which shrouds it, so that it has in the hearts of man a superstition and though its existence is a truth, its practice is a lie. Not having been accounted for on natural grounds it has dwindled down to a physical peculiarity for which man is not responsible, thus putting it entirely out of the domain of reason or intelligence. To separate a truth which has sunk so low in corruption from the corruption, and put it upon the basis of other intellectual or moral powers of man, so that it is incorruptible in principle, must of course lead to new results in the theory of disease. This has been done by Dr. Quimby. His position is new and he has the disadvantage of coming up through the reproaches which ages of superstition and ignorance have thrown around the healing art.

It is much easier to deride a new idea than to give it an investigation and it is much easier to put a senseless construction on the principles that Dr. Q. holds, than to listen with candor to his explanation of them, thus making him responsible for absurdities that it is a libel on common sense to believe. The simplicity with which Dr. Q. describes a patient's disease often disappoints those whose minds are prepared to an explanation, effective and exciting with dangers. This comes from the fact that he pays no respect to it: He neither fears nor honors it and so far as a patient's dignity is identified with his trouble he is liable to feel himself insulted by the want of attention he bestows on their peculiar feelings, then they suppose that he is ignorant of the real conditions they are in. After a while if they persevere, they find out that that was not the point to which his wisdom was directed and in fact it was the very error on which all their misery hung, and that he had patience with them till they corrected it themselves, though the very evidence itself of their disease might remain and give them no inconvenience.

His treatment differs from what was ever experienced by the sick and often seems dark and inexplicable, for he wanders with the patient through scenes and experiences which he is ignorant of ever living through, and finds the world they live in all unknown to themselves and undreamed of by others:

So he either brings to light the mystery of our existence or invents fables to arouse the sick while he deceives them into health; if this last were true it must run out, and as it does not seem likely to do so immediately it is fair to give him the advantage of the former: His principle that man is an intelligence is one admitted in many relations, but it has never been thought to apply to the life he lives in the body: Our life is a confused mixture of chance, providence and primary knowledge all telling in our success or misfortunes—no regulator has ever been discovered which could determine what are the influences that make our destiny: All his knowledge of man is derived by following out this principle with the sick, or correcting their errors and letting them shape their course free from them. The body he has nothing to do with except as it gives him and the patient confidence. His cures are the effect of his faith in the wisdom which he says can undo every evil that man has made. Disease he believes got into the world by ignorance and superstition and maintains its respectable position by the craft and hypocrisy of man and to destroy it is to expose the fallacy and flimsiness of the reasoning which upholds it as a true and living fact: The corner stone of disease is the belief that the body is the fountain of life and from it proceeds the varieties and peculiarities of the genus homo and all the facts of human nature.

Consequently disease is in the body and is all comprehended by the bodily senses. The principle he works on upsets all this by striking at the root of the matter and proving a wisdom superior to matter which rightly understood will produce happiness and progress. Although the former is established by innumerable facts of the bodily senses still it is not the real truth in which the development of man depends, on the contrary it is the error from which all human misery springs. Dr. Q. reasons that man is outside and superior to that he acts upon as an engineer is outside the machine he controls. In science this is true in our belief, and man acts with accurate and exact knowledge, but the knowledge is not supposed to be any part of him–it is arbitrary and independent of man, but under a belief man acts in what he believes. There has never been a truth to teach man to control his body, he has been educated to believe that the body is a prison and he is a prisoner subject to its authority and limitations, therefore he is in it, and as far as he knows every act of his life is controlled by it.

Healing Power, The
[BU 3:0643]

This power, which from the beginning of the world has been associated with the goodness of God, has placed those endowed with it above the masses, like people chosen by God to administer to the suffering of the human race. So the sick, who are always ready to worship the person who cures them, are very loathe to believe such dishonesty. This gives those who had this power a superiority over the sick which they willingly acknowledge to them. In this way religious sects sprang up established by cures, the person claiming that the power was from God. This gave it a religious sanctity and gave these persons power over the sick. Finally the healing power fell into the hands of the priests. Now the power to heal and the right to dictate are two things. The healing is of itself a peculiar gift to the world like any wisdom not reduced to practice. So those who healed were honest, but as soon as their interest came in, there came the deception and as the deception began to show itself, the power ceased. This was the way at the time of Christ. Those who healed had become so corrupt that they were a pest in society, the priests being the worst. A quarrel arose between these two classes and each gave the power to God, so that at the time of Jesus the thinking classes looked upon both as humbugs.

Healing Principle, The*
[BU 3:0213]

It is an undisputed fact that Dr. Quimby cures disease, and that without any medicine or outward application. How does he do it? is the question that agitates and interests the people. If he has any new way, different from the mysterious and superstitious mode acknowledged by others who have appeared to cure disease, by their personal virtue alone. What is it? Where does he say he gets his power?

In the first place, he denies, that he has any power or gift superior to other men. He contends that he operates intelligently, under the direction of a principle which is always his guide, while with the sick, that this principle he follows in practice and in theory, and under it he learns facts of real life, that he could never get at in any other way. He has found the way by which all errors can be corrected, and which he only applies to disease.

Well, what is the principle?

I do not think I could explain it in one word, but it might be called the principle of goodness. It is the highest intelligence that operates in the affairs of man, always producing harmony and makes man feel that he has more to learn and is a progressive being. It is known in all exclusively, intellectual branches, the Law. The natural sciences and all those studies that teach man, that the more he investigates, the more there is in prospect to learn. You see, such a principle does not operate in the affairs of our everyday life. It has been his aim to develop it in relation to human misery and make life a science.

The cause of all misery is in our ignorance of ourselves he says, and in proportion as he develops this higher, happier part of mankind, which he calls Science, he sees through the mysteries of the ills, that flesh is heir to and just in proportion as he sees through them he can correct them. His cures and his philosophy are one thing. What do you mean by that? his cures I have perfect confidence in, but I do not see through his talk. What is his talk good for?

He says, "that his explanation of the patient's feelings is the cure," with a knowledge that all trouble is a false alarm, to truth, that whatever obstructions to health he finds, all rest on a skimpy foundation, some opinion or superstition, he proceeds to undermine the foundation and then the structure gives way. However well established are the facts of any disease, he believes the basis all wrong, and that they are dependent on the opinion of man for an existence, and that these opinions are believed in as truth. So that the facts are merely the expression of the belief. To destroy the belief identified with a patient's feelings, changes the mind and that is the cure.

Then he believes that all disease is in the mind? I should not think he could cure everything by that theory.

He does indeed believe that disease is all in the mind, but then with his experience, the mind is something and embraces a much larger compass of our being than we are taught to consider it. It includes all opinions and religion and everything about us which can change, not that part which is seen by the natural eye, but that which acts upon the natural man. It embraces all excitement and agitation and all the variations of humanity. It is that part that is affected at the contact with a new idea. He says, "mind is matter."

What kind of matter is it and how does he know that it is matter, if he does not see, or touch it and cannot show it to another person's senses?

It is not matter that comes to our bodily senses. It is another kind, which is just as sensible to him as that he touches with his hand. Around every one is an atmosphere of intelligence which contains the whole of our identity, and he has become so sensitive to this atmosphere, that its existence is a fact, and it is with that he operates.

I should think he had discovered a sixth sense.

I cannot say that he has found any one faculty that would answer to a sense. But he has refined and spiritualized those faculties which mankind exercise towards each other till he has arrived at the true way of communicating and influencing minds. For instance, his sympathy for his patients is pure from any feeling like blame or contempt, or discouragement, and is as a transparency to reflect their feelings just as they come to him, with light from a higher source, to account for and explain them to the patient, and his explanation illumines their mind.

Well, how does he know that he has got hold of a true method, how does he know but he is mistaken?

There are many reasons which confirm his belief in his method as a science, one is that he constantly improves, he finds he can cure quicker, and harder cases. Then as he explains himself to others, and they understand, it confirms him. But that, you will say is no proof, and it is not in itself. Admitting that there is a first cause, or God, as everyone does, it is not so hard to demonstrate that Dr. Quimby knows more about him and his wisdom, in regard to health, than anyone else. And unto Him, he, Dr. Q. gives all the glory. He knows that while treating disease he is purely under the influence of the highest truth and all that he says to the patient, admitting the basis is a whole train of consistencies. And according as he follows this method, he comes out of many of the common beliefs that he has in common with other men. He knows that all his peculiar belief is not an invention of his own, for it is all contrary to what as a natural man, he believes–it is not substantiated by anything that he has been taught, but rests on the facts of his own experience with the sick–it is a vital truth that teaches him.

Health and Disease
[Originally untitled.] [LC 1:0610]

Disease is that part of the mind that can be compared to a wilderness. It is full of erroneous opinions and false ideas of all kinds and it opens a field for speculators to explore. The medical faculty, spiritualism and all forms of religious beliefs invite the people to enter under their false ideas; and when I sit by a sick person, he tells me the story of his travels and his experience of the evils that beset him in this wilderness, for it forms a great part of every person. The scientific character is like the prodigal son. It desires to enter this land of mystery to see what it can gain; therefore every person with ambition sets out for the prize and alas! ninety-nine out of a hundred fail and are cast into prison. This is the field for scientific investigation and as health is the thing most desired, to find out how to keep it, and when lost how to restore it is the object of our journey into this territory.

The question may be asked, What is health? I know of no better answer than this. It is perfect wisdom and just as a man is wise, just so his wisdom is his health; but as no man is perfectly wise, no man can have perfect health for ignorance is disease, although not accompanied by pain. Pain is not disease itself but is what follows disease. According to this theory, disease is a belief, and when there is no fear there can be no pain; for pain is not the act but the reaction of something which creates pain and therefore that must take place before the reaction.

But says one, I never thought of pain till it came. Now if it came, something must have started it. Therefore it must be an effect, whether it came from some place or from ourselves. I take the ground that it is generated in ourselves and that it must have a cause. Everyone knows that a person in his natural state is sensitive to what is called pain and if his sensitiveness is destroyed he shows no signs of pain. But to suppose his senses are destroyed because he feels no pain is not correct. His senses may be detached from his body and attached to another idea so that he is not sensitive to any effect on the body which in his natural state would give him pain. This shows that pain is in the mind, like all trouble, though the cause may be in the belief or the body.

For instance, suppose a tumor appears on the body. The person, feeling no sensation or trouble from it, consults a physician who, after examining it, asks the man if he has shooting pains and hot flashes. The man says, "No, why do you ask the question?" The doctor replies that it looks to him like a cancer and then explains the nature and symptoms of such a disease. In the course of an hour, the man feels shooting pains, etc. Now where is the pain, in the tumor, or belief in a cancer? I answer in the belief and as mind is matter a belief is also matter governed by error. Error gives direction to the mind and a cancer is formed just as far as the belief is received by the patient.

If man reasoned from another standard, different results would follow. Every thought is a part of a person's identity, and if it contains a belief, he must suffer the penalty of his acts, for to believe is to act. To illustrate. Suppose while I am talking with you someone comes along and says the small pox is near here. The one who is talking with me never had it; the thought instantly makes his belief in disease and his liability to take it; therefore he is in danger, just as much as he is exposed by his belief. I stand here. I believe that he, as well as the rest of mankind, believes in the disease, but I know that God did not make the disease; therefore being the invention of man, it cannot live where there is no belief. Therefore, I am not affected. To me all disease stands in the same way and just as I have analyzed them, I find that they are the invention of man and they can be dissipated unless the impression is so strong that it is beyond the power of the operator to explain it. Such a case is like the trial of an innocent man when all the evidence is against him. It requires a skillful attorney to get such a case; but when the evidence can be sifted so as to be questioned and destroyed, as it can in nine cases out of ten, there is no danger of losing it.

We all have an influence over each other, and if we know how to direct it, the effect will be just what we want; but if we are guided by a belief, the effect will be just what we do not want when our belief is governed by fear, for our fear affects a person instead of our belief. For instance, a person wishes to influence a friend. If he is afraid that he shall not have the influence he wishes, his fears and not his desire will affect the friend. Therefore it is necessary that man should know himself, for every person is a machine, governed by the owner or someone else. When controlled by wisdom it cannot go wrong, but when guided by error, it cannot go right, for error is not wise, while wisdom is an element of itself, and if our senses are in that, all is right, but if they are in error, discord and misery follow.

To make it understood how we all stand toward each other, I will again compare this wisdom, which is an element in common, to music. Every person possessing it enjoys the pleasure that flows from a knowledge of it. This represents perfect love not of matter. It is harmony without any other character. It is something outside of every other feeling, having its whole happiness in the development of mind; therefore it acts upon man, but ignorance takes it for passion. Then misconstrued and unappreciated it becomes timid. Here is where a great mistake is made. The man that is little above the brute knows no love superior or separate from the brute, while there is a love that does not contain a particle of the animal, the love of the beautiful and wise. This is not appreciated by man and when it comes to him to lead him to a higher state, it is met by the brutal element and a belief formed that it is passion. This cold reception causes a disease and chills the element that flows from the purest fountain. The mistake lies in the false idea of love. Man, being progressive, is not always to remain a brute. His reason must elevate him from the brutal element and lead him to see and feel that the purest love that one can have for another contains no passion nor any of the brutal element. But man began to reason before he came out from the brute and judged the world by his own standard. Therefore to the impure nothing is pure, but those who have passed from the error of matter to the element of love, in which everything lives, can see how it may be misrepresented. The love of parents contains nothing spurious or animal, but let the parent or child be deceived into a belief that they are strangers and then love is changed. Again, let one know of his relation to the other and he in his wisdom discards the error of belief, while the other still is under his brutal belief.

Where then is the brutal element? In the love or in the belief? I answer; in the belief. Let all persons know this and they will understand themselves, and knowing the animal element in the male and female will know their position and safety. Then they will subdue the animal element and lead man into a higher wisdom.

I say it without fear, that religious creeds are based upon this low order of animal intelligence; but as the brutal element is pure, the effect of the belief depends on the intelligence of the person in whom the animal prevails over science.

The reformation of Jesus was intended to separate man from the brutal element that he might rise into that state where ignorance could not enter. This wisdom then will be a light to lead man into the dark and give him power over all unclean ideas and he will become a teacher to those in darkness in whom the light will spring up. This is the light that Paul saw when the scale fell from his eyes. When wisdom becomes common, everyone will use it to draw his friend out of this world into science.

It may be asked if this will not break family ties and destroy marriage contracts? Not at all, for their contracts will be carried into eternal wisdom, whereas they are now made till death. They will then be made for eternity. But says one, If I have got to live with my husband or my wife to all eternity, I shall not believe this doctrine. Let me explain. No two persons are together unless they are agreed. Therefore man and wife are not necessarily together, but most frequently are separate and trying to come together; for as I have said, when two persons agree on one thing, they are together. The difficulty in cases where persons think they are not matched lies in the mutual misunderstanding of the parties. One wants to lead or instruct the other or the one most advanced in wisdom wants the other to share his happiness, while the other knows no happiness outside of this world and cannot see beyond matter. Therefore, this party wishes to control the higher. The higher being capable of receiving the lower wisdom, it becomes deceived by opinions. Under this error it mingles with the lower element and both sink below their level and misery is the result. But cultivate the scientific life and the lower will become subject to the higher.

When two individuals set out on the road to wisdom they will develop each other and their happiness will be one. Their labor will be no greater than to gather gold without much toil. For this science opens such a field to the traveler that he cares not to eat or sleep but his happiness is in investigating the regions that lie open before him. He who enters this country must have a partner, for the whole interest lies in overcoming opposition and developing each other. To be alone in wisdom is like being alone on an island with no prospect of collecting jewels. That which gives me the most satisfaction is to develop a mind capable of improvement. It is like learning music. There is a faculty that gives the operator the greatest happiness. This science is inexhaustible and the more you have, the more you want and you will find this continually exciting you.

1865

Higher Intelligence, The
[BU 3:0358]

Ever since the world began to reason, it has been known that there is a state of intelligence higher than the natural man or brute, but to define it has been the problem to be solved. It has been separated from the lower state by hundreds of names but it has never had a separate identity, for instance, the law and the gospel. Now they put intelligence in the gospel, also right and wrong. Here they admit two kinds of intelligence, good and bad, both in one person. Action and reaction, God and the Devil, Science and ignorance etc. etc.

I might go on to the end of the chapter and never arrive at what all have aimed at. Then what are these two identities that have had so many names, such as health and disease, happiness and misery, etc.? All refer to this same higher state and sometimes intelligence. Yet their separation never has been made, so that the thinking mind can have two identities that they can agree upon. The religious world have tried to give these two principles an identity so they called one God and the other the Devil. This for a time answered, but when men began to reason, these identities merged into one. This has been the case with every theory. Now I propose to find an element that every man will admit whatever his religion or political opinions may be if he is scientific. Every scientific man will admit what is called in mechanics, statics. This includes that class or reason that sees and knows no third power or what is called velocity. It can't reason from cause and effect. It embraces the brutes and natural man. It embraces imitation and cunning, but nothing that relates to dynamics. That embraces a higher power. It sees the errors of statics and cannot overcome them. It is progression or the destruction of error.

Statics also embraces destruction but not construction. Dynamics embraces the destruction of error and the construction of civilization and freedom; both principles admit destruction. All wars are carried on in these two principles. The one to destroy the government is statics, the one to destroy the rebellion and preserve the government is dynamics. This last has to contend with all the ignorance of the lower mode of reason and also the conservative element, that class of mind which is neither dynamics or statics, but a little of both, and not settled in either. They are like sea captains who continue to use a hemp cable upon the principle that an iron one was not strong enough. This was a conservative man. So in all things, the two extremes are the only real identities. Those between are a sort of mongrel that never produce anything but hold back till the men of statics get out of patience and give up the fight.

The conservative rises and says, You both are wrong, and each partially right. This conservative principle is actually of importance. It is like the ballast in a ship. Its weight keeps the ship sometimes from tipping over. But it always acts to prevent the wise, or if there was no ballast the wise would, from the misfortune, become wiser by experience. But to save the lives and property, while the principle is developing, this third element is introduced. Where science is understood, it is thrown away, for it encumbers the ship of science, being nothing but weight or pressure that has no power. Velocity destroys it and so science destroys conservatism. So also freedom destroys slavery and conservatism.

Conservatism shows itself in language. It makes issues where none are needed. It is all grammar and pays no respect to principles. It is power of imitation of sounds. It makes issue on what it does not know. For instance, it admits an error and then sustains it by facts that are used to sustain a true principle. For instance, in the error of slavery. Statics contends it is right; dynamics denies it. Conservatism admits it as wrong, and at the same time denies the right to destroy it and quotes the Constitution to prove that it is right. So conservatism is a sort of looking glass to both. Each can see their reasoning in it.

Now all trouble commences in this lower element which is matter in motion. Conservatism is the first element that is produced, for it is that dead matter that is tossed about by the motion of statics and to get rid of it brings out the higher element of dynamics to calculate power in motion or calculate causes and effects. Freedom is wisdom and slavery, ignorance. Statics never sees nor reflects on the chances, and being ignorant, it comes in that gross matter called conservatism which wants matter to keep still. But as matter is not under the control of statics or conservatism, the latter is as much an enemy of statics as to dynamics.

So the principle if true will keep developing, and dynamics or science will expand till conservatism is used up. For it is but ignorance and shows itself in every development of science. Now as disease commences as a way of accounting for everything upon some false basis, conservatism opposes it. So in every respect this element is of use in a certain state of progression, but beyond that it is a dead weight. For instance, to oppose a truth when it can be demonstrated beyond a doubt is a dead weight to progression. This element is largely developed in religious and political parties and also in the doctrine of disease. Statics has invented all sorts of superstition. The African slaves are a very good example of statics in politics, in religion and in disease. They are famous for their superstition in regard to the other world and believe in all kinds of evil spirits, so that if anyone should say to them that a disease has legs and would come to them, they would believe.

Now it is a fact that this false way of reasoning in regard to all these ideas has a great effect on this still kind of matter called conservatism, and when science shows itself by the working of this lower element, then you hear from the conservative. It is dangerous to meddle with the old established truths (or Constitution) as witchcraft, slavery and all kinds of disease, or the element to create them. You hear the faculty warning the masses (or statics) not to be humbugged. You know, say they, that the old way of practice has been handed down from our fathers who know more than these quacks. Others appeal to the church to prove that our government was founded in slavery and ignorance.

All this is true but they never dreamt that wisdom had another government that came down from on high and is establishing itself in the hearts and understanding of men, founded on the rock of science (called dynamics). This is the pillar that followed Moses when he was leading the people to the land of science and this is the rock he smote that discharged the water that they drank. This rock and water was science. The water was the understanding of it and those that drank in this truth or water were satisfied. The serpent was the doctrine of the statics mind. So as Moses held up their superstition and showed how it acted on the minds and made them sick and gave them pains like the bite of serpents, then those who listened and received the truth were healed or convinced. Now all this kind of reasoning applies to the people of these days, for false science has always existed.

Paul warns the people against these persons teaching science falsely so called. In curing disease, this element called conservatism is all the help the error gets. Let those who know nothing of the cause of disease stand aside and let the medical faculty fight out their own battle and it would be nothing but a mere somersault and the truth would come out conqueror. But the conservative element always sticks to the skirts of the faculty like demagogues or dogs to bark at and hunt the truth and misrepresent everything for the sake of being petted and fed by the faculty. The bolters that are always shifting in a storm to be on the right side after the storm is over, when they can say, "I thought so; it has come out just as I said." Of all matter this is the least.

It is like the lawyer who, when the judge told the court that they must be in their seats when the court began, said, Your honor knows I am the least absent. Yes, said the judge, and the least present. So to wisdom, the conservative minds are the least present or absent. They are a sort of necessary evil that in the progress of truth acts as a stumbling block to science and ignorance. These make up the element of pressure in mechanics. Like the weight of a vessel on the stocks, having nothing to do with getting her off. Wisdom has to overcome it and all the time it says, Let me alone. I was put here and it is against the laws of pressure or weight to be moved for it may stave all to pieces. Statics says, We will shove it off by force. Dynamics says, By the principle of mechanics, by the inclined plane, we get rid of some power or substitute velocity instead. So that if we can start it, the weight or conservatism will be on our side. The inclined plane is the turning point to conservatism. So as the ship moves off, conservatism sings out with science, Here she goes and throws up its cap in triumph, while statics stands in a maze and calls it a mystery.

This is the way with the sick. The doctor stands and looks at his patient that has moved off the stocks by the power of science and all conservatism is shouting, Good. The doctor stands with his thumb in his mouth and when asked if he understands how it was done replies, It (the disease) might have gone before if it had a mind to. It puts ignorance in the body or matter and holds it responsible for their folly. Science has always these errors to overcome. If I could think of a man who has all these elements well defined, I would describe him; but every man has them, some more and some less and no man is free from all, who has the dynamical intelligence. He who has the conservative element may not have the three but he must have statics.

Ignorance or statics puts the highest wisdom in the conservative element. Dynamics puts no wisdom in either but calls them elements in matter to be governed by the laws of dynamics. Statics is the natural growth like all other animal life. Conservatism is the manufactured article. Dynamics is a knowledge of both. The two first are like the clearing up of a wilderness. Statics is the natural growth. Dynamics cuts down the trees or obstructions. Conservatism is the resistance to the power of dynamics. So as cultivation and health come, disease and ignorance disappear.

1864

"Honeymoon, The" Spiritual Analysis of Man and Woman
[BU 3:0860]

Two principles show their practical working in the development of every individual and reveal the progress of wisdom in man. The only true way to show the operation of the higher and invisible intelligence that governs and controls the affairs of the world is by illustration, using natural facts, such as are real to the world, but revealing to the wise a higher development of truth not yet known as such or accounted for. To bring to light the higher and unseen intelligence that overrules the motives and actions of men and yet is unknown, I will use the illustration of a play. Not that the author had the slightest idea of the wisdom that governed him in writing the play, but seeing it, I take it to illustrate the higher truth whence it proceeds.

Every principle of truth and every error assumes a character. Error is generally master in the beginning but truth finally triumphs. Two characters are admitted in the play but only one principle, that of the natural man. The spiritual is so mingled with the natural that its separate existence is not recognized. For instance, love and passion are so interwoven that the world knows only one, while there is as decided a difference as between white and black. Every person is composed of these elements and I will introduce the characters of the play to bring them out. One represents progression, is a well educated, refined and intelligent gentleman. The other, a lady, is aristocratic and overbearing. These two characters are both in different degrees in the lady and gentleman and each is governed by the one which predominates. Therefore several characters are necessary to illustrate one individual. For every person is double, and to bring out the perspective it takes four, for two are only shadows and they change as I shall show.

All plays represent the various characters of one person. Therefore the two characters in the play are really the conflicting and opposite qualities of one individual. The gentleman is one whose finer feelings and intellectual culture overbalances the lower passions of man. The lady is aristocratic so that her higher qualities are subdued by an overbearing and haughty disposition. Money is an emblem of wealth, so they must both be rich. With one, money is riches, with the other, wisdom and virtue are riches and money is a secondary matter. Thus they both hold a high position in society. One uses it to elevate the intelligence, the other, the passions of the world. As these two minds meet, there is a sympathetic attraction towards each other, but with no understanding. For man does not know himself and there must be a discord when the time of life commences. These two typify the development of man into a higher state. In society, the man is superior to the woman, for she represents the scientific-spiritual character, while the man represents the animal. These two do not belong to one or the other exclusively, for man and woman are a compound of them. But in the world, man is the superior. Yet in the play, their wisdom is reversed, for the female in the man is the ruling wisdom, and the male in the woman. Therefore when they sympathize, the male in the woman comes in contact with the male in the man, and the female in the woman sympathizes with the female in the man and they do not understand each other. To make it plainer, I will call it animal and spiritual. The woman loves the man, that is, that part of the woman in subjection to man sympathizes with the higher element in man. The object is to subdue the male that governs the woman and bring it into subjection to the higher wisdom, the female. The spiritual element in man sympathizes also with the same in the woman. The two characters, (The Duke and Juliana) not standing in relation to each other as the world would have them, could sympathize but not harmonize, for their motives were different. At last they marry. Marriage is to agree to a contract in this world.

If I tell a person a story and court him till he believes it, this is a spiritual marriage. If I reason with a person till I convince him of a scientific truth, this is a scientific marriage, sanctioned in heaven where no worldly passions can mar. This is Christ's marriage and to this wedding every person is invited, yet some come without the wedding garment. The marriage of the earthly man is to opinions and that may change, but the great wedding of science is the true wedding, while the other is a contract.

So man is all the time marrying and giving in marriage and getting divorced. To return to the married couple, the man wished to develop his wife or subdue the earthly man. The woman wanted to subdue the scientific man. So when they began to act, they were like Paul when he said, When I would do good, evil is present with me. To develop a person, it is necessary that he should contend with an opposite. So the error in the woman made war with the science in the man. But the truth prevailed, error was subdued, harmony was restored and they became united in one living and true sympathy that knows no dictation.

Now as the female is superior to the male, this has all to be reversed by introducing two more characters that are contained in the play, Leonora and Rolando. Let the man or animal rule and the female is not known in his brutal acts but lies in the soil of the man as a servant, secretly destroying the natural man by her soft tones, speaking through the form of a man. The servant acted in the spiritual element of the man, fostered and fed it in the wilderness till it grew large enough to come forth. There it threw off the earthly garb and assumed the scientific woman. The brutal man cowed down and the spiritual man came forth, became wedded to the scientific woman and the natural man in both became subject to the spiritual man. This is what every person goes through to arrive at the spiritual world.

April 1865

How Can a Person Learn to Cure the Sick?
[LC 1:0559]

How can a person learn to cure the sick? As a pupil in mathematics learns to work out a problem. Every word is supposed to have a meaning. Now words are like nuts. Some are full, some partially full and some are empty. The food or wisdom is in the word, and if the word contains no wisdom, then it is like husks or froth; it fails to satisfy the desire of the person who seeks the substance.

Natural food is to satisfy the natural man and spiritual food or wisdom is to satisfy the inner or scientific man. The child before it begins to know is a blank. It falls into the hands of the natural man and is fed by natural food, while its spiritual food is opinions expressed in words. Therefore, as I said, words contain more or less truth; all are not full and some are empty. But when a person speaks a word that conveys the real substance and applies it to the thing spoken of, that is what is called the bread of Life and he neither hungers nor thirsts for wisdom in regard to that.

The sick have been deceived by false words and have fed on food that contained no wisdom. Hungry and thirsty they apply to strangers for food; they ask for health or the bread of life and the natural man taking bread as a natural substance brings bread to them, but their state or mind does not hunger for natural food, therefore to them is a stone. There is a bread of which, if a man eat, he is filled. This bread is Christ or Science. It is the body of Christ. Jesus said, "Whoso eateth my flesh and drinketh my blood hath eternal life. For my flesh is meat indeed and my blood is drink indeed." The Jews of his day were like the scholars of the present day. Bread is bread, blood is blood and they said, How can this man give us his flesh to eat? They do not understand that wisdom is a body and that opinion is a shadow. The natural man's belief is his body and to eat and drink the world's wisdom is to eat condemnation or disease.

Now I will illustrate a cure. I sit down by a sick person and you also sit down. I feel her trouble and the state of her mind and find her faint and weary for the want of wisdom. I tell her what she calls this feeling that troubles her and knowing her trouble my words contain food that you know not of. My words are words of wisdom and they strengthen her, while if you should speak the same words and the sound should fall on the natural ear precisely as mine do, they are only empty sounds and the sick derive no nourishment from them.

I will describe this food that you may taste it and be wiser for your meal. In order to prove that food satisfies a person's hunger I must find a person who is hungry, and in order to prove that my words satisfy the sick I must take one who hungers and thirsts for the bread of life or health. The lady I have now in my mind felt an uneasy feeling as though she was hungry. Being weak and faint from exhaustion, she applied to a physician for food to satisfy her desire, for she was famished for the want of wisdom in regard to her trouble. Instead of giving her wisdom that would have satisfied her, he in his ignorance gave her these words full of poison. "Your trouble is a cancer in the breast." As she received these words she grew more faint and exhausted till she became sick at her stomach. She ate of this poisonous food till the seeds of misery began to agitate the matter; the idea began to form and a bunch appeared on the breast. As she attached the name cancer to the bunch, the name and the bunch became one body. The physician's words contained the poison, the poison produced the bunch. Their ignorance associated the name with the bunch and called it cancer.

I was called to see the lady and being perfectly ignorant of her trouble, I felt the faint hungry feeling; and as I felt the effect of the doctor's food or opinion on her, I said the food that you eat does not nourish you, it gives you pain in the heart. This I said in reference to the way she reasoned in regard to her trouble. How do you know, she said. I told her then that she thought her trouble was a cancer and she admitted that it was so. I then told her that she had no cancer except what she made herself. I admit the swelling said I, but it is of your own make. You received the seed from the doctor and he prepared the mind or matter for its growth, but the fruit is the work of the medical faculty.

Let us see how much of the idea cancer exists in truth. The name existed before the bunch, then the bunch before it appeared must have been in the mind, for it was not in sight when the word was first applied to it or when you were first told that you had one. You know that you can be affected by another mind? "Certainly," she said. I wish to show you, said I, that every phenomenon that takes form in the human body is first conceived in the mind. Some sensation is felt which we cannot account for; we then conjure up some idea which we create into a belief; it is soon condensed into a form and a name given to it. Thus every phenomenon taking the name of disease is a pattern of some false idea started without the least foundation in truth. Now this bunch I call a phenomenon, for I cannot call it a cancer because if I do, I admit a thing outside the mind.

The senses are the man independent of flesh. That is one thing; the word cancer is another. Now I want to find the matter that the word is applied to. To say a thing exists and to prove its existence are two different things. If any doctor will tell me where that cancer was before it was in sight, I will ask him how he knows. Let him say it was in the blood, that the state of the blood indicates the presence of cancerous humor. Now do you deny that I told you your feelings? Certainly not, she says. Then have I a cancerous humor? No, then there is no wisdom in that argument.

Again he never knew you had an ill feeling till you told him. Then where did he get his knowledge? Not from you, for you never thought of a cancer. It must have been from what you said about your pain. Suppose I had said that I felt these same pains and you had kept your peace; then according to his theory, I must have a cancerous humor. Now I know that I have no humor nor had I an idea or pain till I sat by you; therefore his story of a cancer is a lie made out of the whole cloth without the least shadow of truth. It is like stories of Sinbad the Sailor or some other fable that have no existence in truth. Then you will say, What is this bunch? It is a bunch of solid matter, not a ghost or any invisible thing, but it was made by yourself and no one else. I will tell you how you made it. You will remember I spoke of your having a heat. This heat contained no good or ill but it was a mere decomposition of the body, brought about by some little excitement.

It troubled you for you say your dress fretted the parts. Then your superstitious fears of disease began to haunt you in your sleep creating an action in the part of your breast where the error had made a stand till finally you called on the doctor and got his opinion of what he knew nothing. You commenced then to form the idea till at last you excited the muscles to such an extent that the bunch has appeared. If now I have proved the cure, I have affected it and the bunch will disappear. Do you wish to know why? Yes. Have I not explained that the doctor's theory is based on a lie? Yes. Can the effect remain when the cause is removed? I presume not. How do you feel? I feel easy. How do you feel in regard to your trouble and in regard to what I have said? I think you are right and that it looks more reasonable than the doctor's story. Then your senses have left his opinion and have come to my wisdom. This is the new birth. You have risen from the dead if you are free from the doctor's ideas. This truth has destroyed death and brought life and health through science. Now I say unto you, Take up your bed or this truth and go your way. And when the night of error comes, spread out the garment of wisdom that enfolded Jesus and wrap yourself in its folds or truth till the sun of life shall shine in upon your body or truth and you rise free from the evils of the old belief.

1864

How Does Dr. Quimby Effect His Cures?*
[Originally untitled.] [BU 3:0458]

[*Editor's Note*: These comments were written in response to a letter received from a Mary M. Jackson dated Portland, Nov. 5th 1860.]

The frequency of such instances as the above excite the minds of the community thus a very natural question. How does Dr. Quimby effect his cures? This question will of course be answered by different individuals to suit their own opinions and he is classed accordingly with magicians, spiritualists, humbugs and other inventions of a superstitious belief. We do not wish to disturb those who derive consolation or satisfaction from such theories, but allowing there is any justice in judging a man's wisdom by his acts, we know none who has a better chance to enlighten the question, than Dr. Quimby himself. In his explanation of the phenomena of his cures he stands alone–unsupported by any established theory. He disclaims any assistance from the spirits of the dead and entirely ignores what so many grant him, a miraculous power or gift superior to other men. He contends that there is a principle in curing disease the knowledge of which renders the process natural and intelligent, that the principle is recognized in Sciences, but is not applied to any belief respecting happiness. In his case its development has carried him out of a state of mystery and speculations, to a knowledge where he realizes the origin of the fountain of misery–disease. He does not, as many suppose, deny the phenomenon of disease and refer human suffering to the imagination, but treats it as the result of ignorance, and not as a manifestation of the wisdom of God. In his practice he recognizes a universal principle of goodness which in its operation on mankind individually, produces harmony, while the discords of the sick come from the inventions of man in which this element has no place. This consciousness renders his sympathy intelligent and his system a science.

Portland, Nov. 5th, 1860

How Does Dr. Quimby Stand in Relation to His Patients?–Part I
[LC 2:0663]

He stands as a lawyer stands to his client. He pleads their case before the court of Science or Truth; his pleas are their medicine, their opinions are their crimes, the punishment is the disease and the phenomenon is the prison. The medical men are the mouthpiece of public opinion or error and every phenomenon that takes place must first pass the fire of their batteries and they must give an explanation to everything which is received as truth; so being blind guides, they lead the blind till they all fall into the ditch of error and wallow in their own filth. To get them clear from this mire, which is opinions or disease, is to show that part of them which is diseased is the cause of the misery and the argument is the medicine. I will show you how the medicine works.

Disease is a chemical change. Take the infant, for example. When it is born, its ideas are its body, like the earth in its original state. As the ideas develop the body develops and the original seeds or ideas come forth; these are called mother wit or natural sense. This is the earth spoken of in the Bible. Out of this earth, God or truth made man or opinions and ambition or what is called the natural man without science. It was not good that opinions should be alone, so out of opinions came a higher element. Science is not a natural production of error or the earth or child, but it is from a higher state called God or Wisdom. As the child is the vineyard or earth, the man or opinion is the husbandman and the Science or woman is the wife. So opinions or man thinks he is the wisdom, while wisdom is the owner or proprietor of the whole earth.

The child is like the garden and error or opinions is the man, and wisdom lets out the vineyard to man to cultivate the little ideas or original growth of the earth. As new ideas are sown in the mind, they spring up in the form of reason making the man; and the fruits are opinions etc.; out of this man comes the spiritual or scientific man. This man is not seen by the man of opinions, but he is the real man. I will illustrate these two characters.

A little tree grows up, blossoms and bears fruit. This all comes to the natural sight. The fruit throws off an odor which cannot be seen, yet it is in the atmosphere and can be detected by the odor or life. This life sees in the odor the apple and all its peculiar properties. This is the spiritual senses or the life of the apple tree, so the natural man works out the real essence or property of God into the spiritual or scientific man that cannot be seen by the man of opinions but is the real man.

To understand how I cure is to see yourself outside of the natural man or your opinions, like the odor of the apple, with all your senses or reason; then instead of you, that is the essence being in matter, you will see that matter is in the essence. It is often said that God is in everything. This makes God less than the thing He is in. Now make God the essence with all the senses attached to it; then you have an eternal and everlasting essence without matter or form, a point without magnitude but eternal. Call this eternal Wisdom the Father of all that exists out of matter; see this Wisdom by its will speak the idea matter into existence and everything that man calls life. All these things are in the knowledge of this Wisdom, not the Wisdom in the things that are spoken.

It is the same with man. His wisdom is the living man. His opinions are the body or natural man. To put his wisdom into his opinion is to make an opinion greater than a scientific truth. Disease is an opinion. To put man's wisdom into it is to make the disease larger than the real man.

It is a common remark that after we shake off this mortal coil, the spirit will be set free. This is acknowledging that the body is larger than the mind or wisdom. No wonder that with such a belief men pray to be delivered from this body of sin and death.

Thanks to this wisdom I, my wisdom, can see myself outside of this earthly belief and afloat in the ocean of space, where opinions are like stones and pebbles that men throw at each other, while to me they have no weight at all. All these are in me, that is, in my wisdom and not wisdom in them. I stand in my wisdom to the sick who are in their opinions trying to get out, and the harder they try the deeper they get into the mire. So Wisdom pleads their case, and if I get their case, then opinion is destroyed and health resumes its sway. If you understand this, you can cure.

June 1862

How Does Dr. Quimby Stand in Relation to His Patients?–Part II–Can Dr. Quimby Be in Two Places at the Same Time?
[LC 2:0664]

My answer is I can by sitting by the sick, not the well, for a sick person is one beside himself, and to converse with two persons who are not aware of their own presence, one must be in communication with both. A mesmerizer is only in one place at a time according to his belief, having but one identity, but I have two identities: one in matter and the other out of matter. One can be seen and felt by the natural man, and the other can feel and see the sick man's identity which to him is not visible to his natural man. I will illustrate my two identities. When I sit down by a sick person, I have one identity, the sick has two; yet one is not admitted except as their feelings, but this is not the case. The natural man or identity is the shadow of the real man who is in trouble. When the two separate is when the spiritual man is disturbed and makes his complaint to the world through his medium; but when there is no disturbance, there is but one identity apparent, although in reality there are two the same. For instance, when a person is in a mesmeric state, his real self can be hundreds of miles from his body, yet to him he has but one body and one identity; but to another he has two, for one is seen, and the other is admitted from the evidence he gives of his presence at the place he describes. So with me I am conscious of my own identity; then I am equally conscious of conversing with the sick and listening to their complaints as I am of my own senses. I am conscious of their identity which consists of a body with all the senses of the natural man, with all the intelligence they possess. It can travel and show one things that his natural senses know not of. Their language is their feelings which contain their trouble. It is the touch which Jesus felt. It tells you its trouble. This I communicate to their senses to let them know that their very self is outside of the body and all their troubles are in this self or identity which is not acknowledged. For the sick are like persons in a mesmeric state who want to return home having been carried away by false guides and left alone; being strangers they cling to the shadow of their old identity. This is the identity I see while I retain my own senses as a man. They remind me of a person turned out of his own house where he was born by the dissipation of his parents, driven from his own farm or house, where all his ties of earthly life are, into the world among strangers. Believing they shall have a claim on the old estate, they linger around the old place, sometimes driven away and even put into prison for daring to speak of their wrongs. The child becomes the heir of its own vineyard, given to it by the father of all, so it commences like a man and his wife in a new country. The father is opinions (the child being the vineyard), Science the mother. Opinions are the earthly man and the children partake of both parents. As opinions wants to rule, it is arbitrary and wants to dictate. So as the little ideas grow up, the earth becomes peopled with a race of ideas that are obnoxious to the children of science. So a war commences and the earthly man being more powerful in opinions and these being the standard, the child of science is driven from the land and the land is left to the world of opinions.

This is the state of a sick person brought up under the guidance of parents who have reverence for the opinions of the priest and physician and have no wisdom of their own. The children of these blind guides soon become overbearing and make war with their father, and the land passes into the hands of strangers and they seek a home in the rocks and dens. It may be asked if I believe that man might live forever, as it is called. I answer, No, not that it would be out of a true principle of the economy of life but because man is two beings: one of opinions and the other of Science. For instance, suppose a man and his wife go into a new country and purchase some millions of acres of land, and being intelligent, they have a strong desire that the land should descend to their own offspring. Their children grow up and the females marry men from some other country and all the titles are in the female's (or Science) name, and if the males or opinions marry, their titles are at the will of the female or Science. If this contract or agreement is kept in full force, generations will pass away and still the heirs of the original parents will hold the soil. So it might be with man, if there would be a science that would separate opinions from truth, so that man should not be deceived by false guides whose sole object is to get possession of the science and govern the world; then man would live contented as long as he pleased. But as long as the present theology exists, revolution and misery must follow; there must be a war of opinions against science. Call it aristocracy against democracy, or rich against poor, it is really opinions against Science or progression. Science never makes war; opinions are always making a disturbance and calling themselves the children of wisdom. Jerusalem was called the place where the Lord or Truth dwelt and the Pharisee Jews assumed to be the chosen people of God or Science; this was false science. Paul warned the people to beware of such and avoid those babbling and all opposition of Science, falsely so called.

The Jews had turned the word of God into a false religion and had taken to themselves all wisdom. So to be a religious man was to be a Jew. The Jews being made of opinions were looking for a teacher or ruler who should free them from the Roman yoke or religion. So when this truth made its appearance through the man Jesus and as they claimed to be the wisest people, Jesus went to them, but they could not understand it so he returned to the Gentiles; that is, the truth was first preached to the priests and physicians but they could not appreciate it and condemned it and then it went to the sick who could appreciate it. It is so now. I have tried to make the priests and doctors understand but they have eyes and see not, ears and hear not, and hearts but cannot understand, so they cry out, Crucify it, it is a humbug and they try to set the people against it. Therefore I turned to the sick and found that they can understand what is for their good.

So a new heaven or theory will spring up and a new earth or soil will bring forth from the true vine, for this science is the true vine and its believers are the branches. This science is the stone, which the builders rejected, that will become the cornerstone of the new Jerusalem that came down from heaven and established itself. Then comes the end when opinions must crumble under the tread of progression and their field or false science will be plowed up by the plow of science and their habitation will become a desolate wilderness. The fires of progression will burn up the errors and opinions and the old ideas will become a byword in the land. This is an illustration of the progress of that true science that will free the poor, sick and disheartened beings that have been robbed by the blind guides crying, Peace, peace, when there is no peace.

June 1862

How Does Dr. Quimby Stand in Relation to His Patients?–Part III
[LC 2:0667]

I will show the sick how I make myself known to them in the clouds. A sick person is to himself one person but is looking for his Messiah or Saviour to come and save him. The priest tells him to pray to this unknown God; the doctor also comes to administer to his wants. Each, having no wisdom, are false guides leading the sick and blind till they all fall into the ditch or error together. Now in the clouds of their belief, while wandering around their prison, starving for the bread of life, sick and in despair and given up to die, a voice is heard that speaks, not as man speaks but in that still small voice of wisdom saying, Be of good cheer, your sins or errors shall be explained or forgiven. Then comes a crash of the whole prison, the doors are thrown open, the walls of the prison fall to the ground and the keeper trembles for fear. For he sees the shackles and bolts drop from the prisoner and he hears a voice saying, Come hither! This is the way that this truth acts upon the sick. The prison is the belief, the cords and shackles are the pains and the keeper their belief. My wisdom is the Science or the Saviour. It sees and feels their woes and comes to the rescue, and if they understand this truth, it is wisdom to them; but if not, it does not prevent the cure. It is like a criminal listening to his counsel. If he understands, he is the wiser and better, for he knows better how to keep out of trouble; but if he does not understand, it does not prevent his counsel from getting his case, for the criminal can of himself do nothing. So it is with the sick; nothing is expected of them except to be patient and answer such questions as their counsel shall ask, but if they wish to be posted up so as to keep clear of these deceivers, they must give their attention to the argument of the counsel. But so far as the cure is concerned, it makes no difference, only the counsel will take more interest if he sees his client is interested in his case. But if the criminal takes no interest in his case, it gives the advantage to the opponent which is the disease, for it looks as though the prisoner felt that he was guilty. I find that if the prisoner places all confidence in me or this truth, he excites it more in his favor than if he looked upon me as though I had no higher motive than to plead his case for the little fee I get without regard to his getting clear. When I see this, I take no interest in his case and feel as a counsel does when he knows the prisoner is guilty and has no feeling about his case. Of course, the counsel cannot manage his case with as much zeal as if it were otherwise.

June 1862

How Does the Mind Produce Disease?
[LC 2:1033]

This is a question easier asked than answered. It has often been asked but never answered to the satisfaction of man. It has been answered as far as that the mind has a powerful effect on the body. Beyond this all is a matter of speculation wrapped in darkness and mystery as far as is known to the world. No one has ever penetrated this wilderness of darkness and returned to solve the problem. Thousands are like Moses who stood on Mt. Pisgah and viewed the promised land and saw for others what he was not permitted to enjoy. Or like the peak of Tenerife which saw the rising sun long before it reached the horizon of the common mind. Then the question returns to our mind, can the question now be solved? Can man ever penetrate this wilderness and return like the dove that went out of the ark and brought back the olive branch of peace, showing that the waters were dried up so that man could go forth and till the ground?

October 1859

How Dr. Quimby Cures [I]*
[BU 3:1182]

When anyone explains how an event or a phenomenon is brought about he gives a theory. Theories, therefore have to do with causes and if the author presents facts in support of one, then it is entitled to a hearing from the public, but if he merely suggests a method by which certain things may be produced, without bringing forward any experiments, he gives a theory only and one that cannot be tested. The world is full of such and the very word has become synonymous with mere speculation. It may be thought that a theory is easy to understand, but this cannot be the case when it is new, or when it works out results which the mind is not prepared to receive.

Theories may be true or false, according as they are based on wisdom and supported by facts, or founded on suppositions alone. An entirely new theory of disease is now before the world, and one we venture to say is unsurpassed in the boldness of its position in the novelty of its ideas and the ingenuity of its arguments. It appeals to the humane, the religious and the skeptic, and it declares that the cures by the author are the proof of its correctness.

Dr. Quimby it is well known, cures all kinds of diseases with no external aid of medicine or other appliances and he contends that he cures by a science which can be taught and practiced by others and which when introduced and established in the world, will eradicate from society–that terrible evil–disease.

The principle on which his theory stands, is one acknowledged to be true in philosophy and religion, but false in fact. The superiority of intelligence to matter and the subjection of matter to the purposes of wisdom, is the truth that he carries out in his practice with the sick and it has developed in him a theory so utterly opposed to the commonest facts of our every day experience, that it strikes one as a tissue of visionary ideas. He says that unless there is a wisdom that can analyze and dissolve diseases, he never could cure, and unless he understood that wisdom, he could not give an account of how he cures.

"But" says the scholar "he is an uneducated man and cannot understand the use of language. Then how can he expect to explain himself?" True, he is uneducated, but it is written that "out of the mouths of babes and suckling hast thou ordained wisdom." Disease is a mystery to the world. The first thing we know about it, it is upon us, then when he explains how it got into the world, and how it is nourished and supported, he takes the mind where the light of science, or speculation even, has never travelled before, consequently he is necessarily obscure. Not so much from his own ignorance, as from that of the world.

Dr. Quimby stands before the world not only as a practicing physician, but as a reformer on the subject of disease. His object is to cure disease but his mission is to prevent it. His position that there is no such thing as disease is seemingly untenable, but those who have heard him explain himself are struck with the ingenuity and force of his reasoning and the aptness of his illustrations. To deny disease is to the world, simply absurd, and it is difficult for one unacquainted with him to understand how a man can make any kind of an argument on such a basis. To such, we say listen: "There are more things in heaven and earth than is dreampt of in your philosophy." It is well-known among his patients, that in some cases he talks a great deal with the sick. He says that this is necessary to the cure, that his medicine he gives, is his reasoning and illustrations, which remedy he hopes to give to the world, so that it can be within the reach of all. He contends that disease is an error engrafted in the life of man by superstition and he labors to destroy it root and branch. If consumption is something when it gets hold of a person, (and the world says it is) it is something before and in both cases it is equally a lie. His theory is to show up this lie where it is created and if he succeeds, unborn generations will enter upon life with one less enemy to fear. When he cures a patient suffering with local disease, he destroys it and to them it is as though it never was; it is not driven off the field, or held at bay, but it is killed, played out.

He claims that his mode of treatment differs in every particular, from that of any other practiced, for the only remedy he applies is truth. All medical treatment is mostly the application of certain rules, and every method known to the world, has always admitted disease as a thing independent of the sick person, a thing that can go in the air from house to house, travels countries, crosses oceans, without human intervention of any kind. Its business is to destroy as many lives as it can and as yet, although checked and sometimes held at bay, it has met with no resistance equal to itself. We meet it in everything we eat and drink. We fear it in the air we breathe and like African slavery it is sanctioned by the laws of God spoken in the constitution of man. All this he denies and says there is no such thing as disease. Then sickness is all in the imagination? It will be asked. Not at all–this theory says "As a man believeth, so is he." If a person believes he has a disease causing his sickness, to him this is true and to all those who believe as he does it is equally true, but the Dr. does not have the belief, therefore to him it is not true. "Then all that a man must do is to believe he is well and he is." Not exactly, a person in full health does not think anything about himself whether he is well or not. A sick person, however does think he is sick and he reasons that there must be a cause for it, and that cause, he is told, is a disease, and when he is suffering thus, he is incapable of thinking or believing that he is well. The Dr. denies the disease, not the sickness. He acknowledges the symptoms, feels in his own person the sufferings and sees the danger of the patient, but on the other hand he beholds the truth that is to set him free, and that tells him that there is no disease. This sounds absurd enough when a man is deathly sick with a fever, but disease can be compared to secession. Is secession true because there was a bogus Southern Confederacy–Let a loyal man answer–Truth.

How Dr. Quimby Cures II*
[Originally untitled.] [BU 3:0653]

On what ground does Dr. Quimby claim that he differs from all classes of practitioners out of the regular faculty?

Most persons think that all who heal by the profession of some admitted power in man, are to be classified together and so they put Dr. Quimby in with the rest and whatever honor they render to him as superior and intelligent and respectable, they reason belongs to the whole of the before mentioned class, regardless of his assertions to the contrary. We believe in the right of every man to be heard in explaining his position, but when a man has anything new to offer of course he meets with opposition. When Dr. Quimby's voice shall be heard respecting himself, it will be seen that he is not a Spiritualist, nor a mesmerizer, nor a clairvoyant, nor a healing medium, nor a deceiver of any kind, nor under anything that the most scrupulous aristocrat would object to being himself, that he is an honest and sensible man coming to the sick with a way of curing entirely new, and which in point of intelligence the educated and scientific man would not fail to respect. His principles yield him a theory which can be taught to man as a belief and which being understood and admitted will enable man to correct his own error, understand himself so that he will have no disease. He does not denounce these various classes of healers, nor deny that they cure; but he protests against being associated with them on the following grounds. It is a well known fact among his patients that if he didn't talk he would not cure them, for disease being a mystery it must in some cases be explained satisfactorily to the patient so that he may recover, therefore he says, his explanation is the cure. This is all he claims for his power as it is termed, and in this he differs from all other doctors of any kind.

It may be objected, that the most of his patients take very little interest in what he says to them and do not understand his talk at all, at the same time they have perfect confidence that he can cure. This is true: and it is because of the strangeness of his reasoning: he puts the cause outside the phenomenon, or disease. This he finds in the patient's mind, which contains the knowledge, or as they could term it, the impression or opinion of their disease, and also the effect which the constant presence of this opinion has on them. Then he goes to work to unsettle and break up this opinion which he calls the first and acting cause of their trouble. Under the direction of a principle ruling health and happiness he traces the patients back to the time when they were free from disease and happy and then by illustration and argument enables them to see the process by which they became sick. As they go over these steps they often suffer the same old feelings of their disease, but being protected by another belief they no longer fear a retreat to their old places. Seeing another explanation to all these feelings which is satisfactory and averts or destroys disease they are confident they are on the way to health.

So his modus operandi may be called, arguments proving there is no disease except in the mind, adjusted to the wants of each different case, in which there enters no selfishness whatever.

It is difficult to make the well understand his ideas about disease; they say, if I have the liver complaint there is certainly no mind about that. This comes from a misunderstanding of the term mind. They use the word meaning intelligence and all there is of man independent of his body, also it means imagination when applied towards sickness, and it has a variety of other meanings. He uses the word mind in one sense and says it is something which under certain conditions will produce matter. That it changes and takes form according to the direction given by the acting influences. He places all intelligence outside of it and says it is a medium for truth and error to act through, like a telegraph and that which makes man uneasy, progressive and diseased is the conflict of these two principles.

When error has the reins, disease is made manifest and is supported by every evidence, and working on the ignorance and superstition of man does everything to destroy his powers and render him a miserable being and when it is triumphantly established, the well say, there is no disproving those complaints and in their judgment they crush out the man and kill the body. But the sick can see a distinction between themselves and their trouble and can appreciate the voice of him who proclaims their disease a falsehood fastened on them by a world of ignorance and prejudice, and they can feel in Dr. Quimby's arguments a truth which if more universally understood would break up their diseases no matter what form they had assumed. They only can feel that he comes from a higher intelligence which answers the wishes of the sick by sympathy and unseats the hitherto dark problems of human life. If it is an unanswerable fact to the well that there is no mind about the evil complaint, but that it is a fatal bodily disease it is also an unanswered question which the sick may put to the well, by what right of law or justice do you fasten such a disease upon me to rob me of my health and eat away my life? This is the question which it is the Wisdom of Dr. Q. to answer according to the prayers of the sick, and this he does by destroying the opinions of the sick and showing that the body is not of itself capable of producing disease, but that it is changed from health and becomes diseased by the person experiencing various changes of opinion about themselves, which of course were derived from other persons, whose selfishness, and ignorance rendered them unfit to give the right direction, which would bring about the right change.

How Dr. Quimby Cures III*
[Originally untitled.] [BU 3:0138]

[*Editor's Note*: Previously published versions of this article are written as a third person's account of how Dr. Quimby cures. I found this earlier version in the Boston University collection that is written directly from Quimby's perspective.]

Every phenomenon in the natural world has its birth in the spiritual world. Of this truth however men are ignorant and mistaking shadow for substance, they give credit when credit is not due. No man for example should be considered superior to another unless he proves his superiority by reducing to a science some phenomenon hitherto unexplained. Before musical sounds were reduced to a science they were simply phenomena. People could sing, but he who sang best was not entitled to more praise than any other; for he sang ignorantly. To him only was credit due who reduced musical sounds to a science.

The same is true with regard to disease and its cure. The world is full of sickness arising from various causes; the phenomena are in the natural world while the causes originate in an invisible world. Medical science, being based on opinions, is confined to the natural world where the causes of disease are supposed to arise. This is not the case with the science by which I cure. By a clairvoyant faculty, I obtain a knowledge of disease which cannot be obtained through the natural senses. This being imparted to the patient, changes the direction of his mind and effects the cure. In other words, the explanation of the disease is its cure. I will state a case for illustration. A person calls on me for examination. We sit down together. No questions are asked on either side. I have no knowledge of the patient's feelings through my natural senses. After placing my mind upon him I become perfectly passive and the patient's mind being troubled puts me in a clairvoyant state. As I retain my natural senses I am, it is evident, in two states at once. The history of his trouble together with the name of his disease I now relate to the patient. This constitutes the disease and the evidences in the body are the effect of his belief.

Disease, according to my theory, does not reach to the natural senses; I cannot therefore explain to the well my mode of treatment. The well take no interest in it, for to them my theory is of no use. Then of what use it may be asked is it to the sick? It gives the sick such confidence in themselves that they are not frightened by opinions of disease, for disease itself is an impudent opinion.

Guided by it I throw off the feelings of the sick and impart to mind my own, which are those of perfect health. The explanation I make destroys their disease.

I am to the sick as a Captain to his crew, when storms arise, dangers thicken and destruction seems inevitable. He understands his business, has confidence in himself, inspires the crew with his own spirit and finally brings the ship safe into port.

Jan. 1860

How Dr. Quimby Cures IV
[Originally untitled.] [LC 1:0010]

[*Editor's Note*: I've included this previously published version of this article that was written as a third person's account of how Dr. Quimby cures. This deliberate duplication is offered to show the difference in the "feelings" stimulated in the reader by simply shifting the perspective of the observer. This is also an example of Quimby writing about himself from an anonymous, third person's perspective.]

Every phenomenon in the natural world has its origin in the spiritual world. The world gives credit where it is not due, mistaking noise for substance. No man should have credit over his fellow men unless he shows some superiority over the errors of his age, and to show that he is superior is to reduce to a science some phenomenon which has never been explained, music for an example. Before music was reduced to a science, it was a phenomenon. People could whistle and sing, but no one supposed that the one who made the most noise was entitled to any credit above the rest. Credit was due to him who first reduced it to a science.

Take diseases. The world is full of sickness, arising from various causes; the phenomena exist in the natural world, while the causes originate in an invisible world. Doctoring is confined to the natural world and admits the causes of the disease to be all in the natural world.

Doctor Quimby, with his clairvoyant faculty, gets knowledge in regard to the phenomena which does not come through the natural senses, and by explaining to his patients changes the direction of the mind, and the explanation is the science or cure. To illustrate. Suppose a patient calls on Dr. Quimby for examination. No questions are asked on either side. They sit down together. He has no knowledge of the patient's feelings through his natural senses till after having placed his mind upon them. Then he becomes perfectly passive and, the patient's mind being troubled puts him into a clairvoyant state, together with his natural state, thus being in two states at once when he takes feelings, accompanied by their state of mind and thoughts. A history of their trouble thus learned, together with the name of the disease, he relates to the patient. This constitutes the disease and the evidences in the body are the effects of the belief. Not being afraid of the belief he is not afraid of the disease.

The doctors take the bodily evidence as the disease. Disease with him does not come to the natural senses; therefore he cannot explain to the well his mode of treatment. The well take no interest in it and his theory is of no use to them. Then what use is it to the world? To give the sick such confidence that they will not be frightened by opinions of disease, for disease is itself an impudent opinion. He throws off the feelings of the sick and imparts to them his own which are perfect health, and his explanation destroys their feelings or disease. His belief in this respect differing from any other's is the result of the science of his practice. Therefore when he is with the sick, they feel safe. He is like a captain who knows his business and feels confident in a storm, and his confidence sustains the crew and ship when both would be lost if the captain should give way to his fears.

Dr. Quimby comes to the sick as a pilot to the captain of a ship in a storm or fog when dangers threaten and inevitable destruction seems their doom. He learns the trouble from the captain, and quieting the crew by his composure inspires them with confidence, gives other directions, and brings them into harbor.

January 1860

How I Hold My Patients
[LC 2:1034]

The question is often asked how I hold my patients when I give no medicine and make no applications. I answer, it is through my belief or my knowledge. Then you may ask me where I differ from others. In everything so far as disease and what produces it is concerned. All persons believe in disease and their belief is in the thing believed. For instance, take consumption. People are not aware that consumption has an identity as much as a serpent or canker worm, that it has life or a sort of knowledge. It is liable to get hold of us, and if it does, we cannot shake it off as Paul did the viper from his hand.

All diseases have an identity and the well are subject to be deceived by them and if they once get hold of them, they must surrender arms or compromise. These diseases are in the mind as much as ghosts, witchcraft or evil spirits, and the fruits of this belief are seen in almost every person. These beliefs show what the people are afraid of and what they have to contend with, and make it necessary for them to have some help in driving off their enemies. For if a person cannot conquer his enemy or disease himself, he must have help. Now those employed admit the existence and superiority of their enemy or disease and commence making war with him by first firing calomel, and if that does not start him, the next is blistering or burning, etc. This only enrages the enemy, and a regular battle commences. Finally a council of physicians is called, a suspension of arms takes place, a compromise is made and health yields up all claims to happiness and enjoyment. And the victim has the privilege of going about a cripple and an outcast the balance of his natural life, knowing all the time that he is liable to be caught by any of his enemies at any time, either asleep or awake. This keeps him in a nervous state of mind, not fit for any business, like a man who is in prison under sentence of death. This is just the state of this world.

Now, is it strange that a person is known by this character and is afraid of this state of mind or disease? And when one who has the power of restoring health and destroying these enemies comes up to another who is tormented by these devils, is it strange that he likes him and feels safe in his presence until he himself is perfectly free? This feeling is not always known by the sick, but it is felt. It cannot be understood, for its language is its feelings, and it cannot talk till it learns to speak through the senses. It knows and feels its friend and clings to him as a child does to its parent before it can walk; it is led by sympathy till it can go alone and can understand that it has power over its enemy.

Then its knowledge is its cure. Till then it feels the need of someone who can protect it from its enemy. Now my belief is their protector and my explanation is their cure. My belief is accompanied by my sympathy for their trouble; and like a shepherd who leads his sheep, I lead the sick, by my belief alone, home to health and deliver them to their friends. Then I leave them happy and feel that they appreciate the benefit I have been to them. This money cannot buy. This is what holds my patients. It is what none but the sick can appreciate. The well know nothing of the feelings of the sick; therefore to them it is a stumbling block and to the doctors, foolishness.

March 1861

How the Senses Are Deceived
[LC 1:0488]

Why is it that I run a greater risk of being misrepresented in regard to my mode of curing than practitioners of other schools? I must be allowed to offer my own explanation of this fact because if I were understood, I should not be in danger of being misrepresented and condemned by the guilty. I stand alone, a target at which all classes aim their poisonous darts, for I make war with every creed, profession and idea that contains false reasoning. Every man's hand therefore is against me, and I against every man's opinion.

Man's senses may be compared to a young virgin who has never been deceived by the errors of the world. Popular errors are like a young prince who stands ready to bestow his addresses upon all whom he can deceive. When he approaches the virgin, he appears like an angel of light and wisdom. By soft speech and imposing address, he wins the virgin mind to his belief. Having become entangled in his web or false doctrines, she is carried away from her home or state of innocence into the gulf of despair, there to live a miserable existence or become a slave to fashion. In this state, a false theory holds out to her all kinds of ideas and she becomes a slave to the world. Error favors the utmost freedom in thought and conduct and offers all the allurements of pleasure and enjoyment to the young. Each one is approached with some fascinating idea with which he is carried away and to which he becomes wedded.

These are the ideas founded in man's wisdom and manifested through man. The pure virgin ideas are also shadowed through the same medium, and each is addressed by truth or by error. Error in making up pretense of wisdom assumes an air of wisdom. Wisdom, however, like charity, is not puffed up and it is slighted by error. It is looked upon by the young as an old conservative. They say to it, "Depart for a time while I enjoy the pleasure of error, and when I am satisfied, I will call upon you." Wisdom is banished from the society of the world, and error like a raging lion goes about devouring all whom it can. In the shape of man it approaches the virgin mind and in musical tones commences paying his addresses.

Finally overcome by his sophistry, she is now won to his opinion and is soon wedded to his ideas and they two become one flesh. Her senses are attached to the matter. What is his is hers and she is in all respects the partner and wife of error. She is no longer a virgin but a wedded wife. The belief is the husband. When a person is converted from one belief to another, she leaves her husband and marries another. This was the case with the woman whom Jesus told that she had truly said she had no husband, "for he whom thou now hast is not thy husband." She had served religious beliefs and as each was destroyed by her wisdom, she became a widow. Then she joined herself to another and became a wife. These husbands were creeds, and the virgins were those who cared nothing for religion and had no settled opinions about the future. The beliefs in regard to another world were represented by men, for they were the embodiment of man's opinion. The virgins were those who might be operated upon like the virgin soil.

When Jesus sought to explain the truth, he compared it to a wedding and all who could understand entered in. The ten virgins represented two classes: one having wisdom outside of the natural senses and those who cannot believe anything outside of these senses. When the truth came, they arose and trimmed their lamps, but those who had no oil or understanding could not enter. Everyone who has not risen above the natural man but is contented with being ignorant is a foolish virgin, while those who try to understand are of the other class. Everyone belongs to the former till he becomes wedded to a belief.

There is still another class. Those having professed to belong to a certain sect and having united with it, after a while leave and join another one. These are persons having committed adultery, for they are living with a new belief; therefore they are to be stoned or turned out of the church. This explains the case of the woman brought before Jesus as an adulterer. She had left the world's belief and become interested in Jesus' truths. To the Jews she had committed adultery and had been caught in advocating his truth. As she did not fully understand, she was not lawfully married and her first husband or the church had claims upon her. The Jews, therefore, thinking she deserved punishment, brought her to Jesus to see what his judgment would be. When he heard their story he said, "Let him who is guiltless cast the first stone." They all immediately left and he asked her, Where are thy accusers or thy fears that this is not the true light that lighteth everyone that receiveth it? She replied, "No belief has any effect on me." And he said, "Go thy way and believe in man's opinion no more."

This article was written from the impressions that came upon me while sitting by a young lady who was afraid of dying and also was afraid of being blind. It may seem strange to those in health how our belief affects us. The fact is there is nothing of us but belief. It is the whole capital stock and trade of man. It is all that can be and embraces all man has made or ever will make. Wisdom is the scientific man who can destroy the works of the natural man. Disease is made by the natural man's belief in some false idea. The young are the soil in which to sow the seed of error. The error comes to the virgin mind and makes an impression. The soil is disturbed and the mind listens or waits to be taught. If it is misled, briars and thorns and troubles spring up in its path through life. These all go to make the man of belief. Wisdom destroys these false ideas, purifies the soil and brings the mind under a higher state of cultivation. This is the work of science. When a person has made himself a body of sin and death, truth destroys his death and attaches his senses to a body of life.

1865

How to Make a Belief and How to Correct It
[LC 1:0431]

I will explain how I am affected while sitting by the sick. All mankind act according to their belief without knowing it, so to know how to act intelligently is to correct a false idea. According to our natural belief, man is matter. To my wisdom, matter is an idea that is used like language to convey to another some wisdom that one wishes to explain to his friend. Here is the difference between myself and the world; the world believes in matter and everything out of matter is a mystery. I admit matter, but I call it the shadow of our wisdom, so the natural man's wisdom cannot see itself or matter, nor has any idea of an existence in a state outside of his belief. I admit both, and class them both in this way: science and ignorance.

To make it clear, I will call my mesmeric state the light or world of science and to get into that we must go through the dark valley of the shadow of death. In each state we carry our own belief, so that when a person is in the light, he knows it not as he ought to know; for if he reasons, his wisdom is of the world of error, but if he does not reason, he is like a child, ready to be instructed by science or opinions. To illustrate: I take a child and create in my own mind a dog. I do not speak it to the child, but all the time I am with the child, I have the dog before me. My feelings change the child's mind till our minds mingle or sympathize. At last the child grows nervous. Now I am acting upon the child, but the child knows it not and I may or may not be aware of the fact. Finally the child gets so far under my influence that when in the dark, it sees a dog. When the child's senses become attached to the dog, it becomes a real animal and if I am angry when I create it, the dog will be angry. This produces fear and anger in the child and it becomes fretful; it feels nervous and at times sees the dog in the dark. This is the way one mind acts on another ignorantly.

The science is to correct this error. This has been the study of the ancient and modern philosophers; phenomena take place every day and persons are affected by them, but how to account for them has never been discovered. This is the question, How are all these things produced? We hear people, male and female, talking about some mysterious something. One tells some witch story, another a spiritual experiment that is unaccountable, and some say this is all humbug. There is still another class pretending to be in the secret that warns you against all the above and points you to a God of their invention who knows all things, which He has revealed to them. Others pronounce them bigots and superstitious and say we do not know anything about another world and that it is all a mystery. These are as superstitious as the others. There are some who have their fortunes told who say they do not believe a word of it; yet everything told them was true.

These differences embrace all mankind but do not contain one word of science. They are the working of error to arrive at truth. The child laughs at the superstition of his father and tries to account for his belief in the phenomenon but establishes error almost equal to his father. In this way, error has been changing, not knowing that it has changed. The progress of true wisdom is so slow that the children of one generation do not see the change but speak of the generation of their fathers. The son listens to his parents explaining the superstition of their age, not knowing that the ignorance of the one is equal to the ignorance of the other. So the world goes on from one generation to another. Now I want my children, when I am out of sight to the world of opinions, to say when they hear persons declare that medicine never cured a person "that is just what father used to say; here is what he says about it." When they hear it said that disease is the invention of man and is nothing but a continuation of Salem witchcraft, and that the priests' opinions are the relics of heathen superstition, and Jesus opposed the whole of it, I want them to show how it has been foretold and laughed at. Here is where I stand.

In looking back at the Salem witchcraft, when the judges sat in council judging their fellow men for being witches or wizards, the accused testifying against their best friends, believing themselves bewitched, just ask yourself if these very people rich and poor, low and high, were not like the people of our age. And will not the people of the next generation laugh at the folly of our age? It is twenty years since I first embarked in what was one of the greatest humbugs of the age, mesmerism. At that time, the people were as superstitious about it as they were two hundred years ago in regard to witchcraft. Now see the change; today the phenomena of mesmerism are admitted as much as those of electricity. And those who oppose it stand in society on a level with those who believe in ghosts and witches. The opposers of all science are the material to establish the truth of any phenomenon, right or wrong. In religion, the more absurd, the more opposition and therefore the more material to work with, for to oppose a phenomenon that you admit is to be ignorant of what you oppose. For instance, if a man opposes the science of mathematics, he must be ignorant. And if a person should show him or explain a mathematical problem which he cannot see through, if he is a person capable of investigating, he will listen to the explanation. And if that is not satisfactory, he will not deny the phenomenon, though he may not believe the explanation. I have had some experience in regard to man's belief and I know that the wisdom of man is not properly defined.

Man's wisdom is like his wealth. It does not follow that a man is as rich as he appears, but when he dies and his debts are paid, then you will see how much he is worth. So it is with wisdom; the man who is rich in public opinion today may be a beggar tomorrow; his wisdom is all of this world; when science comes to reckon and test his wisdom, he falls and is buried in the ground with all those minds that make a show of wisdom. I cannot give a better explanation of such wisdom than to quote Paul again, where he says all men have knowledge. Knowledge puffeth up but charity or science edifieth. Charity is a word well calculated to embrace what we call science, for a truly scientific man is never puffed up, but like charity his science is his wealth.

The wisdom of the world is flattery; it puffs man up. Then he continues, If a man thinks he knows anything, he knows nothing as he ought to know, but if he loves God which is science, the same is known to him. The position of the scientific man has neither place nor magnitude. It has length and breadth without thickness; it is in its own element, out of opinion. The wisdom of man has place, a starting point, magnitude and matter. When a man is out of matter or opinion, he is in science. This holds good in all science. Science is to correct all error or phenomena that the natural man cannot correct intelligently. Now when a phenomenon is produced called disease, the causes are unknown; therefore man invents reason to account for it. His reason is the cause of his trouble; his disease is not the cause but what follows. To illustrate, you tell me I "look sick." I say I do not feel sick; in fact I don't know what you mean by the word, so you have to invent some story to tell me or explain by some intelligent sign. I lay my hands on my left side; you ask me what I feel. Now if I had never heard of sickness or disease, I should not know what to say, neither would I be frightened, so it would pass off without anything of any account. But you tell me that people often die with just such a feeling as I have. This starts me, although I have no idea what you mean, my feelings not containing danger or trouble, but your opinions trouble me exceedingly. I begin now to twist and turn, not knowing what to do. This convinces you that I have disease of the heart and you try to explain to me what I have and how it affects a person. By mesmerizing me into your belief you disturb my mind and create the very idea you have invented; and at last I die just as you foretold. All this is disease and you made it. If I had never seen you nor anyone wiser than myself I should not have died.

October 1861

Identity of God or Wisdom, The: Part 1–Ignorance of Man in Regard to the True God

[BU 3:0500]

We are told that God is watching all our acts and that he knows all our thoughts. When we ask if he has an identity, the answer is, No, but he is everywhere. He fills all space and we pray to him asking him to listen to our wants as a child asks a parent. All this is ignorance of the God we worship. There is no person who has the least rational idea of an intelligence independent of man. Yet, all see and will admit that there is something which we cannot comprehend. I have been trying all my life, ever since I was old enough to listen, to understand man's reasoning and see if people understood what they professed to believe. After some fifty years of thinking and listening to people's opinions about God, I have come to this conclusion: that ninety-nine hundredths of mankind are listeners to someone telling a story, like the Arabian Nights in marvelousness, till they get excited, like a mesmerized person, and really create the scenes in their own minds, believe them to be true and will suffer death rather than abandon their belief.

This is the state of society in regard to religion. But as science has progressed, it has explained some of the greatest errors. Still, nine-tenths of every man's wisdom is of that class. I know I was as free from superstition as almost any one, yet I was full enough of it and all the while I was not aware that I had a belief of any kind. For the last twenty years, I have been ridding myself of my old superstitions and am now better prepared to see it in others. I have sat with more than three hundred individuals every year for ten years. And for the last five years, I have averaged five-hundred yearly, people with all sorts of diseases in every possible state of mind. Also I have sat with hypochondriacs and have seen insanity brought on by all kinds of ideas that people believe in. I will name some of the beliefs which have caused insanity.

Religion in its various forms embraces many cases. Some cases have been occasioned by the idea that they committed the unpardonable sin. When asked what it was, no two persons ever answered alike. One had neglected a little child by not sending for the doctor. She herself had lost her father and mother and the doctor had killed two children and she thought she could cure the third herself, but it grew worse and then she sent for the doctor. When the doctor came, the child was quiet but almost gone. He gave it an emetic, which threw it into convulsions and then it died. All this affected the mother who put all her trouble into the idea that she had committed the unpardonable sin by not calling the doctor before. I had to convince her that if she committed any sin, it was that she sent for him at all. I could prove this, for she acknowledged that she believed the medicine the others had taken had been the cause of their death. Here is one of the superstitions of our belief, that if a person does not send for a doctor, he commits a very great sin. This is brought about by the doctor's telling the neighbors that if he had been sent for before, he might have cured the patient. Then the neighbors are down on the mourners, accusing them of being mean and stingy, preferring their friends should die rather than go to the expense of having a physician. This error I am glad to say is dying away and people are not bound by public opinion to send for a physician to torment the dying but let them die in peace. Another error I have tried to correct that has killed many a person is to send for a priest to pray with the sick. This is done more than the former. I have seen the bad effect of it and know how it works.

September 1861

Identity of God or Wisdom, The: Part 2–Showing How the Errors of Our Beliefs Make Up Human Knowledge, Also that We Ignorantly Are the Authors of Our Misery

[BU 3:0501]

Disease is what follows these false ideas. If man had no belief at all, he would either be a brute or scientific as far as his wisdom goes. Now man being a bundle of ideas, his life is affected by his opinions; and as happiness is man's highest aim, it is what we are all striving for. Here is one thing that man is ignorant of, that he is a sufferer from his own belief, not willingly but by his own consent. Not being intelligent enough to judge of cause and effect, he becomes the victim of his own free will. He does the very things he ought not to do and leaves undone that which he ought to do. That is, he takes opinions for truth, which gets him into trouble and he neglects to investigate all things. When a person tells you anything you cannot see, you are not bound to believe it, unless you please. But if you do believe, you convict yourself of a crime that you have acknowledged right. Our belief cannot alter a scientific truth, but it may alter our feeling for happiness or misery. Disease is the misery of our belief; happiness is the health of our wisdom so that man's happiness or misery depends on himself. Now as our misery comes from our belief, not the thing believed, it is necessary to be on the watch so as not to be deceived by false guides.

I will now put a belief in practice. Sensation contains no intelligence or belief, but a mere disturbance of the mind called agitation, ready to receive the seed of error. Ever since man was created, there has been an element called error, which has been busy inventing answers for every sensation. It accounts for every phenomenon no matter where it comes from; in fact it is that power called the Devil. It is a power, for it contains no intelligence, but it is a brow-beating, knock-you-down element in reasoning. It invents all sorts of bug-bears in this world. It has also invented another world and undertakes to account for it and will give you the wisdom about it. This character can be found in all men and can be easily detected in the priest. He appears very sanctimonious, giving you an account of the world of spirits, etc. These two characters give rise to a thousand lesser humbugs, taking their cue from them. As I have said, mind is matter and everything seen by the natural eye is a figure or emblem of the first cause. All things having shape or form made by man is a shadow of the spiritual life of man. All things created for man's misery are the invention of this character called error. You see I have two worlds: one composed of things which we call real matter, but which with wisdom is nothing but an idea. I have nothing to say about this world; it is the world of darkness which the evil of our thoughts has made. It has its priests and doctors and every evil that flesh is heir to. It is the world where all disease is invented. Its actions are in those of the popular doctrines of the day, which are our guides and directors in all things pertaining to our health and happiness.

In fact, it is man as we see him in priest or physician. These men stand to society as a mesmerizer to his subject. It is true they do not always take the patients by the hand, but they take them into the churches and there they mesmerize the audience according to their belief. The patients' minds, being like soil, receive the seed of these blind guides and nourish it in their soul or mind; and when it grows up into a belief, then it is set down as a truth. So all men now believe in these guides of another world and their belief is the fruits of the priests' theory. Now after they are fairly sown in the minds of the people, then cometh the wisdom and warns the people to beware of the fruit. They, knowing that the fruit is pleasant to the eye and much desired to make one happy, eat and then their eyes are opened and they see they are ignorant. I will illustrate what I have just said. Take the weather. Everyone likes the pure air and wants to enjoy it, so they go out for that purpose. Now all action has its reaction, and after returning, a reaction takes place. Then this enemy comes along and says, "You have overdone and taken cold; you should have known better than to have exposed yourself to the air as you have done." Now comes the punishment of your belief. You have been made to believe that there is danger in taking cold. Just as though this God you are called to worship has made an atmosphere tempting you to go out and then seizes you and makes you sick. This is one of the follies of the world. The sensation of cold makes one nervous. The opinions we have of it mesmerize us into a state in which we see the scene of what will follow. We believe that God is a being like man. This may be so, but the people in the Old and New Testament never had such an idea.

God is science, and man not knowing science makes him superstitious, and he has made a being out of science that he cannot understand and called it God. This God has been introduced by the superstition of the world and prevents man from using the reason that wisdom has given him. Hear what Paul said on this subject. The people were superstitious and worshipped idols as they do now, yet not the same idols for there are many idols. "Now as touching things offered unto idols, we know that we all have knowledge. Knowledge puffeth up, Charity edifieth." (Cor. 8:1) What did Paul mean? He means science is not puffed up, but opinions are. So opinions worship idols, but science does not. So if a man of opinions thinks he knows, he knows not as he ought to know (v. 2); but if a man love science as God, the same is known to him (v. 3). Then he goes on to show that there is no wisdom in these and there is no science or God but one and though there be many opinions about heaven and earth, there is but one living and true Science or God.

He also shows there are some who are conscious of this science and eat and drink and worship idols till they die. Then he sums up all this superstition in these words: If we eat, are we the better and if we eat not, are we the worse? But take care that in your reasoning about it, you do not put a stumbling block in the way of those who do not understand. Science is the one living and true God to worship. This is more than all the opinions and prayers of the priests put together. Every man is the medium of these two Gods. Man's opinion is the natural man. Science is the God or Christ. And it is very singular that if there is a God, as all will admit, he is out of existence because he cannot be seen by the natural eyes. It shows that man knows not God. If he did, he would not be so religious, for God is not in their religion; it is opposed to God in every act. Science wants no advocate to sustain it; it can exist without any sect or priest to poultice it up. To learn it is man's happiness and to reject it and embrace religion is to live in sin and ignorance, being in death from fear of the very best friend (science) and all your life subject to bondage.

September 1861

Illustrating the Word "Mind"
[Originally untitled.] [LC 2:0735]

I will illustrate the mind. Mind and matter are like the soil and the earth. The body is the earth and the mind the soil. The earth is the foundation of the soil which cannot be seen by the earth. The soil receives its life from the atmosphere; therefore, that is the real intelligence of man, for the minds of individuals mingle like the atmosphere and every person's identity exists in this atmosphere. For wisdom or belief of every man is the soil as the rose bush is in the earth, but its odor is in the atmosphere. So it is with man. We see him as a tree and his brain as the fruit of the tree. This is his mind or odor which ascends from the earth and contains all the passions and feelings of the tree or natural man. This is as far as philosophy has analyzed man to trace him to earth and there leave him in mystery. David says, "As for man his days are as grass, as a flower of the field, so he flourisheth." Ps. 103:15. Job says, "Man giveth up the ghost, and where is he? As the waters fall from the sea, and the flood decayeth and dryeth up; so man lieth down, and riseth not: till the heavens be no more, they shall not awake, nor be raised out of their sleep." Job 14: 10, 11, 12. Here is where Job ended man, yet he had a vague hope that there might be something after this state. He believed there was a God and he hoped he might see him at the end of the world.

Lucretius, one of the wisest and most learned of philosophers of the Pagan school says, "The nature of the soul we know not, whether formed at the body or at the birth infused and then by death cut off, she flourishes as bodies do, or whether she descends to the dark caves and dreadful lakes of hell or after death, inspired with heavenly instinct, she returns into the brutes." In another place, he says, "If men were once convinced that death is the sure end of all their pains, they might with reason then resist the force of all religion and condemn the threats of poets." Ennius used to say that Homer's ghost appeared to him from hell and bitterly weeping discovered to him the nature of things. Others believed that the souls of ancient poets took possession of some living man, which is the same belief as that of modern spiritualists. All this shows that the soul, which is now called the spirit and was at the time of Jesus called the same, is one and the same thing. I see no difference between the Christian and Pagan in this respect. Both destroy man, but the Christian introduces a belief, which would flow from Job's religion, while the spiritualist would agree with the Pythagorean doctrine. Jesus taught to man a truth which will destroy their philosophies and give them in their place wisdom. I will present some of its characteristics as they come to me in curing disease.

I have said before that man dissolves and passes into space, carrying with him all his knowledge, but as he never has attached his life to wisdom, he only knows himself in matter. Therefore he lives in matter, and this is the belief of nine-tenths of mankind. Jesus tried to introduce a proof that man exists outside of his belief and I have learned the evidence he had of this truth. It is this. Man including his senses, sight, taste, etc., and his wisdom is not of matter nor has he the qualities of matter. Pagan philosophy and religion made them a part of matter and the belief in the transmigration of souls, which is akin to modern spiritualism, observed the more intelligent belief in progression.

Jesus contended that he understood what he said and did, but their prejudice was so strong in favor of his having a power that they could not understand when he tried to teach them that his acts and words proceeded from a wisdom superior to their belief and that it could be taught. To question their belief was to make himself equal with God. In the same way when I say that I know how I cure, this same class of people say I blaspheme and make myself equal with Christ. They do not know how I cure and dislike to admit that anyone else does; consequently they strive to make my explanation as objectionable as possible. I will present the evidence of the faith or truth in me. I know that I can take a person's feelings, and I also know that if I did not come in contact with another, I should not be certain that the feelings were theirs and hence a person's body is not a sure sign that their trouble is in their body or in some other's.

According to my experience, mind or matter in solution is a thing in common which all admit contains life; each person has his senses in this life or mind as a globule of water is in the ocean. So if a sensation is made on the water, each particle is affected and each may locate its trouble in itself. For instance, consumption is as much an enemy to man as a wolf, and man is afraid of it. When a sensation is made on this mind or belief which I call matter and the idea consumption is called up, man's senses see the image in this matter or mind. Fear comes and the reflection is thrown on his idea body and then he believes that he has the disease, while the idea of consumption is a lie started by the error of our own belief and accepted as a truth.

In the same way, when sitting by a patient, I feel the sensation in my mind and immediately a figure or spirit is made which is reflected as an impression on my body. Now if I were not aware of the cause, I might think I was the author or originator of this horrid belief, but knowing that it is only the reflection from my patient's mind, the idea dies. The wisdom that put me in possession of this truth is Christ, the wisdom above my patient. Jesus says, "Fear hath torment and perfect love (or wisdom) casteth out fear." By this wisdom I explain their fears away and destroy their torment and this process is a science. Is it a sin to know and teach this for the happiness of mankind and do I make myself equal with Christ? If I do, then I will submit to the odium willingly.

In writing these pieces, I am often interrupted by patients calling to be examined. I stopped here to see a patient and I will state the case as a proof of what I have written. It was a lady whom I had attended frequently but this time her symptoms were a little changed. She felt as though she had the asthma. When I told her of this state of things, she said she had been so affected but at this present time, she could breathe with perfect ease. Still the fear was in her. I said it was fear, for her body showed no symptoms of it, but I could see her in her mind trying to make it. She told me that she had been up all night with her father who had been very sick with asthma, and she had taken it but was better now. Here was a fair illustration of what I have written. She said I had told her how she felt. I then said to her, If I did not know more than you, I should have thought I was going to have the disease, but my knowledge prevented me. If you had known that your father's fears affected your mind, you would not have had the disease unless you had believed it catching. But I believe it is nothing but a lie condensed into a belief, and we having attached our lives to it are afraid. Here you see the body is nothing, but the trouble is in us, and every man has a body to himself that he places a value on; he looks after it as he does any other property and if the expense of repairing it is more than the value, he will abandon it as a Captain abandons his vessel. He will not lose his life to save his property except to a certain extent.

November 1862

Illustration, An
[LC 2:0807]

An illustration of what I claim to have discovered which the natural man has never had any proof of except by a belief, I will take an egg. Man would never have believed it contained a chicken until he had the truth developed before his eyes. Take a pair of doves, when they are first hatched, and keep them separate from all other doves till they come to maturity. Now will anyone deny but that the female dove has a certain knowledge, instinct or something equivalent to it, that there is something contained in the egg similar to herself, and she will act accordingly, and hatch and protect her young to the best of her ability. Now that something, call it what you will, is superior to the natural man. The chicken is not ignorant of itself as being in the world till it breaks through the shell, for it is possessed of life and will peep and peck.

This wisdom in man is like the unhatched chicken trying to break through the shell of error and assume its real character or identity. The chicken is not ignorant of its identity in the shell, nor is the child of wisdom ignorant that it exists. Although it knows that it is in the shell of superstition, it is beating the hammer of science to break the shell or prison and escape from belief into the land of science. Take a person as we see him; place him in a mesmeric state, then he, to the world, is like the chicken in the shell. His natural senses or shell lies cold and clammy as death, for speak to it and it moves not. You touch it and it awakens no response. Now every person has life and intelligence, not of the body nor within the medium of its senses, for the mesmeric sees and describes things at a distance which it would be impossible to do through his natural senses, and still he has all his senses and will taste and smell and describe what no one present knows anything of. Now here you have an invisible being that exists outside of his senses describing things truthfully which you never saw or heard of. Now let it break through the shell that binds it and awake or pass into this world, and at last it begins to act in another sphere. Now what I am trying to teach is to educate man up to that state where he shall know that he exists and can prove to the natural man what the natural man knows nothing of and has never acknowledged.

1865

Illustration of the Use and Abuse of Language
[LC 2:0747]

No one knows the misery which results from misapplying language to ideas which never had an existence except in man's own brain. Take for instance the word life. The child learns that life is in what he cannot see; he is made to believe that God is a living being, so he naturally supposes that there must be other living beings that he cannot see, for instance the Evil One, who may harm him. In the country bears and wild animals have been made terrors to children. We are also told that our food contains life, that it decays and dies and from this decomposition comes life. This is taught to children and they grow up with these ideas. Now to the child this life contains intelligence, for when we speak of it, it is always associated with some matter we call living. This life that is attached to these invisible forms or ideas which are a terror to mankind is what makes him superstitious because he believes that some invisible spirit is near him and he reasons about it as he would about anything visible that he feared.

This superstition has caused the people to believe that God was present in an invisible form and that sometimes he would talk to Moses and sometimes would affect the people with disease. This kept them nervous and all the time in fear, for their ignorance and prejudice put life into every kind of evil invention which could affect mankind. Hence arose evil spirits which were persons for they could talk and act and consequently they had life. But as Science progressed the spirits changed their characters and appeared in the form of diseases. Now to suppose that a disease could come and attack a person, except it had some wisdom to guide and direct it, is folly. Therefore every person admits a cause which of course must be intelligent and contain life like those people who were tormented by disease which they believed was from the devil. Make life the invention of man and it will not be difficult to convince him that the invisible beings of his own belief are of his own invention and their life is also his own. Let man know that his belief is the cause of his misery and he will cease to embrace evil or beliefs that contain life and learn wisdom for wisdom is not life but the destruction of life.

There is no life or death with God or wisdom for there is nothing to destroy. Matter with God is the same as it is considered by man—that substance, which contains no intelligence, but man, being ignorant, has deceived himself into the belief that his body contains intelligence. So he is to himself what the Irishman was to himself when he awoke from a drunken sleep on his cart and found his oxen gone. He said, "If this is Patrick O'Neil, I have lost my oxen but if it is not, then I have found a cart." So his happiness depended on his own decision. Probably, as he came to his senses, he found that he was Patrick and his horror became his torment. Man reasons about himself precisely in the same way. He finds himself in a dilemma and he begins to conjure up ideas according to his belief and puts life into every idea he creates. Finally he finds himself in the same fix as Patrick and says, If this is myself, I have a disease that will kill me, but if it is Mr. Imagination, he has got himself into a bad fix. A physician is sent for, who is puzzled to know which it is, as they both look alike. He talks to the man to discover if it is he or his imagination and finally concludes that he will give the man a dose of something which will drive away the imagination, and if it is the man, then he is mistaken. Now make man responsible for his belief and give him a rule by which he can detect the imagination from the scientific, then you will find evil disappear.

December 1862

Illustrations of this Truth
[LC 2:1036]

I will illustrate to you the way in which I cure or correct the sick. You know I speak in parables to you. To the well this is of no consequence, for they cannot see any sense in my talk. So it is in every science with those who are ignorant of the meaning the person wishes to convey. This was the trouble Jesus had to contend with. All His knowledge of science must be explained by parables, for the people's belief was in themselves and in the thing believed. Therefore to reduce their belief to a science was a very hard task, for it had to be done by parables of things that each person could understand. When He talked to the multitude it was about the science or principle that was intended to be applied to each person's individual case.

The parable of the sower illustrated the principle like an illustration on some science. It was not intended to be applied to any individual; therefore when the disciples heard the parable, they did not understand it as it did not apply to their case, and they wanted an explanation. Now His explanation to them is as much of a parable to the rest of the world as His parable to the multitude was to His disciples.

So a parable of mine is of no use to the well, for it is not intended for them but is for the sick and must be varied to suit the case that calls it out. Like a lawyer's argument, it depends upon the case to be tried; one plea does not answer for all cases. So it is with the sick; each one's case must be explained to himself. The science can be explained to the well, but not by the same parables that are necessary to be applied to the sick.

I will illustrate. A lady called on me whose feelings were as follows. She felt so weak that she could not keep from stooping over; it was with much difficulty that she could sit up. This feeling I could feel but the woman who was with her could not. Therefore to cure her and make her sit up, the work must be done by an explanation that she could understand, and this must be done by a parable because the lady's identity was in her belief.

It seemed as though I could see the lady sitting in that posture but her body had an identity separate and apart from the earthly body, and this sick (spiritual) body is the one that tells the trouble. This body is the belief, and it seemed to be holding up the natural body till it was so weak it could barely sit up.

These were the lady's feelings. This spiritual body is what flows from or comes from the natural body and contains all the feelings complained of. It speaks through the natural body and, like the heat from a fire, has its bounds and is enclosed by walls or partitions as much as a prison. But the confinement is in our belief, its odor is its identity, its knowledge is in its odor, its misery arises from its false ideas, and its ideas are in itself and connected with its natural body. This is all matter and has an identity. The trouble, like sound, has no locality of itself but can be directed to any place. Now as this intelligence is around the body, it locates its trouble in the matter or body and calls it pain or some other name. Now the sick soul is imprisoned in this prison with the body, which body feels as though it contained life. But the life is in the spiritual body which being ignorant of itself places its own identity in the flesh and blood. This is because the heat from the body contains the identity, and the soul puts such construction as has been taught, and thinks its own trouble is in and a part of the natural body. This is the prison that Christ, not Jesus, entered and broke the walls by His word or power and set the captive free. At this door He stands and knocks, and if we will let Him in, He will explain away the error or forgive the sin and save the soul. He will deliver us from our earthly hell that is made by the wisdom of the world.

March 1860

Illustrations of Immortality
[LC 2:0761]

A river has its head into which little streams flow to supply it. So man has an intellect which is sustained by various streams from the fountain of wisdom. The banks take the name of the river as a man's name is affixed to his bodily form, but both man and river existed before they were named. The river has its Christian name given by man and its surname which comes from its father. For instance, the Penobscot and Kennebec rivers were so named by man but both existed as rivers before their discovery. So with man. His wisdom exists and when it is discovered it is named, and the name is of man. The water of the river is like the mind; both are continually changing and finally they wear out the body or earth. The river empties itself into the earth ready to be drawn out to replenish it as the mind seeks the heights of wisdom that it may draw others to it. Suppose every particle of water to have an identity of intelligence. Its continual motion does not destroy its identity. It is water like in the stream, the lake, the river and the sea; and when it is taken into the earth to nourish and replenish it, it is still water. So man's intellect has its identity whether in one condition or another, and the body is to the intellect what the banks of the river are to the water, an identity to signify that water can be condensed into a form.

Wisdom outside of matter is not recognized, but when it is reduced so that its effect can be seen, it is acknowledged, though not separated from matter. The banks are generally admitted to be the river, and when there is no water in the bed, it is dead. Now the water is as much alive and retains its identity as ever, but man's name is destroyed. In the same way, God in man is not recognized except in the body, and when man sees the wisdom depart, to him man is dead.

Intellect, like water, is always flowing and cutting new channels, and each new channel is like the birth of a child. It receives a name but retains that of its father.

Take the "cut-off" at Vicksburg on the Mississippi. That is like a child who has a name called the "cut-off" or something else, yet with the water it is the same. The difference is in man and not in the water. That, into whatever channel it may flow, has its identity as water. So the wisdom of man is wisdom and his identity is as much in existence as the water that enters into the Atlantic is part of all the moving waters on the globe. It is plain that if each particle of water could speak, it would answer my question concerning the Kennebec or Mississippi or any waters on the face of the globe. It is the same with the intellect of man. My wisdom is in existence as far as I am known, as truly as I am in Portland; and if I was questioned in any quarter of the world where I am known, I, this wisdom, would answer through a medium, although the name that man gives me might not know it.

As the wisdom which constitutes an individual was in existence before it became embodied, so all rivers existed before they were attached to a bed. Let a river have its identity as water as well as its name; then it will be seen that when the name ceases to exist, its identity as water still remains. But man in his reasoning gives life to his own name, and when his idea is destroyed, the life is dead. For instance, if the water of Moosehead Lake should be turned away from the Kennebec Valley, the inhabitants would say that the river had dried up or had died and they would look upon the banks and valley as a thing that once had life but which was now dead. Yet the water might say with the man who knew the facts that there had been no change in the water, that the destruction or death of the river was an opinion of the people, for the water in its identity as a river and as water was entirely distinct from the valley and banks. Man puts wisdom in the matter and not in the principle. So when the matter is destroyed, the principle is dead. Man's wisdom is not of God. God's wisdom is not in matter but outside of it and through it, as the identity of water is distinct from a particular valley. It may be said that this is what all men believe, but actions show that our wisdom is placed in the natural man or matter by our very ignorance. Man has no idea of wisdom identified with anything but his own belief. But if God or Wisdom is the First Cause, everything that is seen is in a representation of Wisdom developed into form. Therefore all identities of man and beasts may exist with the Father, as all the appurtenances of war exist with the government. The contractor of a branch of the war department has all the articles in his wisdom and they are born into the world as fast as they are needed. When one is seen, the world says it is in existence, but it existed before and wisdom brought it to man to name. Thus everything exists with God and man names it; but wisdom has already given it a name which man does not recognize and by that name it will always exist and know itself. Water is water and man may recognize it by a name of river or lake, etc. or may contend that it has dried up; it nevertheless exists in a principle of God's wisdom.

I will try to separate the wisdom of God from that of man. My body sits and writes and all that can be seen is myself and it is my opinion. But the wisdom that governs my opinion that knows what I say as a man is not an opinion. Wisdom has an identity and opinion also. Now what is an identity? Is it in the object that we see or in the wisdom that sees it? There cannot be an identity without intelligence; therefore, man's identity is not in what we see but in the wisdom that cannot be seen and only shows itself through a medium.

Every manufactured article is a symbol of wisdom, but in his reasoning man puts the wisdom in the matter instead of in the cause. Look beyond the body for the created being which is a prior intelligence.

May 1863

Imagination [I]
[LC 2:0656]

What is imagination? It is the word used to convey to another some idea that cannot be seen by the person you are addressing and to him it is nothing but your own fancy. This is an error, for the word is not applied in the right sense. The true meaning of the word if there is any such is this: to create a scene in your own mind by your own wisdom that you know is only the creation of yourself. It is all the while known to you that you are the author, but if you convince another of it, then it ceases to be imagination and becomes a reality to him. But to you it is all the while imagination. Here is the trouble. We take what man believes that cannot be seen for imagination and that which we believe for reality. With God all matter is imagination, for to him it is but shadow, while to man it is a self-evident fact.

Man has the same power of creating things which he knows are shadows or imagination, but to those who believe, they are reality. For instance, to the person who believes it, liver complaint is a reality. To me it is imagination as I define it, for I can make the same idea and know how I make it. But if I believe in disease and make it so plain as to believe it is real disease, then my imagination is gone and I am diseased; this is true. There are two kinds of imagination to the one who imagines, both real to those who believe. Suppose I see a stump really, and suppose I say to a man, pointing to another, "There is a man with a gun." If my words frighten him, he makes the stump into a man. To me it is a stump, but to him it is a man, without any imagination. There is no imagination in either case; we both see according to our wisdom, but I have deceived him and to him my deception is a truth. Again, suppose I become so excited as to affect him so that he sees another object to which he calls my attention. If it is anything that contains life, my fears are excited and the thing is as real to me as anything that exists.

There is no such thing as reality with God except himself. He is all wisdom and nothing else. All other things having form are things of his creation or imagination. His life is attached to all that we call life, and when his life is detached, the shadow to us is dead, but to God it never had any life. There are many ways of illustrating this idea of imagination. I believe this very idea St. John and Jesus tried to explain. Thought-reading was known at that time, for there are many instances recorded where Jesus told them their thoughts, but clairvoyance was rare. All magicians, sorcerers, witches, etc. were thought-readers. Jesus knew that this was the extent of the wisdom of mind known to the priest, and all those who pretended to cure did so on this idea. So when Jesus saw beyond their thoughts, he must be something beyond this power. Thought-reading is what we call knowledge, but clairvoyance is wisdom. The difference is this: the clairvoyant sees by his own light, the thought-reader by the light of another. Therefore Jesus is called the light of the world. Light means that state of wisdom outside of the wisdom of man or thought-reading; it is science. Thought-reading is imagination or reasoning. So when we say a man imagines this or that, it means nothing except that he believes what someone has told him. God is the embodiment of light or clairvoyance and to His light all is a mere nothing. When he spoke man into existence, His wisdom breathed into the shadow and it received life. So the shadow's life is in God, for in this light it moves and has its being and it becomes the Son of God. As Jesus became clairvoyant, he became the Son of God. He said, Although you destroy this temple or thought I, that is, this clairvoyant self, can speak into existence another like the one you think you have destroyed. Jesus attached his senses as a man to this Light or Wisdom and the rest of the world attached theirs to the thought or darkness of the natural man.

February 1862

Imagination [II]
[LC 2:0991]

This is a word which means something or nothing. The way it is used makes it everything or nothing, but if it is applied to the power of invention or imitation, it can be understood. It is wrong, however, to apply it to deception, for a person must first be acted upon before his imagination can produce a phenomenon; otherwise it would apply equally to all operators. But to apply it to one phenomenon and not to another of the same kind is not right.

I tell you a lie and you believe it, immediately your inventive power or imagination commences to create that which I have explained. I explain the operation of a machine to you and your inventive power immediately creates it according as you understand it. This is the power of imagination. In the first instance the world says your imagination has deceived you and there is nothing in it, but in the latter case you are right. This is a misuse of the word and you suffer from it. The power of forming ideas called imagination is one of the highest elements in the human intellect and it is the foundation of all true discovery, yet like all scientific facts it is abused and misrepresented.

To give you a clearer idea of the misuse of this word, I will illustrate it by a religious belief. Church members never use the word imagination in speaking of their belief and their religion. Do they mean to say that they believe without this power of creating the image of their belief? If so, then the power that understands is the power of imagination. The fact is that their religious beliefs are founded in deception and they deceive the people into them. At the same time outsiders are skeptical upon these beliefs and apply the words "imagination" and "superstition" in derision. In this way every person wishing to deceive the masses calls everything imagination that does not coincide with his belief. The medical faculty have assumed to themselves the whole power of creating by imagination every idea based on wisdom and all ideas opposed to them are false. In such ideas they say that the imagination that creates them is a disgrace and belongs to ignorance and superstition.

A physician, for instance, may tell you the most absurd falsehood that his imagination can invent, but it is "true" because it has the sanction of the faculty. If you believe him, you use the power which if rightly applied is one of the best of faculties for the purpose of creating a disease after his description which you have taken for a truth. There is no dispute or controversy about that. But if some outsider should deceive you half as much and you should create an idea, admitted by the faculty, then you are accused of being superstitious and believing everything and imagining all sorts of humbugs.

The word imagination is so misapplied that it has lost all the goodness it ever had, and like religion it has only a name without a meaning covering numerous deceptions applied to weak-minded people. I never use the word as others do. When people think they have a disease which I know they have not, I do not ascribe it to their imagination but to the fact that they have been deceived. A physician tells you what is not true about yourself. If you believe it and he deceives you, that is no disgrace to you, for it shows an honest heart and confidence in the physician. Then follows the creation and appearance of the thing he has told you. As far as you are concerned you are blameless, but the physician is a liar and hypocrite and has used your creative powers to deceive you for his own selfish ends. Now when their hypocrisy and deceit are exposed they cry out, "Humbug, our craft is in danger. This quack works upon the imagination of the sick and makes them believe the medical faculty are not honest."

Let me call your attention to one fact: the word imagination never applies as the first cause. There is a superior power, conception, that originates, and imagination does the work and produces the thing. Error deceives the senses and misdirects imagination. Science detects the direction that is given to imagination and corrects it, if false. All men have gone out of the way, and no one reasons from science. So wisdom classes them all in the dark that it may save the whole by introducing the light of a new mode of reasoning that will separate error from truth. This refers to the subject of health and happiness and not the arts and sciences. The evils that affect the body and mind are included.

1864

Immortal, The
[LC 2:0853]

What is immortal must be solid because it cannot be affected by blows, so that nothing can pierce it or break it through. This I call wisdom. It has no beginning nor ending. It cannot be stretched for it fills all space and there is no place to receive it. So it is like space, and the universe is eternal. But mind is not solid because it is porous; or there is space in all compound beings so that forces applied to it deadens or dissolves it and it passes off in air. Now as the soul is the mind, it must be of matter. If you think she can fly to God and be out of danger you are mistaken for she sickens with disease of the body and things torment her. She is disordered by fear and vexed by cares and the consciousness of crimes committed years ago pierce her through and her crimes are overtaken by the fear of an endless torment after death. All this goes to show that man according to Pagan philosophy is made up of just what the Christians make man in our day. The soul is not a solid because it affects the body and is affected by it; therefore it takes up space like the body. The doctrine of Pythagoras was that the souls were shifted out of one animal into the body of another. Then they must be changed, for when the soul of man entered the dog, the soul must change or the dog would be a man, for the soul must agree with the body which it enters. Lucretius says to his friend, If it be pretended that the human soul passes into human bodies, a man at full age plays the fool in the child. Now if the mind is weak in a weak body, then the mind changes and so things that can be so easily changed cannot be immortal.

1862

Immortality–A Dialogue
[BU 3:0455]

(Pupil) What do you believe about the immortality of the soul?

(Teacher) I have no belief about it.

(P) Do you believe that man has a soul?

(T) I do not know.

(P) Do you believe in death?

(T) What do you mean by death? The crumbling and decay of the body?

(P) Yes.

(T) Yes, I believe in that.

(P) What do you call that which exists after the body crumbles?

(T) I call it the same that existed before the body crumbled.

(P) What is that?

(T) A part of God which can control matter.

(P) I call that the soul.

(T) Well, we will not quarrel about terms.

(P) Where does this something exist after the body dies?

(T) Just where it did before.

(P) Where was it then?

(T) Just where it is now.

(P) Where is that?

(T) Where we are.

(P) Can you see it?

(T) Did you ever see it?

(P) No.

(T) How do you know then that there is one?

(P) Because I see the body moving about.

(T) So do beasts move about. Have they souls?

(P) No, perhaps not. Will you give me your ideas on this subject?

(T) I know that I exist and this truth does not require taste, sight or any of the five senses to prove it to myself. Does it to you?

(P) No.

(T) This fact proves another fact, viz: that we can exist independently of the five senses. This part which exists independently of the five senses is what is immortal, but owing to a vague idea as to what soul means I prefer not to use that term. I will call it the man. This man contains within himself the knowledge of the five senses. He also contains within himself all the faculties of the mind, and by these faculties the man's wisdom forms his own body. This by the world may be called an opinion, but I arrive at it by previous reflection. To this body he attaches the five senses and thus life is given to it. If any accident happens to this body and the man's wisdom detaches his senses and faculties from it, the man has not lost anything, although the world may call him dead. But the world has never seen the man or his faculties, only their representatives or shadow. To the man the change is no greater than if he were to turn from viewing himself in one mirror to viewing himself in another. Life and death are to the world conditions. When the faculties are attached to matter which the world can see, this is a condition of life; when detached from that and attached to what the world cannot see, that is called a condition of death. But with wisdom the whole is reversed. Life and death are merely ideas that may be changed.

Immortality of the Soul, The
[LC 2:0875]

(Question) Do you believe in the immortality of the soul? (Answer) I don't know what you mean by soul. (Q) I mean that part of man that exists after death. (A) What proof have you that man exists after death? (Q) The Bible. (A) Is not all you say a belief? Have you any positive proof of it? (A) The Bible is proof enough for me. (A) Well, it is no proof to me. (Q) Do you believe man has a soul? (A) I never saw one, did you? (Q) No, but I have seen a body with a soul attached to it. (A) That is only your belief about it. (Q) I know it, but do you deny that man has a soul? (A) Never having seen one, I have no belief about it. (Q) Do you believe in the death of the body? (A) Do you mean to include anything in the body that existed before the body had form? (Q) No. (A) Well, I am willing to admit that the body you spoke of may dissolve and if this is death, I know it and have no belief about it, but we were not arguing this point. Can you separate the soul from the body, senses and life? (Q) I don't know as I can. (A) Well, I believe that life, death, senses and soul all belong to the body and are of this world and have nothing to do with the real man, only as a medium. (Q) Then, all beliefs in the Bible to you are false? (A) I have said no such thing, but I do say there is no wisdom in any of these beliefs which can be shown.

(Q) Have you any belief in regard to death and what is called the future state? (A) None at all, as we are taught to believe. (Exit Mr. Question and enter Mr. Atheist.) (Ath.) Please state your ideas in regard to man's future state, as you understand it according to your theory. (A) Well, I will reason with you with regard to my theory and if you wish to ask questions, do so. I know that I am here and that I can exist without the aid of my senses. (Ath.) If you had never had any senses, would you have known this fact? (A) I cannot say that I should, but would that prove that I did not exist? (Ath.) No, it would not prove anything. (A) Well, you must admit that there are certain truths that exist and are known to some persons but which have never come within your senses. (Ath.) Yes. (A) Then, it is not the senses which makes the truth but the truth which is shown through the senses. (Ath.) Yes. (A) You will admit that your natural parents existed before you. (Ath.) Yes. (A) But can you say that they are any older to perfect wisdom than you, except by what you know through your natural senses? (Ath.) No. (A) Then if wisdom is the first cause and matter is subject to it, the body must have been spoken into existence by wisdom. (Ath.) Yes.

Now, if wisdom gives the body motion and keeps it in motion, it becomes the child of wisdom. Parents are the father and mother of their child and they give it an identity though it is really a part of the parents' identity, and their identity belongs to wisdom and their ages are merely the difference in their development.

For instance, if I tell you a truth that has not been developed through your senses, it is no younger by your not knowing it; but when you do know it, you give it birth and it is born to the senses. The child of error takes its identity at its birth, the same as any other idea, and dates its birth from that time. So does any belief, but when wisdom comes it separates the truth from the error and shows that all truths are eternal and that the words life, death, old and young cannot be applied to it.

Take your own existence and remember back as far as you can and you will find your parents can remember back further than you, showing that you existed before you can date your identity yourself. That fact shows that memory is in the mind and is a part of the senses. Not that the principle remembers, for the events may be forgotten, and when they are forgotten, it is to the senses as if these events had never been. This makes man doubt his existence. But when you understand that life and death are conditions of mind like memory, then you will see that as long as you can remember anything, to you it exists; but when forgotten, it is dead to you and I will show why I do not believe in the idea death as it is taught.

Every new development of truth which comes to the senses scientifically is a new birth and its life is dated from that time, although it had existed forever. Man's senses to the mind are like science to the wisdom—to explain whatever comes up within its reach. And truth uses the same senses to prove its existence and thus man, as we say, is the medium of truth and error. Every truth that comes to the senses existed before, while every lie or opinion dates its existence only back to its author. The separation of the bodily senses from the wisdom is not an easy task, for one has to prove what cannot be seen but yet exists, and I know it as well as I know that I have any senses. But to prove it to another is one of the hardest problems to solve; and yet although thousands have known this fact, they have never been able to demonstrate it so it has taken a stand of itself. The existence of a lie or opinion, being begotten in the mind and afterwards developed through the bodily senses, lives just as long as it is believed to be a truth. But when the real truth comes and destroys the lie, it dies, and that is the death of the body.

The body of truth has its natural senses and faculties but you cannot exist in the natural senses at the same time; for you might as well say that light and darkness can occupy the same place at the same time. As all diseases are made manifest through the body, they are treated as though they had their origin in the body. I know that this higher sphere of existence is the habitation of every living person, yet the natural man does not know it, so he lives and dies according to his belief and always will until wisdom burns up his errors by the fire of truth or science. All religion is confined to the natural senses and although all religious beliefs admit an overruling power, they cannot bring one particle of proof of it so as to convince another; therefore their belief is of no use to mankind.

Now man is sick and oppressed and bound down with disease, as it is called, and yet knows not the cause, and his sufferings are more than he can bear, as there is no eye but that of the natural senses, and that can only see the effect on the body. He crawls on the earth, a poor worm of the dust, till his body, mind and soul all return to their original elements. Sometimes it is called fever and revolutions take place till the truth will spring out of the senses by the agitation of the mind and the light will burst in and resume its authority over the natural man's senses. To establish this truth and benefit the world is my great object, but how to bring it about is the question. It may be asked, what advantage would it be to man? It is man himself and to know it is to know himself and be able to keep clear of the evils which affect his senses. The teaching of this truth to apply it to man's trouble is the same as we apply the Science of Christianity to correct and enlighten the world in Science. Disease like all errors must be destroyed by some wisdom superior to that which belongs to the natural man's senses; for the senses may be deceived, but the truth cannot, and the wisdom that can show this fact is above the natural senses.

1864

Intelligence
[Originally untitled.] [LC 1:0281]

You ask me to explain what I mean by that intelligence that is independent of a person's identity as a natural man. I will try to give you the true answer. The natural man is made of the substance called dust of the ground, that is of living matter. This matter is always changing and as it is life it receives into it the essence of wisdom and this essence or identity receives its birth from the wisdom or First Cause. As wisdom is all knowledge it fills all space, so that the natural life or matter is its servant. So as this wisdom spoke the identity called man into existence, essence is in that identity. So that when a child is born, the matter contains this essence. Now I speak of the natural man; he is made of mind and matter; the matter is that part that compares to death; the mind is that which is called wisdom of matter. Now wisdom is the First Cause. The essence is the result or effect of wisdom.

Every living being is made of this essence or idea of matter. This essence is wisdom or progression and as it is attached to matter, it has its father or mother that protects it till it is able to protect itself. But the wisdom of matter has its identity, just as much as the wisdom of God has its identity, so that man has two identities: one of error and the other of science; so as one is destroyed, the other is set free. Each wisdom has no form only as it is attached to an idea. Our wisdom may or may not be attached to things seen by the natural man. Yet it has an identity and is the very substance that makes the shadow we call man. But the natural man is so gross that he cannot see wisdom or light, so that things must be shrouded in darkness. When I speak to you, that which speaks is not the thing that speaks but the shadow of the substance.

I think I hear you say I do not understand. That voice comes from the world of error. But I hear a different voice that speaks from the inner scientific man, saying I understand.

Introduction [I]
[LC 2:0728]

In order to introduce my theory of curing disease, it will be necessary to explain the use I make of a few words to which custom has given a meaning which I am unable to use. For instance the word, mind. All use it as applied to man's intelligence and as the word mind has never been applied to any spiritual substance or any substance whatever, it strikes the reader strangely to hear it as I have to use it. Still I think I can show that the author must have had a different meaning in his wisdom from what is commonly attributed to it. It could not be that he had any idea of any world or existence beyond this life, for mind was considered man's life and all his reasoning powers and at death it ended. Therefore the brain was considered the seat of the mind and now various beliefs show that this false reasoning still holds sway over mankind. The word mind, as it is used and believed, comprises all of man and beast that has life and instinct and at death this all dies, and this is what the author of the word intended to convey.

But as science progressed the weakness of this reasoning was seen and the religious community invested the word with a new signification which the ancients never dreamed of, for with their limitations, it could not explain the life of man as it could not contain the word, wisdom, so a new word was needed and soul was introduced. Now if you will call the soul, science, you will then have a higher development than is included in mind. Let "mind" embrace all matter of the human and brutal creation as the word "matter" embraces all inanimate substances. Then the soul or science, like that wisdom which creates from inanimate matter every manufactured article, will control the matter of the human species that is held in solution and called mind; for mind is always under the control of some spiritual wisdom superior to the natural man.

I will illustrate my meaning with what can come to the senses of the natural man. The wisdom which dwells in matter or mind knows nothing of chemistry for that is a step higher than the natural man or brute goes. The natural man and brute can both see a gold dollar. The chemist by his wisdom can see and dissolve the dollar and hold it in solution. But the mind of the man and brute loses the dollar when it is out of sight. To them, its existence is dead, never to be united in a body called gold, and the brute leaves, not having any interest in it. But the mind of man (I here use the word as it was originally applied to embrace all of man that dies, not science or soul) having set a value on the gold, weeps for he sees it disappear. The difference between the man and brute is here. The latter sees no value in the gold and therefore loses nothing, but the man, through his ignorance, has been made to believe that the gold contains a value which was destroyed with it; therefore he grieves for his loss. The chemist knows that the gold has no value of itself but it is only the representative of value of which it is ignorant. He commences to reason with the man of opinion whose unhappiness is much greater than the brute and this brings up the proverb "where ignorance is bliss, it is folly to be wise." The life and senses of the chemist is in his wisdom while the man of opinion lives in his error. The chemist says to the man, "Why do you weep?" Opinions: "Because I have lost my gold." Chemist: "How?" Opinions: "It is dissolved and destroyed." Chemist: "I can bring it to life and restore the value." Opinions: "How?"

Then the chemist proceeds to condense into a solid the gold that was before held in solution. To opinions this is a mystery from the world of science. He can never enter into that world, for when the science comes, opinion is dead. The gold was matter to the mind of opinion but when dissolved it was nothing; but to the man of science it was matter or gold in both cases. In the same way the man of opinions sees a body called man, and the chemist sees the same, but as in the case of the gold, the former does not see the wisdom that moves, deposits and decomposes the body; he therefore puts life or value in it. The two sit down by a sick person and watch the decomposition of the matter; the man of opinion reasons just as he did about the gold, placing life and value in the matter. But the scientific man sees the value outside the matter which, like the gold, is a representative of a value that is held in solution which the man of opinions knows not. The latter, seeing the value depart, weeps for it, for it has gone from his sight. The man of science or wisdom sees the matter dissolve like any other matter, but the separation of the wisdom from the dross or opinion and its existence, when it can no longer be seen by opinion, cannot be understood. This was the extent of man's wisdom when Jesus appeared.

The Same Subject–Concluded.

Ancient philosophers divided man into two elements: mind and matter, the body being matter and the soul, mind, and one was the offspring of the other. The life of the soul was one thing and the life of the body another, but they both died together. So the word mind embraced all man's life. The intellect of the brute was termed instinct which was included in the meaning of mind. Science never had a separate identity, so that at death all were laid in the grave together; the wise man and the fool, the rich and the poor, all found their level in the grave. The Old Testament says that "a man hath no preeminence above a beast." We have evidence enough to show that what is now called the soul in ancient times had no higher meaning than mind, for we read of good souls and wicked souls. Also that "the soul that sinneth, it shall die." So here is an end to the soul. Such teaching as this is great cause of man's misery.

Everyone will admit that all the qualities of soul which I have mentioned will apply to man's intelligence. They will also admit that mind, according to every definition, can change; likewise that wisdom cannot change, that it is the same today and forever. Now can anyone tell me what there is that is not matter that can be changed? It cannot be wisdom for that does not change. It cannot be any form which can be seen which, of course, must be matter. Then what is it that is not wisdom, not God, not spirit nor matter, and yet can be changed? It is matter held in solution called mind, which the power of wisdom can condense into a solid, so dense as to become the substance called matter.

Assume this theory and then you can see how man can become sick and get well by the change of the mind which is a chemical change making the matter of the man of science, but he is comprehended by the scientific man. Disease is the natural result of ignorance and error, governed by discords of the mind. For instance, friction produces heat, heat expansion, expansion motion, motion disturbs life and life comes out of the motion of mind or matter.

There are various kinds of life–vegetables, mineral, etc. for life is what comes from the decomposition of matter. Wisdom is not life; it is from everlasting to everlasting, the same today and forever; but as life ascends from the lower to the higher kingdom, wisdom attached itself to it in order to develop itself in man. Now life, being the result of a chemical change in matter, must go through a process from the mineral kingdom to the spiritual state till life is swallowed up in science or wisdom.

I will give you the process as it comes to me by this great truth that lighteth every one who comes into it. The elements of the mineral kingdom, by their chemical change, bring forth life. This mingles with its mother minerals and an offspring is produced called vegetable. The life of minerals enters this new kingdom and a new creation springs into life; this again mingles with its parent kingdom and then comes a low animal life called the animal kingdom; one generation begets another till the matter becomes prepared to receive some of the life from the higher wisdom that rules the lower lives. Now man's life comes from his peculiar development, so there is as much difference in the idea man as there is in the other kingdoms, for man is made up of those kingdoms. He combines three parts in himself: the animal, the human and the scientific. Women have more of the scientific element and less of the animal; the latter kingdom makes them strong, the human benevolent and the scientific spiritual and poetical, working in their natural elements out of matter. Their senses are more attached to the scientific life, while man is more brutal and wants to rule and govern the higher kingdoms.

I will give the character of Jesus as He appears to me. He embraced the human and the scientific, was therefore gentle in appearance, for there was no animal element in Him. He came to destroy life, not to save it. All men have a higher development of the animal in them than of the other kingdoms, and this life dies, just as the scientific life is received; therefore if a person could be perfectly wise he would have no life, for everything would be subject to his wisdom; so to lose your life is to embrace the truth, for that destroys life.

The priests and doctors try to save life, for everyone believes he must die to be saved. So man living in this opinion, his life is a life of bondage through fear of death. Jesus came to destroy this fear and break the bands of death or belief and introduce this great truth of eternal progression. Those who believed rose from their graves or beliefs, entered the world of science and attached their life to this great truth. Then they could say, "O! Death, where is thy sting? Matter or grave, where is thy victory? Truth is the death or sting of opinions. Science of God is eternal life in this wisdom. This is the science whose light lighteth the dark dens of disease and leads the sick from their hiding places into that wisdom that will guide them through this world of opinions and land them safe on the shores of Eternal Truth.

Introduction, An [II]
[LC 1:0616]

In the work which I propose to introduce to the public, one of the principal points will be to give the reader an account of the causes and facts which led me to arrive at the following discovery or conclusion, viz:

That man as we see him is a combination of truth and error; that he is as much those two opposites as he is of right and wrong; that the identity of these two characters can be traced through every act of his life and the connections or links can be followed as easily as the progress of science in regard to electricity.

The writings of the Bible have recognized these two principles and the religious world has tried in vain to separate them, for their separation is based on false ideas which are opinions instead of wisdom. They have always regarded the scientific man as a mystery and have thus been trying to divide their own houses or theories and at the introduction of science their theories must fall. Always laboring under a mistake, they endeavor to make a truth out of opinions, which gives rise to parties whose whole business is to have a lie acknowledged as truth and the people made to believe it. This is the full extent to which the religious world has developed man. Death to them is a truth, but the state after death is a question on which there is a wide difference of opinion and is to the Christian world a complete mystery. They do not embrace the true man of wisdom in any of their theories but really disbelieve in everything which goes to identify the scientific man. There are certain elements or principles of life which have an affinity for each other and as these principles unite or come together, certain results follow which vary just according to the combinations formed.

Man as he appears is the machine under consideration and all I say will be to show that he is moved and worked by two agents, science and opinions. But these two agents have no more affinity for each other than light and darkness but each acts in opposition to the other. Error is a combination of matter and has three distinct characters: error, ignorance and opinions, which is all that there is of the natural man, but all these are nothing to the scientific man of wisdom, for wisdom can dissolve them all.

I shall first speak of the natural man, by which I mean opinions, errors, ignorance etc., in fact all there is of man except wisdom, science, and truth. The real or scientific man is made of elements which are eternal principles, everlasting and unceasing, and these principles are what I call eternal life, but when they are united together for certain purposes they are called matter. When the matter is dissolved into its original state, the principles still exist with their own identities. Now outside of these principles exists a superior wisdom which controls them by a medium called science, for by it we prove the identity of wisdom. Science is connected with eternal life or the first principles. Matter or the combination of these principles is also a part of life, but it assumes to be the author of its own existence, while it is but the author of its own acts and it acts in accordance with itself. Man is so formed that he is a perfect image of these two principles. His senses are in his life, but his life is no part of the combination called man but the compound is a union of the principles of life.

The compound has its identity as a machine has life in the inventor. When the machine is dissolved the elements still live in the principles of matter, though the identity of the machine is gone. So the life of the machine is dead. The scientific man's life is his senses and his senses are in his wisdom. The natural man is to the scientific man as a shadow to a substance, simply nothing. Both have their identity, one as a shadow and the other as a substance. But the identity of one depends on the life of the combination of the other.

Take away all science from a man, and you have a complete animal, though not as complete as some. Yet you have an animal that contains all the elements which go to make up an animal and these elements are under the law of matter. The principle of science is not contained in matter or even in its element but it is a part and parcel of wisdom, so that the destruction of matter does not destroy the principles which govern it. Man contains within himself all the elements of matter, but these elements are ignorant of the power that gave them their life or identity. As the natural man becomes purified from the natural element–ignorance, it becomes the medium through which the scientific man develops himself. Matter or the natural man is from above or independent of matter. I will give an illustration showing the nature of these three characters.

A says to B, "I see a spirit," describing it and B believes it. C hears what A says and knows it to be false. C's wisdom is outside of A and B and knows that all that B suffers arises from believing the lie of A. Here we have the three characters: C the scientific man, B the sufferer or natural man and A the liar or first cause. I will call the clergy and medical faculty A, their followers B, while I stand to the sick as C stands to A and B in the foregoing illustration, knowing that what A and B say is false. It is not necessary to confine the identity of the scientific man to any particular branch of science, only to create a man who is capable of detecting a falsehood when it is uttered. For instance, A relates a story affirming that it is true, but B is not bound to believe it unless A can prove or demonstrate it. If the story is based on a religious or medical opinion he cannot prove it and B must use his own judgment about believing it, and if B has been taught to believe in these opinions he must suffer the penalties of his belief, but if he has been taught to understand that all their wisdom is founded in superstition then he will stand to A as C did to A and B, pitying and condemning A for his ignorance and hypocrisy.

I contend that man's happiness and misery is of his own creation after he began to know what it was to be affected and I intend to keep the identities separate, though both are in one. Every thought contains a combination of gases which makes man, the food merely going to satisfy the brutal part, while all ideas go to feed the spiritual or selfish part of A and B. C is not included in these two but he is at the elbow of B to check and develop him and if possible to get possession of B which is but the habitation of A or C. The tempter is B. The disease or elder son is A. The scientific man or younger son is C. B is the body, vineyard, or field and contains the principle of both. And the developing of C is the destruction of A. C is wisdom in B or matter. A is the life of matter changed from one idea to another. I shall call these two characters by various names, sometimes principles or laws of nature, sometimes the natural or spiritual man, good and bad, truth and error, etc. Wisdom is always outside of mind or matter, yet like the seeds in the earth it is growing and coming forth to assume its identity outside of matter. This is the child, science, born out of matter, begotten by wisdom, and kept from the evils of the world till it can speak for itself. All we see of man is a combination of matter or ideas in a living form, having powers like the brute but differing in some respects. Wisdom from some cause best known to herself created man and beast different in their combinations, as the soils of the earth differ in different latitudes.

The products of a tropical clime would die if transplanted to our bleak and cold northern latitudes, yet by introducing a higher element into matter, their transportation can, in a measure, be overcome. It being the design of wisdom that this should be the case, progression was to be the instrument to bring about this change and as man's body like the brute's contains the same elements or soil it was necessary that a different soil be combined with it to bring forth a superior element. Now man being this element, it was into it that wisdom breathed the breath of life or wisdom, and he became a double being; not that man has any preeminence over the brute, for both are of the earth and must return to it again. The brutal element in man will not, if possible, be governed. It makes itself known wherever it is, whether in the wild or domesticated beast or in the cultivated man. It is opposed to everything that interferes with its interests. It is the element to be subject to science and knowing this it makes war with itself and its life is its own destruction. Science is in this principle and is in every thought. It accompanies all the nourishment of the body; it goes with the blood to all parts of the system and is like C as he stands in relation to A and B, to protect the child in B which A wishes to destroy. B is nothing but the shadow of A and they make war with themselves and out of their ashes C springs up. Everything that man thinks about, hears or admits, that thing takes possession of his body and he, that is the machine, is worked by that idea, wisdom being but a silent observer.

I frequently introduce subjects into my articles which do not seem to have any bearing on the subject of disease but they do and could we see what disease is we should learn that it is a deviation from science or truth and that happiness is man's aim. But the roads to it are so obstructed by false lights or ideas that it is almost impossible to travel in the true scientific highway. And Satan has many agents all over the country calling on every person, in every language and tongue, entreating them to listen to their story. Some tell you you are in danger of losing your soul, others offer great inducements for you to enlist in the army of the Lord and fight for their own particular creed, promising you a crown of glory at the end of the war or when you die. So you are deprived of every pleasure you might otherwise enjoy and torment yourself to death, merely for what you are promised at the end of your lives. Your death ends the war and your crown of glory depends on your faithfulness to your leader. Satan has so completely deluded the masses by his deception that his followers "have stolen the livery of heaven" in which to serve him and have established laws as arbitrary as ever did any despot not excepting Jeff Davis. Wisdom has no respect for persons but is like a pair of scales which weighs out to every person his wages for his labor, for all scientific men are laborers in the service of wisdom and their acts are weighed and they receive their wages just in accordance with their acts. But their acts have no effect on the great first cause, wisdom, no more than a person going into business. If he loses all he has, the loss is his and not the government's, yet the government protects all its subjects. So science protects man from error, but it does not protect him by upholding his error. Man stands to wisdom as the child to the parent. The parent is in the child, but the parent's identity is in itself; but had a mother twelve children, each child would have a part of its mother's identity, for the mother's identity is in her wisdom and the wisdom is in the child and the idea matter is in the mother's ideas. So it makes the child of matter and wisdom; not the wisdom of science but the wisdom of the mother. The mother, seeing a shadow of her own belief or ideas, puts into it an identity and gives it a name as though it was not a part of herself. She, by her own belief, makes the distinction between herself and child and this belief keeps her separate from her child. This separation has been going on till man has wandered away from wisdom and become sick and discouraged and Heaven is to bring him back to the knowledge of himself. The knowledge of this is heaven, the ignorance of it is hell or misery, sin and death. It keeps man all his life in fear of death and subject to bondage. What I say is to break the bands or destroy death and let into the prison science, who will open the doors and break down the partition walls which separate us from God or Wisdom, open the cells of disease and let the captives again into the fresh air of health. Now to do this is a science, which I hope one day will be understood. I suppose that all will admit that there really is no wisdom in an opinion and yet there are effects produced by them. All men can give opinions and those who believe are affected by them. This is true, but man's happiness and misery have never as yet been acknowledged to be the result of an effect of our beliefs, but a something we are called upon to get.

We are called upon to get religion to make us happy, admitting that religion is something outside of our belief. We are told that it comes by some mysterious power and this causes people to believe that there are unknown agents working on us of which we are not aware. Now there is a shadow of truth in all this but the explanation is merely an opinion and not from science.

I will here say a few words in regard to matter or mind. Opinions are the life of matter or mind for the time they are embraced, just as the gardener is the life of the garden while he controls it-for the earth would not bring forth the seeds unless the gardener had placed them in the soil. Man is at the mercy of opinions which come and take possession of him and cultivate just such vegetation as they please. So opinions take possession of the mother or native ideas and use them like slaves to cultivate such ideas as they see fit to have sown. They sow the seeds of disease and the native ideas become subject to their direction; this course causes trouble and a war of opinions arises and the doctors or neighbors are called in to settle the trouble, but as opinions are ambitious and the natural ideas are lazy the latter are very easily subjugated by opinion. Science is not known in all this trouble, opinions assuming all the wisdom and that is the exact case with the sick, they being two characters: one, opinions and the other, the natural ideas held in subjection.

Opinions are as cowardly as ignorance, and more so, for they fear science, while ignorance fears error or opinions. Science knows that disease is the effect of opinions and ignorance. Many cures are performed by persons who have no claim whatever to wisdom and it is an admitted fact among a certain class that there is such a thing as foretelling what will take place to some extent and all science does it in a limited sense, but the foretelling depends altogether upon the wisdom of the scientific man. All who pretend to cure profess to tell the effect of their medicine on the patient and that is their science, and it is foreknowledge to the man of opinions. To the true scientific man, the person who pretends to tell the effect of his medicine is a hypocrite and wishes to pass himself off on to the man of opinions as a superior being. He quotes men as being scientific but he knows he is uttering a falsehood. The whole composition of his being differs from the man of opinions. His character is religious in the extreme and his store of information is inexhaustible.

We have not yet arrived at the scientific man. All these characters that I have named are prominent in the world, and are in fact the leading characters of the world, while the scientific man is not known to them at all. Every person has these two characters. I know them both, and I know also that the two, opinions and hypocrites, are consulting together how they may keep ignorance in bondage. For ignorance is the child that is to be purified so as to receive the scientific man and opinions and hypocrites are the two characters that must be destroyed in order to free ignorance. For they are nothing but dross to science, which must be burned up by the fires of truth. They fear the truth as the burned child does the fire. They tremble and the earth quakes and that is their disease, and they greatly fear the light.

I will represent the ignorant man as coming to me for instruction, being in trouble and not knowing the cause of his misery, and the other two pretending to be his friends. I see the other two as plainly as I see him, yet they have no idea that I see them for I do not make myself known to them. Knowing as I do, that they are the enemies of the ignorant man I treat them as I would anyone who I knew was trying to deceive a person with false ideas. I do not trouble them (unless they undertake to uphold their master, error) until I sit with a patient and I come in contact with them. They have their motives and objects as much as science. And if the hypocrite wishes to achieve an object he has to exhibit more shrewdness than opinions, while science has to exhibit more than the three: ignorance, hypocrisy, opinions, or else he will lose his case. Ignorance would not be destroyed for it is the soil on which both these two reside. The reason why I give identities to different principles and ideas, is because principles have as much of an identity as matter. The only difference being that one can be seen and the other can see. One fills all space while the other is space and has its conditions. As wisdom sees opinions, it knows what is the trouble. I talk aloud to the natural man, but he is entirely ignorant of my conversation with the one who governs him, who is in him, as the light is in the darkness.

His fears are the workings of matter and all he says is to complain of his troubles. He is like a person in a quandary, not knowing what to do and afraid of everything. When I enquire the cause of the trouble, I do not ask the person in trouble, but those around him, which are opinions of all kinds.

The sick man is like a stranger in the hands of men who are robbing him of his substance, and he, being frightened, dare not stir. There is, in fact, no end to the torment which the ignorant man endures at the hands of these hypocrites and men of opinions. The sick are in their hands as a mouse in the power of a cat, who will play with it for a while yet will not like it to go free. I find every sick person in the hands of these characters, become as docile as lambs when science approaches, unless they see their reputation is to be questioned; then they will gnash their teeth with rage and try and destroy, not only their own lives, but that of the sick. I have learned how to approach them unobserved. I ask questions to find out the trouble and then expose opinions to the light of reason, which reason is the workings of ignorance. Opinions make false statements from false basis and then labor to prove their statements. They take the very mediums of wisdom to prove their assertions. The only difference is, one is science and knows it and the other is opinions and knows it. I must take the sick man and separate these different identities and also place the scientific man among his enemies. I will call the sick man ignorance and his enemies–opinions, which are like a mob. Each opinion having an identity as much as a person, and it is this point which man does not understand.

Science has its identity in wisdom and is eternal. Opinions reason to save their lives and unless science destroys their reason they live. Ignorance is the soil to be cultivated and opinions believe there is wisdom in this soil. They accordingly reason with themselves according to their belief and operate on the soil to prove that their reasoning is correct. Science is the life of the soil or ignorance and its growth depends upon the developing of the soil. The developing of mind or matter, embraces what opinions call either miracles or humbugs. Either one is but an opinion to science, who sees what will be the beginning and end of all opinions. Take the eclipse: opinions could not see the cause, therefore to them it was a miracle, while science could not only tell the cause but the precise time when the phenomenon would occur. There is another phase of science like this: You see Mr. A tell Mr. B to place his property in Mr. C's hands stating that he will thereby get good interest. Now you know that A and C are leagued together to rob every person they can. Now just as B is about to place his property in C's hands, you, knowing that B will lose it, tell him so and interfere with the speculation. This angers A and C and you are obliged to prove to B before A and C that he would surely lose his property, which if you do, the process is Science put in practice for B's happiness.

It is this science that the sick need to keep clear of the priests and doctors; as the motive of the one is to save the soul, while that of the other is to save the body. Every sick person is in the power of one of these two enemies to health and happiness. Yet, they have such hold on the body that ignorance gives them about one-tenth of their income, while the sick pay about the same as the people did under the Levitical priesthood.

Our religious ideas and beliefs in a future state are all founded on error and they really change man's whole nature. Every truth is not a scientific truth, for were it so we could have no standard to gauge by. Consequently, every man's opinion would be admitted as a truth. The word science represents the name of the process by which man arrives at a truth, while the process itself is science. To illustrate: you wish to know the height of a triangle, the length of the other two sides being given. I will give three ways in which you may arrive at the true answer. First having a correct eye you may possibly guess at it; secondly, you can enquire of one who knows; thirdly, you can measure with a rule; now in all three ways you may arrive at the truth, yet the true scientific answer can be arrived at by a mathematical process in which there is not a doubt, a process of wisdom which is not contained in either of the other three. The science is putting in practice this principle, not that the answer is science but the arriving at it. The correct working of problems by the science of the principles of levers would fail if certain variations were not taken into consideration. For instance, take the first class lever illustrated by a crowbar. If the bar is six feet long and the fulcrum is placed within six inches of the end, then one pound on the long end will balance twelve at the other; and if the weight is raised one inch the other end of the bar will fall one foot. But if the fulcrum should sink or give way, then this same lever becomes a third-class lever where the power is at one end, the fulcrum at the other and the weight in the center. Therefore all this must be taken into consideration or you fail to arrive at the correct answer and the science is to know of the variations and take them into calculations in working out the problem. Suppose again that you and I see a person at a distance and we are in doubt as to who it is. Wishing to ascertain who the person is, we can guess, but we may be wrong; we can get a person to go and see, but he may deceive us, or we can go ourselves. And this last process of finding out is the science by which we arrive at a truth. Science is to labor for what we receive and the reward is happiness. To cure the sick scientifically is laborious, but to cure by books or opinions is nothing. It is merely the science of him who had but one talent which he hid and he got others to think and act for him.

If the world will take an opinion for a truth, then the lazy are on a par with those who labor, and the wise might well say: if opinions are wisdom, it is folly to talk of science. These false ideas prevent man from studying into the wisdom of opinions, which is science falsely so called. Paul speaks of it in his epistle to Timothy, when he says, "O Timothy, keep that which is committed to thy trust, avoiding profane and vain babblings, and oppositions of science falsely so called, which some professing have erred concerning the faith." I contend that disease is the result of the reasoning of this science falsely so called and therefore it is necessary to establish a new mode, or show how man can be scientifically cured of his errors. My method is based on a science which embraces every part of man's reason and which destroys opinions on all subjects which tend to disturb man's happiness. This being my foundation, I assert that everything seen and felt must have a cause and that nothing cannot produce any one thing. Now admitting a cause, the process of finding it is a science and is a labor. I repeat that all there is of us that can be seen is the effect of our belief and our beliefs are matter and can be changed. Everything I write is to either lead or disturb the mind so that the truth can be seen as it were, for it is thus that I destroy opinions and introduce in their place the Science of Health. It is a new mode of religious reasoning, for all belief is the effect of our religious training, the medical belief being a part of it as much as any church creed.

I do not intend to attack any person or persons in particular, but the erroneous ideas of mankind in general. I believe that ideas are something that affect the happiness of mankind and disturb the senses. The senses are affected by opinions, which although not admitted as having an identity, yet they have one as much as heat or cold, and have as powerful an effect on our senses and they contain an odor as disagreeable to health as any atmosphere which man breathes and the individual who has it, has his senses affected just according to his fear. Now the question arises, Does disease exist outside of man's belief, as rocks and trees. I answer, It does not, but the world says it does. Science is to correct the errors which heathen superstition have handed down to us. Ideas are like individuals and live and exist as much as what God has created. The mind is full of these ideas and you can trace their genealogy from the ancient times down to the present date. In every person you will find some trace of heathen idolatry. Now it is these errors and evils that we wish to rid the world of; although they are not seen by man, yet they fill all space. Ideas have life, and both ideas and life have an odor but not a name unless they are attached to the body. Take the disease catarrh; in space it has no form or life but like an odor it may be offensive to a person's senses. It contains no idea so as to make it of any consequence, but attach a name to it, and then the senses are disturbed and we create the enemy which torments us, called catarrh. All false ideas in regard to disease contain the elements which go to make up disease.

Our mind is like the land of a certain lazy man which his neighbors tried to make him till. At last they told him to dig it all over and he would find a treasure buried. This he did, but found nothing. They then told him to plant his land to wheat, which he did. In the fall he went to his neighbors and told them he could not find his treasure, Well they said, go and reap your wheat, thresh it out and sell it and then you will find your wished-for treasure. Now we must work over our minds, looking for a treasure and while doing so rid ourselves of error and find the treasure to be the truth which we get for the result of our labor; else the priest or medical faculty will excite the curiosity by relating some story like that of the treasure which stimulated the person to gain the prize. This excites the mind and the doctors then sow the seeds of disease or tell them some false story which makes them nervous and a phenomenon is produced. When the crop of their own planting is reaped, they show it to the doctor, who says that it is the treasure, which is disease. If wheat or truth is planted we reap truth, if error or disease, we reap disease. In either case, the laborer gets the reward for his toil and if we sow to the wind or believe what the priests or doctors say we must reap the whirlwind. But if we sow to wisdom or science, happiness is the harvest. It behooves every person therefore to test opinions and see if they are based on science or otherwise. For we must be accountable for our beliefs, whether right or wrong and there is no escape from it. Let man understand that he is accountable for his belief and then he will be as careful as to what he does believe as he will be about what he eats or drinks.

Wisdom has never been taken into consideration in regard to man's composition. But man has been looked upon as a machine, set in motion without any wisdom to guide it; as a locomotive let loose to run its race and die when its fires were out. All calculations made in regard to keeping man running are made without considering wisdom at all, but he becomes a machine of opinions, whose owner is error and he is subject to all the errors which error can invent.

1864

Introduction [III]
[LC 2:0908]

In order to understand Dr. Quimby it is necessary to give the reader some idea in regard to how he treats diseases and also some explanation as to the way in which he says they were brought about. To do this I must give his ideas of the cause of disease. These will enable the reader to see some meaning in his otherwise blind writings, for he reasons about things that would seem to many persons as having nothing to do with the cure of disease. His ideas are entirely new to the world and if no explanation or introduction to his writings is made the reader would of course pass over what he says with indifference and condemn it as visionary. It is therefore necessary to set the reader right at the outset lest he should weary in looking for the principle the doctor claims to have discovered.

Dr. Quimby asserts and expects to prove that what is called disease is not a cause but an effect. He says that thoughts are like the shock of a galvanic battery, that they are directed by some wisdom outside of the individual and that these thoughts are deposited according to the direction and bring about a phenomenon. This phenomenon which he calls an idea is named disease.

He says that every idea, whether of disease or of anything else, is a combination of thoughts and that every person is responsible to himself for his ideas and must suffer the penalty of them. Dr. Quimby's theory is to correct these ideas which are false and avert the evil that flows from them. He holds that disease is caused by false ideas over which we have no control and that a different mode of reasoning from that which now prevails will eradicate from society the phenomena called disease.

In treating the sick, Dr. Quimby introduces the subjects of religion, politics and all ideas the discussion of which agitates society. These, he says, contain fear and excite the mind which by a false direction brings about the phenomenon called disease. Thus it is evident, his ideas are at variance with the belief of the world. So he stands alone, his hand against every one's, and all, against his.

He takes every patient as he finds him and commences as a teacher with a pupil, destroying his error by correcting every idea that affects his health. He often comes in contact with pet ideas of the patients, like religion for instance, that are so interwoven with his existence that they have become a part of himself. If these cause the patient trouble it is the doctor's business to correct them.

Chemical changes he talks a great deal about. This phrase he makes use of to give the patient an idea of the change in the system which always accompanies a change of ideas. He says that every idea or belief affects people just in proportion to their capacity to understand. He also says that obstinacy often prevents people from taking an interest in what they hear, thus protecting them from disease.

The doctor shows how fear also affects the mind. He says that false ideas contain some bugbear of which people are afraid and this he has to battle with; and in order to destroy this bugbear which terrifies them, he is obliged to destroy the idea which contains it. Patients, he says, will cling to their ideas as a child to its mother and he sometimes has sharp discussions before they will yield the point. This discussion he calls the remedy, so he says that the curing of disease is a scientific mode of reasoning. His theory is to correct man's errors so far as his health and happiness are concerned.

People not familiar with Dr. Quimby's ideas think that he does not understand the meaning of language and therefore does not express himself clearly upon those subjects which he undertakes to elucidate. It is therefore desirable to determine whether or not he understands his position.

His first principle is that nothing cannot produce something. Life, he says, is not a reality but an idea and in it is the fear of destruction called death, He shows that life and death are no part of wisdom, for the words cannot apply to what never had a beginning or ending. He proves by his theory and practice that every person has within himself the power of creation and at the same time shows that the life given to the creature is not in the thing created but springs from its author. He says that the great creator of all things contains no life nor death, but as long as the thing created remains a mystery, it contains life. Every false idea that man believes in contains life as long as he believes it, but when the error is discovered, the life is gone. Therefore, he says the absence of life is death.

He shows that man is a compound idea without wisdom or intelligence and he appears to have these only when he is acted upon by an identity that has its existence in the great father of all. He shows by his theory that two sets of ideas are admitted in the world, one real and the other unreal; the real being those that can be seen by the natural eye, the unreal, those that cannot be seen.

August 1864

Introduction [IV]*
[BU 3:0410]

Dr. Quimby claims to teach the Science of Happiness. It may be denied that there can be such a science; let me attempt [to] prove that there can be, and is.

That happiness is what men have long sought for but never found, all will admit. Why has it never been found? Because obstacles that cannot be overcome are constantly in the way. If the obstacles can be removed and the path shown plainly, is not the end demonstrated? And is not a demonstration scientific?

But it will now be urged, that obstacles never can be removed; they are one of the inevitable conditions of our finite existence. Mysteries surround us which it is impossible to unravel as well as presumptuous to attempt. In short we are told that evil always has existed and always will exist and that therefore perfect happiness is an impossibility.

It will not I suppose be denied that perfect wisdom would bring perfect happiness. It is equally evident that as we acquire wisdom, happiness follows. All who admit the existence of a superior intelligence admit its power to annihilate evil; who is to limit the development of man's intelligence? Are we not made in the image of God, and as we increase in wisdom and goodness, do we not become like him? Therefore with the same wisdom would not the same happiness follow?

Let us now look into those obstacles which we are told can never be overcome. I. The belief in death is one great source of terror and misery. II. To offset this belief we are told that although the body dies, the soul still lives, and if redeemed it leaves this world of sin and sorrow to take its flight to realms of bliss where innocence and beauty reign. This idea, which at best can be only vague and uncertain is the fruitful source of excitement, and illness consuming, the physician takes the case, and this brings us to the third great obstacle to happiness. III. Perhaps no one evil is more extensively spread, and yields a more immediate and apparent harvest of suffering, than disease. There are almost as many kinds of diseases as there are patients, and physician's principles, like all other lies, are capable of being adapted to the demand. But death, religion and disease are not the only evils that bar the path to happiness. Out of the same material of which these are composed are formed ideas of lesser magnitude, which though not so conspicuous and leading in their character, yet, like a venomous insect, are capable of inflicting extreme torture and are perhaps quite as dangerous from not being so easily apprehended. IV. These ideas are such as spring from social intercourse when human nature is not understood. They are to be seen in the relations of members of families to each other, in friendship, in business and in politics, in love and marriage, in short, in all the relations in which human beings stand to one another. And is it to be said that all these evils are never to be removed? It can do no harm to believe that they can be removed and this theory proves that it can be done intelligently.

<u>Argument</u>

Dr. Quimby asserts that there is no such thing as death. We are taught that the brain is the seat of the intellect, that the organs possess life, and that the body contains within itself the principle of life. Thus we locate the man in the body and believe him to be a part of it. The body is matter formed according to a certain belief, and as such is liable to death. When, therefore, the body dies it is plain that the soul dies also. The doctrine that he survives as a soul is an opinion only, and like every other opinion may be questioned.

I

Dr. Quimby divides man into the natural and the scientific man. The natural man dies and the scientific man is found never to die. The natural man is matter; the scientific man is wisdom. The natural man argues by opinions, the scientific man reasons scientifically; that is he proves his points. The natural man is of ignorance and error, which are liable to death; the scientific man is truth which is everlasting. When, therefore, a man is "born again" he can never die. He then uses matter as a medium and makes himself manifest through it. Thus death is annihilated and remembered as an opinion only, which man was too ignorant to see beyond.

II

The other world, to which we are taught that we shall go, is a belief. The soul is also a belief and as this is something that cannot be seen with our eyes, we are told that it is a spirit. These ideas, which are acknowledged to be mysteries, make people nervous and they give rise to religious excitement, the evil of which cannot be exaggerated. As a weapon with which to enforce obedience to moral laws, people are taught that there is a place of torture to which the wicked shall go, and thus every man is at the mercy of whoever is shrewder than himself. The belief in another world constitutes the basis of religion as represented by creed and is used, sometimes ignorantly and sometimes not, as a means of torment to the ignorant.

Dr. Q. does not accept opinions as truths, for he says that from that false step spring all our troubles. He does not teach the existence of a heaven independent of ourselves, and place to which we exile our friends as dead under the assumption that happiness is there to be found. He teaches that heaven is the happiness which flows from a good act and that therefore we have heaven always within our reach. And the God who rules all things is wisdom which is always in the world, though, in our ignorance we know it not. In like manner hell is the misery which follows a bad act; therefore hell is to be avoided and heaven to be gained by the possession of truth. This truth Jesus came to impart and from this truth were to flow health and happiness.

III

Disease comes within the senses of all, for there are few who have not experienced it and none who are not liable to it. We are taught that the body may become diseased from material causes, and that when the disease arrives at a certain point, the patient will die. This Dr. Quimby regards as an opinion, and asserts on the contrary that the disease does not lie in the body, but in the mind; that the causes of disease, far from being material, are to be sought for in the world of thought, and furthermore that the chemical change we call death is not brought about by any condition of the body.

Dr. Q. does not deny any phenomenon of the body but he does deny any explanation that is given of it. He does not for an instance dispute that a person may suffer and feel sick, but he does deny that the cause of this suffering is to be found in the body. If a person goes to a physician and describes his symptoms, he is told that he has a certain disease, for instance, consumption. Let the same person go to Dr. Quimby. Instead of the patient telling the Dr. how he feels, the Dr. himself takes the patient's feelings and tells him what they are. The Dr. then reasons thus: before I sat by this man I had no such feelings as I have now. I was then well and consumption cannot have taken hold of me so quickly as this. It is proved therefore that one person may have the symptoms without having the disease. Why may not another? Since then the physician's explanation is disproved, viz: that certain symptoms prove the existence of a certain disease, Dr. Q. proceeds to give his own which is as follows.

It will be necessary first to define some words to which a variety of meanings are attached. By mind Dr. Q. means whatever of our natures may be changed, thoughts, opinions, ideas, etc. This he calls spiritual matter, matter because it can be changed, spiritual because it cannot be seen. By intelligence he refers to truth or wisdom, all of these terms which he uses synonymously. As it is necessary for us to have a name for everything that exists, he calls this substance or a solid. Matter he defines as the raw material in which there is no life nor action. He sometimes calls ignorance matter; they are the same in this sense, that to perfect wisdom both are nothing.

All sensation is in the mind. Everything goes to prove this, while the contrary position is a pure assumption. If a man's arm is cut off does the arm ache? On the contrary is it not often the case that after a limb is amputated the same sensation exists as before the amputation? Thus proving that sensation is not in the body. But it is now urged that even if sensation be in the mind, the body can become diseased and the mind affected even to its destruction.

Dr. Q. admits the existence of a supreme intelligence and in reasoning he never ignores the fact that this intelligence is supreme. If then this wisdom is all powerful, can it be affected by matter beyond its own will? Can the weaker control the stronger? An intelligence that is supreme must control matter and in it all things must live, move and have their being. If then these premises are true which all Christendom admits, it follows that the fountain of life and action lies in intelligence. Every phenomenon in the natural world takes its rise in the spiritual world, and is a shadow, so to speak, of that which we cannot see. The causes of disease then, far from being in the body, which is mere inanimate matter, are to be sought for in the mind, which is the machinery by which intelligence moulds matter for its own use.

If then the causes of disease lie "in the mind," the disease itself must also be there. Does not the fountain contain the river? The seed, the tree? Is not every answer involved in its question and does not every cause contain its effect? Furthermore can matter, which is nothing, contain disease which is something?

Since disease and its causes are in the mind, it is plain that remedies must be applied to the mind, and not to the body, which merely, as it were, illustrates the mind. If a picture which illustrates an author's idea be destroyed, no one would claim that the idea which gave birth to the picture was destroyed. The cause, on the contrary still exists, and with material another picture can be made similar to the first. So is disease. If that phenomenon apparent in the body which physicians call disease be removed, the patient does not necessarily recover. The true disease still exists and seeks another way in which to show itself.

In curing a person it is often necessary to explain how the disease is produced. Dr. Q's explanation is this.

In searching after wisdom man gives birth to and meets with ideas which represent either errors or truths. A U. S. one dollar bill for ex. represents so much value: this value we call a truth. A wrong idea may be compared to a counterfeit bill. These ideas to which I refer affect us according to their own character to our belief in them. For instance: If we have a $1 U. S. bill and believe it good and act upon that belief all is right, while on the contrary, if we have a counterfeit bill which we believe good and attempt to pass it we find ourselves in trouble. A currency represents our food and drink in the natural world, so ideas represent our spiritual food and drink, and that both should be genuine is evidently desirable. Society is full of ideas on the subject of disease. Every tree must be known by its fruits and the fruit of the prevailing ideas of disease are apparently in almost every person we meet. A perfectly healthy person is scarcely to be found, and disease is increasing with alarming rapidity. Yet physicians have always had undisputed sway.

But I shall be asked to prove that ideas do affect us. If one hears of the death of a friend, is not the system affected according to one's grief? Is not the frame convulsed and do not tears flow? Or perhaps a rigid stupor seizes the body and every effort to break the spell is unavailing. Who will deny that this is an effect of an emotion of the mind? "Oh but," it is urged, "that is a different case from sickness. We all know that a person by exposure is liable to suffer and be sick." Dr. Q. admits that this is the fact, and that a person usually does pay the penalty of such exposure; but that the cause of his illness lies in the smallest degree in that to which he exposes himself, the Dr. denies. The Dr. says that the cause of his disease is in his own belief. If for instance a person believes that he is liable to take cold on exposure, that belief produces fear. Fear contracts the muscles, and that waste of the system, which in a relaxed and healthy state of the person, passes off naturally, now remains. This must be got rid of in some way and perhaps coughing is the means that nature provides. But a cough, says the physician, indicates disease or a liability to it; and he at once proceeds to put restrictions on the person. These serve to increase the patient's fear and fill his mind with a thousand speculations all based upon the belief that disease is something independent of himself which he cannot control. A person in this state is ripe for any disease a physician may select. When that person began to cough, if the truth could have been explained to him, viz: that an excitement had been produced on his system which was passing off by means of a cough, no fears would have been created, but a quiet condition often would have been maintained and the excitement would have passed harmlessly away. Some may say that this person is made sick by imagination. Were there real trouble it could not be so easily removed. When a case baffles the physician's skill, it is a favorite explanation of his to say that the patient has no disease. Imagination is the only cause of the trouble, and the patient is abandoned with this consoling reflection that his illness is his own fault and he might get well if he chose. This is the charity and liberality of the Science of Medicine. That its mission is of the earth. Earthly, is in no way more plainly proved than by such bigotry.

It would require a volume to take up all the ideas which affect disease and which in curing Dr. Q. is often obliged to explain. This is the reason why he so often talks upon subjects that seem to the patient to have no connection with the disease.

All ideas affect us according to the direction given. Their influence may come within our senses or may not. That we are not conscious of it is no proof that we are not affected. It is the hidden and unseen influences with which Dr. Q. mostly deals and to bring these to light and explain them is the object of his practice.

May 1865

Is Cold*
[BU 3:0766]

[T. Teacher]
[S. Student]

T. Is cold in the person or in the atmosphere? S. In the atmosphere. T. If so, why do not all feel it alike? S. On account of their different conditions. T. The cold is unchanged then but people differ? S. Yes. T. Then the difference is in the people? S. Yes. T. Then the cold they feel is their own condition? S. No, it is the atmosphere. T. You just said the atmosphere was the same, but people differ. What is hot to one person is cold to another. Now what makes the difference? S. The difference is in the people. T. If that is the case then the heat or cold is not in the atmosphere. S. But we all admit that summer is warm, winter is cold. T. That is a belief which does no harm so far as it goes. We <u>do</u> admit that winter is cold and that a certain amount of clothing and fire will protect us from it. So far, so good. But we do not stop here. We admit that the cold weather is liable to make us sick unless we put just such an amount of clothing on and have just so much fire–the standard of which is arbitrarily settled. Now who is to say when a person has on clothing enough except the person himself? Since no two persons feel just alike and you have admitted the difference to be in themselves instead of the cold–Each person should be a standard to himself and no one has a right to tell him he is too warm or too cold. S. Now I feel a cold draft from that door, which you do not feel, yet the draft is there and it is cold and it affects me. T. It may be there to you but to me it is not there, for I do not feel it. If it is there to you then you are the one to be affected by it and not me. If I do not feel it, it is not there to me. S. But it is really there. T. How do you know? S. Because I feel it. T. I might as well say it is not there because I do not feel it. S. Do you mean to say there is no draft simply because you do not feel it? T. No, I say it is not there to me. S. I don't care anything about you–is it there or not? T. How do we know any such thing except as it comes through our senses? What other proof have we that it exists? If half the world thinks it is not there and the other half thinks it is, one has as good a right as another to say how the fact is. So how else can you settle the question except to say that the world is to everyone just as he thinks it is and therefore what is true to one person is not necessarily so to another. S. But don't you admit something to be true independent of all men? T. Yes and about that there can be no difference of opinion. But we have proved that heat and cold is not that thing. Everything is either true or not, what is true we all admit without question, everything else we have different opinions about. We cannot prove that heat and cold are truths of themselves? What then are they? They are ideas that exist in the mind of man.

T. What is a truth? That which exists independent of man and what can be seen with the natural eyes. The earth and all that is on it or in it. Principles and all mathematical truths. Everything else is a belief and is made by man. Does consumption exist independent of man? No. Then what is it? A belief. We believe that cold weather produced disease and that the lungs become so diseased that a person dies. Why should the cold weather produce disease? When God finished everything He pronounced it good. S. We can't always take the Bible literally. T. Then you believe that the air contains something which is injurious to man? S. Yes. T. Then God made man so that it is impossible for him to help being unhappy. If that is the case I do not think man is to blame. S. Man must obey God's laws and then he will be happy. T. What are they? S. The laws of health are among them. T. Where are they? I never saw them laid down anywhere. S. The air is cold and if man does not protect himself from it he must suffer the consequence which is a punishment for his disobedience. T. But sometimes we are placed in such circumstances that we cannot protect ourselves. People are poor and can't buy wood and clothing–are then to blame? S. No, but since the law is matter they must suffer for disobeying it, but the Lord will not punish them in the next world. T. But they suffer just as much here, which is rather hard since they are not to blame. Your God is not a very kind one. S. He may not seem kind to us because we cannot understand all his ways. T. But you pretend to explain them all. S. I rest on the Bible. T. You just said that we must always take the Bible literally. Now who is to decide what part to take literally and what not to? One man has just as good a right as another to give his explanation. You admitted that everything that does not exist independent of man is a belief. Then disease is a belief. S. But it is a fact people are sick. T. Some people are thieves, but did God make theft? No. Then it is a part of man and since it is a bad part, it must have an end, for we read that all evil shall be done away. S. How do you propose to get rid of disease? T. I believe that man has made it himself and if he

338

has made it, he can unmake it. We must see upon what it rests and if we can destroy the foundation the whole thing must fall.

T. Is disease in the mind? S. What is mind? T. It is whatever in man can be changed. Disease can be changed therefore it must be mind. S. But people say it is matter and matter is not mind. T. Cannot matter be changed? S. Yes. T. Then it is not a truth for truth is always the same. S. No. T. Then it is not eternal? S. No. T. Then it is not a part of God? S. No. T. Then with God it is not anything for He fills all space therefore how can anything exist which is no part of them? Therefore man's body is nothing to wisdom and as man becomes wise it is nothing to him. So disease which is a part of the body is nothing to wisdom. S. But we say man suffers, can wisdom suffer? T. Yes, from grief, for Jesus wept over Jerusalem and we weep to see our children do what we know is for their injury, therefore wisdom can suffer. S. Then wisdom suffers for all the ignorance of others, not from its own acts? T. Yes. Man's diseases come we are told from his own acts, therefore his suffering is not that of wisdom? S. No. T. Then if it is not of wisdom it must be of error. S. Yes. T. Then man by becoming wise can annihilate it? S. Yes. T. Do you think the present course had better be adopted? S. Yes. T. Physicians reason that disease takes is origin in matter. Now how can anything take its origin in nothing? God is the Great Originator and to admit that there is a source independent of Him, is to admit a second independent power.

Is Disease a Belief?
[BU 3:0149]

I say it is, for a person is to himself just what he thinks he is, and he is in his belief sick. If I am sick, I am sick for my feelings are my sickness, and my sickness is my belief, and my belief is my mind; therefore all disease is in the mind or belief. Now as our belief or disease is made up of ideas which are matter, it is necessary to know what ideas we are in; for to cure the disease is to correct the error; and as disease is what follows the error, destroy the cause, and the effect will cease. How can this be done? By a knowledge of the law of harmony. To illustrate this law of harmony I must take some law that you admit. I will take the law of mathematics. You hear of a mathematical problem. You wish to solve it; the answer is in the problem, the error is in it, the happiness and misery are also in it. Your error is the cause of your sickness or trouble. Now to cure your sickness or trouble is to correct the error. If you knew the real state of things, you would not call on a person who knows no more than you do if you knew the facts.
November 1859

Is Language Always Applied to Science?–Part I
[LC 2:0743]

Everyone must answer, No; then it must sometimes be applied to error. Language when applied to science is true if it represents the thing it means, but when applied to error, it contains no real meaning but is merely words used to represent what the author thinks is true, which he does not pretend to prove but only states as opinion. This is knowledge; it contains no wisdom but is matter that can be changed; therefore when a man tries to explain what he knows as a science, he is not understood by a man of knowledge. Wisdom is eternal truth, and the language that can explain that cannot be changed, although other words may be used to explain the same truth. Knowledge is seen represented by language which contains no wisdom, and as Paul said, words with no meaning.

Take two persons, one with wisdom or science, the other with knowledge. When the former undertakes to talk with the man of knowledge, he is not understood but is misrepresented by the latter whose wisdom being in his words contains opinions only and not science. Such men are always referring to some celebrated author. For instance, if their knowledge of the Bible is disputed and the absurdity of their opinions shown, they will fall back on the authority of someone who, not understanding, gave an opinion to agree with what he happened to think was right. That will not be admitted by the scientific man who proceeds to give another explanation of the Bible. Then comes the contradiction on language. He is accused of ignorantly perverting the meaning of words and flying into obscurity when the man of knowledge cannot follow him. This last may be true, for he contains no wisdom and to talk science to such a person is like casting pearls before swine. If the man of science will labor with the man of knowledge till he makes him understand his meaning, then the language is without fault.

I have seen this in my own case. The world has no idea of what I wish to communicate; so in his ignorance, each one thinks the obscurity lies in my want of knowledge. While if I excite their muddy brains and create my idea in their mind, then they can see and understand it and my language is correct. This was the case with Jesus. The priests and scribes found fault with his education, for after he had been telling them of this great truth, which they could not understand, the Jews marvelled saying, How knoweth this man letters having never learned? Jesus answered, My doctrine is not mine, but from him who sent me. Here he was accused of being ignorant and he would be now by the same class were he on earth. Jesus taught not opinions but a truth based on eternal science that he could practice which was the science of health and happiness. He called this truth his father, and when it spoke it was not Jesus; therefore he makes a difference between himself as a natural man and himself as this truth or science. He says, If any man will do his will (this truth), he shall know of the doctrines, whether they be of God or whether of man. Again, He that speaketh of himself speaketh his own glory, but he that speaketh His glory that sent him, the same is true, and no unrighteousness is in him.

Here Jesus shows that his doctrine or wisdom was not of man but from a higher power which he acknowledged superior to himself. This the people could not understand for it did not come within their senses, and they said he had a devil; others said he was ignorant, and others said he made himself equal with God. In the same spirit when I say that the wisdom that I speak to the sick is superior to my natural senses and yet I understand if, some say it is all myself. And if I undertake to explain it and they cannot understand it, some say it is from want of education on my part and others say that I make myself equal with Christ. While talking with a Christian, if I contend for my own explanation of the scriptures which differs from their own, this is to make myself equal with Christ. It is the same with the medical faculty. They are the truth or Christ, and if I contradict them and show the absurdity of their theory, then I make myself equal with Christ. Christ is their standard, and if I refuse their explanation which I know is false, then I am accused of making myself equal with them or Christ. Jesus warned the public against false Christs and told the people to test them by their works. The Christ that he taught healed all manner of diseases, while they who profess to be followers of Christ in these days cannot do one thing that Jesus did. Still they assume to be leaders of the true religion which really contains not a shadow of truth. It is made up of forms and ceremonies and sacrifices and can never take away sin or disease that man is suffering from. This is the kingdom I am making war with.

December 1862

Is Language Always Applied to Science?–Part II–Language Continued
[LC 2:0744]

Does language contain any substance? Language is to convey some idea to an individual. The idea is mind combined into a form which holds the substance of the image. For instance, the idea horse is in the mind. This is like a nut or casket. When a person speaks the word horse, it does not follow that he forms the idea because a child may be taught to speak the word and to him the idea is merely a shadow so dim that to his senses it contains no substance. Now if he speaks the word to another child, it contains an empty sound or casket, but if it is spoken to a person who can understand, he will create the idea of himself for the word horse will produce a sensation, for sound is something that can act on the mind and the person becomes accordingly affected. Sound is sensation but not an idea; therefore it must be attached to something to give it an idea that contains a substance. To one person certain ideas may be filled with truth or error, for if they are not attached to a true sound, it is an error and here is where the trouble lies. We all suppose that when we speak anything the thing is conveyed to the person spoken to but this is not always the case, for to speak the truth is a science and every idea contains wisdom, but to speak error is to repeat words without applying them to the idea that brought out the word.

For example, I say Mr._____has the rheumatism. The idea I wish to convey is a perfect image of the rheumatism. Suppose that a dozen persons hear me speak. Each is affected just according to the impression I produce in his mind, and as the word embraces many ideas or forms, I convey as many ideas as there are persons. One has attached the word to a person drawn up and in a state in which he cannot move his limbs and another to a pain in the shoulder and so on, but everyone is affected. Suppose the word rheumatism contained one single idea. Then all will be affected alike so far as the word goes, but now each person is left to create just such an idea as he thinks proper, and if he tells the story, he conveys the word accompanied with his own idea. The world is full of these bogus ideas and they contain a substance that we spiritually eat and by which we are affected. They are as plenty as the locusts of Egypt.

This is true of every word that goes to represent disease. Consumption has as many ideas as there are persons who have heard the word and it is the same with all sorts of fevers and everything which man is liable to embrace. The sick have associated their senses to these ideas each of which, as I have said before, is a nut or casket that contains the wisdom or food of the idea. It is a storehouse to contain the food for the senses. Man lives on this food till it consumes his substance or gets all the life out of the body to feed the mind, so that the body is destroyed by its own friends or ideas. My theory is to analyze these ideas that man lives on which make him sick and show him their contents making him see that they are merely errors started by man without the slightest foundation in truth. And man has fostered and cultivated them into living ideas and given them names that they may go forth and prey upon the children of men. My practice is to apply this great truth to correct the errors of the sick. Therefore when with them, I take the ideas that affect them, analyze them, showing that they are the effect of superstition, and being matter, we make in the body the very image of our idea. This is the child of our own belief, and though it be ever so much deformed and cause us pain and misery, we foster and feed it with the crumbs of superstition to keep it alive.

Let man know that disease is his own make, as much as a mother knows her child is her own, and although the child is deformed, she cannot part with it, (and he will cease from making such children). The child is an idea of the father and mother; it is a child of circumstance, liable to all the evils of its parents. Correct the world of these evils called disease and you introduce a generation of children composed of elements as much superior to the generation of these times as man is superior to the brute. How does man show his intellectual superiority to the brutes? All will admit that brutes have a sort of language by which they communicate and so has man. Then wherein is man superior? So far as language goes, it is not there. A bird sings, each according to his race, but a bird is a bird and is like the first one; he shows that he is not one whit advanced beyond the birds of ages ago. This proves that his language is not to convey any new idea not before known; he lives and dies a bird. So with a monkey. He can talk, but his language is confined to himself and he lives and dies a monkey. His language is never applied to any improvement in science. Take a class of beings dressed like men and women. See what language has done for them, the same as for the brute to show off. Such language has never been applied to one single idea above the level of the brute. Then is language good for nothing? No, when applied to some error or some discovery by which man can advance beyond the world, then language is of some value.

December 1862

Is Language Always Applied to Science?–Part III–Same Subject Continued
[LC 2:0746]

Was it the intention of the authors of language to enslave man or to elevate and instruct him? If those who first reduced words to a language intended to enslave man, then the end was equal to the means. But if it was their design to elevate man and make him superior to the savage, then they have failed to accomplish their object. All man's misery may be attributed to language, for if there had been no language, man would have been but little above the brute. Thus language has developed sciences and at the same time enslaved mankind. Language when used to instruct man in arts and sciences is in its proper province, but when used to deceive and mislead man, it is abused and perverted. All will admit that language is to express one's thoughts and feelings, for if a man had not these to be expressed, language would be of no use.

The beasts have a language for their wants which are selfish and within themselves, but man has feelings which he wishes to express and this desire makes him an inventor of language to communicate his ideas to another. Now language is like all other commodities got up by speculators of very little benefit to the masses. The speculators use it for their advantage to keep control of the market while the masses take it second-hand from the wise, as Lazarus fed from the crumbs that fell from the rich man's table. Such is the food of the masses.

Language that is used by the inventive classes is very simple and constructive, but when it is applied to an invisible world, it is all confined to the intellect of a wisdom that can be seen only by its effects. Look at the amount of language about some invisible something whose existence sprang from the brain of persons who, by their language, have brought into the world invisible evils in the form of diseases and have counterfeited everything that is for the benefit of man, and who have deceived the people into invisible errors from which they are suffering. Meanwhile, their language is to enslave the masses till they have made an invisible world corresponding to this with an army as large and formidable as that of the Potomac, which is marshalled and led forth to attack all scientific improvements in freedom from slavery and from disease. This all comes from the misuse of language. I use language to express the feelings produced on me while sitting by the sick and I find that all the evils that I encounter are from some belief in some invisible thing invented by a superstitious mind and described as true. The people hear the story and eat it, and it comes forth in a belief and their misery is the proof that the story is true. This kind of deception keeps this invisible world in ignorance of its existence in the minds of men.

To rid the world of this kind of imposition is to show man that when a person talks about what is in the dark, he is either deceived himself or is trying to deceive others. It is true that I am talking about things that the patient cannot see, but he can feel them; therefore my language is not confined to what I do not know but to what I do know by my own feelings. This is what I know: that language has been counterfeited. It is only words used to explain our ideas and if a person is made to believe a lie, he uses this medium to convey it to another. This is what makes disease of all kinds. The priests use language to make people believe in their ideas; the doctors and politicians do the same. All their beliefs are without the slightest foundation in wisdom. They are the inventions of error and represented as truth, requiring a language to explain them in order that the people can swallow them. This keeps the people in ignorance of disease and all their lives subject to the power of these wise men whose wisdom is of man and, as Job says, will die with them. These crafty persons use language as a weapon to subjugate the masses, for their proofs come after their predictions; this makes an appearance of knowledge greater than the masses. But if man knew himself he would know that to believe a lie is to create it, and the misery following is our own.

December 1862

Is the Curing of Disease a Science?
[BU 2:0101]

I answer, yes. You may ask, Who is the founder of that science? I answer, Jesus Christ. Then comes the question, what proof have you that it is a science? Because Jesus healed the sick, that of itself is no proof that He knew by what means He did it.

If He healed in the manner reported He must have done it under the laws of science, for there can be no such thing as accident with God. And if Jesus was the Christ or God, He must have known these laws and the way He performed His cures under them. When He was accused of curing the disease through Beelzebub or ignorance, He said, "If I cast out devils (or diseases) through Beelzebub or ignorance, my kingdom (or science) cannot stand; but if I cast out devils (or disease) through a science or law, then my kingdom or law will stand for it is not of this world." When others cast out disease, they did it by ignorance or Beelzebub, and there was no science in their cures. The effect produced was the same, but not knowing the cause, the world was none the wiser for their cures. At another time when told that one had been seen curing or casting out devils in his name, he said, "Forbid him not, for he that is not against us is on our part, but he that is not with us or is ignorant of the laws of curing, scattereth abroad, for the world is none the wiser for such cures." Here Jesus makes a difference between His mode of curing and theirs. If Jesus' cures were done by the power of God and Jesus was the Christ or God, He must have known what that power or science is and the difference between His science and their ignorance. His science was His kingdom; therefore it was not of this world, and theirs being of this world, He called it the kingdom of darkness. To enter into the kingdom or science is to enter into its laws and thereby remove from us the evils of this world. Disease is an evil; it belongs to this world of darkness.

To separate one world from the other is to separate truth from error, and as truth is life and error death, the resurrection of the one is the destruction of the other.

November 1859

Is There Another World Beyond This?
[LC 1:0412]

Where is the proof that there is another world beyond this? All will admit that it is the Bible. I am willing to abide by the decision of this book for proof, but I may differ in regard to man's opinions about its language, for I pretend to say that there is not the slightest evidence that Jesus ever intimated that there was a world separate and apart from man's belief. All he said and did was to show that this other world, as it was believed by the Scribes and Pharisees, was false. If Jesus had lived in these days, he would be called, as he was then, an infidel. I will take the man Jesus as I find him and see if I can gather from what he has said and done what his ideas of another world were. All will admit that he was a very good man, independent of what he taught; but so far as this world's goods went, he had nowhere to lay his head. So his goodness must spring from another source than dollars and cents, as he had none of these. His food or wisdom was not of man; it was above the common opinion of the world. As far as this world's goodness went, he did not make much account of it, for when they were boasting, like all vain men, about their Christian goodness, he said, "If you love and help them that love you what reward have ye? Do not sinners the same?" His goodness was not in anything that man could do as man, for when called to pay his tribute money, he sent Peter to catch a fish and get the money out of it. Here he showed some wisdom to know that the very fish that would bite the hook contained the money. Perhaps the opinions of the wise may explain whether Jesus caused the fish to come round and bite or how it was. I shall not try to explain now but leave it to those who believe it a literal truth.

Now I think I can give an explanation of Jesus' belief. At the time of the birth of Jesus, the people were superstitious and ready to catch at any marvelous thing they could not explain. Jesus, from some unknown cause, had been studying into the laws of mind till he came to the conclusion that the priests were a set of blind guides, talking about what they knew nothing of, except as an opinion, and that they were deceiving the people by pretending to have power from another world. Jesus knew that all their theories and pretenses were based on the ignorance of opinion, but he could see there must be something in all the phenomena. Hearing of John's preaching, he went to hear him, and then saw how it might be reduced to a science. Here was his temptation: if he used this wisdom for moneymaking business, he could not meet with the same results; it must make him selfish. So he concluded that he would risk all the sneers and opposition of the religious world and stand up and defend a science that struck at the very roots of all religious superstition and public opinion and tested all things by one living and true principle.

The Old Testament being their Bible, he had to explain its meaning and show that the writers had nothing to do with religion but that they taught this great truth. So he had to speak in parables. His wisdom being based on science that he could prove, he commenced to put it in practice towards disease; and as disease is made of ignorance and superstition that never had any foundation except in opinions, it must be met by a wisdom superior to an opinion.

All the world's superstition and wisdom was based on an opinion, and to meet it was to spiritualize every one of their ideas. They believed in a literal heaven; to this he gave a spiritual meaning, saying his heaven was not of this world of opinions but of science, and he would bring it down to man's understanding. This they could not understand for his kingdom was science and their opinion of it was their belief, and their belief located it in space and attached their senses to it as a place where this wisdom was and called it a God unknown to the people. But the priests had condensed these phenomena into an identity called God, had given Him power over everything they could not understand and robbed Him of wisdom that explained their ignorance. They created a God after their own heart or wisdom and set Him in the heaven of their own belief. Thus the priests have placed misconstructions on every passage in the Bible which condemns superstition and taken all the wisdom to themselves, while the very science that the Bible contains is their worst enemy. This has made the war spoken of in Revelation, written by John, the Baptist, seem to be written by an insane man. If anyone will look at it, it will be seen that it is a book of the progress of science over the opinions of the priests. It will be seen how he labored to show the people that the priests' ideas bound them and kept them in bondage. But his writings fell into the hands of the priests who put their own construction upon them and turned the guns on the people, who might be taught to see through their wisdom. So the Book of Revelation, like all the others in the New Testament, has been stolen by the priests, turned and twisted and misconstructed to prove that men were writing to establish the truth of the priests' opinions.

Now I know by the cures I make that disease is made by the false constructions of priests and I shall show that not one of the writers of the New Testament ever had an idea of priestcraft; but the priests, knowing that the people fell in with their views, stole the ideas and persecuted the authors, just as they do at this day. The priests came to be the teachers of good morals and order. I shall show that science has had to fight this battle with priestcraft all the time.

Jesus had to establish a kingdom as the priests had done: theirs was based on opinions, his on science, so everything that they believed was only an opinion which his science could tear to pieces. So he begins by saying, "Seek first the kingdom of Heaven"; that is, seek wisdom or science, then all their craft could be explained. Then he says, "The kingdom of Heaven has come unto you and ye will not receive it"; that is, the science is here but you will not try to understand it. In the Old Testament, David called this science wisdom and exhorted his son to seek it first of all. Jesus called it the Kingdom of Heaven and calls on all men to seek it. If this Wisdom and the Kingdom of Heaven were not the same, then Jesus and David had different ideas of wisdom. Does the priest call on the people to get understanding? No. That is what they fear. The priests want them to have religion; that is, to believe in the creeds which cramp the intellect and bind burdens upon them so that they can lead them. They fear investigation, for it is death to their craft.

I will say a word or two about priestcraft. The people mix up priestcraft and religion with good morals, civilization and science. This makes it all confusion, as in political parties. You often hear young men claiming to be Democrats and quoting Jefferson and Madison, not Pierce and Buchanan; their claiming these men as their leaders is like a man quoting the acts of his ancestors who are dead; they are like potato tops, the only thing worth anything is underground. So the ideas of these men who are dead are as far from what they quote as the tops are from the bottom.

Those persons, quoting Christ and claiming him as their leader, are like young voters claiming to be disciples of Jefferson; there is not one idea now advocated that was thought of by any of the Presidents up to the time of Pierce. Men who claim to be Democrats attach themselves to a name that was once attached to a popular party, while the party leaders and principles are long since dead and underground. It is the same with Christians. They attach their senses to the popularity of Jesus and pretend to be his followers but have not the slightest claim to wisdom or goodness.

Religion like politics is undergoing a radical change; men are separating the chaff from the wheat, principles from opinions, goodness and science from religion and superstition and freedom from slavery. This is the warfare, and the general heading the divisions of the armies of wisdom against opinion is science, while ignorance leads the opposite army. The political parties are but one division of this great battle; religion is one and the medical faculty is another; public opinion is the echo of both. All these are in opposition to the Science of Truth, yet in these battles, the truth is left on the field when the leaders flee. These three parties, the priestcraft, political demagogues and medical faculty are marshalled against the Science of Wisdom, and it is not strange that man should falter and turn back.

What claim do the leaders put forth to convince wisdom that they are right and ought to be sustained? In the first place, the priest advances his opinions, claiming to be a teacher of this unknown truth or science. He embodies it in the image of man, called God, gives Him all power his wisdom is able to condense, and calls on all to obey and worship Him. Science sees no wisdom in such a God, so of course there is not sympathy between the scientific and religious man.

The doctor gives his opinion but the science sees it as nothing but the opinion of persons who lived long ago that they quote, like the priests without any scientific wisdom. So it is with the demagogues. These all made the scientific man of no account, for science is not ambitious; it is not puffed up; it wants no office; it asks no prayers or keeps no fasts; it is perfect harmony. It does not want to be dressed up with a military coat and cap and get on a horse; neither does it wish to dictate to the masses.

Is that the case with opinions? No. Opinion is vain; its happiness is in its vanity; its misery is in its exposure; it seeks low company for popularity and gain; it is hypocritical; it has a face for every position where it can see anything to gain; it fasts; it prays; it talks loud at times and very meekly at other times, and it goes for good order where its interests are concerned. Science is its enemy so it sneers at science, calls it visionary and scheming and warns all men to keep clear of it, refers them to the priests and Bible for instructions not to give heed to any science that goes to put down religion. It is very earnest for freedom, based on an opinion, and this must come from the leaders of these classes of the wise, for it is jealous.

One of these parties is in the world and has an identity. The other is in the world and not recognized. Its opinion is matter, it is seen in man; but as science is wisdom, it is not seen, yet it is acknowledged. Opinion looks upon it as a law without any wisdom or anything like itself. So it is, but nevertheless, it is something that man must respect more than anything else. It is to opinion like the wisdom of the dead, respected when attached to matter, but when the matter is annihilated, the wisdom is without an identity, like a thing that once was but now is not.

To give science an identity you must have a resurrection of the body or wisdom so that man can put himself in it and make it his God and himself. Take George Washington. The man was matter. All men speak of him now as the father of their country. Let us see. Washington had enemies. Did they attach their senses to the same man that his friends did? I say, No. His friends were attached to his wisdom and his wisdom is in the American Constitution and Government. Here is where Washington is, and all the wisdom that is in man's breast that sympathizes with Washington is in the Constitution. Where are his enemies now or that class of hypocrites that pretend to praise Washington? They are found just where they were when they were undermining him or the Constitution by electing Jefferson. All their sympathy was buried in the grave of Washington; and ever since they have denied the resurrection of the truths that the people believed in. So Washington or the Constitution is mocked at and spit upon. This Washington of the truth that is condensed in the Constitution is the very Washington, and ever since opposition to it sprang up, wise men and prophets have foretold that the principles of Washington will rise in the form of the Constitution and man will attach his senses and life to it and feel as though it was a part of his very existence. Then it can be said, "Oh, Rebels, where are your opinions?" "Oh Traitors, where are your graves?" Your graves are in secession, your death is in your acts.

The true living Washington will once more appear in the President of the United States and the devil or secession will be cast out. Men will attach their senses to the new constitution of wisdom; the old constitution of opinions or matter must die to establish the new; then men will not be heard denying the very land that gave them birth. Then Washington will be seen in the Stars and Stripes and secession or the devil will be chained to the earth or opinions as a warning to others not to make war against this truth with the idea of governing the wisdom of God by the prince of darkness. Then opinions will be looked upon as emanating from the world of darkness or error and science from the wisdom of God.

To the natural man every man is a shadow, for he is the opinions of the spiritual man. So when you hear a man giving an opinion, the real man or substance is not seen or known, so of course it is an opinion; for if the thing is known, it is not an opinion but a fact. Let this fact be admitted, that life is something that cannot be seen, only the shadow. This shadow is not life but an echo whose cause you do not see, you only hear the sound; and let it be understood that everything not governed by mathematical truths must be wrong, and then men will be convinced that the cause is not inside the wrong, as an opinion. If you give an opinion it shows that you have a doubt, so the truth is outside the opinion.

This something that I call wisdom is something that does not change, while opinions or matter do change. For illustration, I will take a child. A child knows its mother, not by sight or touch but by its mother's wisdom or love. If the mother could be deceived, the deception might act upon the child, for there being no wisdom in the feelings, the senses or life may be deceived because life contains no art or selfishness.

Life has no inventive powers. It cannot see evil. It is all charity. When it hears of evil it does not understand it, for evil contains restlessness. Life does not. Life will not make war. If it is pressed upon by error or opinions, it leaves and attaches itself to some other idea. Its identity is in knowledge of itself. It is love or an element that fills all space. It cannot be any less or any more. This is life. Its character is sight, smell, taste, hearing and everything that is true, everything that cannot be changed or seen by opinions. It is an element of itself not known in opinions at all. Opinions admit it but call it a mystery.

Aug. 12, 1861

Is There Any Curative Quality in Medicine?
[LC 2:0723]

Common opinion would answer that there is, and according to my opinion there is, but it is all owing to the patient's belief, and to perfect wisdom there is no curative virtue in medicine.

I will relate one case out of a hundred to show how medicine proves itself according to the patient's belief or the direction of some other person. I was attending a gentleman who was sick and he thought he had consumption but was not fully settled in his own mind; so of course he was very nervous. Under this nervousness, the glands around the throat were excited and kept him hacking and raising a white frothy substance and also kept him heated, which heat would he thrown off in a perspiration. After I had told him the cause of his trouble, the explanation so far as he understood it relieved him; he breathed more easily and was improving. One day he read in a paper an advertisement of a medicine which would cure the catarrh and prevent the discharges from the head. Thinking it might cure him, he bought a bottle and commenced taking it; but instead of lessening the secretion, it grew worse and he ran down very fast.

My theory explains the fact in this way. His belief admitted that his head was diseased and in the condition of a sore and that the medicine would cure it. Under this belief the glands of the nose were excited and the medicine then proved his belief that the matter was in his head, for it was taken to make the head discharge. His belief did this by exciting the glands and the medicine was taken to throw it off; so when the matter and even blood commenced running, it showed that the medicine was doing what it agreed to do. But another belief came up that I had given him, for I had exposed the absurdity of medicine; and after he saw the effect, he remembered what I had told him. And abandoning his medicine he returned to me again, and in a few days recovered what he had lost. This is how the disease worked. His own wisdom or knowledge produced the phenomenon; his knowledge gave the medicine the praise or blame just as people give God the praise for their own acts while the devil has to take the blame for their troubles. I have observed the effect of medicine and have found that there is more virtue or misery in the advertisement than in the medicine.

Everyone knows how the mouth will water by a desire for something that the person wants and how the mouth and throat will become parched by fear of detection in crime. This was known by the ancients and magicians, and from the fact that the mind could be changed by fear so that criminals could be detected, those who understood it took advantage of it to detect a thief. The magicians made a paste that would dissolve when laid on the tongue of a person in a perfectly calm state of mind; but in case of unusual warmth or feverish thirst, it would not dissolve. So when a theft was committed by the servants, all the people were collected in one room and the magician was sent for. Believing in his power, their minds of course were controlled by their knowledge; and if the thief were present, he knew it and being sure of detection grew nervous. This would prevent the glands from acting and thus bring out his guilt. The others feeling innocent were safe, for if they were nervous it did not produce the state of mind to prevent the past from dissolving. So the mind was the medium to detect the thief and out of his own mouth he was condemned. People put extravagant confidence in medicine supposing that it contains curative qualities. Frequently Indian doctors appear who have discovered an herb or root to cure some disease that man is afflicted with, as though God had made both the disease and its cure. The same class of people say that God has made a remedy for every disease, showing that their superstition is woven into a belief that God made all diseases and made medicines to cure them. This is the belief of mankind and it is not strange that man has gone out of the way.

Now I disbelieve in diseases and remedies as understood by the world and know that diseases and all their remedies are man's invention and the whole effect is brought about by their own belief. Here is my belief in regard to the way diseases are brought about. If you tell a lie or a truth to a person and the person believes it, the effect on the person is the disease. To cure him is to expose the falsehood to his senses. To do this I use my reason for medicine and it acts as a stimulant or alternative as the case may be, while the doctors apply their remedies in the form of medicine.

Oct. 1862

The Same Subject Concluded.

The opinion that God has provided a remedy for every disease gives rise to a belief that there are certain roots and herbs intended by the Creator to cure all diseases. Absurd as this seems, it is the belief of ninety-nine out of a hundred; and this being the case, a door is open to quackery, for new discoveries will come up every day. Dr. Herrick's pills, Ayers' sarsaparilla, and countless others are advertised as the cure-all, being the result of long acquaintance with vegetable medicines and their curative qualities. Then follow certificates of cures and of recommendations from some M.D., and these give the medicines a run. Next a man comes who exhibits the effect of laughing gas and also states that it will cure neuralgia and rheumatism, and the sick rush to him for a time. After he goes, a learned M.D. arrives with flaming advertisements announcing free lectures on anatomy and the digestive organs. He explains the action of these organs and dwells upon the danger of getting sick by over-eating and drinking, receives some fifty dollars from the poor sick and leaves.

Among the throng of humbugs, when all seems dark and despairing, an announcement is whispered in the ear of the sick that God has opened a way for their recovery and sent an angel of mercy who has discovered a flower that will cure everything that can be cured. So here is introduced an imposter who will give Lobelia emetics till they cease to affect the patient, pretending that all diseases must yield to it. This has its day and another comes up. All this goes to show that the mind of man is like an old fiddle played on by every kind of quackery relating to roots and herbs. Now I know all about these things. With my wisdom I understand them all as Job said to Zophar, "What ye know the same do I know also; I am not inferior unto you." I use nothing, yet I could easily use all kinds of drugs. Then Job said "Ye are forgers of lies, ye all physicians of no value. Oh, that ye would altogether hold your peace and it should be your wisdom." This expresses the opinion of Job about the classes I have mentioned. He said at another time "No doubt that ye are the people and wisdom shall die with you." He saw that these wise men and philosophers were an injury to the progress of science. His God was a God of wisdom and proved all things by his science. Therefore he knew all they knew and saw it was only an opinion. So he said their wisdom would die with them, but he know that his wisdom would not, for his life was in his wisdom and that was his science. He could see that all they said amounted to nothing. Job believed in a God but had not really attached his own senses to his wisdom as a progressive being.

I have seen the working of popular belief and know that diseases and remedies are the invention of man, and the very proof which is brought to establish their wisdom goes to substantiate what I say. For instance, an emetic everyone thinks is to clean out the stomach. So when people have eaten too much, they can take a Lobelia emetic; also if they think their lungs are diseased, take a Lobelia emetic, and if they have the dropsy, take the same. Now I will call your attention to what this belief amounts to carried out toward God. What kind of a God is it that made the earth to bring forth trees, herbs and everything that hath life? All this was before man was created; therefore did He make these medicines and the codfish with a liver to cure consumption before the disease was made? This belief would certainly suppose that God made the remedies before the disease, and if He made all the remedies these quacks say He did, He certainly is the greatest enemy to mankind. Absurd as this sounds, we believe it and are affected by our beliefs, and this makes man the most dependent of all God's creatures. He is merely a target to be fired at by every person's opinion. I can show by facts that every person will admit that no kind of medicine has any more effect of itself than almost any kind of food or drink that we use daily, but our ignorance placed some kind of virtue in them as we place wisdom in some one's opinion. The truth which places all disease in the mind can explain the operation of remedies. God is Wisdom and man is opinion; therefore man cannot live in Wisdom and be diseased. But the child of wisdom reduced to science is held in bondage by opinions, and to show that there are diseases according to the belief of man is to show that they are made by circumstances which cannot be controlled except by correcting the error that brought them about, while ignorance would prescribe some medicine that God had made from the foundation of the world.

October 1862

Is the True Issue of the Rebellion before the People?
[LC 1:0575]

Is the true issue of the rebellion before the people? I say, No. The people are arrayed against each other by false issues. Factions and parties have their idea of the rebellion. One set contends that it is a war to emancipate the blacks, another that it is for the constitution and the laws. The North is divided as they always were for the benefit of the South; the North have no real national idea as a body. The Southern feeling runs through the North and there is a subservient obedience to aristocracy and a sort of servile admiration of a Southern gentleman as though he was superior to a Northern man.

Now the South have one idea that is outside of all the Northern party's feeling, that is, Aristocracy or Slavery. To them the true issue of the rebellion is the extension of slavery. To accomplish this is their sole aim, and for this the North is at loggerheads with each other. So false issues are started by the sympathizers at the North. One is that the South want nothing but their rights, and the abolitionists want to get away their slaves. This splits up the North and at this time there are at the North two parties: one that sustains the administration and the other that opposes it for the South, while the administration are really carrying out the measures of its opponents.

The opponents of the administration say they are in favor of the constitution as it is, and the union as it was, and accuse the President of going contrary to the constitution. This is the Southern party. Now, where do they two differ? One party sustains the President in putting down the rebellion outside of slavery and want nothing at all to do with it. Then there is another party that sustains the President but at the same time sees that its personal sympathy is to sustain the institution of slavery. This creates a sort of irritation, for this class sees that the true issue of the war is the extension of slavery. Now this is the true issue, and how stands the country?

The administration goes to put down the rebellion. Now the rebellion contains two issues: one at the North and the other at the South; therefore it requires two parties. The Northern soldiers are employed to put down the rebellion without having anything to do with slavery, but the Southern sympathizers at the North try to instill the false idea that the war is to free the blacks, thus affecting the prejudices of the officers and soldiers. They neutralize their feeling and demoralize their order. This party are exclusively under the power of the government. The other element, the blacks, are arrayed against the true issue, the extension of perpetual bondage of their race.

As the one idea dies out of the administration, of crushing the rebellion and saving slavery, the people get disheartened and say this course can never bring about a peace. Then the element of freedom sets itself against that of slavery, and at last every other side issue will be out of sight and the true issue that was first started by the South will stand out. Then every person must choose between slavery and death or freedom, for there never was any other issue at the South.

Now if the reader will stop and pause a few moments, he will see that the true issue is the extension of slavery. Slavery is the true issue at the South. The party that made war with it is like a little cloud, black, but increasing till the whole heavens are black. Then the lightning will flash and the fire of revenge will fly from one section to another till the whole heavens will be one vast element of freedom. Then those who are in favor of slavery will flee into the mountains and caves to hide themselves from the light that sets the world free. Those that sit in darkness will see the light spring up and those that sit in the shadow of death will be set free from the cursed evil, African slavery.

1863

Jesus' Healing Power*
[Originally untitled.] [BU 3:0467]

When Jesus called his disciples together and gave them power to heal all diseases and cast out Devils, did he give the power without the knowledge how to apply it or did he give the power with the knowledge? If he gave the knowledge so that it could be applied, are not the ones who apply it better acquainted with the power than those who are ignorant of the power and the knowledge?

All admitted Jesus' power–but it has never been explained or been suggested that it could be. If the power of Jesus was merely a gift, why should he be called God or anything else above his followers? And if he understood how he wrought the miracles, it was a knowledge and not a gift, for to call it a gift deprives Jesus of any knowledge superior to his followers. Admit it as a Science that Jesus taught for the happiness of man and then man will try to learn it. How can it be proved a Science? Never till the people admit that mind and matter are the same, both under a direction of an intelligence superior to them. Then man takes a higher stance and is governed by Science and not by error.

Then matter becomes subject to Science and is the medium or power to be put in motion. This medium can be changed into any form and be destroyed, but not lost. All will admit a person can be deceived into a belief which will make him sick and also to correct his error will make him well. This power is all that Jesus ever intended to convey to the world. It is a Science and it can be learned. It is to unlearn what ignorance and superstition has bequeathed to man.

Jesus, His Belief or Wisdom
[BU 3:1065]

Had Jesus, like other men, a belief? And if so, what was it? To suppose Jesus had a belief is to suppose he was not sure of the truth of his words, but to admit that he knew what he was saying is to believe his words were truth and life, for to know what one says is to know the truth. Therefore all men will admit that Jesus knew and therefore had no belief, and the only question to settle is, What did he intend to convey to the people. It must be something invisible, for Paul, I believe, says, "Eye hath not seen, nor ear heard, neither hath it entered into the heart of man to conceive the things which God hath prepared for them that love him." We are told that Jesus was a religious man. If he was, then his religion was in the world before him, for it is said he was baptized of John.

If Jesus was merely a converted man preaching what John had foretold according to the belief of this world, wherein was his superiority to other preachers; for others also cured the sick and performed miracles. We are told also that Jesus is of God. Then where is the God principle in Jesus more than in any man who does the works that he did. To me these stories are all the inventions of the priests. I will try to place Jesus before the people, not as the world places him, but as he places himself, and it will then be seen if he ever taught the doctrines that are attributed to him. In the first place, I deny that Jesus ever intended to teach any doctrine of rewards and punishments or ever hint about a future state, as it is said that he did. If Jesus had no other motive than to tell man of another world, if his words were not applied solely to this life, then his wisdom was a failure. He taught the Science of God which destroyed all religion and introduced a higher wisdom based on eternal wisdom.

The fruits of this wisdom taught by him were in opening the eyes of the blind or ignorant, in loosing the tongue of the dumb, and breaking the chains of those bound by party or priest. I believe that Jesus was the very man prepared before the creation to receive this great truth when the time came, but that he had no knowledge of it, any more than Columbus had that he was the man to discover this continent. Wisdom acts through matter, and matter must go through a certain process of refinement before it can become a medium of any science. At the time of Jesus the world was in darkness in regard to man's future state. Society was divided into sects, and priests by their craft ruled the masses and kept them in bondage, constantly frightening them with what would come after death. Lucretius who lived one hundred and fifty years before Christ gives a true account of the religion of his day which could not have varied much from that of the time of Jesus.

I will quote an extract from his poem. After describing the horrors of religion, he says, "But still I fear your caution will dispute the maxims I lay down, who all your life have trembled at the poets' frightful tales. Alas! I could even now invent such dreams as would pervert the strictest rules of reason and make your fortunes tumble to the bottom. No wonder! But if men were once convinced that death was the sure end of all their pains, they might with reason resist the force of all religion, and contemn the threats of poets. Now we have no sense, no power to strive against this prejudice because we fear a scene of endless torments after death." To suppose that Jesus taught any such religion, as is here referred to, is to put him on a level with the priests. Opposition to the popular religion was sure death and he was forced to come in conflict with it. It is absurd to say he was a come-outer from any sect, for he says, My kingdom is not of this world, but your kingdom is of this world and it must fall. Let the word kingdom represent happiness arising from wisdom, or misery arising from a belief, and then it follows that his wisdom was to make men happy or to establish the kingdom of heaven within them, while their belief made the kingdom of darkness wherein men were sick and wicked.

His religion was based on his wisdom and theirs on their belief. The difference made trouble. He knew that their religion was based on no true foundation, and that their future state was a heathen belief; therefore to them he was an infidel and blasphemer in the same manner as anyone at the present day who opposes the popular religion is an infidel. If Jesus should appear among men now, he would be an infidel to the religious, the same as he was eighteen hundred years ago. It may be asked what was the religion of Jesus? I answer, his life, spent in benefiting mankind. He did not labor to save man from another world but from the evils of this world. He knew that the other world was an evil that the priests had invented to keep man in subjection.

But had Jesus no belief? To himself I think not, but to the world his wisdom was a belief. To him his wisdom embraced all things and he was the medium of it. His religion, if you please to call it religion, was based on an actual truth that could become a practical thing. If a person wishes to teach a science, he explains it by the best demonstrations or proofs he can, for science, like religion, is seen only by its works. Jesus says, "Many shall say, Lo here is Christ, but by their fruits ye shall know them." As I understand the religion of Jesus, it sweeps away all religious beliefs and opinions and leaves man to act on scientific principles of truth. It takes away belief and in its place substitutes knowledge of good and evil. He disbelieved in death, in heaven and hell. He believed in endless happiness and misery and that every idle word should be accounted for at the day of judgment. He believed that just as a man measured out to his neighbor, so it should be measured out to him. And that if a person commit a sin, knowing it to be such, there is no forgiveness; he must be punished for it.

He believed that all manner of sin might be forgiven but that the sin against the Holy Ghost should not be forgiven in this world nor in the world to come. Man must be born again in order to enter heaven. He did not believe that it was intended by wisdom that the child should suffer for the sins of its parents but that it must suffer for its own errors. These are the truths Jesus taught; although I have used the word belief in stating them, I believe them all. Who is there willing to be tested by them? They are also statements of the belief of the world at the time of Jesus, but to these were added the belief that the priests could pardon their sins. Although the same words express both the belief of the world and the truth of Jesus, the difference was that one was based on an opinion and the other on true wisdom.

The priests believed in a heaven, a hell, and a devil and also in the doctrine of salvation by works. These were also embraced in the teaching of Jesus, yet he was in conflict with the religion of the priests and the controversy was upon beliefs. His was a religion of works, theirs of beliefs. One was law, the other was gospel. One was an invention, the other was eternal truth. The priests believed that in order to make man pure and holy, it was necessary to believe in their doctrines. Jesus knew that such a system was false and hypocritical, benefiting only the priests. The idea that a belief was connected with man's health, as cause is connected with effect, had never been presented to the world. Jesus knew that all there is of man that can be affected is his belief, that his wisdom is of God and cannot change, while his belief is of man.

Man makes himself, that is, his spiritual, moral, and mental condition by his belief, and to destroy that is death to the belief, and life to the truth. One religion was applied to man as a belief, while the other applied to man as a principle. The priests reached no higher intelligence than matter. Therefore mind and matter composed the whole man, while the soul was an unsettled question. Jesus divided man into three persons: Father, Son and Holy Ghost; the Christian church at the present time assume to do the same, but there is as much difference between them as between the early heathen beliefs and the wisdom of Jesus. Jesus did not confirm one article of their belief, nor did he in his parables refer to man's future state. Two separate principles are found in his words: the truth which came directly from him, and the error which is the interpretation given by the church. He did not directly attack the mode of worship but brought it in when he exposed the absurdity of their beliefs. Had he lived in these days, he would not have been a religious man according to the church, and yet he taught every element necessary to make a perfect man, not a religious man, but one who would do unto another as he would that another should do unto him.

When Jesus taught this truth, his object must have been different from that of the priest who merely sustained an old system. The very fact that men have such a blind reverence for the Bible shows that there is concealed within its lids something that cannot be seen. It is this something that affects the people, making some insane and some infidels, while there are others who appreciate and reverence it without understanding it. They are affected by the truth, though they do not know it. The Bible cannot speak for itself; therefore all interpretations have equal claims to wisdom, and this is why there is so much skepticism in regard to its true meaning. It is supposed that the learned are best able to explain it, but could they explain it in the days of Jesus? No, for he says his words are foolishness to the Greeks and to the Jews stumbling blocks. Is it the rich? Jesus says it is easier for a camel to go through the eye of a needle than for a rich man to enter into the kingdom of heaven.

When Jesus was on earth, no one understood him but now all think they know his meaning. I, like others, once believed that Jesus came to save man from eternal damnation and to point out the way to another world, but my practice with the sick has produced an entire change in my mind in regard to that subject. If any of Jesus' truth lingers in the religion of the world, it would be seen in the sick, who are just on the verge of another world, as they believe. Yet I have learned by sitting with them that the religious belief is the worst torment one can have at such a time. Although they may say that they rejoice in Christ and are ready to go, they are really afraid and show as much joy when I tell them they will not die as a condemned criminal feels when, kneeling upon his coffin, he hears the words of pardon.

It requires a long time to bring a person into this insane state when he wishes to die. Severe sickness and trouble are necessary to make one ready to leave friends and all earthly ties. It is the same with any fear, diseases for instance. There will be more cases of cholera during a panic than if the presence of the disease was not known. Ghosts are always seen in the dark by those only who fear them. All these evils are caused by the fear of death and it is included in religious instruction that they exist in another world, for men are called upon to accept the summons which calls them to God. This other world contains heaven and hell, with their terrors and rewards, and the Bible is introduced to prove them.

In the days of Jesus, the priests proved these same evils by the Old Testament but he exposed the folly of their belief and showed them that they did not understand the scriptures. His controversy with them makes the New Testament, and the priests of our day will still preach this old belief in another world which they declare is taught by Jesus, while his whole labor was to destroy it in their belief. He failed to do this because of their superstition and their prejudice, yet the truth was in him, and like the good sower he went forth to sow the seeds of truth in man's mind. Some seeds were choked by superstition and were unfruitful, while others fell upon good soil and came forth. The truth could not grow on religious soil, for that stifles discussion. But it grew outside of the church in the hearts of men and shed its light on those who never bowed their knee to the church but who were a law unto themselves.

The other world taught by the church is out of sight and out of the reach to the natural world, but it is said to be the place where all men must go, sooner or later. As it is taught by Jesus, it is a condition corresponding to man's ignorance containing all the evils of imperfect knowledge but differing in every respect from the other world of the priests. They said it was a part of God's Providence. Jesus declared that it existed only in the errors of their belief. According to the priests, the inhabitants of this world are to be transferred at death to the world beyond, there to be dealt with according as their acts in this life demand. The exact limits of the other world were not defined and the idea was started that the inhabitants might return to earth again. Thus arose the belief in transmigration and spiritual communications. Speaking of this belief, Lucretius describes the stately palaces of "Acheron where nor our souls or bodies ever come but certain specters strange and wondrous pale" and how "Homer's ever celebrated shade appeared," etc. Ennius, a Latin poet, who lived a hundred years before Lucretius, held to the transmigration of souls. He affirmed that the soul of Homer was in his body. The ancients held that ghosts were a third of nature, of which together with body and soul the whole man consisted. These specters and shadows of the dead appear or seem to appear when we are asleep or awake and sick and terrify our minds.

It appears from this that there is but little difference between the ancient belief in a future state and the present religious belief in another world. Religious doctrines were the same in the days of Jesus as they are now. There was the spiritualist then, as in modern days, and it can be shown that every modern creed started from the religion which was before Christ and which Jesus opposed. Such ideas as those I have quoted are admitted by every reformer but modified as science gained ground. They cannot be explained away so long as their foundations exist, and they will exist till a new philosophy leads man through the wilderness of progressive knowledge.

What has the religious belief done to enlighten man in regard to his life or in regard to any science? Nothing. Science, steadily developing, has forced the church from its ground, while the church has claimed the credit of the increasing intelligence. Yet it has been an important instrument in civilization because it has held the people till wisdom could spring up in their minds. But it has been a prison and when science burst its bands and freed the prisoners, each assumed a character outside the church. The church is as necessary for the mass of the people as state laws, yet there are those who require no laws of church or state to regulate their conduct. Knowing what is for their good, they live by the light of science and they feel that their religion is their life; and in order to put it in practice, something more than mere profession is necessary. Therefore they labor to develop some truth that is for the benefit of mankind. This is the design of wisdom, and Jesus being the medium of it, I base my faith on the rock on which he stood, which rock is Christ or the Science of God, and no opinion of religion must destroy it.

The church in misrepresenting Jesus has proved itself his worst enemy. Jesus stands to the church as the law to the criminal. The vicious man hates the law for he dislikes to live up to its standard. The church ignorantly worships God because it dislikes the labor of seeking to understand him. All religion is of the law and therefore it cannot save man from sin, but Christ or Science coming through Jesus puts an end to religion and law and introduces a higher principle of wisdom which shall save all who understand.

Jesus was a priest, not after the old priesthood, but after the order of Melchizedek. This was of wisdom; therefore unlike the priesthood of Aaron, it requires no prayers or sacrifices, for in such it took no delight. The religion of the Jews commenced with the creation of man and in applying the principles of wisdom to their religion. Jesus admitted every fact of their belief and interpreted it as a symbol of truth. They started at the garden of Eden, not as a natural garden but as a figure of innocence, representing man in his infancy. Jesus illustrated the condition of man before he began to investigate, by the figure of a child, whose parents were truth and error. The religious people believe that if Adam had not eaten the forbidden fruit, he would not have died. Jesus showed that if the child had not improved since its birth, it would have continued in a brutal state of bliss and would never have gained happiness. Therefore the death of Adam represented the introduction of progression. In the wisdom of Jesus, the word death means simply the change from brutish ignorance to a higher state of knowledge, but to the religious world it is a real thing for the dead never rise. Jesus represents Adam and Eve as two opposite principles in man and his body as a garden, where fruits were the offspring of ideas. True ideas simply nourish the body in innocence but the food from the tree of the knowledge of good and evil causes death to that state of bliss.

The religious world put a false construction on this passage, believing that the act of eating the forbidden fruit was an act of disobedience and that it brought into the world the long train of evils that have followed civilization. Jesus, knowing that this was a false belief, brought a child among them and said, Of such is the kingdom of heaven and except ye become as a little child, ye can in no wise enter the kingdom of heaven. Religion could not enter for it believed that the kingdom of heaven was in another world apart from this world, as two countries are separate from each other. Jesus admitted the two worlds not as places but as conditions of mind. But the people believed that heaven is a place to which the good go at death, and hell where the bad go. So the illustration of the child was a mystery to them. With Jesus the kingdom of heaven is the effect of wisdom, and to enter into it, man must do something that is contained in wisdom.

The child is a representative of the earth and its ideas like seeds in the earth, and its growth like a vineyard. The vineyard, Jesus said, is cultivated by stewards and if the steward is of error, the Lord, when he comes, will put him out and put in the truth. So as error dies, truth lives.

Every man is a representative of the natural and spiritual worlds, as taught in the religion of Jesus and illustrated in his life and death. The natural world spoken of by Jesus is mans belief and the knowledge of the truth is the spiritual world. And as opinions and error (the natural world) died, truth and science rose from the dead; the dead opinions did not rise, for God is not the God of the dead but of the living truth. As man has borne the image of error he shall also bear the image of wisdom. Like other men Jesus bore the image of opinions but he also bore that of God or science.

To the world his science was a belief, but as such it was a mere casket that once contained life. To Christ a belief contained no life or truth but like all matter was liable to perish. So he labored to demonstrate his theory and establish it as a science for the benefit of mankind. Therefore he applied the principles of his wisdom to man's condition. He saw that troubles of every kind originate in belief and in order to relieve these he must change his belief. For this purpose he came into the world, as it is called, not into the natural globe, but into the errors of man. Jesus was all that was seen by the religious world. Christ was never seen. Yet Christ was in Jesus and through him entered the world of opinions to reconcile the opinions to truth and to establish the kingdom of heaven in man's mind as a science. Hence Jesus preached his truth for the healing of the nations from the errors of their belief. Everyone who believed in a doctrine containing punishment was liable to be punished; therefore he urged repentance towards the wisdom that would explain their errors and forgive their sins. Reading the New Testament with this chart, you will see that the world to be saved is man's, the vast domain of man's religious understanding which had been enslaved by the priest, that all men had gone out of the way and none thought right. To save them from their consequent sick and disheartened condition, Jesus opened their eyes to their religious errors, loosed the bands of opinion and prejudice and set the captive free from the prison of his belief.

When he cured the sick he saved them from the other world into which the priest was forcing them, for he never entertained any idea of "another world" as taught by religion, ancient or modern. Christ taught Jesus that man is a progressive being, that his existence is a part of God, that the two worlds were an invention, and death was an error of belief and not a reality of truth. Consequently, life and death being conditions, if a person believes he will die, the belief does not alter the fact, but it keeps a man continually subject to the fear of death. It also taught that man can in no wise avoid the punishment following a wrong act whether he knew that the act was wrong when he committed it or not, for action and reaction are equal and this is true both in matter and spirit.

A man cannot walk into the fire without being burned, and no amount of prayers to God will prevent it, but he is answerable only to himself for his act, not to an offended God. The knowledge of this will save man from the evils that he himself has made and will teach him that the principles of right and wrong are contained in every thought.

If I tell a man a lie and he believes it, he receives the punishment that follows and I too get my just reward, for as we measure out to another so we measure out to ourselves. If I wrong a man, I do not wait for him to repay me; I first wrong myself, for a pure fountain cannot send forth impure water, and neither can an honest man do a dishonest act. He must first become dishonest in order to injure another; therefore Jesus says, "First cast out the beam out of thine own eye and then thou shalt see clearly to cast out the mote from thy brother's eye." These two "brothers" represent the two principles of truth and error in one man. They are also introduced in the passage where Paul says, "If meat make my brother to offend, I will eat no flesh while the world standeth." Here Paul did not refer to any other but himself. Under this interpretation, the passage means: If meat makes my error or my belief in dyspepsia to offend, then I will eat no meat till I explain why I cannot, or work myself out of the error. So when he arrives at the truth, the opinion is destroyed and he has entered the new world where he can eat meat.

Jesus told his disciples that his belief would be destroyed by the religious world but that his science would rise from the destruction. To them this was a mystery, for in regard to life and death they were in their old religious belief. To believe that their idea Jesus should both live and die was a contradiction; it was impossible. He must be dead or not dead; if dead, then the dead must rise. Jesus denied this in his dispute with the Sadducees when he said, "God is not the God of the dead but of the living." But they did not understand him because of their religious prejudices. At another time he said, "Yet a little while am I with you and then I go unto him that sent me. Ye shall seek me and shall not find me and where I am, thither ye cannot come." These words were also misunderstood by the disciples from the darkness of their belief. I will explain them as I understand them.

Christ is that unseen principle in man, of which he is conscious but which he has never considered as intelligence. It is God in us, and when man arrives at that state that he can recognize an intelligence that transcends belief, then death is swallowed up in wisdom. All will acknowledge that every scientific discovery might have been known before, that is, the truth existed before we knew it. We, in like manner, have an existence as active in itself as man in his opinions, but both cannot be seen at the same time for as one dies the other rises.

To put man in possession of this truth, it is necessary to destroy the entire religious belief. Jesus endeavored to do this in order to convince man that his only true living self was the science of God. He also labored to prove that the sympathy that we feel towards each other is a living being with all the attributes of intelligence and that it remains when the natural man is destroyed. This was science to him, and its truth said, "I come again," etc.

I believe that Jesus came to convince man of this truth; I believe it and practice it so far as I understand it. The world, or man's belief, accuses me of making myself equal to Christ as they accused Jesus of making himself equal to God. One of these accusers can visit the sick and with a long face ask God to hear his prayers and raise the sufferer; then if the patient recovers he believes that God blessed the means. But if I attribute my cures to God or Christ, the whole church is against me, and I am accused of making myself equal to Christ. They are not so sensitive about Christ, but it is their own reputation that they fear; they claim to be the ordained instruments of God and if man is saved it must be by their means. Jesus who opposed priestcraft met the same difficulty. It was the duty of the priests to care for men's souls; therefore he must not enter upon that ground, else he make himself equal to them, which was blasphemy.

Jesus opposed the doctrine of another world and taught that man continued progressing; therefore at his crucifixion, when the idea matter was killed by opinions, the Christ that governed it was forced away. The casket or idea was left with the disciples and this to them was death. To see a form of Jesus was either to see a spirit or a resurrection of the old form. To him the science was different. He suffered as a man suffers the penalty of the law. The law of religion said he must die, and when they saw the law of their belief fulfilled, this was the end to the law of man. Now it was necessary that the new revelation of Christ should come to pass and he should show himself to his disciples and others. Therefore the law did what is done by persons now; it put him into a state of unconsciousness, not that he might die, for his belief was that he would return, and the difference of belief made the controversy.

Jesus, like a clairvoyant, went from the idea on the cross to fulfill his promise to the disciples. Unconscious of change, he believed he had flesh and blood and when they thought he was a spirit, he said, "Hath a spirit flesh and bones as ye see me have?" Here he destroyed the belief in death and triumphed over the grave.

Knowledge of God in Man, The*
[Originally untitled.] [BU 3:0418]

You ask if it is by mesmerism or electricity that Dr. Q. is enabled to perform his cures, which to the world seems as miraculous without the aid of medicine or any external treatment? The question presented answers itself before it is finished. The enquirer at the commencement makes use of words as though he understood their meaning and if understood then all questioning is at an end–for what we know we have no idea about, but know it wherever we see it: but if not known, then why use words that have no meaning in themselves, only to give form to an idea or phenomenon that never has been explained, judged only by its outward appearance, accepted on the platform of opinion, and presented to the world as knowledge: thus deceiving the people giving them stone when they ask for bread.

All knowledge which is accepted that has only an opinion for its bases, like the house built upon the sand, is overthrown by the test of investigation, and wafted into oblivion by the breath of true knowledge.

The opinion like a whited sepulcher to hide its nakedness or ignorance, comes forth gaudily arrayed with pompous airs and lordly speech, the fringe of its garment tinged with every idea that ignorance can possibly invent, so to attract by its seeming purity the traveler in his journey, and by so doing, draw him unconsciously to bow at its shrine or belief. And if any do pass it unheedingly by, they are cried out at as Infidels, devoid of all forms of Godliness–I will give you a sketch of the belief of an opinion. It believes in the idea of life and death in the body–it also believes in the idea of disease, and that its causes are all in the natural world, and when man violates any of the laws of the natural world, disease commences its work on the body to destroy its life–so to keep the body alive is to keep disease out, and in order to do this, man must obey all the orders of the Dr. who keeps the rules of health ready and made out; and the name of the disease that will consequently follow if the law is not strictly adhered to.

So man takes this guide book for his life and walks by it, until he finds he can walk no longer–and the world says it's because he did not ask the doctor in time–if he had he wouldn't have got worse–but it's too late now, the disease has gone forth and his days are numbered. Nothing now must be thought of but his soul. So he consults the minister as to what he must do in this trying hour.

He is questioned if he believes thus and so about God, whether he is willing to give up the world and die, that he may go and live with God, who knows what is best or he would not afflict him thus with pain, but when he dies he will be free from pain. If he believes this he is safe and will be forever happy.

So he believes for he dares not do otherwise, and dies a most triumphant death, and his soul goes to God who gave it. Thus is the world deluded by false knowledge into this belief of an opinion of which contains all knowledge but true knowledge, for it gives utterance to no speech as a watch-word from the arms of contention.

Now Dr. Q. differs from all others of his day in regard to the idea called disease–he comes before the world with no belief but his knowledge independent of all form–like a house whose foundation is a rock or truth, against which the wind of ignorance may blow its piercing blast, and the flood of percussion surround its wall, yet it grieves not for it is built upon a principle and will stand a living monument in its Science. For to believe in death is not to believe in life, for death is not life, and to believe in life is not to believe in death–and to believe that life and death is in man, and man is in the body, and that the body dies, is to believe that man dies when the body dies, and to believe that the body is destroyed by disease arising from natural causes–is to believe that the man has no life but in what is seen in a form through the natural senses. So when this form or body is not seen through the senses, man is no more alive, but dead.

Now this belief embraces nothing but death. Its birth is ignorance; it lives in ignorance, and dies in ignorance of the life it has lived. Therefore its death proves nothing of a life after death for ignorance is darkness and darkness sends forth no light to prove that it has any knowledge of what light is; and a knowledge that can't be proved is not true knowledge but false to what it professes and is destroyed by true knowledge which is light and sees no darkness but in its light. These two elements govern man and what is called life in man, as they are directed by the light of each element called soul, and the effect of the light shows itself on the body, which is used as a medium for the soul or light to cast its shadows upon. This light is very sensitive to any light which throws a shadow upon it, and if not understood, it believes it has come to destroy its life, and its belief increases the shadow till it puts all light into its darkness–And this is called by believers in darkness, disease and death.

But when this light is understood to be light, it is not afraid of any shadow that it may meet with, called disease, for it knows its own power, that it can cast out all darkness, but putting its light into the darkness, thereby destroying the darkness or death by bringing it to the light of life. This knowledge is not acquired through the natural senses, but is known only through the sense of the senses. It is not confined to any form or body, but contains all the knowledge of the body, and acts independent of a form and controls the body; and as man understands himself he understands those two lights, and sees the power of one will destroy the light of the other by bringing them both to one great light, which is a knowledge of God or Science–And it's by this knowledge of the God in man, which Dr. Q. has unwaveringly struggled to obtain his power to heal all disease.

For the knowledge of the natural world is foolishness to the scientific world.

March 1864

Language [The King's English]
[BU 3:0580]

How often you hear these words used: Such a person murders the King's English. This I admit is true if you apply language to the things in this natural world, but if it is applied to the spiritual world or ideas that cannot be seen by the natural man, then I beg leave to differ from the knowledge of this world, for I know it is false. In the first place, a healthy person is not a judge of a sick person's feelings. Therefore, if anyone gives a name to a feeling which a sick person has, he names a sensation that he knows nothing of, except as described by the sick. In this there is no standard of right and wrong that the people can agree upon, so everyone sets up his standard of right and wrong, and if a person is ever so sensitive to another's feelings, he must use such terms as the world sets up or he is ignorant of the King's English. So the invisible things must be judged by the visible. Here is the great mistake, for if the learned had to prove to the unlearned everything they said, it would be as hard as for those who are sensitive to these sensations to prove them to the learned. Who is to say what God is? Webster, Worcester or any author, unless he can give some evidence that comes within a person's feeling or senses? Here is where the trouble commences with this idea of God. What is God? This is the question, and let the man come forward and show who and what God is.

The word God is the name of something material or immaterial. If He is material, then God can be seen by material eyes; and if He is immaterial, the natural man cannot see Him. So that if His name sprang from the natural man, he gives a name of something that he knows nothing of, only as is seen in matter or that comes within his feelings. Therefore, one man's opinion is as good as another's till someone can give the substance or impression that caused that word to be applied. Now suppose that man calls wisdom the first cause and that from this wisdom there issues forth an essence that fills all space, like the odor of a rose. This essence, like the odor, contains the character and wisdom of its father or author and your wisdom wants man to give it a name; so man calls this essence, God. Then you have wisdom manifest in this God or essence. Then this essence would be called the son of wisdom. Let wisdom say to God or the son: Let us create matter or mind or man in our own image, or in the likeness of this essence or God. So they formed man out of the odor called matter or dust that rises from the grosser matter and breathed into him the living essence or God, and the matter took the form of man.

October 1860

Language [I]
[LC 1:0405]

Language is the invention of man to convey some idea of a material substance, that can be seen or described. It never entered the mind of the author of language to describe another's thoughts, so that to describe to a person (his own feelings by language) which was never intended for that purpose, necessarily confuses the learned. Everyone knows that as man is developed, he becomes more sensitive to impressions. This makes him superior to the beasts. If man is ignorant of all the influences that act upon him, he is nothing but a subdued brute, but if his higher intellect is developed, it needs a language to explain it. Sickness is the result of the animal or natural man binding burdens on the higher intelligence or scientific mind. The burdens are the opinions of the so-called wise, and language is for their benefit. So the groans and griefs of the sick are heard by the well only as a murmur or unknown tongue.

Having given my attention to their lamentations, I know that they have a language not known by the learned or well, and this language I have been trying to develop that I may bring before the wise the grievances of the sick. So I am forced to use words that will convey the most correct idea of their feelings. This is difficult; some words convey life and yet do not mean anything. For instance, take the word mind. The ordinary definition of that word covers all the wisdom of the natural man. The word death means the annihilation of life. But as man developed himself, he discovered that there was something in him that never had been brought out, and this something gave rise to speculative ideas. When phenomena occurred, the wise were confused. So superstition and reason were introduced to explain the phenomena. They must be explained by the language of the wise and that made confusion. This theory explains all these ideas by applying words to sensations that will convey to the sick that I take their feelings. When I tell them how they feel, I tell them it is in their mind. This of course they do not believe. So to make myself understood, I am obliged to illustrate by parables. Here is one of my parables:

Parable

When sitting by a sick person who had a pain in the left side which I felt and described to the patient, I said, You think you have consumption. The patient acknowledged it, saying that her doctor had examined her lungs and found the left one very much affected. This she believed and when I told her that her disease was in her mind, it was as much as to say she imagined what was not the case. I told her she did not understand what I meant by the word mind. Then taking up a glass of water I said, Suppose you should be told that this water contained a poisonous substance that works in the system and sometimes produces consumption. If you really believe it, every time you drink the idea of poison enters your mind. Presently you begin to hack and cough a little. Would your fears then grow less that the water was poison? I think not. Finally you are given over by your doctor and friends and call on me. I sit down by you and tell you that you are nervous and have been deceived by your doctor and friends. You ask how? You have been told what is false, that the water you drink contains a slow poison, and now your cure hangs on the testimony in the case. If I show that there is no poison in the water, then the water did not poison you. What did? It was the doctor's opinion put in the water by your mind. As the mind is something that can receive an impression, it can be changed. This change was wrought by the doctor's opinion; so calling mind something, it is easy to show that it can be changed by a wisdom superior to an opinion. This wisdom that acts upon the mind is something that never has been described by language, but it is admitted by the wise and looked upon as a superior power. This power gives rise to all religious opinions. Man has tried to condense it into a being called God, and he worships it. My theory is based on this something that man is ignorant of and develops from it a language as comprehensible as any language. It contains no words but speaks from impressions which cannot be mistaken if man knows himself. This language is the feelings of the sick, and to convey these feelings to the well, so that they may have some idea of the misery of the sick and its causes, has been my study for twenty years. I feel now that my labors have not been in vain. Arranging words to convey this truth to the well is a task very few would like to go through. But I think now that I have succeeded so that any person of ordinary talent can see that it is the key to unlock the mysteries of the spiritual world.

Aug. 5, 1861

Language [II]
[BU 3:0815]

In introducing my ideas to the world I labor under the disadvantage as anyone does who seeks to bring into language what has never been embodied in thought or words. In early ages, a celebrated Roman presented his philosophy in a poem and finding great difficulty in making himself understood he thus apologized for his language:

> I know 'tis hard to explain in Latin verse
> The dark mystic notions of the Greeks,
> (For I have things to say, require new words
> Because the tongue is poor, the subject new)
> But your virtue and the pleasure I expect
> From tender friendship, makes me bear the toil
> And spend the silent night with watchful eyes
> Studious of words and numbers I shall use
> To open to your mind such scenes of light
> Which show the hidden qualities of things unknown.

If he, who commenced with man in matter, reasoned him body and soul out of matter, dissolved him into space and finally lost him, found language inadequate to his subject, some sympathy can be had for one who has struggled day and night to rid himself of the earthly matter and rise triumphant into the world of Science whence matter is seen moving as though it contained life. Wisdom is a solid truth and truth cannot be increased or diminished. Therefore, wisdom fills all space. Let us try to identify man in this wisdom that has no matter. A man's wisdom contains his memory of events and his identity of himself as a man. He knows he has a body and this is not matter but wisdom. To make a man lose his knowledge that he has legs is to deprive him of his wisdom as far as his legs are concerned. And if his wisdom is his belief, that can be dissolved so that he cannot have any identity at all; then where is he? An answer in part may be found in Job 4th Ch. where a spirit passed before the Temanite, showing the difference between the spiritual and natural man.

For a further illustration, take two rose bushes, one bearing a white rose and the other a red. Let these represent two children of different complexions. Call the rose the brain or intellect. From each child flows wisdom, as fragrance comes from the rose, and at first it is confined to the brain. The idea of an intelligence outside of the brain is a mystery. But like odors, their intellects mingle, forming a new combination in the mind and this process goes on till the intellect sees that it contains all the elements of the brain as the odor contains the substance of the rose. Finally, the children get to that state where they see and reason that matter dissolved contains the elements of man and here they stop. For in their reason they never count themselves but speak as though matter is the only thing that contains life. Now touch the one who reasons and ask him who it is that talks, the brain or the intelligence. If the odor or intelligence speaks, then it has language, but if there is an intelligence in the odor that speaks, then it speaks in and through the odor and makes itself felt by the rose or brain. I will explain this by what passes while sitting by a sick person.

Every belief contains matter or ideas which throw off an odor like a rose. The white and red roses throw off their peculiar odors. The white is white to itself and the red is red to itself. In like manner, man throws off two odors: one matter and the other wisdom. As wisdom is in the odor of man, it is disturbed by the matter or mind which also has an odor that is like a polished mirror and the fear is the image of the belief. Wisdom sees the image in the mirror, held there by its fear. My wisdom disturbs the opinion. This affects the belief; this deadens the mirror till the image or disease is gone; then this is health.

I find that I am not generally understood when I say mind is matter. Words are not matter but they are the names of something either matter or solid. The word solid cannot be applied to anything that can be changed. Therefore, it must be applied to wisdom because that fills all space and cannot be made larger or denser; it is in and through all matter, which is called solid. I apply the word only to wisdom. Opinions I call matter, for they can be changed. The word does not change but the substance does. All names, as I have said, are to represent something. As this wisdom which fills all space is in all matter, matter seems to have life of itself. But life is in the knowledge of this change, not in the thing that changes. So when I say all disease is in the mind, I do not mean in the word, but in the substance. For instance, all the elements of the rose are in the odor; and if the word matter is applied to the rose or living bush, the odor would represent its mind or wisdom, but the wisdom that spoke the rose into existence is not a part of either; yet it holds it in all its different combinations.

The word wisdom embraces science, for that is the name of wisdom reduced to practice. There is no science or wisdom in opinions or belief so they are embraced in the word mind, for mind embraces all that can be seen of man. I do not believe that because man has invented words to destroy himself, he is destroyed; but that being ignorant of himself he supposes he is something apart from wisdom; and that when he knows himself he will see that the very wisdom that speaks, speaks through the very mind or matter. To illustrate that the eternal principle of wisdom, which is in matter, is not a part of it, but outside of it, as much as a man's sight is outside his spectacles, I once put a lady into a mesmeric state, that the doctor might extract a needle from her arm. I was seated by her. She had every sense and faculty as perfect as in her waking state, but she contained no matter except as an idea. Therefore pain was an idea and she had sympathy according to her wisdom. And being in sympathy with me, she took her arm for mine. According to her belief, to cut my arm must pain me, so she said, Does it not hurt you? I said, No, and she replied, I should think it would.

Here were two persons: one coming within my senses, as a being of mind, the other I was not aware of. This unknown person still lived with all the faculties and wisdom of herself, while the earthly body was as lifeless and unfeeling as marble. This unseen person is the real person and to deceive her is to make her grieve, not for herself but for the man of matter. Every sensation is a disturbance of this mind and every idea is made of this matter. And matter is constantly throwing off particles each of which contains the elements of the idea. Ideas are as separate as living seeds. An apple will not bring forth a pear, neither will the seed or idea of consumption produce liver complaint. But a pear may be engrafted into an apple tree and so can spinal disease be engrafted into consumption. Each disease throws from itself particles which contain the elements of the original idea. This atmosphere or odor is like a mirror and the idea is in it. This is seen by the other life or identity which I call wisdom, which becomes disturbed from sympathy with the person in this odor or belief. To make my meaning plain, I must represent two men, one sick and the other in health; one, a man of opinions and the other a man of wisdom. Wisdom is not science but truth, which reduced to practice is called science. To know that you exist is a truth; to prove that you always will exist is a science, because man has not the wisdom to understand himself. It is a truth that we have a body called matter and it is a truth that we believe it will die, but it is not a truth that it will live again, for this is merely an opinion and must admit a doubt. Wisdom does not admit a doubt, and whether we are of wisdom or of matter is the problem to solve. Here is where man had arrived at the time that Jesus came before the world. Philosophy had reasoned and proved that all which constitute man must change and therefore must be matter. But the religious community believed that this matter was reunited at the end of the world and took its identity.

November 1862

Language–Part I
[LC 1:0513]

One great error that man has to contend with is language. To repeat language is a mere effort of memory and to tell the meaning of words is the same. Now language was invented to convey some idea and not to be used without any meaning. Every word contains either something or nothing and goes to help make up an idea or form or belief in something. There are words used that convey the true idea. The word nothing conveys an empty space and no person expects to see or feel any effect from the word. But there are other words that convey to our senses matter in some form. Yet, when analyzed, they contain not one particle of matter or substance any more than the word nothing. Now I shall show that there are a class of persons who pretend to know all about the original language, yet they use words and give the definition of them so that they have no meaning at all.

All persons will agree on what there is no chance to differ. If I show that words are used as empty of matter as the word nothing, then it will be seen that there is a chance for improvement. Every word that is spoken conveys to a person the idea of something, but the same word may convey to another, nothing. For instance, I say to a child, Did you ever see a bear? Now the word to me contains the matter to make the bear, yet to the child, it is an empty sound. If I do not impart something from the idea to the child, he is profited nothing. If I persist in impressing the child's matter with the idea till the senses become cognizant of the fact, then the child is wiser. But if I do not, the talk is an empty sound. Therefore words, although to me they may contain something, still, if I have not the power of imparting the substance to another, they are as nothing.

Every word is filled with something in the form of matter. This something is thrown out by the person who uses the word and this affects another mind in the form of a sensation. Now if the sensation is not recognized by the person that receives it, then it excites their curiosity to learn the cause. I will suppose a case, for sensation contains no wisdom to the person receiving it till he is made acquainted with the substance of the thing spoken. If a Frenchman should ask a person (in French), Have you ever seen a cat? If the person addressed was ignorant of French, to him the word would contain no wisdom, although the Frenchman had wisdom. But the wisdom was in him and not in the words. While they are talking a cat comes into the room, and the Frenchman says, Voila un chat. Now he has imparted his meaning and both have wisdom in regard to the animal, but the wisdom is in them and not in the cat. Now here is the trinity in the principles of reason. The word is the name of the Father, the cat or matter, the Son or theory and the application of the word to the animal was the Holy Ghost or explanation of the union of the Father and Son. The word God is the word for that substance called the father, Jesus or the matter, the son; the explanation of the union of wisdom and matter is the Holy Ghost or science.

Now here is the introduction of the devil or false reason. A sensation is made that contains no wisdom. The wisdom is in the explanation of the person that feels it and wishes to convey it to another. This is done in two ways: one by sympathy without language, the other by sympathy in the language or using the language to convey the sympathy. One is wisdom and the other is power. In the case of the woman who had the issue of blood, the sympathy of Jesus was given to the woman, not accompanied by any explanation, only a mere word from Jesus to convince her that he knew that he had imparted something to someone in need and he knew the woman was the one. Now to the woman, here was a cure by power; but when he cured by the power of the Holy Ghost, then he explained the fact, or it was no more than any other cure. So the Holy Ghost is the science or language that conveys the idea to the sick or associates the word with the thing. This was heaven and happiness. I will illustrate. I call on the sick; I sit down and receive from the patient their thoughts, not their language but their feelings. These to me are wisdom for I can tell what the cause is or what makes them, for sensation contains the substance of the idea. I know the idea by the sensation just as a person knows an orange by the odor.

When I smell an orange to me it contains wisdom, but if I had never seen or smelled one, the smell would be a sensation without wisdom. This is science: to teach to every person the principles of association (or of attaching the word to the object). For instance, take the word neuralgia. To all who have never heard the word, it only produces a slight shock. As truth is light and error darkness, the word to some is light and to others is darkness. Then the word is in the darkness and the darkness cannot comprehend it. So to darkness or error, it is a sensation. This makes error nervous or excites curiosity to know what it is, and here is introduced false reasoning. Error, taking the word for truth, commences explaining what it is, so he imparts to ignorance his version or someone's else. The patient receives the word with joy, not thinking that it contains the seeds of misery. At last the matter springs up and the patient finds himself nervous and fussy. Fed by this poisonous substance, he goes to the doctor to hear him give it a name. The doctor, being an anti-Christ, says it is neuralgia, so he unites the word to the thing the patient has made and they two become as one twain. This is the false Christ that Jesus told the people to beware of. Now if I have shown how language is used by these two elements or by science and error, then you will see that it is easy to tell the false Christ from the true one, although they both use the same language, for language is only the echo of our thoughts. Our thoughts make the wisdom but our language directs it. So if our wisdom is not of truth, it will show itself by uniting the word to the thing spoken of so that there can be no doubt. But if it is from opinion, it is evil. I will now make an application with this remark first.

Every idea spoken of that cannot be seen, only as an opinion, is to be doubted until some evidence is given to show that it exists outside of man. What state of the world do you imagine would be struck out of existence if the human race should cease to breathe at this instant. The world would exist and everything on it and men's bodies would be lying around and in fact everything that could be seen by the natural eye while living. I am now supposing that man is gone so far as his intelligence goes. All is annihilated. Do you suppose that disease would be prowling round? Would spooks and ghosts be haunting the tombs and dwellings? Would religion be preached by angels? Would heaven be anywhere or hell be in existence? I think I hear someone say this would be the end of all things. Now just suppose that the Great Cause of all things should cause a deep sleep to pass over the frames and there should be a shaking among the dry bones. The flesh should return to the bodies and they should stand up and exhibit signs of life, but no wisdom. All former ideas of everything known was lost: no language, except the original language of sympathy. Do you suppose if a person felt a sensation in the brain, he would call it neuralgia or anything? Now he wants to communicate to his friend how he feels. This he cannot do by language for like those who built the tower of Babel, their language had become corrupt. So that when they called for bricks, they brought them mortar. Therefore, there was a time when language ceased to convey any true idea of sensation.

Now suppose it should enter some one's mind to invent words to explain a sensation. For instance, if a person felt a sensation from an animal running towards him, he might say, "Scared." Now the one who heard the word would have no idea of the sound except as a sensation. So they set themselves to work to give the sensation a name, and as it was in sympathy with both, they called it "Scare." To modify it, it might be called fear or some other word. Now they knew the sensation and applied it to the thing; to them it was wisdom or true. But those that heard the sound and forgot the sensation would attach the word to the sound. And when they heard a sound, it would convey the idea of some horrid thing that frightened them. So you see the very instant man commences using language to convey an idea of sensation, he introduces a false mode of reasoning that leads to all sorts of error and deception. People would become superstitious and false ideas of disease would spring up.

Therefore, all the evils that flesh is heir to are the invention of man. Man has invented every invisible thing that haunts the mind of man. He has created and formed it in this invisible world and these things are as much in existence as the creation of anything in the natural world. As man creates and forms things from the invisible word, so he creates and forms things in the form of diseases and teaches the young and old how to make them. So man forges the fetters or disease that torments him. Man must be taught that he is the author of his own misery. And until that time comes, man will be tormented by his own belief and that of others. This is hard to understand, yet it is true.

Now separate false ideas from the true and then language ceases to have such a sway over the world. But now it is in the hands of the most desperate set of demagogues that ever existed. I am now speaking of that class of words applied to the health and happiness of man. The language of mechanics does no harm, for it means just what it says and so does the language of all science. But when you come to the medical faculty, the clergy and the politician, then language is like that of Babel, a confusion of tongues. It has no application to anything, only the superstition of the world and such superstitious ideas as witchcraft, disease and devils, ghosts and spirits that never have any existence, only in the invisible part of man's being. All of which science will destroy.

These being admitted and man being an inventive being as well as a creative one and his mind being matter, he can create out of his own body or matter any image that his wisdom can be made to understand. So as disease is the greatest evil that troubles him, he creates the image of his own belief and sets it up in his body. And the doctor comes and names it after some invisible thing called disease and says he has caught it or it has got hold of him. So man torments himself by his own folly. I will give a case to illustrate what I have said. Take a man that is in the habit of drinking. He is exciting his system or mind till he gets it into a complete state of working matter, like the potter's clay. Now he is ready to produce any kind of living creature. No one will doubt but he does create the things he sees for they are as real as anything that ever had an existence, but the life of these things depends upon the person. So the whole world is as much a hypochondriac on disease as the drunkard is in regard to his blue devils.

Excitement from study under a false direction brings about a state of mind to create all these devils that the medical faculty produce. So the medical faculty and the priests stand to the people as the rum shop stands to the intemperate: workshops for all sorts of evil spirits in the form of disease, insanity and every kind of misery of the wholesale or retail. Science is opposed to both and to all sorts of false reasoning that leads to misery. My mode of reasoning separates the true from the false. Truth never creates any false images but destroys them all. It never comes to make peace but war, for error is always making trouble. Therefore, science comes to destroy it. Its work is to set one error against another and let error destroy itself. And then peace and happiness will reign and out of the destruction of error comes happiness.

The question may be asked what is wisdom? I will try to give you an illustration. Suppose you invent some new machine for guiding a vessel. Now in illustrating a truth, you must suppose yourself ignorant of navigation, so you apply yourself to the study to learn it thoroughly. You enter a ship as an apprentice for the sake of learning. The word navigation is a word that is applied to a certain kind of wisdom not reduced to practice. The theory is learned and then your senses attach the word navigation to the theory and this is called knowledge, for it admits a doubt whether you know it or not. To know a thing is to put it into practice and know how you do it, while to teach it to others is another branch. Therefore in all this there is no true wisdom. Suppose you take a voyage with me and try to put your wisdom into practice and you fail. Then where do you stand? Your wisdom is not wisdom but a belief based on what you have no proof of. You believed a person could navigate a vessel.

Now I want to put your theory or name in sympathy with the matter or elements or practice of seamanship. So I make the winds and currents and tides and cross seas and every obstacle that a ship master has to encounter, so that you see all this as you see your theory. Now both are separate; each has its identity separate and apart from the other. One is matter, while the other is spirit. Now to unite the two is wisdom. So when I teach you how to apply your theory to your practice so that the two become one, the wedding is called wisdom. Before it was a theory or belief, not wisdom. So now you being one, when you are asked if you believe you can navigate a vessel, you will say I have no belief, I know I can. This is known to you. So knowledge is a belief in wisdom. But when you put your knowledge or belief into practice or apply it to something and it is right, then the two bring forth the element called wisdom. Now as wisdom creates, it cannot act against itself, for the beginning and end is the present. It speaks and it is finished, but belief speaks and then applies itself and when it finds the answer, it becomes wisdom. Now here is the difference. When man speaks, he either speaks the truth or he lies. For instance, when I say I believe that there is such a place as London, do I tell the truth or give my opinion? If I ever was in London and should say I know there is such a place as London, I lie for I cannot see it, and it may be destroyed by fire or in some other way. But if I should say I knew there was such a city called London a year ago for I was there, that is wisdom. But to say I know there is a place called London now may be true and may be false, for it admits a doubt; and if these differences are not made, man gets into trouble. For instance, you feel a little out of sorts and sick and you call a physician. You say I am sick and want you to help me. The physician says, How do you feel? Now apply the wisdom here. Say to him, Tell me how I feel and then you will convince me that you have some wisdom, for his knowledge of your case depends entirely upon the application. If his knowledge depends upon your telling him, then there is no wisdom. But when you apply your wisdom to the thing spoken of, this is knowledge and it becomes wisdom, for all doubts are gone and there is no belief or opinion.

The difference between myself and the medical faculty is in the application of what we know. What they know is just nothing, and what I know is what I feel and my wisdom is in the knowledge of applying my senses to the thing that produced the sensation. I enter a room that is hot; I feel the heat and it affects me; you do the same and both are affected. I know that heat is the cause. Now this knowledge of heat and the knowledge of my feeling produces the state called wisdom. But your knowledge of heat is not sufficient to put you in possession of the fact that your feeling is the effect of heat. So your knowledge is based on a belief and this belief, not being wisdom, makes you nervous, for you want wisdom or harmony. So you call a physician and his wisdom like yours is opinion and he tries to find the cause, so he admits a cause.

Experiments are now tried on you, for in his ignorance he believes it must originate in you. So in the confusion he and you get up another effect which is the reaction of your acts, and you give it a name. He being blind, leading the blind, you both fall into the ditch.

Now I think I have carried you along through this voyage and have now once more landed you on the shore of investigation. Now I ask if you can tell me what it is to get wisdom. I think I hear you say it is applying the name of what you do not know to the thing spoken of. Illustrate. I will. I ask you if you ever heard of a dwarf and you say, Yes. Can you tell me what it is and how it looks. You say, No. I do not know what the word means. So I say, Come with me and I will apply the word to the thing. So I lead you up to Commodore Mutt and say, This is a little dwarf. Now as your senses are attached to the word before you see the matter or thing, when I feel your senses or mind in communication with the matter, out comes another element called wisdom.

So true wisdom cannot be changed and to get wisdom requires the application of science, for science is wisdom put into practice. Now do you think I understand? I will answer in the words of Jesus, Oh, Israel, the Lord thy God is our God, and to love the Lord thy God with all thy might, etc., and thy neighbor as thyself. And the Scribe said, Thou hast answered truly, for there is but one God and to love him is more than all burnt offerings. Then Jesus said to him, Thou art not far from the kingdom of heaven. This God was to put this wisdom into practice and to know that was more than all the offerings of the priests and wisdom of the wise. To know it is heaven and the wisdom gives the happiness.

Language–Part II–Same Subject Continued
[LC 1:0520]

It has been generally supposed that language contains some intelligence, but this is not the case. It is like the raps of a galvanic battery, a conductor of intelligence, containing nothing of itself. An idea is something and to give it to another person requires a medium. So words or language are used to convey the idea. The medium may be used for good or bad purposes like the telegraph. Opinions and science are the two identities that monopolize language. Language is an invention and the person who first started the idea of language gave the first impetus to science, for some sensation, higher than the natural man can understand, wished to make itself known to another person. Now this was the Christ or God manifest in the human mind. The desire to impart something to the world is what has been prophesied. So language is its medium, and every medium is used for good and bad purposes. So language is the medium of science as well as of error. There is no way of getting at the truth by language, for a lie can be clothed in better language than the truth. The least language or clothing truth has, the better, and the pure naked truth, stripped of all language, is the most perfect. So language is not to add words to wisdom but to be used by wisdom to convey itself to another.

Every original idea that has ever developed itself through matter comes to the world or man through language. So the idea is the Christ and the Holy Ghost is the Science or language. And when man is filled with the Holy Ghost or by the wisdom of God or Science, then he speaks not of himself but of wisdom through the Holy Ghost or Science. When it says that Jesus was begotten of the Holy Ghost, it does not mean the man or flesh, but that Jesus was a medium for this great truth to develop itself to the world so that the Holy Ghost was Jesus' father and the Christ is in Jesus. Then Jesus could say that he, that is Christ, had no earthly father but God, made known to Jesus by the Holy Ghost or Science. It required language to communicate this truth to man, but the ignorance of the world, not knowing or feeling the Christ or truth, applied it to the man Jesus and called him Christ. Here was one instance of the misconstruction of an idea, not language. The language was not to blame, for the words were invented long before the idea was developed. Yet, the truth existed before language was invented.

To make it plainer, I will suppose a case. Take the word cancer. Now if a person who does not know the meaning of the word should say to another as ignorant as himself that he had a cancer, there could be no effect produced because the word did not contain the idea. But it might convey some idea and this idea be conveyed to another. Now let one be posted up with regard to the idea cancer; then if he used the word cancer, something would be conveyed to the other by language. Now a belief is a chemical change produced in the mind by language which conveys an idea of an invisible thing that cannot be seen, but described. The image being created in the mind according to description, the matter is kept condensing, a phenomenon is produced on the body according to the belief. Now if there never had been any language, the belief never would have been created and of course no phenomenon would have been produced. Every branch of science is made known to the world through the language of the people and every error is made known through the same medium. To use language scientifically is to correct some error that the people believe in that makes them sick or troubles them. Now through science the error has been destroyed by wisdom through the same medium and corrected by science. Take the belief in the revolution of the earth. The idea that the earth was flat was communicated to the world by language, yet everyone knows it is false.

Wisdom through science uses the same language to destroy the false idea and establish the truth. Take a piano; the same keys that produce discord will produce harmony. So language like the keys of an instrument is directed by a wisdom outside the word or keys. Thousands of persons use words without any meaning. If men knew what they were conveying, their language would be of some force; but they often convey a wrong impression when they intend to convey a right one, from the fact that there never has been a science admitted for the correction of disease. Now let man know that his ills are the effect of his belief and his belief comes through the medium of language, then he will test the belief in science and see what foundation it has in truth. Every truth existed before language was invented. Now can anyone say that disease called Cancer existed before man? Man is not the beginning, there must be some wisdom to create man. So if we believe that disease was before man, then wisdom must create it and man must be more exposed to disease than is in the world. It is true that as the world is at the present time diseases have their identity and are as well defined as evil spirits or devils were in the Old Testament. But we must go back to the first cause, language. Does anyone suppose that if Moses had not known language, he could have given an account of the creation? And if he had not, the world would never have been frightened into the belief that this world would be destroyed. Now as I said before, there is nothing in language of itself. The substance is in the one that uses it.

The substance of which was in Moses and this wisdom he wished to give to the world. If the world could not understand the true idea that Moses wished to convey, it was not for the want of language but because it was not developed enough to receive it. Some persons think a truth is in language. Suppose I speak to you of some scientific truth in Greek, if you do not understand Greek, you receive no value. Suppose I say to you, You will find some food in the basket. Now if you understand men, I have conveyed the truth but not a scientific truth. To convey a scientific truth to another is to explain to them something or give them something that they had no idea of. Suppose I am thirsty and ask for a tumbler of water. If I ask a Frenchman and he cannot speak English, then I have not conveyed my thirst to him, for I have put it in my English and he cannot receive it. Now the science is to communicate the feeling to him so that he will feel my desire for water and give me a drink. Now the medium I use is the Holy Ghost or Christ in me. This acts upon the Frenchman and brings his mind into sympathy with mine and he feels the same desire for drink. Then he, by his wisdom, gives me the water that quenches my thirst. Now this is the truth made manifest in the flesh. This is the Christ that came into the world and took upon itself language to communicate to man what never was communicated to the world before. Now life is a lie and therefore is diseased. The original language is not the invention of man but is God itself. It is sympathy, but man has tried to explain it and created language and lost the original and has set up a false idea and has made the people believe a lie that they might be sick.

When a man speaks, he speaks a lie for he speaks of himself and his life is a belief and not true. Every person believes in the idea of cancer. Now to cure a cancer, the one that undertakes to do it tries to make the person believe that he can cure it, showing that his cure depends entirely on a person's mind. This is true but is not the person that practices the cure a liar? For he will tell you he believes in a cancer independent of the mind and then he uses all his skill to change the mind to cure the cancer. He thus shows that all his practice is deception and only to affect the patient. Now what does wisdom do? Wisdom sees the phenomenon and knows the effect is of the man's belief. So he uses his science or words to convince the man of his error. The science dissolves the error and the man is cured, not of a disease that existed before man was formed but of an error that man has made. So it is language communicated to a person containing some scientific truth, but all the language used to enlighten man in regard to his health and happiness and his future state is worthless and is of great evil to the world. Science will, in the process of time, destroy all these refuse of lies and establish the kingdom of truth in the hearts or understanding of men. Then disease or lies will be looked upon as an evil that has been permitted to deceive the people for some good purpose, like slavery, for they are the works of the kingdom of darkness. Error has its kingdom, as well as science, and as its servants are ten to one of science, it rules the nation.

May 18, 1864

Language–Part III–Same Subject Continued
[LC 1:0522]

As I have shown that language is a medium through which sensations are conveyed, I shall try to communicate to the reader a truth that has never been reduced to practice. When it can be reduced to practice and conveyed to the mind of man, it then becomes a science. Man will then see that what he believes he wants to get rid of, not what he knows. The belief is the casket or bottle that holds the poison that affects him. I will illustrate. In making these illustrations, it gives the person the idea of a sensation and shows whether he understands what he thinks he does. A child can tell a story of what he has read and yet not understand anything of the fact. Now to understand scientifically is to illustrate the idea of some figure of your mind, not to give the identical words, for the words contain nothing. Suppose I tell you that you have scrofulous tumor. Now any person can tell that, but if you have never heard it described or knew there was anything bad in it, you receive no substance. But if you are told your life is in danger, then if you believe it, this disturbs your mind. By what intelligence you have got of this imaginary idea scrofula, you create an image after the pattern. This is the way disease is created. A lie is set in motion as a truth. The minds are excited; fear takes possession of the minds and phenomena are produced. Then the wisdom of the wise or doctors give them a name. This ignorance keeps the minds excited and the wisdom of this class of blind guides deceives the masses through the power of language and keeps the world groping in darkness and disease.

Now make man understand that mind is something that can be affected like the earth, and any false idea may be created by the fear of some lie that originated in some medical school, then he will try to correct his errors instead of embracing more. See the craft of this set of blind guides. Some great medical man in France or England makes a statement of something as false as can be. This is published in the medical journal, a lying sheet in the hands of this set of deceivers. This is sent out as some great discovery. The small fry catch at the bait and like birds distribute it all over the face of the earth. It falls into every person's mind; there it lies and is husbanded till it springs up. Then one of these birds of prey is sent and a name is given, perhaps the spotted fever. The idea and all the misery that follows this disease has been sown years ago so that the person's mind is all ready to produce the disease. Now this fright gives direction, the fluids are changed and phenomenon is produced and all the people pronounce it the spotted fever. Now comes the harvest. The minds are all ripe. The heads are all ready to be taken sick, and in step the reapers or medical faculty who reap a grand harvest out of the suffering of the masses. At last the scene changes and the harvest is over and there is a large number not saved or cured. Then comes lamentation and mourning. At length the cold chill of public opinion commences blowing. And the little streams from the fountain that falls from the eyes are frozen. The soul or mind is left to be at rest till some idea springs up to deceive the people again.

1864

Language of Truth, The
[LC 2:0752]

Language is used in two senses. The natural man uses it to express whatever comes within his senses that can be demonstrated by language. This embraces the belief in what is called true by the learned. But the feelings of the sick and wretched cannot be described by one who cannot feel them, yet they are at the mercy of those who cannot understand their feelings and who attempt to relieve them of something that they have no sympathy with. Now, the Bible was written to convey to such the cause of their trouble, and the New Testament applies more particularly to the sick, so I will confine my remarks to that. The language that Jesus used was not used to describe anything which could be seen or understood by the wisest men of his day, for if what he wished to explain could be seen, then language could have described it. But this was not the fact. The feelings of the sick and distressed was what he wanted to explain, and he had to use such language as would convey to them the fact that he felt their troubles and feeling them knew the causes. The various beliefs of the world was what made men sick, and therefore to cure their diseases was to destroy their beliefs for these were matter and sympathy is not matter but is what is troubled by matter.

To illustrate the use of language in curing disease: A patient has feelings which cannot be felt by another in their natural state and which cannot consequently be described by the natural man, but the latter without any knowledge in himself names a feeling and undertakes to account for it on the ground of local disease. Now, I feel the feelings of the sick and I have to arrange language to convey this fact. I also feel the effect which the words of the doctor have had on the patient. I have to make him understand this and then destroy it all by language. I am then attacked by the natural man because I do not understand language, but when I convince him that a belief and also an opinion are each combinations of mind which, being a substance, constitute the real element of disease, then they begin to see meaning in my language and find that there is a language which has never been reduced to words.

For instance, the feelings of a sick child cannot be described yet everyone is confident that the child feels sick. A doctor is called and the little child is treated according to his ideas which are explained to the mother. If she believes the physician she begins to torment the child by her own mind or belief, which she receives from the doctor. So a new disease is formed that is for the benefit of anyone except the child. That is a creature of circumstances governed by beliefs which are outside his body as much as the opinions of the mother are outside the child. This child's mind (or idea child) is the mother's self embodied in the idea and her life is the life of the idea child. As the doctor changes her idea, they both change the child till it becomes the child of the doctor, still keeping its identity that its mother loves it, that it is her child. To illustrate: The banks of the Mississippi River are one thing and the water another, and he who speaks of the Mississippi speaks of the water, for his remarks apply to the rise and fall of the river. The water represents the mind for other minds to act in, and as the intelligence of the world acts in the water of the Mississippi, not the banks, so people act on the mind of the child; they disturb the mind and the child is affected, as the banks of a river show the disturbance of the water. The doctor stirs up the waters and it throws forth disease and troubles. To cure the child is to say to the water which came from the clouds of error, Be still, and close the windows of the heavens or source so that no rain shall fall on the earth. This trouble is the result of language. To cure the child is to take the feelings and explain them to the mother, showing her how she has been deceived. Then she ceases from doing evil and learns to do right. From sympathy I take the child to myself and soothe it till I calm the waters; the waves are smooth and the wind of opinion goes down and health is established. To do this requires a new language or a new combination of words. Words are to express ideas, and the world never having had such ideas, language is not ready to express them. Language is a combination of words to express an idea, and when a person wishes to express a new idea, he must make a language that will convey his idea to another.

December 1862

Liberty and Equality
[LC 2:0887]

The idea that man is the result of a higher organization of matter and that there is a gradual progression from the mineral to the animal kingdom is true in one sense. But to suppose that man as we see him is superior to the brute or any other living creature is not the case. Man is matter; so are the brutes and all living creatures, and to say that one kind of matter has any superiority over any other matter is false. You might as well say that the soil of California is more intelligent than the soil of Maine. There is no wisdom in the soil of the globe or the soil of man. Man is the soil and wisdom is the husbandman. Now there is a gradual change from the mineral to the animal matter, for all are acted upon by wisdom and as matter is always going through this change, wisdom uses it to develop a truth.

As the earth is developed by man's wisdom for its own happiness, so the matter that contains animal life is also developed. All minerals are sown in dross or error, so truth being in matter, wisdom through itself in the form of science develops the mind or matter of man. Not that the truth is a part of the man or matter, but like the dross, is with it. Gold is not dross, nor matter wisdom. So when we say we purify the gold, it is not strictly true, but we get rid of the dross and leave the gold pure from the dross. So man is the dross and as we purify the wisdom, we destroy the natural man and that leaves the true gold, or man of science. Now the difference of opinions is this. In the development of matter, error puts intelligence in matter. Wisdom does not. So one reasons from the basis of matter, the other from science. Now every man contains these two characters: one matter or opinions, the other science. So science and opinions run along together like gold and dross or any metal and its dross. So wisdom in every development has its dross and the dross of wisdom reasons like the dross of every pure matter. These two principles are known in various characters as freedom and liberty. Freedom is the development of matter, not of wisdom, but the soil error or slavery is to stifle development. But as error is the character to be destroyed, it forges its own weapons to destroy itself. Therefore all progression begins in the element called matter or man.

To the natural man, its own act is not known and it fights itself like an insane person thinking he is saving his friend. I will relate one instance to show how error destroys itself. I was called to see a person that was sick. This person tried to hang herself. She took a rope and ran for the woods, and just as she made the rope fast around the limb of a tree, her husband caught her. Now she told me that she thought her husband was going to hang himself and she was trying to prevent him. Here you see through her own error she was trying to destroy herself. So error in every instance is the first aggressor of its own destruction. All slavery is black, the error is black, the truth is white and pure. Truth is not matter but wisdom. Error is darkness. Darkness is not matter but a state of matter. Matter like soil may be black or white. The color is one thing and the idea is another. Now as I have said in some of my articles, a nation is like an individual, so it seems that our country is a fair representative of the development of wisdom. Now everyone knows the controversy going on in regard to slavery, yet no one has as yet put the idea of freedom on the basis of wisdom, but on the basis of equality. Now equality is not freedom nor slavery but a mere matter of taste. To put wisdom on an equality with error is to admit an opinion as good or as wise as a scientific truth. The question is not whether the black man is as good as the white or whether the white man is better than the black. With error that is the question, and this false idea makes the trouble. Wisdom knows no color; error knows nothing but color and as error has made war with itself, it has bound itself. Now as the United States is the wisdom of the error, it has bound itself and made war with its own house. So slavery is the result of a family quarrel that wisdom has no part in. The children of Uncle Sam are fighting about the soil that gave them life. The soil that has been cultivated is considered the most intelligent, so as intelligence is called white, the white earth or matter is the most intelligent. So the dark earth is only fit for the lower element of brutes. Now these elements are warring against each other to see which shall rule over the other. Out of the two comes another element that contends that one error is right and the other wrong, that is, the black soil is just as good as the white, while the white error contends the white is the most intelligent. Now wisdom stands outside and speaks in this wise. There is no wisdom in either white or black for both are of the earth. Now destroy the idea that man or matter contains any wisdom, then you will make all men equal like the brutes. Now the brutes have their kind, and the birds theirs, and so the Indians. Every race has its identity and are equal to another race, but wisdom is not any part of their matter. Every race of man is like a civilization, just as far as they have progressed from barbarism. The African and Anglo-Saxon are mediums for wisdom to work through. So as you cultivate the soil, it becomes more fruitful, and as the white soil is more fruitful, it is not the soil but the wisdom that takes the praise; but the soil being the error it puts wisdom in itself.

Now the black or wild matter not being cultivated is held by the white error as a sort of soil for the brutal element, but as error never can keep still, it will always make war with itself when it cannot injure wisdom. Now these elements have their identity in individuals, so I shall bring them before you as persons reasoning about the institution of slavery. I will introduce the two extreme ideas. Neither reasons from wisdom but both reason from opinions that are the result of their ignorance of the true issue. Both put intelligence in matter. Here is one reason. He believes that God is the father of all mankind, that he made no distinction of color. The black and white are equal and to enslave the black is a sin, so he goes for liberty and equality. This is the preaching of one set of men. Now as mind is matter, reason and opinions are also matter. And our senses being attached to matter or opinions, a reformation starts up, and the mind like the religious element is excited and persons become fanatical and embrace false ideas and their ideas excite other men and, like the false ideas of religion, break up families and make a great deal of trouble to get rid of an error that is not embraced in any idea they advocate. Then this has its opposite. There are other elements or men that hold that the white man is superior by nature, and that God made the black with a lower intellect or a link between the brutes and the white man. Their intellect is inferior and their natural place is slavery. This is the other extreme. Now out of this error comes a conservative element. This element can't see anything but the destruction of the country; therefore they go for peace that is to heal up the wound full of proud flesh that will at any time break out again. This element in man is all based in matter and contains no wisdom.

Wisdom stands outside of all this and addresses that matter or mind that has been purified by the error, till it is capable of becoming a medium for a higher wisdom than man. I will assume this mediumship and speak as I am acted upon. I see the first person full of sympathy for the poor depressed slave. Their sympathy is guided by their opinions, like the person who sees the drunkard in the gutter and feeling his trouble wishes to convince the world that he feels as though he (the drunkard) was a man, not a beast. So instead of taking him into a house and leaving him till he gets sober, he commences talking to him and helping the drunkard out of the gutter, or entering the shop and lecturing to the dissipated, telling them it is wrong to get drunk, etc. Or he feels a sympathy for such. So in order to show that he is on a level with them, instead of putting them on a level with him, he sits down and drinks and takes part with them. This has an effect to lower him in the estimation of those whom he wishes to influence, and it makes the drunkard more dissipated.

Now I will show how I stand in regard to the black. Opinions of the world is the enemy to the black. Now these opinions are matter and are liable to change by a power or wisdom. Now if wisdom mingles with opinions, it loses its identity and is swallowed up by opinions. So to be respected by opinions and to have your wisdom respected, keep yourself from the error of the world. Then opinions will listen to your wisdom. Instead of letting your body or opinions mingle with error or the slave, keep your wisdom uppermost and address yourself to the wisdom of the wise. Remember that what we see is matter, black or white. Wisdom being out of matter is not seen, and if our senses are in wisdom then we are governed by wisdom. But if our errors are in matter we are governed by matter and are judged by our own works. Now to let your wisdom mingle with the lower animal or lower element is like casting pearls before swine.

Address the higher element of conservatism. That is the purer part of the other two. Then you will receive the reward of your labor. The extremes will listen, and conservatism will be silent and the element of error will melt with the fire of truth. The shackles of the slave will be dissolved, and the error of slavery will be laid low and truth will tear up the roots of superstition. And the blacks will stand as an independent race, like the Irish or Germans, with all their rights as American citizens. Then the superstition against slavery will die and men and women will be left calm and reposed and look upon the dead evil as a thing that once was, but now is not. Then as men and women have their peculiar taste for equality, those that have a taste for the blacks may find someone that will sympathize with them. So the mingling of the colors is not the mingling of wisdom but of opinions. The mingling of wisdom, being outside of matter, it has no part in this wedding. Now that one person is as good as another is not true; if it was, then there could be no improvement. We misunderstand the idea. We mix two opposite ideas together when we say one man is as good as another. That depends on the man we speak of. Paul did not believe that one man was as good as another, and yet they are just as good as far as flesh and blood go. And so one scientific man is as good as another scientific man. The difference is not in the color but in the science.

Science and ignorance are not on a level, but error has made a difference in itself. It is at war with its own, and science has nothing to do with it. Now every person is composed of the two, and the scientific set the error at war, so progression is reformation. All religion is revolution. The truth is not seen but the error is. The error gets into an excitement, like two rogues, and it is an old saying that when rogues fall out, honest men get their due. The scientific man is the honest one, while the Christian is the rogue. When I say Christian I mean all society that is based on opinions. Opinions are the mortar or medium to excite; so as all have opinions, the leaders of all sects or developments act against the democracy or masses and the excitement becomes hot and sharp. Now the slavery question like political or religious excitement springs up and men and women go into it with all the zeal they are capable of. The true issue is not fairly stated. The enemies of Freedom misrepresent the friends of Freedom and the friends of Freedom in their zeal lose sight of the object they wish to obtain.

Wisdom is not known, but there is a quarrel. So after the fight is over, the object or progression obtains the victory. Then the wind of the storm abates and reason takes its stand. The laurels are gathered up and the dead are buried. And those that are wounded in battle go round as objects of the effect of an excitement by which they are the losers and the slave no better. It might be said, if there were none to excite the people to Freedom, there would be nothing done. This is true. Offenses must come, but woe to the one that suffers, that is capable of feeling their suffering. It would have been better if he never had been born or got interested. For when the object is obtained, like a reformation, there are some that are honest but excited who see nothing but the suffering of the slave, that say and do what they would not do in their more sober senses. Now you might say if all were like me there never would be a slave made free. I go for the perfect freedom of the slave to all the rights that the law allows me, or that the law has to do with me. The law does not compel me to associate with any man, black or white, neither does it say I shall not. This is my own right. To have every person free is let the slave free like the whites and turn them into the great field of liberty like all of God's race, and let them mingle according to their taste without any religious excitement, the same as the French or Germans or Irish or any human beings. Then every person will find their level.

If I am inclined to respect one person over another, it must be from some taste of my own, but I want no excitement about it. Then every person will mind their own affairs and will be likely to mingle in society where they feel the most at home. But in political or religious excitements there is no certainty of a man's position. Excitement or opinions take control of wisdom and his opinion leads his wisdom into trouble that he never gets rid of. There are four classes of persons who are affected in this rebellion. One set wants to have their own way, and their way is to compel the ignorant and all others to abandon their opposition to slavery and turn round and mingle with the blacks on a platform of equality. These are few, and if there was no slavery today, the whites and blacks of their own accord would seek their own level and be as independent of each other as ever they were in any community where slavery does not exist. The excess of excitement is disease that Freedom will cure. It will leave the blacks independent and also the whites the same.

Then there is another class that wishes to have their way. This is a political party. They have no principles but a desire for party. They have no sympathy for black or white. They would as soon enslave the whites as the blacks if they had the power and the whites stood in their way. Then there is another class that wishes to see slavery abolished because it is used for political purposes. And although their prejudice is not so strong in favor of freedom for the slave, freedom is the best way of keeping the slave power out of power. Now there are a few, and I am one of this class, that take this view of slavery. I put black and white slavery all on the same platform. Both are opposed to science. Science looks at slavery as an evil that must be destroyed. Now as every party but the party that goes for slavery is a combination of truth and error, the slave party is of that class of mind that has not been worked upon by the wisdom of science. They are of that brutal matter that the light has never penetrated.

Now as the light is lit in men's minds, the minds become excited and the war is in each individual person. Now if their sympathy is with the slave, they are liable to be excited beyond a healthy state. To such, freedom to the slave is heaven and they take the same grounds with the world. If they are deceived into a religious belief, they have a heaven like a world of liberty, and they use all the means to convert the sinner to be saved or to get his liberty, from the sinners of this world. So they make war with everything and every opinion that interferes with man's salvation. So their enthusiasm is the same in both; their motive is good but it is guided by error. Freedom is a prize and those who do not understand what it is would not know it if they had it. It is not freedom to a horse to turn him out of the barn in winter and tell him to shirk for himself. So it is with all kinds of slavery. To say to a man that is bound by the priests, You are a slave, and make him leave the church without enlightening him is as wrong as to hold him in slavery. So it is with disease. To tell the sick man that is kept in slavery by his doctor to break loose and be free, without teaching him wisdom and how to take care of himself, is wrong.

So with African slavery. To mingle with the slave and get him mad with his master without the ideas of liberty is as wrong as the other system. Now the true way to bring liberty to the oppressed is to appeal to the highest tribunal and that is the people. The slaves have no voice in the matter, white or black. Now there have been men and women that think the best way to get rid of slavery is to mingle with the slave, but I do not. The voice of the people is the medium, but there are persons that are like balloons that are full of gas. They rise in the atmosphere long before the great balloon of liberty ascends. These small ones that are filled from the great reservoir go up and burst in the air and keep the people in commotion, looking for the ascension of the great balloon. The question of black and white will be a question of self, not a party question, but an individual idea and this will regulate itself. So I make war with slavery as a very bad and dangerous institution, opposed to the principles of progression and science. I do not go to liberate a disease or free a slave and let the cause remain. Destroy the cause and the effect will cease. So put down the rebellion at all hazards and if any of the institution remains, tie it about so that it can never get its head above ground.

Let every state come back free from the accursed evil or formed so that it will die a natural death. Destroy the party so that no man will ever come up before the people and say anything in favor of the institution. Then slavery is dead. But to mingle on equal ground is to admit to the disease that you exist and I pity you and will try every kind of wisdom to cure you. I say nothing to the disease. The slave is the matter diseased. Now to catch the disease is to mingle with the matter. Stand aloof and destroy the cause. The whites have as much belief in slavery as the disease or slave. Now talk to the belief or whites. Mingle with them and destroy their belief in slavery and then you cure the disease. But to mingle with the slave or black, you catch the disease and you become more offensive than the black disease. So shake off the disease and then attack the cause.

This was Jesus' mission and he says, For this cause came I into the world, to lead those that were sitting in darkness into the light and those that sit in darkness or slavery will see the light spring up. So the only way to kill slavery effectively is by public opinion, through the voice of the people by their votes. There are so many demagogues that want office that they will advocate anything whether they understand it or not. And it would not be strange if the very party at the North will be the party that will go in for the amalgamation of the blacks and whites as soon as they find their days are numbered. But Liberty will be always silently at work to bring about the design that science will destroy every false theory, every superstitious breeze, and will sail over the whole continent of America with the flag of the Union and Liberty forever.

Now the political gas is made from the enemies of liberty who have set fire to the combustibles of their own institution. This creates the gas that is in their own constitutions and is now rising and has caught fire by the fire of Liberty. It will blow up their institution and destroy their laws. It will burn their fences and lay waste their fields and their great men and small men will lament and run from their enemy, for the day of their trouble draweth nigh. Now it is the idea that is to be destroyed, not the color. Therefore to mingle with the black or advocate this is not to change the idea, but to change the idea is to change the constitution of the slave. When I make war with the priests or doctors, I do not attack their character but their platform. Neither do I make the people disbelieve in medicine and acknowledge disease. I strike at disease first that is the institution. So with religion. I make war with the priest, not with the meetings nor with the worship. I go to the cause. I do not make war with slavery or disease but with the institution or principle.

The principle of religion leads to slavery and disease and death. So to destroy disease and slavery is to destroy the cause. Now to talk with the slave is to talk to disease, but to talk to the intelligence of the free is to change the mind and this destroys the principle of slavery. To do this is the work of time. But sometimes the devil makes war in its own kingdom. So when a house becomes divided against itself, it cannot stand. Slavery has been divided against itself and its destruction is sure. So all that the people of the Free States have to do is to take the advantage of their own quarrel and put down the rebellion and the rebellion will destroy itself, for its own fire is slavery and it will burn till it destroys itself, but it cannot destroy the Union. Therefore, to become excited and undertake to mix colors is not the question at all. That would be like destroying all the medicines and leaving the people diseased in mind. Liberating the slave is not the destruction of the idea. The people must be educated up to the standard of Liberty.

1863

Life
[LC 1:0178]

When we speak of life, we speak of it as though it was a thing. Now there are as many kinds of life as there are birds or fish or anything that grows. The life of a plant is not the same as that of a tree. Neither is the life of man the same as that of a beast. All life is matter and it lives on life or matter. Therefore man is made up of life and death. This life is all the time changing, so that we live on life that we get from others. Ideas are matter and of course they contain life. We eat or receive life in the wrong sense. For instance, the Jews, when they ate pork, thought that they ate life, for their belief was that it would produce a disease. So that although the pork was dead, yet its life would rise again in the form of scrofula. So, not to have that life in them, they would not eat pork. Now, as absurd as this idea is, it is the basis of all our knowledge. How often are we reminded not to eat or drink such things. Now just look at our beliefs. We all admit that animal food has life in it. So we eat it as life, for when we say it is so far decayed that it is not good, then we look upon it as poison. So we receive into our stomach life, as though it really added to our life or strength. How often do we talk about fat making us warmer, etc. Now all these ideas are the result of error and the fruits of disease. Does the dog eat meat as though it had life? No. He eats it as though it was dead and expects no bad effect from it. So it is with all living life but man.

Man has reasoned himself into a belief that all he eats and drinks contains life, and this life is his enemy if he does not look out for it. So it keeps him on the lookout what kind of life is in him. Although his life is death, yet his belief is life, and he is affected by his belief. Now when I eat or drink, the life that was in the substance eaten is dead to me and has no life in it. So I am not afraid in eating pork that I shall become a swine, or in eating turkey that I shall become one. Nor am I afraid if I listen and take a person's feelings of scrofula and any other disease that I shall have it, for the life of the disease is in the person who believes it.

Now, what is the weapon that destroys this life or disease? Science! This is eternal, and to have that destroys all other life. This is to the animal life, death. So life, or science, to the natural man is nothing that contains life. It is a sort of principle, but this is the only living and true life. This was what rose from the dead or natural life. Man in his natural state was no more liable to disease than the beast. But as soon as he began to reason, he became diseased, for his disease was in his reason; therefore his reason was his life, which made him afraid of his reason. This, the doctors call nervousness and to prevent this nervous life, they introduce this enemy in everything we eat and drink. Now let man get rid of these blind guides and follow the command of God, to take no thought of what you shall eat or drink as having anything to do with your health. Look first for the science of every phenomenon and pay no attention to your food, any more than the rest of God's creatures. If man was as wise in regard to what goes into his stomach as the beast, he would be much better off. Let the health alone. Seek how to enlighten man in science, and as science is developed, man becomes wise and happy. His life is in his knowledge, and his knowledge is a science. So to put his science into practice for his own happiness is to correct some error that man has embraced, and to prove the science is to take something that man is troubled about, in the form of disease, and correct his opinion so that it changes his health.

August 1860

Life and Death–Two Beliefs*
[BU 3:0162]

Life and death are two beliefs, but one brings health, knowledge and happiness, and the other disease, error and misery. Each state is called our knowledge. To believe in one is to exist in it, for our life is in our belief. A belief in one is (of course) a disbelief in the other for it is impossible to entertain two contrary beliefs at the same time. Death therefore is the destruction of the one (for the time in which this belief prevails) and the life of the other.

Christ came to destroy both beliefs and to bring to light immortality. "He that loseth his life for my sake" he said, "shall find it." It was not meant by this that one should find the same life which is ignorance but a higher life which is science. And upon this rock or science they build their faith and the gates of death shall not prevail against it.

Now your life is in your belief and you are known by its fruits. My life is also in my belief and by its fruits I am known. But your belief is based in ignorance, mine on wisdom. Now as I impart my belief to you it becomes your life. It gradually grows in you to a belief and this is your health and happiness.

Notes

There are three states in which a person may exist; ignorance, error and wisdom. Life is ignorance; death is error while wisdom is a knowledge of them both. It is evident that in this piece the word life is used in two different senses. Life implies death and strictly speaking cannot be applied to what is eternal.

Health, knowledge and happiness means here mere ignorance; those with life. Christ (the truth) must destroy and bring in their place wisdom. The word knowledge applied to both states (life and death) means simply the knowledge of this world, opinions, etc. It is simply ignorance, but as it is used here it is an ignorance that accompanies the happiness of which he speaks.

This piece refers only to those who are saved not from sins, but in them; to those ignorantly well–not intelligently so. He does not in this cure the sick and impart the science, but leaves them like children.

Jan. 1st 1864

Life and Death are Opposite States of Existence*
[BU 3:0163]

Life is wisdom; death is belief. To be in wisdom is to be in health, happiness and eternal life; to be in belief, is to be in error, disease, and death. It was belief that Jesus sought to destroy by bringing life and immortality to light in the Gospel; and that life was Christ.

Therefore they that love their life (or belief) for Christ's sake, shall find it; for they shall find they have life and upon this rock they shall build their faith and the gates of hell shall not prevail against it.

Now your life is in your belief and you are known by the fruits of your belief. My life is my wisdom, and as I impart my life to you, you die to your own life and accept mine, which is health and happiness and life everlasting.

Jan. 1st 1864

Life–Death
[LC 1:0430]

What is death? Man from ignorance has associated truth with error till an error has got to be as true as life itself. For life cannot be seen except as it is made manifest in some idea. This idea is called matter, and it has become so identified with life that life cannot exist without it. This is the way man reasons. To destroy life is to destroy the idea that contains it. Therefore when we see the idea without life we say our life is dead. This would be true if death was life, but it is not so, according to the words of Jesus. He says, "I am the life," and he came to destroy death and him that had the power of death, that is, the devil. Now if the devil has the power of death, death cannot mean what the people think it does.

Let us see what were Jesus' ideas of death and if they are like those of the Christians of our day. What did Jesus mean by these words, "I came not to save life but to destroy it and he that loses his life for my sake shall find it, and he that believeth in me, though he were dead, yet shall he live"? Here you see he used the word death applied to persons that can be seen at this time. So if death means what we are taught to believe, then Jesus knew not what he said. Take it as you please. It either means an idea that can be changed or it means the destruction of life, and then all he said amounts to nothing.

I am certain that I know what Jesus meant to convey to the people, for I have seen death myself and eternal life that he spoke of and can testify that I have passed from death unto life, as he taught his disciples. And knowing this life that is in Christ I teach it to you, not by opinions but by words of wisdom that will destroy death and put you in possession of that true life that will make death only an idea, like all other ideas man must get rid of to enjoy himself. If you will listen to me while I explain the mystery of life, you will see just where the people were at the time Jesus taught this eternal life. The world was in darkness in regard to one thing–that was life independent of a belief. It never entered into their minds that wisdom was not an idea or that their wisdom was nothing but opinions, not life but shadows that depended on the light of this life or science. So as the lamp of science lit up, it dispelled the shadow of opinions and embraced life. Matter, as it is called, with science is nothing but a shadow; life attaches itself to its own belief and as its belief is changed, death is destroyed and life takes its place.

For illustration, take the idea man. We all have been made to believe that we are flesh and blood. I for one do not wish to lose that idea and believe I shall die. So I believe I am flesh and blood and my life is attached to it. I also believe in death, according to the New Testament which is eternal life. I will now put myself in the position of those who Jesus said were dead in trespasses and sin. I believed as all the world did that this body would die, and if there was anything after death, I might be raised and united with my friends in another world, either happy or miserable. Now, all this is under the law. So by the law no flesh can be saved, but the gift of God must be eternal life. In the darkness of this error, the light sprang up and I arose from the dead or unbelief to the light of science, and am now out of my old belief, and my life is still attached to the old idea of flesh and blood.

Perhaps you do not get the idea so I will state it in a clearer way. You once were ignorant of mathematics, then if a person should present you with a mathematical book it would be all darkness to you. But the principle or spiritual wisdom was in the book, and as you began to understand, you had life and your life was in your understanding and you still had a body of flesh and blood in your belief.

As you lose your life or ignorance, you rise from the dead but you still have flesh and blood till the grave or skepticism is destroyed and you rise into the scientific world where those who are in the law or ignorance cannot see you, for the dead know nothing of mathematics. Here is a resurrection; you have risen from the dead and are set down with those who have gone before you.

Instead of being in the book, you are out of it, and to prove that you are out of the book, you say to those who are struggling with the world that you will show yourself to them by your resurrection. So you do a mathematical problem without the book, and then show that they are to be judged by their books; and if they are not found in the book of science, they are dead in their own sins or ignorance. You have a body of flesh and blood in both worlds.

So it is with all errors, death is ignorance; flesh and blood are admitted and unless you are made to destroy it by your own belief, you cannot get rid of it. The world has made an end of life but Jesus was the end of their life. So their life to him was death and his death was the destruction of their belief and their life was in their belief. So I believe in flesh and blood but not in death, for I have passed from that belief into a life that is eternal. I have flesh and blood as you all see and I shall never be without it; but you from your belief may destroy my life to yourself, but to me it is the same today and forever. Here you have the belief of one who has seen the idea of death swallowed up in science; therefore to me the change is not a thing of belief but a truth.

You may ask me if I do not believe in what is called death. I answer, Yes. If I did not, I should not try to destroy it in others. But it is a belief to those who are under it and as our lives are a part of each other, to know that my friends are separated from me on account of their belief makes me more earnest that they shall believe the truth. If your father or mother were carried out of your sight and you thought they were dead, if they knew it, would they not weep for your unbelief? They know they are alive with flesh and blood, but your belief makes a wall so dense that you cannot penetrate your own belief.

October 1861

Life–Death. Conclusion: The Birth and Order of Intelligence in Man
[LC 1:0431]

Life is the substance. Happiness and misery are independent of life. They are the effect of our opinions. Our belief is the earthly or natural man. Science or wisdom is the spiritual man or woman. Adam was the being of opinions, man or woman. Science is the scientific man. The natural man or woman of earth has enslaved the scientific man to the earth and called her woman, has himself received the seed, so that the fruits of the earth are of man. So with intelligence. The natural man or opinion is the woman, and the scientific man is the one that teaches the natural intellect. Now the child is of the earth, earthy, but this mother is not its scientific parent, the father or intellect is its father, for it teaches what it cannot receive from its mother earth or opinions. This was the case with Adam; he was of the earth like all other brutes, but when the science came, he called it woman because it came out of man. Adam or opinions brought forth science and, as opinions rule, they put science down and called it woman. So the natural man is of the woman, and the spiritual or scientific man is woman or the scientific man.

Oct. 1861

Light–Substance and Shadow
[LC 2:0689]

Does man see himself or any other person or any true substance, or is it the shadow of the substance that he sees? My own observation has satisfied me that what I see is nothing but a shadow of some intelligence which is behind the shadow, as a man looking in a glass sees himself, but the substance is not seen by the reflection although you would think life was in the shadow. Everything is reversed by man's ignorance of himself. This reversed shadow is taken for the substance and it has its identity and its life is dependent on the substance and its acts depend on the wisdom that governs it. The substance is the wisdom or identity that contains the life or God. Man is not seen at all but his senses and feelings are shadowed forth in the world of darkness and life is attached to them.

To make myself better understood, I will illustrate by shadows, which all admit have some invisible substance. Present an apple to a person who has lost the sense of smell but who can see and hear; of course he attaches his sense of sight to the apple but to him the odor is nothing. Then give an apple to a man who has lost his sight but has the sense of smell, and observe how these two reason, one reasoning from the sense of smell and the other from the sense of sight. Here you have the two worlds. The man of sight is the shadow and knows not himself; the man of sympathy who can detect odors is the man, for sympathy is true light or sight and would lead the stranger where his eyes would deceive him. Sympathy is the substance of sight, so everything seen by the eye of the shadow is the reflection of the substance which is in the dark. Man (like the apple or rose) has two identities: one the man of sight and the other the man of sympathy. A, by sight, sees the shadow of his friend. B, by sympathy, sees and feels his friend. A has no idea of his friend out of independent sight. B is never absent from him and participates in all his joys and sorrows. A is looking for some change that will restore his lost friend. B is at a loss to know why A should grieve. Here is where the two stand. A is the religious man and expects to see his friend in another world. B is the skeptic of A's belief, for his sympathy is in his wisdom and what is wisdom is known to him, so his friend is always with him. The same is true of Jesus Christ. The religious man worships the shadow of the substance, but I worship what I can sympathize with. The Christian is looking for reappearance of the shadow, so he partakes of the sacrament as a token of his belief that the shadow or substance will come.

I commune with the substance whenever I sit down by the sick who have been deluded with this horrid belief. They have spiritual eyes or sympathy but cannot see, so they rely on their eyes or shadows and being blind they wander about like sheep without a shepherd, and having been deceived themselves, they try to deceive others. Jude speaks of these persons when he exhorts those who have received this truth not to be deceived by these blind guides who have eyes and no sympathy, ears and no wisdom, hearts and no understanding; also to be earnest in contending for this truth that will lead man to health and happiness. He says, "There are certain men crept in unawares, who were before of old ordained to this condemnation, ungodly men, turning the grace of our God into lasciviousness and denying the only Lord. . . . These speak evil of those things which they know not. But what they know naturally, as brute beasts, in those things they corrupt themselves. . . . These are spots in your feasts of charity. . . . They are clouds without water carried about by winds; trees, whose blossoms withereth without fruit . . . raging waves of the sea foaming out their own shame; wandering stars without any light."

Jude was trying to instruct man to attach his wisdom to the sense of sympathy or odor of things instead of the shadow. Every idea is a shadow of a substance, the substance is what the shadow contains and this substance is merely a shadow of some other substance. Trace them back till you find the cause and it will always be found in some sensation where there is neither sight nor sympathy but simply a sensation or disturbance.

When man begins to reason, he either attaches his life and senses to the shadow or to the substance or odor or sympathy. I will state a case. When in the dark, A comes in contact with a rose and having the sense of smell, he enjoys the odor; but B, the Christian, does not until the light comes, and then he sees the shadow. Light makes shadows; the rose was in the dark but the man of sight saw it not. Every idea has its odor and the man of sympathy who has made it his study to reduce the odor to sight or language is a man of science; it is like music reduced to a science. The note A contains no music or sympathy to him who is ignorant of the science of music; nevertheless, every sound is associated with language so that when a sound is made, it is put in the form of a note. And these forms are put together and a body appears visible to the eye to the man of sight. But the music or harmony is out of sight; therefore the man of sympathy can enjoy the music where the other cannot feel it. So with the shadow called man. Thoughts like notes in music are combined into an idea and these contain the substance of the author; the substance is the food for the mind and the ideas are combined into one great idea called man.

So man is the embodiment of his opinions and wisdom, and he shadows forth the fruits of his wisdom like the tree, and the tree is known by its fruits. The judges are the two characters before mentioned. One decides by the looks, the other by the odor, so the standard of judgment depends on the intelligence of the society in which we live. Men judge by the looks. I judge by the odor and in this I differ from all others. I have attached my senses to the odor and have reduced it to language, like sound. If I smell a rose, I know that it is one, from the fact that I have seen the shadow or the substance. So it is with all odors that I have reduced to language, and so it is with disease. Disease is like the apple. If you plant an apple seed, you will not expect the tree to bear pears, but you may engraft a pear. Likewise, if you plant consumption in the mind, it will come up consumption. But as the owner's wisdom is not known in the higher medium of sensation of odors or sympathy, the tree must grow till it begins to bear fruit, till it throws off an odor that can be perceived by the man of true sympathy long before it reaches the horizon of the man of sight. The man of sympathy sees disease long before it makes its appearance. Like the peak of Tenerife, it beholds the rising sun long before it reaches the horizon of the common mind. The odor of disease is as easily seen and known of itself as a blade of grass is known from an apple pip. The man who never saw an apple pip would never think of an apple, but as soon as the man of sympathy sees the pip, he sees the apple, although he might not detect its quality. Science is to cultivate his wisdom so that he may become familiar with every condition of the phenomenon from the first impression to the bearing of fruit, for then it may not be too late to correct its growth. Every disease throws off this odor, and the life and senses are in it, and the body and countenance of the individual is the shadow of his feelings so that "as a man sows so shall he reap." If he sows to the flesh or what he sees as brutes, he shall reap the reward; but if he sows to wisdom or science, he shall reap everlasting life, for his life is in his wisdom.

Ideas are like fruit. If the eye is the judge, then man deceives himself, for sometimes the most beautiful fruit contains the most poison, and some ideas seem so beautiful and desirable that we eat of them. At first they appear pleasant, but soon we find that we have eaten the poison of some idea in the shape of cancer that will gnaw our very life from us. The man of sympathy could detect this loathsome disease or idea by its odor and destroy it in embryo before it takes form and comes forth in the body. Here you see the two characters: one, ignorant of his situation, is living without God or truth in death and disease ready to be destroyed at any time, while the man of sympathy perceives by the sense of smell the stench of this loathsome disease long before it comes to the man of sight or opinions. My theory is to put man in possession of a wisdom by which he can detect these false fruits from the real, lest he should eat of the tree of disease and die. The tree of life will open his eyes and he will see his nakedness and then he will see that all his knowledge is cut off.

April 1862

Love
[BU 2:0424]

What is the strongest feeling in man or woman? Love for the sake of love for others. For this love they will lay down their lives when directed by knowledge, for no passion can follow true love. What makes what is called animal passion? Ignorance or error of ourselves, not understanding the truth. Love contains no fear; ignorance puts a false construction on love. Here lies all the trouble. Love and ignorance are the mother and father of all error or disease. Now to know ourselves is to know the truth of this problem. Love is an element of itself without any form; it has no length nor breadth, nor height or depth; it neither comes nor goes; it fills all space and melts all error down that comes within its power. Its power is its heat, its heat is its love, it is heaven. For this love Christ laid down all his animal life or passions for mankind that they might understand themselves and be saved from the endless hell or misery that follows our ignorance of this power or love. On these two powers, love and ignorance, hang all the law and the gospels.

The gospel is love, the law is error; therefore when you are under the law, you become subject to the laws and penalties. When you are free from the law, it has no power over you. This law of love is that love in mankind that is working in us or error to bring us to truth and set us free from the law of sin or death. The laws of love are the destruction of the laws of error, and they make us a law to ourselves. This law of love has no penalties or prisons, but like the bird that flies in the sky is not troubled with earthly laws but is a law to itself. Its purity is its buoyancy; its ignorance is its weight or stupidity. Each is governed by a sort of intelligence, like science and ignorance. As ignorance and superstition are what are under the law of error, science and truth are their opponents; and the mind is the medium of them both, like the telegraph wire, a medium of truth and error. Love is a substance like food that comes from heaven to feed the soul. Error is matter and contains reason and all the faculties. Love is the true answer to our desire; in our desire is our hope, and when we get that which we hope for, it contains nothing but true knowledge or love-no sorrow, nor pain, nor grief, nor shame, nor fear.

December 1859

Love 2**
[BU 2:0425]

The love which flows from a woman's soul can be compared to the heat from a fire which is thrown equally on all around. It has not the slightest idea of anything in return, for it is impartial, without selfishness or passion of any kind. Like the mother's love to its infant it contains no reason or thought–it is an element of itself. This element is but little understood by the world, for it is not in the world, but the world is in it and the world knows it not. It comes to mankind or the world, and we put a false construction on it. Its language is itself, it speaks not as man speaks, for it contains no matter. It answers our question by an impression that cannot be misunderstood, if man knows himself. This love is what leads man to truth.

When I speak of man I speak of the errors and ignorance of the world and the heat that arises from ignorance is selfishness and contains the character of its author. When these two elements meet, which I shall name man and woman, then comes the temptation, and as love never makes war for gain, it knows no evil, and as error contains selfishness, dishonesty, and jealousy, and disease, it cannot see love or truth in any element but is own.

This element is set in motion by the soul through love to leads us to truth. In this combination of error, it embraces all kinds of disease, all evils of every kind and we all contain these two elements and their separation is the resurrection of the dead or error to knowledge. Now as we embrace one, we destroy the other. True knowledge is in true love—false knowledge is in error and as God is in the former, he contains no matter, and as man is in the latter, he is made up of truth and error. Now as there is a regular gradation from error to knowledge, our identities are in these two mediums or elements, for man has no identities and he becomes subject to the one he obeys. Then how can a man believe in what he never knew? How can he understand unless someone teaches him and how can one teach except he know? Then comes the question is this theory ever taught? I answer, yes. By the mother to her infant, but not understanding the law, she is a law unto herself and does the things contained in this law of love. Now to understand this law is to know how to put it into practice: so that the world can be wiser for the information. This can be learned if any person will give up all their former ideas and surrender to a teacher.

December 1859

Man
[LC 1:0427]

Is man spirit or matter? Neither. Then what is he? He is life. What are his attributes? A knowledge of himself as a living, thinking, seeing and moving being, without matter or mind. Then what is this body that we see? It is a tenement for the man to occupy when he pleases. But as man knows not himself, he reasons as though he was one of the fixtures of his house or body. I will give you an illustration. Take the White House at Washington. The President is the name of the wisdom that governs the man called Lincoln. Suppose in ten years a person inquires what house that is and he is told that it is the president's, does it follow that Mr. Lincoln occupies it? Yet the same intellect is there or ought to be. Now here are three identities in one man: A. Lincoln himself, A. Lincoln as president and A. Lincoln's house. We do not think or know that all there is of us is our wisdom and happiness and misery is what follows our belief. If we had no belief, we should either be fools or wise men, so a belief makes neither but a man of error or matter that can be changed. All these faculties are out of the idea body but one that is error; the Christian character, independent of his senses or life is his stock in trade, as in other persons. I will take him, for he sets such a value on his riches. Religion is called riches and riches sometimes take to themselves wings and fly away. Now there is some standard to test a man's riches to see what they consist in. I will take the Christian. What does his riches consist in? Not in charity, for they have none for any who do not believe as they do.

Here is what Jesus says, If you love them that love you, what reward have you? If you do anything sinners do, you are no better than they. So where is the Christian any better than a man who does as well as the Christian? There is a difference but it exists in the person's belief. Here is all the value of a Christian's inheritance. It is in his belief and all scientific men will see that a belief is worth just what it will bring, and a belief of what you have no proof of is nothing at all. I will assume I am a Christian, independent of any worldly acts. For a Christian according to the people is a gift of God and not of works lest anyone should boast, so it must be a free gift. I will begin and tell what makes me a Christian. I believe the Bible from Genesis to Revelation. I believe that God sent Jesus into the world to save man. I believe God is everywhere and nowhere in particular. He has a form and He is without one. He is three distinct persons and He is but one and He knows all things, etc.

Suppose I believe all this. What does it show? It shows that I have not got wisdom enough to see that in all the above, there is as much wisdom in it as there would be to take in the Arabian Nights as true. If this absurdity makes me happy, it only proves that a fool can be happy in his own folly. To be a Christian is to attach yourself to the above belief. What does it mean to be a Christian according to Jesus' ideas? He is the founder of religion. Let us see what it says in the New Testament. Pure and undefiled religion is to visit the sick in their affliction and keep yourself pure and unspotted from the world. Do the Christians of this age do more of that than the skeptic? Where was Jesus' religion? In his words or acts. Take Jesus as a man, for he was no more than any man and as such, he was not religious. To be religious is to be something more than a man, for the natural man knows not God. So to be a Christian is to be born again. Now religion is a science that can be applied to the happiness of man, but a belief is a belief to the person who has it and no one else.

Here is the difference between the Christian and the natural man; for instance, Jesus and another man just as good in all respects. Let a sick person be the test to discriminate between Jesus and a skeptic. The skeptic is anxious to help his friend. If money would do it, he would give all that he had or suffer his body to be burned, but that can't help the sick man. Then Jesus with no money applies his Christ or religion to the sick and they recover. So religion is that wisdom that can say to the sick and palsied man, Stretch forth thy hand and I will apply the Science or Christ and restore it. Here is the difference. The natural man knows not Science or Christ. To know Science, you must be born of the spirit of religion or truth, but to be a quack is to believe in something that you know nothing of. This makes up the religion of man. It never made man any better. I know it from experience. I do not believe in any God as taught me in my early days, neither do I believe in any religious belief or anything attributed to the Christian. I will admit that happiness is the greatest blessing to man and Jesus taught it. But Jesus' religion and man's religion are as near alike as an abolitionist and a rabid pro slavery man are. One goes for liberty and the other for slavery and it is a burlesque on Jesus for a man to preach slavery and claim to be a follower of Jesus. Jesus preached the true doctrine of Christ or Science: to let slavery alone, not to meddle with it, but preach the truth.

Sept. 12, 1861

Man's Identity
[LC 1:0524]

We often speak of man's identity as though there were but one identity attributed to him. This is not the case. Man has as many identities as he has opinions, and the one his senses are attached to last is the one that governs him. This may seem strange but it is true. Our senses are not our identity, because they cannot change; they are principles. But our belief, thoughts and opinions can change, for they are matter. So when we say a person never changes it is as much as to say he is nothing but a brute, for he really denies the principle of progression because he does not admit such a thing as change. Now we hear of our tastes changing. Does the principle change or our belief? The fact that we are aware of the change shows the change must be in that which can change and this must be matter.

Then what is it that does not change? It is that principle in matter that never moves, or the foundation of all things. It is that which says when we have found out something new, as we think, "Why did you not find it out before?" It says to us when we are investigating certain mathematical truths, "This truth has always existed," and we believe it. This is the something that is wisdom. It does not come nor go, but is like light. You cannot shut your eyes but you see it. You cannot keep it out of sight; in fact, you acknowledge it in every act. But that which acknowledges it is not the something acknowledged. For instance, if you work out a problem and the answer comes out right, you acknowledge a wisdom that existed before you knew it; so you may change but you won't admit the something you speak of, can change. The trouble is to get our senses attached to this something so that we shall not change.

The beast is not aware of this something, for they never acknowledge it in their acts, for they revolve in the same shape their fathers did. But the matter called man has a higher element called dynamics which the brutal man and beast know not of. They know no higher law than the common law of statics. Now the inventive man that changes from statics to dynamics wants to increase his speed, so he invents motions by gearing into the old idea of statics and increases the speed, called dynamics. This develops some new idea and then he says, "Why did I not find this out before?" So here is the beginning of the man of wisdom. His birth is conceived in matter or statics and brought forth in dynamics. This is the new birth. This was the life that God breathed into statics and he became a living or progressive, dynamic being or soul. Each of the two has its senses; one in statics and the other in dynamics and the fruits show their identity. So the senses are the wisdom of each. The senses of the natural man change, for his senses are matter or belief, but the senses of dynamics are his wisdom and this never changes, only develops. So the darkness of statics disappears and leaves the man of dynamics in full possession of all his senses.

1864

Method of Treatment for a Child
[LC 1:0636]

To show the effect of the will upon the mind of a child, I will state the case of one about two years old who was brought to me to be treated for lameness. The mother held the child in her lap and informed me that it was lame in its knee. This was all the information I received from the mother; but when I sat by the child, I experienced a queer feeling in the hip and groin but no bad feelings in the knee. I told the mother that the lameness was in the hip, and that I would show her how the child walked, and how it would walk were it lame in the knee. I then imitated the walk of the child and also showed how it would walk were the lameness in the knee, and after explaining the difference to her, the mother admitted I was right.

I then informed her that to cure the child's lameness I must cure her (the mother) of the disease which was in her senses, while the phenomenon was exhibited in the child. She said the doctor told her the disease was in the knee and ordered it splintered. But to splinter up the knee and keep it from bending would be to encourage the trouble in the hip and make a cripple of the child. I was obliged to explain away the doctor's opinion. When I succeeded in doing that, it changed the mother's mind so much that when she put the child down, she could see that her will guided its motion. This was so apparent to her that she could in some measure counteract the wrong motion of the child. With my own wisdom attached to the child's will, I soon changed its mind so that it walked much better. This is a fair illustration of the ignorance of the medical faculty in regard to the sick, and it is no wonder there are so many cripples in the world.

When this child was teething, it was very nervous which got its stomach out of order, and its food helped to create a nervous heat which filled its stomach and bowels. Now as the heat or gas passed through the colon, it pressed on the veins and arteries in the groin till it destroyed their action and produced a state of numbness in the groin, so that the child could not put its foot forward. So it would drag it or throw its body forward bending the body at the hip instead of bending the ankle, thus keeping the ankle stiff and bending the knee to save moving the hip.

Now all these movements would follow from weakness in the groin and these unnatural motions, by keeping the ankle stiff, created heat in the knee and caused it to swell, and the doctor seeing the swelling thought the lameness must be there. All these errors arise from a want of science on the part of the medical faculty. The doctor's treatment only went to prove his theory and make a cripple of the child.

The sooner people are aware that they are placing their lives in the hands of quacks although "liberally educated" the sooner they will try to understand themselves. The question arises, How can we understand ourselves?

Go back to the beginning and see what man was and how he differed from the brute. Both were on the earth equally ignorant and of course each looked out for himself. Both were equally exposed to the same climate and both got their living as well as they could.

Now no one is foolish enough to believe that disease or its mode of treatment was then in the world or that there was any language greatly superior to the brute's instinct. All ate because they wanted food, not because anyone said eat this or eat that.

This was the state of mankind when God breathed into him the breath of science. He was a wilderness in which to introduce a higher principle of cultivation or science to clear away the error.

1865

Mind
[LC 2:0778]

When I say that all disease is in the mind and that mind is matter, it is to the hearer simply an assertion for he thinks there is no proof of it. All, I suppose, will admit that what we say and believe is attributed to the mind. Again, we say such a person's mind "is disturbed" and "they have lost their mind"; so memory is called mind, and if you forget anything, you say it slipped your mind. Now if I tell you of something you never saw and you believe it, is not your belief mind? Again, is not what a man believes to him knowledge? But should I ask you, if you were ever in London and you say no, yet believe there is such a place or city as London, is not your belief of it, mind, and is not the city in your belief? Now suppose you are standing in one of the parks in London, is that a belief or a fact? If it is a fact, you have no mind about it. Now here you see a city that exists outside of the mind or belief.

Now everything that exists outside of the mind would exist if there was no person to see it, but every person that believes it, to him it exists in a belief. And as a belief is mind, everything that man creates is in the mind and shadowed forth to the mind. For instance, trees exist outside of the mind. When man conceives the idea of making a house, the idea is in the mind, but the timber has no mind. It exists outside, but when the wisdom makes the house, its body represents the idea made in the mind. Now we call the wood of which the house is built matter. Now suppose we think that if we go out-of-doors we shall take cold; the belief is our mind and also the belief that there is something to take or catch. Now this something is like the wood; it is to make something; now all the aforesaid exist in the mind, the same as the wood. The fact that there is something must be a belief for we have not seen it nor felt it any more than we did London, but presently we do feel it; so does it not exist in the feelings or mind? At last we see it and, as we believe, catch it. Now where did it come from? From the cold. Now suppose there never was a person, could that something exist? And if it could not, then it existed in the mind. This shows that the mind is something, call it what you please.

Mind and Disease
[Originally untitled.] [LC 1:0402]

I have often spoken of the word mind as something which I call matter. I use this term from the fact that man cannot comprehend wisdom in any other way than as attached to matter, although they always make a difference between them. We always speak of mind and matter as different; one is something and the other is really nothing or it is like velocity, which is the result of motion. Now velocity is not the result of motion, but is the power that makes the motion. And mind is the weight or error to be moved while wisdom is the power or velocity; and as weight cannot see the power or velocity, so mind cannot see the wisdom that governs it. There is another element called reason, (like friction) which sees the effect, but being ignorant of the cause puts weight and velocity together and calls them one. This reason in man is the result of a chemical change of the mind. We are all taught to believe that mind is wisdom and here is the trouble; for if mind is wisdom, then wisdom cannot be relied on for all will admit that the mind changes.

The ancient as well as modern philosophers knew that this mind or wisdom could be changed, so they tried to separate one from the other, calling one soul and the other matter or mind. Jesus separates the two by calling one the wisdom of this world and the other the wisdom of God. If we can understand what he meant by this world, then we can follow him along. I have spoken of that element in man called reason. This is a low intellect, a little above the brute, which is the link between God and mind and the same that is called by Jesus the wisdom of this world, for this world is another name for matter.

Now mind is the spiritual earth which receives the seed of wisdom or truth and also the seeds of the wisdom of this world of reason. Disease is the fruit of the wisdom of this world, and the wisdom of God or science is the clearing away the foul rubbish that springs up in the soul or mind. This rubbish is the false ideas sown in the mind by the blind guides; priests and physicians who cry peace when there is no peace. Their wisdom is of this world and must come to an end when the axe of wisdom shall strike at the roots of their theories and lay them low. When the fire of truth shall run through this world of error and burn up the stubble, and the plough of science, guided by the wisdom of God and pressed forward by the power of eternal truth, shall root out of the mind or matter every root and stubble, then error can find no place to take root in the soil. Then minds, like a rich, cultivated vineyard shall spring forth that which shall be sweet to the taste and pleasing to the eye. Then man can see and judge of the tree for himself whether its fruits are those of error and opinions, or of science.

July 31, 1861

Mind and Matter
[LC 1:0062]

I often use the word mind as applied to matter and say mind is matter. This is true but then I also use the word mind and apply it to the senses or knowledge. There seems to be a contradiction. So it is, if not explained. I will try to explain it so that you can understand my meaning. Words are used to explain certain ideas that are admitted to exist and when some new idea comes up one must use the same words to explain it. So it is very hard for me to find words to explain my ideas, for they are new to the world. Now as the word mind is used to mean our senses, I have to make another word or I can't explain my ideas of matter. If I use the word soul, I don't give the true idea of soul to the people, as it is understood. So I have to take such words as are used and explain my ideas to my patients as best I can. In this way I can succeed in making my patients understand what I intend to convey to them.

So when I say mind is matter, I mean just what I say but when I use the word mind as applied to the senses, I use it in another sense than when applied to matter; for in the former sense it contains no matter but is the power that controls matter or mind. Therefore when I say my mind understands, I don't wish to be understood to say that matter understands, but the power that governs it. And when I say my mind is diseased, I do not mean my senses are diseased, but the matter or mind that the senses act upon. Here you see I use the word mind in two senses. This appears as though I did not understand the meaning of the word mind. I do understand its meaning, but I can't find any other word to explain my meaning. When the world is enlightened in regard to what mind and matter are, then they will see that mind is matter and can be used like any other matter or moulded into any shape or form by another power that is in man but not admitted, although known and associated with matter and takes the name of mind. Now then this power is separated it is call soul, but when it is in the body, it is call mind and as no one ever saw it, no one knows how it gets into matter nor how it gets out.

It is supposed at death to make a jump and assume the word soul, but this is an opinion. So if the body is sick and the mind ever so much disturbed, the soul is ready to jump out when the mind or body is dead. The word is applied to the body because we often hear that another has lost his mind; when asked what his mind is, they say life, senses or knowledge. So you see the common belief destroys life, soul, mind, and body at death. If the meaning of words shows anything, it shows that the inventor of the same had not the least idea of any existence after death and if there is anything after death, it is not defined by any words giving that meaning. This may seem strange but it is true. Take the word life; it is defined, vitality, existence. You hear this expression that such a person is using up all his vitality or life and at last he dies; so that life is death and there is not a word in use to give the slightest idea of anything after what is called death. Now adopt my theory and you will see that it must take a different word to express my ideas. My ideas are that all the senses are life, not death, and their existence does not depend on a body for their identity, that we cannot teach anyone to see, taste, smell or know, but all their faculties are independent of matter and matter is the medium for their faculties to act upon.

This was Jesus' theory: that although they crucified the man, Jesus, the faculties still lived, and could take a body that could be seen. You may ask for proof of all this, I will give it. All subjects, when in a mesmeric state, retain their faculties and senses and are in all respects just as they are in their waking state, not as is generally supposed, under the control of the mesmerizer. Their mind is influenced by the mesmerizer, just the same as if he should use his power in the waking state. Each retains his own faculties, but one may lose control of himself, just as a person may become drugged or intoxicated. But it is a mistake to suppose the subject is at the mercy of the mesmerizer and has no will of himself. That is not the case, any more than a person in company with a very bad man is under his control. All persons have an influence over each other but some have more than others and this is as it should be. But a tree is known by its fruits: If a person is known to be bad, no one is safe in his company, if the company are ignorant of his character. So it is with the mesmerizer. His character is to be the standard of his power, for zeal is more powerful than imperfect knowledge. If a man is vicious, he can, if he likes, have great control over his subjects or patients and if he is good he has the same influence. Public opinion has the same influence.

Therefore, all men are to themselves just what they think they are, but this to the world is no proof that they are what they should be. Now mesmerism proves this: that man as we see him is all that there is of him but the Scientific man that has examined into the senses finds that there is in the natural man a higher power or law called senses that can act independent.

May 1860

Mind Is Not Intelligence
[LC 1:0003]

I told you that mind is not intelligence. Intelligence contains no thought, no opinion or reason. Mind contains them all. Disease is the off-spring of the mind, not of intelligence. All the above is the result of a chemical change, to bring about or develop some scientific law that will put man in possession of a knowledge of himself so that he will avoid the evils which man is subject to.

Thoughts are like electric sparks. Knowledge classifies and arranges them to a language nearer to itself so as to use them for a medium to communicate an idea to another. This is the state of all men. Under this state of mind all the laws of science have been developed. Every day brings to light some new idea, not yet developed, but bursting forth to the natural world. During this process, the mind undergoes some very powerful effects which affect the body, even to the destruction of the same. But this destruction contains no knowledge; it is only the destruction of the mind. The knowledge still agitates the mind till its end is accomplished. Then the mind returns to its quiet state, and the law is understood.

While all this is going on, as in all sciences, ideas come forth and the minds are affected and try for the prize; for instance, the idea of navigating the air. All minds are excited. Experiments are tried; accidents, as they are called, happen and lives are lost to this world of error. But that which governs the life cannot be lost but must mingle in with the idea of progression–not losing his identity, but what he loses in weight or matter, he makes up in science or knowledge. Therefore, accidents as they are called must happen, and we say, woe to them that are affected; it would have been better, as we think, if they had never been born. This would be true if it were the end of their existence. Now as these laws develop themselves, is the trouble in the laws or in themselves? The accidents, as they are called, are the errors or diseases and correcting those errors and establishing the truth or science is curing the disease or establishing the law.

I have said that when any new idea comes up, a class of persons enter into the investigation of it, but very few are ever able to put their ideas into practice or get the prize, though most all can understand something of the theory. There is a vast deal of difference between talking a theory and talking about a theory. Talking about a theory is like talking about a science we do not understand; it contains no knowledge. Talking a science is knowledge; therefore when a person speaks the truth, it is knowledge, but when he speaks an opinion, there is no knowledge in it. Knowledge contains no opinion, nor language, nor selfishness; and, like charity, has no ill will towards its neighbor, but like the rays of the sun, is always ready to impart heat to all who will come to the light.

Disease is one of the evil results of coming to the truth or knowledge. You will understand that to cure a disease is to understand the law by which that disease was produced. To make it more plain, I will suppose a case. In supposing a case, the person you address must suppose himself perfectly well. Now as thoughts contain a substance that is set in motion by error to form an idea, this substance acts upon another, like a galvanic battery, and keeps up a deposit of thought till the idea is formed in the mind. These thoughts may arise from different causes. I will select one. Suppose you become acquainted with a person. The first impression is a shock from his mind; this shock is kept up until an idea is formed in your mind. The motive or disease is in the idea of the person from whom you receive the shock. To you it contains no knowledge. You receive it as a sweet morsel that you can roll under your tongue. You nurse and foster it in your breast until it becomes a part of yourself. You form a strong attachment for it, and as it contains the character of its father, you become attached to the author. When the idea becomes developed and you find what it contains, you see you have been fostering a viper that will sting you to the heart. Grief, passion, fear and love take possession of your mind; reason enters into the combination, and a warfare commences. Hatred takes the place of love, truth the place of ignorance, firmness takes the place of weakness and a battle ensues. As truth works through this error or disease, knowledge and happiness take its place; the evil is cast out, the author or idea is despised and the mind is changed. You see the deception. Your knowledge is the emancipation of the error and all that follows it; the truth sets you free and happy, which is the cure.

Now sensations can be learned before they affect the body or produce disease so that they fall harmless at your feet. It is necessary that all persons have a teacher till they can teach themselves. The question then arises, How can a person believe in one whom he has never heard, and how can he learn without a teacher, and how can one teach without he be sent?

November 1859

Mind Is Spiritual Matter
[BU 2:0037]

Introduction

It will be necessary to give the reader some idea of what suggested the following article, headed Mind is Spiritual Matter. I found that by the power of my own mind I could change the mind of my patient and produce a chemical change in the body, like dissolving a tumor. (Now the word mind is not the substance, only the name of the substance that can be <u>changed</u>.) The world makes mind intelligence, i.e., direction. I put no intelligence in it, but make it <u>subject</u> <u>to</u> <u>intelligence</u>. The word fire, for instance, don't mean the substance to be consumed but the process of consuming it. So mind is the name of a spiritual substance that can be changed. We speak of a cold fire or a hot fire, yet we do not mean that the fire itself is cold or hot, only that we make it hotter or colder; yet it is fire, subject to our direction. Wisdom I do not use in this piece. I call the power that governs mind, spirit. But you will see that I recognize a Wisdom superior to the word mind, for I always apply the word mind to matter, but never apply it to the First Cause.

P. P. Quimby

Mind is Spiritual Matter

Mind is spiritual matter. Thought is also matter, but not the same matter, any more than the earth is the same matter as the seed which is put into it. Thought like the seed germinates and comes forth, like the tree, in the form of an idea. It then waits like the fruit to be eaten. Curiosity is excited and wants to be gratified; it tastes and then enquires; the answer comes and the spirit is affected in proportion to the answer. Illustration: a thought is sown in the mind while asleep or ignorant; it grows and comes forth. The curiosity tastes; it produces a strange sensation in the throat. The spirit enquires, the answer comes, Bronchitis. The spirit is disturbed and tries to rid itself of its enemy. This disturbance is the effect called disease. Now if no name had been given or fears excited, the idea or tree would have died of itself.

October 1859

Mind Not Wisdom
[LC 1:0511]

Every person admits the mind has a great deal to do with the body and each one makes a difference between them. To such, the mind is the intellectual part of man and the body the servant. In one sense this is true to them, but to wisdom it is false, for they all admit that the mind can be changed and if intelligence can change, it cannot be wisdom.

Jesus made the real man of wisdom. Wisdom cannot change but it can arrange and classify ideas each in its proper place and show where mind falls short of wisdom. To suppose mind is wisdom is as false as to suppose power is in weight.

The natural man whose intellect is linked with the brute and who cannot see beyond matter reasons this way. He is in matter but thinks he is outside of it. He cannot see his absurd mode of reasoning, but it is shown in disease which is the subject of my philosophy. Man is composed of a combination of fluids and gases and also his mind. The mind being the offspring of his body or brain is virtually the same, although in his conversation he makes a distinction between them, but being in matter his intelligence cannot see beyond it. Therefore, he only believes in a superior wisdom as a mystery.

The fact that he admits it as a mysterious gift or power shows that he does not know it. To make man know himself is to convince him that he, his wisdom, is as distinct from his belief as he is from anything that exists separate from him; then he will give to mind an identity embracing everything having a beginning and ending.

Sickness and disease are contained in it but wisdom is no part of it. The sick embrace what they know and no more. Their wisdom is in their senses. The cause of so much mystery lies in the fact that man cannot understand how wisdom can have an identity and not be seen by the man of matter. We put wisdom in matter and if we cannot see it exhibiting life, then no wisdom represents it. If we see a dead person, we have no idea of a wisdom that exists with all the faculties that were exhibited through the body. We try to believe, but our belief is vague. We cannot describe it.

Man is not developed enough to see outside of his idea matter. He is in the idea prophesying of what may come hereafter. I have developed this wisdom which is the real man till I have broken through the bars of death and can see beyond the world of opinion into the light of Science and Wisdom. I can see what things have a being and how we take our opinions for a truth. The sun I will take as a representation of the man of wisdom. Let the light be his senses and the thing we see, his body. The senses embrace all the light and wisdom even its own identity. The idea sun sees the light and, not comprehending its power, looks upon the light as light, without intelligence, while it is the intelligence embracing everything. This is the spirit world.

The moon is a figure of the natural man. Its light is borrowed, or the light of the opinions of the sun. It thinks it has life of itself but the sun's light knows that it is the reflection of the sun's light. The wise man, in like measure, knows that the light of the body or natural man is but the reflection of the scientific man. Our misery lies in this darkness. This is the prison that holds the natural man till the light of wisdom bursts his bonds and lets the captive free. Here is where Christ went to preach to the prisoners, bound by error, before the reformation of science.

1864

Misery
[LC 2:0993]

Man's misery always arises from some error that is admitted as true. We confound our fears with the idea feared and place the evil in the thing seen or believed. Here is a great error, for we never see that which we are afraid of. Suppose, for instance, we see a wild animal lying down in the forest. Not knowing what it is, we are afraid, lest it be a bear or a catamount. This doubt is what makes our fear or torment. If we knew that the animal was securely chained, that knowledge would banish our fears.

Man is constantly tormented through fear of death. We may say we do not believe in the destruction of ourselves, but everything shows us that our lives are destroyed by this king of terrors. Now if it were possible to convince man that the life that can be destroyed is life only because his ignorance and fears make it so, he would then look about to see how he can save himself from the death he so much fears. At night he lies down and goes to sleep. In the morning he rises from the dead or the idea that he lived in eight hours before. Night and day are emblems of man's existence. When man is in doubt, he is in the darkness that he has been warned of.

All men must pass through this purgatory before they can awake to the light of wisdom. In passing through the night of error, shadows appear and the mind is disturbed and anxious for the light of day. In the daytime, we call ourselves awake, but we are just as much asleep to the light of wisdom as in the night. It, however, makes a difference in the ideas we fear. In the day or light of health, the ideas of disease are not near us; but in the night of trouble, we fear the darkness lest we should never again behold the light. These fears arise from our education and they are based on the fear of death, but let death be destroyed by destroying the belief in the evils that lead to it, then it is robbed of its terror. Men are in the dark about death and in this darkness Jesus appeared and brought the light of life.

It is the common opinion that Jesus came to convince man of another world, but this cannot be so for he never proved it. A scientific analysis of the scriptures will reveal the mission of Jesus. He came into the world as a saviour to save man from error and not from truth. Their religion had taught them to believe in another world. He saw the misery it wrought on the people and he made war against it. He saw that, like a serpent, it wound itself around the life of man, running its poisonous fangs through every act. Jesus was mortal like any other man, but Christ was wisdom manifested through Jesus, which could destroy the serpent by binding him with the cords of wisdom in man's own belief so that he could not deceive the people again. This was Jesus' mission: to save man from the devil and teach him to destroy all evil. Christ often comes in the form of some good Samaritan and saves man from the power of the devil. He is the creature of man's belief and he is found in priestcraft and its followers. The church has always fought Christ or science. Their offering of prayers can never take away pain or sin.

1864

Misery Contains Knowledge
[LC 1:0614]

The world has never admitted that misery contained knowledge; nevertheless to the science I am developing, it is as intelligent as any outside expression. Misery is the language of a person who is in trouble and whose trouble comes from the deranged state of the mind. To explain, I have said that every material form from the mineral to the animal kingdom throws off an odor. To me the odor contains no intelligence that I can perceive, though to itself, it may have a language. So every idea of man contains an odor, which is a language that man has learned and taught to others without the use of words. To a person never having heard the term heart disease, it contains no wisdom any more than any strange sound, but both may contain an essence which I can detect. The word orange contains taste and smell, etc., but no intelligence; the term heart disease contains all the feelings and symptoms of a person affected and also the danger of sudden death. To one who never heard of the heart disease, the word would produce a slight sensation, like the odor of something unpleasant; but to one knowing the disease, the odor contains knowledge and it poisons the mind till a being is created after the knowledge of the world. Wisdom detects the difference between the odor of an orange and of heart disease, and the latter affects him, who is in the belief; but if he does not believe, he is not in the knowledge and the sensation produced is like any unexplained sensation. The odor of disease is the belief and that is man's knowledge. Some odors are catching according to the belief. A story that the man in the moon would throw a stone down upon your house and kill you would not be catching to a mature person, but it would be believed by a child and the misery that follows would be the poison of the lie. Children are liable to such a belief, but as they grow older, they learn better.

Make man acquainted with the odors that affect him and no bad effects would follow, while if he remains ignorant, every odor affects him as his knowledge may direct. Each sensation which his knowledge cannot account for is attributed to some mysterious agency from another world. The truth is, man is continually affected by odors coming from things seen and believed, for a belief is as much a reality as a tree. Caspar Hauser was made sick by the odor of a rose. I am easily affected by the odors of disease. When I am in the room with a number of persons and one of them thinks he has the heart disease, I perceive it as easily as I perceive the odor of an apple. It does not always contain knowledge, for to one ignorant of its language, it is not intelligent. If a child who does not understand is told he has the heart disease, no intelligence is conveyed but a sensation is simply produced. We are continually affected by the opinions of the world, and this theory is to make man wiser than opinions and wise enough to understand odors.

February 1863

Mode of Curing Disease, The
[BU 3:0804]

Every person that pretends to cure disease has some peculiar mode or remedy to cure for the idea that disease is something that needs some sort of treatment. Now as disease is believed in as a thing the question is how to get rid of it. So persons come to me not knowing how I cure and have no idea of my manner. And although they know that I give no medicines, yet they are at a loss to understand how they can be cured; so this leads to all sorts of questions by my patients.

For the benefit of those who do not know about my manner of cure, I will relate a conversation that I had with one of my patients.

A gentleman from Boston wrote me a letter asking me if I could cure him, giving me his symptoms as near as he could and saying if I thought I could cure him he would give me one hundred and fifty dollars, if I would come to Boston and cure him for he could not leave his business. I wrote that I never warranted a cure but if he would come to Portland, if I did not tell him all about his symptoms without his letting me know who he was, I would not ask any fee and if I cured him, my charge was two dollars.

In the course of three or four weeks a person came into my office and said he wished to be examined to see if anything ailed him. So I sat down. At the time I sat down with him he had not given me his name nor residence. I supposed he lived in the City. After telling him all his feelings–he said I was right and then told me his name. I then went on to explain the cause of his feelings and showed him the absurdity of his own belief and explained how he had been humbugged by his doctors in Boston and made it so plain that he understood it. After I got through he said, If what you have said is true what need is there of my staying here any longer. I said, If you have understood what I have said and see where you have been deceived, you will be alright. He laughed and said, I feel well now; then said I, You may return in the car; he went down to dinner, paid me, thanked me and returned to Boston the same afternoon, and was alright.

Now this is one case out of a hundred I could bring to prove that disease is a belief and to correct it–all is right.

I will state one more, for it was so easily cured. A lady patient came to see me from out of town some hundred miles, with a lame knee. The knee was swollen quite hard and when she went to walk she complained of it hurting her under the knee in the cord or muscles. I sat down and mentally asked her to walk and I saw mentally where the trouble was. Instead of the knee, it was the ankle; this she could not believe for she had hurt her knee at the time she walked but soon after it became lame. The doctor blistered and cupped it and tried all the remedies in his power to make a white swelling. So I got up and showed her how she walked and showed her that it was impossible for her to walk as she did without limping and hurting her. She looked and saw how she walked, then I told her how to correct her step and made her understand and then said, Now you try. So she tried and walked right off without hurting her. Now said I, Walk as you used to. So when she walked as she did, it had the sore feeling, but when she corrected her error she walked right. So she returned home.

1863

Music
[LC 2:0698]

Has music a body like any substance? Yes, and parents as much as a child. Music is the offspring of wisdom or truth and contains the feelings of its author as much as the child contains the feelings of its parents; and when aroused by an instrument or voice of another, it throws off an odor or atmosphere as much as a rose. All persons take in the tune or odor as much as they take in the rose by the odor, and they take the feelings or state of mind of the author at the time the tune was produced. Music contains as much language as anything else. All the works of nature contain an odor or atmosphere of wisdom with God in it, and everything created by man contains an atmosphere that contains the author. All things must perish and of course decomposition is the proof; so man decomposes and his body or idea like the invention of man decays and wears out. The decomposition of each contains the author and the author is in the odor. Ideas are the invention of man. All the elements of nature are perfect. Man is imperfect. The tree is an illustration of man and his invention. God never engrafts, for he has nothing to add or diminish. He makes man as he does trees and surrounds him with the atmosphere of himself, thus giving him all the senses necessary to develop what man has made of himself. So man sets up for himself like a child out of his time. The child has eyes, so has the father; but the eyes of the child are the mirror of its spiritual sight, so it sees not itself as a shadow. The spiritual sight is not seen at all except as a mystery.

To illustrate the idea, suppose there are two children: one born blind but has the sense of smell, the other has no sense of smell but can see. Both grow up together. One goes by his sight, the other, by his smell. You present an apple to each. One attaches to it the sense of smell, the other, that of sight. Each cultivates his peculiar faculty and each is a mystery to the other. They act in different spheres. One cultivates his sight and looks into all creation, and he sees trees grow and he engrafts and cultivates them. All nature seems to be under his control. He reasons about the blind man as a phenomenon out of the common course of nature. His sight is not deep enough to penetrate the mystery of the blind man's sense of smell, but at last he admits it as a gift coming from some invisible agent. Being ignorant of the cause, he becomes nervous and religious, so he sets up this man as a superior being and refers all things that contain life to his test of his peculiar gift. The man of smell sees no reason for this sort of religious worship and tries to convince the man of sight that his smell is as much a sense as his sight and both belong to the human race, but he, from cause, was born blind and the other had not the sense of smell. This wisdom he gets from his father who has been teaching the child who has this sense that all men have both, but sometimes they are deprived of one or the other. At last the child that was born blind receives his sight. Then he is a natural man and a spiritual man. He attaches his sense of life to the sense of smell or odor when in the dark so that his light is in the darkness of the man of sight who sees it not.

As I have said, all ideas contain an odor of the parent or author, but the man of sight cannot see it nor smell it, so to him it is a mystery. Disease is the invention of the man of sight but, being ignorant of the odor, he often creates ideas that are full of poisonous substances and engrafts them into the idea man. Now as disease grows, its odor cannot be detected by the author till it comes to his sight, as it is sown in the mind and grows and works on the system like a canker worm till it has entered every part of the flesh and shows its skin on the surface as yellow as saffron. Then the man starts as though he was shot and wants to know what kind of a disease has got hold of him. His limbs quiver, his eyes become glassy, his hand trembles, his voice is husky and he almost imagines he sees living snakes crawling over him. When told by the man of odor that he has seen all this long ago, he will not believe it, for he has no idea of the sense of smell. Every living thing throws off an odor and in the odor, like a looking glass, are the senses which take form according to the feelings.

So it is with all vegetables. The healthy and the diseased throw off their odor, and in the odor the body or identity of the vegetable is seen by its odor which is sight to the one that is affected by it. The natural kingdoms are all governed by the law of decomposition, and the science is to replace the affected parts or keep up the health of the system or matter. Man is like all other creatures of God's wisdom. But God has endowed man with one faculty that no other living being has and that is science that can correct an error. This makes man separate from himself. Sympathy cures and all animals are governed by this power, for it is a power until it is reduced to language and can be taught to others. Then it ceases to be a power and becomes a science. The greatest error in the way of progression is that man admits an error to begin with and then tries to prove it is a lie their error makes.

April 1862

My Conversion
[BU 3:1164]

The experience of my conversion from disease to health and the subsequent change from belief in the medical faculty to entire disbelief in it, and to the knowledge of the truth on which I base my theory.

Can a theory be found, capable of practice, which can separate truth from error? I undertake to say that there is a method of reasoning which, being understood, can separate one from the other. Men never dispute about a fact that can be demonstrated by scientific reasoning. Controversies arise from some idea that has been turned into a false direction, leading to false reasoning. The basis of my reasoning is this point; that whatever is true to a person, if he cannot prove it, is not necessarily true to another. Therefore, because a person says a thing is no reason that what he says is true. The greatest evil that follows taking an opinion for a truth is disease. Let medical and religious opinions which produce so vast an amount of misery be tested by the rule I have laid down, and it will be seen how much they are founded in truth. For twenty years I have been testing them and I have failed to find one single principle of truth in either. This is not from any prejudice against the medical faculty, for when I began to investigate the mind I was entirely on that side. I was prejudiced in favor of the medical faculty; for I never employed anyone outside of the regular faculty, nor took the least particle of quack medicine.

Some thirty years ago I was very sick and was considered fast wasting away with consumption. At that time I became so low that it was with difficulty that I could walk about. I was all the while under the allopathic practice, and I had taken so much calomel that my system was said to be poisoned with it; and I lost many of my teeth from that effect. My symptoms were those of any consumptive; and I had been told that my liver was affected and my kidneys were diseased and that my lungs were nearly consumed. I believed all this, from the fact that I had all the symptoms, and could not resist the opinions of the physician while having the proof with me. In this state I was compelled to abandon my business and, losing all hope, I gave up to die, not that I thought the medical faculty had no wisdom but that my case was one that could not be cured.

Having an acquaintance who cured himself by riding horseback, I thought I would try riding in a carriage as I was too weak to ride horseback. My horse was contrary and once, when about two miles from home, he stopped at the foot of a long hill and would not start except as I went by his side. So I was obliged to run nearly the whole distance. Having reached the top of the hill, I got into the carriage and, as I was very much exhausted, I concluded to sit there the balance of the day if the horse did not start. Like all sickly and nervous people, I could not remain easy in that place and, seeing a man ploughing, I waited till he had ploughed around a three-acre lot and got within sound of my voice, when I asked him to start my horse. He did so, and at the time I was so weak I could scarcely lift my whip. But excitement took possession of my senses, and I drove the horse as fast as he could go, up hill and down, till I reached home and, when I got into the stable, I felt as strong as I ever did. From that time I continued to improve, not knowing, however, that the excitement was the cause, but thinking it was something else. When I commenced to mesmerize, I was not well according to medical science; but in my researches I found a remedy for my disease. Here was where I first discovered that mind was matter and capable of being changed, also that diseases being a deranged state of the mind, the cause I found to exist in our belief. The evidence of this theory I found in myself; for, like all others, I had believed in medicine. Disease, its power over life and its curability are all embraced in our belief. Some believe in various remedies, and others believe that the spirits of the dead prescribe. I have no confidence in the virtue of either. I know that cures have been made in these ways. I do not deny them, but the principle on which they are done is the question to solve. For disease can be cured, with or without medicine, on but one principle. I have said I believed in the old practice and its medicines, the effects of which I had within myself; for, knowing no other way to account for the phenomena, I took it for granted that they were the result of the medicine.

With this mass of evidence staring me in the face, how could I doubt the old practice? Yet, in spite of all my prejudices, I had to yield to a stronger evidence than man's opinion and discard the whole theory of medicine as a humbug practiced by a class of men, some honest, some ignorant, some conceited, some selfish and all thinking that the world must be ruled by their opinions.

Now for my particular experience. I had pains in the back which the doctors said were caused by my kidneys, which were partially consumed. I also was told that I had ulcers on my lungs. Under this belief, I was miserable enough to be of no account in the world. This was the state I was in when I commenced to mesmerize. On one occasion, when I had my subject asleep, he described the pains I felt in my back (I had never dared to ask him to examine me, for I felt sure that my kidneys were nearly gone) and he placed his hand on the spot where I felt the pain. He then told me that my kidneys were in a very bad state, that one was half-consumed, and a piece three inches long had separated from it and was only connected by a slender thread. This was what I believed to be true, for it agreed with what the doctors had told me, and with what I had suffered; for I had not been free from pain for years. My common sense told me that no medicine would ever cure this trouble, and therefore I must suffer till death relieved me, but I asked him if there was any remedy. He replied, Yes, I can put the piece on so it will grow and you will get well. At this I was completely astonished and knew not what to think. He immediately placed his hands upon me and said he united the pieces so they would grow. The next day he said they had grown together, and from that day I never have experienced the least pain from them.

Now what is the secret of the cure? I had not the least doubt but that I was as he had described and if he had said, as I expected that he would, that nothing could be done, I should have died in a year or so. But when he said he could cure me in the way he proposed, I began to think, and I discovered that I had been deceived into a belief that made me sick. The absurdity of his remedies made me doubt the fact that my kidneys were affected, for he said in two days they were as well as ever. If he saw the first condition, he also saw the last, for in both cases he said he could see. I concluded that in the first instance that he read my thoughts, and when he said he could cure me, he drew on his own mind, and his ideas were so absurd that the disease vanished by the absurdity of the cure. This was the first stumbling-block I found in the medical science. I soon ventured to let him examine me further, and in every case he would describe my feelings but would vary the amount of disease; and his explanation and remedies always convinced me that I had no such disease and that my troubles were of my own make.

At this time I frequently visited the sick with Lucius, by invitation of the attending physician, and the boy examined the patient and told facts that would astonish everybody, and yet every one of them was believed. For instance, he told a person, affected as I had been, only worse, that his lungs looked like a honeycomb and his liver was covered with ulcers. He then prescribed some simple herb tea, and the patient recovered and the doctor believed the medicine cured him. But I believed that the doctor made the disease, and his faith in the boy made a change in the mind and the cure followed. Instead of gaining confidence in the doctors, I was forced to the conclusion that their science was a humbug. Man is made of truth and belief; and, if he is deceived into a belief that he has or is liable to have a disease, the belief is catching and the effect goes with it. I have given the experience of my emancipation from this belief and confidence in the doctors so that it may open the eyes of those who stand where I was. I have risen from this belief and I return to warn my brethren, lest when they are disturbed, they shall get into this place of torment prepared by the medical faculty. Having suffered myself, I cannot take the advantage of my fellow-men by introducing a new mode of curing disease and prescribing medicine. My theory exposes the hypocrisy of those who undertake to care for the lives of others. They make ten diseases to one cure, thus bringing a surplus of misery into the world and shutting out a healthy state of society. They have a monopoly of the business and no theory that lessens disease can compete with them. When I cure, there is one disease the less, but not so when others cure, for the supply of sickness shows that there is more disease on hand than there ever was. Therefore, the labor for health is sure, but the manufactory of disease is greater. The newspapers teem with advertisements of remedies, showing that the supply of disease increases. My theory teaches man to manufacture health, and when people go into this business, disease will diminish, and those who furnish disease and death will be few and scarce.

January 1863

My Ignorance of English
[BU 3:0814]

Some persons naturally suppose from my remarks to them that I am ignorant of the English language. To the charge, I plead guilty, so far as education goes, and I ask the indulgence that any person requires who tried to explain to another what that person is ignorant of. There never has been and never will be a language by which an editor can be made to understand a scientific fact. Men are all more or less bigoted, superstitious, and conceited, and these qualities are not modified by any kind of literary attainments. On the contrary, education magnifies them in some persons, while if instead of reading and studying from books they had mingled with the world and learned a little of human nature, they might have been more intelligent and liberal.

For myself and my mode of curing, all the language I really need is words to explain to the patient his feelings and the causes. It does not follow that a pilot should know Greek or Latin, or even how to read, provided he knows where he is. If the Captain has all the language at his command and can talk like an orator and is ignorant of the place he is in, it profiteth him nothing. I stand to the sick like a pilot and if the patient places wisdom in the understanding of language, he is ignorant of himself. My wisdom consists in what I know beyond my patient, and if I make issue on language while we are disputing the point, the ship may go to the bottom or on to the rocks. Every person is a book of himself and in most instances a sealed book whose title page the owner has never read and about whose author nothing is known. So when I sit by a patient, I open the book and read the life of the author and sometimes the first impression is so weak that the patient winces, but it is the reflection of his own self, and if it does not please, the fact is not diminished.

Diseases are the effect of disobeying some article of our belief; for instance, we believe that it is a sin to steal, hence stealing is a disgrace, and no one wants to be twitted of it. So it is with every disease not accounted for by some deception or from being made to believe a lie. When with the sick, I come in contact with the life of the patient and expose their hypocrisy which they do not like to have done, so they try to get up a false issue by attacking my learning, assuming that they know more than I do about my business, thus talking about what they know nothing. They suppose wisdom is in words, when these are only sounds. A man may have the whole of the Webster's dictionary at his tongue's end and not know a single fact as he ought to know it. Such a person thinks that he must be wise for he has language, but I test a man's wisdom by what I say when I sit by him, for then I have no opinion but am like an instrument upon which the patient plays his own tune. And if it sounds silly to them, it is their own folly, for I do nothing but listen. But when it is over and each is left alone, then comes the reaction, and if they are as disagreeable to themselves as they are to me, I do not blame them for wishing themselves out of the world. I should wish them the same, if I had no more charity for them than they have for themselves.

November 1862

My Object in Introducing My Work
[LC 2:0839]

My object in introducing this work to the reader is to correct some of the evils that flesh is heir to. During a long experience in the treatment of disease I have labored to find the causes of so much misery in the world. By accident I became interested in what was then called mesmerism, not thinking of ever applying it to any useful discovery or benefit to man, but merely as a gratification for my own curiosity. In this way I went into the investigation of the subject. Being a skeptic I would not believe anything that my subject would do if there was any chance for deception, so all my experiments were carried out mentally. This gave me a chance to discover how far Mesmer was entitled to any discovery over those who had followed him. I found that the phenomenon could be produced. This was a truth, but the whys and wherefores were a mystery. This is the length of mesmerism; it is all a mystery, like spiritualism. Each has its believers but the causes are in the dark.

Believing in the phenomenon, I wanted to discover the causes and find if there was any good to come out of it. At last I found that these phenomena of themselves contained no wisdom, for they were like any phenomenon to be accounted for by a higher power than was in the phenomenon. This led me to investigate the subject, so in my investigation I found that my ignorance could produce phenomena in my subject that my own wisdom could not correct. At first I found that my own thoughts affected the subject, and not only my thought but my belief. I found that my thoughts were one thing and my belief another. If I really believed in anything, the effect would follow whether I was thinking of it or not. For instance, I believed at the outset that mesmerism was governed by the laws of electricity. This was a belief. So whenever I attempted any experiment, the experiment was always in accordance with my belief, whether I was thinking of it or not, the whole would follow. I believed that silk would attract the subject. This was a belief in common with mankind, so if a person having any silk about him, for instance a lady with a silk apron, the subject's hand would be affected by it and the hand would move towards the lady even if she were behind him.

So I found that belief in everything affects us, yet we are not aware of it, because we do not happen to think. We think our beliefs have nothing to do with the phenomenon. Man is governed by his belief but his belief is not always known to him so that often he thinks that the phenomenon has nothing to do with his belief, when all the evil he suffers is from his belief.

Disease is one of the phenomena that follow a belief that we are not aware of. But anything that is believed has an identity to those that believe it and is liable to affect them at any time when the conditions of the mind are in the right state. For instance, take the small pox. Everyone believes in the disease as a living truth. Now those that have had it believe that they are not liable to have it a second time. Now if it is really a fact to them they are safe, but everyone that never had it is liable, according to their belief, so that it is not necessary that they should know that it is in the same place, for minds are like clouds, always flying, and our belief catches them as the earth catches the seeds that fly in the winds. All this I found.

So my object was to discover what a belief was made of and what thought was. This I found out by thinking of something my subject could describe so that I knew that he must see or get the information from me in some way. At last I found out that mind was something that could be changed, so as I believed that nothing could produce no one thing, I came to the conclusion that mind was something and I called it matter. For I found it could be condensed into a solid and receive a name of a solid called "tumor," and by the same power under a different direction, it might be dissolved and disappear. This showed me that man was governed by two powers or directions: one by a belief, the other by a science.

The creating of disease is under the superstition of man's belief. The cures have been by the same remedy, proving that it takes the hair of the same dog to cure the wound for the disease being brought about by a false belief. It took another false belief to correct the first so that instead of destroying the evil, the remedy created more.

I found that there is a wisdom that can be applied to these errors or evils that can put man in possession of a science that will not only destroy the evil but will hold up its serpent head, as Moses in the wilderness held up the errors of the religious creeds in the form of a serpent, and all that looked upon his explanation were cured of the diseases that followed their beliefs. So science will hold up these old superstitious beliefs and theories, and all who will listen and learn can be cured, not only of the disease that they may be suffering from, but they will know how to avoid the errors of others.

I shall endeavor to give a fair account of my investigations and what I have had to contend with and show how I succeeded. I have said many things in regard to medical science but all that I have said was called out by my patients being deceived by the profession. The same is true of the religious profession. Every article was written under a very excited state brought about by some wrong inflicted on my patient by the medical faculty, the clergy or public opinion. All my arguments are used to correct some false opinion that has affected my patient in the form of disease, mentally or physically. In doing this I have to explain the Bible, for their troubles arise from a wrong belief in certain passages. And when I am sitting by a patient, those passages that trouble them trouble me, and the passage comes to me with the explanation and I, as a man, am not aware of the answer until I find it out. So I cannot be responsible for the exact words, but the meaning that the author had I feel certain I shall give. The exact language may not be the same, for language is not used to convey the impression but our ideas or things.

There is a wisdom that has never been reduced to language, for science that never has been taught has never been described by language. The science of curing disease has never been described by language, but the error that makes disease is described and is in the mouth of every child. The remedies are also described but the remedies are worse than the disease, for instead of lessening the evil, they have increased it. In fact the theory of correcting disease is the introduction of life.

I will now introduce myself as a mesmerizer with all the superstitions of a powerful operator, for I had the name of being a very strong mezmerizer. I will give my first experiment. The first trial was with another gentleman or a young man. We all sat down and took hold of each other's hands. Then the gentleman and myself placed our minds on the subject willing him to sleep. So we sat puffing and willing him and forcing the electricity out of us into the subject till we had filled him full according to our belief. Sometimes he would be so full that we would have to make passes to throw it off. At last he came into the right state; then as we had him between us, I wanted to know which had the most power over him. So we sat him in the chair, and the gentleman stood in front of him and I behind him. I willed my friend "B" and he tried to draw him out of the chair but he could not start him. Then we reversed positions and I went in front and I drew him out of the chair. This went to show that I had the most power or will. This ended the first experiment. I then put him into a mesmeric state in less than five minutes. Now as I was a new hand at the business, it became necessary to know how to proceed. So after getting all the information I could obtain, I commenced to try experiments. But I am now satisfied if I never had heard of a mesmeric book nor had any ideas, I should never have had half the phenomena I had, for I believed all I read and proved it by my experiments.

Here I will say a word or two to the reader. If you can make the reader believe anything no matter how absurd it is, he will prove it to be true by his experiments. This proves that our beliefs make us act and our acts are directed by our belief, for the wisdom or knowledge is in the belief. People are not aware of this; this was what Jesus tried to prove so all his acts and talk went to prove the truth of what I have said. Make man responsible for his belief and he will be as cautious what he believes as he is in what he says and does, for he will see that just as he measures out to another just so it will be measured out to him. But does the clergy follow this rule? Do they not dictate to their audience what to believe and what not to believe without the least regard to their health? Now to suppose a man can believe one thing and still have a contrary effect is not true.

If you make a person believe that he is in danger of any trouble he will be affected just according to his belief, so all beliefs are to be analyzed like food or drink to see what it contains and how it acts upon the body, for the belief being in the mind, it shows itself on the body. When Jesus talked he had some object to obtain for the happiness of man. But to suppose Jesus came from heaven to destroy one error and establish another is to suppose that our beliefs alter the wisdom of God or they make a man believe what he cannot understand to insure his happiness in a world that is based on a belief. Now if I understand Jesus, I understand him to condemn all beliefs and show that man is better off without a belief than with one. This I will show. What good is it to me so far as I am concerned whether I believe one thing or another if my belief does not affect my life and if my belief affects my life I get the benefit or misery of my own belief, but it does not alter the wisdom of God nor alter any of his plans. So if there is a world beyond this, my belief cannot change it, but my belief may change me. So if Jesus had no higher motive than merely to introduce a belief, then he was like all others that wanted to establish his own peculiar views or beliefs. Now there was a certain class of people who believed that when a man died he would lie in the grave or sea or somewhere till the end of the world, and then he would rise or the particles would be reunited into a body and he would rise. Now according to the people's belief of our days, Jesus came to change this belief so he said if they would believe what he said they should never die and he that believeth, although he be dead yet shall he live, for he said, "I am the resurrection and the life and he that believeth in me shall never die." Now according to the interpretation of this, if Jesus ever found a believer, he must be alive and also those that were dead could believe. Now how does this last sentence agree with what he said when asked by the Pharisees about the resurrection and he said as touching the dead, God is not the God of the dead but of the living. Now Jesus never meant to speak of what we call death; his death was sin or error. The life was in your wisdom and to lose your opinions and find his truth was life, not death. The wisdom that taught this did not embrace the words life and death. The old Scriptures never talked of death, for their religion was confined to their lives, and when they died, this was an end of them. So they believed in a God, but God required man to obey him here and he punished them here and rewarded them, but he never had any other world until about the time of Jesus. Then it was with a very few and their belief was so much in the dark it had but little effect on the world. Here is a point that seems to slip the minds of the people of these days and they think he came to introduce a new doctrine, but he says, "I came not to bring peace," etc. Matthew 10.

    1863

My Object in Presenting These Facts
[LC 2:0844]

    In presenting these facts to the public, my object is to reach those that have a desire to judge for themselves of the truths of what is called spiritualism. I, for one, contend that no person of any religious belief, infidel or skeptic, can explain these phenomena that are taking place all over the civilized world from the fact that an error has crept into man that prevents him from being outside of the superstition of the world.

    I will show how everyone is a party to his own belief. It is true man's belief changes and this is the error that prevents him from giving an impartial investigation. All men believe in what the world calls death and therefore everyone agrees on this point, yet they differ in some little particulars. There is one class that believes man does not die; he gets out of his body and his body dies and the man lives. Now this is the belief of every person except those that do not believe that man lives at all or they are afraid they don't. Now under these false beliefs they undertake to investigate their own belief, when all they do is to make it stronger. The spiritualists have the advantage of all the rest for all admit the first principle that every person dies. Thus all the experiments are to prove that they live, so they give an explanation of their belief and prove it. They change the skepticism on spiritualism into a belief in it or drive themselves out of one error into another, while those that are investigating run against a stumbling block in the dark and say, "I do not believe that it is all spirits, but there must be something to do with the living."

    So I say that all the above classes cannot solve the problem. It must come from some wisdom higher than any that has yet tried to solve it that the world has known. Now I propose to solve this problem upon an entirely new theory never advanced to the world. It is true there have been flashes of light in the intellectual world but these flashes have never been under any wisdom higher than the church or some scientific man with religious views, and the religious man of all others is the very man to prove it. It is like taking a man that believes in ghosts to account for their appearance in a house. He goes to sleep in the house all alone and he is almost sure to see one. So it has been with all the great professors. They are learned but they are also very superstitious or religious, and if they are infidel, their infidelity is all vapor. They have no proof of it to offer to the world and everything to destroy it. So when they begin to investigate it, their fears that it may be true have the same effect that the clergy does that it may be the works of the devil. Both are convinced of what they do not want should be true.

    It may look like presumption on my part to stand before the world in opposition to every person and contend that all these phenomena are <u>nothing</u> governed by superstition, but if you will listen to what I will bring as proof of what I shall say, then you may judge for yourselves. I will state my principles upon what I believe to be true. It will not be possible to give my theory in full at this time, but I am preparing a work that will explain all these phenomena upon a scientific truth. The object of this discovery is to show, so far as it goes, that man investigates every phenomenon according to his belief; and when he gets stuck he either admits another belief or arrives at a science that will explain his error or belief.

I have no belief in regard to religion of any kind; neither do I have any belief in another world of any kind. I have no belief in what is called death. In fact I am a total disbeliever in any wisdom that ever taught any religion outside of man's beliefs. Then you may ask what kind of a man are you without a belief? I have a belief like all men, but it does not apply to what I have been talking about. I have a belief on all subjects that are agitating the country. My remarks are confined to this one thing-mind or belief in what is called spiritualism or religion. To me both are the same.

I believe there was one person who had these same ideas and to that person I give all the credit for introducing this truth into the world, and that was Jesus. I have no doubt of his being the only true prophet that ever lived who had ideas entirely superior to the rest of the world; not that he as a man was any better, but he was the embodiment of a higher wisdom of that peculiar kind, more so than any man who has ever lived before or since.

Perhaps you do not understand my meaning. Take the discovery of electricity. There were men who had conceived in their minds some of the ideas of Franklin, not that Franklin was of himself the discoverer or the person who reduced it to a science, but this body was the medium that embraced the wisdom of the wise into a sort of focus so that an experiment might be made to prove the principle. Then it took the name of Franklin. The wisdom of the world is not confined to any person, but when it begins to condense into a truth, it must exhibit itself through some medium. This great truth called Christ was exhibited through the man Jesus, the same as this great truth was exhibited through the man Franklin and called electricity. There was a belief at the time of the destruction or overflow of this great truth at the crucifixion of Jesus-that it should rise again. Since then, there has been a constant development of facts showing that there was some wisdom or power superior to man and the superstition of the world has kept it down, as the superstition of slavery has kept freedom in chains.

Now I, as a man, claim no preeminence or superiority over other men but admit my inferiority to the learned and wise, but then it was said by one who was certainly superior to his followers that too much learning had made men mad or superstitious. So learning, when wrongly directed, led to bad results. So it is with the South. Their learning, being directed by the false instructions of their early religious prejudices, led them to believe that slavery was a divine institution, so their learning will be the cause of their own destruction.

I have none of these sins to answer for. I am free from all that false religion. But I have had to contend with the devil or error for more than twenty years before I was free. Now I stand as one that has risen from the dead or error into the light of truth, not that the dead or my error has risen with me, but I have shaken off the old man or my religious garment and put on the new man that is Christ or Science, and I fight these errors and show that they are all the makings of our own mind. As I stand outside of all religious belief, how do I stand alongside of my followers? I know that I, this wisdom, can go and impress a person at a distance. The world may not believe it, but to the world it is just such a belief as the belief in spirits; but to me it is a fact and this is what I shall show. I shall show by letters what I have said, that mind can produce all the phenomena that the world has ever seen and I shall show in my work that Jesus never tried to teach anything different from what I am teaching and doing every day.

1864

My Opposing the Doctors and the Priests
[LC 2:1107]

I am often accused of opposing the physician and priest or the religious creeds. In answer to this I plead guilty, but you must not gather from this that I oppose goodness or virtue or wisdom. I oppose all religion that is based on the opinions of man, and as God never gave an opinion, I am not bound to believe that man's opinions are from God. The difference between man's opinions and God's wisdom is more than one would naturally suppose, but the former is taken for a truth and this makes the trouble that the wise have to contend with. If man knew himself he would not be misled by the opinions of others, and as disease is the result of our opinions, it is the duty of all to know themselves so as to correct their own errors. Now if error is something, as it must be, to correct it must require more wisdom than the wisdom that invented it. So if error is wrong it cannot be the offspring of wisdom, and of course it must be from some other source and that source must be ignorance. Ignorance is the father and disease is the offspring of error; therefore to correct the error is to cure the disease. How do you cure anything but to explain the error to the sufferer so that his wisdom may correct his error?

And as disease is like any other evil that wisdom has to correct, it must be by a science to the natural man, although to a person who has wisdom science is nothing. No one supposes that to oppose the physicians' opinions is to cure the disease, for the opinion is father of the disease or life and to lose your life or opinion is to recover your health. But wisdom is without father or mother, so to destroy your earthly father is to destroy your opinions, and to be with your Heavenly Father is to be wise; so everyone that loses his opinions and arrives at the truth is dead to the natural world but alive in Wisdom or Christ.

When I sit down by a sick person and he or she wants to tell me what the doctor says, to me it is nonsense, for I have not the least regard for their wisdom. Their opinions are the very things I try to destroy, and if I succeed, their opinions have no influence to create disease for they are the very disease I am trying to destroy. Man's profession, not his wisdom, is the standard of his popularity. I stand in direct opposition to all others in this respect and here is the conflict: whether man's opinion is to rule or his wisdom. If the medical profession is based on wisdom, then it will stand the test, and disease must have its origin out of the profession; either this must be true or the opposite. I assert that disease is the offspring of opinion. Ignorance produces the phenomenon or effect as in the brute creation but the perfectly wild brutes, disease or phenomenon differs from that of the domesticated brute. So it is with man. The perfect fool knows no aches or pains; where there is no fear there is no torment. Fear is error, wisdom casts out fear, for it knows no fear. Now does wisdom have an identity? I answer "yes" and so does error. The opinions of man never have admitted wisdom to have an identity but admit it as a power or gift, thus making it merely a servant to error, known by the name of science; but the person who has the wisdom is not admitted superior to the one who admits it.

You often hear persons attempt to explain my cures by their own opinions, not admitting that I have any wisdom superior to their opinions; thus they make themselves out wise by their own ignorance since they deny the very power or wisdom they acknowledge by admitting it as a mystery to them. So they admit a power outside of their wisdom and worship that of which they are completely ignorant. Now I know that this something which is a mystery to them is wisdom to me and that my wisdom sees through their opinions; also that the explanation is the conversion from opinion to truth and health. These two characters, wisdom and opinion, stand before each other and the people choose the one they will obey just as they do in national affairs.

President Lincoln is the representative of health or the Constitution. Jeff Davis is the representative of the head of opinions or disease. All those who follow Davis are those who have departed from health or the Constitution and have followed after false gods or guides. When the armies meet, they come face to face and unfurl their banners. One is the flag of the sun or Constitution, the other is the banner of darkness or opinions. This wisdom has been represented by Joshua and as it says to the sun or Northern armies, "Halt!" and to the Southern moon or error, "Stop!" the leaders seeing the wisdom are alarmed and flee, but the people rejoice in the light of the American Constitution that shall make them well and free them from these blind guides.

This is the way with disease; disease is the offspring of error, and as long as the people will worship men's opinions, just so long they will be sick. To me it is as clear as daylight that if the people could see themselves, they would discard all the priests' and doctors' opinions and become a law unto themselves. All I do is put the world in possession of a wisdom that will keep them clear from these two classes of opinion. You may think I have some feeling against the doctors' character. Not at all, nor do I think that they who know me have anything against me as a man, but they scout the idea that I know any more about curing disease than they do. They have the wisdom and I the power. I stand to the medical faculty in this light as a harmless humbug, perfectly ignorant of what I profess, and all my talk is to amuse the patient and make him believe the disease is in his imagination. If I succeed it is all well, but so far as my wisdom goes, that is all humbug. I am aware that this is my position with the faculty and their opinions have such a strong hold on the people that the mass of people look upon me in the same light, and if by chance someone chooses to see that I am not the person that these blind guides call me, they are looked upon in the same light. I acknowledge that all this is true with regard to my position in society and how do I feel in regard to it? I know that it is all false although my word does not make it so, but I suppose that I have the same right to give my opinion with regard to these two classes as they have to give theirs about me, and I will now give it and let the masses judge for themselves.

The truth that I am trying to establish is something new. All established theories purporting to improve mankind are merely the effect of one set of demagogues trying to get the ascendency over another; the people are no better off, but worse. Disease of a person is like that of a nation; each is governed by arbitrary laws and the governing of both is alike. Disease is acknowledged to have an identity independent of man and man makes laws to govern it, attaches penalties to their disobedience, and calls them the laws of God. Let us see if these laws are not made by ourselves. Take fire for instance. If you put your hand into it, having no wisdom about it, who is to blame? You are. How are you to blame? Because you do not know any better, not because you do not know you are to blame. Is a child to blame for putting his hand in the fire? No. Has he not committed the same sin against the same law? You will say Yes, but he did not know any better. Well, did you? If you did, then you committed a sin of your own making for you put your hand into the fire against a law of your own understanding and your punishment is according to the transgression. But it is not so with the child. He has committed no sin for there is no intelligence in the act. Then the act or sin of ignorance is winked at so that man invents his own misery by his laws.

All governments have laws whereby to govern and in these laws is concentrated the wisdom of the people, the disobeying of which is followed by some kind of punishment. As the laws are our king we obey them through fear and the mediums or officers of the law are condemned or approved so we have no sympathy with the laws except as they keep the people in subjection. This keeps the nation all the time in an uproar like a family of children who quarrel to get possession of their father's wealth. If they respected their father more than they did their own selfishness, all would go well, but a false idea makes the trouble.

The government of the United States was founded on another basis, a higher principle of wisdom that had no laws for its children but whose laws were for strangers. It was based upon the wisdom of the people, on the principle that man was capable of self-government. This element filled the whole of the thirteen states and men and children attached their senses to this wisdom as their father, not as a man of flesh and blood, but an element of love. It was like the love of a good parent who, when the flesh and blood was laid in the ground, hovered around our fears in sympathy and wisdom and comforted us. So the wisdom of the people, gushing through every pore of the signers of the Declaration of American Independence, warms the hearts and limbs of all its children and each child attaches itself to the wisdom, not the President. As the children grew they wanted more land, and strangers coming among us, it became necessary to have a servant to explain the father's will. So we selected Washington, not as a leader or dictator but as a servant or counselor to explain our father's will and see that everyone was rewarded according to his acts. Now in the course of time differences of opinions sprang up and contentions arose; finally the father was denied and the will was broken. At last the wisdom or father was lost and the son became the power and then men began to worship the creature instead of the creator. Now that President is all the government we have and he is the President of a party; the old will is broken and man is like a sheep without a shepherd.

This has been the case for more than forty years till at last a division of the farm came up; this brought up the old will and revived the identity of the father or Constitution. Then the father's sympathy began to ooze out of the pores of his children at the North and adopted sons of the West. A struggle is now going on to see whether the will is good and whether the people still let old principles of our ancestors rule.

Disease began in the same way. Man at first was like a nation, just born into existence with only the laws of life that ministered to their wants from day to day. As in nations, opinions would spring up and as men multiplied, they must enter into a sort of combination for their own protection. This of course brought up a controversy, how to carry their plans into execution and this would lead to parties and leaders. So little by little men bound themselves with fetters of their own making and punished themselves by their own laws for God made man upright and man of himself sought out these inventions. As controversies arose of course men would get excited and troubles would come out of it, then laws and penalties would be introduced leading to superstition and all sorts of error. It then became necessary to select someone to explain the various phenomena. These guides, seeing how their opinions acted on the masses, obtained a power over the people; their next movement was to keep this power in their own hands, and it has always been handed down to this day in nations and individuals.

Man's life is controlled by arbitrary laws. He has no more power over his life independent of the laws of the medical faculty than a State has over the laws of the United States. Both act in accordance with the laws of a superior wisdom. In every act of his life man admits the laws of the medical faculty and dares not depart from them.

It is true that leaders spring up and form parties or theories, but all must admit the old constitution of the faculty, that there is disease independent of the mind. The whole controversy among them is how to kill it. One sets up his standard of warfare and attacks the patient with calomel, blisters, etc. Another approaches the patient with hot crop, ready to play upon the disease if it does not yield. A third advances with a little sugar plum coaxing him to leave. Another commands the disease to leave by power from another world, and so on; but no one undertakes to deny the authority of their father the devil, or the origin of disease.

This was the condition of the world at the time of Jesus. Speaking of the same thing, he says if the old covenant or theories had been faultless there would have been no need of another. So it is with the medical theory; if their remedies were equal to their laws, there would have been no need of another mode but they have created a fire which they cannot put out. So a new remedy must be applied, for the old theories are like an old garment ready to fall to pieces or an old carpet which will not bear to be shaken.

Now I stand alone, as one risen from the dead or these old theories, having passed through all these old ideas and risen again that I may lead you in this light that will open your eyes to the truth of him who spake as never man spake, for he spoke the truth. This truth condemns all man's opinions; it breaks down all creeds and priestcraft and upsets all the medical faculty and brings peace and good will to man. It teaches that man, in order to break off from his wickedness or opinions and learn to speak the truth, must not try to deceive his fellow man by pretending to know what is merely an opinion. Show me the doctor who really believes that his medicine has any curative qualities or any intelligence except as it is associated with his opinion and I will show you a fool, for no intelligent physician would dare risk his reputation on a homeopathic pill to cure a cough supposing that the patient took the medicine in his food and did not know it. This shows that they believe that they work on the imagination of the patient.

There are certain drugs that will act as an emetic or cathartic, so I can act upon a person as these drugs do; but if the patient should take an emetic by accident, it would then make him vomit. Now when the patient vomits if a wrong direction is given, another effect might be produced; so that it all goes to show that the mind must be guided by some wisdom superior to itself. If error directs, nothing certain is known of the effect; if wisdom is at the helm, no medicine is wanted, for wisdom can break opinion in pieces and as disease is the effect of opinion, wisdom is the destruction of disease.

I will illustrate the cures by myself and by the medical man. The medical faculty have through their ignorance created a fire or disease as Jeff Davis has done, and the masses believe that all the phenomena that they see and feel are the effect of a cause outside of themselves and leaders. So they make war with their own shadow and in their insane mind come down upon their best friends thinking they are the cause of their trouble, while their troubles are the effect of their own belief. So it is with the sick. Ignorance, not knowing how the mind can be affected by a direction outside of itself, identifies wisdom with error or matter so that truth is a stranger and it is all the time fighting against itself to get rid of an enemy of its own creation. Now teach man this simple fact–that in all action the wisdom of reaction is in the act, but the act knows it not for if it does, no bad effect will follow. To show these two ideas of action and reaction, it is necessary that the act should be known by some strong power or error that cannot be stayed without some loss. These embrace all the wisdom of the two worlds; one is action and the other reaction and our senses are attached to one or the other; therefore, if we look for the effect we shall find out the cause. But man does not look so far into this principle when applied to himself and here of all others is the very place to apply this rule, for it is the very balance of our existence; it is the principle of eternal life. It is life itself and to know it is to know every sensation, what it is and what will be the effect on our happiness before it takes place, so that we may apply another idea of safety. I will give an illustration to show how this principle is known in part by some and by others not at all.

I will take a child for a medium to explain this principle. The child sees a light. Here is a phenomenon. In it there is no wisdom to the child, so it puts its finger in the light; the sensation frightens the child; this excites the matter or mind and out of the sensation comes reason. It tries it again and the same results follow till fear prevents the child from repeating the act. Now the fire to the child is an enemy so it shuns it, fearing it will produce the same effect as before; thus you see it feels a sort of life or wisdom in the fire till it is taught that the fire is nothing of itself, only a simple chemical action without wisdom. To know that is all that is necessary to allay its fears and when the child knows it that wisdom keeps him from being burned.

Another case: A child will toss a stone into the air, not knowing or thinking that it will come down until it hits him on the head; here is where they fail. As soon as they learn how to apply this principle they will throw up the stone and the wisdom guides them out of danger. This principle runs all through our lives and unless we understand it so as to know how the phenomenon is produced, we do not know the effect.

I will here relate a case which just happened that I shall watch and report at a future time. A young lady whom I had been attending had been stopping with a friend some little time. One day her friend broke out with the measles. She had never been exposed to it she said, but they were in town and the U.S. troops had been sick with them. This was known in the city, so here was the origin of the measles. The soldiers were from the country and were accustomed to soldiers' living, eating, drinking and smoking. These habits and the idea of going to war and leaving their friends acted upon their minds and, being bilious or full of excitement, these different causes produced an eruption on the skin. Here was where the error commenced. The doctors, ignorant of the cause, invented the application of measles to the phenomenon and made the people believe their lie and this created the disease. So all persons, by the laws of these blind guides, who have exposed themselves or who have not were liable to have the disease. This made the disease common and the people gave credit to the doctors for tormenting them with an evil of their own make, just as the South praises the scamp Davis and others for making a disease that will be the means of their own destruction, while they fight the very friends who are warning them of their leaders. This was what Jesus did but the people, like the South, believed him an imposter and crucified the very man who was their friend. This has always been the case and always will till man can apply this test of seeing through the phenomena of this world and looking for causes in the effect. They must not call every new phenomenon the result of a power or gift or unknown cause in order to convince people of anything; but must admit their own ignorance.

I think that I have explained the phenomenon of the measles to the young lady so that she will not be affected by them; but if she is not, these blind guides will say, "It does not follow that a person must catch the measles because they are exposed," then I ask, Why do they catch them at all? Here is the fact. This young lady was nervous. Now see the shrewdness of these blind guides, although I will not give them the credit of knowing the fact. For they are only the mediums of the devil who invents these ideas, and he, like Jeff Davis, acts upon his mediums but see the craft of the old fellow. The measles are slow getting along. This is just as it must be; if you drop a seed into the earth it takes time for it to come forth. So it is with disease. When the devil sows his seeds through these doctors, they scatter the seeds promiscuously; some fall on good ground as it did with the soldiers, others fall on public opinion and are caught by the wise which prevent them doing much harm and some fall on stony ground or where they have had them before, so they do not take root but wither. Like every other error that the devil sows, he sows it in the night or darkness and while men are ignorant or asleep to the little nervous effect the seed is creating, the devil is busy in creating showers of opinion, like rain to help the seed come forth. The minds are agitated for a time to create the disease and when it comes these blind guides are called upon to destroy their own work. So when wisdom or this principle of action or reaction is acknowledged, then the devil and his works or mediums will be destroyed. This is the end of the world as far as disease is understood.

Then comes up a new theory having no consumption or any disease but a wisdom that will explain all these phenomena by the result of action and reaction or cause and effect. Causes not known are a mystery or power, but when known, the effect is known before it comes so that man's life may not be affected by it. In one sense it is foreknowledge; the effect is combined in the cause. The natural man never sees the cause, but when the effect comes he admits a cause, but to him it is a mystery or power that he is afraid of. So he reasons to keep clear of it and in his reason he creates his own misery and here doctors his own errors as though he had caught them from another. In this way man has been acting against his own happiness like an insane man that is always trying to destroy himself by fighting an invisible man, not seen by the well.

June 1861

My Religion
[BU 2:0122]

When I talk to the sick, I talk my theory; when I talk to the well, I talk about it. It is so with my religion. I have no religion independent of my acts. When I am religious, I talk it and put it into practice. When I am not putting my religion into practice for the benefit of the sick and those whom I can help, then if I talk I am talking about it. Here is a distinction that may at first seem curious to some, but if you will look at it rightly, you will see that there is more in it than you would at first suppose. One of Christ's followers made a remark like this in regard to the same distinction, only he called their talk or belief, faith, which is religion put in practice. He said, Show me your religion or faith independent of works, and I will show you my religion or faith by my works. There is no such thing as goodness of itself.

January 1860

My Religious Belief
[LC 2:0838]

In giving to the public my ideas in regard to curing the sick, it will be necessary to correct some false ideas that have been circulated in regard to my religious belief. So I will say I have no belief in regard to any person's opinion or religion or disease. I know they are all based on a false idea of wisdom. I take the sick as I find them and treat them according to their several diseases. As their diseases are the result of their education or belief, I have to come in contact with their beliefs. Their religious beliefs are often the cause of their trouble, but the medical theory causes more trouble than all the rest at the present day. In times of old when the priests led the masses, the causes emanated from the priests, but since the right of religious freedom has been granted to all, the truth has destroyed the power of the priest. It has not, however, enlightened the people but has transferred the idea of disease to the medical faculty, so that now the people have these two powers to contend with, the physician and the priest.

I will not call the power of the priest religion but in opposition to it. All the religion I acknowledge is God or Wisdom. I will not take man's belief to guide my barque. I would rather stand at the helm myself, but the priests and medical faculty have assumed the livery of truth and one pretends to look after the body and the other the soul. So between them both, they have nearly destroyed soul and body, for you cannot find one person in ten but complains of some trouble in the form of disease. All disease leads to destruction or death; therefore death is one of the natural results of disease. So to save persons from what may follow, a religious belief is introduced and another world is made which is to receive all mankind, and then they are rewarded according to their acts. This makes up the whole progression of man's life. Now in all this, progression and intelligence and every kind of goodness is not included. It is true we are told that to live a virtuous life is good, but you never hear that to be posted up on all the wisdom of the world and understanding science gave such a person any advantage over the weak and humble believer who swallowed everything the priest told him; but it is rather the reverse effect. To be a good Christian according to their explanation of religion is to be humble and not be wise at all. Now every person partakes of this belief, and in fact they are all made up of belief, for everything you can think of or remember is such, except principles, and these are never admitted or spoken of in any religion.

Now all things must end according to man's belief, and there never has been any theory yet that has ever come in collision with it. Therefore life and death are the natural destiny of man. It is true that the medical faculty try to stave it off, but their efforts are like those of the Rebels–the harder they work the surer they are to destroy the thing they are trying to save. So man's belief is the thing to be either saved or lost and to this end all their skill is directed. This was just the state of the world when Jesus appeared.

1862

My Use of the Word Mind
[LC 1:0192]

You know I have tried to prove that mind is matter; and if I have proved that, I will now show you that matter is life. This you all will admit so far as vegetation is concerned. Now see if animal matter is not life. If so, you see that man is made up of life. His body is particles of animal life condensed into a form or idea called man, or a living being of life, not science, but life governed by science. Now what is man when he is not man, for you say man dies? So what is he when he is not man? He is science for there is no animal life in science. Then what is science? It is that wisdom which controls life. Is it not life? If it is, then there is no word to define it, for life is matter and matter is life. Animal life is in flesh and blood, so flesh and blood is not science, but science controls it. If science is wisdom, what are wisdom's attributes? Has it an identity? The wisdom of man has an identity of matter in a living form. Can you give any definite idea of what persons mean by soul? The person that invented the word soul must have applied it to an idea that never had an existence, for soul is always applied to life. We read of fat souls and lean souls and saving souls and losing souls, so you see that word cannot explain man when he is not man. For when he is not man, he is not soul so we must get some other word to define what man is when he ceases to be matter.

I will now try to explain what man is and what he is not, and show that what he is, he is not, and what he is not, he is. I will illustrate the two men so that each shall be a separate and distinct identity. I will take for my illustration the man as we see him and science as the man we cannot see through the natural man, for science cannot be seen, only its effects, and show how they differ. The natural man is made of flesh and blood. Science is not. Man has life. Science is life. Man has sight. Science is sight. Man has feeling. Science is feeling. Man has all of the five senses. Science is all of the five senses. Man of himself cannot do anything. Science can do all things. Man is of matter. Science is not. Then what is man, independent of science? Nothing but an idea of life and death. Then where does he differ from the brute? In the idea of science. Where does science make the distinction? It makes no distinction. Who does? The first cause or God. How? In attaching science to the identity called man. Then does science have an identity? Yes. What is it? Wisdom of God. Has it senses? It is senses. Has it soul? No. It creates and destroys the soul. Has it death? No. It destroys death by its own development. When you give it all its qualities, what kind of a creature or person is it? It is the scientific man, not of flesh and blood but of that world where error never comes. It speaks through man. What does? Its life or the wisdom of God. How does it get its food? By the sweat of its brow or the development of itself. Where does it differ from the natural man? In everything. Show by illustration. The natural man is nothing but an idea which science uses to illustrate some fact or problem that is for the development of science. Then what does man gain or lose by death as it is called? Just as much as any matter that is always changing.

August 1860

Nations and Individuals Have Four Characters
[LC 1:0607]

Nations and individuals are composed of four characters. To the world, the natural and spiritual man are united in one body, but science can divide and separate them. The natural lives in truth and also in error and these make two distinct characters. The spiritual man of truth and error the same. Here we have four distinct characters or identities: the natural man of truth and error and the spiritual man of the same and the former is in each case the shadow of the latter.

I will illustrate how these are combined and show how they are distinct and yet united. Let the United States represent an individual or a union of the four. Two of these are seen in political parties. One seeking to govern the nation by slavery may be called disease; the other striving to hold the power over the mind by sympathy for human rights is like health. These two powers are like a man and his wife, one wishing to rule the other who is eager to live in peace. Slavery is that diseased state of mind governed by passion and has its spiritual counterpart in the devil. The opposite desiring to live in harmony is the shadow of a spiritual truth, for they are the offspring of matter. Beyond these, there is yet another being directing and governing all things for the best, Wisdom or God who overrules and provides everything.

The government of the United States I will take as a symbol of this wisdom and by it, I will illustrate how the father or wisdom is bringing about his own ends for the benefit of the world. Slavery and Freedom like heat and cold are necessary to bring about some great result. They are represented by man and woman, and when they unite as in man and wife, it is under a contract and the agreements to bring about the union is the courtship. Like all marriages, this union was subject to certain contingencies. Between slavery (the man) and freedom (the woman), there was no sympathy for each was true to its own element. And when new states like children were added to the union, they partook of their parents' ideas; and as there never was harmony between them, it was not strange that the children should disagree and that they should take part in the family jars. Now the overruling wisdom that I have spoken of is not yet known, but it is in the element which governs the mother, that is love For her children. But the father not partaking of that element does not admit it, yet it acts upon both, in one case to destroy and in the other to purify the mind that is to destroy the earth or ignorance and bring forth the new man or science. The wife or mother is the child of wisdom, but the husband is of the earth. For out of the earth the Lord made man (not woman), and the word man refers to that part of every person that must perish; it is error. The marriage is for the life of the man, but the resurrection is to follow death or the fulfillment of the contract. As the union is now in its last stages and the old man or slavery is about to die, the mother is to come into possession of the estate, and the children being of age claim the privilege of deciding their inheritance and the result is a family quarrel. Those who partake of the mother element are in favor of the union, that is, of holding the property in common, and those who wish it divided are of the father. Meanwhile the wisdom which governs all things is acting silently in the minds.

At last the children begin to conflict, and the slavery power, finding that freedom or the mother element is predominant, becomes wroth and makes war against peace. They fight and out of the ashes of the quarrel comes a peace, corresponding to the mother. Then liberty and peace, neither containing the element of slavery, will mingle and become one. This wedding will embrace a higher class of mind who are capable of being governed by truth and science. The serpent of slavery will be cast out and the love of progress and liberty will mingle with the love of the union; the bargain will once more be renewed and cemented by the bonds of friendship, the Constitution.

Every individual is like a nation and every idea going to destroy the progress of happiness must perish. Sitting by the sick and taking their feelings has led me to investigate the relation of man and wife towards each other. It is often said that certain married couples are not created to live with each other, and if it were not for the law, they would separate. This is the case with half the marriages, but the evil is not attributed to the right cause. It is because of the ignorance of ourselves. Those who feel that they are not mated are in truth mated, but they do not know it, from the fact that they know not themselves. I will try to explain what I know to be the true relation of man and wife, and also explain the error that enters into their union and makes so much misery.

Suppose a lady and gentleman become acquainted with each other and the acquaintance is of the most happy kind. If both are in their proper element, there will be no discord, but if one or the other makes any sacrifice, for instance, if the lady dislikes the natural turn of the gentleman she thinks she loves or the gentleman is deceived in the woman whom he thinks he loves, there must be a concession, as with freedom and slavery. A quarrel follows and one becomes the slave of the other, and if they are ignorant, they both live in a discord. This discord can be overcome by the theory that makes persons one in wisdom. I will suppose that one of the parties knows this science and knows how to practice it, and I will show in what manner it works. This science of love is not of passion; it is always at work whether the person knows it or not. When not known, it produces trouble, but if a person knows it, the same trouble is felt; but governed by wisdom, good results follow. It is like music, the enjoyment of which you wish your friends to share. To compel him with no taste for music to listen would be annoying him, but if he does not listen to the music, it does not follow that he has no taste for it, but for some reason he was not interested.

Individual life is like a book made up of the wisdom and folly of the world, and this science teaches one to read his friend's book. And if he finds that it contains nothing of importance, let him commence and read from his own book and test the qualities of his friend. He must use his own judgment and not get discouraged if his friend becomes nervous, for this shows there is a vein leading to a fountain of purer water than has ever yet been discovered. Therefore, he must not give up the discovery and fall back and parley, causing a delay, whereby the opposition can make a more desperate effort, for if there is nothing to gain, there will be no opposition. I have found in curing the sick that ignorance never disturbs itself to fight. I have also found that I can change the mind so that a person that is hated can become loved, if he has anything to be loved, and also the person that is changed can respect what he never had any respect for. He who knows this science can read his opponent and see whether his mind is worth working, for some persons are like a mine that is soon exhausted, while there are others where it seems the more you dig into their mine, the richer is the ore. This desire to develop mind is God working in us, and if man's senses become attached to this wisdom, his happiness is in the improvement of others. I derive more happiness in developing a person's mind than in all the scientific pursuits I ever followed.

Natural Man, The

[LC 1:0355]

All mankind have respect for wisdom or something superior to themselves that they cannot understand. Man of himself is naturally indolent, brutish and willful, content to live like the brute. He is pleased at any bauble or trifling thing. He has imitation and tries to copy whatever pleases him. In this he shows his reverence for his superiors. As he does not possess wisdom or science, he is often deceived. Thus he is made timid and willing to be led. His courage is the courage of ignorance, and when he sees superior numbers, he curls down like a dog when whipped by his master. Easily led and easily deceived, no confidence is to be placed on his word, for his word is always like the wag of a dog's tail to show his submission. But when his ends are answered, his next act might be to injure the very one that had just saved him from some trouble. He is easy in his manners if all goes well, but if needed for anything he, like the dog, is ready at the whistle of his master or anyone that will pat him, to bite his own master or anyone else.

Now because the brutes can be taught something, it does not follow that they can be taught science. They have their bounds which they cannot pass. So the natural man has his bounds which he cannot pass. But when I speak of the natural man, I speak of that wisdom that is based on an opinion. The brute is undergoing a change by the introduction of the wisdom of man; so the natural man in the same way is undergoing a change by the introduction of the scientific man. The brute is developed as far as the wisdom of man is capable of instructing him; so science takes the man of opinions and instructs him in the wisdom of God or science. Now as every man has more of the wisdom of opinions than of science, he is ignorant of himself, and being ignorant, he can only see one character; for all the wisdom he has is public opinion. He is up today and down tomorrow and knows not the cause of his rise or fall; so he is but one identity that is acknowledged by him. His change is so gradual that he never knows he has changed but supposes that all changes go to prove that he has remained the same. These minds are often found in politics. You will hear a person say, "I was always a Democrat or Federalist and my father and grandfather were before me." Now this is a man of one idea. He is like the old gray-headed veteran who stands on Mount Joy and looks around on Portland and then turns to his young friend and says, "My lad, I remember when I helped cut the wood where the city now stands some eighty or ninety years ago." His young friend says, "You must have changed very much." "Oh! I am older but I am the same man I was then." In reality there is not a single idea about him the same except his five senses. So it is with the political man. His senses are attached to the word "Democrat" and as long as that word lives in the wisdom of opinions, he is a Democrat; and so long as this identity lives in him, he never changes, for his senses never were attached to any principle. So the changes of principle are nothing to him as he never had any. But with the other party it is not the same. The senses of the masses are attached to the word as the Democrats are, but as there is a progressive wisdom that works in man, it finds more affinity in the Federal Party than in the Democrat, for the leaders of the party are selfish and appeal to the one idea Democrat or Federal. This makes up the great parties in all the progress of opinions and science. Now the science, being a stranger to both, cannot work like the demagogues by appealing to the one idea, for the senses are attached to the progression or wisdom that governs both. So as progression is the order of the day the senses of the masses become attached to new ideas and detached from old ones and thus parties are all the time changing, and minds are changing to suit the times. This gives the demagogues a chance to appeal to the masses, and as long as they can lead the masses by one idea, they use any sort of cunning that comes up to suit their convenience.

March 1861

New England

[LC 1:0571]

We are sometimes told that our puritan ancestors were distinguished from other men by one characteristic, viz: a tenacious adherence to a particular religious faith, and that in other respects they were like the society in which they lived. Persecuted on account of religion, they left comfortable homes and faced the dangers of the sea and planted their colony on the barren shores of the new world in order to enjoy, unmolested, the right of worship.

Now if I understand the true feelings of the people, they were men and women who partook of the principle of freedom, for the sake not of monopolizing but of extending it and teaching others to enjoy it. Jealous, therefore, of any social corrupting influence that might lead their flock astray, like Moses they established laws and penalties such as in their judgment would promote the general good. Religion was their peculiar feeling, perfectly simple and easily borne by them; but not knowing that it contained error, yet enforcing it as true, they made it obnoxious to the masses. But opposition awakened their higher faculties, and men and women came forth uniting in themselves these strong elements of character, viz: great intellectual energy, and what gives it protection and efficiency, a corresponding degree of physical strength. These are the characteristics of New England.

As drones always work their way into society, they appeared among this people and affected their intellectual development for being acted upon by the higher element. They, in their intelligence, began to invent and their inventions were counterfeits of those of the higher class because they had no sympathy. Inventiveness is never easy when there is a chance for improvement, but drones having no more respect than savages for improvement appreciated only the worldly advantage derived from them. Gain being the first law of their nature, their eyes were open to the least chance of obtaining the reward of labor without the toil. This desire for wealth became uppermost in the New England mind. But riches are not confined to dollars and cents; there is a purer one and one more difficult to attain.

Wisdom requires the highest development of man, and this the inventive element, when directed to the pursuit of wisdom, produces. Acting upon the natural man, it seeks every opportunity for improvement, while drones are striving to obtain money without intellectual effort. Ambition and love of gain are the two opposite traits of the New England character. They cannot be found in latitudes where the soil requires little or no labor to support populations. The inhabitants of such countries, finding no incentive to ambition or incentive to labor, are indolent and stupid.

If California should lose her gold, the state of society would rapidly improve. For when hard times come to New England, brains will labor and invent, and then thrift and prosperity would ensue. Again let the South become poor; it would at once produce a class of people, industrious and enterprising, who would devote themselves to agriculture and the arts and sciences. New England habits must drive out indolence and establish its own principles of free labor and education all over the country and cause science and industry to be everywhere appreciated. The natural man, who is only a grade above the brute, is proud, overbearing and fond of power. Below him is another class of mind represented in the masses, inferior, because like mortar, it must be molded by some outside influence.

Out of this proceed again the natural man and every evil thing. But when it is refined enough to receive the seeds of wisdom, then New England intelligence enters the field and makes war with the children of this kingdom. This state of things is illustrated in the parable where Jesus says, And they shall come from the East and from the West and from the North and from the South and shall sit down in the kingdom of God. So science shall come into the kingdom of truth. Southern ignorance shall be cast out and a new state of society shall appear.

No community can be thrifty and intelligent except on the basis of labor. In New England every faculty was early brought into action to make money and originate ideas. Every kind of useful implement was invented, manufactured and sold by them to the parties in exchange for land. Opposition served only as a stimulant to their inventive minds. Their wares as well as their ideas were circulated all over the country, and New England itself became a sort of pedlar's cart.

What then is New England? I answer, That portion of the human race that discovers truth, establishes science and cultivates the arts. And also that part of mankind which are skilled in low cunning and craft. The two extremes of moral condition, the subtle act of the serpent and the lofty power of genius meet in the New England character, being the outgrowth, one of the progressive and the other of the brutal elements of man. The latter causes a man to try and gain money without the honest labor of his brain or hands. In such men the highest motive of life is a selfish desire for power and to this end all their energies are directed. They want money, but instead of acquiring it by honest toil or ingenious inventions, they forge lies and appealing to the envy and jealousy of the ignorant try to turn them against all improvement. On the other hand, he, who partakes of the progressive element, brings the fruit of his brains into the market and supports his idle brethren who are too proud to work. A genuine Yankee of the first quality, whether school teacher or professional man, brings his articles into the market and advertises his business. His customers are the indolent and the ambitious. Such are Southerners who, assuming the strut of the turkey and the air of the peacock, live on the degradation of the race. Like bloodhounds they are always ready to spring at their master's bidding. Fed on prejudice they oppose every measure that demands energy of thought. Their leaders, although preaching the doctrine of equality, really stand to their followers as master to slave and find it for their interest to oppose the ambition of superior minds.

Led by sympathy, the early settlers chose localities adapted respectively to develop their peculiar traits. An indolent man in New England and a smart man in a slave community are equally out of place. Ambition and pride underlie these opposite characters and pervade society. The puritan Yankee is opposed in every principle to the Southerner and to the Northern man with Southern principles. The puritan principles of liberty and improvement will penetrate every part of the globe and will always be found battling with indolence and slavery. Although not acceptable at the South, it will one day establish itself on the ruins of slavery. It is indestructible and it would exist if the New England States should be blotted from the face of the earth. It cannot, like matter, be dissolved, for it is God in man. It will reign till slavery is under its foot. Slavery has its God and its religion, but they are in profession only, while the God of New England is in the life of his people. Slavery has its worship, but its worshippers are narrow and overbearing, demanding revenge, while the worship of the lovers of freedom is seen in their works.

February 1863

New Theory on the Cure of Diseases, A
[LC 3:1349]

A gentleman of Belfast by the name of P. P. Quimby has for the last sixteen years been engaged in the investigation of the science of mesmerism, so far as it relates to the cure of disease to see if it could be reduced to a science. After careful investigation he has come to this result: that the cure of disease is as much a science as correcting the error of any other science. His ground is that all the knowledge of disease is in the mind. He calls our feeling the disease; the mind changes the fluids, therefore to correct the mind, you correct the fluids. He believes mind is spiritual matter and by changing the combination of this matter it is shown in the form of disease. He shows the difference between his theory and all others. He explains all other theories on one platform, differing only in the medicines. He says all theories admit of disease independent of the mind. They also admit disease as a thing which can be acted upon by some drug or medicine. He places all theology knowledge from a spirit world in the same category and says that all the above theories have their peculiar medium through which they act upon the mind of the patient. Each and all acting upon the mind of the patient without his having the slightest knowledge of where the trouble lies. They sometimes make a difference between nervous diseases. He describes the medium through which they act. The Allopathic physician approaches the patient through this medium; he admits the error his patient has embraced. I will here take one case to illustrate all the rest, disease of the lungs. This they all admit from the allopath to the spiritualist; this I set down as an error, admitted as a disease by them all. They differ in regard to the means of medicine to be used to get rid of a disease or something that has come upon a person without any knowledge on his part. I said that they all have their mediums. The allopathic physician thinks his medicines contain some healing qualities that can change the fluids of the system and bring about a better state. His first object is to gain the confidence of his patient. This is done in various ways; some by holding out the idea of his superior knowledge over his brother physician; others by running down the old practice by holding out the idea that their medicine is poison. The Spiritualist holds out the idea that he receives his medicine from a spirit world. He admits the same diseases as all the rest though he only differs in the remedies.

Now the patient is left to choose one or the other of the above remedies. His friends sit in and give their opinions. They differ as much as the doctors, each wishing to have his own way until at last a physician is sent for and the experiment commences. One thing after another is tried, until out of patience the physician is discharged and another is sent for. Throughout all of these experiments not one word is hinted at that the trouble is in the mind. When all fails and the patient is left to die, he then sends for Quimby to sit down and tell him how he feels, and at the same time telling him that the trouble is in his mind. This requires proof for it strikes at the root of all the others' theories. He then shows that a proper understanding of themselves will change the mind and bring about the very thing desired. He believes that every word or idea spoken contains something and this something changes the mind of the patient. He sees the spiritual form of the patient whom he converses with and wins it back to itself. This he repeats till the patient is restored to health. His idea of disease is error that changes the mind, truth restores the mind and changes the fluids.

New Truth, The
[LC 2:0836]

I believe now that the time has nearly arrived when the people will be prepared to receive a great truth that gives an impulse to their mind and sets them investigating a subject which will open to their minds new and enlarged ideas of themselves and show man what he is and how he makes himself what he is. It has been said that to know himself is the greatest study of man, but I say to know his error is greater than to know himself, for every person is to himself just what he thinks he is; but to know his error is what ought to be his greatest study. For the last 25 years I have been trying to find out what man is and at last have come to know what he is not. To know that you exist is nothing, but to know what disturbs you is of great value to everyone. The world has been developing itself, and we look on and never think it is ourselves. Through our ignorance of wisdom, we have made a man of straw and have given him life, intellect and a head in the image of our own creation.

To this image we have given the idea man and certain capacities such as life and death and have made him subject to evils such as disease and death. To this man of straw, the words I have quoted are applied. This man of straw has been trying to find himself out and in doing this has nearly destroyed or blotted out his real existence. So in looking for this man, I found it was like the old lady looking for her comb and finding it on her head. I found I was the very idea I was looking for. Then I knew myself and found that what we call man is not man but merely a shadow of error.

Wisdom is the true man and error the counterfeit, and when Wisdom governs matter, all goes well; but when error directs, all goes wrong. So I shall assume the old mode of calling man, as he is called, and make myself a principle outside of man just as man makes all "laws of God," as he calls them, outside of himself. So man admits he is not with God or a part of him. Therefore he belongs to this world and expects to die and go to his God. So he lives all his life in bondage through fear of death. Now this keeps him sick, and to avoid all these fears and troubles that disturb his mind and make him sick, he invents all sorts of false ideas and never thinks they are the cause of his misery. He invents all sorts of disease to torment himself. Standing outside of these ideas I know that they are the works of man because God or Wisdom has never made anything to torment mankind. Error has created its own misery.

Having had 25 years of practice, I have seen the working of this evil on mankind, how it has grown and increased till at the present time there is more misery from disease than all of the evils put together, and every effort to arrest this evil only makes it worse. Within the last seven years I have sat with more than twelve-thousand different persons and have taken their feelings and know what they believed their diseases were and how each person was affected, and I knew the causes. Therefore I know what I say is true: that if there had never been a physician in the world, there would not have been one-tenth of the suffering. It is also true that religious creeds have made a very large class of persons miserable; but religion, like all errors based on superstition, must give way to science or wisdom. So as science progresses, religious creeds give way to a higher intellectual belief and so superstition in regard to religion will die out as men grow wise, for wisdom is all the religion that can stand and this is to know ourselves not as a man but as part of Wisdom. But disease is making havoc among all classes, and it seems as though there will never be an end of it unless someone can step in and check this greatest of all evils.

I have been in the habit of sitting with patients separately and explaining the disease and the cause, etc. till I have come to the conclusion that I can cure persons that are sick if I am in their company, and the number only helps to hasten the cure. I have no doubt that I can go to an audience of one-thousand persons and cure more persons in one lecture than can be cured by all the doctors in the state of Maine in the same time, for I know that one-half my patients I do not see long enough to explain as much as I could in one lecture of two hours. There are a great number of sick who are not sick enough to be cured. Man's life and happiness in this enlightened world is dependent on physicians who have made dollars and cents the cure. So if a man has not these he must suffer. My object is to relieve man of some of his sufferings. I am sent for to go to distant parts of the country and have always found a large class of poor, sick persons not able to be cured, and so they must suffer. I want to relieve this class who are not able to be cured, and also give directions to minds so that this wisdom shall govern the man,

It will be necessary to say that I have no religious belief. My religion is my life, and my life is the light of my wisdom that I have. So that my light is my eye, and if my eye is the eye of truth, my body is light; but if my eye or wisdom is an opinion, my body is full of darkness. Science is the process of getting wisdom.

1865

Nothing and Something I
[LC 2:0796]

I have spoken of nothing producing nothing. I will now show that what is nothing to me is something to the one that believes it. Take a person that believes in ghosts. Now to that person a ghost is something and if the ghost troubles him by tormenting his body with pain, the pain to him is as real as the other pain, and one is as real as the other. Now for me to say that both are nothing is to those who believe, an absurdity, for they think that their feeling to me is all imagination. But this is not the case. I will illustrate it another way. The dark makes some persons nervous, so they want a light; now that light expels the darkness, so when the light is present the fear is gone. Now there is no such thing as darkness to those that have light, so the darkness is in those that have no light. So darkness produces darkness and light produces light. Now to call a belief darkness and call it something and say that nothing produced it, is to light, an absurdity. But to darkness it can't see it, for there is no light in their substance called darkness.

Disease is darkness and all sorts of ghosts exist in this darkness and as the things are real to the ones that live in darkness, the effect on them is real. Now as truth expels their darkness by introducing the light of reason, they will then see that all their troubles are in their minds. For their minds being dark in regard to truth or light, they choose darkness or belief in their error because it looks to them as truth. So they had rather acknowledge a lie than investigate the truth which will condemn themselves. Now these absurdities run all through man's reason, for all his reason is based on this flimsy foundation of darkness; and as there is no light about it, all that ever is seen is the effect on their bodies. And these show themselves to their dark minds in the form of substances and take the name of disease. Now wisdom sees through these shadows and knows the author that makes them.

How often I hear these words. Just take away the pain I have in my head or limb so that it won't come back again and that is all I ask. Now here they virtually admit the pain as some living thing that I may have the power to rid them of; therefore it must have an existence separate from them and then it has an identity. Now where does this belief differ from the belief in Salem witchcraft? The people then believed that these spirits or witches would come and pinch them, leaving the marks of their fingers on the flesh. They also believed that all their pains were from some evil spirit or from God. How often do you hear persons say that God often afflicts people for their good.

Now all these false ideas and thousands more of the same kind are the cause of the evils that man suffers and they are all fruits of the old tree of superstition. So as they begin to trim it up and engraft new ideas into the old stock, it still partook of the old tree. Once it bore all kinds of fruit of misery and good. It first was good and evil. It bore this kind of fruit, but the good became extinct by engrafting all kinds of evil. Now necessity being the mother of invention, man wishes to account for everything he hears or sees. If he feels a pain, he wants to know the cause and being ignorant, he attaches it to something. So he has a name for it, the same as if he saw an animal he would give it a name or he would enquire of someone till he found a name right or wrong. So the doctors being admitted to be teachers of health to warn the sick of their danger, it is supposed they are posted up. So when any of these living things called disease get hold of us, we send for the doctor to tell us what it is and how to get rid of it.

Now if we did not believe disease was a living thing, why do we want to kill it and if it had life, where was it before we got it? So all goes to show that we believe disease is just as much of a living thing as a ghost and witches of Salem times. When the doctor calls, as he is as ignorant as his patient but wants to appear wise, his wisdom looks in the dark. If the patient feels a little disturbed about the chest and tells the doctor, he, that is the doctor, looks very wise into the dark and says your liver is diseased. Now where was this disease or living thing that has gotten hold of you before you knew it? In the doctor and the world. So when you received his opinion you received a lie and this lie brought forth a child, called liver complaint. Now to you the child is really a living being without a father, but to wisdom it has a father, for wisdom knows that nothing cannot produce liver complaint, yet the patient has no idea of its father. But it has a father and he is the belief in a diseased liver. So to wisdom, it is the child of the devil, or one lie begets another lie, or one nothing begets another nothing. But you can only see the effect. This is as far as the natural man can see, but he will always admit that there is a cause. The true cause he never admits as such, yet in his acts he admits it.

Now I find the father and make him own the child or disease and then I destroy both father and child or the devil and his works, for his kingdom is in darkness and his works are brought to light by wisdom. So as mind is matter according to man's belief, belief is matter and so is the effect of belief in disease. But as mind to wisdom is nothing but darkness, the effect on man called disease is the reflection of his belief, and until the light of science lights up his darkness, the shadow to him will be seen. So what to the sick is real, to me is mind.

So when I say that disease is in the mind, I mean that it does not exist anywhere else. For if you feel pain, you know it is you and no one else; if you feel pleasure, does not everyone that is capable of feeling pleasure, feel it? Is it not so with grief? Did you ever hear of a man's liver complaining and the owner feel well? Does a white swelling feel pain? Now if the pain were not in the owner, why does he try to get rid of it? I have seen a great many sick persons and have found that all their troubles they lay to something they want to get rid of. Sometimes they even find fault with their actions and want to act better, and sometimes with their food and they say it hurts them. Yet if they should have their minds acted upon by some excitement, the distress is gone for the time. Now convince them that it is their belief and that their belief is the living thing which has gotten into the stomach and is gnawing them, and ask them where the living thing is outside of their belief. For the thing that gnaws is not the thing that complains, it is the one that gets gnawed, and as they think that they and their stomachs are one, they want to get rid of their enemy.

Now I propose to convince them that they are gnawing themselves, for when I change the mind and allay their fears, the ghost or belief lets go. Now to show the foregoing to be mind, and that although mind with wisdom is nothing, yet to error it is something and wisdom has to admit it as such, and then destroy it, is my object. This sort of reasoning is called the Platonic mode of reasoning. Admit what you know to be a lie and then show your superior wisdom by opposing it. Socrates denied everything and made his opponent prove what they affirmed and his pupil, Plato, took both grounds. So I am obliged to admit what I know is false for the sake of proving it a lie. So with disease. I have to admit the phenomenon when I know the cause is all in the mind and this the sick deny. So to prove it I have to analyze mind in every way that can be conceived of, to show that mind is something that can be changed. When I have proved this, I find facts that will be admitted to prove that minds can act upon another mind. Then comes in this truth that nothing cannot produce any one thing.

So if mind produces any one thing, mind must be something. I then show that mind or thoughts disturb our sleep and strange things arise to disturb us. Now if all this is nothing, how does it frighten man into fits and other diseases as they are called? Now to deny that thoughts are anything and admit that we are affected and that we become sick and lose our sleep and the whole body becomes perfectly paralyzed by a word from another is to admit that nothing produces something. Now assuming that mind or thoughts and reason are something, the way is clear to see and understand how all things come into being and how these strange things like spirits and ghosts and diseases are formed. Again if mind is not something, how can it be changed? Grief is a state of mind and when gayety comes, grief is gone, as when light appears the darkness is gone. Now no one will say that when a person is in the dark and knows it that his mind is not in the knowledge of that fact.

Now dissipate the darkness by the introduction of light and will anyone say that his mind is not changed? His senses are now attached to the light where before they were in the dark. Suppose he was frightened by the dark; when the light comes his fright disappears. Is not his mind changed, and if so what has changed it? If the mind is not something that is capable of impression, how does the darkness impress it? Can there be an effect without a cause? If all men say no, then what is the cause? Give it a name that will represent something that you call nothing. Again if mind is not admitted to be something why do persons take medicine to quiet the mind? Again why are we afraid of things that we cannot see if we do not believe they exist? And if they do exist, they must be something. Again if they are something, they must have life, for if dead they wouldn't be troubling us. Besides if disease was not something that has life, why do we try to get rid of it and believe that it may be killed or destroyed? All man's acts show that he believes in all that I have stated and here is the foundation of man's reason.

Now as I said, wisdom knows that all of this is false, the cause and the effect. The mind is nothing and the effect the same. So to prove that what I have showed is something to the natural man but nothing to the scientific man, is to show that there is something that cannot change; this is a solid or wisdom. So I will try to give some idea of what it can do, and what its properties are and how it acts on this something that man calls matter. So I must suppose a principle or something that exists outside of man or that part called mind. For I take the ground that a principle cannot change so mind cannot be a principle. Therefore there must be a principle that exists outside of mind. Besides, if there is not, why does anything act according to certain principles? Laws are not principles, they are the invention of mind and therefore can be changed to suit any emergency that arises. But you cannot make a pound of lead rise from the ground into the air without some power independent of the principle that keeps it still. It may dissolve and then its weight becomes lighter than the atmosphere. And then it will rise, not of itself, but it is governed by a principle that air is heavier than the rarefied lead, and the principle is, of course, that the lighter must give way to the heavier.

1864

Nothing and Something II
[LC 2:0801]

In investigating the subject of health, I start with the idea that nothing never produced any one thing; therefore every effect must have a cause. Now reasoning from the principle that nothing cannot produce any one thing, it is plain that nothing will produce nothing. If this were not so, everything might produce anything and there could be no such principle as action and reaction, for all things would be springing from anything: animals coming out of the ground, trees bearing fruit in the winter, sleighs running in the summer, flowers springing out of snow banks.

Now we know that all this is not so, so we say that everything has its cause. Call the cause what you will, it must be something. As we see seeds produce vegetation, we may reason that everything has its seed or something that attracts it to its kind. Assuming this ground, I shall try to show that these seeds grow and form bodies and these bodies also produce seeds which form other bodies and all these bodies grow and fill the earth without the aid of man. All this will be admitted by every person. Now all these things must have their origin in something. What shall we call it? I will call it Wisdom. I assume that wisdom is the first cause. We all see harmony in the mineral and vegetable world. All kinds of matter dissolve and pass into the air or earth and out of the decomposition springs life in another form, so that matter of one kind produces other matter of the same kind, and when the matter is dissolved by old age, other kinds spring up.

Take the forest. When the old growth of trees is destroyed, a new growth takes its place, but usually of a different combination. Everything in nature is subject to this law of decomposition, acted upon by some unknown power. We call it old age or decomposition. In this great garden of creation, created by this wisdom, comes another kind of matter called animal which may include any kind of living thing, animals, the finny tribes, the feathered creation, reptiles and every creeping thing. They are another kind of matter more rarefied than the first, yet they are composed of seeds or life, and each seed produces other bodies after its kind. But when old age or time destroys the body, the life that springs out of the dead body is not like the other. So you see that all matter can produce other results of a similar kind, till the idea is destroyed, when the matter assumes another form or identity. Now all I have said is continually going on and yet there is no higher matter developed than the animal.

Now in this garden, wisdom has seen fit to plant another being of matter, not differing so much from that kind that was formed before, yet it is different in this respect. It seems to contain something of the likeness of its father, wisdom. Not a likeness of matter in a form but of wisdom. It seems to have power over the matter of other kingdoms. Now I assume that this superior wisdom is from or a part of the first cause that is to act as an agent to establish a scientific mode of regulating and keeping and preserving the original stock and improving the condition of its race. This agent I call the scientific man or God, acting on matter of all kinds. Now, as I said, matter or seeds produced matter of the same kind, but when destroyed by a natural decay, other combinations spring up. So with the animal creation.

So each kind of matter mingles with other matter and thus the species are kept alive or retain their own identity. Now this matter is devoured by some other matter. The earth and air devours all kinds of minerals and vegetable matter and out of itself comes other forms. So the animals live on animal matter or life, and as this life is seeds or matter, it goes to make the body of the animal that eats it and his character partakes of the food he eats. This either improves the species or destroys it. It generally destroys the original combination. This is called the running out of certain breeds of animals because they are not crossed, as it is said, but it is the natural result of matter. It, and another species, is brought out or another development.

So man lives on all the matter of the kingdom and his matter being a part of every kind, his life is in the combination that governs him. Now as I said before, new developments in matter are always taking place. So man like all other animals goes through this change and would run out were it not for a higher principle that is independent of the seeds or matter for its existence. This is the scientific man that is not seen by the eye of matter, yet he is acknowledged. So as matter has its different kinds of seeds and man being a combination of these seeds, it is not strange that he should express them in his acts. We all know that beasts express certain feelings we call fear and also desire for food and sometimes a sort of tenderness not surpassed by even the higher order of beings. Now in this kind of matter, being separate from the scientific man, you discover superstition or fear. So as language is the invention of this more rarefied matter, it gives the matter or life of that kind, that has arrived at that state to learn a language, to express their feelings by words or language. So then we see by the expression where they stand or the combination of matter they are composed of.

This develops this class of matter called superstition, so as that, like all the other matter, mingles and produces other combinations, it tries to account for that change that is always acting on all kinds of matter called by the name of decay or death. So language gives this matter a chance to throw off its seeds into the world of matter in the form of opinion. These seeds are caught up by the lower class of matter and go to change the composition of their own matter. Now as this class of matter, like the brute, has their identity attached to the matter of which they are a part, the change is not perceptible to them and they think they are the same person they always were, when their combination has changed as much as an apple tree that has had all kinds of fruit engrafted on it. And yet the old stump or body is ignorant of the fruit it produces and holds on to the old identity of the original fruit.

Like the man who calls himself a democrat and claims to be of the old school that every limb and branch has been cut off long ago and nothing remains of the old stock, only the name rubbed into the minds of the people. Now as I said all this kind of matter is the natural result of progression to prepare matter for a higher development of wisdom or science. For as matter contains motion, from the fact that heat is to expand, as matter is dissolved by this heat, it finds itself separated in a large space. Now there must be outside of this matter a sort of foundation for some higher or more rarefied something that can exist out of matter.

So here is where the scientific man resides. After pressing forward by the earnest desire to reach the point from which wisdom flies, he presses on, driven by the pressure of matter. He, like that, rises, till he finds himself beyond the narrow limits of this world of matter. So he passes through this into space, and here he finds what wisdom has created. He then returns to the world of matter and there becomes a teacher of that class of minds or matter that has passed through the fire of superstition and is ready to listen to the voice of reason. Now what is man's mission? To show to the man of matter that his senses are not matter but his life is, and his happiness is, and his happiness is in his wisdom and not in his error. His error is the thing to destroy, so he leaves a teacher to the inhabitants of this world of matter. Now as all things of wisdom's make are in common, man being one of the things created by wisdom, being subject to all the changes of matter, his first creation is fear. So that fear is the beginning of wisdom.

Fear begets action and as from being the result of sensation, it creates heat. This heat is the natural result of fear. Now as this fear rarefies the matter, it becomes a medium for seeds of error and superstition; so where there is fear there must be action. Now language being confined to that class of matter called man, he uses it instead of signs and gestures to convince his friend of danger. So the language is full of the fear. This is the seed called fear that is sown in the soil of man. Now fear like all other seeds is composed of different combinations. So if a man should be bitten by an animal, the language by which he would express himself would be filled with his own fear, not the animal, for the animal has perhaps no fear, but the seeds come from the person's fright. Now as these seeds of fear of the bite spring up in the person, it disturbs the soil of the mind and the animal is seen in the fright, so the person is always afraid of the animal. So his fear with some additions is by language communicated to others till the world becomes a world of fear.

Thus you see that every person's body is continually throwing off from itself these seeds of fear, in all kinds of belief and opinions. Now to wisdom all this is from fear. So as fear is the name of every condition of matter from the brute creation to science, it shows itself in every composition of animal life. But wisdom knows no fear, so perfect wisdom casteth out fear, for fear hath torment. So a man, as we see him, is a man of fear. Now the fear of man differs from the fear of the brutes in this respect. The brutes' fear is confined to such things as wisdom has made but man's fear is confined to such dangers as man has made or invented. Now these things that trouble our sleepless nights and haunt our imagination are among the things of man's invention. Now convince man that at death this is the end of him, then frightful dreams of endless misery after death will fall harmless at his feet. Then the fear of dying will be confined to his natural life. Now the fear of what will be his state after death haunts his imagination or disturbs his mind and strange things appear before his senses that he can't account for by any power of his, and so he thinks they come from the same power that created the things that can be seen.

Thus you see that man by his combination becomes a being of fear. This is the beginning of his wisdom. Then comes the necessity of protecting himself, so necessity is the mother of invention, so he becomes a superstitious man of invention. So in his fright he invents all sorts of ideas and gives them names and talks about them as though they really existed outside of his fears, till at last these ideas are received and believed as much as the things that Wisdom has created. Now among those things are creeds that are invented for man. He believes, so that he may keep clear of some other evil that he is made to believe. Now as I said these beliefs contain the seed or substance and the man of fear eats them, the same as the earth opens to receive the seed, and when the time comes for the seed to come forth, it will come and its growth depends upon the soil. If you sow the seed of witchcraft in the soil of a man of wisdom it will perish, but if in a man of fear, it will grow and come forth and show itself by language or opinion in a belief in witches. So all belief has its seeds, and if the seed does not grow, the fault is not in the seed but in the soil.

The soil is like salt. It will take up just as much as it can receive, but if it has lost its fear, it is not capable of receiving the seeds of error. Then the man of fear looks upon the man of science as an infidel or skeptic and as ignorant as a dog. So when the fear is lost by wisdom, it is cast out, to be eaten by the dogs. So this happens to both. The man that has lost his fear by receiving the truth is free from error, and the man of fear is in his error, and looks upon the other as much beneath him as a dog. So both are satisfied with their conditions. Now the difference between the man and the beast is their belief. The scientific man is not to be included. Now make man as ignorant as the beast and the length of his days would gradually depend on his safety from surrounding objects. Disease could not kill him for it is the invention of a higher development of matter. The natural destruction of matter would apply to him as to the beast but this is not disease in the sense I speak of. Now introduce the man of science from the world of wisdom where fear never comes and he will explain all the workings of matter and how to till the mind or soil so that superstition and all sorts of visionary ideas of disease, etc., cannot grow. Then man becomes upright in wisdom and also in person. He learns that his existence is not in his fear but in his wisdom and all the sacrifice that he offers to this unknown science is lost, for wisdom asks no sacrifices, only that of a pure and contrite heart, free from all fears.

I will take a case to show where fear prevents a man from arriving at a truth, although it is the first step towards it, for if there was no fear there would be no progression. The man of fear reasons in this wise. I will state a case. A lady called on me for examination. I sat down and after a short time I felt a sensation in my side accompanied with a feeling of a tumor. This contained the idea of cancer. So I said to the lady, You have the feeling I have described and she said she had. I then said, You think you have a cancer. She said, I suppose I have. I said, No, you have no cancer only as it exists in the mind. You are afraid of one. She said, No, she had just as lief die as not. I said, Suppose you had, that does not prevent you from having a fear. But she said it came without her knowing anything about it. Now here came in this peculiar mode of reasoning that nothing can produce something, for she believed that her belief had nothing to do with the effect and yet the effect was there and she could not say where it was till she saw it and felt it in the side. So of course she could not find it outside of herself. And as her body contained animal life or living matter and the tumor being a part of her body, it became a part of herself; so of course the cancer had as much life as any other part of her body, and it was eating up the body and yet she said or believed it had no existence that could be seen outside of the body and of course it must have been in her when she was born.

Now this is the way error reasons. Now truth would show that mind being matter and the phenomenon being matter, it must take matter to make matter. And as our beliefs to me are matter, the seed of cancer was in the belief and when her system was excited, the matter or mind was ready to receive the seed; she having it in the soil or belief, it sprang up like seed cast on the snow. When the sun comes out and the snow melts and the earth becomes ready to bring forth, the seed will spring up unless the fowls come and pick it up. So if there was no science to explain away the seed, it will spring up when the mind is ready to bring it forth.

When a man once acknowledges that a belief contains the seeds of disease or poison, then he will learn to analyze beliefs and see what they contain, taking for a standard that nothing cannot produce any one thing. So as a belief to the one that believes it is something and will produce the very thing contained in the belief; to the one that knows a belief is nothing, it produces nothing. So I had to destroy her belief that to her was something, for she believed in cancers, but to me it was nothing. So the belief to me was nothing but what she had made and man can make anything and put life in it and call it his. So it contained neither life nor anything only her belief. To make her understand was the work of a science which is to cure the sick of their fears. This science casts out all their fears and teaches that man is the author of his own troubles.

1864

Obstacles in Establishing a New Science
[LC 1:0460]

The great obstacle in establishing a new science in the understanding of the people arises from their ignorance. Science always has had to contend with this difficulty, and no one has as yet been able to direct the mind of man towards the true mode of reasoning so that superstition should dissolve before the advancing light of science; for man has always been ignorant of himself, and his errors he has fastened upon others.

These are two modes of reasoning, both true to the one that believes them, and neither anything to the person that knows the truth. To the scientific mind, a superstition about anything that science has explained is nothing. But to the unscientific mind, it may be a truth. Now the science to be established is to give a theory based on a truth which can be applied to a false mode of reasoning, which not only can destroy it but can bring about a more perfect and better state of society and sweep away the lies that, like the locusts of Egypt, are devouring our lives and happiness. This cannot be done by any philosophy known to the world, for the present mode of reasoning is based on the very errors the coming science is to destroy. If Satan cast out Satan, then his kingdom is divided against itself. But if wisdom cast out error then the true science will stand. I base my reasoning on a stone which the builders of error have rejected. Mind is matter is the foundation on which I stand, and this is rejected by the world.

Every idea having a form visible to the world of matter is admitted by that world as matter. The reasoning which stands on this basis is one world, and scientific knowledge is another. Science does not make peace with the world; it makes war. It seeks not to save the life of error but to destroy it. It sets ideas at variance with each other, the father against the son. It sets the world of matter in motion, that it may like the earth be prepared to receive a higher cultivation. This has been done in a vast number of ideas, but in the things that concern man's health and happiness, the world is in Egyptian darkness. This subject never has been sounded. The sole cause of man's misery and trouble lies in our false reasoning. It always has and it always will be so till man is convinced that his happiness depends on his wisdom, and his misery on his belief. True, he may be happy for a time in believing a lie, but that is like a man finding happiness in taking opium. It stupefies him so he is not sensible of his trouble, but it really increases his misery. Mind like the earth is under the direction of a higher power which is subject to wisdom. The world calls it God. Now these two worlds, wisdom (or science) and belief, in other words, happiness and misery, have their existence outside the idea matter. To one matter is nothing; to the other it is everything. To science it is an unexplained error; to belief it is a real living substance. I am now speaking of the subject of health. I do not include any true science. But every science not based on the rock I have mentioned must crumble if that rock falls on it, and every idea that is rooted in matter and bears the fruit of misery must be hewn down.

Theories are like trees and ideas can be grafted into them, thereby changing the whole character of the fruit. Jesus engrafted his truth into the understanding of the people by means of parables. Everyone knows that ideas can be sown in the mind like seeds in the ground and that they will grow and bear fruit. The causes of both phenomena are unknown to us, but to the world above matter they are known. To wisdom, these facts are mere ideas, but to matter, they are solid truths.

As I have said, everything having a visible form is matter, but there are things into which the world has put life which bring no danger to man because they contain no knowledge. There are others which breed misery, such as the ideas of disease. These ideas must have their foundation in science or in matter. If in science, why is science called upon to destroy itself? If God made disease and science destroys it, then God's kingdom is divided against itself; but if this world made it, it is not natural to suppose that this world will destroy itself. Wisdom can set the world of errors at variance, and out of the war will come a new theory that will enlighten the mind.

According to the world there is such a disease as the small pox. With God or wisdom this must be a truth or it must be a lie or a belief in a lie. No one will believe that wisdom or science can have the small pox. Therefore its foundation must be in this world and it must be confined to the inhabitants of this world. Wisdom teaches that error can create out of itself another error, the same as a tree can bring forth another tree, and that mind or matter can generate itself. Wisdom cannot create wisdom, for it fills all space. But it can shed its light upon the world of matter, thus destroying the things of darkness and bringing to light things hidden. I have said the small pox is the work of this world and its evils are confined to the inhabitants therefore. This disease is like a tree whose fruits are scattered abroad infecting those who eat them. It is a superstitious idea and like all such it has a religious cast. It had deceived the world so that every person was liable. Therefore Truth or God so loving the world sent (his son) the idea "kine" pox into the world that all might be saved or vaccinated. As far as the small pox was concerned, this was a savior and as many as received the virus (or were baptized with the belief) were saved. Here is introduced another world or a state of progress after death which is deliverance from small pox. To all who have passed from their old belief into the world of vaccination, there is no more death from fear of the small pox but a fear lest they have not been vaccinated with the genuine virus. Now what does their salvation rest upon? It rests on no principle outside the mind. In their ignorance of causes they are satisfied with someone's belief that there is virtue in this savior. Thus their minds are quiet and the fruits are a milder disease; and if the graft is put into a healthy tree (or child), to that, according to their belief, it is a stranger.

This will apply to all diseases. Every disease is the invention of man and has no identity in wisdom, but to those who believe it, it is a truth. All there is of man is his senses and these are nothing in a belief or in wisdom. If everything he does not understand were blotted out, what is there left of man? Would he be better or worse, if nine-tenths of all he thinks he knows were blotted out of his mind, and he existed with what was true? I contend that he would, as it were, sit on the clouds and see the world beneath him tormented with ideas that form living errors whose weight is ignorance. Safe from their power, he would not return to the world's belief for any consideration. In a slight degree, this is my case. I sit as it were in another world or condition, as far above the belief in disease as the heavens are above the earth. Though safe myself, I grieve for the sins of my fellow man, and I am reminded of the words of Jesus when he beheld the misery of his countrymen: "O, Jerusalem! How oft would I gather thee as a hen gathereth her chickens, and ye would not." I hear this truth now pleading with man, to listen to the voice of reason. I know from my own experience with the sick that their troubles are the effect of their own belief. Not that their belief is the truth, but their belief acts upon their minds, bringing them into subjection to their belief, and their troubles are a chemical change that follows.

Small pox is a reality to all mankind. But I do not include myself because I stand outside of it where I can see things real to the world and real with wisdom. I know that I can distinguish a lie from a truth in religion or in disease. To me disease is always a lie, but to those who believe it, it is a truth, and religion the same. Until the world is shaken by investigation so that the rocks and mountains of religious error are removed and the medical Babylon destroyed, sickness and sorrow will prevail. Feeling as I do and seeing so many young people go the broad road to destruction, I can say from the bottom of my soul, "Oh, priestcraft! Fill up the measure of your cups of iniquity, for on your head will come sooner or later the sneers and taunts of the people. Your theory will be overthrown by the voice of wisdom that will rouse the men of science, who will battle your error and drive you utterly from the face of the earth." Then there will arise a new science, followed by a new mode of reasoning, which shall teach man that to be wise is to unlearn his errors. Wisdom cannot learn, but it can destroy.

The introduction of science is like engrafting. Every graft does not live, for some have no life except what they derive from error. When you believe a lie in the form of some disease and the doctor comes, he does not engraft into your wisdom but into your belief, for wisdom will not grow in error, nor error in wisdom. Each must have grafts of their kind. The small pox is a lie and so is the kine pox. It is the offspring of the former, and the senses, becoming separated from the one, cling to the other. Wisdom shows that they are both false and that they are the inventions of superstition. Thus the world is vaccinated from one lie into another, and this is called progression. But the time must come when this false mode of reasoning must give way to a higher wisdom where all things are proved by science.

I tell you a lie which you believe and an effect follows. This does not prove that I told the truth because the effect is seen. For instance, I tell you that you have the small pox. This shocks you and you are really frightened. A phenomenon attends or follows the fright. The physicians are consulted and they pronounce the disease small pox. To you and to the world this is proof that it is small pox, but to me it is only proof that you believed the lie.

Now the question to settle is this. Can a lie act upon a person who believes it so as to make him sick? No one will deny that I think. Nothing then produces something, unless a lie is something, and if it is, where does it start from? Not from wisdom, for if you say it is nothing you must reason in wisdom, for error shows the effect is something. To me the lie and the effect are both nothing, but to those who believe them, both are something. So when I sit by a sick person, I come in contact with what they call "something." This "something" frightens them, and another "something" is produced which they express by aches and pains and other bad feelings. All these they think come from what they call disease. To me this something that they call disease is a lie which they believe, and their aches and pains are the expression of their fears and are like the moans of a criminal sentenced to be hung or shot. Now comes the process of vaccination, or conversion, which is getting them out of one lie into another. The doctor introduces his opinion like a virus which being received into the mind, a change is produced. And if his arguments are heeded, a milder disease is brought forth in the new graft, and finally the person is carried to that state of mind called "safe" or "saved." The priest goes through the same process. First he affirms his belief till the people become alarmed. He then introduces his opinion as a means of safety, and when this is received, the mind is quieted and this is conversion.

The world has been humbugged by these two classes till the sick are tired of life; their substance is devoured; their fields of happiness are laid waste and every kind of enjoyment destroyed. While the people are in this state, another swarm of locusts come upon them to get what is left. These are the political demagogues, the second growth that always springs up after the others get the mind troubled and ready to be affected. These parties are the scourges that pursue society as it passes through the wilderness of error to the land of happiness and science. This journey that science has been traveling is dotted with little opinions where wisdom has cleared up the wilderness and burned up the error. Wisdom never stops; it continues and has now reached the wilderness of disease. And every tree that brings not forth good fruit will be hewn down by the axe of science and burned up by the fire of truth.

July 11, 1864

Obstacles in Establishing a Science
[BU 2:0113]

What has a man to contend with who undertakes to establish a new science? He has the opposition of all the former opinions of the world in regard to it, and all their influence. He will be misunderstood by fools and misrepresented by knaves, for his science will tear down their fortress or belief and they will use all their skill and deception to defeat their enemy. Their weapon is their tongue, and the tongue of a hypocrite is of all weapons the most deadly to truth: for it can assume the voice form of an angel while it is sapping your very life's blood from your soul. Its life and happiness are its own torment. Ever since the world began, science has had this enemy to contend with, and some very hard battles have been fought before error would leave the field. And when forced to retreat into darkness, it would come out when truth was asleep and destroy the happiness of science. Therefore science must keep awake for its own safety. These two powers are in every person, and each one's happiness or misery shows where they are.

If well and happy, it is no proof that they have been through this war of science and arrived at the truth, but that they from some cause are satisfied to become the friend of both powers. In this way they are a kind of know-nothing, but their position is not safe, for their enemy knows their position and only lets them remain while they will keep still or quiet.

What has the truth accomplished? A great deal. It has planted its standard in this battlefield. The standard of mathematics waves its banner to the truth-astronomy, chemistry. These monuments of science, like Solomon's temple, are the place where truth comes to worship, and the true priests are those who can teach these sciences understandingly; and the masses are those whose belief is founded on these teachers' opinions, without knowing the science or truth, but pin their faith on another's opinion or sleeves. This credulity of the people prompts men to selfishness, and there arise false teachers whose aim is to deceive the people and make themselves famous. They throw discredit on their ideas and render them unpopular so that if the same standard should be adopted by a true priest, he would have much opposition to meet with in the minds of those who have been deluded and imposed upon by hypocrites. This places a man in a very bad place to defend himself, and all the influence he gets is from those he cures, and they dare not stand up and face the world and sustain their position, for it is so unpopular that their reputation is at stake. This is the state the two armies are in when the leader plants his standard of science with this inscription, The Science of True Religion is Health, Happiness, and Deliverance.

Dec. 1859

Odours
[BU 3:0760]

You know I have spoken of the odor. It is like the odor of any flower or vegetable and is what arises from an idea. Thought is a chemical change in the fluid, caused by a sensation produced on the mind. The mind is under the direction of a power independent of itself and when the mind or thought is formed into an idea, the idea throws off an odor that contains the cause and effect. For instance, a person is affected; the effect is called nervousness; this contains no knowledge to science, only an effect. Error or the natural man thinks knowledge is contained in it and tries to convince the patient of the truth of this science, which to the true science is false. The patient is more disturbed by this theory, and by the direction of this blind guide, an idea is formed which is held up to the patient's mind to receive a name. The mind or error of the doctor gives it the name of consumption. This disturbs the mind of the patient which like a galvanic battery throws off sparks or ideas. And these ideas being under a false direction are formed into any disease that ignorance and superstition can invent. Now the idea is formed and as it grows it has a sort of intelligence which is not recognized by error but admitted and called instinct. This odor or instinct contains the cause of the trouble and the answer. But to error this is a mystery. So it calls it a power or instinct and never looks upon it as anything that can be reduced to a science.

This odor is the trouble called disease, but the doctors know nothing about that odor and think that what can be seen by their eyes is the disease or trouble. This odor is what I come in contact with. It is the spiritual life of the idea and by the doctors it is called mind. This embraces all they can comprehend and this they make independent of the disease and never treat it as having anything to do with disease. In this way they keep the soul in bondage, for fear of death. This odor is the soul's trouble, imprisoned in error. As the soul tries to escape, it becomes subject to error and as long as error holds it in bondage, it is in death. Truth sets it free by destroying the error. All we see of this is in the prison, and that is not visible to the natural eye. Not one-hundredth part of the misery of the human species is in what is called disease. Ninety-nine hundredths of human misery is in prisons not seen by the natural eyes. This misery is confined to the popular opinions of the day. The common opinion is the prison of the soul. Its destruction is the liberation of the soul from its earthly prison or error. From these prisons the smoke of their tormenting belief ascends and when I come in contact with their grief or odor, I know the cause of the trouble. The trouble is a sort of intelligence and belongs to this world. It is a sort of instinct to the natural man and has nothing to do with science.

July 1860

On Healing Those Who Do Not Understand
[Originally untitled.] [LC 2:0704]

The question has been asked if I do not cure many who do not receive my wisdom and may not even know what my belief is, and why cannot I, who believe that there is truth in you and wish to be taught by you, be cured? To the first question I answer, Yes. I do often cure persons who have no understanding or curiosity about the manner in which I cure them. My wisdom is my remedy and the application to the patient is the cure. It is not necessary that a person who is thirsty should have another teach him where he can find a spring of water to quench his thirst, if the person will be good enough to supply his present wants. But if the person has arrived at that wisdom where he knows there is danger of being thirsty again, then it is necessary that he should be put in possession of a wisdom that will lead him to the fountain so that he will not thirst but where he is to himself a well of water springing up into everlasting life.

The child is satisfied with the present gratification of its wants, never dreaming that it will ever be deprived of what it wants. And a person who is satisfied with having his disease cured without enquiring into the causes is like a child who never thinks that it will be thirsty after it is satisfied. This is the case with the large majority of mankind. Your wisdom can give the child water to quench its thirst, and my wisdom can destroy the error that made the child hunger and thirst after health and happiness. Such hunger and thirst is a disease. The rich man's torment was for water. The thirst made his torment and the wisdom he lacked would have enabled him to get it. This is the case in all diseases, but man is too lazy to think, so he believes what is said without any labor.

May 1862

On Spiritual Medium of Communication from the Spirit World
[BU 2:0012]

I Infidel

S Spiritualist

A Quimby or teacher

Is there a proof of any communication from the spirit world? This question involves two ideas: first, what is spiritual knowledge, and second, is all knowledge, which cannot be accounted for on natural principles? To the last question I will answer, "Yes."

Question: Do you mean to say there are two spiritual states.

A .Yes.

I. Do you believe in a spiritual state?

A. Yes, I believe there are two spiritual states.

I. Do I understand you to say there are two spiritual states?

A. Yes.

I. Can man pass into both while the body is living?

A. No.

I. Do not these communications purporting to come from the spirit world, come from it?

A. Yes.

I. Is there any other spiritual world that does not communicate with this?

A. No.

I. Where is the difference between the two?

A Between the dead and the living.

I. I don't understand you.

A. The spirits of the dead pass through the spiritual world that is occupied by the living, and thence into the higher state, which is a link to connect the two together, like the animal and spiritual kingdoms.

I. I do not understand your answer.

A. To make you understand me it will be necessary to give an illustration.

I. Explain the difference between the two spiritual states so that I can understand where the difference lies.

A. Do you admit there is such a state as is called a spiritual state?

I. Well, I don't know that we have any proof of such a state.

A. What will you admit?

I. I will admit one mind can act upon another mind.

A. Very well, what is mind?

I. It is our thoughts.

A. Can they be seen by our natural eyes?

I. No.

A. Are not our thoughts spiritual?

I. Well, I suppose they may be called spiritual.

A. Do you admit them to be spiritual?

I. Yes.

A. Well, then we agree on one thing, that is that our minds are spiritual.

I. I said nothing about mind, I said thought.

A. Are not our thoughts called mind?

I. Well I will admit that our thoughts and our mind are the same.

A. Well, is it spiritual?

I. In one sense it is because it cannot be seen by the natural eye.

A. Therefore that which cannot be seen by the natural eye must be spiritual.

I. Yes.

A. Then we are agreed in regard to one spiritual state.

I. Yes, so long as we are living bodies, but destroy the body, and where is the mind or spirit?

A. This is not the question in dispute as I understand it. The question is not whether the spiritual state ceases at death or continues after the body ceases to exist, but whether there is a spiritual state or not. This is the question. What is your answer to this question? Do you admit a spirit state?

I. Yes, I admit a spirit state.

A. Well, as you have admitted a spiritual state, I will try to answer your question in regard to the two spiritual states. Shall I explain the first spiritual state?

I. If you please.

A. As there may be some difference of opinion in regard to what constitutes this state, it will be necessary to ask some questions. Therefore I will ask if you believe thoughts have forms?

I. I do not know as I understand your question.

A. Well I will try to put it in such a form as there can be no mistake about it. Can there be an impression without something to impress?

I. No.

A. If you think of a person, do you not form him in the mind?

I. I think of the person and that is all.

A. Is thinking an act of nothing?

I. No.

413

A. Will you please to define what it is if anything?

I. I will give it up and hear your ideas of it.

A. Well as you wish to, I will try to give an explanation. The trouble lies in ourselves. We admit what we don't believe, and then deny that which we profess to believe, thereby showing that we have no belief at all.

I. Explain your meaning.

A. The infidel admits that mind is the result of an organized brain. He also admits that thought is the reflection of the mind. Now he denies that reflection is anything.

I. Well, let the infidel alone and try the spiritualist, and see if his belief is founded on anything that can stand the test. I will assume the character of the spiritualist.

A. You believe that our minds can pass into the spirit world and get knowledge of what the natural man knows nothing?

S. Yes.

A. Do you believe there is more than one spiritual state?

S. No.

A. What do you include in the state you call spiritual? Are the dead and living all together or are they separate?

S. I believe that man while alive cannot pass into the state of the dead, but that the spirits of the dead can come from the spirit world and enter our mortal bodies, and communicate to the living about the dead.

A. Have you any proof of this, and if so please give it.

S. Yes we have positive proof of it.

A. What is it?

S. Communications through mediums. Do you deny that they are spiritual?

A. No. I do not deny that they are spiritual, but I deny that they come from the dead.

S Where do they come from if not from the dead?

A. They don't come at all.

S. What is it that communicates to us through these mediums if it is not spirits?

A. I have not denied that it was spirits, but that does not follow it is from the dead.

S. Please explain where these communications come from that purport to come from the dead.

A. I see you are laboring under the same difficulty that others are who have not investigated the subject.

S. Give your own interpretation of spirits.

A. My interpretation is this. Our bodies are composed of animal life which is called matter, which is a medium for our souls to communicate one fact to another. It is like an instrument to communicate the idea of music. The power can be independent of the body or connected with it.

S. What is the soul? Is it anything independent of an organized brain, or is it the result of an organized being?

A. I believe it is something independent of matter.

S. Can you bring any proof of its acting independent of the brain?

A. Do you admit that the brain is composed of matter?

S. Yes.

A. If the brain is composed of matter does it not occupy space?

S. Yes, but it may be so dissolved as not to seem to occupy space.

A. Well, when in that state is it matter or does it cease to be anything?

S. It is still matter.

A. Can it be seen by the natural eye?

S. No, but yet it is matter.

A. Can it go to another place independent of the body and there take form so as to be seen or felt?

S. Yes, I suppose it must, or I must deny all the proof of the mind acting on the body.

A. This something that sees or feels it, is it a part of it, or is it something else?

S. I cannot say it is the same.

A. Then what is it that feels or sees it?

S. I must give up and hear your explanation.

A. The soul is neither matter nor mind, but is that power that acts upon both.

S. In what way is it connected with matter?

A. The soul fills all space and is in possession of all knowledge.

S. Why is man so ignorant?

A. When we speak of man we speak of something independent of the soul.

S. What is man?

A. Man is a chemical compound of the four kingdoms, and contains in his body all the elements of the same. These elements are under the control of the soul, that power called God, therefore the result of reason is a chemical action like the action of steam to machinery.

S. Is man nothing but a machine?

A. In one sense he is, for he is as dependent on another power to direct his act, as a steam engine is dependent on the engineer. Each is governed by a power independent of itself.

S. Can this power be seen by man?

A. No, from the fact that it does not contain any of the elements of man and therefore is that that is, and is not, and yet is.

S. What is that that cannot be seen and yet is? Please give some illustration so I can understand.

A. You can see yourself in the glass, can you not?

S. Yes.

A. Do you see that that sees you?

S. No.

A. Then there is something that sees and is not seen and yet is. Again, you move your hand–is the power seen that moves it? and yet there is a power admitted. Is it not so?

S. Yes, but that does not prove to me that this power is independent of matter.

A. Is not there a power that can move your body?

S. Yes.

A. Is not your body, matter?

S. Yes.

A. Is that that is moved the same as the power that moved it?

S. No.

A. Then you admit a power that is, that cannot be seen and yet is.

S. Well, what does this power embrace that you call soul?

A. It embraces that power that directs the movements of the mind and body. It also embraces the power that directs all things.

S. What has it to do with our minds and thoughts?

A. A great deal. It is the power that develops all actions.

S. What is the use of a power that makes man unhappy?

A. If properly understood it makes man happy.

S. I thought you said that man was nothing but a machine.

A. In one sense it is so, but in another he is more than a machine. He, that is, his body, embraces what is called mind and spirit. This mind and spirit is the result of power called soul which is independent of the body and uses the body to communicate knowledge, like a lever to communicate power to move weight.

S. Why is man so much troubled with disease if he is nothing but a machine?

A. I see you do not understand what man is.

S. Well, do you understand?

A. I think that I do.

S. Please explain man so I can understand what man is.

A. In explaining man I wish you to distinctly understand that I make no allusion to his bodily form, but his soul. Will you remember that?

S. I will try to.

A. When I speak of man I speak of him as two persons from the fact that they are exactly opposed to each other.

S. I don't know what you mean by two characters in one and yet say that they are directly opposite to each other.

A. I will try to make you understand what I mean. You admit such a thing as happiness?

S. Yes.

A. You also admit such a thing as misery?

S. Yes.

A. Well these are the two characters that I am to speak of.

S. All people will admit such a thing as good and bad, and happiness and misery.

A. I do not admit such a thing as bad of itself.

S. You admit such a thing as good?

A. Yes, but I do not admit bad of itself.

S. Well, what is it that is bad?

A. Bad is the result of ignorance. Of itself there is neither good nor bad.

S. Explain it so that I can understand.

A. Is there anything in fire of itself either good or bad?

S. Yes.

A. What is it?

S. You can use it to make you comfortable etc.

A. I will admit all that. Is it conscious of being good or bad?

S. No.

A. Then good or bad must be the result of a power higher than itself.

S. Yes.

A. Well, then you see that you admit these two powers are in one person good and bad.

S. Yes, and will you explain where they differ?

A. They are both matter and are the result of association. To make it clear to you I will illustrate the two characters. Suppose you should see an object, and you should take it for something very beautiful. This would be good, would it not?

S. Yes.

A. Suppose you should be convinced that it was bad, would not your mind change from good to bad?

S. Yes.

A. Suppose you walked up to the object and see that it was nothing but a statue made of wood, would not the good and bad change or be modified?

S. Yes, but what does this prove?

A. It proves that there is a chemical action in the body, and that it is governed by impressions made on the soul.

S. I thought you said the soul contained all knowledge.

A. So I did.

S. You said that there was an impression made on the soul. Now if the soul knows all things why is it disturbed?

A. Error is not knowledge, neither is impression knowledge, therefore when an impression is made on the soul it is made through the body. This disturbs the fluids of the body and these fluids contain all the elements that make up reason.

S. Do you say the fluids of the body contain intelligence?

A. A sort of animal intelligence which is necessary to keep up a chemical action to develop the laws of the soul or God.

S. I do not know as I understand your reasoning why the soul should be disturbed if it is in possession of all knowledge.

A. The soul is not disturbed of itself, but the body is disturbed by impressions and this produces a sort of chemical action. This action decomposes the nervous system and brings a portion of it into a fluid state which is under the control of this inferior intellect. This creates objects and all sorts of beings that fancy can imagine.

S. Will you illustrate this last idea so that I can understand it more clearly?

A. I will try to. Suppose a person living in the country, happy and at ease, and to all appearance well. Now his nervous system would be quiet, and every thing goes on well and he is happy. This would be called good, would it not?

S. Yes.

A. Well, suppose a person should come in from town and call on this person and ask him how he enjoyed himself. He should first say "I am perfectly happy," and then the man should look at him very knowingly and reply "Men sometimes feel the best when they are in the greatest danger." Would this not be likely to give the man a shock?

S. Yes.

A. Well, then the disturbed man received the first shock to his system and it shows itself in this mind just in that degree that the system is disturbed. The disturber then goes on to relate all the evil stories his mind can invent. The disturbed man keeps up this chemical action under these impressions till he is able to create any that his fancy can imagine. His system changes, his identity also changes, and he becomes a most wretched being. Now this would be called bad, would it not?

417

S. Yes.

A. Well are these impressions a part of the man's feelings or are they something which was independent of the man?

On the Circulation of the Blood [I]
[LC 2:1004]

A great fault in the medical faculty is that they admit certain opinions in regard to the circulation of the blood, as how the air affects it and how the food is carried in it to all parts of the system, etc., all of which is nothing but opinions which cannot stand the test of science. According to them, the blood is composed of certain gases combined together and which are of themselves pure. Therefore to affirm that the blood gets impure is to affirm what is false. It is true it may be loaded with impurities, but the blood or gases are not and cannot be made impure. Now where do these impurities come from? It is supposed from the food. This cannot be the case for some children are born with these impurities, as they are called, who had never eaten anything. That is accounted for by saying the parents eat food and the children are affected by it. If there was not a more sensible way of accounting for it, that theory would answer very well, but I shall try to show that there is a better and more reasonable method.

In all theories of the circulation of the blood, there is not one word said of any intelligence or influence outside of the blood itself, or of man. He is regarded as though he came into existence without a cause, and was then governed by laws that are not admitted as having the least intelligence, and yet the doctors explain what makes strength, etc. They assert that some food has certain chemical qualities which make strength in man, while other kinds of food weaken him. The intelligence is all in what they have admitted contains none. For instance, we say the air makes us feel strong. Where now is the strength, in the air or something else? We also say the same in regard to the blood, though I am not aware that the blood contains any strength of itself. The same can be said of the muscles, thus placing the power in the muscles. All our intelligence is therefore in some organ that the surgeon can hold in his hand, while he discourses at large upon it as though the organ contained the intelligence and power he was talking of. But never does he hint about an outside universal wisdom. This false theory places us in the dark in regard to wisdom and lets opinions rule the destinies of man. I shall endeavor to show that man as we see him is not the real or true man, but merely the shadow.

The medical faculty informs us of all the gases, etc., of which man is composed, yet I never heard of these gases being endowed with the least atom of intelligence. Their theory represents man as a being having wisdom, yet at the same time it deprives him of any by denying that there is any wisdom in the materials of which he is composed, and still calling the materials all there is of him and then giving him a wisdom superior to the brute. Here they virtually admit that nothing can produce something that is wisdom. In all the theory of the circulation of the blood, there is not one word said of anything which makes man except his food, etc. Now if you will follow my reasoning, you will see a different construction put upon the circulation of the blood from that of the medical faculty. All ideas contain a substance as much as the food we eat, and these very ideas are what make us sick. They enter the system and help to make up the body which is itself merely an idea. According to my belief, ideas are imparted to the child before it is born who thus has to suffer for the sins or beliefs of its parents. Not that this was the design of the first cause, but man has wandered away from truth, has invented lies and deceived himself by false ideas till his body has become as corrupt as his ideas that feed it.

All of this the medical faculty pass over as though it has nothing to do with man. The blood is the medium and not the material required to produce strength. The babe has blood but no strength. The man can be so far intoxicated that he has no strength, yet he has blood. The criminal when he hears his death sentence pronounced often loses his strength, yet he has blood. A sick person raising a teaspoon of blood from his lungs, as he supposes, will lose all his strength, while the same person when well may lose half a pint of blood from his nose in a fight; yet if he comes off conqueror, he never minds it in the least. Strength must be in something besides the blood. The same rule will apply to the food, as some persons who eat the heartiest are by no means the strongest. Hearty persons often lie down after eating to rest themselves, being weaker than before eating. It is the same with drink. Persons drink strong liquor to give strength which is absurd, as the weak man will drink one glass of spirits and feel strong while the strong man after drinking one or two glasses will become so intoxicated as to lose all his strength. A glass of water will give a man strength, but is the strength in the water? No, for I have seen sick persons who dare not drink water and a small quantity will take away all their strength. A person complaining of weakness in the knees will be advised by the doctor to apply strengthening plasters, liniments, etc. All these things are believed by the masses and medical faculty, while I look upon them all as deceptions. The strength is not in the remedies but in the belief in them, as the weakness is not in the knees but in the belief.

Strength is outside of medicine, food or drink. Really, what is that which we call strength? It is something outside of the thing acting. For instance, in a lever, the strength must be outside the lever. Just so with the muscles, or they must have something to act on them or they could not act. What this something is, we wish to ascertain. The child must have some intelligence to guide it before it is capable of taking care of itself. If strength is in the food or in anything visible to the natural eye, we could then find the First Cause. But strength is not in what is called matter but it is the effect of something that exists outside of matter. It is wisdom or a consciousness of itself. This wisdom or consciousness is the First Cause of all things. Its identity is itself. It is that principle by which every act is weighed. It gives the specific or relative difference of all matter or acts. It is a body of itself which answers man's every inquiry. It is the source of man's wisdom and man is as one ray of light from the great fountain of light. Darkness is matter and as light or wisdom enters the darkness, it receives its life from the fountain of light till it has grown to a state where it assumes its own identity. Then it stands to the fountain as the child to the parent.

The child receives his strength or will through his mother till he is acted upon by the wisdom of the world, when he assumes a false character and embraces the ideas or opinions of the world instead of wisdom. So his growth is of error and the belief of the world. He becomes as it were a double being and is treated as such, yet considered as but one. A false theory takes possession of the light, and false lights spring up and opinions take the place of science. All the philosophy in regard to the circulation of the blood only tends to mislead man and causes him to embrace errors that he otherwise would not, such as sickness, etc. I shall shortly give the medical faculty's theory of the circulation and then give my own and show that neither has any reference to the real scientific man of wisdom. Their method is not intelligently understood as they do not embrace any wisdom in their explanation of the circulation of the blood but make man a mere machine and a poor one at that, whose machinery runs of its own accord and is under no direction whatever. At the time of the discovery of the circulation of the blood by Harvey, man was far behind the philosophers of our day in regard to the science of hydraulics which was then in its infancy. Of course his explanation was derived from his knowledge of hydraulics, but later discoveries have shown the absurdities of his opinions. The circulation must either be caused by man's own knowledge or by an overruling wisdom which can do all things. If by the latter it must be a perfect scientific system and entirely independent of the aid of man's knowledge.

I will now give the theory of the medical faculty which will show that they do not attribute any wisdom to the circulation either of man or God but make man a mere machine like a pump and breathing upon the principle of a pair of bellows. Their theory is as follows.

"From the right ventricle of the heart the dark blood is thrown into the pulmonary artery and its branches carry it to both lungs. In the capillary vessels the blood comes in contact with the air and it becomes red and vitalized. Thence it is returned to the left auricle of the heart by the veins. Thence it passes into the left auricle. A forcible contraction of this sends it forward into the aorta. Its branches distribute it to all parts of the body. The arteries terminate in the capillaries. Here the blood loses its redness and goes back to the right auricle by the vena cava descendens and the vena cava ascendens. The tricuspid valves prevent the reflow of the blood from the right ventricle to the right auricle. The semilunar valves prevent the blood from pressing back from the pulmonary artery to the right ventricle. The mitral valves prevent its being forced back from the left ventricle to the left auricle. The semilunar valves prevent the backward flow from the aorta to the left ventricle."

This is the explanation of the circulation and not one word is said of any intelligence; therefore it is fair to presume the author understood the power to come from the heart. This cannot be. So far no man can make a machine upon that principle and have it operate well. He tells us of the valves that prevent the reflow of blood to the heart. According to the description it could not reflow if it wished as it is thrown to the extremities and then the power is lost.

I will now give my ideas. I commence at the brain and shall show that man is a perfect machine and so constructed that he is acted upon by a wisdom superior to the blood, and the circulation can go on just as well though the man be asleep and ignorant of the fact. There is a wisdom that keeps the machine in running order and which is not disturbed by false impressions or stumbling blocks. These stumbling blocks the medical faculty do not name, but I shall speak of them in the course of my remarks.

I will now give the modus operandi of the circulation as I understand it. I shall not give the name of the valves and auricles as I do not wish to lead the reader into the dark by using Latin phrases which he cannot understand. But I shall try and carry him along merely showing him the method where the blood takes its rise, where it flows, and how it returns, etc.

The oxygen in the air is imparted to the blood by passing in at the nose where it is received by the capillary vessels and conveyed into small veins and thence into larger ones, and is carried with the blood through them to the upper right chamber of the heart. The heart is divided into two parts which we will call the right and left side and each side is divided into two chambers, the upper and lower. The upper right chamber receives the blood from all parts of the system, from the upper portion of the body through two large veins which unite in one, called the jugular. The lower portions of the body are supplied with small veins which collect the blood and all the impurities which become mixed with it, and empty it into larger ones, which convey it to the upper right side of the heart where it is mixed with that from the upper portions of the body.

The food, after passing into the stomach and undergoing certain changes which I will not describe, becomes what is called chyle and is taken to a reservoir in the lower part of the body called the thoracic duct. The chyle is then carried by the thoracic duct and emptied into the jugular vein where it is mixed with the blood and also taken to the upper right chamber of the heart. This chamber has now reserved the chyle, oxygen, blood and impurities from all parts of the system. The oxygen heating the blood causes it to expand which opens a valve and lets the blood pass into the lower right chamber. As the valve only opens downward the blood cannot return. It then passes through a large vein which branches off and is carried to both lobes of the lungs where the impurities from the blood are deposited and carried off through the windpipe and out of the mouth in the form of carbonic acid gas.

The blood now being free from all impurities is conveyed to the upper left chamber of the heart and then forced into the lower left chamber which acts as a reservoir and holds the blood till it is taken by the aorta and carried to all parts of the system, depositing the necessary quantity to form flesh and receiving fresh supplies of impurities till what remains is carried by the small veins again to the heart to undergo a similar process and be cleansed of its impurities with the new blood which is all the time being manufactured.

I now propose to introduce the agent who although invisible to the natural man yet governs his destinies. I will take the child before it is born. No one will deny but what there must be a circulation of the blood, but the lungs are not needed as there are no impurities to deposit or carried off. The mother supplies the food or intelligence from herself and they contribute to form the machine and get the cars or child ready to receive the freight or ideas of the world. According to my theory intelligence is not one of the elements of mind, but mind is the medium of intelligence. As wisdom speaks mind into existence, its identity is a process of progression. And as wisdom acts through the parent, the child receives its life from the parent as the fruit from the tree till it becomes ripe when its seeds will produce trees which will bear fruit after its kind.

The life of the child is its mother and its body is nourished by the same spiritual or material food of which its mother partakes. But when it is born, its mother ceases to supply its wants by nature or ideas. For now the child receives its food from its mother's breast. This requires a new combination of motions to carry the food to the whole system. Therefore to start the machine, there must be a power. The nose is so constructed that the air can penetrate into it till it comes in contact with the fluids of the head or capillary vessels. Here heat is produced by the oxygen coming in contact with the hydrogen, nitrogen and carbon and this heat is the power that sets the machine in motion.

Now the blood loads up with oxygen and winds its way along through the small veins forced on by the heat in the brain like the steam from a boiler. It then enters larger veins and is still pressed on till it meets the food or chyle, where all is emptied into the upper right chamber of the heart which is called the right auricle. The food, which has undergone certain chemical changes, assumes a milky appearance called chyle and is sucked up by the little capillary vessels and carried by the thoracic duct to the jugular where, as I have said, it meets the blood and is emptied into the right auricle.

Now the air is all the time supplying oxygen to the blood through the nose and mouth. And the brain acts like a boiler; the oxygen, the fuel; and the hydrogen, nitrogen and carbon, the steam or blood.

This constant heat which is kept up in the brain is all the time pressing the blood into the right auricle. The blood is prevented from passing down the thoracic duct by a contraction of the upper end which acts as a valve which can only be opened upward by the chyle pressing up through the duct to empty into the jugular. At the end of every vein or artery and everywhere that you find a valve or contraction, there is an air cell and it is there we get the power which keeps continually forcing on the blood. The heat pressing the blood into the right auricle causes it to expand and this is called the pulsation. When it expands, it opens a valve and the air in the cells forces the blood into the right ventricle or lower right chamber.

The blood which is in the right ventricle is now forced out into a large vein by the pressure from above and carried into both lobes of the lungs by two branches of this vein, where it comes in contact with another air cell which separates the gases and impurities from the blood and forces the blood now freed from all impurities into the left auricle or upper left chamber, while the gases escape out of the windpipe or chimney.

As the blood from the lungs is being continually forced into the left auricle, it forces the blood already there into the left ventricle or lower left chamber and there it is still forced on into the aorta and sent to all parts of the body. When it reaches the extremities, it meets with little air cells there which give it a turn and force it back through other little veins. And it is there sucked up by the little capillary vessels which are continually at work, and it is then conveyed to the jugular which is the great thoroughfare for the blood from the brain and upper portions of the body and also for the chyle that is brought through the thoracic duct. This is the proper course of the blood as it circulates through the body.

I now propose to speak of that invisible wisdom which sees and guides all the foregoing changes. According to my theory, mind is something which I call matter. Our belief is also matter. But the world calls both intelligence. If I believe what I say is true, I make it so to myself whether I wish it to be so or not. For instance, if a mother believes in scrofula, her belief is carried to her child and deposited just where it is directed before the child is born. Now after it is born and becomes old enough to receive ideas from others, it feeds upon them till its mind becomes so much diseased that its body is a mass of corruption or false ideas. Now as it is being fed by the world's ideas, it loses the food its mother supplied before its birth and it becomes like a domesticated animal.

All animals receive impressions from an invisible something. But man being of a higher development is acted upon by two principles: one of wisdom and science and the other of mind and matter. Science is to correct every false direction and point out the true one, and wisdom runs through every act of our lives and through mind or matter. Wisdom is like the nerves of sensation. All these nerves that are mentioned are merely representatives of the scientific man.

To suppose that food is thrown into the stomach and there left to be governed by chance is like supposing that after the coal is thrown into the steamboat furnace it creates steam in the boiler which propels the boat to the place of destination without the aid of any intelligence outside of the engine. Yet we are told that the food enters the stomach where the gases eat or dissolve it and from thence it passes into another reservoir where it receives the addition of a substance called gall. It then enters the small intestines in which there are multitudes of small mouths ready to suck it up and convey it to a fountain that receives it, and then it is sent in a conductor to a large vein which carries it to the heart.

Now here is as perfect a system of regulation as ever governed a railroad, where goods are received at one place and transported to another. And it is as absurd for a person to lecture or write of the circulation, without associating intelligence with it, as to give a lecture on the subject of the railroads out of New York and convey to his hearers the idea that the locomotive starts off with a train of cars and lands and receives freight at the different stations without any intelligence outside of the engine.

Man is like a nation. He is governed by laws but is subject to a higher principle that, unlike laws, cannot be changed. This principle is science, the child of wisdom. The natural laws of a nation are the invention of man. Now science and the laws of man, like the veins and arteries, run side by side, and like the nerves of sensation, one set belongs to the laws of matter and the other to the science of wisdom. The office of the former is to be dishonest and carry out selfish acts, while that of the latter is to keep beside it and hold it accountable for its acts. Thus the two go together. One is wisdom or the guardian spirit who sees every act of the natural man, approving or condemning them as is proper. The other is opinions or evil spirits who act without science, doing as they choose and perfectly indifferent to the principles of science.

The guardian spirit or agent is the invisible man and is called by various names but is harmless, as all principles are. Yet it cannot be annihilated, but the medium matter may be dissolved and destroyed. As I have said before, man is like a nation and governed by his own laws.

Now the great first cause, Wisdom, holds his government responsible for its acts, and it furnished agents to take cognizance of their doings. Every idea is like an individual, clothed with some responsibility. For instance, if I wish to do a certain act, the wish or idea starts off with my authority to do it and wisdom sends an agent to accompany it. Both go together, but my idea is not responsible to the agent for its acts. But the agent is furnished by wisdom to suggest or check the idea if it goes wrong. For I am held responsible to wisdom for my acts, but the agent merely keeps the record which, like the mariner's logbook, tells the tale at the end of the voyage. This agent of wisdom whose name is science is not seen by the natural man, though he often hears him say, "Beware how you act for you are held accountable for your every act."

The natural man is full of deceit and hypocrisy and is only held in check by fear of this invisible agent. And when he hears his voice, it often makes him nervous, for he supposes it is some disease or spiritual influence which is tormenting him when it is but himself. That is the scientific man, prompting the natural man.

I wish to speak of a fact here which is this: that the flesh and blood or the natural man thinks he embraces all there is of him, but he is to the man of wisdom as the child to the father. He wishes his child to grow up good and honest so he permits the child to act as it were on its own account and so he does. Yet he is responsible for his acts. To illustrate. The parent gives the child some money to lay out in something that he may barter and trade. The child invests his capital in something that takes his all, but before closing the bargain he asks his parent's advice, who says to him, The money is yours, lay it out as you please but take care you are not deceived.

The money is invested and it turns out the child has lost by the operation. Now comes his torment. He says to his parent, You should have told me the truth when I asked, but the parent will reply, You must look out the next time; I have no respect for persons. I am not partial to my children and he with whom you traded was your brother.

When you learn that to injure another is to injure yourself, you will learn of yourself to do good and you will break off from your selfishness of your own accord.

Every idea contains two characters: science and error; and the father or agent is in the blood or food. Now as the idea enters the system to establish its claim or deposit its treasure, the agent goes with it to take note of its action.

If you will examine the structure of man, you will see a complete government with all the improvements attendant upon civilization. Each man has his laws which differ according to the ideas introduced. Science's kingdom is in the wisdom of the people but error's is in the laws of the natural man. Nations in their natural state are governed by the law that might makes right. Yet the agent of wisdom is in their acts and prompts them, but the power is not acknowledged till it obtains such a hold on the minds of the masses that they feel its influence. This is a civilization.

All sick people are as much under the law as a savage nation and more so, for as science develops, error also develops. And this ignorance is governed by error and science is not a thing to be feared as its still small voice is heard only to be regarded as an echo to which no attention is paid. Yet it steadily works its way through all the veins and arteries of society and goes with the blood to all parts of the nation called man even to its farthest corner. As a nation develops, it has a seat of government and also avenues of communication. As it becomes more advanced in civilization it has greater facilities for distributing intelligence to all portions of its vast country. It also has its head or leader who transports all of its orders on the thoroughfare over which all other business is transported. Man's hand is the capitol or seat of government for the president, and here sits the natural man and directs the course of events.

The president is elected by the people and he who governs man is directed in the same manner. He who rules his body today may be enthroned tomorrow. Suppose a man is governed by the idea that he can go out into the cold without injury to himself or nation. If he ventures out all the opinions rise and clamor against him and their influence has the tendency to make him unpopular. So he is removed and another idea appointed. When he begins his administration, he acts as though there were no laws but that of might. He is affected by the invisible agent at his elbow who is always checking him by caution. This has a tendency to make him nervous and he becomes despotic and then wars of ideas commence. The ideas form themselves into societies or parties and by controversy create competition which increases the population or makes new ideas.

The ideas of a man are like the population of a nation and being a progressive being, he invites foreign importations of ideas and the ideas, like individuals, come from other nations. Man is a fair specimen of the United States in this nineteenth century. The President of today is the head of the nation but the people are as divided in their opinions as to what will be the result of the war as the ideas in an individual nation. The country is sick and how to cure it is the question. Slavery was forced onto the people and how to rid ourselves of the evil they cannot tell and it is left in the hands of the political faculty or doctors of the law.

So with man, disease is fastened onto the people as slavery is on the nation and the people are groaning under the weight of the evils of their own creation. The body is the battlefield on which the encounters take place, and the circulation of the blood is the means of transportation, and the railroad or canals, and the head the seat of government to which the people rush, causing a rush of ideas or heat to the head, or as erroneously called a rush of blood to the head. The cars are all the time conveying the government stores to all parts of the country at war and they also carry this agent to see that the business is properly executed.

President Lincoln is the medium or embodiment of the ideas of the nation and these ideas are shadowed through him. Now as the ideas or minds of the people change, the medium changes. The President's name is Abraham and he is the medium of the people, but his body is the people or ideas themselves. The majority of the people say through him one day the negroes shall not fight; the next day the majority says the negroes shall fight and Abraham echoes their minds, so that the President is the will of the majority of the people, whether right or wrong. But wisdom all the while sits in the hearts of the people and prompts them to do unto another as they would that he should do unto them. Now the natural man, like the President, is at the head of his body or nation and the doctors, like political demagogues, have stirred up strife among the ideas of man and introduced strangers or new ideas among the ignorant classes till they have got man at war with himself.

Disease is considered an enemy to the scientific man who tries to keep out the false ideas. But these demagogues have made enough proselytes to establish a footing. For the majority rule, and if more evidence can be brought in favor of a lie than of truth, the lie is received by the masses and the truth thrown into the minority.

The medical men, like politicians, have sown the seeds of disease or discord in the minds of the people who kneel down and receive the evil as the camel does to receive the burden. Science checks the progress of error and error checks that of science. Both act against each other, but when error is destroyed, science is saved as by fire, for it passes through the fire of excitement and rises out of its ashes unharmed. Man is in rebellion all the time, that is some portion of his intelligence. The warfare only ceases when truth or mathematics is cultivated, while in other parts of the intelligence of man there is slavery as black as that which blots the face of the South. This slavery is disease and is the blackest part of man's whole being and it has become the enemy of man.

Truth knows that disease is a lie, invented by error while trying to account for some phenomenon of which man was ignorant. Error, to show its wisdom, invented this lie and endeavored to sustain himself by building up a party of ideas. This lie has got man into his present diseased state, so that now every little excitement rouses the thoughts, as the cry that the enemy is advancing rouses the people who rush to headquarters to learn what is the trouble. The ideas arrive from the extremities in the trains and are carried to the heart to await orders. The ideas arrive from the head with orders to receive all the stores and deposit them in the various depots. Now suppose the story is circulated that the heart is to be attacked by heart disease. This is the great storehouse of the nation or body where everything centers. It is to man what Jerusalem was to the Jews, the seat or dwelling place of God's wisdom.

The blood is filled with ideas and they all go to the heart, there to wait until the trains arrive with the products of the nation with which the masses are fed. Here is one city or depot called the right auricle where all congregate, and this vast assemblage produces a stagnation of business or circulation. It is here that you will find all the importers or couriers from other nations, having in charge their ideas on which they keep an eye to see that each of their subjects is respected. At last the trains arrange their business out of this tumult and then prepare to move to the next station, called the right ventricle, in order to clear the depot for other trains which are constantly arriving. The gate of this next city is always closed except when it opens to let in a train. Passing through the city and out a gate at the opposite side, the trains pass on till they arrive at a junction of the road. Here they separate and half the train goes to the right lung and half to the left lung. Here they leave the impurities of opinions or freights and receive orders to pass to the left auricle. Passing through a gate at the entrance of this city, it stops but a moment and then passing a gate at the opposite side it enters another city called the left ventricle.

After all the trains or blood have assembled here, each takes its proper train, all passing out for some distance on the main track or road called the aorta and the different cars switching off onto other roads at every station and going their proper routes and depositing their cargoes at the station all around the road till they reach the extreme limits. When the agent or conductor has got all the freight distributed, they enter the return cars on the back track. Those from the lower extremities start their trains for the right auricle, gathering up freight as they proceed. Those from the upper extremities and head run their trains and deposit their freight into the jugular where they take on board the cargo which arrives over the thoracic duct and then all proceed to the right auricle again.

Now this is as regular a system of intelligence as ever rules a nation and the wisdom which governs all this is as real as that which governs a nation, only it cannot be seen, yet it acts and we perceive the effect. When man shall learn that thoughts and opinions have an effect and that what he says to his neighbor he is responsible for, just as a person is who speaks against the government, he then is responsible to the laws.

When man learns this, he will be careful what he says and how he sows the seeds of disease in healthy minds, as those persons who have sown the seeds of secession in the minds of the loyal. These ideas or seeds are embraced by the people who are alarmed and shaken to their center by every false alarm that is started by the demagogues. Now as traitors and disturbers of the public peace are arrested and carried to prison for saying and doing unlawful things, it behooves us to know what to say before we speak, or what to do before we act.

With disease it is the same. It is a traitor and tyrant, and all who harbor it are liable to be punished. It pretends to be a friend, but there never was a person who acknowledged he wanted to be a traitor to health. But you may see many who are in full communication with these traitors, hugging them up, yet acting as though they were ashamed of their company. You see a man hugging his coat around him in order to hide the traitor called consumption who has got him in his service, soul and body. If questioned hard, he will acknowledge that he has him concealed in his lungs. Now this man is a victim to this traitor and liable to have his whole estate confiscated and be turned out-of-doors, poor and forsaken by this very serpent he is nursing in his bosom.

To believe a thing is a truth merely because someone says it is, is wrong, for you are held accountable for your belief. And if it is wrong you suffer the penalty. Disease is secession and all the evils one can imagine, and its path leads to destruction; while on the other hand, science is the truest friend to man and he who follows its path will find it leads to health and happiness. Truly her ways are ways of pleasantness and all her paths are peace.

Dec. 3, 1863

On the Circulation of the Blood [II]–Illustrations
[LC 2:0871]

In the foregoing article I have shown how the blood circulated through the system or body which I compare to a machine. But man by his ignorance and belief has made a slave of this most perfect of all machines. By the power of his will he has destroyed, or nearly so, the object for which it was built. I took the child before it was born as an illustration of the machine, man, before it was used, as the healthy, well developed child is like the new locomotive just from the hands of the machinist, perfect. Now after its trial trip if successful, it is ready to receive freight. The child when first born is, if healthy, a perfect machine. Its blood, like cars, is ready to be loaded and wait for the staples or products of the country which is our food, while the passengers are ideas and as many are taken as can be accommodated comfortably in the cars. The ideas which the child embraces are like capital stock or profits, for wisdom is riches and ideas pass as paper currency instead of gold, with a discount off.

Opinions pass for truth in the same manner. The child is taught to be prudent and lay up his money. So, likewise, he is taught to store his mind with knowledge which is another kind of riches. So the more ideas he lays up the richer he becomes; this makes him avaricious and like the miser he starves himself by not eating of the wisdom of the wise and lives on the common food of life till he gets rich in the world's wisdom and owns much knowledge in all the kingdom.

Talk with such a one and he will give you an inventory of his knowledge or property. He will begin at his own head or residence and tell you all about the brain, how many have died with the brain fever since he had been acquainted with them. He will then show his riches or knowledge in regard to the spine and will tell you all the different curvatures, name the different parts, telling how each affects the other. And then he will lead you to the heart and here he has laid up great stores which makes him very nervous and fearful lest he should lose them. He takes you to his lungs and also all over his body till you see how rich he is in this world's wisdom. You say to him, Your riches do not appear to add to your happiness. No, he will say, I believe if I had never had a single cent or idea I should have been better off, for now with all I know, I am of all men the most miserable. I have been troubled with the gout in my foot and have been laying up wealth or knowledge trying to learn how to manage it. But it has cost me more than I gained and I have now given up. And with all my knowledge, it has left me lame and dyspeptic. Therefore I say, if ignorance, or poverty is happiness, it is folly to get knowledge or riches like mine.

A child is an illustration of this truth. The body is the earth or natural man. The progressions of the child's mind is science of the medium of wisdom. At its birth the child is like a wilderness; its ideas are of its mother earth. But when wisdom breathes into its nostrils the breath of life or science, it becomes a child of science. Now while it is fed by its mother's ideas, it is like its natural growth which continues till it is ready to receive a different sort of food. The circulation of the fluids before its birth are like little streams or rivulets which wind their way into larger streams or veins. But after its birth the little streams are changed by the introduction of foreign ideas which create war with the ideas of the mother and with progression. The food and all that goes to clothe the body belongs to the earth or Adam, and all the ideas or spiritual food which goes to enlighten the mind to prepare it for a higher state belongs to science, the medium of wisdom or Eve.

The earth produces food, etc. for man, while science the child of wisdom produces and furnishes the ideas or wisdom for the enlightenment of man. Cain and Abel are figures of these two ideas, the natural and scientific man. Cain was a tiller of the soil and Abel was a discoverer or a man of improvement. These two characters are in every man. Cain is the natural brute instinct, the mind, the earth or body and Abel is the higher state in matter or mind which is under the control of the scientific man. And as Cain the natural man is the lawful heir, he does not like to be troubled by his brother Abel or improvement. The child being governed before its birth by its mother's ideas and her ideas all being of foreign importation or transplanted into her mind, the child receives its life from its mother and is born in sin or error. Now after its birth, it is placed under the higher element of its mother who tries to cultivate its growth; but as the food which goes to develop the child's body comes from the lower development of the mind, it keeps the higher development in the minority. So the natural man grows superior to the spiritual man and embraces all the animal propensities which require the food of the natural world. So they grow up like the beast or Esau while science or Jacob, the younger brother is hated. Beliefs, opinions and all fashions are the elements of Esau, while science, progression, love, charity and all the higher qualities belong to Jacob. In the circulation, the lower portions of the body are governed by the natural man, subject to the higher intelligence in the upper portion of the body and brain. The natural man located the seat of intelligence in the heart, while the scientific man uses the brain as the medium of intelligence. Thus you get two individuals: one at the heart and one at the brain.

According to the medical faculty, the heart is where the power or first cause commences, whereas I claim it to be in the brain. It would be natural that the brutal man, not knowing any substance except that which goes into the mouth, should place the seat of power at the heart; but the scientific man does not live by bread alone but by the very words which proceedeth out of the mouth. Wisdom contains no food to the brutal man but to him it is merely superstition, but the superstition is of his own manufacture. Fighting their own shadow is the wars of the flesh, for they make war with themselves, while the scientific man creates fear or destroys the error. All the food which is taken in at the mouth enters as foreign goods into a new country and with the produce of our own country all enter the stomach or market place just as the ideas enter the brain. The freight or food all enters the stomach through the passage called the throat while the or ideas enter the brain through the covered bridge called the nose.

The gases receive the food as the fluids in the head receive the ideas or agents and separate and distribute the food to each part according to the direction of the agents. The stomach employs the bowels and intestines to carry the food along and the little mouths or capillaries separate the good from the bad just according to the direction given them, the impurities being sent out of the body through the proper passages. The lungs receive all the ideas and chyle carries these by the blood, and then the impurities are separated from the blood and carried out through the windpipe, while that part intended for the body is carried to the left side of the heart and from thence taken to all parts of the body.

The lungs and intestines are kept as clear as possible of all impure and corrupt ideas which tend to bring on disease and troubles. Disease is the enemy of which man is afraid and it is this character we wish to consider, for man's happiness depends on the right construction given to this character. He either has or has not an existence. The lower portions of the body admit him to have an existence in the heart, but the truth which dwells in the heaven or wisdom and speaks to man through the brain knows well that such theories are mere inventions of the inhabitants of the lower portions of the body or the regions of false ideas or death. And all my theory tends to dissipate such false doctrines and establish the true ruler of the universe which is wisdom in the minds of man, where his principles will be admitted and turned towards the benefiting of man's health and happiness.

1863

On the Circulation of the Blood [III]
[LC 2:0808]

Man's body, according to the chemist is composed chiefly of carbon, hydrogen and nitrogen which are combustible, also oxygen from the air which unites with the other three. This union produces heat. The oxygen of the air comes in contact with the carbon, hydrogen and nitrogen of our bodies through the nose and produces heat. The nose is so constructed, that the oxygen from the air passes into that organ and comes in contact with the three other substances. This produces heat in the blood. So as this blood receives a portion of the chyle from the stomach it passes to the lungs and leaves a portion of the carbon in the air cells. This is thrown off through the windpipe.

Now as the oxygen from the air is constantly forcing itself through the nose it is very essential that we know the use of this organ and not be deceived by the idea that the oxygen passes down the windpipe. For through this deception we prevent the carbonic gases from passing out of the lungs.

The effect of the oxygen in the air or man's body is composed of carbon, hydrogen and nitrogen. These are of a combustible nature. Now introduce oxygen and this gives life to the blood. Now as the body stands in need of a fourth element to produce calorie or heat, nature has constructed man in such a way that without any effort on his part, this last element is supplied. As the air contains the oxygen, the heat in the brain induces the oxygen to enter. So as the nose is so constructed, the air passes in and deposits the oxygen with the three other elements. This creates heat and eats up the impurities in the chyle that is carried to the lungs to be purified for distribution to all parts of the body. So when the blood enters the lungs it deposits the carbonic gas in the cells, to escape through the windpipe, like smoke out of a chimney.

Now this escape called exhaling and inhaling is when the oxygen is received into the blood or the other three elements through the nose. The idea that the blood receives the oxygen through the windpipe is so absurd that it needs but little explanation to satisfy any thinking person of its absurdity.

I shall show the bad effect on the body by this false theory. It is now a universal belief that the air passes into the windpipe and enters the lungs. This false idea misleads man and he falls into an error that has cost many a poor creature his life. For they, by the power of their will, prevent the very carbonic gas from passing out of the lungs, and it remains in the cells till it becomes so impure that it produces tubercles and abrasions and death.

If man had never heard of such a theory he would have been far better off. What advantage is it to man to know that the blood is carried from the heart to the lungs by a process, that I will give, according to the medical science?

The left side of the heart contains the pure blood and the right side the impure blood. The upper part of the heart receives the blood from the body and the lungs; the lower part sends it out to the body and the lungs. The impure blood from the body is brought by the veins to the upper right side of the heart. The impure blood passes from the upper right side of the heart to the lower right division and then it is thrown into the lungs. Here it deposits the impurities or carbonic gas that is thrown out of the windpipe. This process purifies the blood and then it is fit. [unfinished]

1865

On the Draft
[LC 1:0601]

What will be the effect of the draft on the political parties? The Copperheads intended to turn the draft to their advantage by hypocritically pretending to help the poor, while their true object was to prevent the towns from paying the conscripts. To accomplish this object, the leaders hit upon the idea of making the cities and towns vote to pay each drafted man three-hundred dollars and allow him to keep it and go into the army or pay it into the government and stay at home. This all looks very fair but when you analyze it you will see their true motive. They knew they never could get the loan taken and therefore every drafted man must either go or pay three-hundred dollars himself. This was the plan in order to get rid of paying anything themselves. The deception was so apparent that it soon showed itself and then they turned and said that the cities and towns would never have voted to raise a dollar if they had not driven them to it.

Now let us see how the city stands with those towns that voted to pay every man who was drafted three hundred dollars, when the Copperheads had everything their own way. Portland voted to pay every man who was drafted and went into the army or furnished a substitute three-hundred dollars. Westhook, where the Copperheads ruled, voted to pay every drafted man three-hundred dollars whether he went into the war or stayed at home, giving him his choice which to do. Portland has got her loan taken while Westhook cannot raise hers or the leaders do not want her to and never intended that she should.

Now, Mr. Copperhead, if you are as good a friend to the poor as you pretend to be, why do you not step up and toe the mark as Portland has done and take the Westhook loan and not wait for Union men to do it for you? You never intended to take it and never will. Now how does it affect the poor? In Portland, the poor man who happens to be drafted gets from the city three-hundred dollars, and then by paying out of his own pocket twenty-five or fifty dollars can provide himself with a substitute, instead of paying three-hundred and fifty dollars himself as is the case in the towns where the Copperheads conducted the raising of the money.

Such has been the effect of this deception. It was a trick, laid by the Copperheads and now they are caught in their own trap. Let the poor conscripts call on these leaders and ask them to take the loan and advance the money and show whether they are ready to back up the proposition as the loyal men have done. They have done what they agreed to, and if these Copperheads do not back up theirs you will know it was all a trick and a tool with which to work against the administration.

1864

On the Rebellion
[Originally untitled.] [LC 3:1358]

Now as the rebellion is drawing to a close, the people are settling down to a quiet state of rest, thinking their troubles are all over. They will be in danger by putting themselves to sleep before the serpent is dead. The idea that man is changed when he is overpowered is a false idea. Man convinced against his will is of the same opinion still or a man overpowered may admit his wrong for the sake of his liberty. So it is not to be expected that these rebels and sympathizers have been convinced that the principle of slavery is wrong, only that they were not quite strong enough to conquer and will for the present wait till they get the power; if not in the form of African slavery, they will get it in some other way or try to.

Now the leaders of this cursed rebellion have within themselves the element of oppression. It is their nature with them it is rule or ruin and if they cannot succeed in one way they will try another.

Now religion is a line that is often used by their leaders; when I say leaders, I do not confine myself to the leaders of the Southern rebellion, but to that class of minds who always mingle with the lower classes and set themselves against all progression. It is the finite element in men against the infinite element.

Slavery is finite, liberty and freedom is infinite and will never cease till it has accomplished its work of progression. So every party in religion or politics that goes against this principle of progression goes against God and must come down; but it is not known that every new discovery or revelation that takes place must be developed through blood. But until man can strike at the cause, every agitation will end in the shedding of blood.

Now we suppose that there is no element of political power heating up to set fire to the element of progress to destroy it, but to all such persons I say, Beware, for there is an element, a political element, under the name of religion, that has a greater hold on the masses than African slavery and that is Catholicism; for it is nothing but a political body under a cloak of religion.

Now religion has been considered by every person to be one of the greatest blessings to men and all claim to love it. So the Catholic religion is claimed and yet look at those that believe in it; look at their lives and compare them with any set of beliefs and no person will give them the preference; then what is it that holds them together, although sometimes broken up? This unity, like the Democratic party, holds together and yet there seems to be nothing to hold them; yet you can't change their belief any more than you can a democrat's belief. Now when I say democrat I do not mean one party or another but a certain principle in man to be overbearing; this is slave democracy. This principle is the principle of all political demagogues who use the heresy of heaven to serve the devil with; it is those that know that every person is more or less superstitious and instead of trying to improve the human species, tries to enslave it.

Now they use all their powers to keep the masses in ignorance. The priests of old knew that they had a power over the masses, just as John Smith knew that he had a power over his converts. Now I don't say that they knew what it was, but they knew the fact that they could control the masses. Moses knew it and when he wished to affect any person with any punishment, he used it, but I don't say but his motive might be good. It is the motive of those who use their power to make it good or evil.

Now to suppose that the Catholics do not have a sort of power over the masses is incorrect. The Protestant priests have no such power; they only affect the masses by warning them against some imaginary evil that they believe in. But the Catholics produce miracles and the priests often produce great cures and all their cures are turned to their advantage. And as the people believe in the cures they show them to the priests, like the believers in spiritualism do too. The mediums believe that they have some power from the spirit world, but the spiritualists don't go into a political party as yet; neither does any religious sect but the Catholics and Mormons. All political parties that hold the masses by miracles are dangerous, because the people see results, so you cannot drive them from their belief. But if you can produce the same effect on the people and explain it so that you enlighten the masses, then you disprove their power as a party.

Now disease is an error, and the person that has got it is considered a sinner by the priests, and to be cured is to forgive his sins. The priests are believed to have this power so that they will exercise an influence on their followers that no argument can break. But let some person perform the cures in some other way and show how the priest does it and show how it is used to deceive them, then you destroy their political power and until this is done, man is not safe from this class of political leaders.

I know that they get confessions from the masses that no other persons can get and the persons are not aware of the fact that they do it but feel it is the power of God that acts upon the priest. And this to the sick or sinner is proof that the priest has this power and this gains such a hold on them that they can't be moved by this world's opinion.

Now to break this power is to explain to the masses how it is done and correct an error that is working out destruction to the happiness of mankind. Just get the key that St. Peter has then you can unlock the seventh seal and explain the mystery. Then man will see where to start from. Now we start from a false basis that has been admitted as a truth.

All Protestantism is only a sort of come-outer from the Catholic priesthood, so all superstition is the effect of their doctrine, and all religion admits their foundation the same as allopathy is the foundation of the medical profession and all modes of curing admit the allopathic error of disease.

On the Senses Being outside the Body
[Originally untitled.] [LC 2:0749]

What proof is there that man's wisdom and senses are not in the body but outside of it and in the mind? I will relate a fact which will prove it. I once put a lady to sleep that she might have a needle extracted from her arm and during the operation she said to me, "Does it not hurt you?" The person who spoke was the one who was looking on, for she could describe all that was transpiring. If it should be said that it was myself who spoke through her, I will admit that she expressed my very thoughts, but if I could speak through her body why could she not speak through mine? If so, the body of each was only the shadow of our belief and I thinking it might hurt her and she from sympathy thought it hurt me, we were therefore neither of us hurt from the fact of sympathy. Let her believe that it was her arm that was to be cut and she would make the same ado as though she was awake. This fact holds good in my practice. A patient feels a suffocating feeling and thinks he has the heart disease. If this feeling did not come within his senses, he would not know it. If I am some feet from him and feel it, how can I feel it unless it is outside of the body? If the heat from a coal fire keeps within the stove, no person can feel it.

Let heat represent intelligence. Then the intelligence is in the heat and not in the stove, for where there is no association, there is no knowledge; if the heat is not explained to a person, there is no intelligence. That part of the heat that is in the stove is like the ore latent, hid in the ground, but that which makes itself known is the mind, so-called, or intelligence. So with man, if his wisdom is in his matter, he is like the heat in the stove, ignorant that he has any wisdom outside of himself. Convince him that his wisdom is not in the body; then he learns a fact that will teach him that if he puts his life in what he admits had no beginning or end, then the idea of death is annihilated.

To return to the locality of man's senses. The medium between my body and that of the lady who was undergoing the operation is mind; our senses are there and also all our troubles. There is no matter separate from space. The matter which is seen is the condensation of the matter not seen, which unseen matter is mind and in that are all our beliefs, opinions, emotions, etc. When the mind is disturbed by some opinion or unknown fear, it must take a form before it can affect the body, for the body is merely the shadow which is reflected through the mind; so when the mind is disturbed, the disturbance is shown on the body.

This may seem a mystery to the most of men, for we take it for granted that every pain or sensation is in us and belongs to us. This is not the case. When my subject's ear would burn, he thought it was mine, showing that the sensation was in his mind. His wisdom being in his belief was continually in trouble, which trouble his wisdom located in his mind and my mind being a substance in common, we would be affected bodily alike, the same as two vessels on the water; when the water is troubled, both are disturbed. The mind is like the water, our bodies the vessels and our wisdom the pilot. Our bodies are affected by the sensation as the vessels by the storm; the wisdom is outside the mind and body, as the owner is outside of the water and the vessel. The foundation of the latter is on the land and that of wisdom is on a solid or truth which the waves of opinion cannot break; still his body, like his vessel, is at the mercy of the gales of prejudice and ignorance and he is troubled as a man when his property is at stake. The loss of the vessel or body is a loss, but the pilot and crew are saved or lost according to our belief. If we believe they went to the bottom with the vessel, to us they did, but to themselves, it may be different, and each is affected according to his belief.

To make my meaning plainer, I will compare the mind to the sea, the body to the vessel, and this is the natural man. All Men are in mind as vessels on the sea, tossed to and fro by the gales of the wind of error and those of heaven. The opinions of the world represent the Captain or pilot. The wisdom of God is the foundation of all intelligence and every living being is in this wisdom called God, so the latter stands to each man as the owner of a vessel stands to the master. His property is in his vessel, but his life is not, while the Captain knows no life outside the vessel, neither does the natural man know any life outside his body. When the gale of disease comes up the two stand in this way. The Captain (or natural man) by his belief makes himself a part of the vessel (or body), but the merchant, (God's wisdom), makes his vessel (body) a part of his riches but no part of his wisdom. One grieves for the loss of property, the other for the loss of life and property.

Now make every person rich in wisdom and opinions are but property which, like the birds, may take to themselves wings and fly away. Isaiah says, "The wicked are like the troubled sea when it cannot rest, whose waters cast up mire and dirt." The Christ or truth can walk on the water of opinions and know that it is no part of itself.

I will try to show wherein I know more than my patients. To do this, I shall have to state what my patient knows and tell how it happened that I have discovered more than he knows. Whatever my patient knows and feels, he embraces as a part of himself. To him his body and mind are one; the latter he calls his wisdom, intelligence, soul, and all that he is capable of expressing. His aches, pains and diseases are also himself, all are affected together and all liable to be destroyed. This makes the natural man. This is his wisdom and he is sure of it; to him it is self-evident. Besides this he has a belief outside, which is founded on the Bible, that there is something in him which he never saw and which never will be seen, and that this something leaves earth and goes to heaven; this he calls his soul. The proof of this belief is so feeble and meagre that he is kept in trouble all the time, for his belief makes him responsible for his soul, since if he does not live just so, he may lose that which, notwithstanding his efforts to save, he would never have known he possessed, had not Jesus brought the knowledge to man 1,800 years ago. This soul does not come within the natural senses; therefore it is something that man will have after death if he does not lose it, for there are more chances to lose than to save what he never knew he had.

Here is drawn a Christian. The Atheist has no such belief attached to his knowledge. He lives and when he dies, he runs the risk and waits to know the result. The scientific man has not troubled himself about the matter. Then has any class of persons tried to solve this problem on scientific principles? I know of no one on earth at this time, but myself. I stand alone solving a problem which heathen philosophers and poets in trying to solve have been lost in the floods or error and swept into the gulf of atheism. True minds have penetrated this land or wisdom beyond the natural man and have returned with some proofs of a land outside this ocean of error, but their proofs not being sufficiently certain, experiments have failed and the people are left to wait for more positive knowledge. They are still looking for someone to penetrate the polar region and learn if they can pass through the icy error of death and land beyond in wisdom. Occasionally a breeze or dove from this land comes to cheer the mariner on his voyage of discovery, but more often the icy hand of the error of death chills the very blood and the barque is frozen in the ice or doubt and the mariner makes for the nearest land that he may return home disappointed and die in doubt if there be a passage to the world of science.

I fitted out my barque some twenty years ago and started without chart or compass trusting to the wisdom of my own experience, determined to be guided by the inhabitants of the land where I journeyed and to make my way to the passage that led to the other world or to a new world on this globe. My first intelligence came from a new source. I found a class of persons with no weight in society, a kind of cast off, degraded set who lived on the superstition of heathen idolatry and still held to it. They believed in all kinds of diseases, witchcraft, every variety of misery and were full of inherited superstition concerning this other world. On conversing with them, I found that all mankind had the same belief, but as it had become unpopular, many concealed the fact that they had any confidence in it. Nevertheless by their acts they shew themselves of this belief. By getting into the good graces of this class, I was passed along from one to another, sometimes nearly exhausted and on the point of returning, when a light would spring up or a solitary bird would sing its beautiful notes from the clear sky, while from this light came a mild breath of pure air that would revive my very soul. In this warmth it seemed as though I heard a voice say, "Come up hither." Thus urged, I progressed, till I saw, as it were, a sea like a sea of glass, dotted like the ocean with ships. As I approached I found that these spots were persons and the vapor around them was their garments. As I came up, I was hailed by my old friends with, How came you here? This was to me a mystery, for I thought I had been travelling all over the face of the earth, and when I saw my friends, whom I thought dead, alive, I was struck dumb and wanted an explanation of the phenomenon. Here it is as it came to me.

The earth is round according to our belief and man is ambitious to explain the outside and also the inside of it. So exploring parties are fitted out to discover hidden truths and sciences associated with the earth. But there is a different class of minds who believe there is another world called the spiritual or scientific world, which is as much a world as the natural world and which contains the latter. So the people are all inside the spiritual world together, some disposed to investigate the surface of the interior world or earth, while others like Simms search into the center or bowels of the earth. There is still another class who believe that as the interior world contains strata, so the scientific world contains strata of scientific wisdom whence all science springs. One class goes out from matter into science and the other goes into matter in science and both are together. When this came to light that all I had been doing was to burn up my error by progressing in wisdom and as the light of science sprang up in the mind, I could see men walking on their belief as I was walking on my science. Then I asked, How can I make the natural man understand this? The answer came, The natural man is not of the world of science, but the child of science is in the world of error striving to escape, and this is disease. Then came an illustration of all I saw. Man, as we see him, is a representation of the earth, his eternal structure is the attraction to the natural man to explore, the surface of his body is where he looks to see how he is affected by outward sensations. His wisdom sits in the upper chamber, called his brain, and in the majesty of his knowledge he gives his opinion and all lesser lights bow their heads in subjection to his will. His wisdom being finite affects his acts and the consequence is sometimes a convulsion of the earth or opinions, the power of his life or knowledge is shaken, and his kingdom comes down or departs like Nebuchadnezzar's while another takes its place. This kingdom being all over the world, it rules its subjects, so when the son of science encounters it, a decree goes forth to put everyone to death. Therefore it is necessary that a secret society should spring up in order to undermine it, whose passwords cannot be understood by the king of this world.

Science is light, and the wisdom of this world is in darkness, hence it does not see the light; therefore wisdom governs the natural man although to him it is unknown. It suggests to the natural man, he being vain and dishonest assumes to be the author of his own wisdom. As error is its own destruction, in order that science may reign, it makes war with itself by a power which it only recognizes as a mystery, and in its destruction calls on this unknown power for help. To show how the two powers, opinion and truth, come in contact, I will assume that I am this truth, and my patient is the error, which holds his life and happiness in bondage. Like all demagogues, error pretends to be kind to the poor, especially when its life depends on holding wisdom in slavery, and in this relation of master and slave, error pretends to be the friend of science and is willing to do what science desires should be done. So the error in the sick brings the patient to me. The science which is confined in bondage knows the language of wisdom and secretly tells me its misery, but the natural man or error knows it not. When I tell the error how the sick feel, to him it is a mystery, for error is matter and has no feeling, while sympathy is the language of the sick. As I sit by the sick I feel their pains which is the grief of their wisdom; this is outside of their opinions or body, and my wisdom being outside of my opinions, I, in my wisdom, see their belief, but their errors do not see me. Therefore to them I am a mystery.

Suppose a patient sits by me who has the idea of heart disease; if he believes it, to him it is a reality if he attaches it to himself; but to believe in the disease is one thing, and to believe he has it is another. If he believes he has it, his belief contains the substance or identity of a man with heart disease. From this substance goes an atmosphere like that of any decaying substance. Around the idea is this atmosphere and in it a person with the heart disease. His body is to his mind a sort of mirror which reflects the shadow of the idea; by the doctors this is called disease. I see the original idea and also see the shadow, and to cure the disease I destroy the matter by explaining the error. This breaks in pieces the matter and the shadow on the body disappears. This is my superior wisdom over the patient and all the language I need is to make the patient understand the truth.

December 1862

On Wisdom
[LC 1:0483]

Perfect wisdom embraces every idea in existence, and therefore every idea that comes to the light through the senses existed before to wisdom. Every person who was or ever will be existed as much before he ever came to our senses as afterwards, the same as any mathematical problem or truth. Man's intelligence is a truth that existed before he took form or was seen by the natural eye. Man's body is only a machine and its senses are its medium to wisdom, the same as science is the medium to wisdom. The real man is never seen by the natural senses, but the real man makes himself known through science to his natural senses, as a person who knows a fact can teach it to another. Wisdom or knowledge he teaches through science, and he uses his senses to explain this science, for his senses are all the medium the natural man knows.

The real man is God, or the First Cause. Every idea that man embraces comes through his natural senses, but this real man is not seen, but is truth or wisdom. The natural man may be compared to a checker board, and science and opinion the players. Public opinion or common sense stands looking on and represents spectators. The wisdom that is superior is that which sees and knows the principle of the game. Now opinion makes a move and the natural man or common sense says it cannot be bettered. But science sees the working of opinion, and makes him move in such a way as to compel his opponent to destroy himself, for he knows that opinion knows nothing as he should know it. Every move of opinion suggests his opponent's move. So if one knows his game and the other does not, the ignorant one is beaten every time. But if both are ignorant they think they play a very scientific game. Now there are certain games or arguments which men play called theories that have no foundation or basis, and there is no way to test them because one is not the least above his neighbor and neither can prove anything.

1865

Opinions of Physicians and Priests, The
[LC 2:0823]

Physicians and priests, like politicians, have no idea of the effect of their belief on mankind. All know that they affect the masses or they would not talk and try to change their minds, yet they are ignorant of the effect, for it would seem too much to believe that men would deliberately murder one another. And yet they are causing worse evils than all the accidents by shipwreck and railroad, collisions and every other conceivable thing; and still they seem to be perfectly ignorant of the evil they are making. It is not necessary for me to say anything about the troubles caused by this set of minds in regard to the rebellion, but I will confine myself to my practice. I know beyond a doubt that most of the misery that man has from disease is the result of false reasoning and the world will never be enlightened till the thinking minds are directed to this one fact: that man's diseases, as they are called, are the effect of false reasoning. This can be proved by thousands of instances. I will give some of the instances that come before me in my every day practice to show how disease is created and how little the physicians know of the evil of their opinions. It would seem as though it were intentional on their part, but when I see so much misery produced by them, it must be through their ignorance. But I will give the facts and let the people judge; then I shall take the testimony of patients as they understand the physicians.

I will give the case I had of a lady that came to me for an examination. On sitting down by her, I found her very nervous and she had hot flashes that passed all over her system. Those feelings I always take by sympathy, like all feelings that contain ideas of disease. I can tell them from those that do not as well as I can tell the sensation of water by putting my finger in it. Cold water to a child might make it start, but no effect would follow its putting its hand in it; but if the water was scalding, then bad effects would take place. So it is with the fluids of the body. Now the fluids of the body are the material to be worked upon. This I .call mind and this is the starting point. The senses are something outside of this, but being mixed like gold and dross we take them as one. So when we speak of the mind, we apply it to the senses. But in this way, we deceive ourselves and are liable to get into trouble, because to adopt this mode of reasoning, there is no separating the truth from the error. Now one mode of reasoning combines the matter or fluids and the result is what is called disease; the other mode dissolves the mind or matter and destroys the phenomenon. So I have to explain. Man does not go back to causes.

I have a patient that was very inquisitive and reasoned very fine. And if his basis was good, his reason was correct. Now this man was laboring [unfinished]
Aug. 3, 1864

Origin of Political Parties
[LC 1:0418]

It is laughable to hear people talking about political parties and claiming to belong to this or that party, just as though parties never change their principles. This error arises from the fact that all parties spring up in opposition to some measure or ambition of a few politicians. They get up a false issue and talk about it till the people believe it; then a party is started and the people attach themselves to it without the slightest idea of the principles or whether there is any principle at all.

Let us go back to Washington. All parties claim Washington as the father of our country. Why do they, when the opposition to Washington by the friends of Jefferson was so great that it was with difficulty Washington could be prevailed on to become a candidate the second time? Here commenced the two great political parties. The opposing party after Jefferson came in had no sympathy for Washington, but when Adams and Jefferson, Hamilton and Burr came up, then the Jeffersonians praised up Washington and denounced all others as Federalists. The country was in debt from the war, and Jefferson in reality was opposed to it, and the friends of Washington elected the elder Adams.

The war debt must be paid and a spirit of revolution in the country was kept up by the opposers of Washington and Adams. All sorts of stories were circulated about the latter, and as a direct tax would be unpopular, the enemies of Adams elected Madison. Then came the war with England and parties split up, but finally all settled down on Monroe; so that at his second election there was no opposition. In all these changes, slavery was never mentioned. Its extinction was never advocated. But as there must be two great parties, they must have political food to live on.

When Jackson and Clay, Adams and Crawford came up, they were called Republicans; being in favor of the war, they were said to have brought it on. But be that as it may, the war was popular as all wars are after they are over, and these men being all of one stripe, for all other stripes had faded out, a new era in political parties sprang up. Men had their preferences, some for Jackson and some for Clay, but as Clay gave his influence for Adams, Jackson was defeated, and Adams elected. Adams not making any changes for party preference displeased his friends and they left him, so the next election Jackson came in. Here is where the present dynasty commenced. It began with deception and lying politicians and ended with that traitor Buchanan.

As soon as Jackson came in, commenced the war, founded on the proverb, "To the victors belong the spoils." The people identified their senses with the party, never looking to measures, and the Jackson party took the name Democrat, while their opponents were called Federalists. Yet Jackson never varied one particle from Adams till Calhoun nullified when he put him down, the very next message recommended the reduction of duties on tea, and then the Democrats engrafted free trade and direct tax. This free trade was food for the people. It was sweet to the mouth, but bitter to the belly or purses. But as it never came, it worked well to keep up the steam. But when this died away, another element must be introduced to keep up the party or name and as the North and West were gaining, the democracy saw that they must lose political power so they must get up a false issue to split up the North and South.

The blacks could be made a wedge to drive between the two parties, but to do this it required a party so obnoxious to the Whig or Federal party that they would not unite. So the South starts up a party of fire-eaters, claiming that slavery, according to the Constitution, might spread all over the land. Another party in the South did not want to carry slavery into politics but leave it just as the state had made it and Congress must have nothing to do with it. This hypocrisy of the South inflamed the North and a set of men sprang up actuated by pure revenge for the wrongs heaped upon the honesty of the North. They appealed to the Whigs or Federal party for help, but as the Federal party never had anything to do with slavery, as a party they got no sympathy. This fretted them and the democracy saw this and hugged it like a twin brother. So the Democratic party made a wedge of the abolitionists to split up the Federal party. This gave them the power and they have nourished a viper which has destroyed the Democratic party and it will before long establish the old party of North and South, which always held that slavery was a state institution and the government never had any authority over it, outside the states where it existed.

August 1861

Other World, The
[LC 1:0534]

Suppose every person could disbelieve in another world as it is called. What would be the effect on each individual? Let everyone put the question to himself. Reader, do you suppose that if you could disbelieve in another world that it would put you out of existence as long as you could believe? For as long as you believed, you would be in existence. Now imagine the heavens and the earth and all that in them is, can you doubt that there must be a something that knows more than you do? Then the next question comes up. Where is it? You cannot say in heaven, for you have denied this place. Jesus answered this question of where heaven is by saying it is in you, even in your thoughts. So the kingdom of heaven was in their minds. Now this is my belief. So it is with the other world; it is all in the mind. Now get it out so that the mind does not contain it, then what exists? You exist and that you know if you know anything. You know that you are always learning something new, this you know. You know that matter and mind are always changing. You know that science is progression, and that its truths always have existed and always must. Even if all the people were swept from the earth, still the truth of science would exist. Science in you teaches you that you are a child of science and therefore your identity cannot be lost. So to be a child of science you cannot leave the father and go into a belief of what you can show is nothing but an opinion.

Now where does science look for the God that it worships? In the clouds? No. Does it call it up from the vast deep? No. Then where does it seek it? It looks at the evils of the world and says, How long shall man wander in darkness looking for wisdom when it is in himself and he does not know it? It is the higher principle of our nature. Now let this higher principle rise with me above all the opinions of men about another world, and come up hither and sit on the clouds made by the superstition and look and survey one last space where perfect light and harmony exist. Now turn your eyes to the earth and see men's eyes turned upward to see this world and listen to their stories about it. See them down on their knees begging an unknown God to guide them to this world. So the superstition in regard to it is that the spirits of all those that they have created and believed in come from this vast place, where man never comes, nor ever will come till he breaks the fetters of idolatry, and by the buoyancy of his wisdom, rises by his own wisdom, unfettered by superstitions into the glorious light of science.

1864

Our Religious Instruction is Derived Chiefly from Preaching*
[BU 3:0468]

A minister on Sunday selects a text from the Bible and preaches a sermon upon it. In this sermon he explains the text and the explanation is given as if it were of some value to man. His auditors are not only those who are well but the sick also and it is to these that his preaching is addressed. For the well need no physician. Now what is said to them and how are they affected by it? They are told that it is their duty to be reconciled to their lot. Conscious that they need something different from this, which is a stone and not bread, they leave the church more nervous and unhappy than when they entered.

Was this the case with the teaching of Jesus and his disciples? No; for their object was to correct some wrong interpretation prevailing among the people in regard to health. Jesus never preached to the well. He opposed the religion of his day as the works of darkness and I also oppose for it is the invention of man. Christ is not in it.

Jesus says that a tree is known by its fruits. If the fruits of religion are proved to be bad then the tree that bears them must be corrupt and ought to be hewn down.

Opinions are arbitrary, that is they are beliefs without wisdom, therefore the fruits are as liable to be wrong as right. Every person is responsible for his opinion and must be affected by it either for good or for evil. Religion as it is now taught is an opinion, therefore arbitrary; and this as I have said before is what Jesus opposed. He said nothing to those who were without religion, for he came to save the lost house of Israel.

Out of Matter*
[Originally untitled.] [BU 3:0660]

What is Dr. Quimby's object in trying to get out his theory of curing disease? It is natural to suppose that selfishness is at the bottom of his aims and that all his desire to introduce a new doctrine of health is merely an artful way of introducing himself to the public so that he may get more patients. Still further it may be said that his very theory is merely a cunning invention of his mind to amuse and mystify people who are curious, hear him talk, to know how he cures, while he goes on to make the cure. The world judges in this way of everything and therefore when a person feels it important to give his opinion about Dr. Quimby, his theory and cure it requires no extraordinary compass of mind to pronounce the whole thing a humbug.

However should he feel impelled to inform himself on the subject, one or two interviews with the Dr. would enable him to see that there might be another side to this question. He would see that Dr. Quimby understood perfectly his relation to the world as a doctor, and also the position which the opinions of those awarded him as such, and that his object was to destroy these opinions which measured out his course of actions, endowing him with power without responsibility, and bring to light the motives and principles which make him what he is, to himself. His object is to rid mankind of what he considers to be an error so he lays the axe at the root of the tree, and says there is no such thing as disease of itself, it is all in the mind, and is made of ignorance, superstition, and hypocrisy. Frequently the old tree shakes under the blows of his axe and a reluctance to yield up their opinion to such reasoning takes possession of the patient.

He practices on the principle that the real disease is in man and the visible effect is in the body, and to know it is to know the troubles of the man, their cause and cure. So he describes his feelings and tells him the error he has been led into believing and shows how he has condensed and shadowed his misery into his body, and suffers the penalty of his now belief. The cure consists in making him understand how he has done all this and that it is a wrong course started on a false foundation. Then the patient seeing the error of his ways leaves his old companions and rejoices in the truth that has set him free. There he knows more of himself as a man, in sickness and in health and can understand the condition of others. Dr. Quimby's position is where man never has been and returned though some have explored in the direction. In imperfect language he is in pure spiritual atmosphere where the lives of men with all their mysteries and varieties are transparent to him. He not only sees their thoughts and feelings, but through these to the eternal life that God put into man.

He says he is "out of matter" by which he means that in order to understand where he is, you do not have to embrace any belief of the spiritual or physical condition of man, on the contrary it will be found these very beliefs of which the world is so full, are obstacles in the way of getting where he is, when he can see man stripped of all that arbitrary education has made him.

Outlines of a New Theory for Curing Disease, The
[LC 2:0707]

All medical practitioners claim that their mode of treatment is the best; yet no one has even hinted or dares to risk his reputation on the ground that disease is an invention of man and ought to be treated as an error or deception forced upon mankind by ignorance and superstition in the same way that slavery has been forced upon this country, and with all the attendant evils. Dr. Quimby's theory is that all phenomena called disease are the result of false beliefs originating in the darkness of Egyptian superstition and the effect of certain beliefs is called disease.

African slavery is a disease of ignorance and superstition and is the cause of the present misery in this country; but it is merely the figure of white slavery which has riveted its fetters on the minds of men, while the world of mind lies crushed and humbled by this tyrant of old superstition. Disease is what follows a belief and a belief is like an atmosphere so universal that everyone is liable to be affected by it as one would be by chilly winds. God never made the wind to injure any person, nor has He put any intelligence into it by which man should be afraid of it, but man does not "see it in this light." How often we hear this remark, "Don't expose yourself to the damp, cold air." This belief that God made the air an enemy to man is a part of the clouds that rise in the mind of every person, and when this cloud is seen and felt, all persons, old and young, are affected, for the fear is the punishment of the belief, and it is no excuse that the ignorant have no belief as they must suffer for the sins of their parents. Science is the sun that burns up the clouds or changes the beliefs of man, and a little ray of intelligence springs up and the cloud of superstition vanishes as the true God appears. The people will hail the truth, as the peak of Tenerife hails the rising sun long before it is seen by the horizon of the common mind.

I will bring some cases to show that phenomena that were once produced can never be produced again. This fact holds good in the vegetable as well as in the mental world. Take a primeval forest, cut down the old growth and another will spring up, not like the first, but a more solid, thicker growth. So it is with error; like an old growth, error is tall and porous with a great show. Science is denser and more substantial. Error is the natural growth of man; it is a wilderness filled with all kinds of superstition and everyone is liable to be caught by a native of this land. It is inhabited by every variety of creature: consumption and liver complaint, etc. Science is the axe in the hands of Wisdom to hew down this wilderness and destroy its inhabitants and introduce a better state of society. Like all superstition, error is very religious. Religion and slavery always go hand in hand. Freedom and science also go together and are the same. So religion is in its acts and the other is the same, only when one binds his fellow man, the other liberates him. Where science goes civilization is the purest, but science is not always known. Science in religion has not made much progress except as an indirect result of some other development. Astronomy has destroyed some of the hideous features of religion and introduced a happier state of society, but it was not the design of astronomy to destroy religion. Still it is the natural result of science to destroy error and prejudice. It sometimes comes in contact with the most enlightened state of intelligence, for that is cursed with the shackles of religion of dark ages. You will see religion in its purest state under the most despotic form of government, and you will always find disease under some despotic power of religion; and those who undertake to rid the world of this evil are like demagogues in a despotism. Such is the essence of hypocrisy intended to keep the masses weak so they can be ruled. Starve the masses and you destroy their energy and make them desperate; then the more enlightened will submit to the leaders for their own safety. This keeps in power those demagogues.

So it is with disease. Religion is despotism in politics and disease. The misery of the sick is the torment of their belief. With politics the misery of the South is their religion. The North has more science and less religion. Yet the North has enough to sympathize with the South and bring misery in our midst. Religion makes no compromise; it is rule or ruin. It sometimes takes to itself the name of reform, giving every man the liberty of free speech, and then it subjects everyone to its laws. Just so with the poor slave or sick, for the sick are merely slaves of superstition made so by the sins of our parents. So they, like the African slave, think slavery or disease is of divine origin and the doctor is our teacher. Jesus came out against all this and lost his life. So with every reformer. Let him speak the truth of the church, the medical faculty and political parties or his life is in danger.

September 1862

Parable, A
[LC 1:0145]

How shall I illustrate this spiritual truth or wisdom? I will call it a king, who made a great feast or science for man his son. So he sends wisdom into the minds to call or reason about this great feast or science. They, that is their errors, prevented them from understanding, so he sent other ideas or arguments to convince the error so that it could understand. But the error made light of the truth and went their way and would not reason so that it could not get any foothold as yet. So the error ridiculed any idea that would rise in the minds that this truth ever could be reduced to a science. They discarded from their minds all idea of a science but admitted it as a gift or power. So when the king had failed to reduce this truth to a science because of the errors of the age, it was wroth and it sent forth its power and destroyed these errors that were murdering its science, and by its truth burnt up their old theory or society. Then said he, the wedding or science is ready to be understood by man (or the son).

August 1860

Parables of Jesus, The
[LC 1:0158]

The question is often asked why Jesus spoke in parables to convince the people of another world. Why not tell the simple story and not mystify everything, so that even his own disciples could not understand him. I will admit that there is something in that question that looks dark, but when one understands what Jesus was trying to establish or teach, it will give you a very different slant on his ideas. The first question should be: what was Jesus trying to establish-not take it for granted it was another world. It is generally believed that it was to establish a belief in a future state or world beyond this material world and it was necessary for him to come from heaven to earth in order for him to teach this great truth and to show the people that he really did come from heaven; and to make them believe, he must show a sign or do something a little above the rest of mankind. How natural it is to mystify everything so that the ignorant cannot understand! Men do not want to think; so if they can only get rid of investigating a phenomenon and attributing it to an invisible power so that they stand just as well as their neighbors, that is all they want. There is another class called the wise men, who have been set up as oracles of wisdom. To them everything that starts up must take its rise from their fountain, or they will open their flood gates and overflow the little streams that are trickling over the rocks and pebbles of their superstition.

It is too much labor to be a hewer of wood; so if you take a person of eminence and make him a laborer, he will say like the slothful servant that truth is a hard master. So such persons will hide their talent because they will not put themselves on a level with the thinkers of their age, but rather lie still and cry, Crucify him, for our craft is in danger! The people take the cue and fall upon him with staff and stone or ridicule till they have put him down. Then those wise men rise in their majesty and praise the people for their good sense in putting down the very person who is their friend. This was the case with Jesus; the opposition came from the wisest men or class of men who led the people for their own good. This course taken by the wisdom of this world has always opposed all science ever since the commencement of the world. For when science is established the wisdom of this world has to yield, but a hard battle must be fought before the science is established.

So when Jesus commenced his reform he was despised of all men, misrepresented by fools and construed by knaves and hated by priests and doctors. They thought as they do now: our craft is in danger, so they called him infidel and imposter. When they crucified Jesus they put such a construction on his acts as they pleased and instead of giving his ideas, they gave just such an opinion as anyone would expect from those who wanted to keep the people in subjection and ignorance. Thus they have explained Jesus' meaning just according to their ideas. Now the Bible is in the hands of the people and they can all read and judge for themselves and everyone has a right in this land of liberty to give his own opinion in regard to the Bible. I will avail myself of the same liberty as others. All I ask of you is to lay aside all prejudices and listen to my explanation of Jesus' mission in the world. I will state what I intend to prove, and afterwards, I will prove it by his works and my own and leave it to the people to judge which is the most natural construction–the priests or mine. I will now give my opinion. I take this ground, that Jesus never intended to teach any kind of religion, acknowledged by any religious class of people, but opposed all kinds of religion of his days and ours. Secondly, I say he never meddled with any institution or laws made by the people. Thirdly, he never put any restrictions on man but left him a free agent to do just as he pleased, but subject to the laws of men, for God never made a law. All laws are the inventions of men, not of God and Jesus' kingdom or truth was not of this world but of science. His religion was a science and science was never known to have any connection with ignorance.

There are two standards: one is ignorance of science. It belongs to that class of intellect or wisdom that is of this world and can be detected as easily as you can detect any other error. The difference between the two is this: the wisdom of this world tells what others know. It takes memory of events and the history of the learned for science. But science talks what it knows and stands ready to prove it by works.

Here is the difference in men. A great man is one who can remember anything he ever heard and repeat every person's opinion but has no idea of his own. He stands ready to prove all he says by his standard, so if he is doubted, he shows you his authority. Thus he is a sort of court or town record that is ready to receive any opinion that is supposed to be true, having the court or town stamps–this makes a learned man. A truly scientific man is a book of nature, understood, so that he can prove all he says. He is made not of opinions but of wisdom, and never refers to old authors but proves all things by his science. His memory of events or names or places, he has no shelf to put on, for to him they are only as an amendment. He listens to persons having that knowledge as a parent listens to a child to hear him give an account of some play or story that amuses him for the time. In his leisure hours, he seeks such men as a person goes to a play for the sake of amusement, not expecting to realize any true wisdom. This sort of amusement is of this world and is well expressed by Shakespeare when he says, "All the world's a stage and all men are players," etc. This is the case and as science is a stranger to this world it comes into this world and pays tribute money, to be instructed in all things pertaining to the world.

It pays the clergy for their opinions of truth or science of this world for its own amusement. It asks questions of the wise men about itself as science, as Jesus did, to hear what kind of answers they gave to this spiritual world.

This world is very strict. It worships science as a power not known and is very strict in regard to its followers. It erects standards to this unknown God or science, for it is a God not known to this world, but the world of science is in it. Now as Jesus came from this world of science, he was a stranger in this land and liable to its laws. So that his mission, like all science, being to destroy error, he must come into the world of error to lead the science that is imprisoned in this world of error to the truth or health. Jesus knew that God or science was not in their worship, that all it did was to keep science down and retard it. So he must, like Sampson, throw firebrands into their minds so as to get up a dis-union in order to dissolve the bands or burdens that kept them down. He knew that the people knew not what they did or believed. They never had any science about their belief and had not the slightest idea of what it was or how it could be altered. They never dreamed that to be good was a science, so that all their goodness was based on fear, either of being punished by the laws or being destroyed by the science that they called God. Thus, all their prayers were to this science, not to destroy them. For as the truth came, their life or error was destroyed. So Jesus said in the name of Christ or Science, "He, that is error, that loseth his life or opinion for my sake or science shall find it." So to understand Christ or Truth was to forsake opinions and embrace truth, and not to receive an opinion from anyone who knew nothing about what he affirms.

He told them how to know the difference. If any man say I am Christ and have not the evidence, only resting on an opinion, believe him not, for there shall be many theories and beliefs founded on opinions. So try them and see whether they are based on science or error. (Mark 13:21). If they are based on science they can stand the test of investigation. But if based on error, you will hear a voice like the mighty winds and the earth shall be shaken to its foundation and every idea shall arise and they will make as much ado as the devils did when Jesus told them to depart. Men have to be questioned in regard to their belief, for it won't stand the fire of science.

So they rail and foam, and if that will not do, they escape into the wilderness or run headlong into the sea of public opinion where the common opinion holds them. To attack public opinion is a risk; this Jesus had to run. Now Jesus' world, that God or Science was in, was science. And when he came from science he came to this world of ignorance and superstition. It may be necessary to give some idea of Jesus' knowledge of this other world and where he differed from the leaders of his time. Jesus' two worlds were science and ignorance. Therefore, science can come from its world and go to error and release that science that is bound by error. These are the two worlds and Jesus never intended to teach any other. Now what is the difference between these two worlds? I will try to show.

This world is made up of all kinds of deception, superstition and ignorance, all based on heathen superstition governed by leaders of theories which are based on opinions and do not have the slightest foundation in truth. These two worlds are in and around every one. The natural world is in man, looking out and prophesying about the other world. The scientific world is outside of man and sees all the natural man's ideas of science, as the musician sees the errors of the natural man in regard to music. All science is inspiration and from a spirit world far above the natural man. The natural man has found it out and submits to it as a science. Now in all science God is not known by the natural man. His God is in his ignorance of himself. So when he prays he never prays to any science or wisdom; therefore he thinks all the phenomena he sees are the natural result of the development of man. But being ignorant of science he is not a fit judge of the phenomena that he may chance to see or hear. And being ignorant of himself, he applies the same rules to others. It may be a good rule but there are exceptions to all the rules; so I will make an exception to this, for error is not accountable for its acts as truth is. If a scientific man does wrong he knows it, but if he is wrong from ignorance there is no right in it, so there is no sin to him. Science tells you that fire will burn your hand and you cannot put your hand into the fire ignorant, when you know it. So you cannot commit that wrong without suffering punishment, for your punishment is in your knowledge and not in the fire.

Now suppose you are a child and do not know fire. You see it and as all children do, you want it, or a piece of the red hot coal. Your ignorant desire for the coal excites you and you put your hand into the fire. The sensation frightens you just as much as though you had put your hand into a dog's mouth and been bitten. The sensation produces fright; then comes reason. You reason about the fire as though it contained life and would hurt you, so the fire and the dog are to you just the same. As you stand weeping, someone comes up and tries to soothe you by telling you to keep away from the dog or fire and not get hurt, but makes no distinction between them. So the child sees the dog can move around and thinks the fire is the same as the dog. He shuns them both alike, but puts intelligence in the fire. Now the child grows up with all the ignorance of his youth till he becomes a man. Then he takes his place with other men and knows nothing of science. So it sees a sort of intelligence in everything it does not know and reasons how to keep clear of every phenomenon it happens to see. At last in its ignorance it prays to this enemy; so it worships all things that it cannot comprehend. It puts God into everything; therefore, in its ignorance it gets up a sort of creed or belief to offer up a prayer to this invisible power, to which it has given the name of God and it lives and dies in the fear of it. It worships and pretends to adore it. So when it goes into the water, it prays that the water will not drown it. It sees God in all danger and prays to it to have mercy on it till it can get clear of the enemy it worships. This is the religious man.

Now where stands Jesus as a man? Not Christ. Jesus knew that all this was hypocrisy, fear and ignorance. He made a difference between his God and their God. He knew that their God was a devil, so he said to them, You worship ye know not what; I know what I worship. Again, he says: You are the children of the devil; he was a liar and abode not in the truth. The people in their ignorance want leaders and they will hire them. These leaders know that the people put trust in them and they know that they are not worthy of taking the high responsibility of leading or instructing them. So their first prayer is correct when they say that they are not worthy to take the Lord's or Science's name upon their lips. This is true for God is true and those who worship Him must worship Him in spirit and in truth. So when a person is all the time crying Lord, or Truth, never showing any fruits, beware of such, for they are wolves in sheep's clothing. Jesus told them that all this was hypocrisy and this made them crucify him. The priests never taught the people anything except for the benefit of their craft. The leaders must have a living and a pretty good one. This deception could not be kept up but must go down before the progress of science in the people's minds. All science was confined to the leaders and was of this world. It made them crafty and inventive of all sorts of humbug to keep the people in subjection. This kept the people superstitious and led to sorcery and witchcraft. So deception became the order of the day, so much so that they got frightened at their own beliefs and passed laws to keep it down, just as though the development of science must be under the ignorance of this world.

Jesus saw all this and as the people were groaning under the yokes or beliefs that bound them down, he said, Come unto me all ye that labor and are heavy laden and I will give you rest to your soul by explaining to you the cause of your trouble. When he commenced explaining to the people, the explanation was to save them from the misery of this world of belief and to introduce a science or kingdom, where there would be no offering up of prayer or forgiving of sins but a consciousness or science that would put them in possession of a knowledge of themselves, which the natural man knew nothing of. When Jesus says, Take my yoke upon you, he means my wisdom or science. That is easy, for it contains no restrictions. This, to the people was something new, so they reasoned together like people who want to get some information. This setting the people to reasoning was a stumbling block to the Jews and foolishness to the Greeks, for they had no idea that the people could govern themselves. So he took up the laws of Moses and gave them common ideas of them. Then he showed them a more perfect law of love that bound them together by sympathy, not of this world but of science. The people had never known that a good act must proceed from a goodness that they felt. The priests had never taught such a thing. So goodness was a sort of low wisdom and only applied to the poor. To try to be good without having any reward in view was of no use and the person who put any religion into it was as ignorant as the swine or dogs.

Now here was where Jesus struck at the root of error. He says, Every plant or science that is not planted by wisdom shall be rooted up and goes on to tell the people what his kingdom of heaven was. It was peace and joy in the Holy Ghost or Truth. He explained to them by illustrating the difference in the motives that govern the people. Therefore he said, Except ye become as little children you cannot enter into the kingdom of God or Science. Now every one knows that a little child has no idea of what man calls right or wrong, but might is right. So to become as a child means that you must not be under any restriction that prevents you from doing just as you please.

Suppose you were in this state and Jesus and one of the priests called on you to teach you the wisdom of this world, and you should put this question to the priest. I want my neighbor's ox for my family to eat, can I not take it? The priest says, No. Why not? Because it would be stealing and that is not right. Why? I want it and see no reason why I cannot have it. I am stronger than he is and am not afraid of him. We know that and the wisdom of this world has seen fit to make a law that if you steal an ox you shall pay five oxen back. Well suppose I kill the owner, then there will be no one to tell, what can they do? The Great Spirit will catch you. How? Why he has a place where he puts all who do not repent of their sins. What sins? Stealing from each other. How must I repent? By asking this Great power to forgive you. Will he do it? Yes, if you are sincere. What is that? Say you won't do it again. Is that all? Yes. Well if that is all that is easy enough. Oh, you must confess it to the priest and he will lay your case before the Great Spirit and get your sins forgiven. Why cannot I do it? Because God has appointed certain men to attend to that for his special purposes. Then if I steal, as you call it, I must pay the man four times as much. Yes. Suppose I steal and he never finds it out, will the Great Spirit know it? Yes, he knows all things. What will he do? Just what I told you, if you do not confess to the priest and tell him all you have done. What does the priest get for his trouble? Does the Great Spirit pay him? No. Who does? The person who steals. So if I steal and you are a priest, I must pay you for getting the Great Spirit to let me off? Yes. Then won't he hurt or punish me? No. Does he not have anything to do with the laws of man? No. Then if the laws of man do not catch me, you can clear me from God's punishment? Yes. Well, I understand.

So religion is made up of rewards and punishments, not of good works, lest any man should boast. Goodness is a sort of clever fellow, always in the way of the religious man. An honest man at heart is the

439

greatest eyesore that a Christian can have. He is as bad as a man who never drank or smoked or chewed tobacco is to the temperance party. He must be of them or he is the worst enemy the party has to contend with. So it is with all hypocrites. True goodness, not hypocrisy, is the worst enemy that religion has to contend with. For an honest and upright man is the noblest work of God or Science, but the religious man is of his father, the devil, and his works he will do. Now I do not intend to apply these ideas to any particular man or class of men but to all. We all have religion or error and we all have some science or wisdom of God. Religion is our superstition and belongs to the natural man. Science is spiritual and belongs to the spiritual man. Paul had these two characters; therefore, when he would do good, his old religion was present and that which he would do, his old ideas prevented him; so it was not science that did wrong but his old religion that was in him. Jesus had the same enemy to contend with. If he had listened to the voice of religion of his day he might have been king of the Jews but enemy to all science. Honesty or doing unto another as you would have another do to you was not just the thing, for it struck at the root of all their religion. It made man a responsible being to himself and put into his mind a truth that would show him to act from a higher motive than religion. It teaches us that God is in science and not in ignorance, that might is right for the religious world; but for the scientific world, action and reaction are equal. And just as we measure out to another, just so it shall be measured back to us, and no priest or prayer of this world can stay the hand of this law.

So Christ died for all and Jesus abandoned all his heathen religion and worshipped God or Science, laid down his life or science for the world so that all can enjoy it if they will only forsake their father or their old creeds and embrace Christ or Science. This will wash away all superstition. This was the religion of Jesus. To be a disciple of Jesus you must forsake all these forms and ceremonies, for in sacrifices and prayers he has no sympathy. But to worship this Christ as Jesus did is to worship it in spirit and in truth. This religion was blasphemy. So they crucified him, and parted his garment or Science, and drew lots for it. The doctors took that part which applied to healing and the priests that which applied to preaching. So the people are just about as wise as they were before. Christ or Science is in the world, not in the church or medical faculty but in the hearts of the people, working itself along.

July 1860

Patriotism
[LC 1:0419]

Patriotism is the feeling which prompts man to respect the right of his fellow man, also his obligation to his country and to his God. Every man might say these are my sentiments, but as one opinion is as good as another, we must find a higher principle than opinion to try them by. Now what is that feeling that we call patriotism? This can only be proved by the same scale that all other truths are proved. A nation is nothing but a child; like any child, it contains its father and mother. The father is of the earth or opinions; the mother is the warmth or sympathy of the earth or opinion. Every person takes after his father or mother. George Washington was like his mother; therefore his life was attached to his country or mother. Opinion is the man, wisdom or science is the woman. As each man contains these two characters, to know who is a patriot is to know which rules in man, opinion or wisdom. Each rules its offspring according to its character.

The man rules his child by arbitrary power, the mother by love. Just so in a young nation. The opinion of man rules by arbitrary measures, the higher principle rules by wisdom. I will give the platforms of both. The nation like father and mother has offspring and the inhabitants of the United States are the offspring of the Republic. It is necessary that some sort of an agreement must be entered into to unite the children who contain the wisdom of the mother and the opinions of the father. As a nation grows up, there must be some kind of an organization, for all will acknowledge that the earth produces neither nation nor individuals. Therefore all nations are the offspring of other nations as men are the children of parents. So as a nation commences its growth, it respects its parents just as long as it thinks itself bound.

Children are bound to their parents till they are twenty-one; then they are free. So nations arise from some governments and continue their relations to each other as parent and child. This nation is the descendant of England and as such, they respected their mother country, but it contains another element from other nations. The renegades of all nations came and united themselves with this young province.

They, not respecting the mother but dictated by the father's opinion, became stubborn and had to leave their country. So in the bosom of this country, they found sympathy. As time passed on and opinions came in contact with wisdom or that part of man called science, it, being more subtle than wisdom, made war. For opinions and all that opposes it must come down. So it makes war with the harmless Indians instead of enlightening them. It made war with its father, for its mother or science never made war. At last it conquered its father and established itself. Then it being weak, it was found necessary to enter into some contract that would hold itself together. As the mother or higher principles are always ready to yield, they with opinions came together to establish a government or contract to bind themselves together for their defense. Opinions ruled as they must always do. For it is easier to force people than to reason with them. And they formed the best government that could be formed, for their fears caused their opinions to yield to the subjection of the higher wisdom of the mother.

Slavery was not recognized by wisdom but was created by opinions, which would not yield up this overbearing clause. So the contract was made binding on all so that they should unite themselves like one family for their own protection. Opinions ruled and wisdom sanctioned the bargain and called on the mother of all to attest the agreement and hold the deed. In the course of time, the father commenced war with the sons. They fought and the latter succeeded and in the trade they got more territory. Then the earthly or aristocratic part wanted to increase their power. And as opinions or error must always have a pretext for their acts, they went to overhauling the old agreement of the people made with the contract. Difference of opinions sprang up and each man selected from the old agreements the opinions of their fathers and in their zeal they forgot the wisdom of their mother.

So parties sprang up and arguments were made upon the opinions got from the constitution. All error has its object in view and therefore cannot agree with wisdom, but being a chemical change must beat itself to pieces by its own strength, for action and reaction are equal. The evil of slavery being admitted at first, wisdom held the people to their agreement. But error never wants to be bound but wants to bind everything that happens to affect its progress. Liberty or freedom is the destiny of man, as well as all wisdom. Its heat or love sets error in action. So freedom in religion and every other department of wisdom warms the heart of man, and a chemical change takes place and man throws off the elements of his existence. So if there is more of opinion than wisdom in him, then opinion takes the lead and wisdom or freedom is bound. Wisdom, having nothing to gain and opinion having its life to lose, fights itself like an insane man. Whenever opinions get the better of wisdom, then man is beside himself. This is a demagogue and when wisdom gets the stand, then he is a patriot. Both are tested like all other facts. The true standard is wisdom according to the agreement in the Constitution. So all patriotism that would destroy the Constitution is of demagogues or opinions, not of wisdom. Each man stands on one or the other of these platforms. One rests on the Constitution or agreement, the other on opinions or arbitrary power. One wants the Constitution as it is; the other wants it for the party or to have it destroyed with the idea that they can make another one without the element of freedom.

The Constitution is like a man in the hands of the people. It is passive. It makes no trouble. It is the same today and forever. But parties spring up to get favors from it and as it has no respect for persons, opinions arise; then men argue. The man of opinion leads off, for wisdom never gives any opinion. Wisdom does not move itself, so opinions show themselves through a machine called man. Now when you see a man trying to alter wisdom and turn it to an opinion, he is either a fool or a knave. I do not say the Constitution is true to the letter, but it is true that there was a Constitution which the people admitted right and true and it came as near true wisdom as the people were able to make it. If it is assailed, it must be by someone who thinks his opinion is better than the wisdom of the framers. For they do not say that the framers made any mistake, but they think the people do not understand it. Thus they set up a standard based on opinions and make war with the wisdom or Constitution.

The patriot sustains the wisdom or Constitution, while the demagogue tries to destroy it. The demagogue always uses reason as he calls it; his weapons are getting up false issues, throwing them out like a fisherman to catch the people. When he sees them nibbling at the bait, then he begins to draw in the net. And as there are all kinds of people or opinions, it sometimes happens that the net is torn and all the people escape. So the demagogue gets mistaken; when he thinks the people have swallowed the bait, he commences to draw them up on the dry land where opinions can be seen. And he finds his net full of all sorts of absurdities or impressions that the people cannot receive. Now all a man has got to do is to apply this one rule to allay their argument, to see that their opinions are based on some false issue that the people have been made to believe. The true patriot's duty is to stand firm on the Constitution or mother, never making any false issue, nor any compromise that will rob the children of their inheritance. So as the Constitution is a spiritual truth in the heart of every patriot, sanctioned by the blood of our fathers, never let our earthly passions become wedded to harlots or opinions that will rob us of the blessing that wisdom has bequeathed to us.

August 1861

Phenomena of Spiritualism, The
[BU 3:0631]

According to man's belief, he cannot give a fair account of the phenomena of Spiritualism, from the fact that the experiments are governed by his belief and must be so; but man cannot tell what he believes till the effect comes. His belief is like his courage; he can judge better after it is tested. To say you believe so and so is merely to assent to what someone has said, but to have your belief of any force it must take form. For instance I might say that I believed there never was a spirit seen. Now, to test my belief is to place me where I see or hear something that I cannot account for.

I have found that in experiments everything that rests on a belief is liable to be changed by some other belief or by science. The whole error on which Spiritualism is based is a belief of a world separate or apart from the living into which sooner or later man must enter, and every phenomenon goes to prove the truth of this belief. Now destroy the error and what is man? Some say this is atheism; it strikes at the root of all Christianity. Suppose it does. Must we do evil that good may come? No, let God be true and man's opinion a lie or error.

I will give my belief of man and his progression, leaving the world to judge of the truth of my story. What I know does not rest on the evidence of my own or any opinion, and my opinion I give as such, liable to be destroyed by science. Formerly I believed as all mankind did in regard to death and the state after that change. I believed it was taught by Jesus and that it was all laid down in the Bible. But since I have been engaged in the investigation of man's eternal existence, the truth which I have found has destroyed this belief and has opened to me a light which shows that all my former beliefs were based on superstition. I now stand on the rock of science and prove all things by what I feel and see and not by what others tell me.

I admit the Bible so far as it goes to prove this fact, but the explanation I deny, for I know it is false. My belief is my wisdom, my opinion is my knowledge; every person may say this, but wisdom is of God and knowledge is of man, and that being based on a belief must fail, while the wisdom of God is eternal.

I will mention the articles of faith in which I differ from all classes of believers. To the world what I know is an opinion, so I have to speak of it as my belief and give the evidence of this faith in me, for this truth. To make the difference plain, I will draw out the articles of the Christian faith.

The Christian confesses as follows. "I believe in God and his son Jesus Christ, the savior of man. I believe that man dies and goes to heaven or hell. I believe in a place separate and apart from the living, and sometimes I believe that my departed friends can come and communicate with me through a certain medium. I believe that sometimes men go directly to heaven to be with God. When I die, I believe that my soul will once more join them in heaven, to be united in one great family never to be separated. Sometimes I believe that they never go at all but that when we die there is an end of us. Sometimes I believe the Bible is all a lie and then again it is all the work of inspiration and then I sometimes can see some evidence that my friends can communicate through certain mediums and give tests that they live and know what is going on in the world." This embraces nearly every person's belief about the dead and another world.

Now, as for my belief, I believe all the above is false, but this is only my belief. I know that we both sit opposite each other and can each communicate our thoughts to the other. This is wisdom and not knowledge. We both admit it. I know, also, if you have a trouble in your body or mind, that I can get the fact from you without your knowing it through your senses, and if you know the same, to you it is wisdom, but if you do not know it, it is a belief in what I say, and if you do believe it, it is wisdom. I know that if you go out of sight of my natural eyes and have a desire that I should come to you, that I can go. To me this is wisdom, but to you it is opinion or knowledge, just according to your belief. I know that I can go to a distance and act upon a person and know that I am there and I can make an impression on a person so strong that the person will be aware of my presence. This is wisdom.

I will explain the different meaning with which I use the terms wisdom and knowledge. Knowledge is the word used to define the extent of man's wisdom. Wisdom is what is acknowledged to be true. Now in telling what we know, if this wisdom is based on an opinion and can be changed, then it is knowledge, but if it is based upon science it is the knowledge of God. What I believe in regard to man's capacity and progress is based upon what I know and have no opinion about, but upon science. I believe I can tell your thoughts in regard to your trouble. If this is admitted then you will admit that I have a knowledge of some wisdom superior to a belief or what you know.

Now follow me in this obscure path that leads to light and life in regard to man's capability of progress. If you are cut off from your natural sight and hearing you have no proof that you can come and communicate with me, from your own belief. Is it the same with me? No. Although the partition or veil hides your form from me, yet my spiritual wisdom can commune with you as much as it would if I were in your presence and you were blind. I should know you, but you could not tell unless I made myself known to your natural senses. Yet I know it so from all that I have seen and felt. I know that man begins at his birth to develop this life or science, and his body, like language, is a medium for him to communicate through till a higher life or scientific man comes forth. Then a new heaven and a new earth is formed and man lives in both but does not always know it.

To know this so as to put it into practice is reducing this wisdom to a science. When this is done man lives by his wisdom and learns that his happiness is in his wisdom and his wisdom is attached to the things he knows and not to someone's opinion. Then his old heaven is destroyed and the earth is burned up; his life is in his friends and he becomes a part and parcel of them. Then he will no longer try to drive his dearest friends and relations off to a world made by man or try to make them want to leave all that is near and dear to them and launch Egyptian superstition to look for what he never wanted to find.

This science teaches that there never was nor can be another world, and to separate yourself from your friend is suicide and is as wrong as it would be to turn your child out of your own house because someone has told you it was right.

Your belief separates, your wisdom unites. Each has its effect. If you believe there is no other world, then you do not drive your friend away. When you lie down at night with a belief that you will rise in the morning, you live and enjoy yourself with your friends just according to your belief. It will be just as you believe. If you believe that your friends have gone to another world and come and communicate, just so it will be to you, but your belief is yours and not your friends. Their belief is one thing and yours another. Each is independent of wisdom; it belongs to the natural man and has nothing to do with the scientific man.

Now, you as a natural man who believes in death and that your friend can communicate with you, carry to the medium all that you believe of your friend. But your friend through his senses knows just as much about your going to the medium as you know through the senses, when I come in communication with your spiritual senses.

The medium comes in communication with your belief and the raps and tips come to convince you that your spirits are in sympathy, and this is the language; but outside of yourself and the medium, all is darkness to your friends. I go with you, believing that all this comes from my own mind and I get this truth that the medium can read my own thoughts, and if my superstition is strong enough to move the table then I can see that, but if it is not, then I shall not, and just according to our belief, the effect comes.

August 1862

Poor vs the Rich, The
[BU 3:1160]

Every now and then we hear of the rich oppressing the poor and these attacks come periodically. Now why is it? At times we are quiet and then this disease, as it were, breaks out again. There must be a cause for all this which never has been known, else the disease could be eradicated. It generally makes its appearance just before an election so that the cause must be in the electioneering. Now are the rich so oppressive to the poor or is that a lure to keep some designing politician in office? There is an element in mankind that is overbearing and aristocratic, but it is not confined to the rich any more than it is to the poor. It is an element in us and if we are poor it chafes us and makes us envious. Give us money and it acts like a stimulant. It excites and brings out the aristocratic element and we become overbearing. Our nature is not changed but money stimulates our passions.

If we are poor and have no envious feeling, riches will not change us any. Like intoxicating drink, it excites the ruling passion in man. Some years since there was a political party called The Know Nothings. Now what gave rise to that party? It was because the Democrats let the Irish vote, not because of the envy of the poor towards the rich. There is and always will be a set of demagogues in the country who are too lazy to work and too proud to beg, who are always contriving to excite the poor and envious against the richer part of the community. There is as much aristocracy in the lowest hod-carrier as there is in the wealthy merchant. The one is poor and envious and the other rich and aristocratic. The demagogue knows that his salvation depends on setting the poor against the rich and he makes no distinction in individuals but calls the rich as a class all aristocrats who want to grind the poor, and in this way these demagogues get the votes of the poor.

The foreign population have been worked upon by these demagogues and the Democrats have got nearly the whole of the Irish under their control and that gave rise to the Know Nothing movement. Now let the poor stop and think if it is for their interest to oppose the rich, simply because they are rich. All this talk is just to create an excitement and turn someone out or to get someone into office. The mere getting one or more persons in or out of office is nothing of importance, but to set one class against another leads to bad results. This is seen by the rebellion by setting the whites against the blacks which was only for the benefit of the political demagogues. The rebellion was caused and now they are getting their reward. All demagogues who would set the poor against those who are giving them employment are doing an act that will someday rebound against them.

To say the rich cannot live without the aid of the poor is erroneous. If I have money enough, I can live just as I please, but if I am poor, I must work, beg, steal, else die. Now if a man has capital and is willing to help the poor and thus help and benefit himself, he is the poor man's friend rather than his enemy, and it is as much for the benefit of one as the other for they have a mutual sympathy in the cause and he who would destroy this sympathy between them is a low demagogue and not fit to be trusted by any class. He sets the very element of progression at variance, for if the rich will not employ the poor, it reduces them to slaves, while the rich become an aristocracy. Beware of the demagogue who will set the employee against the employer. You only see them just before an election, at which time they have a great deal of sympathy for the poor, but all they want is some office themselves or are tools of someone else who does. But after election is over and the smoke clears away, you return to your employers ashamed for having abused them when you had nothing in reality against them and merely acted as you did from political excitement.

September 1864

Popular Definitions of the Word "Mind" Confused: Illustrations and Explanations of the Same, Meaning Matter
[LC 1:0421]

Why do people differ so much in regard to the word mind? Every person uses the word and still there is a difference in their meaning of it, although it might seem as though there was no difference of opinion about it. Yet, upon analysis it is found that its meaning is so broad that it gives great scope to the imagination and in reality does not mean anything. Words ought to express what those who use them mean, but such is not the case. Ask persons what the word mind means and they will all differ. Some will say it is the thinking principle. Ask what that is and they will fly off to what a man knows. Ask if man knows he is alive, the answer is, Yes. What is your mind or opinion about it? I have no opinion or mind about it. I know it, if I know anything. Here he makes a distinction between his wisdom and his mind and yet he calls his wisdom mind. This and hundreds of similar cases all go to prove that the word mind does not apply to intelligence above man's opinions. The inventor of the word either meant to apply it to matter or he never had an idea of any wisdom superior to the natural man, for it does not apply to science.

Mind is applied to something that is admitted to have life and dies. This is all that mind can cover, so that when you apply the word mind to that something that proves all things by a standard which all will admit, it fails to apply. The wisdom of man is matter or mind, but the science of life eternal is not mind but science, so that all men are a phenomenon of both. Mind is the something. I will call it a medium or matter in which ideas are sown; each idea is matter of another combination from mind. I will try to illustrate my idea. Suppose we call mind the soil or medium to receive the seed or idea or thought. The body is the earth or man. Now every seed has its own body and every body its own mind. So that when a seed or thought is sown in the mind, it springs up like a tree or plant and its roots embed themselves in the soil of the earth. As the seed grows, it becomes an idea. So as the idea grows, it branches out like a tree and its roots spread in the mind.

Ideas growing like trees take to themselves a character and are known by their fruits and also are detected by the wisdom of the wise. The wisdom of the fruit is like the child's; it contains no knowledge. The beast or natural man eats of the fruit according to his fancy or taste. But the scientific man judges of the tree by its fruits. So of course, the natural man like the beast eats of the fruit and learns what he likes by experiment, but he is guided by his senses which are attached to his taste or sight. The idea or tree or science is a different combination and its qualities embrace a wisdom of all the rest of the ideas. To eat of this tree is to open the eyes of the blind and see the difference between light and darkness. So it is called a tree of the knowledge of good and evil. But there is one more tree that man must eat at some future time, and that is the tree of life; this would make a man live forever. These figures, to explain them literally mean this: if man could content himself to live like a brute, there is plenty for him to live on if he chooses to stay where it grows. But man is so constructed that he won't keep still and the restlessness of his mind is the natural effect if his ideas. So man's combination varies like the varieties of the earth, for all the varieties of the earth are the natural result of wisdom, superior to the earth or mind. Ideas like trees bear fruit; each idea has its mind or soil to sow other thoughts in, like grafting one idea into another. Every idea containing misery or pain is in the fruit, as sweet or sour is in an apple. But the peculiar flavor cannot be detected by looks but by taste, and ideas are the same.

You see or hear of a certain kind of fruit. You cannot judge of its flavor till you have tasted it and then you are affected by it, just according to your own sense of taste. So with disease. Some diseases are not looked upon as catching and therefore we are not affected by them any more than a person is affected by anything that is out of sight and hearing. But bring it within your sight and it affects you. There are certain diseases that are at a distance from us; these do not affect us, except as they come nearer. Our beliefs are another element, which has more to do with man than anyone thinks. Our belief is our senses and according as our life is attached to it, it goes to make up that idea called man. So man is a compound of opinions, belief, wisdom, science and ignorance, all arranged into a temple, not made of wood or stone but of ideas, and the world judges of the architect by the finish and workmanship. So if the ideas are so well arranged that harmony is the result, all is well.

I will make one further illustration. All believe water is matter; but with wisdom, it is not anything, for there is no solid to wisdom, neither is there any space. Opinions are darkness called matter. Wisdom is in darkness or matter and it knows it not, as the seed is in the soil and the soil knows it not. Here you see I make mind something and yet it is nothing but an idea or the invention of man. Man is the offspring of wisdom for wisdom's own happiness, for happiness is not wisdom but the satisfaction of gaining our own ends. Now man being made in the image of God or Wisdom, his happiness like that of God, is to create something that will add to his happiness, so he becomes an inventive being. But as his wisdom is not of God or Science, he does not pattern after the true and living wisdom that acts by science. Here is the difference between the wisdom of God and the wisdom of man.

Every man is a part of each and our senses are attached to both. So when a man speaks of himself as a man, he is in matter; but when he speaks a scientific truth, he is out of matter and so far equal to God. So man's investigations are but an imitation of wisdom's experiments for his own happiness. And man not wanting to be outdone by his father tries to imitate what he sees and hears; this makes man a kind of progressive being. Man invents language from the fact that he cannot be satisfied to let God or wisdom dictate his acts, so he invents language to explain his wisdom. It has been said that language was invented to deceive others. In some cases I have no doubt but the world thinks it does but wisdom gives it another direction. For language acts to undeceive and it often exposes our ignorance.

It is said if a man had held his tongue, people would not have found out he was a fool. By language, man destroys himself, for the life of the man of opinions is in his belief and his belief is darkness; but this eternal life is in his science or wisdom. As man's identity is a knowledge of himself, it is not dependent on a belief, so when man's life is attached to a belief, it does not affect his life except to make it happy or miserable: his life is in his wisdom or in his belief, it does not alter, but his belief is all the time changing. A belief is darkness and opinions are in the darkness. Everyone knows that if you frighten a person in the dark, it is very easy to make him see anything you please. So matter or darkness is our belief; opinions or ideas are also matter or beliefs. So when we are in the dark, these enemies or devils come up and can be seen. Now as the light springs up, the shadows disappear. This is the new birth. Religion is in this darkness and all the belief is of darkness or matter. So when the lamp or wisdom is lit up in science, religion, superstition, ignorance and ten thousand bugbears disappear and the true light of science takes its place. So our life is in both, but when we are in science, we are dead to error.

Aug. 16, 1861

Power by Which Jesus Cured, The
[BU 3:0073]

Why should there be such a controversy in regard to the way in which Jesus cured disease; also what was the real object of his mission to this world? These questions naturally arise in the minds of men and bring up doubts and questionings. By some it is believed that it was to save man from being lost in another world and by others it was to reform this world. All admitted he had a power or gift superior to other men, but what it was has never been ascertained. This was the same in the days of Jesus. The same controversy was going on all the time and in fact it has always been a mystery to the natural man. Phenomena are taking place every day, proving this power or gift and all admit it, but it has as yet never been reduced to a science so that it can be taught and learned. Yet its opponents speak as though it was governed by natural laws, but when asked to put these laws into practice they get off by saying that it is nothing but Mesmerism. When asked to explain Mesmerism they say it is psychology. Then if you ask what psychology is, the answer is Mesmerism. So you see the world is just as wise as it was before. No person has undertaken to reduce this power to a science. Mesmer tried to explain it on the ground of electricity. Others have done the same. But not one single step has it advanced since Mesmer. Those who believe it is governed by some law attribute it to Galvanism or electricity. The religious vary. The Spiritualists ascribe it to the spirits of the dead. Christians, when speaking of Jesus, ascribe his miracles to the power of God, but when they speak of this power in man, they attribute it to natural causes. Some say that it is the power of the devil; others, Mesmerism, etc. In the days of Jesus the people admitted it and reasoned about it just as they do now, for when Herod, the king, was told that Jesus was performing these cures, he said that it was John the Baptist, that is, that his spirit came and took possession of Jesus and cured diseases. That was as the Spiritualists of this day believe. Others believe that it was the spirit of Moses acting through Jesus. When the Pharisees asked him where it was from, he said if they would tell him where the power of John came from, then he would tell them how he performed his cures. This they could not do; so you see it has never been explained nor even suggested that it could be. Now settle this one point and you establish a basis for investigation. As it stands, it puts Jesus on the level with all of the Spiritualists of his day and all ages.

If it is a gift or power, why should he be called God or anything else above his followers? And if he knew how he wrought the miracles, then it is a knowledge and not a gift and to call his wisdom a gift or a power is depriving Jesus of any knowledge superior to that of his followers. Admit it as a science that Jesus taught for the happiness of man and then man will try to learn it. Then the inquiry will be made: How can it be proved a science? I answer, never, until the people will admit that mind and matter are all the same and both under the direction of an intelligence superior to matter. Then man takes a higher standard and is governed by a science and not by error or mind. Then matter becomes subject to science and is the medium or power to be put in motion. This medium or matter can be changed into any form or state and be destroyed, but not lost. The identity of a thing can be put out of this world, as it is called, and only remains as a thing that once was, but now is not.

I will give an illustration. Suppose a person believes he has a tumor in his left side. His knowledge or error believes in the idea of tumors independent of his knowledge. He thus admits an error to begin with. Now his knowledge gives direction to the matter and the matter is formed. This is proof that there is such a thing as a tumor. No one will deny that one is a phenomenon brought about by false knowledge and true knowledge or science can destroy that tumor or idea and establish a knowledge of truth that will prevent a person from ever being deceived into that error again. All will admit that a person can be deceived into a belief and his belief make him sick. They will also admit that to correct his error or belief will make him well. This process is all that Jesus ever intended to convey to the world. This is a science and can be learned.

Its opposers are ignorance and error. Its science is in unlearning what ignorance and superstition have bequeathed to man. Our belief makes ideas out of our identity of a body. Our bodies are nothing but an idea of matter that is under the control of error or false knowledge, and happiness or misery is the wages of our investigation. If truth or science reigns, all goes well. If error reigns the wages is death, for all the acts of error lead to death. Death is an idea or matter and all the acts of science destroy death and lead to life and happiness.

May 1860

Prayer I
[LC 1:0021]

Can any good come out of prayer? I answer Yes, but not in the sense that is supposed. A phenomenon can be produced in the same way that is brought about by mesmerism, and the world is put in possession of a fact but no knowledge, for there is no knowledge in the church prayer. It is the effect of superstition and ignorance. It is not of Christ but from a lower superstitious mind which is ignorant of itself and God. No man prays but he who expects to get a favor or be rewarded for more than he deserves or perhaps has more of this world's goods than his neighbor. Witness the effects of the prayers of this world– of those who pray to the earthly man. They belong to the begging, hypocritical, lowest class of mankind. No man of character will beg or pray for the sake of gain.

Prayer is the desire of the heart and if the heart is right the prayer will be answered. For as the heart is only the figure or emblem of our knowledge, a true heart or mind must be scientific knowledge of ourselves and a corrupt heart or mind must be full of superstition and ignorance, deceit and hypocrisy.

It is generally admitted by most of the world that prayer is of divine origin, but if it is to be offered to God this is not the case. If it is of the devil, I will admit that it is as old as its father, for we read that the devils prayed, and the devils asked prayers as when the devil wanted Christ to worship him. So do all men of narrow, contracted minds like to be worshiped. One great argument in favor of prayer is that Christ said, He who humbles himself shall be exalted. What is required of a person to humble himself is to get down on his knees and hold up his hands and in a hypocritical cant ask of God some favor which he is not entitled to. God rewards everyone just according to his acts and He knows our wants before we ask. So to ask of a Being whom we acknowledge knows our wants is either to curry favor or flatter Him with the idea that we think He will be pleased to see how much we honor Him. This is the wisdom of this world, but not the wisdom of God, for God asks no such worship. To worship God is to worship Him in Spirit and in truth, for He is in the truth but not in the error. Our reward is in our act and if we act rightly and honestly, we get the reward. If we act selfishly we get the reward also. He who expects God to leave science and come down to ignorance and change a principle for a selfish motive to please him is either a knave or fool and knows not God. God does not act at all but is like the heat or fire that throws heat or fire on all around. Those who will come can enjoy the heat or love, but if we choose to stand out in the cold, we cannot expect exclusive privileges; for He has no respect to one over another. I have no account with God. He pays me as soon as my work is done and I ask no favors of Him out of His principles. If I act wrongly He will not step out and correct me. I must do it myself. If I act rightly I get my reward, for our happiness or misery is in our acts; and as we are a part of each other, our happiness is in our neighbor, and to love our neighbor as ourselves is more than all burnt offerings and sacrifices. If you understand this, Jesus said, You are not far from the kingdom of heaven. Jesus had no sympathy with the hypocrite's prayer. He warned his disciples and the multitude against all such prayers. His prayer was that God would forgive them for they knew not what they did. A desire to know God is a desire to know ourselves and that requires all our thoughts to come into that happy state of mind that will lead man in the way to health. This is a science and is Christ's prayer. The ignorance of this is superstition and belief in all sorts of evil spirits. This is the effect of this world's prayer; both will be answered but one contains no knowledge and the other contains science the world knows not of.

March 1860

Prayer II
[BU 2:0067]

The question may be asked, How I look on prayer? I answer as I do on all other errors that have been invented to govern mankind and keep the people in ignorance of themselves and God or Science. You may ask if I would destroy prayer. No more than I would the law for murder or theft; but I would put into man a higher law that would teach him to worship God as a God of science and knowledge and this law would put the law of man or ignorance to death. For prayer is the law of man, not of God, and makes God nothing but a mere sorcerer or magician to frighten the ignorant and superstitious. It puts Christ on a level with all the jugglers of His day. The construction upon the parables shows the state of intelligence of the church. It makes Christ's mission here of little consequence to the world of science but puts Christ on a level with the sorcerers of His day.

Take for instance the parable of the wedding. The turning of water into wine is quoted as some great thing, as though God took this way to convince men of His power. But if there could not be a better explanation of this parable than the church gives them, Christ is merely a magician. The church's explanation has been the means of making more sickness and death than all the evils flesh is heir to.

Why should the explanation of Christ's mission, which was to "heal the sick, destroy death and bring life and immortality to light," be left to a set of persons who have no sympathy with the sick, but who by their interpretation of Christ keep man in sickness and ignorance of himself? Of what advantage has Christ been to the sick according to the common opinions of mankind? Do the priests relieve them of any burdens? If not, where is the benefit of the church prayer? It is right in contradiction to Christ's own teaching. What was Christ's idea of prayer? He called it hypocrisy and a blind guide to lead the blind. He warned the people against those who prayed in the streets, told them to obey all the laws, but not to believe in the doctrines, for they laid burdens upon the people grievous to be borne. Now, if these burdens were their belief, Jesus must have explained them away in order to relieve them, and His explanation was their cure. Therefore He said to them, "Come unto me all ye that are weary and heavy laden, and I will give you rest." Jesus' explanation was His religion, but their belief was their religion and that religion was founded upon the old superstitions which contained all the superstitions of Egyptian darkness, prayers, sacrifices and burnt offerings.

Jesus did not condemn any of the above, but he had a knowledge of the errors that man is subject to and His mission was to bring life and understanding to light or science, in regard to our ignorance or darkness and to put man into a state where he might, by relieving the sufferings of his fellow men, be of some advantage to himself and to the world. His religion was not of this world, and the world knows Him not. Christ is God or Science, and to know God is to know science and put it in practice so that the world can be benefited by it.

This tells the rules of action. They are not left to the natural man, but they must prove themselves on some subject that is in need of it. The same subject is in the world now that was at the time Jesus put His theory into practice. He gave His disciples knowledge to put the same into practice for the benefit of mankind.

Who art thou, oh man, that shall say to the poor and sick, lame and blind, that the person who can help you is a humbug or acting under the direction of the devil? If the devil will take your aches and pains and relieve you, cling to him, and at the end of your disease you will see that the devil is the same one who was crucified eighteen hundred years ago, by just such enemies to the sick as they have now. I, for one, am willing to be called a humbug by all such people. I have the same class to uphold me that Jesus had, which is the sick. The well opposed Him and the well oppose me. I do not set myself up as an equal to Jesus, or any other man, but I do profess to believe in that principle that Jesus taught, which I call Christ. That I believe in and try to put into practice as far as I understand it, and the sick are my judges, not the well; for as the well need no physician, they cannot judge me. Neither am I willing to be judged by the church creeds till they can show me that their power or belief is above their natural power. I shall not take their opinions of what they know nothing about. I will draw a line between the professor of Christ and myself and leave the sick to pass judgment. As I have the Bible I have the same means of judging as anyone, for we all have the same Bible and everyone has a right to his opinion concerning it. Yet his opinion is nothing but an opinion and only valuable in indicating the source from which it comes. There is no truth in it unless it can be put into practice as Christ put His into practice. Then it becomes a fact.

What does Jesus Himself say of this power? He admitted it, for He says, "Of myself I can do nothing," thus admitting a power superior to Himself; and also when asked a question by His disciples, He said, "No man knoweth, not the angels in heaven, neither the Son, but my Father only." At another time when asked by a scribe who had been listening to Jesus, while he reasoned with a Sadducee, "What is the first commandment of all?" Jesus answered, "The first commandment is Hear, O, Israel, the Lord our God is one Lord." Here He admits a supreme power and says, "Thou shalt love the Lord thy God with all thy heart and thy neighbor as thyself."

The young man said unto Him, "Well, Master, thou hast said truly, for there is one God, and there is none other than He, and to love Him with all thy heart and soul is more than all burnt offerings and sacrifices." Jesus saw that he had answered discreetly and He said unto him, "Thou art not far from the Kingdom of God." These questions and answers were given before the whole multitude, and I see no reason for disputing Jesus' own words by putting a mixed misconstruction on some passage and making Jesus something that neither He nor anyone else ever thought of. He was accused of making Himself equal with God, but that was their ignorance which gave that construction, and if I had not been accused of the same thing a hundred times, I might put the same construction on Jesus as others do. But I can see and show to the sick beyond a doubt the difference between Jesus and Christ, and the difference between the two words gives a very different meaning to religion. The church construction makes our acts and lives one thing and our religion another. Jesus made our acts the effect of our knowledge of Christ or truth or science and in proportion as we understand science we understand God and acknowledge Him in science and in truth.

This science separates us from this world of sin and death and brings life and science to light, and this life or science was in Christ or was Christ and was what Jesus taught. The ignorance of Christ or Science or truth put "Jesus" and "Christ" together and called it "Jesus Christ." For ignorance and superstition could not account for any of the cures that Jesus made except it be from heaven, and although Jesus tried all in His power to convince them to the contrary, He could not. The religious people of Jesus' day like the Christians of this day made heaven and hell places independent of man, and although some may deny it, their acts give the lie to their professions.

All persons pray to a being independent of themselves, acknowledging a state or place where God is, independent of themselves, and when they pray, supposing that He listens, ask Him to hear their prayers and relieve their wants. This is precisely what the heathens did, and Jesus called them hypocrites and condemned it, for He said this offering up of prayer and sacrifice year after year could never take away sin or error so that the world could be benefited by such forms. But once in the end of this world of superstition, Jesus sacrificed His own opinions of all superstition and embraced Christ or Truth and laid down His own life for the happiness of mankind. Before this, the world knew not Christ or Truth. This truth Jesus taught and His teaching was the healing of the nations, and if this truth had not been misconstructed, the world at this time would have been rid of thousands of errors it now has. This was Christ's truth or belief, for a truth to a person who cannot understand it is a belief. So Jesus' truth or Christ was to the people a mystery and of course embraced a belief. But to Jesus this was science and He labored to convince the people that it was, that the fruits of it were seen in His practice and that it could be taught; for He made a difference between His cures and His disciples' cures and the cures of the rest of the world.

The magicians and sorcerers cured by their belief. They thought their power came from a spirit world, and they acted upon this belief. They believed that sickness was sent into the world to torment mankind. The priests had the same belief. Each one's prayer was to his own God to keep him clear of his enemy. The priests held up to the people the idea that they must do something different from living honestly and dealing with mankind as though we were one family, that a certain belief was necessary to keep us clear of hell which itself had been invented to torment man.

This doctrine kept the people in ignorance of themselves and made them nervous, giving rise to a sort of belief in evil spirits. As mankind are all the time inventing ideas for their own interests, it finally led to the introduction of the medical faculty. Now it seemed to cover all the ground that ignorance and superstition wanted; it put the masses into the power of the two classes—the priests and the doctors. The priests would offer up prayers to their God for the salvation of souls, and the doctors would offer up prayers for their business. The people are, in the meantime, in the condition that the prophet told of when he said, "The prophets prophesize falsely, and the priests can rule by their means, and the people love to have it so, but what will they do in the end thereof?" Now it is just so with the clergy and the medical profession. Both are an evil and Jesus opposed both by destroying all their ideas. This He did, or tried to do, but they destroyed Him before He established the science so that it could be taught.

Jesus wanted to introduce this science, which He called Christ. This science gave the lie to all the old opinions of Jesus' day. He had no heaven or hell out of man, no happiness or misery outside of us. His God was in Him and us, and His prayers were in Him and in us, and His life and ours was in this Christ or belief, and this belief was the law which He put in all of us. If this law could be understood, it would rid us of all the evils that are bound on mankind. It would not keep man in ignorance of himself, but would exalt him in the natural world. It would rid him of the superstition of the world, would make men worship God, not as a man who could be flattered by our hypocrisy but as a God of knowledge, as a science that gives to every man just what he learns. Those who seek Him in prayer desiring to learn His laws will be rewarded just in proportion to their labor. He asks no prayers for His good, and a prayer made up of words is all lost unless accompanied by some good to someone, and if we do good to one another our prayer is in the act. When Jesus said to the righteous, "Come ye blessed for I was naked and you clothed me," they were not aware that they had done any good, but He said, "Inasmuch as you did it unto the least of these my brethren, you did it unto me," or God, and in His answer to the wicked, "Inasmuch as you did it not to them, ye did it not to me." He put the good and bad in the acts and not in the words. So true prayer is in our acts, false prayer is in our words and by their fruits ye shall know them. For He said, "Not all those who say, Lord, Lord, shall enter into the Kingdom of Heaven or Science"; not those who say, "I understand it," but those who put it into practice so that the world shall be the wiser for the knowledge. Now you see that if this is so, "it is easier for a camel to go through the eye of a needle than for a rich man" or one learned in the world's knowledge to embrace this Truth or Christ. But I say to all, strive to understand.

March 1860

Principles of Progress, The*
[Originally untitled.] [BU 3:0645]

In the world of intelligence there are certain leading principles that affect the growth of a new idea in the community; they show themselves at the commencement and during its development and acting through different people influence the progress of mankind in different ways. One is fair and independent; the other is cautious, blind and selfish.

It is a time honored custom as ancient as it is respectable for the learned and educated classes to put down everything that they cannot at once comprehend. Thinking that they possess the keys of all knowledge they deny every fact that does not come through the legitimate development of their ideas and oppose en masse the possibility of intelligence coming from anything but books, and literary and scientific research. So when a question comes before the people originating outside of their education it is met with every species of opposition, runs the gauntlet of abuse and misrepresentation and contempt before it reaches a successful stand. Therefore to obtain a candid hearing for a subject not understood or admitted is impossible. The very first mention must be met by an unbelieving and unreasoning people with distrust and it must be looked upon as an absurdity.

The experience of Dr. Quimby has not been an exception in this respect. Curing disease without medicine has so long been considered a humbug by the leading minds in society, that it has no place of respect in the world. Yet it comes forth in this case claiming public respect and attention. He is of course misunderstood and distrusted by many because they class him where he does not belong and the objection which is felt by those towards him may be traced to opinions which they hold respecting him and which are in themselves open to objection. For instance some persons hold that he cures by power from the Devil, and consequently have no respect for him on that account. Now from their acquaintance and knowledge of the aforesaid personage, they conclude that the Dr. must be as wicked, as well as powerful, as he, so it is reasonable that they consider him a questionable character. This style of judgment is the basis of the prejudice which exists in the community against him. There are however others who are willing and desirous to hear what he has to say himself supposing that he ought to know as much as anyone about his way of curing disease. He insists that disease arises from a belief based on an opinion, and that it is all the invention of man like any other belief. When a person feels sick he consults a physician that he may know what to believe respecting his trouble, and whatever the doctor tells him is received with as much confidence as though it was a direct revelation from heaven. This belief acts upon the sick like truth, "for as a man thinketh so is he" and it soon becomes evident in the flesh. Dr. Quimby has no belief in treating the sick any more than a lawyer has respecting a client whose case he pleads. He knows that there is an over ruling truth that can set free the sick and diseased and he yields himself entirely to the guidance of that truth so that in curing he is not beholden to any opinion of man. He says the voice of the sick is not heard in the world. It is the construction and opinions of the well about them, that gets the public ear, while they posture, the suffering and helpless are completely controlled by the influences coming from the knowledge of those whose duty it is to cure them. He also says that the well know nothing of themselves about the sick, consequently their judgment is uncharitable and fallible. The operation of Dr. Quimby's system brings to light the unexplained mysteries of disease and shows up the powers that influence the sick, so that man can be freed from their dominion. The basis and leading principle of his theory is that mind is something and under given directions will produce given effects, that every wrong action or trouble in the body got there through the mind and consequently must be removed through that medium; that thought is a living vital matter, and takes effect on the sick when applied to them as certainly as any matter that we see. It is his duty to get the sick free from the charges made against them by the well. So he takes up their feelings which stand as evidence against them and explains them in a way which destroys what they would prove disease. Therefore he is the sick man's friend and treats them by a knowledge of their feelings.

Statements made by him to the sick have a strange sound to the well and need an explanation to render them intelligible, for he often tells a person they have no disease when nothing is plainer than that they have. Here comes in his peculiar belief which to him is knowledge. He does not trace disease to a hidden or mysterious source, or no source at all. Neither does he pay any respect to it as though he reasoned that it came from God. He refers it directly to man himself under the dominion of errors invented by man and believed in as true, and of an independent origin and to cure disease intelligently in the most beneficial way to man is to correct the error on which it is based. There in the first place he lifts disease from its accustomed basis of truth and places it on the basis of error. Consequently in his reasoning disease is not the ruling power, and he does not admit it except as a deception. And in demonstrating this position he comes in contact with facts which are held to be as true as the eyes in our head, and in many cases meets in opposition to his process the strong and bitter religious prejudices which are so common in the community. He cannot admit a disease and then cure it any more than a court can pronounce judgment on a criminal and then try the case. Dr. Quimby gives the sick the same chance for their health as an accused has for his life, and if he can analyze his symptoms and destroy that evidence of disease then the patient is free. In this he follows no track trodden by man and ventures a field entirely unknown and unexplored as an intelligence. So he cannot be ranked with any society or association of believers. ** See note

He does not put disease on the presumption that it is imagination and if a person chooses to think he will get well, he will do so. The anguish of the body is as real as anything, but it does not mean anything of itself, and is dependent on the construction of those who do not experience it to receive a name and a character, determining the condition of the organs and the danger of the patient's life. He says our body does not act of itself but is acted upon by the owner who is also acted upon by others who know about as much of us as we do of them. The intelligence is what controls the man we see and that is not seen, but it is known and felt in a medium of itself, which when once known is unmistakable. It is his work to separate the workings of the natural intelligence from the action of the man who thinks he controls himself, and put it upon an independent ground so that man may know himself. With the sick the reverse is true in common belief. The body is sick, suffers and dies, and very little is known of the owner. To the sick the body is a cruel tyrant, the organs all conspire together or singly to kill him. The lungs say he shall not have any air, the stomach refuses to give him food in peace. There is a general confusion of threats and compromises, the body haggles and encroaches. Man becomes cowardly and is finally overcome; gives up to whatever the body agrees upon; disease has the day and where is man? Where is his ambition, his self-respect, his power of taking care of himself? He has become a weak, complaining being that he would despise in the day of his health. This is the being that Dr. Quimby cures and according as he restores to him a sense of his lost rights and makes him feel that he is or right to be master, just so the body ceases to be a tyrant and becomes a servant subject to direction.

Then when it is asked by what power Dr. Quimby cures disease, I answer by the knowledge of the wisdom that puts man outside of his body and the understanding of which gives him control over it, making his destiny not disease and death, but progression in knowledge. Just according as man walks in the knowledge of this truth, he is wise and happy–but any direction which admits matter superior to man creates an error which really imprisons him. Ages of education have condensed these errors into living facts and now nothing is plainer to those who have lived a quarter of a century than the irrefutable approach of misery, sorrows and trials. To lift the burden of life of one of its greatest evils and to open the way for greater works in the same place is the effect of the establishment of Dr. Quimby's system. In order to satisfy the world that it can be done he holds on to his works and his principles.

Jan. 11th, 1862

** Note: Dr. Quimby is unjustly accused of being a Spiritualist. This is not so, his mode of cure bears no resemblance in theory or practice to this class. He has nothing to do with the spirits of the dead: his work is entirely with the living. While treating the sick he is not asleep or unconscious, but is at all times himself as much as every regular physician. He says disease is in the mind, and to cure it–he changes the mind. In this process he is supported by no authority of man and cannot be called a clairvoyant, or healing medium, or eclectic doctor any more than he can be called an allopathic physician.

Proof that a Person Can Be in Two Places at the Same Time and Be Aware of the Fact
[LC 2:0896]

What proof has Dr. Quimby that a person can be in two places at the same time and be aware of the fact? I suppose that no one will deny that a mesmeric clairvoyant can be away from his body and describe things not known to his natural senses, as it is called. Although the clairvoyant is to himself in but one place at the same time, yet the company believes he is in two, for facts show that he is with them, and at the same time he is in another place. Now if this is admitted, I will state another fact, viz; that they can all ask questions of persons at a distance and the persons are not aware of the fact through their senses. This is so clearly shown that I suppose that no one will deny it. This goes to prove that every person has two identities: one called the natural senses and the other the real man or God or Wisdom. Now the real man is not matter nor spirit but wisdom acting on matter. This is the man that always will exist and is conscious of his own existence, although to the natural man he is, if admitted at all, a spirit. This error by the Christian world causes all the false theories about another world. This was what Jesus tried to prove and would have proved it, if they had left the natural man Jesus in the tomb. Then the man called Christ, when he showed himself to his disciples, would have been the proof to them, for they thought he was a spirit. But when he said, Hath a spirit flesh and bones as ye see me have, then they believed that the man Jesus had risen. So when they found the body gone, what other conclusion could they come to but that, if they believed anything at all?

But there were some who knew better and this got up a controversy among the believers for Paul says, "If Christ be preached that he rose from the dead, how say some among you that there is no resurrection of the dead?" So you see in those days, thirty or forty years after the crucifixion, there was a difference of opinion among the people. Now if the body of Jesus had been left in the tomb, this controversy would never have come up, for Jesus never believed or tried to prove that their idea Jesus should rise, but that this Christ or Wisdom would take to itself a body to prove to them that man lives when the world calls him dead, and a knowledge of this is the other world. Now you may ask why I undertake to tell what Jesus meant to convey. Paul undertook to explain this mystery, and all the clergy in the country, and why should I not have the same liberty? Paul says after going on to explain to the people, "Last of all he was seen of me also, as of one born out of due time." Now it seems to those who believe that Jesus rose, that Paul was talking about the man Jesus, but not to me. He was trying to show that there was a difference.

Now to show what was meant by Jesus and Paul, I will give you my own experience of this same Christ or Wisdom that Paul speaks of, and to prove it, I must refer to the sick as Jesus did, for he never proved anything to the well, from the fact that a well person wants no sympathy, but the sick are among strangers and have fallen among thieves and have been robbed of their substance. Jesus often compares the priests or doctors to thieves and robbers, not that he meant to say that they would steal a man's pocketbook, but they would rob him in another way by making him listen to lies, knowing that by this way they would rob him according to law. So it is now; the laws are made more for this set of robbers than any set of men.

Look at the medical faculty of the army. See their influence. All outsiders are shut out. No matter what are the cries of the sick, you are told you must be attended to by the regulars. It is so with the priests but the truth is working out a revolution in the minds of the people and the white slaves as well as the black will be free from those slaveholders. This rebellion, before it is over, will open the eyes of northern Christians and show that the profession of religion is all a deception to gall the masses, as is the profession of the South towards the Union. Christ is not known in either. It is the working of the natural man to develop a truth higher than slavery of blacks or whites. Each is in bondage and to those Jesus preached and put his preaching into practice. So his preaching went to condemn all the popular theology of his day, showing that it was as wrong as slavery and wars, for it bound those that were free like Paul and others, but the slave he never meddled with.

He told them, like servants, to obey their masters but to those that were borne down by the priests or doctors, he said, "Come unto me, all ye that labor and are heavy laden, and I will give you rest. Take my yoke (or theory) upon you and learn of me." Now how did he lighten their burdens but by removing their sins or error by explaining their feelings. And to do this, it was necessary to take upon himself their feelings or sins. So he says he took our sins that he might lead us to God or truth. Now the explanation was his cure; then they were liable to fall back or be sick, from the fact that they were not aware of the mode in which it was done. So to them it was a mystery or a power. I do the same, I sit down and when their feelings become condensed into a form, the life is in the form and this life is the real person. This person is not known through the natural man, only through the natural medium, but I see the two. There is but one real man. The other is the shadow. Every person knows that language is the expression of thought and is an act of the will. Man or a child learns to produce certain noises called language, but if the idea is not in the sound, if ever so perfect, it conveys no meaning. Therefore language contains no sounds to the natural man. The natural man is the echo of the true man. Now when the true life of man is disturbed by a disturbance of his spiritual matter, it takes a form just according to its feelings and its feelings are itself. So to destroy its feelings is to destroy the life of the error or disease.

Now if language is itself like the odor of a rose, it tells you the state of its health by its odor. So it is with all animal or vegetable substances. This is all the language it has. Now to learn and analyze all the variety of sensation, so as to know a person's feelings by the language that makes no sound in the world like language, is not a very easy task. This is what all the pagan philosophers tried to reduce to a science, but in all their investigations, they had one stumbling block. That was to prove it to others. Their philosophy was true in theory but it required someone to reduce it to a science. This was never done. To them they knew it was true. So their whole aim was to reduce man's life and happiness to a simple truth or science so that he might keep clear from the errors man was liable to fall into. So in fact, their wisdom consisted in the fact that the greatest good was the greatest happiness. So every act that brought pleasure was good, not that it was right or wrong, for right and wrong are arbitrary, but to analyzed every act to see the effect, believing the answer was in the act, so to do an act, thinking that the opposite result might take place, was not in their philosophy. But every act must bring its reward sooner or later. It is like forcing a ball from a gun at any distance on a horizontal line. The ball will fall just as fast as though it had no lateral pressure.

Any thought that affects us contains the happiness and misery and may be calculated on as well as the force of a ball. Science is to reduce every act of our lives to a science so that man can get the most happiness out of the least labor. Science reduces manual labor by introducing mechanics. So wisdom saves a great deal of misery by seeing the causes and effects of our acts. So as we learn wisdom we shun misery, for misery is the fruit of error and happiness the effect of ignorance or science. Thus wisdom analyzes every idea and it finds man's misery arises from some fear of some belief that contains some opinion of man. All religious opinions are false and cannot stand the test of investigation. Science is God's religion and opinion is man's religion. So God shall reign till man's religion is put down. Then comes the end of superstition and then comes the religion of science and God. This measures out to every man just according to his wisdom. So to be a God-like man is to be a scientific man, not a man of opinions. When man makes his highest motives his greatest pleasure, then he will make his happiness the greatest treasure of his life. This is true religion, not the religion of any one man, nor does it belong to anyone, but it is the outpouring of every living being. It is called sympathy. But sympathy is language and when a person can attach his senses or wisdom to this sympathy, then he will act in harmony with himself. But when his senses are attached to opinions, then he is at the mercy of everyone's opinion, like a man tossed about by every breeze of opinion.

I was attending a child with what the doctor called neuralgia. The pain, as he said, was so great that he resorted to morphine to make the child sleep. This opinion of the doctor's had an effect on the mother and of course the doctor carried the mother from the child. This of course made the child nervous and called insane.

June 9, 1863

Proof That There Can Be A Moral Science*
[BU 3:0471]

Moral Science is that which, when understood will enable man to be good Scientifically; that is, that virtue and happiness will as necessarily flow from certain causes as bad acts must follow as the effect of selfishness and dishonesty. This may be denied. Has not every event a cause? Let us then trace an event back to its cause and see if different circumstances might not have prevented a different result. Take a professional murder for example. The act of murder is the result of previous education. So in every act, there is a something which prompts us to do right or which deters us from doing wrong. None would suppose that one who had always lived a virtuous upright life would, in a same condition, commit murder. This act then needs [The article abruptly ends here. –Ed.]

Prophecy Concerning the Nation, A
[LC 1:0557]

It is based on the principle that mind is matter, also that nations and individuals are governed by wisdom or error, and the effect shows which power governs. Upon this wisdom I make this statement or what might be called a prophecy. I admit the United States is a child or man not fully grown with passions like all other children. The President is the servant of the wisdom of the child or people, for the people are the body and their wisdom is their strength. Now as foreigners come among us, their ideas affect our government or mind; this creates imitation, for error is uneasy and is never still in man or nation and it is always getting up something to destroy itself, for its life is its own destruction. Slavery is admitted by the people, for the Constitution says nothing about it and they have it in their power, the Constitution neither admitting nor denying it. The error is free to put such a construction upon it as they please, and as error is never right, it always works out its own destruction.

I will take Jeff Davis as the head of this error or disease; for such it is, and it must be treated accordingly. I give no medicine but I explain the truth which destroys the error and kills the disease. Jeff Davis is the patient and Abraham Lincoln is the physician. His disease is of the head, brought on by over-excitement of the mind. His wisdom, not being equal to his ambition, the excitement affects his body or the South. The South is the body and Jeff is the brains. And in a fit of delirium tremens he assumed the Government, and the people thinking him sane, listened to his story. In a fit of rage he undertook to destroy himself and the government or father; his pretended father, who was not in reality his father, got frightened at his insanity and offered him the whole of his wealth. But the rest of his brethren protested against it, so they commenced to check his career. Now an insane man is a coward and Jefferson Davis is a mixture of man and mule.

I will give his character, as he seems to me. He is a coward and a fool. I will show you how he is a fool. He cannot see the end of his schemes; his wisdom leads him to destruction and he thinks by his error, to control the North and West. Here he shows his courage in his ignorance. As soon as he sees his error his courage fails, for it was based on ignorance and infused into the people; his error expanded to the surface of the border states. But as in health or disease, man is like a stream running into the ocean. When the tide sets in, the stream rises; so as the Northwest current sets towards the South, the tide of the border states rises and the lowlands of the states are in danger of being overflowed with their own stream.

Now you can see Jeff Davis paddling from one point to another to check the tide. He will try to throw up a dam around the border states to prevent the North West navies from influencing the South. But when the Southeast winds come with their ships and he sees nothing but death on one side and the halter on his own, then his courage will prove sham. And he will, if not destroyed, flee with all he can get, and leave the South to take care of itself.

454

April 1861

Proverbs
[LC 1:0422]

A body without soul is a man of opinions without science.

Man is made of opinions and therefore is matter.

Wisdom reduced to practice is the spiritual man or Christ.

Life is self-evident–not matter or mind.

The senses are a knowledge of sensation, with or without science.

Science is a wisdom superior to opinions, it is not seen or known by opinions, it is harmony.

Language is the invention of opinions to communicate to another opinion what wisdom knows.

Do animals reason like men? This question cannot be answered categorically, it is like thousands of other questions asked by those who know not what the question involves. Error is not science, it uses language to try to explain what it does not know. In this way the standard of opinions is based on ignorance or matter.

How do animals communicate with each other? Here is a question that opens a wide field for the wisdom of opinions, with no proof of wisdom above the person that asks the question. After some arguing, they settle down on the opinion that animals reason and have a language. This is all an opinion without the slightest evidence or wisdom above the animal.

Can there be any wisdom above the opinion of man to explain the actions of animals. As all give their opinions, I will give my knowledge of the human species.

Instinct is a mystery to opinion and is not admitted as intelligence or wisdom and is not superior to opinions, but inferior to them. Now opinions divide wisdom into two classes, instinct and knowledge. Science also makes two divisions, but not like opinions; it makes opinions neither science nor instinct, but a sort of mixture of ignorance and error.

How does wisdom act on animals? By the law of harmony. Wisdom has its bounds that man or beast cannot pass. Science is wisdom reduced to self-evidence, which has an identity, so that science is a child that grows like any other growth and receives wisdom according to its capacity to take it up, or it is like water that takes up salt, it is capable of taking up just so much and no more. Man and beast, fish and foul and every creeping thing that has life, but the scientific, sceptical man, have their bounds that they cannot pass and when they arrive at perfection, they either recede or assume a wisdom superior to their race. Man is the only one who has ever been capable of teaching a science or of proving it by self-evident wisdom.

Take the dog. He will trace the various and winding routes of his master till he finds him. Suppose the master leaves the dog in the house and travels in a straight direction till he comes to three roads that all meet. When released, the dog will come to these roads, and try one or more of them a little way when he will return and take the other, as though he reasoned that if his master had not gone two of the roads he must have taken the third. If that was so, why did he not keep on? But he went a little way and then returned, not seeing his master on any other road. So there must be some better explanation than that.

I will give an explanation according to my wisdom of scientific facts. The dog, when with his master, was like a mesmerized subject. The master held the dog by sympathy, just as a mesmerizer holds a subject. When the master left home, the dog went with him as the subject under this wisdom of harmony. When the dog was let loose, his wisdom was drawn by this master till he came to where the three roads meet, then reason entered and the dog hesitated. But as he left the right road his sympathy was disturbed and he returns to the spot where he feels in harmony with the wisdom, then goes another road and meets with the same result, returning he starts on and his sympathy grows stronger. He follows the dictates of his own feeling until the object is obtained.

Animals are a combination that act according to their organization. Their wants are few; happiness is all their aim. The gratification of their appetites and rest is all that they want, so they eat and drink, not from any reason but from a simple desire to gratify themselves. This is perfection in the beast. They also have imitation to a certain degree, but it is not of their combination but a higher combination. Left to themselves, they soon return to their native element. This imitation, opinion calls intelligence, so it is the intelligence of the man of opinions, but not of God or Science. A monkey is a monkey, you can teach him to imitate, but science can never be learned by him. You can make an automaton chess player, but he cannot go beyond his limits and it is so with the brutes. Man is another combination, higher. But the man of opinions is no more a scientific man than the brute; like the brute he is capable of imitation to a certain extent, but if he goes beyond that he ceases to be a brute and becomes a living scientific being.

Woman is not matter but science or truth. Man is matter or opinions, so that everyone is of these two elements and by their acts are to be judged.

Man is made up of opinions. Science is the woman, so when they are united then you see the man and woman or Jesus Christ. Now destroy the man of opinions and the Christ lives in the flesh and if you destroy the Christ, man becomes a brute.

Man after the fashion of opinion is the offspring of Father and Mother. Wisdom defines them in this way. The father is of opinion, the mother is science. So the child being the offspring of its father or opinions, receives the wisdom of its mother or science. Here are the two.

Science and opinions never have agreed and never can; their identities are as opposite as light and darkness. Although opinion has always been trying to take to itself wisdom, wisdom has never acknowledged the union and never can. These two identities are all through man's life, not one act of his life is independent of both. Science admits nothing but facts; opinion knows nothing but error. These two characters are as plain in the world as light and darkness. I will give you some names that they have been identified with since the wisdom of the world has discovered the two, and will show how every phenomenon has been acknowledged by both. I will commence with the Old Testament. This book shows a state of society and wisdom and progression far above the wisdom of opinions. So that science or wisdom had made considerable progress in the world of error at the time the Old Testament was written. So if the Bible was not for the development of some wiser truth than the masses had, they never would have accepted Moses as a leader. According to the account, Moses taught his wisdom to the people. What motive had Moses in taking the course he did if it was not to convince man of a more excellent way of making them happy than they were taught in Egypt? If so, then we must expect Moses must have been a better man even than he is represented. One thing is certain: that at the time of Moses all nations were very religious and superstitious, for these two elements, superstition and religion, have always gone hand in hand. So have science and progression gone along together.

Moses and Aaron were representatives of these characters: Saul and Paul, Adam and Eve, the law and the gospel, the rich man and the beggar, the tares and wheat, the prodigal and elder son. All symbolize these two elements in man, the religious man or sinner and the scientific man. Just as a man breaks off from his superstition and embraces wisdom based on science, just so he is not religious. Religion belongs to the man of opinions who, not knowing God, worships something he is afraid of. While the scientific man worships God in wisdom and sees nothing but love and harmony, and his love or wisdom casteth out fear, for fear hath torment.

I will introduce you to a religious man of the world of opinions, reasoning with a man not of the same dispensation in religion, but a man of wisdom and science without any religion. The former I will call Christian and the latter Skeptic.

(S) Is there any such substance as matter?

(C) Everything we see goes to prove that fact.

(S) Is matter a solid substance?

(C) There is matter that is solid and there is matter that is not.

(S) Is there any matter so solid that light cannot penetrate it?

(C) Yes, I have no doubt of that.

(S) Do you admit a wisdom that can penetrate all matter, substances?

(C) Yes.

(S) Suppose you should be in a prison where there was no light or any chance for matter to penetrate. Do you believe there is a wisdom capable of penetrating your prison and communicating to you any intelligence? You may call it God or anything you please. Do you believe it?

(C) Yes.

(S) Well, is it matter?

(C) No.

(S) Then it must be something not matter.

(C) Yes.

(S) You admit it intelligence?

(C) Yes.

(S) Then you have intelligence in prison where matter cannot go. You believe it?

(C) Yes.

(S) Do you believe it is aware of its own presence with you?

(C) Yes.

(S) Would your belief prevent its coming?

(C) No.

(S) Can there be a wisdom that can be at any particular place and know it without a consciousness of itself?

(C) No. [unfinished]

August 1861

Prove to Me that Mind Is Matter
[LC 2:0679]

You will admit that I am at a distance of some hundreds of miles from you according to your belief. Now if your senses are your mind and then if I act upon them, I must act outside of your own wisdom. My wisdom, being attached to my senses, does not admit space except as an error, so that distance is an idea, not truth; and according to error, I am at a distance from you. But I am now sitting talking with you and although you have eyes, you cannot see, ears and you cannot hear, yet I am trying to make you understand that I am with you even in your very thoughts and I will tell you how you may see and understand. Suppose your senses were an instrument and my wisdom wished to communicate to your wisdom some truth.

I come to your senses and use them to communicate to your wisdom the fact, but as your wisdom is of this world, you are ignorant of the author and think that the ideas are your own. So watch your feelings and see if there are not some vibrations or strains that pass through the senses that will make the whole body tremble so that you will say that your mind can be affected; then you will see that mind is matter and that it can be changed.

Belfast, July 11, 1862

Questions and Answers**
[LC 3:1302]

[*Editor's note*: There are three copies of *Questions and Answers* in the Library of Congress collection. A notation immediately below the title of this particular copy states: "George A. Quimby's writing below.–E. Q. P." Presumably E. Q. P. is Elizabeth Quimby Pineo, who is George Quimby's daughter and one of P. P. Quimby's granddaughters. All three copies of *Questions and Answers* have the "Preface" at either the beginning or end of each copy.]

The Science of Man or the Principle which controls all phenomena.

Soul's Inquiries of Man

Jesus was the name of a man and Christ was the "truth." This truth was a part of God and the principle of the idea of Jesus.

Preface

Dr. Quimby's writings are not to establish any religious creed or bolster up any belief of man, but they are simply the outpouring of a truth that sees the sick cast into prison for no other cause than a belief in the opinions of man, there to linger out a miserable existence, driven from society into the dark cell of disease where no friend is allowed to enter to soothe their woes. The knowledge of this condition is known to him from their own feelings and calls forth his place in their behalf. He stands to the sick as an attorney to a criminal, a <u>friend</u>. This is what he believes Jesus intended to communicate to the world when he said they that are well need not a physician, but they that are sick. So he pleads their cases and destroys their opinion, breaks the bars of death and sets the prisoner free. This was Jesus' religion, that he believed, taught, and practiced.

Answers to questions asked by one of my patients.

Ques. 1ˢᵗ You must have a feeling of repugnance towards certain patients; how do you overcome it and how can I do the same?

<u>Answer</u>. In order to make you fully understand how I overcome this repugnance, it will require some little explanation of my mode of curing, for my cures are in my belief or wisdom, and the patient's disease is in his belief or knowledge. Now my wisdom is not knowledge, for what a man thinks he knows is knowledge or opinion, but what is wisdom to a man, he has no opinion about. As God is wisdom, wisdom is science and we call the proof of getting science, knowledge, belief or reason, but when the answer comes, our knowledge vanishes and we are swallowed up in God or wisdom. The sick are strangers to this wisdom, being led by false guides without it, who have eyes and see not, ears and hear not, and hearts that cannot understand, therefore like strangers they are at the mercy of every one's opinion. Having a strong desire for wisdom or health, they call on every one for their food or wisdom. So when they ask for bread they receive a stone, or for water they receive vinegar, and thus they are driven like sheep to the slaughter, not daring to open their mouth. This is the state of the patient who asks the above question. My wisdom sees their condition, feels their woes and comes to their rescue, but to get them from their enemies is often an arduous task. The repugnance of which you speak is not towards their personal senses, but to the ideas their senses are attached to. As the ideas are knowledge to them, they are a person beside themselves and it is the identity disease, that I first come in contact with. This is what I have to annihilate, and at first I sometimes feel a repugnance towards the sick such as a man would feel in entering a penitentiary to rescue a victim, who has been innocently confined. The disturbance of the rescue, sets the house in an uproar the victim not knowing the cause is as much frightened as her enemies. But when I succeed in destroying her enemies or opinions and get her to wisdom or self, she receives me as one who has saved her from the jaws of death. This to her is health and happiness. You say how can I do the same? If you believe this wisdom is superior to opinions, and that opinions are nothing but error that man has embraced, then when you come in contact with a person diseased, your wisdom will throw the mantle of charity over their errors, if it is for the restoration of their health. But if the repugnance arises from some unknown cause, examine yourself, and see if the fault lies at your own door, if not you may be sure it is some false opinion in the person that troubles them. So to overcome their evil or error, pour on coals from the fire of love or charity in the form of right reason till you melt down the image of brass that is set up in their minds, and they will leave their errors and embrace the truth. This is heaven.

Ques. 2 You say when you know a thing it is not an opinion. I can understand that, but how may I be really sure I know a thing, I have felt perfectly sure of a thing and still afterwards found I had been in error, or had been mistaken.

Ans. Knowledge as I have said is not wisdom, but it may be harmony and it may seem like wisdom. Yet there is a discord, so discord is harmony not understood. To know how to correct this harmony or knowledge that it may be wisdom is the question to consider. The first part of your question where you say "I can understand that" is contradictory to the last paragraph showing that you do not understand. Here is the discord, you say you have been perfectly sure of a thing and yet found you have been mistaken. Now if your wisdom had been perfect in the thing you thought you knew, it would have revealed the discord or error. So to purify yourself from error, so that you may know the truth or wisdom is a process of reasoning outside of matter for there is no wisdom in matter. So that when you have arrived at a truth, if you find it attached to a belief, you may know it is not a truth, for it may change, but this is a truth, that a belief may be changed. God is truth, and there is no other truth, and if we know God the same is known to us.

I will now try to attach your senses to God, not the God of this world or Christian's God, but the God of the living and not of the dead. My God is my standard of truth and as I know God, the same is known to me. I know I am writing this if I know anything, but to know that I shall finish it admits a doubt, and to know that you will understand it, admits more doubt. This doubt, is not wisdom but belongs to that class of man's inventions called reason, knowledge, etc. God is not seen in this question perfect, except as far as I see, but He is seen in the clouds of my knowledge. When you read this if you understand it, then you will see God face to face but not as Moses did. I await your answer, to know whether he does appear to your understanding; if so, then here is your proof that you are born of God in this one thing! Then you cannot know anything more so far as this question goes. Man's God is all the time listening to our prayers and settling all sorts of trouble.

My God does not act at all, he has finished his work and leaves man to work out his happiness according to his own wisdom. I will give you the attributes of my God. The wisdom of God is in this letter, and if you understand, you will hear his voice saying I understand this. So the understanding is God, for in that there is no matter, and to understand is wisdom, not matter, and to know wisdom is to know God, for that is wisdom.

I will give you some ideas of God, reduced to man's knowledge. All sciences are a part of God, and when man understands science the same is known to God, but the world's God is based on man's opinion, and right and wrong is the invention of man, while God is in their reason, but not known. Here is an illustration. The bells are ringing. I walk to church and take a seat. The minister opens the Bible and reads the text from John. The fact of going to church, and seeing the minister is known to me, but there might be a doubt in regard to the Bible, for it might be another book. This last I admit with a doubt, and also the verse and chapter is a doubt. He reads the thirteenth chapter of John, 36th verse, where Peter says, "Lord, why cannot I follow thee now? I will lay down my life for thy sake." All the above as far as words go is true, but when he comes to explain where Jesus went, when he came back, or if he went at all, his wisdom was knowledge and he reminded me of Paul's words, "All men have knowledge, knowledge puffeth up, charity (or wisdom) edifieth." I could see nothing but an opinion of what he had no wisdom; a parable of something which he might know as a belief but not wisdom. The explanation of the Bible is founded on man's opinion, and not on wisdom. The Bible contains wisdom, but it is not understood and to prove a thing is to put your proof into practice, for all men can give an opinion.

Jesus came into the world not to give an opinion, but to bring light into the world, upon something that was in the dark. What was it? Where was it? How did he describe it? And what was the remedy? He tells the story himself, where he called his disciples together and gave them power or wisdom. Now if it was power and not wisdom, then he knew not what wisdom was. So far as I can see, it admits a doubt, but I have no doubt of what he meant to command them to do. In Matt. Ch. 11th he went to preach, and put his preaching into practice. John was cast into prison for preaching the coming of someone who would put this great truth into practice, so he sent one of his disciples to Jesus to inquire if he was the one that was to come, or do we look for another. Now what was he to come for?

Jesus answers this question when he said, go tell John the things you have seen and heard, how the blind receive their sight etc. After telling how John or this truth had suffered, how it had been put down by force, he made a parable of the ignorance of his generation. "We have piped unto you and ye have not danced." Then giving a statement about errors, he says, "Oh Father, Lord of heaven and earth; because thou hast hidden this truth from the wise and prudent and revealed then unto babes, even so is it. All things concerning these errors are revealed unto me by my Father. No one knows the truth but the Father, save the son Jesus, and those to whom he shall teach this truth." Then he says, "Come unto me all ye that labor and are heavy laden and I will give you rest, take my yoke, and learn of me, for my burden is light." You see that his labor was with the sick and not the well, and all his talk was to explain where the people had been deceived by the priests and doctors, and if they learned wisdom, they would be cured. The knowledge of man puts false construction on his wisdom and gets up a sort of religion which has nothing to do with Jesus' truth. Here is where the fault lies. If you do not believe the Bible as they explain it then you are an infidel. So all who cannot believe it as it has been explained, must throw it away. I do not throw the Bible away but throw the explanation away, and apply Jesus' own words as he did, and as he intended they should be applied, and let my works speak for themselves, whether they are of God or man, and leave the sick to judge.

Ques. 3 Our spiritual senses are often more acute than our natural ones. What is the difference? What do you call spirit-world?

Ans. I will try to explain the difference between spiritual and natural senses. If I had never seen you and wished to write you a letter on some worldly affair, I should address your natural senses, and you would attach yourself, to my knowledge. Suppose you believe what I say then your belief is founded on my knowledge. This belongs to the natural world and your happiness or misery is in your belief. But I have sat by you and taken your feelings, these are your spiritual senses, not wisdom, but ideas not named or classified. In the spirit world there are things as they are in the natural world, that affect us as much, but these are not known by the natural senses or wisdom. The separation of these is what Jesus calls the law and the gospel. The natural senses are under the law governed by the knowledge of the natural world, subject to all the penalties and punishments man can invent. The spiritual senses have their spiritual world, with all the inventions of the natural world, but the communication is not admitted by the natural man except as a mystery.

There is just as much progress in the spiritual as in the natural world, and the science I teach is the wisdom of God to the senses in the spirit world. So it requires a teacher to teach the wisdom of God in the spirit world, as well as that spiritual wisdom, that has been reduced to man's senses in the so-called sciences. Paul says, "How shall they believe in him of whom they have not heard? And how shall they hear without a preacher?" And how shall they teach unless they be sent or understand how to teach? I am now talking to your spiritual senses, standing at your door, knocking with my wisdom, at your heart or belief for admittance, if you can understand, then I will come in and drink this truth with you, and you with me. This is the spiritual world or senses. Suppose you are sick, and feel you need a physician, then is the time you in your spirit, will call on me or my spirit, and when I come, if you know my voice or understand, you will open the door, and when you do understand, I am with you.

Question 4 Is not one's own experience wisdom to him in a certain sense?

Ans. Wisdom is not knowledge but the answer to our knowledge, but in error knowledge is wisdom till wisdom comes, for example: suppose I make a sound, that is not wisdom, but a sensation. Suppose you try to imitate it, this process is called knowledge or reason. When the sound is in tune with me, this is wisdom not understood, so we call it wisdom, but when we can make the tone intelligently and teach it to others, then the tone is the effect of wisdom, and wisdom comes out of the discord. Wisdom is always the same, it is the point of all attraction and everything must come to this,: it is harmony. This is the Christ. True wisdom contains no matter, false wisdom is the harmony not understood. I will illustrate: Suppose you tell me a story that you say is true, but you get your information from another. I believe it and to me it is wisdom, but you see it is not wisdom, for there is a chance for deception. But wisdom leaves no loophole, it can be tested. This was the controversy of Jesus. The priests thought their opinions were wisdom, but he knew they were false. To test their wisdom was to put it into practice, so every one was to be known by his works, whether they were of God or man. Jesus showed his wisdom by his works, for when they brought him the sick, he healed them. So did others pretending the same way. If Jesus knew how he cured then the kingdom of heaven had come to their understanding; but if he did not, then he was just as ignorant as they were and the world was none the wiser for his cures. His wisdom was from above, theirs from man's ignorance. These made the two worlds, science and error, and as man has borne the one, he shall also bear the other.

Question 5 Is it possible for one to condense his spiritual self so as to be seen by the natural eye of others, as Jesus did?

Answer. This question is not properly stated. Jesus never said he had a spirit, but said, spirit hath not flesh and blood, as you see me have. Here was the rock that they split upon. Jesus' wisdom knew that it was not in the idea body, their knowledge made mind in and a part of the body. So each reasoned according to their wisdom. Their wisdom was their opinion about what persons had said a thousand years before without any proof but merely as an opinion, this they called knowledge. Therefore Jesus' wisdom or Christ was a mystery to them. So when Christ or wisdom spake through Jesus, saying though you destroy this temple I will build it up again. This that spoke was the wisdom, so the builder was not destroyed, but the temple. But they believed as all the Christians of our day do that the temple and the builder were the same, so that when the former was destroyed, they had no idea of what Christ intended to do. Here comes in your question. The Christ that acted upon the idea Jesus, admitted flesh and blood as well as his enemies, but his wisdom knew it was only an idea that he could speak into existence and out. So when they destroyed the idea Jesus, they destroyed to themselves Jesus Christ, or mind and matter. Now when this wisdom made himself manifest to them, they thought he was a spirit, for they believed in spirits, but Christ to himself was the same Jesus as before, for Jesus only means the idea of flesh and blood or senses, or all that we call man. Now Christ retained all this and to himself he had flesh and blood. This was to show that when you think a person dead he is dead to you, but to himself there is no change, he retains all the senses of the natural man as though no change to the world had taken place.

This was what Jesus wanted to prove. Man condenses his identity just according to his belief, this all men do, some more than others. I cannot tell how much I can condense my identity to the sick, but I know I can touch them so they can feel the sensation. To me I really see myself but I cannot tell about them. I will try to prove the answer to you. When you read this, I will show you myself and also the number of persons in the room where I am writing this. Let me know the impression you may have of the number. This is the Christ that Jesus spoke of. How much of the Christ I can make known to you I wait your answer to learn. Read the 14ᵗʰ Chap. of John, he speaks of this truth that shall come to the disciples as I am coming to you.

Question 6 If I understood how disease originates in the mind and fully believe it, why cannot I cure disease?

Answer. If you understand how disease originates, then you stand to the patient as a lawyer does to a criminal who is to be tried for a crime committed against a law that he is ignorant of breaking, and the evidence is his own confession. You know that he is innocent, but you can get no evidence, only by cross-questioning the evidence against him. Disease has its attending counsel as well as truth or health, and to cure the sick is to show to the judge, or their own counsel, that the witness lies. This you have to show from the witness' own story, then you get the case. The error is on one side and you on the other, and out of the mouth of the sick, comes the witness. I will first state a case. A sick person is like a stranger in his own land, or like an ignorant man not knowing what is law or right and wrong according to law. Both are strangers, and both are liable to get into trouble so each is to be punished according to the crime they have committed. Now the man ignorant of state laws, wants a horse, seeing one, he takes it, not knowing that he is liable to any punishment, but as a matter of convenience, and when he has used him as much as he pleases he lets him go. Now he is arrested for stealing and he being ignorant is cast into prison to await his trial.

I appear against him as state's attorney, and you appear for the prisoner. All the testimony is on my side, but if you are shrewd enough to draw from me an acknowledgment that the law cannot punish a man that is ignorant of the law (and not know it) after I have shown the testimony and made my plea, then if you can show that the prisoner has been deceived, and led into the scrape by me, I having received pay from him, then the court will give you the verdict, and arrest and imprison me.

A sick person is precisely in this very state. The priests and doctors conspire together to humbug the people, and they have invented all sorts of stories to frighten man and keep him under their power. These stories are handed down from one generation to another, till at last both priest and doctors all believe they are God's laws, and when a person disobeys one he is liable to be cast into prison.

Suppose you are a doctor of the law of health as it is called, and you find a person perfectly ignorant of disease or your law, so you call on her and commence explaining the necessity of being acquainted with the laws pertaining to health. She being ignorant or like a child sees no sense in your talk, but you continue to explain, and as she grows nervous you keep it up till she shows some sign of yielding to your opinion. Then you tell her she has the heart disease, or lung disease, and it will soon be found out, and then she will be punished with death at any time the Judge sees fit to call her. In her fright, she acknowledges she is guilty, then you enter a complaint against her. She is arrested and cast into prison, there to await her trial. You are the devil or error's attorney and he is the judge, she is brought into court to be tried by error's tribunal. Now I appear, for I have learned her story, unknown to the judge or attorney. I have the evidence and see that the very attorney against her, is her deceiver and the author of her trouble. This I keep to myself till I draw from the judge that a person cannot be tried for a crime which they were forced to commit. This being done I commence my plea for the victim, and show that she has never committed any offense against the laws of God and that she was born free, etc. Then I take up the evidence and show that there is not one word of wisdom in all that has been said, also that she has been made to believe a lie that she might be condemned. In this way I get the case. Disease being made by a belief or forced upon us by our parents or public opinions, you see there is no particular form of agreement, but every one must suit <u>his</u>, to the particular case. Therefore it requires great shrewdness to get the better of the error, for disease is the works of the devil or error, but error like its father has its cloven foot and if you are as wise as your enemies, you will get the case. I know of no better answer than Jesus gave to his disciples when he sent them forth to preach the truth and cure. Be ye wise as they were, or serpents, and as harmless as doves, that is not get into a rage. In this way you will annoy the disease and get the case. Now if you can face the error and argue it down, then you can cure the sick.

Ques. 7 I can see this belief places man entirely superior to circumstances, but will it not therefore take away all desire for improvement and cause invention to cease and the whole go back rather than progress and cause us also to become indifferent to friends and social relations, and say of everything that it is only an idea without substance, and so take away the reality of existence?

Answer. The answer to this is involved in the last. You can answer it by your own feeling, when you plead the case of the sick, condemned by the world, cast into prison with no one to say a cheering word, but left to the cold icy hand of ignorance and superstition, who have no heart to feel and whose life depends on its destruction. If you can be the means of pleading their case and set them free from their prisons of superstition and error, into the light of wisdom and happiness, there to mingle with the well and happy, knowing that you were the cause of so much happiness, would it not be enough to prompt you to continue your efforts for the salvation of the sick and suffering till the great work of reformation is completed? You may answer for yourself, and say if it does not place man superior to the interests of this world, and instead of taking away the reality of existence, it makes man's existence an eternal progression of joy and happiness and its tendency is to destroy death and bring life and immortality to light.

Ques. 8th Suppose a person was kept in a mesmeric state, what would be the result? Would he act independently if allowed? If not, is it not an exact illustration of the condition we are in, in order to have matter which is only an idea seem real to us, for we act independently?

Answer. I think I understand your question. God is the great mesmerizer or magnet. He speaks man or the idea into existence, and attaches his senses to the idea and we are to ourselves just what we think we are. So is a mesmerized subject, they are to themselves matter. You may have as many subjects as you will, and they are all in the same relation to each other as they would be in the state we call waking. So this is proof that we are affected by one another, sometimes independent and sometimes governed by others, but always retaining our own identity, with all our ideas of matter, and subject to all its changes, as real as it is in the natural or waking state.

Ques. 9th What do you think of phrenology?

Ans. As a science it is a mere humbug. It is at best a polite way of pointing out the soft spots of a man's vanity.

Ques. 10th What is memory or that process by which we recall images of the past?

Answer. I have explained memory in that class of reason called knowledge. It is one of the chemical changes to arrive at a fact, matter being only a shadow. When the senses are detached from it we forget the shadow, till it is called up by another. This is memory. If there was no association there could be no memory, and those that have the greatest amount of association and least wisdom have the greatest memories. Those who rely on observation and opinion as the laws of reason have great memories, for their life is in their memory. But the former retain their reason, as it is called and are forgetful of events. Memory is the pleasure or pain of some cause or event that affects our happiness or misery, or it is something ludicrous. For instance, a judge heard one tell another "his coattail was short," and the other replied, "It will be long enough before I get another," attempted to repeat the joke, but he forgot the sympathy or music in it and said, a man told another, his coattail was short, and he replied, it would be a long time before he got another one. The company failed to laugh and he said, I do not see anything to laugh at myself, but when I heard it I laughed heartily. Memory is the effect of two ideas coming in harmony so as to produce an effect that leaves a scene of some idea either ridiculous or otherwise embracing so many combinations that it brings up the scene. Memory is one of the senses of man, and will exist so long as the idea matter exists.

Ques. 11th What became of the body of Jesus after it was laid in the ground, if you do not believe it rose?

Answer. Jesus is the idea matter, so those that believed that Jesus and Christ was one, believed that his body and soul were crucified. Now came their doubts whether this same idea should rise again. Some believed it would, others doubted. So far as Christ was concerned, all their opinions had no effect. Christ was the wisdom that knew matter was only an idea that could be formed into any shape, and the life that moved it came not from it but was outside of it. Here was where their wisdom differed. The disciples believed that the wisdom of man would rise out of the error or idea man or matter, and matter comes under the head of memory. How far their idea of Jesus went I am unable to say. Some said he was stolen, others that he rose. There is as good reason for believing one story as another. Now Jesus said nothing about it. Now I take Christ's own words for truth when he said touching the dead that they rise, God is not the God of the dead but of the living. He knew that they could not understand, but to himself Christ went through no change. To his disciples he died. So when they saw him they were afraid because they thought he was a spirit, but Christ had not forgotten his identity Jesus, or flesh and blood, so he says, a spirit hath not flesh and bones as you see me have.

If Christ's believers of this day could have been there with their present belief, I have my doubts whether they could have seen or even heard any sound. Yet I believe Christ did appear and show himself as dense as their belief could be made, but their unbelief made the idea so rarefied that it was a spirit. These are my ideas of the resurrection of Christ. But Jesus, the world's idea (if the people were as they are now) was without doubt taken away, at any rate, their idea man never rose. Christ lost nothing by the change. Every person rises from the dead with their own belief, so to themselves they are not risen and know no change, and the dead, as they are called, have no idea of themselves as dead.

Ques. 12 Do we receive impressions through the senses and do they acting upon the mind constitute knowledge?

Answer. This question is answered by Paul to the Romans although he did not use the same words. This belief means faith, the peace in the truth was through their belief. Hope is the anchor made fast to the truth. Belief is the knowledge that we shall attain this truth, so that we glory in the tribulation or action of the mind, knowing that it brings patience, and patience confidence, and confidence experience, that we shall obtain the truth. Knowledge is opinions, so when an impression is made on the mind it produces a chemical change. This comes to the senses and opens the door of hope to the great truth. This hope is the world's knowledge or religion that is used like an anchor to the senses, till we ride out the gale of investigation and land in the haven of God or truth.

Question 13 How is matter made the medium of the intelligence of man?

Ans. There are two ideas, one spirit and one matter. When you speak of man, you speak of matter. When you speak of spirit, you speak of the knowledge that will live after the matter is destroyed or dead. This is the Christian's wisdom. With God, all the above is only opinions and ideas without any wisdom from God or Truth. All the above is embraced in his idea as an illusion, that contains no life, but lives, moves, has its being and identity in his wisdom. So that to itself it is a living moving something with power to act, to create and destroy. Its happiness and misery are in itself. So when its shadow is destroyed to B and C, he is dead. A loses nothing but is the same as before, but to B and C he is dead. So the shadow is the medium of truth and error. To error it is matter, but to truth it is an illusion.

Ques. 14 Do I err in thinking knowledge the effect of some influence on the mind, instead of something independent of the whole individual?

Answer. No but you err in thinking that knowledge is wisdom. Knowledge is the effect of an influence on the mind and is the medium that carries the senses to this great truth.

Ques. 15: Can anyone bear any amount of excitement and fatigue without a reaction?

Answer. No, no more than a mathematician can solve every problem without a reaction, but as he becomes master of the science, the reaction diminishes till all error is destroyed.

Portland, Feb. 1862

Quimby's Method of Treatment
[Originally untitled.] [BU 2:0024]

It may be somewhat strange to you to know something of the mode of curing disease by a person who does not believe in any disease independent of the mind. I am acquainted with a person who does not give any medicine at all, and yet he is in the constant practice of curing persons afflicted with all diseases that flesh is heir to.

He not only discards medicine but disease also, contends that all disease is in the mind, and that the cure of disease is governed by a principle as much as mathematics, and can be learned and taught. His ideas are new, not like any person's I ever heard or read of, and yet when understood by the sick they are as plain and evident as any truth that can come within a person's senses. His ideas are compared to that which troubles the sick, not to persons well; for those who are well need no physicians. He is not a spiritualist as is commonly understood, believing that he receives his power from departed spirits. But he believes the power is general and can be learned if persons would only consent to be taught. He has no mystery more than in learning music or any science which requires study and practice. It cannot be learned in a day nor in a month, yet nevertheless it can be learned. He has spent sixteen years learning and yet he has just begun.

I will here state what has come within my observation. A friend of mine by the name of Robinson, of North Vassalboro, had been sick and confined to his house for four years, and nearly the whole time confined to his bed, not being able to sit up more than fifteen minutes during the day. Hearing of Mr. Quimby, for this is his name, he sent for him to visit him. He arrived at Mr. R's in the evening and sat down and commenced explaining to Mr. R his feelings, telling him his symptoms nearer than Mr. R could tell them himself, and also telling him the peculiar state of his mind and how his mind acted upon his body. His explanation was entirely new to Mr. R. and it required some argument to satisfy Mr. R that he had no disease; for he had been doctored for almost all diseases.

His eyes were so swollen that it was impossible for him to see. His head had been blistered all over, and large black spots came out all over his body. Therefore to become a convert to his theory was more than Mr. R could do. But Q told him he stood ready to explain all he said, and not only that but to prove it to his satisfaction; for, said he, the proof is the cure, and R was not bound to believe any faster than he could make him understand, and the cure is in the understanding.

So Mr. Quimby commenced taking up his feelings, one by one, like a lawyer examining witnesses, analyzing them and showing him that he had put a false construction on all his feelings, showing him that a different explanation would have produced a different result.

In this way Quimby went on explaining and taking up almost every idea he ever had, and putting a different construction till R thought he did not know anything.

"Mr. Q's explanation," said R, "was so plain that it was impossible not to understand it. Not one of his ideas was like any that I ever heard before from any physician; yet so completely did he change me that I felt like a man who had been confined in a prison for life, and without the least knowledge of what was going on out of the prison, received a pardon and was set at liberty. At about ten o'clock I went to bed, had a good night's rest, and in the morning was up before Q and felt as well as ever. Q and I went to Waterville the next day. I had no desire to take to my bed and have felt well ever since." This is R's own story.

I was well acquainted with Mr. R and know this story to be true. This is the case with a great many others where I was not acquainted with the parties, and I was induced to go to Belfast to see if he (Quimby) could talk me out of my senses, for I thought I had a disease. At least it seemed so to me, for I had had for the last ten years a disease which showed itself in almost every joint in my limbs. My hands were drawn all out of shape. My neck was almost still. My legs were drawn up, my joints swollen and so painful it was impossible to move them without almost taking my life. I could not take one step nor get up without help. It would be impossible to give any account of my suffering.

When I arrived at Belfast I sent for Mr. Quimby. He came, and after telling me some of my feelings, said, "I suppose it would be pretty hard to convince you that you had no disease independent of your mind." I replied I had heard that he contended all disease was in the mind, and if he could convince me that the swelling and contraction of the limbs and the pain I suffered was in my mind, I would be prepared to believe anything.

He then commenced by asking me to move my legs. I replied that I could not move them. "Why not?" he said. Because I have no power to move them. He said it was not for the want of physical strength, it was for the want of knowledge. I said I knew how to move them but I had not strength. As he wished me to try, I made an effort, but without the slightest effect. He said I acted against myself.

He then went on to explain to me where I even thought wrong, and showed me by explaining till I could see how I was acting against myself. In the course of a short time I could move my legs more than I had for three years. He continued to visit me and I am gaining as fast as a person can. I have been under his treatment for two weeks, and I can get up and sit down very easily. I can see now that my cure depends on my knowledge. Sometimes he asks me if I want some liniment to rub on my cords or muscles. I can now see the absurdity of using any application to relax the muscles or to strengthen them. The strength is in the knowledge. This is something that he has the power to impart. But how it is done is impossible to understand. Yet I know the knowledge he imparts to me is strength, and just as I understand so is my cure.

Quimby System, The
[LC 3:1363]

The Quimby system is applying a new mode of reasoning to an old mode of reasoning, by which the former corrects the errors of the latter and shows how the old philosophy has brought about the evils that man suffers, called disease. His philosophy shows that matter, of which the body is formed, is created by the wisdom that controls it, and this wisdom is governed by two principles, right and wrong or light and darkness. The light is Christ and the darkness Jesus, or human and divine. All error is human and is governed by human laws. All divine or science is wisdom and not human. He shows how humans create their troubles or disturbances and how the human is governed by human laws or beliefs, which is one and the same. So he says, to know one's self is to know that man, like Jesus, has two natures: one human and the other divine. Then he is subject to the one that lives, that is his body, for the body is the medium of both. So to know how to correct an error is to know how to make it.

There has never been a philosophy reduced to a science to cure disease. Men have philosophized about diseases but never has their philosophy been put to the test intelligently. Now he professes to show how man makes his disease, as it is called. Man has never got to the point of progression to admit he is a creative being and until he is educated up to this point he cannot see that he is his own creator. He thinks he is made and fashioned by some power independent of his existence, but this is an error. Man makes himself and is responsible to himself and no one else. Therefore, anything he may do can't change the divine; so the human may create and destroy but the divine is not changed. Now to make the human subject to the divine is to make man know himself.

Relation of This Truth to the Sick, The
[BU 3:0257]

What course of argument must be used to make the masses understand this truth by which I correct the errors that make man sick? What relation has this truth to any one and how does it stand to the sick? It is the sick man's friend, and those who can understand it are related to those who do not understand as a teacher who wishes to make his pupil understand the principles of mathematics. He is not to teach mathematics but to explain what the rules mean, so the pupil is not to copy a mathematical work because that gives him no wisdom in regard to the truth; the disciple is not to be above the science, nor the teacher above the truth, but the latter is to explain the science by the words of the truth.

To illustrate, I stand to this Science as the teacher or expounder of it, not as the Truth itself. So when the Truth says through me that all disease is in the mind, you want me to explain what it means. You ask the question because you do not understand what is meant by the mind. It is this: all opinion, belief, reason and everything that can be changed originating in man–all these are included in the word mind. Thought is a seed or an effect of this great ocean of mind. The word mind covers all man's reasoning as the word wood covers all vegetable substances. A chair is made of wood but it is an idea made out of wood. In the same way mind is the material and disease is a manufacture made of the material, but the wisdom that forms the idea is called something else. Here you see that mind embraces every part of man but his wisdom, and here is the distinction which the world makes only in a different sense. The world calls the parts mind and matter. I call them wisdom and matter. Therefore when I use "mind," I use it as matter containing no intelligence, but it is like sound connected with something to which we attach intelligence.

October 1862

Religion [I]
[BU 3:0072]

It has been generally taught that there is a resurrection of this flesh and blood, or that this body should rise from the dead. Now if death is anything independent of ourselves, then it is not a part of our identity and if death is the annihilation of life, then life dies and if your life dies, then it is not life. This absurdity arises from the fact that man began to philosophize before he understood himself. Man is superstitious from ignorance. He sees through a medium of ignorance called matter; therefore he sees nothing outside of his belief. This belief is his matter and his reason is a part of his belief; therefore he is to himself just what he thinks he is. But his belief makes his life and death the same identity. Therefore when he speaks of life he speaks of saving it or losing it, just as though it were matter and must go through a chemical change before it could go to heaven or get separated from itself.

Thus we are taught to believe that our lives are liable to be lost or cast into some place of torment if we do not do something to save it, just as though life were a thing independent of ourselves and we must look out for it or we should lose it. Absurd as this is, it is the belief of all mankind, infidel or Christian.

Now you see, this is the matter or belief that is in matter reasoning about something outside of itself that may be lost if it is not seen to.

Therefore we are taught to believe that Jesus came to make all right, suffered and died and rose again to let mankind know that they should rise. Let us see what was really accomplished by his mission according to his followers' opinions of him. We are told that man had wandered away from God and had become so wicked that it was necessary that something should be done or he would be in danger of being banished from God's presence. What was required of him in order to be saved was to repent and return to God, only believing that he should never die. Therefore his life depended on his belief, for if he did not repent or change his mind, he would be damned. Now, what are we called upon to believe? In the first place, you must believe that Jesus, the man, was Christ or God and that he died on the cross and that the man Jesus rose from the dead and went to heaven, there to appear before God and sit down with God in heaven. If we believe this we shall be saved. If we do not believe it we must be damned. Now you see that our lives are in our belief and our belief is made up of someone's opinion who knows just as much as we.

I, for one, do not reason in that way. I know that man has two identities: one in this state called Christian or diseased, and one in the spiritual or scientific state. Each is governed by its own belief, and when one has the ascendency, the other is the servant. Death and life are the two identities. Life is the knowledge of our existence that has no matter. But matter is its servant or medium. Death is the name of that state of mind that reasons as man reasons and the brutes and all of God's creatures. The life of this state (death) depends upon its reason. It reasons that life is in it and a part of it, and at the same time acknowledges that life is something that can be lost or saved and reasons about it as one man reasons about another. Death reasons also with the idea that it is saving its life and invents all sorts of diseases which destroy its state or self. It prays to be saved, it fasts and observes forms and ceremonies. It is very strict in its laws to protect its life. Knowledge is its destruction, so it fears God or Science as its destroyer. Its life is not destroyed but its opinions are, and its opinions are matter. The destroying of its opinions is death, but not annihilation of matter, but of error as far as it goes. The matter returns to its former condition ready to be formed into some other idea. These beliefs are from the knowledge of this world and are the inventions of man, but the wisdom of this world is foolishness with God or Science. This world is made up of the above beliefs and is subject to a higher power.

The wisdom of God does not go into the clouds to call truth down nor into the deep to call God up, but shows us that God is in us, even in our speech. It sees matter as a cloud or substance that has a sort of life (in appearance). It sees it move around. It also sees commotion, like persons running to and fro upon the earth. It can come into this state called this world and reasons with its followers or science, who are in this world, imprisoned by a belief, for science not understood is not safe unless it has an identity. Its identity is a knowledge of itself, for if you should do right ignorantly, you are not safe. To be clear from this world is to know that an opinion is not knowledge; and when this is found out, the opinion is destroyed and knowledge or science takes its place and the identity or opinion is not in this world only as it is remembered. I will give an illustration. I am now speaking of the wisdom of this world.

You see your friend walking about and you talk with him. Finally he dies, as you say. Now his identity with you is that he once lived, but is now dead. But you do not know but that he may live again, though this is only an opinion. You follow him with the same opinion or belief and so on. So you never enter into the world of science, for flesh and blood cannot enter truth, nor can it enter Science. It cannot understand the separation from this world or belief.

Now where do I stand? I do not stand at all. I know that all the above is the reasoning of matter and when people learn the truth, they will make matter subject to science. Then the wisdom of this world will become subject to the scientific world. This world calls the world of science a gift. To call it a gift is to say that those who practice it for the benefit of man are either ignorant of this science, are humbugs or are fools talking about what they do not know. Those who call Jesus' knowledge of this science a power or gift place him on the same level with all the sorcerers of his day.

April 1860

Religion [II]
[BU 3:0031]

What is the true meaning of another world? It is supposed that man dies and goes to God or a spirit-world. This is the general belief and if this is true, why should it be so strange that some persons should believe that their friends return to earth and appear to the people? This was the belief of a large class of mankind in the days of Christ. If all this is called truth, it is founded on an opinion that there is another world and the Bible is quoted in proof of it. Now all the above is to me error based on ignorance of science. Science would never have led man to that belief. Paul said that all men had gone out of the way, none doeth good, no not one. Now where did they go?

It is said that man had wandered away from God and become so wicked that he was in danger of eternal punishment. What does this mean? Man is here on the earth as he always was, so it does not mean that he got off the globe. To wander away from God is to suppose that He had some locality, and to be in His presence is to return to His place of residence. This place could not be in another world, off the globe. It must be somewhere in this world that God resided because it says, Christ came to lead man back to God. Now if God is in another world and Jesus came from that place down to the earth to lead man there, or to open a way whereby man could get there himself, then it is to be supposed man had been in heaven in the presence of God but had wandered away and could not get back. All this looks very silly when we think of asking men to believe it, but we don't think of half we believe, embracing it without giving it the least thought.

Man is made up of thought and ideas. There is nothing about man unchangeable but his science, for science embraces a principle and principles are not matter or ideas but a knowledge of them. Life is an evidence of science and science acknowledges it. So is feeling, taste, etc. All the senses are admitted by science to exist independent of matter because matter is accident and can be changed. Ideas are matter. Our bodies are an idea and the senses are applied to the idea, but the senses can act independently of the idea of body. So the senses are all there are that cannot be changed. They may be obstructed by error but not destroyed. To separate these two ideas explains the true meaning of life and death. The people all believed in death, Jesus did not; therefore, his arguments were to prove that death was a false idea. If we believe in death, we are in our belief, and if we know it is an error, we are in life. And if we believe in either, it is proof that we are alive. Now Christ wished to prove that what we called death was to him nothing but a separation of his truth from the people's belief, they of course being in their belief, the crucifixion of Jesus was death according to their belief.

Jesus never intended to allude to the natural body, for it is an idea that belongs to the natural man or error. So when he speaks of a resurrection, it is from the dead, not that the dead rise, for that would go to show that he was still a believer in matter and if he believed in matter, he must believe it dies and then rises again. But if he believed that it is nothing but a medium for the senses to use and control, then all that he meant was that his senses should rise from the dead or error of the people, who believed that the senses are a part of the idea called body. Here was where the difference was. Now to prove his truth was to show himself to his disciples after they had seen him, as they supposed dead, alive again. This to them was a resurrection of the dead, not Christ or Jesus' teachings. Jesus' teaching was to show that Christ was a truth of God or a higher knowledge that separated science from ignorance, and this Christ was in the idea Jesus, that Christ was all that ever could exist without changing and that Jesus was nothing but the idea of matter that could be changed or made into any form.

Christ is the man that should rise from this superstitious idea. So when the people saw their idea or form destroyed, their hope was cut off; but when in the clouds of their ignorance they saw this same Christ or truth take form again, they were afraid, and as it became dense enough to be identified, it was recognized as Jesus' body, but it was not the body or idea that they had believed in some days before.

Now the people called this identity Jesus Christ. This is where the trouble lay; the people's mind was changing but not scientifically and they were left in a more nervous state than before, for now they thought Jesus' body rose and if Jesus' body rose, it went to show that his ideas were not changed from the common belief. It amounted to nothing at all, for no man has ever risen since and there was no proof of Jesus' soul being separated from his body.

So man gets up a belief in opposition to the Bible's belief or he must believe that Christ went to heaven with a body of flesh and blood; this man cannot believe, so the common explanation of the resurrection leaves it worse than before. Now look at it in a common scientific way and see if I cannot explain it so that the wayfaring man, though a fool, need not err therein.

Take the man Jesus as a man of flesh and blood, like all other men. Give him the knowledge that mind is matter and that matter is under the control of a higher power that can act independently of matter or ideas and that he, Jesus, could be in two places at the same time and be outside of the body or idea called Jesus, then it would not be very hard to believe that this knowledge called Christ, which Jesus had, should say, Although you destroy this idea of Jesus, he, that is Christ, should rise or make himself known to the people. For this Christ or truth had the power to assume any form that it pleased, and as the people knew it not except as it came within their senses as the natural man, they could not believe till it took the form of Jesus as a man. This form the people called Jesus; therefore it went out that Jesus rose from the dead, and it has always been believed by those who call themselves disciples of Jesus that the man or idea Jesus rose from the dead.

Now here is my belief: I believe in Christ or the truth. This truth taught this, that although the people thought that when they crucified the idea Jesus, they crucified Christ, Christ knew that they knew not what they did. Therefore he said, "Father forgive them for they know not what they do." This same power was not in the idea the people had but just so far as this power or knowledge was made known, just so far it could make itself manifest to man. And those who believed that Jesus would rise, just so far this Christ could make itself known. But to those who saw it, it was Jesus, for they never had any true idea of Christ independent of Jesus.

Now to believe that the idea, Jesus or flesh and blood rose is to believe that the dead rise. This Jesus denied when he said that that rises from the dead not that the dead rise, but that that rises from the dead, never marries nor is given in marriage, but as touching the dead, that they rise, he says, that God is not the God of the dead, but of the living, for all live to God.

May 1860

Religion [III]
[LC 1:0541]

What does Jesus mean by the Kingdom of Heaven? We all know the common opinion was that heaven was a place. Now some suppose it to be a state of mind. Had Jesus either of these ideas? I say he did not, and will show what his ideas were. God is represented as all wisdom and love. Now love is not wisdom, but a desire for wisdom; therefore, a desire to get wisdom for the sake of happiness that follows is the highest love. This is heaven and to be deprived of this love is to be out of heaven. The sick are strangers to this heaven. It is true they have a sort of love but it is governed by a false love or wisdom. It is the light or wisdom of man. This leads to death but to have the true love or desire that leads to wisdom, this is heaven.

Now as I have said, the sick are strangers to this truth and being strangers, they are deceived into a false belief that lulls them to sleep. To cure them it is necessary to arouse them from their lethargy and show them their errors. To get a person out of an error is to destroy their error. This can be done in two ways, one by ignorance, the other by science.

I will now give the true conversion of a man of this world or sick man converted to the religion of Christ or cured intelligently, and also one converted from one disease or error to another. I call all error disease that leads to death, and the remedy is religion or a knowledge of the truth that will save us from the evils that flow from our sins. To illustrate the different forms of religion is to show the different modes of restoring the lost child of disease to health and happiness. To show how Jesus differed from all others is to show each religion separately and how the belief affects mankind.

All will admit that Jesus opposed all the religion or modes by which the medical men and priests used to save the people from their sins or evils called diseases. For to be diseased was an evil and the sick were dealt with accordingly; and the false idea that the sins or diseases of the parents are visited upon the children is handed down to this generation. This was the belief of the people in the days of Jesus and to save them from their sins was to cure them of their disease. For this cause Jesus came into the world, suffered and died and rose again that all that believe might be saved from these sins and enjoy the presence of God which was heaven. This was the doctrine Jesus taught.

Now what was the idea the world had of heaven? People never had such an idea as the Christians have now. They never believed in any other world, but their suffering was their evil and to be cured was their heaven or happiness. For this object they employed every means in their power according to their belief. The people were taught that there were certain rivers and pools the angels would disturb and those who visited them were healed. Certain diseases were held so sinful that the victims were kept aloof from the people till the priests cured them. So their religion was all for their health or happiness. This idea of preparing for another world never entered into their minds. It is true that there was a small class who believed that at the end of the world the dead would rise. This belief has been handed down from generation to generation so that religion was in that mode which was used to restore them to health. This of course made them happy. This to them was heaven.

So all religion was for the happiness of man, but their religion never extended to any state after death. Now Jesus opposed their religion or belief so it was necessary to destroy them to cure the sick, for these beliefs made them sick. To do this he had to show them the absurdity of their own belief, so he called them to him and said, Beware of the doctrine of the Scribes and Pharisees for their doctrines bind burdens on you. It made them superstitious, made them believe in ghosts, spirits and all sorts of juggling. This kept the people under the rule of the priests who invented all sort of craft to deceive the people, pretending to take away their sins so that God would not torment them with evil spirits and disease. Jesus knew it was all in their beliefs, and if he could introduce a higher principle or a better mode of reasoning or priesthood that could take away their sins or errors so that they would be more enlightened he would be doing them a great favor, and would establish a universal truth that would work out a more excellent law. To do this it was necessary to bring proof of his superior wisdom. So it is said, He came into the world, suffered, died and rose again. He was talking about this great truth called God that governs every true and scientific mind. He made two worlds: one the natural or superstitious man that they were all; the other the scientific man. Now the scientific man was to rise from the earthly or superstitious man. This he called a resurrection from the dead. Not that the dead rose, for if you cannot get a man out of his error, there is no resurrection. As Paul says, If Christ (or this science) be preached that it rose from the dead (or error), how say some among you that there is no higher truth than man's opinion? As science is spiritual, it must be explained by literal things. So he used parables to show how this truth grows in the minds, for he makes the mind matter and sows the seeds of wisdom in the mind. So he takes, for example, a little child before its mind is filled with the errors of priest, as a figure of heaven. Not that the mind contains any wisdom, but like the soil of the earth it is pure from foul seeds or error, ready to receive the true seed of wisdom, guided by a higher development than the priest. He says, "Of such is the kingdom of heaven," that this truth could live and grow in the child. Not that the heaven or kingdom was happiness, but the happiness was in the one that got into it. But as the kingdom grew, false ideas would creep in, for it is not to be supposed that Jesus ever intended to make his kingdom perfect till every enemy or error should be destroyed. So he likens it unto a great many things, to a sower in a field, and an enemy sowing in the same field. Here you have good seed and bad seed, truth and error, good and evil. But the good was good, and the bad was bad, and they never mingled.

I will take a person as he would come to Jesus, and show how he preached to them the kingdom of heaven. Take the little child that was tormented by the devils that would throw him into the fire and water and on the ground. See what he does. See if he ever said anything about another world, but ask the parents when they said they had carried him to the disciples and they could not cure him. The cure was what they wanted. So here was the cure: Jesus asked how long the child had been in this way . When told, he said, Do you believe all things possible with God? They said, "Yes." So then he cured the child, not by a "power" but by his wisdom, for he knew what he was about. So their faith in him kept the child from having any more fits. All his cures went to prove his theory of the mind. This theory of Christ was what he talked about. It was a science. So he preached it and illustrated by parables, and proved it by showing himself to the multitudes after they believed him dead. This truth was called Christ and when Jesus spoke it he spoke

Christ and the identity of it was a body and the doctrine was its blood. So when he says, "If you eat not my flesh nor drink my blood, you have no life in you." But the ignorance of the people thought he meant to eat the man Jesus.

I will give an illustration. Suppose a person comes to me to learn navigation. I say, "You must be born again, for your ideas of navigation are all false." He says, "How can I learn or be born again when I am so old?" I answer, "You must be born in the science, of navigation." This he cannot understand, but still he wishes to learn. So I begin to explain. As he begins to learn, this is called the love that is spoken of with which he so loved the world, etc. Now the love for wisdom prompts him to learn, and as he learns his happiness is full. This is entering into heaven. This is the heaven that God has prepared for everyone who will try to learn, and if everyone will search for God or Wisdom, God will not cast him off.

I will apply this to disease. To me the disease is a lie or burden bound upon you by the errors of the world. I take upon myself your infirmities that I may lead you to health, for health to you is heaven. The love for health prompts you to come. My love for you prompts me to lead you to health. This I do by teaching you the errors of your belief and showing you where you have been deceived. The truth, like love, leads you to see your error, and the happiness of your recovery is heaven. People believe that religion is one thing and health another. This is a false idea, and if you look at it you will see that to be happy is the chief end of man. And now what is happiness is in what we think we have obtained. Take the religion of our day: but that is a poor illustration of happiness, for the misery it occasions is twice the happiness. We are taught our belief is one thing and our health another. But it is not so. Man's belief is his heaven or his hell. You may not be aware of the effect of your belief.

Disease is one of the evils that follow our belief. For instance, I will cite a case. Take a young lady. Begin to tell her that her happiness depends upon her having religion. She has no idea what you mean. So to convince her you give an account of what religion is and show that she must get it or be eternally lost. This makes her nervous. So you tell her to come to Christ. This to her is all blind. You say Christ is standing with his arms extended to embrace her. Now for her to fall into the arms of a stranger is more than she can do. So she weeps, not knowing what to do. She becomes unhappy. This you tell her is the conversion of her soul. At last she is made to believe she is not worthy to be a Christian. Then come the soothing words of the priest and his words soothe her aching head and she quiets down. Then you tell her this is a change of heart. Now she is in a state to get religion.

What has been brought to pass? The young lady has been deceived into a belief that has cost her all the happiness she had. It will be said her religion had nothing to do with her health, but this cannot be the case for our life is nothing but a belief and when this fact is known then people will begin to be cautious what they believe. For every person is responsible to God or Wisdom for his belief, and must take the consequences of his belief.

Now as I said, religion is a belief and disease or happiness is what follows. So as all men have sinned or got a belief, the sentence of death has been passed upon them, for all have sinned and come short of the truth. So this truth came into the world of opinions to open the eyes of the blind, or appeal to a higher intelligence to lead them to the truth that would cure them of their sins or errors. Now a religion or a theory was to explain to the masses to keep them out of their trouble. We suppose that Jesus wanted to convey the idea that man was in danger of being destroyed after death, but if he would believe in Jesus he should be saved.

So our belief depends upon our beliefs. Now what was Jesus' idea? Let us see if Jesus' belief was founded on man's opinion or on the scientific fact that man through his belief in the priest had been deceived. This deception had brought on evils that were unable to destroy. The leaders of the South who have deceived the people and brought forth all the evils we are now suffering from. They have a God and a religion which upholds them in their wicked belief. The North also have their God and their religion. Now Jesus' religion or belief was different from this. He had no words or ceremonies but a love for the higher development of the human soul. This was Jesus' religion and he put it in practice by his acts upon the sick, not by giving an opinion of what he knew nothing but by showing that their sickness was the effect of their belief. Now see if you admit that mind is matter and to change the mind you remove the burden.

How often have you heard persons say that they are not nervous and they never change their mind. That is as much as to say that they have no wisdom, for wisdom changes the mind. Make a person believe a thing. The belief being matter or mind is an obstacle to wisdom. This obstacle must be removed before the truth can shine. If there is not wisdom enough to remove the obstruction we say such a man has a strong mind. It is true he has a strong error to be overcome, but his mind embraces just as much intelligence as a stumbling block in the way of a train of cars. That must be overcome by wisdom. The dissensions among the passengers represent the contrast between the strong-minded and the intellectual man. One sees no way to remove the obstacle and concludes that it cannot be overcome and settles down in the strength of his mind, while the wisdom investigates the chances and sets himself to work to remove the burden. As the intellectual man works, his mind changes; while the strong man sits and contends that he knows, and when he makes up his mind nothing can change it. The other is fickle and therefore has no mind or stability.

This is the case with disease. The belief is the burden to be overcome. In any disease the strong mind means a man deficient in mechanical wisdom who can't see whether the world develops him or he develops the world. The strong-minded man is a man whom the world develops and he, not knowing the fact that change comes with the growth, and therefore he never changes. While the man of God or Wisdom develops the world, for the world is one universal truth, while matter is one universal error. These two principles of truth and error make up the extremes and every identity is in the one called truth, but the controversy arises about the sensation made on this mind or matter. The strong-minded man's foundation is in what has been handed down from one generation to another. This to him is truth and the disciples of this are his leaders. So his wisdom is based on their opinions and these, being false, are the burdens that the scientific man has to remove, so that the conflict is not to establish an opinion but to destroy an error. The error is the disease and the destruction of the error is freedom from the disease. But the strong-minded man reasons as though you wanted to destroy his belief and make him embrace yours. But truth reasons in this way. Truth is a universal element of God and the destruction of error leaves the man this element without an opinion, but with wisdom.

I will give an illustration. Suppose someone should say that a messenger had just arrived and said that Washington was taken by the Rebels. Now the minds of men would be disturbed and their wisdom would begin to create in themselves burdens according to their mode of reasoning, except those who were bound before. This class would begin to throw off their burdens, so each one's mind is in action directed by their wisdom, governed by their love of party. So this love or enemy would destroy or create trouble. Now when the mind is disturbed the ignorance of our wisdom rises from what they know, and as the lower kind of reason comes from error, there is no wisdom but fear or submission. This is the element that man is afraid of. This is the element man worships and bows down to and prays to. He worships it not because he loves it but because he is afraid of it.

May 1, 1864

Religion Analyzed: Part 1
[LC 1:0437]

The difference between a truth based on an opinion and on wisdom is this. Wisdom backs itself up by science; opinion gives no proof but someone's opinion. Here is the difference. Man who is under the wisdom of opinion has no idea on what his opinions are based. All controversy springs from this error. It is the basis of all our knowledge. Strip man of this and you leave him a mere skeleton. All that men talk about is what they know nothing of, only that someone said so. Look at religion. How often we hear this remark. It is a good thing to have religion or such a man has religion; I would not give much for such a one's religion, etc. Everyone hears this kind of talk and yet they never think to analyze it or see if there is any science to prove it. No, that won't do; you must believe in religion as though it was something that had an existence independent of man and he must get it.

Let us see what man gets when he gets religion, for I will admit that he gets something. It cannot be wisdom, for they say they are willing to be called a fool for religion's sake. So it must be something to get which they are willing to sacrifice all the pleasures of the world and become a mean despised being, laughed at, spit upon, and hated. Now what is it? If you ask one that has it, they will tell you, You must pray for it; that God will answer your prayers and if you will comply with certain laws and regulations, break off from your sins and turn to God, then perhaps you will get it. I will take a sinner or one who wants to get religion and show you what he gets and how he gets it. You never heard of a man getting religion who never heard of Christ or the Bible; so religion began at the commencement of the Christian era.

It seems there was a man called Jesus who the people believed was God, at least some of them did and some denied it. Like all other phenomena, the people wanted proof that he was God. So, of course, in all phenomena that appear which are the invention of man, not of science, opinions spring up. Everyone will admit that Jesus was a man of flesh and blood. To be a Christian was to believe he was God. For if men should not believe so, they should die in their sins and where he went they should never come. So to go to heaven or where Jesus went was to believe that he was God and then you should be saved. Therefore, a belief was necessary to get to heaven. At that time, heaven was a place separate and apart from earth and man's salvation depended on his religion to insure him a passage to it. Religion, when you get it, is just what you get from any belief that man invents. At that time, it was a cross to admit such a number of absurdities as was required of a person to believe, and it was not strange that they should be called fools. Are not the Mormons and the Millerites called fools? Yet their belief is not half as absurd as that of the people eighteen-hundred years ago. Now there never was and never can be a belief that is perfect; it must admit a doubt. Science holds no doubt. It is that wisdom that proves all things and holds fast that which is good.

Paul shows the difference between true and false religion. He says if a man thinks he knows anything, he knows nothing as he ought to because it embraces a thought or doubt; but if he knows science, that wisdom is known to him. The above religion is nothing but an opinion. I can take three out of ten and make them believe in just such a religion as I please and they shall meet with a change of heart, talked of by the religious or superstitious world.

Nov. 15, 1861

Religion Analyzed: Part 2–Jesus and His Teachings
[LC 1:0438]

You may ask me if I deny that there was such a man as Jesus. I answer, No. I do not doubt there was, any more than I doubt that there was such a man as Washington. But I have doubts that Jesus was the author of the Christian religion or had anything to do with it. Its author lived in heathen ages and it has been modified as science developed itself. I believe it is a stain on the character of the man, Jesus. I will here give my ideas of Jesus and the introduction of Christ, which was Jesus' teacher or the God in Jesus, or God manifest in the flesh. At the crucifixion of Jesus, there was not much account of him. It is said Josephus speaks of him, though that is denied. Therefore, there could be but very little excitement about him at that time. All we hear from him is the account gathered some years after his death. Paul's conversion took place thirty years after his death and at that time, he was so unpopular that Paul was destroyed.

Everyone knows that religion has been a thing like politics, changing like the Democratic party. Yet, its disciples claim to be followers of Jesus as the democracy claim to be followers of Jefferson. Now there is not one single idea advocated by the parties of either Jesus or Jefferson that was ever thought of by these men, yet they claim to be followers of Christ. Go back to the Puritan fathers and you will find the Christians hanging the Quakers and burning the witches. Still later, you see these very Puritans fighting every sect differing from them. The true followers of Christ at this day are disciples of Wesley, Calvin, etc. Now their religion is a creed and nothing else and unless you subscribe to it, you are not a follower of Jesus. Jesus was the man who brought this true light or Christ to light, which the priests have crucified. It came to them first and they refused it. Then it turned to the Gentile or scientific world and has since then been working in the hearts of the wise, and will always, till priesthood and superstition have been blotted out of the natural man.

Return with me to the days of Jesus and see if I do not give his mission a higher character than what is claimed by the priests and all the religious wars made by the priests. Everyone who reads the history of Jesus will see that he never intended to get up a party on his own account, but tried to enlighten the people on such subjects as would be for their happiness. The people were groaning beneath the Roman yoke and led by priests who ruled them by a rod of iron, robbing the widow and fatherless by pretending to pardon their sins. In fact they were a complete engine of deception, playing upon the superstition of the masses without the least regard for the people's happiness. This was the state of the people at the birth of Jesus. Many groaning in their captivity were prophesying for someone to deliver them, but no one came. Now when this promise had so matured in the hearts of the people, it must come forth; a child must be born capable of receiving the science, just as it is in the discovery of any new knowledge, the discovery of America, for instance. The minds of the people must be excited so that a certain chemical change will produce a child that can receive this wisdom. So Columbus was born, not with a knowledge of his future life; but when the time came, it came forth, and the people called it America.

Franklin was also born after a certain change in the soil of the mind, preparatory to the production of a new idea or science. Eighteen-hundred years ago, the world had become so disturbed by their religion that a child was brought forth to all appearances like other children, with this peculiarity: his mind was preparing to receive this great truth called Christ. But the child Jesus was as ignorant of it as Franklin, Columbus or Fulton were of their future. All new sciences come when they are the least wanted by the wise, for they are disturbed in their position; therefore, they must expect to meet with opposition. This is as it should be, for there will arise false lights that will deceive, so there should be some way to test them.

When Jesus came of age, he was informed with regard to the religion of his day; and as John the Baptist was preaching, it was not unlikely that the young man would go to hear him. As he heard him telling of a truth that would strike at the roots of this heathen wilderness and every tree or theory that could not stand the test of such a blow must come down, he was excited then by the Holy Ghost or this truth and was carried up into a wilderness where he could see all their craft and hypocrisy. Like all men who get a new idea or truth into their heads, they want to make the most of it, but there is a point where selfishness gives way to sympathy for his fellow man. This was the case with Jesus. His wisdom knew no bounds and to cramp it would be to betray it into the hands of its enemies. To declare it would be to run the risk of his life. He came to the conclusion that it was his duty to listen to the voice of those poor sick ones bound down in prison by the priests and come out and separate himself by standing up and denouncing the political engine that was crushing the poor to death. His first act was to do good. So he started out and called on men who were fishing to follow him. Then he went preaching this science and proving it by his works. In this way he saw that the priests' opinion made the people sick and affected them in many ways. So he preached the truth by showing how they had been deceived. This the people gladly received and were healed. So he cured all manner of diseases by the word of his mouth.

Nov. 15, 1861

Religion Analyzed: Part 3–Comparison between Christians Eighteen Hundred Years Ago and Now: Science and Ignorance Illustrated
[LC 1:0439]

Here is the difference between the followers of Jesus, who was crucified eighteen-hundred years ago, and the disciples of Calvin at this day. One believer disbelieves in everything that cannot be substantiated by cures and the other believes in nothing but forms and ceremonies which Jesus denounced. One's works are their religion, the other their belief. This difference was the same in Paul's day and he says, Show me your religion without works and I will show you mine by my works. To be a disciple of Jesus is to put his wisdom into practice, not to be calling yourself a Christian, but by your acts, to separate yourself from opinions and beliefs that can never make a man happy or wise and to enter into that world of Science where opinions never come. The world's religion is a belief, that of Jesus is his acts.

A belief is merely a belief in some idol or man. Paul says of idols, We know that an idol or belief is nothing in the world and that there is no other truth but one, that is Science or God. I will here relate an incident. A lady came to see me who was troubled with what she called neuralgia in the head and neck, running into the shoulders. She was a person with what would be called an expansive mind. She reasoned from cause to effect and was quick to understand, but. she was very religious. She had imbibed this error in her youth and never tested it as she had tested other things. Now a person is known by the company he keeps and public opinion is the judge by which we are judged. So man's opinions and ideas of science and superstition are tested by the wisdom of science and science respects science, but it has no dealings with opinions; therefore, a religious man and one purely scientific have no more dealings than the Jews and the Samaritans. The Jews represent the religious man of opinions and belief, the Samaritans, the scientific or infidel. Jesus was a scientific man and the woman at the well was also a Samaritan. But she mistook him for a Jew or a man of opinions, for when he asked for water, her answer showed this.

Now if Jesus had not shown himself superior to an opinion, there would have been no explanation, for one opinion is as good as another. But was that the case? No, for he said, If you knew of whom you ask water, I would be a well, etc. Here were some dealings whereby she was to receive something and you see she did, for she went away into the city and told all he had said and then inquired if he was the true Christ—not a Jew. Jesus knew her thoughts which was her character and the good he appreciated, while the bad he despised. All men are made up of good and bad and carry the two characters with them in every capacity in life. When you are talking with a person of opinions and scientific subjects are not named, the world that sits listening is as wise as it was before. They may have some new ideas but they are like sounding brass; they contain no wisdom that the world is put in possession of. Ask for proofs you get an opinion or ask for bread and you get a stone. A politician will talk all day and night, yet he will never say one word that cannot be found in someone's speech; still he talks of his wisdom. Listen to the priest. He repeats some old story that never had any science or wisdom above opinion and you leave as hungry as you entered. True you may be amused by his talk, so you might in a barroom. The only difference is made by the public opinion; neither advances the science of wisdom.

These two characters appear in the sick; so when they come to me, Satan comes also. Now Satan is error or opinions and his honesty and religion are all hypocrisy, and science knows it. I always address myself to the scientific man. This rouses the dignity of Satan, for he expects to be respected and when he finds he is discovered by me, he assumes a sort of dignity and appears very religious, etc. This is returned by me with a sort of scorn. This contempt often rouses the disease. Then it leaves and I am the persecuted one. For it will rail and call me everything bad, but if it is kept in check by reason, it is modest in its denunciations of me. When I say me, I mean this truth. The world knows no other character than one, so if they speak a truth, it is all the same. Here is the mystery; man as we see him is not the man but the shadow. No one sees the creator of the thing created. You see a man walking, but the man that moves the form that walks, called man, cannot see the man that makes him walk. We see the automaton, but the wisdom cannot be seen for it has no matter. The two men are not seen at all, yet they have an identity and the body is the instrument of both. Everybody contains the two: the father and son. The father is science, the son is matter and opinions; when the father speaks, he speaks through the son. Now when the science is the son, that is the offspring of the father, through the matter or son.

When the child science is born, it is nursed by the son or matter till it comes of age or understanding; then it speaks for itself. But its father being wisdom and its mother being matter, it takes its mother's name. So Adam was the son, wisdom the father, and the science or rib taken from Adam was another offspring, for God saw that it was not good that matter should be alone. Science then came forth and matter called it woman. Here is the generation of man. Adam means earth in Hebrew. As God or wisdom spoke man into existence in this form, he called it Adam or earth. That form of Adam is man, not science. So as God saw that earth was not fit to be alone, he takes from it a higher element, science—the rib and shows it to the earth and the earth calls it woman or science.

I will give another illustration. Every idea that man has is either the offspring of science or error. Each is a character of itself, but as science cannot be seen by error, error does not admit it except as a principle or mystery. Each has its senses and each its life; error has its death, but science never dies. So life is to be wise and happiness is the result of true wisdom. I will try once more to make the above plain. The natural man speaks of man, woman and child; this is the trinity: father, wife and son. But when I speak of the generation of the scientific man, I have nothing to do with error or the natural man; the latter is at enmity with the scientific man. This scientific man is not subject to the man of error nor never can be. Every man is in fact four persons; wisdom is the father and mother of all. When he created Adam or earth, it was without form; but when he formed man out of the earth and breathed into him science, then man became a living soul. So man being of Adam was of the earth, earthy. Now the life of the earth or Adam must come forth. So wisdom caused a sleep in Adam, took the rib or science and explained it to him and he called it woman because she was taken out of man. Therefore, science is the woman; ignorance, the Adam or man.

Here are two characters: science and man and woman, separate from wisdom. Adam says science or woman is bone of my bone and flesh of my flesh. Therefore, shall man or ignorance leave his father or Adam and cleave to science or woman that they may be one flesh or life? The wedding of science and ignorance brings forth a son called error or Cain, which means a possession in Hebrew. Abel was the brother or spiritual son of Science, for Abel in Hebrew means vanity or vapor or breath. Here you have the spiritual and natural son of Adam and Eve: Cain the natural man, Abel the spiritual man or woman. When the two sons brought unto wisdom the fruit of their labors, the wisdom had respect for Abel or science, but for Cain or error, he had no respect. So Cain or error was wroth as all error is with science. Then wisdom says to error, Whom are you wroth with? If you do well, you will be accepted, but if you do evil, sin liveth at your door. While Cain or error and Abel or Science were reasoning together, error rose up as it always does and fells science down or slays it. So when wisdom asks error where science is, it answers, Am I my brother's keeper? Then wisdom says for this act you are cursed or separated from the earth or ignorance which might receive you. So when you investigate or till the ground or matter, it shall bring forth not science but error and thou shalt be a fugitive and vagabond on the earth. This is the character and science would slay it, and wisdom would not have it slain but let it kill itself, so error undisturbed will destroy itself. The death of Abel or science means the smothering or cramping of the truth, as they did with Jesus. And as science cannot be killed, its place is in the hearts of man. It has never risen from the dead or error, but the time will come that it will rise from the dead and there are persons standing here that shall not die or denounce it till they see it coming in the clouds of their minds. Then every scientific eye shall see it and opinions shall flee. Science will then take her place in the world of opinions and opinions will worship it like all other sciences.

Nov. 15, 1861

Religion Analyzed: Part 4–How the Error of Disease Is Made
[LC 1:0441]

All ideas are matter and those that contain danger contain also fear and are of the same class. I will illustrate the differences of disease and show how they are created. A child creeps towards the fire, the heat affects it and the sensation on the child is called fear. There is no wisdom in the sensation, but there is fear. So it creeps nearer and is more affected, but there is no intelligence in the child. At last a sort of intelligence comes, enough to make the child creep out of the fire. Now the burn is called disease. Here is a disease without any intelligence; it is simply the reaction of the act. Give the child wisdom and the fear is gone, for there is no danger. This is one class of diseases, or cause and effect without any wisdom and here is another class. In order to keep the child from getting burned, you tell him the fire will burn him to death if he goes near and frighten the child by telling him stories which he will believe. This makes the child see danger, when it exists only in the mind of his parent, which his parent tells him of to prevent him from running any risk. This danger contains fear and just as you make danger the reaction is fear and disease. Here is where disease commences, in the danger of opinion; the other is not a disease but a phenomenon without intelligence.

You may trace nine-tenths of all disease to danger created by parents when children are small. The religion of this world is the effect of the danger of something of which we know nothing and to keep clear of it is religion. Religion, like fear, is the result of a belief in some idea that contains danger. I will make an illustration that will explain the two kinds of religion, for works are not a religion but a belief is. By faith, you are saved and not of works, lest anyone should boast; but if you believe so and so, you shall be saved and if not, you shall be damned. So religion is a belief and here is the explanation thereof.

Suppose a dozen children were playing and a stone should be seen by one of them coming down directly over their heads and he should show it to the rest. Now down it comes and it frightens them. The children are taught that heaven is up in the skies; don't you suppose that they would think that God sent the stone down to frighten them, if they were in mischief? While they are pondering, some person tells them that they must be good children and obey their parents. The children believe and the priests have made this danger through their ignorance or belief. While they are talking and the priest is giving them good Christian advice, a clap of thunder comes and the lightning strikes a tree. Now they are frightened again and apply to the priest to explain. He tells them the Lord is angry and has sent a thunderbolt to show them that they were not good children. This frightens them. The wind blows and it becomes dark, or perhaps an eclipse of the sun takes place. This is explained in the same way and so on till every phenomenon that could happen is explained. The belief in all the above is admitted as true and this is religion. To believe that, you will believe all the above and ten times as much more, and to repent of everything which the priest says is wrong will gain for you a place in heaven when you die; otherwise you must go to the opposite place. The Christian is one who believes all and so shapes his course as to keep clear of all till death and then he is landed in heaven.

All of the above belongs to the priests. They are the teachers of the young and this nursery is to fit them for another class of hypocrites worse than themselves, the medical faculty. One is sent for to see a child made nervous by the false ideas of the priests. He finds the child laboring under nervous excitement. He feels the pulse and inquires what they have been doing; the answer is nothing except listening to the priests' explanation of the dark day. As the doctor believes just like the priests, he does not make him the author of the trouble but introduces the same subject himself. So looking very grave he says, You have committed a sin against the laws of God or health. For if you expose yourself to the cold, you are liable to take cold, be sick and die of consumption. This makes the patient more frightened. The doctor is sent for again; he finds the patient dangerously sick and says that the brain is affected, that there is a collection of water on the brain and he must die. The minister comes and talks with the child to prepare his mind to die, telling him that he must believe that God will forgive him and receive him to heaven. The minister prays and the friends all weep violently, all exciting the child and then he is told that God will receive him. By this time the child is so nervous that it wants to go to heaven and at last exhausted, he pants and dies. Here is the beginning and ending of the Christian religion. It was born in ignorance, grew up in error and died in the same. This is one side of life where I used to be, but now I have turned over the leaf and will present the religion of Jesus.

While all the above was going on, there was a certain set of infidels who said that the priests did not know any more than they did. But they could not account for the darkness, nor thunder nor water on the brain and did not believe the doctors could. Some a little wiser began to believe that there must be some natural cause for all these things as well as for others that were known. Some began to talk this way. At such a time as this, John came out of the wilderness or darkness and told the people that someone would come who could explain the falling of the stone, etc. So the child Jesus, being of a certain combination prepared by the great truth, would of himself, like all other children, without knowing why he did it, listen to the priests' belief. He could see that it was all inconsistent with wisdom and that it made the people nervous and sick. So he investigated the phenomena and he was often found in the temples disputing with the doctors on these subjects. At the age of thirty, hearing of John, he went to hear him preach, was baptized into his belief and it became so clear to him that the priests and doctors were the cause of nine-tenths of man's misery that the heaven or this truth was opened to him and he saw the true explanation or Holy Ghost; and it came to his mind and he heard the voice of science saying, This is my beloved son in whom I am well pleased. Then he was led up into the wilderness or into all the priests' and doctors' opinions and saw there was nothing but hypocrisy and priestcraft to humbug the people. After he had fairly investigated the whole subject so that he could see that all their misery was their religious belief and the doctors were in league with them, then he came to the conclusion to come out from among them and preach the king of truth or that science that would explain all their troubles. His first act was to take some witnesses with him. So he called on Simon Peter and Andrew, his brother, to follow him and as he went along or talked, others followed him. So Jesus went all about Galilee teaching and curing all manner of disease among the people. And his fame went out through all the country and they brought unto him all sick people to be healed.

Nov. 15, 1861

Religion and Science
[BU 3:1034]

It has generally been supposed that the authors of the Old and New Testaments were inspired to write an account of another world off and apart from this globe. Under this belief strange ideas arose in the minds of men. In the old scriptures is given an account of the formation of a literal earth and the creation of man. Then it goes on to tell how man became so wicked that God caused it to rain forty days and flood the earth, destroying all the inhabitants except Noah and his family, who after the floods dried up came forth and commenced to till the ground. All this story is believed to have a literal meaning and all who question this belief are called infidels or deists. Now after Noah and his family began populating the earth, you see an account of the generations of Noah. Then the world became wicked again, but God promised not to destroy it by water a second time but by fire. Here follows a description of the final destruction of this earth and its inhabitants by fire and a promise from God of a new heaven and earth where there shall be no more death nor weeping, where all shall worship God day and night, where the wicked shall be destroyed and God shall reign eternally. Now this is explained literally. It is believed that all this was communicated to Moses on the Mount and that God came down and talked to Moses, giving him a code of laws or belief that man must accept in order to gain a place in this new heaven. This theory God caused Moses to write down and it was called the commandments of God, given to Moses for the happiness of the children of Israel, to be taught to them while he was leading them through the land of Egypt into the land of Canaan.

This belief was to counteract some false idea that the people had, for they were very ignorant and full of all sorts of superstition. There were no principles regulating their conduct towards each other but might was right. The strong oppressed the weak and there was nothing to prevent their perpetrating any abuses. It was Moses' aim to stop these abuses and free his people from their bondage and degradation. So he instituted a more just and liberal code of laws attaching penalties to abuses that he could not prevent and putting restrictions on men to bring about a better state of society. He did not try to instruct the people but only sought to bring them under his standard by which their oppression would be lessened and their condition improved. Neither did he attempt to establish any kind of worship or belief about God, but his regulations appealed to the interests of men and were as good as the people could carry out. They made man more cunning and crafty and overbearing, but they did not analyze motives, leaving them as arising from the natural world. This state of things continued for a long time. Religious doctrines never entered into men's heart, but the wise men were engaged in developing the mind of man. All evils that were suffered were from their acts and their acts were the offspring of their belief and their belief was made by the leading spirits of the age.

If the person who gave direction gave it intelligently so that it could not be bettered, then the world was wiser or better for their opinions. But if directed by ignorance and superstition, then the people had to suffer for their belief; for our happiness or misery is in our belief. Now as the belief of the people did not embrace any kind of a religious opinion in regard to another world, they could not get sick on that subject. The evils that troubled them were of this world and confined to the laws of Moses. These made them nervous but did not create disease. Now as truth progresses, it has to contend with error. And as Moses put restrictions on the people they murmured and complained. So in order to keep the people in subjection, the leaders had to invent all sorts of beliefs. Therefore, prophets were introduced and the priests and prophets led the people, but truth or science is not under the control of either. It moves along like the rising of the tide. It is the only enemy that priests and doctors have to contend with, for it is death to both, and life and happiness to all who get it. Happiness is what follows our belief and the life of the priest and doctor is in their belief and their interest is in the misery of their belief. For if the people have no belief, they would have no disease, as disease is their belief. So it is the intent of the above classes to keep the people posted up on all their beliefs to insure them a good living.

One of the old honest prophets knew this trick and said that the prophets prophesied falsely and the priests ruled by their means and the people love to have it so and what would they do in the end thereof? (Jer. 5:31.) As science progressed, the priests had to give way, for there never was one particle of knowledge or progression in either of the above theories. Science only leads the world in true philosophy, never making man sick or diseased. Disease is not the offspring of science but of error, and as priests and doctors have taken that part of philosophy into their hands, all other sciences in regard to all other facts have let the science of life alone, supposing it to be in the hands of scientific men. All knowledge of the scientific world has had this error to contend with and the priests and doctors have been driven from their ground and have taken their stand just where public opinion places them. They do not lead science, but science leads them. There was a time when they led but as their craft became so apparent to scientific minds they had to yield. If anyone will just follow along the progress of the development of the human mind since the laws of Moses, they will see a steady progress of science and an annihilation of priestcraft. Error has assumed more forms than the colors of the rainbow and to every form the misery is shown in its believers. It has shown itself in all kinds of superstition but it has had to yield to more liberal belief.

All error in the Bible has been modified by the wars of its own party. Its opposers were of that class of minds that could tear down if it could not build up, but in the tearing, science made some progress. For when rogues fall out honest men get their due.

All new theories in the Old Testament were illustrated by some phenomena that the people were acquainted with. So the science advanced and showed itself in some leading spirit of its age, as in Noah: his theory was represented by a flood, for it swept away all the old world or superstition of his age.   Then Moses' theory was leading the children of Israel out of Egyptian darkness into the land of truth or science. But as Moses never entered the land of science, he saw for others what he never was permitted to enjoy. So science crept along in the hands of some of the prophets and other theories are represented by altars and the science of truth was the sacrifice. There was Balaam; his theory had false prophets who knew just as much as some physicians in our day. His ass spoke and so do such now. When Joshua showed the absurdities of the people's theory, they left it and followed him, so the magicians and sorcerers and all such deceivers had to fall back for the true science.

In the case of Nebuchadnezzar, the magicians and sorcerers had complete power over the masses and as the king was in advance of them, he saw that all their pretended knowledge was false. When he was sick and sent for his magicians and sorcerers to interpret his dream, they said, as the quacks of these days, Tell us how you feel, or your dream, and we will tell you what the matter is or give the interpretation. But he said, No, tell me my dream or how I feel, first. This they could not do and complained at such an unreasonable request. And when Daniel told him his dream or how he felt, these magicians put him into a fiery furnace, which means they put him through a course of questions which he answered, showing knowledge superior to theirs. This made them angry and they tried, as the doctors do now, to put it down with contempt. They did not stop the investigations for when Darius came into power, they tried to smother this truth and persuaded the king to pass a law that no person such as Daniel should practice. But Daniel took no notice of it and he was cast into the lion's den or company and when the meat was thrown in to test the science, these lions' mouths were shut and Daniel came off conqueror.

Thus truth has had to fight error step by step and the truth has been revealed to the wise and opposed by fools and the ignorant; so wisdom crept along till the time of John, the Baptist. Here was a new development of truth, far above anything reached yet. It held out a new motive to man, placing him above the superstition of the world or error. At the time of John, the world had been embracing false doctrines, not in regard to another world but to this world. They had a vague idea of a world after death and the priests, to strengthen their authority and hold on the people, invented all sorts of ideas, pretending to be empowered with authority to pardon their sins. They held out to the people that the dead should rise at the end of this natural world. All this was not taught by Moses but crept into the church, which itself is only a sort of popular religious opinion and carries sway in men's minds even to this day. The church contained the belief of the people and as science was developed, the priests lost power over the people. And at the time Jesus appeared, they acted as doctors and cured the diseases of the people. When John appeared his teaching struck at the root of all this error and he said, The axe of science is laid at the root of the trees or theories and every tree or theory that cannot sustain ideas must be hewn down or destroyed. The fire of truth would burn them up. Their beliefs made people sick, just according to the penalty attached to the crime or belief. For instance, the Jews believed that eating pork would produce scrofula; therefore they would not eat it and those who did eat could not help being disturbed by this belief. Where this error started I cannot say. Only, it was to satisfy the ignorant, so they would be better off not to eat the meat. This was for the poor at first and the aristocracy took advantage of it, just as the priests lay restrictions on the people but do as they like themselves. So you see scrofula was the result of their belief and the remedy was total abstinence from pork; but as priesthood went down and their theory was exploded, the idea that pork produced scrofula was absurd. This last belief was worse than the first, for it made this disease a thing independent of pork and therefore the people were afraid of it. Here you see one disease let loose in society. Now to get rid of this disease, mankind must get nervous and wrought up to a very high state of excitement, ready to embrace any idea that the priests could invent. And as the priests lost their hold on the people, medical men were introduced. And at the time of Jesus, it was the complaint that the poor paid all they had to the priests and doctors and got no relief.

As the doctors got control of the popular mind, they invented diseases to humbug the people as the priests had done. At last they made a sort of compromise, the priests taking the souls of men into their charge and the doctors their bodies and between them both they almost destroyed body and soul. This was the state of society at the time of Jesus' appearance. John saw all this humbug and warned the people against this pretense and foretold that someone would come who would put an end to all this priestcraft and doctoring. He did not know that disease was all in the mind, but thought that the mind had a great influence upon it. Jesus hearing of John and knowing that he taught a new theory went to hear him explain his ideas. This was called baptism. So John baptized or explained to Jesus his ideas of priestcraft and its effect on the mind, but its remedy had never occurred to him. When Jesus heard John's thought or was baptized, as he came from the water or understood his ideas, the heaven or truth was opened unto him and its voice descending from God or Science, said, This truth is the Son of God or Science.

Then he was led up into the mountains of his belief to be tempted by the errors of the world for the people were all ready to embrace him as king and the temptation he had to go through was against his interest as a man, for preaching this truth and opposing all the errors of his age was not a very pleasant thing. But he overcame them all and took his stand in opposition to all the world, denouncing the priests and doctors as a set of quacks who opposed the people, bound burdens on them and robbed widows and orphans. This made them sick and nervous and the doctors came in for their share. Thus they suffered by these blind guides. Here is the difference between Jesus' ideas and the rest of the world. The belief of the world was confined to matter. They had never been taught that the senses were a separate identity from the body's identity but they believed that man as you see him is all there is of him and when the body ceased to act it was dead and this ended man till the resurrection at the end of the world. Some had a different belief but they were all confined to this world.

To keep man in subjection to the laws, certain penalties were attached to every act, thus putting restrictions on the people for the benefit of society. These restrictions were called burdens and the people complained. They had no idea of right and wrong as we have now, but their only interest was in keeping clear of the laws or lash. If a person wanted anything belonging to his neighbor, he did not reason as we should, but like the beast, sought how he could get it without being caught. They reasoned like any person running a risk where dollars and cents are concerned. Not that their happiness or misery was involved in the act, but how to get what they wanted. How shall I get it was the question, not is it right or wrong, but shall I get caught and if so, how much shall I have to pay. So it was a speculation. The happiness was in stealing and evading the punishment and the misery was in paying the fine. This was the whole story and all their study was to take advantage of each other. Their religion was their laws which were all confined to their lives. So when they died they were free from the law and death ended their religious opinions and everything else. Therefore the living mourned for the dead and often hired others to help them mourn. Not that the dead knew anything, but that the living lost something. Neither was this mourning because they loved them, for they would kill anyone to make a little money. In the case of selling Joseph to the Ishmaelites, they cared nothing about his life. Money was their God. So it was with Judas. He cared nothing for Jesus' life; money was his object, for he had not yet the Christ or truth that Jesus taught.

Now where does Jesus differ from all other teachings? In every particular. His belief is founded on truth and is not of man, but of God or Science. Therefore, his priesthood was not of this world and contained none of the church forms or ideas but taught that misery would follow our acts. His theory was that the senses were not a part of our body and that they were affected by our belief, their happiness or misery being in our belief, which belief was matter and could be changed by a power independent of itself. The science was to put people in mind of this fact, so it was necessary to produce cures on the people independent of anything but his word, for his words were the destruction of matter or disease. This showed man that his belief made his trouble, so he warned them against the bread or the doctrines of the Scribes and Pharisees, for they made them sick.

This was his mission—to show that if they robbed or otherwise injured their neighbor, rendering an equivalent would never cure the evil, but that their neighbor like themselves had eternal life. And just as they measured out it should be measured to them again, for action and reaction are equal and the knowledge of the result is in the thought or idea. For instance, if you want to put your hand in the fire, the knowledge of the result is in the thought. So it is in every act or desire of our lives. If we desire to get something from our neighbor without returning an equivalent, the answer is in the desire and the misery is in the answer. It will be as certain to follow, as a weight thrown in the air is sure to return with as much force as it received. Jesus tried to teach this and that was all, for his other world was this truth—that although they destroyed his identity of a body of flesh and blood, this Christ or science would exist and could take a form again. This truth is what he strove to teach his disciples and when he was about to be betrayed into the hands of his enemies, he sat down and performed his last act by talking over this new theory.

When he broke the truth and gave it to his disciples, he said, Eat this bread or theory for this is my Christ or truth. And then he said, Take this cup, or the result of our belief, which is the life of this truth or Christ and as long as you are interested and think about it, you do it in remembrance of me or Christ, till the Science is established on earth as it is in heaven. This was his last conversation with his disciples. Now how long did his disciples continue in this belief and how much did they understand of what he said? How much of a reform did he effect through them according to his desire? Time has shown. The very moment he was arrested they left him and denied their action with him.

Judas had an idea of what he taught but it did not penetrate to the destruction of his old belief. His senses were in the two beliefs and when Christ or Jesus' belief was in him, his old belief of dollars and cents was present, prompting him to make a little money. So he betrayed Jesus into the hands of his enemies.

Jesus saw and knew this at the time he was talking over his belief in the form of a supper. He saw that Judas was honest but ignorant of Christ when he said, He that dippeth his finger in the cup shall betray me. Judas tried to understand more than all the rest and thought he did. Jesus knew that he did not understand and knew that when the time came for him to stand up and defend the truth he would shrink. This was to him perfectly plain and so it was in regard to them all. The fact was that Jesus taught a new doctrine so hard to understand that it was impossible to teach it to the people. The disciples thought they understood it, but when asked to prove it they were unable to explain, and so denied him. But the females who always have more sagacity than the men, though of more delicate physical structure and of silent influence, understood him. They were the ark wherein were deposited the tablets of stone or Moses' laws and all of the rules of the world in regard to spiritual knowledge that the wisdom of men do not contain. So they had more to do with the crucifixion of Jesus. Then women bore the ark in Moses' day. They have always been a sort of reservoir to hold the new ideas that the world has brought forth in their ignorance. They are the first to catch any new ideas and the last to let them go till every particle of truth is drawn out, as the humming bee finds honey in the flower where the wasp sees none. Now at the time when Jesus was put to death, he had been teaching this truth, that the senses of men were not confined to this body, but could act apart from it, and what a person believed, he, that is the power that governs the senses, could put his senses into and then the senses would be affected just according to his belief. So that our happiness or misery is in our belief. This is what he tried to prove and did, but the disciples did not understand it till he put this part of it into practice. Then their minds were changed. They saw him dead; to them this was all there was, the end of all men, as they were taught. Now to see him rise again was the introduction of the new heaven or belief. This was a very exciting thing. If he did not rise, then their talk was all in vain and all Jesus said went for nothing. The people could eat and drink as they had done and there was no proof that the senses were not really confined to flesh and blood.

This of course excited mankind and this was the great problem to be solved, but how it was to take place was a mystery. So various opinions came up as to how the dead should rise. Now in all this excitement there were some enthusiastic persons, who never get anything right except what they cannot help. These often try to help a matter on, as the Spiritualists help on the communications from the dead when they are produced with difficulty. It was so with this problem. There were those who did not understand that Jesus never alluded to his flesh and blood but to his senses (which was all that ever had any life), that they should take form and be seen by his disciples to prove that all men had the same senses as Jesus had. This they could not understand, so they did what all crazy-headed enthusiasts would have done. They stole the body of Jesus away, for fear that the body of Jesus should not rise and then all this new theory would be exploded. So when the Christ or Science took form and showed itself to the people they were afraid and trembled. This was natural, but when assured it was the Christ taking the form of the man Jesus, they believed. This would lead some to suppose that the crucifixion was all a humbug and that Jesus was not dead. So they went to the sepulchre to see if the body was there. Now if Jesus' body had been there, as it ought to have been, then the problem would have been solved, but lo! and behold! the body was gone! This left the people in the dark and gave them a chance to call up doubts whether he was really dead or not and these doubts which exist to this day commenced the controversy on that subject.

Paul speaks of it and it has never been explained if these enthusiasts had left the body of Jesus in the tomb, there was proof enough, to establish the truth of Jesus' doctrine: that the senses could exist independent of this idea or body. Now if the senses exist independent of the body, then the body is nothing but an idea that the senses are attached to. So when the senses are attached to anything, they are a part of the same. When we attach the senses to anything that has life, its life or identity has around it an odor or heat that is the prison that the senses are confined in. And to liberate the senses is to destroy the prison or atmosphere, that they may act freely. As all our unhappiness arises from our belief, it is necessary that we should understand what influence is controlling us. We are told that God brought to man all living creatures to see what Adam would call them and he gave names to all of them so that to every sensation made on the mind, the senses had to give a right explanation in order that man should not be led away by false explanations. The science is to separate the error from the truth or the law from the gospel.

The laws of Moses have passed through many modifications and some have been repealed, others modified and amended to suit society, up to this day. The laws of Jesus are the same today as they were when they fell from his lips and in all his teaching no word ever escaped him that put any restrictions on man. If Jesus ever gave an opinion, he gave it as such not as a truth but as an opinion of the man Jesus, but when he spoke of Christ, he spoke no restrictions or commands. I will give a few of the teachings of Christ, showing the difference between his opinions of mankind and the religious opinions of the world. These last never imposed any moral restraint: an eye for an eye and a tooth for a tooth. Self was the ruling passion and all laws were made with the idea of restraining the people to keep them under so that the rich could ride over the poor. This made them jealous and crafty. The priests never instructed the people in the idea of taking care of themselves, but bound burdens on them in the form of beliefs. These beliefs embraced all kinds of evil spirits. This made them nervous and according to my belief would make them create in their minds all kinds of evil spirits, thus making them more nervous. This was worse than the old Mosaic law, for that put the misery in the penalty and their penalties only made the misery.

The priests found that their laws were not sufficient to lead the people, so they invented evil spirits or ghosts to frighten them so that they could control them. I will show you how to form an evil spirit and how it will get hold of you. Take a child whose mind is all right.

You have something that the child wants and the law says if I take it I must pay four times its value. Now the child wants it and contrives every way to get it. This makes it nervous and it grows more and more nervous to have its desire gratified. It knows no principle of right or wrong and thinks it has a right to whatever it sees. It is under no restriction except the law and this law is of no force to the child. So some evil or ghost is invented to frighten the child into submission. Now the introduction of this last evil has given rise to more evils than all the laws of Moses, for then if a person wanted to steal anything, the punishment was in the detection or fine. If the child stole a thing of no value the law could not take cognizance of that, so they were obliged to get up some other humbug to keep the young in subjection. This brought out all the talent of the wise who invented all kinds of evil spirits or introduced the old Egyptian errors into the world again and now you will see relics of Egyptian superstition.

Moses tried to free his people from it, but as his laws never reasoned at all, the people obeyed them through fear. So the world has been humbugged even to this day by blind guides leading the blind. Ignorance and superstition have invented all sorts of beliefs and as the senses are something independent of our belief we put them into our belief and all the misery that we suffer is the heat or odor that arises from our belief. This heat or odor is matter and our senses are in it like a person in prison. And when I come into this prison or atmosphere it affects me just as it does the person who is in it. This atmosphere is the prison or place of torment and this is heated up by their belief. So when I change their belief the fire of ignorance or the heat subsides and their senses are relieved from a burden that binds them down.

As disease is a belief, it has never entered into their minds or senses that their belief is the cause of their trouble. Let this be made plain to the people and then they will not say one to another, Know you this truth! but it will be so plain that any person of ordinary ability can see it. These beliefs will give way to Science and superstition and bigotry will be driven out of the minds of men and the Bible will stand on the rock of Science. Then when a person undertakes to say to you, Believe this or that, the people will say to such, Show me your belief by your works to the sick, as Jesus showed his belief in his day. Then all hypocrisy and deception will be driven from the land. The minds of men will take a more elevated stand and men will be just what their works show them to be. Then when a doctor comes to you and you have to tell him all your feelings and your health is in his belief, you will see that his belief is not one whit better than the priests, who tell you a story about what they have not the slightest evidence of in truth. Then the people will take their beliefs into their own hands and will purge their minds from all these false superstitions that lay burdens on them and bind them on their shoulders in the form of rheumatism, neuralgia and a thousand other diseases for the benefit of the profession.

The people will see that God never bound anyone, only by love for one another and this love knows no ill-will towards its neighbor. It calls no one master but one and that is God or Science and Science never made man or child unhappy to know it. It sometimes makes them unhappy in getting it. This is where all the trouble is. Men who are lazy would rather give an opinion on a scientific subject than to investigate it. All religious opinions are embraced without the slightest investigation, for if they try to investigate, it makes them nervous. This makes them create in their mind the identity of their belief. They attach their senses to their ideas and their misery is in their belief. So it has always been; men would always rather give an opinion than investigate a principle. Phenomena have always taken place which the wisdom of the world has undertaken to explain. So when such take place, they are handed over to the wise men to explain as though God's laws depended on man's wisdom or intelligence for an explanation.

All new theories are opposed by the wise who never admit them, till the truth of them is so apparent that their opinions are not wanted for their success. Then they come in and steal the thunder, claim the discovery, cheating the inventor out of his birth right by pressing him till he, like Esau, will sell all for a mess of pottage. This is human nature. It was just so in Jesus' days. The priests and doctors tried to buy him out but Jesus told them that to put his ideas or truths in theirs would be like putting new wine in old bottles, and their bottles being of leather would burst and the wine would run out. To the priests he said that their theory was like an old worn garment and to put his truth into theirs would be like mending an old garment with new cloth. It would tear out and make the rend wider. So when they saw that they could not do anything with him and that he was going to make his theory or doctrine popular, they were afraid and said, Our craft is in danger. So they got the people enraged by telling lies and representing him as their enemy while he was their best friend. They cried, Crucify him, for our craft is in danger!

The silversmiths would lose their chance of selling their gods, for his ideas struck at all idolatry. So they crucified the man Jesus, thinking that they were destroying the Christ, but when this same Christ appeared again, they were afraid. Jesus' belief was very simple but the people's superstition has put a false construction on it and it was a stumbling block to the Jews and to the Greeks, foolishness. But truth proves itself.

It was then and is now believed that Jesus was trying to prove another world apart from this. Now there is not the slightest evidence that he ever hinted at a world independent of man's senses. On the contrary, all his acts went to show that he never harbored such an idea. I will now state what I believe Jesus' belief was and the people may take it for what it is worth. Jesus never believed in any world at all as the people do now. The old world was the old beliefs of the Old Testament and no one believes that the writers of that refer to anything but their beliefs, for their own safety; for at death all was ended. Jesus believed that our senses were not a part of this natural body; that death was an unbelief and that the senses lived. So if the people could understand that their senses lived, then death was swallowed up in victory and that belief vanished.

This was all taught as doctrine. This if believed would put away all superstition and upset all forms and priestcraft, so they said, Crucify him! It would not do to have such a fellow among us. And after the deed was done, the priests and doctors gave a turn to public opinion and explained Jesus' ideas on their own ground, and the people could not see the cheat but embraced it. So what is religion now? It is about as near Jesus' ideas as democracy is near the old-fashioned republicanism of Jefferson's day. And if the disciples were here now, hearing the ideas advanced, it would be as new to them as their ideas would be to the people in our days. Religion like politics is undergoing a change all the time and has just about as much to do with enlightening the minds of the men as political parties. It is like a sort of irritation to keep up investigation, like any error. The church is good in its place and like laws will act upon the simple and ignorant till they are ready to embrace Christ's truth of doing to another as you would that another should do to you. As this is understood, the religion of man goes out of fashion. But it will be a long time, for they have decked it up like a fashionable saloon equal to Solomon's temple.

If Jesus was here now he would not be permitted to talk in the churches. And if he had the privilege he would not find that class of people that he associated with when on earth, for they can't attend meetings; it is too expensive. It takes quite a sum to hire seats for a whole family so only one or two can afford to be religious; the rest have to stay at home or go to a cheaper kind. Like saloons, there are all kinds of religions to suit customers and like doctors, they want to make something by their profession. So you see it is the same as it was in Christ's day. They have turned the houses of the Lord into houses of merchandise and fancy goods and preach for doctrines the commands of men. They thus show that there is not one particle of truth in all they say, for if it was true it would not change and religion like all other fashions changes every year, showing it does not contain one single true idea or one atom of science. Now let Christ or truth be preached: that man's senses will always exist; that he is just what he makes himself and that his happiness is in his belief and his belief contains his character. It must be taught that man's act are governed by his belief, his happiness or misery being the fruits of his belief. His belief is the two worlds. To be in ignorance or error is in one world, misery and pain being the fruits. Science and truth is the other and happiness and peace is the reward. So man has these two worlds in him and he is the subject of the one he obeys and God rewards everyone according to his acts. I find no allusion to any world independent of man's senses, only in the brain of a superstitious world.

1860–Summer–

Religion for the Well and the Religion for the Sick, The
[LC 2:0673]

It is customary for the clergy to open the Bible, read a chapter, make a prayer, and then after reading a passage as a text, preach a sermon. This is the fashion of the day, and everyone who preaches from the same text explains it according to his views, as though his explanation was of some value to man. Suppose a number of persons who are sick and in pain sit listening to preaching; instead of receiving any spiritual food or drink to cool their feverish tongue, they get nervous and are told to be reconciled to all that happens and not complain of their suffering, so they leave the church more nervous than they entered it. Now was this the case with the preaching of Jesus and his disciples? No, their preaching was from some wrong impression that the people had in regard to their health. Jesus never preached to the well. The priests of his day preached to them to make them religious, and when they got a convert, they made him ten times more miserable than before. This is the same in our day. All sermons are preached to make men more religious, and when they have succeeded, men are ten times more liable to disease.

Jesus opposed such works as the works of darkness, and I oppose this sort of religion as the invention of man and shall show that every word they say is false and contains not a word of Christ or truth. Jesus says a tree is known by its fruits. If I show that the fruits of religion come from a corrupt tree, then it ought to be hewn down. Everyone will admit that when a minister preaches from a text, he gives his opinion as to what it means, and his opinions make up his religious discourse, the fruit of it is the good it does to the hearers. Everyone knows that opinions are arbitrary or a belief without wisdom, so how can the fruits coming from a religious opinion be anything but bad? It must be so, for every person is responsible for his opinions and must be affected by them either for good or evil. All religion is arbitrary and was opposed by Jesus, for he had nothing to say to those who were without religion, for he came to save the lost house of Israel. You will find that all his disciples were from the church and religious, being Jews. So, being a Jew himself, his remarks were to his own people and everything was for the benefit of the suffering sick, who had been robbed of their health and happiness by the religion of the priests and left like the prodigal son, to eat the husks and crumbs of their own labor or wisdom or common sense.

This kind of food was to the priests and religious people a dry morsel as it is now. If a person undertakes to question the opinions of the priests and doctors and to think for themselves, such a person is denounced by both classes and their wisdom laughed at and ridiculed as dry food and worthless. As I said at first, all preaching is religious but not of the religion of Jesus. It was the very religion he opposed, for he saw that it contained nothing but opinions that were forced upon the people, making them sick and unhappy. Jesus' religion was Christ or truth, not opinions. So when he spoke the truth, he spoke God or Wisdom and that would burn up the priests' opinions and destroy the misery that followed them. So all his religion was to the sick, made so by the priests. The sick are the only ones who are in danger, for if a person is not sick, he needs no physician. So to make anyone sick is to get him in danger of something. If you cannot make him believe he has a disease, you can make him believe his soul is in danger of being lost. This is the same. One is an effectual as the other; either makes a man miserable and is the effect of our belief. When Jesus commanded his disciples to go forth and teach all men and cure all diseases, he never told them to go to the well and preach the doctrine of the Scribes and Pharisees but to go to the lost sheep or those who had been made sick by the priest, to call on them and cast out their corrupt ideas that they got from the doctors. So by their fruits they were to be known, and instead of making the young sick and crazy by false doctrines, they showed the absurdity of their religion and expounded the living truth which broke in pieces their opinions.

Their test came when they had something to perform; for instance, when Paul went to Athens, his text came up by the state of society. He saw that their religion was all vanity and it made the people sick and wicked, so he said, I perceive that in all things you are too superstitious or religious. You often hear this text preached from Acts 17:22-23. "I found an altar with this inscription, To the unknown God. Whom therefore ye ignorantly worship him declare I unto you." Paul knew the people were very religious, for when he was a religious man, he was very religious and persecuted all who disbelieved in his religion. But when he saw the truth or Christ, it lit up his wisdom so that he saw that all his religion was of man and he condemned it as superstition, etc.

Religious worship is all the invention of man; there is not one particle of the wisdom of Christ in it. It is only the superstition of the old church that Jesus opposed. Jesus had got rid of his religion before he undertook to preach the Christ or truth. This is the difference: one teaches what he believes about something he knows nothing of, and if he succeeds in convincing others of this belief, this is religion. They are convinced of all kinds of errors and are put under a great many restrictions so that fears of something horrible get them nervous. This is called religion, and their feelings are the fruits. Therefore religion is to make men more miserable than before and this is always so, although at times it may seem different. Shall we do evil that good may come? Now let truth be truth but every man or opinion a liar. The idea of opinions being true is what causes all the controversy. All medical skill is based on this sandy foundation. Religion is based on the same, so when minds of wisdom blow and the waves of truth beat upon the house of opinion, its foundation is washed away and it falls.

Science, like rain, has been dropping upon superstition or religion until it is nearly crumbled to pieces. And as the tide of wisdom sweeps along the shores of superstition, it will wash out the errors and leave the shores of time clear from the rocks and ledges of religious bigotry. So when the wind of life springs up, the soul will glide away down the stream of life to the great ocean of wisdom, there to float free from all harm till time shall be no more. You may say that this time may never come. I will answer in the words of Jesus spoken on a similar occasion. As in the day of Noah, they were eating and drinking in heathen superstition and the floods of wisdom came and those that entered into this truth were saved; so shall it be now. The heavens or minds are black with error and the sun or wisdom gives no light or truth. The stars or teachers fall from the heaven and the powers of their theories are shaken. Now as this truth cometh from the east and shineth to the west, so shall this great wisdom come and thou that understandest shall enter in and be saved from the evil that follows the belief of the priests and doctors. The truth shall come in the clouds of error, and every eye of wisdom shall see it, and it shall sit on the throne in the belief of man where it will judge the world and separate the truth from the error. Then every theory of man, based on an opinion, shall fall and the Son of God or Science shall reign on the earth as it does in heaven; then there will be a new heaven or science and a new earth or belief, for the old theory of opinions shall be burned up by Science.

Truth and wisdom shall reign till error shall be known as a separate thing from wisdom. Wisdom or Science shall test all opinions, and when a man gives an opinion, it will be taken as such and truth as truth. Religion will then give away to a higher wisdom that will prove itself as Jesus proved his wisdom when on earth.

Jesus was the founder of this great truth and his field was the mind of man. His labor was not among the well or in any known science, but it was with the sick, and his sermon was to correct the error that made the people sick. Therefore all he said was to destroy religion because religion was a sin, based on an opinion. If a person can show where a sermon corrects any error that the sick have so as to relieve them from any suffering, then I will admit the preacher is a follower of Jesus. Jesus never preached without having some object to obtain. But you may go to the church forever and gaze on the dead bodies of sin and error and offer up prayers to this common God, and it will never take away sin and error. But once in the end of these things, the truth will come out and explain all and the sick will be made better; but never will the truth shine till error is shown up in its true character and its cloven foot of ignorance is seen. Then it will cease to be error to mankind.

April 1862

Religion in Disease
[LC 1:0491]

The question is often asked why I talk about religion and quote Scripture while I cure the sick. My answer is that sickness being what follows a belief and all beliefs contain disease, the belief contains the evil which I must correct in order to cure the patient; and as I do this a chemical change takes place in the mind. Disease is an error for which the only remedy is truth. The fear of what will come after death is the beginning of man's troubles, for he tries to get some evidence that he will be happy and, fearing that he will never arrive at that state of happiness, he is miserable. Another fear is the chance of losing his life which is constantly multiplied as the medical faculty creates new diseases which, like the locusts of Egypt, are in everything we eat and drink. What I shall try to show is that these beliefs do really produce the very evil we are afraid of here.

We are taught to believe that if we pray we shall receive an answer to our prayer. A superstitious person, believing this, is ready to believe he may be punished by prayer for someone may pray that God may remove him. Each army prays that God will direct the weapons that will slay their enemies. In Biblical times did not God answer the prayer of those who wished to destroy their enemies and did they not die? These facts prove that what we really believe may follow. We really believe in disease and as we create what we believe, disease is the result of our belief. People never seem to have thought of the fact that they are responsible to themselves for their belief. Therefore, to analyze their beliefs is to know themselves, which is the greatest study of man. All theories for the happiness of man contain more misery than happiness, either directly or indirectly. Destroy the beliefs of man and leave him where God left him to work out his own happiness by his own wisdom. One-half of the diseases arise from a false belief in the Bible. It may seem strange that the belief in the Bible affects us but it is so for every belief affects us more or less and I now propose to show that diseases are the effects of our belief directly or indirectly.

I will relate a case where the religious belief affected the patient and caused the disease. The lady was aged. She was so lame and bound down that she could hardly rise from her chair, and could take only a step by the aid of her crutches, feeling so heavy that she dare not step. In this condition she had lived some years, and all the happiness she had was in reading and thinking on the Bible. She was a Calvinist Baptist and by her belief she had imprisoned her senses in a creed so small and contracted that she could not stand upright or move ahead. Here in this room of Calvin her senses were laid, wrapped in her creed; here she was confined by the narrow limits of her own beliefs, yet in this room was Christ or Science, trying to burst the bars and break through the bands and rise from the dead.

She labored to be free from the bands and no one came to her relief. When she would ask for an explanation of some passage the answer would be a stone, and then she would hunger for the bread of life. At last in her misery she called upon me and I found her as I have stated. I knew not what caused her trouble. She thought it was from a fall, but this I knew was not the case. After explaining how she felt, I told her her trouble was caused by a series of excitements from studying upon what she could not reconcile. She thought upon religious subjects, and not seeing the Scriptures clearly, her mind became cloudy and stagnated. This showed itself on the body by her heavy and sluggish feeling which would terminate in paralysis. She said she could not understand how her belief could make her so numb. I explained this fact to her as follows.

I said to her, You will admit I have described your feelings. "Certainly," she replied. What do you suppose Jesus meant by these words, "A little while I am with you, then I go my way," and "You shall seek me and where I go ye cannot come." Do you believe that he went to Heaven? "Yes," she replied. Now let me tell you what I think he meant. I had told her before that in order to cure her I must make a change in the fluids and produce a healthy circulation, for she by her belief had produced a stagnation of her system. You have admitted that I have told you your feelings. Then I was with you as Christ was with his disciples in sympathy, and when I go my way I go into health and am not in sympathy with your feelings. Therefore, where I go you cannot come, for you are in Calvin's belief and I am in health.

This explanation produced an instantaneous sensation, and a change came over her mind. This mortal put on immortality or health and she exclaimed in joy, "This is a true answer to my thought." I continued explaining Scripture, as I shall describe, and a complete change took place. She walked without her crutches.

Her case is so singular an example of my practice that I will give the substance of my reasoning. It seemed as though all her feelings were in her belief, and if I wished to give an idea of them, I would make a comparison from the Bible; therefore, when I wished to convey the idea that I was with her, I took a passage in the New Testament to explain my being with her and being away from her; she was, as it were, dead in sin or error and to bring her to life or truth was to raise her from the dead, for she believed that she never would be well till God had raised her from the dead. I quoted the resurrection of Christ and applied it to her own Christ or health, and produced a powerful effect upon her. I commenced in this way.

Your belief is the sepulcher in which your wisdom is confined. The world is your enemy. Your opinions and ideas are your garments, and the truth is the Holy Ghost or angel which will roll away the stone and heal your grief. The God in you will burst the bands of your creed and you will rise from the dead or your religious belief into the truth. You will then walk into the sitting room and the friends will start as though you were a spirit, and you will say, "Hath a spirit flesh and bones as you see me have? Give me a chair." Then the friends will inquire where the Christ is. The truth will say, "She has risen from her religious body of sin and death and gone to meet her friends in Heaven." Then comes the false ideas, and as they cannot see the truth, the body being changed to them is gone and they report it stolen. You leave the body of belief and take that of science and rise into health. This is the resurrection of the dead.

This with other explanations produced such an effect on the lady that she could rise from her chair as quickly as any person of her age.

The natural world is full of figures that may illustrate man's belief. The silkworm spins out his life and wrapping himself in his labor dies. The infidel and brutal man reason but they do the same. The caterpillar is a good illustration of the natural man groping in the dark, guided by a superior wisdom that prompts his acts. When his days are numbered, wrapped in the mantle of this earth he lies down to sleep the sleep of death; but the wisdom that brings forth the butterfly also develops its science. In order that truth may come forth, error must be destroyed; and science groping in darkness bursts into light and rises from the dead as the butterfly, not the caterpillar.

All men have sinned or embraced beliefs so all must die to their belief. Disease is a belief; health is in wisdom. So as man dies to his belief he lives in wisdom. My theory is to destroy death or belief and bring life and wisdom into the world; therefore, I come to the sick not to save their beliefs or life in disease but to destroy it. And he that loses his belief for wisdom will find his health or life.

I will now give what I conceive to be the ideas of Jesus on the resurrection. I address my words to the sick for I cannot make illustrations to the well, for they are not affected by their belief. According to the Scriptures sin is a transgression of the law. What law? It must be of God, for it says, "The soul that sinneth shall surely die." So sin is death, and the law to which man is liable whose penalty is death is God's law. Therefore, God is supposed to make laws to punish man for his thought, for every idle word is to be accounted for. This law breeds countless evils and it is the part of wisdom to correct it; for to believe that God is the author of our evils is as absurd as to believe that he made the remedies and laws before he made man. How often do you hear this remark: "There is a remedy for every disease." When we ask what it is, we are referred to some root or herb, but no hint is ever given that disease can be cured by the power of truth.

Did Jesus employ such remedies? On the contrary, had the sick whom he cured tried them? He said: "My words are life eternal, and by my words I cure all manner of diseases." If disease was a thing that required a chemical change, Jesus must have been ignorant to undertake to talk to it. If the palsied limb was the thing to be cured, why did he say to the owner, Stretch forth thy hand, and immediately it was made whole? Why did he not apply some remedies to the arm? The fact was that Jesus knew that the arm was not the cause but the effect, and he addressed himself to the intelligence, and applied his wisdom to the cause. He "spake as never a man spake," for he spoke to the cause, but when man speaks he gives an opinion. All the acts of Jesus were based on truth, while man acts from an opinion and chooses darkness rather than light, for the light of truth will show him his error. He therefore shrinks from investigating his own belief since he knows it cannot stand the test of science.

Truth and error both produce a chemical change in the mind, therefore it is folly to apply an inanimate something to cure an inanimate disease, for neither contains any intelligence. If a man's face is dirty and he is satisfied there is no disease but if it troubles him, the trouble is in him and not in the dirt. To cure him would be to tell him to wash. If the person believes he is cured, the water proves that what was told him was true.

The war between my patients and myself is here. They make the dirt the disease. I make the dirt the cause. They put intelligence in the dirt. I put intelligence in the person. To cure him I must convince him that the dirt is nothing that need trouble him, and that water will remove it. By knowing the truth they are able to remove the cause. The doctors put the trouble in the dirt as though the trouble and the dirt were one and the same. They never address the intelligence, but the opinions, while the cause, being unintelligent like the dirt, affects the intelligence and is reflected on the body.

1865

Religion of Jesus
[Originally untitled.] [LC 2:0726]

Was the religion of Jesus a belief or was it a truth? Who is to say? Must the answer come from a professional believer or from the works of someone? Suppose a man should discover the truth in regard to a certain fact and should render his wisdom practicable, we should call that a science, should we not? The world who saw the effect and knew not the science or cause must acknowledge it a mystery. This class would talk about it, but the author would not talk about it, but would put it in practice. Here are two kinds of wisdom, one reduced to a science and the other an opinion about it. Jesus put his wisdom into his works. The world talked and preached about Jesus and this was religion but it amounts to nothing for it contained no wisdom.

The religion of Jesus was to put his wisdom into practice and it is what the world knew not of. It was the light that lighteth everyone that cometh into the world of wisdom; therefore to be a follower of Christ is to break from your errors and learn to understand the truth. This truth weighs all things. It balances every act and rewards everyone according to his act. Its labor is to convince man of his errors for his happiness, not to browbeat him into a belief, but to teach him that all men were born free and that error has bound them. Religion upholds slavery, science destroys it. The religion of Jesus, which was Christ, destroys slavery and convinces man that a slave is an emblem of his error. Wisdom is the master, so when the servant or error is above the master, evil reigns. Here are two separate identities. Error had religion to oppose the scientific man and stifle progression. Science also has a religion which liberates the prisoner. The religion of the priests was to bind the masses and keep them in subjection. Both of these characters, science and religion, are in every man, and it is hard to separate them, for the error will often assume the form of an angel.

October 1862

Resurrection
[BU 3:0812]

I have written much to try to show that the principal error in man's belief that Jesus sought to destroy was the heathen idea of the resurrection of the dead. Many facts prove that this was the case and among the following is strong evidence; those who held to that doctrine were the very ones who murdered Jesus. Consequently Jesus must have opposed their popular religious opinions, and he silenced even the Sadducees in regard to the resurrection. Jesus denied the resurrection of the body but he taught the resurrection of the science of life from the opinion of error. The belief that man lies in the ground till the last day or till time shall be no more was absurd, as it led men into all sorts of wickedness, and caused the thinking classes to disbelieve in any God whatever.

The Pagan philosophers were the only men who had any real idea of a wisdom that governed all things. They believed in one Great First Cause, and they reasoned that life was attached to matter, which decomposed and returned to its original elements, and that the soul escaped and entered some living form. Popular superstition contained the ideas of heaven and hell and many believed that at the end of the world, the particles of the body would be united and the soul would take possession. Lucretius describes the popular religious belief, which was too grossly absurd for wise men to accept; therefore such looked forward with delight to the change, for under their theories man had no hope after the body was dead. It was not strange therefore that as age advanced, they should like to fall asleep. The Christian was not reconciled to giving any peace to the man of sorrow, so he believed that man was again united with a body and sent to some place to be punished. This made some insane, while some killed themselves from despair.

As time rolled on and science progressed, these ideas looked more absurd, but as persons were afraid to investigate, they were nervous when their ideas were disturbed. Yet reformers came up changing the ideas of death, till at the time of Jesus the world had almost become believers in the supernatural and spiritualism was quite general. These beliefs showed that the people's minds had been exercised with the idea of man's existence after death and that they were ready to receive a truth that would explain it. Jesus sought to bring them out of their beliefs in harmony with his wisdom. Herod showed his belief in spiritualism when told that Jesus was performing miracles, by saying that it was John the Baptist, when he knew that both the persons had been alive at the same time. Jesus had this belief against him. His idea of spirits was different from that of the world. The latter arose from ignorance, while their belief produced the phenomena as is done in our days. The wisdom of Jesus, being of a higher order, showed him that the people's wisdom was based on a belief that could be destroyed; therefore in communicating to them he spiritualized all their ideas and only handled their beliefs to illustrate his wisdom which was of the First Cause, and could consequently control all phenomena and explain all beliefs.

The people, in their ignorance, would produce phenomena to all appearance the same as Jesus did, and they accounted for it on the doctrine of the agency of departed spirits. He knew that to apply his wisdom to the healing of the nation and the individual was a science, while the miracles they wrought were from a belief in a power that neither the person who operated or the one who was cured could explain. Under this error, the world was kept in ignorance of themselves, and all their life subject to disease and death. Those who made a difference between the cures of Jesus and those of the people, when they bring no proof to substantiate or explain it, make a distinction without a difference.

My object is to show that Jesus denied any difference in the cure; it was the same whether performed by him or them, but he did make a difference between the two modes of cure. The world received wisdom from the cures of Jesus, else he differed not from the magicians. The idea that Jesus derived his power from the spirits or from the devil or from any agency independent of wisdom was an error so strongly planted in the popular mind that the people would not receive his explanation. I will illustrate the trouble by my own case. I perform cures and so do others and the people admit both, and seeing no difference in them, judge me by others. Consequently, I am made as ignorant as they are, for they do not pretend to explain their cures but attribute them to the spirits. Now I know there is a difference and I can explain to the sick that it exists in the wisdom of the operator. It is the same in music. A person may play on an instrument by rote as well as another who plays scientifically and the world in its ignorance cannot see any difference, yet there are those who can see a difference, who may not be able to explain it, and whose attempted explanation may lead the people still further into error.

This was the difficulty with Jesus, and he told whom he cured to show themselves to the High Priest and rulers but say nothing. The blind man followed his counsel and merely said, "Whereas I was blind, now I see." Jesus saw a truth that led man out of matter into wisdom, and when this wisdom was reduced to practice, it became a science and the necessity of performing cures was the field for this science. As man's opinion made the people sick, his wisdom could explain the error and change the mind and out of this change the cures came. This wisdom put man into possession of a truth by which the mind becomes subject to it. Man's wisdom being in his mind, which to truth is matter, consequently dies with the matter. Job says, "Ye are the people, and wisdom shall die with you." So at death man dies with all his wisdom. Jesus' life was not in man's wisdom but in God's wisdom. Therefore to him, their wisdom was matter. This matter I call mind, which is matter under control of this wisdom or Christ.

When Jesus said this Christ should rise, he meant that this wisdom should rise from the errors of mankind and should subject mind to this truth. According to Jesus, mind could not cover the word wisdom, for wisdom is wisdom and nothing else. John says, "In the beginning was the Word, and the Word was with God, and the Word was God." So this was the name of something that could not be changed. All matter is changing and subject to death, for death is the change of matter from one state to another. Mind, matter, soul and life apply to these various changes. In the days of Jesus, people had begun to reason about a resurrection. There had been some glimmering of the soul's immortality, but the idea that the body rose was not held by heathen religion, so the people had to reason out this belief. Job says, 19:26, "And though after my skin worms destroy this body, yet in my flesh shall I see God." Still the doctrine of the resurrection was unknown to the wisest heathen; it was peculiar to the Gospel or disciples of Jesus. Still as they had some idea of immortality, they had begun to reason on the subject. The Sadducees asked Jesus whose wife should the woman who had seven husbands be in the resurrection. If the scriptures had taught a resurrection of the dead, this was a fair question, but Jesus knew that it was not taught by any writer of the Old Testament.

November 1862

Revelation*
[BU 3:0511]

Can the idea of revelation be explained so that it can be understood by man? I think it can. Revelation is to explain some phenomena not understood by the natural man. Therefore some idea must start up, then opinions and discussions arise concerning it, and then comes the revelation that shall explain it to the natural man, if adopted the explanation is revelation. Now religion is claimed to be a revelation from God, to man through the man Jesus eighteen hundred years ago. How much of God's wisdom revealed to man is explained by the clergy? For nothing is claimed by science as a revelation. All that is claimed is this: that God made himself manifest in Jesus, to tell or explain some belief that man must have in order to be saved.

This salvation depends on certain forms and ceremonies that men set up and claim to be of God. This is the sum and substance of revelation and the people put just as much stress upon it as the South do upon the King Cotton. Just as though cotton was all that ever God intended to protect, and man must worship that at the expense of all other interests. It is just so with the priests; they have got up a king that all must bow down and worship, called a creed. The followers are the Christians, just as though every science and good act of man is nothing compared to their king or creed, while the science of astronomy has done more to enlighten the world than all King Cotton or the priests put together.

Oct. 1861

Right and Wrong [I]
[BU 3:0453]

Do the words right and wrong convey to man any true standard of justice? Are not those words arbitrary and do they not convey to the world the idea that man is to take some person's opinions in regard to the meaning? The words were never intended to apply to the leaders of any party or sect. It must be admitted that they are right and what they say of right and wrong does not apply to them but to the masses.

Now let us see if it is not so. Take the Bible as a test. We are told that this book defines the words right and wrong. Now the Bible does not define anything, but certain men set themselves up as the standard of right and wrong to judge others, but they do not come within that sphere. In political parties, each party leader explains what is right and what is wrong for the masses to believe. So with the medical faculty. The leaders are never reckoned into the progression, only the masses. Now the idea is so absurd, although the masses do not know why it is so, it causes controversy, and up spring parties and every party or sect has its leaders, and every leader has his right and wrong for his followers.

This false way of reasoning can never cure the evil. Enlighten the masses and let them see, that the answers right and wrong are not to apply to the leaders but to themselves. Then they will see that one man has no more right to set up a standard of right and compel others to bow down to it than another man has to set up a standard for him. Now I set up no standard, neither will I bow to any person's standard of right, for the man that made the word made it to judge others and not to be applied to himself.

Here is where I stand. All men will admit that animals protect themselves by their strength or with some weapons that are given them and they use it and are all selfish. Now man at first came very near the character of the animal, and he has got a great deal of the animal about him at this day. Ask a man if he believes slavery is right and he will say, Yes, and another will say, No. Now I will suppose that both are honest and both appeal to the Bible. Now I say one is just as right as the other according to the definition of the words right and wrong. Now is there some way to get rid of the evil that separates them, for if you can make them both agree as touching one point the thing is settled. So let the word right go, and ask them if they would be willing to submit to the slaves to rule them if they should get the power; let them put it to their own selves and if they say they would, then they are honest but not intelligent. For every person knows that whoever is not willing to do by another as he would be done by, is not honest.

Now if to be honest is right and dishonest is wrong, then reason out what is honest, and what is right. Now every man has his own identity which God gave him and to enslave him because you have the power is doing what you would find fault with if applied to you.

But if man is enslaved for the good of the community to protect the masses, as you would chain a wild beast, that would be honest and good. But to admit that you are not afraid of them and then enslave them for your own good, is not honest, and is bad. So to enslave man's opinion in regard to creeds or diseases is as bad as approving slavery.

Right and Wrong [II]
[BU 2:0279]

What is right and wrong? The question involves more thought than a person at first would suppose. We often hear persons using this expression: this or that is right or wrong. When asked to define the word wrong, they use some comparison admitted by some old superstitious opinion, all without any authority. All persons claiming to be Christians always appeal to the Bible for the proof of all goodness, believing that the Bible is the foundation of all truth. I am willing to abide by the decision of this great book, believing it is the best authority to decide all questions in dispute, but I am not willing to take any person's opinion on a subject where he cannot show any wisdom above his followers, only that he has read and studied more than his neighbors. The Bible is in the hands of the people just as much as the science of mathematics is in the hands of the people and all will admit that this wisdom is known by its works. So it is with the Bible. The Bible is in the hands of the people and they will give their verdict just according to the evidence that is placed before them.

Now what idea does the Bible give us in regard to right and wrong? All will admit that God has no use for such a word as right, for he never made anything wrong. So he is not the author of right and wrong; for when he had made all things and finished them, he pronounced them good so that there was no wrong at any time. But there was not a man to till the ground, so that right and wrong commenced after the formation of man and good and evil was of man, not of God. To create evil was to deviate from good, so that right and wrong were the invention of man; for one man cannot make right and wrong–there must be two to be in opposition to each other. The natural man knows no right and wrong, for he is but little above the brute creation. The brutes cannot do wrong according to their organization for might is right with them. The natural man is on the same platform with the brute, neither is responsible for their acts, but both are governed by two powers superior to themselves. These powers are might and science. Might is law, science is sympathy or charity or a knowledge of both. Science is not expected from the brute, so that they being ignorant of science, it holds them in subjection. Man, who is a little above the brutes, shows his wisdom or power in the same way that the brutes do, by enslaving his fellow man. All of this is the natural man and belongs to this world. It does not come under any law except the law of might. It has never heard of science in its acts.

Man is made up of these two characters: might and science, so that all laws to the natural man are arbitrary and overbearing, but as might or law is right man must submit. Although he may see the error, he cannot correct the evil. Now what is right and wrong and how came such a standard in the world and is it needed for the happiness of man? This was the question in the days of Jesus. He called these two powers the law and the gospel. The law was might and the gospel was Christ or Science, so that what the law failed to do was left for science to accomplish. Science or Christ in Jesus entered into the world of might and introduced a higher law that put an end to the law of might.

I will now show how naturally the idea of right and wrong came into the world. As man and beast were in the world together, the beast having more physical strength than man would overpower him unless the strength of the beast were counteracted by some shrewdness of man for his protection. So in the course of human progression it became necessary for man to establish some sort of agreement that would bind them together for the protection of their lives. This agreement, if made in good faith, with the full knowledge of the good that would follow, and admitted by all, was the introduction of the wisdom of God into the hearts of all those who acknowledged it good. Now to them this was binding, for it produced a chemical change that made man different from the beast. Thus they introduced the wisdom of God into man and called it right and to vary from this agreement was wrong. This was the origin of right and wrong. This agreement contained no law, for it was of God. It contained no punishment, for it knew no fear.

As wisdom in man is science, it is progression, so that the development of this wisdom is progression. As man progressed, it would not be strange for him to violate this agreement, which violation was not a violation of law but a breach of honor. They were a law to themselves. But other men were not bound to their agreement; so as people multiplied, it became necessary, so they thought, to introduce laws. As laws have penalties they are burdens to all who are under the law. So as the law entered, the love of God or Science grew cold. At last the wisdom of man took the place of science and science was not known in the hearts of men. Then man set up a standard of right and wrong according to his wisdom and attached a penalty to each act according to his best judgment. To disobey the laws that man set up, they had to suffer the penalties.

Now as the world became populated, the laws took cognizance of the people's acts, and as they knew no law, to them these laws were arbitrary and overbearing and they murmured for they had no voice in the making of the laws. Thus man invented the words, right and wrong. This wisdom has been kept up and has been placed in the hands of the priests and doctors. They bind on the people their opinions and call them laws of God and to disobey them is a sin. These laws have placed man in bondage and kept him ignorant of himself. God never made a law. Might is right with the beast and when man wants to govern his fellow men he has just as much right to do it as any other beast. Both are under no law but man and if they are sincere, they have no more feeling than any other brute and it becomes the duty of Science to make some law for its own safety until a higher law can be introduced within their hearts that will teach them that action and reaction are equal and to injure another, we injure ourselves; to teach them that man and beast are born equal and that the natural man has no preeminence over the brute, but all were of the dust and must return to the dust again.

So man when he was first introduced into the world was on a level with the brute and as a tree is known by its fruits, so is man known by his acts. Now as science has proved to all persons understanding it, that the true wisdom of Science is progression, to oppose progression is to oppose science. As disease is an enemy to truth or science it is a hard master and the sick person is a slave, and while I pity the sick person or slave, I detest the law which holds them in bondage. I would not destroy the evil by killing the master, but persuade the sick not to believe in him, as Jesus did when he told the people to do all that the law compelled them to do but not to believe in the doctrines. For their doctrines are of this world's opinions and are not binding on strangers. And to admit them as truth is to acknowledge their punishments just. There are two kinds of punishments. Everyone is either punished by the laws of agreement or the condemnation of their own free will.

I will now try to separate these two agreements or laws, for all laws are made by man and in all I say I do not allude to God at all for God is not known in the natural man, while the scientific man is a part of God and to talk about God is to talk about something you do not know, while to talk science, is God. Now science talks or applies itself to the errors of the world. Error talks about itself and talks about God or science as a stranger or a being to whom they pay tribute. So they think it is necessary for the happiness of mankind to keep up a sort of form or ceremony to promote his kingdom. Therefore, certain laws are established, accompanied with penalties for the good of the community. These laws were for those who were strangers, while those who agreed to the contract and understood it were free. I will give you one illustration of the truth of this contract called law and show where the injustice is. Suppose that the state of Maine should vote that murder was wrong and pray that the legislature should abolish the law for murder. The legislature comes together and takes up the petition giving it a thorough investigation. It comes to the conclusion to send it to the petitioners to see if they in their wisdom are prepared to adopt it as their rule of action.

Here is the contract. "We, the science of God or the representatives of Him and you, after a full and deliberate investigation of the wisdom of this world, have come to the conclusion that the time has arrived when man shall throw off this old law of this world and substitute a higher and better law that shall be set up in everyone's heart, to do unto others as you would that they should do unto you. Therefore, we, as well as you, do hereby agree and bind ourselves, not strangers but ourselves, the people of Maine, that we will respect each other as far as your petition goes and call science to witness that if we violate this contract we shall be judged guilty of one of the most disgraceful acts ever done by man. This law shall be placed in the forehead of all those who come into this contract, and the punishment for murder, according to this act, shall not be binding on anyone who signs or comes into this agreement. So that everyone who commits murder according to this act is judged of himself and the world as a murderer, having forfeited all claims to honor and is looked upon as a murderer and outcast by the world and by the signers of this contract. The old law shall be kept in force for strangers or persons coming among us, but we shall not be punished by the old law of this world. All persons who see fit to murder one of the signers of this contract shall be punished as a murderer and shall be delivered up to the authority of the old laws to be dealt with according to their laws. But if a murder is committed by one of the signers of this contract, he shall not be punished by the old law. But if he escapes from the state or is protected by strangers, his name shall be published to all the world as a murderer and outcast from the state of Maine and of course is liable to the laws of any other state and his membership shall not be introduced as proof of good character."

Belfast, September 1860

Right and Wrong III*

[Originally untitled.] [BU 3:0769]

Two things exist: Right and Wrong. The Right is God, it is truth, it is perfect wisdom. The Wrong must be subject to the Right and some time or other will be controlled by it. Man is made in the image of God therefore there is some of this Right in him. When an infant is born I do not believe it is wicked for it never thought a thought nor committed an act. Thus the evil it does in after days must have been acquired. The evil therefore must have existed independent of the child and have been learned by him. The evil then is a different character from himself. Then after he has secured the evil into himself he becomes a double person, one evil and one good. The evil then is to be cast out by the good and that is the question, how is it to be done?

If evil is not of God it must be of man. If the man has made the evil that torments him he can correct it. How has he made it?

It is a fact that we affect each other, that we take feelings, thoughts, and opinions etc. from each other without knowing it. These are incorporated into ourselves and become a part of ourselves and their effects are seen in the acts of our lives. An opinion then contains within itself its own effect. If it is good the effect is good–if bad the effect is evil. We then must learn to discriminate between the good and the bad so that we can select only that which is for our good. But if those opinions do come without our being aware of it, how can we learn? Here is where man's ignorance is his own enemy.

Scenes from the Belief in Death and the Belief in Life–Part I
[LC 2:0731]

I will suppose three persons standing over a sick person who, as they all believe, is dying. First let us sum up what there is of the man. He knows that he is in bed and that he is about to take his departure to the world of spirits. This is knowledge; let us examine his belief and see what there is of him independent of it. He believes he is now going to die, that his body will die, and that he must leave all that is near and dear unto him (for life is his belief) and he believes that he shall lose that. So accordingly, he is entirely gone at death, mind, body and soul, for he believes his soul is his life, so there is not one particle of him outside of his belief.

His Christian friend looks upon what is his belief. He sees the man wasting away, he sees his life dying out like a candle, and at last it is gone. All this he knows to be a fact, yet he believes his soul has gone to God who gave it. The Atheist and the Spiritualist both see the light of life burn out and they return to their peculiar belief which neither can prove. The Atheist says, "Well the poor fellow has got through with his troubles." The Christian and Spiritualist assent, but the latter insists he still lives and to prove it, he goes to a medium and gets a communication from the dead, giving the particulars of the death, precisely as they all believe. To the other, this is all a humbug, for each holds to his belief. I have seen many such scenes, have attended the sick and dying man, have told him at various times how he felt, and I know that death as it appears to these classes and to the dying man is only the phenomenon of their religious belief.

Then what is my belief of man. I have none to myself, but to those who are looking on, my wisdom is a belief, for if I cannot bring any more proof than my word to them, my wisdom must be a belief. I will compare their belief with my wisdom and give some proof of the latter so that the reader may judge between them. All the aforesaid persons make the man just what they see of him; his life is in his body and like the life of a plant grows with the body and dies with the same. They have no life that cannot be seen by the natural eye so death closes their life. All the life that I admit is my wisdom and what a man knows contains no mind nor matter. So it is not life but a truth. Wisdom is eternal with no beginning or end. My senses being in my wisdom are myself. Memory also belongs to my senses. My belief is what I do not know and that is attached to matter, for when wisdom comes, our belief is at an end. According to my wisdom, man does not die for so long as he has the belief that he shall die, so long he is not dead but going to die. So when he says through a medium that he is dead, he does not tell the truth, for the very fact of his saying so proves that he is alive.

Wisdom has no life for it has no death. It is the parent of life. So when a person attaches his senses to wisdom, he then lives in what never had life or death and he becomes a progressive being. This is what I know to be a truth. So as I sit by the sick man, I look upon him as a chemist looks on and sees a lump of gold dissolve. The friends of the sick man not being chemists see the value or life depart with the gold, having placed value in the gold as it circulates among men. They never think that the value was in them, while the gold is only a representative of value, but the chemist knows that he can condense the gold into form again. They weep to see the gold waste away, their hope is gone, for they have lost the value that they have put in it; so they mourn just according to their loss, not knowing that the gold still lives in wisdom or science.

The spiritualist expects the gold to assume a new body and they all reason according to their belief. But the chemist says you grieve for your ignorance. The gold still lives, with all its qualities, as it did when you carried it with you, although your ignorance cannot see it; the real value that you put into the gold was in yourself and the gold was the shadow of it and was only a representative of value, never knowing any in itself. The value is the wisdom you can reduce to practice, so you can dissolve the metal and speak it into a solid at pleasure and teach the same to others.

I will now show you a miracle. The gold is dissolved and held in solution, so that no one would know it from pure water. Then applying his wisdom, he restores the gold to a solid form. To them this is a miracle, but to him it is a science. This is done to show that although they see the gold decomposed, it still exists in that wisdom that numbers the hairs of our head. This is the way with the sick man. I know that the value is not in the matter; it is in the individual. Ignorance weeps because he has seen the matter in a form like the gold and as he could not see the owner, he supposed life or value to be in the matter. But like the chemist, I saw the owner outside the matter or his belief, and as I saw the matter dissolve and their opinions and hope disappear, I could see the person living as though nothing had happened to him.

1862

Scenes from the Belief in Death and the Belief in Life–Part II
[LC 2:0732]

I was called to see a young lady who was dying, as it is called. She was seated in a rocking chair, and after sitting by her a few moments, I knew she was about to leave the body and just as I was going to ask her if I should not lift her on to the bed, she said to me, "Shall I now lay you on the bed?" I said, Yes, and took her in my arms and laid her on the bed. She then said, "Now I will place your head so you will be easy." I placed her head on the pillow and she said, "Now I will cover you up." I did as she said, and she then remarked, "I will now sit down by you and make you quiet, so you can go to sleep." So I took my chair and sat down by her, and in less than five minutes she had ceased to breathe. This young lady was as much detached from her body as I was and she grieved for me instead of herself. She believed that I was sick, so her happiness was in helping me. But her life was in her wisdom, for she knew she was alive and was trying to comfort me, since I felt grieved to see her leave, as I had then the same idea which the world has. This is one of the many cases I might mention to show that when persons are leaving the body, they have all their senses, but to those who are looking on the person appears insane.

I was sitting by a patient whom I had put to sleep that she might have a needle extracted from her arm and while the surgeon was performing the operation, she said to me, "Does it now hurt you?" I replied, "No." She said, "I should think it would." Here was a person awake to all that was going on, who at the same time took my body and arm for the one in which the needle was. When I mesmerized my subject, if his nose itched he would say to me, "I wish you would scratch your nose," and if I did, it would satisfy him. I know that every person like the gold exists in the solution with all his life qualities of wisdom and opinion and is happy or miserable according to his life.

I will now say a word to those persons who are so anxious to have their friends know they are dying. To me this is horrible, and if they only knew what I know, they would never forgive themselves for the misery they inflict on those who would like to stay with them. There is no worse punishment I can inflict on a mesmerized subject than to mentally carry him away and leave him among strangers. Everyone who has ever mesmerized knows this fact. Now see how the dying like to embrace their friends. The army nurses will tell you that the dying man will get as near you as possible, and that they like to have you soothe them till they are separate from our belief of life, for that is what torments them. I have seen a great many when their friends cut the cord that held them to their belief of life and I know how it acts upon them. According to the Christian belief, it is necessary to prepare the dying to go to heaven. So the minister comes to create a heaven in his own mind, far off, and to impress the dying man of it; and as he grows nervous, he creates one according to his own belief and starts for it under the direction of his pious friend.

The scene is as trying as it is to tear a child from its mother and lodge it in some dungeon and then say good night. Both are as full of grief as they can be, but the dying get to that pitch which grief cannot reach; then they become as marble, and their friends console themselves by saying they are calm. I have seen all this many times. This is what I want to impress on the friends. If you want the satisfaction of having your friends with you, never even hint that they are going away, for you will drive them from you, but sit by them just as though you were all together and you will see a scene that you will always greatly remember, for you will always feel this life of your friend or child mingling with yours, not to be separated by a belief. These are the proofs of that wisdom which teaches me that my life, senses, and everything near and dear to me in this world of solution, which is God, and in it we all live and move, although by our belief we all live without God and in bondage through fear of death, and the knowledge of this wisdom is the new birth. Disease is a departure from this wisdom which will dissolve the error that holds the life in bondage and set them free from death. To be free and know it is to know this great truth and put it into practice. Therefore to cure disease as I do, it is necessary to believe this, not as a blind belief but as a wisdom which is a light that sees through the error of man's belief.

October 1862

Science
[LC 1:0150]

The word science is frequently used but so loosely defined that its true meaning cannot be understood. Ask a person what science is, he answers, "It is knowledge, a collection of general principles." This leaves it just where it finds it. So everyone sets up his standard of a collection of general principles.

Let us see if the word can be explained so that everyone may know. Science embraces something that is spiritual or a revelation from a higher state of mind than that of the brutes, so to me science is the name of that wisdom that accounts for all phenomena that the natural man or beast cannot understand. To illustrate. You throw a ball into the air; every child will soon learn that the ball will return. This is not science. But to know understandingly that it will return with just as much force as it received is science. To acknowledge it simply as a fact is not science, but science is in the act, not known, as God is in the world and the world knew Him not.

This principle or science Jesus tried to teach to man. The acts of man were sometimes according to this law but the actors knew it not. So they, being ignorant of the science, were a science to themselves; but as they did not know the motive, they could not teach it to others.

Paul, speaking of this science, says some have not heard of it, and how shall they believe in what they have not heard of, as a science, when it was never taught, and how shall men know about it unless someone teaches them, and how can a man teach a science that he knows nothing of? So, he says, How beautiful are the words of that person who can teach science but all cannot understand. He uses the word charity for the same wisdom that we use science and goes on to tell that although we give all our money to the poor and suffer our bodies to be burned and do not understand science or charity, it is of no use; it profiteth nothing. The world is none the wiser. To understand science or charity so as to put it into practice so that it becomes a science is not an easy task. Well might the disciples say, This is a hard saying and how can a man believe or understand? Many shall try but few can understand. Therefore, if they cannot understand, must the wisdom of God or science or charity be of no effect? Wisdom says, No! Let science be true but every man a liar. This science was in the minds of people, but the priests and doctors led the people and explained it according to their own notions so that when Jesus came to establish this truth as a science, to them it was a stumbling block. The wisdom of this world never has put science into goodness but thinks goodness is cultivated or a dispensation. It never thinks it is a revelation from a higher power that distinguishes man from the other living creatures. This wisdom or charity was known by some to have an identity, but was never admitted as a creature or anything independent of the natural man. So goodness was considered by the priests as a sort of subjection to the rulers. A good person was like a good dog, ready to obey his master; then his master would pat him and call him a good dog, although he had just torn another dog in pieces or had done something to please his master.

This was the way with the Christian Church–to be good was to persecute all who would not bow the knee to the leaders and all who had the boldness to speak their opinions were heretics or infidels. The priests patted the heads of their dogs and set them onto the swine or those who oppose them, so that to steal or rob from one of these skeptics was a virtue rather than a wrong. I have seen this effect in my own practice. There are persons who are honest according to their religion who will come and tell me a lie, as I call it, to deceive me into a belief that they mean just what they say. I have just as much confidence in their honesty as I have in a bull dog who looks as innocent as a lamb when you have something that he wants, and after he gets it he will bite you as soon as your back is turned. This all arises from smothering the science or charity or revelation from God. And this is done by the priests. The priests make their goodness a sort of self interest and charge people a fee to pardon their sins which the honest part of the community would look upon as a wrong. The priest flatters them with the idea that they are doing just right so they worship the priest as the masses worship the leaders and every person knows that a leading demagogue will uphold any crime his party is guilty of and applaud the actor for his goodness or honesty. Charity has no friend with any of these leaders; it finds no foothold, therefore, like the dove of the ark, after trying to find a place to rest, it returns to its house and is gone to the world. This was the case in the days of Jesus. He came to establish this science or charity. This word science not being used to explain this truth, it was called by Jesus, "Christ" and by Paul it was called "charity" and by the wise men who admitted it, it was called a power or gift, but it never was admitted to have an identity, to the teaching of which, the senses were attached. This was Jesus' religion, so that he talked his religion, not talked about it. Because to talk wisdom is wisdom, whereas to talk about wisdom is to talk about an unknown God.

Now Jesus tells just about where the people stood in regard to this truth. There were none who understood it but many who acted according to the principles. These he called persons who, being ignorant of the law, were a law to themselves because they did right and did not know why they wanted to do it. He describes their minds as half wise and half foolish. But the wise were ignorant of the cause of their own wisdom, so that in trying to make people understand this truth, which he called the greatest of sciences or the kingdom of heaven, he spoke in parables.

He commences by a parable of the foundation of this science or the ground in which it is sown, and then shows its growth by parables. So when he was asked for an explanation of his science or power or kingdom, he took a little child in his arms and said, Of such is the foundation or kingdom of heaven. Now everyone knows that a child is a blank as far as virtue or vice is concerned and with it might is right. Now the growth of this child's wisdom depends entirely on the direction given to its mind. Then he says, What shall I compare its little wisdom to? I will compare it to a grain of mustard seed that a man sowed in his garden.

So God sowed wisdom in this little child's mind and this wisdom, if properly developed, would teach him that his body, like the earth, was the casket or loom for this wisdom to develop itself in.

As it developed itself, it would leave its mother earth and derive its life from a higher and more perfect mother that had no matter but which, like the air, was perfect so that it lifts one above all the fog or atmosphere of earth and the decomposition of matter or ideas that contain all sorts of evil. The growth of this wisdom was liable to be destroyed, for Herod sought to kill it. But its mother hid it in the ignorance or bushes in the sea of superstition till it could grow in the hearts of the people. So when its branches began to put forth and the fowls or theories began to build nests or attack it, then came the devil and made war against it. Then the priests and doctors joined in and stirred up the multitude to search out where the true wisdom was, that they might take counsel together, how they should put it down.

When Jesus appeared at the common age of man, ready to defend himself, John sent to him to know if he was this science or Christ or must we look for another. As Jesus began to preach this truth or science, it struck at the root of all their old superstitions and it troubled them. This was the very thing that people had looked for. The prophets had prophesied that the time would come when man should act from a higher motive than dollars and cents, when goodness was virtue and virtue could be appreciated, for virtue was nothing to the priests. They looked upon all virtue as passion and treated it as such. Thus sympathy or love was misrepresented by these blind guides so that people acknowledged and thought that they were born dishonest and all sorts of vice and passion were elements of our nature. When Jesus began to separate vice from virtue the war began.

This separation was his religion, for vice and passion were the inventions of man. It was a sort of appetite and made the people brutish. I will not say brutish for that is a stain on God or goodness, for the brutes act as they were intended to and to compare them to man, who debases himself below the brute, is a stain on the noble character of the horse, for instance. I have seen a thing driving a horse who looked more out of place than he would if he were in the hills, and the horse had the reigns. This sort of intellect, which is made up of the lowest passions of men, is as much beneath the brute as the hawk is beneath the dove. These two characters make up man. One is ignorance, superstition and all kinds of passion, to gratify the lusts of a low, contemptible mind which cannot see honesty in anything except as a restraint upon the appetites; so he looks upon all restraints as burdens and oppressions. This is the wisdom of this world. This wisdom has always been in the ascendancy. It has been the enemy of truth or science. So when any new development of truth comes up, this brutal intellect catches the seed or idea and puts a low construction on the acts. This causes the war of error to see which should get the mastery. Science comes as a natural result of the quarrel, for the truth never makes war for anything; all the fighting is done by ignorance and superstition.

Now as I have already said, the beasts were made perfect as they were intended to be; no change is visible in each succeeding generation. The combination of the natural brute is perfect. But it does not contain science or wisdom. Man, that being who is called the noblest work of God, has a higher development and shows that there is something outside of matter that can control matter. This something is what the world has always been looking for. It is not in the beasts, for it is not life and that the beasts have; nor is it reason, for the beasts have that; nor is it passion, nor is it love nor temper, for all of these the beasts have. Then what is it that makes man above the beasts? Science or revelation from a spiritual world, higher than the natural world. And this wisdom or science is, like all other wisdom or science, progression. Although it is in the beastly man, in some it is never developed, yet in others it has.

Wisdom or science makes the distinction in man by this figure: man is of the earth and is earthy or brutal; yet in him, like the grain of mustard seed, was this science in the form of a rib or this higher power and the science called it woman. And this woman or wisdom is to lead man or ignorance to truth and happiness. Now, neither the woman nor the man had any science, so you see that the man, like the beast, was willing to live under restriction, as all other animals did; for God placed all other animals under the law of might. But it was not so with the rib. The rib saw farther ahead than the beast; it had more sagacity and, like the serpent, said to it, Here is a tree or knowledge of good and evil or judge of right and wrong, and if you eat it or investigate, you shall be like the father of it, more than the brute. Here you see the true character of wisdom. It shrinks not from investigating, although it is unpopular and has the whole world to contend with. It fights its way regardless of danger. So it ate or investigated whatever it saw.

Now I will suppose the tree. All theories are called trees. John says every tree that beareth not good fruit shall be hewn down. In this sense, a tree means anything that man wants to investigate. You must go back to Adam and Eve or to a little child, as Jesus said when he undertook to explain the same idea. So of course it had no reference to man and woman as we see them now but to the development of knowledge above the brute. So he takes man and woman as figures of truth and error and shows that the mind of woman is better calculated to receive seed or investigate than man. They have more endurance and have more patience to investigate any new science than man, but their wisdom is not of this world but of that higher power called science. When they give their idea to man, he then eats or understands and then goes to work to form the idea that has been given to him by the woman. It has always been the case that all spiritual wisdom has been received through the female. The oracle of Delphi was a woman. As men's minds are more brutal and less scientific or spiritual, they never believe till they can see with the natural man's eyes. To them science is shadow. Now as man is of matter and his thoughts are a part of himself, he lives on his ideas and forms all of his plans in matter and carries them out in matter; thus the natural man knows nothing above matter. The spiritual man, or the woman, is not of matter and sees all the changes of matter. These two characters are in every man and the way they can be distinguished is by the answer. If the answer is true, it can be shown; if the person has the wisdom of science, and if the answer is to be proved by an opinion of the person or others, it is of this world and is of no force, if true.

Paul, in trying to separate this wisdom from the natural world, called it charity and said, Though I speak with the tongues of angels and have not science or charity, it is of no force; the world is no wiser. And though I have the gift of turning tables and everything else upside down and have all faith that it is of God or spirits but have no knowledge or science, it amounts to nothing. And though I give all my goods to the poor to establish this science and even go as far as John Brown did to establish his opinion in regard to slavery, there was a truth in it, but his act was governed by an opinion; and although he might be honest, as I have no doubt he was, yet it all amounts to nothing, for it does not embrace charity or wisdom. And this has been the way with all fanatics. Although they may be honest and give all they have and at last sacrifice their lives, it is only their opinion of a science that they worship; the science they know not of. Science or charity does not act in that way. Science suffers long before it becomes a fact. It envieth not other science, it praiseth not self, is not puffed up, doth not behave unseemly, is not easily provoked, thinketh no evil, rejoiceth not over trouble but rejoiceth in the truth. Science never fails but prophesies. The knowledge of this world fails but science never fails.

July 1860

Science Is Freedom–Error Is Slavery
[LC 2:0711]

This principle applies to all things. Religion is slavery. Science is the doctrine of Christ. Jesus' religion was proved by science, the world's religion by opinion. Science never holds any truth in bondage. Opinion enslaves every truth it can. Might is right with opinion, but Science says try and prove all things and hold fast that which is good. Science is strong, opinion is weak. Therefore it is timid and dares not investigate. It goes for keeping down all investigation. It is cowardly and despotic, seeks low and vulgar company, becomes popular by its own folly. It is the demagogue in everything. It is the vilest passion in man. It is a coward because it has no wisdom, so its strength is in its fear, like a man holding a maniac, not daring to let him go. Slavery is the result of ignorance and fear. The slave is held in bondage by fear and submits to his yoke from fear. This is the way with disease. The sick is the slave, the master opinions; each is afraid of the other. Call them two persons: one opinions and the other science. Now when opinion gets the advantage of science, it is like a dog in the manger; it won't let the ox eat nor eat itself. Opinion will not investigate, nor let anyone else, lest it should be destroyed, so it holds its victim when it holds itself by so doing.

As I have said a sick person is a slave, bound and cast into slavery. The disease is his master, the doctor is the medium of opinion and consulted by the man of error. To illustrate the idea, I will take a case I had a day or two ago. A man came to see me who was very lame in one of his legs. It was somewhat crooked and very painful in the knee and he limped very badly. When I sat down I perceived that the man was laboring under a very bad impression or master. I said to him, You are afraid. You have been told that you have a white swelling and that you must keep your leg bandaged and perfectly still. To do that, you must submit to be on your back and remain perfectly still till you get well. He said all that I told him was true. A physician had told him that very thing a week before and he felt discouraged. Here you see a man led along like an ox, bowing his head to receive the weight of the yoke. So from fear he let the doctor bind fetters on his leg to bind him down to the bed, there to be punished for some crime that he never was guilty of committing. Thus he became a slave to his own belief or fear.

Now what was my mission? It was to loose the man that Satan had bound and let him go. How did I do it? First by telling him how he got where he was when telling his feelings. These were the punishment of his belief. So disease is a belief or sensation; this confines our senses in the belief. It may be said a child has no belief. A child has fear of the fire when it burns him; no one will dispute that he may not know the cause. Now thought or a belief is as real as the fire, and a child is as susceptible to a person's belief as to anything that comes within its natural senses. So to know the child is to destroy the evil. This is often done through ignorance more than by science. It is done by our own belief, just as our belief makes us sick. Fear is the beginning of wisdom, for if there were no fear, there would be no development of wisdom. So fear worketh out wisdom, wisdom worketh out love, and love casteth out fear.

I will illustrate. Man is either under one or the other of these two, fear or wisdom. To make it plain, I will suppose a case. Take a person who thinks he has the heart disease. His disease is in his belief, his belief is the master and his wisdom is the slave. The man of belief holds the child of wisdom because he is afraid. The child of wisdom is afraid of his tormentor, so each is afraid. But the child of wisdom is not born. It is in the opinion, struggling to be delivered from its earthly bonds. Therefore it is not wisdom reduced to science but wisdom in the earthly man or belief. Now comes the man of wisdom who has passed through this new birth and is outside the man of belief. He takes the man in this state of disease, and addresses himself to his belief which is the tyrant that holds the child in bondage through fear. He convinces the man that the child of wisdom will not injure anyone. So as opinion gets rid of his fear, he looses the bands that bind the wisdom, and the wisdom not knowing the fear of opinion is frightened; but as they begin to understand, wisdom assumes its stand and belief gives way, and science yields up its authority and becomes the servant.

I will separate a sick person and make him two distinct persons, one superior in physical strength and the other stronger in spirit or science. The former is the man of opinion and being stronger physically, he attacks the small man of wisdom and by his greater strength deprives him of his freedom. Each is afraid. The small man is afraid of the animal man and he is afraid of the scientific man. This is precisely the state of the sick man. I come to the man of opinions and say, Why do you enslave this little man? He replies, Because he will injure me, and I hold him in slavery for my own protection. I then say to the small man, What are you afraid of? I fear that his ignorance will never let me go. I say, Do you want to harm him? No, is the reply of the scientific man. Then I say to the strong man, Loose your hold, you shall not be harmed. After being convinced, he releases his hold of the scientific man, and each sees that neither wants to injure the other. Now the tables are turned. The brutal man becomes as docile as a lamb, and the child of wisdom leads him by his science. The lion and the lamb lie down together and a little child shall lead them. The lion is the physical man, the lamb, wisdom, the child, science. This is health and happiness.

September 1862

Science Is One Character of God

[Originally untitled.] [BU 3:0747]

Science is one character of God. Error is another character, not of God. Science or God applied to man or beast is perfect in its own sphere. Wisdom of God is that which feels the error of this world. To illustrate how the two are connected together as the vegetable and animal are connected together: this discord of science is divided into two classes. Matter is under the wisdom of God, not known to itself. Matter to God is an idea that contains no science but is like fire or water. Air is another idea. The earth is an idea differing from the sea or water; the air or fire has the same difference. So the wisdom that governs the sea attaches the identity of life to the fish, but it does not attach wisdom or science to it. It is like a machine or automaton that moves by its own power. That power is a part of the wisdom of God that is perfect in the thing made, but subject to a higher organization, so that the higher contains more of the wisdom of itself than the lesser.

So by degrees, matter is changed till it is capable of receiving its author or creator, or wisdom of science. Then man stands in the world of matter, in perfect form and perfect combination of matter, arranged like a perfect instrument ready to be placed in the hands of science or ignorance. Each can play, but one is the natural development of the matter; the other is the author of matter or idea. Now when man is ready to receive this science, he then becomes equal with his father, or science, in every error that he corrects scientifically.

I will try to give an illustration. A lady called on me who had been paralyzed. Now if she had been born so, the matter of the body would have been part animal and part vegetable, or some sort of matter that would not have been perfect, but as she was not born so, her body was subject to the science of God's wisdom. Now becoming one half paralyzed, she is in discord with the other side, but as the other contains no science nor ear for correcting the discord, it wants an instrument that can receive the wisdom of science so that it can disturb the dead or deranged state of the paralytic side and bring it in tone with the well side. This wisdom is not of man but of God, and when applied to man is not his servant but his master, and its kingdom is not of this world of matter but is a world of itself. Its father is the author of its own existence and mankind are its sons and daughters. So as this son of God is in man, its growth is its wisdom, its happiness is its knowledge. Its mission into this world of matter is to govern and control all the developments that matter is liable to pass through; its happiness is in the chemical changes that it produces in the human mind, for the that are corrected in the two kingdoms of error and science. The wisdom is to be able to correct any error that man's matter may go through so as to restore it to harmony. This is the science of God, not of man.

August 1860

Science of Man, The

[LC 2:0907]

The greatest good that can be bestowed upon man is a knowledge of himself. This puts man in possession of a wisdom superior to circumstances. Man, without this wisdom, is a creature of circumstances, tossed about by every man's opinion. Religion is what flows from our belief and the misery is its torment; happiness is what follows our knowledge of God or truth. To illustrate the idea, I will suppose a case. Jesus took water as an illustration of this great truth or God; so I will take the same and show how our religion works, for true religion works by love or wisdom and purifies the heart of man. False religion is like a canker worm or poison that poisons the whole fountain.

Now suppose you are drinking out of the living waters of life. You drink and are satisfied and the satisfaction is your religion. The happiness is the fruits of it. Being ignorant of the goodness of the water or God, you worship it ignorantly. So where ignorance is bliss, it would be folly to get into an error. But man is a creature of progression. He is a sort of chemical change. So as he begins to reason, he gets into error and then he becomes the child of error. So in his error he calls for water to quench his thirst; but someone that pretends to knowledge tells him to beware of the water, for there is a slow poison in it. Now talking about what he knows nothing, he condenses his error into a belief that the water contains slow poison. Now he drinks with fear. The belief is his religion, his feeling is his misery, his pains are his torment. So to save him from hell or pain is to destroy the poison or belief. This is what I do. For I have no belief that God ever injures anyone, and my knowledge of him keeps me from the torment of a belief.

Jan. 30, 1862

Science, Woman, the Spiritual Rib

[Originally untitled.] [LC 1:0181]

I have shown that there is no matter independent of mind or life. It is proved by geologists that matter is going through a process of change which is called life. Then life is in the atmosphere or space. And if life is in a state invisible to matter, it may fill all space. Now in this space there must be a diversity of matter or life, viz. the life of minerals, and the life of vegetables and the life of animals. And all these lives are in the atmosphere, like the mist that went up from the earth at the creation. Thus matter or life is in an invisible state to the visible matter but governed by the same God. This makes the material earth or natural world. God made matter and condensed it into certain forms and elements so that it should contain all of the elements that were necessary for man. And to be a combination of these, it was necessary that there should be a chemical union of all matter dissolved into space before man could be formed. For man is made of the dust of this living matter. Now as man contains all the elements of this material world or life, he is a miniature world of himself and contains all the elements of the original world or matter. This matter or life, under the wisdom of God, forms the identity of what is called the natural man. So that man, spoken into being, was made up of all the elements of the old world. Now you have an identity of matter, or life, formed from the mist or dust of all material life, in the form of a man. Thus the natural man partakes of those elements of life of which he is largely composed. He is a sort of phenomenon to the natural world or life, and he commences his life in a higher state of matter. The field or garden in which he is placed is with all the creation of animal forms, and he is liable to all the evils that his life is capable of knowing. This makes man composed of all combinations of living life, thrown together in human form. It is not strange that queer forms and characters should be in the world, which can be traced to the animal creation with which he is most identified.

All phenomena or diseases are the effect of the life that man receives from this atmosphere of animal life, and as man is like all other living matter, a chemical change or progression is constantly going on and he embraces what is called annihilation. And as his life is a life of destruction, he is at war all the time. So with man as with beast, might is right. As man's life is a sort of purifying process, it has to contend with all the grosser life or matter of the animal. So with life, might is right with man and beast, but as man is the rib or purest part of animal life, it contains more of the element thought, for this the lower life does not contain. Thought is one step higher than life, yet even in this state science is a stranger. Man, like the earth, is throwing off a vapor or life, and that contains all the life, or matter, of his perfection. Out of that vapor or life comes a more perfect identity of living matter, more rarefied than the former, but being in danger of being devoured by the former; the latter life is less gross but more spiritual. So that what it loses in gross life or its physical strength, it receives from a higher power, called God or science. This science is the wisdom of God that controls this pure life that is subject to the lower or grosser life. This is another phenomenon of wisdom.

As the earth is composed of different kinds of soil adapted for certain kinds of vegetable life, the rest of the earth is wanted for some other use. So as man is of that kind of earth that bears more of the food to sustain the lower lives, he must not find fault with a more pure soil or life that can produce a higher kind of living food that gives man more pleasure than he receives from the lower lives, and this life or soil is the spiritual rib or lives that arise from man. This is a more perfect matter or soil. This is the soil called woman. This is that pure soil that has gone through all the changes of life from the mineral kingdom to the spiritual or scientific world, or the kingdom of heaven, where God or science is.

Now I do not mean that woman means every female, nor do I pretend to say that man means everything of the animal, but that the life or matter of a female contains more of that life of love that is required to receive the higher development of God's wisdom than the life of man; for this soil or life is pure love or life, which has been purified by this chemical change that life has gone through. No intermediate space has ever been where this soil was rich enough to bear the fruits of science to satisfy the natural man. Phenomena have always occurred in the form of science, as though man had once been far advanced beyond his present condition, but it cannot be so from the fact that science is wisdom, and wisdom is superior to error. As error has more physical strength, it is counteracted by a higher power called science. These two elements are the life of man. The male creation feeds on the lower order of life. It makes the higher order a sort of pet for a while, as the cat plays with the bird for a while, then in a sort of playful way devours it. Thus all life in the lower animals sports and plays with its prey. So the natural man sports and plays with the female; at the same time his weapons of destruction lie concealed in his breast, ready to be used at his own pleasure; and while the purer part of his nature is sympathizing with its own love in a higher life or soil, the animal life is prowling around to devour the little pleasure that is striving to grow in this barren soil. This keeps science down and regards it as an enemy, for it is not known to the natural man.

Now, put this science into the life or soul of the female, and then she is safe from the lower animal life, and it puts her in possession of a science that the natural man knows not of. It separates her from matter and brings her into that spiritual state that rises from all animal life with a knowledge of its character. She then stands as a chemist among all sorts of matter or life which are under her control and which she has the power or knowledge of changing. Then she becomes a teacher of that science which puts man in possession of a wisdom that can subject all animal life to his own control and separate the wisdom of this world from the wisdom of God. Then woman becomes a teacher of the young and man stands to woman as a servant to his Lord, ready to investigate all phenomena by a science. The woman is the very one who gives all the impressions to the child. The female is always the most respected among the animal or feathered race. But man, from some cause, probably having more physical strength and looking upon all things as inferior to his own wisdom, is not content to subject all the brute creation to submission to his will but must subject the very creature that his best life or nature adores to submission, and in this way woman is deprived of carrying out the science that God intended. By this physical force woman is kept down and does not have the stand in the world that God intended. But I do say that at the time that matter or life becomes pure enough for the science to reign over ignorance, then science will become the master and ignorance the servant. This will as surely take place as that there is a chemical change going on in matter.

Mind is only another state of matter called life. Life is only a state of matter that is purifying itself to receive a higher life that will never end; that is science. And as man is nothing but a living animal, he lives on such living life as his appetite craves, and as he separates the animal from the spiritual, his appetite or passions change till he is completely carried away by the spiritual life. Here is just as much a phenomenon as any of the rest of the world's phenomena, for science teaches man that although he is not of this world, he is a teacher in it and, being a teacher, he is a soldier in the hands of science. To fight the error of life like a soldier and contend for the truth or science requires more courage than it does to fight for your own bread. Like the deist, the beast's courage is for what it can eat. It fights for that, but man ought to have a higher motive than the brute. I am sorry to say that, give man all his beastly appetite craves, he, like the lion, would lie down and sleep till roused by hunger. Then look out for his teeth; but the female is more wide awake and like the hen who scratches for worms to feed her chickens, while her husband is either fighting some political battle or strutting round like the rooster. I do not mean to say that every man is a rooster, or every female a hen. There are some hens that care nothing for their young, and if it were not for their mates, the chickens would starve. So it is with male and female of the human species. There are exceptions to all rules, and as science and error are so combined, it is impossible to draw the line of distinction.

As the mind of man is like the soil, it is composed of all sorts of soil or earth. So as California is the place the minds are directed for gold, so the wisdom of God or science is more abundant in the soil or life of the females, but it does not follow that their life is all the soil that is capable of producing science, but it contains more of the spiritual wisdom than is found in man. This is as it should be, and if it could be admitted by man so that woman could have her place in the life of man, the world would in a short time be rid of the scourges that infest the land, that is, the medical faculty and priests. Women are religious from science, naturally, and if man had not instructed them, the world would have been now free from superstition and evils that follow our belief. Woman is not one half so superstitious as man. They have three times as much courage and endurance as men. Their sympathy is almost inexhaustible. While men get out of patience and would leave the sick, woman will cling to the sick as much as to say to death, You shall not have the life. Now where is woman placed? Just where man puts her to satisfy himself. She has nothing to do with her situation, but she must be content with what man chooses to assign her. In wisdom he, of course, is to be the great center of attraction, and although he has no light only as it is thrown from the sun or higher part of his wisdom, the woman, he never thinks while he is surveying the solar system of his wisdom that the very light enabling him to distinguish between light and darkness or error and science is derived from a higher power superior to himself. You may infer from what I have said that I want to place the female above the male. This is not the case, for a female coming forward in public to advocate man's ideas is as much below the male as the male, who leaves his standing and takes the character of a brute for the gratification of a set of men and women, is below the brute itself. Neither is in the place designed by their creator. The woman lowers herself, and the man becomes worse than a brute.

Then it may be asked, Where is woman's true position? I answer, As a teacher of the science of health and happiness. This is what man does not want to do. It is too much like labor to toil over the little children and sit by the sick and take their sufferings upon yourself. This man will not do, but he is very willing to bind burdens on his neighbors which they will not lift one finger to remove. You may ask how they bind burdens? By teaching false doctrines whose effect on the people they do not know, therefore keeping alive errors which keep the people in bondage and all their lives subject to death.

I will now tell what these are that we fight and where science steps in and puts an end to the war. I have shown that life is matter and this matter belongs to the three kingdoms: animal, vegetable and mineral. These all have life. This life is thrown off like the mist that went up from the earth, and the life is itself and it makes war with its own father and lives on itself. Now as man is that combination of matter or life that is condensed to form an idea, in his natural life he is the life of all living life before him. He becomes a sort of living matter and is subject to all the living laws of life or matter, so that man lives on life just the same as all other living things who slay and eat each other. Thus, might is right. Man throws off from himself a more perfect life or matter. It at last becomes more refined and becomes the medium of a higher life, the life of science or everlasting life where there is no death but where all things are tried by science. As science grows in this matter, its life is its wisdom, and to get wisdom is to make war with its enemy. So its weapons are the wisdom of God in science.

The war is the evils of the world. These are the old superstitions of the world, and as they are the life of the old heathen idolatry, the priest and doctors cultivate these ideas and feed the multitudes so that they get so raving for some spiritual food that they attack each other. Therefore everyone's hand is against his neighbor. We live on each other's lives, for our ideas are life. Now when the science comes, this life or error makes war against it, for science is its destruction, and sometimes a hard battle is fought before the enemy is destroyed.

I will illustrate one battle. Take the Devil. He was just as much a terror to his generation as Robert Kidd was to the mariners of his day. Now science was the only enemy he had to fear and all who dared to attack him were in danger of their lives. What crippled him? Science, not known, has chained him to the earth, but his power is not stopped. His voice is yet heard in the darkness of bigotry. But when the true science that can show the true answer to all the inquiries in regard to him shall come, then the error will be annihilated, and life eternal will take the place of this life or belief in the Devil.

August 1860

Scientific Interpretation of the Following Passage: I Cor. 8:1, 2, 3 Verses
[BU 2:0486]

"Now as touching things offered unto idols, we know that we all have knowledge. Knowledge puffeth up but charity edifieth. And if any man think he knoweth anything, he knoweth nothing yet as he ought to know. But if any man love God the same is known of him."

Now what did Paul mean by all the above? He begins by saying that we all think we have knowledge concerning offerings to idols.

But this knowledge puffeth up, so it is not worth much. What does Paul mean by knowledge? He means that wisdom that man has which is brought out in trying to account for all phenomena. Man sees, hears or feels a sensation; being ignorant of the cause he undertakes to account for it. This is knowledge and it makes him vain and puffed up. Paul says such a man knows nothing as he should know, but if he knows science, then his wisdom is known of him. So Science is God and God is one of the names of Science. Wisdom is the only living and true life.

Why should all persons appeal to the Bible? The Bible contains no intelligence of itself. If you wanted to know anything about mathematics or any science the world admits, you would not go to the Bible. Then what is the Bible good for? There must be some cause why everyone should admit a book that everyone should explain. If we consider the believers in the Bible, we shall find them of all classes of minds, all differing in regard to the meaning and yet no two agreeing what it is good for. Suppose the Bibles were burned up, would it have any effect on you as an individual? I think I hear you say, No, but it would have on some others. Suppose it would. Then it is of some use, like the law to keep man in subjugation. This is the fact and Jesus had the same idea of it. So he says, What the law has failed to do, science will do.

Science has destroyed opinion or law just as far as it can be proved. It has enlightened man in all the arts and sciences. The Science of Health and Happiness has not been admitted as yet; still, happiness is what all wise men have been trying to establish. The ancients thought they had discovered it, but owing to the superstition of the world, the people could not understand it. They required that every phenomenon should have a mysterious source. So the wisdom of the wise was interpreted by the opinions of the ignorant and as ignorance is increased, the wisdom grew cold and the wise men were believed when they spoke. Now the ideas of the writers of the Old Testament are not known to the world, being enveloped by opinions about them which are taken for truth, while the authors are winked out of sight. The writers of the Old Testament were scientific men, far superior to the men of our age in regard to the subject on which they wrote. I shall show that the Bible was never intended as a religious book according to the opinions of the world.

But it is a scientific explanation of causes and effect, showing how man must act and think for his own happiness and teaching us how to unlearn our errors that lead to misery and disease. It has nothing to do with theology. The whole aim of these ancients was to teach man how to be happy by wisdom, for happiness is what follows our acts. Man acts according to his wisdom and if his wisdom is of opinions he is liable to get into trouble, but if it is of science, he gets his reward of his study and the happiness is what follows. So the Bible is the wisdom of certain men condensed into a book like any other mathematics. This book if rightly understood would give man an idea of all the superstitions of the world and the right understanding of the authors would explain the absurdities of superstition and show that ignorance is the theory of the day. At the time of Jesus, these were misrepresented so that not one of these ideas were admitted, but a literal construction put upon their writing when they never intended to have them understood as literal facts.

September 1861

Scientific Man, The
[LC 2:0848]

I will try to define what I mean by the scientific man or a man outside of matter. To do this I must assume myself in relation to mind as God stands to all creation. The natural man is only an idea made by God's wisdom, like a shadow. After this shadow goes through a certain change, like any other matter, it is then in a state to be a medium of a higher power than itself. God sends an identity of his wisdom to take control of the medium and carry out his own design and bring man to a knowledge of the father. This identity that he sends is science or the son of God.

It is very difficult to illustrate to a person what you may know for the want of wisdom in the person you address. Like this: You cannot make a child understand what you say till it arrives at a certain state of mind. Every person is a child in what they cannot understand. So to illustrate, I must use a strong figure so you can get at my meaning. For if you do not do the thing God does, then you cannot be the son of God unless you do His will. Christ was called the Son of God. Now why was He called the Son of God? Because He did the will of His father that sent him. Now to be a son of God, you must do His will, and His will is to subject your errors to the truth so that you can know that you are born of God.

Now I will suppose God, when He spoke man into existence, knew that man was His own idea, and if He made him, then nations were all of God, not of the idea. Now call these nations a chemical change that was going on for a certain time, for a certain effect till man became of age, or that men became ready to be governed by a higher principle than matter. Now science is wisdom put into practice. So science is the son of God or Wisdom. Now science being the son of Wisdom it is a part of Wisdom. Now give this science an identity with a knowledge of its father and then you have a son, ready to take possession of man or matter, when matter becomes purified or a chemical change takes place, so it can be governed by an independent power.

Now for proof of what I have said. I know that I can create an idea of some kind of animal and make it appear to have life, but the life is in myself or my own knowledge of this wisdom. Now suppose I give the created animal to another. He sees it and sees that it has life and moves. He knows it has life. Now to him it has life, but to me it is nothing but an idea of my own make. His wisdom keeps life in the animal just according to his belief.

Now suppose I teach that person how to create the animal so that he can create one himself, then I impart my own wisdom to the matter or idea man till a son or scientific identity arises, and this son is equal to his father so far as he acts according to scientific wisdom.

And to show that he is equal to his father is to do the things his father does; thus he is the master of the matter or idea man. This son or science is not seen by the natural man, so the natural man thinks his life is in this belief. Now to come to the knowledge of this is the new birth. You may ask what benefit all this wisdom is to man if man lives right along without any change. It is of vast importance to man. Suppose man had no idea of progression, then [unfinished]

1863

Senses
[BU 3:0037]

I have spoken of the senses as something that can exist independent of our natural body. This is new to the world or it has never been admitted, for all the senses are attached to and a part of the body, and the idea of their being separated is something which has not dawned upon the intelligence of the world. It may be a belief among some persons but it is not admitted among the scientific. To have a knowledge of this science is to know when an impression is produced on the senses. The senses contain no knowledge of themselves. When a sensation is produced on them, if the soul or identity is aware of it and knows its true meaning, it does not produce the same sensation as though the soul was ignorant of the true meaning. It is very hard for me to define what I want to communicate to you, for there are so many meanings to the same words and they all mean the same thing and contradict each other, that I do not know how to explain what I mean by the senses. I will try to classify them.

In the first place, I believe matter to be nothing but an idea belonging to the senses, but the natural man does not recognize this idea. I believe mind is matter used by that power that controls the senses for a medium, and used to form any idea that is desired to bring about a truth or specific fact. The senses do not embrace of themselves any idea of good or bad, but are simply the act of seeing, hearing, smelling, tasting, and feeling. All these are independent of knowledge, for the beast and child contain them. Mesmerism proves the life of all of them independent of the body, so I set them down as senses, not matter, or mind, but life or the medium of the soul. The soul or wisdom of the senses is what has never been acknowledged to have an identity but is embraced in the word senses. Here you see I have identified two powers or something independent of matter and independent of each other.

Now the senses are life and are sensitive to impressions, not through flesh and blood but through the medium called senses. This fills all space and contains all sight, smell, etc., all these are light and light contains all the elements of the senses. The senses may be compared to particles of light. Now suppose God to be the fountain of senses or light; this light contains particles and each particle contains an identity, and the particles are made up of these senses governed by a higher power. Now the strength of the light or senses is the expansion of its light or senses and the diminishing of its senses is the contracting of its light till it can be embraced in a bushel.

Jesus says a wise man will put his light on a bushel instead of under it. Now as each person is a particle of this great light or senses, and the knowledge of it the soul, it knows that its life is not in the contracting of its senses but in the expansion of its life or senses. Therefore the life of the body or ideas is the knowledge of its senses, and the senses are called the eye of truth. So if the eye or truth be single, the whole body is full of light or truth, but if the senses are darkened or contracted or evil, the whole body is full of darkness. Now as the senses like light expand, the error or darkness is annihilated. And the knowledge of the senses is not confined to the idea of matter, like itself in the bushel, but sees itself outside of the idea or bushel and sees into this darkness or world of superstition. So that life or light is in darkness but the darkness comprehendeth it not, and as man is evil or ignorant, he chooses darkness rather than light. For the light would condemn him and destroy his life or ignorance. This truth composes all the life that will exist as a science but the wisdom of darkness reasons in its own element. Its light is its ignorance; its knowledge is matter; its soul is its knowledge and its knowledge is its life and its life is in itself and itself is matter and matter or life is like water so condensed to take the form of solid or ice.

Science dissolves the solid or ice and decomposes it. Each globule takes its own identity and looks at the solid, as the senses look at the body as an idea of mind so that there is no science or truth or soul; then the whole body or identity is full of darkness. Now take the natural body and compare it to ice and its warmth or cold, its knowledge. You see just how far its eyes or senses can go. It sees its body but it is not acquainted with its destroyer, the sun or science. But as the sun throws its rays on its cold, icy form, a chemical change takes place and decomposition commences. The particles or identity of which it was bound by error is dissolved. It rises and each globule assumes an identity, not that it is ice but that it has broken away from the prison and is now free to assume any form it pleases. This is an illustration of the science man. Man is made up of ideas like globules of water, the cold or ignorant state of the world like north winds has condensed his ideas into a form or body containing all the ideas of disease and all other bad effects.

In this state, like the ice, he sees no light of the science and like the particles of water, reasons as though he was the very identity and wisdom of the world and when this body shall be dissolved, it ends its identity. The ice reasons just so, if it reasons at all, but science reasons in this way. Although you dissolve this ice or body you only set the particles free from the error that binds them together and they have a house or identity, not made by the hand of error but eternal, in the science.

1	2	3	4
wisdom	medium	to be acted upon	condensed
SOUL	SENSES	MIND	MATTER

May 1860

Senses, The [I]
[LC 1:0272]

Why is it that mankind has settled down on the fact that man has five senses, no more nor less? The wise say the spiritual man has two more, making seven senses. Now, what is a sense? We often speak in this way: Such a thing comes within my senses. If senses means what the wise say it does, why is man set down above the brute? Let us see how they both compare. The man sees, hears, tastes, smells and feels and so does the brute. As far as the five senses go, man and brute are alike. Neither shows any preeminence of wisdom over the other. When you ask where is man's superiority, you are told that man reasons and the brute does not. Ask for proof and they can show no difference. Only as they make it in their own minds, for if you place them both together, the brute is a little the shrewder. Now all will admit that there is a vast difference between a wise man and a brute, but the brutal man is as much below the brute as the latter is below the wise man. This wisdom that makes man above the brute is not of this brutal world, but it must come from some higher source. I have so much confidence in the wisdom of the wise men of old that I have no doubt but they solved that question; and I have so little confidence in the wisdom of this world that I disbelieve every truth founded on man's opinion. All science is susceptible of proof, so that an opinion is of no force to the scientific man.

We often hear of the laws of God, but when we ask for wisdom on the subject, the wise fail to give us the information desired by the scientific man. They can give their opinion and as that contains no knowledge, the scientific must look for wisdom elsewhere than to the wisdom of this brutal world of five senses. So I will leave man and brute with their five senses and search out some other source to solve the problem of the senses.

I will ask anyone if seeing is matter, or is it something independent of matter? For instance, you see a shadow; is that which sees any part of the shadow? All will say, No. Then the shadow comes in contact with something. Now what is that something called—sight or one of the senses? Is it matter? The natural man cannot answer that question any more than the brute. If it is answered at all scientifically, it must come from elsewhere than the natural man. The natural man says that the eye is the sight. Jesus says the light of the body is the eye. So the natural man and Jesus differ, for the natural man puts sight in the natural eye. Settle this question and you get one of the five senses defined so that there can be no dispute between the scientific and natural or brutal man; and as the natural man has failed to satisfy the scientific man, let the latter try to convince the natural man of his error. The scientific man makes all sensation outside of the idea of matter, so that to him all sensation must be made on something independent of the natural man's idea of senses. All will admit that God knows all things. If you do not own it, you must admit it, if you are above the brute, else you, admitting that the brute knows nothing about God, put yourself on a level with the brute. So I take it for granted that this question is settled that God knows all things. So God sees. That is one sense. All will admit that God is equal to man, at least in regard to wisdom; so if he can show that man's five senses can act independently of his natural body, besides having other senses, no one will allow that man's wisdom is superior to God. So if it can be shown that man or this wisdom is not of matter but of God, then we will divide him into as many senses as is necessary for his happiness or that of the scientific world.

What is necessary for the natural man's happiness is to eat, drink and enjoy himself in the easiest way he can. The savage is a fair specimen of the natural man and the wild beast the natural specimen of the brute creation. One has no preeminence over the other. Might is right. Each is happy when not disturbed. If never disturbed they would be like the fool, without even error, so that disturbance brings into action other senses, and as wisdom is developed, it gives man a knowledge of himself above the natural man of five senses. Thus the wisdom of the scientific man sees the man with the five senses a little above the brute, trying in error to free himself from his earthly matter or ignorance and arrive at the knowledge of the phenomena that keep him in a state of sin or disease and death. So I will leave the man of five senses in error to talk to the scientific man about the other senses.

He is not embraced in one idea. A man may be scientific in many sciences-chemistry, mathematics, astronomy, botany—all that are acknowledged and admitted by even the natural man, though not understood. But the Science of Happiness is not acknowledged by the wisdom of the five senses, so it requires more senses to put man in possession of this Science that will teach him happiness. As happiness is what follows a belief, it is necessary to know whether our wisdom is of this world of opinions or of the world of science. This world sees nothing outside of its senses. Wisdom sees nothing inside of the natural man's senses but ignorance, so that the wisdom of this world is opposed to the Science of Happiness. Let us see what will be admitted by all. I believe that it will not be denied that there is such a phenomenon as mesmerism. If it is denied, then those who do so may enjoy their own opinions, and I will turn to those who admit it. This embraces a large class of the scientific world, so taking it for granted that the phenomenon can be produced, I will show how many senses a person has in a mesmerized state.

I have put many persons into this state and none, with one exception, had any idea of seeing through their eyes. There was one who thought he saw through his eyes but all experiments show that it is not so. This shows that sight is not through the eyes. It is also proved that breathing, as it is called, is one of the faculties. In fact, a mesmerized subject is all that a person can be in his waking state at the same time. He is another person separate and apart from his earthly identity. He can feel, fly, walk and pass into the sea and describe things lost and can find things that he knows not of in another state. Now where and what was this invisible something that could pass in and out of matter? He could eat, drink and even get so intoxicated that he would show it through his natural senses. And all these effects would be produced without his natural senses being addressed in any way.

Now what is this something called mesmerism, clairvoyance or spiritualism? It is the mystery or power that has troubled the wisdom of this world to solve. Solve this problem and you give a knowledge to man that the world has always admitted but not understood. To understand this phenomenon is to go back to the first cause and see what man was. As language is the invention of man, we cannot get at the cause of the introduction of that by the analyzing of it, so we must go back of language to find the cause that prompted man to invent it. So let us go back of language and we see living beings going round like beasts not seeming to have any way of communicating with each other. Then each acted on his own responsibility, eating and drinking as it pleased himself. Now the desire for food prompted the mind; and as food has the sort of odor that arises from it, man like the beast is drawn to the odor from a desire to have this sensation gratified. So that the odor attracted the man like the beast not by sight, but by smell. Here is one sensation but with no name; it is the same in man and beast; they eat and are satisfied. As they eat, taste comes. This opens the mind to see what the thing is. This brings sight or knowledge so they go on till all the faculties are developed in man and beast. As the faculty of smell was more important than even sight, it would be the one they most desired, for it not only attracted the animal to the thing smelt, but warned him of danger of being destroyed; so that all animals cultivate this sense for their own safety. The fowls would cultivate it to protect themselves by their wings when any animal or man came near them. So by experience all animals have learned to keep clear of each other by the peculiar faculty of smell. As they associated sight with the odor, then when the odor came in contact with their sense, they would create the thing contained in the odor. If it was an odor from some living thing that they were afraid of, they would fly or run till they were free from their enemy. So little by little the wild beast settled down on a sort of basis that gave each one some faculty to counteract some other faculty in another. The lion depended on his smell and so did all animals who were inferior to their enemies; so that if the lion imitated some other animal, for instance if he was quick in his motions, he would not be so acute in his smell, so the victim could keep out of his way and yet remain in his sight. The atmosphere of the lion was certain death to the other animals so that their fright threw off an odor that did not attract the lion till the object of his prey came in contact with his sight. So all things went on in this way and man was at the mercy of the wild beast. His sense of smell was as acute as that of the wild beast, but his physical strength was less. Now, necessity is the mother of invention and it became necessary for man to introduce something to counteract the wild beast, so it would be natural for man to make signs or have some way to give his fellow man a warning of his danger. For men in these times, like all other animals, would go together in herds or parties, for although each might not know each other's ideas, they all had a fear of their enemies. This state of progression must lead to a sort of language, so that language was invented for the safety of the race. Now, the sense of smell was the foundation of language, and as language was made to apply to some sensation, it must take some time to introduce it for the odor must be so defined that a person perceiving the thing named could describe it. So at first it must be partly smell and partly acted out by gesture, so that the person could understand what was intended to be communicated to him. For instance, the sense of smell for food must be named, so that one could convey the idea to another. Now when man wanted food his sense of hunger excited his sense of smell more than the one who was not hungry, so that the hungry must be drawn to the food by the odor that arose from the food desired. To communicate the food to another must be done by bringing the food to the other or by accompanying the other to the place; therefore the name was given to some odor that could be smelled, for instance some vegetable or root. So when the name was mentioned, the person would create the thing named.

This created the power of creating. So the odor contained the thing created as there was no call for creating anything but food and drink to sustain life. Man would naturally give names to all the odors he liked and the names would correspond to the pleasures that the food produced, accompanied with gestures of joy; while those odors that contain frightful things, although they could eat them, were represented by gestures of a frightful kind, for instance, the odor of a beast that they could kill when perceived by someone. To communicate the idea to others, he must create the beast in his own mind and so change his matter that an odor would arise from him so strong that it could be perceived by the person affected. This would introduce the art of language and make man shrewder than the beast. As language was introduced, the sense of smell became more blunt till it, like other instincts, gave way to another standard. So as man became shrewder than the beast he became more savage, till at last man's superior shrewdness would make the beast afraid of him. Man, having imitation like all other brutes, would imitate and invent some new thing, thus bringing a new faculty into play; and as men excited this faculty, that of smell was confined to a narrow sphere. As imitation was developed, the practice of thinking would increase, so that thinking came to be as much of a sense as smelling. Forming thought into things or ideas became a sense; the power or sense of imitation brought up the sense of motion, so that man's thought when put into an idea would move and seem to have life. All of the above was spiritual and it could not be seen by the natural man or beast, so the natural man would imitate his idea in some way that it would be seen and felt by the natural man; thus invention of things in the spiritual world was shadowed forth in the natural world. As this invention was received, the spiritual senses were not relied on for the safety of man, so the invention of weapons would give a person an advantage over a wild beast.

This warfare was kept up till man could invent castles or some place of defense. In the progress of the world, men would form themselves into parties or tribes and then rivalry would spring up and aspirants would come forward to lead off. And as hunting would be the only sport or amusement, the hunting ground would be a bone of contention. That would lead to fighting among men and the invention of weapons of some kind, till wars would become the order of the day. This would increase the power or faculty of thinking which would lead to inventions of different things and at last there must be some laws or regulations introduced to feed those who could not fight. The ones who stayed at home would be those of the weaker portion of the race, including the females, the aged and children. So some laws must be adopted for their support and safety and penalties attached to the disobedience of these laws. The officers of the laws would be taken from the most aspiring and cunning part of the tribes. This placed the leaders above the masses so competition sprang up which increased the leaders' perceptive faculties to invent all sorts of stories to keep the people quiet. As language was what they all wanted, those who could teach it would be looked upon as superior to the rest. Phenomena would then, as now, take place and the wise would be called upon to explain. This would introduce astrology and priestcraft so that at last there came up a sort of craft among the leaders, like politics of our day. Then all sorts of inventions would spring up to keep the people in submission when they grumbled at their leaders, not as they do now, for we are born slaves and they were born free. Therefore it required more strict laws then than now. All sorts of ideas were started and among them the power of creating objects that could be seen; that faculty was cultivated for the benefit of the wise. This introduced spiritualism among civilized tribes, at first for the benefit of the leaders, so superstition became the power to worship; and as it was necessary that someone should explain the phenomena, persons would be appointed, and thus priests and prophets sprang up. These men must be paid and cared for and the people were taxed to support them. At last the tribes formed themselves into nations and kingdoms and gave the power to the priests, so the priests stood at the head of the nation.

As the priesthood was founded on superstition, it was necessary to keep the people superstitious; so all sorts of inventions were made to keep the people ignorant. And as science was invented or discovered, all the discoveries were kept a secret from the people so that any chemical or mechanical effect could be produced and the people thought it came from God. Astronomy was discovered; the priests kept it as a revelation from heaven and all their astronomical calculations were made, not as a science for the masses but as a direct revelation from God to bring about some great design. This kept the people in a state of nervous excitement and made them excite the idea of spiritual sight, knowing that whatever they could make the people believe, they would create. So all they had to do was to start the storm of evil spirits, and the people's superstition would produce the very phenomena wanted. This was proof that evil spirits did exist. Then it was not hard to make them believe that the spirits would get hold of them, so that at last it became a matter of fact, so much so that at the time of Saul there were some fifty ways of getting communications from God, and how many ways of getting it from the devil, I know not.

December 1860

Senses, The [II]
[LC 1:0495]

Are our senses mind? I answer, No. This was the problem the ancient philosophers sought to solve. Most of them believed the soul, senses and every intellectual faculty of man to be mind; therefore our senses must be mind. The translator of Lucretius says Lucretius attacks the ancient academics who held the mind to be the sole arbiter and judge of things and establishes the senses to be the arbitrators for, says he, "Whatever can correct and confute what is false must of necessity be the criterion of truth and this is done by the senses only." This difference is true in part. Both were right. But they confused mind and senses into one, like the modern philosophers who make wisdom and knowledge, mind and senses, Jesus and Christ, synonymous. Now mind and senses are as distinct as light and darkness, and the same distinction holds good in wisdom and knowledge, Jesus and Christ. Christ, Wisdom and the spiritual senses are synonymous. So likewise are Jesus, knowledge and mind. Our life is in our senses; and if our wisdom is in our mind, then we attach our life and senses to matter. But if our wisdom is attached to Science, our life and senses are in God, not in matter, for there is no matter in God or Wisdom. Matter is the medium of Wisdom. This difference has been overlooked by the ancients, and modern philosophers have put mind and soul in matter, thus making a distinction without a difference. Now according to modern philosophy, the soul, mind, life and senses are all liable to die; but according to this truth mind is matter, that which is not true is matter, the life of a lie is matter and all matter must be dissolved. Wisdom is not life. Our senses are not life. A truth is not life. But all these are solid and eternal; and to know them is life and life eternal. Life is in the knowledge of this wisdom, and death is in the destruction of your opinion or matter.

I will give some experiments of the man of wisdom acting through the man of matter and dissolving the man of matter so the man of wisdom can escape. This process is the Science of Wisdom. Take for example two persons, or you and myself. One wishes to communicate to the other some fact. You feel a pain. I also feel it. Now the sympathy of our minds mingling is matter, but there is no wisdom in it, for wisdom is outside of matter. If we both feel the same pain, we each call it our own for we are devoid of that wisdom which would make us know we were affecting each other. Each one has his own identity and wants sympathy, and the ignorance of each other is the vacuum that is between us. So we are drawn together by this invisible action called sympathy. Now make man wise enough to know that he can feel the pains of another, and then you get him outside of matter. The wisdom that knows this has eternal life, for life is in the knowledge of this wisdom. This the world is unacquainted with.

Now Jesus had more of this life or truth than any other person, and to teach it to another is a science. And although one may know it, he may not be able to teach it. If you know it and can teach it, then you are a teacher of the truth; but if you know it and cannot teach it, then you are a follower of the truth. Now the knowledge of this truth is life and the absence of it is death. There are a great many kinds of life. Man begins at his birth. Mineral life is not vegetable and vegetable life is not animal life and there is another kind of life that is not understood, and that is the life that follows the knowledge of this great truth. The word life cannot be applied to Wisdom, for that had no beginning, and life has. The word death is applied to everything that has life. All motion or action produces life, for where there is no motion there is no life. Matter in motion is called life, but life is not wisdom but a chemical change of matter, and that is called animal life. Life is the action of matter, and to know it is a truth and to know how to produce it is wisdom. I will now show how to produce eternal life. It was possessed by Jesus, for he says, "My sheep hear my voice and I give unto them eternal life. I and my Father are one."

I shall show that Jesus was not life but life or Christ was in him, and he taught it. He says, "Whosoever will save his life shall lose it, and whosoever shall lose his life for my sake shall find it." Then people believed their life to be in themselves, but Jesus knew their lives were in God, for if they lost their opinions and found this truth, then they had lost their life and found it.

I will now take my own practice to explain what life is according to Jesus. I said if two persons were sitting together and each felt a pain, each would call it his own. Now this pain is life, for it contains our senses, and this life is in matter. So the pain is in our mind, and our mind, senses, and life are all the same according to the world's wisdom. I know I can take a person's feelings, and this knowledge to me is a truth, and to know it is life, and this knowledge the patient does not possess. He knows he has a pain and this to him is a truth so that his knowledge is life, but this life is in his belief and his belief is his knowledge and his knowledge is his mind and his mind is matter. So his life is liable to be lost by his losing his mind. My life is in my wisdom and my wisdom is not matter; so that to know this is a truth outside of my patient's belief. And this truth contains my life. To get his senses out of his matter into this truth is to give him eternal life. I want to give him eternal life to save him from the sufferings occasioned by his belief that he shall lose his life by disease of the heart. My wisdom acting on matter is in matter but it is no part of it. So what to him is death is to me matter that can be changed and there is no wisdom in it. His ignorance keeps his senses in fear of death and all his life subject to bondage through this belief. I will try to teach him the truth which will free him from the fear of death and give him eternal life which is this truth.

I commence by describing to him his feelings. These he admits; but how I can tell them is to him a mystery. This I know for I see him in his error, yet he cannot see me in his wisdom, for wisdom is outside of error and error cannot see outside of itself for it is in its own prison. It wants me to explain how I can see it and how I know how it feels. I will suppose you, the reader, to be the patient, and that you acknowledge that I tell your feelings and what you think is your disease. All this I get from you without your knowledge; therefore you do not know how I do it. So I will inform you. Everyone is made of matter and matter is continually going through a chemical change; this change is life, not wisdom, but life like vegetable or mineral life. Every idea is matter, so of course it contains life and is the name of something that can be changed. Motion or change is life. Ideas have life; a belief has life or matter, for it can be changed. Now all the aforesaid make up man, and all this can be changed. As I am trying to convince you how I take your feelings, I must use such illustrations as you can understand, for my life is in my words; and if my words cannot destroy your life or matter, then I cannot give you my life or wisdom.

I will now take a rose for an illustration. You are like a rose. You throw from yourself an atmosphere or vapor. When the rose is dead, all outside of it is darkness to the germ of the bud. This is the child. As the rose opens, it expands and unfolds itself to the world, the same as a child's brain; as it expands, it opens the folds of its understanding. As the rose comes before the world of roses, it takes its stand with the rest of its kind. So it is with man. As he unfolds his knowledge, he is classed with other minds of his kind. As the rose throws off its peculiarities to the air, the world judges of its odor. So as man throws off his peculiar character of life or health or disease, the world is to judge of his happiness or misery by the fruits of his belief.

Take a person with consumption. The idea consumption is matter, and it decomposes and throws off an odor that contains all the ideas of the person affected. This is true of every idea or thought. Now my odor comes in contact with this odor thrown from you, and I, being well, have found by 20 years' experience that these odors affect me, and also that they contain the very identity of the patient whom this odor surrounds. This called my attention to it, and I found that it was as easy to tell the feelings or thoughts of a person sick as to detect the odor of spirits from that of tobacco. I, at first, thought I inhaled it, but at last found that my senses could be affected by it when my body was at a distance of many miles from the patient. This led me to a new discovery, and I found my senses were not in my body but that my body was in my senses, and my knowledge located my senses just according to my wisdom. If a man's knowledge is in matter, all there is of him is contained in matter; but if his knowledge is in wisdom, then his senses and all there is of him are outside of matter. To know this is a truth, and the effect is life in this truth, and this truth is in wisdom. So the man who knows all this is in wisdom with all his senses and life.

Then where do I differ from you? In this respect: my wisdom is my health, and your wisdom is your disease; for your wisdom is your belief, and my wisdom is my life and senses, and my senses teach me that your trouble is the effect of your belief. What is light to me is darkness to you. You being in the dark stumble and are afraid of your own shadow. I with the eye of truth see you in your darkness or belief and you seem to me blind, or like the rose you cannot see the light, while I being in the light see through the clouds of your ignorance and see your senses and all there is of you held in this ignorance by this error or matter and trying like the life of the rosebud to break through and come to the light.

You have eyes, taste and all your senses but the clouds are before them and as Jesus said, "Ye have eyes and see not and have ears and hear not and a heart but cannot understand." Now what is the reason? It is this. Your eyes have not seen, your ears have not heard and your heart has not understood what happiness there is in knowing that your life, senses and all there is near and dear to you is not part of matter, and that matter is only a belief or casket to hold you in till wisdom dissolves the casket and lets you into the light of science. There you hold life in the form of the rose and live in a world of light where all the sorrows of Hell Eternal and disease can never come, where you can sit and see that what man takes for a reality is only the dross of heathen superstition. Then you will not be afraid of disease which leads to death.

You may observe if all I say is true, what is it good for if it is only a belief like all religious beliefs? If it is nothing but a belief, then I will admit that it is of no more value to a person than any religious belief. But it is not a belief and my practice proves the truth of my assertions. You may ask for proof that will give some light upon the subject. I will give it, as near as a man who has eyesight can explain colors to a blind person.

When I sit by a patient, if he thinks he has disease of the heart, the atmosphere surrounding him is his belief, and the fear of death is in the density of the clouds of his mind. Now knowing he is in the clouds somewhere, I, as it were, try to arouse him, but it appears as though he were blind, so I shake him to arouse him out of his lethargy. At last I see him aroused and look around but soon sink back again. By my talk I seem to disturb the clouds and this sometimes makes the patient very nervous, like a person coming out of a fit or awakening from a sound sleep. What I say is truth, and being solid, it breaks in pieces his matter or belief till at last he looks up to inquire what has been the trouble. My explanation rouses him and gives another change to his mind, and that is like a thunderstorm. When it thunders and the lightning flashes, the patient is nervous. When the cloud of ignorance passes over and the light of truth comes, then the patient sees where his misery came from, and that it was believing a lie that made him sick. My arguments are based upon my knowledge of his feelings, and this knowledge put in practice is the Science of Health and is for the benefit of the sick and suffering.

1861

Senses, The [III]
[LC 2:0807]

What are man's senses? The common opinion is that man has five senses and these are so well defined that it won't be necessary for me to mention them. According to my theory of this truth, the senses are only a representative of what man and beast are. When reason enters the child, it is not supposed that he has more sense. Now if senses are not what is called knowledge, then knowledge can exist without senses. I make the senses our knowledge, so when our knowledge is gone our senses are gone for knowledge is what can be destroyed, but wisdom is what will stand; so the changing of our knowledge is the losing of our life or senses, but the finding of wisdom is an eternal truth. Then instead of having senses we are wiser and better. This makes man different from the brute creation. The brutes have senses and a knowledge, but they have shown no proof that their knowledge has ever led them to show wisdom over their predecessor.

Senses Detached from the Body, The
[LC 2:0779]

I will give some experiments to show how a person's senses may be detached from the body and yet be as active as ever. I have said that mind is matter and our senses are not matter. As ideas are matter, the idea man is matter in a certain form and our senses being attached to the matter they become one. This is called man, or the inner and outer man. Now the connection to man is a mystery, yet experiments show that they can be separated and both have an existence. This is shown in mesmeric experiments, and often in fevers, etc. The body can be in one place and the senses can be in another. This connection of the two is the mystery to solve.

My experiments for the last twenty years or more have carried me through the idea matter till I have landed beyond the influence of this narrow sphere and risen into that state where matter is created. I know how it is spoken into existence and I can return to the earthly man who thinks his body and senses are one and the same and show him what is real and what is false and how the idea man is attached to the idea matter.

I shall take some patient that I have cured, to prove my assertion. I will take a captain that had lost the use of his limbs. He had been in the army, and being under great excitement, when he would lie down to rest, the anxiety that he felt by the danger that surrounded him kept his mind excited, and the fear of being aroused at any moment kept his mind in constant action like a steam engine, all ready to move at any time. His senses being attached to his belief and his belief being matter and containing all the elements of war, he would fight in his sleep. This would create dangers and he would have his company out to prepare for the fight. So he kept his senses attached to a body that he had made with his company and detached his senses from the body that lay sleeping on the ground. So he became like a person mesmerized. His senses had become detached from his body and his body was like a person's body in a sound sleep or dead. So when I sat by him I found his senses were away from his body. I could hear persons walking so far off that it would be impossible for a person in a normal condition to hear them. Every sound started me and this was the way with the young man, and his body was as lifeless as a dead man's. He had no pain in it, but it was perfectly useless. The doctors pronounced him past cure and so he was to all medical treatment. Now to cure this man was to put his senses or self in communication with his natural body, for he had a spiritual body, and when he was asleep he to himself was awake and then his mind was as active as any person's, and he would drill his company and give off his orders as though he was in the field.

Now how could this cure be brought about? Not by medicine, but by a science which I felt I knew. So I sat down and let my senses follow his, and this brought me away from my body. So after being under his influence, I attached my senses to his body and addressed myself to that. At last I made him see his new body, like waking a person from a sleep till he could balance his arm, till it rested on his elbow and use a little power to direct it. This excited him and a warm perspiration started. That aroused him and his sense of hearing became less sensitive and then his senses came nearer to his body and as quietness was darkness, he could not find the company, so his fear decreased and his anxiety left and he began to improve from that very hour, and in a few weeks, he began to walk and finally got well.

Now the science was in putting the theory in practice, like a man putting the theory of navigation into practice. He may teach the theory; this is one of the Godhead. The vessel is another. Now to attach his theory is to embrace the holy ghost or application, and when that is done, this is wisdom. This is what is meant when Jesus said, Go ye into Jerusalem and tarry till the holy ghost shall direct you. Jerusalem was the theory or learning of the world. So the theory of navigation is Jerusalem and the person must go into that in a vessel and stay till the holy ghost or application teaches him how to apply it.

Now man like a vessel is under a captain and his voyages are sometimes along shore. Most men make the voyages along shore without the least knowledge of navigation and the pilots or doctors are of that class of persons that can teach the points of compass and how to take the sun, but when the storm of life begins and it is necessary to know where you are, then the cloud thickens and darkness sets in, the lightning flashes and thunder rolls and the wind whistles through your ears and the whole body is in a trembling condition and your mast or legs spring and everyone is working and the cry is, Breakers ahead! Then you call on the Holy Ghost or that third power, practice, not theory. This is the state of the sick. The doctors are very good fair weather pilots but when your vessel is in danger they are of little account; you will do as well to clew up your sails and heave to and lash your helm and lay still till the storm is over. And if you are lucky, you will come out all right. So don't put your trust in man's theory but try the theories and see if they will stand the test in the day of trouble.

I have said that all disease is in the mind. I will try to explain it more clearly. I will separate the mind from the senses and the senses from the thing called disease. Now to cure a trouble is to know how it is made. As men reason, they reason upon mathematical principles, but as they stand on a false basis, they will land sooner or later in trouble. Disease is the effect of one kind of reason. The cure is the opposite kind of reason. One is based on science and the other on belief or opinion. To give the reader an idea of my manner, I will take the case of a lady that came to see me. I will show how I changed the mind and how the cure was affected. I sat down by the lady and she affected me in this way. I felt a heat in the back of my neck accompanied with pain. This affected my shoulders and the pit of my stomach. Now all this pain or heat of itself contained no wisdom, only the state of mind. This is mind and out of this everything grows or is made. This was the condition of the lady.

Now she had a belief that she had a cancerous tumor and in fact thought she had one coming. The belief was in this heat for the heat was the mind or soil to have the cancer. Now her beliefs contained the elements of a cancer to her, so she received the belief, and this made the disturbance in the mind. Now who was it that made the disturbance? Not wisdom but the devil or error. Now the sensation made her inquire what it was, and some error or ignorant physician gives his opinion that it is a cancer. So she believed this opinion, and went to work to make the phenomenon. So now I had to change her mind and destroy her belief. This set her senses free from the error and this was the cure. As my reasoning is from what I consider a false report taken for a truth, I have to make the change by illustrations. So I said, Your disease is all in your mind. You think you have a cancerous tumor. This she said was a fact and not in the mind, so I went on to prove my theory and put it into practice.

So I began by a parable. Suppose I ask you if you ever saw a quince and you say, I don't think I have. I said, will you tell me how it looks, how it smells and how it tastes? This you cannot do so you admit your ignorance. Then I commence to explain how it grows on a tree like a small pear tree and I describe it to the best of my ability. You listen. Now all the time your mind is going through a chemical change and you really create a quince after my description. Now this quince is a spiritual one but it has a real name, so you start up excited to find a quince, and as fruit is known by names, you approach a fruit store and look at the various kinds of fruit. At last your eye strikes on the kind you think is a quince, so you buy one and come and show it to me and say, I have found a quince. I say are you sure? You say pretty sure. Have you not a doubt? Why, I cannot say certainly, but I am as sure as I can be without being certain. So I say to you, It is a quince. Now this is wisdom, but in the quince there was no life nor wisdom, and in the name, there was no life nor wisdom to you. But when I put your senses and the name to the thing called quince, then out of this came life or a truth. This is wisdom.

Now for the application to you to cure your idea cancer, for that is what you are afraid of. But first I will say that all reason contains three elements of the trinity. Wisdom contains them all and so does man's opinion and science the same. Now man's trinity is the word, the flesh and the opinion. Science is the word, the flesh is the thing, and the theory is applying the thing to the thing named. Now I shall speak of man's trinity that creates diseases. When you heard the name of tumor or felt the sensation of heat, of course being a little excited and your curiosity awakened, you went to find the cause of your trouble so your senses would enquire of everyone what it was. At last you got the idea of cancerous tumor. Now of course you would look for it the same as you looked for the quince, so your senses would look all over the body, and of course you would be very anxious to find where it generally located itself or stopped. At last you settle that you have found it by the direction you have had from me so you come to me and say, I have found it. I ask you where, you say in the stomach. I ask you when you got it and how it came there. This you can't tell, only that it came without your knowing it. So I say you have made it yourself by listening to the devil or error in the opinion of the medical faculty or public opinion. This you can't believe, so I then commence to explain the trinity of disease.

As I have already said, the belief is a lie, the effect and the explanation. I shall give the elements of error, or the three principles. One is a lie or an old superstition or belief in a disease. This is the idea called the devil. He was a liar from the beginning and he is the father of all disease. So he tells a lie out of his own self and explains it on some scientific principles according to his belief. Now as he is very pious and religious, he has introduced every kind of fashionable ideas and being very unassuming he has now the good wishes of all the people. So much so that his word is now the law of the land, and all that do not bow down to his will, he will smite with some disease of his own make. So his kingdom is of this world of opinion and if you will just look, you will see that every idea of his is in his heaven. Not one thing he ever said is true, but all say he is the author of death and hell and heaven. He created angels, made spirits and witches, and made a great throne up in the heavens and invented all kinds of disease and every sort of misery that can be imagined. So his kingdom is a kingdom of darkness.

Now if every person should cease to exist, his kingdom must fall, for it is all built in the air, yet he is reverenced and prayed to and the people kneel down and ask him to have mercy on them. His laws are the laws of the land; in fact he is the God of the world and his opinion is law. So when you disobey his opinions you disobey a law. Now see where the God of science stands outside of all this deception, and see that all this sort of worship is all idolatry and superstition. But as science never acts but for good, its kingdom is not of this world, for to be good is to be wise and this goodness is health and happiness and is the destruction of error and disease. Now wisdom knows from the beginning that everything that is comes from his wisdom. So man's wisdom can make the distinction between the wisdom of God and the wisdom of the devil or opinion. God created the earth and every living creature that is in or on it, and he created the skies but he never inhabited them except as birds inhabit.

The devil's kingdom is in the air or out of sight and all its inhabitants are spirits of those that had an existence in or on the earth. It has all kinds of physicians and all kinds of diseases and they are both spirits, prowling around seeking whom they may devour, and they have their agents through whom they communicate their will. So in any trouble in this world that affects the human family, the spirits of this devil are ready to administer to their wants. So as they, through their mediums, invent all kinds of evils, they give the evil to the people by a sort of description or illustration. For instance, this devil wishes to destroy you by one of his evils. He commences by telling you about some idea that exists in the world or mind, for the mind is where the prince of darkness dwells.

I will stop here and say a word or two about a young man that first called to see me. I sat down and found him very much frightened and nervous from a little sensation of suffocation. He thought he had the heart disease, and when I told him what it was and all it amounted to, he was all right. Now if it was not for this evil in the mind, there would not have been any cause of alarm, and if I had not explained, he might have died at almost any time, for he said it would wake him up two or three times in the night. Now I say that science calls these evils lies, and the sick have been made to believe that the very things or evils that they bring on themselves by their own acts are something that has come upon them without any of their action, when in reality they are the author of their own existence.

The word cancer is a lie, and the devil or error is the father of it, and it originates in his brain and this residence is in man's mind. His kingdom is in the opinions of man. Now to get a description of his lie, he gives the symptoms so that the symptoms are accompanied with language that will illustrate the evil in such vivid terms that it is almost impossible to deny its existence. So then you begin to have your curiosity excited to know all about it, as the young would sit down by the chimney corner and listen to some ghost story till the ghost would haunt them all night, and they would wake up in the morning all exhausted by some foolish story that never had any existence outside of the mind.

Now as mind is matter, this direction becomes attached to the senses. Then the senses are under the direction of this blind guide and he commences to create in the mind an image after the one the doctors set up. So in their ignorance they watch the growth of the seed sown in the mind. While asleep or ignorant, it grows and is nourished by the person till the proof begins to appear in the form of symptoms; then the fears are further excited and the doctor is called, and after he hears the story or description, he says he thinks you have a cancer. Now of course you are excited to fight the evil and get rid of it. So you inquire where the locality is, and the doctor asks where he seems to dwell the most to you. You say sometimes in the head and sometimes in the shoulder and in the side and over all the chest and in the stomach and runs up to the throat and feels hot. Then says the doctor, that is he, it is a cancer in your stomach; so now you are directed to that locality. This makes you nervous and the next thing a new disease, and so on, till you use up all your mind creating the evils the devil has invented. So your senses being attached to them, you reason that you and your belief and your senses are all one. So this makes up the devil's trinity: the word, the flesh, and the devil. The devil is the author of his own words and the flesh is the phenomenon. So that when he speaks a lie, he speaks of himself for he is a liar and abideth in it. To cure is to show the Father is in the belief.

1864

Senses, The (Sight)
[LC 2:0879]

When we see an object do we see it or do we not see it, or is it only the shadow of the object we see? We often say we know a thing and find we are mistaken. This kind of reasoning comes within the comprehension of every person. There are things that cannot be seen by the natural eye and yet which are seen by some persons and believed to have an existence as much as the seen. The distinction of things seen and things not seen causes all the controversy of the world, for what all agree to, there is no controversy about. To make it clear I will illustrate.

The things that are natural are attributed to God, and man being one of the many natural objects of God's work, he reasons in his own element which is matter. Yet God knows that every living thing is nothing but his own creation and wisdom is the author. Wisdom speaks into existence certain ideas and man is one of them. To wisdom they are all as dross or shadows, and man, like all the rest, reasons that his natural life is his real existence. Everything that God has made comes within the sphere of man and this makes man's material world. Yet to wisdom it is nothing but the shadows of ideas and every idea having the power to create other shadows. Therefore, the idea earth is the foundation of man's reasoning. Now out of this reasoning comes a more perfect man invisible to the earthly man, for the reason of the latter is the foundation or earth for the higher development of man. Now the invisible man begins his foundation on the highest development of the natural man. In this world every idea that has formed in the natural world is conceived or shadowed forth in the natural world so that everything that is manufactured or shows the hand of man is attributed to some being or animal. Now as God has made fish in the sea, so man has made ideas that lie out of sight of the natural world and yet they are believed to have an existence as much as the fish or wild beast of the forest and man is as liable to be devoured by them. I will name some of the evils or enemies that man has to contend with. The things that God has made are all harmless unless they are interfered with and then they defend themselves according to the law of their lives. For matter is all for man's good but if we wish to confine or direct it, we must do it intelligently or bad results will follow. So with the brutes; all can be controlled by a higher power or wisdom for man's happiness.

Now to govern and control them man is endowed with a higher development called genius, or an inventive power so that he can create by his wisdom ways and means to subject the wild. This makes man an inventive being. Here he steps out of the brutal element to a higher state. There is some sagacity in the animal creation that mingles with the human as the vegetable does with the mineral. The mineral is the foundation for the vegetable, and the brutal for the animal and the animal for the intellectual and the intellectual for the scientific kingdom. This last will rule till all the others are subject to science. Then will this science give up its kingdom or authority to wisdom and wisdom will answer all things.

Now as Science is the kingdom that will break in pieces all others it would be well to understand where we as individuals of the lower kingdom will stand. Now man is the embodiment of all the kingdoms of the world and must be subdued by a wisdom higher than that of the natural man. Therefore every act must be weighed by science, for science is the axe that will hew down every error. The kingdom of darkness is the natural world; the kingdom of light is the scientific world. All mankind are in darkness trying to get to the light, so darkness is a state called death and our senses, which are no part of man, are attached to the idea man in the darkness or ignorance, and they are brought to the light or life. Then he is in life. So that life and death are conditions and have nothing to do with the real man, except as a state of happiness.

Death is the state that man dreads and every condition of mind that embraces error embraces death. So disease is a condition of death and truth or health, the condition of life. To be alive therefore is to be wise and happy. Ignorance of wisdom is a state not of happiness but of brutal satisfaction or a passive state. It can't be happiness for there is nothing earned, and happiness is a reward for something. It is riches that are gained by toil or labor for the benefit of mankind. It is the reward of knowing that someone is benefited by us. The knowledge is happiness or heaven, the wisdom of which is our senses. Life or light is to know it; then we are in the life or light. This is happiness.

Now our senses cannot be seen for there is nothing back of them. They are the beginning and ending of all things. They embrace all that ever can be or ever has been. They are the real man. They can create and can destroy. They speak into existence everything. Wisdom is the father of our senses, and man is the embodiment of just as much wisdom as he is wise and the embodiment of the wisdom of mankind is God. Thus God and man are the embodiment of wisdom so far as wisdom is understood. So man like God is a creation subject to wisdom. God's wisdom is not man's wisdom. Man gives to God all the wisdom that creates all things, but it does not give God the creation of man's invention.

Do we see the real object or its shadow? It admits a superior wisdom that acts upon man. God creates in heaven or himself everything that has form and then forms it, or condenses his idea to form. And to every form he gives life but not the same life. Now as man's identity is one of the forms (and life is in the form), it is like a shadow that depends upon the light for its existence. So he attaches a part of his own self or senses to it. As a rose imparts to every living creature its odor, so man becomes impregnated with wisdom, assumes an identity and sets up for himself. As a child, when forced from its parent, becomes a man, so wisdom develops itself and sets up on its own account and becomes a God or creative Being. Then it wishes to imitate its father, so to stimulate it to action wisdom holds out rewards in the shape of happiness for every act that is for the benefit of man. Now there must of necessity be a correspondence or opposite to everything, a right and a wrong. So goodness with wisdom is right, money with the shadow is riches; with wisdom, to do good is happiness and with the opposite, to get money is happiness. The real must destroy the shadow. The working of the shadow introduces the light and destroys itself. But as I said, money is error's God and wisdom is science's God. Error is more active, for its life is its own destruction. So it invents all sorts of ideas by which to explain itself to others. But the ideas, like habits, are handed down as having an existence. These are explained to error till error can create them by its own power. When error believes them he creates them and when he creates them he sees them and he believes that they had their existence at the beginning of the world, when in fact they only existed in a story or a name. So the evils that torment man are the invention of error, spurred on by the love of gain, for the happiness of evil is in what it gains.

The natural man thinks his happiness and misery is in the idea man. For instance if a person has a white swelling, as it is called, he thinks the pain and all he suffers is in the knee, and so it is. Yet the knee is one thing and the man is another. Call the knee darkness and he is in the dark. Now the darkness is one thing and the senses another, so they are in the dark. But the trouble of being in the dark is in the senses not in the dark. So the knee is the darkness and the senses being in the knee or attached to it, it gives this pain or that condition of mind called pain. Now to cure the man is to detach the senses from the idea white swelling. This is the cure. So the science is to detach the senses from the idea of what troubles the man and this is the cure. To make it plain, suppose you are sitting in a room. You cannot see a mountain with your natural eyes, for the walls of the room prevent your attaching your senses to the mountain. Now close your eyes and think of the mountain, then the walls are gone and the senses are free to look, but open your eyes and your senses are obstructed by the walls. This is the condition of a person that is afraid of being blind. Their fears are the walls of their prison and to see through the walls is what they are trying to do. I tear down the prison or belief by the weapons of wisdom. This sets fire to their error and burns up their prison and their senses are set free.

I will give one more illustration of the senses. Suppose you think of a meeting house in some village that, to one standing in front of it, hides the sight of some object. Every time you stand and look at the meeting house the object is lost. Now you cannot think of this scene but what you must change your position in order to see the object. Suppose someone comes and tells you that there has been a fire and burned up the meeting house, giving a minute description how the fire commenced, how it burned first the belfry and windows till you see nothing but the bare frame and that all in a blaze. Now the building becomes transformed and without changing your position you can see through the flames and see the object that was hidden before. So disease is an obstacle in the mind that darkens the prospect of happiness and health and it must be destroyed by the fire of truth, and when the error is destroyed the senses are relieved from their trouble and are once more free from error and in the light of health. The natural man's reason is the obstacle that wisdom has to overcome and the senses are liable to be attached to these evils. This is disease. Now see the obstacles in the way of your seeing what you would like to see. Now shut your eyes and rise in your wisdom into the light or air, far above the object of the invention of man. Then you, like the dove, can soar aloft and look down on the errors that imprison your senses. This flight is the scientific man that has labored to rid himself of the errors of the natural man and risen from the darkness of superstition and death to the light of life, there to tell of what is real and what is not and how the things that seem real are nothing but the shadows of what cannot be seen.

September 1864

Separation of Myself from All Others Who Treat Disease, The
[LC 1:0452]

Feeling it a duty I owe myself and others to define my position as a man and a doctor so that I may not be misrepresented, I take this method to lay before the public my ideas so that they, being my judges, can decide the merits of my claim. For three years, I have been in this city attending to the duties of my practice without interfering in any way with the world outside of my business. I have given my whole attention to the sick, believing that my method of healing is entirely new and unknown to the world, and my object is to reduce it to a science so that it can be practiced by everyone for his own good. This is the sole reason why I remain here. I seek no favors of any one. I do not write this to get patients, for I have as many as I can attend to, but to separate myself from all others who see fit to assign me a place among the humbugs of the day.

It is in my wisdom that I differ from all others. The world puts the wisdom in the body and when that dies, the soul jumps out, if there is any, and it goes just where their wisdom admits it. You may not understand just where I am, so I will make an illustration to show how I am equal to God as people say and how I am equal to Christ. Suppose the reader is sitting in a parlor; of course all that he sees comes within his wisdom, so he sees himself. If I should be sitting with you, you would see me and you would allow that I could see as much as you see yourself. Now am I not in your wisdom with every other article in the room and are not you in my wisdom as much as all the other articles? So you see I am in you and you in me. You will not say that the great wisdom of all is less wise than me, so is he not in you and you and I in him? And are you not equal to me in what you know and am I not equal to you in the same? And are not both of us equal to the wisdom that knows all things, as far as we know? When I make any remark in regard to God, it is in this way.

As to death, I do not believe in it, for wisdom cannot die; but if my wisdom is in my body and a part of it, then I die according to my belief; but my wisdom is not in my body, my body is my wisdom. Now disease is in the wisdom of the patient and of course his wisdom is in his body. So he puts his disease in his body according to his own belief. The doctors' opinion is their belief and I being in my wisdom see the sick or their opinions. To destroy these, I make them wiser and their wisdom breaks their opinion and sets them free. To make it clearer, I will show you how to make a disease and how a person gets into it, like a prison, and how I get them out. Tell a person he has the heart disease. At first you cannot get him into that belief or prison, but at length he acknowledges it and then he is in this disease. So far as he believes, he leads himself in this disease. As my wisdom is not an opinion of disease, that is in my wisdom like any other opinion that I know is false, so my wisdom can see through his opinion, and when I convince him that his suffering arises from his own belief, the truth decomposes his opinions and the separation is the cure.

All I want to show is that I do not belong to any sect or creed. As I used to mesmerize, some think my mode of treatment is mesmeric, but my mode is not in the least like those who claim to be mesmerized subjects or spiritual mediums. I have nothing to say in regard to persons curing by the spirits. I know all about that way of curing. Neither have I anything to say about mesmeric treatment; I know all about that. I have been over twenty years investigating the subject. And if I had no other aim than dollars and cents, I would close my eyes, go into a trance, tell the patient how he felt and call some Indian to prescribe by making out the patient sick of scrofula or cancerous humor or of some other foolish disease and impress upon the patient the necessity of having medicine ordered by the spirits of my own getting up to the value of several dollars of which I should receive for my own benefit or they never would get well. If I should do this, I should do what I know to be wrong; and if anyone in a trance or mesmeric state, making it his profession to cure diseases first tells the patient that he is ignorant of what he says and that he recommends a medicine of his own invention, he deceives the patient.

I have had a clairvoyant subject long enough to know that when a person is unconscious of what he says, that he has no selfish motives, any more than a person in a dream. A person is either asleep or awake and if asleep, he will never recommend medicine for his own advantage. If awake, he should be honest and let the patient know it. I sit down awake and tell the feelings and have confidence in my wisdom to cure without medicine. But people are superstitious and if any person purports to come from another world, it has a great deal to do with his cure. His cure is in the belief of the patient's confidence in the spirits that recommend medicine. I ask no aid from any source outside of that wisdom which is given to all men in all branches of science. Wisdom never acts in that way. If the spirit was wise, it could cure without medicine and if not wise, it is not of God.

Portland, March 1862

Shadow and Substance
[Originally untitled.] [BU 3:0575]

I will make one illustration to you to let you know how I get you into heaven in the presence of God or Science. You know I told you, you were in a vacuum. I will now explain. When I speak to you I do not speak to this shadow but to the substance or your senses. Your senses make the shadow. You see this shadow on the wall–this is a shadow of a substance. But you take the shadow for the substance and attach your senses to it, not knowing that it is a shadow but believing it to be a living moving substance. So it is with every substance or idea that has been acknowledged to have a material form. Man by general consent has made matter, but God, not being man, has no matter, only as an idea. So matter to God or Science is a medium of communication to the natural man in his own language or semblance.

Now all admit that they cannot imagine a thing so divided, that it may not be divided again. They cannot see it so small, that it cannot be divided. So it is with wisdom; what comes in contact with your sight or touch is wisdom of this world. Everything that you cannot see and feel is belief, although it may be so near and the veil so thin that you would risk your life that it is true, yet there is a mist. In this mist lie all the mixtures of error and ignorance. Ignorance sees no mist, but is blind. Error sees a light, but it is a false one.

So science sees error's light and knows it is a false one. Now error being superstitious always sees through this mist and foretells future events. It creates all kinds of bugbears on earth as it does in heaven. The earth is its mother. Its ignorance is belief, so ignorance takes error for its guide. As error is superstitious it makes to itself a belief and to it attaches its senses. As it is very fond of instructing the ignorant in all things pertaining to this world of mystery, (for its opinions are of no force; it has to prove them by science) it gets up a false standard and if it can succeed in deceiving itself into a belief that it sees through this fog of its own make, then it has a basis for its belief.

So it has at last succeeded in making itself and the ignorant believe that in this fog or darkness is a land of pure delight like Pike's Peak. And if man will leave all things here below and take this chart or belief, they, like the children of Israel, will reach that land where there is no sorrow, where gold is as thick as gravel stones and where they can lie down on beds of down and walk the golden streets, never to get into any more trouble. These are the arguments of the speculators of endless error. Their lives, like the speculators of the natural world, are constantly displaying their tracts or cards, holding out great inducements to the people to leave their homes of health and go to that land whence no trouble ever returns, to bring back even an olive leaf. This is the land for which the prodigal son set out. And when he had spent his substance, he would have given his whole life as a servant to return once more to his father's house or health. But none of the speculators would even give him a husk to keep him from starving.

These speculators excite the people for their own benefit, till they are insane enough to leave house and home and all things dear to them, and like lost sheep, wander away from happiness and friends among strangers, where no friend comes ever to give them a cup of cold water to quench their thirst. Then they come to their senses and say like the rich man, Go tell my friends at home that I have been deceived; as there is so great a distance between you and me, I cannot go if I would and I do not want you to come to me into this place of torment. The speculator says all of this is false. If he had been steady at work he would have done well. So he refers them to Moses and some others who made money and says, if he had listened to them he would have succeeded, but as he did not listen to such, he failed.

November 1860

Short Chapter on Disease, A
[LC 2:0713]

What is disease? It is the punishment of our acts or belief. Can it ever be blotted out of the mind of man? I answer, When man acknowledges that happiness is the greatest aim of the human soul, and everything that goes to mar our happiness is wrong or evil. When man learns that his misery is in his belief and his happiness is in his wisdom, then he will cease from doing evil and believing in what he has no proof of and learn to do well or act rightly. Man must understand that mind is matter, that thought, reason and argument are all the same and are all a belief, and that the reality of them is that it is true that we all do believe it. But wisdom is not in any of the above. A man, body and mind is like the earth and the skies. The earth could not bring forth anything without air; so when the air is affected, the earth is likewise affected. So the body of itself is like the earth. Every sensation in the body is first made in the mind and this is thought, which is of the earth or body called mind. And all disease of the earth originated in the mind or clouds.

September 1862

Showing How the Opinions of Physicians Operate on the People
[LC 1:0456]

No one knows the mischief or the misery that physicians of all kinds make by their opinions, and this never will be known till man learns that his belief makes his trouble. For instance, a person feels a slight disturbance at the pit of the stomach. Ignorant of its cause, he applies to a physician. Here comes the trouble. The physician assumes a false character. His practice makes him either a simpleton or a knave, for if honest he would know that he could not tell anything about the patient. If he were blind he could not even tell that the patient was sick, so that all his knowledge is gathered from observation and questioning.

Therefore he is doctor only in name. He dare not risk his reputation by sitting down by the patient and telling his feelings as I do. Therefore he knows he is acting the part of a hypocrite. The patient is in the hands of a deceiver whose business it is to deceive him into some belief that happens to occur to him. At this time the physician stands to the patient like a tailor ready to fit him a garment. If rich he will persuade him he has the spinal complaint, or bronchitis, or some other disease that fits the patient's fears. If very poor, and there is no chance for a speculation, he will fit an old pair of worn-out lungs onto him, just enough to keep him breathing a short time. This is the way the regular faculty humbugs the people. Now when the people are educated to understand that what they believe they will create, they will cease believing what the medical men say and try to account for their feelings in some more rational way.

I know that a belief in any disease will create a chemical change in the mind, and that a person will create a phenomenon corresponding to the symptoms. This creation is named disease, according to the author. The idea disease has no effect on a person who has no fear of it. The small pox, for instance, produces no effect on a person who has had it, or has had the varioloid, or has been vaccinated; but on another it is not so. The doctor can produce a chemical change by his talk. It makes no difference what he says. A phenomenon will follow to which he can give a name to suit his convenience.

For instance, a person gets into an excited, heated state and a doctor is called. He gives medicine which affects the patient and he feels better. That then was what the patient needed and the doctor has the credit. If the patient grows worse, the medicine makes him sick; the doctor says he has the symptoms of a fever, while in reality he himself has been the cause of nine-tenths of the trouble. Give men the knowledge of one great truth, that man is constituted of two different principles: wisdom which is seen in science and error which is seen in matter and in opinions. The latter is governed by no principle known to man but is simply the action of cause and effect. If wisdom is the cause it goes with the effect, but man who sees only the phenomenon puts wisdom into it, for the cause is never seen. Wisdom is always the real cause. To the natural man this is a mystery and it is not taken into account.

I will illustrate it. Take the small pox. The first sensation upon the patient contains neither opinion, happiness nor misery, but it is like a breath of air blown upon your face. The cause was one of the natural results of motion which might be traced back through many changes containing no more harm than any breeze that reaches man at any hour, but it gives a start to the mind like the fall of a weight. This shock, although containing no intelligence, disturbs the senses which is the real man. I will drop this illustration here and undertake to describe the senses or the real man and separate them from what seems to be the man.

The senses are all that there is of a man. Therefore when he changes his senses, it is necessary to know what he gains or loses by the change and also what he embraces. To suppose a man has but five or seven senses is as absurd as to suppose that he has but a certain number of ideas. His senses are himself, what he knows and what he thinks he knows. Paul divides man into two identities: wisdom or what could be proved by a science, and knowledge or what man believes to be true. So when a man says he thinks he knows or believes he knows, it is sure that he does not know as he should. But if he can prove his knowledge by science, then his science is known to him.

A man's senses embrace these two characters, which are natural opponents, to both of which life has been attached. The scientific man sees and knows himself, and he also sees and knows his opponent, but the man of opinion can only see the scientific man in a mystery. As wisdom advances in man, the effect is to destroy the senses which are attached to knowledge. When knowledge overbalances a man's wisdom, his error reigns, but if wisdom is in the ascendency his knowledge becomes subject to his wisdom. In mathematics, chemistry and all the arts and sciences that can be demonstrated, knowledge submits to wisdom, but that part of man's senses attached to knowledge that is not subject to science is in the ascendency in religion, disease, and politics. These are false sciences based on opinions. They are the same that Jesus denounced as false prophets, evil and blind guides who deceive the people. These errors embrace that part of men that believes in sickness, death, another world, and all kinds of superstition. They beget tyranny and selfishness in man, and slavery and democracy in nations. It is the mission of science to destroy these, and science will be developed till they are destroyed.

Therefore when man's belief in these opinions is at an end, his senses will seem to be annihilated, but in reality he will be like the young eagle which has burst its shell and soars aloft on the wings of wisdom, where he looks down upon the earth and sees the natural man crawling like a reptile, waiting to devour the child of science as soon as it is born.

Every development of wisdom, whether applied to creeping things or to the element of freedom, is a child of God. Concealed in the egg of slavery, wisdom is kept warm by the heat of discussion, but now it has broken its shell and assumed a character and the enemies of freedom, like those of Christ, stand ready to devour it as soon as it is born. But the mother of freedom will receive the child to its bosom and will flee into the wilderness till the time arrives when the senses of man will be so changed that slavery will be chained to the lowest grade of brutality and there in the wilderness it will die and be forgotten. The error of disease will go through a similar revolution, for it has been hatched by the church, kept concealed by the medical faculty, while their absurd opinions are the very food that has fed the child of science whose heel shall bruise the head of the serpent, disease. These two characters, science and error are separate and yet they act together and always will till truth reigns over all the dominions of opinion. They are embraced in every man and their separation was the science that Jesus taught. To understand the separation is eternal life in Science.

Jesus came into the world of error, not into Science, for he was there with Wisdom. All science was with Wisdom, but when it comes to the world it comes as Jesus did. It first comes to the educated but they, having no light to distinguish between truth and error, cannot receive it. So it turns to that class which has no prejudices, and here in the wilderness it develops itself until it has attained its growth and then it comes forth. Then commences the war between the educated who are ignorant of the truth and the science. While science is growing in the minds of the people, its opponents are eating and drinking, gloating over their spoils, till the tide of popular opinion sweeps away their foundation and they never seem to realize their danger till their house falls over their heads. This has been the case with the Democratic house; while they still hold to the idea that slavery will be tolerated, the thunder of freedom is shaking the temple to its foundation, and they hide themselves in the crevices of their belief, claiming, "I was always opposed to the extension of slavery, but the Constitution must not be violated." That is, you must not break the egg by the heat of discussion and let out the bird of liberty, for if you do, democracy is dead.

The medical faculty reasons in the same way. "Do not destroy the medical constitution," they say, "for you will let in a swarm of quacks that will get the world in a horrid state. The regular physician will have no standing and sickness and death will triumph over the land." The ministers also exclaim, "Do not touch the divine institution, for religion is all that keeps the world from going to destruction." Wisdom replies, "I will laugh at your fears, and I will pour out light like wrath and cut you off from the face of the earth and give the earth (or mind) to a more enlightened people who will obey the laws of science and teach others to do the same, and you shall be cast into everlasting mystery." This is progression and it is the religion of Jesus. It is the stone of science that the builders of religion rejected. It is the star that guided the wise men to the only true God. Its body is wisdom, its blood is its life and unless you eat it and drink it, you have no life in you. Happy is he who, when a cloud of disease comes, for the Lord is always in clouds of error, can say, I fear not, fear hath torment and perfect wisdom casteth out fear. He will rise from the clouds and meet Christ above the opinions of man. Then when the science comes you will not be harmed.

I wish to make you understand these two characters, science and opinions. Give to each an identity like a man and separate one from the other, and then see which you follow; for you must follow one. You cannot serve both at the same time. If you serve science you are in your wisdom and know it. If you serve opinion, you have no wisdom but your life is in a belief that can be destroyed. So you will live all your life subject to bondage through fear of death. But if you have passed through death or opinions to the life of science, death will have no power over you. Disease is death and the belief is the fear; therefore if death is destroyed the fear is gone. It becomes us then to search into the causes of the phenomenon called disease and find if it is not an image of our own make. The Jewish people were making all sorts of false beliefs that tormented them. So God through Moses says, "Thou shall make no graven images" to represent any false idea which they had been taught, nor worship any superstition, for truth was jealous of error. It always condemns our error and rewards our scientific acts.

Disease was conceived in priestcraft and brought forth in the iniquity of the medical faculty. The priests prophesied falsely and the doctors flourished by their lies, and the people love to have it so. Then the question arises, What can you do to prevent it? I say, repent all, and be baptized in the Science that will wash away your sins and diseases with your belief. Come out from the world of opinion; and when a doctor says you have so and so, make him prove it.

July 16, 1864

Sickness Is What Follows the Belief that Disease Is an Independent Life
[LC 2:0646]

There are certain phenomena that man is afraid of which do not contain life. These include accidents. For instance, if a person breaks his leg, no one is afraid of the person who broke his leg because the thing that broke it is not attached to the leg. But if any disease attacks and eats off the leg, then the person is frightened because he has attached intelligence to disease. We think that we do not attach intelligence to disease but all our beliefs prove the contrary. There is not a person who believes in a Supreme Being called God but also believes in a supreme being called the Devil, and all persons who believe in ministering angels from heaven admit evil spirits from hell. Let them say what they will, actions speak louder than words. If they do not believe in a devil and evil spirits, why do so many place so much power in their minister? It certainly is a great sacrifice for them to attend meeting and pay the minister; they will often pay three times as much to support the gospel as they will give to the poor. If they thought all will be well after death with them, you would not see them so interested. All facts go to show that man believes in a heaven and hell. It is true some undertake to deny one and establish the other. The liberal Christians pretend to believe in heaven and disbelieve in a hell, but this is as absurd as the other, for if the Bible teaches one, it does the other. Every act of the liberal churches shows that if they act in obedience to a belief in heaven, the same belief makes them act to keep from hell.

As I have said, if one is right so is the other, and whoever believes in one believes in the other. The same book that teaches heaven teaches also hell. To disobey heaven was a sin and as Adam sinned, death entered into man's belief, so all men have sinned. To sin is to transgress some law, and as the torment came from the devil, man has been taught to keep clear of him. As no man has seen God, we have attached our senses to a being which has never been seen, but the devil has been seen as much as the sea serpent and we often hear of his evils tormenting man. There is not a Christian who honestly believes in God's angels but who at the same time warns people to keep clear of the evil influences of the devil.

Many try to make the people believe that my cures are the works of the devil. Some go so far as to say that they would rather their friends should die than come to me. Now I ask which power such a person is most afraid of? This fear shows how much they believe in the devil. All such persons attach their senses to the effect produced, so if I affect a person, that person is under the influence of the devil and all they say is to make the people keep clear of him. If the devil can be transferred from one to another, it shows that torment is of him and not of God. These very persons have more to do with the devil than God, for God does not ask any sacrifice as they offer. According to their belief in the devil, God has nothing to do with those who are well and happy but is occupied with tormenting the sick, for they seem to be the ones who are tormented. If God is so kind to those who are all the time trying to destroy the devil and are keeping you from him, why does he let them suffer so much, since there is three times the amount of suffering by those who are afraid of the devil than by those who do not care much for him.

Once this devil tormented men by entering them and burning their life out. Then he changed to the form of witchcraft and now he assumes a more respectable character. He appears in the most fashionable society in the form of neuralgia, spinal disease, heart disease, rheumatism. The medical faculty are always ready to inform the people of his coming and insist that he has made his appearance long before he is realized by the patient. Soon after he is acknowledged, they very modestly offer their services to drive him away. They commence the battle with their various inventions of war: blisters, linament, calomel, etc., and fight the devil out of the sick. This is upheld by the clergy and physicians. They are the very agent of the lying influences that started thousands of years ago and have been fed and nourished by the church till the world is overrun (like the people of Egypt) with false doctrines, and they have taught furthermore that God is at the cause of all this hypocrisy.

I stand apart from all this. All their Gods and Devils, their heaven and hell are humbug to me. Their religion arises from the fear of their belief. There is not one particle of sincerity, but it all comes from ignorance. They believe that disease is catching. A broken leg is not catching, but a lie is, and if you make a person believe a lie, they are affected just according to the danger, and their fear is their torment. So as the priests have made the people believe a lie, their torment is the result of their belief.

Here is my belief founded on practice. My God is all wisdom, no matter but solid, full of love, compassion and every attribute that wisdom can suggest. The devil is all matter, all error, hypocrisy and every evil that man is capable of inventing. His intelligence is only opinions and his life is in his superstition and ignorance; his death is in the wisdom of God or Science. In fact, the devil is a chemical change that every son of God must pass through, as man passes from matter to science, there is a chemical change, his ignorance puts wisdom in the change and thinks life is in it. By this ignorance, death came into man's belief because he saw matter moving around and could not account for the cause. He attached his senses to this shadow or matter, not knowing that the substance was not in the shadow, so that to him everything that moved contains life. To me everything that moves is matter and there is no life in it. Life is not matter nor is it in matter. All disease is made from the belief in another world. I have no other world. My world is one living, progressive world, and man is in the world of matter and ignorance and to get out of error is to get out of one world into another, so I have one world in progression. Do I believe in rewards and punishments? I do not believe; I know. I am as sure that everyone will be rewarded according to his works or thoughts as I am that I am writing this article. It is as sure as that action and reaction are equal.

God is the rewarder of every scientific truth. Every error is a chemical change, like the solving of a mathematical problem; when the answer comes right, then comes the reward. The life is in the true answer and we attach our senses to the truth; this is an everlasting truth. But error attaches itself to the error, and when the true answer comes the error dies; the misery is what follows the investigation and the happiness is in the knowledge that you are right. To show how my religion works on me is to show how I feel when I am sitting by a patient. I seat myself by my patient and his feelings become mine. I know that these fears arise from some idea based on an opinion. As they have attached their senses to some invisible life in the form of disease that I know is false, their fears to me are all in their belief and I know that they are the cause of their own misery. My religion is to impart to them the evidence that their trouble is in themselves and their torment is seen in the shadow or body.

Now make man sensible that there is no misery or happiness for him except he earns it by his own act, that if he is slothful, he will be rewarded for indolence; then he has some stimulant to excite him to do well. But if his acts are to be governed by rewards outside of his acts, he then becomes selfish and wants more than he deserves; so it is with his misery. Make him know that there is no forgiveness for sin or error and that he must take the consequences of his acts not from anyone else, then he becomes the judge of his own self. As sure as man lives, his punishments will follow his thoughts and acts in the body in the form of pain or trouble whether he is conscious of committing error or not. So if you believe what a person tells you and it contains rewards or punishments outside of your acts, it is false and you will get the reward of your belief.

Dec. 23, 1861

Spirits–Are They Substance or Shadow?
[BU 3:0862]

Is a spirit a reality, i.e., a truth, or is it the work of superstition? I affirm that it is the work of superstition. There is just as much truth in a spirit as there is in the belief that spirits do exist. If a person believes a lie, to him it is a truth, not that the lie is a truth, but the belief is a truth to him and he is affected by it the same as though it was a scientific fact capable of demonstration. The belief in the real existence of spirits is so universal that every person admits it more or less. Let us examine whence this spirit comes.

The process of mind called thinking is a sort of sketch or draft for an idea or thing. For instance, a man wishes to construct a machine; he creates it in his mind and this creation can be seen and described by a very sensitive person. Under the excitement of a superstitious fear of the dead, a man will create a being after his own idea. This also might be seen by another. I know this to be true for upon this principle, I cure disease. Ghosts and spirits, like diseases, are the invention of man's superstition and the wisdom that can destroy one can destroy the other. Man, not knowing that the things he sees are ideas of his own or of someone else's creation, calls the thing seen a spirit. This gives rise to the idea of spirits of the dead, for the living have no disembodied spirit. God casts no shadow of himself, but when his wisdom is reduced to man's understanding, that casts a shadow; therefore true wisdom is not seen. Spirits are not produced from either of these causes. They come from superstition. Destroy the superstition about death and the process of thinking of other things would stand. So long as people think about the dead, so long there will be spirits, for thought is spirit, and that is all the spirits there are.

May 1862

Spiritual Communication, A

[BU 2:0145]

[*Editor's note*: This is a transcription of a communication between Phineas Parkhurst Quimby and his second-born child, William Henry Quimby. The date recorded on this document is December, 1859, or two years after William's passing on August 14, 1857. "Mother" referenced in this conversation would be Quimby's wife, Susannah Burnham (Haraden) Quimby; and "John" would be their oldest son, John Haraden Quimby, who was still living at the time of this communication.]

"William, will you give me your idea of death?" "I can give you my opinion, but you would say an opinion is no proof, and therefore is of no force." "Well, tell me what you think." "Well, if you want me to tell you what I have no proof of and what is only my opinion, I suppose I can do it if it will be of any use. You remember when I was sick in bed and one night when you were sitting by me, you know I was very weak, and you all thought I was worse and I thought so. Mother thought I would die, and I thought sometimes that I should; but don't you remember that I told you to put me to sleep?" "Yes." "Well, that was to get rid of that feeling, and when I went to sleep I felt a little nervous, I suppose, and I had a dream that I never told of before because it troubled the family and it made them feel badly. I dreamed that I was dead and you wanted me to go to Bangor and stay till the trouble was over, and I seemed to go there, but I knew all about it. But as it was a dream, and the association made me feel so badly, I could never speak of it to mother, for it seemed they had the same dream, so I kept it to myself." "How long did you sleep?" "Till the trouble was over, and when I woke up, it seemed like a reality." "Did you have any sort of knowledge in this sleep of your opinion while awake?" "Yes, I reasoned I was with you, just as you and I used to be when you would talk me to sleep before, but I never was conscious before of the idea of death having so much effect on a person. For I could reason with myself, and I am satisfied if I had been taught to believe as some people do, my belief would have governed my dream, and I should have been ten times more unhappy; for when I woke up it did not affect me so long, from the fact that I knew it was only an opinion. And you say that is no proof, and I always remembered that. But I know how to pity those who take an opinion for a truth, for an opinion is as real to the person who believes it as though it were true.

"As I have reasoned myself into the belief that man never dies, I shall not try to give myself any trouble about others' beliefs. If people believe that they die and their spirits come back and talk with their friends, I have no doubt but what they do. But it is their opinion, and that is of no consequence except to lessen their belief that there is such a state as death; perhaps it gives them some happiness. But as far as I am concerned I am satisfied with my belief." "Suppose I should believe that you were dead?" "Suppose that you should, would that make it so?" "No." "Suppose I should believe that you were dead, what would you say to that?" "I should say, if I knew anything, I know I am alive." "Well, can't you be as charitable toward another as you would like them to be towards you?" "Yes, but I can't believe that you are dead." "Did you ever know a dead man to speak?" "No, but you know that we all believe that the body dies and the soul lives." "Yes, but did you ever see a soul?" "No." "Then why do you believe the soul lives when you say an opinion is of no force?" "Have you any proof that a person is alive when you see him dead?" "No, only my belief." "You say that your belief is of no force, for it contains no proof, is it not so?" "Yes." "Well, suppose I admit that I am dead, will that make you any better satisfied?" "No." "Well, what shall I admit?" "I don't know, but I wish I really knew that I was talking to you." "Don't you believe your own senses?" "Certainly, but you don't come within my senses." "Why not?" "Because I can't see you." "Then because you think you can't see me, I am dead?" "Yes." "Can you see John?" "No." "How do you know?" "I think he is alive." "That is nothing but an opinion which you say is of no force." "Will you give me your opinion about it?" "I have no opinion about it. I know that I am here now, and that is all I care about it. If I am dead, it is news to me. I don't know any more about it than Lucius knew when he was asleep, that he was asleep. So if death is only a mesmeric sleep, it is not much to go through."

December 1859

Spiritual Communication between the Living
[BU 3:0633]

If the fact can be established that a person may know another's thoughts without that other being aware of it, then you have a starting point to reason from. Then it will be seen that man is double or has two identities, one seen by the natural eye, and the other seen by the intelligence which is not confined to any sense or organ. I call the last the spiritual or scientific man. The difficulty of establishing the fact of a personal identity outside and apart from the natural man lies in the fact that error sees no science in anything, for when error sees science, it is not error. So when the spiritual man knows himself, he is not the same man as before but another. This makes him one real man and another in remembrance. And when the child grows to manhood, the man sees himself as a child in remembrance but attaches his life to it. So it is with man's existence.

Man's life is eternal and is a part of God or wisdom but cannot be seen by the eye of man, for that sees the medium and only the medium. We call the medium ourselves, yet there is no more wisdom in ourselves as a medium than there is in a galvanic battery or any other material. Yet destroy the medium and you destroy all communication with each other as far as the natural man's intelligence goes. To illustrate. Suppose two blind mutes are sitting in the same room. The natural man would reason that their distance from each other was just as far as their bodies were apart, not having any idea of a sympathy that is mingling, because ignorance is the sight and the eyes are the medium of his wisdom. But the scientific man sees that although these two blind mutes are like two stumps to the natural man, yet there emanates from each an atmosphere which mingles together and of which the natural man knows not, and all it wants is a medium to communicate it to each other. Here is where man stands towards himself. The natural man, or skeptic, is the man who has never been developed at all. So he thinks he knows himself as he appears. He is as certain of what he cannot see as of what he can see, for his opinion is as true as sight, and whatever he believes, no matter how absurd, to him it is true. He denies everything that he cannot see, and when he sees it, he never investigates but gives his opinion, and to him, his opinion is true. In such a man there is the seed or child of wisdom confined in the prison of this earthly man, struggling like all other science to be delivered from this body of error. From the prison of such an error I have been laboring for twenty years to free myself, and the discoveries I have made I will give to those who are within the sound of my spiritual voice and can see with spiritual eyes through the clouds that there exists something besides his opinion or belief. I will write in the form of a dialogue that it may be seen how far I am from the world and what I know.

You may call yourself A, and I will call myself B. (B) Will you admit that we can communicate our thoughts to each other by language? (A) Yes. (B) Will you admit that I can think of Boston without your knowing it? (A) Yes. (B) Will you admit that I can communicate the fact to you by language? (A) Yes. (B) Then we have established the fact that we can think independent of each other? (A) Yes, I admit that. (B) You also admit that we can by language convey our thoughts by language to each other. (A) Yes. (B) Will you admit that you know what I am thinking of without language? (A) No. Do you? (B) That depends on circumstances. (A) What kind of circumstances? (B) I will tell you. Sensation is not ideas but is merely a shock, like that of a galvanic battery, and rouses the person, but there is no language in that. (A) I can't understand. (B) I will try to illustrate what I mean. Suppose I had never seen nor heard of a steamboat and you had seen one. You could think of one, could you not? (A) Yes. (B) Could I? (A) I suppose not. (B) Could not your thoughts affect me? (A) That is what I want you to prove. (B) I will do so. You know you had a pain in one of your knees. (A) Yes. (B) Did I not tell you of it? (A) Yes. (B) Do you doubt that I told you the truth? (A) No. (B) Then you must affect me without language? (A) Yes, for I never told you. (B) Yes you did, or I never should have known that it came from you. (A) What way did I tell you? (B) Precisely as though you spoke it. (A) I do not understand. (B) I know you do not, and I will try to make it clearer. Sensation is not intelligence to a person till it is associated with some medium. For instance, I never saw or heard of the steamboat, so of course I could not make one in my mind and if I did, I should not know for I have no language to express it. But you have seen one and have language to explain. Your language excites my mind and you create the boat and attach my senses to a steamboat. So when you speak of one again, you convey to me the language. (A) You do not make it plain. (B) You know I told you that you had a pain in your knee. (A) Yes, you said so. (B) You deny this? (A) No, but I don't exactly understand how you know it. (B) I thought so. (A) Won't you make it clearer? (B) I will try. If you had been alone you would have had the pain, you don't doubt that. Then I did not make the pain. (A) I do not know that I gave you the pain. (B) Suppose you had no pain. Could I have felt it? (A) No, but that doesn't satisfy me that you might not have a pain in your knee. (B) Well, what will satisfy you? (A) You see Mr. G. coming along. If you will tell him how he feels without his saying anything to you, then I will believe. (B) Well, call him in and I will try.

Mr. G. enters and says, I am sick and want you to tell me how I feel. I sit down and tell him how he feels and what he thinks and even tell him what he has been doing, etc., and Mr. G. acknowledges that I have told his feelings better than he could. Then A says, I will admit that you can tell a person's feelings, without their telling you. (B) Will you tell me how much you really understand? (A) I understand that you can tell the feelings of another. (B) How do you know? (A) Because I know that you told me my feelings. (B) Could you not be deceived? (A) Not in what you told me. But you might have guessed and if you did you are good at guessing. (B) Then the real fact of my telling your feelings is a belief in what I said? (A) Yes. (B) Could you have any stronger proof? (A) I don't know as I could, but more proof would strengthen my belief. (B) Have you any positive proof that might not be changed? (A) No, for it may be all guesswork and deception. (B) What would be positive proof? (A) I do not know. I have seen enough and if I have been deceived, I should be deceived all the more. (B) That is so. I can tell you that if you knew one thing then you would have the proof. (A) What is that? (B) If you knew you could tell my feelings, then you would have the proof in yourself. (A) Yes. (B) You will now admit that I tell your feelings? (A) Yes, but I cannot see how you do it. (B) Then your wisdom is based on what I say. (A) Yes, for I have no better proof than your opinion. (B) Then to you my opinion is knowledge, but to me it is wisdom and here is the difference between knowledge and wisdom: knowledge is based on a belief in what we do not know without a doubt, and wisdom is the science of the thing we speak of. So I think now I have shown the difference between yourself and me. (A) Yes, I think I can see that what you know is wisdom and what I think I know is an opinion, so that my knowledge contained no wisdom. (B) I want you to go with me to the Spirit-rapping mediums to convince you that all the knowledge comes from man's wisdom. (A) I do not believe in the spirits at all. (B) Why not? Do you believe it all a humbug? (A) Yes. (B) Don't you believe that there is another world beyond this? (A) I do not want to discuss that question now. Wait till another time. Finis. They agree to go to see the spirits tomorrow.

Spiritual Communications from the Dead
[BU 3:0635]

Interview with the spiritual medium, the next evening.

(B) Good evening. Are you ready to go with me? (A) Yes, but I tell you frankly I am a perfect skeptic in all this sort of humbug. If there is anything after death, I do not believe our friends can come back on earth and communicate with the living, but I am willing to go just out of curiosity. (B) That is right. Here is the house, let us go in.

We enter and are seated by a table. The medium tears up some pieces of paper in small strips and requests us to write the name of some of our friends who have died. He then leaves the room. We both write a few names. The medium comes in and says, I see the spirit of your grandmother. A starts and says, what is her Christian name? The medium answers, She seems to say it is Jane. Is that her name? (A) I believe not. Other communications followed to A which were correct.

The medium says to B, I see a spirit who wishes to communicate with you. Will you please to ask him what his name is. I ask the name and my mother comes through the raps. The medium asks if it is right. I say, yes. Another comes and another, till four or five have made themselves known. All spell out their names by the raps. Finally someone raps that they will write their name on the medium's arm, and the name of my mother appears. Then comes another spirit who seems very glad to communicate with me and spells out the name of G. Q. I ask if it is my son and receive the answer yes. The medium says, Your son wants to give you a test. He hands me a piece of paper and a pencil and requests me to place them under the table. I do as I am requested but with the privilege of looking at the paper. But the medium would not grant it. So I sit up to the table and lose sight of the paper for some seconds and when I look again the paper was gone. The medium says, Perhaps it is in your hat or pocket. This diverts my mind from the floor and when I look there again I see a piece of paper folded up. I examine it and the name of my son was written on the paper. We then leave.

After leaving I say to A, What do you think of that? (A) I can't say. It upsets all my philosophy. (B) How? (A) I never believed in anything after the death of the body, but this looks mysterious. (B) Why? (A) Because there are some things which I cannot account for. No one knew what was told through the medium except myself and my friend who is dead. (B) Well, because you can't account for it, it must be spirits. (A) No, I won't say it is spirits, but these are the facts that I cannot get over. (B) Can you get over my telling you about your knee? (A) No, but that is a different case. I never told anyone what was communicated to me. (B) Did you ever tell anyone that you had a pain in your knee? (A) But I cannot see the similarity of the two cases. (B) Suppose I explain. (A) I do not see how it can be explained. I went in, a perfect skeptic, and had not the least idea or thought of my friend, for I had not thought of him for years, and when he rapped out his name and told me of a fact that no living person besides myself and him knew, how could I doubt it? The fact speaks for itself. (B) Yes I know that, but the accounting for it is the thing we are after. (A) I don't care how you account for it. There is the fact. Call it spirits or works of the devil. I don't care. The fact is all I want. (B) You get excited and run after the shadow and forget the substance. If you will listen and not get too much excited I think I can explain the phenomenon on a principle of truth that you will admit. (A) I can't see any principle that explains a fact that explains itself. Here you sit and the raps come, and you hear from your friend who is dead. This you know and it needs no explanation. Your explanation only makes it darker. I know I had a friend who died so, and so here come the raps telling the whole story. (B) Then, why deny the fact that the spirit came back and told the story? (A) I cannot account for it on any other grounds. (B) So I thought. (A) Can you? (B) Yes, but you cannot understand any more than you could about the pain in your knee. You know just about as much about one as the other, and when you understand one you will the other. (A) Well, make me understand how these raps come. (B) If you cannot understand how I can tell your thoughts, it would be impossible to make you understand any physical experiment, from the fact that the power which makes the thoughts makes the raps. (A) I can't see how it is done. (B) I will try to explain. You know I told your thoughts? Well, thought is nothing but rarefied velocity. When I say "nothing" I do not mean it exactly, but the weight is so light of itself that it comes next to nothing, like electricity. What is lost in weight is supplied by velocity. You bring thought into velocity, for every person knows that they do think. If thought is a chemical action, it is set in motion by the will or belief, and you can see how by the belief it can be formed under a certain wisdom for good or bad results, for man is like clay in the hands of the potter to be worked according to his own will. When a man thinks, he shows mechanical skill in putting his thoughts to some account. So an idea is formed. This is the effect of thought governed by some will superior to the thought or idea. To illustrate. Take a rich man of ordinary talent but selfish. Such a man can create a great many small minds from the fact that his power is in his money, but his motive governs his power, although everything seems to give the appearance of disinterestedness. Still everything acts for his own benefit. This is done by the knowledge of human nature. He sees that man, like dough, can be molded into anything; for when it gets a little dry, all that is necessary is to moisten it by that substance that can be taken up and absorbed. This puts the clay in good working order.

Now spiritualism, religion, and politics and every kind of phenomenon are brought about upon this one fact that one person acts on another for good or evil. (A) Suppose you are right. How can it be helped? It has always been and always will be. (B) I will admit it always has been and that it always will be until men's true motives are known. (A) Well, neither you nor I can change man. (B) That is a fact, but there is another fact that man is not aware of that is working in the world of man's mind that will bring about the very thing I am talking about. It is not an opinion, so I shall only show the principle and the problem works itself out, not by any supreme wisdom but by a chemical change that is taking place in the minds all the time. So changes must take place. Men's minds will run to and fro and knowledge will increase, but wisdom is not known. Parties and theories spring up, but these are the beginning. Men attach their senses to the change, and their lives being in their senses, principle is not known. To illustrate the change of mind, I will take this rebellion. Before it broke out, the minds of men had been worked up by the leaders to this pitch that the South were set against the administration party. This was brought about by the leading men, North and South, belonging to the Democratic Party, for sake of the loaves and fishes. To bring this to perfection, the North must set the people to quarreling about slavery and the South would make a handle of their arguments to convince the people that the North wanted to destroy their "peculiar institution"; this would unite the South and divide the North. Of course a fire cannot be kindled without some kindling and that was supplied by a few fanatics at the North and South, so the fire burned till all the country or mind was on fire. Meanwhile the Democratic Party was kept in power by these two elements: a united South, held by the false idea of slavery, and a divided North. Finally the North applied reason or water, cooling the flame of the northern masses and Lincoln came in president. Here is the state of the public mind. All the above is past and now the end cometh. Yet in all that has passed there has not been any wisdom and neither will there be in what is to take place, but there is a law of action and reaction and upon this ground I have my belief. So I will predict as the country now stands, it is, so far as observation goes, just where it was when Lincoln was elected, only to the natural eye it looks a little darker. But I see the light and it seems to me it will come in this way. The Democratic Party will split at the North and assume a new name, perhaps the Union or people's party, and out of this party a child must come which will devour the Republican Party almost. It will try to hold out the olive of peace to the South, but the Republicans won't agree. The South will grow wroth and a hatred will spring up and the democracy will unite with the Republicans under a new name. So the North will be united with the exception of a small party, and their word will go forth, Union forever. And if slavery stand in the way it must come down, and it will, for the North in their zeal will employ every means available to accomplish its end. So slavery dies without even a watcher to close its dying eyes, but its death must come through the elements of the Democratic Party, and if Mr. Lincoln is not the one, then another will rise up. But I think it will sprout from Abraham, for in him and in his seed shall all the earth be blest.

Sept. 4th, 1860

Spiritual Interpretation
[BU 3:0830]

What is the element that receives all sensation? Love for ourselves. This is the ground mark or foundation of all our acts, to gratify its own element. It is the mortar or dough in which all sensation is made. Of itself it contains no knowledge. It is perfect harmony. Its element or language is its perfection. It embraces all the senses but not wisdom. It is the power that wisdom uses to bring all things into harmony with itself. This to this world of error is not known but admitted; the matter or ideas of this world is put into this element. So it is like the ocean. It can hold all sorts of ideas and, like the ocean, disturb error to its lowest depths and then calm by wisdom, so that not a ripple on the surface can be seen. But in the depths of this ocean of love lie all kinds of evil spirits that are gnawing the life of the soul, that are identified with it. This is the disease in the mind.

When the storm of ignorance and superstition was raging and all the ships or minds were tossing to and fro, and even Jesus' disciples were in danger of being swamped by the errors of the age, when their barque or belief was just sinking into heathen idolatry, and when their enemies disturbed the walls or belief, then in the darkness of the night or error, when there was no eye to see or heart to feel, no arm to reach out or voice to be heard, Jesus was seen walking upon the water of their belief saying to the waves, Be still, and the winds and waves obeyed him and there was a great calm. This was the state of the minds in the days of Jesus. The people's belief was their disease and to embrace their errors was to take their disease. Then misery was what followed their belief and their happiness was the unlearning of their errors. Their ships were their theories and the water was their mind and their ideas, their danger. Their wisdom was of this world of matter, while the wisdom of God could say to their wisdom, Be still, and their ideas of wind and mind or matter would obey. Now the introduction of Jesus' ideas was a new heaven or wisdom and a new earth or belief. The new heaven, under the direction of the wisdom of God or science, could create a new belief wherein could be peace and happiness that the old heaven or wisdom knew nothing of, where there should be peace and power in the Holy Ghost or explanation of this new world, where no errors nor selfishness nor strife could dwell, so that all ignorance and superstition should be cast out into outer darkness, never to return.

Now, as Jesus was walking by the seaside of the belief of the leaders' ideas, he saw two men, Peter and Andrew, spouting or fishing in the old Mosaic laws or sea and said to them, Follow me and I will make you teachers of this truth to man and not slaves to the priest. So they abandoned their nets or old belief and followed him. They went on and saw others in their ships or beliefs, mending their nets or creeds, for their nets, like the priesthood, had weak places and were like a garment ready to drop to pieces. They also left their father or old belief in their ships of error and followed Jesus. So he traveled all through the land preaching the kingdom of heaven and curing all kinds of diseases, and his fame went through all the land

and great multitudes followed him. And he went up into the higher state, into the science, and opened his mouth to them in truth or parables.

Now the laws of Moses had a tax on the people to pay the priest for forgiving their sins and the doctors had a fee for curing the sins that affected the body. So all persons who were not of their belief were strangers and needed teaching, or needed to have their eyes opened to the truth of their belief and their ideas or opinions were like fish in the great sea and they asked tribute money or an answer to all of their questions to pay for teaching strangers. When Jesus came into Capernaum, they that received the tribute money, or gave information in regard to the truth, asked Peter if his master paid tribute money or wanted any information in regard to their religion and Peter said, Yes. So as he came into the house or belief, Jesus asked of Peter, Who paid tribute money, the children or the believers, or the skeptic or the strangers? He answered, Strangers. So Jesus said, Lest they be offended, let us ask a question for them to answer. Go to the priest or sea and cast in a hook and put a question and catch an idea or fish and open it and you will find a piece of money. Go and give it for you and for me. Now the sea or belief was the ocean in which was all the wisdom of the world, so the preachers or spouters fished in it, and the ships were the little society or church where the people congregated to catch some spiritual food or fish. When Peter and Andrew left their father or belief and their nets and society or ship and followed him, then they left all for his sake. When the young man came to Jesus and asked him what he should do to inherit eternal life or wisdom, he said, Keep the commandments. The young man replied, This have I done from my youth upwards. What lack I more? If you would be perfect, go give all your old religious ideas away and follow the Science or Me. So as he could not understand, he went away sorrowful for he had much wisdom of this world. When the disciples heard this, they thought it a hard saying, so they said to him, We have left our old ships and nets and even father and all for your science and what shall we have? Jesus answered, If they could understand all his truth so that they could teach the people, then they should sit on twelve thrones, judging or teaching the twelve tribes of Israel. But this they could not understand; so when they were called upon to stand up and defend the science, they all forsook him and there never has been a person since Jesus who could throw one particle of light on Jesus' science. As soon as Jesus was crucified, the disciples were driven away or killed; so all of the teachings of Jesus fell into the hands of men who knew nothing of Jesus' science, and they took the record and put just such a construction as they pleased. So you see that all we have is the opinions of men who lived hundreds of years after the crucifixion of Jesus.

Now as they could not cure any person, the teachings of Jesus must be explained in some way that did not require proof; so right in the face of Jesus' teachings, where he gave his disciples power or wisdom to teach and told what would follow, that they should cure all diseases as he did and greater cures should they perform, the priest had to get over this by saying the days of miracles are past. The people believed these blind guides so they have crucified Christ in every way that error could invent. Now Jesus stood alone in the world with no living man of flesh and blood, feeling the sorrows of this world of flesh and blood, weeping over their sins or errors that bound them down and well might he say as he did, Oh! Jerusalem, thou that stoneth the wisdom of God and hated those that teach it to you, how often would I have gathered you together in love for each other, as a hen gathers her chickens under her wings of sympathy, and runs the risk of her life for her young. This to them was all without meaning. They could not see any sympathy outside of dollars and cents nor feel another's woes. So he said to them, Ye have eyes but cannot see and ears but cannot hear the voice or misery and no heart to feel another's woes. Now they did not want to understand, for it would make them break off from their sins and turn to the truth and become honest and good. Jesus' sea was love for the sake of the world's happiness. This love he laid down for the sins or beliefs of man and received into the bosom of this love or sympathy, which was pure, not a selfish idea, independent of all, but a love for the sake of all.

Jesus, as a man of flesh and blood, as we all are, purified his own life, received this eternal life in the name of Christ and took all our opinions that would have killed him if he had been ignorant of the truth, rose again, pure and clean from all priestcraft and superstition and then denounced the priests and doctors as the enemies of the happiness of man. Now to be a follower of Christ is to do the things that he did, but to be a believer in Christ embraces what you know nothing of, only as a belief. There is a vast difference between a belief and knowledge. Knowledge is wisdom and does not contain a belief. A belief is error or the wisdom of this world and the only way to tell them apart is to detect them by their work or fruits.

I will give you the key to heaven or science as far as correcting the errors in regard to your health is concerned so that you cannot be deceived by the errors of the world. I will give you a sign so you can tell the difference between my theory as a teacher of Christ or Science and my opinion as a man, so you shall not be deceived by false teachers, who will come and say to you, I understand; I do just as Dr. Q. does. It is all spiritualism. I can tell your feelings just as well as he can. If you know me then you will say, By your fruits I shall know you. Now if they tell you how you feel and locate disease, offering any opinion in regard to your diet or advice concerning what you shall do, if they give a name to your trouble and tell you that your feelings are the symptoms of some disease of a serious nature, thereby giving you a glimpse of a long train of troubles which you are liable, to such you can say: That is not like Dr. Q. You are known by your fruits. Now if he had been a true disciple of me, he would have taken upon himself all your feelings. These feelings are my knowledge of your trouble as they are yours, but to me they contain the true answer and when my explanation satisfies you, then your difficulty is gone and you are happy. Jesus knew that all the troubles of mankind arose from ignorance of immortality and Christ revealed to the people that man was spiritual and his unhappiness lay in a wrong belief. This belief amounted to this–that the natural world is all there is and as man required something higher to satisfy him, the spiritual world was admitted and made to contain all sorts of witches and frightful things to keep the people in subjection. So this spiritual world, as it is called, has never been investigated as a science and all revelations from it and allusions to it are steeped in mystery and superstition. Thus most of us are in this mystic land. We only know our bodies and further than that we are in the dark. Christ is that revelation, a science of the spiritual world which is a knowledge and cure of all the ills flesh is heir to.

The people are divided in two classes: followers of Christ and followers of Jesus. This is a great mistake. To illustrate the difference between Jesus and Christ, I will take myself. There are a great many persons who believe in my healing power but know nothing of the truth of it; so they make me as a man responsible for all my acts and belief in all things. Thus my private character is brought into my belief just as though I could not be a teacher of truth unless my character as a man was in harmony with the errors of the world. Now I stand before the people, judged according to my outward acts by one class and by my science by another. So if I should put on the cloak of hypocrisy and attend meetings, pay tithes and be very strict in all things pertaining to the wisdom of this world, then I am received by the wisdom of this world, but the scientific world looks upon me as a hypocrite. Jesus' private character as a man had just about as much to do with Christ as P. P. Q. has with his cure. Jesus, as a man, knew nothing of Christ as P. P. Q., as a man, knows nothing of this wisdom or truth, but when he feels it, he speaks not as P. P. Q. but as the patient's trouble is revealed to him. So this science in P. P. Q. takes the trouble or sins of the patient and the answer is accompanied with the feelings. Thus P. P. Q. is the medium of the truth to correct the errors of the world, just as Jesus was the medium of God or truth or Christ to convince man of his errors and lead him to Christ or health or truth. I will now give you an illustration to show where the followers are and where the disciples are.

I will take myself as a figure. Suppose that music had never been reduced to a science and I discovered that it could be taught to others and undertook to teach it. Suppose I called the science Christ, then it would be P. P. Q.'s Christ or theory. Suppose further that you should try to learn it so as to teach it; would my character as a man have anything to do with my Christ or theory? All will say, No. If I am a very good man, that has nothing to do with my science; it may make it more admired or perhaps it might make persons give more heed to what I say. Now suppose that I am as bad a man as I can be. Does that prevent me teaching my Christ or science? Now suppose the wisdom of the world sits in judgment on me; they will all admit that I play very well but I know no more about it than they do. So they say he has a power but it is of God, but I know nothing of it myself; so they put all the power in me as a man and call my name P. P. Q.'s Music. Now suppose that I am a very good man and a pattern in society, kind in my manners, possessed of every quality that belongs to a good man of this world. There are two classes: one the scientific and the other the aristocratic or ignorant. Each professes to believe in me and as they can't agree, it is left for me to decide. So I decide in this way. All you that believe in me as a scientific musician or a Christ and understand the science shall do as I do; and all you that don't understand but believe that I, the man P. P. Q., have a power that you acknowledge shall be called followers of me; so you undertake to follow me by acting as I do and trying to imitate my character, while those who are the disciples of my theory care nothing about my character except as a secondary thing. Of course we all would like a person that is amiable and pleasant if he is a teacher of any science, but it is not absolutely necessary that he be a good or a bad one. Now as far as Jesus stands, I for one, do not pretend to be or not to be a disciple of Jesus, for I let my life and acts as a man speak for themselves. I do not pin my belief on Jesus' character nor care anything about it, any more than he did himself. Like all other men who are willing to be judged by their acts, he let his character speak for itself. It was the Christ that Jesus was proud of; so all men ought to be proud of any science that would make the world wiser and better. I believe the same, so I profess to be a disciple of Christ, not of Jesus or the man. I let my man speak for himself, but I believe in Christ and put Him in practice on all those who live in this world of misery without this science or truth. So all my prayers are offered up to Christ, not to Jesus. The world prays to Jesus but Jesus prayed to God to forgive them or teach them for they knew not what they prayed to.

Now this Christ is in this element of love or sympathy that contains no error but is pure love that will wash away all error that chances to get into it. It knows no evil, it sees no wrong, and in itself it is perfect harmony and attraction. It contains our senses. So it is, as it were, our life and all that is good and harmonious. It seeks the wisdom of this world of error as a person seeks gold to purify the gold from the dross. Its happiness is the developing of God's love or science. It analyzes all misery and trouble to liberate the soul that is bound in this world of error.

July 1860

Spiritualism [I]
[LC 1:0527]

Who are to judge of the phenomena of spiritualism; those who see the phenomena or those who can produce them? It seems to be the opinion of those who see the experiments and cannot explain them that they must be brought about by spirits. So all explanation that is given which goes to show that it is the works of the living cannot be true, for these men, wise in their own conceit, cannot admit what these narrow minds cannot comprehend to be true. So this set of wise men must give their opinion, and the world is bound to believe what they know nothing about, for they admit it is only their opinion. Now I fall in company with such persons every day and have conversed with them, and they cannot give one single fact to prove their theory, only those based on a belief in spirits of the dead. This error is so common and is believed by nearly every person, that to deny it is to deny our own existence. Now every person that believes in spirits of any kind is a believer in spiritualism although he may deny it. Yet he is ready to believe at the first phenomenon that takes place that he cannot account for. So it is with disease. All men who believe in disease admit it as a thing or spirit outside of themselves, like spirits, and so they are liable to catch one when they are in a right condition to take a disease or see a spirit. This is the same with religion.

Every religion embraces these evils. Now to suppose that Jesus was a believer in this is to make him a spiritualist which he positively denies. For when he was accused of being a spirit, he denied it and said, A spirit hath not flesh and bones as ye see me have. Now Jesus had a different idea of spirit from the rest of the world. His spirits were of this world. They were a belief not of wisdom but what flowed from a superstitious mind.

I will give one parable of his, the parable of the spirits leaving the man when he wanders about and at last returns and finds the house swept and garnished and then goes off and gets other spirits more wicked. Then he returns and takes possession and then he sees the last state is worse than the first. Now in this parable we shall see what Jesus thought of spirits, how much life they had and what injury they could do. I will now make a proper illustration. Take a sick man who believes he has consumption or any disease. His belief is himself a spirit, not the spirit of truth, but of disease. Now let a person sit down and explain away his belief and the spirit or fear leaves him and wanders around like a man's mind when he is convinced of an error. At last it comes back in the form of a doubt, but everything seems to be cleared up and his house or belief seems to be completely swept of every error or doubt and he wanders around for happiness. At last he runs against a doubt or bad spirit. This excites him and more doubt comes up and these are spirits, so at last they return to his mind or house and enter. Then comes the conflict with truth.

If the spirit of error gets the advantage, the truth is enslaved and error or evil spirits rule and this last state is worse than the first. This is spiritualism and this was Jesus' spiritualism. But the religious spiritualism is the belief in dead spirits, good and bad, that inhabit another world. The only difference in them is whether they come and converse with the living or not. Now Jesus never had any such belief. He labored to convince the world of a science in regard to the working of the mind, showing that the mind is capable of changes and that in these changes is what we call reason and thought. And the science is to cultivate these thoughts for they take form and if we do not understand that they are the creation of ourselves of some other person, then our superstition calls them spirits. So the act of thinking is the foundation of spiritualism, for if there was no thought, there would be no improvement. This is the case with brutes. Their power of thought is limited to their race, but if the brute be placed under a wisdom superior to themselves, their matter or mind is lifted up, producing a higher state than the original one. This is the same with the human species. Man is a thinking machine. His thoughts are spirit or matter, like the shock of a battery controlled by this wisdom. If his wisdom is of science, his thoughts are to him the reflection of his wisdom, but if his thoughts are from his belief, they are spiritual.

So a corrupt fountain cannot bring forth pure water, nor a belief explain a scientific fact. The science is to change the man or wisdom, not that you can bring a clean thing out of an unclean thing, but there is such a thing as sound to those who can hear and there is an echo. Call the sound the real and the echo the spiritual, like action and reaction. The echo is opposed to the sound. Reaction is the man of opinions and contains nothing but noise, yet it has its identity and name and ignorance puts as much life in it as he does in action. For those who see no reaction cannot see action, so when the action is not seen, to such the action is dead. But to the scientific man, reaction is a spirit or the echo of his own act. Now there is no life in the belief that wisdom is in the shadow or reaction. Make man understand that what he sees is not himself but the shadow or reaction and then he will not put life into the vessel, but will see himself outside of the thing or world looking into it instead of being in the thing or vessel or body looking out.

Here is the difference. The man of belief is in his belief; the man of wisdom is in his wisdom. One is looking out of his belief to find wisdom and the other is in wisdom looking into the belief to put wisdom or the real man. Such is the difference between the religious world and Christ. The religious world is looking for Christ to come, but Christ is outside looking into their beliefs, saying, "I am with you even in your own beliefs or hearts and you know me not, so repent and break from your belief and rise in the truth." So the diseased man is in his disease or spirit, for a spirit is a belief whether of disease, of God, of witches or of the other world. All are of this world and science will destroy them all.

Our feeling is a state of mind like water. Cold water is expressed by some intelligence outside the water. Hot water and all the varieties of heat are expressed by language which expresses the change in the water. This is the same with ideas. Like water, they affect man and the misery or pain depends upon his fear and his fears are the result of his error. Let man know that his thoughts are as harmless of themselves as water and he will not be getting into trouble as he does. Disease is one of the troubles that follows his ignorance. Make him learn that any spiritual idea is the out-bursting of a fountain and that the water contains nothing bad but is a mass of water let loose, and he will be better off.

So with mind that is under the direction of a belief. It lets off a volley of matter or opinions in the form of every evil that can be imagined. To the wise it is as harmless as the water but to the ignorant it contains what is bad and frightful. So wisdom separates the wheat from the chaff and the separation is the end of the world or the error, and this is science. As I give my wisdom to one particular branch of this wisdom, that is the correcting of the false ideas of the sick, I have to make war with every idea that affects them and the effect is shown on and in the body through the mind, as it is called. Now the natural man treats the body as the man and knows nothing of the owner. So he enters his neighbor's house and upsets everything that is in harmony and sets up his kingdom of darkness or opinion. So the children of darkness destroy the house. But when the true master or wisdom comes, then he turns out the children of false ideas and puts in a more intelligent set of ideas that will render unto the truth a better offering.

1864

Spiritualism [II]
[BU 3:0552]

As there is much excitement on the subject of spiritualism, and those who have undertaken to write against it do not seem to throw any light upon the subject but rather fan the flame by calling it a humbug and a deception; now to call it a humbug is to call all those, who from honest opinion are bound to believe certain facts which come within their own senses, deceivers; and if persons must give up their opinions from facts which come within their own knowledge to persons who cannot give any reason, only that it happens to be contrary to their own opinion, then man is not a free agent but must have someone to tell him when or what to believe. This setting up a standard for others to fall and bow down to, I, for one, cannot do it. The Bible says, "Try the spirits and see if they are right, if so embrace them, if false discard them, but treat your opponent like a human being, who you think is in the wrong."

I am very far from believing that it has anything to do with the dead, but I think that a large proportion of its converts are honest but are misled for the want of some better proof. To explain to them the truth that they have witnessed, if this can be done in such a way as to come within their senses, they are bound to believe it, but if it cannot, the fault is not in them; it is in the person who undertook to lead them.

Now if my explanation does not convince those who may chance to read it, the fault is in me and not in them, for I believe if any person knows a fact, he can make it understood if he has the patience to reason with his opponent. But we often give our opinions and think others must believe them, whether they are right or wrong. This is asking more of others than we are willing to give ourselves.

I ask no more of my opponents than they may ask of me. I have been investigating the subject of the mind for the last sixteen years and, after careful investigation, have come to the following conclusion which I shall give as follows.

We are all acted upon by early impressions which prevent us from investigating subjects of this kind without being biased by those early impressions. A large majority of mankind are taught to believe in a superior being and also in some religious creed. These creeds all teach the locality of two places: heaven and hell. It is true that some believe the locality of the latter to exist in the heart, or mind of man, yet the fruits of the latter belief is left unexplained; if the idea ever was believed in the locality of a hell and the wicked were doomed to that, then it would not be strange for persons to believe in evil spirits. This same is true of the former place; therefore good and bad spirits are believed to have an identity in this world.

Now with such a belief it is not strange that any development of the mind should disturb mankind. This belief was what Christ had to contend with; it was not his belief, but it was the common belief of the people of his day and he condemned it in all his sayings and doings. These ideas were believed by the Jews and other nations, only differing in some little variation.

Most all believed in a resurrection of the dead, but it was at the end of the world. This idea Christ opposed by correcting Martha when she said to him, "If thou hadst been here our brother would not have died." Christ answered her by saying, Thy brother shall rise again. She replied that she knew he would rise again at the last day, at the resurrection, showing that she believed in a resurrection at the end of the world. But did Christ sanction this belief? No, he said, I am the resurrection and the life, he that believes in me shall never die. Now where did Christ's belief differ from the rest of the people? In this: He knew what the people's belief was concerning a resurrection; they believed that the dead would rise again; he knew that there was no such state as death, but man continues along and is just what he makes himself. Now here was a difference of opinion. Their opinion embraced all of the errors of the Egyptian darkness. It embraced a belief in a located heaven and hell; it also embraced a devil and evil spirits which were let loose in the world to torment man. It also embraced the belief in disease and all its bad effects; besides these exist hundreds of other beliefs which affect the people.

This was the state of the world when Christ commenced his reform, and this was what he had to contend with. These beliefs were called yokes and the priests and rulers would not lift their finger to lighten their burdens. Therefore Christ said to the people, Come unto me all ye that labor and are heavy laden and I will give you rest; take my yoke upon you, for my yoke is easy and my burden light.

Now what was Christ's yoke? It was his belief and the burden was truth and truth condemned all these errors; therefore to take his yoke upon them, the burden would be in proportion to the yoke. Therefore if they believed in Christ, they would throw off the Egyptian yoke or burden and all. Now the burden borne by the yoke or belief was their opinions in regard to a located heaven or hell. This belief Christ opposed and tried to convince the people that these places were states of the mind and that there was no such a being as a devil, independent of the person affected.

Take mankind as they are, believing some in good, some in bad spirits and some in none at all and it is not strange that any excitement produced by the development of the mind should disturb mankind. If the people would settle down on some belief on which they could agree, in a short time they would not be tossed about by every wind of doctrine; but I shall take the world as it is and show that all of these developments are the effect of the mind and have nothing to do with the dead. I will admit all that is claimed by the spiritualists but must differ with them in their explanation of the facts. Where does the idea arise that it is the spirits of the dead, from what is said while in this trance? The medium when aroused from the trance remembers nothing of what he has been saying. When asked by someone of the company if he was conscious of what he had been doing, his answer is No. The company are then left to argue the subject and then adopt a belief.

This arouses all their prejudices in regard to spirits of the dead and at last leave the scene just about as their former beliefs were. This is the same in regard to mesmeric experiments. The medium's belief is founded on his friend's opinion and his friend's opinion is founded on what he said in an unconscious state. This state is produced in various ways. The oracle of Delphi is an example. The shepherds while watching their sheep discovered that they would go to a certain place and hold their heads over a chasm in a rock from whence issued forth a sort of vapor, this would make them spring, jump and cut all manner of capers. This fact was made known to the priests, who took advantage of it and erected a house over the chasm and also placed a stool perforated with holes over the chasm on which the medium was placed. The vapor would rise and the medium would be convulsed and at last fall into an unconscious state and then foretell future events. This was believed by the people to come from the spiritual world. All persons know that there are certain people affected by religious excitement and will go into a trance, but very few believe that they get any knowledge from the spiritual world.

Therefore it is no proof because some persons can go into that state themselves, nor is it the result of some spirit. See how many ways a trance can be produced by mesmerism. I can produce it in a great many ways by taking the patient by the hand and also by giving them a piece of money or some other substance and also by sending them a handkerchief or glove. I have produced it on a patient at a distance without their knowing anything of my design of affecting them. I have for the last ten years produced a state of mind in a person who to all appearances appeared to be wide awake. It does not follow that persons in a mesmeric state must have their eyes closed. Some have their eyes open, some hear, others do not. Some cannot say a word while others can talk. Some can throw themselves into a trance, others cannot. You can teach nearly all to, if you please. Therefore the getting into this trance is no proof of its being brought on by the spirits of the dead. Then where is the difference? I am at a loss to say where they differ, only in the opinion of the people. I will now compare some of my experiments with those claimed by the spiritualists.

I profess to be a medium myself and am admitted to be so by the spiritualists themselves; therefore before I give my explanation, I will relate one little circumstance to show what confidence they have in their early impressions when they are not aware of the fact.

I was talking with a friend one day upon the subject of spiritualism. He was a strong believer in the doctrine. We differed in regard to the explanation of the phenomenon. He contended it was from the dead; I, that it was confined to the living. At last I said, Will you admit that I am a medium? He said, "Yes!" And a seeing medium? "Yes." Well, can you see the spirits, said I? "No," said he. Then you admit I can see the spirits and talk with them and you cannot. "I do," said he. Then said I, "I tell you they don't come from the dead." "Oh, you are mistaken," said he. Therefore, you see he denied what he had admitted, but this I laid to his early impressions, and reasoning from false basis, his conclusions must be false. You cannot reason with persons from the fact that the whole of their theory is founded on some idea that never had an existence, only in the mind. Destroy the idea of the spirits of the dead and you destroy their theory. Where is the proof of the spirits of the dead? I find none but can bring sufficient proof that the spirits of the living are with us.

I will now explain what I mean by the spirits of the living. The animal spirit is living matter, acted upon by another power which does not depend on an identity for its existence, which cannot be seen even by spiritual eyes but is admitted. This power I shall not undertake to explain, but in all I say, I acknowledge its existence.

Now as man is animal matter, for some wise purpose he is left to develop himself. Like everything else, matter cannot develop itself unless there is some chemical action. So it is with man. Man when excited develops some new principle which could never have been brought about in any other way.

Jesus was a medium, and through him, that is his natural body, some laws were developed to man that never had been before. Franklin and Napoleon were mediums, far above the errors of the age. So it is with all others who show some knowledge superior to the errors of their own time.

The development of man is to correct some error that exists in the natural man, for if he did not develop himself, he would be but little above the brute, but the undeveloped man is full of error, superstition and ignorance. Now to develop oneself is to unlearn that which superstition and ignorance have bequeathed to him. Now as this is spurring man forward to develop himself for some wise purpose, the ignorant oppose it like all other science, calling it by various names. Some oppose it as the works of the devil, others as proving their old theory of spirits, etc. Each of these classes only act as a clog to prevent investigation.

I will now try to explain where the error lies. Those mediums who undertake to explain lose their own consciousness, so how can they then be responsible for what they say while in this state? Their opinions are founded on the opinions of others. As for myself I have no opinion. What I see I know; if I cannot believe my own senses I cannot believe others. One great fault in mankind is this. There are certain ideas admitted to be true which exist only in the mind, among them the idea of a located Hell. Now to admit the idea independent of man's mind is to admit its inhabitants. Admit this and I see no reason for opposing anything they can bring forward. Their foundation and arguments are good, but I for one cannot see their reason. I admit the fact and will show that they can be brought about by the living.

When I first commenced mesmerizing, I often saw experiments that I was not able to account for in any other way than to believe it came from the dead; but since I have become a medium I have changed my opinion. I can see where I was deceived by my early education. I was not aware that man had this power to create ideas so that they could be seen by another. I had no idea of what was called imagination, but I found that the word imagination could not cause all the phenomena. Therefore I was left to find some other way to account for all I would see and on investigation I found that ideas were something.

The next thing then was to find out what they were. This I did, and found that ideas when condensed into a form contained a portion of our own natural body. It is the heat that arises from the fluids of the body under a nervous excitement. For instance, a lady came to see me who was sick. She appeared like a person who had the dropsy. I took her by the hand. Her mind then left the body (as it appeared to me) and I followed it, although it seemed as though I was in two places at the same time, for I was still sitting in my office and at the same time I could see a scene which I will now describe. I seemed to follow her some distance over the water, the wind blew a gale, the water seemed very much disturbed, the sun looked as though it was near 11 o'clock A.M. At last I saw a brig under full sail; my attention was then fixed on that. I saw a man on the bowsprit dressed in an oil cloth suit; at last he fell overboard, the vessel hove to, but the man sunk. This seemed as plain to me as though I had seen it with my natural eyes. I have asked spiritualists to explain this. They all say it is the spirits of the dead. My explanation is this: The lady lost her husband five years before. He was in a brig off the Bahamas and lost as I described. On hearing of the death of her husband, it produced a nervous shock, producing a chemical action upon her system, which threw off this heat and in this heat, as vapor, she created the cause of her trouble. This was to her the remembrance of some trouble which she could not be reconciled to. This heat is the secret of all the phenomena that has heretofore been a mystery to mankind. It shows itself in a thousand ways. It is the foundation of all superstition and ignorance. Out of this men form images that frighten them. Persons in fevers create all the scenes that trouble them. It is the material used to create all the ideas and forms of all our false ideas. This is taken for the spirits of the dead. This the spiritualists jump over.

I shall give some examples of various kinds to show that the mind can produce almost any phenomena that can be imagined. I will here show how disease is created. Take for instance the heart disease. I take this because there are a great many who think that they are laboring under this disease and as I am a skeptic in regard to disease independent of the mind, I will show how this heat is used to bring about this disease.

Ignorance as well as truth has its identity and when an idea is admitted, whether true or false, it will have its effects upon mankind. Now the idea of disease, independent of the mind, is like the idea of hell believed by almost every person; therefore admit disease independent of the mind and you keep man in ignorance of himself, all his life subject to bondage. Now disease like evil spirits is admitted. Therefore the priests warn the people to have nothing to do with the devil and the doctors endeavor to keep the people clear of disease.

Christ denounced both as error and proved it by his works. He showed that evil spirits and disease were one and the same and that both existed in ourselves, for when he cast out devils, he cast out disease also and when he cast out disease, he cast out error.

It may be asked, "Where is disease?" In the mind. I will show how it is in the mind. I spoke of disease of the heart, that idea is admitted and all the symptoms accompanying it. The fluids of the body are excited, and the mind creates an identity corresponding to its feelings and differing from its healthy body. In this respect it sees itself, that is its spirit with its heart disease, just as it thinks it is. This to itself is as real as any idea can be; this keeps up a constant excitement till the natural body becomes changed, so as to be called disease. Now destroy the idea of disease independent of the mind and evil spirits also, and it will teach man to look within himself for the evil that troubles him instead of any other source. The ideas are both founded on error and cause nine-tenths of the misery of the human family. It is the stepping stone to insanity, for man deceives himself into a belief that evil spirits are around him, talking to him, spurring him on to commit some evil deed which he would not do if he properly understood where the author of these thoughts reside. I shall now give some illustrations to show how people deceive themselves.

I was called to see a lady who had become insane by this false idea of spirits of the dead. The lady had been with friends and as usual the subject of spiritualism came up and as there was a medium in the room, she was requested to try some experiments. After various experiments were tried, the spirits wrote that Mrs. C was a writing medium. It is a trick of the trade. It has this effect on the person whom the spirits select; it makes them nervous and brings their nervous system into a state to be affected by their own thought. This is the same in mesmerism. I always found that if my subject pretended that anyone could be mesmerized I could most always produce the sleep. It is a tendency to excite and as persons are more or less disturbed by their early impressions, they cannot help being affected. This was the case with the lady in question. She had lost her husband some twelve months before. This would naturally excite her and when she returned home, she thought she would try the experiment. Her father and mother were present. She sat down by the table and took her pen in hand and waited the movement of the spirits. In a short time the hand began to shake. This of course would excite her and she ventured to ask if there were any spirits present? Answer, "Yes." She asked if it was various persons? Answer, "No." At last she asked if it was her husband? Answer, "Yes." Are you happy? "No!" By this time she became much excited, more questions were asked, but no answers were received but, "Yes" and "No." At last she asked when will you be happy? When God takes you to heaven. "When will that be?" "Soon."

The father then interfered and broke up the sitting. The lady went to her room and retired. This was about nine o'clock. About ten she got up, came downstairs, asked her mother where the matches were. "Are you sick?" asked her mother. "Yes, and going to die." This frightened the parents and they arose. She seemed in great distress and her father went for one of the neighbors. When they returned she was running around perfectly insane. She said if they would leave her alone for a few moments God would take her to heaven. She pleaded so hard that they went out, but looked through the window. She went to her husband's chest and got a large knife. They rushed in just in time to prevent her from taking her own life. She then became a raving maniac. A physician was called but to no purpose. She continued in this way for more than a week, when I was called to see her. After some time I quieted her mind, explained to her the cause of her trouble and she became sane and has had no more trouble from the spirits. She is satisfied that she herself was the cause of all her trouble.

I went to see a lady who had cut her throat under the direction of the spirits. She had become insane and was told to kill two of her children. She resisted and left them and went to a neighbor's house to stay. She retired to bed, but the spirits kept telling her to go and kill the children. She arose and tried to find a rope to hang herself, but could not. She then went to the room where the man and his wife were and entreated them to protect her and keep her from killing herself and the children. They rose, telling her to lie down there in their own room. She saw a pair of scissors, took them and placed them under her apron. She then laid down with her clothes on and covering her head, cut her jugular vein. Her friends thought she had gone to sleep. After a short time she threw off the clothes with her arms and asked where she was. They went to her bed and found her covered with blood. She asked if she was dead. When told no, she asked what she had been doing. The artery had closed so that the blood had stopped. A doctor was sent for and the artery taken up, but the mind was completely deranged.

I was called to her about a week after the deed was done. She was then laboring under a strange delusion, feared she would be carried to the insane hospital and thought I came to kill her. I succeeded in restoring her to her reason and satisfied her that what she saw and heard was the effect of her own mind. She understood it and her understanding was the cure.

Now can any person believe that spirits from the dead came to her persuading her to take the lives of her children? If there is, it is an error of the mind which should be corrected, founded on some false idea.

Some persons would explain these two cases upon imagination, but that is not the fact. The things seen and heard are as real as anything that comes within our senses. Ideas are formed by the mind and as often destroyed before they are put in force or ever developed to our senses.

Spiritualism and Mesmerism [I]
[LC 2:0813]

Mr. Editor:

Thinking that my experience in mesmerism may give some light on the phenomena of spiritualism, I will state my experience for twenty-five years. It was about that time I first gave my attention to the subject of mesmerism and I have followed it up to the present time and have seen the workings of the phenomena in all its phases, from putting a person into an unconscious state to the experiment called spiritualism. It is true that there is a class of persons who try to show that spiritualism is not mesmerism, but to me they only show their ignorance of mesmerism. For mesmerism is not confined to one set of experiments but is the working of the mind under various influences. And as I have given my whole time to the investigation of the subject, I will relate some of my experiments and leave the candid reader to decide which is the most reasonable.

My first experiment was to put a person into an unconscious state called mesmeric and my ideas about it were these: that I contained more electricity than the subject and by the power of my will I charged him so full that he came completely under my will. Now I had no idea that my belief had anything to do with my subject and myself. But experience proved to me that all my experiments were governed by a belief and not by wisdom at all. I knew that if I sat down and took hold of the hand of certain persons they would pass into this state, but the whys and wherefores I knew not. So to make myself acquainted with the phenomena, I consulted every author I could hear of to know what to do. There was a work written by a Doctor Townshend of Europe and I read it but had no idea that what I read had anything to do with my experiments; but time showed me that all I ever read or heard gave direction to my experiments.

I will here state what was the common belief at the time and show how the experiments went to prove it. There were certain conditions that must be complied with and if they were not complied with, the experiments would fail. But the failure was never attributed to spirits but unbelief, etc. Among the conditions influencing the experiments was metal. If I had any steel about me, it affected the subject. This was my belief, and if it rained, my experiments would fail. This was also according to the belief in electricity. So there were a great many conditions of weather and persons necessary. If a skeptic was too near, it affected the patient. So I went on like all mesmerizers getting into trouble and out. And after some three years I found I had produced a great many phenomena, but I was as ignorant as when I began and I have never seen the person that has as yet got out of the darkness. Yet old mesmerizers are as ignorant about the phenomena of their days as the new converts and will always remain so till they investigate the subject with different ideas from what have ever been advanced. As I never had read any writing upon the subject before I commenced, I only had to get rid of what I got from reading after I commenced.

It would take me a long time to give a birds-eye view of what I have experienced for the last twenty-five years, but I wish to lead the reader along, so that he will be prepared to understand me when I come to the phase of the phenomena called spiritualism. Now I was prepared for the experiments of spiritualism, though not exactly the way they came. But I was prepared to see matter moved by the power of man's will, for I had experimented on this idea for months all alone trying to move an object suspended by a thread. So when I heard of the Rochester Rappings I was myself trying the experiment. Now why did I try the experiment? I will tell you. I was trying some experiments with my subject and they were never better, and I experimented till past twelve o'clock and never failed. When I closed, I went to the door and found it was raining very fast. It had clouded up while I was experimenting and if I had known the fact, I could not have had one experiment. They would all have failed. To me this was a complete stunner. I retired and lay and thought it all over and came to the conclusion that it was all my fault. The experiments were in accordance with my belief. I then determined not to read any more nor take any opinion but launch my barque on the ocean of thought and be governed by no one's opinion but by the sensations made on me by my subject. And I have kept my vows and now I will give my own ideas, not my opinion but my experiments.

I had arrived at that degree that the subject could read the thoughts of persons and could travel and explain what the person knew, and also see and describe what the person nor anyone else in the room knew. I say I had arrived at that point. But I was just as ignorant as I was at the first experiment I had so far as knowing the whys and wherefores. To show the similarity between the experiments then and now under the so-called spiritualism, I will relate one or two of the many I used to show. My mode was first to put my subject into what I called a clairvoyant state and then request one of the company to give me the name of some individual and the boy would find him. I did not care whether dead or alive. So a name was handed me. I can't remember what it was but I will call it John Brown, for I think it was that. I passed the name to the boy who was sitting blindfolded by the committee. He read the name aloud. I told him to bring the person.

My mode was to make him ask questions so that the audience would lead him along. So I said, Enquire who he is, a man or boy? He said, a man. Is he married? Yes. Will you tell me if he has any children and how many? He said he had a wife and three children. Well, find him. He said he left town between two days. Well, find him. So he traced him to Boston, and by enquiring, he followed him to the interior of New York and found him in a cooper's shop. Now all this was literally true, and I suppose the audience knew the fact, but the boy nor myself knew nothing of it. Well, what became of the man? He said he was dead. Well said I, find him and bring him along. Well said he, he is here, can't you see him? I then reminded him that he was mesmerized, for in that state everything was as real as in the waking state. So I said, Give a description. He then went on to give a general description. Now these general descriptions amount to nothing, for everyone will make it fit their case. So I said, I don't want that; if there is anything peculiar about the man, describe it. There is one thing peculiar. He has a hare lip. This was the fact. Now I asked that question so that if there was anything peculiar the audience would create it.

Now what was the conclusion they came to? Those who believed it was the spirit of the man, believed he came. Those who believed it was clairvoyance or thought reading continued to believe so. Some said that I had hired the committee to give the name. So they all left with their minds just as I had found them. Now these experiments convinced me that man has the power of creating ideas and making them so dense that they could be seen by a subject that was mesmerized. So I used to create objects and make him describe them. At last I could take persons to all appearance in the waking state and make them see anything I chose. I found that I could stop persons while walking. This led me to the fact that I could act on living matter without contact. I could hold people down so that they could not rise and could keep them from rising. This showed me that man has an unconscious power that is not admitted which governs his acts. This is not recognized by his natural senses and this is the mystery that hangs over the world. I must say a word or two about this mystery.

Words are used to convey some idea of something that can be seen, but if a word is spoken that should wound another's feelings, there is no language to explain the peculiar sensation. Now my experiments and investigations have educated me up to this state that I feel this peculiar sensation that is made on persons and I feel and know how they feel and convince them of the fact. Now this is the state that embraces all the phenomena of spiritualism, disease, religion and everything that affects the mind. So every person's belief affects them. Now there are persons who are sensitive to this state and are acted upon by the influences of different beliefs. As there is a certain class of persons who believe that spirits come back, as it is called, to them they do come back, just as the man I spoke of. Some persons believe it is the works of the devil, and it is to them the works of Satan; and as good spirits and bad are believed in, so the experiments go to prove their belief. Now I know that all of what I have said is true, but it is all the natural working of man's belief. Convince man that every act or belief that he embraces has an effect on his body and just as he measures out to another it will be measured back to him and there is no escape, he will be cautious what he says. Now I have seen the experiments in spiritualism and I know that they are the workings of man's own belief and I have proved it to the medium. I knew a very excitable medium who was very susceptible to impressions. I tried some experiments with her. I told her I would convince her it was her own belief that governed the raps. So when the spirits came, I asked certain questions that I knew she did not agree with me upon, nor indeed any of the company; such as: if I could be two places at the same time and whether I could make myself known to certain individuals without their knowledge. All this the spirits denied and said I could not. I then said I would not trouble the spirits any more. Then I went on to explain how I could do these things and I knew I changed their minds. So I said I would come again and convince them that I was right.

So in the course of three or four days I called and found the same company and said, I will now convince you that I was right. They all laughed and I sat down by the table and the raps came and the question was asked if the spirits were present and it rapped, Yes. I then repeated what I said and it rapped; I was right in every one of my questions. When I asked them what made them give such answers, they said they were mistaken. Now this is the state of the case. As people become educated, the ideas change; this keeps the mind all the time excited. In a short time, the superstition or fear will change and all the phenomena of today will cease and some new phase will spring up, just according to the wisdom of the world. And this sort of superstition will keep up till man finds that true happiness is in true wisdom, and wisdom reduced to a scientific mode of reasoning will place man where he never was placed before. To be happy, he must do something. For that happiness that comes from a belief or ignorance may be blissful; but if the happiness of that man who labors to make others happy is of no more value that the happiness of one that sits and folds his hands and says, All I want in this world is to be let alone, so don't disturb me, Let me be happy, then I agree with the one who said of this sort, If ignorance is bliss, it is folly to be wise.

Spiritualism and Mesmerism [II]
[Originally untitled.] [BU 2:0008]

How does spiritualism differ from mesmerism? The word "mesmerism" embraces all the phenomena that ever were claimed by any intelligent spiritualists. The spiritualists claim that they get knowledge from the dead through living mediums.

Do not mesmerizers do this? Surely. Then what is the difference? In the ignorance of the people.

I will give some facts which have come under my own observation. When I first commenced mesmerizing about sixteen years ago, the most of my experiments were of the following kind. After getting my subject in a mesmerized state, I would try some simple experiment, for instance, imagine some person or animal which he would describe. I would then put him in communication with some person of the company, and let that person carry him to some place which he would describe. In these experiments it would often happen that he would get intelligence from some person of whom the company knew nothing. At other times the audience would like to have me send him after someone's lost friend. This I used to do but tried to make them understand that it was the reflection of their own thought.

In these experiments I had an opportunity to see and hear the different opinions and beliefs of mankind in regard to whether he really saw the person that he would describe or not. I found that my own opinion could have but little effect upon the mind of the audience. Their opinions would govern in most all cases. Sometimes, when the experiments would embrace the friend of an infidel, I would confuse him some; but I found that nearly all persons were inclined to believe just about as their religious opinions will. I also found that my subject's religious opinions were just about like the person's opinions that he was in communication with.

If they professed religion to the world and were a hypocrite at heart, the subject would find it out, and the same was true of the subject. I had one subject who was very religious when awake, but when asleep was just the opposite.

I will here relate an experiment when on the Kennebec. I had my subject in the sleep. I then requested any of the company to bring me the name of any individual dead or alive, and the subject would find him. A name was accordingly handed me. I passed it to the subject. He took the paper on which the name was written and read the name aloud. At this time the subject was blindfolded so that it was impossible for him to see with his natural eyes. I then told him to find the person. I will relate his own story.

He said, "This is a man." "Well," said I, "find him and talk with him." In a short time he said, "I have found him." I asked, "What does he say?" He answered, "He was a married man, had a wife and three children, was a joiner by trade; left his tool chest in a barn, and left between two days, went to Boston, stopped a time, left for the state of New York, worked there for three years, and then died; he has been dead three years."

I told him to bring him here and describe him. He went on to give a general description of a man, and I told him that if there was anything peculiar in his appearance that differed from all others to describe him. "Well," said he, "there is one thing in which he differs from anyone else in the room. He has a hare lip." This was a fact.

Now as there is no knowledge among the people of the principle by which this was done, the people were left to their own judgment. So I left them arguing, some trying to prove it was the man's spirit, some calling it humbug and collusion. Others went away and told what they saw and heard.

This kind of an experiment I was trying almost every day for over four years.

I then became a medium myself, but not like my subject. I retained my own consciousness and at the same time took the feelings of my patient. Thus I was able to unlock the secret which has been a mystery for ages to mankind. I found that I had the power of not only feeling their aches and pains, but the state of their mind. I discovered that ideas took form and the patient was affected just according to the impression contained in the idea. For example, if a person lost a friend at sea, the shock upon his nervous system would disturb the fluids of their body and create around them a vapor like a cloud and in this cloud they create the essence of their trouble. This cloud being a part of their nervous system acts upon the body. Now unless the scene can be destroyed, it will destroy the body. This cloud embraces all the phenomena of spiritualism, mesmerism and all other excitements differing according to circumstances.

Every person has around them this cloud or vapor and in that are all their ideas, right or wrong. This vapor or fluid contains the identity of the person.

Now when I sit down with a diseased person, I see the spiritual form, in this cloud, like a person driven out of his home. They sometimes appear very much frightened, which is almost always the case with insane persons. I show no disposition to disturb them and at last they approach me cautiously, and if I can govern my own spirit or mind I can govern theirs. At last I commence a conversation with them. They tell me their trouble and offer to carry me spiritually to the place where their trouble commenced.

I was sitting by a lady whom I had never seen before until she called upon me with her father to see if I could help her. The lady had all the appearance of dropsy. I took her by the hand. In a short time it seemed as though we were going off some distance. At last I saw water. It seemed as though we were on the ocean. At length I saw a brig in a gale. I also saw a man on the bowsprit, dressed in an oilcloth suit. At last he fell overboard. The vessel hove to and in a short time the man sank. This was a reality, but it happened five years before. Now to cure the lady was to bring her from the scene of her troubles. This I did and the lady recovered.

I often find patients whose disease or trouble was brought on by religious excitement. I went to see a young lady during the Miller excitement. She was confined to her bed, would not converse with any person, lay in a sort of trance with her eyes rolled up in her head, took no notice of any person. The only thing she would say was that she was confined in a pit, held there by a large man whose duty it was to hold her there, and she said to me, "I shall never die, nor never get well." She had been in this condition for one year, refused all nourishment, and was a mere skeleton at the time I went to see her. This was her story when I got her so as to converse. I sat down by the lady, and in about an hour I saw the man she had created, and described him to her, and told her that I would drive him away. This seemed to frighten her, for she was afraid for my safety. But when I assured her that I could drive the man away she kept quiet. In three hours she walked to the door, and she recovered her health.

I could name hundreds of cases showing the effect of mind upon the body. Some will say it is spiritualism. Others will say it is not. When asked to explain where the difference lies, the only answer is, that the mesmeric state is produced by some other person on the subject, while the spiritualist is thrown into this state or trance by spirits. Now the fact is known by thousands of persons that this mesmerizing oneself has been common ever since mesmerism has been known; therefore there is nothing new in that. So it is with questions put to any spiritualist.

Let us now examine the proof of its being from the dead. A person is thrown into an unconscious state. While in this state, the spirit of some person purporting to come from the dead enters the body and addresses itself to the company, telling some story which the company knows nothing of. When aroused from the trance, he is asked if he is conscious of what he had been saying or doing. To this question they nearly all say, No. The company is left in the same condition as in the mesmeric experiments. Some call it mesmerism, some spiritualism.

I will now show the similarity between this experiment and spiritualism. A person sits down and throws himself into what is called a spiritualistic state or trance. He then commences talking to someone in the audience. When asked what he has to communicate he replies, "A friend wishes to communicate with Mr. A." Mr. A. then asks who wishes to communicate with him. The medium replies, "Your brother." He then asks, "Will you give his name?" The answer is, "John." "Ask him how long he has been in the spirit world and what was his business while in the body." The answer, "I was a joiner by trade, had a wife and three children, been dead six years." This is true. The medium knew nothing of the past before. The company is left in the same state as in the former experiment. Some believe it is a spirit of the dead, some believe it is humbug and others it is mesmerism. My experience explains these two to be mesmerism. After practicing for six years with a subject, trying all kinds of experiments, I then became a medium myself. The spiritual medium after going into a trance speaks to the patient thus.

My name is Sarah B, your sister and guardian spirit. I come to communicate some facts in regard to your health. The medium then goes on to explain the patient's feelings, describing some located disease and then prescribes the remedy. The patient asks, "Can you give me some proof that you are my sister?" A slate and pencil is called for. The medium's hand is then raised by the spirit and she writes this communication. "You were not aware I left home when I intended to go, but I took a steamer for Liverpool. Five days out the steamer sank and all were lost but fifty passengers."

This is looked upon as certain proof that it is from the spirit world. The company is then left in the same doubt as before. The spiritualists contend it is spirits, but they can't describe the diseases of the sick; here they fall far short of what they profess. They all contend that the time will come when diseases will be cured without the aid of medicine, yet all the mediums I have ever known or heard of locate diseases the same as any physician and then go on to prescribe medicine, and this is done nine times out of ten by some Indian who purports to have been dead some hundred years ago.

I will here relate one instance to show that these communications are in accordance with their prejudices. I had a patient who thought she had a white swelling on her knee. This fact was known to certain persons at one of the sittings. The medium was very much excited and wished to communicate some fact to the company; it purported to be the name of an Indian. The amount of his communication was to tell the company that there was one lady at Belfast very sick who begs Dr. Quimby to come and heal her. Now these are the facts; there had been a lady here who I had been treating with what was called white swelling also, and this fact was known to the medium too that she, "my patient," had left for home three weeks before and she had not the white swelling about the knee when she left.

As I have been investigating this subject I sometimes try experiments to see if any knowledge that the medium should get in regard to me would make any difference when in the trance or under the spirit guidance. As facts are what I want to get at, I take my own way to collect them.

I had had quite a number of patients sent me by an old German physician who communicated his knowledge through a certain medium and located diseases that the patient never heard of. I became rather suspicious in regard to his skill and I contrived to let the medium know it to see how it would operate on the old German doctor. And in a short time he found it out, probably by the medium and like all other persons whose opinions are ridiculed, he ceased to send me any more patients and became a sort of prophet. The medium, not giving her own name but assuming the name of another person, said that I was a medium but was too proud to admit it and the spirits would take the power from me. This was what I expected. I have tried other experiments with less success. This was exactly the case with my mesmerized patient; if a person was a skeptic or had any hard feelings against me or my patients, I could not get him to have anything to do with him. That shows that the mediums are affected like all mesmerized subjects. I will here relate an instance that happened while I was in Boston.

I went with a friend to see a medium. I think it was the medium that R. J. Shaw used to communicate through. When we arrived at the house, we were informed that there was a gentleman there to be examined who was sick. And as the gentleman I was with was acquainted with the medium, he asked if we could not sit down at the same time, and being informed we could, we took seats at the table. The medium was a young lass, about sixteen years old, a very pleasant appearing young person but not much knowledge in the medical profession. In a short time the raps commenced. The doctor gave notice of his presence by loud raps. He was then asked by the sick man, What was the matter. The lady medium wrote out the trouble, but as I had my doubts in regard to her skill, I was troubled for her. This affected her and her hand stopped writing and shaking and moved towards me. My friend asked what that meant. It was not for me to tell. I then asked the medium if I was a medium and the answer came, three loud raps. I then asked what kind of a medium; it wrote, a healing medium, and I then went on to help the young lady out of her trouble and everything I said to the old man in regard to his health was backed up by raps or writing. This experiment was just like mesmerism. I then told my friend that if there was a medium in the sitting that was a truthful medium I could prove to him I was a healing medium.

We then went to another medium that was a lady who could produce the raps and was a writing medium also. We sat down to a large table with a number of others. The questions were nearly all asked mentally. After quite a number of ladies and gentlemen had got communication from their dead friends, it came to my turn. I said that I had nothing of importance to ask so it passed to another. The communications were of that character that affected the ladies very much and I was very much surprised that the company could not see how exactly it agreed with mesmerism.

At last it came to my friend's turn; he replied the same as I did. But it was unsatisfactory to the rest, as he was a strong believer. I then touched his toe to put him in mind of what I was to prove to him without letting anyone of the company know that I could see the spirits. He then asked if there was any medium present. The answer came by raps, "Yes." "What kind of a medium?" The alphabet was then called for and spelled out "seeing medium." This seemed to astonish the whole company. He then asked if he was the medium. The answer was "no," until it came to me. When asked if I was the medium, loud raps signified, "yes." I then asked if I see you, the raps came "yes." I then said, "If I will describe your person and dress, will you say to the company whether I am right." The raps came "yes" to every remark I made in regard to her person or self. The answer to all was "yes." I then said to my friend, "What do you think of that?" He replied, "I don't believe you see the spirits." "Do you hear him?" said I, and loud raps followed. "Do you hear that, my friend?" "Yes, but I don't believe it." The raps came very loud to prove I really saw the spirit. I then asked my friend to explain it. He said it was mesmerism. "Well," said I, "so is all the rest." He would not agree to that. He said, "All the other experiments were spiritualism except mine."

Spiritualism and Mesmerism [III]
[Originally untitled.] [LC 2:0715]

Can the phenomena of spiritualism be explained on the theory of mesmerism? I answer, No, not so far as the development of Mesmer goes. Mesmerism is as much in the dark as spiritualism. Neither has ever been explained and they are both one and the same governed by differences of opinion. Those who believe in mesmerism and write about it stand precisely on the same basis because neither has any wisdom, but only a belief that certain phenomena will occur, while the causes are in the dark and man is led by what some person said about it. For instance, I found I could put a person into a mesmeric sleep, and others could do the same. Then I wanted to do more, so I procured books and read about it and I found that the authors accounted for it on the principle of electricity. Of course, I believed it and all my experiments went to prove the truth of my belief. At last I found that instead of electricity governing my subject, he was governed by the minds of myself and others.

So I discarded all this false theory that I was told and discovered that the subject had an identity of his own and had as much of a being as the one who governed him. He was governed by the principle of argument as much as any other person. The subject sat down for the purpose of being mesmerized and if the operator has the idea of what he wants to do, he can do it. A sits down with the intention of putting B to sleep. B sits down with no other motive than to see if A can do it, so their minds mingle. A's will is determined to accomplish his object. B gives up his will and becomes passive. The only way in which this process has been accounted for is that A fills B full of electricity. This is all a humbug. Their minds act precisely as two persons sitting down, one listening to the other admitting that he knows more than himself and the advantage is first tested. No one gives up his opinion to the other unless he thinks the other is superior to himself. I found that out.

The sight is what is the mystery, the eyes not being the medium. The subject is in another element separate and apart from his natural self, but in his natural belief. As a man in the dark travels by another's light, the subject sees the idea of his mesmerizer, but the sight is in the odor of the idea. This is new to the world and man cannot understand it. Therefore I will give some examples. If A thinks of an orange, B will see it, everyone knows this. Does he see it as we see it? No, he sees it in the odor, for the odor is the light of the idea. So it is with everything that has form, and the background makes the object, for if there were no light at all, the object could not be seen. It is so with thought. Thought takes form and the wisdom that makes the thought is the light of its body. The light is felt like the odor and contains the knowledge of itself. This is the light the subject is in, for the mesmerizer makes the light by his own belief. It commences in total darkness, is first blue, then grows light and when it is the color of gaslight, this is the light the subject is in, and it compares with daylight.

Whatever the subject is asked to see, if the mesmerizer can form the idea, it is seen in the light. This is clairvoyance. But it is in the blue light or darkness that the subject sees by sympathy or odor. It is called thought-reading and is the state persons go into when they are "entranced by a spirit." Then if you see a friend, the friend is formed but cannot be seen very distinctly but is described like an apple or pear by the odor. All this is governed by our belief. If you believe in another world and believe your friends are with you, the belief may so affect the subject and carry him into the clairvoyant state and, if he believes in this state, he sees all the living and the dead and they are with him according to his belief. When he awakes however, it is all dark and he is sure he has been to another world. All this is as plain to me as daylight for daylight is clairvoyance and twilight, thought-reading. I have been in both places with both my natural senses, have seen the sun, land, water, vessels, heard the winds blow, and felt the warm breezes. When I sit by the sick I see, but not always so plainly, unless the patient is sure he has a certain disease. Then I see it in every particular. All this teaches me that my belief no matter how absurd can produce phenomena to prove it; therefore I believe the writing on the arm, the moving of matter, the spirit hand, but the medium must be of a peculiar combination of matter. It needs a man whose eyes will stand out when you tell him the moon is inhabited by people forty feet high, and make him believe it. Then he can see anything.

1862

Spiritualism (Death of the Natural Man)
[LC 1:0357]

I am often asked where I differ from a spiritualist. In everything, but as this is an opinion to you, I will try to make it clear. The spiritualist believes in the dead rising and they sometimes say there is no such thing as death. Now let us see what their works show. What is life? All will say it is what a man knows. So his senses are attached to his wisdom, his wisdom is made of opinions and his senses are attached to his opinions. His opinions embrace all beliefs. So to destroy his belief, you destroy his senses, for they are in his belief and a part of it.

Let us see what his belief embraces. In the first place, he believes in matter, called living matter, that has life, for he says that life or matter must die or perish. Now here is the contradiction in the spiritualists' belief. They deny that the dead rise but if the dead do not rise, what are the dead? You are pointed to a man lying motionless and to all appearances, even according to a spiritualist, dead. Now is he dead or is he not dead? The spiritualist may answer, The body is dead. Was it ever alive? You must say, Yes, for I point to a man moving around and ask you if that man is dead and your answer is, No. Then he must be a living man and according to your belief we have a living man and a dead one. Now where do they differ? Here is the mystery. Their belief, like all others, flies right back to the old superstition which they all believed, that the dead rise and in this fog they get lost like all others. Now let me help you out of your belief. You are a man of opinions and your senses are attached to your opinions and your belief makes no separation between your wisdom and your belief. Your belief is matter so that when the matter ceases to act, the senses also cease, for you have no wisdom above the opinions of man.

I will show where I differ from spiritualists and in fact all other sects. My theory is founded on the fact that mind is matter, and if you will admit this for the sake of listening to my ideas, I will give you my theory. I assert that according to man's belief there are certain facts admitted and established beyond a doubt, and as my wisdom is not of this world or belief, only in part, what I know I have no opinion about. All knowledge that is of man is based on opinions. This I call this world of matter; it embraces all that comes within the so-called senses. Man's happiness and misery are in his belief; all the wisdom of science is of God and is not of man.

To separate these two kingdoms is what I'm trying to do, and if I can succeed in this, I have accomplished what never has been done but what has been the aim of all the learned philosophers ever since the world began. The secret of life and happiness is the aim of all mankind and how to get at it is the mystery that has baffled the wisdom of the world. Now I should never undertake the task of explaining what all the wise men have failed to do but for the want of some better proof to explain certain phenomena that come under my own observation which have never been explained, from the fact that the error exists now as much as ever. The remedies have never destroyed the cause nor can the cause be destroyed by man's reason, for science cannot admit what cannot be proved. Until some better proof of what we see and hear and feel can be produced, the world must grope in darkness and skepticism. My object is not to strike at any science that is established. I admit such for fear I may be misunderstood.

I will separate the two worlds of which I am now speaking and show what one has failed to do, and also that the other is not acknowledged independent of the first. The world of opinions is the old world, that of science is the new world, and a separation must take place and a battle must be fought between them. The world of error and opinions has held science in bondage ever since man began to act independently of the savage life. The child of science has been nourished in the bosom of its mother, in the wilderness of error, till it grew up so as to assume a character; then when it has undertaken to assume its rights, it has always been met with the thunder of error. But as it is so much of a friend to the happiness of man, the enemies or error could never prevent its growth, for that was in the scientific world. That world has no matter or it is so rarefied that the error cannot see through it. So the scientific man can pass through the errors and instruct the child of science till it bursts forth and becomes a man or law. Then the natural man or error destroys its leaders and falls down and worships the scientific laws and acknowledges them as king of this world. So as the science is now acknowledged, the kings of the earth are cut off and the kingdom is divided against itself; the leaders with their armies flee into the wilderness, there to rally for another attack when any new science is started. Now the Science of Life and Happiness is the one that has met with the most opposition from the fact that it is death to all opposers. It never compromises with its enemies nor has any dealings with them. Its kingdom is of science, not of error. Therefore it is not of this world of matter.

I will give you a declaration of its laws, how much it admits, how much it condemns and how it puts its laws in force. Its habitation is in the heart of man. It cannot be seen by the natural man for he is of matter and the scientific man is not matter. All he has are his senses; there is his residence for the time. He has no abiding city but is a traveler or sojourner in the world of matter. His house is not made with hands but is in the scientific world, so his whole aim is the happiness of man. Now as man is of matter, his belief embraces all there is of him. The scientific man sees through this matter which is nothing but an error acknowledged as a truth, although it is to the natural man a reality. Now as error holds on to all territory as under its power, it keeps the scientific man in slavery or bondage. So to keep the Science of Life down, they invent all sorts of humbug in the shape of invisible things and attribute life to them while they pretend to be the people's guide to wisdom. It is almost impossible to tell one character from another as both communicate through the same organs. As the scientific man has to prove his wisdom through the same matter that the natural man uses, he is often misrepresented and put down by false stories, representations of the errors of the natural man. This was where Christ found so much trouble in his days, for the people could not tell who was speaking.

The scientific man was called by the natural man, "angel." So if an angel spoke they would listen. The natural man, being superstitious and ignorant, is easily led by the cunning errors of the world. The leaders, being crafty and superstitious, believe in every phenomenon which is produced and they attribute it to the invisible world. The locality of this world is the mystery, and so all kinds of speculations are got up about it. It opens all the avenues of matter through which to give the inhabitants communications, but the natural man has possession of the mediums so that the scientific man is misrepresented in nine-tenths of all he says. Now to be in the scientific world is not necessarily to be wise but to acknowledge a wisdom above the natural man which will enter that world where wisdom sees through matter. This is the condition with those persons who are thrown into a clairvoyant state. To them matter is nothing but an idea that is seen or not, just as it is called out. All of their senses are in this state but are under the control of the natural man. So it is always hard to establish a fact in this world that goes to destroy the power of the natural man. All the explanation of this scientific world is given by these blind guides who have eyes but cannot see, ears but cannot hear and hearts that cannot understand science. They are afraid of the truth lest it will destroy them, for their death is the introduction of the Science of Life and Happiness.

To show you the two characters conversing through one medium I will take myself as the medium of the scientific man and also of the man of error or of this world. When two persons argue, it is supposed that they have some object in view or there would be no need of reasoning; but nine-tenths of all arguments are about nothing, from the fact that error contains no wisdom but a belief which is started by some crazy brain and acknowledged by the ignorant as true. Ignorance is roused into action. This produces error and error is not confined to any particular mode of reasoning but is always attaching its senses to some opinion which has been acknowledged as a truth. As opinions are always changing, error does not see the change, for its senses are not in the change but in the opinion. The scientific man attaches his senses to science, not to opinions. For instance, eighteen hundred years ago there was a man called Jesus. All admitted the fact that he was a man. His theory of action was reasoning to mankind, so a controversy sprang up in regard to the man; the man of opinions attaches his senses to the opinions about the man. The scientific man saw nothing to affect him in any way; so when Jesus was brought before Pilate, Pilate heard the stories, but seeing no proof of any superior wisdom beyond any man said that he found no fault in him. So he attached his senses to the man, Jesus, as a man. But the superstitious were divided, as they always are. One class claimed that he came from God, the other, that he had a devil. So these two classes were at war with each other and in their zeal they attached their senses to the acts of Jesus as proof of their wisdom. One party wanted to show that Jesus came from God and they introduced his cures as proof, for no man could do as he did except God be with him. Their ignorance never saw that his cures proved nothing except that he knew more than they did, which did not prove that he came from any place, only that he did the cures. But no man is bound to believe this because they say so, any more than they are bound to believe that a person who cures another gets his power from the spirits. The ignorant say if it does not come from the spirits, where does it come from? Thus the skeptic is either bound to take their explanation and believe it is the spirits or he is an infidel or unbeliever.

So it is with the ignorant about Jesus; they assume as a fact that you must believe that Jesus came from God. If you believe and acknowledge his cures, that will not do, but you must believe what you and no other person has any proof of and which rests only on what a certain number of persons say. So the controversy among the people was about something which never had anything to do with Jesus. This is the way with all persons who attached their senses to an opinion of some other person without proof. Jesus, like any other man, was in the hands of the people and they gave their opinions about the man so that the writings of the Old and New Testament contain opinions about the man Jesus and others. Man now takes the opinions as the words of Jesus, while Jesus had not the ideas which were attributed to him. As he had no one to speak for him, I will try to give his ideas as a man. Jesus always wanted to make a difference in regard to his opinions and what he knew as a science. To show how he separated himself as a man of opinions from the Scientific Man or Christ, it was necessary to show something as proof, and the sick was the problem to be solved. This separation was a mystery to the people and their superstition was called into action, and instead of listening to Jesus when he talked the Christ or Truth, they attributed his works to a power from God and all the cures were taken to prove that fact. If the people could believe that he came from God it was of no use to know how he cured, for if they knew this, it would destroy the belief that he came from God and so upset their religion. Therefore the leaders labored to prove to the people that Jesus had a mission from heaven to earth to save souls, and the cures were only to prove that he came from God. Now the believers are in the opinions of man and not in Christ, for Christ was Jesus' science and this gives the lie to all the former. Jesus stood before the world as I do, with this exception; my own case will explain both. The two parties who sat in judgment on Jesus were divided on this point. One party thought he came from heaven; the other thought that the spirits of the dead talked through him, and they hoped to introduce dissension among the people, enough to put down the established religion. Jesus was in the hands of these bigots and could not explain what he intended to have the people believe. It is so with me. One class calls me a spiritualist but a hypocrite; another calls me evil or the devil. The third says I am an infidel or a disbeliever in Christ. A fourth, not the least, say I am a harmless humbug. The sick is the only class who know anything about what I teach. They say it is a science and can be learned. But as it is in the world of error and superstition and my judges belong to this class, I am accused, as I have stated, and of course my works are my proof.

Now as I have said, when men argue they think at least that there is some point to start from or they would not reason. As the standards of parties are established by error, it is almost impossible to introduce any new science unless it is explained on some of the theories of the natural man. Thus all phenomena are thrown into the hands of these blind guides who have pronounced judgment upon everything that has appeared. So whenever anyone shows a phenomenon, the priest and doctor catch the idea out of the mouth of the author and explain it on some theory known to the people. The theory of health is one that has come up many times and failed because of the blindness of the wise, so that it has now almost become a terror to the one who has boldness enough to stand up and face the blind leaders of the blind. You see that Jesus could not stand up against so powerful an enemy, for the instant he spoke, they would put a false construction on his every word. So they turned the word of God to no effect by their theories and traditions. Thus you see that with the people the wisdom of the science of life had no foundation but was like a house built upon the sand; when the wind of science blew upon it and the tide of public opinion came, it must fall and be destroyed. But unto this science men have raised altars with this inscription: "To the unknown God." I will say to these guides, This science that you ignorantly worship, I will declare unto you. First of all, you know that mankind are in the dark so far as their life is concerned; that man is all his life subject to disease and death; also that it was foretold that Christ should come and lead man back to God. This same Christ that you crucify by your theories is the same that Jesus taught eighteen hundred years ago. It was taught by the prophets of old and has always been in the world but has never been applied to the curing of disease, although false Christs have arisen and deceived the people, and the true Christ has been crucified by the priest and doctor till this time.

I will now try to establish this science or rock and upon it I will build the Science of Life. My foundation is animal matter or life; this, set in action by wisdom, produces thought; thoughts, like grains of sand, are held together by their own sympathy or wisdom or attraction. Now man is composed of these particles of matter or thought combined and arranged by wisdom so as to make a form called man. As thought is always changing, so man is always throwing off particles or thoughts and receiving new ones. So man is a progressive idea yet he is the same man although he is changing all the time for better or worse. As his senses are in his wisdom and his wisdom is attached to his idea or body, his change of mind is under one of these two directions, either of this world of opinions or of God or Science, and his happiness or misery is the result of his wisdom. As the idea man has always been under the world's wisdom, the scientific man has always been kept down, from the fact that no man has ever risen to that state where the scientific man could control the wisdom of the natural man. This has always kept man in a war with himself. These two powers make up man, and the science is to keep the natural man in subjection to the scientific man. In this warfare, if the natural man rules, disease and death is the fate of the scientific man; if the latter rules, life and happiness is the reward.

Now I stand on this rock fighting the errors of this world and establishing the Science of Life by my works. What is my mode of warfare? With the axe of truth I strike at the root of every tree or error and hew it down so that there shall not be one error in man showing itself in the form of disease. My wisdom is my knowledge and not matter or opinions. It decomposes the thought, changes the combination and produces an idea clear from the error that makes a person unhappy or diseased. You see I have something to reason about and this something is Eternal Life and this life is in the science. This was what Jesus tried to establish so that man could have a starting place, but the wisdom of this world tries to account for all phenomena on some principle founded on man's opinion, letting the world grope in darkness.

If I can show that man's happiness is in his belief and his misery is the effect of his belief, then I shall have done what never has been done before. Establish this, and man rises to a higher state of wisdom, not of this world but of that world of science that sees that all human misery can be corrected by this principle, as well as the evil effects of errors in any science. Then the Science of Life takes its place with other sciences, then is brought to pass, "Oh death! (or error) Where is thy sting! Oh grave! Where is thy victory!" The sting of ignorance is death but the wisdom of science is life eternal to all who believe it.

I have said that to reason there must be something to reason about. I will show the world's reasoning and how I reason. I will take the oracles of the world, for all science of this world of opinions has oracles. These oracles of which I speak are those who pretend to instruct the people in regard to health and happiness. The first is the clergy, for they lead off in everything pertaining to man's happiness. I will ask them what they think of Christ, his mission if he had any, and of what advantage it was to the world? They reply that the world or man had gone so far astray that it was necessary to send Jesus Christ into the world to convince man of a future state of rewards and punishments, that he might repent and be saved. If this is true I ask, Why did Jesus devote so much time to the sick? (Oracle) To show that he came from God. [Q] What does that prove? If I cure a person, does it prove that I came from God? (O) No, but do you make yourself equal with Christ? [Q] Have you any proof of anything that you never saw and is only an opinion? (O) The Bible. [Q] Does the Bible speak for itself or does someone explain it? (O) We must take the Bible as our guide of truth.

Let us now sum up this oracle's wisdom. All of his wisdom is founded on an opinion that there is another world and that Jesus Christ came from that world to communicate the fact to the inhabitants of this one. This is all an opinion sustained by no proof. On the contrary, everything goes to prove it is false, for the happiness of man is not increased by this false theory because this oracle cannot cure the sick. Now Jesus cured the sick and said if they understood him they might do the same. We want a theory like that of Jesus, not of talk but works, for talking a theory that will not cure is worthless. So if I set down the priests as belonging to the false prophets, the sick are no better for them. Next are the medical oracles. These number as many as the former and are on the increase. How much knowledge have they independent of an opinion? None! Yet they have given the people to understand that their wisdom is far above that of the masses, but their knowledge is all opinions and the sick pay them as though it were wisdom. The people have been cheated into a belief that these oracles have more wisdom than they have. This I admit, otherwise they could not humbug the people out of their money and deprive them of their health and happiness.

My oracle is Jesus. He proves the goodness of wisdom. Jesus was the oracle and Christ the wisdom shown through this man for the happiness of the lost or sick who had been deceived by the other two classes: priest and doctor. God or wisdom has seen how these blind guides had robbed the widow and the poor of their little goods, deserted them and left them forsaken and despairing, dependent on the charity of a wicked world. This wisdom developed itself through the man Jesus and he fearlessly stood up and denounced these guides as hypocrites and devils. He showed how their theories affected the people and also that they were in direct opposition to all science and good feeling, and he introduced a new theory, a more excellent priesthood or science which had no sacrifice of feeling but took upon itself our infirmities and explained them for the happiness of man.

What was it that Jesus wanted to communicate to the world? One simple fact that man was a progressive being, that his happiness and misery were of his own make, that his belief is his wisdom and if it is founded on an opinion, it was liable to make him unhappy. To separate the truth from the error is a science, the knowledge of which teaches how to correct an error or disease and in this knowledge is eternal life. Jesus never intended to teach the people a belief in another world. His words and acts showed them that their beliefs were false and that they were the cause of their misery. But this they could not understand, and being in their belief, their belief became a part of their identity. As they were taught to believe in spirits, their misery was attributed to them. And as error begets error, the people were tormented by their own belief. It never entered into the minds of these blind leaders that as a man sows, so shall he reap, for action and reaction are equal. The knowledge of science was not general and that the belief of man had anything to do with his health was a thing not dreamed of. All that was believed was something that could not be seen, so the prophets prophesied of someone coming from heaven. Now if heaven was not something that the people believed in, away and apart from this earth, then it would not have been in the prophesies. So this heaven was an established fact and all their controversies were in regard to it. They introduced all sorts of mediums that purported to come from and have communications from that place. There was the dwelling of God and all religious theories were based upon the belief that there was another world where God dwelt and where He ordered all things according to His own will. Absurd as this is, man is made of this composition, for man is only a mass of matter or ideas, combined together by a wisdom superior to the matter of which the ideas are formed. Science is not recognized in this belief. For it belongs to that class of minds which have never risen to a state where they can discern that man can perceive anything independent of his natural senses. To this class of minds whatever is not established is a mystery. If a lead ball is thrown into the water it sinks to the bottom, that is a fact. If a wooden ball is also thrown into the water it floats, and then comes the mystery. A medium from the other world is required to explain the phenomenon. Argument is of no force. The explanation must come from God, and thus it is with every mysterious phenomenon–supernatural power only can explain it. Thus man is kept constantly excited to understand every little thing that happens. He never has thought that heaven and hell were a part of his belief and consequently a part of himself, but he believes that these two places are independent of himself and he is liable to go to one or the other after he is dead. So he lives in hell all his life, trying to get to heaven, but never gets there for it is always at a distance, and he is always looking for a savior to save him from hell.

How often we hear very good people say that they are weary of this wicked world and they long to be with Christ, showing that they are not there now, but hope to be. You see that their faith contains a belief, not a substance. The faith that is of man is merely a belief in something not obtained, for when the substance is obtained, then faith or belief is lost in the substance and they have what they hoped for. Was Jesus' faith a belief? No, His faith was the substance of our belief and that substance was Christ. Jesus put his faith in practice for the happiness of man. This substance or Christ or faith is something intended to be applied to man, and Jesus put this in practice for his happiness. The question arises, Has it an identity? Answer, it has; it is all that ever had an unchangeable identity. It is wisdom itself but the Christian's faith is an opinion about this wisdom. I have said that Jesus' faith had an identity and to this his senses were attached. This Jesus could say to his faith, "Father forgive them for they know not what they do." What did this Christ strive to do? It strove to enter the heart of man and teach him how to break away from his errors and learn the truth. Jesus taught Christ and put it in practice by his works. Do the Christians do the same? No. They preach about it, so their faith is not of works but a belief. The world is no wiser or better for it. To prove your faith in music is to play a tune on an instrument by your faith or science, not to talk about music, telling about how beautiful it is. The Science of Health which Jesus taught was practiced by his faith or wisdom and his instrument was man. He took man after he had been beaten, bruised and deceived by the priests and doctors and applied his science or Christ to put him in tune, so that he could sing psalms to the one living and true science and appreciate Jesus as the medium for "he hath opened the seventh seal" that can correct the errors of man who shall be saved from disease and misery. How does Jesus stand by the side of his pretended followers? He talked and taught his Christ to the people. Priest and doctor talk about it. Here is a vast difference. Jesus put intelligence in the Christ or science; the Christians put no intelligence in Christ or science but apply all the intelligence to Jesus, calling the Christ a power. The difference has always been kept up; the natural man cannot see intelligence in anything he cannot understand. Therefore Christ or intelligence of Jesus is to him a power or mystery and he wanted to know whence it came. This ignorance on the part of the priests and people originated all their speculation about Jesus. The Christ or higher intelligence was shrouded in darkness to them, for they could not see why he, merely a man, should be more than a man.

Everyone knows that a clairvoyant state is different from the natural state. Let me illustrate what all will admit. Persons in a clairvoyant state can talk, using the same organs as when awake. They also have every faculty which they have in their waking state, independent of the natural body, and space and time may or may not be annihilated. They act entirely independently of anyone and when awakened may not remember anything that has been going on. Here you see a being acting independently of the natural body or the identity of flesh and blood, with all the organs and senses of the natural man. Now where is this identity when the natural man is acting, for both cannot be acting at the same time? Everyone will perceive that if a man could retain his reason and natural senses and at the same time be conscious of the other state, he would be a man beside himself, thus making two living intelligences in one identity, acting through one medium. Thus the clairvoyant man could correct the errors of the man of flesh and blood and keep him in subjection to his wisdom. This was Jesus Christ.

To have this Christ was to be born again or receive the higher wisdom. This wisdom or Christ was the mystery to mankind. This was the Christ that should reign till all error should be subject to it. Disease, being the off-spring of error, deceives the people, making them nervous, sick, and liable to death, for all this is matter and belongs to the man of flesh and blood. But it is the design of wisdom that matter should be the servant of this clairvoyant man or science; therefore when Jesus received this wisdom, he became God and man. When the man spoke, it was like anyone else, but when the Christ spoke, it spoke not as a man, for that is of God or wisdom from above. Jesus taught the people to distinguish by their works the true Christ from the false. It must have proved its source by works, for he says, "Not everyone who says I am Christ is so himself, but he that doeth the will of the wisdom that sent me."

Let us see if a test can be found such as Jesus laid down. When he called his disciples together he gave them power over all unclean spirits and sent them forth to heal the sick. Here is the test of the clairvoyant or Christ power or wisdom. How did he apply it when he cured disease? Of course, if he was in this state all the time, all things were present to him so that not a sparrow could fall to the ground unnoticed by him, not Jesus, for although the Christ was made known through Jesus, it was only made known according to the necessities of the time when he, Jesus, lived. I will take one of his miracles to show that Jesus and Christ acted together. When the centurion came to Jesus to tell him that his servant was sick, Jesus was not aware of the fact but immediately became subject to his clairvoyant state, saw the servant and administered unto him. Then he said to the centurion, Go thy way, and according to thy faith so it shall be unto thee. So the centurion left and the servant was healed in the selfsame hour. Now this is as plain to me as any cure I ever performed. This was not a power but a higher wisdom that the world knows not of. I will now introduce myself, showing that I cure in the same way.

Everyone knows that there is a difference in clairvoyance. Subjects differ in the direction of their minds. I do not practice clairvoyance except with the sick and I will show others how to be clairvoyant like myself. I said that a clairvoyant does not remember what he says in his sleep. To put a person into a clairvoyant state is to change him from one state to another; so as he loses his natural senses, he embraces the other senses or clairvoyant state till he is completely lost to this world of matter. I will show how I first discovered this state. This state is progression, not imitation, but independent clairvoyance.

When I first began to mesmerize and as I became interested in the experiments, I found that the subject could see through matter. I could not help believing this and it showed me that matter could be seen through by a clairvoyant; so it became not an opinion but a truth to me. I also found that all that man's senses embraced could be seen and felt by a person whose bodily senses were dead, if we judged by the body. All this became a wisdom, not a belief, but a part of my identity. So what is a belief to the world concerning these things was to me a truth. My next aim was to become a clairvoyant myself, and as I became convinced that matter was only a medium for our wisdom to act through, I could see how it could be transformed and the senses or clairvoyant state be attached to any idea the natural man might think of. The two kinds of reasoning make up the natural man. Both modes of reasoning can be carried into the clairvoyant state for this does not embrace reason.

To make a good clairvoyant, one must, beginning on earth, rid himself of all beliefs in every theory of man; and as he sees the absurdity of his own opinions, he becomes lighted up in another atmosphere where he feels the discord of this world. He then becomes sensitive to the errors and opinions of man; they affect him and make him nervous. All his senses become entirely independent of his natural will or senses; then he is two persons. This is my state as far as regards the sick. When I sit by the sick and take them by the hand, I feel a sensation. This affects me, and the sensation is produced by something coming within my senses as a man of flesh and blood. This excites the spiritual or scientific man and the senses being freed from matter or opinion see the natural man or opinion that causes the trouble. As I retain two identities, I see the error and explain it to the natural senses. These are set at rest and harmony is restored. I cannot find language to explain this so that you will understand it. I will take the science of mechanics to illustrate these two principles. The word statics is used in calculating stationary powers as weighing on scales, hoisting from a vessel by a cable, dropping a dead weight, etc. All this combines action and reaction. They constitute and come under the head of statics. The natural man and even the brutes have a knowledge of this. The principle of dynamics is from a higher wisdom known only to statics as a mystery. Here is where the foundation of science commences. Dynamics, like clairvoyance, puts man in possession of a higher wisdom, so that a man understanding the science can see through the statics or natural man.

An experiment of this wisdom is seen in a person standing on board a vessel, hauling her up to a wharf with the line made fast on shore, while one standing on the wharf hauling in the vessel by a line made fast to the vessel acts upon statics. The difference is just one-half. The one on the vessel with half the power of the one on the wharf will be twice as long as the other, for he travels with the vessel. So it is with everything where the power moves with the weight or body to be moved. This is dynamics and it makes all the controversy in calculating powers that are in motion as steamboats, locomotives, etc. Man, being matter, is always in motion, for in this is his life. Like a steamboat, his time is calculated and the steam kept up by supplying food as the mind uses it up. His life depends upon two principles. The wisdom of the savage or natural man is all statics, or might is right. As he begins to progress, his life and happiness will be governed by a higher principle of wisdom. So as he loses in error, he must be supplied by wisdom or his force will destroy his body. For he is now a locomotive man instead of a sawmill. His machine is in motion and his sawmill calculation will not govern it. This holds good in every department of life. The dynamical calculation is based on progression. Statics or demagogism is different. Statics is darkness. Dynamics is light and the people are under one or the other of these two classes. All nations have shown that the principle of statics has governed, for as yet no nation has stood the test of time for all have broken to pieces when they have got up the steam. The regulator of dynamics has never been attached to the engine of wisdom, and until that is done, revolutions must take place. Then comes anarchy, confusion and tyranny, and the people have to yield to a superior power that keeps them in subjection till their fears are forgotten. Then they fire up again and blow to pieces. This principle holds good in nations as well as in individuals. Disease is the natural result of demagogism.

March 1861

Standard of Law, The
[LC 1:0386]

In my article of the standard of men's acts, I showed the political standard but did not give the true standard, from the fact that it is not recognized as such. It is known as judgment; therefore, any man's judgment is a standard. If his judgment happens to be popular with the masses, then his standard is true, so it returns to the first idea that each man is his own standard. Yet everyone knows and acknowledges that there is a difference in deciding any problem, whether it is decided by a mathematical standard or an opinion. All will say that the people are not wise in regard to the standard of law. Law is one thing and the judges another and their duty is to decide any troubles that parties get into which they cannot decide themselves. The people make the laws and agree to sustain them, so the judges listen to their stories and decide the case according to their own laws.

Now as troubles often come up where the law is not defined, the judge makes a decision, which is an opinion, not law, and the people are not bound by it, as for instance, the Dred Scott case. The people are not bound by that decision, for it is the opinion of a majority of judges and they are not supreme law. The people are the law and the judges its expounders. The expounding of the law is like the expounding of any other problem. It is as necessary to have an expert for a judge as it is to have an expert in a bank to detect the spurious coin. These persons must be selected by the banks, not by the people. And as it is for their happiness to have the law properly executed, the court, like the bank, ought to have the right to select their own judges. The people must not have the power, for in selecting a judge, they do not stand in the same relation to themselves as in making a law. In making a judge they make him by a party without regard to his merits as an expert in law; while the law is made for the whole people, the judge is made for the party. This defect makes trouble and is felt in the whole country. It makes man act upon a political standard and is the basis of men's reasoning. The same error runs through all the troubles in government and party opinions have been the ruin of nations and statesmen.

As I have said, man is a nation and is his own judge and juror. A man, ignorant, is like a nation in a savage state. As error enters a man, his error commences, and the first law is self-preservation. Then arise opinions as to how to preserve the peace and health. This brings up parties and man, being a nation, governed by the same law of opinions, truth has never been acknowledged by them. Opinions spring up in man, bringing everyone into the field and each man is a government of himself, governed by the opinions of his friends. Now political friends are one thing and friends to the government or health are another. And when a person is in trouble, it is hard to tell who is the cause of it. The sick or president makes his grievances known to his friends, as he thinks. And if they are the friends of the government or health, then no harm is done by their acts or opinions. It is well to know the officers of man's health, so we shall know them in nations. The military are known by their dress. The priests were formerly and so on down to the police. And the officers of man's health are under as good discipline as those of the nation, the one being as corrupt as the other. I will analyze man as I have nations, for he as a nation, is of all corrupt beings the worst. There is no good in him that can be heard. His officers are deceptive, hypocrisy and all kinds of evil, and they are prowling round seeking whom they may devour.

This makes up that element in man, corresponding to the lowest passions of the masses in a nation. This party has their leaders and they are as easily detected by their wisdom as they are in a nation. I will give the foundation of each man as a nation and men's acts as combined into a government, as a nation. The child's mind is a new territory not explored. An adult is like an old world. The child's mind or soil in a natural state brings forth the fruits of its mother's mind. As it is naturally rich but uncultivated, it holds out great inducements for strangers. So strange ideas are sown in the mind. And as its mind is under none but the first law of nature, might is right and all kinds of ideas spring up in anarchy and confusion. Each stranger wants to cultivate the mind according to the prejudices of his father. This makes confusion and as in all governments, a convention is called and a constitution is formed. Some concession is made to suit the rabble and some to suit the more sober classes. But science is not taken into the treaty at all, nor ever hinted at in the constitution of child's mind.

Now health and happiness are the first articles in the constitution of both the government of man as man and nation as a nation and of course there must be leaders and teachers for each. So a certain set of men come up as teachers for this young nation and a controversy springs up as to what kind of laws are best to keep this child in subjection till it shall get large enough to take care of itself. Meetings are called, arguments are brought forth and parties are formed. At last a set of laws are agreed to by the majority but opposed by the minority. These laws are placed in the hands of certain party leaders and the nation or child is to be governed accordingly. And the first act is to bring the child into subjection to these laws. These laws are based upon opinions that happen to arise in the minds of the old world or people who wish to govern the young child or nation according to the wisdom of their fathers. And to carry out the design, men are appointed to instruct the young in all the religion of their fathers. Here is almost the first false move, implanting in the mind of the child our religious opinions. As they spring up, other opinions also come forth and a discord ensues. This fills the mind or soil with foul seed or opinions and the mind becomes disturbed and someone is selected to settle the difficulty. Another set of political guides is selected to make peace with the religious or diseased opinions. This set are office holders to the priests. For if they opposed the priests' opinions, they would be unpopular. So it is for their advantage to acknowledge the priests' right and not lay the trouble to their opinions, but to disobeying their laws.

This class is called doctors, who make their living as I have just said. And thus the people are kept under by these blind guides. Their minds are kept disturbed and the doctors call it disease. Their diseases or troubles increase; their burdens are multiplied till rebellion springs up. Then a war is started by the unbelievers of the two classes. A suspension of hostilities takes place; judges are appointed through the influence of these blind guides and they decide according to the party that is in power. This makes more trouble, so it goes on from one generation to another coming up and flourishing for a time, then followed by wars and rebellion and death. This is the case with disease and nations are only the whole people's mind concentrated into one body called nation, having its feature and growth like a man. The health or disease of the people shows the health of the nation, not the intelligence but the health. Wisdom is not health, for if it was, the beast would be wiser than the human species and this is not the case. So there must be some defect in our bringing up, for if man's life is limited to seventy or one-hundred years, then it may be compared to a bubble. This is the world's reasoning. But science is a kingdom not of this world of opinions. It has no dealing with the opinions of man but tests all things by a standard, not of man but of science, which does not say, Believe this or that but shows its opinions by its works. It does not ask you to believe what your fathers believed if it is false, but proves all things so that the natural man will believe. This kingdom has its government, its law and teachers. I will give you its form of government and describe how it is establishing its power or wisdom on earth unobserved, yet rising like the flood.

While the people of this world are eating and drinking, giving opinions and marrying in parties, the kingdom of science will come to sweep them all away into the death of eternal oblivion. You may ask for a sign, that you may tell when these things will be. I will give you the signs of the times. Take one individual as a fair specimen of a nation. A diseased individual is like a diseased nation, each is under false leaders. The sick are under the hands of the priests and doctors, just as the government is in the hands of the politicians. Public opinion in politics is the opinion of the leaders of the parties. And national disease is the effect of error as is the disease of an individual. The masses, in each case, are under a silent influence that is not organized. So they think they are their own judges and you will often hear this remark from them, "I have an opinion of myself," as though they were the authors of their opinions. When questioned for proof, they refer you to someone's opinion. To understand the signs of the times so you may not be deceived by specious appearances, you must test each opinion by the standard of science. Ask how they know and you will see them squirm and gnash their teeth. Then in a fit of rage they will leave you and enter the swine or their old superstition and are lost to the world.

As I have said, I will give you the foundation of the spiritual or scientific kingdom. It is not built by man's opinions, but it is a kingdom of science to test all the kingdoms of the earth. Unlike all other kingdoms, it never commences war, nor meddles with men's opinions. It is the scale or higher court to which all other kingdoms refer their troubles. The court sits in the hearts of all the people and just whatever parties agree to it, it obliges them to perform. It has no parties or sects and no religious worship; it judges of all and measures out to everyone just as they measure out to another. It has no laws but judges man by his own laws. Its reasoning is to show the parties the folly of their own reasoning. It asks questions to see if opinions can sustain themselves. It never argues but always listens to hear the arguments of opinions. It shows no matter. It is unchangeable. It is the same, today and forever. You may ask how we shall know it when it comes by its wisdom. It judges no man but leaves all judgment to the reasoning of opinions. Thus man judges himself and he must be punished according to his own laws. For the punishment is in the law; the law is the will of the people and the judge administers the law. I will give you one or two cases showing how the judge decides in this kingdom. This kingdom is not matter. But the kingdom of opinions is matter. So when a subject of the spiritual kingdom sets up his kingdom in the earthly man, he is liable to be overpowered by the children of darkness or this world; and if he is overpowered, his kingdom is let out to the kings of this world.

When a person is sick, he is in the hands of the children of darkness, and his mind, like a nation, is taken possession of by the enemies of health. He is in the same state as Job. His enemies are compassed about him and he is denied assistance. Thus beaten and bruised till a reaction takes place, he is left to die of his own accord. I will take such a one and bring him before the tribunal that renders to everyone his due. This tribunal is invisible to the natural man and cannot be seen by the natural sight. But the other senses are awake to its power and it uses the natural organs to influence the natural world. As you may not be acquainted with the inhabitants of this other world, I will try to compare them to two persons conversing about these two worlds and their beliefs respecting them. I will show that the natural man is ignorant of the spiritual or scientific world and to be born again is to get out of the world of opinions into the world of science. Imagine yourself listening to two persons conversing about religion. The natural man is religious, not scientific. The scientific is not religious. The conversation is from the world of opinions or religion to the scientific world; this is no easy thing. Both have their identity: one in the world of opinions, the other in science, and to separate them more plainly, I will call one matter and the other wisdom. The world of matter is governed by opinion; that of science, by wisdom. So the thing talked about must first start in the world of opinion, for wisdom never starts anything. Every sensation is made on the senses and if they are attached to wisdom, a scientific answer comes. But if a sensation is made on the senses attached to opinions, then disease and misery come.

These are the two worlds. The man of opinion asks the question, Do you believe in death? The man of wisdom says, No. (Opinion) What do you believe? (Wisdom) I have no belief. To bring these more clearly to your belief, I will assume the character of the man of wisdom and you the reader, the man of opinions. (O) Do you not believe that the soul leaves the body at death? (W) I have not said that I believe in death. (O) Of course you believe that the body dies. (W) You say I do but I do not say so. (O) Well, what do you believe? (W) I have no belief about the other world; I know it. (O) Then if you know it, do not men die before they get into the other world? (W) Why do you wish me to admit death when I have told you that I do not believe in it? (O) You do not believe that your body can go to the other world? (W) Yes, I do, but not in the sense that you do. Each world has the same ideas. The only difference between us is that your world is made by superstition and your ignorance is the matter. My wisdom is in your matter or ignorance, and your error cannot see it. You being blind cannot see the light of wisdom or science, so that my world is to your world a mystery. (O) I do not see any sense in what you say. (W) I shall not quarrel with you on that score; it looks to me as though you do not understand yourself. (O) I can make nothing out of your ideas. (W) Can you make anything out of your own? (O) I think I can explain it better than you have done. (W) I have not tried to explain at all; I cannot explain what never had an existence. (O) You do not deny that man dies. (W) I do not admit it, do you? (O) Yes. (W) Will you tell me how you know that a dead thing has life? (O) I do not mean the soul, I mean the body. (W) Has your soul senses? (O) Yes. (W) Do you mean that your senses die? (O) No. (W) Then the body only dies, as you say? (O) I do not know. (W) I agree with you in the last statement. (O) Have you any proof that you will have any senses without a body? (W) Yes. (O) What is it? (W) If you wish me to tell you what I know of myself, I can do so, but if you believe in death, why do you not show it so that I may have some idea of it? (O) I suppose that you do not deny that man dies? (W) You have asked that question a number of times. It seems as though you never would know what I do believe, so I will ask you to explain your belief about death. Do not tell me what I believe or disbelieve, but tell me what you believe yourself. (O) Well I believe that this body dies and that the soul or life or something lives independently in another world, or this world or somewhere. I cannot tell exactly where, but I do not believe that when man dies that is the end of him. (W) All this is a belief, is it not? (O) Yes, I admit that I have no positive proof of it. (W) How can a man have proof that he is dead? (O) The living have the proof that he is dead. (W) Then the living are the judges of the dead? (O) Yes. (W) Then because you say a man is dead, he is so? (O) Everyone will admit that he is dead. (W) I wish I could make you stick to one thing, that is, what you mean by dead and not dead. (O) All the Christian world believe in death. (W) Well, because all believe in death is that proof to any one that does not believe it? (O) No, but the Bible teaches it. (W) Then because the Bible, as you say, teaches it, it must be so, of course. I must take an opinion of someone who knows nothing at all, for a truth. Just look at the absurdity of your own belief; there is not one single idea of truth in all your opinions. If you will listen to me, I will tell you facts, demonstrable, that will explain all your error; for yours is an error, arising from heathen superstition and I will show you where they lie.

(O) Well, I will listen, if you will not fly off from the point. (W) I will try not to. (O) You are a clock-maker by profession? (W) Yes. (O) Do you understand how to calculate the train of wheels and the length of any pendulum to fit any case of a given length? (W) Yes, I do not care what length of pendulum you give me, I can calculate the number of vibrations in a minute and calculate a train of wheels to correspond to the beats so the clock will keep correct time. (O) Did you always have that power? (W) No, I do not call it a power. (O) Why not? I do not have that gift or power. (W) It is because you will not try to obtain it. (O) I have prayed and talked and used every means to get it and have finally concluded that it is a gift or power which derives from some higher power which you do not acknowledge. (W) How do you know? Can you calculate a clock? (O) No, I have not the gift, but I know just as much about it as you do, in fact no one knows. We see clocks run and keep time and that is all we know about it. To talk about a science is all nonsense, for it is mystery. (W) Then because you cannot see there is a science by which a clock can be calculated, all these clocks are made and kept in order by a power or gift that a man knows nothing of? (O) I will admit your power, but to admit that you know more about it than all the rest of the world, I cannot. Because if it could be taught and learned, every person could teach it; this shows it to be a power.

(W) Do you admit that I can make a clock and repair old ones? (O) Yes, I know you can but I do not believe that you know anything more about how you do it than I do. (W) What is your business? (O) I am a musician, a violinist. (W) How long since you had the gift or power? (O) It is not a gift. (W) What is it? (O) It is a science. (W) You do not know any more then about the power than I do. (O) Can you play? (W) No. (O) Then how do you know that I do not know any more about it than you do? (W) I judge you by the same standard that you judge me. (O) I do not judge you at all. (W) You said you know as much about a clock as I did. So why should I not know as much about music as you do? (O) Perhaps you do, but we cannot agree and when doctors fall out, we must leave it to some person whom we agree has more knowledge than either of us. And as we are sick or out of tune, we will call a physician to get his advice, for we both acknowledge the medical skill.

A physician is called and, looking very wise, he listens attentively to each story and after a careful investigation makes the following report.

Man is like a machine or clock; his power is in the pendulum which makes so many vibrations in a minute. The clock will keep good time, but if it gets out of order, you must send for a scientific man to repair it, not a quack. You are both right. There is no correct rule to make a clock. Careful investigation by scientific men show that it is impossible to make any accurate calculation in regard to a science, from the fact that on examining clocks, all lengths of pendulums are found also, all sizes of wheels with a different number of teeth in each wheel, and very few are alike. Therefore, I have come to the conclusion that a clock-maker cannot tell with accuracy about a clock any more than a physician can about a man; they are both mysteries in the world.

It is true the world has given the medical faculty the credit of wisdom or power superior to the clock-maker or musician. But I am free to admit that the medical men labor under the same trouble with the rest of the world, that is: that there is no such thing as science. It is true that men can play on musical instruments, but it is folly to say that there is a science by which it can be taught and learned. Listen to the bird that sings; there is no science about that. One bird learns from another by sympathy. To set up a standard of science shows an amount of general information that the common people lack.

Here is the trouble. The masses, like the brutes, have the power of imitation. See the beavers, how perfectly they arrange their houses and their young have the same imitation and so on. The clock-maker does and the medical men too; only, medical men have been selected as teachers to the masses. This gives them more power, for the power of the profession is in the confidence of the people. If there had been any such thing as science, the medical faculty could not have stood one year, from the fact that all their power is in the position that the world has given them. It does not come from wisdom in their profession but from their opinions being acknowledged as superior to such men as you. You have given them the charge of your lives and they are bound to preserve them to the best of their ability. But so far as my wisdom is concerned in calculating any theory to cure diseases by a science, it is just as erroneous as to undertake to say that there is a science in music or in clock-making. In conclusion, I will say to you both that all the science in our three cases lies in making the masses believe that we have a science. But here is where we, as medical men, have the advantage of you, as the common class. We do not recognize anyone without a diploma. This all cannot get, from the fact that the deception must be kept from the people, or the faculty is ruined. No one has any respect for your mechanical power; it is too much among the masses and your musical power is in the same category. But we, when a man undertakes to step in, cry out, Humbug, Quack, and the people are so loyal that they put down all opposition so that all we have to do is not to appear to notice them.

(O) Do you not think there is some science in it? (PHY) Oh, yes. Or that some men have more sagacity than others. This you see is the profession. To be a good professional man is to keep aloof from the masses, for otherwise he loses his dignity, and his wisdom will not sustain him. So popularity and not wisdom is the medical science. Wisdom never was popular, for it had no identity. So hoping I have settled your troubles I leave. (Clock-maker and Musician alone)

(Clock-maker) What do you think of the doctor's opinion? (Musician) He has shown that he knows nothing of music; what do you think of his opinion in regard to your science? (CM) I have come to the conclusion that he knows nothing about clock-making and we are in the same predicament that we were before. If a man could be found who is a clock-maker, musician and doctor, then I think we could get at the right answer. (M) I think I know just the one, so if you please we will have his opinion.

Here is introduced a third person. (CM) Have you read the doctor's report on our cases? (Wisdom) Yes, but I saw nothing in what he said, showing that he knew anything about his own business or yours, for I happen to be acquainted with all these powers as he calls them and he showed entire ignorance in regard to them all. (O) Can you explain where the truth is? (W) Yes. The word science has never had life attached to it but has always been looked upon as a power that never had life. So that when we speak of science, we never have attached any of the senses to it. Therefore, science is not known by the natural man, yet he has science but knows it not and it has no place of respect in his heart or senses. I will try to give it a foundation that you both will admit. Before you knew how to calculate a clock, the calculation was a mystery; but as soon as you learned it, the mystery was gone. Your senses left the mystery and attached themselves to the wisdom you obtained. And the mystery to you was like an opinion that never was true. So when the musician called it a mystery, you could see where his senses were attached, also that he was in the dark. But your senses being attached to the light or wisdom, you could see through his darkness or error. The difference between you was this: his senses were in his error, and error's light is a false light. Your senses, being attached to the true light that lighteth everyone who is scientific, it was a mystery to his light, his senses not knowing the true light.

You both are right and neither knows it, from the fact that science has never been acknowledged by opinion to have any wisdom, while science is wisdom. And as fast as a person finds wisdom, he finds science, for the word science is the name of the wisdom that sees through the opinions of man. As far as the doctor's science went in his explanation, you could both see that his science was ignorance in regard to your cases. And as far as the sick, his wisdom is just the same. Here is the mystery. Science, as it is called, is something that the natural man worships. He looks upon it as coming from some superior power, independent of himself, when his own wisdom is all the science he knows of. For to the fool who knows nothing, there is no science.

Your wisdom in regard to making a clock is one thing, but if you can calculate it and know by what principle you do it, that wisdom is not of this world but of God or Science. It has never entered man's senses that his senses are his wisdom and his body is an idea that his senses are attached to. He admits it himself, when the very senses are not recognized by itself, but speaks of itself as a third person. This is the case in sickness; the senses often speak of themselves as another person. I will try to illustrate. Suppose we should differ in opinion on some subject, for instance, about a certain man's complexion. Suppose I said he had black eyes, and you insisted that his eyes were hazel and we argued to convince each other. We are both certain we are right, but ours is the wisdom of opinion. We cannot agree, so we refer our differences to a person who decides that his eyes are black, so the one in error gives it up. In all this, no science or wisdom is displayed. Now suppose I am called to decide their controversy. They do not tell me the thing in dispute, but ask me to tell them what they are disputing about. I tell them they are disputing about Mr. A. How do you know, they ask. Because I see him here and the thing in question is his eyes. Turning to Mr. B, I say, You think he has black eyes and Mr. C thinks they are hazel, but I know you both are mistaken, for his eyes are blue. They are not bound to take my opinion as such because I say so; but if I tell them what they think, and they know that I have no knowledge of it through my natural senses, they believe. This belief was founded on my telling them what they thought. This to them was stronger proof than they could give me, so they admitted it was a truth although it was still to them a mystery.

I will try to give a stronger proof that I knew more than they did and show that my power was wisdom. Their minds excited mine till I could see the man in question. His eyes were blue. I also saw another man with hazel eyes. The man with blue eyes was in harmony with me, but the one with hazel eyes was not; neither was the man with black. As I convinced them of their wisdom, their error disappeared and at last there stood a man with blue eyes. Now to the world of opinion, this is a mystery or power, but to me it is wisdom, just as much as it is to the clock-maker or musician. Let science be looked upon as a character and opinion as a character, and every man may be as these two principles. Then man can measure himself by his own wisdom, but now he is weighed by the scale of public opinion which is not science. Every science that is acknowledged is wisdom to those who understand it. Why should it be an impossibility that a person might see and feel another's feelings? Is not this the case in every branch of wisdom? Does not the musician feel the discord of his pupil, and does not his wisdom correct it? If the mind is not something that can be corrected, then there is no wisdom or science to be applied. Now man is a machine, acted upon by one of the powers, opinion or wisdom. The discord is made by a sensation on the mind. If the sensation is rightly directed, then the effect is harmless, but if not, then it embraces an opinion. For instance, take two persons. One knows the cry of murder; the sensation following it depends on the wisdom or error of those who hear it, for otherwise all would be affected alike by every sensation, for it contains the basis of wisdom or error. Now if error is aroused, discord and disease follow, but if wisdom feels or sees it, it amounts to nothing.

May 1861

Strength
[LC 2:0817]

Does man put strength in his legs when he undertakes to rise from a chair? Everyone will say he does. Now this is not the case. When a person rises from a chair he weighs nothing to himself, any more than his arm. Now just lift your hand and see if it requires any strength and you will find it does not. It is as easy to raise it as to put it down. Now take a ten pound weight in your hand and it requires some force to lift it. Now is the power put into the arm or weight or neither? I say it is neither, but you exercise a will outside the body and weight just equal to the weight. The words weight, power and motion as used are all applied to something that has no wisdom. If you wish to move a table, you do not put the power in the table but in the weight or resistance, and then you use your judgment to move the weight. Now the thing to be moved is called weight or resistance.

Now comes in the science to know how to move the weight. The natural way is for the power to come in direct contact with the weight. This is the natural man's reasoning. The scientific man's reason suggests some purchase by which he can move the weight with less power, so he invents or develops purchase. This embraces another combination called time. This is often lost sight of by those that have learned the benefit of the lever. They know that by the use of the lever they can raise a weight that they can't lift by their physical strength, but they are not aware that they have gained nothing by the lever. The lever is for convenience and the loss of time is equal to the gain of power.

I will illustrate. Suppose you have a body to raise one foot that weighs one-hundred pounds and your strength is equal to lifting twenty-five pounds. Now if the weight was in four parts, the quickest way would be to lift twenty-five at a time with the hand. But as the weight is all together, you get a lever that is four times as long as the height you wish to raise the weight. Then place a fulcrum one fourth of the length from the weight to be raised, so that the long end will be three times as far to travel as the weight. And then apply your strength which is twenty-five pounds to the long end of the lever and it will just balance. Then one ounce will raise the weight and your twenty-five pounds will drop three times as fast and the one hundred will rise. So three times as much velocity must be applied to twenty-five pounds to balance three times the weight. So that what you have gained in one case you have lost in another. This makes velocity and weight equal.

Now although these principles are known, man never acts upon them when he reasons about his body. He reasons as though his body and power were all one, and in this way he acts against himself. I shall give some illustrations to show how absurdly man reasons about his body. If he knew he was affected by his own reason and that his body was as much a weight to him as he believed it to be, and by false reasoning he acted against himself, then he would learn to reason correctly.

I will show you how man reasons about his body and also show how he ought to reason. To reason right man admits his body is heavy or weighty, but he also admits that the power is in the weight to raise itself and if it can't raise itself then the legs or lever are not strong enough to raise the body. So you will hear them say, My legs are too weak for me to raise my body. This is the way the sick man reasons. The well man does not reason at all. If he wants to get up he can, and he does not know how he does it, nor does he care. Now the sick man cannot rise and he begins to reason and if he fails, he applies to some physician who knows just as much as he does, and both together know nothing, they reason after this way. There is no strength in your knees and your back is weak. It must have something to strengthen it. So they rub on some liniment or apply a blister or something else. To me this is as absurd as if a man should put a green tree under a rock and wait for it to grow so that it might be strong enough to raise the rock. In fact it is not wise at all. It is the height of ignorance.

Man is just what he believes himself to be and if when sick he believes he is heavy, he is so to himself. Now he is in a diseased state and it requires someone to get him out of this dilemma. To reason as he reasons would be like the blind leading the blind. I reason according to scientific principles with the sick man. I say to him his body to him is like a weight to be raised; the power is his will and the application or reason is the lever. The body is the weight or disease. So to destroy the idea weight is to change the mind or get up an action like reasoning and show him that as long as he waits for his body to grow strong he is doing nothing. The strength is in his own understanding and this is outside of his body or disease as the doctors call it. The weakness is in his error or mind and that weakness reasons as though the body was weak.

Now when you will to rise, you make the same effort as though you were raising any weight outside of yourself. You feel as though you must put power in your limbs. And you also feel as though you were taking hold of a wooden man and lifting him up on his feet and getting him balanced. Then it is time enough to put motion in him; but the first is to feel as though you were a second person lifting another. But if you feel as if you were lifting yourself, it is like trying to lift yourself up by taking hold of the straps of your boots as you sit in your chair and see if you can lift yourself out of your chair. One is just as absurd as the other. Just feel as though you were outside of the weight and lift it up, only leave the feet on the floor and hold the body up and do not let it press on the limbs and knees and you will get it so light that when you say, Rise, it will obey your will. Then you have overcome the error, cured the disease and the weight is gone.

If you put a weight on your limbs by your own reason and then undertake to make your legs grow strong so they will raise the body, the limbs will become as heavy as the body and another power will be needed to raise the legs. So apply your wisdom to the idea body and raise the weight as you would any weight till you have got rid of the idea that strength is in the body. In this way you will purify yourself from error and by the power of will, which is velocity, will raise the weight of error and subject it to your own control. Remember that one grain of weight or the tooth or a crown wheel of a clock is enough to raise a fourteen pound weight on the barrel. Now divide the fourteen pounds into grains and then you get a lever equal to the weight so that one ounce on the long end of the lever will be equal to fourteen pounds on the short end. Therefore, 48,384 times the velocity of fourteen pounds is equal to the weight. It is as much quicker than the fall of a weight as lightning is quicker than an ox team. So that if the will is anything, velocity is everything, if it is put in action.

Now call this velocity the spiritual man with all his wisdom and the weight or matter to be moved and the obstruction the mind or false reasoning. Then you will have a perfect man outside of matter or mind that controls the other three. Then you will see that just as a man is wise he is spiritual, or velocity, and his velocity is made superior to his weight as much as lightning is more powerful than steam. This velocity is the man or wisdom that governs and rules all things. Its weight is its density; its buoyancy is its power. Identity is its wisdom and when they are all combined in perfection it is the great first cause and as man departs from these truths he becomes weighty, ignorant and diseased.

1864

Strength; Whence Is It, of Matter or Wisdom? Errors and Misery Resulting from the Misapplication of the Word.
[LC 1:0443]

What is strength? This question sounds as though it might be easily answered, but on consideration, it is not so easy. Words are so misused that it it impossible to get at the original meaning of the person who applied the word or at the feeling or state of mind when the word was first introduced. If you choose to apply the word strength to machinery, then I have no fault to find with the definition. But if it means will, then it is wrongly applied, for will is independent of the thing you call strong. If you say, "That is a strong lever," then it does not include the force that is applied to it. If the person who first used the word applied it to his wisdom as a powerful intellect, then it will only apply where there is some intellect, the quality of which is not taken into account. This confusion of meaning makes a great deal of trouble, for we put intelligence into everything that has resistance instead of in the intelligence having the strength. As far as man is concerned the word strength has no meaning at all unless you call it will. A man's legs are a combined lever, and if you mean that they have strength you might as well say that a lever has strength, for one is as much alive as the other, and neither of itself can do anything.

The word strength does not convey the author's feelings when he made the expression. He either meant to apply it to wisdom or to matter. If the author meant to give a name to the phenomenon called will, then it makes a vast difference in reasoning about strength. For instance, a person is "weak," as it is called, in the back or limbs. Now the medical faculty goes to work to rub on all kinds of strengthening medicines just as though there were intelligence in the medicine and it imparted strength to the weak part. This absurd idea is carried out all through our lives, and it deprives man of the true wisdom that might make him happy and intelligent.

My theory gives the lie to all the above, for I have seen that the word strength is a mere word with no more meaning than to lead man astray and the whole medical science is based on this word strength. This or that thing is said to give a person strength. In the case of a fever the whole invention of the medical faculty is brought to play to discover some medicine that will give strength. The chemist is employed to discover the chemical properties such and such things contain, and numberless articles are said to contain strengthening virtue. The food is strengthening, the air is strengthening and you can find no end to the strengthening things given to the sick, and all the while they are growing weaker. This false idea should be corrected.

Everyone knows that animals have more strength than the human species and it cannot be their food; for a man fed on grass would die according to our belief, while the animal will live, and he will live on the same food as man and still grow no stronger. Man puts the construction on the word to suit himself. It is used to work some piece of machinery, a carriage for instance, as though it had intelligence. If the word applied to man's will is called strength, the thing that it is applied to should not be called strong. You may ask what this has to do with the curing of disease. I will tell you, for it is the very thing to correct. Apply the word strength to man, not to matter, for wisdom has life and the matter has none. There is such a term as resistance and this is the opposite to strength. For instance, you wish to raise a stone. That wisdom that wants to raise a stone is one thing, and the stone is another. So if wisdom chooses to apply its strength through the arms, its motive or will is applied just according to the amount of resistance. If a horse is attached to a dead weight, it applies its will or strength just according to its wisdom; and if it fails, it makes another effort to overcome the resistance, and as it gets deceived it loses its power or strength. Strength is intelligence; it embraces all man's wisdom, and if this wisdom is of this world, his strength is in his muscles; but if his wisdom is of God or Science, his strength is in himself and to be wise is to be strong.

I will illustrate my idea of strength as I apply it to the sick. When I use the word I couple it with skill. These two are governed, either by the brutal wisdom or the scientific wisdom. I will state a case of my own experience. I treated a man who had lost the use of his lower limbs. He could not move them when he was sitting in his chair. The doctors called it a spine affection. When he attempted to rise, he had not strength in his spine to keep his body erect. He would give out at the pit of the stomach, and this took all the power from his legs. This was the doctors' theory and the man believed it and applied his will or strength according to this wisdom. His hope was cut off. He believed the spine was diseased and so did all his friends and physicians.

According to my theory his body was like the weight to be moved; his will or strength was applied to his body just as it would be to a lever that you believed would break if you applied too much power to it. His reason directed the power, and being deceived he could do nothing. To cure him, or make his legs strong and his spine well, was to first convince him that there never was any strength in the idea body and that strength came from some other source.

Everyone knows that, the will being put into action, an effect is produced called strength. For instance, a person by the power of his will can hold another; this is called strength. What is the grasp? Strength? or is it the will applied to the hand? No one supposes that the hand would catch hold and grasp unless it was directed by another power. This other power is the will governed by the wisdom and the effect is called strength. Strength is the name of the phenomenon; it is an act, so will without an act or motive is no will or strength and availeth nothing. So to sit till his legs grow strong would be as absurd as to make a steam engine and after it was ready to work, sit and wait till the wood made its own fire, its steam, and let its steam on to the piston head. For a man that has lost his strength to sit still and wait for it to come is just as absurd as to put clay into a mortar bin and then wait for it to make itself into a vessel. Such an idea of strength is so absurd that it takes away a man's reasoning faculties. Let man know that his weakness is the want of right direction to his ambition, then his strength is in putting his will into action; both are the result of his wisdom. Destroy a man's prospects and happiness, and you destroy his strength. So as you rouse his ambition and will, his strength comes. The course taken by the medical faculty in their mode of reasoning destroys man's natural powers and makes him a mere tool in the hands of a quack. Every man who reasons that strength can be made by food, air, or rubbing, or any liniment is a fool, although he may be honest.

I have tried the experiment and know. I do not guess at it when I say that there is not one particle of virtue in any sort of medicine that people take to give them strength. Neither is there any strength in one kind of food more than another, but it may be all summed up in this: the gratification of man's desires embraces all there is of him, and these vary according to circumstances. All men have a desire for happiness, and this desire creates an appetite, and the desire wants to be gratified. This brings up this feeling called will, and then it is forced on by wisdom to accomplish a desire. The wants of the animal are limited; therefore it is lively and happy, for it acts according to its will. It is often said that the beasts are sick. Granted, but man takes their freedom from them as well as from the human species. Let both be wild and you see a bold race.

Look at the uncultivated savage and you will not see him creeping around as though he had done some mean, dirty act, like the civilized man. Of all mean looking things, a human being that is completely under the medical faculty is the lowest; he is as much a slave as the Negro at the South, and in fact more so. Look at a sick female suffering from some opinion that the doctors have made her believe. In her mind she is completely under the doctor; she is not allowed to eat or drink or even walk or think, except as the family physician gives direction. The sick have given their souls to the priests and their bodies to the physicians. They then tell about the good doctor, how much he has done for them, showing that he has deprived them of all noble, manly feelings, left them sick, feeble in mind and body, while the doctor struts around like the slave driver, and the sick curl under the lash of their tongue, as the negroes under the lash of their masters.

This may seem strange, but it is God's truth that the sick are a mere tool in the hands of the medical faculty to be treated just as they please. It never will be any better till the sick rise in their wisdom and declare their independence. You may say I am making war for my own gain, but I think I can convince anyone who is out from under these slave drivers that I could make ten dollars where I now make one. My object is to raise my fellow man to his original state. I am a white abolitionist. The blacks, it is true, are slaves, but their slavery is a blessing compared with that of the sick. I have seen many a white slave that would change places with the black. The only difference is that white slavery is sanctioned by public opinion. But make the slave know that he is one and you will see a difference in the result. It is hard for me to keep myself within bounds when I think of the groans of the sick, knowing that it is all the effect of a superstitious ignorance. Does not the South quote the Bible to prove that slavery is of divine origin? Do not the priests and doctors quote the old heathen superstition to bolster up a weak and feeble edifice just ready to crumble and crush the leaders? Is not science raising her voice and crying aloud to the people saying, How long shall it be till the old heathen idolatry shall come to an end and man shall learn wisdom and be his own master and not a slave.

November 1861

Subject of Mind, The
[LC 1:0336]

From time immemorial the subject of mind has been a theme of ancient and modern philosophers. Now if the idea of mind did not embrace all our reason and philosophy, man would not be all the time trying to investigate its nature.

Mind is always associated with something else. Moses used the word wisdom in the sense of mind when he said God created the heavens and the earth, which means mind and matter.

The philosophers of our day separate matter from mind and call matter material and mind immaterial, so that matter is not under the control of mind and as mind is immaterial it is nothing. Now can nothing produce something? The philosophers of our day may answer. Lucretius divided mind from matter in these words: body and space or void, void being mind. He also called it space and vacuum, so all philosophers have gone back to matter and tried to trace it up to that point where it ceases to be matter. Lucretius makes no difference in matter but calls it all matter. This includes mind, for he says in Book fourth, four-hundred and forty-first page, "Sound is substance as experience shows, since to the sense impulsively it flows." Now why all these different applications of the same term? If mind is matter, what is life? To show that mind is matter we must illustrate it by something that men will admit. But what is it to man whether mind is matter or not? I say it is of vast importance to the world, for if it can be shown that mind is matter, it will be seen that even mind is under the control of a wisdom possessed by man, so that wisdom acting upon mind changes the mind and produces another idea. Now if I speak and the sound is substance, it must come in contact with some other substance or fill some vacuum in the mind.

I will show that matter is a medium for wisdom and when I say matter I embrace mind in it, so it is not necessary to repeat the two every time I allude to mind.

I will now show that there is no such a substance as weight nor gravitation in wisdom, that even the earth is not governed by wisdom according to man's philosophy, for if it was, God could not see all around a globe at the same time. And if the globe is matter independent of wisdom, then it fills some space. So that man on the globe is not in the center of space; therefore he must be on one side and all the planets that are at such great distances from the earth and each other cannot all be in the center of space.

Let us see how this theory holds out and analyze it. All persons have noticed when the skies look dark they are nothing but shades. Now as the particles of matter are set in motion by some invisible power, they are separated and driven before a more powerful substance; this brings them into a more solid form, so at last they can be seen by the eye. Then as they are driven against an opposite power or atmosphere they become more dense till their density is seen and felt. This is called snow; forced still closer together, it becomes ice. It is now called matter; this gives rise to a new philosophy. The world has been divided into three classes of philosophy. The Grecian experience shows that it is dangerous to search too deeply into science, for as all things must be proved by wisdom, the invisible things must be proved by the visible. So that although a person's theory may be true, yet not having the wisdom to put it into practice, only in their own lives, the ignorance of the world, while it gives to the author the credit of honesty, sets him down as a fanatic and thus misrepresents him when his very philosophy is true.

We at this time boast of our philosophy as though it was a late discovery, but when tested by the philosophy of the Greeks, it vanishes like dew before the sun. They searched for wisdom beyond the narrow limits of the human mind and soared above the idea that this world is all there is. And they went on to dissolve all matter and hold it in solution.

All of this is true but it wants to be brought to the understanding of the natural man. They went so far as to believe that they had not only discovered the wisdom that governs all things but they were accused of discovering life itself and it taught them to apply it to man for his happiness. This required proof to sustain it and as their wisdom stopped at the fact it gave their opponents the advantage of them and they were looked upon as visionary theorists. So the wisdom of this world established new things based on things that could be seen and felt.

As I stand alone, separate from all these things and all theories, I have a right to introduce a new and more perfect theory based on facts produced by my own wisdom and admitted by my patients.

This wisdom gives to every theory its just due and condemns all error. It proves all things and holds fast that which is true. I shall show that the Grecian philosophers were correct and so was the Copernican system and that all former philosophies did not believe the earth was flat but they spiritualized all things for the happiness of man.

Now there are two philosophies that will bear the name of wisdom: one is founded on the idea of matter, etc. and on the present philosophy of the day, and the other is the philosophy of wisdom. One admits all that is governed by their philosophy and looks upon all wisdom that cannot be accounted for as a mystery or gift.

I shall try to separate the one from the other and show that the philosophy of this world is based on the phenomena of the scientific world.

The scientific world is in opposition to the natural world. Each world proves its works but the natural world is the shadow of the spiritual world and is governed by a lower class of minds too gross to rise to the substance that is attached to the shadow, so that every truth has its shadow and the two modes of reasoning prove their works. One reasons out of matter, the other reasons in matter. So the philosophy that is founded on the basis of matter has the majority, like all other errors. Every truth is in a minority and is opposed by the majority. The principle of this world is that the majority is right, and so, of course, as error is always in the majority, it must be right.

Now let us see if it does not hold good. Is it not so in religion and politics? The truth is not acknowledged at all as an opposer of error, but a mere balance to weigh each man's opinion.

Opinions are the substances that are weighed. Truth is nothing but the balances. It has no existence in this world because it is of the world of wisdom and that is a stranger to matter. Now these two worlds or philosophies split up the world of matter, for one reasons in matter and the other out of it. One has laws, the other has none; one has religion, the other has none. One has the wisdom of matter, the other the wisdom of God and each proves its science. Now man is made out of the wisdom of matter, and matter has its God, and all of its laws are found in matter, and as disease is a transgression of these laws of matter, man is punished by the laws. Now to punish a man for disobeying a law, is to suppose the law existed before the offense was committed, for where there is no law, there is no transgression. So this world's God supposed that man would do wrong and so made a law in advance. The disobeying of this law was sin. "So by the law came sin and by sin came disease and by disease came death." So everyone is under the sentence of death, for all have sinned. This is one of the majority reports, and to get clear is to do something to get rid of nothing. For the law is the enemy to get rid of and that is made of nothing. It contains nothing, for the same majority says that where there is no transgression, there is no law.

So then, if there is no act, there is no law. This makes it just as the wisdom of God makes it. Every act contains the law of action and reaction and that is all the law that wisdom ever had, but the wisdom of man puts the other construction on it, namely that the effect comes before the cause. This holds good in all of this world's philosophy and I shall show that all their philosophy is based on phenomena that take place in the spirit world or above the natural man, and man in his ignorance gets up a philosophy to explain his ignorance of the phenomena.

This causes the misery that human persons suffer and is the ignorance of themselves. Man invents his misery and lays it to God. Being ignorant of God or wisdom, he sets up a standard based on an opinion.

For instance, how often we hear this saying, "Wrap up so you will not take cold." Now if you go out in the cold under certain conditions, you transgress one of God's laws. Now I ask the question if winter and summer heat were not made before man? All will say, Yes. Will any person stand up and say that anyone going outdoors alters the weather? No. Then the cold does not forbid a person going out or have anything to do about it. So if a man goes out, he goes according to his belief and he is affected just according to it. We will take two persons: one believes in taking cold, his fears excite him; the other is accustomed to the cold and never knew anything bad about it. Now I ask anyone if they think these two persons go out under the same feelings? All will say, No. Then the one that is always catching cold would be the most likely to be affected? Yes. Now God made a law that if a person exposed himself to the cold and he disobeyed this law of health, he must be punished. You may say the healthy man was not really exposed, for he was not in feeble health. Then the man in feeble health is the one to be punished or take cold.

Now see how absurd such a belief is. According to this experiment, and this holds good in every case, the great Father of every good and perfect gift is all wisdom, knows all things, and sees the effect before it happens, governs all our acts, not a hair can fall without his knowledge, made all laws for the happiness of man and had such great love for us that he exposed himself to his own laws and took the penalty to save us poor sinners. All this is taught by the clergy.

Now listen to me for a short time till I set all this right. This law, it seems, was not to embrace those that did not catch cold, for they could not have broken the laws; for if you disobey the law in the least, you are guilty. So the law was for them that disobeyed it. So it is for the sick, these poor weak creatures that can hardly get a breath of air without transgressing a law that these benevolent gods have made and punish all that break them. Now strange as this crazy idea is, it is the belief of 99 in 100 foolish men! How long will you be deceived by false teachings! It is just as impossible to disobey God's wisdom as it is to cut your finger with a razor and say you were ignorant that a razor would cut, when you got it for that purpose. God cannot have a law, for a law presupposes a disobedience, and if God was not wise enough when he made all things to know what would be the end of every act, then he is not the God the Christians claim him to be. And is he dead? No. Then he certainly has respect for persons and gives preference to the well, for all the laws that are attached to God by the Christian world are to punish the sick; for the well are not punished at all. So to keep clear of his laws is to have nothing to do with him, for the weak flourish under his government like the green bay tree and the Christian finds it a hard road to travel. And if it was not for the leaders exciting and driving them on they would all turn back and become as bad as the rest of the world. Now what infidelity and hypocrisy there is in the world in this 19th century, yet we boast of our religious wisdom!

If any person can show me one single idea in any creed that ever Jesus subscribed to I should like to see it. Religion now is just what it was 2,000 years ago; all the Grecian philosophy opposed it and some were imprisoned and some killed. Jesus opposed it and they murdered him and destroyed his theory and kept up the same old theory only as it has been broken in two by come-outers. It has always been opposed to science. It imprisoned Copernicus and has persecuted all investigators ever since the pagan philosophers blew it up and showed its hideous form and bloody bones. It is founded in ignorance and superstition and is the greatest evil that ever invaded the human mind and were it not for science the world would have at this time the places of torment.

All of this error is the effect of the philosophy of minds. The wise have never established their philosophy by experiments. Error has, and so as one is established, the other becomes the subject. Now establish the true philosophy or goodness and happiness, and then you have a heaven on earth. Then Jesus' words will come to pass when he says, I will create a new heaven or philosophy and a new earth or matter where there shall not be any darkness but all will be light. Now this is the new heaven or philosophy that was foretold in the days of the wise men and repeated by Jesus 1800 years ago. Now I will show you the new philosophy or Jerusalem that man is destined to enter, where there shall be no more sickness or death, where old things are done away and all things become new. Now this philosophy was for man alone, for he had wandered away in the dark and had become so gross that he could not see anything but gross matter. So Jesus said to such, "Ye have eyes but cannot see, and ears and cannot hear and hearts but cannot understand."

Now I shall show that there is a philosophy that has nothing to do with the common philosophy of the day and that our philosophy and religion causes all the evils we mortals suffer. Now if man knew the true philosophy, the shadow could not do any harm; but man worships the shadow and loses the substance. I shall show this and prove it, for I do not mean to give my opinion when I have the truth in hand. My object is the good of mankind independent of all religious sects or creeds. It is a philosophy which, if understood, will make man free and independent of all creeds and laws of man and subject him to his own laws, being free from the laws of sin, sickness and death.

Being once freed I know how to teach others, so I will tell you what must follow this new science, and what it teaches man and how far he is bound. And his binding is a free offering and cannot be altered it he knows the truth or philosophy, so that no one shall enter in blindfolded so he will want to retract before he understands. I will give you my experience as one that believes what he says and is ready to be judged by his patients, and if the world finds fault, I will listen to them; and if their philosophy does more good to the sick than mine, I will consider it and give it the preference. So I will give mine or the philosophy of health and ask my questions of the world. Are not words sound and is not sound something? For if it is not something it could not produce something. Then this something in the form of language is something. Now two somethings of the same kind cannot produce another something, so that one something must act on another something and then a third something can be produced. So if sound is something, it does not act upon itself and if it acts at all, it must act on something else. Now one of these somethings I call God or wisdom. Now as wisdom is a substance that cannot be changed, it cannot fill any more space than all space. It cannot act separate from itself, so it is in all and a part of all; it knows no bounds nor time, it is eternal. Now as every substance throws a shadow, the shadow must have a background of something and this something I call mind or matter and as this something acts on matter it does not act on itself. So of course that that acts is not the same as that that is acted upon, so that that acts is this substance that cannot change but is under two somethings that act upon the same something.

As it may confuse you to understand these somethings I will classify them. The substance acted upon is mind or matter. This I will call No. 1. The substance that acts upon No. 1 I call essence or God and this I will call No. 2. Now the two somethings that govern and direct No. 2 I call wisdom and error. Now as wisdom is all light, it knows no matter, and as error is made of matter, or animal life, it acts upon itself. So as error excites No. 1, error's light produces a shadow, and its shadow is its own making. Now the world's wisdom is in No. 1 and the wisdom of God or the essence is in No. 2. Now there are two directions: one the wisdom of God or essence, the other the wisdom of animal life or matter. Animal life or matter is always changing, so science or wisdom's essence or God is always progressing. Man is in these two somethings; wisdom is the seed sown in matter or ignorance, and as matter is animal, it is disturbed by the child of wisdom and tries to get rid of it. Therefore in its ignorance it is excited and this excitement brings out the child of error, so the children are conceived in the same matter and grow like the two spoken of in the Old Testament, Jacob and Esau.

"Jacob (or wisdom) have I loved, but Esau (or error) have I hated." The same characters were in the parable of Cain and Abel. Cain was the error. Abel was the wisdom. So all through the Old and New

Testaments you can trace the two characters and know their generation from Adam and Eve down to the present day. Error is the older, science is the younger, so that the error is always before the truth in this world of matter, but truth is eternal with the fathers of wisdom. Jesus illustrated these two characters by himself, the flesh and blood or mind and matter or animal life. The essence or child of wisdom was Christ or God, so as the Christ grew in the likeness of the father or wisdom, it threw off the error or natural man and became perfect or wisdom. Yet the Christ used the servant or earthly body as a medium to communicate to the natural man; but Jesus, the natural man, knew not Christ, only as Christ made himself manifest in his works.

Now these two characters were mysteries to the natural man, so the natural man is called the Christ, a power. So it is now. People often ask if I "can impart my power to anyone," and when I tell them it is not a power in the sense they mean, they cannot understand it. So I have to let it go. I have a power and all that call it a power are in the same state that the people were that were looking for a second coming of Christ. Jesus said he was near you, even in your thoughts and you do not know it. When I say I can teach this wisdom, I mean that there are a great many persons who can learn this wisdom, and when once learned, the wisdom is a power; and to put wisdom at the root of a tree or error hews it down like the axe strikes at the root of a tree.

This wisdom is to error or disease like fire; it burns up root and branch.–PPQ

Superstitious Beliefs
[LC 1:0378]

Man, to understand himself, must know how he stands in society, for public opinion is the standard of all our acts. Now to know ourselves is to see where we, as one individual, stand to the surrounding influences that act upon us. For we are mere machines in the world to be moved and regulated by the wisdom of God or science or by the opinions of mankind. These opinions are what cause all the misery in the world; so to know ourselves is to know science which proves all things. I will show where every man ought to stand and to show more clearly where I am, I must take the two extremes of man's belief. The first is the religious belief of another world. This class embraces all those who are affected by it and all false ideas based on phenomena that cannot be explained. Many of these ideas purport to come from the dead or are opinions; so it takes in all the superstitious who bow down and worship this belief. If a man believes that his power comes from another world, then all who embrace this belief are ready to acknowledge the standard. This standard of the priests had its full sway in early ages when the priests cured all diseases. At last opposition arose, as in all humbugs, and a more learned class of humbugs sprang up who led the more sober part of the people. They admitted the religious error and made a still more religious belief. So you may trace the grand scheme of humbugs from Judaism down to the present day. When new phenomena appear that affect one, they also affect the other. Just keep the two before your eyes. You will find the same reform as it is called in these two humbugs.

The spirits of the dead and all kinds of superstition have been battled by science and their standard driven from the dark ages of heathen idolatry step by step, sometimes appearing in various forms of assumed wisdom, again splitting into parties and settling down into deception. This will always be until man sees himself in the true light of reason, not of opinion. To show the two extremes of humbug, I will take one that is established and is as real to those who believe it, as that the sun rises; this is the allopathy practice of medicine. This is the very foundation of man's belief and to give it a character and standard, it must have a religious belief as erroneous as its father, the old church. These two go hand in hand and their absurdities have called out another class, the spiritualists, accompanied by their physicians. These are at war with each other and what looks absurd to one of these parties is true to the other. Each has its standard of belief to which it bows down and worships and which is as real to them as their own existence. I will show that they are the two standards of the world.

The standard of science never goes back to precedents for its proof but shows its science by its works. If it goes back, it is to show that the world has progressed, not to rake up some wisdom but to show that the world has progressed every day in science. The science of life contains the two classes above mentioned. As I have said, the spiritualist goes back into the dark ages of Judaism where the belief of heaven and hell and spirits of the dead were invented, together with every kind of heathen superstition, to seek wisdom by which to correct the errors of the age, supposing that the world was wiser then than now. And showing that any foreign intelligence purporting to come from abroad is worth more than what they get at home. Now, does science go out of the way? No. Chemistry is here just what it is everywhere and the chemist is always showing his improvements and so it is with all sciences. But that science founded on opinions is proved by referring to some one's opinions. And when you go to the opinions, you are sent to another and so on. It is like chasing a jack o'lantern to find the basis independent of an opinion. The science of health is in the hands of these blind guides. There is no difference between them. They are the two extremes of humbug. One belongs to the upper crust, the other to the lower. And if there chances to be a person not under one of these two classes, directly or indirectly, I should like to see where he stands.

Disease is one of the heathen inventions and has had as many names as any political party ever had, but is always the same thing. The serpent was its author or inventor when it made Eve eat the forbidden fruit. As that was a sin, it poisoned all the human family, as is believed. And as sin is disease, all men became diseased, for all have sinned, the Bible says. The apple that brought on the first disease could not have been eaten by the inhabitants of the world, so that they must have caught it from our first parents. Thus catching diseases originated, but Jesus condemned this idea when he said, The old proverb was done away with, that the father had eaten sour grapes and the children's teeth were set on edge, showing that it was a lie. But the people believed it. As the serpent was lost or metamorphosized into the Devil and the people were made to believe it, it became necessary to have a place for him to dwell. So hell was invented as his dwelling place. And as he still held his old grudge because he was driven out of the garden, his whole power was aimed against mankind. We next hear of him tormenting Job with boils, so that disease was his invention. He used to send out young devils or evil spirits, and sometimes the Lord employed them, as when he wanted to deceive Ahab. These devils could enter man and make him do all kinds of things. They tried it with Jesus but they could not deceive him, although he recognized their existence, for he used to cast them out. These devils had teeth and they could also talk. The Bible is full of accounts of their tormenting man and if it is true or the Christian explanation of it, then there were evil spirits at the time the Christian era commenced, eighteen-hundred years ago.

Now, where are they? If man is not affected by them, who is the author of our troubles? Man is affected more than he ever was. These same devils reigned in the time of Jesus and he sent forth his disciples to cast them out. He said that they would be destroyed at the end of the world, for then the Devil and all his works shall be destroyed and death itself. Then there should be no death nor hell. They were to be cast into the lake of fire. Jesus put the power of destroying these evil spirits in the hands of his disciples. Now let us see what they have done. First we find the priests persecuting them, hanging them and casting them into prison till all the disciples were destroyed and they got the power into their own hands. If these devils were the priests that crucified Jesus and all his disciples, then we can trace them along. But if they were evil spirits which the Devil sent into the priests and prophets, we can also follow them down. The people were divided on this point. The priests taught that they were the chosen ones to put down the evil spirits, not that such were in them. And here is where the war commenced. The priests, like the demagogues, had power over the masses and as the people believed in these evil spirits, of course there would be different opinions about their power. The most superstitious were the easiest led and as the priests had full possession of the minds of the masses, it was very easy to interest them in their favor.

So all opposition came from a more liberal quarter, but yet governed by the same belief in the spirits of the dead; so science had nothing to do with the religious quarrel. The quarrel commenced about a false opinion, existing only in the minds of political demagogues and science is as much a stranger as in any political quarrel. Still they hold out to the people that they are their friends and thus they have got the world to admit their wisdom. What do these parties propose to the people? To restore order and happiness to man. I will give their platform. They have established the fact that there is another world, which constitutes one plank. The return of spirits to earth is another. Also the Devil leading the wicked into trouble. These and a still larger number of grievances are laid down as facts. What do the leaders propose? To get up an army and attack this devil and in the name of goodness reform the world, drive the devil out of existence and establish the kingdom of heaven on earth. This is the appeal to the people and as this is a spiritual war against the devil's kingdom, it is necessary that the people should know what they are fighting for and who are their leaders, etc. The priests like the demagogues have made the people believe that they have been deceived and that it is necessary that they should do something to get out of their trouble, while the troubles are the effects of their beliefs invented by man and all the warfare is to fight down their own beliefs. So it is with the sick; the devils are the priests' opinions and the disease is the punishment of their belief. So the people pay the priests for the opinions and get the reward thereof in aches and pains.

These are the profits of the priests, for they know that the people know not the author of their misery. They offer their services to fight down the very evil they have created. In spiritual as well as in literal wars, there must be opposition parties, some for the health and some for the disease. As the war is in the minds of the people, the destruction of life is what is aimed at. Health and happiness being the land of science, the destruction of either cripples both, so all their aim is at this land. All will admit that this land is overrun with every kind of devil in the form of disease. How to destroy them is a matter of opinion, so parties spring up and make war in their peculiar way. The priests are for driving them out by prayer, while every prayer goes to create more devils. This is seen by another class called educated or more scientific, the doctors. They calculate more scientifically for their own benefit and have induced the people to give up to them all those who are killed by these devils in order that they should examine and discover the place of rendezvous.

Thus the people have given them this power over all who fall by disease. So when a person is attacked by one of these children of their own make, they commence war against it. If he attacks them in the side, the doctor claps on a blister. If he flies to the head, he also follows him there. If he goes to the stomach a dose of calomel is sent after him. This generally starts the devil and ruins the man and his house being shattered to pieces, he gives up the ghost and leaves. Then the doctor claims his prize; so he cuts up the head like a vegetable, hanging up one part and preserving the other in alcohol. They contend this is all for the benefit of the people and like the priests in Egyptian theology, instead of lessening the evil, they create ten times as many more. Finally, the people in despair, like Saul, have left their oracles and sought witches or those having familiar spirits, to enquire how to get rid of these Philistines that are overspreading the land and devouring their lives and substance. So in the darkness of night, they disguise themselves and are seen making their way to some woman having a familiar spirit to inquire of her how the battle is going on with their friends, for the doctor is fighting the battle. In a trembling voice, they ask if the spirit will respond; a faint rap is heard denoting yes. Then the communication is open and the spirits have the field. Here is war between the living and the dead. A revelation commences, but as both are in the devil's employ, it makes but little difference to the scientific man which gets the day.

April 1861

Symptoms of Disease, The
[LC 2:0098]

I will give the symptoms of a person who called on me to be examined. The upper part of his body above his hips felt so large that his legs were not strong enough to carry the weight. Therefore he complained of weakness in his knees. This idea of weakness etc. was his mind for there never was any strength or knowledge in his knees of themselves any more than there is power in a lever of itself. If the lever or legs had to create its own power, his body would never move. Therefore if his body ever moved, it must be by some power independent of his knees or legs.

There is such a thing as pressure, but pressure is not power, for if it moves it is not pressure, for it contains motion and motion is another element independent of pressure. These two elements together are called mechanical power, so mind or matter agitated is called spiritual power. Neither matter nor mind contains any knowledge. Now as this man's mind or matter was in a state that it contained motion or error, for error is motion not knowledge, it was not all pressure. Now as health is the enjoyment of all our faculties, any foreign substance trigs the wheels so as to retard the motion; so error trigs the mind or retards the motion. This was the state of this man's body. Now to put this man in full possession of his faculties is to remove the burdens that bind him down. These burdens are the effect of error having control of the mind or matter. These errors are made of mind or matter first formed into an opinion; then comes reason; then comes disease or death accompanied with all the misery the idea contains.

October 1859

Taking a Disease
[BU 3:0751]

I will try to define what I mean by taking a disease. Mind is matter and is under the direction of a power called the senses. The senses embrace no knowledge of themselves, no more the mind, but the soul or intelligence is some way connected with the senses, like the power with the direction. This same combination runs through all mechanical science; the direction is the wisdom that directs the senses. The senses cannot act at all of themselves–only as they are acted upon by this power called wisdom. This wisdom can act upon the body or independently of the identity. This is all there is of man. The senses are under the direction of wisdom, either right or wrong, that controls them either by science or error, or for good or evil. As matter is an idea, I shall class it all together but attach the senses to it in some cases and detach them in others.

I will illustrate. Suppose I think of Niagara Falls; my senses are no part of the falls, nor are they attached to them. Now suppose a person should undertake to throw me, that is, my bodily senses, over the falls; my senses are attached to my body and both are matter, but one is under the senses and the other is independent of my senses. The trouble lies in my knowledge of the result of being thrown into the falls; that is drowning, which is losing my identity, senses, matter and all there is of me. Now put me in possession of the fact that my senses will not be lost, if the identity of my body is, then death is swallowed up in truth. As our knowledge is progressive and a higher power than ourselves, we know God only as we know ourselves, so that eternal life is in the dark. Our knowledge is in our belief and we are taught that our body contains the senses; we have no proof that they can act independently of the body's identity.

So when I am afraid that my life is in danger I am afraid just as much as my knowledge sees any danger of losing my life. So I stand nervous and trembling for fear that I shall be thrown into the falls. The fear is not in the falls, nor in my knowledge, but in the ignorance or idea that I shall be lost if I fall into the water. Now suppose I escape. The idea is now a part of my bodily identity, not the falls, but the danger. This is my disease. By the doctor this is called nervous, but is all the disease there can be. This is being bound in heaven or the mind. Now till all this is cleared up, the mind, as in a dream, is groaning over the trouble, fearing to be destroyed. This trouble, being a part of the matter, throws off a heat or atmosphere and the soul or senses are in the scene. Every person who comes within this atmosphere affects me because I am afraid. This knowledge or fear, for it is fear, is not known to another as knowledge but as fear or a peculiar state of mind which they construe falsely, giving a false interpretation to my acts because they know not my trouble. Now if the fear changes my bodily identity, producing a deranged state of matter which can be seen through the bodily senses, this effect is called by the profession, disease and treated as such. So their explanation is like Aaron's priesthood, where sacrifices are offered up every year but which could never take away sin or error. Therefore to cure man of disease or error, it must be done by a new priesthood, not after the order of Aaron that can never explain it away but after a higher and more excellent priesthood that can take upon himself our infirmities, can bear our burdens and lay down his life to save the sick.

Now return with me to the falls and behold a young person standing trembling, with flushed cheek and quivering lips, with cold and clammy perspiration starting, urged on by her friends to make the last leap, never to return. Urged I say, for error is always urging us on to destruction. Now in the midst of all this confusion, a voice is heard out of the clouds of error saying, "Be not afraid, there is no danger." They all stop and lo! I appear before her enemies, for it happens to be a young female, sentenced to be cast into this lake never to return. There stand all her earthly friends, weeping and forcing her along. Just as she approaches the precipice, I seize her by the hand and command her enemies to desist. A sort of parley takes place and I propose to run the risk of my own life to save the lady. This being agreed, I then say a few words to the friends. I tell them there is no danger of her being lost and will run the risk of my reputation to convince them of their errors in regard to her disease. This act washes away her sins or error and establishes the doctrine of eternal life, which is to them a mystery. So I step forward to the brink and in I go–now lost to sight and gone forever. In an instant I am seen on the surface perfectly calm, with not a ripple to be seen. This, to bystanders, is a miracle; so I repeat it till the fears of that danger are passed. Then I return the young lady to her father's house where all will rejoice, as all fears of the danger are gone. Health is returned and again she is ready to embrace some other errors of the priests and doctors.

The errors of these two classes of mankind give rise to all the evils that flesh is heir to. They are separate and apart from all science and do not embrace one single truth but are the stumbling blocks for the truth to overcome in arriving at science. It is true that they were once necessary evils, but it is time now that man should look about and see if there cannot be a higher mode of worshipping God or science from a higher principle than fear. For say what you will, the whole foundation of the creeds is based on fear. This fear causes all the misery in the world and I will show how it is grafted into the mind.

All mankind have a kind of reverence for something they call God. No matter what name you give it, most admit it and their fears of it depend on the idea they have of this power. For at the same time that they call it God, they call it a power–supposing that God is in the power, whether it is good or bad. Man in his wisdom has undertaken to give an explanation of God's wisdom and define what is good and what is bad or what is right and what is wrong and has tried to make the people believe that they are the true oracles of God. So they get up certain laws and forms of obedience to God, just as though the father of wisdom had condensed his wisdom into a little shell about as large as a coconut and required of man certain acts for his own gratification. If the child will obey these laws, he holds out to him all sorts of happiness, like a toy shop, where they can get just as many playthings as they desire. This is in one hand. In the other he holds out a direful rod, with all the horrors that a crazy brain could invent. These, like the pillar of fire and cloud of smoke that went before Moses while he was leading the people of his age, go before the people in our days. And the people now as then murmur and complain at the food that they receive from these spiritual guides.

July 1860

Thought
[Originally untitled.] [BU 2:0003]

Thought, like the blossom of the rose or tree, contains all the elements of the tree or rose. Now as the law of vegetation governs the tree or rose, so the law of mind acts upon the idea or spiritual tree, known by the name of good or evil. Now although this tree differs from all other trees in the garden of man, it cannot be detected except by its fruits, and as the fruits appear pleasant to the eye of the mind and are supposed to make men happy, it is cultivated without knowing the peculiar properties it contains.

Now as this tree grows it sends forth its thoughts like blossoms, and as it is looked upon as a fruit much desired to make one well, it is received with joy and cultivated in the garden of our minds. Now in the beginning of the creation of man this tree was a tree that differed from all others in men and was very like the tree of life. The fruits of this tree have been the foundation of all the philosophy of man ever since man was created.

Now as man's natural body contains the soil for this tree to grow, as the earth is the soil for the rest of the trees and herbs and creeping things that have life, it is the duty of man to investigate this tree and see what its fruits contain. The tree is to be known by its fruits. This tree is an idea like all other ideas in man, but differing in one peculiarity, happiness and misery. All the rest of the trees of knowledge contain right and wrong without any regard to happiness or misery. This is the difference between the trees.

Now as this tree can bear the fruits of other trees, it is another reason for its being cultivated, but to understand the tree or idea is to understand its fruits or thoughts.

I shall now call this tree an idea which contains happiness or misery and also truth and error. Now as error, like the serpent, is more subtle than any other idea in man, it acts upon the weaker portion of our thoughts and ideas and engrafts them into the idea of happiness and misery. Now as this idea grows and sends forth its fruit, it is conveyed by error to other trees or ideas in others, and thus spring up false theories, false doctrines etc. Now as this tree or idea sends forth such a variety of thoughts or fruit, it is like Joseph's coat of many colors, hard to tell what was the original color or idea. This throws man into darkness and doubt and he wanders about, like a sheep without a shepherd, running after false ideas. Being blind, he is not capable of judging for himself and suffers himself to be led by the blind.

Now as the tree of knowledge of good and evil was an idea of happiness and misery, it is easy to detect its fruits. All other ideas are spiritual, and the fruits or thoughts are spiritual and are not perceived till they come within our senses. We are very apt to get deceived by them, for they come like a thief in the night when man is off his guard. Now as health and happiness is the greatest blessing that can be bestowed on man, and this was the original fruit of the tree, it can be very easily detected from the grafted fruit or ideas. The original fruit is spiritual and cannot be detected by the eye, for it does not contain even spiritual matter.

Its qualities are sympathy, harmony and peace; the fruit of evil contains matter, and has form and can be seen and felt.

To the Old Whigs
[LC 1:0434]

How often we see editors accuse each other of their party being the cause of this trouble. The Democrats accuse the Abolitionists and the Republicans accuse the South. Now when there is a difference of opinion it may be that neither is right. Every person, sixty years of age, knows that formerly there were two parties, the Federal and the Republican party and that the South was divided like the North. How came the whole South or nearly the whole South to change and become united against this party now called Republicans? My first vote was thrown for Jackson. Adams was elected; Calhoun nullified the tariff and was put down. The Democratic party at that time never advocated free trade. Now it is one of their measures, so Democracy covers that, but it is one of the new Democratic features. At that time the Whigs advocated the tariff as the Republicans do now.

There was at the North and South another party kept up by the leaders of the Democracy; this was the ultra party. The Democrats had their hobby to keep their party together, while the Whigs advocated the constitution and equal rights to all. The Democrats, after the free trade policy became grafted into their creed, commenced the cry of aristocracy and tariff, that the people were taxed for the benefit of the rich and the duties came out of the poor. This bugbear had its effect on the South and they kept up the cry that it was to build up the rich at the North at the expense of the South. By this kind of deception the defeated party got into power and thus deceived the people into free trade. Now how does it happen that foreign nations are opposed to a tariff in our country if the consumers pay it? What difference to them is it if we pay the duty? But that is not the fact. The tariff, like all other competitions must reduce the prices if it is not so high as to act as prohibitive. You cannot name an article, with one exception, that is manufactured that has not fallen, and that is liquor. That is a democratic doctrine of free trade.

I will admit that liquor has risen by competition, for when there was no competition, foreign liquors were high and yet were retailed at three cents a glass in all saloons and at the first class houses it was but six cents; now there is forty times as much and not half as pure. And yet under the Democratic doctrine of free trade, it has risen to three times what it formerly was. Now the poorest N.E. rum is six cents and logwood brandy is ten cents a glass. This fine free trade doctrine has got up a feeling against the two sections of the country. It is one of the bugbears of Democracy and another is the negro question. That has had its effect and is still harped on by the Tories of the North, who are the very ones that have caused the destruction of the political parties. The Democratic party is the cause of all this trouble. When the Whigs of the North and South were in sympathy with each other, the northern Democrats were accusing the Whigs of being Abolitionists for the purpose of uniting the South.

The Democrats at the South were telling the Southern people that the Whigs were against them at the North. This deception of the Democrats of the South drove all the South together and split up the North by aggravating a few fanatics that always voted so as to throw the power into the Democrats' hands till it broke up the Whig party. Then the honest Democrats united and commenced making war with the two parties. The Democrats attacked them as they did the Whigs by calling them Abolitionists. This enraged them and it led large numbers of their friends to leave the Democratic party. The Whigs who believed this humbug thought that all who joined this new party must be Abolitionists, so they abandoned their party and went in for the extension of slavery, when it never was a question at the time of the two parties. The Republicans of this day are on the same platform that the Whigs of the North and South occupied thirty years ago and then the Democrats did not dare to advocate the doctrine they do now. Here is the beginning and end of all Democracy. It was born in sin and its growth has been its own destruction. It has finished its work and given up the ghost; its leaders will go year after year to the polls and look on the party that has transgressed all honor and patriotism. And their consciences will burn with guilt and they will become the outcasts of society and the abhorrence of all the parties.

Now let every old Whig ask himself this question. What did the Democratic leaders accuse you of; was it not that you were Abolitionists? You know whether you were or not. This has been all the trouble at the South. It was for political power. Do not these Tories accuse you now of being Abolitionists? Does not the Argus try every way to identify Republicans with Abolitionists? Read that paper about the first of September 1861, quotations from Henry Clay about the Abolitionists, and then turn to the time he made the speech, and in that same lying sheet you will see that the same paper that now quotes him, there called the Clay party, Abolitionists. Here is the inconsistency of the Democratic party. The Whigs never were and never will be Abolitionists; they were for letting slavery alone and for having Congress do the same.

Sept. 10, 1861

To the Reader [I]
[LC 2:0850]

In introducing this work to the reader, my motive is to correct the false ideas that are in the world or man's mind in regard to his health and happiness. I take the ground which the wisest men who have written have made the basis of their reasoning. They have searched into the hidden mysteries of the mind to find what it is and in their researches, they have found themselves at last in despair and some have ended their lives by their own hand. Others have been made insane, all because they could not solve this one idea, mind, for the word mind is applied to all the intelligence of man and embraces soul and life. My object has been ever since I commenced investigation to see if it was possible to find out how far the wisest philosophies had penetrated the dark recesses of this unknown science.

One of my first objects was to ascertain what mind is, for if the mind dies with the body, then all the fuss and trouble of living and using our minds to be of importance hereafter would be of no value. So I made it my first object of inquiry. Of course I took for my basis the old scriptures and found that the mind was ourselves and at death there was the end of man. Then I found a soul spoken of, but when I looked for that, I could not find that any person had ever seen it or heard it. So I went back to the heathen philosophers. I found they were in the same dilemma in regard to the soul as they were to the mind, and both according to their own philosophy ended at death. For death was admitted by both Christians and Pagans to the soul and body; for how often do you hear this passage quoted by professors of religion: Fear not those that can kill the body, etc., but rather fear those that can destroy both soul and body in hell.

Now then, if the soul can be destroyed, I came to the conclusion that Paul did. If there was not anything based on a more solid foundation than the opinions of certain men, then I for one would not believe anything. So at one sweep I discarded the Bible and all sorts of religion as the invention of man and came to the conclusion that man like a clock was made to run about so long, more or less, and then run down. As I never could find anything of man independent of the machine, I, of course, like the rest of mankind, by my belief took it for granted that when the machine ran down, it had finished its work and must be laid away.

Yet, there was a sort of nervous restlessness in my mind that if there were not a first cause why should he not have someone to keep these machines running. I knew that I could make a clock and if I sold it to another, I put him in possession of wisdom enough to keep it wound up even if he could not repair it when it got out of order. But as I never saw anyone that seemed to repair man when he got out of order, but rather increase his misery, I came to the conclusion that Job did when he said, "Mine eyes hath seen all this, mine ear hath heard and understood it. What ye know, the same do I know also: I am not inferior unto you: surely I would speak to the Almighty, and I desire to reason with God; but ye are forgers of lies, ye are all physicians of no value. O that ye would altogether hold your peace! and it should be your wisdom." Job 13: 1-5.

I had come to the same conclusion with the wisdom of man in regard to man's happiness: that all his wisdom only went to make man more miserable. So I launched my barque out into the ocean of thought trying to baffle the winds and waves of the wisdom of this world till death should settle up all my accounts. A disbeliever in everything as far as a future existence went, I lived a stranger in a strange land, till the waters of public opinion were stirred in regard to mesmerism. I floated around, not moored to any person's opinion in regard to creeds or religion but still a believer in the medical science; for I never employed a quack nor took a particle of quack medicine in my life, neither had my family. So I was clear from that sin, as it was called.

When mesmerism first started, I, of course, being independent of all prejudices, went to see some experiments. I shall never forget seeing a boy thrown into a state perfectly unconscious to all surrounding objects, cold, lifeless and still, at the mercy of the operator. Here was the first rock that my barque struck. This gave me a sort of shiver and a cold chill passed over my whole frame. Twelve minutes before I had seen him walk on the platform, now cold and insensible to pain and yet under the control of another. This set me to thinking and being very fond of investigating every new phenomenon, I tried the experiment and succeeded in getting a person under my control. This was called mesmerism, but being ignorant upon the so-called science, I commenced to read upon the subject to inform myself. I obtained the best works at the time and read them to find out what it was.

I learned that it was electricity, etc.; so all my experiments went to prove it was governed by the laws of electricity. When it rained, I could not produce any experiment. This was according to my belief and my belief was based on someone's opinion that knew just as much as I did. They had more experiments but no more wisdom, for I found after a while that the more I thought I knew, the less I really knew. For at one time when it rained as hard as it could pour, I being ignorant of it had some of the best experiments I ever had in all my practice. So I came to this conclusion in regard to mesmerism: that man had begun to philosophize before he understood anything about the subject he was trying to teach others. So I put my barque out to sea again, determined not to run onto the rock of the "science of mesmerism," for I had found that all this wisdom was of man and they called it wisdom of a science, not understood. So I found that it was knowledge, not wisdom. Then I made up my mind that if there was anything in mesmerism, I would know it but I would not be led by man's opinion. So I became an infidel to their religion or opinions, not in the phenomenon.

I found a young lad some fifteen years of age that I put into a mesmeric state and when with him I found that all I had learned, I had to relinquish, for it was the effect of my own ignorance. Among the things I had to lighten my craft of was phrenology. This is one of the humbugs of the day. I shall show that there is no foundation in truth for it. You can judge after reading my experiments. Lightening my craft, I made sail for what was uppermost in my mind, to see whether there was any wisdom outside of what we call man. My first experiment was made before I knew what I wanted to prove. For when I put my subject to sleep, after trying a few experiments, I thought I would leave; instantly the boy jumped up, went to the table and brought my hat. This was unexpected, but it was just what I wanted to know, if he could read my thoughts. At first I was all aback, but after recovering myself, I said to myself, If you will replace my hat on the table, I will stop a little longer. Without saying a word, he sprang up, took my hat and returned it to the table. Here was another fact I had gotten, not an opinion but a truth.

1863

To the Reader [II]
[LC 1:0535]

In introducing this work to the reader, my only excuse is the existence of evils that follow the opinions of the world in regard to man's health and happiness. My practice for 20 years has put me in possession of facts that have opened my eyes to the misery of mankind, from ignorance of ourselves. My object is to correct the false ideas and strengthen the truth. I make war with what comes in contact with a person's health or happiness, believing that God made everything good, and if there is anything wrong it is the effect of ourselves, and that man is responsible for his acts and even his thoughts. Therefore it is necessary that man should know himself so that he shall not communicate sin or error that will rebound to his disadvantage.

All my writings are the effect of impressions made on me while sitting with the sick so that my book is of the lives and sufferings of my patients, their trials and sorrows, and my arguments are on their behalf. It may seem strange to the well that I write upon so many subjects, but when you take into consideration the great variety of persons and the peculiar state of literature varying from the most cultivated to that of the lowest intellect, it would not be strange if my writings did not excite the curiosity of the reader.

For instance, one is all full of religious ideas and becomes almost insane, and some are entirely so. This excites me, and my thoughts run upon religion. Another will be almost insane upon spiritualism; then I have to battle that or show the absurdity of that belief. Some are excited upon Millerism and believe the world is coming to an end. This brings up arguments to refute their belief, some upon witchcraft. Now their minds are continually dwelling on all these subjects and on the Bible. So to cure, I have to show by the Bible that they have been made to believe a false construction. My arguments change their minds and the cure comes. This is my excuse for what I have said upon the Scriptures.

Some people are lovesick and disappointed. These are not a great many. Minds are affected in various ways. Some are shipmasters. Their sickness is caused by various things. But all mankind must be reached by parables so I illustrate by such parables and symbols as they can understand. All my illustrations are called out by the case I have to treat. Females are more spiritual than men; therefore with them my illustrations are drawn more from the Bible than from any other work. The medical science I have to use rather hard, for the sick have the most bitter feelings towards the physicians and the religious teachers. These two classes I have to come in contact with. The fear of these two classes makes the patient sick. I have found this out by the effect the patient has on me. I have been so provoked when sitting by the sick, with the physician and also with certain classes of disease, that it was with the greatest difficulty that I could keep my temper, and I had never seen the doctor or minister. But I always found that when I would get the patients clear from their opinions, they would express themselves in as strong terms as I had. I thought the fault might be with me, but I am now satisfied that I was only the scapegoat to carry off feelings they dare not lisp out but could not tell why. Therefore, as far as I am concerned, I have not the slightest feeling as a man towards any person but error. That I have no sympathy with. It is a hypocrite in myself and in everyone else.

You may say that I have gone out of the way to attack religious denominations. If I have, the fault is in my patient. Everyone knows that some very pious persons, when sick, are the most profane and talk the worst about the Bible. This is because they are the most in fear of it; this is the cause.

With these remarks, I will leave this part of my subject and say a word or two in regard to words. I differ from all persons about some words. One is "mind." Mind to me is not wisdom but spiritual matter. And I think before you get through my book you will think so too and be convinced of the truth of what I say. So far as my education is concerned, I need make no apology. If I have learning enough to explain my theory, it is all I want.

1864-65

To the Sick
[LC 2:0902]

Dr. P. P. Quimby takes this way to give the sick and those who need his services a short illustration of the manner of treating diseases, as they are called by the medical faculty. My mode of treating the sick is entirely new and original with myself. I have no similarity or affinity with any other mode of practice. Therefore, when others undertake to identify my practice with any other, they not only misrepresent me but show their weakness by so doing. For everyone that I treat that can understand me at all will see that I am entirely different from any other person. Those that have some selfish motive to identify me with mesmeric practice use this argument: it is nothing but mesmerism, etc. Others that wish to class me with the spiritualist say it is spiritualism, but I won't own it.

Now this mode of misrepresenting me I, of course, can't help, only as I make my patients understand. And as it is easier to let it go that I am a spiritualist or anything else than to explain, they let it go by, saying I don't care what you call it if I get well. So it makes it very hard for me to separate myself from others who claim me as one of their kind, but I can see and explain where I differ from all others. All persons of every rank and profession believe that disease is a thing independent of the mind, and also that it can affect the mind. Now all classes agree in this that there are curative properties in certain medicines and that certain kinds of food give strength and also certain exercises, etc. In fact a sick person is a complete slave to the medical faculty, to be acted upon just according to their little narrow, contracted wisdom, narrowed down to a certain belief. Now all of the above is to me superstition and ignorance. If every man and all sorts of drugs were out of existence, it would not be twenty years before a race of people would spring up healthy and happy, if all other sciences and improvements went on.

I have been twenty years in the practice of curing disease and learning, the causes and I have learned that nine-tenths of the sick at this time would be well and hearty if the medical faculty were annihilated. Neuralgia is one of the commonest diseases of the day, but this is giving way to a new invention called the spine disease. And there have been such improvements that this has almost lost its identity in the new inventions of human diseases. This has opened a field for the medical faculty. There cannot be a female of any respectability but she must be insulted by these quacks with the idea that she has this disease in some form or other. Now all the above cases I can treat and cure almost at once, from the fact that of all humbugs, it is the greatest, and the medical men know it, for they are not blind. Look at the cures performed by the mediums and the quacks as they are called and you will see that eight out of ten belong to the class of diseases above spoken of. And they are got up by the medical faculty. These men lead the people and give direction to their minds and in this way, they gall the people and they rob them of their health and get the people sick and in despair. And in their trouble they seek a witch or those that have a familiar spirit to enquire of them.

Now what I am trying to do is to convince the sick and all those who want to keep well that my mode of treatment is entirely in opposition to the above. What they call disease, I call an effect of deception; this deception I call the disease, and the effect that follows, they call the disease. I will give some illustration. Take a healthy person, if you can find one, tell him some exciting story which makes him a little nervous. Now here is the ground for the medical sower to sow his seeds of disease. He commences by telling the patient that he or she is liable to have the consumption, so some humbug is started in the form of inhaling into the lungs. This makes the patient nervous and then a new improvement is introduced to inhale into the stomach. This prepares the way for all variety of diseases, like falling of the womb, internal ulcers, ovarian tumors, weak spine, heart disease, etc. Now I say and stand ready to prove that all the above diseases are made by the medical faculty for their special benefit. A more miserable humbug was never invented and men and women pay their money to these quacks for what never had an existence outside of the profession. These diseases were never known to the people seventy years ago, but now every female is liable to be affected by these diseases. The medical faculty have been the means of lowering the female character, for they feel guilty and ashamed of themselves. For they have been made to believe a lie and they can't help it. Now I never make any examination, nor apply any remedies of any sort, but simply tell the patients how they feel. I know they have been misled by these quacks and deceived into a belief and this belief is the cause of their troubles and to correct it is the cure. This is a very easy task, for the deception is so apparent that it does not take much sagacity to correct it.

Then there are other classes of diseases that cannot be cured so easily. Rheumatism that affects the legs so much that the joints become stiff. Such I would advise to stay at home if they think to be cured at one or two visits. All bedridden persons that have the use of their limbs but can't walk from weakness, I have cured very soon. But those that are paralyzed on one side or both had better stay at home for the expense will be more than the good they will be liable to get. Persons smoking or chewing, if they have any disease that they would have me treat, independent of tobacco, I can cure; but if they are well and choose to smoke or drink or chew, it is none of my business. It is a matter of their own. But if they are sick, then if I find that tobacco hurts them, I almost always cure them at the first sitting. If any person is nearly gone with consumption, I should advise him to stay at home, unless it is to be relieved of their distress. So it is with a great many kinds of disease. This circular is to send to those that write for information. With this is a circular giving some idea of my method of curing.

1864

To The Sick–[A Printed Circular]
[LC 3:1470]

DR. P. P. QUIMBY would respectfully announce to the citizens of _____ and vicinity that he will be at the _____where he will attend to those wishing to consult him in regard to their health, and, as his practice is unlike all other medical practice, it is necessary to say that he gives no medicines and makes no outward applications but simply sits down by the patients, tells them their feelings and what they think is their disease. If the patients admit that he tells them their feelings, etc., then his explanation is the cure; and if he succeeds in correcting their error, he changes the fluids of the system and establishes the truth or health. *The Truth is the Cure.*

This mode of practice applies to all cases. If no explanation is given, no charge is made, for no effect is produced. His opinion without an explanation is useless, for it contains no knowledge and would be like other medical opinions, worse than none. This error gives rise to all kinds of quackery, not only among regular physicians but those whose aim is to deceive people by pretending to cure all diseases. The sick are anxious to get well, and they apply to these persons supposing them to be honest and friendly; whereas they are made to believe they are very sick and something must be done ere it is too late. Five or ten dollars is then paid for the cure of some disease they never had nor ever would have had but for the wrong impressions received from these quacks or robbers (as they might be called), for it is the worst kind of robbery, tho' sanctioned by law. Now, if they will only look at the true secret of this description, they will find it is for their own selfish objects–to sell their medicines. Herein consists their shrewdness, to impress patients with a wrong idea, namely, that they have some disease. This makes them nervous and creates in their minds a disease that otherwise would never have been thought of. Wherefore he says to such, never consult a quack. You not only lose your money but your health.

He gives no opinion; therefore you lose nothing. If patients feel pain they know it, and if he describes their pain he feels it, and in his explanation lies the cure. Patients, of course, have some opinion as to what causes pain. He has none; therefore the disagreement lies not in the pain but in the cause of the pain. He has the advantage of patients, for it is very easy to convince them that he had no pain before he sat down by them. After this it becomes his duty to prove to them the cause of their trouble. This can only be explained to patients, for which explanation his charge is_____ dollars. If necessary to see them more than once, _____ dollars. This has been his mode of practice for the last seventeen years.

There are many who pretend to practice as he does, but when a person while in "a trance" claims any power from the spirits of the departed and recommends any kind of medicine to be taken internally or applied externally, beware! Believe them not. "For by their fruits ye shall know them."

[1860-1865]

To the Sick in Body and Mind
[BU 2:0005]

Dr. Q. has been induced by the great number of cases which have come under his care within the last twelve years to devote his time to the cure of disease. His success in the art of healing without the aid of medicine has encouraged many persons who have been suffering from sickness of long standing to call and see him for themselves. This has given him a very great advantage over the old mode of practice and has given him a good chance to see how the mind affects the body. He makes no pretension to any superior power over ordinary men, nor claims to be a seventh son, nor a son of the seventh son, but a common everyday man.

He contends there is a principle or inward man that governs the outward man or body, and when these are at variance or out of tune, disease is the effect, while by harmonizing them health in the body is the result. He believes this can be brought about by sympathy, and all persons who are sick are in need of this sympathy.

To the well these remarks will not apply, for the well need no physician. By these remarks I mean a well person does not know the feelings of the sick, but the sick alone are their own judges, and to every feeling is attached a peculiar state of mind which is peculiar to it. These states of mind are the person's spiritual identity, and this I claim to see and feel myself.

When there is discord in these two principles, or inward and outward man, it seems to me that the outward man or body conveys to me the trouble, the same as one man communicates to his friend any trouble that is weighing him down. Now all I claim is this, to put myself into communication with these principles of inward and outward man and act as a mediator between these two principles of soul and body; and when I am in communication with the patient, I feel all his pains and his state of mind, and I find that by bringing his spirit back to harmonize with the body he feels better.

The great trouble with mankind is this. They are spiritually sick, and the remedies they apply only serve to make them worse. The invention of disease, like the invention of fashion, has almost upset the whole community. If physicians would investigate mind a little more and medicine a little less, they would be of some service; but this inventing disease is like inventing laws; instead of helping man, they make him worse. Diseases are like fashions, and people are as apt to take a new disease as they are to fall in with any new fashion. Now if there was a law made to punish any person who should through any medical journal communicate to the people any new disease and its symptoms, it would put a stop to a great deal of sickness. Seven cases out of ten throughout the whole community of old chronic cases are the effects of false impressions produced by medical men, giving to the people the idea they have spinal disease, or heart or kidney or liver disease, or forty others that I could name, to say nothing of the number of nervous diseases.

Now all of these ideas thrown into the community are like so many foolish fashions which the people are humbugged by. I do not dispute but that any of these diseases may be brought about through the operation of the mind, but I do say if there was no name given to diseases, nor symptoms, there would not be one-tenth of the sickness there is at this day. I have taken people who have been sick with all of the above diseases, as they thought, and by describing their symptoms and state of mind without their telling me their trouble, have satisfied them what the trouble was and they have recovered immediately. A person sick is like a person in a strange land, without money or friends. Now there may be someone nearby who would be glad to receive such persons, but they are ignorant of them. The sick are not in communication with themselves, nor anyone else. They feel as though no person could tell them how they feel. [unfinished]

To the Sick: The Conflicting Elements in Man
[LC 1:0424]

A sick person is two beings: one of which is opinions and the other Science. The senses or life is attached to both so that man is not seen at all, but the result or idea is seen by the idea matter. Wisdom is what is called progression; opinions are aristocracy. These two powers are acting in opposition to each other. All they agree in is an identity called themselves or a kind of marriage or co-partnership, like man and wife. The idea body is called man, but each claims the right to act through it in their own peculiar way, like a telegraph company. It is the medium of both unless in times of war when the strongest power controls the company. Now a man sick is a deceived man, for wisdom never deceives anyone, while error is always in trouble. So after man is once set in motion, he is then like a ship ready to receive the master. Every state of mind is under the control of these two elements: one is caution and the other is recklessness. The regulator is wisdom or science. This never acts except when the other two get into a quarrel. Then it acts by harmonizing the two, not by compromise but by convincing recklessness of its error and caution of its fear or ignorance.

I will try and illustrate. Take a person with the hip disease. He is a man of opinions called hip disease. This is one person; science is the judge; progression or recklessness is the other person. Progression wants to go ahead; opinion is afraid of the danger; it reasons according to its evidence. When the man was well, he was neither one nor the other but a natural progression. When started or excited these two characters are at war and each wants its way. I will take this combination of individual and suppose him one man at first, well or in harmony with himself, that is, having no opinions or ambitions. At last something starts him. Progression wants to get rid of the enemy; opinions want to stop and argue. While in this quandary, another man of opinions comes along and asks the trouble. Opinion states that there is trouble in the leg. Opinion wants to reason. Progression does not want to reason but to go on, let what will come. They halt. The man of opinions or doctor looks very wise and asks all kinds of questions of ignorance until he gets the entire story and sees that the opinions of the sick man are based on ignorance or no opinions at all.

Then he gives his wisdom based on the opinion of ignorance that the sciatic nerve is affected and the inflammation may spread and reach the hip joint, which would cause disease. In that event, amputation and possibly death may follow. Ignorance receives this as true and now the man is made of opinions and ambition, although the latter is ignorance as long as it is held in check by opinions. Now ambition wants to walk, but opinion says, "Don't step; it will injure the limb." So these two are at war till someone wiser comes to help. The wisdom of the man listens to the arguments of the two. I will take the lame man, as he is seen, and myself talking to him. I say to him, Won't you try to walk? This is addressed to the man of opinions or the natural man. He makes an effort and then says, "I can't. My hip pains me and I can't step at all." Now I know there is no pain in the hip, so I say, The pain is not in the hip, it is in the mind. This sometimes makes the patient angry, for he thinks it is in his hip. I commence to reason; this makes him nervous and he says his hip pains him. I then ask him what idea he has of the hip. He says the doctors have examined it and have pronounced it hip disease, accompanied by an infection of the sciatic nerve.

I then say this name is the cause of all your trouble. He says "Oh, no! I felt the pain long before I saw a doctor." Well, suppose you did, is there any intelligence in the pain? (P) Yes. (D) What? (P) Why, when I have a pain I know it. (D) Who knows it? (P) I myself. (D) Then you yourself exist when you have a pain? (P) I suppose I do, I know my hip aches. (D) Would your hip ache if you did not know it? (P) Yes. (D) Does your other hip ache? (P) No. (D) How do you know? (P) Because I do not feel it ache. (D) Then because you do not feel it ache, it does not ache? (P) Yes. (D) Then if you do not feel the lame one ache, does it ache? (P) I do not care anything about your reasoning. I know my hip aches and that is all I can say and if you can stop it, that is all I want. (D) You get nervous? (P) Well, you make me so nervous, you make my leg ache. (D) I have not touched your hip, have I? (P) No, but your talk makes it ache. (D) I know that and that is just what I want to convince you of. (P) Well, if that is what you want to do, you have succeeded. (D) Now I want to show you how your hip became as it is.

In the first place, God never made any intelligent ache or pain. The intelligence is attached to the intelligence of man. I will give you an illustration. Suppose you should have a lead pipe leading from a well to your house and that you should drink the water. You admit that the water in the well is good, but if it runs through a lead pipe it is poisoned; the one who tells you that story disturbs your mind, but the disturbance contains no intelligence. Yet, as you reason his belief into you, you become poisoned and you put your belief into the water, so that according to your belief, you poison yourself. You now become diseased with your own belief or the doctor's. You said my talk made you nervous, so it did, and so did the doctor's and my controversy is with the doctor's belief or poison. So you listen to my controversy with the doctor or your disease and I address myself to the disease as a person independent of yourself, as a man of health. In this way, I say to your disease, it has deprived your life or senses by its opinions and disease denies it and asks for proof. I say you have told him his hip is diseased. Disease will ask him if his hip is not lame. Of course, he will say, Yes, for he believes it true.

September 1861

To Those Seeking the Truth
[LC 1:0435]

This is written to show you how you stand in regard to this truth and how I stand in regard to you. This applies to all persons seeking after the truth. I will liken it unto a treasure in the wilderness of which you have heard and go in search of. You start in your search with no guides but what you have seen and enjoyed. You hear of men embarking in the enterprise, but not having found it shortly return to their own opinion. You listen to their story and learn as far as they are concerned they have never seen one who has entered that land of light, where disease never comes. They all after a short time return and live and die in their own belief. This makes you feel gloomy; then one comes along saying, I have felt the warm atmosphere of the place; it invigorates me and I felt as buoyant as though I had been in the air. This gives you courage and you pray that you may be guided by this light that you see now and then dimly and so you travel on, sometimes in the dark, guided by a power that you cannot see, sometimes by the light of Wisdom and then you take courage.

Now in the darkness of the night, you hear the cries of the sick who are tormented and you halt, not knowing what to do. Then some unknown hand reaches out and in a whispering voice says, Fear not, pass forward; then come the groans of the dying and you tremble. At last the voice of the sick dies away and the light of Wisdom springs up and you see the prize you are seeking for in the darkness. So you tread lighter and lighter till you become so buoyant that you feel as though you did not weigh anything. Now you are standing in this place between opinion and Wisdom and looking at everything as you see it, but not knowing the names of things you meet. You hesitate, but you have gone so far that you cannot get back, yet not far enough to feel sure that it is the land of the living. So you are surveying the land and reasoning about it. At last, shadows will appear before your eyes and your senses will be brought into play. The shadows will take form, then life will enter. Voices like the rushing winds will salute your ears, and you will look and individuals will arise of flesh and blood. Then you will know that you have passed from death unto life; your belief is lost in sight, you will not doubt. Your grief will be turned into joy and you will see that all your misery is in opinions. And as you grow, you will see the error of the world's opinions.

I will now tell you where I am and how I am leading you along. You are in the old world or testament. I am in the new world or testament, not P. P. Quimby but this truth. It is the light that lighteth everyone that cometh into this world and to make you understand it, it takes upon itself flesh and blood. So when it speaks, it speaks not as man speaks, but it speaks the truth, not opinions. The natural man is opinion, not wisdom; the scientific man is not flesh and blood but wisdom. And where wisdom is recognized by the natural man, then the natural man is not far from the kingdom of heaven. To gain the kingdom of heaven is to gain Science. There are many kinds of science, but they are all from one great wisdom. And science is the name of that particular application of wisdom to a particular phenomenon. For instance, chemistry is the name of a wisdom reduced to practice and the practice is called science. Now man looks upon chemistry as something separate and apart from him as much as religion, while chemistry is one of the elements of his own existence, for it contains no matter. So it is with mathematics and all the sciences that ever have been developed. Man is just as large as he is wise in Science, so science is that solid that will break in pieces all opinions. There is one development of wisdom that has never been acknowledged by the natural man and when that is acknowledged, the natural man then becomes subject to a higher power. This is the Science of Wisdom whose fruits are health and happiness. This is the foundation of all other sciences. It is the rock of wisdom and man is made of it. Opinion is its servant and when the servant becomes the master, then the wicked reign and the people mourn.

It may be asked if health and happiness is a science, how can it be put into practice for the benefit of man? I answer, Just as you put into practice any other branch of wisdom for man's good. All wisdom that has been reduced or developed is the growth of the scientific man. And as wisdom is developed, it is put into practice for the happiness of man. Opinions or beliefs are the natural man, and as he dies, the spiritual or scientific man takes his place. Just as the wilderness is the natural man and civilization clears away the trees and cultivates the soil, so the natural man is full of brutal and false ideas warring against himself. And science lies and sees the wicked do wickedly till their wickedness is destroyed by the weapons of their own make. As the wisdom is developed that sees through all the evils of the world of opinion and belief, it corrects the error and establishes the truth. This changes the natural man into a man of wisdom that will see that human misery is based on an opinion. Let a person just look at himself as the image of his maker and he will see that man is a complete image of the very God he ought to worship.

I will make the one living and true man: the father, the son and the Holy Ghost. The scientific or wisdom is the father; the idea man or matter the son, or flesh and blood; the explanation of the unity is the Holy Ghost or wisdom. These three make the one living and true man. The father or wisdom will reign through the son or matter by the word or Holy Ghost till all enemies are explained through the son. Then the son shall become subject to the father or science and wisdom shall reign all in all. In the days of old, this wisdom spake through the prophets. At last, it spake through science or a wiser medium, but it has never spoken to the sick in prison. But ancient and modern philosophy has looked for the true Messiah or Wisdom that shall open the prison doors, burst the bolts and bars, break the chains of superstition and set the captive free. When this comes, there shall be a time such as was never seen before, when the priests and doctors shall hide their faces from the people to keep from being ridiculed for their superstition and ignorance. They will be set down on a level with the old Salem witchcraft. Their power shall be taken away from them and they shall be turned out to eat the fruits of their own labor. Then to be religious is to show the world that you can correct some of the diseases that have been invented by these blind guides. As man knows himself, he learns that all he is, is his life, and his senses are in his life, that opinions are mind subject to his life. His life embraces all his faculties and his happiness is in knowing that he is no part of what is seen by the eye of opinion. The world is the shadow of wisdom's amusement. All that is seen by the natural man is mind reduced to a state called matter.

October 1861

Trinity of Opinions and the Trinity of God or Wisdom, The
[BU 3:0243]

Man as we see him combines two trinities, although he is ignorant of it. I will try to condense one into a personal identity. Error is the father, belief is the son or body, wisdom is the Holy Ghost or reason. To make it clear, I must take a person where the trinity is the plainest. I will take a sick man for his is the plainest one. The error is the tyrant, the belief is the son or offspring of the father. The error wants to hold the truth in subjection, for the truth is the wisdom of God in man, not developed. So error disturbs the mind and a belief is formed. This belief contains the penalties and these beget fear. Here you have opinion, the father, the belief, fear or punishment, the son and the knowledge of all, the Holy Ghost. This is the world's trinity.

The trinity of God is wisdom or God, the father; health, science or wisdom in practice the son; and the explanation of the two, the Holy Ghost. These three are one and the same in power and wisdom. And to be born of the spirit of wisdom is to break from your wickedness or opinions and turn to the truth. The new birth is to put off the old man, that is error, with all his belief and put on the new man or Christ. It is to destroy all the old superstition of the old world and enter into the world of science where opinion and belief never come. In this world there is no more death or sighing, for the old things are explained away. Death and hell and he that hath the power of death called error is cast into the lake of fire or science that will burn up all the chaff or error, and the new Jerusalem shall be established in the hearts of men. Then the sun or wisdom will light up his new world; there will be no more night or ignorance, and all will bow down before the throne of wisdom and sing the song of everlasting life. The error has its creeds and religious worship, for it worships this great truth in a mystery; so it reasons about the other state or world because it does not know what it reasons about. Therefore it makes to itself a God just according to its knowledge. It lays down its articles of belief for opinions have now become a belief. Truth or wisdom is not in its creeds, but a firm belief in the error.

The first article is to believe in a First Cause. Not knowing what it is, it calls it God and believes that the man Jesus is his son, and the Holy Ghost is the power that God gave his son Jesus. So in their blindness, they pray to this unknown God, to whom they have attributed all the faculties of man. They believe that he requires certain duties of man for his own special benefit and if they will fulfill those laws that he has given them, they will be received into his kingdom and if not, they will be cast off. You see there is not the first word of wisdom in all the foregoing but a simple belief founded on someone's opinion. Long before all this belief, people were religious but their religion had no heaven nor hell, and in fact they nearly all disbelieved in anything after what they call death. There were a few who believed in a resurrection of the dead at the end of the world. Therefore the other world had but little effect on people's lives for they did not believe that God would reward them after death. If they did wrong, however, they were punished by some plague or evils that would affect the body such as leprosy, scrofula, etc. Their religion consisted in forms and ceremonies, temples and altars, etc. all of which could never explain away their superstition.

But the tide of progression rolled on, and wave after wave swept away some of the old landmarks of superstition and the people were carried off on the waters of science, flowing from the great ocean of truth. Yet they were like fog tossed about by the winds of superstition, not knowing where to fly. In this ocean of progression, the voice of John was heard crying in the wilderness of error, for he had kept up with the current but was not carried into the sea like some others. So he broke the silence by the voice of his reason and exposed the hypocrisy of the priest. Now Jesus being posted up on all the theology of the day went to hear John.

As I have said, the idea of a science to test man's goodness was never dreamed of by the wise men of his age. The truth had made its way along in every branch of the sciences except goodness, and goodness being what follows our acts, to know how to have it and to attach the wisdom to our acts is a science. So religion is the nursery of disease. The belief made men sick and unhappy but the idea of another world had no hold on the people.

October 1862

True and False Science
[LC 2:0683]

Man's belief makes him what he is and he is subject to all the errors of the world as far as his life and happiness are concerned. This science of happiness embraces all sciences admitted by scientific minds, but the knowledge of it separates the real from the spurious science. It proves that a belief in any science that can be proved never makes a man sick, but one that is based on an opinion is false. For example, all religion is based on an opinion. The healing art must be a science or an error, and when its advocates claim it as a science, the people have a right to call for proof. So it is with any new question; it must be demonstrated to skeptics on an admitted principle.

There are persons claiming wisdom or science, and when asked for proof, they give their opinion, while every scientific man knows that any opinion is merely a babbling about what is not understood.

Nebuchadnezzar understood this and when he besieged Jerusalem, he gave a command that they should bring certain of the children of Israel and of the kings and of the princes, children in whom was no blemish but well favored and skillful in all wisdom and cunning in knowledge and understanding science, and such as had ability in them, to stand in the king's palace and whom they might teach the learning and tongue of the Chaldeans. Here Nebuchadnezzar knew that there were babblers or men of pretense among them even in his own palace, so he found that such science as theirs was only opinions about what they knew nothing. Paul warns Timothy and says, "Keep that which is committed to thy trust, avoiding profane and vain babblings and oppositions of science falsely so called." Ever since the world began, there has been a war in error. But science never makes war nor has any hand in it; it never dictates but reasons what it knows. Error is Science falsely called.

Now I claim that my cures are done by a true science and so do all others the same. This was just the same in the days of Jesus. The false science or saviour or Messiah claimed the same power as Jesus, but the latter contended there was a difference. The world has never been shown where it is and the false science has had the day up to this time. Now I profess to show where my practice differs from all others and also to show that their professed science is nothing but an opinion based on an error. My science consists in proving that this is only an error and their misery is what follows the error. To prove this, it is necessary to show that man is made sick by his belief and cured by it and that all there is of man is error, ignorance and science. His life and senses are in these and they make up man. So when a man goes to a doctor, he is in one of the two, ignorance or error; he cannot be in wisdom, for wisdom cannot be ignorant or in error. Error is opinion, reason is knowledge and is always showing what it knows. Ignorance is the child disturbed. I will take for illustration one who is sick and a spiritualist. He sits down and after I have told him how he feels and he admits it, I begin to tell the causes. This requires his attention and, in listening, he grows nervous and says, "I don't want you to talk; that won't cure me. I came to be cured." Well I answer, "That is what I am going to do and I want you to listen while I tell you what has made you sick." "I don't care what has made me sick. I want to get well. I believe you can cure me and that is all I want. I don't want to hear you talk. I am a spiritualist and so are you, but you won't admit it so it does not make any difference. Just cure me and let your talk go; you cannot change my mind." "What do you believe," I then ask. He answers, "I believe you get your power from the spirit world." These believe that I have a power. This belief requires no reason or thought, only a belief in a spirit world which has all the spirits of the dead. To reason is to get them nervous, for they cannot understand. It is much easier to admit an error than to try to understand it. Such a person stands in relation to a doctor as a scholar who comes to his teacher with a mathematical problem and wants him to work it out for him. The teacher tells him where his error is, and then goes on to explain how he got into it and to teach him how to get out of his error. But the pupil says, "I don't want you to explain it; it makes me nervous. I only want to get out of my trouble." The teacher replies, "I want to make you understand that there is a science." But the pupil says, "That is all nonsense." The same is the case with the spiritualist. He says to me, "You have a power which all men have not; some men have more electricity than others." I answer, "Electricity has nothing to do with it." "Well," he says, "It is of no use for you and me to argue. I know it is all spiritual electricity, so just correct the evil and that is what I want; you cannot change my mind." So I cure them in their own belief and save them in their sins or ignorance, ready to get into trouble again the next day. This is the case with a great many. They want to hold on to a belief and then be cured of it. They want me to admit a disease and then want me to cure it by my spiritual power, so their belief makes them sick and their belief makes them well. My wisdom cures and they are none the wiser.

There is another class of minds like the following. A person comes to see me. I commence to tell him how he feels, and he admits it. I then say your mind is affected; this makes you nervous and you believe you are troubled with dyspepsia. He answers, "I have the dyspepsia but my mind is all right." I then ask him why everything looks so dark and gloomy and why he feels so alone in the world. He says, "My dyspepsia causes it." I say, "I have no dyspepsia and yet you make me feel as I have described." He answers, "I don't know why." I then say, "It is caused by your religious belief. You cannot understand, so it makes you nervous, and you put your trouble into your food." "My religion does not make me nervous," he answers, "it is the only thing that gives me happiness. I cannot give up my religion. I would rather die than give it up ." "I do not want your religion; I only want to show you how afraid you are to "have it touched." "I did not come to have you talk to me about religion. I came to be cured of the dyspepsia."

Here is a person with whom I have to argue until I change his mind. His mind is the disturbed state of his matter. His belief is the bugbear that frightens him, and his fright changes his mind. This is the disease and the misery is the complaint or feelings. As I am not afraid of such a belief, I stand to a person like the above as a pilot stands to a captain when he is in trouble and calls for one. I know my business, and if the captain won't listen to hear me tell him how he got into his trouble, that does not prevent me from getting him out of his trouble, but the captain is none the wiser.

The next kind of patient is the lawyer. Jesus could not make much out of this class of minds, for their wisdom is all arbitrary. They never argue from scientific principles but from law, and everyone knows that law is arbitrary. I sit down by the learned lawyer just as I do with all others and tell him his feelings. Sometimes he will admit them and sometimes he will not, except as a guess. I commence to explain and he breaks out with, "I know what the matter is, I understand the structure of the human system. I know the liver is turgid, the lungs are irritated, etc. I understand my difficulty. Do you think you can give me anything to help me?" "I never give anything for disease; I believe all disease is in the mind and my explanation cures." "Well, my mind is not troubled; I have a local disease." "That is your belief, and that is just what I must change." "But you don't understand," the lawyer insists. "I have a disease of the liver; I understand my trouble." I answer him, "If you understood yourself, you would have no trouble or belief. I explain your feelings in my way and by enlightening you and showing you the cause of disease, I make you see that you have embraced an error which is the cause of your misery. When you see this, you will lose your belief and gain knowledge." "Poh! This is humbug. You need not think to come such game on me. You do not use words correctly." Then he goes on to quibble about words and puts me down on the ground that I have no education. There he has the advantage certainly. He quarrels all the time with me and seems very much afraid I shall gain some advantage over him in argument. His native intelligence is cramped by law and his opinions are molded with the intention of getting the better of his opponent in some little matter. He is blind and deaf to the fact that there is an intelligence superior to an opinion. Still I cure him and he goes on browbeating and blackguarding, pleased with coming out ahead in such warfare.

April 1862

True Christ and the False Christ, The
[BU 2:0120]

I will try to explain or separate the true Christ from the false Christ and show that "Christ" was never intended to be applied to Jesus as a man, but to a truth superior to the natural man, and this truth is what prophets foretold. It has been called by various names, but is the same truth. There is a natural body of flesh and blood–this was Jesus. His mind like all others was subject to a law of truth that could be developed through the natural man. This power Jesus tried to convince the people of, as I am trying to convince the people that there is such a state as clairvoyance, that is, that there is something around us which the natural man is unaware of that has an identity and can act upon the natural man. When this power acts upon his senses it acts in the form of an idea or thought. The natural man receives it like the servant, but acts as though he was the father of the idea. The world gives him the credit for this superiority over his fellowmen.

But unwilling to admit this power, the world attributes it to some unknown cause as the best way to get out of their trouble. They would rather have it a miracle than a science, for otherwise it would lower them in the estimation of themselves and cause their own destruction, as all truth destroys error. This belief in an intelligence independent of ourselves has always been admitted, but attributed to some miraculous power from another world.

1860

True Life is Health
[BU 2:0103]

True life is health, knowledge and happiness, all in this belief. Death is disease, error, misery and pain, all in this belief. Each of the above is called our knowledge, and to believe in one is to disbelieve in the other, for our life is in our belief. Death is the destruction of the one and the life of the other, or the disbelief of the one and the belief of the other. Christ came to destroy death or belief and bring life and immortality to light, and this life or belief was in Christ. They that lost their life or belief for his sake or belief should find it. Upon this rock or belief I build my faith and the gates of death cannot change me. Now your life is in your belief and you are known by the fruits. My life is my belief. Now as I impart my belief to you, it is your life or health; and as you receive my life or belief, you die to your own; and my life in you grows to a belief and this belief is your health or happiness.

November 1859

True Love*
[Originally untitled.] [BU 3:0771]

True love is pure above all earthly feelings. It would lead one to lay down one's life for a friend and what more can one do? It is independent of all we see with the natural eyes. Its attraction is not of this world. That feeling is a part of us, then there is a part of us that exists independent of what we can see. That is the real man. He is eternal. He never can die. Forms may change. He is independent of forms. This is love—a spark from the great love that fills all space and is the beginning and end to all things—from whence all things rise in which we all live and move and have our being. It lights and warms, it comforts and consoles. It is tangible because we can feel it.

Then that which feels it is not the body because this love does not address itself to the body. This proves then that the sense of feeling is not in the body. So all our senses are independent of the body, but we locate them there.

Now this love is the Creator of all things. For his own pleasure he made the world. He created the matter and then put it into form. He gave to everything its own life. The mineral, the vegetable and the animal world all have their allotted spheres or action. They fulfill their destiny and then dust returns to dust and the spirit to God who gave it. But to man, God gave something higher. He breathed his own breath into man and he became a living soul. All other created things have their limit, a circle as it were in which they move and generation after generation they come around to the same spot they started from. But man improves. He investigates and understands science, which makes him a king, a God, so far as he understands it. Now man takes his place as a ruler—and here begins his trouble. He does not know nor acknowledge his higher nature. He reasons as the animal does if he reasons at all, that matter contains all intelligence, that life is _in_ the plant and death the end of life—that all action, all heat and vitalities are generated in the material form. He does not know in the first place that he exists outside his body, that in a world which we cannot see with the natural eyes everything material takes its source and is a shadow of the hidden substance. He not only denies his own higher nature, he denies his God every day of his life as if a plant contains its own intelligence and knows how to take care of itself, what need has it of any other care? So with the body. It is just a machine it is true, but can a machine oil itself? Now the Lord has freed us so that the oil is supplied if we act in accordance with the true principle of life. What is the true principle of life? It is that from Him springs our life, not some other, that from Him we derive heat, action, sensation, intelligence, happiness—everything that we are capable of feeling. That is the real man. God is not ashamed to acknowledge us as a part of himself—why should we hesitate to accept the position? With this mode of reasoning we accept our bodies as a house given us to live in and the intelligence which keeps the house in order is no part of the house itself, but independent of it and which we must try and understand if we desire our own happiness.

True Wisdom
[LC 1:0416]

Let me give you an idea of true wisdom and how it acts on man. True wisdom is like heat. Now you know that heat in the soil of the earth brings forth vegetation. Vegetation is like ideas. Wisdom warms the heart of the mind or matter. This puts vegetation or thought in action so the mind brings forth food or ideas; these being forced by the heat or activity of the soil, they grow like a tree, and the root or fibers take root in the soil or mind. As it grows, it derives its life from them and the mind being fed by the wisdom of the world, the tree takes up the particles it receives. The earth brings forth all creeping things, everything that has life as well as all diseases. They grow in the mind like a tree.

August 1861

Truth [I]
[LC 2:0811]

Words are sounds to represent something that contains matter or form or they are applied to some imaginary thing. Now the word truth is applied to either of these two ideas. So when a person says a thing is so and so, if we believe it, this is a truth. Now separate those things that we can't see clearly from those things that are in the dark, and then apply the word truth to such as have a substance according to man's belief and those that have no substance only as a belief, and then you will know what is truth and what is not. For instance, what you know, you are not a part of, but it is yourself; but the thing known is something, not of you, but outside. For instance if I say to you, did you ever see a house? Now you see you are no part of the house but outside of it. But if I ask you if you ever saw a man come to you after he is dead according to your belief, you will say, No, but if I ask you if you believe he has a spirit, you say I believe he has. Now don't you see this belief contains no substance only a shadow and it requires darkness to produce it.

So ignorance is darkness and truth is light. So as you come to the light or science, the spirit or belief or darkness will vanish, for there is no substance in it. So every word is nothing of itself till it is attached to some idea that contains a substance. So to separate the truth from error is to correct the error that makes the trouble called sickness. Now I class all the troubles of man among those truths, based on a false mode of reasoning, for when a person knows a thing his opinion ceases and he comes out of the dark and stands in the light. So everything we don't know beyond a doubt has a shade of darkness. For instance if I ask you if you can see the figure five, you will see it plain in your mind, but if I ask you, if you see the answer to 75 added to 5, 13, 19, 6, 31, 100, 99 and 75, now you are in the dark and you see no answer till after you add them up in your wisdom and set them down in the mind. Then your wisdom can see the answer in the mind, but before this there must be a chemical process to develop the mind so the answer would come out, and when it is out, the opinion is gone, and you stand outside looking at the answer.

So with disease, the seeds of opinion are sown in the mind from a belief of man, for as I have said, mind is matter and governed by his belief which is matter, and the wisdom is also matter and is all a part of the same and the truth destroys both. So when the world gets wise enough to learn that what cannot be seen outside of the man is nothing, if the thing seen is the effect, then it is not certain that it exists at all. For instance all diseases like religious opinions admit something that you cannot see. This is all as far as man's health and happiness is concerned, for if he admits it as a truth, he certainly is liable to create the misery of his folly.

For instance, heathen superstition is now believed to be all fiction or nearly so, even the city of Troy, the siege of Babylon and lots of others. We get as good and correct an account of them as we do of London and why should we not believe one as well as the other? Just because we know persons that have told us that London exists, but no one who had never been to London, but was transferred to London in his sleep and then awakened, dare risk his life and wisdom to say that he knew it was London. Therefore if he was as sure as he could be without asking when he was told that it was London, this would not make him any more sure. After getting satisfied, his belief is gone, and he stands outside in his wisdom. So it is with all these old fables. They are accounts of all kinds of diseases and how the people died and the symptoms have been handed down to this day. The plague of Egypt is one, although all the history is based on a fabulous account of what never had an existence. Yet we hear of this old disease being in existence. So all this goes to show that whatever has been handed down for history and been believed is as catching as the evils that are invented by the medical faculty of our days. Modern fables or stories are as popular as the fables of the ancients. Neither have an existence outside of the mind.

1864

Truth [II]
[LC 1:0525]

How are we to determine what is a truth? The dictionary says it is conforming to facts, veracity, certainty, exactness, faithfulness, etc. Now all this does not settle the fact how to tell what a truth is. We wish to find some ways of testing facts in order to know how to define the truth so that persons won't ask what is a truth. Now the truth is like the word right; neither would be needed if there were not something to change; but as changes are continually taking place, the discord is called wrong. When all is harmony, that is called right. So right is a truth and wrong is a discord. To apply the word truth to discord or belief is using it in another sense. If two persons agree upon anything, they call it a truth, but the truth is in them and not in the discord or thing believed. For instance, two persons believe that there is such a thing as a ghost. Now if they believe it, it is a truth to them, but it is not certain that the ghost exists outside of themselves. The word truth used in this way applies to all sorts of error. But there is another mode of testing the word scientifically. I will give a case where the right and wrong truth came in, for the word is only to assent to what one or more believe. I will show how I test the word.

A patient calls on me; I sit down by her. I feel a sharp stinging pain in my breast. This I tell to the patient as her feelings. This she says is true. So here is a real truth without a belief for its basis. I now tell the patient that she thinks the pain arises from a cancer coming on the breast. The patient says, Yes. Now here is another combined truth, for it combines the two: the fact that she believes she has a cancer and that I know she does. But in this there is a discord, for I know there is no truth in it, but the truth is in her belief. So the discord is in these two truths. It is also a truth to me that there is no cancer. Now to destroy the belief of a cancer is what I try to do. My reason is to destroy one truth that is founded on a belief and establish health and then she will enjoy it. This is a truth and we both agree to this last result as a truth, that she never had a cancer, only as a belief.

Language was invented to communicate a sensation from one person to another. Now if there never had been any sensation, there need not have been any language. So as sensation is the first action in matter or mind it required some way to describe it. So of course discord would make the idea. Then the opposite is harmony. So every word must conform to this rule of discord and harmony. Discord is disease; harmony is health and every person starts from one or the other of these two bases. The word truth is applied to both, but if there was not any discord, there would be no need of harmony, for before there was discord all was quiet. So that it is a truth that there is such a state as discord in the mind, but the discord is in us and not in the thing spoken of. The discord is not in the tune but in those that hear it, for if there were no one to hear it, there would be no discord.

Now there are certain things that would exist if there was not a man on the face of the earth and certain things and conditions that would not exist, for instance, our senses. When a man dies, as it is called, if his senses die with him, then everything that pertains to man ceases. But no one would say that if every man was blotted out of existence that everything that existed would go with man. But if we look at it in the right sense, destroy the wisdom that man has and you destroy creation. For with wisdom they are all as dross. For everything that moves and has life is in wisdom and there is nothing outside of him. Now as wisdom sees through everything, matter is to wisdom a shadow, but to man it is a substance and yet man creates things that to the one that creates them are shadows. So the ideas that man has created and brought into being, which cannot be seen, are the things I shall speak of as being of that class I call discord, to which the word truth is applied. The invisible world or the things believed in that have their existence in an invisible world are as real to those that believe them as those things that are seen and felt by the natural senses. And both have the same identity in the natural world and are called truths and here is the error in language. To make it plainer, I will illustrate.

Suppose I tell you a story that I know is a lie and tell it as a truth and you believe it. Now to you it is a truth and you believe it, yet I know it is false. Now the question is how shall man distinguish between the two? One is based on a belief and the other on a fact, yet you cannot show the difference between them. Here is the lack of language expressing the true meaning of what a person wishes to express. It all arises from admitting a lie at the beginning. Then someone began to account for some sensations after his own thought and told them as if they were true. This error, once introduced, started up a sort of false reasoning, based on an opinion or false basis. And from this false basis has sprung up all kinds of theories of another world and God and disease. And as men have received them as living truths, man assumes them as facts and all his wisdom is based on them. This is called the Bible and if this false theory is not admitted, then you disbelieve the Bible. So now the question arises, what influence prompted the writer of the book or did they have any higher object than those men that wrote about the rebellion of our day? We know that there are certain events spoken of that happened before the New Testament, but did the people who wrote the book believe that they themselves were inspired from any superior power over their followers that they could not learn? Now to me every man when he writes has his two influences, but when he has nothing to test his wisdom by, it is of no value to the world.

1864-65

Truth and Error
[Originally untitled.] [BU 3:0131]

Mind is the medium of a power or powers superior to the natural man. In speaking of mind we naturally embrace this power, as in speaking of a lever, we often embrace the power that controls it. In the latter case the mistake arises from our ignorance of mathematics, for if we understood the science of mathematics we should never confound the lever with the power moving it. So in regard to mind, the body may be compared to dead weight, the mind to a lever, both governed by a superior and intelligent force. There is no intelligence in the body or in the mind but only in the higher power that governs them. The natural man cannot understand this and as happiness or misery follows our acts and our acts depend upon our knowledge of ourselves, it is not strange that we are often in trouble.

All men admit the existence of these two motive powers, truth and error, but not as powers independent of the mind and superior to it. Every development of science reveals the higher one to man; he sees and recognizes it in particular instances but never as the one controlling power which shapes and governs all our right actions. The other, or lower one, is animal power and a servant of the first. To know ourselves is to separate and distinguish these powers from the mind which they govern.

Truth, Day and Night
[LC 2:0810]

Truth like fire is an element of itself. It cannot be divided. It embraces every element of itself. Error is a compound of ideas or mind. The senses are in self-existence or a knowledge of itself. All the foregoing exist in an invisible state and can only be seen through a medium. Yet it contains within itself all the power and wisdom that exists. It speaks matter into existence. It gives life to what it creates. It sets bounds and makes laws. It creates and destroys. I am now speaking of man as we call him. He is God on a small scale, and yet he is but one ray of light from the great fountain of wisdom. I will now try to show how he, that is this wisdom, creates matter or disease, for I shall show that the phenomenon called disease is matter according to our belief. Divide man into light and darkness or matter and wisdom. For example, we speak of tomorrow just as though there was another day separate from today. Now the word conveys the idea of two different days as much as though you saw a man yesterday and you also saw him today, showing there was space and time between the two events.

Now the man was the same but the space and time was in you. So it is with day and night. We divide up the year as a man divides a wheel. The surface of the globe is divided into twelve spaces and each space into equal parts according to their length. The spaces are called nights and the parts called day. So in fact the earth is a great wheel whose circumference (in round figures) is 25,000 miles. This is divided by twelve, not in equal parts; then each part is divided into days and the spaces are nights. Now this we all believe, not exactly as I have stated, because we never stop to think of it, yet we speak of day and night as though there were two separate days. Now if we are on the day called Monday, for we must be on the day, if on anything, when do we step off on to the day Tuesday? I can't see myself stepping at all. The day I make by my education. The earth is like an apple and man is on it and if he lies down and sleeps and wakes he is on the same spot as he was, and if he chooses to call that sleep, night, to him it is night, but the earth has no such idea.

Now suppose a man could get his light from some source independent of what he believes and the sun's light had nothing to do with his light, would he divide the earth's surface into three-hundred and sixty-five days and just as many nights? No. Then you see that night and day are conditions of man. Now this looking for tomorrow is like looking for disease. Neither exists outside of the one that is looking. Then what need of being troubled about what you know does not exist only as you make it. We are not aware that we are affected by our belief. So if we do what we believe is wrong and our error will come to light, then we fear the morrow because we have transgressed some belief. So disease is what we are afraid of. We fear the morrow lest it come. Now true wisdom destroys the darkness or night and it becomes all day or light. So wisdom destroys the darkness of disease and we see its existence was in us. Then we shall not be afraid of this imaginary day. Then we say, Sufficient unto the day is the evil thereof. Let the morrow be as a condition of progress. See what will develop, the progress of progression.

1864-65

Truth, How Determined?
[BU 3:0289]

What shall I liken truth unto? I will liken it unto a schoolmaster who calls his pupils around him and delivers unto them a mathematical problem, and to everyone a problem according to their several abilities, with directions how to work it out, and then goes his way. And when he returns he calls his pupils around him and inquires of them the answer. The first comes and says, Master, you delivered me this problem and here is my answer. The Master, or truth, sees that it is right and gives him the prize, and then calls on another and another till he calls the youngest of them all. Then he says, Master, you gave me too hard a problem and I could not do it; here it is. Then the truth gives the problem to one that can do it and casts the unprofitable direction into outer darkness and gives to the child another that it can understand. So everyone that understands the true directions will arrive at the truth, but he that understands it not will be misled and the evils or misery that follow are the result of the matter, and the destroying of the matter or error is the changing of the direction and the hell or misery is the name of the effect that follows our act, and the heaven or happiness is what follows the same. Therefore, we cannot serve both masters at the same time. How shall we know whose servant we are? I will give you a sign. When anyone comes and says, I know the truth, ask for proof, and if you find that it is based on an opinion, do not believe it because he says so but listen to inward answer. In this way you will steer clear of a great deal of misery.

1864

Two Brothers
[LC 1:0577]

There once were two brothers who looked very much alike. They were in the same business, dressed alike, were both lame and each had a pumple foot. Their names were John and William R. A gentleman wished to find John, but could not recall to mind his given name and he asked a friend if he had seen Mr. R. Which one? There are two brothers. The lame one. They are both lame. Well, the pumple-footed one. They are both so. Well he is a pedlar. They are both so. Well, this man trades too. So do both. Well, my man is a Democrat. So are they both. After thinking awhile, he says, He wears a buffalo coat and drives a lame horse. So they both do, replied the other. Well, said he, I will give up and wait till I can see him. The difficulty was that the gentleman was not aware that there were two brothers. As soon as he learned the fact, he must find out the name in order to discover the right one.

Wisdom is the surname and Science and error the given names. Science is the Christian name of wisdom and error that of ignorance. Neither ignorance nor wisdom act, but as matter is the medium of both, it is difficult to distinguish them unless you know their surnames. All through the Old Testament, these two opposites are found as Adam and Eve, Cain and Abel, Jacob and Esau. And in the New Testament, Jesus and Christ, Paul and Saul, etc. These two characters are in every person, but the natural man recognizes only one. Both can create, God or Science through the scientific man, and error through the natural man. And if you do not know their names, you will be liable to be deceived.

Opinions is the man that can invent stories and give false directions, that is, creating disease. Wisdom never creates an idea that tends to make man unhappy. Wisdom is outside of matter while opinions are in matter. The masses of the people are the medium to act upon. An error exists in the masses which sets the mind at work and after error has created a disturbance, it has not wisdom enough to guide it. Being in ignorance of its wrong ideas, it finds fault only with itself and guides and controls the storm by what intelligence there is in matter. Error will fault but cannot show any reason for its acts. After the storm has raged and destroyed the country, as those out of matter had prophesied, then the same ones who caused the trouble commence a war against the expenses the government have been to, to put out the fire these same persons have kindled. Error commences the trouble by exciting the minds till a phenomenon is produced. And while science is all the time trying by mild means to correct the lie, error is attributing the cause to science. After it succeeds in correcting the lie, then error berates it on account of the cost it has been to for nothing, trying to show that had the capital been spent in another way, how much better it would have been.

This is a fair example of how error works. When error is so subdued that science takes the lead, then the two characters will be recognized and kept separate and the acts will determine which is of science and which of error.

In order to show how error can invent a lie and have it admitted as truth, I have only to refer to the rebellion. Every intelligent person will admit that had there been no slavery in this country, we should not be engaged in the present war. Here we have a starting point–slavery. Now the idea slavery exists in the minds of man and every man individually will admit that he wants his liberty; yet, if everyone had his liberty as the world is now, there would be no liberty at all, for by abolishing all laws, perfect liberty would be granted everyone. Then might would be right and man is so constituted that the stronger would enslave the weaker. A compromise must be made between liberty and slavery. In this compromise, man has no right to bind or enlarge its bounds beyond the contract which is confined to what the parties agree to.

The United States has great extent of territory and it embraces the two brothers–freedom and slavery. To act on the agreement of equal rights as far as possible, an agreement was made that the majority should decide which brother should govern them when any new territory was annexed to the old homestead. As the party for freedom increased, as it always will, slavery being the opposite contracted with aristocracy and wanted that which it could not get by the agreement. These two brothers are elements in every person and the government is the voice of the one or the other. They are chosen as President or oracle to utter the voice of the people, and the people are the matter to be acted upon. Slavery is advocated and wants its power extended and all the elements of the institution are brought to bear to help its progress. Freedom also appeals to the people to prevent the spread of slavery. Now as freedom and slavery are wedded together, as it were, a family quarrel ensues and the children take sides with one or the other of their parents. Slavery is the father or brutal man. Freedom is the mother. As slavery has the brutal strength of the father, it endeavors to crush out freedom. But freedom having the sagacity of the mother is shrewder and keeps herself more on her guard, while slavery having no other motive than to rule tries to govern by its will.

Freedom is more powerful and is always on the lookout, while slavery being a brutal element has no regard to self preservation. Its motto is, Let us eat, drink and be merry and take no thought of the the morrow. So it does eat and drink till the flood of liberty comes and washes it away. Man's life, his health and his happiness is as much a science as chemistry and his errors will submit to wisdom as much as they do in chemistry. Tell a person or a multitude of persons that you can raise a ship upon the hydraulic principle with a gallon of water and they will laugh you to scorn. You tell them, I do not wish you to believe what I say merely because I say it, as I can demonstrate it. Then when you show the experiment to be true, their mouths are closed and they bow in reverence to the law or principle.

When man can be shown scientifically that his life is one that can be lengthened or shortened by scientific computation, or changed from good to bad and bad to good, then he will bow to that principle. The good does not change to bad nor the bad to good, but science destroys the bad and the good lives, while error only creates bad and covers up the good. Man's life and happiness are the things to be attended to as that is for his happiness. For if he is unhappy and without health, he is of all beings the most miserable. It has not entered man's mind that his happiness is an effect and not a cause. In mathematics when a person is working out a problem, if it is difficult, he is unhappy until he arrives at the answer. Then if the answer is correct, he is happy and his error is swallowed up in science and his science becomes wisdom. Man has analyzed everything but himself which to him is a complete wilderness and full of false ideas which run wild and destroy all his prospects. He rises in the morning apparently safe from these wild beasts or ideas but before night, he is caught and devoured, else his estate is mortgaged to the devil for a ransom to get rid of some error that he has been accused of, such as going out of doors and taking cold, contrary to the laws of his God. Man becomes a slave to the medical and religious world and is all his life subject to their laws. This is the way that science is punished by its own. It comes to its own and its own receives it not but turns and opposes it. All the happiness that man has, has had to pass through the fire of excitement before it could establish its claim; yet, there never has been a person who has been able to resist this wicked generation that holds the life of man in slavery. Let man's wisdom once get its standard established, that he must fight his way through the rebel armies of medical and religious ideas before they will abandon the field to him; then he will buckle on the armor of God or wisdom and fight the battle of liberty from religious and medical slavery and establish the Science of God in the intelligence of man. Then opinions will be cast out and man will live by science, for opinions lead to death and misery, while science leads to health and happiness. Then he will see that disease is the creation of error and that the introduction of science is its destruction.

Man's happiness is in his wisdom and as he frees himself from the medical faculty and their opinions by analyzing them, he destroys the phenomenon of disease which he has built in himself, and this edifice or disease is matter and is made by error and can be destroyed by science, for wisdom does not recognize any matter and man's life is in it. Science is the light of his life with which to light up the lamp of wisdom, and as the light springs up, the error dissolves. Now admit this truth as a science and then the man will walk by science or light, instead of error or darkness. Then he will learn that this world which contains all kinds of disease, evil spirits and every miserable idea that makes us unhappy is of our own make and created by our beliefs.

We can create this idea called matter and condense it into any form that our belief is capable of forming. And if our power of imitation is sufficient, we can form any idea we choose. Every disease is a manufactured article of our own make and children being but a lump of our own ideas, their mind or matter is as much under our control as their education. We can teach our children to be just what we wish and even give form to their matter and certain actions to their bodies. So we can create tumors, coughs, and every disease that flesh is heir to. Mind or matter is like mortar or potter's clay. And no one can deny that the clay in experienced or scientific hands can be made into better vessels than in the hands of an unscientific person.

Mind is like the clay and wisdom and error are the potters. Error can make vessels which wisdom can destroy. For error is merely an apprentice to wisdom, as it were, and when wisdom molds the clay, error stands aside. The two characters are spoken of by different names. Paul spoke of them as the inner and outward man. If there is not some way to distinguish one from the other, how are we to know which one speaks? The word science is not used but once in the Old Testament and once in the New Testament. The people knew that there was a difference between a truth and an error, but the two characters could not be known except through the oracle or medium through which they spoke. The natural man or error put the wisdom in the oracle, but the scientific man puts the oracle in the wisdom. This makes two invisible beings acting through one oracle. Therefore to know which one spoke, it was necessary to have them named. They named one and the other when it became old enough to have a being. Science was never applied to the inner or the outer man by the world, but science is the one and error is the other.

The natural man is composed of gases and these gases must have a separate identity. If the gases ever had identities, they must have had them in their original state. If the gases separate, are the two characters of man, then man can have an identity when he is separated from the gases which make what is called flesh and blood. If oxygen is the life of man, then there must be life outside of matter, for the oxygen cannot be destroyed or changed. Therefore the oxygen is the outward man. Now divide the gases into two characters. One, that character called truth or wisdom, the other error, and then the element embracing truth cannot be changed; it includes all intelligence without matter. The other element is under the control of wisdom which is the element I call God. It cannot be seen, for it is all wisdom. The other element is the gases which compose the natural man. These elements are the gases which are combined together to produce certain effects. For instance, oxygen and nitrogen united go to make up the air. Then there are elements called carbon and hydrogen, the carbon being a solid and the hydrogen being a gas. Water is formed by the combination of oxygen and hydrogen in certain proportions. Could we take away oxygen from the water, what remains, being hydrogen, will burn. Now the caloric is the invisible principle that we call heat. This principle is something, but we do not find any intelligence which man admits except these gases when they are combined into the form called body. Then the life is visible or the body has motion.

If these gases when combined produce wisdom and when separate are nothing, what was it that made the gases whose combination makes wisdom? The element of caloric does not seem to belong to any of these gases, yet it is a power or principle which cannot be seen. Oxygen is not water, neither is nitrogen; yet when mingled together in certain proportions, these two produce water. Water is matter and the two gases which are not matter can produce it; therefore nothing can produce something. Remove the oxygen from the water and what remains burns, so according to this theory, oxygen is water and nitrogen is fire. It is certain that everything animate or inanimate, matter or solid dies or dissolves and passes out of sight. Now if each and every one of these endless bodies or beings that are formed by the combinations of these gases, when resolved into their original state do not hold their distinct identities, then there can be no First Cause.

I assume that every element when disturbed is combined with other elements to produce some idea and when the idea is destroyed, the elements of which it is composed return to their original state. If life is a combination of elements which when they are dissolved destroys life, then life is not an element of itself but a result of a combination. And let me ask what was it that made the elements a combination? It must be something that is outside these gases. I contend that wisdom contains all this and everything in the form of gases or fluids are subject to it. Then we have an endless space filled with invisible matter and governed by an invisible wisdom which sees things that are invisible to our eyes. Give wisdom an existence outside of matter and give it a being and then you can have something which will exist when opinions are gone.

I assume wisdom to be the father of all and science the son of wisdom, and those of us who know science or the son know wisdom or the father, for wisdom and science are one. Science is the Christian name of wisdom. Error is the child of ignorance, and the generation of ignorance will roll on till it destroys itself; and out of its ashes rises science, the child of wisdom. Wisdom and error are both in the world together, but error being the elder, it keeps science in subjection as long as it can. But as science grows, it expands and error loses its hold of science. Now these two distinct identities have been kept up ever since wisdom began to act; yet, they have always been applied to matter and the world has always been trying to convert the one into the other.

The religious world have made a man of matter and endowed him with these two principles, thus making the word of no effect by their doctrines, for wisdom is not of this world. Man is ever trying to make a wheat out a tare but Jesus never confounded the two together. He called them by various names: sometimes the rich man and the poor man, the law and the gospel and sometimes the difference was made in one person as Saul and Paul. Jesus was one character and Christ was another, but the religious people of his day and the Christians of ours had the same opinion of Jesus. They considered Jesus Christ was like George Washington, that is a single person with a double name. So it was with Paul. His other name was Saul. No one believes that Saul was the surname for it was the Christian name and Paul was the other, yet, they did not belong to the same character and we have Paul's own words to prove this testament correct.

We also have Jesus' own words to prove that he was not God but Christ was. Paul tried to show the difference between himself and Saul whom he called brother for he says, If meat make my brother to offend, I, that is Paul, will eat no more meat while the world stands lest I make my brother to offend. Here are the two ideas error and wisdom in one body. Wisdom says if meat or argument on false ideas offend my brother, error, I will not argue any more so long as these false ideas stand. In other words, cease from arguing about what you do not understand till you learn what you are talking about.

The people have no idea of God at all. It is true they have a belief about God but it is as absurd as their belief in heaven, and they cannot locate him either in heaven or earth or under the earth and yet they believe in Him. The great fault is in the first state. Man has been taught to believe that matter is intelligent and that matter can be developed as science can. This is an error, for when science is developed, it is done through matter, not that there is the least wisdom in matter, however. The old idea that beauty and ugliness, good and evil, strength and weakness, pleasure and pain is in the thing spoken of causes all the trouble. There is no intelligence in anything that can be seen by the eye; one can only see the working of intelligence in matter. With pain, the pain is in the invisible, while the effect is apparent in the visible, the visible being one character and the invisible another. Science has one character and is not seen, but its brother is seen in matter or the natural man. For instance, science acting through matter or man's body gives to the world some scientific fact and the matter is the brother and science can only be seen through its brother. Aaron has an impediment in his speech. So has science and it makes its brother or Moses speak for it. Error has the same brother to speak through, so the brother becomes the oracle of the two, yet in fact they are all separate beings.

When wisdom is acknowledged to contain every idea and it is acknowledged that nothing can exist without its knowledge, then although man, as we call him, cannot admit it because of his unbelief, it will not prove that it does not exist. Teach this truth that matter is nothing but gases combined together by wisdom for certain purposes and directed just according to the will of wisdom, then he will see that although he, that is the Christ or the Scientific man, is not seen by the natural man or Jesus, yet he exists with all his wisdom. He will find that errors and opinions exist and he can see them, yet they cannot see him. All that you know scientifically is God or Wisdom and to prove what you know so all will admit it is science. For instance, when the idea first started that a steamer could cross the Atlantic, error disputed the fact. The ignorant said nothing, the scientific believed, but even their wisdom had not rid itself of the old garment of error. When the voyage was accomplished, then science threw off the old garment of error and arrayed itself in the white robes of wisdom which shone like the star of science in the heaven of wisdom. This light threw its rays on the world of error which caused its dry bones to shake, and those that had been dead in the grave of doubt came forth, saved by the everlasting truth. Some of these false prophets were in the City of Gotham, lecturing to the people that the steamer never could cross the ocean. And even while they were eating and drinking at the feast of error, the steamer arrived at their very city. Then those that were dead were resurrected and those that slept, awoke, some to everlasting shame and others to life.

This was the first resurrection of steam and those that rose at that resurrection never die again. We never have been taught to believe that what we see is not that which sees. Being ignorant of ourselves, we have put all our wisdom into matter and believe that matter can bring forth life. All the theories of the ancients prove that what we call intelligence was the result of the combination of gases formed into what is called man. The Christian believes the same, but they have a superstition of the ancients of a light. But as to what it is or where it goes, they are as much in the dark as ever. Every generation has made a distinction between good and bad and truth and error, but they have never given either an identity. If man would call them elements like light and darkness and admit that every person is in one or the other, then he will easily learn to distinguish between the two. All kinds of evils are darkness and science from the least to the greatest is light. Man should choose light rather than darkness, but he has got so far in the dark that to come to the light or science is a greater cross than he can bear, and rather than be the subject of conversion, they remain in the dark. For then they are in company with their own flesh who are the children of darkness and whose father was a liar in the beginning and abode not in the truth. The elements of error are as real as that of darkness and no one disputes the fact that there is darkness, but take it and bring it to the light, and it vanishes. So error vanishes when brought to the light of science.

These two characters spoken of in the Bible are contained in the present rebellion, Freedom and Slavery. Slavery is the natural working of error, yet it seems hard that these wars must take place. There is such a thing as ignorance and that begets ignorance. At last they get quarrelling among themselves and out of the war comes error. Science is an element that is kept in reserve till the time of reformation comes and matter must go through certain processes before it can be molded by science. For instance, take paper; cotton is the matter, rags is the error. The rags go through a process to destroy their identity and then comes the pulp or ignorance. Then comes a higher process. The pulp goes through a number of changes. All the error or impediments are removed and the wheels of time set the rocks of freedom in motion, and the hand of science guided by the power of wisdom rolls out the white scroll which John held in his hand when the angel wrote the things which shall shortly come to pass. This is the parable of the end of slavery to the African race.

There are many other rebellions yet to be battled before man can sit by the throne of wisdom in every department of science. The nation like an individual embraces these two characters, science and error, and both are elements. Science is the element of freedom in the lawful minds and error is the element of slavery in the slavish minds. These two elements have been acting together like white lead and oil, but each element or substance retained its own identity. Slavery or the brutal element has tried to keep freedom in chains, but freedom expands while slavery contracts. Therefore, the bands that once bound freedom are broken and the cry has gone forth from the temple of liberty to those that are bound to prepare for the battle, and the word of freedom has gone forth to all the world even to the whole length and breadth of the kingdom and will not return till every one shall acknowledge the rights of the enslaved at the cradle of liberty.

Two Principles Acting on Man, The
[BU 3:0772]

You know that I have said that in every desire or thought, there is an answer either harmonious and scientific or false and erroneous. For instance, the ox wants to drink. The intelligence or harmony and error is in the desire, not in the water. For the word or idea water is not known to the ox. If the truth gives direction, the desire is gratified and peace and harmony follow. If error gives direction, reason, opinions, calculation and every element error is capable of inventing is set to work to gratify the desire or produce harmony. For when the science or answer is discovered so that the desire can be gratified, opinion is gone and truth takes its place and mind becomes the subject to soul or science.

Suppose a lady wants to sew two pieces of cloth together so they won't pucker. Now the true answer and the false one is in the desire to do it right, but it may not come to the light; therefore it is in the dark. The true answer or science is in the desire but the desire knows it not, as God was in the world and the world knew it not. The world of darkness is error and disease and its light is darkness. The light of science is health and happiness and its light is its truth and the length of its days. These two lights are truth and error and science is the knowledge to harmonize the discord in error. I will try to illustrate science.

All kinds of belief are error, for truth has no belief. You are taught to believe that the earth is flat and try to convince me of the reasonableness of this belief. I admit your belief and also that the earth rested on a shaft which lets it turn around horizontally and that the shaft is stuck in the ground perpendicularly. Now, we believed these ideas to be true and so they are to us and therefore founded on a science to us. So that the knowledge of our science was in our belief and not in the earth. Suppose someone should come and dispute our belief. Are we bound to believe them because they contradict us, giving no reasons only that it is not in harmony with their ideas? All will say, no. Now, minds are excited and the whole thing is agitated, and it is found that there is not one single particle of harmony in our beliefs; and in the chaos of mind, a new idea springs up that it is round and our theories are knocked all to pieces. Like political parties, we all fall in and embrace the new idea as truth. Now it becomes our duty to prove it and the science is the knowledge of the old idea and the belief is the new. To put the new science or belief into practice so as to change the belief is to establish harmony and to do that is to reason away all the opinions of the old theory. And this is done by seeing the answer to all the questions and desires of the people so as to satisfy them.

Now as disease is admitted as a truth which is matter, it has form and is as much in existence as the earth is. Now to introduce a science that will destroy the earth is not much harder than to destroy disease. You see it is not an easy task to destroy this earth or disease, but when I tell you that the earth is the Lord's and the fullness thereof and that man is nothing but an idea that can be changed and that the process is a science or knowledge of what matter is—when I tell you this, it is much easier said than proved. This science I prove on the sick when I correct their errors.

A patient consults me who has a sick body and whose sensations are accompanied with certain ideas which "wise" authority has established. They are her knowledge but they do not satisfy her or she would not seek other advice. Now to cure her would be to destroy her ideas and introduce others which are in harmony with her desires. If I succeed in doing this, then she is happy and disease and the matter which formed it is annihilated. This is not very easily done, for to give an answer which will destroy ideas the most reasonable and obvious possible and which we have all been brought up to believe and do believe is something that carries one into an unexplored region of truth. In the first place one must feel that the reality which everybody sees is not right and that he has an intelligence which can destroy it. In the next place he must argue out his knowledge against the patient's and this places him in opposition to all the wisdom of the world, for of such wisdom is disease.

Here is the phenomenon in the natural world in the form of heart disease or tumor and here I stand with my knowledge which tells me that the disease is a lie. Then I prove that matter disturbed is mind and that the material of which disease is made is superstition, opinions and a complete ignorance of God. If man did not reason, he would never be sick any more than the brutes, but it is the design of God that knowledge should be developed through man. Now when man asks a question about himself, there come two answers; one is in matter and sets up its standard in the natural world; it condemns man to be the result or emanation of matter and subject to its laws. This, apply it as you may, is discordant with our highest desires. The other answer comes in harmony with the desire and makes man an intelligence which can control matter and create his condition. It satisfies the desire and destroys his trouble and the whole thing is done intelligently so that the same question will not come up again and he is ready for another and new question. This makes man progressive and places his happiness in his knowledge. But in elevating the spiritual man, the standard of the natural man is destroyed and his wisdom is good for nothing. This is not flattering to man's pride.

So with ignorance and vanity it would not work. But a man with true knowledge would give not only the benefit of his knowledge, but the knowledge itself to the world and become a teacher to mankind. Now his works are his proof that he is what he pretends to be, and they in their appearance are the same as the works of men who have no such motive as his but who labor to create their own fame. Their judgment of him, of course, is the reflection of their own policy and their believers follow their opinions. So when I undertake a sick person's case and tell them that their trouble is in their mind and my explanation helps them, these doctors and wise men think I am telling them a lie and curing by a trick which I conceal for my own benefit. And my patients, many of them, come to me with the idea that I shall insult them by telling them that they have no trouble and it is all imagination. These men think the only way in which the mind can affect the body is through the imagination and that I affect my patients through that faculty. Now, I show that man is spiritual or scientific and if he does not receive a satisfactory answer to every thought or desire, he is troubled; and the wisdom of the world, making man the result of organized matter, locates every trouble he may have in the body, thus creating the very trouble he wants cured. This gets him farther into trouble and he wanders in darkness through the troubles of the body to get an answer to his first unsatisfied desire.

Two Sciences
[LC 1:0014]

There are two sciences: one of this world, and the other of a spiritual world, or two effects produced upon the mind or matter by two directions. The wisdom of this world experimenting, acts in this way: it puts its own construction on all sensations produced on the mind and establishes its knowledge after the effect is produced. For instance, a child feels a pain in its head. The child has no idea what it is, and if the mother is as ignorant of its origin as the child, no effect of any amount is produced. But the wisdom of this world arrives in the form of a lady. She hears the account of the pain from the mother, and assuming a wise look gives her opinion in regard to the trouble, and says the child is threatened with dropsy of the brain because she shows the same symptoms of another child who died of that disease. This account excites the mother, whose mind acts upon the child. The explanation of the wise lady gives direction to the mind, and presently the work commences to show that she is right. A doctor is called who is as wise as the lady, and not being willing to be outdone by her, he puts in a few extras, like congestion of the brain, etc. and says the lady was right but did not get the whole of the matter. So he has two chances after the child is killed to prove his superior skill over the lady.

It sometimes happens that a controversy arises between the two parties, each trying to establish their own opinion so as to have the disease turn their way. In the mean time the patient is left to her own self and gets well. This is all the good result I ever saw from such a controversy. The patient is a mere tool in the hands of these blind guides who attempt to cure her. While this controversy is going on, seeing that all each party wants is to establish their own way, the patient sends for me in her dilemma. I arrive and a fire-brand is thrown in between the combatants. I contend that the child has no dropsy of the brain but only some slight shock upon its mind, and quieting the child is all that is necessary for a cure. Here the controversy ends. If the mother employs me I prove my theory and the child gets well. If they prove theirs, they kill the child; and an examination is made which establishes their theory, and I am a humbug or quack. If I take the case and the child gets well, then the child was not sick, only a little nervous.

December 1859

Unknown God, The
[BU 2:0395]

When Jesus asked Peter, "Whom do the people say that I am?" Peter and the disciples said, Some say, John the Baptist, some Elias, and others Jeremiah or one of the prophets. Now all of these were dead; therefore they did not mean to confound the man Jesus with them. But they believed the spirits of these men came back and entered the living and talked to the people. Jesus knew that this was their belief and they knew it. When Jesus asked His disciples the question, He never intended to convey the idea that He wanted to know who He, Jesus, was, but who this power was. They thought it must be the spirit of some person who had been on earth and when Peter said it was the Christ or God or Truth or Science, this was a new idea, and Jesus answered, "Flesh and blood hath not revealed the explanation to you," and upon this explanation He, Jesus, would build His Christ or Church or Truth, and the gates of error could not prevail against it. He, that is, Jesus, would give Peter the keys or explanation so that he could understand and practice it for the benefit of mankind. This knowledge would give him power to loose those who were bound in heaven or in the mind, and loose those bound in their earthly body. The idea that the man Jesus was anything but a man was never thought of. Jesus never had the least idea of such an explanation.

The prophets had foretold of a Messiah that should come and when the child Jesus was born, the people believed that David's spirit had come and taken possession of his body. So they called Jesus the son of David. But they meant to be understood that it was David's spirit speaking through Him, Jesus, and some called him the Son of Man.

Now, everyone admitted the power that Jesus had, but there was a difference of opinion in regard to it. All men have a power, but to have a power superior to the natural man has been a question ever since the world began. Upon this question the people split. To believe is to believe in a power the natural man cannot explain. If Jesus had a power, we must admit a knowledge superior to it, that governs and directs it, and if we do admit it, where does it come from? All will answer, from God. All will admit that there is another power that affects man for evil. There must then be a sort of bad knowledge or false Christ that governs it. Then we must admit a true knowledge and a false knowledge which act upon His power. Now how are we to know the good from the bad? Only by the fruits or direction. If we must take an opinion, then we have no standard; for everyone has a right to his opinion and by doing so we throw away Christ's or Jesus' opinion when He says, By their fruits men ought to be judged. We judge them by their works. What are their works? I suppose Jesus knew what He meant and He meant to give His disciples the true idea of His meaning when He called them together and gave them the power to heal all sorts of diseases and cast out devils. Did He mean to give the power without any knowledge how to apply it, or did He give the knowledge with the power? If He gave the knowledge so that it could be applied, are not the ones who apply it better acquainted with the power than those who are ignorant both of the power and the knowledge?

I will try to illustrate what Jesus meant by these powers when He was accused of curing by ignorance. You may have seen in the papers an account of a young lady being cured by the prayers of a Mormon preacher. I have no doubt that he raised her up by his prayers and the belief in Mormonism would naturally be established in the young lady's mind. This cure, as far as it goes, is to establish Mormonism. Now if the Mormons established all their beliefs and that is right, why do not all people who believe in prayer embrace Mormonism and all that the Mormons preach?

When the disciples said to Jesus, We saw men casting out devils in thy name and forbade them, He said, "Forbid them not, for they that are with us are not against us, and they that are not with us scattereth abroad." Here Jesus made the difference between His knowledge and theirs in using this power. They cured, but the world was not any wiser for their cures, so they scattered abroad. The cure was right, but it was done through ignorance.

This is the way with prayer. Prayer contains no knowledge and only leaves men in ignorance and superstition. Seeing this account in print and knowing how it was done, I thought I would try the same experiment on a lady myself according to my way of curing disease. I have no creed or belief. What I know I can put into practice, and when I put it into practice I am conscious of it and know what will be its effect. I sent to the lady (the subject of my experiment) who lived out of town a letter, telling her I would try my power on her from the time I commenced the letter which was Sunday, and visit her at different times until the next Sabbath; and on the next Sabbath I would come between the hours of eleven and twelve and make her rise from her bed where she had been confined by sickness, unable to walk for nine months. At the time appointed I went and used my power to restore her to the use of her limbs and to health. On the Wednesday following my letter, her husband wrote me that on Monday night she was very restless, but was better the next day. On the Monday following that, I received a letter from her saying that at the time I appointed for her to rise from her bed, she rose from her bed, walked into the dining room and returned and laid down a short time. She then rose again, dined, and also took tea with the family, rested well that night and continued to do well. Now I suppose all of this transaction would be accounted for by the religious community by the power of the imagination of the patient. Suppose you do give it that explanation. How was the lady cured by prayer? On the same principle, I suppose. If so, how was it with the centurian who came to Jesus, saying that he had a servant lying sick with the palsy, grievously tormented? Jesus said unto him, "I will come and heal him." The centurian said, "Speak the word only and my servant shall be healed." Then Jesus told him to go his way and the servant was healed in that self-same hour. Now who cured the servant? Jesus, or the centurian, or the servant's own imagination? Settle this question among yourselves.

Another case: when Jesus came into Peter's house, He saw the mother of Peter's wife lying sick of a fever. He touched her and she arose and ministered unto them. Now if you cannot tell how this was done and yet admit it, you must admit a power that you cannot explain or understand, and if you cannot understand it, it is an unknown power. Now to exist in any individual this power that you admit and from which you hope to derive benefit is to worship an unknown God or principle. This principle which you ignorantly worship, this I declare unto you by explaining it.

March 1860

Vaccination according to the World and according to Dr. Quimby*
[BU 3:0219]

To vaccinate a person is to inoculate him with the virus of the cow pox. A sore is formed where the vaccine is inserted and then the patient has had the kine pox. This prevents the person having the small pox. The solution of this is that the virus conveys its disease to the body, which becomes infected with it.

I will try to give what would approximate to Dr. Quimby's explanation of vaccination, according to his theory that all disease is in the mind and that mind is matter. The first assertion is that the vaccine matter is no different from any matter and that the effect on the body, called vaccination, is not the effect of the matter, but of the change of the mind, (which is matter). That which renders vaccine poisonous and infectious and also a preventative to the small pox, does not dwell in the matter, but in the mind of those who employ it. Irrespective of its relation to the human body, it is like any other matter, its color, form and substance, are admitted of themselves, but simply its power, its virtue, in regard to its effect on man, is no part of itself, but exists from the fact that the whole civilized world believes it to be there. It does no infect the system, of its new power, but from the power of the belief that it produces disease. The force of universal belief renders it a perfect agent of the belief and it will always provide the effect till the belief is shaken.

The world believes that the body, being matter, acts like any other matter independent of the mind, therefore when a foreign substance enters the body, both act on their own hook without any control of the man. The Dr. says that man's body is a shadow of himself, and that man reasons about a phenomenon till he finds a belief that nearly satisfies him and that this he calls the truth. But as he reasons his mind changes and his body sooner or later, also changes, so that when he arrives at a belief which he thinks is truth, the body is ready to produce the fruits of the belief, and perhaps has already done so by the time that he discovers what his belief is.

According to the world the matter is poisonous of itself, and made by God capable of producing kine pox and of preventing small pox. The Dr. makes it the simple agent of man's belief that it is poison, etc., and hence the effects follow according to the force of the belief and not according to the law of God.

The world says man is matter and like any matter must decay and perish. The Dr. says man is of matter, which must change, but he is also of wisdom, and the problem of life is to subject matter to the understanding of wisdom. By the world the body is believed to be a living house for man to inhabit with appetites, passions, and diseases independent of the man. The Dr. says the body is well of itself, its ills and diseases are those which follow the belief that the body acts of itself and has independent existence; therefore it is the duty of man to seek wisdom that he may correct the errors of his belief and learn the truth.

It may be asked if he objects to vaccination. Not at all—no more than he objects to the law for murder, but nevertheless it is doing evil that good may come, it is destroying one error by another not quite so great. Instead of repealing the law against murder, he would put into man's heart a higher principle of wisdom, which, by teaching man to understand his own motives and desires, would render the law of man of no effect. So with disease, he would not do away with the precautions and means of cure now within the reach of the sick, but he would introduce this theory which makes disease the invention of man. So that man could look to his own belief for the cause of his misery, and correct his errors by another mode of reasoning.

The cause of vaccination is fear of the small pox, which acts upon man as the fear of ghosts acts upon those who believe in them. It brings about the phenomenon that he dreads.

Various Ideas Come Up Sitting with Patients
[BU 3:0639]

I am often asked questions by my patients in regard to children and idiots, because I say disease is all in the mind, having told them many times that mind is the medium or material used by wisdom to bring about a result. Then they will say, I had no mind about it. That is just like a man who has made a pair of boots and someone says to him, you must have given a great deal of thought or mind to come to the knowledge of making a pair of boots. No, says the shoemaker, I never had any mind about it. I merely took up the leather and knife and immediately the boots were all cut out. While I was talking about their wear, I looked and the boots were all made and I never had any mind about it. To me, one is as plain as the other. The man's mind and thought were one and the leather and material, the other. Now he would reason that the boots made themselves. Everyone can see the folly of this kind of reasoning in everything but disease, from the fact that the people have been made to reason from a false basis.

Men of opinions have led the world, when the fact is that they are only a stumbling block to science. Man who reasons is in the dark or he would not reason, for if he knows a thing, he can prove it. Someone says, I believe there is such a place as London, yet I never saw it. His belief is based on some one's wisdom. To those who have seen London it is a fact based on sight. You may have a thousand proofs like the former, yet it is an opinion, and opinion always admits a doubt, if it is ever so small. This doubt is the very thing to overcome. It is like a dead point in a steam engine. Get rid of this and you have perpetual motion. It is so with the mind. Lift the curtain that hides you from an object and it is present. This is where man fails; his wisdom is in his sight; that of the wise is in their wisdom. So to be wise is to see by the eye of wisdom; then you do not have to ask. When my patients cannot understand, they think I do not know myself. It is hard to convince by talk a blind man who was born blind that you can see what he cannot. The blind man must admit what he cannot see before he can have his spiritual eyes or wisdom open; so it is with my patients; they must admit what they cannot understand as in all sciences. There never was nor ever can be a science without a phenomenon. My theory is like all the others; no theory was ever established on nothing; even the theory of religion has its phenomena.

September 1862

What Calls Out My Arguments
[LC 1:0502]

It may be necessary to explain what calls out my arguments. All that I write is intended to destroy some belief of the patient. A belief is what I call disease, for that embraces the cause and it sets the people to reasoning until their systems are prepared like the earth to receive the idea. And when the phenomenon is brought forth, the doctors call that disease. The belief in an idea that cannot be seen by the natural eye is as real as the belief existing in the natural world. For instance, every person who has not been there believes there is a rebellion at the South and every day brings evidence to prove the truth of their belief. But those who are there have no belief; they know it.

Everything that does not come within the natural senses must be a belief. Disease is one of this class. The phenomenon is admitted, and to make man admit it involves a belief that it exists. It does not follow that he is diseased any more than it follows that a man is in the war because he believes there is one. Yet he may be liable to be caught though there are some exceptions. War, like some diseases, has its exempts, for instance, small pox. A man can procure a certificate from a physician that he has had it or has been vaccinated. So the belief makes the thing to the person believing it, and as the belief becomes general, every person is affected more or less. Children are not exempts. They suffer, if they are in the vicinity of the disease, for their parents' sins. Their diseases are the effect of the community. The children at the South had nothing to do with this rebellion and neither do children have any part in the belief in the evils that come upon them in the form of disease. These come from the older inhabitants who embody the superstitions of the world, and they are as tenacious of their beliefs as they are of their lives, for their life is in their belief.

See how the South fights for slavery under the belief that it is a divine institution. The people believe the same of disease and each one will fight for his peculiar disease till truth will exterminate both. One is as dangerous as the other and each has its sympathizers and traitors. Take a person sick under the law of disease which he knows will kill him if the law is put in force. He or she is as anxious to condemn himself or herself by insisting that they have a certain disease as a Rebel is to swear that a Yankee is an abolitionist. Each is working to have the victim condemned. Both may be summed up as the effect of man's belief.

Religious sects fight for their various beliefs which contain not a word of truth and the world has to suffer the consequences. The medical faculty, spiritualists, and every class who have wit enough to have a belief keep up a warfare all the time to keep their beliefs alive that they may obtain a living. But when these are cut by science or truth, they wither and die out and from the ashes comes freedom or science. War is always engendered by beliefs. Slavery is only the name for all evils that have affected man, of which disease is one. They all have to pass through a sea of blood before their heads can be crushed and they can be handled by reason. Religious opinions have waded through blood before reason could control the mind, and then the warfare is carried on in words. Universal freedom has not yet gone through this sea of blood but is now in the storm and God only knows how it will come out.

The belief which makes man bind his fellow man is very strong, for it appeals to the religious prejudices, and they really are the bottom of all evils. The natural man believes slavery is right and he is religious in this belief, although in everything else he is governed by party interest. Every sick person is suffering either directly or indirectly from the effect of some belief; therefore my arguments are to show the absurdity of the beliefs whatever they are, for beliefs are catching. For instance, who would believe that any sane man at the North would catch the belief of secession, yet it is quite common. I have to come in contact with many persons' beliefs, either directly or indirectly. The child is a mere tool in the hands or belief of the parent, just as the Southern child takes its parents' beliefs without knowing the consequences. Therefore the child is affected by its parents' beliefs, which are just as real an enemy to health as slavery is to freedom. Science is the true man. Belief is the enemy to happiness, for everyone knows that a man will die before he will give up his belief. So when a person has a belief in any particular disease, he will not give it up until it destroys the body, although he knows that fighting is his own destruction. A belief always makes out its own destruction. When I sit by persons, I find them either like a child or a person in a belief. If they have no ideas that come within their senses, they are like one affected by surrounding circumstances, as a child whose parents are fighting is frightened and perhaps killed by the parents' evil acts.

When I have a patient who is frightened by some feeling in their system which they have not named, they are like a spectator in a riot who finds himself attacked and violently abused when he has been quiet all the time. But he knows that every person is liable to be affected by the company he keeps. I have to reason with such persons and convince them of their error; and as they learn the truth, they are safe, for to know a truth is to get out of an error or disease. I take the same course with such as I should with a stranger who had ignorantly got into a mob and was violently attacked. I enter the crowd, take the man by the shoulders, lead him out and then befriend him till he is safe.

A belief in disease is like a belief in any other evil, but there are those who, putting entire confidence in the leaders, accept certain beliefs. Such are honest and are the hardest patients to cure, for they attach a religious respect to their beliefs which are their very life. They often say they would rather die than lose their belief.

A belief going to establish any religion is held onto as a child holds onto its mother when it is afraid of strangers. I frequently have a hard battle with such before they will relax, and they will sometimes weep and lament as though I were really going to take their life. As I have no belief to give them, I try to show them the absurdity of their own.

It will be seen that in all I write, my reasoning is to destroy some belief that my patient has. Rheumatism or that state of mind affecting people in that way is caused by various beliefs. Their minds, as I have said, are deceived into bad company and they have to suffer the consequences of their acts, although their intentions may have been good.

I will state a case. A man uses tobacco freely, both chews and smokes. His wife, being of a sympathetic nature, enters into his error to try to reform him. This brings her into the same company that he is in. She is regarded as bad as her husband. She is beaten until blood starts out of her elbows, shoulders, and limbs, and her hands become swollen and sore so that she cannot work. Meantime her husband appears as well as ever. This is taking a disease from sympathy and it shows that such evils are catching in the world. To such I stand in this way. I take the symptoms and know who is the devil. I expose him and when I make the patient know him, the devil leaves, the error is cast out, the belief leaves and the patient is cured. This is a process of reasoning from cause to effect, not from effect to effect. The world reasons to make one disease in order to cure another. I destroy the disease by showing the error and showing how the error affects the patient.

A number of my pieces are on some religious belief and they were written to convince the patients of some error in regard to God which they had embraced and which troubled them; therefore it was necessary to change their belief and destroy the evil that tormented them. And when they saw how inconsistent their belief was, it changed their minds.

December 1862

What Has My Writing and Talking to Do with Curing?
[BU 3:0827]

It is natural to ask what has all my writing and talking to do with the curing of disease. Having the right to explain my own theory, I will try to show that by this very theory which I talk and write I detect the causes of disease while the remedies are similar to those used to correct any false idea that can be changed by a true explanation. Every man is made of truth and error and the change from error to truth is a progression; accordingly, each man's senses show his grade by his acts and reasoning. Some are so equally balanced that it is hard to tell which preponderates. I will introduce different characters showing the working of this theory on man. The natural man is a being without ambition, whose wants are confined to his appetites and are therefore easily supplied; docile, easily ruled, he makes a good slave or waiter, but a poor steward, for he has no pride to be gratified. Although he walks upright, this man contains more of the brute than the human species. The next in order comes the servant. Vain like the peacock, he is pleased to make a show. This man has the seeds of ambition and is a compound of the brute and the vanity of error, with no wisdom higher than opinions and not always that.

These two classes are healthy, for they are too ignorant to be fearful or too much taken up by their vanity to be interested in what makes disease or to counteract any opinions. After these comes another set of minds of a different combination. They are conceited and at the same time brutal; they embrace a large class and are hard to rule, except when their prejudices are appealed to and then it is easy. It is only necessary to attack something beyond their opinions. This is the masses whose mind is the field in which another class of higher development act. The latter contain a superior element; governed nevertheless by the intelligence of the masses; therefore, their whole reasoning is based on the prejudices of the lower order of minds and they do not give their thoughts to scientific research but become as prey to low and selfish motives. Hence the finer and higher feelings of the people are blunted and they gratify their appetites in a lower circle even than the leaders. Low and desperate, their health corresponds to their belief and when overcome by some misfortune which cramps their spirits, they wilt down and give up easily. Through their low, ignorant state this class is healthy. This takes in the Irish and the dissipated of all classes. They become stupid and consequently are not liable to disease but they are superstitious and are just the subjects for epidemics. This applies more to males than to females, for the latter when degraded are generally out of the reach of diseases. All these are not so liable to disease as a higher class, for they lose all self-respect and respect for others.

There is still another class constituting the higher element in the development of mind who are governed by another set of rules as dishonest as the former and whose effect on the masses is still more dangerous. While the masses are kept in ignorance and brutal degradation, the latter is kept in bondage by spiritual chains that torment their souls. While the former only suffer like the brutes in dirt and poverty, the latter is kept in pitiful servitude and cast into prisons of a spiritual nature; thus they are kept sick by the leaders. To this class or lost house, I come to preach this theory, to open their eyes and break their prisons and set the captive free. Their torments or disease are the effect of their blind guides, and to explain away their belief is to put this new theory in practice. Therefore, everything I write goes to destroy some idea which we have, for we live on our wisdom and our health depends on our reason. Therefore if we reason wrong, we suffer the penalty of our own reasoning. Those who do not reason are more brutal but less sick. This is as far as man has arrived. Now let the wise learn that to be healthy is to seek the true philosophy of health. Then health and wisdom will be the father and mother of peace and happiness.

Dec. 1862

What I Impart to My Patients
[BU 3:0543]

The question is often asked me do you impart anything to your patients when you talk? I answer, I do and I will try and make you understand how. To do this I must give you an illustration in language applied to something that you wish to know and which gives you trouble. The trouble is the disease, and the phenomenon is the effect.

To make you understand I will illustrate. Suppose you are purchasing goods and in your hurry you lose your wallet containing all your money. You do not miss it until you go to pay your bills and then you find that you have lost your cash. Now the shock excites your system or mind, just according to the amount you are disturbed. Now you become excited and very nervous. This is accompanied with a feverish state of mind or body, for the body is only the reflection of the state of the mind. At last you let your trouble be known to some person and you begin to look for the money. You cannot find it and borrow the money to pay the person assisting you. This adds to the trouble and at last you take to your bed and send for a physician. He feels your pulse, says your head is affected and orders your head shaved and a blister applied. This only aggravates the nervous excitement. So you keep on until you finally give up and dismiss all the doctors and come to the conclusion that your money is gone and you must make the best of it. The next day you feel more reconciled, and your doctor calls as a friend, finds you better and says the medicine you took had a good effect on you.

Now the question arises who gave the medicine? Not the doctor, but wisdom took possession of the man and he began to reason, and this contains something, but not all, so he sends for me. I know nothing of his trouble but I have found a pocketbook containing $10,000 and am going to advertise it. At the sight of the pocketbook he starts and says that is mine. The shock changes the mind and the cure is made. Now who imparted the cure? The $10,000 I gave him?

So this is the way I cure. The person has lost something that he cannot find or has got into some trouble that he cannot get rid of. Now he wants something to satisfy his desires, and whatever that is, it is the same as the money, and the one that can impart it gives to him the remedy. Suppose a person receives a shock from falling into a river in the winter. This produces a shock and he returns home excited like a cold. This produces a cough. Now as there are many ghosts in the form of disease, he feels some of them may get hold of him. So he goes to a doctor and lays his case before him. The doctor says you are very liable to have consumption. Now of course you are troubled, and are all the time like the man who was looking for his lost money. So he enquires of every person what is good for a cough or if they can tell where his money is. So every person gives his opinion, and there is just as much in one opinion as there is in another. Both are husk and contain no food. At last in despair he gives it up and now I am sent for. Now I will show how I really give the sick person something he needs.

I first tell him what he is afraid of by telling him how he is affected. Here is something he cannot get from the doctor. This makes him feel more comfortable, and then I go on to show him how he has been living on husks or opinions about an idea that never had an existence, only in the superstition of the people. Now as the patient is full of these opinions, I have to give him something in the form of truth that will dissolve the error and satisfy the patient. Now the something that satisfies the patient is the substance, like the money, for the money contained no value in itself but was a representation of value. So health and happiness is what every man wants. So the substance is the representative. The wisdom that I impart to him by my words, filled with the substance that he longed for was to him like the money, and his soul was satisfied. Now if I had no more wisdom about his troubles than he had, my substance would have been like chaff or opinion, containing no food. Here is the difference; it is my own wisdom that is superior to his. As in every case of trouble, opinions never impart any wisdom, and science never imparts opinion but truth.

So the scientific man, in whatever he does, imparts to the world some substance, while the man of opinion never imparts anything but what must be destroyed. One reasons from the basis of statics and the other, from dynamics. These two principles are seen in chess and checkers. You will see two persons playing a game. Here they show power: One that can play both sides while the poor player cannot play either. Now take two poor players; they really believe they show as much science as the very best players and they will look as long and make as great calculations as they think is the very best, when they show no kind of sagacity or science. While the other has both set before him and he is at a loss to know how to move at first until he finds his strength or wisdom of his opponent and then he feels his superiority. Then he moves with confidence.

1863

What Is a Belief?
[LC 2:0771]

What is a belief? It is that combined substance which throws off an atmosphere capable of chemical action, by which the thing believed can be made and thereby affect the body. If man's life is exposed to the danger of wild beasts inhabiting the wilderness, his fears excite his mind and from his mind-body is thrown off an atmosphere in which is seen the wild animal; therefore his trouble is the effect of his belief. Clearing up the wilderness destroys the danger from wild beasts and clearing away the error of disease rids man of the fear that he may be caught by some of the thousand diseases which attack human life. A story which is believed is nothing, and the result is disease, and people are affected just as they believe themselves liable to be caught.

For instance, a slave and a union man run away from the rebels; the latter is safe when he enters our laws, while the danger to the slave is increased when the law for returning slaves was in force. Repeal the law and convince the black that he also is free and then he is safe. It is the same with disease. Disease is a story which follows some act or excitement. The desire for freedom prompts a slave either black or white to make his escape and the belief that he may be caught and the story of what would follow is the disease, while the pain is in proportion to the danger of the punishment. All this is in the belief. Disease is classed by the world into two kinds: disease of the mind and disease of the body. I believe disease to be all in the mind for I know that <u>mind is the matter affected</u>. The senses are not matter, but man in his ignorance, when reasoning beyond the natural man, makes mind, matter, life and senses synonymous or confounds their meaning. Therefore in explaining the truth that disease is a lie, I have to admit a lie in order to reason it out of existence.

For instance, every disease is admitted as a truth. Knowing it to be a lie, I am obliged to admit it for the sake of proving it a falsehood; consequently I seem to maintain two contradictory statements and I stand to the world which makes disease a truth as a man in error. The ancients embodied the foregoing position as follows. "When I say I lie, do I lie or do I tell the truth? If I tell the truth I lie, and if I lie, I tell the truth." This was never solved from the fact that they did not know what the truth was, their truth being merely an opinion of what truth was, and giving way as science advanced. Consequently, as truth was not known, it was impossible to tell whether a man spoke the truth or a lie. Every development of science proves the world's wisdom to be a lie, for as it advances it opposes, face to face, some popular error that the world believes true and which leads man astray. In early times, men reasoned and had opinions about the heavenly bodies, what they were and what their purpose was, but when the truth was made known through the science of astronomy it conflicted with the popular opinions and proved them to be errors. Science has always been fought by error in every branch of learning, but the field that has been travelled over and plowed up with the most diligence by the learned as well as the uneducated in the hope of discovering the truth is religion. Many have thought that they have found the pearl of great price, but when tested by universal application, it has failed as a truth and only remained as a belief.

To discover a science which will teach man to be master of his own health and happiness is to find a truth by which man's thoughts can be tested and their character analyzed. To do this requires a new revelation of wisdom, for all tests heretofore tried have failed and their foundation has crumbled away. Religion has been undergoing a change ever since the minds of men have been roused by scientific discoveries. Its basis has been undermined by the progress of intelligence and has been swept into the valley of despair where its seeds have been picked up by eagles and carried to the remote parts of the land and there dropped into the soil of man's mind, to spring up in some creed having the ancestral features of its father. The world's religion is constantly decaying and eagles in the form of demagogues of every kind live on it. Jesus says, Where the body is, there shall the eagles be gathered. So when people are ignorant and superstitious, every kind of enemy to science abounds. The effect of science on general intelligence is to destroy the influence of this class of leaders; therefore they hate it and oppose its progress all they can. But science has conquered these enemies in every branch except in this one of man's life, and they have departed to some error which under their husbandry yields minds who return to society as hypocrites and demagogues and sap the very life and virtue of the people.

From the darkest ages of Grecian philosophy, there have been men who have waged war with this class of minds whom I have mentioned. But if they fight on the enemy's ground or admit their principles, they are soon surrounded and disarmed of their weapons or arguments by these corrupt minds and their truth taken from them to make their enemies more specious and more crafty in their error. But having obtained a victory over truth, they commence to quarrel among themselves and in their rash zeal, they expose the rottenness of error so that the truth shines upon their motives and under this light men see for themselves. Then, as they cannot bear the light, they flee into darkness or more dense superstition where the lamp of science has never burned.

There is a solid basis on which the scale of science can balance the body of truth with the carcass of error, and thereby show that error weighed with truth is nothing, merely a lie invented to account for some sensation which has taken place in the mind. I will describe this scale and with it weigh the common ideas of health and happiness. The ground on which I shall base it is this. The medical science from beginning to end is an error, and that it is so is shown by the absurd attempts of the faculty to bolster it up. The religion of today exposes the absurdity of the pagan religion and that derived its little truth from heathen mythology. These two systems of religion do not contain a particle of science. These two errors, religion and medicine, are what truth wants to have weighed to see if they are what people want for their happiness.

For as man's happiness depends in a great measure on his diet, if his food hurts him, he is not happy; so ideas being food for the mind, it is necessary to know the quality and quantity which man needs to make him feel the best. If man eats froth, he soon gets faint for something more substantial; consequently his food ought to be weighed by some standard. (There is a kind of food which grows spontaneously and which feeds large multitudes; it is the food of public opinion. When this is put into the scales with truth, it sometimes outweighs the latter. I will explain how it is done. Public opinion supplies ideas to certain worthless minds, a figure of whom can be found in large cities hanging about eating saloons and eating the soups set for the customers who come to buy the solid. Such vermin are always ready to bark at any reform which comes up and when there is a breach made in the world of intelligence by the advance of new discoveries, this class is always thrown in like mortar to fill up the breach. Their ideas being so offensive and contemptible to truth, truth rather than parley retires and leaves them the field. Eager for anything that will satisfy their craving appetites, these birds of prey feed on the body of truth which is left them. After eating and drinking, they lie down to sleep; when they awake, the light of truth shines upon them and being blind, they cannot bear the light and in the darkness they lead the blind, till they both fall into the ditch. This illustrates truth and error and where error weighs the most.) Truth is not science, for a man may tell the truth without knowing it, but if the truth comes from wisdom, the process of getting it is a science.

I will illustrate. I say to you, If you do not go into the house, you will take cold and you do not go into the house and do take cold. This shows to you that I am right, while the fact is, I have only given an opinion based on the belief that the atmosphere contains danger to which I am also subject. Let us weigh this idea in the scale of science and see if it contains any truth. God made the air not for man or beast but for some wise purpose. He placed man and beast on the earth and so constructed them that the air was necessary to them. Therefore the air is to them a great storehouse, containing all that they want to make them enjoy life.

Now to make man afraid of the atmosphere is to do him a great damage and subject him to fear. Science asks the man of error what there is in the atmosphere which God made that should hurt him and why he should be afraid of God's works? The man of error is vexed at this question because he cannot show that his opinion contains any substance; he feels that it is a bubble and as it bursts, it makes a breach in his knowledge. Then comes the mortar of public opinion to fill up the breach saying, "We all know that we take cold in the air." The world being on a level with error, the breach is stopped and science is overpowered. But as wild beasts venture sometimes near the habitations of man and are caught and tamed, so error ventures into the field of science and is overcome, not made wiser, but is like a person who admits what he cannot understand. So error, like the lion, can be led to truth in wisdom by science as the little child. This little child was in Daniel when he was thrown in the lion's den. It makes the lion as docile as the lamb. It cannot be made of error, but as truth destroys error, from its ashes will rise the phoenix of science.

1862

What Is a Belief?–A Fragment*
[BU 3:0740]

It is taking what someone tells you as your own knowledge and acting upon it. For instance you desire to find out the way to steer into a certain harbor, you ask someone and he without any explanation gives you certain directions, which you follow.

What Is a Clairvoyant Person?
[LC 1:0416]

It is a being, conscious of his own existence as a living, thinking, seeing, intelligent creature. All this is not seen by the natural man. Then what is the natural man? He is the shadow of the clairvoyant; neither is conscious of the existence of both at the same time. Why do you speak of two when one is only a shadow? The clairvoyant is like a man who is just where he thinks he is. The natural man is governed by a belief. Reason does not enter into the combination of the clairvoyant for if he reasons, he is not clairvoyant. Where is my consciousness? I am conscious of my senses in both states at the same time. I see the substance and shadow at the same time and change the former. I do not see my own shadow, but I see myself as I really am to myself and knowing that I am not as I ought to be, I change that knowledge by comparing myself to health till I feel it. Health is the standard by which we judge ourselves and just as a man deviates from this standard, he is in the dark and makes shadows. These shadows are the feelings of the sick and are called disease.

September 1861

What Is a Spirit?
[BU 3:0630]

A spirit is the shadow of a person's belief or imagination. Fear produces a chemical change and out of this fear comes phenomena and these again produce fear. This fear creates fearful things or spirits. Perfect wisdom casts out all fear and then the spirits are gone. Man's belief is the basis of his spiritual sight. For instance start a story that ghosts are seen in a certain graveyard; every person believing in spirits, good or bad, is just as liable to see a ghost as he would to be affected by any belief on a religious subject. When Miller prophesied the end of the world, ninety-nine out of a hundred were affected to some extent. This was shown by the count taken by the churches. Even the Unitarian Universalists had their evening meetings and men and women spoke who never spoke before and probably never will again. But it showed what man's belief can do.

I have said that fear produced a chemical change in man's belief, and as matter is one element of his belief, this is liable to take form according to the belief. It has always been impressed on children that ghosts are seen in the burying grounds. This belief makes an atmosphere over the dead like a cloud on a mountain, and in a certain state of mind, certain persons can make a ghost as easily as a certain state of the atmosphere will make the borealis which always keeps just so far from the traveller. So it is with spirits. When you get where they are, they are gone, but the atmosphere still remains and persons may feel it. I once visited a sick man. It was about eight o'clock in the evening when I visited the room. Immediately upon entering, the atmosphere of the room produced such an effect on me that I felt as though my hair stood on end and it seemed as though the room was full of spirits. As I approached the bed, he seemed frightened. I said, You are frightened to death. Why do you lie here? He said he couldn't get up. I said, You are afraid of these devils. They scare you, and when I came in, they left and are now standing out among the apple trees. He said, They scared you a little. This was a fact. He then said, These devils have taken me by the nape of my neck and seat of my pants and laid me here, but I never told of it before. I told him to get up and I would keep them away. He did so and got well.

These devils followed me over two miles before they left and then they parted and flew to the woods. They seemed like a swarm of bees. They varied in length from six inches to two feet. Each seemed to have a separate identity and all the idea they had was to follow me. So all that was necessary for me was to keep up courage enough. These were spirits. The man had become sick from some nervous trouble and was made to believe that he was full of humor. As he philosophized, he contended that the body was made of animal life and this living humor was eating his very vitals, so the heat that passed off from his body was full of living devils. As I came in contact with his belief, the atmosphere I felt was the company or devils that he was with, and in the atmosphere, I saw the spirits or shadow of his belief. And as I took in the atmosphere, I was impregnated with it, but the devils were to me shadows of his own make. So as my system threw off this heat that I inhaled, I could see these imps, and I never shall forget how earnest and determined I was to keep up, for it was the passing off of the disease from me.

May 1862

What Is Death?
[LC 2:0900]

What is death? It is a belief. For if it is a fact, there can be no evidence of its coming to life. A person is alive or he is dead. He can't be both, although we hear of the living telling how they died and what they went through. Now if a person can tell all it is said they can, it is proof that they are not dead. Now first settle what a man is of himself after he is dead. According to the spiritualists' mode of reasoning, he cannot be a spirit for they say he is the same person, wears the same clothes and is flesh and blood. Now Jesus says flesh and blood cannot enter heaven, so accordingly these spirits, as they are called, cannot be flesh and blood; if they are, they cannot be spirits, for the same author says spirits have not flesh and bones. Jesus would not allow that he was a spirit but that he had flesh and bones as he had before he was crucified. So he either told a falsehood or his dead body rose, and if that rose, he did give people to believe a lie, for he said as touching the dead, God is not the God of the dead but the living. He also said, They that rise from the dead, not that they rise, etc. Now all this seems like a contradiction. So it is, if you take the Christian's explanation. But if you will take Jesus' explanation, it is clear, for he never had any idea of death as the Christians say he had; his ideas were at variance with all the world. He never taught any other world as was believed by the religious Jews. He made man up of ideas.

To make a man like Jesus' ideas, you must take a child. The child according to his ideas was a blank so the child's existence was not dependent on itself nor a belief nor an opinion. It was a living fact, a child with an identity susceptible of progression. Now as the child's growth of body depended on food, so the growth of its intelligence depended on wisdom or opinions. As the child began to learn, its identity became attached to its knowledge. Now its knowledge embraced flesh and blood and memory and all the senses and everything it learned. Now to lose its memory of what it was would be to destroy its life for its life was a part of itself but its wisdom can create all that it knows. Knowledge is a created element but wisdom is infinite and eternal. It is God, and every person is a God just as far as he is wisdom. To know this is life, for this wisdom will teach man that wisdom is from everlasting to everlasting. Here is the trouble. The knowledge of man is finite and must be forgotten and destroyed, but wisdom not being matter cannot be destroyed.

Now man is a living principle of God, like mathematics. Mathematics is wisdom reduced to practice. The effects of mathematics must be destroyed while the wisdom remains. For instance, take a steam engine. All the principles must exist when the engine is torn to pieces. Now man reasons as though the engine were the living principle and when that is destroyed, the principle or identity of mathematics is dead; but if we stop to think, we shall see the folly of this. Now every machine and every mathematical calculation that has ever been reduced to practice existed before it was formed. Now the wisdom was as separate from each other as the results are. For instance, see the art of printing all over the world. See the amount or identities or wisdom acting upon matter, each having its own identity of wisdom as well as of matter. See the varieties of all sorts of wisdom.

Now suppose that every printing office in the natural world should be destroyed at one blow. Is there any life of printing in existence? The ignorant would say all is dead, but every identity of the printing world would know that this is not so. Each has its own identity. So with man; his body is a machine shop or scientific world carried on by the wisdom of God in the identity of man. Each identity claims its own self. The matter is the fruits of its development. If it does not develop itself, it does not make itself any the less out of existence but it is like the idiot; it is behind the times. It exists, it must exist, and the destruction of the matter does not destroy the principle called man. Now to me I know I live in the principle, and the principle is like all other principles capable of progression; and as I believe in that, I know that the natural man is ignorant of himself as the child is of any science. Science to the natural man has no identity of wisdom. It does not embrace the properties of thought and reason. Yet everyone knows that everything that has form must have its first start in the First Cause.

Now just raise yourself from the earthly man and wander on the globe and look around and see if you are not with all your faculties, having an identity of your own, leaving the spot but not your identity. This is to the world death, but to wisdom, science and progression. Now what proof is there of what I have said, if proof was wanted to establish the foregoing? Volumes could be written to establish this one fact: that a person sitting in his chair or lying on the bed in a state of unconsciousness to the natural world can be at a distance conversing with persons explaining what was going on. Now the objection is that the person is alive for he comes back. If the body is destroyed, then there is no evidence that what I say is true. This false mode of reasoning arises from our ignorance of what man is. When we find that man, like his God, cannot be seen by the natural eye but is like a principle put in practice, then we shall see just how learned or wise we are. What we see has as much to do with the man as the engine of a steamboat lying at a wharf in Portland with the intelligence of the maker in New York. How many people ever saw Franklin, the father of electricity? Yet he exists as much as he did one hundred years ago. Franklin is the name of that wisdom reduced to practice through a medium of flesh and blood, and a body of galvanic batteries. His wisdom was as much in his experiments as in his body and more so, for his body was not the machine to exhibit his wisdom. So he had to create new bodies to illustrate his truth. Now to suppose this truth existed in his batteries or body is to deny the existence of any wisdom outside of man.

1863

What Is Disease? I
[LC 1:0041]

The theory of the doctors and other leaders of the people (if there is any theory to it) is it is a certain something (I would not attempt to describe their views) that comes in various shapes and on various accounts or causes and attacks people in various parts of the body and with various results. Indefiniteness and uncertainty characterizes all their ideas about it and their ideas go no further than a belief. They believe it to be a something, they can't tell what. When a doctor speaks of the case of a sick person he gives his opinions. It may be founded upon what is to him very much evidence, including much experience. Still, in all cases it is after all an opinion which he gives, and this cannot be infallible and sure, not truth and sure and therefore good for nothing) because two opinions (there is an old saying that when doctors disagree or have different opinions) about the same thing cannot both be right. The same uncertainty about disease is allowed and winked at in the practice. But what is disease? If it is true that it is a thing of itself, did anyone ever see it? In all the post mortem examinations and dissections of bodies which has taken place, has the thing disease ever been found in the body?

A tumor or any disarrangement of the system is an effect, called by Dr. Quimby a phenomenon, or result of some cause. The question is, What is the cause? (This determines the disease.) To each of these questions you answer, No. Then I say, You know yourself that if it is not a material thing of itself it must be a property depending upon another thing.

It must be either a live thing like a fox (and twice as cunning) in order to come of itself and attack us, and furthermore, it must have intelligence or else it is a dependent characteristic of some other thing and if the latter, what is that? We hear the name animal life given to something in the body. We are told also that the body is under the control of the mind and we see daily illustrations of the fact. What then is the use of the second power called animal life? Did anybody ever see that? Is that a thing of itself or does it like [?] belong to something else? Oh, one cannot tell. That is something that no one can fathom is the answer invariably to this. How did they find that out? But this "life" is of the body I suppose. Now if the body is matter, has matter life? Again, did you ever see the body of any kind of an animal move without displaying intelligence? You know there is intelligence with every man and every animal and that intelligence guides each man and animal in all his movements. This intelligence needs no proof, but that animal "life" spoken of can neither be proved nor defined.

On the other hand, take away from a man or animal all knowledge, intelligence, or instinct and conceive if you can of any movement that he would make. What could there be a movement for? Nothing! There could be no object; the thought shows an inconsistency. Watch the very lowest brutes or the very smallest insect and you will see intelligence displayed in their movements. And again watch yourself and you will see no act or movement that is contrary to your will, but every stir or slightest motion is the result of your direct volition. What then can be the use of the animal life? If the mind has the control of the body as I would have the control of a hammer in my hand which would be no more a tool than the body is to the mind, of what use would be that second, indefinable, indescribable opinion of a thing or power called animal life? And if it is a thing of itself, why is it never seen nor found, and how can it go out of existence? But if it is not a separate thing of itself but a property of another thing how can it, being a live or active quality, be a property of a dead or inanimate thing, such as we see matter to be? You may say that is its life. How can it die then? If life dies, then it is not life. Again if disease is not a thing of itself, it must be a property of some other thing that has life and animation and intelligence of itself else it would produce no action or bad result. What then does it belong to? If to the body it could manifestly continue its operations after the spirit left the body. But we have not and cannot prove that the body has any life or animation or intelligence of its own, or independent of the mind; the evidence is all the other way. Then we have only the mind left to which to ascribe the disease as a property or how may it exist in the mind? I answer in the form of a belief, and the body being under the control of the mind, a subject of its influences is moulded and affected just in proportion to the state of mind in its belief.

A person is to himself just what he thinks he is and he is in his belief, sick. If this were not so, if it was not true that all disease is in the mind, not one of the hundreds of cures that have been made by Dr. Quimby, and are constantly being made, could have been accomplished by him, and the old time administers of pills, calomel, and error would still have undisputed possession of the field of sick and wounded. Again, take it another way. You complain of a pain in your side, is it you that complains or your side? You perhaps answer that it is your side complaining through your mind. But I ask, Has your side knowledge? And can it notify your mind that it may speak for it? Is not the knowledge in your mind and is it not your mind that complains? How much pain would you have if you did not know it? How much pain is there in a dead body? Why doesn't pain continue after the soul or mind leaves the body? It is known by all persons that the state of mind or belief influences a person's health. Why is it? How far does it go?

You see that there can be no action or motion without an intelligence behind it and you know that your body has no intelligence. I will quote a few lines from Dr. Q's writings "_____" [sic]. There is nothing animate in the body, so when the body is injured by what we call disease, it is by an error of the mind, the body being subject to the mind, so when the mind is corrected of its error, the truth is established which is its health.

What Is Disease? No. 1
[BU 2:0096]

What is disease? Disease is what follows the disturbance of the mind; this mind is spiritual matter. When I speak of disease I do not mean to confine the word to any particular phenomenon or disturbance of the mind, but that the mind or matter is simply disturbed like the soil of the earth, ready to receive the seed or disease. This disturbance contains no knowledge or thought, any more than a house on fire would disturb the inmates or spirits who flee out, not knowing the cause. It embraces mind without truth or error, like weight set in motion without direction. Weight like mind could never set itself in motion, but being set in motion it is called mechanical power. So is mind set in motion, spiritual power. Both are governed by laws of truth or error; the fruit shows which of the two powers govern.

If it is directed by wisdom or God, no bad results can follow; but if directed by error and ignorance, as ignorance is the mind and error the enemy to truth, the truth will show which governs. As there is no knowledge in error, it sometimes follows that some good results follow, as it did in the case of Joseph being sold to the Ishmaelites. They, it is said, meant it for evil, but God meant it for good. Truth does not work in that way (that is by accident). Truth works by laws, like mathematics, error like chance.

The answer may come right or may come wrong (in error); in either way, it contains no law by which the world is any way the wiser. Ignorance is its life and truth its death. So by error comes disease and death; so by the destruction of error comes the introduction of truth or science or health; and as error is matter or mind, it is the instrument of its own destruction. The matter is not annihilated, but the mind is.

That combined substance that shows itself in persons in the form of an opinion indicates its character by a peculiar show of wisdom, superior to its followers. And when disturbed by wisdom or truth, it dies; but when not opposed, its opinions are sown into the minds of others, like seed in the ground, and comes forth in some form.

This which follows the disturbance of the mind the doctors call disease. Here is where all error lies; they take the effect for the cause. We confound the error and truth together; we take an opinion for a truth, which is an error for what we know we have no opinion of.

If opinion is knowledge, then there is no knowledge, for every person has an opinion. Now if opinion is knowledge, then why is reason introduced? This very fact proves that knowledge is the destruction of an opinion or disease, for what we know, we have no opinion about. Now disease is what follows an opinion. It is made up of mind directed by error, and truth is the destruction of an opinion.

These ideas and hundreds of others have been given to explain the effect of the mind. All of them admit disease as one thing and the mind another. This theory that mind is one thing and disease another has left the people in darkness and caused more misery than all other evils put together. It has always been admitted that a theory that cannot be put in practice is not very good.

The mind is a spiritual matter which, being agitated, disturbs the spirit. This disturbance contains no knowledge of itself, but produces a chemical change of the fluids of the system. These disturbances may be produced in various ways, for instance: by the death of a friend, or by religious excitement, witchcraft, etc. All of the above contain what is called knowledge, which is communicated to the spirit and sets it to work to form disease after the form the spirit gives the mind. The mind being the matter under the control of the spirit, it is capable of producing any phenomenon.

October 1859

What Is Disease? No. 2
[BU 2:0104]

What is disease? It is what follows the effect of a false direction given to the mind or spiritual matter. The body is composed of matter, not mind, but when agitated, that part which is called heat and is thrown off is mind or spirit. It is not intelligence but a medium to be used according to the direction given it by a power independent of itself, like that direction given to mechanical power. The effect of this direction, call it what you please, on the body, is to destroy itself, for its life is its own destruction.

December 1859

What Is Disease? Part I–Disease, Love, Courage
[LC 2:1115]

What is disease? This question is often asked and it could be very easily answered by a physician of the old school by simply pointing out a person coughing and saying this man has consumption. Here is a person who coughs, raises, and etc. Now instead of calling that phenomenon by a name, explain how it came. This the doctor does not do except by another phenomenon as much in the dark as the former, so you may chase him from one lie to another till you are sick and tired and at last you only find it a mystery. Where do I stand as far as disease goes? I know that the bottom of all these phenomena is a lie in the beginning and started by a liar till it was received as true; then the phenomenon is called disease when it is the fruit of our belief.

Every idea is the embodiment of an opinion resolved into an idea. This idea has life or a chemical change, for it is the offspring of man's wisdom condensed into an idea and our senses are attached to it. For instance, you see something that you would like, an apple perhaps. You attach your senses to the idea and then the value is in the idea in the shape of love or worth or anything you may chance to have. If it is love, it is not in the idea but in the essence or author of the idea or owner. I will try to make it plainer. You see a person; at first sight you are affected and you attach your senses to the idea in the form of love. You may or may not be deceived, for love is not matter but solid, and passion is matter governed by error, and subject to love. Love is wisdom, passion is error acting on ignorance. Science is to keep the two separate or error in subjection to wisdom. When two persons meet we think that the first impression comes from the idea or person but this is not the case. The atmosphere around the idea is what is affected and this is not known to us, so we reason from a false basis not knowing ourselves.

To give you a clearer idea of what I wish to convey, I must take myself as one person and my patient as another. When I sit down I am one person, that is, I am quiet of myself, perfectly at ease, not afraid of any impression from my patient, feeling my superiority to them, and this is like strength. My wisdom is my strength; my opponent's wisdom is his error for if he knew the truth he would not want me. So there are two persons in one body or two wisdoms acting through one medium, and as the error is a coward, it assumes a sort of courage but it is the courage that arises from error. I do not know how to describe true courage, for wisdom needs no such word. I never knew that God showed any courage. It seems to be a sort of braggadocio element. If a dog shows courage, it is based on the assumption that he is not afraid, for when he is overpowered his courage fails, so it shows that what is called courage in us is an element not perfectly understood. Take away the fear of danger, then man has courage. Some men see danger where others do not and as no two men reason alike, so no two men's courage is alike. I know of no way of giving you a test of courage as well as to take myself.

When I first commenced my practice, I thought I had courage as much as my neighbors or others, but as I found that I was liable to be affected by another's feelings, my courage failed. So I used some sort of stratagem to get the advantage of my patients, and being rather reckless, I ran risks which the world would call courageous. For instance, I was not afraid of an insane man if I could get his eye; to the world this looked like courage, but to me it was wisdom. I had no fear, for I saw no danger nor harm. Here is where courage is made known. It may be classed like the mechanical powers, pressure and power. Pressure is one element of mechanics. Power is another and embraces both pressure and velocity. So courage is based on one of the elements of action, not seeing the other element reaction. Here is the difference: if you

601

see the reaction, your courage is lost in wisdom. Now I have been trying to get wisdom in regard to the diseases of mankind, for a disease is like the rest of the evils that come within our senses.

When I first used to take the feelings of patients, it took courage to keep me from taking the disease. I know this sort of courage, it was a sort of fear lest I might be called a coward, so I would pluck up courage. But now I see that if I had known what I know now, I should not have been in any more danger than a person in a boat where the water was not over three feet deep. But my courage admitted the water twenty feet deep, rough at that, and myself in a leaky craft. Now as I began to touch bottom or get wisdom, I found that the depth of the water or the danger was in my patient's mind and I believed his story without looking for myself. This made him two men to me. After I had found out the trouble, his fears were one man and his wisdom was another. His error had possession of his wisdom that was based on error and his courage turned to fear. To make courage out of fear was to make him believe there was no danger, then his courage would come, and to destroy both let him know the truth. (To make courage out of fear was to make him believe that there was no danger.) I know that disease is the invention of man, therefore it requires no fear to prevent my saying so. It requires no courage, for there is no danger. Danger is the thing that calls out fear, and courage is the element to face it. So just as a man's fear is, so is his courage. Some never see danger, so their courage is not courage but a kind of artificial mock pride, a desire to be praised for what they do not feel, for their ignorance destroys their fear.

This was the way with myself. My ignorance made me bold for I knew no danger, but as soon as I found that I was liable to be affected by the sick, my fears came. Then just as I saw danger, my fears increased and my courage failed. But I would feel the same reckless propensity to kill disease; so I would be more cautious and more artful till I found my enemy had the same fear that I had. At last it became a sort of warfare between myself and my patient. I found that my courage was my protection and that error was an element or odor that arose from ignorance and fear was what arose from that. So I came to this conclusion: that ignorance begets error, error begets fear, fear begets courage and wisdom destroys all the above.. So as man grows wise he grows strong and his wisdom makes him happy and good, for goodness is wisdom and wisdom is the religion of Jesus, not the Christian religion, but the opposite of that.

One is the invention of man, the other is the wisdom of God which Jesus illustrated by taking a little child. I will do the same to show that goodness is a science and also that religion is a science, and all religion based on man's opinion must come down. One can be proved, the other cannot. I will show the two by the child. Everyone will acknowledge that the child's character somewhat depends upon its bringing up. If this is admitted, it shows that if the parents could see what was best for the child's happiness, much of its misery might be avoided. So you see that it is admitted that the child's bringing up had something to do with its goodness. Here is a fact like all others in science. Sometimes it works well, sometimes ill, but when it works ill, we see how it might be avoided, showing that if we had more knowledge we could better it. This shows that science is wisdom reduced to practice. So as goodness is the result of our training, it is certain that to be good is a science, and as goodness is religion, that is a science. It is all summed up in this: that the world is made of ignorance, disease, religion and error, hypocrisy and all sorts of evils, and to be a follower of Jesus and believe in the Christ is to separate yourself from all the above and stand alone in your wisdom. This will teach you that man without wisdom is of all things the most miserable. He is liable to get into trouble by every act of his life.

1861

What Is Disease? Part II–Same Subject
[LC 2:1118]

What is disease? This question involves a great many speculative ideas. Some suppose that disease is independent of man; some that it is a punishment from God for the wrongs of our first parents and others think that it comes from disobeying the laws of God. Now let us analyze the above and see if there is any truth in these statements. If there was not a living creature on earth, then there could be any disease, or disease must have an existence before man was created. If so, then God created it for some purpose and if man's opinion is of any account he reasons that disease is his enemy and if God created an enemy to destroy him then God is not man's friend as is supposed. So you see that the idea that God had anything to do with disease is superstition; then the question comes up again where does it come from? I answer, it does not come, it is created, not by God but by man.

We have not a true idea of God. God is not a man any more than man is a principle. When we speak of God we are taught to believe in a person, so we attach our ideas to a person called God and then talk about his laws, and teach man how to obey them and the disobeying them is our trouble. How often we hear these words, if man would obey all the laws of God he would never be sick. Now the acknowledgment of this error is the cause of nine-tenths of our sickness, for all laws are arbitrary and binding, and when a law is so severe that man is liable to be cast into prison for committing an act or even thinking a thought that is not in accordance with the law, no wonder the people grumble and complain. The Christian's God is a tyrant of the worst kind.

God is the name of a man's belief and our senses are attached to our opinions about our belief or God. The savages' God is their belief, the Mohammedan's is theirs and so on to the Christian's God. You see that the Christian's God, like his follower's, is like a house divided against itself. The God of the North and the God of the South are as much at war as the Christian worshippers; each prays to their God for help and each condemns the other. Thus it is plain that God is a mere farce, and all our worship is from superstition and fear of a tyrant whose name we dare not take in vain.

The time will come when the true God will be worshipped in spirit and in truth, for God is a spirit and not a man. When I say spirit, I mean that invisible something that like the earth is ready to receive the seed of wisdom or error. Wisdom is the sower and man the vineyard, and as man is made in the image of God his mind is spirit and receives the seed of wisdom or error.

Wisdom has no laws, it is the true wisdom or light. The law of man is the invention of evil thoughts and wisdom is not in it, for as wisdom is in us the law is dead. So to be wise is to be dead to the law, for the law is man's belief and wisdom is of God which is science. Now if we could understand the true idea of causes and effects, we could learn where the cause of disease originates.

Man has invented a God according to his belief so that God is the embodiment of man's belief. As man's belief changes, so his God changes, but the true God never changes. So the wisdom of man condensed into a being called God is set up for the ignorant to worship, and as all men have been made to acknowledge what they have no proof of, the idea of a personal God is believed in, so that no one questions the identity of such a being. This God was made up of the wisdom of the heathen world and we have reverenced and worshipped it not from love but from fear. Its only opponent is science, so as science enters, this God gives way but not without a struggle. The true God is not acknowledged by this, man's God, but it is in the hearts of the people, working like yeast till it affects the whole lump. It is called by the children of this world of opinions Infidel and Deist, etc. To be an infidel is to question that God of man's opinion; for if a man questions a certain class of opinions, he is an infidel. Jesus saw through all this hypocrisy, that the God of the heathens was not the God of peace but of war, and this same God is worshipped now as then. He is called on now more than he has been since the Revolution. He is one of the most convenient Gods I know of. He listens to the North and the South and leads their men on to battle, and from the prayers of his followers, He is as much interested in the victory as the winning party. All this kind of cant is kept up with a certain solemnity and form as though there were real truth in it. But the time will come when all this must give way to a higher worship, for it is a vain worship that shows itself in every church in Christendom. They worship they know not what. This false idea is the foundation on which the world stands, and the evils that flow from this fountain are corrupt, for when the fountain is corrupt the stream is also. When the angel of truth disturbs the waters, they throw forth every kind of corruption. This poisons the minds of the multitudes and makes them sick. The true wisdom, like science, explains away this earthly God and brings man into a more happy state where opinion gives way to facts.

Aug. 1, 1861

What Is Disease? Part III–Its Process and Cure
[LC 2:1120]

In the above article I asked the question what is disease and in that I gave the causes. Now I will describe how it is brought about and the cure. I said that God was the embodiment of man's belief or opinions. These opinions have been forced on man like burdens till the people have had to yield to their weight and make the best of it. Yet they murmur and complain but dare not raise their voice in support of the God of wisdom. Opinions embrace nothing but false wisdom. They of themselves have no element of adhesion, therefore their life depends on coercion or force, so laws are established and penalties attached and if the people grumble, laws and penalties are applied, sanctioned by God, and God being only the embodiment of these opinions reduced to law. You are told of the laws of God. Disease is the result of disobeying these laws. So man is made to believe a lie that he may be condemned by sickness. For instance, we are told that if we go out and expose ourselves to God's cold or law, we shall be sick. Here man makes God the author of his own act that he sometimes cannot help and then punishes him for disobeying it. If he exposes himself, he dare not find fault with the punishment, so he lives all his life subject to a tyrant that will take every advantage of his ignorance to torment him. This belief makes him a servant to sin and to man's opinion. So his life is in the hands of the priests and doctors to be handled to suit their convenience. Thus man is a mere lump of clay in the hands of these blind guides and whatever they say the people believe; their belief disturbs the mind and the doctors sow the seed of disease which they nurse till it grows to a belief. Then comes the misery.

Now the God I worship has no fellowship with man's opinions. So to cure the disease is to break in pieces the opinions. This places man on his own wisdom independent of man's God or opinion, then he sees the one living and true God who rewards everyone according to his acts, not his belief. To believe in this God is to know ourselves and is the religion of Christ, it is Christ in us, not opinions that we are in. Just as we know this truth, we are of and a part of God, then we become joint heirs of God and will be guided by the wisdom of the father of all truth. This purifies and cleanses our minds from all opinions and leads us into the world of science where opinions never come. Then one man shall not lead us by his opinions, but if one says, here is the truth, let him prove it. This raises man to a higher self-respect, and if man does not respect himself he cannot find fault if others do not respect him.

[1861]

What Is Disease? Part IV–The Christian's God
[LC 2:1121]

I will now sum up the substance of these two chapters by introducing the Gods of the two above theories and as one of them is only man's opinion, I will introduce a priest, a doctor and the law as the God-head, for the three are equal in power. The priest is the father, the law is the son and the doctor is the Holy Ghost or explanation of the law. All these make up the God-head of the heathen idolatry. These two give the people their beliefs which are sanctioned by a sort of divine wisdom and so acknowledged by the wisdom of the father of all. Strange as this may seem, it is the foundation of all the misery that man suffers. Although we are taught to love and respect this man's God as the giver of everything we receive, yet if one-half of what we attribute to Him was true, He would be the worst of all tyrants. If we should look upon a parent as we are taught to look upon God, we should hate and despise the very name of God.

Let us see what kind of a God He is and how He compares with a parent. In the first place God is represented as knowing all our acts and having a watchful care over us as a good father. Now if any parent could have half the power that they say that God has over His children, they would curse Him to His face and treat him like a tyrant. Now all this talk about a God who reasons and makes bargains, accompanied with rewards and punishments, is so much like the natural man's wisdom that no one can help seeing that our Christian God is the embodiment of man's wisdom, when man was far behind the present generation. No attribute of their God shows any wisdom but a sweeping idea of everything. When His wisdom or acts are spoken of, it is like a military officer or some grand monarch or king. He is King of Kings, Lord of Hosts, the great High Priest. Once it was the height of honor to get a feather in your hat, for a military man was the greatest of all men; therefore God must be a military man for He had war in heaven.

The devil was the first secessionist we find and he was driven out of heaven. You never hear God compared to a statesman or any other learned man. It is true when He came to earth some eighteen hundred years ago he was not represented as a military man, but He was far inferior to the wisdom of the wise. He was called a very simple man, uneducated, full of sympathy, so He must have come down since the writers of the Old Testament. How natural it is for men to court the company of the great men, especially military ones. This was the reason why the aristocracy would not have anything to do with Jesus because he had none of the military turn of mind. Their superstition could not account for his cures and his life was so plain and simple it was not worth knowing, so they had no claim on him. The wise of this world who base their theory on opinions steal all they can from their neighbors, and when Jesus was crucified, they stole his ideas and engrafted them into their aristocratic creeds. This kept them aloof from the masses, so God was not permitted to associate with the people but could only communicate through the priest. Therefore all the intelligence we get from God is through the wise priest and he does not condescend to communicate through the masses, so the people pay the priest for what information they get from heaven.

We all really believe more of this stuff than we are willing to acknowledge and this keeps the people in bondage under the priests. The burdens of false ideas makes men nervous and superstitious. This gets their system in a condition for another swarm of hungry dogs, called doctors, that invent diseases, make the people admit their opinions, and after they admit their belief they are ready to bring about any disease that can be introduced to them. As people cannot see how disease is made, this false theory has led the people ever since and it always will till the true idea is explained how disease is made. According to my theory, all of the above can be explained on scientific truth so that man can be his own doctor and priest, and he shall not say to his neighbor, know you the Lord? But all shall know Him from the least to the greatest. My theory will explain all the phenomena. If you will read the first article in vol. 1ˢᵗ you will see that according to that, mind can be changed, and any kind of an idea produced; so to apply this truth to the mind you can cure or correct the error and establish the truth.

Aug. 3, 1861

What Is God?
[BU 3:0665]

What is God? God is the name of that essence that flows from wisdom. It fills all space and contains all the identities of this natural world. Man is created in this essence and formed out of the dust or error of the earthly ideas. Happiness and misery are the invention of the natural or earthly man or ignorance. I will try to illustrate how happiness and misery come into the identity of man. God is not the author of misery, for misery is what follows our belief. To make it plain to our understanding you must suppose yourself ignorant of what I shall illustrate.

I will show the absurdity of this world's wisdom. We all say and believe that God made the world in six days and rested on the seventh. Now no one supposes that God in these six days was trying experiments, but worked or acted scientifically and after all was accomplished according to his wisdom, he or his wisdom sat down to rest. This rest was called the seventh day and in it he neither worked nor did anything else. So that man was to do the same. Now let us look at it in a Christian manner and see if we do towards God as we would like that he or anyone else should do to us. I labor all the week for the benefit of man's happiness to explain to them the science of health. Now on the Sabbath I want to rest and I want the privilege of choosing my own amusement. I do not want people coming and laying before me their troubles on that day. The Lord sat down to rest after six days of labor. Man labors all the week for his own selfish ends, for the world's goods and when he cannot make any more money he is uneasy and unwilling to sit still; he fixes up some place to go to get rid of the day that annoys him. All those who have been laboring in the vineyard of God or science want that day to rest from their labors. But the wisdom of this world knows nothing of God but, like the foolish virgins, spend all that day knocking at the door of the Lord praying him to listen to their hypocritical story, expecting to learn something on that day so they can have all the rest of the week to serve the Devil in. Now if God is what their ignorance would make Him, where does he get any rest? For they call the seventh day the Lord's and if there is any day in the whole seven when he could not get any rest it is the seventh day. On that day they call on him, laying before him all the fraud and deception, asking him to forgive their sins, without doing anything themselves except to humbly and hypocritically get down on their knees and say over some words which amount to nothing. So you see the wisdom of man is all the time tormenting God according to their creeds.

Now, how do I worship God? In all that I do scientifically, and when I have labored scientifically all the week, I want to rest. So I let God or science rest. So the God I worship is not known in the religious world. If their God sits on the seventh day and listens to their stories, he would become as hard-hearted as a New York judge who sits on Monday and hears the story of the miserable creatures brought from the

Tombs to be tried. The Christian's God is placed in just such a place and he is just about as good, for his verdict is governed by public opinion and where he gets the most support. So that money makes the good Christian and ignorance makes the convert. The rich are saved with money and the ignorant are saved by grace, not by money for they have none. So the rich set up the religion to guide the poor and pay the priest for teaching it; therefore God is not in their week's work, but on Sundays. So if the priests take care of the masses Sunday, the rich will look out for them the rest of the week.

As there are so many kinds of Gods it is necessary for a person to know what kind of a God he worships. There is the God of war and the God of peace, the God of love and the God of hatred. All of these added to the heathen Gods make quite an army of Gods. Now all of these require obedience to their laws; therefore we pray to the God of battle to sustain us while we are fighting battles for his glory, and if ever a hypocrite was sincere, it is the prayer of the murderer who prays to his God to sustain him in his bloody act, then after the act is done returns thanks to his God as though God has sanctioned his bloody deeds. Oh shame! Vain man! This is the wisdom of this world. I have no fault to find, for the God that I worship is not responsible for this world's God. My God is one God the living and true God who is the same today and forever. This God is not the Christian's God. The Christian's God is the God of persecution, envy and malice; he asks tithes and observances, has certain rules and ceremonies, requires long prayers and is very strict. He is very scrutinizing and not one hair of your head can fall to the ground without he sees it. He knows every one of your acts, stands outside them and sees all that you do, rewarding every one according to their acts. This is the Christian's God, but this is not my God. My God is wisdom and has more intelligence. He acts in this way: when I ask my God if it is right to injure another, He asks me what I think about it and says do you think it is right? and lets me answer my own question, my happiness or misery being in the answer. If I should say, is it right to do wrong? He answers, What do you think? Do you not have any power over me? No. Why not? Can you not judge what is right? No. Then you must learn. Suppose I wish to steal. Well, suppose you do. Would that make you any happier? Yes, if I knew you would not punish me. Did I ever punish you? No, not that I know of. Did you ever do anything you knew was wrong? Yes. Did not you feel guilty? Yes. Was not that feeling punishment? Yes. Where did that come from? You, I suppose. No, I never punish anyone. Then who does? The one that does wrong. Then I punish myself. Yes, if you are punished at all. Well if all that punishes me is myself, that shall not punish me anymore. If you do not punish me why should I punish myself? Because you agree to. How? Do you want me to punish you if you do wrong? No. Then why do you want to do wrong if I do not wish to punish you?

November 1860

What Is God? Part I
[BU 3:0707]

I have said that according to the religious world, God is the embodiment of man's belief. All nations have a God according to their belief and show their God in their religion. The belief contains no wisdom but is a shadow of something that cannot be seen and is worshipped by man who knows not what it is. This something is what the world of opinions reasons about. The Jews prophesied about it and attached their senses to it, looking for its coming as for a man of great power who would free them from the Roman yoke. Heathen nations had a vague idea of this something. They incorporated it into their beliefs as a monarch or king, so it has always been in the world or in man's belief, but man knows it not. Language was never invented with the idea that it could be felt or described and to the wise it is a stranger. It has no place in their hearts or in the religious world except as an unexplained mystery. It comes to man's senses but man knows it not. It stands knocking at the door but it is not recognized as having an identity; so it is mocked at, spit upon, hated and despised by all men. Yet it is always the same, calm and unmoved, sympathizing with its friends who are bound down by the opinions of this world's belief.

Now, what is it? It is an invisible wisdom which never can be seen through the eyes of opinion, any more than error can see truth, for when the truth comes the opinion or matter is a shadow of this light or substance that I call something. Again what is it? If I should tell you what it is you would ask for proof, so I will give the proof of it from your own opinions, for opinions always admit but cannot understand it. So when opinion is convinced what it is, opinion is not opinion but is this something. Still what is it? It is what never has been acknowledged to have an identity. Then what is it that has been admitted but cannot be seen and yet is not acknowledged to have an identity? Can the reader answer? "Yes, it is God."

I ask, Is God without an identity? You say no. Then it is not God. What then is it? I will try and tell you and bring the opinions of the world to prove my answer. It is a key that unlocks the innermost secrets of the heart in the prison of man's beliefs, and it leads the prisoner who has been bound a captive to health. What is that that you call the key? It is wisdom, not opinions, and this I will prove. Opinions are like a shadow, the substance is God. True wisdom is attached to the substance; false wisdom to the shadow. Language is attached to the shadow, wisdom to the substance; therefore language is not in harmony with wisdom; the discord is in the opinion; the senses are life or wisdom. If the senses are attached to opinion, when opinion is lost, man loses his opinion but saves his life, for his life is his wisdom of self-existence. This life is embodied in our senses and the knowledge of sensation, so if all sensation is dead, life is still life but not active. The sensation is made in this world of matter and all religion is the result of man's opinions. This makes up the Christian and his senses are attached to his opinions. The errors of their opinions are the misery of their life, it being subject to the world's opinion.

Now this something is a knowledge of this wisdom which puts man in possession of a truth that he can explain to another. It does not come to the man of opinions. This shows that every man has two selves, one of knowledge by the natural man, the other by the spiritual man. Here is the proof. The sick will admit that I can tell them how they feel better than they themselves can do. This shows that I know more than they do and also that this wisdom is not known by the natural man. If so it must be superior to his wisdom, and what is it? It must be proved by an admitted fact, for simply telling it would be no proof.

I must make the reader detach his senses from a God of man's belief and attach them to this invisible wisdom which fills all space and whose attributes are all light, all wisdom, all goodness and love, which is free from all selfishness and hypocrisy, which makes or breaks no laws and restrictions but sanctions men's acts according to their belief, right or wrong, without respect to persons. For the natural man is only a shadow of man's wisdom, and if the shadow is from this world of opinions, it will be destroyed when the light of the wisdom of truth comes. But the life will be saved by wisdom and when the senses shall be attached to this wisdom, then shall be brought to pass that saying, "Oh, death! Where is thy sting! Oh, grave! Where is thy victory!" Death is robbed of its victim; the grave gives up its idea of death. Then life rises to that happy state where death, hell, and disease and the torments of existence find no place from whence no traveler ever returns but where man knows himself. This knowledge teaches him that when our senses are attached to opinions of any kind, we become the subject of that opinion and suffer according to the penalty attached to it, unless forgiven or the debt paid by the truth.

This is the new truth spoken of by Jesus; to know this is to have eternal life and the life is the wisdom that can enter the dark prisons of man's mind and find his life imprisoned by the opinions of this world and there hear his groans, feel his sorrows and break the prison walls of his belief and set him free. When a person gets this wisdom and attaches his life to it, then his life is to him a blessing, for it is of use to man. Then he is happiest when relieving those who have fallen into the hands of thieves, been robbed of their substance and imprisoned in a creed, there to languish from the wounds of the priests and doctors till the angel of wisdom or the tide of progress forced along by popular opinions shall beat against the walls of this superstition and break down the medical opinions, lay priest-craft low and overflow the superstitious world with science and good order. Then all men will be judged by what they know, not what they think they know, and all can prove themselves by this standard.

Aug. 9, 1861

What Is God? Part II Concerning Human Standards
[BU 3:0709]

Every science has its standard based on knowledge, not on opinion. I say nothing about such, for they prove their wisdom by their works. But it is of false standards with no evidence of truth except the misery they produce that I shall speak of. The two most dangerous to the happiness of man are those of the medical science and the priests. These two classes are the foundation of more misery than all other evils, for they have a strong hold on the minds of the people by deception and cant. They claim all the virtue and wisdom of the nation and have so deceived the people that their claims are acknowledged in war and peace.

Let us analyze the beliefs of these guides. Take the medical man, what is his science except that of killing human beings? Is the world wiser by his opinions? Do not the very medical men themselves recommend to the people not to read medical works? Does the mathematician warn the people to keep clear of mathematical books? Is not the world wiser, better and more enlightened by them? Is the world made wiser or better by quack medicine or opinions of the faculty? Are not these opinions like the locusts of Egypt in everything you eat and drink? Science and progression have had to fight both theories ever since the world began to think and act.

It is a common saying that the religious or Christian souls are the foundation of God's moral government, but let us see if it is not the reverse. Take the North and South of this American Republic as specimens of mankind. According to religious statistics, the South is more religious than the North, for all religion is confined to sectarian creeds. For instance, how long is it since the Unitarians were admitted as Christians? And even the Universalists are scarcely admitted within the pale of Christianity. The religion of which I speak, and with which science and revelation have had to contend includes more of the liberal classes. Show me where the people are called the most intelligent. It is in New England. This mixing up of religion and science is like establishing honor among thieves. Religion and politics always went together, but science, progress and good order never had anything to do with either.

Religion is what crucified Christ. Pilate's wisdom found no fault with him, but the religion of the priests said, "Crucify him." Paul had this idea of religion when he said to the Athenians, "I perceive you are altogether too religious or superstitious." Then he goes on to show them how their religion led them to worship this same something of which I am talking, so he said, "This something that you ignorantly worship, I declare unto you." Here you see that Paul was not a religious man, but was converted from a man of religious and superstitious opinions to a man of science and progression and he showed that this something was not far off, but the religious world did not know it. This always has been and always will be the case till wisdom separates religion and politics from the scientific world. All science is spiritual and is not known by the priests and demagogues or doctors. The theories of these three classes are not based on wisdom but on opinions. Wisdom is the solid or substance. Matter or mind is the shadow of the spiritual wisdom. Now put man in possession of this wisdom so that he can make an application of it for the benefit of the suffering community, then this wisdom will soon separate the chaff from the wheat.

Aug. 9, 1861

What Is God? Part III Comparison between Two Gods
[BU 3:0710]

All the parables were intended to illustrate the two principles, truth and error. Truth is the wisdom of God; error is the god of opinions; and the two have no dealing with each other. Each has his disciples, the god of opinions and the god of Science or Love; but their acts are so different that their characters can be easily explained. I will give you the religious or political god. He is represented as watching the movements of the armies and dictating to the heads of the nation. No one approaches him except the ordained priest. He takes particular care of the President and the heads of departments; in fact he is the ruler and dictator of all things. But he must be approached with as much reverence as the President or General Scott. The South has another god, not so great, according to the account of Jeff Davis; he seems to be of a lower intellect, for he sanctions this low guerilla warfare and a kind of cruelty which is only practiced by the Indians. These are the gods of the religious world.

Now where is my God? He is in the hearts of the people. How does he act? He is not a man, nor a being, nor has he form. He is neither male nor female. I will give you some illustration of his wisdom. If you see a man in trouble, you are or you are not bound to help him. If you have ever admitted it is right to help a man in distress, he will put you in mind of your agreement. Then if you neglect your duty, punishment must follow, for action and reaction are equal and the truth never varies. This embraces the law and the gospel, and on this hangs all man's happiness and misery. If man is governed by this truth, it develops his higher wisdom and enables him to prove all things by a standard based not on opinions but on what can be proved. It shows that all man's happiness and misery are in keeping or breaking this agreement. Now if a man is in trouble, although you may bind yourself to help him in the best of your ability, if you do not know it you cannot be punished. This is the law of opinion, so it is with the higher law. This higher law is not known as having any responsibilities, but it is the most perfect of all laws. It is very little understood, and not at all intelligently. To understand it intelligently is to make it your rule of action with the sick, or those in trouble, for the well are not bound by it.

I will show you how a well person is not bound by this higher wisdom. Suppose a person is sick and in great distress. A well person sees the sick one but cannot feel his aches and pains. Then he is not bound to relieve him, for he is ignorant of his feelings. To bind him so he is responsible for his acts, he must be born again, as it is said of Christ, so that he can feel another's feelings. Then he knows what the world of opinions is ignorant of. Then he stands in relation to the sick as one man stands to another who is in trouble of the natural world of right and wrong.

I will take myself as one risen from these dead ideas or opinions into that higher kingdom of wisdom where my acts have as much restriction over my life as my acts toward the well. My wisdom shows me the sick in prison; it also puts me in possession of their troubles and the causes, and if I listen and agree to help them out of their trouble, the agreement on me is more binding than any obligation towards the well.

I will here say a word or two which the well must take as an opinion but which the sick will admit as a truth. The sick are imprisoned for their belief; the imprisonment is what they suffer. When I come in contact with them they affect me not in the way one man of opinion affects another. Their language is different. The well speak in my own tongue, but the sick cannot do that for the language of the well cannot describe the feelings of the sick. Thus they are prisoners in their own land, among strangers and not understood.

Aug. 9, 1861

What Is God? Part IV The Process of Sickness
[BU 3:0711]

I will illustrate the manner in which the sick express themselves. Ideas or thoughts are matter or opinions. These opinions are in the world of matter and our senses or life are attached to our belief or opinions. As opinions are something believed and admitted, they become matter according to the wisdom of this world and are subject to all the laws of the wisdom of this world. Thus the priests invent creeds with penalties attached to their disobedience and the doctors invent diseases with other penalties. The teachers of the young are instructed to establish the sayings of the priests and doctors in the children's minds. Now everyone knows if he will stop and think that if a child when it is first born is given to the savages it will grow up one and with all the peculiarities of one or nearly so; this proves that the life or senses of the child is attached to the belief of the savage and the child has become subject to its teachers.

In the same way religion or a belief in another world is binding on the child and the penalties of the doctor's beliefs are also binding. Suppose you bring the same child into this country at the age of a man, will anyone say or believe that he is bound in his conscience to obey the laws of our priests and doctors? I think not. This then shows that the child's mind or wisdom can be molded into a savage and if this can be done it will not require a great stretch of imagination to make a disease. Just admit this child's mind is matter. According to common belief every form of matter can make a shadow under certain conditions of light. Disease having a form makes a shadow according to its identity or description. For instance consumption is a belief; this belief is matter and throws off a shadow; this shadow is the atmosphere of a belief and life is attached to the shadow. As life is the senses and the senses are in the mind or matter, they are all associated together; here is where the mistake lies.

I will make an illustration to show where the mind affects the senses or life and yet you will see they are different. Suppose you are ignorant of the effect of a charcoal fire. You sit down in a room, the heat affects the mind or body or matter; all this contains no intelligence. At last the life is disturbed, just as the cold would be and would wish to rid itself of the sensation of heat. The senses, being attached to life, will become disturbed. Opinions enter which are like more coal and fan the heat or excitement. Reason, which is another element of fire, fans the flames till life and the senses are so affected that they will not remain. This is disease.

Suppose I come in. The instant the heat affects my mind my wisdom communicates to my senses the cause and the remedy. My senses become composed, my wisdom directs my senses, and they act on the body; the door is opened, the trouble is explained, the patient is saved from his torment, his mind or opinion is destroyed, but his life is saved and his trouble is at an end. Opinions are the elements used to torment life or senses. They contain no wisdom above the brute but are matter and can be destroyed. All the opinions of the priests are condensed into a solid according to their belief, and although they cannot be seen by the natural eye, the eye of opinion can see them and lead the senses that are attached to the opinions to the locality where these beliefs are.

For instance the priests tell their hearers that there is another world separate and apart from this. They give such a glowing account of it that their opinions like fuel set fire to the audience and a chemical change takes place. Their minds are disturbed like mortar and their senses are affected by the opinions of the priests and a plan or expedition is fitted out to go to this world, which is actually created by the priests' opinions. The minds are so disturbed that the life, losing its relish for this world, is persuaded to embark for the world of the priests' opinions, to which their lives and senses are attached. Their senses are held between two opinions, not knowing what to do; this is called by the doctors "disease of the mind." They, not knowing the cause of the trouble, take the story of the patient who, also being ignorant, is ready to be deceived by the ignorance of the doctor. So the doctor, like the priest, gets up a false idea or disease and engrafts into the patient's belief a new idea of some disease that affects the body. Then he reasons till it takes root in the mind and comes forth in the image of its father. The life or senses are then attached and the thing is brought to the doctor to receive a name. So after he examines it he gives it the name of cancer. The patient now wants to know what is to be done. The doctor gives the punishment of such a disease; this troubles the life or senses so that life wants to leave the opinions of the doctor or cancer and escape to the priest's world where they are told that diseases never come. Here they are halting between two opinions; this last stand is called a real disease of the body. Now these two blind guides quarrel with each other. The doctor accuses the priest of frightening the patient and the priest accuses the doctor of the same. Between the two a war is made and the whole world is affected by their opinions. Parties spring up, reason is brought to inflame the minds and the weaker portion of the people are disturbed till the whole world of man's mind is overrun with false theories.

Aug. 9, 1861

What Is God? Part V The Cure
[BU 3:0713]

In the darkness of this superstition when all are either sleeping or ignorant of the danger that awaits them and the sentinels on the watch tower of those minds that see their craft are warning the multitude of the danger, when the enemies of science and progression are mustering the thoughts of the scientific world and casting everyone into prison for their belief, I enter this land of darkness, light the lamp of liberty, search out the dark prisons where the lives of the sick are bound, enter them and set the prisoners free. These prisons, like the prisons of this world, can be detected by the atmosphere or description. I have said all diseases were opinions condensed into an idea of matter that can be seen by the eyes of wisdom. In like manner, all ideas of the priests can be seen by the eyes of wisdom; each throws off its shadow or spiritual matter, and each has its particular sense, so that it can be detected as easily by the eye of wisdom as an apple or an orange can be detected by the eye of opinion. The wisdom of opinions is ignorant of any wisdom that cannot be seen by itself, yet phenomena are admitted by them which cannot be understood.

To be in a state to become a teacher of this unknown God is what never has been acknowledged by the opinions of man's wisdom. Thousands of persons have undertaken to penetrate this land of mystery and have returned with the idea that they have made the discovery and thus have deceived many people, broken up families, led the weak and timid and stimulated the strong. Till the people, like the children of Israel, have left their happy land or state of mind to follow these blind guides, till they have wandered so far from health or home that they have lost their way and fallen among strangers or doctors, who pretending to be their friends have robbed them of their happiness and left them like the prodigal son, sick and disheartened in this land of superstition. Like Moses, I enter this land and lead them out, and as I pass through the sea of blood or beliefs of these blind guides, I feed them with the bread of wisdom and smite the rock of truth and the water or wisdom gushes out and cools their parched tongues. I go before them in this wilderness, holding up the priests' serpents or creeds, and all that listen to my explanation are healed from the bite of these creeds. The people murmur and complain, some call me humbug and quack; others want to return to their own old ideas of religion, but I stand up and entreat them, stimulating them to press forward and not to give up till I have restored them once more to that happy land of health whence they have been decoyed away. So I am hated by some, laughed at by others, spit upon by the doctors and sneered at by the priests, but received into the arms of the sick who know me.

Aug. 9, 1861

What Is God? Part VI Conclusion
[BU 3:0714]

Perhaps by this time it would be well to sum up all this journey describing how I got into this land and how I got out of it. I will do so in a few words.

After I found that mind was matter I found that ideas were matter, condensed into a solid called disease, and that it contained all the wisdom of its author, like a book. Seeing the book (for sight with wisdom embraces all senses, hearing, tasting, etc.), I open it and see through it. To the patient it is a sealed book but to wisdom there is nothing hid which cannot be revealed or seen, nor so far off that it cannot be reached. So I read the contents of the book to the patient and show that it is false, then as the truth changes his mind the darkness of his mind is lit up till he sees through the error of disease. The light of wisdom dissipates the matter, or disease; the patient once more finds himself freed of opinions and happiness is restored and all is quiet.

What I said above is produced on me by the patient, by lighting up the mind and making the patient clairvoyant so that his own senses see through the priest's and doctor's opinion. This dissipates the opinion, for it is nothing but a shadow taken for a substance and the misery comes from mistaking the opinion for a truth; here is the trouble that arises from opinions. Now let men cease from giving opinions or let the people understand that there is no wisdom in one, then you shut the mouths of these barking dogs, howling night and day, which keep the people in constant excitement.

Look at these barking editors, they do more harm than the army. If Congress would muzzle these apes so they should not tread down fields of wisdom and let in the swine to prey upon the corn of government the people would be glad, for the government is as much diseased as the individual.

If the prescription of the President is equal to the disease, then amputation of some of its limbs will not be needed; but if these blind editors, speculators and Northern politicians are allowed to prescribe for the patient I am afraid that it will linger along till its blood is so far gone that it will go into a decline, lose its identity and become a den of thieves.

There is no doubt that the government is bilious and needs purging to rid itself of the aristocracy that wants to rule after the manner of these opinions, for these opinions are the disease and the government was born with this infirmity. But disease, being an aristocracy founded on opinion, cannot be truth; so in darkness it tries to spread over the whole body and it always makes trouble to save its life, for if it keeps still the tide of progression will overflow it and it will be lost. So the South or disease tries to hold its power and it takes weapons that will be sure to destroy their object, for the extension of slavery is the disease and to carry out the idea is to destroy it. They being ignorant of the wisdom of the North have got up false issues and have been successful in making the people admit them, till finally driven to their last extremity they have shown their cloven foot, so that the North and West have stopped to examine into their troubles.

Seeing no chance for escape or getting up any more false issues they show their shrewdness like the opossum by lying low and crying out, "Let us alone, we want nothing to do with you." Thinking by proceeding thus the North, rather than quarrel, will propose something by way of compromise.

The timid and weak are pressing the North and West to build up something but the President says, If you have wrongs, lay them before Congress; and the South whines and says, "Let us alone." This is to get up a sympathy in the North and meanwhile they steal from the government till they have shown their true character and have obliged the North to pass laws for their own safety which must destroy the very institution which the North has never opposed, that is slavery. The very acts of the South will destroy slavery and it cannot be helped.

Aug. 9, 1861

What Is Happiness?
[LC 1:0020]

What is happiness? It is what follows any act of the law of science, but it is not always understood. Sin and misery are the effects of our belief put in practice, governed by a law of sin and death. Man is the medium of these two laws; the one, chance or ignorance, which is of this world; the other, God or Science, which is of a higher. The wisdom of one is called the law; the knowledge of the other is the gospel or science. These two laws enter into all our acts. Mathematics contains the two laws. The solving of a problem does not establish the science, although it may be right, but it develops a phenomenon for a more wise and excellent law called science so that the world may be benefited by it. So by establishing the law of science we destroy the law of ignorance. This holds good of all the laws of science; the introduction of the one is the destruction of the other, to all who understand. To such there is no offering up of sin or sacrifices but a fearful looking for judgment or acting wrong that will get us into trouble. This keeps us on our guard. Now, it has not entered into man's heart to conceive a more excellent law whereby man may be saved from his sins or errors that bind him down by the laws of sin and death. To introduce a science that can explain the errors that keep us in trouble is what prophets foretold and wise men have looked for ever since the world began. This knowledge has been called by various names. It was called the New Jerusalem that came down from heaven and it was called the kingdom of heaven. This is the law that was written in the hearts; it is the knowledge of ourselves that can see the evils of our own misery.

It may be asked, how can we distinguish between the two, for everyone has a right to his own opinion. That is true, but science does not leave it answered in that way, but proves it so that there can be no mistake. Now as disease is an error, so the mind, as in any error, must be corrected by a power independent of itself, and this power must be governed by a science in all cases; though it may not be necessarily understood by the person applying the power. As science, like God, never acts except like a balance which judges correctly, it contains no thought or reason but judges everyone according to his worth. As error is a chemical action and contains all of the above, it is like two rogues at war with itself. There is an old saying, and a very good one, that when two rogues fall out, an honest man gets his due; so when error is at war, it develops some truth or science. As the degrees from total darkness or ignorance are progressive, they embrace all kinds of talents, like teachers from the lowest classes of this world to the highest of the spiritual world. All science to the natural world is looked upon as a mystery, witchcraft, sorcery, etc., because it cannot see anything beyond itself. But there is a mind that can teach it and another that can learn it and so on until it reaches a science. Then comes the end of the world of error and the introduction of a more excellent law of God or science. As a person's happiness is the effect of his knowledge, to be good is the first of science. All religion that embraces creeds is of this world and is governed by laws and contains rewards and punishments; therefore holding out inducements to be good with one hand and retribution with the other is not the religion of Christ. He is in us, and a part of us, and to know ourselves is to know Christ and to preach Christ is to help each other out of our troubles, destroying the enemy that has possession of us.

Thus to lay down your life for your friends is not so easy a matter as some might think. It is easier to talk about religion than to talk it. To talk it is to put it into practice, and to put it into practice is to give it to those who ask, for to give them a stone when they ask for bread is what anyone can do, as then you part with nothing. To give to everyone that asks of you some spiritual food or knowledge that will cool their feverish tongue or soothe their excited brain, and lead them like the good shepherd to their home of health where they can rejoice with their friends is not so easy as to sit down and thank the Lord that you are not like other men. To be a follower of Christ is not an easy thing but to be a representative of the kingdom of heaven is not very hard; it only requires one to become as ignorant as a child. The majority of men have not much to sacrifice to become a representative of the kingdom of heaven, but to become a follower of Christ is not so easy a task.

To call yourself a follower of Jesus is to call yourself a pattern of goodness and that was more than Jesus said of himself, for he never sounded the trumpet of his own praise. We are called upon to become followers of Christ or science so that the world may be benefited by His truth. This is our happiness and the happiness of others, for we are all workers of the same truth. Therefore forsake error and embrace the true science or truth and fight the enemy of health, like a soldier of science.

February 1860

What Is Happiness and Misery?
[LC 2:0734]

We are told that religion makes happiness. Let us see what it is. There cannot be such an element as happiness of itself nor such a state outside of man's wisdom. Then happiness must be the result of either our wisdom or our belief. If it is from wisdom it becomes a part of ourselves but if it is from belief it becomes adopted and we may lose it. We often hear a person say that religion makes him happy. Now if religion is anything outside of ourselves then it contains neither happiness nor misery, but if we seek this something we call religion we are happy when we get it. Can any person define what they get that makes them happy except that it is a belief and that belief which will make one person happy will make another miserable.

Look at any religious society and you will find that the individuals cannot all agree in belief. So those who do agree are slaves to those whose authority they admit as their rulers.

A church has its pastor, its deacons and other officers, also its forms to which its members must subscribe, and they, being numerous and each having an opinion of themselves, are either led or ruled into submission by the pastor. This sometimes makes the yoke grievous to be borne for the burdens are heavy, while they who bind them are happy for they rule and their power is their happiness.

The poor soldier who fights for the leaders sinks under the burden bound upon him. To keep up his courage the officers hold out the idea that he is fighting for a great and good cause, and a crown of glory in heaven awaits those who die upon the battlefield. This is all the happiness the privates get. So they fight to keep society from ruin while their reward is the satisfaction of fighting the devil and supporting the officers, and their happiness is what follows their belief.

Reverse the tables, making the priest the laborer or soldier, and tax him to pay the former soldier for his instructions, then it would be shown how well their principle of action, which they preach to others, applies to themselves.

In this war let the officers and politicians become soldiers and laborers and peace would soon triumph. I will illustrate happiness. Suppose a person is told that certain food if eaten will produce certain effects. He then eats the food and the effect is produced; this is proof that the food produced the effect for he reasons that if he had not eaten it the effect would not have occurred. This he lays to the food, but that, containing no happiness or misery, is not really the author of his misery; therefore it must be in himself. Suppose I eat the same kind of food and feel well; the food does not contain that feeling so that is in me. Suppose furthermore I say to him, The food is not the cause of your trouble but the opinion of the person who told you it would hurt you is the author of the mischief and he had been deceived and believes the food contained something that was hard to digest. You from sympathy became affected and you were nervous when you ate the food. You then attached your senses to the fear and lay your trouble to the food. Here you see misery is what follows a belief, and happiness is that state that follows our belief or wisdom. If our wisdom can give us a science that will correct our opinion, this is happiness that the world knows not of.

November 1862

What Is Human Life?
[Originally untitled.] [BU 3:0882]

It is an element of itself that fills all space. Then what is man? It is a knowledge of this life condensed into a form called man. Life being something that fills all space, independent of ideas, what is it and how does man know he has it when his idea body is destroyed? As we acknowledge man, it is impossible to prove that there is any life outside of him. To the natural man, this cannot be done, yet it is a fact and can be shown so plainly that even the natural man can have few doubts. I will try to explain life outside of matter or what is called flesh and blood. Follow me in your thought into space, outside of everything that has form, and see what kind of a creature you would be. To illustrate, pass into a garden filled with all kinds of flowers with all their peculiar odors. Man has given a name to each flower but God has given to each a peculiar odor; its life is in its odor and each odor is attracted by its kind. Man enters and to him it is like a confusion of tongues. He perceives no distinction of odors and to him they have no identity of odor, but the flowers have their own identities. Put as much wisdom into the life or odor of each flower as you put in each flower and you have a garden full of living life, with all the wisdom of each flower outside and apart from the natural eye, yet living and acting in space with all the knowledge of each flower.

In this chaos of wisdom, each odor is attracted to itself and can mingle and harmonize with its peculiar kind. And when these kinds come in contact with each other, the result is a mingling or union of feelings that does not disturb each other; but if another odor comes, the repulsion is so great that a discord is produced. This is harmony not understood, and it keeps each odor in its proper state. It is the same with the brute creation, but man, that is his life or odor, has a higher development. In this odor or life is all the wisdom of God, not reduced to practice, but like the odor of the rose, not acknowledged by the natural man. The natural man is like the uncultivated forest which often throws off some of the most beautiful odors from the uncultivated flowers. So man in the forest state often throws an atmosphere from an original idea or flower that fills the whole earth with fragrance, and the people become impregnated with it for good or evil. As the man of life or odor contains all the wisdom, he cultivates the natural man or vineyard. And mind being the soil to cultivate, experiments are tried. So wisdom being the man of life, he becomes the husbandman of his own vineyard. In the earth or natural man is where all seeds or ideas are sown; so it brings forth all kinds of creeping things that have life and the office of wisdom is to keep the vineyard in good order so that its fruits will produce happiness.

By the deception of error or ignorance, man has wandered away from science or spiritual life and, like Esau, has made his way into the wilderness of matter and recognizes no life outside of his own little vineyard. So he lives in death, never dreaming that he is the cause of his own misery. Now rise up with me into space, like the odor of the rose, and sit down on the clouds of error and see men walking and blown like trees by every wind of opinion, sometimes torn from the earth by a hurricane and hurled into the air, the tornado being started by some political devil and blown up by his imps.

Each of these men, who are affected by the disturbance of the earth or man, has his identity in this atmosphere. This is disease and everyone is liable to be affected as much as the rose so that the man of life will sometimes say, The life of a savage is preferable to that of a civilized person. This is disease. He is not intelligent in the wisdom of that great life that teaches him that all things that man creates must come to an end, but that part of man which is true wisdom lives forever. The ignorance of this truth is disease.

While I am sitting here away from the little flock I once used to lead through the valley of disease, while the winds of error are blowing the odor of disease into your very nostrils, I think I hear you say, "Oh had I the wings of a dove, I would fly away and be where I could rest, where my sorrows could be turned into joy." Now as you are putting up your petition to this great truth, I am standing by you cheering you up by my words and driving away your enemies who come in the form of doubts saying, I shall not get well, etc. I am with you and know this and feel it is eternal life. To teach it is to adopt a language that will convey it to another; this is what I am trying to do. I will try to give you the true man standing by you at this time, not myself as a man in Belfast but myself as a teacher of this truth, who is with you in whatever condition you may be placed. I will try to give you some idea of myself as your teacher or physician. To your natural eyes, I cannot be seen; then how am I seen and felt through the senses? The senses are nothing more of themselves than a musical instrument is an idea matter. To you I cannot be seen in matter, so if I am with you, I must be something independent of matter. What is there that all will admit must exist independent of matter? Take the senses of man and see if there is any matter in them. All will admit that God is not matter, for if God sees all things, his sight penetrates the darkest places and not a thing can be hidden from his sight. So it is with all the senses of man and there is no matter in them. A knowledge of these senses condensed into an idea, spoken into existence with all the senses attached to it, is man in the image of his maker. Make this image the medium of God or Christ to speak through and then you have the natural man. To know himself is to know that he, that is his life or senses, can be transferred from one idea to another without the knowledge of the natural man. When you believe this, then you can see and feel that I can be with you although, according to the natural man's idea, hundreds of miles apart. According to this truth, if we are in harmony, we are together; but if there is a doubt, that is separation or discord and the gulf is not widened on account of the idea distance. For two persons may be sitting together and the space be as great as the space between the rich man and Lazarus.

Sympathy annihilates space, discord makes it, and man is in one and Christ in the other. To be with Christ is to be in harmony with wisdom and his wisdom will keep us from the evils of man's opinions. This is the theory. How can it be applied to man and what is the use of a truth that cannot be applied to the evils that flesh is heir to? This truth is talked of by Paul: 1 Cor. 4:5, for we preach not ourselves but this truth that is in us. What was this Christ? If Christ is God, then God was in Paul and Paul was the servant or medium. Everyone may see that I am of God or that my words are true, but there is but one living and true God or Christ and all the other Christs are false. Then how are we to know what is truth? When our senses are attached to truth, then we are heirs of Christ, and when attached to error, we are heirs of this world. The Christ is to separate the error from the truth, for truth is harmony and error discord.

We often hear it said that if man did not disobey nature's laws, he would not be sick. What does nature command man to obey that he must suffer if he disobeys? A law is to protect the innocent from the insult of the strong, but facts are not laws. Laws have penalties attached to them, and when there is no law, there is no transgression. If God made a law before he made anyone to disobey it and then made man subject to it, to disobey God's laws would be right, for when he made all things he pronounced them good. I cannot find any law that God ever made. God's law is truth, and that is right or law, so it is right or lawful to do good on the Sabbath day. The Jews made law and not God, for God cannot make anything that will conflict with another. He is the harmonizer, and when man tries to explain it, he calls it a law of honor that harmonizes right or law. Whatever men agree to do, the agreement is law, for they have agreed that it is right.

A law supposes two parties and an agreement, and the binding of this agreement is right or law; but man made it, not God. If you throw a stone into the air, it returns with just as much force as it received. This is a truth and of course a law. But God has nothing to do with the reaction, for that was contained in the act. This is also a truth or law and contains no reward or punishment. But if you from your ignorance let the stone fall on your head, you have not obeyed or disobeyed a law and deserve no reward or punishment, but from your ignorance you have learned a fact. A stone will come down on your head if you get under it when it is falling, and that is a fact. It is false that God makes laws that man disobeys. Man makes lies and we believe them, and the misery that follows is the reaction of our own act. Therefore we agree to torment ourselves by our own belief. Jesus knew all this and said, Let your communication be yea, yea, nay, nay, and whatsoever is more than this cometh of evil or opinion. If man would tell what he knows and no more, he would not deceive his neighbors; then there would be no transgression for there would be no law or opinion. We mix opinion with truth and we call it law, but all the laws of God are nothing but truth. Man's laws are not God's laws, so sickness is not the disobeying of God's but man's laws, and this brings sickness and death.

Belfast, July, 1862

What Is Man?
[BU 3:0641]

There is a great difference of opinion in regard to this question. For my part I believe that every substance throws a shadow. Now is man the shadow or the substance? I contend that what the world calls man is not the substance of man but the shadow, and, if he is the shadow, what is the substance? Wisdom is solid and man is the shadow. Then how it is that the substance, shadow, has a form? By the design of wisdom. God is the name of the great wisdom that decides and governs all things through the medium called mind, which becomes the shadow.

Wisdom or God speaks the idea and it takes form according to direction. Man is the plant or tree created in this medium. So as it grows, it receives its light from the great father of all, wisdom. As this life enters the plant or shadow called man, it becomes the son of God. The original child of God is perfect, but its shadow is to the child, matter. So the matter or mind called man is the tree or plant that receives the life. This life is the real man; the shadow is the medium or mind and that is the changeable idea or tree called mind. Man or the son of God or wisdom is not seen in the shadow, no more than God is seen, but the whole creation speaks His name and shows His power.

So all created things or shadows show by their motion and act that there is an intelligence that governs and directs them. Man is the name of that wisdom that directs all the acts of the human species and also which governs and directs the brute creation beyond what is natural. The natural brute is like the natural fruit; the cultivated brute is the effect of man; the natural man or savage is like the natural fruit; the cultivated man is the developing of the original seed, the scientific man or God. The grafted fruit or ideas is the development of the scientific man.

Life is not intelligence but is the ocean in which wisdom lives. Matter or mind is the shadow of life; so as wisdom is in life it speaks ideas into existence. It shadows forth life and knowledge, but not wisdom, for wisdom is the substance and knowledge the shadow. So a man of wisdom and a man of knowledge have two separate identities. The sick man is the effect of knowledge or opinion and to cure him is to destroy his opinion.

It may be said a child has no opinion and yet it has a disease. A disease and an opinion are one and the same, for they are both in the mind and neither contains any wisdom, for wisdom destroys both. It is true that you cannot see the effect of an opinion on the body always, neither can you see a disease, as it is called, at first, but after a while you see the phenomena. This is the way with an opinion. There are certain facts, as they are called, that are true and every one will admit them as such. A certain poison, arsenic, is admitted to be a poisonous substance. Who made it poison? It must be God or wisdom. If the wisdom of man is a part of God, can it not make a poison by a certain direction of the mind? For mind is the substance wisdom works in. Mind is matter and all kinds of matter is the result of wisdom and if man knows himself he is capable of making matter from the invisible mind. Everyone knows that stones are found in the bladder. So the mind of man contains all the elements of the vegetable and animal kingdoms, so these must be under the same control that man's body is.

August 1862

What Is Religion?
[BU 3:0761]

This question is more easily asked than answered; for when you ask to have it defined, it vanishes as a thing and only remains as a belief. All persons have a right to a belief, so all persons can have religion if they have any desire to get up a belief. I have tried to find if there is any such thing defined in the dictionary, but I find the definition of religion to be, "A system of faith, worship and pious practices." Then pious means "religious, godly," so you get right back where you started from, just as in thousands of errors founded on error.

The definition of mesmerism, for instance, is fully as intelligent and satisfactory. It is psychology and that is magnetism and magnetism is a power which one man has over another. What is that? Why, mesmerism. It is the same in defining a disease. Ask physicians what disease is—they begin to give an opinion. For instance, ask them what causes pains in the shoulders or side—answer, rheumatism. What is that? Neuralgia. What is that? Nervous affection. So they will go on from one thing to another till you get them angry and drive them back where they started from. So it is with all theories based on ignorance and superstition. Is it so in science? No. The chemist does not give an opinion. He tells the truth and if you do not believe, he shows you the facts so you have no doubt. Now in all the above theories there are phenomena which cannot be accounted for by the natural man, for they do not come within man's reason. Man reasons in matter and all his experiments are proved in matter for all phenomena are developed in matter or the natural man. The natural man never can understand the things of the spirit and all these are governed or created in the heavens or spiritual world, and this spiritual world is science. And in all I say, I never mean to give any other meaning to spiritualism than the phenomena produced in developing science.

In chemistry, phenomena are produced and not always according to the known laws of chemistry, but they are accidents as they are called. When these accidents are produced, men look for the cause and then they reason and have opinions. This is the religion of this world but when the science or truth comes, wisdom takes the place of religion and this world of opinions gives way to the scientific world. Then is established Christ's kingdom or science or religion in this world as it is in heaven. This world means just what it did in Jesus' day; the natural world of Jesus' day was all the wisdom of the Mosaic laws or religion. Their religion was their belief. They had some wisdom in regard to science. Jesus knew all their beliefs, and then as now, the people were discussing all sorts of theories and beliefs and when some new idea or theory started, it came from the sea or belief of the old school. The old school was like the river Jordan, and to

wash in that or understand, you could withstand all the enemies' fire or darts. So the sea was the great popular belief and all the little streams ran into it, just as the old allopathy is the sea, and all other doctoring runs into it and that swallows up all the rest, for it is made up of all these little streams and when they can't stand the tide, they fall back and mingle with the great sea of allopathy. So it is with religion. The Mosaic priesthood is the great ocean of religion and all the streams or creeds run into that and the fishes or ideas that swim in that sea have kept the people in food ever since it was discovered.

1860

What Is Spiritualism?
[LC 2:0702]

Spiritualism is the name of a belief in the immortality of the soul. Its believers rank it among the sciences. I will analyze this claim by asking the spiritualists a few questions, being myself the skeptic. When I speak, is it I or my spirit? If it is I, do I think also, and if I think, when do I cease thinking? If I lose my organs of speech, etc., belonging to the body, where am I? Am I anything? If I am a spirit, when was I not one? How came I flesh and blood and then a spirit? I am either a spirit all the time or else I am not, and if I am one, what becomes of flesh and blood? When is the change called death? What dies? If the spirit is not dead, how can it give an account of what never happened and if it does not, what do you make of these communications given and purporting to come from the dead? These questions are in the dark and can only be answered by a person's belief about a hereafter, and that is founded on the fact that they want to have it true; but being ignorant of what they pretend to believe, they deceive themselves and others.

I will state my belief and bring proof to substantiate it as true. Spirit is only matter in a rarefied form, and thought, reason and knowledge are the same. To wisdom all these are only shadows of wisdom. Memory is the same. Our existence does not change. That is a self-evident fact. Memory is attached to this existence; it is not eternal but belongs to the idea matter. Life is composed of light and wisdom; everything having form contains an odor, and life and wisdom give it quality or body as it pleases and to every idea its own peculiar body or odor. Man, as we see him, is composed of these odors just according to his knowledge. The wisdom that keeps the body together is not seen nor admitted but is an identity of itself. All mankind is one body of wisdom, each having a self-existence in this wisdom. Matter is the medium, and error is the material that is employed to work out the problem.

I will made an illustration. Freedom from error is the great problem of man's destiny, so he ventures on investigation with fear. Fear is darkness of the truth, but truth is in the fear. Error is only a state of mind that is not really anything but commotion. Man is two beings. God is one and man or God is in his works and he, being ignorant of his God, leaves him in ignorance of himself, so he reasons as though his body had life. This error makes him two, yet he is but one. And when he learns that matter is nothing but error, that he has to get rid of or have it at his will, then he will begin to understand what he is and how he stands in relation to others.

As I have said freedom is science, slavery error; each acts outside of what is called matter by error. So error tries to control the truth and make it subservient to its will. It therefore establishes its science by authority, not science. This error makes a sort of atmosphere that fills the whole earth like the air and, at times, it gets so condensed that it darkens the heavens or wisdom so that the light of truth seems to have gone out. But truth like lightning flashes through this darkness and like a thunderstorm destroys the cloud of error. Then the light of freedom once more shines out and lights up the heavens with its wisdom of freedom, and science takes one more step towards perfection. Every living being is affected by this change. It is the outpouring of error striving for the ascendency and its life is in its own destruction. Property, character, bodies and every destructible thing must be changed and the owners lose their place in the world and give way to a higher class of mind. But their identity is not lost except as a power and they take their places where ruined politicians and demagogues stand. This is illustrated by the present rebellion. The error or secession element, North and South, will be driven from this land of freedom and will mingle with the vilest class of minds. Their memories will be held in contempt and they will be called liars and traitors.

May 1862

What Is the Relation of God to Man?
[LC 1:0417]

What proof is there of a God according to the popular opinion of the day? Is there one single quality of wisdom in the God that man worships? Is not all the worship confined to an intellect far inferior to the natural man? And is not the true wisdom of justice, sympathy, love, good order and intelligence set aside or looked upon as a secondary thing? Are we not told that religion is something independent of man? It is true there is a wisdom higher than the natural man. For the natural man is superstitious, bigoted, overbearing, proud, vain, full of cunning deceit and all the passions of the beast. He is very religious under some circumstances: fear of death for instance; bold when there is no danger and only kept in check by fear. This is the religious man, but this is not the religion or wisdom of the wise. All religion is of man and the trouble lies not in the religion or belief, but in the separation of opinions from the truth.

I will not quarrel with any man's religion or opinions, but only see if his religion or wisdom is of this world of opinions or of the wisdom of God or Science. I will try to separate these two religions and to do this, it is necessary to show to the religious man the absurdity of his religion. This cannot be done except by a knowledge of the religion that these vain men worship. They, being ignorant of the true wisdom, set up a standard of worship and bow down and worship an unknown God or wisdom. Now this unknown God or wisdom is not in their worship at all. He is not in houses made with hands, nor in temples made of stone, nor is he in the field of battle directing the opinions of man. He requires no offering of silver or prayers and has no laws outside of wisdom. In fact he is no man's God but the God of all who admit him.

I will now try to explain to the natural or superstitious man the living and true God whom he ignorantly worships. All admit this God is not a part of themselves nor is his kingdom of this world of opinions. But it is in the skies or clouds of their ignorance. They admit that his coming must be in the clouds of their ignorance. They admit that his coming must be in the clouds, so of course he is not with them but is to come. The God of wisdom says, You need not look for him in the clouds of your ignorance nor in the foundations of your temples for he is near you, even in your own hearts. But you know him not and crucify him every day by your vain worship. Therefore I say, Repent of your vain worship and worship the true and living God that is not made in the image of man's identity of matter but in wisdom that can be shown by his acts. I will give you the true God that I worship and thousands of others who know him not and yet are a God to themselves, who do not know that they worship any God, when they are the very children and heirs of God. But being strangers in the world of opinions, they are wandering alone in the world, like sheep without a shepherd, subject to this world of opinion.

Let man become aware of these two principles of truth, based on mathematical fact and the other based on an opinion. Then he is ready to test the Gods to see whether they are from man's opinions or wisdom. Each has its God and its world, but the natural man not knowing how to account for the phenomena that often occur makes to himself a God like himself. As the wisdom of truth progresses, it has no identity independent of Science. As it contains no superstition, it contains no religion, for it has no identity of God or man; it is either admitted as a science or one of the laws of this God of opinions. This the scientific man will not admit. So a warfare is kept up by the opinions of man trying to convince the scientific man that all his wisdom is from their God of opinions. This he will not believe, so he is an infidel to the man of opinions. For he disbelieves in his God and knows it is the invention of heathen superstition and has no wisdom above the natural man.

To which of these classes did Jesus belong? Let us examine the writings of the New Testament and see if they will give any light on the subject. Jesus called these two characters Law and Gospel. The law is the natural man or opinions. The true science or wisdom is the gospel; there was where he differed from the world. The new birth was to search into that Science that would destroy opinions, so he called upon all men everywhere to repent of their sins or belief and prove all things by Science. For their false science or beliefs had deceived the people and bound burdens on them that their mode of reasoning could not remove. So it was said that which the law or their opinions had failed to explain, this truth in the form of a science took upon itself that the errors might be explained. Opinions knew not this Science, so it was a stranger and they said, Crucify it. So they spit upon it, stoned it and finally made it so unpopular that it ran out. Then the men of opinions stole the body or truth, parted it among them and reported it was all a humbug. To this day, it is looked upon as a humbug by the Jews. So Christ's wisdom lost its identity at the crucifixion of Jesus and has never been acknowledged by man's opinion since.

False Christs have sprung up and deceived many and at this day all mankind are worshipping these false gods who can never take away the sins of their ignorance. But the true Christ or Science will come in the clouds of their ignorance. Every eye shall see him. He shall sit on the throne of wisdom and judge the world of opinions; then he will reward everyone according to his truth. There are some standing in the high places, who shall not see nor even believe till it comes. Then they will hide themselves in the rocks of their opinions and creep into their beliefs or dens to hide themselves from the great truth of scientific progression. Then Science will take a God to itself and man shall worship it day and night. There will be no darkness. For the light of wisdom will light up the dark dens of superstition. The evil or ignorance will be cast out and the truth will prevail. Then the truth will bind this old serpent, the opinions or devil, and chain him to the earth or superstition, so that he shall not deceive the child of wisdom by his smooth tongue and false doctrines.

August 1861

What Is the True Meaning of Life and Death and of the Two Worlds?
[LC 2:0694]

How came man to reason that there ever was a world beyond this life? And what is the evidence of a world independent of man as we see him? Life is a self-evident fact that needs no proof more than each individual has in himself. Death is an opinion of what life is; therefore man's life is in death or opinion, so he lives in bondage through the fear of death. If man knew himself, he would know that death is ignorance of himself and this ignorance is the cause of the greater part of his trouble. The life of death is an opinion, so all men must die for all men have opinion. To lose their opinion is death and the knowledge that you have changed is life. Life embraces the true wisdom that can prove all things. Our senses are one of the attributes of life. They are not the life but the medium. Where our senses are is where we consider ourselves to be. So if our senses are attracted to some opinion, we think that something has life, and as all opinion must die, we are afraid of death. This fear is our death for its life is opinion. This wisdom of this error is the destruction of death. The child knows no death nor fears it; therefore he has no opinion.

Life is a point without space; all things start from it. When it is attached to matter as an instructor, it acts through that medium of God's laws called the senses, so life and the senses are all that make man; his wisdom is what he acquires by his own effort. If he never places his senses higher than an opinion, then he is subject to death; but if he can see that his life and senses can be detached from an opinion and live in the Science of God, then he loses the fear of death as a destructive element but tries to solve every problem of death for the sake of what he can gain. These two worlds are science and opinion. How shall a man know he is in each? By his wisdom. If it is of this world, he shows it by his belief; if it is of God, by his science. Every thought is of this world and also every opinion, but every scientific fact is of God and is known to the person who knows it, and he is just as far advanced in another world as this fact is known to him and he can make it known to others.

Beware of false sciences for there are many; try and see if they are of God or man. If from God they can be shown or proved, but if from man, they rest on some opinion. All our acts spring from one of these sciences and act either for or against us, for man can act only according to the law that governs him and this is either God or Error. Suppose a man to be God, and his children the Sons of God. All will admit that the children are a part of their parents or father, yet there may be a doubt who the father is but there can be none as to who is the mother. So I will use the mother God. Suppose she knows all things; then she knows all about her child, but this the child does not know, for its wisdom is limited to itself and acts in its mother's wisdom and knows it not. The mother acts upon the child and the child knows it not. The child is the offspring of two ideas: one called its father and the other, its mother. Ignorance and superstition have changed these two characters, and by making brute force the leading power have made the father the wiser, the mother, the weaker. But according to true wisdom, this is reversed.

The child is the offspring of the earthly element called Adam and the spiritual Eve or mother, and it is in these two elements. So as one must give way to the other, it makes war with itself. The mother is its real life and the child lives in her, while the father or brutal part tries to keep the spiritual life in subjection to itself. When Paul broke from the earthly father and mingled with the spiritual mother, the father would come and tempt him. So he said, When I would listen to my mother, my father was present with me; when I would obey my mother, my father would not let me, so it was not the mother but the father that governed me.

These are the two worlds; to rid ourselves of the earthly man is what we need to make us happy. God is not of the earthly but of the heavenly or higher intelligence called Science. Man's identity is embraced in every faculty. When we speak of man's senses, we speak as though each man had sight of his own, and between him and his neighbor there was no sight, and so with all the senses, but it is not so. Sight is not a thing but is one of the attributes of God, like light. Tasting is not a sense confined to the body, but life and all the senses fill all space with no variation. This is the God of all wisdom. He spoke matter into existence and gave it life eternal. Like the child, man acts either by the sympathy of his spiritual mother or the dictates of the earthly parent. Each individual is composed of these two identities; our life is in both and our happiness and misery depend upon which we follow. If we follow the mother, all is harmony; there are no laws to oppose us. But if we follow the earthly or brutal element, we become a slave to the evils that the earthly man is capable of inventing. We are subject to the laws and penalties, rewards and punishments, and every kind of disease that ever was or will be invented, for such is the kingdom of the earthly man.

The new birth is to know the wisdom that makes man sensible that there is a higher life of his identity than that of the natural man or brute. When I compare men to brutes, I do not mean to say that brutes will cease to live, but they have no anticipation of anything except their daily wants. They take no thought of the morrow, the morrow to them is nothing. They are ignorant of another world, yet they are wiser than the Christian, for all his belief of another world is founded on an opinion in the ignorance of this wisdom I call Science. This never teaches another world of space or spirit, and the man of science is as ignorant of another world as the brute, but he is wiser in cause and effect. He sees progression in everything except death, and that is a superstitious fear of what will happen only in our belief.

Let man settle this great truth, that his life, senses and memory is all there is of him, and these are not his exclusive right, but they are all in the mother of wisdom, like the child who cannot get out of sight of the parent. Our life is her life, but our ignorance makes us unhappy. When we lose sight of this principle of sympathy, we are under the influence of the earthly father and we become his child. Yet the sympathy of the mother is still in us, but we know it not till the reaction of our acts comes, and then comes the reward of our acts. All liars must have their portion in this lake of wisdom that will burn up the lie or explain it; so disease being what follows a belief, it is too late to repent after the disease comes. The phenomenon is the result of the belief. The disease or misery is what follows. For instance, if I make you believe that strychnine won't hurt you, your belief is nothing till you put it in practice; then comes the reaction of your belief, and the effect shows just what you really believed. If no effect took place, then my belief neutralized the poison so that it acted according to direction. But if the reaction was bad and caused disease, the feeling is the misery and the misery is the disease.

May 1862

What the Parables Taught
[BU 3:0850]

All the parables that Jesus made were to establish the kingdom of heaven or God's science in this world of man's mind. This science was to put man in possession of a knowledge superior to the natural man, so to the natural man it was a mystery. They could not understand how there could be any power which could see the workings in the natural man's thoughts. So to establish this was not an easy task. This cannot be told literally to the natural man because it is not of matter. The only way it can be taught is by illustration.

It has generally been supposed by all the wisdom of this world that Jesus wanted to teach a resurrection from his body and that man should go to a place independent of this globe. This being his belief he had to illustrate it by parables. Now as absurd as this idea is, it is the belief of nine-tenths of the people of this world. Now let us look at it one moment.

If there is another world independent of this natural world, then I have no doubt that the parables were intended to refer to it; but there seems to be in the minds of all those who believe in this old theory another idea warring against the old one. It is like this: that the other world is only a state of mind and that Jesus never intended to teach the resurrection of the body and that heaven is not a place but a state of mind that will follow us after death. So you see that even with this idea all believe in death. This places man in the same state that Paul was after he was converted to the truth of science. He would often find himself talking or thinking upon these truths and his old superstitious ideas would come and nearly upset him. So that at the time he would exclaim! When I would do good or think right, my old ideas are present with me and that truth that I would like to understand I cannot, for my old ideas or evil thoughts are present with me. So it is no more I, the man Paul, but the old theory, Saul, that is present with me.

So you see that most of the writers of the Old and New Testaments are explaining the difference between good and bad or error and wisdom. Error and misery make up one character of man, ignorance another. Wisdom is science and has a character of its own unlike all others. It contains no sensation; it is wisdom and nothing else; that is God. Man is in the other two characters and is made up of matter, with this wisdom in it; so this wisdom is in the matter or mind and the mind or matter knows it not. This wisdom is like the chicken in embryo. It grows and breaks the shell and then assumes a character in another element. So science is in ignorance and it grows till it bursts through the shell of superstition and then assumes a character. These two characters are not known in the natural world. The scientific world of wisdom knows the two, but the natural man knows it not. These two characters are in every person and are the cause of all the trouble in the world. The standard of science is not admitted in the natural world and never will be as long as knowledge is looked upon as a gift or power. So long as this state of mind exists, it keeps up a warfare of opinions. I will give an illustration to show where the trouble is. Wisdom is not puffed up; error is. Wisdom is not vain of itself, error is. Wisdom is not dependent on matter for an existence; error is. Wisdom cannot be destroyed; error can. Wisdom is God; error is matter. And as man is matter, God put Wisdom into matter to control matter for its own happiness. God contains neither happiness nor misery of himself. Happiness and misery are in the act of matter, not of wisdom.

August 1860

Where Does Dr. Quimby Differ from a Spiritualist?
[BU 3:0642]

In everything. All spiritualists, as well as all religious denominations, believe the brain is the origin of the mind and that the mind is the man or soul; the seat of the brain is man's residence while on this earth, and at the death of the body, the soul or life leaves and enters another state independent of the man of flesh and blood.

It is true that there is some difference of opinion in regard to this state. The religious believers acknowledge that man dies and then they try to show what becomes of him after death. Some say he goes to heaven, and others cannot tell exactly what does become of him but take the Bible for authority and let men read and decide for themselves. The Spiritualists differ in one respect from other classes of believers.

They think their friends by some means get out of their body, as a blade of grass springs out of the seed which dies, retaining all of their ideas, knowing how they left the body and died. And still they did not die, knowing that they are in another state and also that they are in the same state as they were before they entered the other side, or, in other words, before they died. Ask if they believe in death? No, but the body dies. So they fly about and return just where the whole religious world stands in regard to the dead.

To me all this is what follows our belief handed down to us from generation to generation without the least foundation in truth. I differ from it all in every respect. My belief is what follows my practice and I cure with the wisdom that I shall use to explain where I differ from every other person that I ever heard of or talked with. My wisdom teaches me that instead of mind being the man, it is the medium, and the brain is like a galvanic battery acted upon by wisdom. This wisdom sets the brain in action and mind is the result. The mind throws off thought governed by wisdom, directed to some point which is some idea to be made. So the deposit from the thought made from the matter or brain is called mind and knowledge. So when wisdom comes, mind ceases.

Where Do I Differ, Etc.*
[BU 3:0477]

Nothing can take a form in the material world without its correspondent idea which is its cause in the spiritual world; so no disease can show itself in the body without the idea be first developed in the mind. This is because intelligence is outside of matter. If disease is independent of the mind then there is a power in matter and if so there must be two antagonistic powers in the spiritual world–spiritual I say for power itself cannot be material; the power that moves anything cannot be seen or touched but must be independent of matter, which proves the point that power is independent of matter. If disease is independent of the mind the cure must be, hence the medical science. Physicians act upon the principle that there is an intelligence independent of man, but we are taught that man is made in the image of God. But how can a cure be independent of the mind? If it is independent of the mind it cannot come through our intelligence, hence matter must act upon matter and if that is so where is God?

The belief that disease is independent of the mind is founded on the false idea that mind is wisdom, that is, that man is made up of wisdom and matter, wisdom being subject to laws of its own, but which in fact we pretend to know but little about, and matter being its own laws, which we say we understand, at least to some extent. They make no provision for that intermediate state which Dr. Q. calls mind, but which we confuse with soul and whatever is eternal. This they do not recognize as different from wisdom which of course cannot change.

Mind cannot exist of itself but is dependent for its life on wisdom. It is everything that holds that middle place between tangible matter and an eternal truth. It is that part of us that can be changed, not that part that changes by decay as wood for example, but that part that is changed by the direct influence of a superior power. For instance, when one experiences a shock of pleasure or pain the condition of the system changes from the effect of it and that, that is changed is called mind.

When a person cries the system goes through a change that results in tears and that change is mind–that change is what we call our feelings and is mind.

With regard to Salem Witchcraft: The Drs. admitted the phenomenon and called it witchcraft which the people believed, and acting upon that belief "for as a man thinketh so is he" they would first become nervous or excited on the subject; that excitement of itself would produce contractions in the system and some other unusual states which they would at once ascribe to the influence of someone whom they would think bewitched them. This would all arise from ignorance and the belief which they had been made to receive from the learned. The instant one felt an unusual sensation (such was their excitement) that their fears prevented them from overcoming it as they would in a natural and relaxed state and they believed themselves bewitched. When that conviction once took possession of them they were under the influence of their beliefs just as much as a mesmerized person is under the mesmerizer's influence. Their fears took away their control and they were subject to the influence of public opinion. Their own minds acted upon the minds of others and thus kept the waters disturbed. This would go on either till someone wiser than the rest destroyed their house built upon the sand, or until they spent their excitement.

Where Do I Differ from All Others in Curing Disease?
[LC 2:0657]

In the first place, all mankind admit disease is a living thing independent of the mind; therefore the cures must be brought about by some agent also independent of the mind. So all sorts of inventions are produced to cure the disease. Some believe in prayer, some in Bandrith's pills, some in the spirits of the dead, others in Poland water, some in travelling in foreign countries, etc. All these claim a power beyond man's reason and are believed to contain a virtue far superior to man himself. To me they are all humbugs from the allopath to the prayers of the Mormon. They are all founded on one false idea, that mind is wisdom. I employ none of these aids; I believe they are the medium of disease, and instead of lessening the evil, they increase it. It is like Salem witchcraft; instead of explaining the phenomenon, they create disease by their ignorance.

This is my theory. Mind is matter or the medium of wisdom and has no more wisdom in it than iron or brass. It is a material for wisdom and error to manufacture into any idea that comes up. So mind, being the material called man, is a shadow or machine whose owner cannot be seen, like a corporation. You see the building and the laborers and the machine but the corporation you cannot see. In like manner, you see the machine called man but the owner is out of sight and never can be seen by the shadow, but it is all that contains what is called man. Now when the machine gets out of order, I tell him, not the machine where the trouble is and convince him of the fact; then we (not the machine) go to work to repair the damage. I have been twenty years repairing these old machines and have never called to my aid spirits, mediums nor any of those agencies I have mentioned. I appeal to the owner of the body or machine, and if he has not sense enough to understand what to do, I have to do it myself. With children I always do it myself, for their little minds are like mortar that can be molded into whatever form of health and happiness you may please if you know how to do it. I should as soon think of stopping the revolutions of a steam engine by throwing coal on the fire as stopping the operation of the mind by a box of Bandrith's pills, or curing a disease by medicine. Disease is what follows a belief. There is a vast difference between a disease and a phenomenon. A fool with a large head and no brains is not diseased, for it is perfectly satisfied with itself. Tell a bright child that if it does not do so and so, it will be like a fool; and if you succeed in making the child believe, then the wisdom or child will commence with its mind to make a child or shadow like the pattern. The misery you have produced on the senses shows itself in the shadow, and this is what the world calls disease. I call it the effect of the disease and the shadow shows the misery in the belief.

Here is where I differ from all others. I use common sense; my medium is my wisdom. So is theirs, but they put their wisdom in their remedies, and so do I. The Spiritualist puts his wisdom into the dead. The Christian who believes that prayer can cure puts his remedy in prayer. They all have something which works the cure. The homeopath puts his wisdom into a pill and it must be powerful. I have nothing to get into. My wisdom is outside of the cause and sees right through it and sees that medicine is all useless unless it satisfies the patient till nature restores the mind to a quiet state; then the doctor claims the cure. Ever since the world began, certain men have led the masses by their wisdom which has been merely their opinions, and they make the people believe they are the wisdom of the world. In ancient days, these were among the Chaldeans. Nebuchadnezzar, when he besieged Jerusalem, took certain of the wise men favored in knowledge and understanding science to stand in the king's palace where they might teach the learning and the tongue of the Chaldeans. Here is the first and only place in the Old Testament where wisdom and learning were called a science. Paul in 1st Timothy 6:3 says, If any man teach otherwise and consent not to wholesome words, even the words of our Lord Jesus Christ (or Science) and to the doctrine which is according to goodness, then he says such a man does these things knows nothing but doting about questions and strifes of words, whereof cometh envy, strife, railing, evil surmisings, perverse disputings of men of corrupt minds and destitute of the truth, supposing that gain is godliness; from such withdraw thyself. In the 20th verse he says, "O Timothy, keep that which is committed to thy trust, avoiding profane and vain babblings, and oppositions of science falsely so called, which some professing have erred concerning the faith."

December 1861

Where Do I Differ from Others in Curing?
[BU 3:1155]

Wherein do I differ in theory and practice from all others who cure the sick?

All mankind, with possibly a few exceptions, have admitted the existence of disease as something independent of the mind; the cure, therefore, must be brought about by some agent also independent of the mind. Various measures and inventions are accordingly resorted to as remedies in the treatment of disease. Most people believe in medicine as a remedy; some believe in prayer and in the influence of departed spirits; mineral water and sea bathing, mesmerism and foreign travel are often recommended for the same purpose, all of which claim a power independent of man's reason and are believed to contain a virtue far superior to man himself. To me, however, they are all deceptions, from the drugs of the allopathist to the prayers of the Mormon. They are all founded on one idea, viz: that the body contains intelligence. I employ none of these aids; I believe they are the medium of disease and instead of lessening the evil they increase it.

This was the case, for instance, in the Salem witchcraft; unable to explain the phenomenon, the people in their efforts to suppress the disease only extended it.

My theory is this. Mind is matter and the medium of wisdom. Like iron or clay, it contains no wisdom in itself but only is a material to be molded into ideas by wisdom or error. Mind (being the material called man) is a shadow or machine whose owner cannot be seen. Man may be compared to a corporation: you see the building, the machinery and the operation, but the corporation you do not see. In like manner, you see the human body, but the power that works it, though it is the real man, is invisible.

Now when the machine gets out of order, I do not address myself to the machine but to the intelligence that controls it. I do not call to my aid mediums, spirits, electricity or any of the popular agencies of the day, but I appeal directly to the owner of the body and seek to enlighten him as to the cause of the difficulty and the means of correcting it. If I succeed, then the patient himself effects the cure, and the cure is a permanent one, for the same influence that destroyed the disease will prevent a repetition of it. This is what Jesus meant when he said: "Whoever drinketh of the water that I shall give him shall never thirst." With children, however, and those who are not able to understand the truth, I am obliged to apply the correction not to the intelligence but to the mind; but I should as soon think of checking the operations of a steam engine by throwing coal on the fire as of changing a patient's mind by a dose of medicine. Let me illustrate this further by a galvanic battery. Call the battery the body and the liquids the mind. When the battery is set in motion, certain results follow. Electricity, like thought, is thrown off and if wrongly directed a bad result is produced. This is illness. Now, in order to correct the difficulty, a doctor would give his attention to the battery as though the cause of the difficulty resided there; I would give mine to the operator, for I deem the ignorance of the operator the disease and the supposed difficulty simply its natural effect.

There is a vast difference between a disease and a phenomenon. Idiocy, for instance, is not a disease, for a fool is perfectly satisfied with himself. But tell a bright child it is becoming a fool, repeating the assertion till the child believes you, and it will commence to create a mental image like the pattern given to it. The misery you have produced on the child's senses shows itself in the image and this in turn produces some disturbance in the body. This the world calls disease; I call it the effect of disease, the natural result of the misery contained in the belief.

I will cite a case in point. I was called to visit a little girl who was sick. I found her lying on a lounge in a kind of stupor, utterly unmindful of what was passing on around her. She had been in this condition nearly a year. Her parents, having previously consulted a physician, told me that she had water on her brain and that she was losing her mind in consequence of it. After two or three visits I became convinced that there was no water on her brain but that the child's insensibility was caused by her parents' belief in the fact assumed. The result proved that I was correct. I gradually awoke the child from her stupor, changed the direction of her mind and restored her to her health. In this case it was clear to me that the parents had communicated their belief, which they had derived from the doctor, to the child and were making her an idiot.

I make use of my own intelligence as the sole medium of my cures; others ascribe efficacy to external remedies. The homeopath puts virtue into a powder which must be powerful. The Spiritualist puts intelligence into the dead. The Christian who is taught that prayer can cure believes the remedy to be in the prayer. All have something external to themselves in which to locate the curative power. I have not. The wisdom by which I cure, being superior to the cause of the disease, comprehends it and knows that all medicine is useless except as it satisfies the patient while nature restores the mind to a quiet state. The doctor then claims that the medicine has cured.

Why Are Females More Sickly than Males?
[LC 2:1064]

This question is often asked. The answer comes; they have nothing to employ themselves about so they sit down and talk over their aches and pains, and in this way they make themselves sick. Now if sickness is a thing independent of talk, why should talking about it make it? Suppose a farmer sits down and talks about commencing haying. Would the grass be mowed by talking about it? There is more in talking than people think, for if disease is independent of the mind, then talking can't affect anything. Now everyone knows and acknowledges that by talking or thinking about a disease they can make it, or at least aggravate it and to aggravate a disease, it must be something connected with the mind or the mind cannot make it. Everyone knows that females have more inquisitiveness than men; they want to see more, they have more curiosity than men. If you do not believe it, go with an intelligent female into a carpet factory or any manufactory. Or go to Saratoga or any other place, and if you do not find that you cannot gratify all their inquiries, then I will give it up.

I know from experience that females think and bring more to pass in one week than men do in four. There is a difference in the word thinking but not difference in the acts. If I think of a horse, that is all; so it is all if it is not accompanied with some knowledge of this world or science. Here is the difference between the male and the female. Not one man in ten thinks mechanically. To think mechanically is to analyze the thing thought of. To hear a thing named and not investigate it is the wisdom of this world, but to think from the wisdom of science is to investigate and understand. A person cannot think without having some curiosity to be gratified. Thinking mechanically so that the world can be put in possession of something new requires labor, and the person who puts another's thought into practice is an operator, but to repeat another's thought requires no thought but memory. The mocking bird or parrot can do that, but to build a belief from another's thought requires as much labor as to discover a science.

So you see, man never has as yet been able to establish Jesus' science. In Jesus' day, he never got anyone to teach it. False Christs have appeared and have deceived many as he foretold that they should and we see it fulfilled to the letter. Now Jesus warned the people against these false guides, for they contract the understanding and imprison the senses or knowledge in theories and beliefs which are of their own invention. In regard to disease, the wisdom of these guides accounts for all bodily aches and pains as arising from some local disease. So when women feel badly, they have a curiosity to analyze their sufferings for themselves and they have a fear of coming under the law of disease. Between both of these feelings, they are much excited and disturbed. If they are unfortunate enough to make a disease, then they have proved man's theory of disease and are delivered up to man to be cured. If they do not succeed in making any local disease, they must be encouraged that they can or will be called nervous, spleeny or hypochrondriacal and receive no sympathy from anyone. If they had less intelligence, they would follow in the wake of public opinion and make a disease accordingly. But having some knowledge that they have nothing to thank the men for, they hold on to it sometimes with great tenacity, even when the law of disease threatens them on every hand. Now when some person comes to them and attempts to claim this intelligence and release it from its imprisonment where man's wisdom has enclosed it, sometimes they recognize it as a superior wisdom and receive it with joy and thanksgiving. And sometimes they are so wedded to their opinions of disease that they will not recognize any intelligence or even virtue, except as coming through some advocate of disease. In such a case, the disease is long and intricate. The little wisdom that has fought against the various approaches of disease has been overcome and fails to recognize its true friend at first.

August 1860

Why Do I Not Cure All with Equal Ease?
[LC 2:0668]

That I do not cure all who come to see me as easily as I do some seems strange to the well. The reasons are plain to me and I can explain them to the sick, but to the well it is a mystery from the fact that they are under an influence that is adverse to the sick. For the well have no sympathy with the sick and every dollar they pay comes as hard as though they had contributed to some charitable object that they took no interest in, but from fear of being called mean they would subscribe a small sum. All mankind are affected by these feelings, and when a sick person is brought to me, the real person is not known in the controversy but the error or person that brings them. So I have to address myself to that character, called by this world our natural man, but the victim is not known and has nothing to say.

Every case is a variation of these feelings, and I know the difficulty I have to contend with, while the well or those in error do not, and to make the world comprehend I must explain by such natural figures and emblems as they can understand. I divide man into two characters. One governed by selfishness and the other by sympathy, and every man's senses are attached to one or the other of these elements. Truth is an element of itself but error is a combined substance under a false direction and our senses are attached to one or the other.

Suppose fire is an element of itself and your senses are attached to it and you live and move in it. Now cold is a chemical element composed of various substances. The senses of the man who lives in the fire are out of his natural element in the cold, and he knows no other except as a mystery. Occasionally a warm substance passes through the element cold and it affects him. He looks for the cause but not knowing whence it came, it is a mystery that cannot be explained. In this flash is intelligence that penetrates the cold, icy mind and melts his error; so for awhile he really believes it comes from the sun or some superior power so that he begins to set himself to work. Motion creates friction; friction creates action, action heat, heat expansion till the icy band of superstition breaks like ice and the soul or truth rises into the element of heat. As heat contains light or wisdom and cold is transparent or error, the light penetrates the cold but the cold knows it not till it melts or dissolves by the power of heat and is absorbed in the light or wisdom; it has its own senses but its error is burnt up and its wisdom is saved by fire.

Disease is in this element, not in the senses; neither is the heat wisdom but the element that wisdom lives in, so the warfare is not in the heat but in the cold; fear is cold; death is the medium of all misery and as it is the combined element of disease, it is the king of terrors. So all combinations that lead to disease are like little streams that run into this ocean of death. As all men live and move in their belief, their belief is like a house or barque, either in the ocean of death or the rivers that enter into it. Men find it hard to stem the current when the tide of public opinion is running so fast that they are in danger of being driven onto the rocks and ledges that are under the water or their wisdom. The pilots who are waiting to get a call are found to be under the pay of the master of the seas, the devil. So the streams or rivers are filled with false lights to deceive mariners while sailing on a voyage of discovery. This may seem strange to the well, but I can make it plain to the sick.

These two oceans are invisible to the natural man but they are as real as the earth we stand on. When a mariner is tossed about on the ocean, he is like a man in an idea or belief tossed about by the opinions or waves of public opinion, and in ancient times peoples' beliefs were compared to havens or places of safety. Noah's theory or belief was illustrated by an ark floating on the ocean of death. Noah was one thing, his ark another, and the ocean was the sea or world that we are all on or in, more or less. This truth descends like a fish hawk, and it dives into the sea and rescues the drowning who have been washed overboard from their old superstition and are being carried down the gulf of despair till they are released by someone like the fish hawk and are carried into the ocean of science or light. Every person is in these two elements but is not aware of his characters, and being ignorant, he wanders into the dark till he loses his way and is carried by the rapid stream into the ocean of death.

Spiritual wisdom is always shadowed forth by some earthly or literal figure. Thus the Bible is spiritual truth illustrated by literal things, but the world accepts the shadow or literal explanation and knows nothing of the spiritual meaning. These remarks are made to show how little the well know of the sick, and in fact, the sick if you judge by their talk are as far out of the way as the well. And they were brought out by some patient that I had under my charge. The difference of feeling in each patient and the influences that affect them and the burdens I have to overcome cannot be understood by the world. The sick are a burden on the well, and if it were not for a certain sort of pride which would object to being looked upon as a low-minded person, the sick would be thrown onto the cold, icy hand of the world there to be dealt with as the public law provides. When the poor ask food of the rich, the latter will frequently send them to the overseers of the poor saying, "They will help you," and shutting the door, feel very nervous and say, "I do not like to be troubled by these miserable creatures." This is literally true. I know it from my own experience with the sick. I have often used my efforts to restore them to health when their friends would drive them away as though they were strangers, but fashion and pride cover a multitude of sins. I do not like to blame the well, but we are so constituted as to look upon disease as an evil and the sick person afflicted that we cannot help being affected by it. Disease is like the natural man. The Christian has no sympathy with his neighbor's children if they do not walk up to the mark, while his own children are provided with a seat in heaven because he is a pious man.

This hypocrisy runs through every vein in the natural man, yet it is not known. I will cite one case for illustration. A child of about 11 or 12 years was brought to me by its parents to be cured; it had lost the use of its lower limbs. The child of course had nothing to say so I had to be governed by the parents. They were affectionate and tender parents but the earthly man had the advantage in them and he was the one with whom I was to come in contact. The question of course came up if I thought I could cure the child, and a categorical answer was expected. This placed me in a very unpleasant position, for if I said I could help the child, then I became responsible to the parents for the cure. And if I should say I could not, then the child would feel very badly, for the child would think I might. I cannot act independently from the fact that there has been so much deception that the well look upon the medical faculty with suspicion, and well they may, for the people have been humbugged out of their money and health. People do not stand in relation to each other as they should, owing in a great measure to our religion.

Religion, instead of soothing down the rough paths of life, throws stumbling blocks in the way of man's happiness making him selfish, superstitious, penurious, narrow-minded, dictatorial and overbearing. This gets up a counter reaction and brings in another set of skeptics that look upon all men as selfish and imposters so that the wise men of the ages have used their wisdom for their own personal advantage and have no idea of pure sympathy, and their lives have been the guide board for others to follow till the masses have lost all confidence in them. It is therefore hard to correct this evil that has crept into the church. Money, it is said, is the root of all evil, but this is not the case. Pride, selfishness and power are the evil. This creates the desire for money in order to obtain the power and influence so much coveted by man.

Now let man be made acquainted with his true character and his relation to his fellow man and you will not see so many miserable creatures without friends or money. But as long as the present theology stands and the medical men have sway, misery and disease must follow.

To return to the case I have mentioned. In order to cure the child, it was necessary to have her with me or where I could see her often. This would of course be expensive to board her and her mother at a public house. I was aware, but the parents were not, that I could not have the same control over the child by letting them dictate the terms of her cure for their fears lest she should not get well, in which case they would lose their money and place me in a relation to them as a sort of money maker. They could not help this, and I knew it, so I must give them security by an opinion that I could help the child or they would have their doubts about leaving her. The child had nothing to do; its life and health was the same as an old mill. If it did not cost much to have it repaired, the owners would have it done; but if there was a doubt, then comes in the cost and how it could be done the cheapest. Competition came in and the poor old mill was cut to pieces and none the better.

Let the well know that there is a higher power in man than dollars and cents, and that is the wisdom that sees the misery of the sick, and it is for their interest as well as the sick that it should be understood. Then instead of my coaxing the sick or their pretended friends, they both would coax me and excite my sympathy in their favour, and instead of putting me to the trouble of running after the sick, they would run after me.

March 1862

Why Do I Talk to the Sick?
[LC 2:0855]

The question is often asked, "Why does not Dr. Quimby make his cures and hold his peace, for his talk only confuses the mind of the patient and makes hard feeling and it does no good." In this way he is misunderstood, from the fact that his ignorance of language makes it hard to get the idea which he would convey for he has never been educated. Upon the whole, his explanation upon what he knows nothing about is against him. If he had an education, he might have been a very smart man, but my advice to him is to hold his peace, at least so far as the explanation of scripture is concerned. He had better let people believe what they please, cure the patient and let religion alone.

This is the opinion of nearly all mankind who know anything about me. Now to all the above I plead guilty and I will plead my own case before the world and my accusers, as they are my judges. So far as electioneering for proselytes in religion is concerned, I am innocent. That I try to establish my religion is not true. My religion is my life and my health and every idea that goes to destroy my health and happiness is evil and it must be destroyed or health cannot be enjoyed. As I am permitted to speak for myself, I will commence by calling your attention to the first sentence where it says, Why does not Dr. Quimby make his cures and hold his peace? Now from the above, it would seem as though disease was something that a person had gotten and to get rid of it was the cure. This acknowledges a something outside the patient, for the patient would not want to get rid of nothing, so disease must be something. Now is this something a living thing or is it not or what is it? We often hear of people catching a disease or a patient has gotten this disease. Now if they send for a doctor, what does he do? Does he not talk, and must not the patient answer certain questions that the doctor asks him, and is it necessary that the patient should have an education to answer? For if the patient would not tell the doctor how he feels, the doctor would be left to find it out and a poor investigation would follow. Therefore it requires that the patient should talk and so should the doctor.

Now who talks in parables, the doctor or the patient? The patient can say I have a pain in my side. Now if the doctor knew it himself by his feelings, there would be no need of deception, but not knowing, he must deceive the patient by his Latin that to the patient is words without meaning; and of course the words without an explanation to the patient who does not know the meaning is like sounding brass and tinkling cymbals. For instance, the doctor says, The pericardium of the heart is thickened. The patient does not know what he means. The doctor's wisdom is in his words and he thinks that words mean something without any explanation. Now a word is the name of a substance that has life or something, so disease is the name of some substance that must have life according to our interpretation of it, for we say we catch it or it will come upon us. To use a word without attaching it to the thing that the person can see either by the eye of the mind or through the senses is no wisdom in the person who uses it.

It is like a dentist who had been making a set of teeth for a lady. After putting them in her mouth, she asked him if she could chew her food with them. The dentist, not satisfied to say, Yes, which would not show that he was a man of letters, must make a great palaver of words that to the lady meant nothing and wound up with this sentence–that with these teeth she could masticate any kind of food. This kind of explanation was of no use to the woman and there was no wisdom in it, for the wisdom was in the knowledge that the dentist imparted. By her reply, we get the wisdom of the dentist, for she said, Oh, yes I know all that, but I want to know if I can eat with them. How often do people laugh at persons because they do not understand what another says. There are two ways to it. If a person does not know that his wisdom is what he wants to communicate to another, he may deceive himself and also deceive others by his words. But when plain words are used to express one's feelings, if a person does not understand, it is either that the person has [The article ends abruptly here.]

1862

Wisdom Is Eternal*
[Originally untitled.] [BU 3:0480]

Wisdom is eternal, without beginning or end, and has no death, so when a person attaches his senses to wisdom he becomes a progressive being. Disease is the natural result of ignorance and error, and is the punishment of our acts or belief. The popular religious beliefs also, are a great cause of our misery and suffering, and what follows these beliefs, is the material or medium that is worked into diseases of the body, and is ascribed to the body. The religious belief, prepares the mind for the medical belief, thus the mind, like clay in the hands of the potter becomes molded into disease, misery, and death. In the life of man's circumstances, apparently so insignificant as not to excite the least attention, may from the construction put upon them, exercise a lasting influence upon his character, from good or evil according as his thoughts may be guided. But the influence of thought in the operations of the bodily organs and in their disarrangements called disease is not admitted or acknowledged. To admit this theory, and explain the errors which cause bodily suffering, disease, and death, and to reveal to man these influences, which guide or control his spiritual nature and which determine his happiness or misery has been and now is the study, investigation and practice of Dr. Quimby.

In asking what is the nature of matter you strike at the root of the whole thing. When we understand that, we shall have learned the rudiments of the "theory" and then extend and apply reason to them as far as we are inclined.

Word Life and Its Common Application, The
[LC 2:0733]

The word life in all its applications is attached to matter. It begins, grows to maturity, then decays, and at last dies; this makes life matter of itself, for anything that grows to a certain stage and then decays is matter. The expression is often used, Life has its bounds which it cannot pass, and man's life is considered three score and ten, and the exception proves the rule. The wisdom which teaches my theory, teaches that life has no matter except as it exists in our belief. As matter is deposited into various forms, for example, into a tree, man calls the process a growth and applies the word life to the growth. After it has reached a certain state it commences to react and decompose and this process is called death. Then the dust returns to the dust as it were, and the life to man who placed it in the tree. Still this life is not known, for man cannot believe in life independent of matter. Man reasons in this way about the body. A child commences to grow and he calls the growth of the child, life; when it has reached a certain maturity it begins to decompose and die like the tree; then the dust returns to dust and the life of the body to the belief of the living. No such ideas as these come from wisdom, for wisdom puts life in the senses, and they having no matter contain neither life nor death. As life is in the senses if we attach these to wisdom, our life is in our wisdom and as that never dies, our life does not die. Happiness is contentment not life nor death; misery is discord, not wisdom but error and belief. If then you attach your life to an error, like putting life in the body, your life is unhappy according to the loss or disturbance.

I will explain more clearly. Life comprehends all that man thinks of and his happiness is in his life and that being attached to ideas called matter, he puts life or value in the matter. For instance if he should lose his watch, he grieves just the amount of the value it contains to him, while the value is really in himself, for he does not grieve as though he had lost a friend. A slave holder owns a slave who is worth to him one thousand dollars. He feels the loss of the black but owing to his education he cannot see that the slave is different from any other piece of property of the same value. He also has a son, who instead of being an income, is an expense to him, but should he lose him, the value being in his love for the child, it is not measured by dollars and cents. The love is in him and not in the boy. The slave has life and so has the son, and just as the father deals out to each, so shall it be dealt back to him. If the father considers the slave mere property and the son a loving being capable of enjoyment then his happiness is the son's and the son's the father's, but the slave receiving no such sympathy of course cannot return the same, so discord springs up in the slave and the sin of the father is visited upon the son. Correct this error, the slave becomes a servant and is contented. It is the same with disease; drive the sin out of the father and a more healthy atmosphere surrounds him. Truth corrects the evil, for it is an evil.

November 1862

Works–the Fruit of Our Belief
[BU 3:0250]

What proof can be brought to show that a man is just what he thinks he is? My answer is: his works. Man is known by his works, for they are the fruit of belief and where there is no fruit there is no belief; and in that case man is either perfectly ignorant or perfectly wise, and stops work because he is God and God has finished His work. Now man is not supposed to be either of the two, God or an idiot. So he must be a being between both. That makes him a man of opinions and belief. To show whether the works are of God or error is the great aim of each kind of man. Both cannot be of God, for one reasons from what he believes and the other from what he knows.

I will introduce a man of error who bases his knowledge on others' belief, still thinking he has an opinion of his own. The effect of his wisdom or belief is seen by its fruits. The younger son is he who listens to the reasoning of his brother and sees him contradict himself and shows him his absurdity. This is the scientific man and he is not known, for when the man of opinions is destroyed by the scientific man, he is not seen at all. Take two persons talking about mesmerism; one never heard anything, the other is posted in all things pertaining to the law of mesmerism. Let A be the wise man and B the ignorant man. A sits down and expounds the principles of mesmerism. He reads from those who have written on the subject, how a man sits down, takes hold of another's hand, looks him in the eye, and at length the man is affected; his eyes close and he goes to sleep. Then B asks how this is done. Here comes the mystery or science of A.

A, not knowing what to say, commences to tell that the mesmerizer has more electricity than the subject; and the former being positive and the other negative, B receives from A this electric fluid till he is charged and is perfectly under A's control. This story is unintelligible to B so A proceeds to convince B of the truth of his reasoning. A subject is obtained and A sits down and takes hold of him. I will call him C. Shortly C is fast asleep. A commences to show B the science. He takes up a book and asks C what he sees. C answers, The book. B asks him how he sees the book. A says the electricity passes from me to C and I impress on his mind the book. B says he understands this though he cannot explain it to himself but admits what A says.

Another experiment is tried to prove it is by a magnetic principle. A magnet is placed close to C's hand which immediately moves, proving that the magnet moves the hand.

Another is tried, the magnet is concealed and A says to C, Go and get the magnet. C, being blindfolded, starts off and returns with the magnet. B is surprised and says he would like to hide the magnet. A is a little disconcerted but yields to B so he hides the magnet; then A sends C to find it and he does so. Here is A's explanation: when I hid the magnet, C read by thoughts but when you hid it, he was clairvoyant. This is a higher state. B, being unable to explain the phenomenon, admits this explanation and these experiments go to establish the science of electricity and magnetism. So machines are made to take the place of mesmerism and persons are put into a mesmeric state.

Some time after these experiments A asks B, What do you think of mesmerism? B, I do not know. I cannot account for it but I cannot help thinking that there is something in it, though I do not believe anyone knows what it is. A, Why, don't you see it must be electricity. B, I do not see how that made him find the magnet. A, Well, there is a great deal you cannot understand, but when you have seen as much as I have, you will believe it. I want to show you something far beyond what you have seen. B: Well, I will go.

So they obtain the subject C. A says, I have learned that the subject can go to a distance and tell what you know to be true. B, I should like to have him tell what I have in my parlor and then I will believe. C is thrown into a trance and is put in communication with B who takes C to his house. C describes all the family and says, I see a man with spectacles sitting and reading a newspaper. He is a stranger. B, that is a mistake, there is no one in my house but my family. A, That is strange but sometimes I do make mistakes and imagine what is not true. Here they stop and each leaves for home.

When B gets home, he finds Mr. H. reading the newspaper just as C described. Here comes the mystery. All night the phenomenon runs through the head of B and A is in the same state, for his science had not explained this phenomenon. In the morning B starts off for A and meets him. Then he tells him that C was correct and asks A to explain. Another explanation is given and B becomes a perfect believer in mesmerism.

Experiments are tried to prove if the subject can penetrate the earth and find treasure, so they put C to sleep and send him to look for treasure. He finds a great many. B carries him to the moon to see if he can tell what kind of inhabitants live there. All these experiments prove their own belief and a little more.

Finally it enters the head of A to go to the world of spirits. Here is a large field for operation. C finds the dead and explains about them to A and B. By this time they have become so wise that their light has lit up the whole world of spirits so that everything is perfectly plain. Here is as far as they can go, for the whole world stops here and here ends mesmerism according to the world's belief. At last there comes a report that spirits made their appearance at Rochester, and raps and table tipping take place. Then B asks A how he explains these things. A: "It is by the power of electricity." B: "I cannot believe that, I want to see something of it." So they go to a medium and everything goes to prove the belief of the medium that it is spirits. One rap means "yes" and two means "no," and these prove the spirits. B asks A what he thinks of that. A says, it is a development of animal magnetism. B says, No, I believe it must be spirits. Here is a difference of opinion. B is as well posted as A. The medium agrees with B and so does another person whom we will call G. B believed A till A showed his ignorance; then B embraced the opinion of the medium and G. So it goes on. One opinion is believed till some other phenomenon comes up that cannot be explained; then someone states an opinion and the multitude follow.

Like the rest of the world I began with no belief or opinion. Like a child I went to see. I did as B did and asked A's explanation and took it; then I went to work to prove it and did prove beyond a doubt it was governed by electricity. At last I ran against a stumbling block which upset all my theory and left me without anything but the bare experiments. I then went to work to prove my belief, and my experiments proved anything I believed, and I concluded that man is to himself just what he thinks he is. I have waded through the mire of ignorance, crossed the river of superstition, have walked on the water of my belief and at last landed on the shores of wisdom, where I have found the olive branch of truth that tells me that the water or error has dried up so that the dry land of reason is ready to receive the seed of wisdom into the earth or mind of man. As I have passed through the fire of superstition and been baptized in the water of error and belief, I have come up out of the water and the heavens or wisdom are open to me and I see the wisdom in the form of a dove or sympathy saying to everyone, "Behold, the truth hath prevailed to open the book of superstition; it hath broken the seal and introduced a new form of reasoning."

1862

World Does Not Understand, The*
[Originally untitled.] [BU 3:1080]

Dr. Quimby's remedy for disease does not come to the senses. That which cures is never seen, and nothing in his doctoring can be imitated. Men reason from what they see and seeing nothing to imitate and hearing nothing to believe in his treatment they cannot understand that there is anything to learn. He often has occasion to talk considerably with a patient who though annoyed and wrought up by what he says, is at a loss to know why he so persistently brings up subjects, that seem to have no connection with her. She thinks his talk can be of no benefit to her, for she neither understands nor believes him and what he says is merely trash. Now why should she condemn as trash, that which she admits she knows nothing about? There is no justice in such a decision and yet it is precisely on such opinions that his reputation as an intelligent physician rests. The question is, does he, or does he not know what he is about? If he does not then the world is right, and he is wrong, but if he does, then his writings mean something that the world does not understand.

1863

World of Science, The
[Originally untitled.] [BU 3:0383]

What progress has the wisdom of this world made in the world of science? I answer none at all and in making this bold statement I will try and explain what I mean. Ever since the remembrance of man, phenomena have taken place in the world, the origin of which has baffled the skill of the most profound scholars of the age. They see the shadow and treat it as though intelligence was contained in it. Its form, locality and growth has occasioned much doubt and questioning among the people. And the wisdom of this world, not wishing to be considered unable to give satisfaction to the various repeated enquiries, comes forward with all gravity due to the profession to still the troubled waters by presenting the fact to the world in the form of an opinion which says: The problem is beyond the power of man to fathom and in order to give proof that no further investigation may be deemed necessary, he is followed by priestly robes who displays them to the gazing multitude by repeating the psalmist's words, Thy knowledge is too wonderful for me, I cannot attain unto it. And the people with reverential awe say, "Amen." Thus conceived, born and baptized into a belief is man's opinions, and its offspring is the shadow or idea, the life of which is its light; and if its light is darkness or ignorance, then the more fearful and dense is the darkness, and its ignorance or false knowledge, which is seen, makes the shadow or trouble, and the world calls it disease.

That which is made was made. Then if it was made, it did not make itself but must have been made by a wisdom or knowledge outside, or independent of what was made; and the wisdom that made it must be in what it made, under whose government it lives. If under the government of this world or man's opinions, then the shadow or disease is its offspring. And if man cannot recognize that which he has made and sees, how can he teach his brother man the wisdom of God or science which he has not seen? This world sees nothing without a form and in order to make a form, there must be something to make the form out of. The mind, it is said, changes; therefore it must be matter and is capable of assuming any form or idea it pleases according to the direction given. In wisdom or science there is no matter or form. We cannot see God or wisdom in a form or idea. There is no darkness in it but perfect light which destroys all darkness or shadow by filling all space. A knowledge of it leads this world out of its false ideas or disease to perfect knowledge or health, which is the world of science.

January 1864

Wrong Construction on Words
[BU 2:0144]

We often use words, putting upon them a wrong construction, and think that a person is bound to believe what we say because we say it. For instance, you often hear a scientific person make this assertion, that there is no such thing as weight, that weight is attraction, that its true scientific explanation is attraction. Now this is easy to say, but hard to prove when we admit that a fifty-six pounder is heavier than a block of wood of the same size. When we ask what the difference is, we are told that it is attraction, that there is no such thing as weight. So you see you cannot convince a man of what does not come within his senses and he will not believe it because someone says so.

Neither party is right, and both are nearly right. If you place the two weights in an exhausted receiver, they will both fall at the same time. This proves attraction. Take them into the open air, and then the iron weight will fall the faster. Now is it attraction, or must you introduce another word? Why do they not fall in the same time as in the receiver? Because they have to fall through a medium called atmosphere or air. This medium is more dense near the earth, but as it recedes from the earth, it becomes less dense, and bodies are weighed or measured in this medium. So attraction is of no use except to show that all things have a tendency towards the earth. To suppose that the attraction is in the thing attracted is wrong, and so is the idea that the weight is in the matter attracted. The word weight is the name of matter that is in motion, for when there is no motion, it is called pressure. Weight in motion makes mechanical power, and as velocity increases, weight diminishes until weight is lost in velocity; then the whole is under the law of attraction.

Now as the human body is matter and mind is weight, the natural man knows no law of attraction any more than the metal knows of the attraction that governs it. The law or science that governs man is as much in the dark to the natural man as attraction is to weight. Attraction knows weight is ignorance. As the mind is like the weight and the soul or truth is like the attraction, as we gain in knowledge, we lose in mind or ignorance. So as perfect velocity casts out weight, perfect knowledge casts out mind or ignorance, and truth reigns in all. God is the attraction of both. Ignorance, like the brute, sees no higher law than itself; therefore the ignorant act in accordance with their belief. Man, who is a little above the brute, has discovered that there is a law of attraction, and that same knowledge sees in man a higher and more intelligent law of knowledge that the natural man knows nothing of. This teaches man that as he loses in ignorance by embracing the truth, he leaves this world of error and takes truth for ignorance. So as he learns science, he disregards error till all error is swallowed up in truth. Then one shall not say to another, Know you the truth, but all shall know it from the least to the greatest. Then disease shall be destroyed and truth shall reign all in all.

March 1860

Your Position in Regard to the World
[LC 1:0012]

What is your position in regard to the world or the errors of the world? You cannot embrace both. If you embrace the world you embrace its errors and become a servant to its laws, and the spirit or truth departs to the God that gave it. But if you hold on to the truth, the world is in subjection to you and instead of becoming a servant, you become a teacher of truth to the world and lead other minds to the truth.

Instead of your happiness being in the world, the world's happiness is in you. Here is your true position and this is the struggle you will have to go through. Shall the world lead you, or shall you lead the world? This is the point that is to be settled in your mind.

Now I will give you the signs of the times. Many shall come in the name of the truth and say, do this, or do that—music, dancing, and all sorts of amusements. But truth says, Beware, be not deceived; seek first the truth and all the above will be a pleasure to you. To know whether you are born of the truth, the truth shall show just your position in the world. Then you can take the lead and the world will listen to you.

Then the kingdom of this world has become subject to the kingdom of heaven, for error has become the subject of truth.

This is a trying scene to go through. It seems as though you must leave all the world's pleasure and seclude yourself from society. But this is not the case; you will like society all the better. For where the carcass is there will all the eagles be gathered; so where error is, truth will go to lead the captive free. This will make you love amusement for the sake of doing good. Then you will rejoice with those that rejoice and weep with those that weep and your happiness is their happiness. Then you will be loved and respected for your love or knowledge and you will draw around you those minds that are in harmony with yours. Then will the old ideas come and knock at your door for admittance, but the truth will say, Depart from me, ye cursed, for when I wanted truth you gave me no answer; when ignorant or naked, you gave me no truth or clothes; therefore depart ye cursed, into everlasting darkness where ignorance and error dwell.

December 1859

Your True Position towards Truth and Error
[BU 2:0062]

Question: "I understand you to say sometimes that mind is matter and at another time you separate them by showing that the mind leaves the body and goes to a distant place, sees and describes objects that are not known to any person present."

Answer: Certainly, and I will give you the proof. The mind is a medium of a higher power that is not recognized which is independent of the natural man. Therefore when we speak of mind we embrace this power as we often do when we speak of a lever, supposing the power in the lever, not thinking that the lever or mind contains no knowledge or power, for knowledge is power.

This natural mistake is attributed to our ignorance of mathematics. The science of mathematics separates the error from the truth. The same mistake exists in regard to mind and matter. The body may be compared to dead weight, the mind a lever. Error puts knowledge into the lever. Here is where all the mystery lies. The natural man cannot see beyond this standard and as all our happiness or misery is what follows our acts, it is not strange that we are all the time getting into trouble. Now, separate the power from the lever or mind and the mind becomes subject to this independent power and acts upon another's mind in the same way that the natural man may suggest to his friend the best way of applying his power to the lever to move matter. As our bodies are the machine to be moved like a locomotive engine and the mind is the steam, it is kept in action by a power independent of itself, for the mind or steam contains no knowledge, any more than the body or engine. Now all men will admit these two elements: one called right and the other wrong. These two powers are the powers not understood or admitted to have an existence independent of the lever or mind, yet every development of science shows one of these powers and it is acknowledged by all, but its place of residence is not known nor acknowledged. It is looked upon as something mysterious and miraculous till it shows itself and is understood as a science. Then it is acknowledged but not recognized as that power which governs all our right acts. The other is animal power and is a servant of the first. These two powers govern the mind and body as the engineer governs the steam and engine. Knowledge of ourselves as spiritual beings separates both.

Jan. 1860

P. P. QUIMBY–LETTERS PATENT

By the Editor

Phineas Parkhurst Quimby was issued three Letters Patent individually for his inventions and another Letters Patent jointly with a fellow Belfast, Maine resident by the name of Job White. I've been unable to make a connection between these two persons, but as Phineas' mother's maiden name was White, it is quite possible that other gentleman was related to him.

As Quimby was always interested in anything mechanical, his several occupations and interests tended to overlap. The Letters Patent are:

1. White & Quimby Circular Sawing Machine–Patented Sept. 12, 1829
2. Quimby's Chain Saw–Patented June 3, 1834
3. P. Quimby, Permutation Lock–Patented May 23, 1836
4. Quimby's Patent Steering Gear–Patented March 19, 1850

Before examining P. P. Quimby's inventions and improvements to mechanical devices, we should consider some historical background of the pertinent years surrounding the patents. Some of the records published here for the first time are incomplete due in part to the "Great Patent Office Fire" of 1836.

The fire occurred on the morning of December 15th at the Patent Office, which was then located at Blodgett's Hotel in Washington D. C., and consumed an estimated seven thousand models and nine thousand drawings of pending and patented inventions. In the years leading up to the fire, the United States government had issued approximately ten thousand patents.

In an effort to restore those records, the U. S. Congress stepped in to authorize the reconstruction of the records and more valuable models from private files. Out of the ten thousand patents effected, only two thousand eight hundred forty-five were restored. A piece of our American history and ingenuity was forever lost in that fire.

In 1975, Mrs. C. C. Pineo, a direct descendent of Phineas Parkhurst Quimby, deposited additional materials in the Boston University collection. Dr. C. Alan Anderson created a numbered list of the materials on October 1, 1975, which states in part: "…along with three patents, two sheets of steering gear drawings, wrapper for patents, and box for papers… The box in which the papers are contained probably came from Erroll Stafford Collie; the December 1946 date on the box (presumably the expiration date of some photographic paper) most likely indicates approximately the time when Collie and Ervin Seale borrowed the Quimby papers."

This supplemental collection of materials is comprised of forty-six items beyond the three Letters Patent, including four pieces of P. P. Quimby's writings (three of these are the only examples of Quimby's handwriting found in the entire Boston University collection); writings of Mrs. P. P. Quimby (Susannah Burnham Haraden Quimby); a school composition by George A. Quimby; a letter from a Quimby cousin (Susan); writings of people outside the Quimby family; and miscellaneous poetry and quotations.

White & Quimby Circular Sawing Machine–Patented Sept. 12, 1829

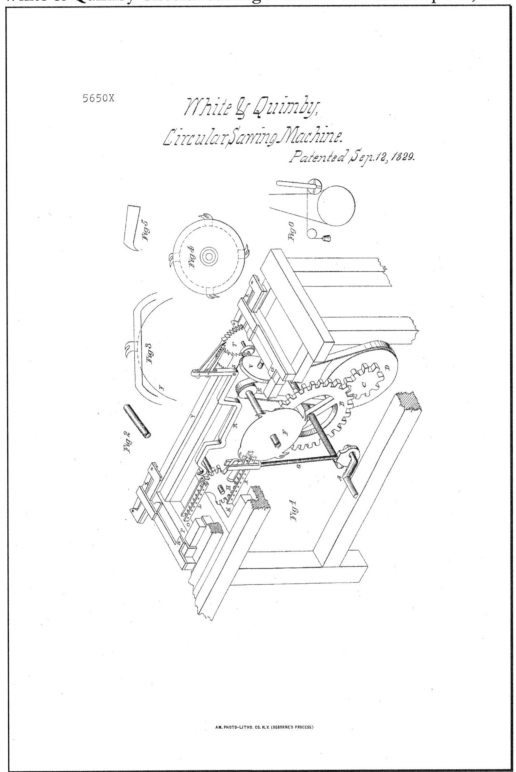

As of this writing, this single image is all that is available from the U. S. Patent Office for this patent. Joseph Williamson wrote the following in his 1877 book *The History of the City of Belfast in the State of Maine*: "A valuable machine for sawing coach-panels and veneer from the circular surface of timber was invented by Job White and P. P. Quimby, in 1829; and with improvements is still successfully used."

Quimby's Chain Saw–Patented June 3, 1834

The U. S. Patent Office doesn't seem to have a record of this patent, and most likely the formal record was lost in the Great Patent Office Fire of 1836. Although there isn't a mechanical drawing of this machine, Dr. Quimby did have his own copy of the Letters Patent, and his heirs placed it in the Boston University collection in 1975.

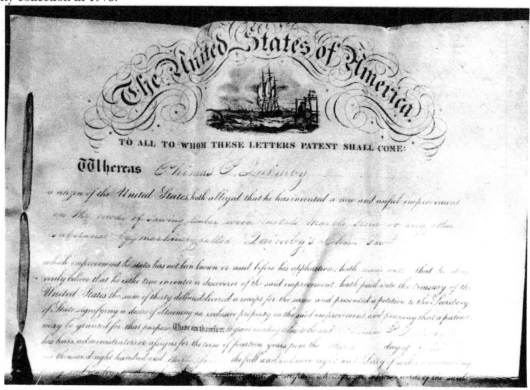

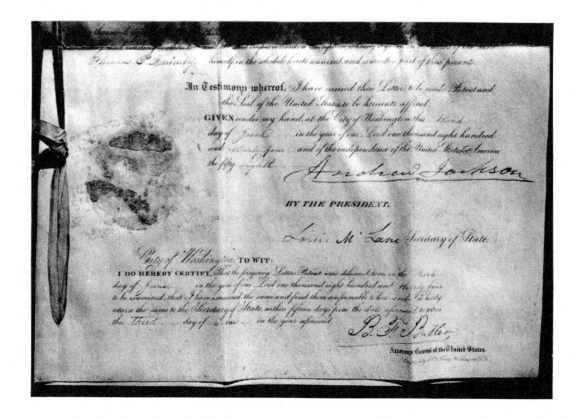

The patent states:

The United States of America

TO ALL TO WHOM THESE LETTERS PATENT SHALL COME:

Whereas Phineas P. Quimby,

A citizen of the United States, hath alleged that he has invented a new and useful improvement in the mode of sawing timbers, wood, metals, marble, stone or any other substance, by machinery called "Quimby's Chain Saw,"

Which improvement he states has not been known or used before his application; hath made oath that he does verily believe that he is the true inventor or discoverer of the said improvement; hath paid into the treasury of the United States the sum of thirty dollars, delivered a receipt for the same, and presented a petition to the Secretary of State signifying a desire of obtaining an exclusive property in the said improvement, and praying that a patent may be granted for that purpose. These and therefore to grant according to law to the said Phineas P. Quimby his heirs, administrators or assigns for the term of fourteen years from the third day of June one thousand eight hundred and thirty four the full and exclusive right and liberty of making, constructing, using and lending to others to be used for the said improvement a description whereof is given in the words of the said Phineas P. Quimby himself in the schedule hereto annexed and is made a part of these presents.

In Testimony whereof, I have caused these Letters to be made Patent and the Seal of the United States to be hereunto affixed.

Given under my hand, at the City of Washington, this third day of June in the year of our Lord one thousand eight hundred and thirty four and of the independence of the United States of America the fifty eighth

[signature] Andrew Jackson

BY THE PRESIDENT,

[signature] Louis M. Lane Secretary of State

City of Washington, TO WIT:

I DO HEREBY CERTIFY, That the foregoing Letters, Patent were delivered to me on the third day of June, in the year of our Lord one thousand eight hundred and thirty four to be examined; that I have examined the same and find them conformably to law and I do hereby return the same to the Secretary of State, within fifteen days from the date aforesaid to wit on this third day of June in the year aforesaid [signature] B. F. Butler, Attorney General of the United States.

There are four handwritten pages of description or schedule annexed into the patent:

The Schedule referred to in these Letters Patent and making part of the same containing a description in the words of the said Phineas P. Quimby himself, of his improvement, in the mode of sawing timber, wood, metals, marble, stone, or any other substance by machinery, called "Quimby's Chain Saw."

To all to whom these presents shall come;

Be it known, that I, Phineas P. Quimby of Belfast in the county of Waldo and State of Maine have invented a new and useful improvement in the mode of sawing timber, wood, metals, marble, stone &c. by machinery called "Quimby's Chain Saw" and that the following is a full and exact description of said improvement as invented by me.—

My improvement consists in the peculiar construction of the saw, and of the carriage on which the substance to be sawed, is placed, the latter being contrived so as to adjust itself by the motion of the machinery, but for the better understanding these I will describe the whole machine.

The frame consists of four upright posts of sufficient length and strength, connected on the opposite sides in pairs by rails, and by four cross girths, two at each end, which form bearings for the support of the machinery, here in after described.–

First. The Main shaft to which the moving power is applied, has its bearing on the lower side-rails, and on it is fixed a large cog wheel near its centre, which meshes or works into a spur-wheel placed in the middle of the shaft which bears the band wheels hereafter described; also in that end of the shaft towards the front side of the machine, is fixed a drum pulley, designed to bear the band which turns the pinion of the rack, which causes the carriage to recede.–Second. Parallel to and at a short distance from the main shaft and on the same rails for its bearings, is fixed the shaft of the main band wheels, in the middle of said shaft is the spur wheel worked as just described above, by the large cog-wheel on the main shaft, on each side of said spur-wheel–are the large band wheels or pulleys, the bands from which turn two smaller ones on the upper or lower saw shaft as hereafter described.–Third. Still further on and parallel to the last mentioned shaft, is the lower saw shaft, bearing on the same rails, and on the centre of which is a grooved pulley around which the saw passes, which might be of iron cast or wrought.–Fourth. Immediately above the last described shaft and parallel with it is the upper saw shaft, having its bearing on the upper front side rail and one of the carriageway rails, on those two points opposite the band wheels on the second shaft described, are two small band pulleys and near the centre another grooved pulley corresponding to that hereinbefore described round which the saw passes.–Fifth. The Saw is composed of a number of Links, the length of which Links and the number to be employed to be such as to suit the use to which it is to be applied, each link to be flattened, and to contain one tooth or more at the pleasure of the maker and each tooth to be made of suitable materials and being separately inserted into the link and fastened in by a screw or pin or welded fast or if better liked, the tooth or teeth of each link, and the body of the links to be solid and composed of one entire piece of metal.– These Links are to be connected together like the fuzee chain of a watch, or to be inserted into each other and play as upon a joint, and all then brought together, so as to make a ring or endless circular chain; each tooth is to be made thicker at the cutter edge or front where it cuts, and the plates composing the links are to be made something thinner, at their front ends so that they may not catch as the saw moves forward though this precaution may be unnecessary since the teeth being made thicker in the front will make sufficient room to obviate any difficulty on this score, moreover the heads of the rivets confining the links are to be countersunk, so as to form a smooth surface.–This saw is to be placed around the grooved pulleys hereinbefore described by which it is made to revolve.–If desired more especially in large saws the bottoms of the grooves in the pulleys may be notched so as to catch firmly in the links of the saw similar to the method used from revolving endless chains in common use, but I prefer them without.–Sixth. The railway of the carriage consists of two bed pieces, parallel to each other, so as to rest on the top cross girths at the ends of the frame, for the carriage to run on, immediately over the main shaft on the inner one of these rails forming the ways and the front top rail of the frame are the bearings of the short shaft on the end of which is fixed the pinion that works the rack of the carriage hereafter described upon this shaft are a fast and a loose pulley, which receive a band from the drum of the main shaft, as hereinbefore mentioned, and are intended to cause the carriage to recede from the saw.–On the front end of this shaft is also fixed a drum or grooved pulley with cams on which winds the chord of a weight suspended over the end of the frame by means of extending pulleys fixed in any way most convenient, the intention of which is to draw the carriage towards the saw, but a constant force, whilst the band is running on the loose pulley.–Seventh, the chain-carriage consists of two bead pieces that slide on the ways, one of which contains the rack on its underside, by which the carriage is made to advance or recede and two substantial end pieces into which they are halved the end pieces are notched on their inner sides so as to form a rectangular groove in which the transverse carriage is bedded, at the bottom of the notch is also a horizontal groove, in which the tenons of the transverse carriage play, next the rear ends are two horizontal mortises, extending half their length or more to admit the oblique or wedge-like planes, which press the transverse carriage forward as hereafter described.–The front bed piece is produced a short distance past the end piece towards the farthest ends of the machine, and then turns obliquely towards the front, on the front edge of this oblique part are raised two cams for knobs, one immediately at the end and level with the upper surface of the piece, the other at the beginning of the bend and level with the lower surface, the object of these knobs being to throw the rack in and out of gear by their action on the following contrivance viz. On a line with the band which drives the pinions pulley and in the top girth of the far end of the frame is fixed by means of a beveled mortise and screw, so as to admit of its end moving laterally, an arm branched towards the end that extends to the band of the above mentioned pulley and the other passing a short distance beyond the girth; the lower arm of this fork is supplied with a friction roller, that bearing on the band serves to tighten it whilst the upper is simply notched, for the purpose of catching the band, from the top side of the arm near the band rises another arm the top of which is supplied with a friction roller and is on a level with the nearest or lower knob of the bed piece above described, which acts upon it laterally when the carriage is receding and the effect is to throw the band on the tight pulley of the pinion shaft, and cause the carriage to recede from the saw till the other knob or cam of the bed piece strikes a similar upright arm with a friction roller situated on the projecting end of the arm beyond the end girth which reverses the motion and throws the band on the loose pulley again leaving the pinion shaft free to be acted on in an opposite direction by the cord and weight heretofore mentioned by which the carriage is drawn against the saw, a small catch is fixed to the front top rail which catches in the first arm when the arms are operated on by the knobs for the purpose of steadying it whilst the band is shifting.–

Eighth, the transverse carriage consists of an edge or front plank with tenons at the ends that slide in the horizontal grooves of the end pieces above mentioned and a floor or bed piece, to the front edge of which it is attached, on the upper side of the floor and towards the rear edge thereof are made two rectangles notches to admit two rectangular planes attached to a straight slide resembling saw teeth, the tapering ends whereof as well as of the notches lie towards the far end of the machine these tooth like planes pass through the long mortises in the end pieces of the carriage above described and the effect of moving them forward is to press the transverse carriage towards the saw and vice versa by means of the tongue or pin on the underside of one of the triangles or teeth, which works in a corresponding groove in the bed of the carriage, parallel to the oblique side thereof its reverse motion serves to reverse the motion of the carriage when desired; This connecting slide and its triangles are moved forward by the following contrivance–upon the lower side and nearest the rear edge of the triangles, is a rack the shaft of whose pinion has its bearing on the rear side or bed piece of the main carriage, and a projection or addition formed on the side thereof, the shaft extending beyond this addition receives first a ratchet wheel and secondly an iron lever with a cylindrical knob at its extremity, and suspended thereto a weight.–the end of the cylinder or knob rests on the inner edge of the top rear rail of the frame, and when the carriage is moved from the saw, it moves the knob along the rail for a short distance, then it commences to rise gradually up an arched inclined plane, the upper end only of which is to be made fast to the furthest rear post, until just as the knob of the bed piece of the carriage is about to act on the arm to shift the band of the pinion of the rack of the carriage, it arrives at a notch in the edge of the plane which lets it pass through and the following of the weight causes the lever, by means of a small hook or hand attached to the lever, and kept down on the ratchet wheel by a spring, to draw or revolve said wheel one notch or more by which means the triangular planes are advanced and of course the transverse carriage moves or wedges towards the saw and the substance to be sawed being made fast on that carriage is thus brought to the saw during each backwards motion of the main carriage.

Operation. The substance to be sawed is fixed firm on the transverse carriage by any convenient fastenings, so as to project sufficiently, past the front edge thereof –

The carriage having been drawn to its proper place in front of the saw or towards the furthest end of the machine, and the pinion shaft being out of gear, the main shaft is then revolved and communicates its motion to the main band wheels by means of the large cog wheel and spur wheel, by means of the band wheels and bands, this motion, multiplied to any degree desired, is given to the saw shaft, the chain saw is thus set in revolution, which it may be proper to mention will revolve, particularly in large saws with a momentum proportional to its weight, similar to that obtained in the rim of a balance wheel and the carriage being under the pressure of the suspended weight, the substance to be sawed is pressed by a constant force against the saw with which it is kept in constant contact, when the cut is finished, the cam throws the pinion partly into gear and the carriage is carried back until the other cam throws the pinion out of gear again, simultaneous to which the weight attached to the lever of the ratchet wheel on the back part of the carriage, falls through the notch in the inclined plane, and the transverse carriage is moved or wedged one thickness nearer the saw, or in other words, performs the setting of the machine; and these operations continue till the work is finished. - - I have omitted giving dimensions of the parts in the above description as these will depend chiefly on the purpose for which the saw and other machinery are to be used.

I will also mention here that although I have described the saw as operating in vertical position, I do not intend to confine myself to that position alone, but intend it to be also operated either horizontally, obliquely or in any other way best suited to the purposes to be accomplished or in which saws are used.

Now what I claim as new and my own invention, and for which I ask Letters Patent, is the saw in form of an endless chain, made and applied as herein described and specified, together with the contrivance of the wedge like or rectangular planes, and the combination of the rack pinion, ratchet-wheel, lever, catch, inclined plane, and weight by which the motion of the transverse carriage herein described is obtained.–

In Testimony that the foregoing is a true specification of my said improvement I have hereunto set my hand….. at Washington this 27th day of May 1834.

Phineas P. Quimby

Witnesses

Charles Palmer
Robt. Clarke

A newspaper article published in the *Bangor Courier* was republished in the *Belfast Republican Journal* on August 3rd, 1834:

NEW INVENTION.–We witnessed, at the shop of P. P. Quimby, at Belfast, the present week, the operation, upon a miniature scale, of a machine patented by that ingenious mechianie [sic] for sawing lumber. It is extremely simple in its contrivance and the construction of the saw is entirely new, being similar, somewhat, to that of a watch chain, the teeth connected by rivets and the saw so constructed as to pass round cylinders grooved for the purpose, and turned by means of a single wheel and band. This little machine, worked only by hand, cut, while we were present, several pieces of wood with such wonderful exactness and celerity as seemed to demonstrate the adaptability of the machine to purposes of great utility. It is plain that very little power is lost by friction, and the power required may be supplied by horse, steam or water. We invite those who feel an interest in the progress of improvements to call, in passing through Belfast, and examine for themselves and to hear from Mr. Quimby an explanation of the nature and properties of his invention. –*Bangor Courier.*

[This article is continued by the *Belfast Republican Journal* reporter.] We have also seen the saw, above named, recently invented by our ingenious Towns-man, and think it will rank high among the improvements of this age. It is put together much like a watch chain. The teeth are separate, and new ones are added as easily as teeth can be *set* in the common saw. It runs over two cylinders with groves, and saves more than one half of the time and labor of the strait saw, as it is constantly operating and it moves like a circular saw. It saws back and forth, and thus saves all the time occasioned by the necessity of carrying back the car-carriage of the common saw. It unites most completely all the advantages of both the Straight and Circular Saw, and promises to make a rapid and complete revolution in the whole business of sawing wood, marble, &c. We have seen the model, or rather the miniature in successful operation, doing its office with surprising precision and beauty. A Patent, we hear, has been secured, and a Saw on a large scale will shortly be put into action. It has attracted much attention from many curious and practical observers of its principle and work, and will well reward the trouble any one may take to call and examine it.

P. Quimby, Permutation Lock–Patented May 23, 1836

The U. S. Patent Office does have the mechanical drawing and handwritten description or schedule of this patent, but not the actual Letters Patent. This is a photograph of P. P. Quimby's copy:

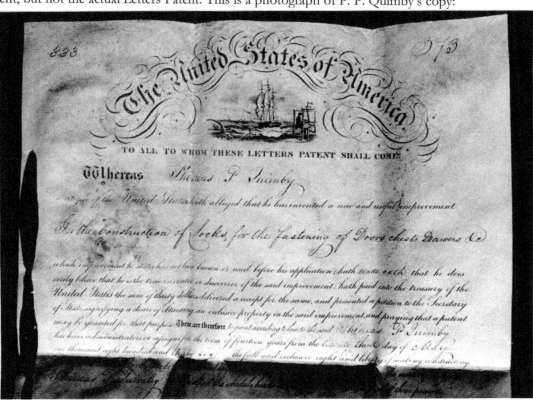

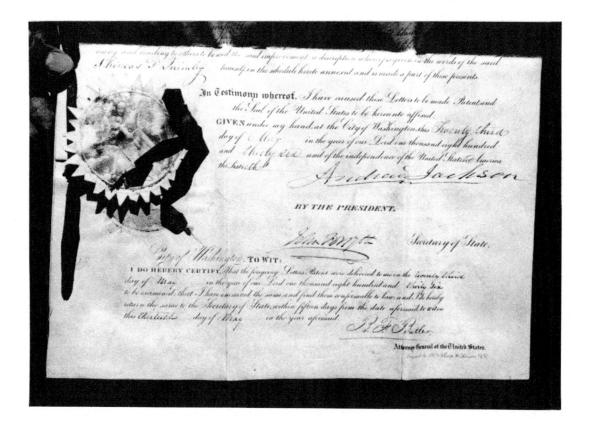

The patent states:

The United States of America

TO ALL TO WHOM THESE LETTERS PATENT SHALL COME:

Whereas Phineas P. Quimby

A citizen of the United States, hath alleged that he has invented a new and useful improvement

In the construction of Locks, for the fastening of Doors chests Drawers &c.

Which improvement he states has not been known or used before his application; hath made oath that he does verily believe that he is the true inventor or discoverer of the said improvement; hath paid into the treasury of the United States the sum of thirty dollars, delivered a receipt for the same, and presented a petition to the Secretary of State signifying a desire of obtaining an exclusive property in the said improvement, and praying that a patent may be granted for that purpose. These are therefore to grant according to law to the said Phineas P. Quimby, his heirs, administrators or assigners of the term of fourteen years from the twenty third day of May, one thousand eighteen hundred thirty six, the full and exclusive right and liberty of making or constructing using and lending to others to be used the said improvement; a description whereof is given in the words of the said Phineas P. Quimby himself, in the schedule hereto annexed and I made a part of these patents.

In Testimony whereof, I have caused these Letters to be made Patent and the Seal of the United States to be hereunto affixed.

GIVEN under my hand, at the City of Washington, this Twenty third day of May, in the year of our Lord one thousand eight hundred and thirty six, and of the independence of the United States of America the Sixtieth

[signed] Andrew Jackson

BY THE PRESIDENT,

[signature] John Forsyth Secretary of State.

City of Washington, TO WIT:

I DO HEREBY CERTIFY, That the foregoing Letters Patent were delivered to me on the twenty third day of May, in the year of our Lord one thousand eight hundred and thirty six to be examined; that I have examined the same and find them conformably to laws; and I do hereby return the same to the Secretary of State, within fifteen days from the date aforesaid, to wit on this thirtieth day of May in the year aforesaid.

[Signed] B. F. Butler

Attorney General of the United States

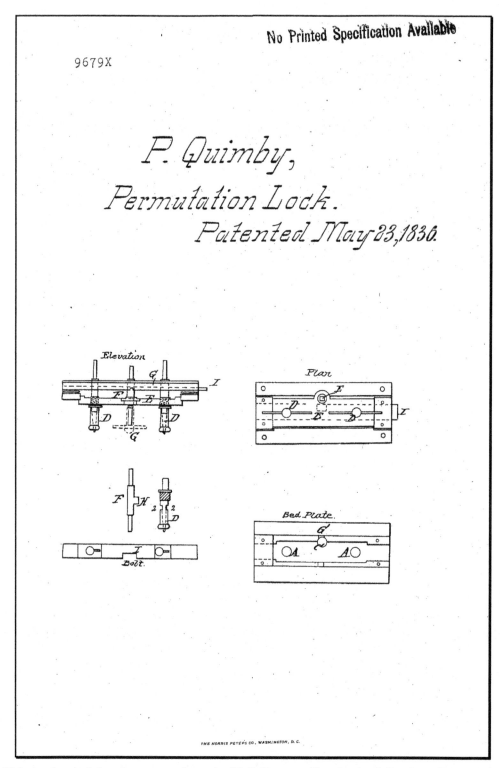

This mechanical drawing comes from the U. S. Patent office. In the following photograph, it can be seen that Quimby's copy of this mechanical drawing simply says, "Phineas Quimby's Lock." Within his written description or schedule he identifies this lock as a "Combination Screw Lock."

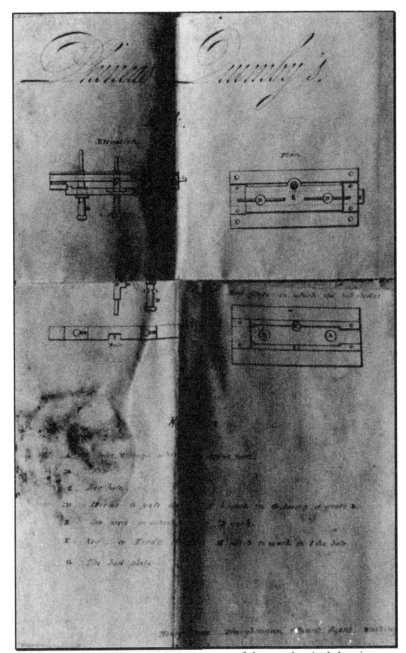

Photograph of P. P. Quimby's copy of the mechanical drawing.

The handwritten description or schedule states:

Phineas P. Quimby of Belfast, Maine.

Letters Patent.

The schedule referred to in these Letters, Patent and making part of the same, containing a description in the words of the said Phineas P. Quimby himself of his improvement in the construction of Locks for the fastening of Doors, Chests, Drawers, &c.

To all persons to whom these patents shall come.–Be it known that I, Phineas P. Quimby of Belfast in the county of Waldo, & State of Maine have invented and made a new and useful improvement in the construction of Locks, for Doors, Chests, Drawers, &c. and the same have made, constructed and applied to use, and which operates on a principle heretofore unused and unknown called the "Combination Screw Lock" specified in the words following viz: The Lock in addition to the case in which it is enclosed, and which may be in the shape of a door, chest, drawer or padlock, consists of a bolt or bolts with two or more holes through it, through which two or more screws are to pass connected with said holes in the bolt on two or more slits in the bolt to receive the screws at the place in the same screws which are grooved: also, two or more screws with one or more grooves in them to admit of their passing onto the slits in the bolts the bolt to contain a mortise or gap in which the key plays: the bolt to be impelled with or without a spring in order to place the bolt in a situation to be moved, the screws must be raised or lowered until the grooves in the screws come in a line with the slits in the bolt. After the bolt is moved a turn of the screws, either or all of them more or less times, prevents the movement of the bolt until the screws are restored to the position in which they were before they were started. In the drawing which is herewith transmitted the holes marked A. are those through which the screws pass. The holes marked C. is the key hole; B. the bolt. What I patented and especially claim as my own invention and for which I ask an exclusive right to use is–1st The constructing of locks either of wood or metal with bolts containing one or more holes and slits for the reception of screws with grooves in them.–2nd The application of screws to said bolts and such way and manner, as to impede and prevent the movement of the bolt in some position and not to impede or prevent it in others.

In testimony that the above is a true specification of the improvements I have invented and claim a patent for, under the name of "Combination Screw Lock" as above named, I have here unto set my hand this thirty first day of March AD 1836.

Phineas P. Quimby

Witnesses

C. F. Angier
W. G. Crosby

Quimby's Patent Steering Gear–Patented March 19, 1850

Once again looking to Joseph Williamson's 1877 book, *The History of the City of Belfast in the State of Maine* we find: "In 1850, a new apparatus for steering vessels, by means of a screw and a compound lever, was patented by P. P. Quimby, the inventor. It was first applied to the bark 'Lillias.' "

The *Lillias* was built in 1849 in the Belfast, Maine shipyards of John Haraden, who was P. P. Quimby's father-in-law.

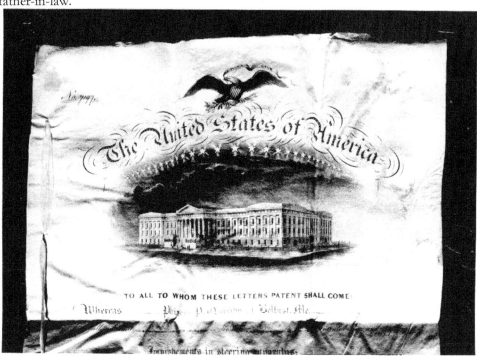

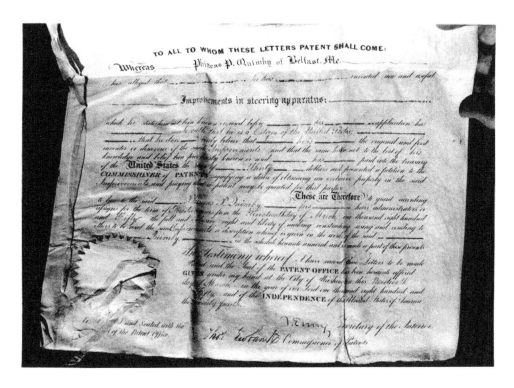

This patent states:

The United States of America

TO ALL TO WHOM THESE LETTERS PATENT SHALL COME:

Whereas Phineas P. Quimby of Belfast, Me., has alleged that he has invented new and useful Improvements in steering apparatus; which he states have not been known or used before his application has made oath that he is a Citizen of the United States; that he does verily believe that he is the original and first inventor or discoverer of the said, Improvements and that the same have not to the best of his knowledge and belief been previously known or used; has paid into the treasury of the United States the sum of Thirty dollars and presented a petition to the COMMISSIONER of PATENTS signifying a desire of obtaining an exclusive property in the said Improvements and praying that a patent may be granted for that purpose. These are Therefore to grant according to law the said Phineas P. Quimby his heirs administrators or assigns for the term of Fourteen years from the nineteenth day of March; one thousand eight hundred and Fifty the full and exclusive right and liberty of making, constructing, using and rending to others to be used the said Improvements, a description whereof is given in the words of the said Quimby, in the schedule herewith annexed and is made a part of these patents.

In Testimony wereof I have caused these Letters to be made Patent and the Seal of the PATENT OFFICE has been hereunto affixed GIVEN under my hand at the City of Washington, this Nineteenth day of March, in the year of our Lord one thousand eight hundred and Fifty, and the INDEPENDENCE of the United States of America the Twenty-fourth.

T. Emery, Secretary of the Interior.
Tho. Eubank Commissioner of Patents.

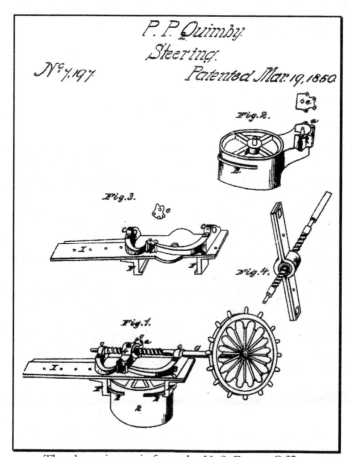

The above image is from the U. S. Patent Office

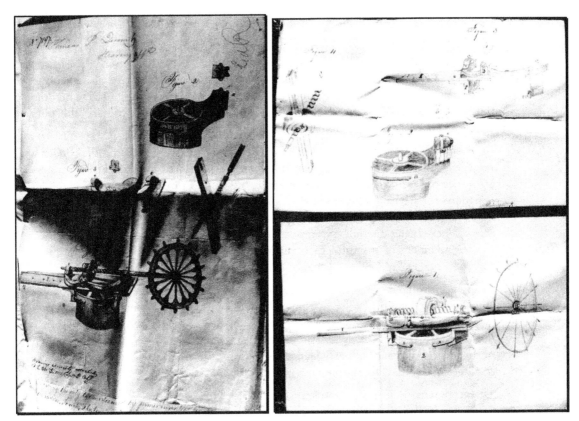

The two photographs above are copies of the mechanical drawings retained by P. P. Quimby.

The description or schedule of this patent states:

The schedule referred to in these Letters Patent and making part of the same.

To whom it may concern:

Be it known that I, Phineas P. Quimby of Belfast, in the County of Waldo and the State of Maine, have invented a new and useful machine for Steering Ships and Steamboats which is entitled "Quimby's Patent Steering Gear" And I do declare that the following is a full clear, and exact description of the construction and operation of the same, reference being had to the annexed drawings, making part of this specification, in which Figure 1 is a perspective view of the whole machine. Figures 2, 3, and 4 are detached parts of the same, with reference showing the mode in which the same goes together, as follows. Fig. 2 Is a band attached to the rudder head with a pintle in the center, as shown in the drawing.

A. Is a socked joint in fig. 2. B. is a flange on Fig. 2.

Fig. 3 Is a half circle or bow, with a hole in the center crosspiece, which fits onto the pintle in the center of Fig. 2. C. C. are boxes at the ends of the crosspiece of the bow 3. D, is a socket joint in Fig. 3 corresponding to a similar one in Fig. 2 (marked a). E, E, are caps for said socket joints. F, F, are dogs attached to the underside of Fig. 3 which plays in the flanges marked B. on Fig.2.

Fig. 4 is a lever made in two parts with half rounds in the center which when together make a circle to enclose the revolving nut which is fitted and held in by trunnions inserted in the circular part of lever above and below. The lever is fastened together with two screws. At each end of the lever is a groove or slot which receives the pin in the socket on bow 3 and band 2.

Letter G is the screw (to which is attached the steering wheel) which turns in the boxes on the ends of the center piece of bow 3 marked c, c.

Letter H is the nut (through which the screw passes) in the center of lever 4 fitted in with trunnions which play in the circular part of the lever.

Letter I is a continuation of the center piece of bow 3 by which the machine is secured to the deck of the vessel. The whole to be made of cast iron or other metal. I am aware that a screw placed athwartships and acting upon a turning and traveling nut attached directly to the tiller or its equivalent on the rudder head, has been employed for the purpose of steering vessels. I therefore do not claim the invention of that arrangement.

In my apparatus I introduce the lever Fig. 4 for the purpose of moving the rudder with the same length of tiller, through a given space with less turns of the wheel than can be done in any other way with the same pitch of screw, by which I obviate a great objection in former apparatus for steering, to wit: the want of command over the rudder by reason of the great number of turns of the wheel, or the great friction produced by increasing the pitch of the screw. These being the only two modes used by former inventors for obtaining the velocity in the movement of the rudder, to wit: shortening the tiller or increasing the pitch of the screw.

In my apparatus any required velocity in the movement of the rudder may be obtained with the same length of tiller by diminishing or increasing the length of my lever, without increasing the pitch of the screw, as increasing the pitch of the screw or shortening the tiller makes it operate stiffly and unnaturally. And in fact I am enabled by the introduction of the lever to obtain that particular combination of power and velocity which the exigency of all occasions may demand in an apparatus for steering vessels.

Therefore what I claim as my invention and desire to secure by Letters Patent, is—

Attaching the nut acted upon by the screw, to an interposing lever, arranged substantially as herein described by which arrangement I am enabled with the same pitch of screw and the same number of revolutions of the wheel to move the rudder through a larger arc than in the old apparatus.

P. P. Quimby

Witnesses:

Andrew P. Palmer
Wm. John Bowman.

REFERENCES

Primary References

Microfilm of the source documents that comprise the writings or transcriptions of Phineas Parkhurst Quimby. The collection was divided in 1930, when a portion of the documents was placed in the Library of Congress, Washington D. C.

The Library of Congress, Washington D. C.

This collection of source documents was microfilmed by the Photo Duplication Service of the Library of Congress in 1969. There are three microfilm reels recorded at shelf number "Mss 14,301." The identification on the microfilm is:

Quimby, Phineas Parkhurst, 1802-66.

Pagers, 1859-66. ca. 100 items.

In Library of Congress, Manuscript Division. Mental healer. Handwritten copies of essays, notes for essays or lectures, and drafts of letters by Quimby on such subjects as wisdom, happiness, health and disease, spiritualism, science, Christ, religion, life and death, and mind and matter, as well as accounts of his experiences in healing. Included are letters, 1862-65, from Mary M. Patterson (Mary Baker Eddy) to Quimby.

Gift, 1953.

Reel 1: The last four digits of the microfilm frames are numbered 0001-0643. The contents of this microfilm reel include 7 commercially bound copybooks that are identified as Volumes 1-7.

Reel 2: The last four digits of the microfilm frames are numbered 0644-1152. The contents of this microfilm reel include 4 commercially bound copybooks that are identified as Volumes 8-11.

Reel 3: The last four digits of the microfilm frames are numbered 1153-1474. The contents of this microfilm reel include various handwritten manuscripts penned in Quimby's own hand; three handwritten copies of the document identified as "Questions and Answers"; handwritten correspondence from Dr. D. Patterson and Mary M. Patterson; and newspaper clippings from the press.

On September 29, 1970, Mrs. Elwyn Seelye, a direct descendent of Phineas Parkhurst Quimby, added the personal journal of Lucius C. Burkmar to this collection. Lucius Burkmar was Quimby's subject in experiments and demonstrations of mesmerism. This personal or private journal was microfilmed by the Library of Congress Photo Duplication Service in 1982. The shelf number is listed as "Mss. 18,619." The formal description is:

Quimby, Phineas Parkhurst, 1802-1866.

Papers, in part, 1843-1845. Addition, 1 item
Private journal of Lucius D. [sic] Burkmar, 1843-45.
Microfilmed 1982.

It should be noted here the Library of Congress has subsequently removed the individual pages of the commercially bound copybooks and placed them into sleeves.

Boston University, Boston, Massachusetts

In 1962 a second portion of writings by and about Phineas Parkhurst Quimby was loaned to Boston University Libraries for microfilming by Mrs. Elizabeth Quimby Pineo, of Belfast, Maine, who was one of P. P. Quimby's granddaughters. The microfilming was achieved at Chenery Library on May 8, 1963 by the Micro Reproduction Service of Boston University. Four reels of microfilm were produced:

Reel 1: The early writings of Phineas Parkhurst Quimby identified as "Lecture Notes" by Horatio W. Dresser in his 1921 publication of *The Quimby Manuscripts*. There are eight small handmade booklets numbered Volumes 1-7 (there are two copies of Volume 1). These booklets were not microfilmed in sequential order. The last four digits of the microfilm frames are numbered 0001-0163.

Reel 2: Nine commercially bound copybooks of articles by Quimby. The last four digits of the microfilm frames are numbered 0001-0576.

Reel 3: Miscellaneous small notebooks, articles, poetry; letters, etc., that are mostly written by Quimby. The last four digits of the microfilm frames are numbered 0001-1240.

Reel 4: Lucius C. Burkmar's personal journal was also microfilmed for the first time on this occasion prior to being relocated to the Library of Congress in 1970.

An informational notice at the beginning of the microfilm states:

WRITINGS BY AND ABOUT PHINEAS PARKHURST QUIMBY

Loaned to Boston University Libraries

For microfilming, 1962

By Mrs. Elizabeth Quimby Pineo, Belfast, Maine

Errol S. Collie told C. Alan Anderson, October 17, 1962, that he (Collie) in the 1940's marked some of the manuscripts as follows: "QM" followed by a page number refers to the page of the first edition of THE QUIMBY MANUSCRIPTS where the marked item may be found.

The fraction-like mark refers to volume and page of bound Quimby notebooks placed in the Library of Congress in 1930 where the item may be found.

"S of H" refers to the first edition of Collie's processed SCIENCE OF HEALTH AND HAPPINESS containing articles in the 1930 Library of Congress Quimby collection but not published in THE QUIMBY MANUSCRIPTS.

This microfilm does not include Quimby material in the Library of Congress or Harvard University Houghton Library as of the date of microfilming.

The materials on this film have been roughly divided into three groups:

I. Early Writings by Quimby, called "lecture-notes" by Dresser in THE QUIMBY MANUSCRIPTS.

II. Bound notebooks of articles by Quimby.

III. Miscellaneous material–largely articles by Quimby.

Harvard University

Six copy books are located in Houghton Library of Harvard University presumably placed there by members of the Dresser family. In preparation for this publication, the printouts of the microfilm were digitalized, indexed, and compared with the materials from the other two institutions. The materials in this collection are essentially a duplication of the materials found in the Library of Congress and Boston University. The formal listing of these materials is:

57M-38 80-
Quimby, Phineas Parkhurst
[essays concerning mental healing]
MS. by various hands; [n.p., 188-]
<u>6 volumes</u>

ARCHIVAL NEGATIVE FILM ON FILE IN HOUGHTON

Secondary References

Beta, R. (ed.). *Talk With God–Quimby Quotes. Direct Quotes From the Original Writings of Phineas Parkhurst Quimby. Compiled by The Quimby Group of Miami.* Miami: The Awareness, Inc., 1983.

Collie, Erroll Stafford. *Quimby's Science of Happiness. A Non-Medical Scientific Explanation of the Cause and Cure of Disease.* Marina del Rey, CA: DeVorss & Co., 1980.

Collie, Erroll S. (ed.). *The Science of Health and Happiness by P. P. Quimby.* (Three red binders containing mimeographed typewritten pages, self-published and distributed by E. S. Collie.) New York: private publication, 1940.

Collie, Erroll S. (ed.). *The Unpublished Writings of Phineas Parkhurst Quimby.* (Essentially a re-issue of his 1940 publication.) Ft. Pierce, FL: Douglas James, 1981.

Dresser, Julius A. *The True History of Mental Science. A Lecture Delivered at the Church of the Divine Unity, Boston, Mass., on Sunday Evening, Feb. 6, 1887. Revised with Additions.* Boston: Alfred Mudge & Son, 1887.

Dresser, Annetta G. *The Philosophy of P. P. Quimby, with Selections from his Manuscripts and a Sketch of his Life.* Boston: Geo. H. Ellis, 1895.

Dresser, Horatio W. (ed.). *The Quimby Manuscripts Showing the Discovery of Spiritual Healing and the Origin of Christian Science.* 1st ed'n. New York: Thomas Y. Crowell Co., 1921.

Dresser, Horatio W. (ed.). *The Quimby Manuscripts.* Second Edition. 2nd ed'n, 3rd printing. New York: Thomas Y. Crowell Co., 1921.

Hawkins, Ann Ballew. *Phineas Parkhurst Quimby. Revealer of Spiritual Healing to this Age. His Life and What He taught. (Based on the Quimby Manuscripts and original letters in the Library of Congress.)*, 7th printing. Marina Del Rey, CA: DeVorss & Co., 1951.

Seale, Ervin. (ed.). *Phineas Parkhurst Quimby: The Complete Writings.* (3 vols). Marina Del Rey, CA: DeVorss & Co., 1988.

Additional References

Abercrombie, John. *Inquiries Concerning the Intellectual Powers, and the Investigation of Truth.* New York: Harper and Brothers, 1842.

Dods, John Bovee. *Six Lectures on the Philosophy of Mesmerism, Delivered in the Marlboro' Chapel, Boston.* New York: Fowlers and Wells, 1847.

Dods, John Bovee. *Spirit Manifestations Examined and Explained. Judge Edmonds Refuted; or, An Exposition of the Involuntary Powers and Instincts of the Human Mind.* New York: De Witt & Davenport, 1854.

Dods, John Bovee. *Thirty Short Sermons, of Various Important Subjects, Both Doctrinal and Practical.* Boston: Thomas Whittemore, 1845.

Hall, Spencer T. *Mesmeric Experiences.* London: H. Bailliere and J. Ollivier, 1845.

Hall, Spencer T. (ed.). *The Phreno-Magnet, and Mirror of Nature: A Record of Facts, Experiments, and Discoveries in Phrenology, Magnetism, &c.* London: Simpkin, Marshall, and Co., 1843.

Poyen, St. Sauveur, Charles. *Progress of Animal Magnetism in New England. Being A Collection of Experiments, Reports and Certificates, from the Most Respectable Sources. Preceded by a Dissertation on the Proofs of Animal Magnetism.* Boston: Weeks, Jordan & Co., 1837.

Sunderland, La Roy. *Pathetism: Man Considered in Respect to His Form, Life, Sensation, Soul, Mind, Spirit; Giving the Rationale of those Laws which Produce the Mysteries, Miseries, Felicities, of Human Nature! Psychology, Phrenology, Pneumatology, Physiognomy, Pathognomy, Physiology.* Boston: White & Potter, 1847.

Townshend, Chauncy Hare. *Facts in Mesmerism, with Reasons for a Dispassionate Inquiry Into It.* London: Longman, Orme, Brown, Green, & Longmans, 1840.

Unknown, Author. *The History and Philosophy of Animal Magnetism, with Practical Instructions for the Exercise of this Power. Being a Complete Compend of All the Information Now Existing Upon this Important Subject.* Boston: J. N. Bradley & Co., 1843.

Upham, Thomas C. *Elements of Mental Philosophy, Embracing the Two Departments of the Intellect and the Sensibilities. In Two Volumes.* Vol. 1, 3rd ed'n. Portland: William Hyde, for A. Hyde, 1839.

Williamson, Joseph. *History of the City of Belfast in the State of Maine. From its First Settlement in 1770 to 1875.* Vol. 1. Portland: Loring, Short, and Harmon, 1877.